UNTOUCHABLE

Also by Randall Sullivan

The Price of Experience

LAbyrinth

The Miracle Detective

UNTOUCHABLE

The Strange Life and Tragic Death
of Michael Jackson

RANDALL SULLIVAN

Grove Press UK

First published in the United States of America in 2012 by Grove/Atlantic Inc.

First published in Great Britain in 2012 by Grove Press UK,
an imprint of Grove/Atlantic Inc.

1 3 5 7 9 8 6 4 2

A CIP record for this book is available from the British Library.

Hardback ISBN 978 1 61185 603 3
Export trade paperback ISBN 978 1 61185 597 5
Home trade paperback ISBN 978 1 61185 576 0

Printed in Great Britain by the MPG Books Group

Grove Press, UK
Ormond House
26–27 Boswell Street
London
WC1N 3JZ

www.groveatlantic.com

For Elaine Veronica Sullivan

CONTENTS

Author's Note

The inception of this book was an e-mail sent to me by Will Dana, the managing editor of *Rolling Stone* magazine, in late June 2009 that read, "Are you ready to drop everything and do the big Michael Jackson piece?" After thinking it over for twenty-four hours, I said yes, and flew to Los Angeles, where Michael had died just a few days earlier. During the next several weeks, and in the course of conversations with editors at *Rolling Stone*, I realized that most people thought they knew quite a lot about the life Michael Jackson had lived up until the time his criminal trial on charges of child molestation ended with an acquittal in June 2005, but that he seemed in their minds to have disappeared into some sort of twilight zone during the four years afterward, at least up until the time of the announcement of his "This Is It" shows at the O2 Arena in London during March 2009. So the idea became to provide an account of those last four years that would somehow also be the story of his life, with the details of his first forty-five years "brush stroked in," as somebody—maybe it was me—put it.

By the time I realized that what had begun as a magazine article was turning into a book, I was committed to that structure and it still felt right to me. I knew, of course, that I would need more than brush strokes to tell the story of the first nine-tenths of Michael's life in what purported to be a biography, but I still wanted the story of his final five years to be the crux of the work.

I began to imagine the structure of this book as a spyglass telescope, made of three sections, or tubes, that fitted over one another, and could be extended or retracted as needed. The first tube, the one closest to the eye, would contain the lens that examined those years after the criminal trial, when Michael was a kind of Flying Dutchman wandering the globe, his three children in tow, searching for a new home he never found. The second tube, a bit further from the eye, would need to be fitted, I thought, with the lens I used to study the circumstances that led to the criminal charges against him, including the Martin Bashir documentary, *Living with Michael Jackson* that ran on ABC, the raid on Neverland Ranch, his arrest, and his trial. Then I realized that this second tube would have to reach at least back to 2001, when his "30th Anniversary" concerts coincided with the 9/11 terrorist attacks. Finally, I understood that the length of this second tube was really the twelve years between 1993 and 2005, when Michael's life, and his public reputation, were gradually destroyed by two very public accusations of sexually abusing children.

The Michael Jackson who existed after August 1993 was a different Michael Jackson than the one who had existed before then, so the story of those years is key to understanding his life, and needed to be told in some considerable detail. I would have to research and write a chronicle of the two main events that bookended those years, the Jordan Chandler scandal that broke in 1993 and the criminal trial that took place in 2005, that both encompassed and eclipsed anything previously published.

The third and most distant tube would house the lens that provided my view of Michael's life up to 1993, the first thirty-five years of his youth, his rise to fame, his reign as the King of Pop and his transformation into the person the tabloid media called "Wacko Jacko"—in other words, the story of Michael Jackson that most people thought they knew. It would be necessary to rely largely on the public record for this section that I would be telling as, essentially, backstory, but I would have the advantage of filtering this through the two other lenses of the telescope and thus through the sources that had helped me construct them, some of those being people whose relationships with Michael had lasted decades. Plus, circumstances had arranged themselves in such a way that I was provided with a level of access to the inner workings of the Jackson family in the post-Michael era that no writer had ever or was ever likely to be granted again, and that was a blessing.

This last development was concurrent with my realization that there was a yet a fourth piece to my telescope, and that this was the perspective of all that had taken place in the months and years after Michael's death, the celebration of and the struggle for his legacy and his estate. This fourth piece I came to imagine as fitting snugly over the first tube and thus becoming the part that was pressed against my flesh, containing the concave eyepiece that created my telescope's magnification.

So in a way, I told myself, I was writing four Michael Jackson biographies. I could even claim that the total was five biographies, or even six. Knowing that many people might wish for a more conventional account of

Michael's life, I created the timeline that I consider an essential aspect of this book, laying out the story of Michael Jackson in chronological fashion, from beginning to end. And then there are, of course, my chapter notes, which not only describe how I wrote the book, but how I sorted the mass of conflicting information about Michael Jackson to deliver what I hope will be a definitive chronicle.

So there you have it, as good a description as I can offer of what I've done, and why.

PROLOGUE

For someone who so often professed his loneliness, Michael Jackson spent a remarkable amount of time avoiding people. He lived most of his life behind gates and walls or in surreptitious transitions from one hiding place to another. He wore disguises, broke off relationships, and changed telephone numbers constantly, but still paparazzi, process servers, delusional women, and desperate men pursued him wherever he went.

The saddest part of his situation, though, was that the people Michael took the greatest pains to elude were the members of his own family.

In the late summer of 2001, they were after him again. It was just two days before his scheduled departure for New York, where his "30th Anniversary" concerts were to be staged at Madison Square Garden on September 7 and September 10. Jackson's friend and business partner Marc Schaffel, in collaboration with producer David Gest, had assembled a collection of performers who would stretch across the years since the recording of Michael's first solo single, "Got to Be There," in 1971. The gamut ran from Kenny Rogers to Usher, and included such disparate talents as Destiny's Child, Ray Charles, Marc Anthony, Missy Elliot, Dionne Warwick, Yoko Ono, Gloria Estefan, Slash, and Whitney Houston. Samuel L. Jackson had agreed to serve as master of ceremonies, while Michael's friends Elizabeth Taylor and Marlon Brando were recruited to deliver televised speeches.

Michael wanted his family in New York as well; his brothers to perform a medley of hits from their days as the Jackson 5, while his parents sat in special box seats. The Jacksons, though, insisted that they should receive appearance fees. David Gest agreed to honorariums of $250,000 for family members, even those who would be there to watch the show rather than performing in it. Schaffel thought it was "pretty weird" to be paying Michael's own family to attend his anniversary concert, especially the ones who weren't even going to be onstage, but Marc advanced money to pay the Jacksons out of his own pocket. Just days before the first concert, though, Jermaine Jackson read an article that said his brother would be making as much as $10 million from the two concerts and convinced his parents that Michael should pay the three of them another $500,000 apiece. Jermaine and his father Joe actually drew up a contract and, with Katherine Jackson in tow, chased Michael around Southern California to try to get him to sign, threatening all the while not to show up in New York unless he did.

Michael took refuge for several days at Schaffel's house in Calabasas, in the hill country at the far western edge of the San Fernando Valley. The day before their scheduled departure for New York, though, Michael said he needed to make a quick trip north to Neverland Ranch to collect some clothing and other personal items for the trip. He and his two young children, four-year-old Prince and three-year-old Paris, had barely set foot inside the main house at Neverland when the security guards alerted Michael that his parents Joe and Katherine, and his brother Jermaine, were at the main gate, saying they had some papers they needed Michael to sign and demanding to be admitted. Michael told the guards to tell his family he wasn't at the ranch and to send them away. Joe Jackson, though, refused to budge. "I'm his father," Joe told the guards. "I need to use the bathroom. His mother needs to use the bathroom. Let us in."

Frantic, Michael phoned Schaffel and explained the situation. If they got through the gate, his family would hound him to sign this contract agreeing to pay each of them another $500,000. But still, he couldn't keep his mother locked outside when she was pleading to just be allowed to use the bathroom, Michael told Schaffel. What he was going to do, he explained, was instruct the guards to tell his family again that Mr. Jackson was not on the premises, but to admit them to the property so that they could use the facilities.

As soon as Joe and Jermaine were through the main gate, though, they drove straight to the main house and pushed their way inside to search for Michael. "They literally ransacked the place," Schaffel remembered.

Michael retreated with the kids to a hiding place that was concealed behind a secret door at the back of his bedroom closet and phoned Schaffel from there. He was in tears by then, literally whimpering into the phone as he asked Schaffel, "You see what they do to me? Do you understand now why I don't want anything to do with my brothers, why I hide from them and refuse to answer their phone calls?"

"I've supported my brothers, supported them all," Michael cried into the phone. "I've put their kids through school. But they still come after me, still wanting more. It never ends. And my father's worse than they are."

Michael choked up and couldn't continue for a moment, Schaffel recalled, then sobbed, "The worst part, the part that kills me, is that I have to lie to my own mother."

"Do you understand, Marc?" Michael asked. "Do you understand now why I am the way I am? How else could I be?"

PART ONE

EAST

1

On June 29, 2005, sixteen days after the not-guilty verdicts in his Santa Barbara County child molestation trial, Michael Jackson came to the end of a journey that had taken him across the country, above the Atlantic Ocean, over the Mediterranean Sea, and into the Persian Gulf, where his private jet landed at Bahrain International Airport in Manama, eight thousand miles from his former home in California. He had to go that far to get relief and even there it wouldn't last long.

Those who met him on the tarmac were pleased to see that his appearance was markedly improved from the withered wraith he had become during the final stages of his criminal trial. "Near the end, he went days at a time without eating or sleeping," remembered his lead defense attorney, Tom Mesereau. "He would call us in tears at three or four in the morning, worried about what would happen to his children if he was behind bars. In those last couple of weeks, his cheeks were sunken to the point that his bones looked right on the surface." By the time he arrived in Manama, Michael had put on nearly ten pounds and looked like he could dance to the terminal if he had to. Bahrainis greeting him at the airport agreed he appeared far less strange in person than they had imagined from photographs. And the size of those hands, *Allahu Akbar*.

Mesereau had been among the crowd of people who gathered at Neverland on the afternoon of the verdict. Michael repeatedly thanked the attorney but seemed capable of little more than hugging his children and staring into space. Some observers described Michael during the trial as sinking gradually into a drug-induced delirium as he raved about the conspiracy against him but Mesereau insisted that it was only on this final day that he encountered a Michael Jackson who seemed "less than lucid."

A handful of people knew how thin the star had been stretched by the jury's deliberations. One was the comedian-turned-activist Dick Gregory, part of the crowd that accompanied Jackson from the courthouse to the ranch on what everyone thought might be Michael's last trip to Neverland.

The gaunt, white-bearded Gregory had been in and out of Jackson's life for years, but Michael was especially adamant about having Gregory present while he awaited and received the jury's verdict. Later in the evening, after Mesereau and others had taken their leave, Michael asked him to come upstairs to his bedroom, Gregory recalled. Michael clung to him on the stairs, Gregory said, and he could feel the entertainer's bones jabbing through his clothes. "Don't leave me!" Michael had pleaded. "They're trying to kill me!"

"Have you eaten?" Gregory asked. The comic purported to have been the one who taught Michael to fast, claiming he had coached Jackson through forty days without food. A person had to drink gallons of water to go so long without eating, Gregory had instructed him then, but Michael appeared to have forgotten that part of the regimen. "I can't eat!" Michael answered. "They're trying to poison me!"

"When was the last time you drank water?" Gregory asked.

"I haven't," Michael replied.

"You need to get out of here," Gregory told him.

Within an hour, Gregory, along with a small security detail, escorted Jackson to Santa Barbara's Marian Medical Center. Jackson was immediately put on an intravenous drip of fluids and sleeping medication. The doctors who treated him told Gregory that Michael would not have survived another day without medical attention. As his family prepared for his "victory celebration" party at a nearby casino, Michael himself lay in a hospital bed drifting in and out of consciousness, wondering at one point if he was in jail and at another if this was the hereafter. He was released from the hospital only after spending nearly twelve solid hours on an IV.

He made one more trip to Neverland to pack, then left the ranch for the last time. Mesereau had advised his client to get out of Santa Barbara County as soon as possible and not to return. The district attorney's office and the sheriff's department were obsessed with Michael Jackson's destruction, Mesereau believed, and would be especially dangerous now, after being humiliated by the verdicts. "I told Michael that all it would take to open the door to another criminal charge was one child wandering onto the ranch," Mesereau recalled.

Michael spent most of the week following his acquittal recuperating at his friend Deepak Chopra's Center for Wellbeing in Carlsbad, California, on a bluff overlooking the Pacific Ocean, between Los Angeles and San Diego. He was joined by his children and their African nanny Grace Rwaramba. Slim and attractive, with an orange-tinted Afro and large, round eyes so dark brown that they appeared black in anything other than direct sunlight, Rwaramba had been Jackson's employee for almost twenty years. Now in her late thirties, she had fled a Uganda decimated by the murderous warlord Idi Amin right around the time she reached puberty and had spent her teens living and studying with the Catholic nuns at Connecticut's Holy Name Academy. Among her classmates, Grace had been best known for her vast collection of Michael Jackson pictures, postcards, T-shirts, and gloves, and for her emotional proclamations of love for the King of Pop. In the 1985 Holy Name yearbook, each graduating senior was permitted a "prophecy." Hers read: "Grace Rwaramba is married to Michael Jackson and has her own generation of the Jackson 5."

It was incredible how close she'd come to living her high school dream. After earning a degree in business administration at Atlantic Union College, she met the family of Deepak Chopra, who personally introduced her to Michael and arranged for her to obtain a position on Jackson's staff during the *Dangerous* tour. As personnel director, she had been tasked mainly with organizing insurance arrangements, but Grace moved steadily up the ranks at Neverland, becoming Michael's most trusted employee. When Michael Joseph Jackson Jr. was born in 1997, Michael appointed her the infant's nanny. She had taken charge of each of the next two children, Paris-Michael Katherine Jackson, born in 1998, and Prince Michael Joseph Jackson II, born in 2001, growing so close to them that all three children called her Mom.

Her relationship with their father was more muddled. Over the years, Grace had developed a certain "be careful what you wish for" cynicism about Michael that strained her devotion to him. The only person on his staff who ever dared to criticize or challenge him, she had been dismissed several times but each time had been brought back almost immediately, mainly because the children cried for her. Tabloid and Internet reports of Michael and Grace's impending marriage regularly surfaced, but a rarely mentioned obstacle was that Grace was already married to someone named Stacy Adair. She had wed Adair in what was described as "a ceremony of convenience" (presumably to protect Rwaramba from problems with the immigration authorities) in Las Vegas in 1995. Adding to the confusion was that those who spent time around Michael characterized Grace in ways that were wildly contradictory. Chopra invariably referred to her as "a lovely young woman" and said she was "devoted" to Michael and his children. Others reported that she was principally dedicated to the power she wielded as Michael's "gatekeeper" and spent much of her energy attempting to insulate him from anyone who might attempt direct contact.

Though she had grown up as one of fifteen children in the Ugandan village of Ishaka, Grace had spent most of her adult life living in either fabulous mansions or the presidential suites of five-star hotels, developing an outsized sense of entitlement along the way. "The most powerful nanny in the universe," was how *Time* magazine described her, because of the sway she held over Michael's children. Tom Mesereau acknowledged that Grace's self-importance was a contributing factor to his subsequent resignation as Michael's general counsel. "I got really, really tired of dealing with her," he said. Many reports linked Grace to the Nation of Islam but in truth she had undertaken a course of Bible study during Michael's criminal trial and was said to have joined the Jehovah's Witnesses. In the only public comment she made during Michael's criminal trial, Grace replied to a question about who was behind the molestation charges by answering, "Satan, the devil." Jackson's spiritual advisor among the Witnesses, Firpo Carr, said he heard her described as "this woman in the background with all of this power, flexing her muscles," but that in his personal encounters with Grace he had found her to be "one of the most humble people I've ever met."

That mixture of modesty and might was regularly tested in her dealings with Michael, whom she often treated like the fourth of her juvenile charges. When Michael finally gave in to her demands to get his own cell phone, he lost the device within a day, and went back to telling people to call Grace's number if they wanted to speak with him. He and the nanny regularly bickered over Michael's wasteful spending. Nearly all the revenue from Michael's catalog holdings, record sales, and song royalties was going directly to his enormous debt payments. Yet even as he lived hand-to-mouth, Michael continued to insist on booking the most expensive hotel suite in every city they visited. When there was no money to pay the bills, they stayed with one of the many "friends" the star had around the world who offered hospitality. Michael possessed so little grasp of his finances that he had whatever checks came his way deposited into Grace's bank account, then asked that she dole cash out to him as needed. He grew peeved or suspicious whenever she told him the money was gone.

On June 17, four days after his acquittal, Jackson's passport and the $300,000 bond he had posted to meet his $3 million bail were returned to him by Judge Rodney Melville, who had presided over the trial. Two days later, without advising even those who were closest to him, Jackson flew with his children and their nanny aboard a private jet to Paris, then traveled by limousine to the Hotel de Crillon, part of the magnificent palace complex at the foot of the Champs-Elysées. The $300,000 he had pocketed upon his release from bail would cover the cost of ten days at this pinnacle of privilege. Lodging in a presidential suite at the Crillon was almost impossible to obtain on short notice, committed as such accommodations were to the various heads of state and high-ranking government officials who typically occupied them, but for Michael Jackson the Crillon's management had been willing to make adjustments. During these ten days he could not only rest and continue to recover, but also give himself something that he had been denied in recent months—the trappings of royal status. He was still the King of Pop, something more than a mere celebrity, a personage of such importance that he could have the Crillon's fabulous Leonard Bernstein Suite, where his children could frolic on the famous wraparound terrace with its spectacular views of the City of Lights while he tickled the keys of the maestro's piano.

A single item of good news encouraged him: Mediabase, which monitored airplay for the radio and recording industries, reported that spins of Michael's records had tripled in the first two days after the "not guilty" verdict in Santa Barbara County.

Peace and privacy were promised in Bahrain. Upon arrival at the airport in the capital city, Jackson and his children were transported directly to the staggering palace of their host, Sheikh Abdullah bin Hamad bin Isa Al Khalifa, the thirty-year-old, second son of the king of Bahrain. For most of the past decade, Abdullah had been not only the governor of Bahrain's southern province but also the hardest rocking oil sheikh in the entire Middle East. A devotee of Led Zeppelin and Bob Marley, the portly Abdullah kept a second home in the Kensington section of London, where he was known for riding around on his Harley-Davidson motorcycle, often in flowing robes, occasionally with a guitar strapped to his back. An aspiring songwriter whose family wealth and Islamic faith had imbued him with a sense of transcendent possibility, the sheikh's plan was to revive Jackson's career (and launch his own) through 2 Seas Records, a music label the two would own as partners. Abdullah's palace was fitted with the finest recording studio in the entire kingdom and Michael would have full use of it for as long as he liked, just as the sheikh had assured him during a series of phone calls between Manama and Neverland Ranch during the criminal trial.

The Bahraini prince demonstrated his seriousness during those months of the trial with ample financial largess. Introduced to the entertainer through Jackson's brother Jermaine, who converted to Islam in 1989, Sheikh Abdullah from the first had lent more than a sympathetic ear to Jackson's woeful tale of legal bills that were eating him alive. "He would say, 'What can I do for my brother? What can I give the children?'" recalled Grace Rwaramba. In March 2005, just as the prosecution began to present its case at the criminal trial in Santa Barbara County, local utilities had threatened to shut off service at Neverland unless the cash-starved singer paid his overdue bills. Abdullah, who had never met Michael face-to-face, responded by immediately wiring $35,000 in cash to her personal checking account, Rwaramba recalled. She was "flabbergasted," but the sheikh merely apologized for the paltry amount, promising "next time it will be more." A month later, Michael asked for $1 million, Rwaramba said, and "it blew my mind" when Abdullah sent exactly that amount. By the first day of summer, Abdullah had promised to pay the $2.2 million in legal bills Jackson would accumulate by the end of his criminal trial if the singer took up residence in Manama.

Sheikh Abdullah was aching to show off his prize, yet insisted that the media hold Jackson's presence in Bahrain as a sort of open secret for nearly two months. Various publications reported that Jackson was in the country as a guest of the prince, but added only that, according to the royal family, "Michael wants to lead a normal life and does not want to be hounded by the media." The sheikh and his famous guest did not venture out in public together until they traveled to the emirate of Dubai on August 20, and even then they did not make themselves available to reporters until another week had passed.

One Middle Eastern story after another celebrated how "happy and healthy" Jackson appeared in the photographs taken at his first public appearance since the trial, in Dubai on August 27, 2005, two days before his forty-seventh birthday. Dressed in an electric-blue shirt and a black fedora, Michael smiled tentatively but sweetly as he and the jowly, droopy-eyed Abdullah posed with the legendary Arab rally driving champion, Mohammed bin Sulayem, while cameras clicked and rolled all around them.

The photo session took place in the corporate offices of Nakheel Properties, the megadeveloper responsible for several of the projects that had transformed Dubai into the world capital of architectural adventurism. Luxury real estate and appointment shopping were what drove the local economy these days and Michael had contributed his part earlier in the week when he ventured out in disguise and behind blackout windows to the absurdly opulent two-story retail complex known locally as "The Boulevard." When the photo session finished, Nakheel executives took Michael and Abdullah on a boat tour of the Dubai shore, skimming over iridescent blue waters alongside the white shell and coral beaches that had once been the tiny emirate's main attraction. From the water, Jackson could see each of the skyscrapers that sprouted from Dubai's fabled sands like petrodollar silos. The Jumeirah Emirates Towers were the twelfth and the twenty-ninth tallest buildings on the planet, he was told, but mere scratching posts compared to the Dubai Tower, where construction had begun almost a year earlier and which, at 2,684 feet, would be the tallest man-made structure on earth by the time of its completion in 2009.

The destination of that afternoon's cruise was the emirate's ultimate engineering feat, the Palm Islands, where more than a billion tons of rock and sand were being used to create a residential community of artificial islands, each in the shape of a palm tree topped by a crescent. Here a world of make believe was being brought to life on a scale that would make even Neverland Ranch seem quaint by comparison. While Michael once again assured all present that he was serious about settling down in Dubai, Abdullah delighted the trailing reporters with his announcement that "Mikaeel" planned to build a grand mosque here in his "new home," dedicated to English-language instruction in the principles of Islam.

Jackson had not actually become a Muslim, but was "on the verge of converting to Islam," according to the Arab-Israeli newspaper *Panorama*. The story would soon be picked up by CBS News, then seized upon by *New York Sun* columnist Daniel Pipes, who observed that "it fits into a recurring and important African-American pattern." That Jackson appeared to welcome being addressed in Bahrain by the name of Allah's great angel, Mikaeel, gave the conversion claim credence in the minds of those who did not know that during his criminal trial the entertainer had several times escorted his children to services at the Kingdom Halls of the Jehovah's Witnesses in both Santa Barbara and Los Angeles and was permitting his mother Katherine to instruct all three kids in church doctrine.

Mikaeel would keep his religious ambivalence to himself while dwelling in the Middle East, and especially when he returned with Abdullah to Manama for a public greeting by the sheikh's father, King Hamad bin Isa Al Khalifa. After His Majesty and Mikaeel withdrew behind closed doors, the king's staff announced to waiting reporters that Mr. Jackson had just acquired a "luxury palace" in Manama and was donating "a huge amount of money" for a second mosque to be built in Bahrain's capital city.

The palace was being rented by the royal family, though, and the millions Jackson had "donated" for the two mosques were an empty pledge. The entertainer would live on Abdullah's dole throughout his stays in Manama and Dubai but even the oil sheikh's pockets weren't deep enough to fill the hole that Jackson was in. The vast assortment of problems— legal, financial, personal, and professional—that had chased him to the Persian Gulf were not only following Jackson, but stacking up against his narrow back.

Two weeks before he celebrated his birthday in Dubai, Jackson had been fined $10,000 by a district court judge in New Orleans for his failure to appear at a hearing prompted by a particularly specious sex abuse accusation. A thirty-nine-year-old man named Joseph Bartucci was claiming that, while watching coverage of the trial in California, he had recovered the suppressed memory of an assault on *him* that had taken place twenty-one years earlier, during the 1984 World's Fair. According to Bartucci's complaint, he had been "lured" into Jackson's limousine and taken on a nine-day ride to California in which he was forced to consume "mood altering drugs" while Jackson performed oral sex on him, cut him with a razor, and stabbed him in the chest with a steel wire. Bartucci could offer not one piece of evidence to support his allegations, while Jackson's attorneys had provided irrefutable proof that their client was in the company of President and First Lady Ronald and Nancy Reagan during some of the days when Bartucci claimed to be his captive. Yet Judge Eldon Fallon allowed the case to go forward even when it was revealed that Bartucci was an admitted bigamist who had been party to eighteen separate civil suits and criminal complaints during the past seventeen years, and was arrested for stalking a woman in 1996. Infuriated that his attorneys in New Orleans had run up a $47,000 bill without obtaining the dismissal of a fabricated lawsuit, Jackson fired them while he prepared for the trip to the Persian Gulf, then simply turned his back on the Louisiana litigation. Now Judge Fallon was demanding that Jackson show cause why he should not be held in contempt and a default judgment entered against him. Jackson would have to answer, even if he did so from halfway around the world.

It was but one legal predicament among many. During the past twelve years, Jackson had paid out almost $100 million in settlements and attorney's fees to deal with the scores of court filings, both frivolous and not, against him, and dozens remained pending. Of all these claims, by far the most expensive—in every sense of the word—had resulted in the payment of more than $18 million to the family of a thirteen-year-old boy named Jordan Chandler back in 1994. According to Mesereau, Michael had come to realize that making a deal with the Chandlers was "the worst mistake of his life." It was the size of the settlement that convinced much of the public and many in the media that Jackson was, more likely than not, a child molester. What sort of innocent man, people asked, would pay that kind of money to a false accuser? "Someone desperate to get on with his life," answered Mesereau. "Michael had no idea how people would interpret his decision to try to make the whole thing go away." The consequences of that decision had multiplied exponentially as one lawsuit after another was filed against him, with various grifters lining up for their piece of the entertainer's rapidly shrinking fortune.

On September 23, 2005, Michael flew to London with Abdullah, Grace Rwaramba, and the children, booking an entire floor at the Dorchester Hotel. It was his standard operating procedure when traveling, he explained to the sheikh, who was footing the bill. Jackson made the trip to deal with what was perhaps the most piercing of all the legal claims currently pending against him: a lawsuit filed in November 2004, in the midst of his criminal trial, by Jackson's former business partner and erstwhile "dear friend" Marc Schaffel.

The thirty-five-year-old Schaffel had emerged as a public figure in late 2001, when he suddenly became the most visible among a crowd of advisors jockeying for position around Jackson, mainly because he had been charged with assembling a choir of superstars to sing with Michael on a charity single titled "What More Can I Give?" The song had originally been inspired by a meeting with South African president Nelson Mandela but was subsequently intended to benefit Kosovar refugees. Then, in the wake of the September 11 atrocities, "What More Can I Give?" was hastily rewritten with the intention to raise money for the families of those who had died in the terrorist attacks. The evolving project had turned into an almost perfect example of how and why virtually everything that in recent years had been initiated from within what the media liked to call "the Jackson camp" was destined to end in a fiasco of finger-pointing and litigation.

Schaffel had been popping up in Jackson's life since August 1984. Just eighteen back then, Schaffel was a freelance cameraman for ABC television, which sent him to Detroit to shoot footage of the Jackson 5's *Victory* tour. Schaffel arrived at the Pontiac Silverdome late and was mortified when the Jacksons' security detail denied him permission to join the rest of the media in front of the main stage. "They put me in a room backstage to wait," he recalled. "So I'm sitting there feeling really stupid when I hear the door open. I assume it's one of the people that's going to usher me outside, but in walks Michael, who closes the door, and it's just the two of us." Jackson took one look at the enormous camera sitting next to Schaffel and stepped over to inspect it more closely. "This was back in the time when they were switching from film to video, and I had one of the first ENG cameras around," the thickly built Schaffel explained. "It was a huge thing with a separate flash for video, and Michael was fascinated by it. He asked, 'Can I look at your camera?' and I was like, 'This can't be real.' He asked, 'Can I pick it up?' and I said sure, but I was a little concerned, because this was one big-ass camera, very heavy. But he just reached over and lifted the camera up like it was made of cardboard. I was amazed by his strength." As Jackson began to fiddle with the camera's lens, Schaffel could hear people shouting "Michael!" outside the door, calling out to the star that he needed to make a costume change. "I don't think Michael even heard them," Schaffel said. "Finally, he says, 'We have another show to do here. Can I call you later and use the camera, try it out?' I said sure, and gave him my number, thinking I'd never hear back. But the next day I get a call asking if I can come by the hotel where the Jacksons were staying. Michael was that interested."

The two ran into each other again in the mid-1990s at a fund-raiser for the AIDS research foundation amfAR in Beverly Hills. "Michael points to me and says, 'You were the guy with the camera,'" Schaffel remembered. "He didn't know my name, but he knew my face." He and Jackson didn't have their first real conversation, though, until the year 2000, when they met at the home of the famous dermatologist they shared, Arnold Klein, a friend of Schaffel's who became a significant figure in Michael's life over the years, involved in aspects of the entertainer's life that ranged from financial management to the conception of his two oldest children. "Michael was staying at Klein's home after a procedure," Schaffel remembered. "He used to stay at Arnie's house quite a bit." The two spent most of that evening in conversation. "Michael testified later that he liked Marc's enthusiasm and ideas," Schaffel's attorney Howard King would recall.

"He especially liked that these ideas didn't involve singing and dancing. Michael was intent on finding a way to make money that did not involve being onstage or in a studio."

Jackson's longtime publicist, Bob Jones, recalled that Schaffel had appeared on the scene at almost the very moment when the people who had done Michael's film work over the past several years were breaking with him amid complaints that they weren't being paid. Boasting of his background in film production and flashing a bank account that approached eight figures, Schaffel pledged to organize Michael's various film and video projects through a company the two formed, called Neverland Valley Entertainment. There was talk of building a movie studio at the ranch, of making short films, perhaps producing an animated television series. But Schaffel was swiftly drawn into the preparations for Jackson's "30th Anniversary" concerts, which were scheduled to take place on September 7 and 10, 2001, at New York City's Madison Square Garden.

Pulling together a list of performers Jackson considered worthy of the event had proven a complex task, but Schaffel quickly demonstrated he could contribute. Working as Jackson's liaison with concert producer David Gest and writing a series of checks drawn on his own accounts to cover Michael's cash flow problems, Schaffel helped secure the participation of many of the stars who would perform at the two concerts. Schaffel's talent for massaging Michael's ego would prove as much of an asset to the anniversary concerts project as his organizational abilities. When Michael began delaying his arrival in New York, "David was calling and screaming at me like it was my responsibility," Schaffel remembered. "'You gotta get him on a plane and get him here!' David wanted him to have five days of rehearsal and Michael said, 'I don't need that. I'll do one or two days.' Michael wanted to go on a private jet, and David was trying to get him to fly commercial because they got comp seats on American Airlines. So Michael just waited him out. See, Michael just really wasn't that psyched up to do the show. I mean, he thought it was neat, but . . . when something is Michael's idea, he's in it 110 percent. If it's not his idea, if it's something he's *got* to do, he feels it's work, and he starts dragging his feet."

Still, when word came that, despite the highest prices in the history of show business, tickets for the two Madison Square Garden shows had sold out within five hours, Michael wept with gratitude. CBS agreed to pay a licensing fee in the seven figures for the rights to edit the concert footage into a two-hour TV special and Jackson was now guaranteed a take of $7.5 million for his appearance at the two concerts, money Michael desperately

needed. VH1 would later calculate that for the time the entertainer actually spent onstage, his pay totaled $150,000 per minute.

Jackson at the time was living on what he described as a "restrictive"
budget that had been imposed on him by his record company, Sony, and
his main creditor, Bank of America. He complained constantly that because
of his huge debt he had no ready access to his enormous wealth. "It was
not difficult at that time for Marc to withdraw as much as a million dollars from his bank account," King explained, "so he began to make cash
advances to Michael. Generally, they were paid back a short time later,
when other funds of Michael's came in." The first sum Schaffel handed
over was $70,000, in July 2001, to pay for the shopping excursion with
which Michael celebrated the news that he was about to receive a $2
million loan advance to create a charity record. When Michael said he
"needed" something, Schaffel understood by then, he was not speaking of
necessity as most people understood it, but rather about "a psychological
state that he required in order to function."

That first cash advance was repaid in short order, Schaffel recalled.
Money was constantly flowing to Michael from sources that were spread all
over the globe. He didn't keep a bank account for fear that some creditor
might try to attach it, so all payments were made in cash. One of Schaffel's
main duties soon became acting as, literally, Michael Jackson's bag man.
"Michael's other advisors, associates, business partners, patrons—whatever
they were—would get him money by actually transmitting the payment to
Marc, who would deliver it to Michael in cash," King explained. Schaffel
had made the first such delivery to Michael in a paper sack from an Arby's
fast food restaurant. Michael thought that was hilarious and began referring to the money coming his way either through or from Marc as French
fries. "They'd have conversations where Michael would say, 'Bring me some
fries, will you? And supersize it,'" King recalled.

A month after handing over $70,000, Schaffel wrote a check for
$625,680.49 to cure a default on Michael's Bank of America line of credit.
Repayment continued to flow into his bank accounts, but the sums were
not exactly congruent with what he was paying out. Still, Michael's business manager said the debts would all be evened out over time and Schaffel
had no reason to doubt it. "Marc not only adored Michael, he trusted him
completely," King explained. Schaffel made two more French fry deliveries to Jackson in August 2001, filling one bag with $100,000 in cash that
Michael wanted to shop for antiques, and another with $46,075 that
Michael needed to pay for appraisals of a $30 million mansion on Sunset

Boulevard in Beverly Hills, a property Jackson insisted he could afford to purchase after learning that the Madison Square Garden concerts had sold out. In early September, shortly before the concerts, Schaffel made two more payments, the first a relatively minor sum of $23,287 for the supposedly "free" concert tickets that Michael had promised to his personal guests for the anniversary concerts. The tickets turned out to not be free after all, and to avoid the embarrassment of explaining this to friends and family, Michael paid for them out of his own—that is, Marc's—pocket. The second payment was for $1 million that Michael needed for his "best friend," Marlon Brando, who demanded that sum in exchange for agreeing to make a videotaped "humanitarian speech" to be shown during the first of the two concerts. Michael's other advisors all argued that it was ridiculous to pay Brando so much for a speech no one wanted to hear, but Michael insisted. "Marlon is a god," he said. The naysayers would be proven right when, less than two minutes into the great actor's incoherent comments, the crowd started booing and didn't stop until Brando did. Well, it was only a million dollars, Michael said, not that much money, really.

In the days immediately before the concerts, Schaffel gave Jackson $380,395 to pay for a pair of customized automobiles he wanted, a Bentley Arnage and a Lincoln Navigator, as well as a check to cover the interest on the $2 million loan Michael had taken out to finance the charity record.

By this point he had received reimbursements of $1,750,000, Schaffel recalled, but that amount didn't quite cover the $2.5 million he had paid out. The remaining debt was secured, though, because Michael had signed over the rights to "What More Can I Give?" Schaffel agreed with those who said it was the best song Jackson had delivered in years, with a soaring melody and a lyric that was as moving as any Jackson had ever written. By the beginning of September, the two of them were already talking about using it to produce a charity record that would rival the success of Michael's "We Are the World" project back in 1985. Survivors of the next major humanitarian catastrophe would be the beneficiaries.

The 9/11 terrorist attacks took place just hours after Jackson finished his "Billie Jean"/"Black or White"/"Beat It" medley at the end of the second anniversary concert. Up to that moment, Michael had imagined that the ugliest part of his stay in New York would be the nasty argument he had gotten into with Corey Feldman backstage during the first concert over Feldman's plans to write a book about their relationship. When he was awakened after only an hour or two of sleep in his suite at the Plaza Athenee just in time to watch the World Trade Center towers collapse,

"Michael was completely freaked out," Schaffel recalled. "He thought there were terrorists loose in New York and he wanted to get his kids out immediately. We had a lot of police working as security at the hotel he was at, and they helped us get across the Hudson River to New Jersey before the bridges and tunnels were closed." The next day, when Michael insisted he needed $500,000 in case he and the children were forced to "go underground," Schaffel drove to a bank and withdrew exactly that amount in cash. Jackson holed up for two days in New Jersey, then summoned Schaffel and the rest of his entourage to White Plains, New York, where the airport was about to reopen for a few hours. Sony arranged for a private jet at one of the hangars. Michael was en route from New Jersey when a new problem developed. The actor Mark Wahlberg had been shooting a movie nearby and was at the White Plains airport also, with *his* entourage, trying to get on the same plane. "So we had this big spat over who had priority," Schaffel recalled. The two camps stood on the tarmac shouting at one another until Sony ruled that Michael Jackson was the ranking celebrity. Wahlberg was informed that he would have to wait until another jet could be located, and he stormed off. "But then at the last second Michael decided he didn't want to fly," Schaffel recalled. "He said he was going to go back to California by tour bus. So he told the rest of us to just get on the plane and go, before Wahlberg came back." Within minutes a bus had been hired but by the time it got to White Plains, Michael had changed his mind again. He loaded his mother and other relatives on the bus, sent them off toward 287 West, then got Sony to find yet another private jet, and flew back to Santa Barbara aboard that plane with Grace and his kids plus a pair of bodyguards.

When they reconnected back in California, Jackson and Schaffel immediately began to talk about using "What More Can I Give?" to raise money for the families of those who had died in the terrorist attacks. In October, Schaffel rented a suite at the Beverly Hills Hotel, where he met with senior executives of the McDonald's restaurant chain to discuss the "What More Can I Give?" charity record idea. It had taken only a couple of hours to strike a $20 million deal, after McDonald's execs calculated they could sell at least five million copies of the record through their U.S. outlets alone.

Schaffel felt like he was surfing a tidal wave of good fortune during those days, when he worked as Michael's main intermediary in setting up the recording sessions at which the likes of Beyoncé Knowles, Ricky Martin, Mariah Carey, Carlos Santana, Reba McEntire, and Tom Petty contributed their voices and instruments to the "What More Can I Give?" project. It was the most fabulous experience of Marc's life. He had gotten everything on videotape and couldn't wait for the world to see Celine Dion after her first performances of "What More Can I Give?", cheeks bathed in tears as she explained how much it meant to her to sing with Michael Jackson. One great talent after another had reacted similarly. The immensity of it was breathtaking. "Michael was so excited about the project," Schaffel recalled. "I didn't have to beg him to get to the studio, he would come in on his own. He really, really, really wanted to make it happen. He was like a different person when he was like that. He was convinced, and so was I, and so was everyone else, that we had two number one hits here, the English version and the Spanish version, which is actually the better of the two."

Then things began to unravel, as Schaffel would learn they tended to do in the decaying orbit of Michael Jackson. On October 13 the *New York Post* printed the first story about the "What More Can I Give?" deal. McDonald's was startled, then overwhelmed, by the bombardment of complaints from American moms outraged that a so-called family-food chain would consider distributing the music of a suspected pedophile. McDonald's executives phoned Schaffel two days later to say they were backing out of the deal.

It would get worse. Several of Jackson's financial advisors were upset by their discovery that Schaffel had obtained the rights to "What More Can I Give?" and they contacted John Branca, Michael's longtime attorney. Branca had been a recurring figure in Jackson's business affairs for more than twenty years, negotiating many of the entertainer's most lucrative contracts. At times, he was Michael's closest advisor. Relations between the entertainer and the lawyer had been cooling again recently, as Michael became increasingly suspicious that Branca was using him to profit from other business deals. The attorney imagined that Marc Schaffel might be part of a growing problem with his prize client. Branca, as well connected as anyone in the entertainment industry, needed only a few days to determine that Schaffel had made most of his fortune as a gay pornographer, producing and directing films with titles like *Cock Tales* and *The Man with the Golden Rod*, as well as operating several pornographic Internet sites. The attorney promptly phoned Jackson and set up a meeting at which he showed him a tape of Schaffel directing a gay sex scene. Soon after, Schaffel received a letter informing him that his contract with Michael Jackson was being terminated because "information about Mr. Schaffel's background, previously unknown to Mr. Jackson, has just been discovered."

"That was all complete bullshit," Schaffel said. "Everybody knew about my past, including Michael. At Arnie Klein's house, Michael and Carrie Fisher and Arnie all made jokes about it, in front of many people. [Sony Music Group CEO] Tommy Mottola knew, too. He brought Usher to the studio to sing on 'What More Can I Give?' and Tommy was sitting there joking with me about some girl in the porn business he knew, to see if I knew her, too. But now suddenly everyone is acting like they're completely shocked."

He knew Michael had no issue with his homosexuality, Schaffel said, or with Arnold Klein's, or with anyone else's. Still it was a relief, Schaffel admitted, when Michael phoned him a few days after the termination letter was sent and said, "Don't worry, Marc, this will blow over. Just go with the flow."

Unfortunately for Schaffel, Branca and other Jackson advisors were actively lobbying Sony to kill the charity project by refusing permission for any of its stars to appear on the record—at least until Michael was able to recover his rights to the song. "And then Sony and Tommy Mottola became concerned that if they let us release 'What More Can I Give?' Michael wouldn't finish *Invincible*," Schaffel explained. "And he *was* dragging his feet about getting that album done. We would go to New York to record, then to Miami, then to Virginia. We would go here and we would go there. And Sony was paying all the bills. What it all came down to was that Michael wasn't into it. Then when we started on 'What More Can I Give?' Michael was one hundred percent into that and zero percent into *Invincible*. Sony had tens of millions invested in their record, so they decided to shelve ours." To try to ensure that the song stayed on the shelf, Sony put out the bogus story that "What More Can I Give?" had been considered "too weak" for inclusion on *Invincible*.

Schaffel pressed on, attempting to stage a concert in Washington, D.C., to raise money for the families of the 9/11 Pentagon victims that would be filmed as a video for "What More Can I Give?" Michael failed to show up. On June 13, 2002, Schaffel faxed a letter to the Japanese chairman of Sony Corporation, Nobuyuki Idei, begging Idei to either release the single or permit its release through an alternative distributor. "It would be a tragedy almost as great as the first one to let corporate greed or politics stop the movement of people working together in the healing process," Schaffel had written. He received no answer. Schaffel persisted, selling various rights in the "What More Can I Give?" project to an assortment of partners, contingent upon Michael Jackson's participation, and waited for a chance at rapprochement.

He saw that opportunity in the debacle that engulfed Michael in the months after the late 2001 release of the long-delayed *Invincible*. Sony had recognized within two weeks that *Invincible* was going to be the first full-fledged flop of the singer's career. Like all Michael Jackson releases, the new album had gone straight to the top of the charts, but the 363,000 copies it sold in that first week was still less than a fifth of the 1.9 million units that 'N Sync's *Celebrity* sold in the first seven days of its release that same year. And *Invincible*'s sales had dropped off precipitously. Sony was estimating that it would sell only two million copies of the album in the United States, less than a tenth of what *Thriller* had done, and only three million copies overseas, less than a fifth of the number *Dangerous* had racked up. Reviews of the album ranged from lackluster to dismissive. Only one single from *Invincible*, "You Rock My World," reached even the top ten in the United States. Mottola and Sony believed that Jackson's refusal to support his new album with a world tour had doomed *Invincible* internationally. The company's executives also complained that Jackson had failed to show up at a series of promotional appearances both in the United States and abroad.

"There *were* a lot of events scheduled," Schaffel recalled, "and all of a sudden Michael didn't want to do them. That pissed off Tommy, who thought it was all because of 'What More Can I Give?' And a lot of it was. Michael wanted them to use 'What More Can I Give?' to promote *Invincible*, but Sony thought, 'You'll sell millions of copies of your record but hardly any of ours.'"

Sony was mortified by reports that it had spent $51 million on the production and promotion of an album that was selling so poorly. In early 2002, an unnamed company executive told the *New York Daily News*, "Charges of pedophilia have really spooked a lot of American record buyers." Within days, Jackson and his record company were locked in a battle that would become both public and vicious.

The opening volley had been fired before the album's release, when Jackson demanded that Sony renegotiate his contract. Michael wanted possession of his master recording catalog within three years rather than the seven specified in the current agreement. Also, he asked that Sony throw another $8 million behind *Invincible*, with most of that money going to pay for the album's third video. After Sony refused both requests, Jackson contacted his friend, songwriter Carol Bayer Sager, to ask if her husband Bob Daly, the former head of Warner Bros., would investigate whether the record label was cheating him. When Daly reported back that he saw no evidence of this, Jackson not only cut off contact with Bayer Sager and her husband, but proceeded to make what was perhaps the biggest miscalculation of his musical career—accusing Tommy Mottola of being biased against black entertainers.

Al Sharpton was with Jackson when he showed up outside Sony's New York offices in July 2002 surrounded by a chanting crowd bused in from Harlem, waving photographs of Mottola drawn with horns and a pitchfork. Encouraged by Johnnie Cochran, the former O. J. Simpson attorney who represented Jackson during the Jordan Chandler affair, European fans had been bombarding Sony's corporate offices with faxed sheets of black paper in a campaign coordinated to support the racism charge. Speaking to the media assembled outside Sony's offices on Madison Avenue, Jackson not only described Mottola as "very, very devilish," but branded the entire music business as "racist," and announced that he intended to form a black artists union to combat discrimination. Michael was furious when Sharpton and Jesse Jackson, who had been egging him on for weeks, began to backpedal. Sharpton actually told the assembled media that he had never known Tommy Mottola to be anything but sympathetic to black causes. By the next day, the backlash against Michael Jackson throughout the entertainment industry was ferocious. Almost instantaneously, Michael found himself despised by the people whose support he needed most.

Schaffel chose that moment to speak up for his estranged friend, telling the *Los Angeles Times*, "If you ask me, I think there are people who don't want to see Michael on top." Some of those people were at Sony, Schaffel suggested, and had been behind the scuttling of the "What More Can I Give?" project, because they knew it "would paint him in a different light than how they want him to be seen. They don't want Michael to succeed. And they're using my background as an excuse." Jackson, who had almost no one else defending him publicly at that moment, was so grateful that he immediately brought Schaffel back on board. In what was for Schaffel a delicious bit of irony (and for John Branca no mere coincidence), Marc's return to the fold would coincide precisely with Michael's decision that he was done with his longtime attorney. Branca's animus toward Schaffel afterward was considerable, but this bit of palace intrigue had actually been wrought by Michael's new German managers, Ronald Konitzer and Dieter Wiesner. "Dieter and Ronald had brought in an outside auditing firm that did a complete examination," Schaffel recalled, "and the paperwork Michael was shown attacked Branca for his relationships with Sony and Tommy Mottola."

The paperwork was a dossier that had been prepared by the Manhattan-based corporate espionage firm Interfor, Inc. The company's director, an

Israeli émigré named Juval Aviv, was regarded as a dubious character in many quarters. *The Village Voice* had once published an article about him under the headline "Secret Agent Schmuck," debunking Aviv's reported claims that he had been the lead assassin of Israel's state intelligence service, Mossad, in avenging the massacre of Jewish athletes at the Olympic village during the 1972 Summer Olympic Games in Munich. Nevertheless, rightly or wrongly, Michael believed the claims in the Interfor report that Branca and Mottola had been involved in transferring funds that belonged to him into offshore accounts at Caribbean banks. It fit with suspicions he had been harboring for years about Branca's too-cozy relationship with Sony. "Michael hated all lawyers anyway, including his own, and he made the decision that Branca should be fired," recalled Schaffel, who was assigned to facilitate Branca's dismissal, and then to replace Jackson's longtime attorney with David LeGrand, the same Las Vegas lawyer who had contracted the Interfor report.

As the long process of Branca's dismissal unfolded, Michael invited Marc to accompany him on a trip to Berlin in October 2002. Jackson was traveling to Germany to be honored at the country's most prestigious entertainment awards ceremony, the Bambis, with a special Millennium prize that recognized him as the world's "greatest living pop icon."

The celebratory trip swiftly turned into a nightmare. First, while being serenaded by the huge crowd of fans gathered outside his Berlin hotel, the Adlon, Michael had impulsively displayed his nine-month-old third child, Prince Michael Joseph Jackson II, by dangling the infant over the balcony railing of his third-floor suite. The images of him holding a baby in a blue jumpsuit, its head covered by a towel as its bare feet kicked the air forty feet above a cobblestone sidewalk, shocked and outraged parents worldwide. Child advocacy groups seized the opportunity to join in an orgy of public castigation. The British tabloids that had, for nearly two decades, called the star "Wacko Jacko" now were delighted to change that to "Mad Bad Dad." Several commentators in Germany suggested that perhaps Michael Jackson should face criminal charges. Michael, who had never before been deplored on this scale, was forced to issue the first public apology that he had ever offered for his erratic behavior: "I made a terrible mistake. I got caught up in the excitement of the moment. I would never intentionally endanger the lives of my children." Later, he even attempted to explain for the first time how his youngest child had become known as "Blanket." It was derived from an expression he used with his family and his employees, Michael told a reporter: "I say, 'You should blanket me or you should blanket her,' meaning a blanket is like a blessing. It's a way of showing love and caring."

Jackson was subdued at the Bambi Awards ceremony and when he was called to the stage to pose with a fellow recipient, actress Halle Berry, he could barely whisper the words, *"Berlin, ich liebe dich"*—"Berlin, I love you." News reports suggested that the "painfully shy" performance was the result of his humiliation and remorse over the baby-dangling incident. What the journalists didn't know was that, shortly before Jackson took the stage, Schaffel had alerted him that something far worse was coming his way from across the English Channel.

To support the career comeback he hoped to launch with *Invincible*, Jackson had agreed to cooperate with a documentary by Martin Bashir, a British journalist to whom he had been introduced by their mutual friend, psychic spoon bender Uri Geller. Bashir seduced Michael, according to Tom Mesereau, among others, by boasting that he had been a confidant of the late Princess Diana. "Michael wanted to hear all of Bashir's Diana stories," Geller recalled. Jackson had tried for years, unsuccessfully, to form a relationship with Diana. She and Jacqueline Kennedy Onassis, in fact, were just about the only two famous people he ever met who chose to keep him at arm's length, which had only deepened his fascination with each of them. Bashir's Diana anecdotes had persuaded Jackson to consent to what was about to become the biggest public relations catastrophe of his life.

"Bashir told so many stories about her, and Michael was completely charmed," Dieter Wiesner recalled. "But then I heard from people in the UK that Bashir wasn't Diana's friend at all, that she felt he had tricked her into talking about her affair, and that she felt used by him—as Michael did later. So I was worried."

Footage of Bashir's documentary *Living with Michael Jackson* had gotten loose in London, and friends were phoning from England, Schaffel said, to warn him that Michael was about to be painted as a freakish pervert. After reading transcripts of the documentary's rough cut, "Marc knew what a disaster this was going to be," Wiesner remembered, "and Michael could see it in his eyes. After that I said, 'Michael, this is going to be terrible.' And he didn't believe me. He said, 'Dieter, Dieter, please. I don't think so. Don't think bad.'"

Almost a month passed before they flew back to Florida, where Bashir was supposed to personally screen the documentary for Jackson. "Michael was still waiting for him, because he should have the last approval," Wiesner remembered. "More people were calling from UK, telling me this is going to be a bad thing. Then Bashir shows up with the whole camera team. He wanted to show Michael everything, but he wanted to have his reaction on tape, and I knew that would be used against Michael also."

Bashir had arrived for what was to be their final interview shortly after the first of the year. Within seconds of sitting down with the star, the formerly unctuous director began to confront Michael with a series of acid-laced questions about his physical transformation. It was a particularly sensitive subject for Jackson at that moment in his life. Less than a year earlier, Michael had been preparing to shoot a video for the *Invincible* album when his then-manager, Trudy Green, sent someone to the star's trailer to make a mold of his face. "She told Michael it was something for the makeup artist to use," Schaffel remembered. "But Michael wanted me to ask her what it was really about. And Trudy told me, 'Well, you know, he's not looking too good right now, and we think we should make this mask for him to wear in this video.' When Michael found out Trudy had said this, he just broke down and sobbed. It was one of only two times I ever saw him do that. I mean he was just heartbroken." Michael stopped production of the video immediately, then fired Green, replacing her a few days later with "the Germans," Wiesner and Konitzer. He was still distraught about the incident, though, which perhaps explained why he blatantly lied to Bashir about the extent of his plastic surgery, insisting there had been only a couple of operations on his nose, nothing more.

Bashir ramped up Jackson's discomfort with an observation that his two oldest children, Prince and Paris, claimed they had no mother, then got Michael to contradict his earlier statement that the mother of his third child was someone with whom he had a relationship by admitting that Blanket was born to a surrogate. When Bashir discussed the subject of children who regularly spent the night at Neverland, often in Jackson's own bedroom, the end was at hand. After admitting on camera that the ill or disadvantaged children he invited to stay on the ranch often slept in his bed (while he slept on the floor) Jackson grew agitated as Bashir pressed the subject. At first he said it was natural that family friends like Macaulay and Kieran Culkin would sleep in his bed; then he blurted out that "many children" had slept in the same bed with him. In his denial that there was any sexual motivation for this, Jackson uttered a line that would be replayed in countless news broadcasts: He told Bashir, "The most loving thing to do is to share your bed with someone."

Bashir returned to the UK "without letting Michael see a thing," Wiesner recalled. Jackson was still in Florida when *Living with Michael*

Jackson—introduced by Barbara Walters—was broadcast by ABC on February 6, 2003. "I was sitting with Michael on his bed watching it," Dieter Wiesner recalled. "And he just broke down like I never saw before. He couldn't believe that something like this was coming up again. He looked like he was gonna die. He couldn't talk. He couldn't make a word come out."

The Bashir documentary "rocked his world," said Santa Barbara County district attorney Tom Sneddon, who by the end of the year would ask a grand jury to indict Jackson on ten felony charges of child sexual abuse. After the documentary aired, Michael was so distraught that he took to his bed—alone—for days. Publicity-seeking Los Angeles attorney Gloria Allred and her associate, Beverly Hills psychiatrist Carole Lieberman, promptly filed nearly identical complaints with the Department of Social Services to challenge Jackson's custody of his children.

With Jackson incapacitated, Schaffel took charge of damage control. The former pornographer swiftly demonstrated his media savvy by assembling a collection of videotapes about Bashir's time with Michael Jackson that the British director did *not* control. Before agreeing to cooperate with Bashir, Jackson had insisted that he would have his own camera crew on location to shoot Bashir shooting him. "Despite how he's portrayed," Tom Mesereau observed, "Michael is no fool. He's actually one of the most intelligent people you'll ever meet. And he knew that he should have his own record of what was transpiring during those Bashir interviews. It was probably one of the smartest decisions he ever made."

How smart wouldn't be clear until almost two years later, when Jackson was in the midst of his criminal trial. On the Jackson tapes, Bashir was seen lavishing praise on Michael as both a father and a humanitarian, saying at one point that he had been moved to tears by his subject's sensitive approach to parenting and was even more touched by Michael's kindness to seriously ill and underprivileged children. A juxtaposition of those remarks with Bashir's condemnation of Jackson in his ABC documentary as "dangerous" to children, Schaffel recognized, would be devastating.

Schaffel's own stroke of genius was to set up interviews with a young cancer patient named Gavin Arvizo whose relationship with Michael Jackson had become the centerpiece of the Bashir documentary. A child psychiatrist and a child welfare worker were recruited to interview the boy, his mother, and his two siblings, all of whom defended Jackson vehemently. Gavin himself insisted on camera that he had never been touched inappropriately and that Michael was "completely innocent." His sister Davellin and brother Star supported their brother by saying that during sleepovers at Neverland they always spent the night in Michael's bed while he slept on the floor nearby. Their mother Janet Arvizo told the interviewers, "The relationship that Michael has with my children is a beautiful, loving, father-son and father-daughter one," and threatened to take legal action against Bashir. Schaffel also delivered an interview with Debbie Rowe, the much-maligned mother of Michael's two oldest children, whose generous assessment of her ex-husband's character stood in marked contrast to what was being reported about their relationship in the media.

Though Schaffel was not able to include the interviews with the Arvizo family in what he was calling "the rebuttal video" (the cameraman who had shot those tapes was refusing to release them, claiming he had not been paid—at least not enough), executives at ABC's rival networks were wowed by what they saw. Debunking the Bashir documentary might generate ratings that rivaled or even surpassed those that ABC had garnered. Fox eventually made the highest bid for what it would title *Michael Jackson Take Two: The Footage You Were Never Meant to See* and broadcast "the retaliatory special," as *People* magazine called it, on February 23, less than three weeks after ABC aired the Bashir documentary. The Fox special not only stemmed much of the condemnation coming Michael's way, but made him millions of dollars at a time when, as one associate put it, "he was dead broke on a cash basis."

Schaffel put together a deal with Fox for a second documentary, this one titled *Michael Jackson's Home Movies*, that would be broadcast in April, featuring family and friends such as Liz Taylor describing the sweetly naive man-child they knew and loved. Schaffel's spreadsheet showed that Jackson would earn at least $15 million from the two videos, and perhaps as much as $20 million. Under the terms of their agreement, 20 percent of that money was Schaffel's.

While waiting for the checks to arrive from New York and points east, Schaffel resumed his cash advances to Jackson. The first was made in February when Michael wanted to celebrate the Fox deal with a shopping spree. The paper bag he gave Michael was filled with $340,000 in cash, Schaffel said, because he knew how pent up Michael was, and knew also that nothing had a more calming effect on him than making an extravagant purchase. Schaffel gave Jackson another $100,000 for a shopping spree in March, then wrote Michael a check for $1 million in April. He needed $638,000 to pay for a piece of jewelry that Liz Taylor was demanding in exchange for agreeing to the use of an interview with her in the *Home Movies* video, Michael had explained, and another $250,000 that his mother Katherine insisted upon for *her* appearance in the video. The remainder was required to make the deposit on a new Rolls-Royce Phantom that he absolutely had to have. A week later, Schaffel gave Jackson an additional $130,000 to help him pay off the Rolls.

Of course it all sounded strange to outsiders when their relationship spilled into the courts four years later, Schaffel would say, but you had to understand the extraordinary character of Michael Jackson. Michael's over-whelming charisma was combined with a detachment from conventional reality that made him at once enormously powerful and utterly helpless. During a trip to Las Vegas in 2003 they had checked into adjoining suites at the Mandarin Oriental, then headed to a business meeting in a conference room downstairs. Schaffel recalled: "After the meeting, I had to go to the bathroom, so I told Michael, 'Just wait here a second.' But, of course, Michael doesn't want to wait, so he decides go back to his room on his own. But he doesn't remember the room number or the floor or anything. He probably doesn't even know what city we're in. So he just walks up some stairs and starts knocking on doors, waiting for the bodyguards to open one." As he raced to catch up, Schaffel remembered, he could see the hallway filling with excited people who were following Michael Jackson down the hallway. "I mean, the entire hotel is in an uproar," Schaffel recalled, "and Michael just keeps moving from door to door, knocking on each one, getting more and more frantic to escape the crowd gathering behind him. I finally run up to him and say, 'Michael, my God, stop!' Then I have to lead him to the elevator, with all these people still following us, and get him upstairs. The point is, Michael would have just kept going until somebody showed up to take care of him. Like a lot of people, I wanted to be the one."

Schaffel still trusted Michael implicitly but by May 2003 he was begin-ning to grow antsy about the wait to be paid his share of the profits from the sale of the two videos. On top of that, repayment of the money he had advanced to Michael was arriving behind schedule. Not wanting to bother the star with such petty concerns, Schaffel took them to Jackson's attorneys. The lawyers at first said the money was coming in from Fox more slowly than anticipated and that nothing had been received so far from foreign distributors and DVD sales. When Schaffel pressed, saying he knew that Michael had received at least $9 million to date, the attorneys answered that Michael had other debts to pay and that they weren't sure Schaffel had a valid contract to collect 20 percent of the video money anyway. Eventually, an agreement was struck that would pay Schaffel $1.5 million for his work on the videos: a $500,000 payment immediately, followed by ten installments of $50,000 each. Less than a month after Schaffel received that first half-million, though, Michael complained that his funds were already depleted, that creditors were hounding him, and that Bank of America was gouging him with a ridiculous rate of interest. What Michael "needed," Schaffel knew, was to spend money; he gave Michael another $250,000 to go antique shopping in Beverly Hills. "Bear in mind that Marc was still receiving repayments and the installments he had been promised from the sale of the videos," King would explain. "He understood Michael's situation as a simple cash flow problem."

"I knew better than anyone how much money was coming Michael's way, just from the deals I made for him," Schaffel said. "Besides the two videos I had done for him, I had signed a deal with one of the broadcast networks to do a one-time concert of all his hit songs that would pay $15.5 million. Plus, I had another deal for Michael to do his own television reality show. This was before the explosion of reality shows. We had an oral agreement with a network to do this show that was basically just about his everyday life. And that was going to be worth $5 million per episode, with the foreign rights and everything. I knew that could become a real money train. So the point is, I wasn't worried about getting my money back, and then some."

Schaffel gave Jackson another $100,000 for a shopping spree in August. Periodic repayments continued to be deposited in his bank account, and the $50,000 installment payments for his work on the rebuttal videos were arriving on schedule. On September 18, 2003, Schaffel recalled, Michael's personal assistant Evvy Tavasci phoned to say that Michael needed $500,000, half of which would go to a Beverly Hills antique dealer who was threatening to sue him for nonpayment. Marc delivered another supersize order of French fries.

The late autumn of 2003 was shaping up as a turning point in Jackson's life and career. Michael finally negotiated a break with Sony by agreeing to release a series of compilation albums. The first was to be called *Number Ones* and would include every song of his that had hit the top of the charts. Sony had also agreed to finance a series of music videos—Michael insisted they be called "short films"—that would accompany the record's release in November 2003. As production for the first of those short films geared up, Schaffel and Wiesner were negotiating with Peter Morton, founder of the Hard Rock Cafe franchise, to do a show for him in Las Vegas sometime the following year. The real excitement in the Jackson camp, though, surrounded the six-month trip combining work and vacation that Michael planned to begin on November 22. He and his core entourage—Grace and the kids,

Schaffel, Wiesner, and Michael's publicist Stuart Backerman—would begin by heading to Europe, where, between scheduled events in Germany, Austria, and France, Michael planned to spend the holidays at Elizabeth Taylor's Chalet Ariel in Gstaad, Switzerland. From there, he would be heading to South Africa to participate in the Nelson Mandela Tribute that U2's Bono was organizing, then flying to Brazil. City officials in Rio de Janeiro had given Jackson permission to stage the first nonathletic event they had allowed in years on the grass floor of Maracaña Stadium, a nighttime performance of "One More Chance" in which Michael would be surrounded by two hundred thousand people holding lighted candles. Rio officials also wanted Michael to perform a concert on the beach for an audience they estimated would number two million people, "and we were negotiating the terms of that even as we prepared to leave for Europe," Schaffel recalled.

Schaffel, Wiesner, and Backerman were all with Michael at the Mirage in Las Vegas during the third week of November, spending hours every day on the phone as they prepared for Michael's departure, completely unaware that they were being listened to the entire time by deputies from the Santa Barbara County sheriff's department. "They knew that Stuart and I would be leaving two days ahead of Michael to help set things up in Europe," Schaffel said. "They probably even knew what had happened on the video with the Cascio kids."

Jackson had come to Vegas accompanied by Eddie and Marie Nicole Cascio, the younger siblings of his longtime aide Frank Cascio. The family had been a big part of Michael's life since the late eighties when he had met patriarch Dominic Cascio at the Palace Hotel in New York, where Cascio was working as concierge to the luxury suites. The Cascios were the sort of big-hearted, full-throated Italians Michael had been drawn to for as long as he could remember. He had fallen in love with the entire clan, recognizing them as the close-knit, loving family he had always wished he came from. The Cascios responded in kind, enveloping Michael in a rare experience of human connection that was at least slightly independent of his celebrity. Dominic and his wife, Connie, allowed Frank and Eddie to travel with Michael from the ages of thirteen and nine. Over the years Frank had worked for Michael in a variety of capacities, ranging from roadie to personal assistant, both on tour and at Neverland Ranch. Eddie and Marie Nicole had visited Neverland often as well, sometimes with their parents, sometimes not.

"There was a level of trust with the Cascios that I don't think Michael had with anyone else," Schaffel recalled. "They were *his family*." It was the Cascios' home in Franklin Lakes, New Jersey, to which Michael had retreated with his children after the 9/11 attacks. "They were who he went to whenever he wanted to feel safe," Schaffel said. With their parents' permission, Eddie and Marie Nicole had been removed from school (to be tutored privately at Michael's expense) while they learned the dance routines that Michael had planned for the first video he would shoot for *Number Ones*.

"Michael promised the Cascio kids they would dance with him in the video," Schaffel recalled. "The two of them worked so hard and were so excited about it. But after we met with the director and looked at the costumes and stuff, Michael said, 'Ooh, I don't know.' He thought the whole idea lacked originality. He dragged Dieter and I into the trailer and said, 'I can't do this.' We knew why—the director sucked. But then Michael said, 'All right, I'll just get it done and make Sony happy.' Mainly, though, he didn't want to disappoint the Cascio kids. But when he brought the kids in to dance with him, the director said, 'Who are they?' And Michael said, 'They're going to be dancing with me.' So the director left and he got on the phone with Sony. Then he came back and asked if he could speak to me privately. When we were alone he told me, 'We have a problem. Sony says they don't want Michael in the video with kids.' I said, 'Well, I can tell you that these aren't just dancers. These are what Michael considers his family.' He says, 'Are you going to tell Michael?' I said, 'Why am I telling him this? Sony should be telling him.' So a short time later Tommy or someone from Sony calls, and the next thing I hear, five minutes later, is Michael shouting, 'Marc, come to the trailer right now!' Michael was so distraught. I mean he was bright red, he was pacing around the trailer, and then he just started picking things up and throwing them. And he said, 'I am not doing one other thing if I can't have these kids in the shoot with me. I'm leaving. We're not doing this. Tell everyone they can go home.'"

On November 17, *Number Ones* was released to immediate success. Sony, realizing that the record would sell close to ten million copies worldwide—nearly half of those in the United States—immediately became solicitous, offering to assist Michael in any way it could during his six-month trip abroad. Things looked bright again.

"We were all still at the Mirage in Vegas," Schaffel recalled. "I was in one of the penthouse suites, and Michael was in one of the villas down below. We were having a great time. We did an autograph signing at this novelty store at the Aladdin called the Art of Music, and we did the Radio Music Awards, which was where 'What More Can I Give?' was played in public for the first time. The crowd loved it. Michael was really happy." Then, just as the entourage was preparing to leave for Europe, "the shit hit the fan," Schaffel recalled.

On the morning of November 18, 2003, the Santa Barbara County sheriff's department staged a massive raid on Neverland Ranch looking for evidence that would support charges of child molestation. A warrant was issued for Michael Jackson's arrest that same day. At the Mirage, "it was absolute chaos," Schaffel remembered. "Michael went nuts. I could hear it even up in my penthouse suite. Michael absolutely destroyed the villa he was in. I mean he threw everything in the place. He broke lamps, he broke furniture, he broke the art on the walls, you name it. He threw things through windows. He made so much noise that the Mirage sent its security, which got into it with Michael's security. It was completely insane. And that, I would say, was the beginning of the end for Michael. I mean, that was the worst I'd ever seen him, by far. No comparison. Michael was a very strong person, very resilient. I'd seen him be upset, seen him cry, but he would bounce right back up. This time there was no bounce back. This time, I saw him break. Not just break down, but *break*. After the scene in the villa he didn't even have the energy to get angry again. I'd have to call it a mental breakdown. He literally just lost it. You could wave your hand in front of him and he couldn't see it. And it wasn't drugs, not at first. The drugs came later, of course."

So did the Nation of Islam. "They arrived on the scene pretty quickly and just took over," Schaffel recalled. "One of Michael's brothers called them. Leonard Muhammad came, and then Louis Farrakhan himself showed up. And they were feeding Michael this line that, 'The Nation will never let anything happen to you. We will protect you.' And Michael was so helpless that he just put him himself in their hands. It was a huge mistake."

Schaffel flew back to LA that night. "When it first came out that they were talking about 'a complainant,' we knew who it would be," Schaffel explained: Gavin Arvizo, the featured child in the Bashir documentary. "I knew I had video of Michael and [Gavin Arvizo] and his family, and I figured there was stuff on it that would help. But meanwhile Michael has to get out of the Mirage. They're calling the cops to throw him out," Schaffel said. Michael and his security staff were in Schaffel's Lincoln Navigator, driving around Las Vegas, being followed by camera crews in satellite trucks, with TV helicopters whirling overhead. It was all over the television, even in LA. "He was like a hunted animal," remembered Schaffel, who found Michael and his entourage a place to stay. Marc had become friends with the owner of the Green Valley Ranch, a hotel and casino resort just south of Las Vegas, in Henderson, while scouting the place as a location for one of Michael's videos. "I called, and the guy was as nice as could be," Schaffel remembered. "He extended every courtesy to Michael for the next three days." Michael phoned him a couple of times from Henderson, but was incapable of conversation, Schaffel recalled. "He still sounded completely broken, completely hollow. All he could say was, 'How can they do this? How can they say this?' I don't know if the Nation was talking to him, or telling him not to talk to me, but he was completely distracted by whatever was going on around him. I had a real sinking feeling."

Grace Rwaramba and Dieter Wiesner phoned later that evening to ask if Schaffel would wire $30,000 in cash because the security guards were threatening to quit for nonpayment of their wages. "You have to send the money to me, not Michael," Grace told him, according to Schaffel, "because Michael will use it to go shopping instead of paying the guards." Schaffel wired the cash but it was the last order of fries he ever delivered to Michael Jackson.

By the end of that week, Jackson was forced to report to Santa Barbara County for arrest. Schaffel would not see him again until almost three years later, in London. Michael did phone him one more time, though, from some place where he was staying in Los Angeles. "He said, 'The Brotherhood'—he always referred to the people from the Nation as the Brotherhood—'the Brotherhood feels that—no offense to you, Marc, I love you very, very much—but the Brotherhood feels that I need to only communicate with other people in the Brotherhood. But it's just temporary, and it's something I need to do because they're going to protect me. Don't take it personally.' I got pretty concerned when he told me what they were telling him. Michael said, 'You know, I'm not going to have a problem.' And I said, 'Why is that?' And he said, 'Because the Brotherhood said that if they indict me, and if they try to find me guilty, that every black person in the country will riot in the streets.' I said, 'Michael, I really think you need to reconsider this advice that you're getting.' But he said good-bye and hung up on me a moment later, and he never called me again."

Dieter Wiesner ran into similar problems with the Nation of Islam. "For the first days, I was still with Michael every day and every night," Wiesner recalled. "I even brought him to the police when he had to be arrested, but then the Nation of Islam took over. Michael was scared and they used that. Leonard Muhammad had complete control of him for a while. They wouldn't let me see him or even speak to him. So I went back to Germany. And Michael called and said, 'Dieter, did you hear from my mouth that you are out?' I said no. And he said, 'You should come back.' So I did. But then Muhammad and his people brought him to different places and wouldn't let me go to Michael. It was worse than Sony. So I went back to Germany again and I didn't get to talk to Michael after that. I was his manager. I had the contracts. But I couldn't even speak to him."

Schaffel bided his time for months while still collecting the $50,000 installment payments he was owed for the rebuttal videos. "Marc honestly thought that Michael was just waiting for the smoke to clear, and that he'd be in touch when he could," Howard King explained. In June 2004, though, Michael's brother Randy Jackson became Michael's new "chief financial advisor," and immediately stopped the payments to Schaffel. By that point, according to Schaffel's accounting, he had received a total of $6,283,875 from Jackson, which left him $2,275,889 short of the $8,559,764 he had given Michael out of his own bank accounts.

"We filed our lawsuit almost reluctantly," King said. "Marc was convinced that Michael didn't know they weren't paying him." Be that as it may, Schaffel demonstrated that he intended to get his money back, whatever it took, in November 2004, when he lodged a $3 million claim against Jackson. The timing was what gave the court filing such a sharp edge: Michael had just been indicted by the grand jury in Santa Barbara. In Schaffel's lawsuit, he charged that "Jackson's frequent excessive use of drugs and alcohol impelled him into irrational demands for large amounts of money and extravagant possessions."

It was King's idea to have Marc go on *Good Morning America* for an interview by Cynthia McFadden during which a series of taped phone messages Michael Jackson had left for Schaffel would be played to the American public. "We were trying to make people aware that Marc wasn't just some guy who passed through Michael Jackson's life in a week," King explained. "And that he was seriously involved with Michael. We had thirty phone messages in all. Most were Michael asking Marc for money. 'Marc, I really need . . .' 'Marc, I really want to buy . . .' Some were very strident, very militant, very contrary to the soft-spoken high-pitched voice we know. 'I'm *insisting* that we must do this. We *must* capture this opportunity.' He sounded a lot more like a high-powered business executive than the meek and mild superstar." The ones ABC preferred were those that had Michael pleading for money. "Hello, Marc, it's Michael," one message began. "Please, please, never let me down. I really like you. I love you . . . Marc,

I really need you to get, um, seven million dollars for me as soon as possible . . . Seven, seven and a half, um, as an advance."

Now that Michael knew he hadn't been paid, Schaffel insisted to King, the money would arrive. There was no reply to Schaffel's TV appearance, though, and all the filing of the lawsuit brought was a cursory denial of the allegations by Jackson's attorneys at the courthouse in Santa Monica where King had positioned the case. "Michael didn't even show up at the first two depositions we scheduled," King recalled. "So we go to court to get an order. Mesereau is there, and suggests to the judge that if we would go to where Michael was at they would pay all the expenses. The judge sends us out into the hallway to talk, and I tell Tom, 'Look, I'm Jewish. I'm not going to Bahrain. But I'll go anywhere in Europe that has a nonstop flight so long as we're talking four first-class tickets so that I can bring an assistant and Marc can bring an assistant. And you guys pay for everything.'"

It was agreed they would meet in London. The "assistant" King brought with him was his wife Lisa. Schaffel's traveling companion was Dieter Wiesner, someone "who adored Michael more than anyone alive, including Marc," as King described him. It was intimidating, King admitted, to step off that elevator at the Dorchester and realize that he was about to depose a person who had an entire floor of one of the world's great hotels all to himself. "They usher us into this absolutely spectacular suite," the attorney recalled, "and I learn that Michael's own suite is right next door. He comes in just a moment later, dressed all nice, and sits at the table, but then begins to complain about the lighting. He doesn't want the sunlight on his skin or in his eyes. So it takes about five minutes to get the drapes adjusted the way he wants, and then we're ready to go." But first Tom Mesereau insisted that Dieter Wiesner could not be in the room. "Dieter has come all the way to London, and the whole way there all he can think about is what it will be like when he finally gets to see Michael again," King said. "I mean, he still loves the guy."

"We knew Wiesner was probably going to file a lawsuit against Michael at some point," Mesereau countered, "so it just wasn't appropriate to have him listening in."

"Dieter had to go down to the lobby and sit there drinking coffee for the next ten hours," King recalled. "It broke his heart." Upstairs, Jackson was cool to Schaffel. "He said hello, but didn't shake Marc's hand," King recalled. Schaffel grew especially glum when Jackson answered a question about his "discovery" that Marc had directed and produced gay porn films. "I was shown a videotape by the lawyer [Branca] and I was shocked," Michael said. "He was in that whole circle, and I didn't know."

"I saw Marc was hurt," King remembered, "and told him, 'It's war, baby.'"

Schaffel had imagined that when the two of them saw each other again, all the good memories would come flooding back and somehow everything would be put right. "We had so many great times together," Schaffel explained. "Michael used to stay at my house in Calabasas all the time. Grace and the bodyguards would come with him, get him set up, then leave, and either Michael by himself or with the kids would stay there alone for days." Michael used to love to stroll over to the Commons, a large mall lined with restaurants, theaters, and shops that was just down the hill from Schaffel's home. He wore disguises, but not the kind that would call attention to himself. "No veil or surgical mask," Schaffel said. "Just a baseball cap he wore with his hair tucked up into it, and sunglasses. Part of why it worked was that no one would expect to see Michael Jackson in a place like this. He would go into that movie theater right over there, all by himself, walk all around here, all by himself. He loved being able to do that."

His favorite memory of having Michael at the house, Schaffel said, was the time he stepped out into the backyard and saw Michael with his head thrust into the shrubbery on the border of the property. "The neighbors below me were having a birthday party for one of their kids and Michael was snooping through the bushes," Schaffel remembered. "All of a sudden I hear some kid scream, 'Hey, Mommy, look, it's Michael Jackson!' And Michael backs away from the bushes like a little kid who's in trouble. I hear the kid still telling his mom it's Michael Jackson. So I look through, and the mom says, 'Oh, no, that's just our neighbor Marc.' Michael laughed for an hour afterward."

It was all business, though, around the table in the suite at the Dorchester. "I don't think [Michael] even looked at Marc," remembered King, who was asking all the questions. He tried to fight it, King said, but found himself being much more impressed by Michael Jackson as a witness than he had anticipated. "Michael is very poised, very charming, very aware of the camera," King recalled. Jackson insisted that he be allowed a break every hour to change his shirt and "refresh." "The guy spent the first three shirt changes knowing nothing," King recalled. "But then I had all these phone messages he'd left, plus all these documents and letters he signed. I will say that Michael, to his credit, said right off the top that if Marc was owed money he should be paid. He said he just didn't know if Marc was owed. And Marc believed him, still believed him. I didn't. I had recognized by then that Michael is *way* smarter than he's made to look in the media. No way he didn't know. Still, he handled the questions really well, and was very witty throughout. I have reading glasses and when I took them off to look at him, he said, 'Howard, I know when you take off the glasses you're *really* serious.' He's very charming, and of course, he's *Michael Jackson*. It affects you."

Mesereau thought King was oblivious to the poignancy of the situation. "The thing that struck me in that deposition, as Marc Schaffel sat across from us, was the sadness in Michael's eyes," the attorney explained. "It really hit me then that Michael went through life knowing that anybody he developed a relationship with was eventually going to sue him. And yet he kept hoping it would turn out differently each time."

During one of the breaks, King's wife pulled him aside and said, "I think you don't want women on that jury." When her husband asked why, Lisa King answered, "The whole time, I felt the need to hug him and be his mother. He looks so sweet and vulnerable sitting there that you want to take care of him."

For King himself, the moment of insight came during the last break of the day. While Michael was off changing his shirt and refreshing himself, the attorney happened to look down at the floor beneath the chair where Michael had been sitting. "And I saw that with his feet he had chewed up that carpet mightily," the attorney recalled. "I mean he had literally dug a hole in it with his heels. And it sort of shocked me. Because all day he had looked as cool and calm and collected as you could imagine. That was absolutely how he appeared on camera. But, like us, the camera had only seen what was above the tabletop. Somehow, Michael had managed to channel this tremendous amount of tension he had in his body into his legs and feet, every last bit of it, so that from the waist up he looked perfectly serene." He stared in wonder at that fist-sized ball of carpet nap beneath Jackson's chair for several moments, King recalled, "and I thought, 'Wow, this guy is good.'"

2

He had been performing almost as long as he had been alive. Michael Joseph Jackson, born August 29, 1958, was still in diapers when he began to entertain his mother by shaking and shimmying to the rhythm of the washing machine at the family home in the sooty industrial city of Gary, Indiana. As a five-year-old, he brought down the house at a Garnett Elementary School pageant with an a cappella rendition of the *Sound of Music* tune "Climb Ev'ry Mountain" that made his kindergarten teacher weep. By age six, he was the lead singer of a group called "The Ripples and Waves Plus Michael," which included his four older brothers. The Ripples and Waves had become the Jackson Brothers by the time they answered an advertisement in a local newspaper for musical groups to perform at a fashion show for a local modeling school. More than two hundred groups showed up at the audition, but six-year-old Michael Jackson stood out even in a crowd that size. "All of the brothers were talented, but Michael was magical," recalled Evelyn LaHaie, the school's owner, who chose the Jackson Brothers to perform as her modeling students walked the runway at the Big Top department store in Gary. On Michael's seventh birthday in 1965, his song-and-dance routine during a performance of "Doin' the Jerk" led the Jackson Brothers to a first place finish at Gary's "Tiny Tots' Back to School Jamboree." A little more than six months later, what was now the Jackson 5 won the annual talent show at Gary's Roosevelt High School behind a lead singer who was in the second grade. Even at that age, Michael Jackson was an astounding mimic who could produce eerily exact replications of Wilson Pickett's shouts and James Brown's yowls.

The Jackson 5's first real gig was at a local club called Mr. Lucky's, where they earned seven dollars for their performance. Not quite eight years old, Michael was fronting a band that now performed regularly at small black clubs, strip joints, and the occasional private party all over northwest Indiana and East Chicago. The group was still obscure enough to enter amateur contests and in early 1967, when Michael was eight, won the biggest talent show in the midwest at the Regal Theater in Chicago for three consecutive weeks. In August 1967, the Jackson 5 was awarded first prize at the biggest talent contest in the country, Apollo Theater's "Amateur Night." Within a year they were signed to a contract at Motown Records, and a year after that delivered a debut record that shot to the top of the *Billboard* Hot 100.

The father that drove this success was a shrewd, vain, domineering brute who in the process of advancement so wounded the most sensitive of his six sons that the controlling force of Michael Jackson's adult existence became a determination to be as little like Joseph Jackson as possible.

Up until the time he found a way to live off his sons' talent, Joe had been a busted-out boxer and bluesman who supported his sprawling family by working the four-to-midnight shift as a crane operator amid the grime and grit and blast furnace heat of the Inland Steel Mill. He earned just over $8,000 in his best year, barely enough to sustain the Jackson family home—a tiny, aluminum-sided cube without landscaping or a garage—in which eleven people shared a single bathroom. In the spring of 1964, when the Jacksons began performing publicly, Joe's five older boys had the smaller of the home's two bedrooms, where they slept in a triple bunk bed, with six-year-old Michael and seven-year-old Marlon squeezed together on the middle mattress, while nine-year-old Jermaine squirmed to make space on the upper bunk he shared with ten-year-old Tito, so that the oldest son, thirteen-year-old Jackie, could sleep alone on the bottom. The two oldest girls, Maureen (called Rebbie by her family), who was not quite fourteen, and eight-year-old La Toya made their beds on a convertible sofa in the living room, with two-year-old Randy asleep on a loveseat nearby. The youngest Jackson, Janet, would not be born until two years later, in 1966, and joined her sisters on the sofa as soon as she left her crib.

Thirty-five years old in 1964, and already the father of eight children, Joe Jackson was an inch and a half shy of six feet tall, with heavily muscled shoulders and a cheek mole; he was handsome in a heavy-lidded way, and more ambitious than anyone outside the immediate family realized. Determined to mold his sons into a musical act that would achieve the success he never did, Joe pushed them relentlessly. Michael's memories of those early rehearsals all centered on the father/manager who brandished a belt and bellowed at them constantly, smacking his sons on their backsides or throwing them into walls if they made a mistake. Being locked in a closet was the punishment for repeated failure.

Joe's own rhythm and blues band, the Falcons, had disbanded a couple of years earlier after failing to obtain more than a handful of bookings in local bars. The guitar Joe loved more than anything else he owned sat on the shelf of a clothes closet that little Michael considered "a sacred place," mainly because he and the other children were strictly forbidden from entering it. Their mother Katherine would take the guitar down from time to time when Joe was out of the house to teach the children her favorite country and folk songs. Tito was seven when he began sneaking into his parents' bedroom to borrow Joe's guitar, playing it for the oldest brother, Jackie, who had just turned ten, and six-year-old Jermaine, who harmonized as Tito picked and strummed. The three of them were learning at least one new song a week until Tito broke a string on the guitar and was discovered by his father. The whipping he got for that "tore me up," Tito remembered. It was a phrase all the Jackson boys used to describe the beatings their father gave them when he was in a fury. As he sat crying on his bed afterward, Tito insisted to his father between sobs, "I can play that thing." Joe demanded that the boy prove it, and Tito did just that, with Jackie and Jermaine sliding in beside him to sing along. In that moment, Joe Jackson decided that the steel mill would not be the end of his road. He brought home a new red guitar for Tito the next day, then told all three boys they were going to "rehearse," which they would swiftly learn was not at all the same as "playing."

Five-year-old Marlon was soon added to the group, at his mother's insistence, even though he possessed little if any musical talent (though he was a terrific dancer), but nearly two more years went by before Michael was let in and changed everything for everyone. None of them, especially Joe, wanted to acknowledge that it was the sublime talent of the band's youngest member, and that talent alone, which would make the Jackson 5 a star attraction.

Michael figured it out, of course, and by the age of nine he was the only one of Joe's children who dared to fight back against his father—"just swinging my fists," as he remembered it. "That's why I got it worse than all my brothers put together . . . my father would kill me, just tear me up." The other boys would say that Michael deserved the beatings he got. He was defiant, they said, and brought a bad attitude to rehearsals, demanding to know why they had to do things this way instead of that one. Joe's other sons followed their father's lead—right into adulthood—but Michael never would, not even as a very young child. Once, when he was three and had just received a spanking, Michael pulled off one of his shoes and threw it at his father's head. Joe responded by snatching the boy up by one leg and holding him upside down as he administered a whipping so severe that it became a family legend. During his first couple of years with the Jackson 5, Michael caught the back of Joe's hand more times than he could count, and was regularly whipped with a strap or a switch. The older boys were increasingly baffled by their little brother. On the one hand, it was obvious that Michael took the abuse their father dished out far more personally than any of them did, and that he was much more deeply hurt by it. On the other hand, he refused to stop saying and doing the very things that he knew would result in another beating. It wasn't a lack of fear, Michael would say: He was so afraid of his father for most of his childhood that he could taste vomit in his mouth whenever Joe came near him. Anger welled up beneath that fear, though, and fermented into hatred. Shamed by a sense of powerlessness, he found only one weapon he could use against his father—the threat that when it was time to take the stage he would refuse to sing. It worked once in a while, when Joe could see that Michael truly meant what he said, but more often the result was a beating worse than the one before it.

For all that, Michael never failed to admit as an adult that there had been two main ingredients in the success of the Jackson 5: his own ability and Joe's will. By the time the Jacksons began performing professionally, Joe had choreographed their movements down to the smallest detail. "He told me how to work the stage and work the mike and make gestures and everything," Michael recalled. The price of Joe's attention to detail, though, was that, "If you didn't do it the right way, he'd tear you up."

Like his own father, an Arkansas schoolteacher named Samuel Jackson, Joe was a humorless taskmaster who discouraged—even disallowed—socializing with anyone outside the family. He wasn't going to allow any "bad associations," as he put it, to distract his sons from their primary mission of showbiz success. The Jacksons were among the few children in their neighborhood who looked forward to going to school, because lunchtimes and recesses were the only opportunities they ever got to play with other kids.

As it had been for Samuel, the distinction between discipline and cruelty was largely lost on Joe. On more than one hot summer night he popped through the boys' bedroom window wearing a grotesque fright mask that left Michael and Marlon crying in bed long after he'd pulled the disguise off, chuckling at its effectiveness. His purpose, Joe would explain, was to make sure they didn't put themselves at risk by leaving the damn window open. He was *protecting* his boys.

Joe never stopped working on his sons' act and wouldn't allow the boys to slack off either. During the week, he rehearsed his sons twice a day: in the morning before school and in the afternoon when they got home. Kids from the neighborhood who already despised the Jacksons for shunning them would stand outside throwing rocks and taunts at the house, telling them they thought they were special but really, "You ain't nothin'!"

Once they began to get bookings at talent contests and in dive clubs, Joe would have the boys doing as many as five shows a night on weekends, all over the Gary and East Chicago area. There were lots of nights that ended when Joe would roust them out of bed at three in the morning to go to work. "I'd be sleeping and I'd hear my father—'Get up! There's a show!' Michael would recall thirty-five years later. "We'd have to perform." He would whine sleepily the whole drive there, but once he took the stage Michael always seemed fully awake. He loved performing that much, and loved it almost as much when people threw money at the stage afterward. He and his brothers would run around madly collecting coins from the floor and stuffing them into the pockets of the pants they had learned to wear with belts cinched tight to help support the weight of all that money. He spent most of his "earnings" on candy, Michael would remember. Joe kept the fees, which were becoming the family's main source of income.

Weeknights, when the kids went to bed, Joe would be in the audience at nearly every performance of every important musical act that came through the Chicago area, always sitting with a notebook in his lap, jotting down a description of each dance step or act of stagecraft that was worth stealing. The next morning, he'd make his sons learn this new move or that one. They had to get it right, of course, or out came the belt. He'd use the buckle on anyone who made the same mistake twice.

By the time Michael was eight, the Jacksons were good enough to play what was known as the "chitlin' circuit," a loose association of two- or three-thousand-seat theaters located in inner-city neighborhoods that stretched from Kansas City to D.C. As soon as school let out on Friday afternoon, the boys would "line up for inspection" next to the Volkswagen bus where their equipment was piled into the luggage rack on top, then depart for a weekend of work that often wouldn't end until they rolled back into Gary early Monday morning, just in time to eat breakfast and head off to school. They were opening for acts that included the Temptations, the O'Jays, Jackie Wilson, and Bobby Taylor. Sam & Dave became big supporters. On the chitlin' circuit, it was Michael who studied the other entertainers. Joe, like his older boys, loved to socialize backstage, but Michael hated that even as a boy. "It makes me shy," he would explain. "I don't know what to say." Instead, he would stand at the back of the theater, watching the acts he most admired. James Brown was at the top of that list, a performer who left puddles of sweat on the stage and a state of ecstatic exhaustion in the crowd. Timid as he was offstage, Michael constantly probed the adult performers for tips or advice. He pestered the notoriously prickly Etta James in her private dressing room, persisting even when she told him to scat. I just want to learn from the best, Michael would say, and, like James, most of the chitlin' circuit's stars couldn't resist the compliments of such a cute kid.

The Jacksons were catching more and more eyes. Some of the other opening acts grew resentful of the group, complaining that those kids wouldn't be so popular if they didn't have a damn midget as their lead singer. It seemed the only way to explain Michael Jackson, who at the age of eight was already using his voice to convey an impossibly complex range of adult emotions, from love and loss to hurt and betrayal to disillusion and yearning. He had no idea where it came from and neither did anyone else. Yet he got no compliments from Joe. "If I did a great show, he'd tell me it was a good show," Michael recalled. "And if I did an okay show, he'd tell me it was a lousy show." His father also never told him, not even a single time, that he was loved, Michael remembered. He was aching for something he didn't even know existed, until he began to see it among some of the families they met in hotels.

Sam & Dave did say they loved him, though, and the kings of call-and-response finagled a spot for the Jacksons in the country's most prestigious and competitive talent contest, the "Superdog," held at the Apollo Theater on West 125th Street in Harlem. Backstage, the boys touched the fabled "Tree of Hope," a pedestal-mounted log that had been cut from the tree that stood outside the most famous restaurant in Harlem, the Barbecue, where Louis Armstrong and Count Basie had used the rehearsal halls upstairs. Then the Jackson Brothers went out and won the Superdog to a standing ovation. It was August 13, 1967, two weeks before Michael's ninth birthday.

Their triumph at the Apollo helped the Jacksons land their first recording contract. Gordon Keith, one of five partners in Gary's Steeltown Records, arranged for an audition at the family home. "They set up right in the living room," Keith recalled. "The furniture was pushed back. They and their equipment took up pretty much the entire room. The whole family was there; Janet was a babe in arms. They were getting ready and there was a thick cord stretched between two of the amps Michael was near. It came up to his chest. From right where he was standing, without a running start, he jumped straight up from a flat-footed position right over this cord to clear it. He had all my attention from there on. I knew I was looking at a boy who was superhuman. When they sang, Michael sang like an angel . . . but when Michael danced, all while singing, he blew away James Brown, Jackie Wilson, Fred Astaire, and anyone else you can name . . . I was flabbergasted. Knocked out. Blown away. Speechless." On January 31, 1968, Steeltown released the Jackson 5's first single and one week later the whole family sat around the radio in the living room, stunned and giggling as they listened together to the first time "Big Boy" was played on WWCA, unable to quite grasp that they'd come to this. By the summer of 1968, the Jacksons were opening for the Motown acts Gladys Knight & the Pips and Bobby Taylor & the Vancouvers at Chicago's premier venue, the Regal Theater. After watching Joe Jackson's boys from the wings, both Knight and Taylor phoned Detroit, urging Motown's executives to take a look at these kids.

Even though Joe hated white people, he hired one—a lawyer named Richard Arons—to help him manage the group. Others had already contributed to the Jacksons' development, people like Shirley Cartman, the junior high school orchestra teacher who persuaded Joe to replace the weak drummer and lead guitarist he'd recruited from the neighborhood with a couple of talented local musicians named Johnny Jackson (no relation) and Ronnie Rancifer. At Cartman's urging, Tito moved up to lead guitar, while Jermaine switched from rhythm to bass. The result was a band that was tight enough to give Michael's soaring boy-soprano vocals the structural support they needed, yet fluid enough to accommodate the dramatic pitch changes that the child seemed to pluck out of thin air. And it was that local talent agent in Gary, Evelyn Lahaie, who had convinced Joe to change the group's name to the Jackson 5. "So many groups at that time that had names that ended in 'Brothers' or 'Sisters,'" LaHaie remembered. "It was too common. I knew that they should have something different."

Joe never surrendered even the tiniest percentage of control over his sons until Berry Gordy came into their lives. Joe had shown the boys just about everything you could get done in business when you combined ruthless with rough. Berry Gordy taught them how much more effective a man might be when he knew how to mix ruthless with smooth.

Like Joe, Gordy had a parent who was a schoolteacher, had tried to make his mark first as a boxer and, failing at that, had joined the blue-collar labor force. Gordy was still working on the assembly line at a Lincoln-Mercury plant when he opened a store called the 3-D Record Mart that featured jazz music. When that went under, he was reputed to have worked briefly and unsuccessfully as a pimp before going partners in a company called Rayber Music that recorded cheap demos for aspiring musicians. He was also writing songs by then, and one of them, "Reet Petite," became an R & B hit for Jackie Wilson in 1957. That was the same year he discovered a group called the Matadors (later called the Miracles), whose lead singer, Smokey Robinson, encouraged Gordy to invest his songwriting royalties in music production. By 1959, Gordy had coauthored four more songs that were recorded by Wilson, including "Lonely Teardrops," which not only topped the R & B chart, but rose as high as #7 on the pop chart. He founded what became Motown Records in a bungalow on Detroit's West Grand Avenue in December of that same year. One of the first records the company produced, "Shop Around" by Smokey Robinson and the Miracles, not only hit #1 on the R & B chart in 1960, but climbed to #2 on the pop chart. A year later, Motown's release of "Please Mr. Postman" by the Marvelettes reached the top of both the R & B and pop charts.

By the summer of 1968, when the Jackson 5 auditioned for the company, Gordy had a roster of talent that included the Supremes, the Temptations, Smokey Robinson and the Miracles, and Stevie Wonder. Motown's artist development division, which educated performers in subjects like etiquette, grooming, and fashion, had helped make the label's black acts more successful in white America than any before them, and the Supremes' lead singer, Diana Ross, was in a class by herself as a crossover talent. Nothing Gordy accomplished so amazed the rest of the music business, though, as his uncanny ability to create a sense among his artists that they were members of "The Motown Family" while at the same time effectively robbing them blind with the stingiest royalty rates in the business.

Gordy wasn't even present at the Jackson 5's Motown audition on July 23, 1968. After all the child labor law headaches he had suffered for signing Stevie Wonder, Gordy was reluctant to take on another underage act. When he saw the 16 mm black-and-white film his aides had made of the Jacksons' audition, though, Gordy sent back word to sign them immediately. The contract Joe Jackson executed on his sons' behalf paid each of the boys slightly more than 1 percent of what their records earned, which would come to about two cents apiece per album. Berry Gordy made a lot more from their music than the band ever would during the years the Jackson 5 recorded for his label.

This disturbed Joe far less than Gordy's insistence that Michael was the star of the show and that his brothers were merely a supporting cast. The Motown chief had made his position clear from the moment of the Jackson 5's public debut during the late summer of 1969 in Southern California, where Gordy was determined to relocate both his primary residence and his company. The press release-slash-invitation that announced the event was prepared by Gordy personally, even though it was "signed" by the young woman who had become Motown's signature asset: "Please join me in welcoming a brilliant musical group, the Jackson Five, on Monday, August 11, 6:30 to 9:30 p.m. at the Daisy, North Rodeo Drive, Beverly Hills," it read. "The Jackson Five, featuring sensational eight-year-old Michael Jackson, will perform live at the party. Diana Ross." Joe fumed, concerned that singling out Michael would not only create dissension among his boys, but further undermine his authority over them.

The major impact Gordy made on Michael with this event, though, was what he taught the boy about the malleability of so-called reality. When Michael tried to tell Gordy and Ross that they'd made a big mistake in the press release because he was ten years old, not eight, Gordy explained that it wasn't a mistake, and it wasn't a lie, either, because a lie wasn't a lie when you told it for the purpose of public relations. "It's for your image," chimed in Ross, who was already going along with Gordy's story that she had "discovered" the Jackson 5 at a benefit concert for the campaign of Gary's first black mayor, Richard Hatcher. "I thought I was going to be an old man before being discovered," Michael had breathlessly confided to one interviewer after his performance at the Daisy. "But then along came Miss Diana Ross to save my career. She *discovered* me." When a suspicious reporter told the young performer she had heard that he was almost eleven (his birthday was in eighteen days), Michael vehemently denied it. So how old are you, the interviewer asked. "I'm eight," Michael answered.

Whatever his age, Michael's performance at the Daisy wowed the crowd. *Soul* magazine's reviewer hailed the Jackson 5's lead singer as "an eight-year-old boy who became a man when a microphone was in his hand."

Gordy was already finding other ways to separate Michael from his family. Joe and his sons endured Gordy's cheapskate accommodations for more than a year after their signing with Motown, sleeping on the floor of Bobby Taylor's apartment while they recorded fifteen songs during weekend sessions at the company's studios in Detroit, driving up from Gary every Friday evening, then driving back during the predawn hours of Monday morning, all at their own expense. When Gordy moved them out to Los Angeles in the summer of 1969, he put them up at Hollywood's most notorious palace of sleaze, the Tropicana Motel on Santa Monica Boulevard, where most of their neighbors were hookers and drug addicts. After a month, he moved them into an even more run-down motel on Sunset Boulevard. Gordy was himself ensconced at his stupendously opulent mansion in Bel Air, where the walls were covered with paintings of him dressed as Napoleon and Caesar.

A little more than a month after the Daisy show, though, Gordy arranged for Michael to begin living with Diana Ross at her lovely home in Beverly Hills. Gordy was just about to release the Jackson 5's first single and, confident it would be a hit, urged Ross to help Michael understand that a star had to think of himself differently than other people. "Wherever you go from now on," Ross told the boy, "people will be watching you." Though Michael meant far less to Diana than the boy wanted to believe, she instructed him simply by letting herself be observed. When they were alone in the house, she usually wanted the boy to draw pictures and leave her alone.

Michael was still spending his days, and many of his evenings, with his brothers at Motown's West Coast studios, where the five of them were working under the command of Deke Richards, the songwriter and producer who, as Motown's creative director of talent, was running the company's West Coast operation. With A-list songwriters Freddie Perren and Fonce Mizell, Richard and Gordy had formed what they called "The Corporation" to craft the songs and package the performances that would make the Jackson 5 a hit. Gordy and Richards, along with their producers, invested a remarkable amount of time and money in the recording and engineering of the song that would be the group's first release, "I Want You Back." The demands on his older brothers were not nearly those made of the group's eleven-year-old lead singer, who was spending as many as twelve hours a day in the studio. His strongest memories of that time, Michael would say later, were of falling asleep at the microphone, and of staring out the windows between takes at the children on the playground in the park across the street: "I would just stare at them in wonder—I couldn't imagine such freedom, such a carefree life—and wish more than anything that . . . I could walk away and be like them."

Gordy and Richards and just about everyone else at Motown, though, were mesmerized by the seventy-pound boy standing in front of them. Watching Michael step to the microphone and summon up emotions that seemed to befit a forty-year-old man who had done a lot of hard living, then as soon as the song was finished go looking for somebody to play hide and seek with, was both eerie and enthralling. Gordy would talk to the press about Michael's "deep and intuitive understanding" of things, but not even he seemed to have a clue about what its source might be. The things Michael did onstage were obviously practiced—anyone could see that he had copied and combined the moves of James Brown and the stage drama of Jackie Wilson—and yet he somehow owned the result entirely. Diana Ross had taught him about the power of the "oooh," especially when it was used to put an exclamation mark on a lyric, something everyone agreed Diana did better than anyone ever had—until they heard Michael do it.

"Never seen anything like him," Smokey Robinson would observe of Michael. And the whole world seemed to agree, in October 1969, when "I Want You Back" was released and shot straight to the top of both the *Billboard* and *Cash Box* pop charts. Shortly after the song's release, the Jackson 5 made its national television debut on an ABC program called *The Hollywood Palace*. For Michael's brothers, and for his father in particular, the experience was one more hard lesson in the reordering of their reality. Diana Ross was the special guest host for that episode of the show, but whenever she came backstage, Ross spoke only to Michael, whispering encouragement that was for him alone, and entirely ignoring the other boys. She introduced the group by saying: "Tonight, I have the pleasure of introducing a young star who has been in the business all of his life. He's worked with his family, and when he sings and dances, he lights up the stage." Sammy Davis Jr. came bounding out from behind a curtain wearing an excited smile, only to be politely rebuffed by Ross, who explained to the audience that she was talking about "Michael Jackson and the Jackson 5." Stepping onstage in the lime green suits they wore with matching gold shirts and green boots, the same outfits they had appeared in at the Daisy, the other Jackson brothers looked stunned. Joe was incensed, demanding to know if Berry Gordy was trying to rename the group. Not at all, said Gordy, who stood with him backstage, but Michael was "obviously the star." Surely Joe could see that. "They're all stars," Joe retorted, but what he thought really didn't count anymore and deep inside he knew it.

The older Jackson sons absorbed another blow to their pride when their first album was released a month after "I Want You Back" came out. Under the title—*Diana Ross Presents the Jackson 5*—the other boys were pictured holding instruments they had not been allowed to play, on an album to which they had contributed little more than a chorus of backup vocals. The truth was that Jackie and Tito possessed only modest musical talent, and Marlon had none at all. No one had ever told them this, though, until they were about to become big stars. The process by which Michael had been separated out from the others was perhaps hardest on Jermaine, who had a perfectly adequate singing voice but just not one that was remotely in the same league as Michael's. Jermaine had suffered at the age of nine when he was replaced as the group's lead singer—his family believed the spell of stuttering that followed was a direct result—but tried to accept that he was, as his father put it, the group's "second soloist."

Diana Ross wrote the liner notes for the Jackson 5's first album. She began with the declaration that, "Honesty has always been a special word for me—a special idea," then repeated the lie that the Jackson 5 was "five brothers by the name of Jackson that I discovered in Gary, Indiana." By this time, Michael seemed to actually believe this was true, and more than a few of those who promoted the album were unnerved by the boy's capacity for blending fiction and reality so seamlessly that lines of demarcation seemed utterly erased.

His brothers were back on their game by December 14, 1969, four days before their album's release, when the Jackson 5 made its first appearance on *The Ed Sullivan Show* wearing huge smiles and swaying in perfect rhythm behind their little brother as he took the stage in a crimson cowboy hat and delivered a performance of "I Want You Back" that had the girls in the audience pulling their hair from the first note to the last.

Satisfied that his investment would pay off, Berry Gordy moved the Jacksons out of the motel where they had been living and into a home he had leased on Queens Road in the Hollywood Hills, with a living room that offered more floor space than their entire house back in Gary, and a view of the Los Angeles Basin that after dark looked like diamonds spilled on sable. At Fairfax High School, where they had begun attending classes in September, Jackie and Tito were all but worshiped. Fourteen-year-old Jermaine saw the junior high girls from his classes literally fighting to sit next to him. It was not so difficult to nurse a bruised ego, the other boys found, when the whole world loved you.

In February 1970, the Jackson 5 released its second single, "ABC," which also went to #1 on the pop charts, displacing the Beatles' "Let It Be." Like "I Want You Back," it sold more than two million copies. The Jacksons' third single, released that May, was "The Love You Save." It hit #1 too, bumping the Beatles' "The Long and Winding Road" from the top spot. They had become the first band of the rock era to send their first three songs to #1. Their second album, *ABC*, was released that same month and was even more successful than the first had been. In July, the Jackson 5 concert broke every attendance record at the Los Angeles Forum, and a screaming crowd that was largely composed of young black women got so out of control that the boys were hustled off the stage before they could finish their set for fear that the security staff would not be able to protect them. On October 10, 1970, just as their fourth single, "I'll Be There," was being released, the Jackson 5 sang "The Star Spangled Banner" at Game 1 of the World Series in Cincinnati's Riverfront Stadium. "I'll Be There," would provide a further revelation of Michael's gifts. Even white critics who had dismissed the Jackson 5 as "bubblegum soul" loved "I'll Be There," which sold more than any of the three singles before it, and made the Jackson 5 the first group ever to send its first four releases to the top of the pop charts.

Michael Jackson, a twelve-year-old pretending to be ten, had become all but iconic in what seemed the blink of an eye. When he and his brothers flew back to visit Gary, it was for a ceremony at which the street where they once lived was renamed "Jackson 5 Boulevard." That April, Michael had become the youngest person to appear on the cover of *Rolling Stone*, with a headline that read, "Why does this eleven-year-old stay up past his bedtime?" He was four months from his thirteenth birthday, but the delayed onset of puberty helped the lie about his age remain viable. "Here you have the chief child, the new model, the successor to James Brown and the Tempts and Sly, the cherubic incarnation of their sum," Ben Fong-Torres had gushed inside the magazine. The most memorable anecdote from Torres's article was about Michael telling a concert audience that he could sing the blues because he knew all about them, then describing how his heart had been broken by a girl he met in the sandbox, only to see it all go downhill after "we toasted our love during milk break."

He kept his cover by holding fast to the enthusiasms of childhood, far more excited about the premiere that September of a network cartoon show called *The Jackson 5ive* than he was about the cover of *Rolling Stone*. Even though the voice of the animated character named Michael Jackson was not his, "I woke up every Saturday morning" to watch, he would remember. "I felt so happy, you have no idea . . . I think I felt more special about that than the records and the concerts and everything."

The Jackson 5 kicked off its first big national tour that October in Boston, where, even with a large security staff and a twelve-foot-high fence protecting them, the boys had to be pulled offstage before they were mobbed by an audience of young women who had gone completely berserk. At Cincinnati Gardens, thousands of girls who had been turned away when the concert sold out staged a near riot outside the stadium, while those who got inside the gates crammed the aisles and shrieked themselves into a near delirium, even as local disc jockeys took turns pleading for calm. Fourteen girls had to be carried outside unconscious after fainting. Girls collapsed in the aisles at every stop after that, and by the hundreds clamored and chanted afterward outside the Jacksons' hotels.

Michael seemed to enjoy the attention at first, but his pleasure quickly diminished. Halfway through the tour, he didn't want to leave the hotel except to perform, and what he seemed to love most about their stop-overs were water balloon and shaving cream fights with his brothers. That stopped when first Jackie, then Tito, and then even Jermaine, grew more interested in the girls gathered at the stage door after a concert than they were in fun and games with their little brother.

When the Jackson 5 left the United States in October 1972 for a twelve-day European tour, they discovered that the white girls there were just as crazy for them as the black girls in America. A full-scale riot erupted in the streets of Amsterdam when it was announced that the Jacksons would perform only one night in the Dutch city. On their way to a command performance before Queen Elizabeth in London that would launch the tour, the boys were nearly crushed by the screaming mob of girls who awaited them at Heathrow Airport. Plugs of Tito's Afro were ripped from his scalp within seconds of his stepping off the plane. The shrieking inside the terminal was so intense that it brought tears to Marlon's eyes. The five brothers were swiftly separated by the surge of the crowd and had to scramble and shove their way separately to the limousine waiting at the curb outside. Michael, still not five feet tall, was nearly strangled by girls who grabbed opposite ends of the scarf he wore, and had to work the fingers of one hand up under the scarf to push it off his larynx, using the other hand to protect his eyes from the fingernails that clutched and slashed at him from every direction.

"Sheer pandemonium," was how a release issued by the delighted executives at Motown described the scene. Their English fans barricaded the entrance to the Churchill Hotel, where the Jacksons were staying in London, and had to be dispersed by bobbies firing water cannons. The next day, a nine-year-old girl tried to force her way into Michael's room at knifepoint. Dozens of other girls brandished knives at the police outside the hotel; one girl swung a sledgehammer to try to get inside. The Rolls-Royce limo that carried the group to their performance that evening was dented and scraped in dozens of places as it crawled through the swarm of young girls who scratched at the windows with their fingernails, smashing their faces against the glass. While the boys were performing inside the Talk of the Town nightclub, the limo was stripped to its frame and they had to ride back to their hotel in taxis.

The older Jackson brothers surveyed the mad scene that surrounded them with fear and wonder, but for Michael only the fear was real. He was a prepubescent boy standing four feet, ten inches tall and weighing less than eighty pounds—"round eyes, round dimples on a round face, under a round Afro," was how Ben Fong-Torres had described him in *Rolling Stone*—who had no way of understanding the sexual frenzy he elicited from the young women who charged and clutched and clawed at him. "They were so big," his mother Katherine would explain. "And he was so small."

3

In London, Michael had decided to turn the trip forced on him by Marc Schaffel into a three-week holiday for his children. Prince and Paris got a taste of their father's London experience when they ventured from the Dorchester with him on October 7, to visit Abbey Road, the studio where the Beatles recorded the majority of their songs. A relatively small crowd of fans and photographers outside the hotel had done their best to create a mob scene, pushing up against Michael's security team in a crush of clutching arms and contorted faces that terrified his kids. When they got to St. John's Wood for a tour of the studio, Michael recalled recording "Say Say Say" here with Paul McCartney back in 1981, but the children were a lot more excited about their father's promise to take them to see the movie *Wallace and Gromit: The Curse of the Were-Rabbit*.

First, though, they would meet up with Michael's old friend Mark Lester and his family to see the musical *Billy Elliot* at the Victoria Palace Theatre. Almost forty years later, Lester was still best known to the world as the young actor who had played the title character in *Oliver!*, the musical that had won the 1968 Academy Award for Best Picture. Back in the days when he and his brothers were just beginning to become recognized as recording stars, Michael explained, he used to open teen magazines and see pictures of himself and Mark on opposite pages, as if facing off against one another, "the positive and the negative, the black and the white." They had not actually gotten to know one another until late 1982, shortly before the release of *Thriller*, when Lester got a call from someone who said Michael Jackson would like to meet him, and arranged an introduction in a suite at the Montcalm Hotel in Park Lane. Lester had ceased acting as a young adult and was now almost completely obscure outside Gloucestershire, the county west of London where he worked as an osteopath and ran an acupuncture clinic in the spa town of Cheltenham. He and Michael, though, had remained in close contact for the past two decades and rarely went a year without seeing one another. Mark was godfather to all three of Michael's children, as Michael was to at least two of Lester's four kids—who had made multiple trips to California for stays at Neverland that were the envy of their schoolmates.

The Lester kids seemed as excited as ever about seeing Michael in London, but their father was distracted by the thought that he might be the biological father of at least one of Michael's own children.

Back in 1997, while married to Debbie Rowe, Michael had asked Mark to donate sperm at a clinic in California. Lester had wondered ever since if his sperm had been used to impregnate Rowe with her daughter Paris, he said. And now, in London, he was struck by the "uncanny likeness" between seven-year-old Paris and his own eleven-year-old daughter Harriet. He chose not to press the subject, though, and accepted that living with doubts was the price one paid for a relationship with Michael Jackson.

Lester knew far better than most people how "traditional" Michael's avowed value system was, but even he had been taken aback by his friend's reaction to *Billy Elliot*. The foul language was totally unacceptable, said Michael, and he would never have brought his children to see it if he had known how bad it was. At age forty-seven, Michael still refrained from cursing. While he no longer insisted that people not use swear words in his own presence, he demanded that they refrain when his children were around. He was a far better father than he was given credit for by the media, in Lester's opinion, not only refusing to let his children be spoiled but dealing with them very firmly when he saw some sign that they thought they were above ordinary folk.

Still, the Jackson kids did have the run of an entire floor at the five-star Dorchester and were used to such special treatment as having Madame Tussaud's wax museum closed to the public so that they could join their father on a private tour. They marveled at the figure of him twenty years younger, frozen in the middle of a dance step and outfitted in the sequined black suit, white V-neck T-shirt, and red-banded black fedora. When they went shopping at Harrods three days later, the kids were greeted by the store's then-owner, Mohamed Al-Fayed, "Princess Diana's father-in-law," as Michael preferred to call the father of the boyfriend who died with Diana in the 1997 Paris car crash. Prince, Paris, and Blanket were allowed to sit with a crowd of regular people when they saw *Wallace and Gromit* but only after being ushered into the theater during the opening credits to seats that had been saved for them in the back row. Two days after that, they were loaded onto a private jet and flown back to Bahrain. For all the children knew, this was how everyone lived.

*   *   *

On the same day he left London, Jackson's attorneys filed a countersuit against Marc Schaffel in Santa Monica, alleging that he had misappropriated funds, had failed to pay production costs for "What More Can I Give?" and had continued to represent himself as Michael Jackson's business partner long after the relationship was "terminated." The suit also accused Schaffel of keeping $250,000 worth of sculptures and paintings that belonged to Jackson.

The answer to Jackson's court filing came swiftly and painfully. In November, Schaffel's attorney Howard King provided *Good Morning America* with a recording of Michael Jackson that would paint him as an anti-Semite: "They suck—they're like leeches. I'm so tired of it. [Recording artists] start out the most popular person in the world, make a lot of money, big house, cars, and everything, end up with—penniless. It is conspiracy. The Jews do it on purpose."

It was an area of vulnerability for Michael and the entire Jackson family. He had been beset by allegations of anti-Semitism since 1995 upon the release of his album *HIStory*. The controversy was ignited by the lyrics of his song "They Don't Care About Us," which included the verse: "Jew me / sue me / everybody do me / Kick me, kike me / don't you black or white me." Even as he insisted the song was a protest against racism and ethnic discrimination, the Anti-Defamation League had mounted protests that forced Michael ultimately to add percussive sound effects that obscured the words "Jew" and "kike" in subsequent issues of the album.

Many in the entertainment industry had heard, as well, the stories of an anti-Semitism that ran rampant in the Jackson household; based largely on quotes attributed to her by her daughter La Toya (who later retracted these claims), Katherine Jackson had been accused in particular. Jermaine's public conversion to Islam, combined with the family's involvement with Louis Farrakhan and Michael's move to the Middle East after leaving the United States, further cemented the impression of anti-Semitism many had.

Howard King admitted his doubt that Jackson truly disliked Jews: "I think at the end of the day Michael was pretty tolerant of everybody." The attorney seemed only too happy, though, to see his legal adversary pilloried once again by the Anti-Defamation League, which on the morning after the "leeches" recording aired on *Good Morning America* demanded a public apology from Michael Jackson "to Jews everywhere."

What it all meant, at a minimum, was that Michael would not be returning to the United States in the near future. By the middle of November,

Sheikh Abdullah had invested more than $5 million in Michael Jackson. That included paying the entertainer's numerous attorneys who were attending to assorted civil matters. Abdullah's own attorney Ahmed al Khan was helping Jackson handle his negotiations with assorted major creditors. The sheikh had covered all the costs of Michael's living and travel expenses since his arrival in Manama and had spent a substantial sum to arrange and coordinate recording sessions that linked Jackson with studios in Los Angeles. He provided his guest with the use of both a Rolls-Royce and a Mercedes Maybach, and bought him jewelry, watches, and a statue made of solid gold.

Abdullah still seemed to believe it would all pay off. The Bahraini media swallowed Sheikh Abdullah's latest press release whole, turning it into a series of rapturous stories about how, days after his arrival in the country, Michael Jackson had recorded Abdullah's original composition "He Who Makes the Sky Gray." The people of his country would be hearing the song "very, very soon," according to the sheikh, who promised that "proceeds will go to relief efforts in different parts of the world to help victims of wars and natural disasters." What he and Mikaeel would offer was "a song created in Bahrain," Abdullah went on, "to show the world that this region is not about wars and conflicts."

Jackson "thrilled the nation" when he traveled to Dubai with Abdullah in mid-November to attend the Dubai Desert Rally Awards, according to the November 14 edition of the *Khaleej Times*. Mikaeel had tried to be inconspicuous while he ate lunch with the managing director of the Dubai International Marine Club, Saeed Hareb, according to the newspaper, but those in attendance were beside themselves when he stepped forward to present the trophies to the winners in the Desert Rally's automobile and motorcycle categories. "Reports have surfaced," the newspaper account added, that Jackson had just paid $1.5 million for a lot at Bahrain's manmade Amwaj Islands, where he planned to construct the palace that would replace Neverland Ranch as his primary residence.

The Persian Gulf's pride in Jackson was torpedoed the very next day when the UAE's largest afternoon daily, *Evening Post*, ran a banner front-page headline announcing that "Wacko Jacko" had been caught inside a ladies' toilet at Dubai's Ibn Battuta Mall. Jackson had been costumed in an abaya, the black full-length gown, face veil, and head covering traditionally worn by Arab women, when he ducked into the bathroom and removed his headdress to apply what the newspaper described as "much-needed" makeup. A woman emerging from a toilet stall squealed in horror at the sight of Jackson's "mangled" face and began snapping photos of him with her cell phone. Shoppers at the mall heard shouts and screams, then saw Jackson's bodyguards wrestling with the woman outside the bathroom as they forced her to hand over the cell phone. Jackson was then driven off with his bodyguards in a vehicle with blacked-out windows.

One day after the *Post* report, Arab newspapers were filled with demands that Jackson receive "appropriate punishment." A Syrian housewife was quoted as saying, "This man shows his immoral character pretending to be a woman. He should be punished severely." Jackson must go to jail, chimed in a Sudanese nurse who promptly changed that to "a place worse than jail, so that it would set an example." A young Egyptian mother declared that Jackson had insulted not just Muslim women, but the entire Muslim world and demanded "stern action."

The Al Khalifas responded by getting Michael out of the country. Rather than address the mall incident directly, though, Sheikh Abdullah explained to Jackson that his uncle, the king's brother, was returning from overseas and would need the use of the home in which Michael and his children had been staying. Along with Grace, they were sent off to neighboring Oman, where a dinner had been arranged at the home of the U.S. ambassador. The traveling party had just checked into the Al Bustan Palace hotel when word came that Jackson's longtime chief of security, Bill Bray, had died in Los Angeles. Bray, a retired Los Angeles Police Department officer, had begun protecting Jackson when Michael was the ten-year-old lead singer of the Jackson 5. In the years that followed, Bray became the fiercely protective father figure Michael yearned for, literally carrying the young singer through the shrieking, scratching crowds of young women that so terrified him as a preadolescent. A breach had opened between the two during the *Bad* tour, though, when Bray, in an attempt to secure his financial future, prevailed upon Jackson to sign a document that for a few weeks made the aging bodyguard the CEO of MJJ Productions, Michael's principal business arm. Bray surrendered the title after Jackson realized what he had done, but for the first time doubts about Bill's motives had been seeded in Michael's mind.

Those seeds sprouted a year later when Bray became involved in the so-called "Moonie Fiasco." A representative of the Unification Church of the Reverend Sun Myung Moon named Kenneth Choi had been assigned to persuade Michael to join the other Jackson brothers in a series of concerts to be staged in Seoul, South Korea, under the auspices of the *Segye Times*, a newspaper owned by the Moonies. Choi had gone to absurd lengths to make what he called "The Jackson Family Reunion Concerts" happen, spending money in prodigious amounts along the way. Michael's parents, Katherine and Joseph, were flown twice to Korea, once with their oldest daughter Rebbie, and shown the most extravagant level of luxury that Seoul could provide. Michael's manager Frank Dileo was offered two cashier's checks totaling $1 million by Choi if he could convince Michael to participate in the concerts (and he was fired three days after he discussed the situation with Jackson). Joe and Katherine's representative Jerome Howard got a new Mercedes as an incentive bonus to make the "Family Reunion" concerts happen. After complaining that "these are my boys, not Jerome's," Joe Jackson received a Rolls-Royce Corniche and $50,000 cash, while another $35,000 cash went to Katherine. Jermaine Jackson got a Range Rover for being (supposedly) the brother Michael trusted most, and the Moonies sent the star himself not only a new Rolls-Royce but also a truckload of artwork and $60,000 cash. He would receive $10 million if he performed at the four concerts, Choi promised Michael, in addition to his share of the $7.5 million that was to be split among the Jackson brothers. Eventually, the Koreans were buying expensive gifts for seemingly anyone who claimed to be able to influence Michael Jackson. The farce hit bottom when Bill Bray's girlfriend persuaded Choi to hand over the keys to a 560 SEL Mercedes, simply for claiming she had Michael's ear. Bray himself somehow came out of it all with $500,000, and when Michael heard about that, things were never the same between the two of them. Bray was not invited to live at Neverland when Michael moved to the ranch, and in 1995 his position with MJJ Productions was terminated.

The press release issued on Michael's behalf after Bray's death was brief: "I am deeply saddened by the passing of my dear and longtime friend, Mr. Bill Bray. As I traveled the world, Mr. Bray was there by my side. Bill Bray will forever have a special place in my heart." He hadn't been able to face seeing Bill old and shriveled and dying, Michael admitted to those who were with him, then cried alone in his room.

Michael was still recovering from the news of Bray's death when two days later he learned that his former manager, Dieter Wiesner, had just filed a $64 million lawsuit against him in Los Angeles. Wiesner had spent nearly a decade at Jackson's side, beginning with the *HIStory* tour in 1995, when he traveled with Michael to 120 shows around the world. Much of the bond they formed during that time, and after, resulted from Wiesner's sympathy for Michael's wish to escape the music business. "He said on the *HIStory* tour that he would never do this again, that touring was over for him, forever," Wiesner recalled. "He said, 'I don't want to be doing the moonwalk on stage when I'm fifty.'"

4

On March 6, 2001, Michael Jackson traveled by car from London with his friends Uri Geller and Rabbi Shmuley Boteach to add his name to the list of illustrious and celebrated figures (including several U.S. presidents, the Dalai Lama, author Salman Rushdie, and actor Johnny Depp) who have addressed the Oxford Union Society. He opened his remarks with an observation that he had been making in one form or another for going on twenty years: "All of us are the products of our childhoods, but I am the product of a lack of a childhood."

It was the central fallacy of his adult life. He had *had* a childhood, just not the one he wished for. This dissonance between what he imagined and what he had was the primary source of both his creativity and his unhappiness. It made him rich and famous and lonely all his life. He owed his mother Katherine for it every bit as much as he owed his father Joe, but of all the truths Michael avoided, that was at the top of the list.

Katherine Jackson was born Kattie B. Scruse in Alabama, to a family that on her father's side had been listed as "mulatto" in an early twentieth-century census. Stricken at eighteen months with polio, she either wore braces or walked with crutches until she was sixteen, and suffered merciless teasing by her classmates in East Chicago, where her family had moved when she was four. She grew up as a child apart, painfully shy and quiet except when she got the chance to sing or make music. She and her sister Hattie were each members of their high school's orchestra, band, and choir. Kate, as her family called her, played both clarinet and piano, and possessed a sweet and rich soprano voice that more than one person told her should be heard on records. She and Hattie adored a Chicago radio program called *Suppertime Frolic* that played nothing but country and western music. The two sisters adored especially the songs of Hank Williams, and it was an early dream of Kate's to become the first black female country star.

By the time the braces came off and the crutches fell away, Kattie B. Scruse had grown into a lovely young woman who dreamed of a career in show business, either as an actress or a singer, but never found the self-confidence to strive for such a life. Instead, at nineteen, she was terribly smitten by the dashing local ladies' man, recently divorced twenty-year-old Joseph Jackson. They married only a few months after meeting. She had legally changed her name to Katherine Esther Scruse not long before the wedding, but never quite got over the feeling that a poor crippled girl like "Kattie B. Screws" (as the other kids had called her) was lucky to land a man so many other women admired. The whispers of Joe's infidelity started early but Kate ignored them for as long as it was possible.

She seemed far more accepting of their lot in life than Joe did, making many of the children's clothes herself or shopping for them at the Salvation Army store. She worked at Sears part-time as a saleswoman to supplement Joe's earnings at the mill. Religion was the anchor of her life. She was raised Baptist and became a Lutheran but abandoned both churches when she discovered that the ministers of her local congregations were conducting extramarital affairs. Right around the time that Michael made his famous kindergarten performance at Garnett Elementary, Kate was converted to the Jehovah's Witnesses by a pair of proselytizers who were going door-to-door through the neighborhood. She was determined to get the entire family involved, forcing them all to dress up each Sunday morning and walk with her to the local Kingdom Hall. Joe lasted only a few weeks, and her older sons fell away soon after that. Only Michael and her two older daughters, Rebbie (who was an ardent Witness) and La Toya, fully embraced the principles of Kate's faith. The others, though, all accepted the tenets that separated the Witnesses from American society. There were no birthday celebrations in the Jackson home, and no celebrations of the "pagan" holidays Christmas and Easter, either. Even Jackie and Tito refused to engage in the idolatrous practices of saluting the flag, singing the national anthem, or reciting the Pledge of Allegiance, but none of the Jackson boys made a display of their defiance.

Though indifferent to the religious practices of the Witnesses, Joe appreciated the discipline and structure that his wife's faith imposed on their children. Witnesses were taught to think of themselves as sheep, and of those who surrounded them as goats. When the battle of Armageddon was fought (any day now), the goats would be slaughtered and only the sheep would survive, resurrected to a life on earth as subjects of the Kingdom of God, ruled over by Jesus Christ. Joe had no interest at all in the spiritual dimensions of his wife's faith, but it pleased him immensely to have his children indoctrinated into the belief that they must remain separate from the "goats" of their depressed and declining community.

Rebbie, La Toya, and Michael would accompany Katherine when she went door-to-door through the neighborhood each week to witness her faith and distribute copies of the *Watchtower* magazine. Perplexed by his father's refusal to attend services at the Kingdom Hall, Michael was more deeply bonded to his mother than ever by their shared beliefs, and became in some regards her special favorite by being the only one of the boys who would join her in regular Bible study. Katherine had always given him the love and affection he craved, though she was also quite willing to smack any of her children across the face if they talked back to her, or in some way offended God. The only real trouble between Katherine and Michael had arisen out of his habit of filching pieces of jewelry from her dresser drawer to give as presents to his favorite teachers at Garnett. His mother had him whipped for that, and yet covered up for some of his other transgressions, especially when she knew that Joe was in the mood to administer a truly terrible beating.

A strange, even insidious ambiguity developed out of Katherine's enthusiasm for Joe's push to make his boys into a successful singing group. Early on, she would sew the boys' costumes and drive them to their local engagements when Joe was unavailable. Later, she seemed to relish their success every bit as much as her husband did. They all could see that she loved the money and the attention, and yet she was constantly reminding them that wealth and fame weren't what mattered—that only preaching and proselytizing were important in the eyes of God. An implicit and troubling hypocrisy became an undercurrent of Katherine's character; what she said and what she did seemed to grow further and further apart.

This was nowhere more evident than in the blind eye she turned to Joe's infidelities and in the exposure to the more sordid aspects of sexuality she permitted her six-year-old son after he became the Jackson Brothers' lead singer. Many of the clubs the Jacksons played in the early days were strip joints. Michael's memories of those dates were a large part of why he was so uninterested in clubbing when he got older: "Fights breaking out, people throwing up, yelling, screaming, the police sirens." He stood in the wings watching women undress before a rowdy mob of drunken men any number of times as he waited to go onstage and sing for the same crowd. Forty years later, he could still vividly recall "the lady who took off *all* her clothes." Rose Marie was her name, remembered Michael, who watched her at the age of seven with a stricken fascination as the young woman twirled the tassels attached to her nipples, lashing with them at the men who groped her from the front of the stage, then stepped out of her panties and threw them into the audience, where "the men would grab them and sniff them." Returning home in the predawn light with a father who had enjoyed Rose Marie's show as much as any man in the audience, to a mother who preached that such licentiousness was satanically inspired and would result in exclusion from the Kingdom of God, Michael defended his soul with a prudish romanticism that in years to come would not merely inhibit his sexuality, but simultaneously crush and distort it.

Michael saw less and less of his mother when the Jackson 5 hit the chitlin' circuit and began to travel throughout the Midwest and Northeast with their father. Those absences became prolonged after the signing with Motown, and Michael went weeks and months without seeing his mother—"the only person who made me feel loved"—at the ages of ten, eleven, and twelve. An early experience of severe turbulence made him terrified of flying and his father had to carry him onto the airplane kicking and screaming when their concert schedule forced the Jackson 5 to take off in a storm. Joseph "would never hold me or touch me," Michael remembered, "and the stewardesses would have to come and hold my hand and caress me." He cried all day before their first trip to South America, Michael remembered. "I did not want to go and I said, 'I just want to be like everyone else. I just want to be normal.' And my father found me, and made me get in the car and go, because we had to do a date."

He had long been denied the right to make friends outside the family, and now, constantly on the move, he began to experience all new relationships as fleeting. "You meet people on the road, somebody on your floor, could be a family," he recalled, "and you know you have to have as much fun as you can in a short time, because you are not going to see them again."

Michael was shocked and appalled by the attitudes of the groupies who swarmed around the Jackson 5 when they became a big act. They bore no resemblance at all to what his mother had told him about the fairer sex. He was every bit as shocked, and even more appalled, by how his father and his brothers took advantage of young women who would do anything for a little attention from a famous family. From the first, Joe made no effort to hide the way he reveled in all that available young flesh, saying good night to his sons in their hotel rooms with both arms full of girls half his age, at once showing off his boys to the girls and the girls to his boys, then cackling as he headed off down the hall to enjoy the sweet fruits of success. Michael and Marlon, the two youngest members of the Jackson 5, were especially wounded by the constant betrayal of their mother, and in some way felt betrayed themselves by her unwillingness to hear about it. The older Jackson brothers, though, learned well from their father, and in almost no time Joe was accepting sloppy seconds from his strapping, handsome oldest son, Jackie, while Jermaine stood third in line. The hurt and shame and impotent angst were all still audible in Michael's voice twenty-five years later when he described what it was like for him as a prepubescent, pretending to sleep in his hotel room bed while his brothers thrust away at groupies who lay on their backs or bellies right next to him. On more than one occasion he tried to convince the girls who gathered at the backstage door that they should go no farther, warning that they would be used and discarded. When they went ahead anyway, he was confused and frightened at first and then, over time, disheartened.

Between tours, Joe and his sons returned home to a two-acre estate on the north face of the Santa Monica Mountains, with a private driveway off Hayvenhurst Drive just below Mulholland in the affluent enclave of Encino. It had become the new Jackson family home in the spring of 1971, a five-bedroom, six-bathroom mansion that was supposed to be Katherine's dream house. Her sons' friends called it "The Big House," more because it felt like a prison than because of its size. Janet Jackson's first husband, James DeBarge, gave the Hayvenhurst mansion its most resonant nickname: "The House of Fears." Their new home was as far removed from the house the Jackson boys had grown up in as their former neighbors in Gary could have imagined. There was an Olympic-size swimming pool, basketball and badminton courts, an archery range, a guest house, a playhouse, and servants' quarters, all contained within a gated compound that overflowed with citrus trees and flowering shrubs. The driveway was filled with luxury automobiles and the walls of the family room were lined with gold and platinum records.

Joe's already nasty personality darkened during those years. He bitterly resented that Berry Gordy now seemed to have more control over his sons' careers than he, the father who had molded them into a professional act, and he went to maniacal lengths to remind the entire family that he and he alone was the boss around the house. A five-minute limit was imposed on phone calls and Joe enforced the rule with a leather strap that he used on even his teenage sons. He had refused for years to be addressed as "Dad" by his children, demanding that they call him "Joseph." Some imagined that it was his way of instilling a professional attitude in his brood, but Michael saw through that to the truth: "He felt that he was this young stud. He was too cool to be Dad. He was Joseph." The boys were regularly reminded that Joe thought of himself as their manager first, and as their father only when all else failed. Michael would remember the chill that went through them all when Joseph told them, "If you guys ever stop singing, I will drop you like a hot potato." Inside the Hayvenhurst compound, what Joe called "discipline" became more ritualized and sadistic. He would make you strip naked first, Michael remembered, then slather you with baby oil before bringing out the cut-off cord from a steam iron that he was using now instead of a leather strap, and crack it across the back of your thighs, so that when the tip struck it felt like an electric shock. "It would just be like dying," Michael remembered, "and you had whips all over your face, your back, everywhere . . . and I would just give up, like there was nothing I could do. And I hated him for it, *hated* him. We all did."

Their Bible-reading mother did little to stop it. "She was always the one in the background . . . I hear it now," Michael recalled. "'Joe, no, you're going to kill them. No! No, Joe, it's too much!' And he would be breaking the furniture. It was terrible." They would all beg Kate to divorce him, but, "she used to say, 'Leave me alone.'" Katherine's defenders would describe Mrs. Jackson as an abused woman who had been constantly bullied, threatened, and intimidated by her husband, and whose religion taught her that breaking up a marriage—any marriage—was a transgression against God.

Terror would run through the Hayvenhurst house the moment they heard Joe's car in the driveway, Michael said: "He always drove a big Mercedes, and he drives real slow. 'Joseph's home! Joseph's home! Quick!' Everybody runs to their room, doors slam." More than a few times, he either fainted or retched when forced to be in his father's presence. "When he comes in the room, and this aura comes and my stomach starts hurting, I know I am in trouble." Michael and his little sister Janet used to play a game of closing their eyes and picturing Joseph dead in his coffin, Michael remembered, and when he would ask if she felt sorry, Janet's answer was always the same: No.

It was worse when they were on tour. The scene Michael dreaded most was the one Joe created after a performance, when he would send his sons into the room where a buffet dinner was set up, then bring in perhaps a dozen girls that he had selected from the group at the stage door. "The room would be just lined with girls giggling, just loving us, like, 'Oh, my God!' and shaking," Michael remembered. "And if I was talking and something happened and he didn't like it, he'd get this look in his eye like—he'd get this look in his eye that would just scare you to death. He slapped me so hard in the face, as hard as he could, and then he'd thrust me out into the big room, where they are, tears running down my face, and what are you supposed to do, you know?"

The more Motown elevated Michael above the others, the angrier Joe seemed to become. There was nothing he could do, though, to prevent Gordy and his executives from launching the solo career that they saw in Michael's future. Michael's first solo single, "Got to Be There," was a sweetly innocent love song that was released in October 1971 and by Christmas had hit #1 on the *Cash Box* chart. The song became the title track of an album that was released in January 1972 and sent two more singles into the top ten. One of them, Michael's chirpy cover of "Rockin' Robin," actually sold better than "Got to Be There," rising to #2 on the *Billboard* pop chart.

The first Michael Jackson solo track to become a *Billboard* #1 was, in essence, a love song to a rat. Released only a few months after the *Got to Be There* album, "Ben" was the theme song for the movie sequel to the popular horror film *Willard*, about a meek social misfit whose strange affinity for rats leads ultimately to his being devoured by them. The leader of the rats, Ben, returned in the sequel, adopted by a character with whom Michael would identify: a lonely boy without friends who finally finds a companion in the superintelligent rodent. Michael, who kept pet rats himself, delivered a haunting, sentimental theme song for *Ben* that was both weirdly moving and astoundingly successful, not only reaching #1 on the *Billboard* chart, but nominated for an Academy Award as well. Michael sneaked into theaters on at least a dozen occasions to watch the film from the back of the audience, waiting until he could hear his song during a credit roll that included his own screen-size name.

The "normal life" that Michael repeatedly said he longed for was slipping further and further into impossibility. He had tried to follow Marlon to Emerson Junior High but being mobbed in the hallway made that difficult. Girls lined up outside his classrooms, trying to get a look at him through the tiny glass windows in the doors. A jealous boy made a death threat and that was the end of Michael's public school experience.

He had turned fourteen the month the album *Ben* was released and finally hit puberty around the same time. Reporters began to catch on to the lie about his age. Rumors about his sexuality were spreading by the time he turned fifteen. Publicly, Joe and his other sons countered with the laughable story that Michael was so promiscuous they had to keep the groupies away from him. The other male members of the Jackson family persisted in trying to convince Michael it was time to surrender his virginity. According to his sister Rebbie, one of them had tried to shake Michael's sexuality loose with some Jackson-style shock therapy, locking him in a hotel room with two adult hookers who left him scared, shaken, and still a virgin. The prostitutes were pretty rattled themselves; Michael had resisted their attempts to undress him, they said, by picking up his Bible and reading passages from Scripture aloud to them.

The loneliness that would become an increasingly chronic condition for Michael worsened year by year. He felt abandoned by his older siblings, who were all using marriage as an excuse to get places of their own and escape Joe's oppression. Rebbie had been the first to go, just eighteen when she announced that she intended to marry another Jehovah's Witness named Nathaniel Brown. Joe was adamantly opposed. Rebbie was a looker who had the biggest voice of all his children, and the richest, except for Michael's. She possessed everything she needed to be a star, Joe said, but instead the girl wanted to marry a man who was even more religious than her mother and become a housewife. For one of the very few times in her life, Katherine had opposed her husband and supported the marriage. Tito left in 1972, marrying at age eighteen—just like his older sister—a pretty seventeen-year-old of mixed black and Hispanic background named Dee Dee Martes. The wedding of nineteen-year-old Jermaine one year later made big news because the bride was Berry Gordy's oldest daughter Hazel. The year after that, twenty-three-year-old Jackie married Enid Spann, a mixed black and Korean beauty whom he had been dating since she was fifteen. In August 1975, shortly before Michael's seventeenth birthday, his eighteen-year-old brother Marlon secretly married a young fan from New Orleans named Carol Ann Parker, but didn't tell his parents about it until four months later.

The Jackson 5 was by then in an increasingly steep professional decline. After scoring consecutive #1 hits with their first four single releases, the group's fifth release, "Never Can Say Goodbye," would peak at #2. The Jacksons sent one more song to the top of the charts later in 1971 with "Mama's Pearl," but the group managed to chart in the top twenty only three times in the next several years, with 1971's "Sugar Daddy," 1972's "Lookin' Through the Windows," and 1974's disco number "Dancing Machine." Both at Motown and throughout the record industry, the Jackson 5 were regarded as a dwindling resource. Joe and his four oldest sons all blamed Motown's refusal to let the members of the group mature as artists. Though they played their instruments onstage, the music on their albums was still being made by either Motown's sizzling in-house studio band, the Funk Brothers, or by the Wrecking Crew at Hitsville West. The Jacksons had produced at least an album's worth of material at their home studio in the Hayvenhurst compound but Gordy's reluctance to let them perform their own songs either in the studio or onstage meant that not one of those songs had been heard by the public.

The group was being squeezed between Gordy's money-grubbing resistance to sharing songwriting royalties with his artists and the opinion of the man who was really running Motown, Ewart Abner, that the Jackson 5's time had passed. Michael was becoming as frustrated as his brothers. His third and fourth solo albums, *Music & Me* and *Forever, Michael*, had peaked on the pop charts at 93 and 101. Joe was furious that neither Michael's solo albums nor the newest Jackson 5 albums were receiving much promotional support from Motown and began to tell his sons they should leave the label. The executives and producers at Motown insisted that Joe's obnoxious attitude and clumsy incompetence were the problems; nobody wanted to work with the Jacksons because nobody wanted the stress and irritation of having their father around.

Amid the mounting tensions, sixteen-year-old Michael amazed everyone by phoning Berry Gordy personally and demanding a meeting, at which he let the Motown chief know just how unhappy he and his brothers had become. Gordy flattered and cajoled but made no promises. Joe and the other Jackson brothers were indignant when they learned that Michael had "gone behind our backs." Though outwardly apologetic, Michael was inwardly thrilled. He had asserted himself as never before and in the process won more respect from Gordy than his father ever did. It was the first of many indications to come that, for all his apparent social and sexual timidity, he could be as aggressive as necessary when it came to business. Things were different between him and his brothers—and especially between him and his father—from that day forward. Still, Michael went along with Jackie, Tito, and Marlon when they voted to leave Motown and let Joe look for a better deal at another label. Jermaine was excluded from the vote, and not just because he was out of town at the time: His marriage to Hazel Gordy had divided his loyalties and his brothers feared that he might stick with his father-in-law if things came to a head.

By the summer of 1975, Joe had negotiated a deal with CBS Records that provided the Jacksons a ten-fold increase in their royalty rate, a $750,000 signing bonus, and a $500,000 "recording fund," plus a guarantee of $350,000 per album, more than they had received for their most successful releases at Motown. The Jackson brothers were also given the right to choose three of the songs for each album, and to submit their own compositions for consideration, something Gordy and Abner had never permitted. Still, Michael said, he only signed the CBS contract after Joe "cajoled" him "with the promise that I'd get to have dinner with Fred Astaire . . . My father knew that I loved Fred with all my heart. He knew I would sign without reading the contract . . . It broke my heart that he did that. He tricked me."

Jermaine, though, not only refused to sign the CBS contract but immediately informed Gordy that the brothers were leaving Motown. He would be the president of the company some day, Gordy told his son-in-law. "I believed in Berry, not Joe," Jermaine explained to a reporter. At Gordy's insistence, Jermaine left the Jackson 5 thirty minutes before a scheduled performance at the Westbury Music Fair. Michael was nearly as upset as Joe when they learned that Gordy had successfully separated one of the brothers from the family. The difference was that Michael believed some of the blame was his father's.

Berry Gordy wasn't done making his displeasure felt among the Jacksons. His opening salvo was the announcement that a clause in the group's Motown contract gave him ownership of the name "Jackson 5" and the brothers would not be allowed to use it at CBS. Gordy also enlisted Jesse Jackson to raise whatever fuss he could about CBS "stealing a black act from a black record label." Finally, he sued Joe Jackson, the Jackson 5, and CBS for $5 million. Gordy let it be known that Motown would also begin compiling albums from some of the 295 unreleased Jackson 5 recordings that were still held in Motown's vaults. Joe and Richard Arons were convinced that Gordy would go as far as having them killed; the two actually began checking under the hood for bombs before they would start their cars and took roundabout routes whenever they drove in Los Angeles in order to avoid Gordy's supposed assassins.

Now recording for CBS subsidiary Epic Records as "The Jacksons," the brothers replaced Jermaine with fourteen-year-old Randy, and one year after signing with the company they celebrated the announcement that the five of them, along with their three sisters, were about to become the stars of the first television variety show in American history hosted by a black family. *The Jacksons* would run on CBS television for less than a year and was ranked last in the Nielsen ratings at the time of its cancellation in March 1977, but the show was seen as seminal nonetheless, launching the career of the one Jackson who showed any ability as a comic actor, ten-year-old Janet. She was subsequently hired by Norman Lear to play the role of Millicent "Penny" Gordon Woods on his sitcom *Good Times*.

The Jacksons was also the title of the brothers' first album for CBS. It went no higher than #36 on the charts, possibly because Gordy had confused the public by releasing his own Jacksons album, the weak *Joyful Jukebox Music*, at almost the same time. Jermaine's first solo release for Motown, *My Name Is Jermaine*, did far worse, peaking at 164 on the top two hundred. *Billboard* called the album a bomb. Disgusted that Joe reveled in Jermaine's failure, Michael began to look for some way to get time away from his family and his father to think about where his career was headed. The opportunity to do just that came along in the summer of 1977 when he was offered the role of the Scarecrow in the all-black cast of *The Wiz*, a musical film based on L. Frank Baum's *The Wonderful Wizard of Oz* that would be directed by Sidney Lumet. Shooting would take place in New York at the Astoria Studios in Queens.

Production of *The Wiz* was burdened from the start by the casting of Diana Ross as Dorothy, a role most of the public identified with Judy Garland's performance in the 1939 classic film *The Wizard of Oz*. Ross was thirty-three, twice the age that Garland had been when she played the twelve-year-old Kansas farm girl. Stephanie Mills, the young actress who had been Dorothy in the Broadway production of *The Wiz*, had just signed a recording contract with Motown and was the preferred choice for the part, but Ross wrested the role away from her, overcoming even the resistance of the film's producer, Berry Gordy.

The Wiz was a commercial disaster but not due to any fault on Michael's part. He'd pushed himself hard during the 1978 production, collapsing with a burst blood vessel after nearly dancing himself to death on set—the critics took notice and Michael was credited with the film's one really strong performance. Joe had vigorously opposed Michael's decision to act in *The Wiz*, fearful that becoming a movie star would set the Jacksons' lead singer even further apart from his brothers. Michael's decision to go to New York and work on the film anyway was the boldest declaration of independence that he had made up to that point in his life.

Michael was now openly questioning his father's abilities as a manager. Joe's abrasive personality was already making relations difficult with the producers and executives at CBS, whose help the Jacksons needed if the group was to make a comeback. Lots of people in the record business by then didn't like Joe, in part because he refused to hide his disdain for people with light complexions. That bothered Michael almost as much as Joe's tendency to repeatedly go for the short money, the sure thing, instead of planning for the long term. His father's foremost concern continued to be the Jacksons franchise, even as it was becoming increasingly clear to everyone at CBS that Michael's solo career was the future. Jermaine's absence from the group was making that fact obvious. The pretense that the brothers were a package of major talent had gradually dissolved as Jermaine's solo career at Motown floundered. His second album, *Feel the Fire*, had performed even worse than the first, evidence for many that backing his little brother was the best use of Jermaine's singing voice. Jackie's sweet but thin high tenor had been exposed in the one solo album he was allowed to record for Motown, *Jackie Jackson*, which failed to chart. Tito continued to be no better than a journeyman guitarist, and everyone knew that Marlon, the funniest and friendliest of the Jackson brothers, was just along for the ride. Joe wanted that ride to continue for all his sons, but especially for himself, and had never offered more than lukewarm support for Michael's solo career, which he foresaw as the demise of the group. Joe did battle with CBS to win the company's approval for a new album that the Jacksons would write and produce, but for him that meant *all* the boys, equally. CBS executives, though, were beginning to recognize that Michael wasn't simply the best singer and dancer among the Jacksons, but also the best writer. The one notable song on the Jacksons' second album for CBS, *Goin' Places*, had been "Different Kind of Lady," a jittery R & B/ disco hybrid penned by Michael that was hugely popular in the dance clubs in both Los Angeles and New York. Even as CBS's new president, Walter Yetnikoff, confided to other company executives that he was inclined to drop the Jacksons from the label, he was urged by some of them to let Michael put together a solo album of his own compositions.

Michael's increasing confidence in his abilities as an artist was undercut by the shame he felt about his appearance. Around the time of his fifteenth birthday, he had begun to suffer severe acne. He was already self-conscious about his looks, especially his wide nose. Nothing wounded him more during this period than the expression of disbelief he so often saw in the faces of those who were introduced to him at the Hayvenhurst house. Strangers "would come up and ask if I knew where that 'cute little Michael' was," he explained to the *Los Angeles Times* music writer Robert Hilburn. People actually shook their heads when they realized that "cute little Michael" had been replaced by this awkward teenager with erupting skin. He began refusing to leave the house when he didn't have to, and was unable to look people in the eye when he was forced to go out in public. His mother would say that the difficulties of this period, in particular the blooms of acne that circled his face from forehead to chin, actually changed her son's personality: "He was no longer a carefree, outgoing, devilish boy. He was quieter, more serious, and more of a loner."

Shortly before his sixteenth birthday, it struck Michael hard that he had never in his life made a real friend. His attempt to rectify that confused everyone around him, especially the members of his family. At the 1974 American Music Awards ceremony, Michael and Donny Osmond had served as cohosts with six-year-old Rodney Allen Rippy, a child actor who had appeared in several feature films, including Mel Brooks's *Blazing Saddles*, but was best-known for a series of sickly sweet Jack in the Box commercials that had featured his frustrated attempts to get a grip on a Jumbo Jack. The boy had been taken aback when Michael asked for his phone number, and was stunned when the pop star began to call him every Saturday morning, at exactly ten o'clock. They were buddies, nothing more, as Rippy would take pains to make clear later: "Michael would give me advice about how to handle myself in show business, about smiling at people and shaking their hands. It was just stuff like that we talked about. Very ordinary. It absolutely amazed me that Michael Jackson was interested in what was going on in my little world."

Even among those who did not know that Michael's best friend was a boy who had just started elementary school, questions about his sexuality were proliferating, and he took these more and more personally. He was especially stung by the false rumor that his father was having him injected with female hormones to keep his voice high. In the months before moving to New York to work on *The Wiz*, he had attempted to normalize his image by dating Tatum O'Neal, then a thirteen-year-old Oscar winner for *Paper Moon* with a woman's body and a wild thing reputation. They'd "taken up," as Michael would put it, after an encounter at On the Rox, a small satellite club attached to the Roxy on Sunset Strip, where they happened to be seated at adjacent tables one evening in the spring of 1977. Without warning or introduction, Tatum had reached out to hold Michael's hand as she sat with her father, actor Ryan O'Neal, while Michael chatted with a pair of publicists from Epic Records. For him, this was "serious stuff," Michael would explain: "*She touched me.*" Their first date was the next evening, when Tatum invited Michael to a dinner party hosted by Hugh Hefner at the Playboy Mansion, where the girl suggested they go hot-tubbing together—naked. Michael insisted on swim suits. "I fell in love with her (and she with me) and we were very close for a long time," Michael would write later in his "autobiography" *Moonwalker*. That wasn't exactly how O'Neal recalled the relationship. Tatum told friends that

Michael could barely bring himself to speak to her, let alone make sexual contact. The affair, to use the term loosely, would finish in an infamous fizzle during a party at Rod Stewart's house in Beverly Hills. According to a story that was repeated throughout Hollywood and reported later in the tabloids, O'Neal and a female friend of hers had tried to pull Michael into bed with them. He had not only refused sex, it was said, but dashed from the house blinking back tears, chased by the taunts and jeers of other guests. Whispers about the young man's sexuality grew into a murmur of innuendo and ridicule that would increase in volume over the next decade.

The worst part for Michael might not have been how he left the party, but his realization that he had nowhere else he wanted to be. The closed circle of his family was making him feel more and more claustrophobic and life at the Hayvenhurst house had become all but unbearable. His brothers had married, but their brides were never really admitted to the Jacksons' inner circle. Katherine referred to them collectively as "the wives," as if to make clear they weren't quite the same as those she called "the family." Michael was still phoning Rodney Allen Rippy every Saturday morning but longed for someone to share his thoughts with on the other days of the week. Instead, he was forced to substitute the rats and snakes and birds he kept in cages in the playhouse.

In New York, he had discovered the joy of being in disguise. Concealing his identity (and perhaps more important, covering his acne) with the full makeup that transformed him into the Scarecrow while he was working on *The Wiz* had allowed Michael an opportunity to hide and hold his head up high at the same time. He reveled in the discovery of how freeing it could be to meet people when you were wearing a mask. Members of the crew would say later that they had to literally drag him off the set each evening. When he went out at night as Michael Jackson, he now at least had a ready explanation for his bad skin—all that makeup he had to wear. And he was going out a lot that autumn in New York.

Michael became a regular at Studio 54 just as the disco club was reaching the crest of its popularity. Watching the floor show there was the closest he had ever come to forgetting he was a Jehovah's Witness. People were shoveling cocaine up their noses at Studio 54, spilling more on their shoes than could be found in some small American cities, then following the coke with chasers of amyl nitrate. Upstairs, the "Rubber Room" was the stage for a disorganized orgy, with people having sex of every conceivable variety under no more cover than a darkened corner, and lots more having sex on the catwalks overhead. Michael came in many nights with Liza

Minnelli, who had befriended him at the club and took him regularly to the so-called VIP room in the basement, a dingy little space bordered by chain-link fences where celebrities sat in white plastic lawn chairs laughing about what the people who couldn't get in imagined it must be like down there. On the main floor, Michael was often seen at the same table with Andy Warhol, who like him was much more interested in watching sex than having it, and who didn't expect him to make conversation. Truman Capote, another companion, described Michael and his sister La Toya as "oases of innocence" amid the debauch of Studio 54. The two didn't drink, didn't use drugs, and certainly didn't have sex. Michael would watch people acting out sexually, Capote recalled, but did it the same way that he watched James Brown dance, like he was studying what he saw in order to put it to use at some later time.

Michael's greatest breakthrough in New York had come when he secured a promise from the executives at Epic Records that he would have creative control of his next solo album. He wanted to start work on it as soon as he returned to Los Angeles. But the brothers all insisted he had to wait until they had finished the next group album, *Destiny*, and outvoted him four-to-one. They proceeded with apprehension, though, deferring to Michael's opinion in ways they never had before. Even Joe was walking softly, fearful of alienating the one group member they all knew was indispensable.

Michael had come back from New York skinnier than anyone had ever seen him, speaking in a peculiar breathy falsetto that made people lean in close to hear him. At the same time, he exuded a new authority and seemed reluctant to share his thoughts with anyone in the family. He was itchy and irritable around the house, snapping at even his mother for the first time any of them could remember. Joe responded to Michael's moodiness by demanding that CBS and Epic give his boys the same sort of control of the Jacksons' new album that had been promised to Michael as a solo act. He knew how much was riding on *Destiny*. Joe was concerned enough about the Jacksons' future, in fact, to hire a couple of white comanagers, Ron Weisner and Freddy DeMann, to ensure not only that CBS kept its promise about letting his sons write their own material but also that the company would push for crossover promotion, giving just as much attention to securing a white audience for the boys as it did to satisfying the Jacksons' black fans.

The result was the best album the brothers Jackson had so far released, either at Epic or at Motown. Throughout the music industry, it was agreed that there wasn't a weak song on *Destiny* and that Michael Jackson had delivered a tremendous performance on the album. The range of his voice, combined with his ability to adapt to varying styles and tempos, was what most amazed people. Ever since passing through puberty Michael had been dealing with questions about whether he had a voice that would work for him as an adult. Ben Fong-Torres observed how skillfully Michael was coping with his vocal slippage "by switching registers in the middle of phrases and by changing the keys," but there was still a feeling that his best performances as a singer might have been delivered before he turned fourteen. On *Destiny*, though, Michael had transitioned with seeming effortlessness from the lush ballad "Push Me Away" to the snap and crackle of "Shake Your Body (Down to the Ground)," handling each masterfully. The latter song, written by Michael with his younger brother Randy, was a huge hit, hailed from the first as one of the handful of truly great disco numbers ever released. There was perhaps more to Michael Jackson, several reviewers observed, than anyone had previously realized.

Michael, though, was more embarrassed by *Destiny* than proud of it. He was especially upset by a jacket photo in which his brothers, egged on by Joe, had posed behind the studio control board as if they were writers and producers of the album. Mike Atkinson and Bobby Colomby had actually produced the album, but only Michael among the five brothers voted to give the pair credit. Atkinson and Colomby (the latter more responsible for persuading Walter Yetnikoff to give the Jacksons another chance than anyone at CBS) had to obtain affidavits from the engineers and musicians who worked on *Destiny* in order to win their executive producer credits.

The disappointing release of *The Wiz* in the midst of the *Destiny* tour was little more than a footnote in the swirl of discontent that surrounded Michael in early 1979. The depth and intensity of his wish to become a movie star was something Michael would not share with his brothers or with Joe. He agonized in private over the one plum part he was offered after the release of *The Wiz*, that of the transvestite dancer in the film version of the Broadway hit *A Chorus Line*. Michael turned down the role, concerned he would be seen by the public as "that way." It was an old wound. *Jet* magazine reported as fact the gossip that he was considering a sex change operation so that he could marry actor Clifton Davis (who had written the Jackson 5 song "Never Can Say Goodbye"). When J. Randy Taraborrelli, the *Soul* magazine reporter who would become the chief chronicler of Michael's youth, had felt compelled to ask him if he was homosexual, it upset him further. "I am not homo," Michael snapped in reply. "Not at all." As a devout Jehovah's

Witness, he was required to see homosexuality as an abomination. "What is it about me that makes people think I'm gay?" Michael demanded. "Is it my voice? Is it because I have this soft voice? All of us in the family have soft voices. Or is it because I don't have a lot of girlfriends?"

Michael worried also that his movie star ambitions would be hindered by his appearance, a subject that made him even more uncomfortable than questions about his sexuality. He was still fighting severe acne outbreaks and increasingly bothered that he had the darkest skin among his siblings, who teased their brother during Taraborrelli's visit to the Hayvenhurst estate a week before Michael's twentieth birthday by calling him "Big Nose" and "Liver Lips." He was most deeply injured, though, by one his father's typically cruel remarks. "I was going through an awkward puberty when your features start to change, and he went, 'Ugh, you have a big nose. You didn't get it from me,'" Michael recalled in a conversation with Rabbi Boteach. "He didn't realize how much that hurt me. It hurt me so bad, I wanted to die."

By the time Michael returned home to Los Angeles from the *Destiny* tour in the spring of 1979, the tension created by a constant effort to counter deep insecurities with towering ambitions was fueling an obsessive focus on the solo album he had deferred for nearly a year now. His brothers wanted to work on the album with him, but Michael refused, even when Katherine attempted to convince him that he owed them. The balance of power had shifted for good. This new record was nothing to worry about, Joe assured his other sons. Michael's first two solo albums, made when he was still a prepubescent boy soprano, had charted well enough, but the two made after his voice changed were miserable failures, and this new one would most likely be the same.

Michael was receiving a good deal more support from Quincy Jones, the musical director from *The Wiz*, whom he had chosen to produce his new album. He had asked if he could produce Michael's next solo album, Jones would recall, while they were preparing to begin principal photography on *The Wiz*. "At rehearsals with the cast, during the part where the scarecrow is pulling proverbs from his stuffing, Michael kept saying 'So-Crates' instead of 'Socrates,'" Jones recalled. "After about the third time, I pulled him aside and told him the correct pronunciation. He looked at me with these big wide eyes and said, 'Really?' and it was at that moment that I said, 'Michael, I'd like to produce your album.' It was that wonderment that I saw in his eyes that locked me in. I knew that we could go into completely unexplored territory, a place that as a jazz musician gave me goose bumps."

The young man's oddities and uncertainties were on full display when they began work on the new album in Los Angeles nearly one year later, but Jones could see that they were more than matched by his effort and ambition. Michael was coming into the studio better prepared than any artist he had ever worked with before, Jones said. "Driven" and "determined" were the two adjectives the album's producer would most often use to describe his young star. On top of that, Michael was more willing to accept criticism than any other performer he had seen, Jones said, even when distraught over the announcement that only three of his own compositions had been selected for the album's final cut. Throughout the production, "I saw his sensitivity and his focus," Jones recalled. "There was such an innocence, but he didn't miss a thing."

Anyone associated with the record who would later claim they knew it was going to be a big hit was "a flat-out liar," Jones would say thirty years later. "We had no idea *Off the Wall* was going to be as successful as it was, but we were thrilled. Michael had moved from the realm of bubble-gum pop and planted his flag square in the heart of the musical pulse of the '80s."

The three songs from *Off the Wall* that Michael had written would turn out to be among the albums most successful numbers. Michael's falsetto funkfest "Don't Stop 'Til You Get Enough," in fact, was the biggest hit of an album stocked with them, becoming his first recording to reach #1 on the pop charts in more than seven years. The pulsating "Rock With You" (written by Rod Temperton) also hit #1, while two other cuts from the album, "Off the Wall" (also by Temperton) and "She's Out of My Life" (written by Tom Bahler), reached the top ten, making Michael the first solo artist in pop history to put four singles off the same album into the top ten. Reviewers were almost unanimous in praising the record, agreeing that there wasn't a weak number on it. The buying public agreed: *Off the Wall* would sell nearly five million copies domestically, and another two million in the foreign market.

Jackson had his publicist send a letter to Jann Wenner, *Rolling Stone*'s editor and publisher, suggesting that Michael should be on the magazine's cover in light of *Off the Wall*'s success. Wenner wrote back, "We would very much like to do a major piece on Michael Jackson but feel it is not a cover story." Furious, Michael said it was because editors believed that putting a black person on the cover resulted in fewer sales at the newsstand and vowed to prove them wrong. When *Off the Wall* won only a single Grammy, for best R & B album, Jackson sobbed around the house for weeks, then repeated his vow to deliver another solo album as soon as he could, to "show them."

Michael turned twenty-one shortly after the release of *Off the Wall* and celebrated his legal adulthood by announcing that he intended to hire his own attorney to examine his business affairs and explain to him where all the money was going. Joe was incensed and confronted his son but Michael refused to budge, and the two stopped speaking to one another. Katherine tried to intervene, urging her son to believe that his father was working in his best interest, but Michael held firm.

His search for new representation was a short one. Michael had been deeply impressed by the very first attorney he interviewed, a thirty-one-year-old corporate tax specialist named John Branca, who was at that time best known for being the nephew of Ralph Branca, the former Brooklyn Dodgers pitcher who had given up the playoff-deciding "Shot Heard 'round the World" to the New York Giants' Bobby Thomson in 1951. Branca offered to organize Michael's finances and promised to renegotiate his contract with CBS. The attorney proceeded to do just that and was soon reporting back to Michael that from this day forward he would receive the highest royalty rate in the business as a solo artist, 37 percent, the same as Bob Dylan. Not only that, Branca added, but CBS had agreed to let Michael leave the Jacksons any time he wanted, without affecting his brothers' relationship with the company.

Branca would say later that he had motivated himself during his negotiations with CBS by recalling something Michael told him right at the start of their first meeting: "I intend to be the biggest star in show business, and the richest."

"Thriller Time" was how Michael Jackson would refer to the two-year period of his life that followed the release of his seminal album, as if recalling an alternate dimension of temporal reality. Thriller Time changed everything, certainly, and just as certainly, changed nothing at all. In those twenty-four months, and in the twenty-four years that followed them, Michael Jackson would demonstrate as completely as any person ever has that the central truism of the celebrity experience is that getting what you want will never make up for not having what you need.

All Michael knew for sure in early 1980 was that the success of *Off the Wall* had not satisfied him. His *next* record, he assured everyone around him, would sell *twice* that many copies. He would have to wait to prove that, though, because his family had already made sure that the next Michael Jackson record would belong to them.

Released in July 1980, the Jacksons' *Triumph* was, all things considered, a major success for the group. Critics called it the strongest album the brothers had ever put out, and the public was only slightly less enthusiastic. Three songs (all either written or cowritten by Michael) from *Triumph* charted in the top twenty and the album itself was certified platinum within six months of its release. Michael sang lead on nearly every number, but even during those recording sessions had scarcely concealed his frustration at being forced to delay work on a new solo album. His brothers, on the other hand, could barely contain their excitement about the impending *Triumph* tour, scheduled to visit thirty-nine cities beginning in July 1981, in spite of Michael's reluctance to accompany them.

He certainly didn't need the money; *Off the Wall* had made him wealthier than the rest of his family put together. For the first time in his life, he was acquiring assets, among them the house his parents lived in. Joe surrendered his interest in the Hayvenhurst estate to Michael in February 1981. In his determination to prove to the world (and to Berry Gordy in particular) that he could stand on his own as a businessman, Joe had dug himself a hole so deep that in the end there was nothing to do but cry out for help. It had started in 1974 when he formed his own record company, Ivory Tower International Records, planning to build the business around a female quartet from Ohio that called itself M.D.L.T. Willis. The group and the label went nowhere. Joe would sign, manage, and produce several other singing groups during the next seven years, and they all fizzled as well. By the beginning of 1981, he was hugely overleveraged and so desperate for cash that he offered Michael half of the Hayvenhurst estate for $500,000. It wasn't long after that before Joe sold Michael half of the half of the property that the parents had tried to keep for themselves, leaving Katherine with just a 25 percent interest in the estate and Joe with the understanding that he was now his son's tenant.

Joe still had his share of the management fees from *Triumph* coming in and would receive about 5 percent of the net profits from the *Triumph* tour—if Michael agreed to participate. As usual, Joe counted on Katherine to make that happen. Despite having filed her second divorce action against Joe just a few months earlier, Katherine did what her husband and her other sons begged her to do and persuaded Michael that he owed the family a piece of his enormous success. Half of whatever Joe got out of the deal, after all, was hers.

It was understood from the beginning that Michael would be the stand-alone star of the show on the *Triumph* tour. The grandest productions and the biggest applause at each stop came whenever he performed one of his solos from *Off the Wall*. The last number of every show would be "Don't Stop 'Til You Get Enough," which ended with Michael disappearing into a giant smoke screen created by Doug Henning, the magician who was accompanying the Jacksons on the tour. Neither the audience nor his brothers would see him after that. Michael not only refused to socialize with anyone connected to the tour but issued strict instructions that no one was to use swear words, make sexual references, or tell dirty jokes while in his presence. Still upset that he had ended the *Destiny* tour with a bad case of laryngitis, Michael declined to speak except when he had to, sipped a brew of lemon and honey constantly, and insisted that air conditioners be turned off whenever he was in a room—even if it was ninety-five degrees outside. All he wanted, Michael made clear, was for this tour to be over. "I will *never* do this again," he told *Soul* magazine's Taraborrelli. "Ever."

Robert Hilburn interviewed Michael in the back of a tour bus after the show in St. Louis and found the star to be quite different in person from "the charismatic, strutting figure" he had seen onstage. The Michael Jackson he met face-to-face was "anxious," the *Los Angeles Times* writer recalled, "frequently bowing his head as he whispered answers." At one point Hilburn asked Michael why he didn't live on his own like his brothers. Unbeknownst to the writer, Michael had bought a condominium near the Hayvenhurst compound back in February 1981, but rarely slept there. "I think I'd die on my own," Michael told Hilburn. "Even at home I'm lonely. I sit in my room and sometimes cry. It is so hard to make friends and there are some things you can't talk to your parents or family about. I sometimes walk around the neighborhood at night, just hoping to find someone to talk to. But I just end up coming home."

Michael was making such admissions more often in interviews, as if he wanted people to understand how strange he was, how strange his life had been, and how strange the world *they* lived in was to him. "See, my whole life has been onstage," he explained to Gerri Hirshey when she interviewed him for *Rolling Stone*, "and the impression I get of people is applause, standing ovations, and people running after you. In a crowd, I'm afraid. Onstage, I feel safe. If I could, I would sleep on the stage."

CBS president Walter Yetnikoff had been quick to recognize Michael's vulnerability and quicker still to exploit it. "He had no social skills," Yetnikoff would recall later. "Sometimes I felt like he was still six." On his first visit to the CBS corporate headquarters, Yetnikoff remembered, Michael interrupted a meeting to say, "Walter, I have to tinkle. Can you take me to the potty?" At another meeting, Michael confided how hurt his feelings had been by Joe. "He said, 'You know, I've accomplished a lot,'" Yetnikoff recalled. "'And my father has never told me that he's proud of me.' And I became Daddy, and I said, 'Come here, Michael, let me give you a hug and tell you how proud everyone in the pop music field is of you.'" Soon after, Yetnikoff began to point out that if he really wanted to show Joe who he was, breaking away from the Jacksons to continue his solo career was the way to do it. It was exactly what the young star wanted to hear.

Michael returned to Los Angeles in spring 1982 prepared to impose his will. The Hayvenhurst house had been demolished at his instruction during the *Triumph* tour and rebuilt into a Tudor mansion with beveled glass windows and clinker brick chimneys. On the grounds, he assembled his first full-scale menagerie, buying black and white swans for the ponds out back, a pair of peacocks named Winter and Spring, two llamas named for Louis Armstrong and Lola Falana, a couple of deer he called Prince and Princess, a giraffe he dubbed Jabbar, and a ram he named Mr. Tibbs. All the animals slept in a stable at night but were free to roam during the day. Neighbors would complain about the stench when summer came.

The centerpiece of this early attempt to create an environment tailored to his fragile psyche was a small-scale version of Disneyland's Main Street U.S.A. (with its own candy store) next to the garage. Even as he fussed over every detail of the Hayvenhurst house reinvention, though, Michael's bedroom on the upstairs floor of the house continued to look as if he had just moved in or was about to move out. Books and records remained stacked in knee-high piles and clutter was everywhere. He never bothered to put a bed in his room, preferring to sleep on a thick green rug by the fireplace. His one effort to personalize the space was a multicultural collection of five life-size, female mannequins—one white, one black, one Asian, one Latina, and one Middle Eastern—all of them elaborately dressed in the latest fashions. He gave the mannequins names and introduced them as his friends.

His mother complained that Michael never seemed to eat and La Toya, whose room was just down the hall, swore that he never turned the lights off at night. Michael was up reading long after she went to sleep and she was often awakened at two, three, or four in the morning by the sound of him laughing hysterically at a Three Stooges video he had seen ten times before. He was working in there all the time, too, though, filling the notebook he carried with lyrics, humming melodies into a tape recorder, or studying the songs other writers had submitted to him, like a mad scientist locked up in his laboratory.

The recording of the new album began at Westlake Studios in Los Angeles during April 1982. He and Quincy Jones gradually winnowed a list of thirty songs down to the nine that would appear on the album. Michael had decided that "Thriller," a spooky, feral number enlivened by the catchy hooks that were songwriter Rod Temperton's specialty, would be the title track. "This is going to be a *big* album," Jackson declared more than once during the engineering sessions, and Jones suspected that might be true. "All the brilliance that had been building inside Michael Jackson for twenty-four years just erupted," Jones told author Alex Haley in an interview for *Play-boy* magazine. "I was electrified, and so was everyone else involved in the project." Musicians and engineers were so caught up in the drama of it all that during one recording session they kept cranking the volume up higher and higher until suddenly the speakers overloaded and burst into flames. "Only time I saw anything like that in forty years in the business," Jones said.

Yet immediately before *Thriller*'s release on November 30, 1982, Jones was among those who warned Michael not to expect too much. The country was in the midst of the worst recession in more than twenty years and record purchases, like every other form of discretionary spending, had dropped off dramatically. Selling two million units would be a big success in this market, Michael's comanager Ron Weisner advised him one day when engineers were putting the final touches on the album. Michael sputtered in fury for a few moments, then stalked out of the studio. The next morning, he phoned Walter Yetnikoff and said that if the people he trusted had so little faith in him, he didn't want to even release the album. Yetnikoff played him perfectly: "Who cares what they say?" the CBS Records president told Michael. "You're the superstar."

Thriller's release two weeks later was a tsunami that caught the entire music industry by surprise. The first song from the album released as a single was the weakest cut on it, Michael's sugary duet with Paul McCartney on "The Girl Is Mine," which rose to #2 on the *Billboard* Top 100. The second single, "Billie Jean," was a song into which Michael channeled his disturbances with astounding skill and unnerving passion. Randy Taraborrelli popularized the notion that "Billie Jean" was inspired by an obsessed female fan who had tried to convince him to join her in a double suicide. Plastic surgeon Steven Hoefflin claimed that "Billie Jean" had been inspired by a beautiful young woman Michael spotted in a crowd gathered at the gates of the Hayvenhurst compound. Hoefflin said that Michael told him he'd been in a car with two of his brothers and wrote the entire song during that drive, later sketching the girl's nude form and giving it to Hoefflin as a gift.

Michael himself would insist that he wasn't thinking of any one girl in particular when he wrote "Billie Jean" (in three minutes, according to Hoefflin), but had created a composite of the especially persistent groupies whom he and his brothers had encountered while touring over the years. This claim probably had some truth to it, but in the end "Billie Jean" was more about Michael himself, as if he'd observed his own impending nervous breakdown and responded by creating the most danceable therapy imaginable. Katherine was as much a catalyst of the lyric as any groupie or fan, the mama who warned him to "be careful who you love." The girls Joe and his brothers had used and discarded on the road floated like ghosts through the lyric and so did the young women who had tempted Michael along the way.

"I knew it was going to be big when I was writing it," Michael said of "Billie Jean." He was so consumed by the song, Michael recalled, that he failed to notice his Mercedes catch fire on the freeway one day while he was driving to the recording studio, and was alerted only when a young motorcyclist waved him over. Quincy Jones didn't get "Billie Jean," though, and wanted to keep it off the album. When a stunned Michael insisted it remain, Jones suggested changing the title to "Not My Lover," because he worried that listeners would think Michael was referring to the tennis player Billie Jean King. Jones then demanded that Michael cut the song's lengthy percussive introduction. That was the part that made him want to dance, Michael said; it stayed. The dispute between the two turned nasty for a couple of days, but might ultimately have served "Billie Jean." Jones instructed engineer Bruce Swedien that if Michael insisted upon opening the song with thirty seconds of drumbeats, then they had to be the most memorable drumbeats anyone had ever heard—a "sonic personality," as Jones described it. Swedien, who usually mixed a number just once, mixed "Billie Jean" ninety-one times in order to create the percussive platform from which the song arose, adding a bass drum cover that came in after the first four bars of kick, snare, and hi-hat, then taps on a flat piece of wood that were filtered in between the beats. Swedien's removal of reverberation from the opening drum sequence gave "Billie Jean" a stark, emotionally naked quality that grew gradually into a kind of euphoric hysteria as notes were doubled by a distorted synth bass that turned sharply staccato, underlaid by a deep echoing throb.

Michael's voice came in softly, accompanied by finger snaps as it increased steadily in volume and intensity. By the time the violins and guitar solos entered, a seemingly random series of shouts, screams, and spectral laughs (overdubs made by Michael singing through a cardboard tube) began to sound in the spaces between notes, like a sort of viral insanity trying to gain entry to the listener's mind. Michael accompanied the eerie, disembodied chatter with a series of what sounded like musical hiccups, as if he were trying to cough up some evil spirit, while the propulsive bass line just kept moving ahead toward some inexorable reckoning that everyone who heard the song knew would not have a happy ending. Michael would never again deliver a song that was either so relentless or so revealing.

People moaned and shrieked when "Billie Jean" first began to be played in the clubs of Los Angeles, as if the song had infected them with a compulsive fusion of madness and glee, pouring onto dance floors and demanding that it be played again. The level of sexual display it inspired was unprecedented. Reviewers called the song "scary," "bizarre," and "eccentric," then added that they absolutely loved it. "Billie Jean" went to #1 on the pop charts almost overnight and stayed there for weeks, followed shortly by "Beat It," the first true rock song Michael had ever recorded, a cut included on the album because he wanted to prove that no genre was beyond his grasp. Quincy Jones had suggested trying the song and recruited Eddie Van Halen to contribute a guitar solo that sounded like the flapping wings of a metal bird in a wire cage. By March 1983, Michael was among the handful of performers who had ever placed two songs in the top five at the same time. The critical mass that created would sustain *Thriller* commercially for sixteen months, as seven of the album's nine songs were released and became top ten singles, from the edgy "Wanna Be Startin' Somethin'" to the symphonic "Human Nature" to the sassy "P.Y.T.," which was the biggest hit among black audiences. By April 1983, *Thriller* was selling as many as 500,000 copies per week and putting up numbers the music business had never seen before, recession or no recession. Michael became, as *Rolling Stone* put it, "quite simply, the biggest star in the pop music universe."

That star was about to go supernova. On March 25, 1983, two weeks after "Beat It" reached #1 on the pop charts, an invitation-only audience at the Pasadena Auditorium was present to watch the taping of the *Motown 25: Yesterday, Today, and Forever* NBC television special. Like Diana Ross and Marvin Gaye, Michael had nearly refused to participate in the program, which was meant to honor Berry Gordy. The gradual realization of how poorly he'd paid them had alienated many of Gordy's Motown stars, forcing the proud mogul to make a series of pleading phone calls. Michael withheld consent until he was promised a solo spot after he performed with his brothers, and even then refused to sing one of his Motown hits, insisting instead that his solo would be "Billie Jean." Much as he wanted to say no to that, Gordy knew he couldn't. He would be glad he didn't.

Jermaine was back with his brothers when the Jackson 5 went on before an audience that had already sat through performances by Marvin Gaye and Smokey Robinson. The Jacksons' "reunion" began with Michael singing lead on "I Want You Back" and built momentum right up through his moving duet with Jermaine on "I'll Be There." The brothers exchanged hugs before the adoring crowd, then trotted offstage—all except Michael, who seemed to hover in darkness for a moment, until the spotlight settled on him. He looked different than people remembered him. He had always been slender, but now he was lithe. The macrobiotic diet he'd adopted and whatever dermatology treatments he was receiving had vanquished his acne. His skin was lighter, but still dark, his nose a little narrower, but not altered in a jarring feminine way. His high, stiff Afro had settled into soft curls.

The costume he wore would become a trademark ensemble, but that night was the first time anyone had seen the sequined black jacket (borrowed from his mother's closet) with spangled silver cuffs that matched his shirt and the black tuxedo pants hemmed above the ankle to show off his glittery white socks and shiny black Bass Weejuns. And of course there was the rhinestone-studded glove worn on his left hand. He seemed diffident at first, as if unsure what to say or do, speaking softly as he paced the stage, restlessly shy, and thanked the audience for letting him share those "magic moments" with his brothers. No one watching could have imagined that every bit of what he did or said was rehearsed. "Those were the good songs," Michael said, as he approached a curtain at the edge of the stage and grabbed a black fedora from someone's hand. "I like those songs a lot," he continued, moving back toward the center of the stage. "But especially I like . . . the *new* songs."

Louis Johnson's splatting bass guitar riff from "Billie Jean" kicked in at that moment, as Michael stuck the fedora on his head and began a rhythmic pumping of his pelvis so pronounced that it looked almost cartoonlike. An audience that consisted mostly of music executives, music writers, and music makers sat rapt, mouths open, palms on cheeks as they watched Michael Jackson translate the language of his song into dance. There were people present who would swear that he levitated when he brought his performance to a climax with his unveiling of the "moonwalk," a reverse toe-to-heel glide that moved him—magically it seemed—backward across the stage, before he finished by spinning into a pose balanced on the very tips of his toes. What he got in return was more than a standing ovation. People actually climbed onto their chairs to applaud him. Weeping and laughing, members of the audience congratulated one another for having been there to see it.

The rapture of the crowd was palpable even through a television screen when *Motown 25* aired on May 16, 1983. The day after Michael Jackson's performance was seen by an audience of fifty million Americans—more than had ever viewed a musical special before—he found himself standing atop the Mount Everest of adulation, alone at a summit of fame and fortune that no solo performer other than Elvis Presley had reached before him. And he wouldn't have to come down for at least another year.

Billboard listed *Thriller* as the #1 record in the country for an unprecedented thirty-seven weeks and the album remained on the charts for two solid years. Everyone who was anyone wanted to meet Michael Jackson. The matinee idols of his youth reached out to him from every direction. Fred Astaire wanted Michael to come over to the house and teach him the moonwalk. Elizabeth Taylor phoned to ask for tickets to his next concert appearance. Marlon Brando invited him to drop by for lunch.

The crazy velocity of it all kicked into a still higher gear in December 1983 when the "Thriller" video premiered. The project had been initiated when Michael saw the film *An American Werewolf in London*, then phoned the movie's director John Landis to say, "I want to turn into a monster. Can I do that?" Landis brought makeup artist Rick Baker along to his first meeting with Michael and the two showed the star a big book of Hollywood creatures. Michael was frightened by the images, Landis would recall—"he hadn't seen many horror films"—but nevertheless asked the director to write something that featured a combination werewolf–cat person character. CBS balked at the extravagant script for the video that Landis submitted. Nearly a year after its release, the *Thriller* album was beginning to slip down the charts and shooting from this script would cost a fortune. Landis persuaded Showtime and MTV to ante up the money for the video's budget and began putting together his cast and crew.

MTV's participation in the production was yet another triumph for Michael. Only a few months earlier, he had broken the young cable network's de facto apartheid when MTV began playing his "Billie Jean" video, one of the first starring a black performer it had ever aired in heavy rotation. Now MTV was cofinancing his new production. Along with Rick Baker, the creative team assembled by Landis included choreographer Michael Peters, composer Elmer Bernstein, and horror film veteran Vincent Price. Landis wanted *Playboy* centerfold Ola Ray to play Michael's sexy, strutting date in the video, but knew he would have to run the idea by his star, who seemed confused when the director asked if it was okay to cast a centerfold in the part. "I don't think he even knew what I was talking about," recalled the director, who was amazed once again by Michael's naïveté, but relieved to obtain his consent. The most difficult conversation Landis had with Michael came when the director explained a scene in which Michael asked Ray to go steady, then presented a ring, warning her, "I'm not like other guys." Michael didn't understand his dialogue was supposed to be a laugh line.

The premiere of the fourteen-minute "Thriller" video at the end of November 1983 was a Hollywood event that rivaled the release of the biggest budget theatrical film, with Marlon Brando, Elizabeth Taylor, Diana Ross, and Cher all in attendance. Made on a budget of about $500,000, "Thriller" became the highest selling music video ever, eventually shipping nine million copies, and continued to hold that position for the next quarter century. Music videos were never the same after its release and neither was MTV, which began to play more and more black performers. Sales of the *Thriller* album climbed again after the video's release and Michael Jackson's stardom seemed to have crossed some sort of cultural threshold. There had never been a success on the order of the one he was experiencing.

Yet in the weeks before the video's release, Michael was demanding that it be destroyed. The elders at the Encino Kingdom Hall of the Jehovah's Witnesses had gotten wind of the "Thriller" video's concept and summoned Michael to a meeting at which they expressed concern about "the state of Brother Jackson's soul." He at first resisted their attempts to force him to change the video, but when the elders threatened him with a "defellowship" that would have resulted in expulsion from the church, Michael wilted. His membership among the Witnesses was, he believed, the most stabilizing force in his life, both the strongest link he had to an experience of ordinary life that he craved and the fundament of his relationship with his mother. Even at the height of *Thriller*'s success, what he looked forward to most each week were the "pioneering" expeditions he made with the Witnesses. Michael loved everything about it, including the disguises he wore when visiting the shopping malls and suburban neighborhoods of the San Fernando Valley. His favorite getup combined a fake mustache and beard, a pair of glasses with clear lenses and thick black rims, and a wide-brimmed hat that he pulled low on his forehead, all worn with a pullover sweater and a neatly knotted necktie. The adults on whose front doors he knocked almost never recognized him when he offered a copy of *Watchtower*, Michael said, and neither did the grown-ups he approached at the malls. Kids, though, often spotted him right away.

"Like the Pied Piper of Hamelin," he recalled, "I would find myself trailed by eight or nine children by my second round of the shopping mall. They would follow and whisper and giggle, but they wouldn't reveal my secret to their parents. They were my little aides." Michael also continued to forswear alcohol, tobacco, and profanity, as a devout Witness was expected to do, and accompanied Katherine to the Kingdom Hall four times each week when he was in Los Angeles. "Church was a treat in its own right," he would explain. "It was a chance for me to be 'normal.' The church elders treated me the same as they treated everyone else."

That became a problem, though, after he admitted the "occultism" of the "Thriller" video. He was already on shaky ground with some of the church elders, who were not only critical of the "worshipful attitude" shown by his legions of fans, but concerned as well about the increasingly provocative queries he was making during the question and answer sessions at the end of services. Michael had been particularly obstinate on the subject of the Genesis story, saying repeatedly that he didn't understand why Adam and Eve should have been tested with forbidden fruit. If God was God, Michael reasoned, then He must have known the choice that Adam and Eve would make. And if God knew their choice, then why would He be angry at them for choosing it? It didn't make sense. Furthermore, he wondered if Cain and Abel were the products of incest. "And they were two boys," he noted, "so how did they have children, anyway?" He was unsettled as well by what he had begun to recognize as a sort of, well, *contradiction* in his mother's adherence to their religion. Like her, Michael continued to reject Christmas and Easter as pagan holidays, even though he always found himself aching to participate in the festivities when they rolled around. He had also accepted for his entire life that he should enjoy no birthday celebrations. So it troubled him that each May 4, Katherine would accept birthday gifts, as long as they were presented in brown paper bags rather than wrapping paper. But she was so good otherwise, "a saint, really," as he would often say, that this seemed a minor transgression. And he did not want to lose the connection the two of them had formed around their faith, or his place among the one group of people he knew who treated him like a regular human being.

The morning after his meeting with the church elders in Encino, Michael phoned John Branca and demanded that the tapes of the "Thriller" video, now held at a local processing plant, be shredded and discarded. The befuddled attorney pointed out that Jackson had already spent half a million dollars of other people's money on the video but Michael refused to be dissuaded. By the time Michael phoned his office the next day, Branca had the tapes sitting on his desk and an idea that he hoped might preserve them. He'd been reading a book about Bela Lugosi, the most famous of the movie Draculas, Branca said, and was surprised to discover that Lugosi was a devout Roman Catholic who believed that playing a vampire in the movies had no effect on his personal faith. With that set up, Branca suggested a disclaimer at the beginning of the video explaining that nothing in it reflected Michael's religious beliefs. Grateful to be offered a way out of this corner he was in, Michael quickly agreed. John Landis, though, refused—at least until Branca convinced him that without the disclaimer the video would never be released. It was Landis himself who eventually wrote the sentence that was inserted at the video's beginning: "Due to my strong personal convictions, I wish to stress that this film in no way expresses a belief in the occult.—Michael Jackson."

The disclaimer only added to the swirl of rumor, innuendo, and mystique that surrounded Michael at the beginning of 1984. "If 1983 wasn't the year of Michael Jackson," Dick Clark had observed during his annual New Year's Eve television special, "then it wasn't anyone's." He was being given a level of public permission to live in his own world that had never before been extended to anyone, celebrity or not. The dissonances of his personality actually *contributed* to the fascination with him. People marveled at the sexual energy that this twenty-five-year-old virgin generated onstage, especially when he danced. "Aided by the burn and flash of silvery bodysuits, he seems to change molecular structure at will," a short article in *Rolling Stone* observed, "all robot angles one second, and rippling curves the next. So sure is the body that his eyes are often closed, his face turned upward toward some unseen muse. The bony chest heaves. He pants, bumps, and squeals." Michael would later describe it this way: "I am like caught up in a trance with it all. I am like feeling it, but I don't hear it. I'm playing everything off feeling . . . It just empties you out. You are above it all. That's why I love it, because you are going to a place of nothing nobody can do. It's gone, the point of no return. It's so wonderful. You have taken off." His need for the experience had become an addiction he had to feed even when he wasn't touring. Each Sunday he would not only fast in accordance with the requirements of his religion, Michael explained to *Rolling Stone*, but also would lock himself up alone in his room to dance to the point of physical collapse, until he was laid out on his back, bathed in sweat, laughing and sobbing uncontrollably, utterly spent, and finally free. Free of what, the magazine's reporter had asked. Free of myself, Michael answered: "I love to forget who I am."

That was becoming more and more difficult. On February 7, 1984, Michael was the guest of honor at the Guinness Book of World Records induction ceremony staged at New York City's Museum of Natural History, where *Thriller*, with twenty-seven million copies sold already, would be certified as the biggest selling album of all time. Wearing one of the quasi-military jackets, replete with sequins and epaulets, that had become the staple of his wardrobe, Michael arrived with actress Brooke Shields on his arm. It was their first date—and her idea. The centerpiece of the party was an eight-foot world globe studded with lights that spelled out, "Michael Jackson—The Greatest Artist in the World." Walter Yetnikoff read a telegram sent by President Ronald Reagan and his wife, Nancy. The First Couple had saluted Michael by writing: "Your deep faith in God and adherence to traditional values are an inspiration to all of us."

Three weeks later, on February 28, the Grammy Awards ceremony at the Shrine Auditorium in Los Angeles was the Michael Jackson show from start to finish. Brooke Shields was again Michael's date, but this time had to share him with Emmanuel Lewis, the twelve-year-old, three-foot, four-inch-tall star of the hit TV show *Webster*, who spent most of the evening perched on Michael's lap, while Shields sat next to them wearing a dazed expression. The crowd was giddy to the point of delirium with the weird charm of it all, as Michael was summoned to the stage again and again, accepting a record-tying eight of the gilded gramophone statuettes in all. Each time Michael's name was mentioned, or even when his image appeared on the studio monitors beside the stage, the fans in the balcony erupted into a cascade of applause that was more frenzied and sustained than anything those in the orchestra seats had ever witnessed at an awards ceremony. The biggest stars on the planet were like extras in his home movie. For the first time in his life, Michael seemed beyond caring what anyone thought about him. Backstage, the press eagerly asked him what was his favorite song and Michael promptly answered, "'My Favorite Things' by Julie Andrews." The reporters began to laugh, thinking it was a joke, but then in the next instant realized he was serious, and stood with frozen grins as he literally skipped off down the hallway, singing the song at the top of his lungs. The after-party was held that year at the downtown restaurant Rex il Ristorante, where Michael and Brooke looked down from their balcony table on a crowd of commoners who included Bob Dylan, Arnold Schwarzenegger, and Eddie Murphy.

Michael was the main attraction even at that April's Academy Awards ceremony. When he showed up with Liza Minnelli at the most exclusive annual affair in Hollywood—legendary agent Swifty Lazar's party at Spago—"The stars were reduced to mush," as a *USA Today* columnist who was there put it, "as if the evening hadn't been about the movies, but about Jackson instead." The world-famous celebrities in attendance literally stepped on one another's feet trying to get close to him.

Even after the Grammys and the Oscars, even when he had been worshiped by fans who seemed to regard him as a sort of walking, breathing deity, he still had to go home alone at the end of the evening and wonder why he was so unhappy. "I was so lonely I would cry in my room upstairs," he would remember of that time. "I would think, 'That's it, I'm getting out of here.' And I would walk down the street. I remember really saying to people, 'Will you be my friend?' They were like, 'Michael Jackson!' I would go, 'Oh, God! Are they going to be my friend because of Michael Jackson? Or because of me.'"

"Michael Jackson" was now somebody else, the character he played in public. "I hate to admit it, but I feel strange around everyday people," he told Gerri Hirshey. Alone, in private, he was nameless, a little boy lost. The only relief from the overwhelming sense of isolation he felt at that time, Michael would remember, came when he made his way down to Encino Park and sat in a swing among the kids on the playground. They didn't know who he was and, more important, they didn't care.

Those walks to the park were ended by the crazed fans who literally camped in the bushes outside the gates of the Hayvenhurst estate. The expressions on some of their faces terrified him. "Oh, no, I can't go out there," he told one journalist who asked if they could conduct their interview at a nearby restaurant. "They'll get me for sure. They're around the corner, and they want to get their hands on me." More and more often he was surrounded by bodyguards when he ventured forth from the Hayvenhurst house, burly men who were instructed to let no one who was not a child get near him.

He tried to explain himself, as best he could, to the occasional interviewer who seemed sincerely interested. "I am a very sensitive person," he told Robert Hilburn at the *Los Angeles Times*. "A person with very vulnerable feelings. My best friends in the whole world are children and animals. They're the ones who tell the truth and love you openly and without reservation." And he was more and more wary of adults. He explained his increased reclusion to *Rolling Stone*'s Hirshey by describing himself as "just like a hemophiliac who can't afford to be scratched in any way." When Hirshey asked about being on tour, Michael let her know precisely how unlike other pop stars he was: "Girls in the lobby, coming up the stairways. You hear the guards get-ting them out of elevators. But you stay in your room and write a song. And when you get tired of that, you talk to yourself. Then let it all out onstage. *That's* what it's like." He disliked parties and hated clubs. "I did that when I was a baby," he would explain. "Now I want to be a part of the world and life I didn't have. Take me to Disneyland, take me to where the magic is." He made trip after trip to Walt Disney's original park in Anaheim, where the security staff would usher him through the secret passageways that connected rides, so he could avoid the people in lines. Pirates of the Carib-bean was his favorite attraction at Disneyland. He would cruise through those dark grottoes again and again, in disguise, praying that no one would shout, "There's Michael Jackson!" and wishing at the same time he could join the laughing children in the boat next to him. He was yearning desper-ately, Michael told one interviewer, for something he could identify only as "playtime and a feeling of freedom."

Emmanuel Lewis continued to be his closest companion. When he wasn't giving him piggyback rides, Michael enjoyed carrying the twelve-year-old dwarf in his arms like a toddler. Visitors to the Hayvenhurst estate stood stunned, forcing polite smiles as they watched Jackson and the boy playing cowboys and Indians on the front lawn like a pair of five-year-olds. Those who knew him couldn't help but be touched by the fact that there was at least one thing in his life that seemed to make him happy.

Michael's determination to retreat into a second childhood was never more evident than when he visited the White House in May 1984 as the guest of President and First Lady Reagan. Promised that he would be meet-ing just Ron and Nancy and a few children of staff members, Michael was dismayed when he stepped into the Diplomatic Reception Room and found it filled with excited adults. He immediately fled down a hallway to a bathroom just off the White House library, locked the door, and refused to come out until a White House aide ordered his assistant to round up some kids and make most of the grown-ups leave. "It's all so peculiar, really," Nancy Reagan would remark. "A boy who looks just like a girl, who whispers when he speaks, wears a glove on one hand, and sunglasses all the time."

He still didn't know a single adult he could call a friend and it was becoming more difficult for him to connect to his family. The joint man-agement contract with their father and Weisner and DeMann that Michael shared with his brothers had expired back in March 1983 and he had been formally without representation ever since. The brothers were waiting to see what he would do next, and Joseph was hanging in there, hoping to hold on to some percentage of the family superstar's future. Joe tried to distance himself from Weisner and DeMann, but in the process only deepened the contempt Michael felt for his father. "There was a time when I felt I needed white help in dealing with the corporate structure at CBS," Joe explained to an interviewer. "And I thought Weisner and DeMann would be able to help. But they never gave me the respect you expect from a business partner." Weisner and DeMann responded with a statement that they had "no problem with Michael or the Jacksons"—other than Joe. "True, we don't have a good relationship with him," DeMann conceded, "but I don't think he enjoys a good relationship with anyone whose skin is not black." Michael weighed in with the most public expression of scorn for his father he had ever permitted himself, telling *Rolling Stone*, "To hear him talk like that turns my stomach . . . Racism is not my motto."

Any doubt about Joe's future was erased in June when he received a letter written by John Branca that informed him that he, Joe, no longer represented Michael Jackson and should refrain from suggesting that he did in any further business contacts. The brothers, nearly as upset as Michael that Joe had responded to Katherine's most recent divorce filing by deliberately concealing assets, followed suit with letters from their own attorneys telling their father that he was no longer their manager. It was the first time anyone in the family saw Joe cry.

Michael had already spoken to Frank Dileo, the promotions director at Epic Records, about leaving the label to work as his manager. The squat-bodied, staccato-speaking Dileo had been credited by many for orchestrating the release of singles from *Thriller* in a sequence that resulted in songs appearing among the *Billboard* top ten at the same time, creating much of the synergy that lifted the album to its stratospheric success. Frank was a Technicolor character whose hardscrabble hustler persona provided an odd sort of balance to Michael's image of ethereal weirdness. Dileo cast himself as a roly-poly phoenix raised from the ashes of multiple disasters, including the death of his uninsured father when he was a teenager, a misdemeanor conviction for working as a bookie for college basketball games, and a house fire that cost his family everything they owned. Sporting a skinny ponytail and a fat cigar, the big-bellied, loud-voiced Dileo was affable but not easily intimidated, especially by the likes of Joe Jackson.

Joe still had some steel in his spine, though, and was as canny and calculating as ever. He knew from past experience that playing the boys against one another was a winning strategy, five against Michael. What a great idea it would be, he suggested to Jackie, Tito, Marlon, and Randy, to capitalize on the tremendous success of *Thriller* by including Michael in a "reunion tour" that would celebrate Jermaine's return to the group. Michael still hadn't made plans for a *Thriller* tour, Joe pointed out, and could fold his solo performances into the Jacksons' stage show, turn it into something really huge financially for them all.

Jermaine was in the moment the idea was put to him, but Michael resisted more tenaciously than before. He was tired of touring, he said, tired of all the attention, tired of travel and hotel rooms—tired of his family, period. What he didn't say was that there was nothing he could gain by continuing to associate professionally with his brothers. Much as they needed him, he didn't need them at all. The brothers first tried using guilt to sway him. Marlon was going through a nasty divorce, was in real financial difficulty, and couldn't even make his mortgage payments. Maybe he should sell that house and buy a smaller one, Michael suggested. The brothers then called a meeting at which they showed up with a life-size poster of Michael and told him they were going to put it onstage in his place. Michael still wouldn't relent. It was time to play their ace in the hole.

Katherine was still the only woman in Michael's life. The dates with Brooke Shields were just a show. Brooke had tried to kiss him a couple of times, Michael confided to one of his brothers, but he was grossed out when she put her tongue in his mouth. With Katherine, though, it was true love. And true love was the only thing that could change Michael's mind. During a private meeting Katherine requested with Michael, she implored him to join his brothers on the reunion tour. They needed the money, badly in a couple of cases, she told her son. This was family. Finally, when all else failed, she pulled out the big gun: "For me, Michael, please?"

It was a choice between the only two things Michael had, his mother's love and his career. He chose his mother's love, of course, but did not fold completely. He insisted that his involvement in *Victory*, the album that would launch the tour, be kept to a minimum: two songs that he would write and sing. One of them, a duet with Mick Jagger titled "State of Shock," would be the only hit the album produced. That was fine with the brothers; this album and the tour that followed were about money for them and they intended to fill their pockets with as much of it as possible.

An unanticipated problem developed when several promoters said they were afraid to book the Jacksons into the large outdoor stadiums they planned to pack with paying customers for fear of the crush of fans who would try to get to Michael. "I could not guarantee the safety of those in front of the stage," New York promoter Ron Delsner told reporters.

"I don't think anybody can—if they do, they're liars." "Michael Jackson whips people to a fever pitch," chimed in Atlanta's Alex Cooley. "His fans are the root of the word 'fan'—they're fanatic about it. So, yeah, there're problems." Joe and Katherine joined forces to suggest a promoter who was not troubled by such concerns.

Best known for his electroshock hair style and for staging championship boxing matches (including the Muhammad Ali–Joe Frazier "Thrilla in Manila"), Don King had served four years in an Ohio prison for killing a man in a Cleveland street fight. He was loud, coarse, controversial, given to outrageous and racially loaded statements. King had showed up for his first meeting with the family wearing a white fur coat and a gold necklace with a pendant on which a gold crown was topped by the name DON. Michael despised the man from the moment he met him: "Creepy," he called King, and let everyone know he wanted the promoter kept away from him. After King forked over a $3 million cash payment he called "good faith money"—a pittance to Michael but a fortune to his brothers—King said the forty shows he had planned would gross at least $30 million, which, after expenses and the 15 percent management fee that he and Joe agreed to split, would leave about $3.4 million apiece for the brothers. King's next coup was the negotiation of a deal with the Pepsi-Cola company to sponsor the tour for $5 million dollars, ten times what the Rolling Stones had received from the same company for their 1981 tour. Michael resisted, saying he didn't drink soda, didn't need the money, and didn't want to appear in a commercial. Once again, the family pressured him into accepting.

The dreaded Pepsi commercial was filmed on January 27, 1984, at LA's Shrine Auditorium, which was filled with a crowd of 3,000 to simulate the atmosphere of a live concert. With his brothers, Michael was to sing the lyrics of a jingle titled "You're a Whole New Generation" set to the music of "Billie Jean." Paul McCartney warned Michael that appearing in a TV commercial would leave him "overexposed" and hurt his career in the long run. Bothered by the idea of shilling for a product he didn't believe in and filled with a sense of foreboding about the shoot, Michael agreed to only a single four-second close-up.

At 6:30 that evening, the Jacksons were beginning their sixth rendition of "You're a Whole New Generation," the highlight being Michael's descent down a staircase to the main stage through a pyrotechnic arc of brightly colored explosions. He was posed at the top of a platform above the staircase when a magnesium flash bomb went off about two feet from his head. As he descended through the smoke and began to spin at the bottom of the stairs, he felt a hot spot near the crown of his head, but assumed it was the stage lights. As he finished his third spin and rose onto his toes, Michael realized his hair was literally on fire and fell to the stage floor, pulling his jacket up over his head as he shouted for help.

Amid the screaming chaos, many of those in the audience believed that there had been an attempt on Michael's life. Jermaine, standing less than ten feet away, thought his brother had been shot. Videotape of Michael being loaded into an ambulance, with one sequin-gloved hand poking out of the blankets, led all three national news broadcasts that evening. (Michael had told the ambulance attendants to leave the glove on so people would know it was him.) At Cedars-Sinai Medical Center, doctors found a fist-size second-degree burn on the back of his head near the crown, with a spot of third-degree burn about the size of a quarter in its center. For his recuperation, he was transferred to Brotman Medical Center, which recruited six volunteers to answer phone calls about Michael's status. Tens of thousands of cards and letters arrived, including one from the president of the United States. Pepsi paid Michael $1.5 million to avoid a lawsuit, all of which he donated to Brotman to establish the Michael Jackson Burn Center, earning an incalculable amount of goodwill from the city of Los Angeles in the process.

Two negative effects of the accident on the Shrine Auditorium set, though, would endure far longer than the good publicity. His hair never grew back in fully on the spot where the third-degree burn had been. More important, after first refusing to take painkillers, Michael swallowed a Dilaudid pill that was the first narcotic ever to enter his system. His discovery that the drug not only eased the pain on the surface of his body but numbed an ache deeper inside would change him over time in ways that no one then could have imagined.

His more pressing problem in the summer of 1984, though, was the runaway greed of his father and brothers, and Don King's encouragement of it. The brothers and King had decided that tickets for the *Victory* tour concerts would be priced at $30 apiece and be made available to the public only by mail order in lots of four. This was at a time when the highest priced concert tickets in the country, for shows by Bruce Springsteen and the Rolling Stones, went for $16 a seat. News that no one who couldn't afford to shell out at least $120 would get into the Jacksons' shows not only roused the media to charges of gouging, but shocked and angered the group's core fans: inner-city youth. Michael had opposed setting the ticket prices so high and objected to making them available only by mail order, but was again outvoted five to one.

As the star of the tour, Michael suffered the brunt of the negative publicity. In the end, he had no choice but to threaten his brothers and King that if they refused to change the ticket policy he would refuse to perform. Shortly after they yielded, Michael announced that he would be donating all of *his* earnings from the tour to charity, dividing approximately $5 million between the United Negro College Fund, a foundation for cancer research, and Camp Ronald McDonald for Good Times.

The tour itself was sheer indignity from start to finish. At the first stop in Kansas City, Jermaine told a reporter, "Even though Michael is very talented, a lot of his success has been due to timing and a little bit of luck. It could have been him, or it could just as easily have been me." Michael steadily distanced himself from his brothers as the tour progressed, refusing to stay on the same floor with them at their hotels and insisting his attorneys be present at the business meetings that, within the first few dates, became the only conversations he had with his siblings. The other Jacksons traveled to their concerts in separate vehicles before the tour was half finished and insisted upon collecting their payments immediately after each show. The brothers saw a chance to double their money when a producer offered millions for the right to tape the tour and edit Michael's footage into a home video, but Michael threatened not to perform at one more show if his brothers agreed. By the time the tour arrived at its final stop—six dates at Dodger Stadium in Los Angeles—the stress was so great that Michael had all but stopped eating, his weight falling to an all-time low of 110 pounds. Joe and Don King were already negotiating a deal to take the *Victory* tour to Europe, but when Michael learned of it he informed them there was no chance. No one in his family, though, was prepared for the shout-out Michael gave from the stage on December 9, 1984: "This is our last and final show. It's been a long twenty years and we love you all." Michael looked at the shocked expressions on his brothers' faces and couldn't quite suppress his smile.

Michael was still flush with the phenomenal success of *Thriller* in 1985, well on his way to earning more than $200 million from sales of the album alone, when he taped a sheet of paper printed with "100 million" on his bathroom window that would remain in place during the two years he spent recording his follow-up to *Thriller,* 1987's *Bad.* The note would become the artifact of a self-inflicted curse that shadowed the remainder of his career. "This has to be bigger than the last one," Michael repeatedly told the musicians who were working on the album with him. "If it sold a hundred million copies, I don't think he'd be totally satisfied," *Bad*'s coproducer Bruce Swedien confided to *Rolling Stone*. "But he'd hold still for that."

Jackson was no less determined to create a private life that corresponded to the scale of his public success. Having grown up in a world where indulging one's whims was the license of stardom, he increasingly insisted upon living without limitation. During the *Bad* world tour, he demanded that a bus, a plane, and a helicopter be available to him at all times, regardless of cost. Michael hired Martin Scorsese to direct the "Bad" video after Steven Spielberg and Francis Ford Coppola proved unavailable, then spent an unprecedented $2 million on the project. Such grandiosity could be justified when *Bad* went on to become the first album ever to produce five #1 records and racked up domestic sales of seventeen million units, plus another thirteen million internationally. The *Bad* tour grossed $125 million and the star of the show walked away with $40 million of that. *Bad* was an astounding success by the standards of almost anyone else, but a crushing disappointment for Michael Jackson. *Rolling Stone*'s review argued that *Bad* was "actually a better record than *Thriller*," but other critics were less enthusiastic.

The "Bad" video was greeted with outright derision. Scorsese shot from a script by gritty New York City novelist Richard Price, based on the story of Edmund Perry, a young black man from Harlem who had gone to prep school on a scholarship, only to be shot dead by a plainclothes police officer who claimed the kid had tried to mug him. Scorsese, Price, and Jackson all envisioned the Perry character as a solitary figure struggling to maintain footholds in two very different worlds where his isolation was bracketed by snobbish preppies and menacing street toughs. The story would come to a climax with the young man's transformation into a rebellious badass intent on dishing out every bit as much pain as he had absorbed. Jackson and his dancers spent hours watching *West Side Story* and Michael intended to model his performance in the video on the one delivered by George Chakiris, who in the movie had played the leader of the Puerto Rican gang, the Sharks.

The project appeared to be shaping up into a music video that would be every bit as big as "Thriller," but the reaction of most viewers when Michael strutted onscreen in his tough guy getup had been to nearly suffocate on a simultaneous eruption of gasps and giggles. It wasn't simply the black leather that encased the star from head to toe but a blinding array of metal accents affixed to every tuck, fold, and surface. The absurd silver heels and buckles on his boots were the most understated part of the costume, outshined—literally—by the glinting studs, buckles, and numerous zippers that decorated his wristband, belt, and jacket. Radio stations across the country held contests that challenged listeners to guess just how many zippers and buckles there *were* on the jacket. More startling was Jackson's appearance. Pale-tone pancake makeup was slathered onto the surgically altered features of an androgyne who bore little resemblance to the young black man who had gazed pensively from the cover of *Off the Wall* only eight years earlier. The general public's response to the star's new album and video was encapsulated by the headline on the cover of *People* magazine: "Michael Jackson: He's Back. He's *Bad*. Is This Guy Weird or What?"

The world's reigning pop star had officially become a freak. Recognizing what he was up against, Jackson had taken the stage at the following year's Grammys to deliver a blistering live performance of "Man in the Mirror," then spent most of the rest of the evening sniffling in a front-row seat, barely able to blink back tears as he was shut out of the awards and watched the ceremony turn into a coming-out party for U2. By then his plastic surgery makeover and "Wacko Jacko" image (the nickname had become a staple of the British tabloids) were alienating more and more music lovers. In the United States, Jackson issued instructions that photographers at press conferences use only a medium telephoto lens with a shutter speed of 1/125, an f-stop of four, and film compatible with tungsten lighting, rules that were meant to disguise Jackson's multiple plastic surgeries but only served to infuriate and disgust the media.

In 1988, even as his three-and-a-half-octave tenor reached the peak of its power, *Rolling Stone*'s readers voted him "worst artist" in almost every category of the magazine's annual poll. Still the biggest selling recording artist on the planet, Jackson felt massively unappreciated, especially by music critics. Bruce Springsteen ("He can't sing or dance") was called "The Boss," while various newspaper and magazine polls were naming Madonna ("That heifer!") Artist of the Decade. Don King, whom Jackson initially despised, finally got Jackson's ear by telling him, "The white man will never let you be bigger than Elvis."

5

A week before Christmas, in 2005, a group of Sony executives flew to Dubai to meet Michael Jackson face-to-face. Along with several of Sheikh Abdullah's financial advisors, the execs assembled in Jackson's $9,000-per-night suite at the emirate's sail-shaped Burj Al Arab hotel. Sony CFO Robert S. Wiesenthal endured only a few minutes of chitchat before explaining to Jackson that he was on the brink of a bankruptcy that threatened the corporation's bottom line.

Late in 2003, concerned that Jackson had missed several seven-figure payments he owed, Bank of America sold his loan to Fortress Investment Group, an "alternative asset" management company accused of being one of the most predatory on the planet, specializing in the exploitation of financial distress. As Fortress began to ratchet the interest rate on Jackson's debt up past 20 percent per annum, both Neverland Ranch and, more important, Jackson's half of the Sony/ATV catalog were put into play. Then on July 11, 2005, just two weeks after his arrival in the Persian Gulf, Jackson was sued for $48 million by Prescient Acquisitions Group, a New Jersey financial services company that claimed it had brokered the deal with Fortress.

What compelled the Sony executives' trip to Dubai was their discovery that Fortress was about to call in Jackson's loan. If that happened, Wiesenthal and the others gathered in the suite at the Burj Al Arab explained, Michael would be forced into bankruptcy and his half of the song catalog thrown up for grabs to the highest bidder. Sony, which for years had been maneuvering to take complete control of the catalog, could not let that happen.

Jackson was remarkably subdued and compliant, with little to say beyond a few marveling murmurs about how the ATV catalog was saving him once again from financial ruin. It was quite a change from the Sony executives' last encounter with the star. Although Jackson's music had generated as much as a billion dollars in profits for Sony since the 1980s, the performer was increasingly seen by the company as more liability than asset, and the public relations catastrophe that had followed the release of *Invincible* encouraged that point of view. Sony had permitted Jackson to record eighty-four songs at the company's expense—from which he selected the sixteen that appeared on *Invincible*—and in the process to run up production costs that were more than double that of any album ever before released by the company. Jackson had then called Sony Music Group's CEO a racist for refusing to spend even more money on *Invincible*.

Relations between the company and its erstwhile recording artist improved after *Number Ones* was released in late 2003 and sold ten million copies. Sony had been prepared to negotiate new agreements for loan guarantees and other compilation or anniversary albums when suddenly Jackson's life and career disappeared into a two-and-a-half-year-long crisis of trauma and catastrophe. Sony watched Martin Bashir destroy most of what was left of Jackson's reputation, then saw Tom Sneddon put him through the ordeal of a criminal trial that had left Michael, in Tom Mesereau's words, "psychologically shattered." The not-guilty verdicts at the end of that trial had done little to restore the entertainer's public standing.

What was now at stake was not simply the most valuable asset Jackson owned, but the most valuable asset ever owned by any recording artist. Jackson had purchased the ATV/Music Publishing Catalog in 1985 for what then seemed an astounding price of $47.5 million. Twenty years later, it was worth a billion dollars.

As would be the case with his later purchase of Neverland Ranch, Paul McCartney was the catalyst for Jackson's acquisition. McCartney's impact on Jackson's life was far out of proportion to their relatively brief relationship. The former Beatle's fascination with cartoons and animation had served for Jackson as an enormous source of validation and encouragement. The revelation that a cultural icon of McCartney's magnitude cherished and collected Woody Woodpecker cartoons not only eased Michael's embarrassment about the hours he spent watching animated shorts but offered the first solid evidence he had seen that a determination to remain childlike was shared by other geniuses. Jackson's later discovery that Steven Spielberg and George Lucas were also major cartoon collectors pleased him tremendously, but it was McCartney who had provided Michael with a retort to the taunts he had endured for years from his father and brothers. Michael especially enjoyed telling his family that he and Paul had written their duet "The Girl Is Mine" while watching cartoons together.

During the summer of 1981, Michael was staying at McCartney's house in London while the two worked on their duet "Say Say Say" for

McCartney's album. Over dinner one evening, McCartney revealed that not only had his cartoon collection proved a solid financial investment but added that his collection of song rights (he owned titles that included such standards as "Stormy Weather" and "Autumn Leaves," as well as most of the Buddy Holly catalog) were incredibly profitable, spinning off hundreds of thousands in profits each and every year. Music catalogs were the best way he knew to make "big money," said McCartney, who was then forced to admit that he didn't own the rights to his own Beatles songs. He and John Lennon had sold those when they were young men, and now 251 titles—including "Yesterday," "Hey Jude," and "Let It Be"—were included in a catalog of more than four thousand songs held by the Australian Robert Holmes à Court's ATV Music. McCartney had tried to buy the ATV catalog earlier that year but failed to persuade John Lennon's widow Yoko Ono to go in as partners with him and was unwilling to put up the entire $20 million cost alone. If it became available a second time, though, McCartney added, he intended to make a bid. He had no idea, Paul would say later, that Michael, who mostly listened silently, was looking for ways to put this tip to use.

When Jackson returned to the United States, he instructed John Branca to look for song copyrights he could purchase. By the end of that year, Branca arranged for Jackson to buy the entire Sly Stone catalog, which included his classics "Everyday People" and "Stand!" (a song Michael had performed with his brothers the first time the Jackson 5 appeared on *The Ed Sullivan Show*). Branca later helped Michael purchase the copyrights to Dion's two biggest hits, "The Wanderer" and "Runaround Sue," as well as Len Barry's "1-2-3" and the Soul Survivors' "Expressway to Your Heart."

In September 1984, Branca phoned Jackson to say the Beatles song catalog was back on the market. After a bidding war that lasted eight harrowing months and involved a series of tense conversations with Mc-Cartney and Ono, Branca closed the deal in May 1985. McCartney was furious when he learned that Jackson now owned most of the songs he had written as a Beatle. It was "dodgy," he complained, to "be someone's friend and then to buy the rug they're standing on." Michael was "the kind of guy who picks brains," Paul said and didn't make that sound like a compliment. Jackson then began to license Beatles songs for commercials, beginning with the use of "Revolution" in a Nike sneaker ad. "I don't want 'Good Day Sunshine' to become an Oreo cookie ad," McCartney protested, "which I understand he's done. I think that's real cheesy." McCartney was equally incensed when Jackson collected $240,000 from Panasonic for the rights to use "All You Need Is Love" to sell "a friggin' loudspeaker system." Not my fault that Paul was too cheap to buy the catalog himself, retorted Michael, who then hired people to begin developing a series of films based on four Beatles songs: "Strawberry Fields," "Back in the USSR," "Eleanor Rigby," and "The Fool on the Hill." He also intended to design a series of musical greeting cards and music boxes that featured songs from the Beatles catalog, Jackson announced.

After several years of sniping and estrangement, Jackson and McCartney met in 1990 to discuss what Paul described as "this problem" between the two of them. The very next day, McCartney's attorney phoned Branca to say that Michael had agreed to pay Paul a higher royalty rate for his songs. No way, Jackson told Branca: "He's not getting a higher royalty unless I get something back from him in return." McCartney threatened to sue, but in the end decided that his only recourse was to cut off contact with Jackson. The "problem" continued to irk him, however. As late as 2006, McCartney would tell an interviewer, "You know what doesn't feel very good is going on tour and paying to sing all my songs. Every time I sing 'Hey Jude,' I've got to pay someone."

What neither McCartney nor most other people understood about Michael Jackson, Branca would explain, was that beneath the breathy voice and halting manner, he was as shrewd a businessman as any artist who had ever lived. "Part of him may be a ten-year-old, with all the enthusiasm that implies," Branca told a London newspaper, "but the other part is a sixty-year-old genius." Frank Dileo described him to the same paper as "a cross between E.T. and Howard Hughes."

Branca and Dileo had made those observations back in the 1980s, in the halcyon days when the ATV catalog was supposed to be the jewel in the crown of Michael Jackson's financial empire. No one imagined then that it would become the crown itself. Securing the ATV catalog was crucial for Michael. During his criminal trial, he had raved that the charges stemmed from a conspiracy between Sony, Tommy Mottola, and Tom Sneddon, among others, to gain control of the catalog. He was surrounding himself with Nation of Islam guards, Jackson told a number of people, because he was terrified that Mottola would put out a contract on his life.

At their meeting in Dubai, Wiesenthal informed Jackson that Sony had set up a preliminary deal with Citibank that would refinance Michael's $300-million-plus ATV debt on much better terms than Fortress was likely to offer and that Sony was willing to agree to a new dividend policy from the publishing company that would cover much of the interest on the ATV loan. In exchange, Sony would require greater freedom to make investment decisions without Jackson's approval, a right of first refusal on any sale of Michael's stake in the ATV catalog, and an option to buy half of his half of the catalog for approximately $250 million. Also, he would have to drop the demand to reclaim his master recordings. Negotiations would drag on for more than two years but the deal in principle seemed to offer the glimmer of hope for a life beyond Dubai and Bahrain. At the height of the holiday season, Michael was suddenly in a mood to celebrate.

Christmas had almost been ruined on December 9, when the *National Enquirer* ran a story that Jackson had nearly killed himself with an overdose of drugs and alcohol and was "in a critical condition in Bahrain." Quoting an e-mail from "a high ranking police official" in Santa Barbara who stated that the entertainer had overdosed at least twice since arriving in the Middle East, the *Enquirer* cited "sources who said Jackson was shooting himself in his leg with a syringe filled with Demerol." Michael's PR spokesperson Raymone Bain denied the story, telling the *Enquirer*, "I spoke to Michael on the phone today (Friday) and I can tell you he sounded fine. He is not abusing any drugs. He is continuing to work from Bahrain on his Katrina relief song." When the mainstream media neglected to pick up on the story, Michael heaved a sigh of relief and happily prepared for what he described to his children as "a family gathering."

On December 21, 2005, Sheikh Abdullah gave Mikaeel $250,000 to shop for Christmas gifts and to entertain his guests, who would be arriving within days from England and the United States. The sum raised his investment in what Abdullah continued to call their "partnership" to more than $5 million. Michael hurried to Ashraf's Department Store in Manama the very next day, spending $40,000 in what was little more than a walk-through. He bought $35,000 worth of high-end electronics at Manama's Panasonic store the following day and awaited the arrival of Mark Lester's family from London that evening. They would have an old-fashioned Christmas in Bahrain, Michael had decided, with a big tree, piles of presents, and lots of excited children to open them. He was overjoyed when Frank Cascio and his family arrived from New York a short time later.

Now twenty-four, Frank had been part of Jackson's life since he was in elementary school. During those years he had become, among other things, Michael's favorite "pranking" partner. When they were on tour, Cascio was put in charge of the arsenal of stink bombs and water balloons that Michael regularly set off in meetings or threw at cars from hotel balconies.

Frank loved, almost as much as Michael did, the water balloon fights at Neverland, which were always organized into a red team and a blue team and usually ended with a bunch of fully dressed people in the swimming pool. He got a kick, too, out of Michael's superlong-range laser pointer, capable of shooting a red dot from a hotel suite on a high floor to the sidewalk in front of an unsuspecting pedestrian a mile away. Once, when they were in New York at the Four Seasons, police officers had followed the laser's strobe all the way back to the suite and Michael had to hide the thing to keep the cops from confiscating it.

In 2004, Tom Sneddon attempted to make the case that Michael had served wine to Frank's fifteen-year-old sister Marie Nicole and twelve-year-old brother Eddie. Only when Dominic and Connie Cascio made it clear they were ready to testify that any wine their kids drank at Neverland had been served by themselves and that as Italian Americans they had been taking a sip of wine at the dinner table since they were very young—it was part of their culture—did Sneddon drop the matter. The Cascios insisted they loved Michael Jackson as much as they ever had and that he was welcome in their home, where he had visited many times, whenever he wanted to stop by. Tom Mesereau questioned just how loyal the family really was after the Cascios refused to let their younger children testify for Michael at his criminal trial, and for a time let it be known that he thought a lot less of them than his client did. Still, in the run-up to the criminal trial in Santa Barbara County, Frank spoke to the media on Michael's behalf, telling reporters that he had spent many nights in Jackson's bedroom as a boy and that it was like crashing with a buddy in a college dorm room, not even remotely sexual. On television, he came across convincingly as a no-nonsense New Jersey guy who was sick of all the sleazy opportunists trying to make a quick buck, denouncing Michael's accuser and the two other boys who, over the years, had claimed to be molestation victims as "nothing but liars." And in spite of his attorney's reservations about them, Michael still enjoyed the company of the Cascios far more than he did that of the Jacksons.

What the Lesters and the Cascios understood better than anyone else was how much it meant to Michael to be able to share a sense of extended family with his children. They traveled in a party of eighteen to the Seef Mall on Christmas Eve to see Peter Jackson's remake of *King Kong*, then took a trip to the International Italian Circus courtesy of Abdullah's money.

His guests had to return home on New Year's Day, though, leaving Michael not only lonely but facing the problem of Sheikh Abdullah's mounting impatience. Many projects had been initiated, ranging from a so-called "comeback album" to what was planned as the first release of 2 Seas Records, featuring Michael singing a duet with his brother Jermaine. Nothing had moved forward.

The most pressing issue was Michael's much-ballyhooed "Hurricane Katrina song," now four months overdue. Katrina devastated New Orleans on Michael's birthday, August 29, and eight days later he announced that he would release an all-star charity single within two weeks to provide relief for the Big Easy's huddled masses. By the end of 2005, quite a few people were wondering where that record might be. Not to worry, said Abdullah, who spoke for Jackson in a telephone interview with the Associated Press: "The record is coming along great. We've been taking our time to perfect it."

Aware that his toxic reputation made it impossible to assemble the polyglot choir of superstars who had collaborated with him on "What More Can I Give?" Michael decided to use only black performers on his Katrina record, which was to have a "gospel feel." The two biggest names among those who had thus far contributed vocals belonged to a pair of performers quite familiar with criminal charges and bad press: Snoop Dogg and R. Kelly. Ciara, Keyshia Cole, and the O'Jays were among the singers who had recorded sections of the song in a Los Angeles studio in November, with Jackson producing it by phone from Bahrain. A number of the other voices promised back in August—including those of James Brown, Jay-Z, Mary J. Blige, and Missy Elliot—were still missing from the mix. The main reason for the delay, Abdullah insisted to the wire service, was that more artists had come forward to ask if they could contribute. Asked to name those artists, the sheikh demurred: "I'd like to keep that as a surprise." Abdullah quickly added that Michael had already laid down "a wonderful track" that would serve as the baseline of the song. "His voice is phenomenal," enthused Abdullah, who added that the working title was "I Have This Dream." Asked if the Katrina song was the harbinger of a new Jackson album, Abdullah replied with a laugh, "I will just say we've been very busy. This is a raindrop before the thunderstorm. He's getting ready to come out with a lot of bells and whistles. He's so energized. It's explosive." Abdullah promised that "I Have This Dream" would be delivered before the end of February.

It had now been more than six months since Michael's arrival in Bahrain and nearly six million dollars of the Al Khalifas' money had been spent on him and his various projects. Abdullah's father, the king, was beginning to wonder what exactly the family was getting in return for all their generosity to Mikaeel.

Increasingly restless and dissatisfied with life in Bahrain after his friends from England and America returned home, Jackson abruptly departed with his children for Orlando, Florida, explaining that he intended to secure the production facilities he needed to finish his Katrina song. "I'll be back," he told the sheikh, who certainly hoped so.

As a regular visitor to Disney World, Michael had been renting houses in Orlando for years. He made no concession to cash-strapped circumstances on this trip, leasing a twelve-bedroom, nineteen-bathroom mansion owned by timeshare mogul David Siegel that featured a sixty-foot pool bordered in real gold. Located on a four-acre private island inside the guarded gates of the Isleworth enclave, the home featured 1,700 feet of shoreline and rented for $15,000 per week. Michael's presence would rouse media snoopers in ways that neighbors like Shaquille O'Neal and Tiger Woods never would, so privacy was key. Siegel agreed not to tell a living soul but was taken aback when Michael appeared in plain sight on the roof of the house with his children one day after moving in. "He said he'd take it under the condition that nobody knows he's here," Siegel recalled. "I didn't tell anybody. He moves in. Within a day he's up on top of the house waving at boaters."

Jackson was in Orlando mainly to meet with boy band impresario Lou Pearlman, whose success with the Backstreet Boys and 'N Sync had financed the construction of his state-of-the-art Trans Continental Studios out on Sand Lake Road. Pearlman had been supportive during Jackson's criminal trial, telling CNN that Michael should "get back to the music" as quickly as possible: "What I'm saying is, ignore the personal side of it . . . because he's never going to eradicate the good, bad, or indifferent of what's been happening in the media. Let's talk about the King of Pop. Let's talk about how he dances, great songs. That's where he's got to go."

Monitoring the Orlando meetings was no doubt stressful for Sheikh Abdullah, who received reports that Jackson and Pearlman were talking about a deal to record Michael's "comeback album" in Florida rather than in Bahrain. About all Michael would accomplish during his brief stay in Orlando, though, was to dodge a bullet. Lou Pearlman was about to be exposed as one of the all-time monsters in an industry famous for them.

Federal investigators were already putting together a case that would charge Pearlman with swindling more than a thousand investors out of $315 million, in addition to $120 million fraudulently taken from banks. Within a few months, the impresario would flee the country to avoid arrest and remain on the run for nearly a year before being captured in Bali, then detained in Guam and extradited back to the United States. Facing a federal fraud trial scheduled to begin in March 2008, he would plead guilty and accept a sentence of twenty-five years in prison.

For Jackson, of course, a greater concern was the steady leak of allegations that Pearlman had committed dozens of sex crimes against the members of his boy bands, many of whom were living at his Florida mansion when the molestations took place. None of the teenagers were ever formally identified, but Jane Carter, the mother of teen idols Nick and Aaron Carter, told *Vanity Fair* magazine: "Certain things happened and it almost destroyed our family. I tried to warn everyone. I tried to warn all the mothers. I tried to expose him for what he was years ago." Being in business with a man who had been so publicly outed as a pedophile would have been catastrophic for Jackson. Aside from the fact that both Carters had performed with Michael on "What More Can I Give?" Aaron Carter had been a regular guest at Neverland while in his early teens.

Michael got wind of the sex abuse claims within days of arriving in Orlando and immediately broke off what Pearlman had described in the media as "negotiations." Jackson returned quickly to Bahrain, knowing he was lucky to get out of Florida before the media learned that he and Pearlman were meeting. Abdullah welcomed him with open arms, relieved to learn that the recording of the Katrina song would be completed in Bahrain after all.

Or perhaps not. Michael seemed to be dragging his feet about finishing "I Have This Dream." What concerned him most was that the legacy of "We Are the World" would be tarnished. The success of his first great humanitarian anthem was something he treasured but at the same time felt haunted by. "In the same way he doubted he could ever make another album as good as *Thriller*," Dieter Wiesner explained, "he also didn't think he could do a record as important as 'We Are the World.' And he knew that everybody would compare."

"We Are The World" was Michael's real follow-up to *Thriller*. The pinnacle of success he had achieved with the album created a daunting level of public expectation about what he would do next. Early in 1985, *Rolling Stone* published an article that described recent months as "a black hole for Michael watchers, who witnessed the most spectacular disappearing act since Halley's comet." Kids were already trading in their sequined gloves for Masters of the Universe action figures, the magazine reported, as "remainder tables groan beneath unsold Michael calendars and a Fifth Avenue store was palming off clothes for the Michael Jackson doll as outfits for Ken."

The unveiling of "We Are the World" in March 1985 would not only put Michael front and center again but elevate him to savior of mankind status. The song made pop stars the point persons in global humanitarian efforts. An initial shipment of 800,000 records sold out in three days. In all, three million copies of "We Are the World" were purchased before the end of the year, and the song raised almost $40 million for the starving people of Ethiopia. As much as this success inspired him, Michael wanted to make sure he got credit for it. When Ken Kragen put together a domestic antipoverty program called "Hands Across America" and commissioned a theme song that was to debut at halftime of the 1986 Super Bowl, Michael objected, and eventually convinced Kragen that his own song "should *always* be the anthem" of celebrity relief projects. He was overjoyed when "We Are the World" was declared the front-runner for Record of the Year at the Grammy Awards ceremony, scheduled to take place one month later, but annoyed to discover that Quincy Jones had been chosen to accept the prize. He promptly concocted a plan to upstage Jones. A young woman was hired to play the part of an adoring fan who would run in from the wings while the award was being presented to throw her arms around Michael as he stood next to the producer. It would make the front page of every newspaper in the country, Michael enthused, and nobody anywhere would remember Quincy's acceptance speech.

The core of essential beneficence in him was increasingly covered over by the accretions of egomania. Ever his enabler Walter Yetnikoff grew tired of it. "I could not have a conversation with him that did not revolve around Michael Jackson and his records and his shows and how wonderful he was." He grew so out of touch with the world around him that he often did not recognize newly minted celebrities. When he showed up on the set of the movie *Space Jam*, which featured Michael Jordan at a time when the NBA star was at the apex of his fame, Michael found it very difficult indeed to believe that *a basketball player* might be more famous than him. Jackson needed one of the young boys who accompanied him to explain just who exactly this other Michael was.

6

He had become convinced that it was time to "take control of my own life," Michael Jackson announced as the end of the 1980s approached. Almost immediately, he began to shed the very people who had been the architects of his enormous popular success. Among the first to go was Quincy Jones, the producer of his three previous solo albums. Jackson resented the credit Jones had taken for *Thriller*, especially since Jones had tried to keep "Billie Jean" off the album. Jones believed there was a simpler explanation: "I think at one point he felt I wasn't in touch with the market anymore," Jones would tell CBS News anchorwoman Katie Couric in 2009. "I remember when we were doing *Bad* I had DMC in the studio because I could see what was coming with hip-hop. And [Michael] was telling Frank Dileo 'I think Quincy's losing it and doesn't understand the market anymore. He doesn't know that rap is dead.' This is 1987. Rap hadn't even started and by 1992 it was all rap and at that time Michael was going after all the big rappers, Teddy Riley, all the rap producers, to spend five times what they were paying me to produce his records."

Michael then discharged Dileo. As his manager, Frank was adept at massaging Jackson's ego at the same time he emerged as one of the very few people who could disagree with Michael and make it stick. The best-known story about the two involved Jackson chasing his manager around a hotel room by brandishing his pet boa constrictor; Dileo reportedly pulled out a gun and threatened to shoot the damn snake if Michael didn't put it down.

The five-year run of success that Jackson and Dileo enjoyed together ended with a thud, though, in early 1989. The media reported that Dileo had been fired for botching the domestic release of Michael's ninety-minute video *Moonwalker*, which would not be distributed theatrically anywhere but in Japan. The Jackson family was furious with Dileo for letting Michael spend $27 million on the project; twenty-five people had worked for a solid six months on a four-minute-forty-five-second section constructed around "Leave Me Alone." Dileo was prominently featured on the *Bad* album jacket, appearing with Michael in a large photograph that bore the caption "another great team." When *Bad* failed to become "the biggest record ever," as Michael had predicted publicly and often, he began to divest himself of everyone associated with it, Jones and Dileo among them.

John Branca was the next to go and his departure foreshadowed Jackson's future even more ominously than the exits of Jones and Dileo. David Geffen was the agent of this specific dismissal, but the pattern was perhaps more important than the particulars. Again and again, Michael would allow a new and exciting voice not only to catch his ear, but also to cancel out the advice of a proven familiar. Anyone who knew how he had been raised understood that loyalty was of little value among the Jacksons. Branca, though, had been instrumental to Jackson in securing the ATV music catalog. He had a handshake agreement with Robert Holmes à Court in the spring of 1985, Branca would recall, but then the Australian "fucked me" by making a more lucrative deal with rival bidders Charles Koppelman and Martin Bandier. Branca maneuvered behind their backs with a phone call to Irving Azoff, chief of MCA, which was putting up the money for that deal, convincing Azoff that a favor to Michael Jackson at this particular moment would be repaid many times over. When Azoff pulled the funding for the Koppleman-Bandier deal, the catalog was sold to the next highest bidder, Jackson. The only concession Branca had to make to Holmes à Court was an agreement that the Australian's daughter would retain rights to "Penny Lane" as what, according to Branca, Holmes à Court termed a "souvenir." Five years later, though, Geffen began whispering that Michael should have a better deal at CBS Records and that Branca's close relationship with Walter Yetnikoff was the main reason he didn't. In the years since closing the ATV deal, Branca had made Jackson tens of millions in various sponsorship and merchandising deals. The copromoter of the *Victory* tour, Chuck Sullivan, had paid Michael $18 million in 1985 to develop a clothing line. A year later, Branca negotiated a deal with Pepsi that paid his client $15 million for the rights to sponsor a Michael Jackson solo tour. In 1988, Branca secured an advance of $10 million from a company called L.A. Gear to endorse its sneakers. A year after that, he salvaged the *Moonwalker* debacle by negotiating a ridiculously lucrative contract for Michael on rentals and sales of the video, a deal that resulted in Jackson's actually earning a profit on the seemingly doomed project. Michael began to resent the attorney, though, when Geffen and others explained to him how much of that money Branca was putting in his own pocket, and how he was using his relationship with Michael Jackson to feather his nest with other clients. In late 1990, it was announced that John Branca was being replaced as Jackson's lawyer by a team of attorneys who were closely associated with Geffen. Yetnikoff was fired by CBS Records' parent company, Sony, a short time later.

All of this had occurred while Michael was sinking deeper and deeper into a self-imposed isolation. He had separated from both his family and the city he had called home from the age of ten when he purchased Neverland Ranch in 1988 and left Los Angeles to live in the Santa Ynez Valley, more than a hundred miles up the coast, just north of Santa Barbara. He had first admired the property while Paul McCartney and his wife Linda were staying there during the filming of the "Say Say Say" video in 1982. It was called Sycamore Ranch back then, nearly three thousand acres where Figueroa Mountain Road wound through lush rolling hills to an estate that had been built to the lavish and exacting standards of a wealthy California developer named William Bone. The 13,000-square-foot main residence, set among one of the most beautiful groves of live oaks in all of California, was a hybrid Tudor mansion and Dutch farmhouse, with brick and masonry walls built around massive wooden beams that framed leaded glass windows, topped by a beautifully gabled roof. There were seventeen rooms on the first floor, sixteen rooms upstairs, and an enormous wine cellar below ground. Branca had handled a lengthy negotiation with Bone, eventually reaching a deal that allowed Jackson to buy the estate for $17 million, a little more than half the asking price. Jackson rewarded his attorney with a Rolls-Royce convertible. Almost immediately after taking possession of the property, Jackson renamed the place Neverland Valley Ranch and made it over into a signal declaration of wealth, success, and the power to create a private world in his own image.

The ranch in Santa Barbara County, just a short drive from Ronald Reagan's "Western White House," was far enough removed from the home he had grown up in—for his first ten years, anyway—to support the Jackson family's rags-to-riches story's most mythic dimensions. By the time the *Bad* tour was over, Michael's personal fortune had grown to considerably more than $100 million and he was looking for something that would awe his visitors in the same way he had been awed when he first saw Berry Gordy's staggeringly luxurious Bel Air palace, or Paul McCartney's stunning spread in East Sussex. Neverland Ranch would amply serve that purpose.

Branca warned Jackson that he was unlikely to recoup the $55 million he had invested in "improving" Neverland if or when he sold the place, but Michael was by then indifferent to such concerns. Reporters invited to tour

Neverland during its 1990 public unveiling most often began by inspecting the towering statue of Mercury (the Roman god of profit, trade, and commerce) in the driveway outside the mansion, then climbed a hill out back that led to a near replica of the Main Street train station at Disneyland, with a floral clock that was barely less magnificent than the one Walt Disney had designed for his own park. There, they caught a C. P. Huntington–style train out past a two-story fort outfitted with water cannons and a nearby Indian village replete with teepees, a totem pole, and full-size-replica Native Americans, to the amusement park where a carousel with custom-made hand-painted animals awaited young visitors. There was also a Ferris wheel, a bumper car arena, a three-story-high slide, and Michael's favorite, a roller coaster called the Zipper. Nearby was a zoo where horses and zebras ran together, and buffalo roamed among ostriches, deer, llamas, and giraffes. The "rec building" housed two floors of arcade games, while Neverland's private lake offered kids the choice between a swan boat, a canoe, and a red dinghy. The train's final stop was the $2 million Neverland Cinema, with a fully stocked candy counter and a glassed-in viewing booth with reclining beds to welcome seriously ill youngsters.

"Michael Jackson is very fond of children," *Rolling Stone's* Michael Goldberg observed in his report of the trip to Neverland, without a hint of hidden meaning. Goldberg was shown a room on the upstairs floor of the main house where a canopied bed was covered with dozens and dozens of dolls along with jack-in-the-boxes featuring each of the major characters from *The Wizard of Oz* sitting on shelves beside it. Another room was jammed full of children's games and toys, coloring books, and crayons. The "train room" featured an enormous and elaborate Lionel set, surrounded by cardboard cutouts of Bart Simpson, Roger Rabbit, and E. T. A pile of Peter Pan, Mickey Mouse, and Bambi quilts lay on the floor, in case the kids staying over wanted to have a slumber party. Goldberg was clearly more captivated by the "exquisitely furnished" first floor, which included an oak-paneled library stocked with rare editions of Charles Dickens, Mark Twain, and Rudyard Kipling, a living room anchored by a custom-made Bosendorfer rosewood piano, and a den warmed by a stone fireplace. *Rolling Stone's* reporter refrained from mentioning the numerous life-size paintings of Michael that hung on the interior walls of the main house. Nearly every one showed him striking a heroic pose while costumed in brightly colored but vaguely military uniforms that suggested the dandified garb of nineteenth-century European royalty, replete with cape, sword, ruffled collar, and, very often, a crown.

Goldberg was among those who insisted that one couldn't fully appreciate the magic of Neverland unless you saw it at night, when the whole place looked as if it had been "sprinkled with a kind of high-tech fairy dust." Strands of white bulbs ran up the trunks of the oak trees and out the limbs to the branches, blinking on and off at intervals so that the glittering trees seemed to materialize out of thin air one moment, then vanish the next. The sound of music was nearly deafening. After its release in 1995, Michael's song "Childhood" played constantly on the carousel, while cartoon soundtracks blared from the speakers astride a JumboTron the size of a drive-in movie screen. Songs filled the air even when one wandered off to explore the grounds; on lawns and in flowerbeds, speakers disguised as gray boulders poured forth show tunes until nearly midnight. A winding yellow brick road illuminated by recessed gold-color lights led to an amusement park that was lit against the night sky, while the main house, the lake, the bronze statues of young boys beating drums, playing accordions, or shaking tambourines were lit with strobes that lent the entire scene a sense of Brigadoon-like appearance and disappearance.

Michael's favorite place in Neverland was the three-turreted tree house that could be entered only by climbing the trunk. It was there, at a spot overlooking the lake, that he had written most of the songs for his new album, *Dangerous*. The entire music industry was in shock at a report that Jackson had spent $10 million of CBS Records' money on the production of *Dangerous*, five times what it cost even the most profligate bands to make a record. Michael publicly reveled in the commercial success of *Dangerous*, even as he privately winced at the mixed critical reception. The attempt to replicate his earlier successes was painfully obvious to those who panned the album. The song "Who Is It" was filled with sonic hooks almost identical to the ones Michael and Quincy Jones had used on "Billie Jean," they said, while "Heal the World" seemed like little more than a rewrite of "We Are the World." The *New York Times* called *Dangerous* Jackson's "least confident" solo album. The *Los Angeles Times* asked, "How dangerous can a man be who literally wants to please everyone?" Still, *Dangerous* debuted at #1 on the *Billboard* album chart and remained in the top ten more than a year later. Record company executives were most impressed that more than three-quarters of *Dangerous*'s sales had been made outside the United States.

Michael Jackson was the most international music star ever and in recognition Sony had secured his future with a contract that was the most lucrative in the history of the entertainment industry. The $65 million guarantee was but an advance on a deal that could be worth $1 billion to Jackson, according to the Sony press release that announced it. Jackson had become the first artist in any medium to be given 50 percent of profits, or even close to that amount. That was on top of the 25 percent royalty he would receive for each retail sale, plus a signing bonus of $4 million and $1 million per year to run his own record company. Sony had also agreed to put up an additional $2.2 million per year in "administrative costs," plus more than $10 million to pay for music videos, and honored the singer's ambition to be a movie star by including provisions that guaranteed him a fee of $5 million for every film he appeared in, plus a large percentage of the gross receipts. "Michael is the greatest superstar in the music industry," Sony senior vice president Ron Wilcox told the *Los Angeles Times,* "and the contract is justified by his past achievements, existing talent, and future potential."

Jackson was now wealthy almost beyond imagining. The ATV catalog was doubling in value annually, spinning off millions in earnings. Dollars were flowing out of his accounts in prodigious amounts, but still not nearly as rapidly as they were flooding in. Michael was watching his fortune grow, keeping a constant eye on cash flow, and paying close attention to accounting statements. "The bookkeeper we hired during *Invincible* was the same bookkeeper Michael had back in the *Thriller* days," said Marc Schaffel, "and she told me that back then Michael would check the complete balance down to the dollar in his bank account, every day. That she would write the checks and deliver them to Michael and he would sign each one personally. She said there were times he would see a bill and he wouldn't sign the check, that he would call the vendor and ask them, 'Why is your bill $50,000? You're charging me too much.' And then he would go back and tell her to make the check for $40,000. She said he knew every dollar that was going in and out. It amazed me because he was so far removed from that when I met him."

Michael was in Asia, near the end of the *Dangerous* tour in the summer of 1993, when word came that he had been accused of sexually molesting thirteen-year-old Jordan Chandler, and that authorities in both Los Angeles and Santa Barbara counties had initiated criminal investigations. He canceled his remaining dates and soon after checked into a rehabilitation facility to deal with what was said to be a prescription drug addiction, then returned to the United States several weeks later to discover that the floor had fallen out from under his entire life.

It was Michael's misfortune that this first "child sex scandal" had broken the year before O. J. Simpson cut his wife's throat, at the very moment when cable news and tabloid culture were recognizing their perverse synergy. Jackson's singular strangeness seemed to make anything possible, and the dollars dangled by various editors and producers attracted a slew of "insiders" who sold the entertainer out for whatever they could get. Two former Neverland security guards received $100,000 to tell *Hard Copy* that they were fired because they knew too much about the singer's relationships with young boys. Later, in court, both men admitted they had made up most of their story. Jackson's former maid Blanca Francia took $20,000 for telling *Hard Copy* that she had seen Michael naked with young boys, including her own son, then contradicted that claim in interviews with the police and Jackson's attorneys. Francia later threatened to file a lawsuit that squeezed a $2 million settlement out of the singer. Jackson's former secretary Orietta Murdoch and his ex-head of security Robert Wegner sold separate stories suggesting that Jackson had been sexually involved with a pair of Australian kids, who each adamantly denied it.

Being stabbed in the back by those he let close to him changed Jackson in ways that would prove profoundly destructive. He began to lose faith in everyone around him, and to reach out for the kindness of strangers who wanted only to get their fingers in his pockets. In a search for reassurance that grew as ceaseless as it was unsuccessful, he became prey to every sort of charlatan. Inspecting his bank statements and reviewing his accounting reports was now next to impossible. He cycled in and out of an addiction to the synthetic opiates he had begun to take while recovering from the Pepsi commercial fire in 1984. His need to numb himself became consuming in 1993, after he endured the most mortifying experience of his life, being forced to strip naked from the waist down so that police could photograph his genitals. The purpose of the exercise was to compare the results to pictures and descriptions provided by Jordie Chandler. Now, even the short length of this painfully shy celebrity's pubic hair was part of the scandal that engulfed him.

Jackson found it more and more difficult to work. He was paying out huge fees and making enormous settlements to try to contain an avalanche of litigation, and was billed tens of thousands every month by the PR consultants he hired to counter bad publicity. He was increasingly susceptible to flatterers and enablers. Millions of dollars were still pouring in each year but now even more was pouring out.

He did manage to complete his double album *HIStory* for a 1995 release but was not encouraged by the reception. Worldwide sales were barely more than half of what *Dangerous* had done. *HIStory* was the first album ever to sell twenty million copies and be considered a failure. Some major critics were openly dismissive. The *New York Times*'s Jon Pareles built his review around the assertion that, "It has been a long time since Michael Jackson was simply a performer. He's the main asset of his own corporation, which is a profitable subsidiary of Sony."

At Sony they were starting to wonder about that last part. Jackson had spent most of the millions allotted for his future video productions on the "teaser" he shot for *HIStory* in Hungary. "The production company would call me in the middle of the night and say, 'Michael wants more troops,'" his marketing executive Dan Beck told the *Times*. By the end of that year, Jackson found himself so short of cash that he was forced to sell Sony a half-interest in the ATV catalog for $100 million, about a quarter of what it would be worth a few years later. He had been able at least to retain 51 percent of the catalog and control of the most profitable part, the Beatles songs, and in the years that followed Sony added any number of classic songs to the package, material that reached across a range stretching from Bob Dylan's "Blowin' in the Wind" to Joe Diffie's "Third Rock from the Sun." Sony also guaranteed Jackson a minimum income of $6.5 million per year from the licensing rights to the catalog's songs. In 2001, when *1*, a collection of the Beatles' #1 hits, sold more than twenty million units worldwide, Jackson's share of the profits was $9 million. It still wasn't enough to keep him afloat.

His dreams of movie stardom had died in the Jordan Chandler drama but Michael refused to accept it, writing one six- or seven-figure check after another to pay for video projects such as a thirty-five-minute film called *Ghosts* that he cowrote with Stephen King and shot in 1997 with special effects wizard Stan Winston, only to see it dismissed by critics as a "vanity project." All told, he would spend an estimated $65 million on video productions during the 1990s and receive little in return but more bad press. Despite a net worth that had been estimated as high as $1 billion, he was struggling to service an increasingly massive debt. Branca made a deal with Sony that netted Michael a quick $25 million in cash, but the price was a reversal of their ownership positions in the ATV catalog. Now the company owned 51 percent of the song titles and Jackson was the minority partner. By 1998, Michael had depleted a $90 million loan from NationsBank taken out two years earlier and was forced to bring Branca back to negotiate a new $140 million loan from Bank of America.

That money was gone before a year had passed so Jackson negotiated a $30 million line of credit with the bank that was maxed out within a few months. In 2000, he managed to have his B of A loan raised to $200 million, but now the bank was taking advantage of his financial distress by demanding higher rates of interest.

He began to oscillate wildly between a series of financial advisors, many of them either inept or on the make. One of those who tried to organize his affairs was Al Malnik, a superrich Florida attorney who was best known for his past association with organized crime kingpin Meyer Lansky. Even Malnik, though, couldn't convince Michael to curb his spending. "There was no planning in terms of allocations," Malnik would explain in a deposition connected to one of the many lawsuits filed against Jackson. "For Michael it was whatever he wanted, at the time he wanted." Jackson seemed "bewildered" whenever he tried to discuss money matters, said Malnik, who had tried to explain to Michael that flying to London for a weekend of shopping was one thing, while renting a private jet to carry an entourage and renting an entire floor of a five-star hotel to house them while he did so was quite another. By Malnik's estimate, Michael was spending about $8 million per year just on travel and antiques.

At Neverland, it was costing the star $4 million per annum to keep employees who ranged from carpenters to snake handlers on the payroll. Michael's advisor Rabbi Shmuley Boteach got what was for him a shocking display of Jackson's extravagance in December 2000 when he learned that Michael, who was staying with his entourage at the Four Seasons in New York, had continued to rent an entire floor at the hotel during a nearly month-long trip to Neverland for the holidays. Why didn't you vacate the rooms while you were gone and save yourself a few hundred thousand dollars? Boteach asked. "What were we supposed to do with our stuff?" Michael wanted to know.

Shopping and spending had become for Michael as addictive as any opiate. Those who worked for him described seeing Jackson leaf through a magazine and order every single product advertised in it. He ran up a bill at Celebrity Costumes for just under $100,000 in a single year. In 1998, he reportedly became the first to place an order for a $75,000 per bottle "limited edition" perfume being licensed as "the ultimate symbol of indulgence." The "heavenly scent" confected from roses, chocolate, and musk would be sold in a flask made from platinum, gold, and diamonds, packaged in a walnut box manufactured by the same company that did the woodwork for Rolls-Royce interiors, a container that could be opened only with one of the gold, diamond, and ruby keys that Graff jewelers was crafting for that sole purpose, according to the press release announcing that Michael Jackson had already placed a deposit on two bottles, one for himself and one for his dear friend Elizabeth Taylor.

In 1999, Michael paid $1.54 million at auction for the Oscar that producer David O. Selznick had received for *Gone with the Wind*. Less than a year later, Beverly Hills jeweler David Orgell sued Jackson for nonpayment on a $1.9 million Vacheron watch. The entertainer tried to return the timepiece but Orgell said it was scratched. They settled in 2001, and the very next day Jackson used the Vacheron as collateral on another loan from Bank of America. Soon after this, he submitted the winning bid at auction on a pair of nineteenth-century French paintings but was forced to return the art when Sotheby's sued him for the outstanding balance of $1.6 million.

Jackson had shown such remarkable business acumen as a young man, skillfully selecting collaborators, representatives, and advisors. Now approaching middle age, he seemed irresistibly drawn to projects that most of the press and much of the public found laughable. In 1996, Jackson flew to Paris to meet the Saudi prince Al-Waleed bin Talal and join him in the announcement of a "family values" global entertainment empire whose projects included plans to create a theme park home for all British bovines afflicted with mad cow disease. Soon after, the singer showed up in Warsaw, where he announced the $500 million World of Childhood amusement park he planned to build with the cooperation of the Polish government. According to Malnik, Jackson's serial advisors managed to lose $50 million of his money in the 1990s alone on a series of "bizarre" projects that never came to fruition. Two of those advisors were Dieter Wiesner and Ronald Konitzer, who had collaborated with Jackson on a series of grandiose near misses that began with the marketing of a sport cola they called "Mystery Drink." Wiesner and Konitzer went on to use the singer's name in promotions for a giant resort near Victoria Falls in Zimbabwe, and for a huge "Majestic Kingdom" theme park in Detroit. By the end of 2000, the press openly mocked any announcement that involved Michael Jackson.

For years, virtually every contract involving Jackson had been freighted with assorted side deals in which various "representatives" pocketed enormous fees for persuading him to sign this or that agreement. Hundreds of thousands of dollars changed hands, almost always under the table, while huge fees were taken off the top by a carousel of attorneys and managers.

In 2001, when Michael LaPerruque became Michael's new chief of security, he discovered that most of the guards at Neverland were doubling and tripling their salaries by offering to go shopping for Jackson, using Michael's name to purchase duplicates of the high-end items he wanted, ranging from electronics to jewelry, then having the seconds sent to their own homes. After LaPerruque left Neverland in 2004, he was replaced by Chris Carter, a handsome young African-American man whom the entertainer had spotted while strolling through a Las Vegas casino. As his new head of security, Carter was principally useful to Jackson for his ability to obtain the antianxiety drug Xanax under an assortment of fictitious names. Within the year, Carter's next-in-command was an eighteen-year-old surfer named Joey Jeszeck whom Jackson hired upon meeting him in a skateboard shop near Neverland. After Jackson dismissed Carter, Neverland's former security chief readily agreed to testify for the prosecution at the 2005 criminal trial, but was unable to answer when called, having been arrested in Las Vegas on an assortment of felony charges that included armed robbery and kidnapping.

The atmosphere around Jackson grew murkier still when his brother Jermaine introduced the Nation of Islam into his life after the filing of the criminal charges in 2003. Various insiders who found themselves suddenly on the outside claimed that Louis Farrakhan's son-in-law Leonard Muhammad had not only taken charge of Jackson's security detail (forcing out LaPerruque), but was also managing his business affairs. The tensions this created boiled over in late 2003 when Jackson's "chief spokesperson," Stuart Backerman, abruptly quit his job, citing "strategic differences." It was widely believed that Backerman had refused to work with Muhammad and the NOI. Later, the PR man admitted this to a London tabloid, the *Sun*: "I quit because the Nation of Islam had infiltrated Michael's world. I was the only one who was left standing at this point, because Michael wasn't in his right mind."

Stories linking Jackson to the NOI and suggesting he shared Farrakhan's anti-Semitism further eroded the singer's shrinking public support. In the media, mentions of Jackson's career were now almost always coupled with the word "decline." What may have been Michael Jackson's saddest career moment came in August 2003, three months before the raid on Neverland, when he celebrated his forty-fifth birthday with a public event that only served to emphasize his reduced status. While hundreds of young people from South Central, East LA, and the San Fernando Valley paid upward of $30 per ticket for seats in the old downtown Los Angeles movie palace where the concert celebration was held, nearly every one of the spots inside the velvet ropes up front reserved for A-list guests remained empty. Instead of Stevie Wonder and Diana Ross, Jackson's fans found themselves being entertained by obscure performers who lip-synched his greatest hits. And when the birthday boy himself took the stage at the end of the evening to lead a rendition of "We Are the World," he was accompanied not by the likes of Bruce Springsteen and Ray Charles, but by an assortment of Michael Jackson impersonators.

Unable or unwilling (even those closest to him weren't sure) to generate any fresh stream of income, Jackson was falling further behind financially. More and more of the people he did business with were not getting paid. Some of those who said he stiffed them not only took the singer to court, but also used the media to gain leverage. No one did more damage in that regard than Myung Ho Lee, the South Korean–born financial advisor who claimed to have managed Jackson's business affairs from 1997 to 2001, and sued the singer in early 2003, demanding $13 million in back pay. In papers filed with the Los Angeles Superior Court, Lee described Jackson as "a ticking financial time bomb waiting to explode at any moment." The singer fought back with a countersuit against Lee in which he claimed his signature had been forged on a contract and that it was Lee who owed the millions, siphoned from Jackson's bank accounts. Michael complained to those around him that Lee had made unauthorized and disastrous investments in various dot-com ventures (most notably the gaming company Tickets.com) that cost him a fortune when the boom went bust. Lee answered by collaborating with Maureen Orth on an article for *Vanity Fair* that convinced hundreds of thousands of upscale readers that Jacko really was Wacko. In the summer of 2000, Lee told Orth, Jackson had paid an African witch doctor named Baba $150,000 to conduct a "voodoo ritual" in Switzerland that was intended to result in the deaths of twenty-five people on an "enemies list" topped by the names of David Geffen and Steven Spielberg. Though Orth didn't report it, quite a few people in the entertainment industry knew that Jackson *had* fallen out with Geffen and Spielberg and this added an undercurrent of credibility to the story. Baba's curses had been sealed with the blood of forty-two ritually sacrificed cows, according to Lee, who claimed to have wired payment for the slaughter to a bank in Mali.

Though Jackson nearly had Lee's lawsuit thrown out, the Korean's attorneys successfully scheduled a deposition of Michael Jackson in June 2003, at which the singer's finances would be fully explored. The day before he was to be questioned, Jackson settled out of court for a sum said to be "well into seven figures." He refused payment, though, to European concert promoter Marcel Avram, who had filed a $22.1 million suit against Jackson for backing out of two 1999 "Millennium Concerts" in Sydney and Honolulu. At the end of a 2003 civil trial in Santa Barbara County, a jury of Jackson's neighbors awarded Avram $5.3 million, but the concert promoter was still chasing his money two years later.

A "forensic accountant" appointed by the Santa Barbara County Superior Court to examine Jackson's finances reported that the entertainer's annual budget was $12 million for personal expenses and the maintenance of Neverland, but this amount was a pittance compared to the $54 million a year it was now costing him to service his enormous debt. Yet Jackson continued to stay in $10,000 per night hotel suites and to rent an entire floor of standard rooms for his entourage.

"Michael would believe somehow that Sony was paying for it all," Schaffel explained, "and they were. But they were charging it to him. Anything he did, whether it was hotels or private jets or whatever, they paid, but they charged him for it. So he was using up more and more of his income and going deeper and deeper into debt with Sony. Sony never really said no. Anything Michael wanted, Sony would say fine, but they would just keep racking up the bill. They had no reason not to, because they had the catalog to cover the cost. Michael was losing more and more of the catalog instead of gaining more and more. And he wouldn't want to hear about any of that. All he wanted to know was how much cash was in his pocket that day. He would say to me, 'Look, I don't want to work my ass off and get nothing out of it.' That was a lot of the problem with *Invincible*. The expenses were so high, he owed so much, and he was so far behind on his payments to the catalog, that he felt he'd never see a dime out of the album when it was released. I would say, 'Michael, if you make $20 million on this deal, you're paying down your debt to Sony.' He said, 'That's not my money. Everybody's putting their hands in—the lawyers, the accountants.' He'd say, 'They all take their piece of my money and what am I left with?'"

Of course, Michael Jackson tended to look at money a little differently than other people, Schaffel acknowledged. "I remember this time in Vegas when he wanted to buy something that cost a hundred grand and he wanted me to get him the money. So I went to the Mirage and some casino manager called me back and said, 'For you, because we know you, we can give you fifty thousand if you want to come down and get it. But because of the time of night and we're not a bank, we can't give you a hundred.' So he gives me the fifty grand. Dieter is with me, and we hurry up to Michael's suite, because we know he's antsy and wants to go buy something. He had the Cascio kids with him, and a couple other kids who were traveling with him. And he said, 'Oh, did you get my money?' And I said, 'Well, I have fifty grand. It's all I can get late at night like this.' And he looked, kind of not happy, through these stacks of ten thousand apiece. He's pouting, and he says, 'It's no good. I need a hundred.' And then says, 'Oh, forget it.' And he says, 'Kids, come here.' All the kids come over, and he hands each of them a stack of ten thousand and says, 'Go out and entertain yourself for an hour.' Dieter and I just looked at each other like . . . 'Only Michael.'"

7

By late January 2006 Sheikh Abdullah could sense in Mikaeel a new restlessness, a mounting dissatisfaction with life in Bahrain. And Abdullah was more and more uneasy. He had planted a story in the *Gulf News* that was intended to show that the star was settling into his new life and had paid $8 million for a home in Sanad (about ten kilometers south of Manama) where he and his children were now living. The house, of course, was provided by the sheikh. Abdullah got the same newspaper to report on Mikaeel's surprise appearance at a traditional Arabic wedding involving a member of the prominent Al Gosaibi family who had befriended him during his months in the Persian Gulf. Mr. Jackson had watched from the sidelines, the *Gulf News* reported, for fear of distracting from the nuptials, and requested that no one take photographs of him. Only the Lebanese pop singer Ragheb Alama, who had performed at the ceremony, was allowed to have his picture taken with the King of Pop. Abdullah confided to the *Gulf News* reporter that Mikaeel would be vacating the mansion in Sanad soon but planned to keep it for his relatives and friends when he moved into a more impressive home by the sea.

Just five days after the wedding story ran, Michael again departed from Bahrain, bound this time for Hamburg, Germany. He and his children were headed for what they hoped would be a private visit with the Schleiter family, whose twenty-three-year-old son Anton had been a special friend of Michael's for more than a decade. Jackson had dedicated a song on *Invincible*, "Speechless," to Anton and his younger sister.

Anton Schleiter was frequently mistaken by the American media for Michael's other Anton, Anton Glanzelius, who at one time had been the best-known child actor in all of Scandinavia. Shortly after his appearance in Lasse Hallström's 1987 film *My Life as a Dog*, Anton Glanzelius received a phone call at his parents' home in Gothenburg, Sweden, from someone in America who identified himself as Michael Jackson. He wanted to let the boy know how much he had enjoyed his work in

Hallström's movie and invited him for a visit to California. The Swedish Anton had no idea who Michael Jackson was, but judging by the reaction of his family knew this must be someone important and ran to a neighbor's house to ask if they had any Michael Jackson albums because he wanted to see what the star looked like. Anton Glanzelius and his mother made the trip to Los Angeles later that year and visited the Hayvenhurst estate, but only got to spend a couple of hours with Michael, whom the boy described as "very polite" but also very quiet. The biggest thrill of the visit, Swedish Anton said, was meeting Michael's pet chimpanzee Bubbles, who came downstairs wearing a diaper and shook his hand. A year later, Anton Glanzelius received a second call from Michael, who said he would be in Sweden the next week and invited the boy to spend the day with him at Liseberg, the largest amusement park in Scandinavia. He had visited Liseberg several times before, the boy said, but never like this. The park's management closed Liseberg to the public for the day so that he and Michael would have the entire place to themselves. They rode Michael's favorite ride, a roller coaster called the "Loopen," twelve times and spent nearly an hour driving bumper cars, where Michael was "laughing constantly," the boy remembered. It was so much fun that after a while he barely noticed the photographers who lined the roofs of nearby buildings. He spent that night in Michael's hotel room. When recalling the sleepover twenty years later, Anton Glanzelius said there wasn't the slightest hint of a sexual advance. Instead they talked "about everything from football and fame to girls and love." He had been amazed at how "kindhearted and humble" Michael was during that day and night, and even more amazed that Michael kept in contact afterward, regularly sending packages filled with presents and videos. Then, in 1993, when the Jordan Chandler scandal broke, Michael had cut off all contact.

The German Anton, Anton Schleiter, had entered Michael's life two years after the Chandler affair, when he met Michael during a taping of Germany's hugely successful Saturday night television variety show *Wanna Bet?* That Michael had appeared on *Wanna Bet?* several times over the years was a testament to both his popularity in Germany and his comfort level with the country. No fans in all of Europe adored him so passionately as the Germans. When the Jordan Chandler accusations first surfaced, thousands of his German fans organized sign-waving "solidarity marches" in Berlin, Hamburg, and Cologne. An astounding number inked themselves with "Michael" tattoos to express the depth of their support.

Jackson answered their love by returning to Germany again and again, visiting the Phantasialand amusement park near Cologne in consecutive years during the late nineties. One of the most touching, disturbing, and emblematic photographs of him ever taken was shot when he attempted to ride the park's carousel. Michael's stricken expression as he had tried to sit astride a hand-carved wooden horse that was far too small for him was pathetic to some people, heartbreaking to others. Jackson's relationship with the German media changed after the baby-dangling incident at the Hotel Adlon; when criminal charges were filed in California one year later a number of the country's columnists took to calling him "the King of Flop."

His German fans, however, demonstrated their continued fervor when the nation's biggest newspaper, *Bild*, published a front-page story on January 26, 2006, reporting that Michael Jackson and his children were ensconced at an ordinary redbrick house on Garstedter Weg in Hamburg's middle-class Niendorf district. Michael was in fact making one of his regular attempts to vacation in "normal life," and had hoped to give his children the private experience of a happy, healthy suburban family. The Schleiter household didn't fit so snugly into that category these days, even without the fans and police outside. Anton's father, Wolfgang Schleiter, an executive at the Sony subsidiary BMG who refused to offer support for Michael when contacted by reporters after Jackson's 2003 arrest, had recently separated from his wife.

When word circulated that the *Bild* story was true the crush of fans that surged into the snow-covered streets of Niendorf created an unprecedented level of chaos. Squads of police were dispatched to put up a barricade and restrain the screaming fans who stood outside the Schleiters' house begging for Michael to appear. Some in Hamburg demanded to know why Jackson wasn't being made to pay for the extra security, as many visiting celebrities were required to do, but a police spokesman explained that neither the pop star nor the Schleiter family had "encouraged the public to come."

Shortly thereafter, Anton left with Michael, Grace, and the three children for Venice, Italy. The young German was still among the traveling party when Michael checked them into the Excelsior Hotel in Florence. Because of its exquisite antique shops, the city had long been Michael's favorite shopping destination. He was unable to bear staying there for more than a couple of days at a time when he didn't have money to spend, so the group moved on to stay for five nights at the Villa Savarese on the

Amalfi Coast. The six of them stopped over for two nights in Rome after that, then flew to London so that Mark Lester and his family could be with them on February 13, when Michael hosted a large gathering at storied Cliveden House for Prince's ninth birthday.

Returning to Manama on March 11, Michael had exhausted both his allotment from Sony and the remainder of the $250,000 that Abdullah had given him for Christmas. Several emerging controversies back in California had distracted from his holiday during that last week in England and Michael came back to Bahrain more convinced than ever that the American media was out to get him. Tom Mesereau had withdrawn as his attorney on February 23, and reporters in Los Angeles were doing their best to frame the announcement as yet another case of Jackson wearing out the loyalty of an indispensable ally. In fact, Mesereau said, "there was no problem at all with Michael." He just couldn't bear dealing with Raymone Bain for another day.

Bain was a curvy, micro-miniskirt-wearing PR powerhouse from Washington, D.C., who, before becoming involved with Michael Jackson, had been best known for her professional relationships with Marion Barry and Mike Tyson. She was prone to labeling adversaries as racists and her insistence on doing so during Michael's criminal trial in California was what led to the first falling-out with Mesereau. "Raymone is all about Raymone," Mesereau said. He wasn't terribly fond of Grace Rwaramba, either, Mesereau admitted, and found watching Grace and Raymone battle for control of Michael almost as grating and tedious as dealing with them individually. By early 2006, Mesereau was fed up with it. "But I still felt fond of Michael," insisted the attorney, who had done what he could to convince a disbelieving media.

In Manama, Sheikh Abdullah was working feverishly to protect his family's investment in Michael Jackson. Jermaine, meanwhile, was maneuvering desperately to get a piece of 2 Seas Records, on the one hand promising Abdullah he would deliver Michael, and on the other urging Michael to remember all the sheikh had done for him. Worried by Michael's obvious restiveness, the sheikh imported John Legend and Chris Tucker to Bahrain. Michael was interested in working with Legend as a producer. Tucker, best known for the *Rush Hour* movies, had been, along with Macaulay Culkin, the most loyal of all Michael's celebrity friends during his criminal trial; they were the only two who had agreed without hesitation to take the stand on his behalf. He was suitably impressed by Abdullah's palace in Bahrain, Tucker said, and absolutely awestruck by the sheikh's mansion in

Dubai. "Even Michael was blown away by the place," Tucker said. "They had to kick me out." He was encouraged by how much better Michael's condition was than when he had last seen his friend, Tucker told *Playboy* shortly after returning from the trip: "Michael is a genius, a creative being in a whole other reality . . . We're going to see a lot more from Michael."

Abdullah wanted badly to believe just that. The sheikh's final attempt to put Michael back to work on the Katrina record came when he flew Tony Buzan in from Singapore. Buzan was an intellectual hustler of the highest order, a cofounder of the international Memory Games competition who now sold his services as a motivational guru to a global assortment of wealthy dilettantes. He had been working in Singapore when Abdullah ("an old friend") phoned him one evening and said, "A fan of yours would like to speak to you." After a short pause, Buzan heard someone with an American accent say, "Hi, it's Michael." It had taken Buzan some time to realize that it was Michael *Jackson*, mainly because the masculine voice he heard was nothing like the wispy murmur that the entertainer used when he spoke in front of television cameras. Jackson had just finished reading one of Buzan's books and was enthused about applying some of the concepts in it. "I'd love to have you explain your ideas to my children," Michael said, "and teach them how to think." After Abdullah got back on the line, letting him know that Michael would be his primary student and that he, the sheikh, would be paying, Buzan caught a first-class flight to Bahrain, checked into a suite at the Burj Al Arab, then spent the next nine days commuting to Michael's mansion in Sanad.

Buzan was frequently identified in the media as the inventor of mind mapping, but that was hardly the case. Mind maps had been around since at least the third century, when Porphyry of Tyre began using them to try to illustrate the concepts of Aristotle. The American psychologists Allan M. Collins and M. Ross Quillian created extensive mind maps in the early 1960s. Buzan's innovations were so dramatic, though, that he had virtually *reinvented* the field, as he told it, by incorporating such elements as the semantics of Alfred Korzybski and the science fiction novels of Robert Heinlein. What he did for his clients, Buzan said, was help them create a diagram of their individual consciousness in which words, ideas, tasks, or goals were arranged around a central word or concept. The result was a kind of "graphic note taking" that encouraged people to solve problems by using the brain's vast, untapped potential, the 99 percent of mental ability that most of us waste. Buzan charged his clients $37,000 per session, a fee that Abdullah paid without hesitation.

The sessions would proceed, of course, as Michael Jackson wished them to. Jackson mainly wanted to talk about Leonardo da Vinci. Michael was fascinated by geniuses and by the whole idea of genius. He wanted to imagine what a map of da Vinci's mind must have looked like, and how it would be different from the mind maps of Alexander the Great or Charlie Chaplin, two other figures he was especially obsessed with at the moment. Since he understood that Michael had been raised as a Christian, Buzan found it unusual that in their discussions of the great historical figures, his host never once mentioned the name Jesus. Yet for all Michael's eccentricity, Buzan considered him to have been "probably the best pupil I've had."

Buzan was only slightly less impressed by Jackson's two oldest children, Prince and Paris, whom he described as "fast learners like their father," with the same ability to focus intensely on whatever engaged their attention. While it appeared obvious that Michael bore no biological relation to the two light-skinned older children, he suspected Michael might be Blanket's natural father, because the youngest child had a much darker complexion than Prince and Paris. All three kids, though, were remarkably attached to their father, Buzan observed: "I would watch them coming and going from the international school every day. They left happy, and came back happy. On their return, those three kids could not run any faster from the car to get to hug their daddy."

The children were "greatly amused" by the larger-than-life-size photographs of themselves that their father had hung among the prints of portrait paintings by various Renaissance masters who included Leonardo, Michelangelo, and Raphael that covered the interior walls of the house. Buzan noticed there were no photographs of the Jackson family in the house, not even a picture of Katherine.

In the long days and evenings he spent with Jackson, Buzan said, Michael made only a single reference to the scandals that had engulfed him in recent years, the baby-dangling incident in Berlin: "Michael was indignant. He said, 'I'm a dancer, one of the fittest, strongest people in theater. I lift and carry adults with no difficulty.'"

Buzan saw no signs that Michael was abusing drugs except once when they were making a trip by car and the sun struck him at an angle that bypassed the dark lenses covering his eyes. "Michael cried out in pain and involuntarily ducked his head." Such hypersensitivity to sunlight, Buzan knew, was among the more common side effects of regular opiate use, caused by the shrunken pupils such drugs produce. Just a few days later, a person identified as Michael's "aide" was stopped at the Manama airport carrying a suitcase stuffed with synthetic opiates that included hundreds of OxyContin pills. The ensuing scene was an enormous embarrassment for Sheikh Abdullah, who was forced to involve his father in suppressing a criminal investigation, freeing Michael's drug courier and keeping the arrest out of the newspapers. Once again, Abdullah swallowed his anger, even helping Michael to arrange a lavish party for Paris's eighth birthday on April 3.

The sheikh's apprehension spiked again on April 13, when the *New York Times* published an article under the headline "Michael Jackson Bailout Said to Be Close." "After months of talks that spanned the globe, with meetings from Los Angeles to New York to London to Bahrain," the *Times* reported, Fortress Investments had reached a rough agreement with Sony on a deal to refinance Jackson's debt at an interest rate of around 6 percent, only a little more than one-fourth of what they had been forcing Michael to pay since buying his loan from Bank of America. That deal wasn't quite as close to a conclusion as the *Times* suggested, but the agreements in place were solid enough to suggest that within a matter of months Michael would be enjoying a level of solvency—and cash flow—he hadn't known in several years. Among the many questions it raised was whether he would see a continuing need to remain in the Middle East.

Abdullah pressed as he never had previously for a public agreement to secure the future of 2 Seas Records. On April 18, Michael obliged, dispatching Raymone Bain to announce that Guy Holmes, the former chairman of Gut Records, a successful UK indie, had been hired to serve as 2 Seas CEO. "I am incredibly excited about my new venture, and I am enjoying being back in the studio making music," Michael had said, according to Bain, who promised reporters that on November 21, 2 Seas would release a new Michael Jackson song, coproduced by Bruce Swedien, under the title "Now That I Found Love." Michael's first album for 2 Seas would follow in "late 2007."

The problem was that Michael wasn't really "back in the studio." He seemed, in fact, even less interested than before in working on his new album, and did little more than tinker with the Katrina song. For the first time, the sheikh let his annoyance show, pointing out that he had now "advanced" Michael more than $7 million and needed to see him get serious about his work. What was the point of the $343,000 he had paid to Tony Buzan, Abdullah wanted to know, if Michael was still as lacking in motivation as he had been before the mind mapper's arrival? Michael answered with his own complaint that Abdullah had taken advantage of his exhaustion at the end of a long and grueling criminal trial by manipulating him into agreements that weren't really in his best interest and quite possibly violated his contracts with Sony.

Tensions between the two mounted all during the first two weeks of May. Michael had been asking Abdullah to build him a house in Bahrain since his arrival in the country, but now he began to demand it, insisting to the sheikh that he couldn't continue to move his children from one Al Khalifa property to another, that both they and he needed something more permanent, a home they could call their own. Abdullah replied that Michael first needed to demonstrate that he intended to honor his promises. In response, Michael announced that he would be forced to fly to London to give a second deposition in the Marc Schaffel case on May 22. From London he would be traveling to Japan to accept a "Legend" award at the MTV Music Video Awards ceremony in Tokyo, Michael told the sheikh, and when he returned he expected to have a home of his own waiting for him. Abdullah swallowed his indignation and made an effort to part as friends, embracing the singer as he said good-bye, wishing him safe travel and securing a promise that he would return to Bahrain soon in order to finish what they had started.

It was the last time the prince of Bahrain ever saw Mikaeel.

PART TWO

NORTH

8

They had never stopped loving Michael in Japan. Hundreds of fans stood in a downpour, holding signs welcoming him back to their country on May 27, 2006, when Jackson walked the red carpet at Tokyo's Yoyogi Olympic Stadium, where he would accept his MTV "Legend" award. After being introduced as "the King of Pop, the King of Rock, and the King of Soul," he grew emotional onstage, thanking "all the people who believed in me," then told the Japanese, "I think you are a very sweet, generous, and kind people."

He kept repeating "Aishiteru!" ("I love you!") during the five days he spent in a country where no one breathed a word about the molestation trial that had ended less than a year earlier, not even when he visited a Tokyo orphanage run by Catholic nuns. During his visit to the Seibi Gakuen children's home in downtown Tokyo, a crowd of excited orphans performed traditional dance and music, then swarmed him afterward. A day later, Jackson showed up "unannounced" in the TV studio where the enormously popular band SMAP was recording. The dropped jaws and bug eyes of the boy band members appeared to amuse Michael enormously, though he only stayed long enough to give them all high-fives. The president of Avex Records threw him a party hosted by the socialite Kano Sisters, who introduced Jackson to the singer Yoshiki and surrounded him with "glamour models." He visited a Pachinko parlor long enough to play on a machine that featured a Michael Jackson character and promised the clutch of cameras that he would return to the Land of the Rising Sun for a "Christmas party" in December.

The Japanese had long appreciated Jackson in ways that would never translate across the Pacific. While the country's young idolized Michael as the ultimate pop culture icon, Japan's intellectual elite embraced him as a Kabuki theater performer of the highest caliber. Without the slightest awareness of it, he had adopted a stylized persona that seemed to combine the *onnagata* and *wakashu* roles of *yar o kabuki* (young man kabuki): the exotic and androgynous garb, the heavy layer of white-pallor makeup, the smooth, shoulder-length black wig, and the high-pitched falsetto voice. Michael could project the qualities of profound hurt and deep sadness that was part of every major Kabuki performer's character, as well as the sense that he held a deep mystery in his core.

After brief appearances in Singapore, Shanghai, and Hong Kong, Jackson stopped in Brunei to attend the sultan's birthday party—then he fell off the radar. Sheikh Abdullah certainly couldn't find him. Every day the king's son had been phoning the contact numbers he had been given, and every day he was told by those who answered that Michael would get back to him quickly. Abdullah never received a return call.

During his absence from Bahrain, someone Abdullah would identify only as "an American in the music business" gradually convinced the sheikh that Michael had been merely using him to mark time, that he would never come back to Bahrain from Japan, and that the Al Khalifa family was not going to get anything at all in return for the $7 million it had invested in Jackson. When Jackson did in fact fly back to Manama that June, Michael discovered not only that the sheikh had failed to provide the home he asked for, but that he had moved Michael's possesions out of the mansion in Sanad, packing them into suitcases now in storage at the Ritz-Carlton Hotel. The jewelry he had left behind and nearly a million dollars in cash, Jackson was told, were secured in a bank safe. Michael, Grace, and the children spent less than twenty-four hours at the hotel, feeling menaced the entire time by members of the kingdom's "public security" police, who followed them wherever they went. The next day, Michael once more put on his abaya, raised the veil, then traveled to the Manama airport disguised as a woman before joining Grace and the kids aboard a private jet that had just flown in from Paris.

They departed without saying a second good-bye to Sheikh Abdullah. The money and the jewelry were left behind.

Less than twenty-four hours after leaving the land of the Al Khalifas, Jackson was the guest of an equally wealthy Arab, his friend Prince Al-Waleed, who was hosting Michael, Grace, Anton Schleiter, and the children aboard the Saudi prince's gargantuan $200 million yacht, *Kingdom 5KR*, anchored in the Mediterranean just off the Côte d'Azur. When money from Sony arrived, Michael moved the traveling party to Versailles, where he gave a deposition in the Prescient Acquisitions case, then led the group to the New York Hotel in Paris.

Jackson looked so healthy on a foray with the children to Disneyland Paris that it seemed there might be truth in Jermaine's claim that Michael was doing three hundred push-ups a day to get in shape for a comeback world tour. Being chased by a raucous crowd of reporters and photographers from one attraction to the next at the park, though, seemed to wear the entertainer out. Two days later, he was photographed looking wan and weak as he was pushed about in a wheelchair, shielded from the sun by a big black umbrella while on a tour of the city's botanical garden, Jardin des Plantes. Carried behind their father by security guards, Jackson's children wore long black gowns and face veils that made them look like mini-mourners at a funeral.

Word that Michael Jackson had arrived in Cork on the afternoon of June 23 set off a wave of frenzied speculation that spread from southern Ireland across the entire country in a matter of hours. The most widespread rumor was that Michael would be making a cameo appearance at Bob Dylan's concert the following evening in Kilkenny, most likely to perform a duet of "I Shall Be Released." What Dylan made of the "We want Michael!" shouts that came at him out of the Irish darkness the next night only he knows.

Sony executives were incredulous that Michael had flown from Paris to Cork aboard a regular Aer Lingus flight instead of one of the private jets he typically leased. Perhaps, it was suggested, the reality of his fiscal circumstances had finally registered with Jackson. This hope dimmed, though, when word came that, once on the ground in Ireland, Michael had hired both a stretch limousine and a cargo van to transport his traveling party and the twenty-seven designer bags filled with his wardrobe to an eighteen-room castle he had rented as his temporary residence in the country. Blackwater was set on its own private woodland in southern County Cork's Castletownroche. Michael might've told Sony that Blackwater was relatively affordable as castles go, costing a mere 7,500 euros per week in high season. For that you got a piece of living history that went back at least as far as the Iron Age, maybe even to the early Mesolithic. History mattered to Michael Jackson, as Blackwater's proprietor Patrick Nordstrom would discover within hours of the star's arrival. Jackson was full of questions about the fort of Cruadha that had stood on the site before the castle's construction in the twelfth century and about the eighth-century Sheela na Gig that was among the fort's remnants.

Nordstrom was struck within a day by how little resemblance the Michael Jackson he was hosting bore to the bizarre character depicted in London tabloids. While the castle's owner agreed with those in Bahrain who had remarked that Jackson was far less strange-looking in person than in magazine and newspaper photographs, it was Michael's regular fella demeanor that made the more memorable impression. He was shy, curious, and exceedingly polite. What the Michael Jackson living under Nordstrom's roof seemed to want from life were simple pleasures, like porridge in the morning and afternoon walks in the woods. The privacy and serenity of the fifty-acre estate that surrounded Blackwater were why Michael had rented the castle. He loved that its grounds were a nationally protected nature reserve and that a lengthy stretch of the River Awbeg was enclosed and secured by Blackwater's boundaries. Watching the pop star and his children frolic along the pathways of the castle's fifteen-acre woodland maze was marvelously touching, Nordstrom recalled. Under that canopy of leaves, Michael revealed a personality that was far different from the one that most of the world knew, Nordstrom observed: "The shyness left him and I saw a much more boisterous and loud spirit who loved playing with his children."

Be on the lookout for leprechauns, Michael told Prince, Paris, and Blanket. He truly believed in the little-old-man fairies, as he admitted to anyone who asked. Shortly after his arrival in Ireland, a British publication reported that Jackson was in Ireland specifically because he was determined to meet a leprechaun. London's *Daily Mirror* followed this with a report that Michael was planning to open a five-hundred-million-euro leprechaun theme park in County Cork. "He loves the whole idea of leprechauns and the magic and myths of Ireland," an unidentified source was quoted as saying. The theme park story was bogus but that last remark was quite accurate.

Michael had told his children on the plane ride from Paris that there was no better place to chase magic than Ireland in the summertime and the two oldest kids knew this was a big statement. "Magic" was the most fraught word in their father's vocabulary. The way Michael used it (and he did so constantly), "magic" might refer to a movie star's charisma or to a fairy-tale ending or to the spells cast by one of the witch doctors he consulted. "Magic" could be his description of a ride on Space Mountain at Disneyland or of a James Brown spin and slide. "Magic" was anything that made Jackson marvel, made him gasp, made him laugh like a child or tremble with fear of the unknown. "Magic" was wonder, superstition, and the suspension of disbelief. It was what he had substituted for the religious enthusiasm of his youth. To call a person "magic" was the highest compliment he could bestow.

He admired those who practiced magic almost as much as he did those who possessed it. Michael followed the careers of the top stage magicians with an almost fetishistic intensity, and arranged to see and meet them in nearly every city he visited. He had become close friends with Siegfried & Roy during the early 1990s when he was often Steve Wynn's guest at the Mirage, even writing the duo's theme song, "Mind Is the Magic." As soon as Patrick Nordstrom mentioned that he had a magician friend in Cork, Michael urged his host to call the man and invite him for a visit.

Liam Sheehan was on the road with a packed bag within half an hour of receiving the call, "driving like I was in a dream," he remembered. He had anticipated that Jackson would be traveling with a huge entourage, Sheehan admitted, and was taken aback to discover "it was just Michael, the kids, their nanny Grace, their teacher, and Michael's friend Anton." Michael and the kids were finishing their grub, his friend Nordstrom told Sheehan upon arrival, but Grace Rwaramba came out to greet him a moment later, and immediately produced the nondisclosure form the magician would have to sign before settling in at the castle. "Grace told me straightaway how difficult it was for Michael to trust people," Sheehan remembered. "She told me about how they had gone on a helicopter trip to the home of a so-called friend, hoping to find a little peace and quiet, and as they were landing, they saw that there was a huge crowd of people gathered outside the door to the place, and that the field below them was swarming with paparazzi. Grace told me that people were always trying to get something from Michael, and he knew it. She said he was betrayed constantly. It was a sort of sobering way to begin the evening."

Michael and the kids were grinning excitedly, though, when they followed Grace into the drawing room a short time later. Sheehan, who specialized in what he called "walkabout magic," led the group around the first floor of the castle, performing tricks as he went. He wowed them all with his special version of the card-to-ceiling trick, but was most affected himself by how Michael's daughter responded to the fish production trick. "I borrow some money—a fifty-euro note in this case—and the fish comes out of the money," Sheehan explained. "And then I put the fish into a glass—no worries, the fish will be okay. But as we moved into the bar, Paris came in behind us holding the fish in her hands. She said she didn't want it to be alone. It was very innocent. That's what all three of those kids were: very, very innocent."

Like millions of people worldwide, Sheehan had been horrified by the images of Jackson dangling Blanket over the balcony at the Hotel Adlon in 2002. That, "along with all the rest," as Sheehan put it, had led him to imagine that Jackson's children would be "pretty weird." In fact, the magician said, "they were as bright and polite and delightful as any kids I've ever been around." He was especially touched, Sheehan said, by how close Michael seemed to his eight-year-old daughter, and marveled as well at the girl's composure and intelligence. "The very first conversation we had," Sheehan recalled, "was when Paris came up to me and asked, 'Do you know my dad's name?' 'Michael,' I said. She shook her head. 'Michael *Jackson*,' I told her. She shook her head again. I was baffled. 'His real name,' Paris told me, 'is Michael *Joseph* Jackson. His middle name is the same as the first name of his dad, my grandfather.' She seemed very proud of that. I saw then, and again and again over the days that followed, how determined Michael was to give his children the feeling that they were part of a big, happy family." Sheehan felt almost ashamed of himself when he discovered that Michael did not call his oldest son Prince as the expression of some ridiculous royal fantasy, but because that was the first name of his maternal grandfather.

The three kids spent most of every day "in school," as they put it, shut up in one of the castle's rooms with their teacher, and it became obvious to Sheehan that they were learning at a more than respectable rate. When the magician performed his best-known trick, which involved having the children select a word from a book that he would identify by a process of deduction, Sheehan had suggested that either Prince or Paris might want to pick a word for little Blanket, who was just four. But Blanket insisted upon choosing his own word, Sheehan recalled, and then afterward upon demonstrating that he actually knew what "actually" meant.

All during the two weeks he spent with them, Sheehan remembered, Prince and Paris kept trying to get him to run a footrace against their father: "Paris told me, 'My dad is really fast. He just ran a race against a doctor in Dubai and beat him by a huge distance, so I know he'll beat you.' She told me the doctor was thin, meaning, without saying it, that I was a trifle fat." Grace Rwaramba confirmed the story of the footrace in Dubai. The doctor had questioned Michael's physical condition and Michael, offended, challenged the man to a race, then beat him so easily that the doctor couldn't stop talking about it for the rest of the day.

The woman who identified herself as the children's nanny was clearly more than just that, as Sheehan had realized within his first week under the same roof with the Jackson family. "Michael's personality was meek and mild," the magician recalled, "but Grace was very direct and quite assertive. She looked so ordinary in her T-shirt and jeans, but you had no doubt within a few days that she was the one in charge. She wasn't just taking care of the kids, she was taking care of Michael, too. She was the boss, and you felt it."

Behind closed doors, Grace was complaining constantly about Michael's financial mismanagement. She had been furious for weeks over how her employer had handled the windfall of a seven-figure payment he hadn't been expecting near the end of their stay in Bahrain. "Instead of buying a small house, so that we won't go from one hotel to another or stay with friends, he told me, 'Grace, you have to go immediately to Florence and buy antiques.'" She had used her own credit card to pay for the trip, Grace said, but when she arrived in the Italian city to inspect the collection that Michael wanted, she was less than impressed. "I called him and said, 'This is not worth anything.' Michael wouldn't listen to me. He said, 'Buy it. Buy it.' We didn't even have a home to live in so we had to put the antiques in storage." Just a short time later, before the trip to Japan, she had warned Michael not to believe the promise of a million-dollar payday he had been given, Grace said. "I told him, 'Michael, by the time everyone takes his cut you will end up with a very small amount.' He didn't want to hear. He flew to Japan. By the time everyone took their share, he ended up with just two hundred thousand dollars." She would not be returning with him to Japan at Christmastime, Grace said, to watch the whole thing happen all over again.

Grace may have talked like the boss in front of Liam Sheehan, but Michael never forgot that the real power was his, as he made clear more than once in private discussions of the biggest issue that existed between Grace and him that summer: how to deal with Debbie Rowe.

Prince and Paris's biological mother was, to put it kindly, a quirky character. A big (five-foot-ten), beefy (two-hundred-plus pounds) Germanic-looking blonde, Rowe had been raised as the adopted daughter of a millionaire Jewish couple from Malibu. Sheltered as a girl, she didn't have her first boyfriend until she was thirty, but within two years was a "biker babe" tricked out in black leather who swore like a sailor and drank like one, too. Rowe had gotten to know Michael Jackson back in the early 1990s when she was working as a nurse for the entertainer's skin doctor, Arnold Klein. A certain intimacy had developed between the two when Michael dripped a skin-bleaching agent on his scrotum and Debbie attended to his burns. Jackson bought her a car to show his gratitude. Klein and Rowe eventually began traveling with Jackson; when he toured Debbie would give him massages.

In 1996, just as Michael's nineteen-month marriage to Lisa Marie Presley was ending, he confided his distress over Lisa Marie's refusal to bear him children. Rowe said she would be happy to take the job. She was already pregnant (by in-vitro insemination) in November 1996 when the couple married at the Sheraton Hotel in Sydney, Australia. Michael's publicist Bob Jones would claim that Michael had only married Debbie because he was deep into a business relationship with Prince Al-Waleed and the Saudi royal had not been happy that Debbie was pregnant and unmarried. The best man at the ceremony was an eight-year-old boy. After exchanging pecks on the cheek, the couple retired to separate suites and never slept in the same bed.

Michael Joseph Jackson Jr. (soon to be known as Prince) was born in February 1997 and rushed directly from the hospital to Neverland so the baby would not be able to bond with his mother. Michael had a team of nurses watching the infant around the clock, Jones recalled: "He measured the air quality in the room every hour." She had "never seen Michael so happy," said Rowe, who offered to serve as a surrogate a second time. Paris-Michael Katherine Jackson was born in April 1998 after a complicated pregnancy that left Rowe unable to bear more children. Protected by a prenuptial agreement, Jackson divorced her in 1999, securing sole custody of the kids with a deal to pay Rowe a reported $8 million and buy her a house in Beverly Hills.

In 2001, Rowe signed a court order terminating her parental rights, but in 2004, after Jackson was criminally charged in Santa Barbara County, her attorneys filed a motion to reverse that decision. Her main concern, Rowe stated in court documents, was Jackson's involvement with the Nation of Islam: "Because she is Jewish, Deborah feared the children might be mistreated if Michael continued the association."

Jackson and Rowe reportedly reached a settlement of their custody dispute in late June 2005 but when Debbie's attorneys read the fine print of the contract prepared by Michael's legal team, they realized that their client was about to be shut out of her children's lives entirely. The lawyers' concern mounted when Michael and the kids left the United States and took up residence in a country that was not a signatory of the Hague treaty, meaning Rowe's legal rights were unenforceable. Debbie refused to sign the settlement agreement and threatened to go back to court. Hoping to assuage her, Michael agreed in August 2005 (two months after his move to Bahrain) to allow Grace to take Prince and Paris to meet their natural mother at a Los Angeles hotel. Debbie was infuriated when Grace told her she would be introduced as a "family friend" because Michael didn't want to confuse the kids, then had to sit through the meeting hearing Prince and Paris repeatedly address Grace as "Mom."

Less than a month after Grace took the kids back to Bahrain, Debbie filed a lawsuit demanding money for legal fees, support, and increased access to the children, who she claimed had been "abducted" to the Middle East on fake passports. The February 15, 2006, announcement that the California Court of Appeal had reinstated Rowe's custody rights made headlines across the country. During the next several months, Debbie's lawyers began to play rough, submitting court filings that for the first time made public what everyone already suspected: Michael Jackson was not biologically related to either Prince or Paris, despite his claims that the children had been conceived "the natural way." Rowe's attorneys also disclosed some details of the original deal with Jackson, revealing that she had agreed, among other things, not to speak to anyone about her ex-husband's physical condition, drug use, or "sexual behavior"—boiler plate language that raised eyebrows when it was applied to Michael Jackson.

Debbie and her attorneys became even more aggressive when they learned that Michael and the children were now domiciled in Ireland, which *was* a Hague signatory, filing a suit in Los Angeles Superior Court that demanded $245,000 in missed payments while pressing forward with Rowe's custody and visitation claims. If Grace hadn't let the kids call her Mom in front of Debbie, none of this would have happened, Michael grumbled. It was Michael's fault for not keeping his promises to the woman, Grace answered.

Neither Nordstrom nor Sheehan had even the slightest notion that there was any drama involving the kids playing out across the pond during the Jacksons' stay at Blackwater, even as they lived under the same roof with them. Michael continued to enjoy sitting by the fire with Nordstrom during the evening to pepper the master of the house with questions about the castle's history. Sheehan remained amazed that "Michael was so normal to talk to. At the castle, he used to come down in the middle of the night for a bowl of apple crumb and he absolutely loved being able to do things like that."

The Jacksons' stay at the castle ended on July 4, which happened to be the magician's birthday. "The kids all jumped into a waiting limousine," Sheehan recalled, "but Michael made them get out and thank each and every one at the castle for their hospitality. I think that tells you right there what sort of father he was."

9

Not one of the people who attended to Michael at Blackwater had been aware that cable news networks back in America were providing nightly coverage of the *Schaffel v. Jackson* civil trial at the Los Angeles County courthouse in Santa Monica. Michael barely seemed to have been aware of it himself. The only appearance he made in court was via the videotaped deposition that Howard King showed the California jury during Jackson's fifth day in Ireland.

"I played some of it that first day just to buy myself time," King recalled. "I really wasn't prepared to go to trial, to tell you the truth, because I just didn't believe there would ever be a trial. I thought this would be settled right up until the moment they brought the jurors in. All the accounting had been done, so it was pretty clear. Some of it was embarrassing to Marc. He wasn't quite as pristine as we had thought, and so we were ready to settle." King had already whittled his original demand of $3.8 million down to $1.4 million and would have taken half that to avoid a trial. "But they wouldn't offer any money," King remembered.

What King didn't know was that the day before the scheduled trial date, Raymone Bain had announced a massive "restructuring" of Michael Jackson's business relationships that involved the dismissal of his attorneys in both the United States and Bahrain, and the termination of his relationships with 2 Seas Records, Sheikh Abdullah, and Guy Holmes. Bain, who had orchestrated the entire thing, was now Jackson's "general manager" and in that capacity had hired New York–based entertainment lawyer Londell McMillan to supervise the "turnaround" of Michael's affairs. McMillan, whose other clients included Prince, Stevie Wonder, and Spike Lee, would be taking charge of all financial and legal matters involving Michael, effective immediately, according to Bain.

"All I knew," King recalled, "was that Michael suddenly had this new attorney, Londell McMillan, who was running things, and that Londell was committed to being a hard-ass: 'Michael doesn't have any money and he's not paying.' Even the judge was like, 'Are you crazy?' The judge, God bless her, spent two solid days with us, trying to get this settled. She said, 'Do you really want all this dirty laundry aired?' And Londell's answer was yes. What was obvious was that here was another new advisor who felt he had to prove to Michael how important he was. And prove it by showing how tough he could be with Michael's money and reputation. I got used to seeing it in their eyes, the next in the long line of people who think they are going to be Michael's savior and his advisor for the rest of his career. I'm thinking, 'Yeah, right.' But I have to deal with it so off to trial we go. I was shocked, but also delighted. I mean, there was a lot of press. I was on CNN every night. It couldn't have been better for me."

It couldn't have been much better for them, either, most of the reporters in the courtroom agreed: Liz Taylor insisting on a $600,000 bracelet, Marlon Brando demanding a million in cash, Celine Dion in tears, Marc Schaffel delivering his supersize fries. They had Michael only on video and in tape-recorded messages, true, but that was enough to support the "Two Jackson Personalities Emerge" headlines that appeared in newspapers across the country after the first day of the trial. Michael had whispered "meekly" that he wasn't sure when or how Schaffel was paid, according to the wire service story that became the most widely distributed account of his deposition testimony. Yet only moments later the jury heard the tape of a message Michael had left for Schaffel in a voice that was much louder and deeper: "Marc, call Al Malnik. I do not want any ifs, ands, or buts about releasing 'What More Can I Give?' at this point. Do it now!"

Hearing these two very different voices "left those who listened wondering if they had any idea who Michael Jackson really is," one TV reporter breathlessly informed her viewers. Fans, critics, and creditors alike were startled and amused by the revelation that for the past several years one of Jackson's main sources of spending money had been earned by leasing hundreds of acres of pasture at Neverland for cattle grazing.

Schaffel himself took the stand on July 5, the day after Michael and his children left Blackwater Castle. On cross-examination, he was immediately confronted by the fact that he had backdated eighteen checks totaling $784,000 after receiving a termination letter from Jackson's attorneys on November 21, 2001, and that he had used $54,000 of that money to make a prepayment of the rent on his home. When Schaffel was questioned about his claim that Michael owed him for the $300,000 he had delivered to a "Mr. X" in South America, he could produce neither a receipt nor a canceled check to show the jury. Schaffel claimed he had taken the money in cash from a safe in Brazil where he was keeping it and without prompting told the jury about being asked by Michael to find children in South America who could join his family. Several jurors squirmed; one shielded her eyes.

The full panel delivered a "split verdict" on July 14, 2006, awarding Schaffel $900,000 of the money he claimed to be owed and Michael $200,000 that jurors agreed had been skimmed by Schaffel. Raymone Bain and Londell McMillan fell all over themselves declaring victory. The jurors had "turned back" Schaffel's claims against Mr. Jackson, said Bain, while McMillan declared, "It's a new day for Michael Jackson. We were unwilling to pay one penny more than the amount Schaffel was owed, and the verdict proved us successful."

His client had won a net judgment of $700,000 and immediately placed a lien on Neverland. King pointed out: "I guarantee you I was better paid for my time than Michael's attorney was."

The three jurors who spoke to the media after the verdict were unsympathetic to either the plaintiff or the defendant, saying that neither was "the most upstanding character," as one put it. A young woman from Tarzana who was now a nursing student at Brigham Young University said she hadn't held Schaffel's background against him because of what she believed about Michael Jackson: "I have issues with adult entertainment, but I also have issues with child molestation."

Jackson and his traveling party spent the last ten days of the Schaffel trial at Ballinacurra House near Kinsale, a harbor town on Ireland's south coast. Though not a castle, Ballinacurra was an even more gorgeous property than Blackwater, surrounded by ten-foot-high stone walls and, beyond that, by thirty acres of woodland and lawns. The residence offered its own ballroom, formal dining for ninety-six people in its Garden Room, and twenty-two bedrooms with sleeping accommodations for as many as fifty-three guests. Michael's group numbered only seven persons, three of them children, but he took the entire place. The entertainer spent much of his time in the African-theme bedroom he had chosen for writing songs, while his children were "in school," then joined the kids in afternoon walks along the banks of the Whitecastle and Ballinacurra creeks. He had not left the grounds at Blackwater once during his two weeks there, and seemed similarly disinclined to venture forth from Ballinacurra. Michael sent the house's proprietor, Des McGahan, on several runs into Cork to pick up what had for years been the staple of his diet: KFC original chicken with mashed potatoes and gravy. One day, though, Michael had decided to venture into Kinsale proper, where his costume of silk pajamas and a surgical mask did little to discourage the attention of townspeople. "A furor," McGahan described the ensuing scene. "People were all askin' one another, 'Didjya see Michael Jackson around town in his pajamas?'"

Other than that one mad excursion into town, Michael seemed to be seeking at Ballinacurra the same simple pleasures he had found at Blackwater. After a week or so, he and his wife began to feel sorry for the man, McGahan said: "He was lookin' for a home. He was tryin' = to look for normality." Still, the most memorable moment of his famous guest's stay for him, McGahan would recall, had come late one night when he ventured into the garden to satisfy his curiosity about why Mr. Jackson insisted that the outside lights be left on between dusk and dawn: "I popped my head through the hedge and saw him moonwalkin' across the lawn. I thought, 'This can't be true. Michael Jackson is dancin' on the grass.'"

Michael would rent a number of Irish castles and country homes during his six-month-long stay in the country. Back in the United States, though, gossip columnist Roger Friedman wrote that Jackson was "mooching" off *Lord of the Dance* creator Michael Flatley at the tapmaster's CastleHyde during his summer in Ireland, and that claim would be repeated in "news" stories for the next four years. But if the entertainer and his children stayed with Flatley at all (Flatley claims they did), it was a *very* short visit, because by the beginning of August 2006, Michael, Grace, and the children were ensconced at the most luxurious of the properties they would occupy in Ireland: Luggala Castle in County Wicklow, on Ireland's east coast, just south of Dublin. The six-thousand-acre estate included not only the exquisite lake Lough Tay and a beach of imported sand so white that it looked like granulated sugar against the black rocks of the Irish Sea's shoreline, but also a two-mile-long driveway that wound up what the Irish called "Fancy Mountain" to the magnificent Gothic Revival house where the "Golden Guinness Girls" had once cavorted. Luggala rented for a reported 30,000 euros per week, which meant that Michael Jackson had paid upward of $300,000 for the eight weeks he occupied the castle. That price included use of a chauffeur-driven Rolls-Royce but not the cost of the helicopters Jackson was using to scout out recording facilities where he could continue work on what Raymone Bain persisted in calling his "comeback album."

In the last languid weeks of the Celtic summer, Luggala offered Prince, Paris, and Blanket a variety of outdoor adventures boasted by few other properties on the planet, but their father swiftly discovered that he couldn't go outside himself unless he was covered head to toe in netting, because the midges swarmed to him in clouds, gorging on his blood wherever they found a patch of exposed skin. Retreating indoors, he probed the chefs, butlers, and cleaners for stories about previous guests like Mel Gibson, then asked what they would say about *him* when he was gone, and laughed when they answered, "Oh, nothing at all, sir." The Rolls-Royce took Michael and the children to Wicklow town for visits to cinemas and restaurants and Michael created his largest local stir when he stopped at a store in Dun Laoghaire to buy a book of Beatles lyrics. Paris got a book about fairies.

Like everything in his life, of course, this peace was fragile. On the morning of August 29, word came that a towering brush fire had broken out at Neverland, near the amusement park. A firefighting helicopter extinguished the blaze; beyond burned ground, damage was minimal, but the Santa Barbara Fire Department was unable to say how the inferno had been set off. Michael naturally suspected arson. He pictured the ranch falling into decay, its windows shuttered, the grounds around it blackened. The news from Neverland was not an auspicious beginning to his forty-eighth birthday. If Michael had learned anything during the past few years, though, it was compartmentalization, and he said nothing about the fire to his children as they helped Grace prepare their father's "surprise party," or when he joined them for a trip to the Lambert Puppet Theatre in the coastal village of Monkstown, just outside Dublin.

It was Grace who finally found the ideal place for Michael to resume making music, in the Irish Midlands of County Westmeath. Viewed from the main road between Dublin and Galway, Grouse Lodge looked to be nearly as far removed from the splendor of Luggala Castle as the Jackson family dwelling back in Gary, Indiana. All that showed from the unsigned entrance just outside the village of Rosemount was a gravel driveway filled with bumps and potholes that wound through a screen of trees, then disappeared behind the stone walls of a three-hundred-year-old Georgian estate that appeared to have fallen into a sad state of neglect. It was here that Jackson would make the most serious sustained effort at producing new work that he had managed in years.

Proprietor Paddy Dunning was a renowned sound engineer whose Temple Bar studios in Dublin had served U2 and many others. Working with a family of local stonemasons, along with assorted other skilled tradesmen, Dunning and his wife Claire had spent nearly five years converting the assorted cowsheds and other outbuildings of Grouse Lodge into a unique collection of cottages assembled around a grassy courtyard filled with flowering plants. The manor house was now outfitted with two state-of-the-art studios where the slab-cut stone created acoustics that, since 2002, had delighted recording artists as diverse as REM, Manic Street Preachers, and Shirley Bassey.

During her visit to Grouse Lodge in the late summer of 2006, though, all Grace Rwaramba would tell the Dunnings was that on behalf of some-one she would identify only as "an A-list pop star" she wanted to book the larger of the two studios plus a three-bedroom cottage that had once been a cowshed for at least a month and perhaps longer. They had ab-solutely no idea who this new lodger might be, the Dunnings would say later, until the day when a bus rolled down the gravel driveway, pulled up outside the main building, and opened its doors to release three excited kids who were followed by their shy but smiling father, Michael Jackson. The stunned couple waited for the rest of the entertainer's entourage to emerge from the bus, but the only other passengers were Grace Rwaramba and the children's tutor.

From the day of his arrival, Michael made it clear that he thought of himself first and foremost as a father, Paddy Dunning would recall. What had sold him on Grouse Lodge, Jackson explained, was that it offered an atmosphere that encouraged "family living." The Dunnings and their staff were known for protecting the privacy of their guests, and Claire's repu-tation for fabulous home cooking was another major draw. He wanted a place where his children could eat well and find plenty to do while he was working, said Michael, who seemed every bit as interested in the estate's big indoor pool, archery range, billiards, and Ping-Pong tables, along with its close access to horseback riding stables and fishing platforms, as he was in the recording equipment at Grouse Lodge. He didn't even want to go into the studio until he had set up a school for his children and organized their schedules, Paddy Dunning remembered.

During the weeks that followed, the Dunnings and their staff would say later, they witnessed none of the Wacko Jacko antics they had been reading about in newspapers for years. "We just saw a pure and utter gentleman who was an extremely great parent to his kids," Paddy Dun-ning said. Even though he had no real idea of how miserable Michael had been during the past several years, Dunning couldn't help but be touched by the joy his new guest seemed to be experiencing in Ireland. "He ate well here, and he looked healthy," said Dunning, who saw no indication that Jackson was strung out on drugs as had been reported only recently in the English papers. Michael began taking long walks in the Westmeath countryside within days of arriving at Grouse Lodge. Dunning accompanied him at the beginning and was impressed by how fit the supposedly ill entertainer seemed: "Michael could move really quickly—I've never seen anyone move so quickly. He was like a ballet dancer." Jackson was both astonished and delighted by the willingness of the local people to let him wander freely through the fields, allowing him to pass by with no more than a wave. Dunning had ordered his staff not to tell anyone that Michael Jackson was staying at Grouse Lodge, but was especially touched by the willingness of his neighbors and the shopkeepers in nearby Rosemount to join in the conspiracy of silence that surrounded the most famous visitor the area had ever seen.

Scattered rumors of Michael Jackson sightings circulated after Michael and his children ventured into the nearby villages of Moate and Kilbeggan. The Dunnings and the Grouse Lodge staff denied all knowledge. "If someone told me, 'I've heard Michael Jackson is there,' I would tell them, 'Yeah, so is Elvis Presley,'" Dunning said.

Actually, Elvis *was* in the area. Dunning had purchased the dilapidated National Wax Museum in Dublin earlier that year and was in the process of rehabilitating it. Unhappy with the likeness of Presley that was among the most featured items in his collection, Dunning had ordered a new Elvis made, then carted the old wax figure back to Rosemount, where he stuck it under a tree out back of Grouse Lodge and forgot all about the thing. He would never forget the shaken expression on Michael's face, Dunning said, when Jackson returned from one of his afternoon walks and breathlessly told him, "Paddy! I just met my father-in-law in the woods!"

After a month in the converted cowshed, Michael and his party moved into a more luxurious accommodation nearby. The Dunnings also owned Coolatore House, a neighboring estate where fifteen acres of gardens and woodlands surrounded a one-hundred-and-fifty-year-old Victorian country home that the couple had restored to high standard.

Like Patrick Nordstrom before him, Dunning was at once surprised and impressed by how constantly inquisitive Jackson seemed to be. Michael read the *Irish Times* cover-to-cover every day and could discuss the booming economy of the "Celtic Tiger" as well as any business executive Dunning knew. He had been fascinated by the discovery that the legendary hills of Cnoc Aiste and Uisneach were each within walking distance of Coolatore House, and read extensively about the two rises, thrilled to learn that Uisneach was the traditional geographical center of Ireland, home to the "Stone of Division" that had been used to mark the nation's original provinces.

Michael's love of Irish music was at least equal to his fascination with the country's history, said Dunning, who was constantly being encouraged by his famous guest to invite as many traditional performers as possible to play at Grouse Lodge. Michael was enthusiastic about performing with every one of the musicians who visited, and invited Dunning and the members of his staff to join in the jam sessions that became an almost nightly occurrence. He was utterly flabbergasted, Dunning would say later, to discover "just how incredible Michael was at playing any instrument." He had not a clue beforehand that his celebrity lodger was an outstanding drummer, Dunning confessed, but was even more astonished by Jackson's demonstration of his abilities as a guitarist who could play both lead and bass. It was when Michael sat down at the piano, though, Dunning recalled, that he the rest of the staff at Grouse Lodge were truly blown away. Jackson had traveled with a Casio keyboard for years, including the old beat-up one that he was using in Ireland. Before he played piano for them, Dunning and the others assumed that Michael's keyboard was essentially a songwriting tool, something he noodled on while working out melodies. It was well known that Jackson had produced most of the early songs credited to him by first writing out the lyrics longhand, then singing the melody or humming the rhythm line into a tape recorder that he handed off to someone he paid to put it on paper. He had no formal music training and couldn't write notes. Michael had taught himself to play keyboards, though, and for more than a decade now had been using them to work out tunes. How far he'd advanced in that time was revealed to the people at Grouse Lodge the first time he sat down to perform a medley of Beatles songs. The sing-alongs that formed around Michael's sessions at the piano were the highlight of his stay for most of the people who worked at Grouse Lodge, even though the rest of the room regularly went silent so that everyone could listen to his solos. "You can't overstate his singing voice," Dunning would say later. "Pitch-perfect."

Will.i.am, whom Jackson had chosen as his principal collaborator on the new album, agreed. "As far as [Jackson's] vocal abilities are concerned, he's still killing everybody," the Black Eyed Peas front man told *Rolling Stone* shortly after returning from a week with Michael at Grouse Lodge in the autumn of 2006. Within a month of Jackson's arrival in County Westmeath, a slew of high-profile collaborators were streaming toward

Rosemount aboard helicopters and limousines and many more were making their appearances at Grouse Lodge via satellite hookups. "New Jack Swing King" Teddy Riley, who had worked with Michael on *Dangerous*, coproduced at least a couple of new Jackson songs in the Grouse Lodge studios. Shortly after Riley's departure, his onetime protégé Rodney "Darkchild" Jerkins, now one of the most sought-after producers in the world, jetted into Dublin and made his way to Westmeath to talk about what he and Michael might do together. Jenkins had produced Jackson's one hit single from *Invincible*, "You Rock My World," which had garnered Michael his first Grammy nomination since 1997's "Earth Song." Michael was meeting with as many as a dozen other producers, feeling them out, searching for some sign of inspiration that would convince him he could deliver another *Thriller*. Akon, RedOne, Syience, and Giorgio Tuinfort all received either requests for transoceanic phone conferences or invitations to visit Michael in Ireland. Top hip-hop talent manager Charles "Big Chuck" Stanton not only flew to Ireland with his nephew, producer Theron "Neff U" Feemster, for a series of meetings with Michael, but also had the temerity to tell the *Los Angeles Times* about it afterward, assuring the newspaper that Michael was more focused than he'd been in years. "He's ready to take over the world," Stanton told the *Times*. "He's got some hot records . . . We're giving Michael a lot of edgy street records. He's putting melodies to some hard party records."

Jackson only really got down to business, though, when will.i.am arrived at Grouse Lodge. The two of them had been speaking three times a week before he flew to Ireland, will.i.am recalled: "He'd be like, 'I need you to dig deep inside! Do something that's unprecedented!' He'd hum a little melody over the phone or something. Eight song sketches were conjured out of phone conversations." Three of those sketches became finished songs during the week will.i.am spent at Grouse Lodge, though only one was tracked—a number Michael had titled "I'm Dreamin'." They would spend a solid month together in January, Michael promised, and work out the rest of the material. Will was almost as impressed as Paddy Dunning by how Michael seemed to have taken to Irish country living. "One day I was like, 'I'm hungry,'" he remembered. "And Michael goes, 'Take the horse. Take the horse and pick apples. It's wonderful. We love doing it. The horses love going apple picking.' I'm like, 'Allll righhht.'"

As his sense of being in a protected space grew, Michael explored farther and wider. Dunning hired a local taxi driver to drive Michael and Grace and the kids around Westmeath in a borrowed van with blacked-out windows. They made regular trips to the cinemas in the surrounding towns of Mullingar, Tullamore, and Athlone. In Rosemount, Michael could even walk into the pub unannounced, take a seat without being fussed over, and get some feeling for what normal life must be like among the locals. Upon returning to Grouse Lodge, Michael commented again and again on how incredible it was to be staying in a place where people seemed delighted to see him, but at the same time perfectly willing to let him be. He'd never experienced anything like it.

Dunning himself drove when Michael wanted to visit Dublin. "We'd pull up to a red light and Michael would look out the window, because he'd be sitting up front with me, and a person would not believe their eyes," Dunning recalled. "They would go into semishock at the sight, not knowing what to believe—is this Michael Jackson that's pulled up alongside me on Dame Street?" As they drove back home through the Irish countryside, the two of them sang duets, recalled Dunning, who especially enjoyed their rendition of "The Girl Is Mine." Michael sang the Paul McCartney part, Dunning remembered, "and I did Michael Jackson."

One of Michael's regular stops on his trips to Dublin was the Ailesbury Clinic in Merrion Court, where he spent many hours with the clinic's medical director, Dr. Patrick Treacy. For going on two decades, it had been Michael's practice to cultivate relationships with cosmetic surgeons in any city or country where he spent significant time. The enormous number of procedures that had been performed on his face required constant maintenance, and the trust he invested in the physicians who did this work for him inevitably resulted in something that resembled friendship. He tried to become familiar with the doctors he sought out even before they met. In researching Patrick Treacy, Michael had been pleased to learn that the doctor was not only an advanced Botox, Dysport, and dermal filler trainer who instructed physicians worldwide, but was also renowned for his implants of permanent facial prostheses and for his skill with radiofrequency lasers. During his visits to the clinic, Michael usually made a beeline for the glass room where the high-end cosmetic creams and lotions were stored, Treacy recalled. His famous patient would fill his pockets with tiny bottles of Nicholas Perricone, Agera, and Matriskin potions that cost as much as $200 apiece. "What have you got?" the doctor remembered asking Michael one day when he arrived at the glass room just as Jackson was coming out. Michael, looking sheepish, laid out what he had collected on the counter. "Well, you certainly have good taste," the doctor said, "but there'll be nothing left for the Irish ladies." Michael apologized, grinning "mischievously," Treacy recalled, then said, "Just put them on my bill." Of course, he didn't think of what Michael had done as "stealing," the doctor was quick to say, because, well, he was Michael.

Treacy traveled to Grouse Lodge almost as often as Michael came to Dublin. The two also drove together to the Crumlin Children's Hospital, in a suburb north of the city, where Treacy was attending to a brother and sister, ages five and seven, who had been horribly burned by a gasoline bomb set off during a gang war in Limerick. Michael wouldn't stop asking about these two children, Treacy remembered. "He continually asked me, Were they in pain? Would they be given morphine? Would they be scarred? Why could he not go in and see them?" This last question came up again and again. He refused, Treacy explained, because "it could be read totally the wrong way by seeing him go into a pediatric hospital so soon after the pedophilia case." Michael, though, refused to take no for an answer. "Do you think I would ever harm a child?" he demanded to know, and the doctor knew they had come to a pivotal moment in their relationship. He most decidedly did *not* believe Michael would harm a child, said Treacy, but he still refused to let Michael come into the hospital with him.

Michael's excursions were almost always made in the afternoons or early evenings because while his kids were "in school" he spent nearly every minute working. Only after dark would he let himself truly "play." He recorded dozens of songs in Studio Two, where he loved the acoustics. The only disquieting note was that none of the tracks were finished. It was as if Michael wanted to start as many new projects as possible to avoid reaching the end of any of them.

By the time Michael had been in residence for a couple of months, Dunning was practically convinced that Jackson would be settling down permanently in the Irish Midlands. Michael was in contact with at least a couple of property agents who were showing him estates in Westmeath and the adjoining counties. When Dunning bought a derelict Georgian estate called Bishopstown House about a mile down the road from Grouse Lodge, his famous guest visited it with him and the two discussed in detail what sort of renovations should be done, all with an eye toward Michael settling in for at least a long visit at some future point. "He found a comfort here in Westmeath," Dunning recalled. "I felt he didn't want to leave."

The idyll had to end, of course, as Michael must have known all along. The tabloid press still didn't have a fix on him, but they were closing in. Unconfirmed reports of Michael Jackson sightings in nearby villages captured the attention of local journalists, who were especially intrigued by stories about the big-time, bling-wearing rap producers who were being ferried into Westmeath County from Dublin's Shannon Airport. Three guards had been posted on rotation at the top of the drive at Grouse Lodge, put there to intercept unwelcome visitors, according to the *Westmeath Independent*, which in October 2006 took note of the "heavy security presence" in Rosemount.

Jackson was actually given some cover by the embarrassing imbroglio that flared up in the south of France during the second week of October, when assorted British tabloids and the *New York Daily News* published photographs that purported to be of Michael dressed as a woman out shopping with his daughter Paris on the sidewalks of Saint-Tropez. The slightly blurred images of a slender figure outfitted in high-heeled shoes, a short-sleeved silk top, skinny jeans, and a floppy women's sun hat, while carrying a fluorescent orange handbag and holding a young girl's hand, were accompanied by stories that breathlessly informed readers that it was the first time one of the entertainer's children had been seen out in public without a veil. "In keeping with Jackson's love of the eccentric," as one of the British papers put it, "Paris was dressed almost identically to her famous father." Within days of the shots' worldwide publication, however, the photographer who had snapped them admitted that it might not have been Michael Jackson after all, and the public was left to ask, as it had been doing for years, "Who knows?"

Perhaps in response to the Saint-Tropez photos, or maybe because Raymone Bain and will.i.am combined to convince him that it was time to "do some publicity," Michael agreed a few days later to allow *Access Hollywood* to send its correspondent Billy Bush to Grouse Lodge with a camera crew to shoot tape of the world's most famous missing person working with will.i.am. on his new album "at a remote location in Ireland." Michael clearly did not want Bush's visit to turn into a full-scale interview and insisted upon answering questions as obliquely as possible while seated at a studio control panel, seemingly absorbed in mixing a song. Bush tried several times to create a conversation about Michael's "comeback," but gained little traction.

"Do you see something big with the music that you make again, or getting that groundswell going?" Bush asked. "Doing clubs and intimate things and getting it bigger and bigger and bigger?"

"You know, I'm not sure, on that level," Michael said.

Fortunately for Bush, will.i.am was not so reticent. "Big!" was his reply to the question about the scale of Michael's plans for the future: "Something needs to put a jolt back in the music industry. And the only thing that can do that is the jolt itself. The energy that sparked the imagination of the kids that are . . . me, you know, the Justin Timberlakes, we're all products of this [man]. So the only person who can put that jolt back into that monstrosity of entertainment and music is the one who created that."

"Are you writing new material?" Bush asked Michael.

"I've never stopped," Michael answered softly, with a smile. "I'm always writing a potpourri of music, you know. It's how it is." He turned his head and moved away before Bush could follow up. Bush was so desperate for footage that he sought out Paddy Dunning, who told him, "Michael gets up in the morning and makes breakfast for [the kids], usually porridge and fruit."

The most revealing moment of the *Access Hollywood* crew's visit to Grouse Lodge had come during the setup that preceded Bush's attempted interview, when Michael and the cameraman discussed how he would be lit. "Less shadow," Michael suggested.

"Less shadow," the cameraman repeated. "It's more frontal. You like that?"

"I like that, but can you pump more?" Michael asked. "Like a little hotter?"

"You mean warmer?" the puzzled cameraman suggested. "Like a little hotter?" "No, brighter," Michael told him. "Take away the shadows. I'm trying to look like I slept," he added with a laugh, "and I need your help."

The insomnia that plagued Michael Jackson for more than two decades had grown steadily worse since the airing of the Bashir documentary two and a half years earlier. Before discovering drugs, he had tried to put himself to sleep with bedtime stories. During the *Triumph* tour in 1980, he traveled with a custom-calibrated recording machine with three separate clocks that switched on in the middle of the night to resume playing whatever book on tape he was listening to at the time. He almost always awoke within two or three hours of closing his eyes. He began to use pills or injections to sleep after the Chandler affair in 1993, but built up tolerances that required higher and higher doses. Frank Cascio, who was working for Jackson full time by then, recalled collecting his employer's stashes of Xanax, Percocet, and Valium and keeping them with him every night before Michael went to bed. "I wanted to always make sure I had them with me and not have anything in his room where he didn't wake up and say, 'I can't sleep tonight,' and not realize what he's taking," Cascio explained.

By the time the Chandler case was settled, Michael was going days at a time without slumber. "Lisa I truly Need This Rest I Haven't slept litterally (sic) in 4 Days now," Michael had written to Lisa Marie Presley in a sprawling sloppy scrawl that filled up an entire sheet of legal notebook paper at one point during their relationship, explaining his failure to communicate. "I need to Be Away from phones and Business people."

Only after prescription drugs began to fail him as soporifics did Michael discover the one medication that gave him everything he wanted in a sleep aid. The syrupy white liquid propofol (marketed by AstraZeneca as Diprivan) is a short-acting, intravenously administered hypnotic agent better known as "milk of amnesia" among the medical professionals who use it as an anesthesia for day surgeries. Its many benefits include the fact that patients wake up (or come to) after a propofol injection in a state that is both alert and euphoric. This latter result has produced an archive of amusing anecdotes that date back to the time that the drug was still in its testing stage. Dr. Mike Roizen, the Cleveland Clinic physician who performed one of the earliest clinical studies of propofol, recalled that the first patient to give informed consent to be administered the drug was a young woman who came out of anesthesia after a knee operation, promptly grabbed her surgeon, and gave him "perhaps the most sensuous kiss I've ever seen in an operating room." Similar reports emerged from other studies, but so, also, had concerns about the drug. Propofol was limited by a very narrow "therapeutic window": a medical way of saying that taking even a little more than the recommended dosage could stop a person's breathing. Among those who had discovered propofol as a recreational drug—somewhat like ecstasy in its effect—there had been a number of deaths, some of them classified as suicides.

Michael had begun using propofol to sleep in 1996 while on the HIStory tour. Reportedly, the drug was administered either by a Beverly Hills doctor who was traveling with Michael, or by a pair of German anesthesiologists whose inclusion in the tour was arranged by Dieter Wiesner. Wiesner insisted the latter story was not true: "There were doctors there but I did not bring them. I was completely against it." However the doctors who gave it to him were hired, Michael came to rely on the propofol drip they fed him because it allowed him to go unconscious for hours every night no matter what his travel schedule and wake feeling refreshed each morning.

The propofol drips stopped, though, after the *HIStory* tour ended. Jackson again resumed the use of antianxiety medications and painkillers to get him through the night. His sleep disorder not only persisted, but was exacerbated by the bedsores he'd developed during the two-plus years between the airing of the Bashir documentary and his acquittal at the criminal trial in Santa Maria, a period when he had spent days at a stretch on his back in an immobilized drug haze.

Although he'd regularly resorted to OxyContin and Demerol while living in Bahrain, Michael's use of synthetic opiates was more restricted during his months in Ireland than it had been at any time during the previous three years. The price he paid for the last concerted effort he ever made at weaning himself off painkillers and antianxiety medications was a steady increase in sleepless nights. And yet, according to Patrick Treacy, Michael resisted asking for Diprivan or even Demerol with more determination than he'd managed in years. "The only prescriptions I wrote him were for minor things like colds," the doctor said.

Treacy and his colleagues at the Ailesbury Clinic *did* use propofol to put Michael under during an operation on his nose in 2006. Afterward, Treacy visited Michael at Coolatore House and found his patient in extreme discomfort: "He was running around the room covering his face and saying, 'It hurts! It burns!'" Yet Michael did not ask for another dose of Diprivan, Treacy said, and even refused the doctor's offer of other pain medications to see him through the week. Michael also did not ask for anything to treat his insomnia, according to Treacy, who claimed later that his patient had made it clear he understood the dangers of using propofol without an attending anesthesiologist. "Michael would never have done so," the Irish doctor insisted.

Without the drugs, though, Jackson was sleeping no more than a couple of hours a night. Amid the lawsuits, the scandals, and the tabloid gossip, not to mention the urgency he felt about restoring his finances and reviving his career, it was nearly impossible to make his mind rest. On top of that, all his best ideas came to him at three in the morning, Michael said.

One of those ideas was triggered by a question Billy Bush had put to him about a "second chapter" to *Thriller*, given that the twenty-fifth anniversary of the album's release would arrive in late 2007. "It's a great thought," Michael had said at the time. Sony agreed. After the meeting at the Burj Al Arab in Dubai, the company had become quite receptive to the idea of another Michael Jackson retrospective. His criminal trial in Santa Barbara County had been bracketed by the enormous success of *Number Ones* in 2003 and the impressive follow-up of *The Essential Michael Jackson* (six million copies sold) in late 2005. Only a few weeks after will.i.am flew back to the United States, the Black Eyed Pea signed on as executive producer on a special anniversary edition of *Thriller* that would include remixes, duets, and perhaps a few new songs. They would title the project *Thriller 25*, Michael and Sony agreed, after the company agreed to release the album on its reissue label, Legacy Recordings. This decision would ease at least a little of the pressure he felt to deliver what was now being described on six continents as his "comeback album," Michael realized, and earn him some good credit at Sony if it sold even a million copies. More important, it offered him the opportunity to show the music industry that his best work was relevant to young artists even a quarter century later. That all sounded a lot better than risking another experience like the one he had endured upon the release of *Invincible*.

This happy development did not change the fact that Michael was becoming more and more restive as the end of October approached. The weather was turning chill and damp. Darkness came sooner. Worst of all, Billy Bush had shredded his veil of privacy. Right after shooting the interview at Grouse Lodge, Bush stopped over in nearby Moate, where "he told the men, women, children, and dogs in the street where Jackson was," as a reporter for Britain's *Observer* described it. "Stupid man," a sorrowful Paddy Dunning would say.

The paparazzi and tabloid reporters asking about Michael Jackson in the pubs and shops of County Westmeath multiplied steadily after that. Michael was moved to tears when he heard about a local farmer who had threatened to empty his slurry trailer on the car of a paparazzo who was trying to sneak a snapshot from a neighboring property. He knew it was only a matter of time, though, before one of the photographers succeeded. Sure enough, during the last week of October, a grainy image of Michael entering the main building at Grouse Lodge appeared in several Irish newspapers. In the days that followed, drive-by gawkers on the Dublin-Galway road stalled traffic like nothing ever seen before in Rosemount. For the first time since his arrival at Blackwater Castle back in June, Michael was implicitly criticized in the Irish press, on October 28, when one of the small Midlands newspapers published an article about his visit with the children to a Tullamore play center called Jumping Jacks. Michael Jackson had come in dressed all in black, it was reported, wearing a cowboy hat outfitted with a veil as he watched his children play with six or seven local kids. One mother complained that Mr. Jackson's burly "minder" had asked rather sternly if another woman was taking photographs of Michael's children; later she herself had been followed outside by the same man, who wanted to know if she was making a phone call. Even the *Westmeath Independent* became so desperate for Michael Jackson news that it built a story around a sighting of the star carrying a Mickey Mouse bag as he left the studio after an all-night recording session.

Word of Jackson's stay at Grouse Lodge went worldwide after the *Access Hollywood* segment aired in early November. The inns and pubs of County Westmeath crawled with people who carried cameras and microphones. There were no more walks in the countryside.

Michael's nerves were not calmed by thoughts of his impending appearance in London on November 15, at the World Music Awards ceremony, where Beyoncé was to present him with the fifth-ever Diamond Award (for selling more than 100 million albums). From the moment he accepted the invitation, Michael began to dread the event. His performance would be broadcast to one hundred and sixty countries worldwide and on top of that he was "terrified of having to meet the queen," Patrick Treacy recalled. Jackson's deepest fear, though, was of Fleet Street. There was no place on earth where he had been subjected to either so much adulation or so much ridicule as in London. The English tabloids couldn't get enough of Wacko Jacko. They would all have their knives and forks out by the time he arrived, Michael knew, waiting for the feast to begin.

10

In July 1988, when he arrived in England at the climax of his *Bad* tour, Michael had been treated literally like royalty. Ahead of the first of his seven scheduled concerts at Wembley Stadium, Jackson was honored with a dinner at Guildhall, the historic town center of the city of London. The centuries-old building had survived the trials of the Gunpowder and Overbury plot leaders, and a fire from a World War II Luftwaffe raid that burned off its timber roof, but it had seen nothing like the visit of Michael Jackson. Dressed in a bright red-and-blue tunic that was likened by reporters to the uniform of a military dictator, Michael had become (with the permission of Queen Elizabeth II herself) the first commoner in history admitted to Guildhall through the building's royal entrance, his arrival heralded by the trumpeters of the Life Guards cavalry. Amid the memorials to Lord Nelson, the Duke of Wellington, and Winston Churchill, dancers dressed in Olde English costumes scattered rose petals at Michael's feet as he was escorted to the head of the long table in the Great Hall where so many affairs of state had been conducted over the centuries. A huge platter of roast beef was paraded through the room by the Corps of Drums of the Honourable Artillery Company, but Jackson never touched it, instead nibbling at a vegetable salad prepared by his personal chef.

After the meal, the star was led into the courtyard with Frank Dileo and the ten-year-old boy who was his constant companion on the *Bad* tour, Jimmy Safechuck. He saluted as the band of the Corps of Royal Engineers marched past, then walked up and down a line of liveried troops, as if sent by the queen to inspect them. Michael began to dance when the band broke into its version of "Billie Jean," then turned, startled by the sound of hooves clattering upon cobblestones as a knight in armor rode into the compound astride an enormous steed. Leaping from the horse, the knight pulled a sword from a stone, went down on one knee before the American pop star, then handed him what was supposed to be Excalibur. "Do you realize that you've just become the King of England?"

one of the entertainment writers in attendance called out. "Gee," Michael replied. "A king? I never knew."

Nothing would surpass the London event for pomp and ceremony, but similar deference was shown to Jackson at virtually every stop on the *Bad* tour. The press dubbed him "Typhoon Michael" in Japan. Six hundred reporters and photographers clamored and jostled upon his arrival at Narita Airport in Tokyo; nearly three hundred remained to meet the cargo plane that touched down more than an hour later with Bubbles aboard. In Japan, he dedicated each performance of "I Just Can't Stop Loving You" to a five-year-old boy named Yoshioka Hagiwara, whose recent kidnapping and murder had traumatized the entire nation. Dubbed "Crocodile Jackson" by the Australian press, he sold out stadium dates in Sydney, Melbourne, and Brisbane weeks in advance. Frantic camera crews followed him on a round of visits to seriously ill children in the Sydney suburbs and he made the front page of every major newspaper in the country when he tucked several sick children into bed after hearing pleas from their mothers. Visits to orphanages or to the children's wards of hospitals, as well as charitable donations, were principal features of Jackson's stay in each of the cities he visited on a sixteen-month-long world tour that included a hundred and twenty-three concerts in fifteen countries.

Michael Jackson was a phenomenon like nothing the world had seen before him, greeted outside the United States with a level of crazed enthusiasm that far exceeded what Elvis and the Beatles had generated decades earlier. The nearly four and a half million tickets purchased made the *Bad* tour the largest grossing concert series in history. References to "mass hysteria" were part of the press coverage at every stop. "There was a peculiar religiosity to his concert reviews," entertainment writer Simon Frith would write for his "Brit Beat" column in *The Village Voice*, "as if people were going to Wembley (a common setting for revivalist meetings) to be redeemed." A granddaughter of Emperor Hirohito attended the first concert in Tokyo; in London, Charles and Diana, the Prince and Princess of Wales, were among those in Wembley's private boxes. Meeting with Michael before the concert at Wembley, the princess urged him to perform "Dirty Diana." Bob Dylan and Elizabeth Taylor were among the crowd at the concert in Basel, Switzerland, where Michael met privately with Oona O'Neill, the widow of his idol Charlie Chaplin. Headline writers in every country he visited felt compelled to give him a new nickname—"The Earl of Whirl" or "The Peter Pan of Pop"—but in England the adulation went hand in glove with open ridicule.

The *Sun* had started it with the 1986 headline that asked, "Is Jacko Wacko?" Jackson's reputation for weirdness dated at least as far back as the *Destiny* tour, and was rooted in his remarkably earnest curiosity. In 1980 he had spent time on Los Angeles' Skid Row, a largely abandoned downtown stretch of Spring Street where a large number of the city's homeless population gathered and lived. He had gone in disguise, of course, in a stubbly fake beard, a battered old hat, and the tattered clothing that he imagined would allow him to blend in. All he wanted, Michael said, was to get a feel for what life was like for the people down there. A year later he was wearing the same disguise when he wandered into an Atlanta antique store and, for some reason, tried to conceal himself inside an antique armoire. He was spotted by the owner, who made the scruffy-looking fellow for a drunk. The owner ordered him to come out and leave the store but Michael refused to budge. The man called the sheriff's department, which sent a deputy who walked into one of the strangest scenes he had ever encountered: The proprietor was holding the bum in a headlock as the man thrashed about wildly, trying to explain that he was *the* Michael Jackson. The deputy arrested both men, one for criminal trespass and the other for assault. No charges were filed but it was the first public record of Jackson's determination to cope with fame by going undercover.

He went incognito throughout the eighties. He delighted in playing with makeup and costumes, and continued to experiment with disguises when he went out "pioneering" for the Jehovah's Witnesses until he broke from the church in 1987. In 1985 he was spotted pedaling a bicycle along Ventura Boulevard in what *Rolling Stone* would call "a daringly thin disguise": faded jeans, a white T-shirt, and a khaki cap with desert flaps jammed down over the hood of his windbreaker. Jackson had also taken to going out in public wearing a gorilla mask. "I love it when people stop and are scared," he offered. "And I love it when they don't know it's me inside the mask." And yet at the same time he *wanted* them to know. The producer, arranger, and songwriter David Foster, who began working with Jackson as early as *Off the Wall*, would recall a visit of Michael's to New York in which the star prepared for a surreptitious trip to the movies by permitting Foster's children to dress him in their own clothes; baggy jeans, a scarf, and a cap turned to the side, "gangster-style," with his hair tucked up inside it. However, when the kids told him he had to push the curled lock of hair on his forehead into the hat as well, because it had become such a signature look, Michael refused. "It was a dead giveaway, but he was adamant," Foster remembered: "'No, no, I've got to have my curl out!'

I thought that was very telling. He didn't want to be seen, but he kind of wanted to be seen."

The confusion about the difference between telling lies and doing public relations that Berry Gordy and Diana Ross conspired to lodge in Michael's mind at the age of ten had morphed into a belief that there was no such thing as bad publicity. He began to idolize P. T. Barnum and planted a story himself that he was sleeping in a hyperbaric chamber so he'd stop aging, posing inside one of the $200,000 contraptions for a photo that ran worldwide. When a rumor started that he was trying to buy the bones of Joseph Merrick, Britain's famous "Elephant Man," Michael made an actual offer in order to give the story legs. He collaborated with the *National Enquirer* on articles reporting that he refused to bathe in anything but Evian water and had been carrying on conversations with John Lennon's ghost. Frank Dileo was Michael's chief aider and abettor in planting such stories in the tabloids, going so far as to *insist* that his client be described as "bizarre" in a report by the *Star* that ran under the headline: "Michael Jackson Goes Ape. Now He's Talking with His Pet Chimp—In Monkey Language." Most people were unaware that Michael's chimp companion Bubbles (who had been rescued from a cancer research laboratory) lived most of the time with his trainer, Bob Dunn.

The problem with such strategies was that the tabloids began to print almost anything about Michael Jackson and felt they could get away with it. This included such concocted items as Jackson paying $1 million for a potion that would make him invisible so he could go shopping with his pet chimpanzee and not be stared at. An *Enquirer* report claimed that Jackson's musical rival, Prince, was using ESP to drive Bubbles crazy. "Prince has gone too far this time," the *Enquirer* had Michael saying. "What kind of sicko would mess with a monkey?" His supposed terror of the HIV virus was made into a tabloid treat and an invented story that he had refused to kiss the Blarney Stone on a visit to Ireland because he feared catching AIDS gained so much credence that it was printed as fact in *Rolling Stone*.

What would make Michael's "Wacko" image more ominous than amusing was, of course, his insistence upon seeking out young boys as his closest companions. After the Jordan Chandler scandal broke in 1993, the game played by a media that for years had been titillated by Michael's strangeness turned scary and mean. Back in 1988, though, when he came to England on the *Bad* tour, there were many mentions of Michael's "young friend" Jimmy Safechuck in the British press that summer but virtually no insinuations of impropriety. Reporters who trailed the two of them on an after-hours trip to Hamleys, the seven-story toy shop on London's Regent Street that was Michael's favorite shopping destination anywhere, were giddy with the queer charm of it all. Jimmy had on an exact replica of the stage costume Michael wore (one of several the star had ordered for his ten-year-old friend) and seemed neither more nor less excited than the nearly thirty-year-old man who led him by the hand through the store. Many in the press knew that Jimmy's parents had been provided with their own limousine and a blank check to eat at expensive restaurants or attend West End shows so that their son and the star could be alone. Some even knew that Michael and Jimmy slept in the same hotel room, yet the images that this conjured in those days were of battery-powered car crashes and scary story telling at midnight. It was *understood* that Michael Jackson sought the company of prepubescent males because he yearned to be one himself, longed to go back in time and make his life into what he believed it should have been, in those days when he had been a ten-year-old himself, staring out the studio windows at the playground across the street, imagining himself on swings and slides and merry-go-rounds with the other kids his age.

It wasn't as if Jimmy had been the first of Michael's young friends. Few knew about Rodney Allen Rippy, but the whole world had watched Michael's relationship with Emmanuel Lewis play out on national television. Shortly after the 1984 Grammy Awards ceremony, Michael, Emmanuel, and Brooke Shields were again a threesome when they arrived at the American Music Awards, but it was only the boy whom the star carried to the stage with him as he accepted the prize for best song and told the audience, "Important to me in writing songs is inspiration, and I'm holding one of my inspirations, Emmanuel Lewis." The diminutive boy visited Jackson not only at the Hayvenhurst estate but also at the Westwood condominium known among Michael's employees as the "Hideout," the one place in Los Angeles where he could escape both his fans and the media. Rumors went around about the two but those who visited the Hideout said that all they ever saw was Michael playing games with Emmanuel or teaching him to moonwalk. Reporters' ears pricked up when word got out that Lewis's mother had pulled the boy away from Jackson in late 1984 after the two checked into a hotel as father and son. A story (later confirmed by Jackson publicist Bob Jones) circulated that the entertainer's security guards had been ordered to purchase baby bottles and nipples each time Emmanuel visited. After the Chandler scandal, there would be public speculation about what sort of perverse sexual activities must have been involved. Then, in 2005, *In Touch Weekly* published photographs that had been taken years earlier of Jackson and Lewis lying in bed and sucking milk from bottles. For Michael this was barely less mortifying than the accusations of molestation, though perhaps it was easier to let people believe that he might be sexually abusing Lewis than to acknowledge what they were *really* doing, which was being babies together. How to tell the world that he wasn't trying to be heterosexual or homosexual or even asexual, but rather *presexual*, was a problem he could never solve.

After Emmanuel Lewis, Jackson collected an entire tribe of lost boys, including both of the young stars of the hit TV show *Silver Spoons*: Alfonso Ribeiro and Ricky Schroder. Much would be made later of his supposed preference for white boys but he had actually favored Ribeiro (who, like Rodney Allen Rippy and Emmanuel Lewis, was a fairly dark-skinned black kid) over the blue-eyed, blond Schroder. Michael met Corey Feldman in 1985 on the set of *The Goonies*, which was being produced by Steven Spielberg. They were shooting a scene that required an expression of shock and Spielberg had gotten it out of him, Feldman recalled, by blurting out that Michael Jackson was coming for a visit. He gave the star his phone number, Feldman said, but didn't expect a call. Michael phoned that evening and spoke with him for two hours, telling stories about Paul McCartney. They talked at least once a week after that, according to Feldman (who had begun to dress up like Jackson long before Jimmy Safechuck did), and went on any number of trips together. Feldman not only scoffed at suggestions that Jackson had made sexual advances toward him, but recalled a trip to the Disneyland Hotel where Michael offered him the bed and took a cot for himself. All Michael had ever really surprised him with was kindness and generosity, Feldman said, a statement that would be echoed by one boy after another who got to spend time with Jackson. The kids who visited him at Neverland would come back with stories of pillow fights and food fights, reporting nothing worse than that they'd been allowed to gorge themselves on candy and stay up past midnight watching movies.

Michael's eccentricity was remarked upon in the media far more often than his friendships with young boys. "Why doesn't this guy want to grow up?" was the question reporters asked about him, not, "Is he a pedophile?" Whatever nasty remarks editors made about him behind closed doors, they had to admit that stories like the one about him hiring the little people who played the Seven Dwarfs at Disneyland to come to the Hayvenhurst estate to frolic on the lawn in full costume for his entertainment made great copy. Before 1993, people found that stuff charming, not creepy.

Most of the mockery Michael was subjected to arose from his fake romances, the continuing need he seemed to feel to pretend that he was hot and heavy with some young woman whose hand he'd held. Tatum O'Neal and Brooke Shields were both pretty forthright about it. "No big romance," Shields would say of the relationship. "We have a lot of fun because we just joke like we're in kindergarten or something." Eddie Murphy was hilariously wicked on *Saturday Night Live* as an ultra-fey Jackson, bragging about his imaginary exploits with various women. Michael laughed at that himself. He continued to be highly reactive, though, to suggestions he was homosexual. He asked Joan Rivers to stop telling her "Michael Jackson is so gay he makes Liberace look like a Green Beret" joke, and when she wouldn't, planted a story in the *National Enquirer* that he was thinking about suing the comedienne. Hardly anybody paid attention to the fabricated tabloid report that Jackson was having an affair with British pop star Boy George, yet Michael insisted on holding a "major press conference" in Los Angeles that served little purpose other than to draw attention to the story. After warning that any such future "false allegations" would be met with a lawsuit, Jackson's publicist read a statement in which Michael denied taking hormones to keep his voice high and having cosmetic surgery on his eyes. He was speaking out, the statement read, purely to protect the children who admired him.

Michael *did* enjoy the company of older women who had become famous themselves at a young age and who didn't threaten him sexually: Diana Ross, Liza Minnelli, Katharine Hepburn, and Sophia Loren among them. Jane Fonda had been the first to tell Michael he was born to play the role of Peter Pan. During tours, one of his employees was assigned to create a Shirley Temple theme in each hotel suite Michael occupied, decorating it from one end to the other with photographs and cutouts of the former child star, "so that when I walked in I would see her," Michael explained. He even insisted that a picture of her at age five or six be taped to the mirror in his dressing room. When he finally met Shirley Temple Black, by then a former United States foreign ambassador who was thirty years his senior, "we said nothing to each other at first, we simply cried together," Michael would recall, because they knew each other's pain, knew what it was to mourn a childhood they felt they'd missed.

It was Elizabeth Taylor, though, with whom he grew closest. During his purchase of Neverland Ranch, Michael confided to the real estate agent handling the sale that he planned to adopt twenty-nine children and marry Elizabeth Taylor, then reacted emotionally when the woman said Taylor could be his grandmother: "But I love her!" The shared personal mythology that had collected around a core of common childhood experiences would keep their relationship going for nearly a quarter century. They had met in December 1984 when Taylor asked for fourteen tickets to one of the Jackson 5 concerts at Dodger Stadium in the final days of the *Victory* tour. The seats she was given were in a VIP box so far back from the stage that "you might as well have been watching it on TV," recalled Taylor, who had led her large party out of the stadium before the concert was half over. Michael called the next day, crying over the phone as he apologized profusely. They talked for three hours that day, according to Taylor, and the calls between them continued for months as "we got to know each other on the telephone." On the day Michael finally suggested dropping by, he asked if he could bring a friend. He showed up a short time later leading Bubbles by the hand.

The root of the connection between them was the similarity between their upbringings. Each had become the family breadwinner before the age of ten, pushed by a parent/manager (in Taylor's case, her mother) whose investment in them had more to do with money than with love. Taylor understood Michael's tortured relationship with Joe Jackson in ways few other people did. "I was a child star at nine, had an abusive father, and that kind of brought us together in the very beginning," Taylor would tell Oprah Winfrey in their 2005 interview. "Our fathers were very much alike, tough, hard, brutal," Michael had explained to Rabbie Boteach five years before that. Sorrow and self-aggrandizement were fused in each of their psyches, and it produced a relationship that was both tender and toxic.

They defied their imprisonment in fame by doing things like sneaking out in disguises each Thursday afternoon to take in a movie matinee, sitting in the back row with a tub of popcorn between them, holding hands. Taylor was a regular visitor to Neverland; she and Michael even had their own special picnic spot on a cliff overlooking the amusement park. Liz bought Michael an elephant for his zoo, and he returned the favor by presenting her with a bejeweled elephant bauble the size of a soccer ball at her birthday party in Las Vegas. On the whole, Michael did a lot more giving than she did, presenting her with assorted necklaces, bracelets, and pendants created by her favorite jewelery designers and regularly showing up at her door with bottles of the world's most expensive perfumes. In 1991, Michael hosted and laid out a reported million dollars for Taylor's eighth wedding, to Larry Fortensky, a mullet-wearing construction worker twenty years her junior, in a Neverland gazebo. It was widely reported that, at Neverland, Jackson had created a sort of shrine to Taylor where a television surrounded by photographs of her played the actress's movies twenty-four hours a day, seven days a week. This was not true, but there *was* a large portrait of Jackson hanging in the hallway of Taylor's Beverly Hills home on which he had written, "To My True Love Elizabeth."

Just as Michael had broken eventually from the Jehovah's Witnesses, Liz had separated from the faith she was raised in—Christian Science—to convert to Judaism, before her marriage to producer Mike Todd. Taylor embraced the mysteries of the Kabbala long before Madonna did and convinced Michael to wear a red string as protection from the evil eye during his criminal trial in Santa Barbara County. "We like the same things," Michael had told Paul Theroux when the author asked about his relationship with Liz. "Circuses. Amusement parks. Animals." What he left out, of course, was drugs.

In the early eighties, when Michael and Liz were first getting to know one another, Taylor had received more than a thousand prescriptions for sleeping pills, tranquilizers, and painkillers. Many of those prescriptions were written by Taylor and Jackson's mutual physician and friend Dr. Arnold Klein, who regularly provided Liz with both Dilaudid ("cream of heroin," as it's known on the street) and an assortment of powerful tranquilizers. Strictly to aid in recovery after medical procedures, Klein said. Friends said that Taylor regularly overdosed, passing out with her eyes open, barely breathing. Paramedics who weren't entirely sure if she was dead or alive had to rush her to the hospital on multiple occasions. After she was revived and released, Taylor would use a flask of liquor to wash down more pills during the ride home. She was in and out of rehab during the next fifteen years, a period in which Klein had written many prescriptions for his other friend and patient, Michael Jackson. One of the drugs he gave Michael was Demerol, Klein would acknowledge, for "pain management." Associates of both Taylor and Jackson said that the two regularly traded pills. Liz was Michael's date when he arrived at the American Music Awards ceremony at the Shrine Auditorium in Los Angeles in January 1993 and numerous witnesses described Taylor as "teetering," her eyes so glazed that she couldn't recognize people who were standing right in front of her.

When Theroux suggested that Elizabeth was Wendy to his Peter Pan, Michael replied, "She's Mother Teresa, Princess Diana, the Queen of England, *and* Wendy." Mother Teresa and Princess Diana were who he always mentioned when he spoke about what sort of woman he imagined marrying some day, someone "classy and quiet and not into all the sex and the craziness," as he put it to Rabbi Shmuley Boteach. It was the same way he had described his mother Katherine, telling Boteach, "She is like a saint." Elizabeth Taylor was no saint, and her sexual adventures were the stuff of legend in Hollywood, but Michael saw her as fundamentally innocent. "She's playful and youthful and happy and finds a way to laugh and giggle even when she's in pain," he told Rabbi Boteach. "I know if we ever did anything romantically, the press would be so mean and nasty and call us 'The Odd Couple,'" Michael lamented to the rabbi. "It would turn into a circus and that's the pain of it all." So they would remain simply "very good friends," the same description he gave to the young boys who were at his side from the late seventies onward.

In 1986, Michael had starred in *Captain EO*, a $20 million 3-D film produced by George Lucas and directed by Francis Ford Coppola that was both the most expensive and the most promoted short film in the history of the movies, despite being shown exclusively at Disney theme parks. On the set, only three people were permitted to speak to the star: Coppola, Liz Taylor, and ten-year-old Jonathan Spence, and of these Michael seemed closest to the boy. They were seen any number of times nuzzling and hugging, and seemed to love playing patty-cake with one another. People thought it was innocent, if a bit odd. When Santa Barbara County authorities contacted Spence years later, he assured them that nothing inappropriate had happened between Michael and him. Jackson's secretary, though, said Spence continued to call the MJJ Productions office occasionally, asking for airline tickets, and once for a new car, which he received.

Jimmy Safechuck and his family would do far better, and this time Michael's generosity produced the first rumblings of suspicion. After Jackson purchased a Rolls-Royce for the Safechuck family in London, Frank Dileo warned him that reporters would find out about it and start asking questions. Hurt, Michael asked, "Who cares what they think?" and carried on with the relationship. When the *Bad* tour moved on to Dublin, a group of reporters drinking in the bar at Jurys Inn began to speculate about where wee Jimmy might be that night. Hotel stationery and an envelope were requested by the journalists, who laughingly wrote out a note telling Master Safechuck that he could be rescued if he was being held against his will. It had seemed a great joke at the time because no one thought seriously that there might be improprieties involved.

There were whispers, though. Quite a number of people had been mildly scandalized—or at least put off—by the crotch grab that Michael had begun to do onstage. The move had first showed up in the "Bad" video, and was carried over into the *Bad* tour. Michael at first insisted it was "choreography," but what he was doing onstage looked blatantly masturbatory to some in the audience. And, well, really, those *were* stroke motions he was making. When his story changed—what people saw was a reflexive move he made in response to the music, Michael said, and he wasn't even conscious of it—people who doubted him grew more outspoken. Those were pretty sexual gestures for a guy who was supposed to be Peter Pan. There were murmurs that maybe he was hiding something.

Only a handful of people knew in 1988 about the single credible claim of inappropriate conduct that had been made against Michael Jackson and most of those people were in England. The story involved a boy named Terry George who had been twelve when he approached Michael at London's Lanesborough Hotel in 1979 and asked if he could do an interview for his school newspaper. Charmed, Michael invited the boy to his hotel room, where they spent most of the time "giggling and laughing," recalled Terry, who realized during this first encounter that Michael preferred the company of kids to that of adults. It seemed a dream come true, especially when Michael called the boy at home the following week. By early 1980, the star was phoning him three times a week, occasionally collect, always at exactly nine at night, London time, the boy recalled, an hour when his parents were often out playing bingo. He and Michael would chat for hours "about silly stuff," Terry said. Sometimes Michael would sing to him over the telephone.

Then one night Jackson called and sounded different. The line went quiet at one point, and he asked Michael if he was still there, Terry remembered: "Out of nowhere, he asked me if I masturbated, and that if I did, did I use cream?" He really didn't understand the question, said Terry, who "could hear down the line that [Jackson] was making strange noises." The conversation left him feeling "confused and uncomfortable," said Terry, who made it clear that Michael had never touched him when they were alone. His conversations with Jackson ended soon after, when his parents discovered that he had run up a huge bill, Terry recalled, and forbade him from using the telephone. He went to Michael's hotel again when the star came to London in 1981 but this time his friend was "frosty," and all contact between them ceased.

Terry eventually told his parents about the masturbation conversation with Michael and they told some acquaintances. Word spread, but slowly. It was still just people from their neighborhood who were aware of it when Michael came to London on the *Bad* tour in 1988. But during the next five years the story would somehow cross the Atlantic Ocean. In 1993, Terry received a phone call from a Los Angeles Police Department detective who said that he believed Michael's "bad behavior" had started with him. He didn't believe Michael was a pedophile, Terry told the detective, just "a very confused person."

11

Michael Jackson's expected arrival at the 2006 World Music Awards ceremony was being framed by the newspapers in London as a shot at recovery, if not redemption. Jackson's last appearance on an English stage had been almost ten years earlier, at the 1996 BRIT Awards, where his performance of the best-loved number from the *HIStory* album, "Earth Song," was disrupted by a particularly memorable protest against celebrity self-importance.

HIStory's $30 million publicity campaign had been launched in the summer of 1995. When the executives at Sony met with him in the spring of 1995 to discuss how they would promote the album and the world tour that was to follow, Michael suggested, "Build a statue of me." Sony built nine statues, each one a thirty-two-foot-tall construction of steel and fiberglass that depicted Jackson in his familiar pseudo-military garb with a bandolier strung across his chest, fists clenched at his hips as he gazed off into the distance. They were distributed in dramatic fashion to strategically selected European cities in June 1995. The scene that surrounded the giant crane that had lowered the Michael Jackson statue to the Alexanderplatz in Berlin was surreal to say the least, but even that didn't compare to the sensation created by the giant Jackson statue that was floated down the River Thames aboard a barge in London. "Excessive" and "over the top" were among the milder criticisms made of the statue campaign; critics in several countries declared themselves "nauseated." The distribution of the statues was followed shortly thereafter by the release of a "teaser" video that had cost $4 million and showed the real Michael Jackson costumed in the same way his statues were as he strode regally past hundreds of hired Hungarian soldiers who were surrounded by thousands of frenzied fans. "The clip doesn't just stop at representing previously known levels of Michael mania," wrote Chris Willman in the *Los Angeles Times*, "it goes well beyond the bounds of self-congratulation to become perhaps the most baldly vainglorious self-deification a pop singer has yet deigned to share with his public, at least with a straight face."

That summer's publicity campaign had included a joint interview of Michael and his new bride, Lisa Marie Presley, by Diane Sawyer for ABC's *Primetime Live*. Seen by some sixty million viewers in the United States alone, the Sawyer interview demonstrated that Jackson's ability to attract an audience was undiminished. The undisguised point of it all, though, had been to answer the questions that lingered after the settlement of the claims made against Michael by Jordan Chandler, and in this the interview had failed miserably. The most memorable moment had come when Michael told Sawyer that he saw no reason to abandon his sleepovers with children. The deer-in-headlights expression on Presley's face produced a public outpouring of pity for her.

The 1996 BRIT Awards were held for the first time at London's Earls Court. A significant minority of the audience had gagged on Bob Geldof's introduction and presentation of a special "Artist of a Generation" award to Jackson: "When he sings, it is with the voice of angels. When his feet move, you can see God dancing." Singing and dancing amidst a multi-colored collection of clapping, chanting children, Jackson had struck what appeared to be a Christ-like pose as he stepped onto a platform and was hoisted above the crowd. Many of the audience's younger members began to shake their heads. Just as the performance of "Earth Song" came to a crescendo, Jarvis Cocker, front man for the band Pulp, "invaded the stage," as it was described in newspaper stories, to pantomime what appeared to be a highly stylized fart directed at Jackson.

Bundled off the stage by security, Cocker was detained and questioned by police on suspicion of assault but eventually released without being charged. The initial condemnation of Cocker's "rude display" was swiftly overtaken by congratulations for his nervy defiance of an overblown idol. Many applauded when Cocker answered criticism in the press by stating, "My actions were a form of protest at the way Michael Jackson sees himself as some kind of Christ-like figure with the power of healing." Noel Gallagher, leader of what was then Britain's biggest band, Oasis, promptly suggested that Jarvis Cocker should be made a Member of the British Empire. The nation's most influential music magazine, *Melody Maker*, also demanded that Cocker be knighted. Pulp's record sales soared, even as "Earth Song" began to fall from the charts, and a $50,000 waxwork statue of Cocker was placed in London's Rock Circus. Over the next few months, Jarvis Cocker became an icon of cool in England while Michael Jackson turned into a symbol of all that was passé in pop music.

Now, nearly a full decade since the BRIT Awards debacle, Michael was returning to Earls Court. Even before his arrival in London the city's tabloids were reporting that Jackson had infuriated World Music Awards organizers with a half-million dollars of last-minute demands that included twenty first-class plane tickets and the erection of an eighteen-foot-high temporary wall around the Hempel Hotel in Bayswater, which he and his entourage had taken over at a cost of $80,000 per night.

At Earls Court, Michael's failure to appear on the red carpet to greet the thousands of fans who had come out to see him got the evening off to a bad start. Tensions mounted when the crowd discovered that Jackson would not be joining Chris Brown's performance of "Thriller," as had been promised in the newspapers. The disappointed audience drowned out Brown's solo and several performances that followed with boos, claps, and chants for "Michael!" When Jackson finally took the stage (after being introduced by host Lindsay Lohan as "a god") to join a choir for a gospel-inflected version of "We Are the World," he seemed "overawed and petrified," as an audience member quoted by the *Mirror* put it. Michael sang only the chorus of the song before abruptly stopping, throwing his Roberto Cavalli jacket into the front row, then repeatedly telling the audience how much he loved them. There was little love coming back. Boos rained down from every corner of Earls Court as he surrendered the stage to Rihanna, whose performance of her hit "Unfaithful" was largely drowned out by the raging crowd. Critics savaged Jackson in the next morning's newspapers, describing his performance as "embarrassing" and "a shambles." Michael's inability to explain what had happened—he told reporters only that it had all been "a misunderstanding"—further irritated the media, which mocked him for days afterward.

"Michael Jackson is beyond hope," wrote one London columnist, and plenty of his colleagues seemed to agree. There was a new level of unattributed nastiness in the reporting on Jackson. One story described him as "a truly macabre figure" who was "so prone to panic attacks that he cuts himself off from human contact for days." British press reports also called Jackson a "germaphobe" who hadn't appeared on the red carpet at Earls Court because he was terrified of being touched by fans. An anonymous associate said Michael had become so lacking in self-confidence that he couldn't bring himself to speak aloud.

The catastrophe of Jackson's appearance at Earls Court chilled his relationship with Raymone Bain, who had served as his intermediary with the World Music Awards organizers. Bain did her best to put out the story that Michael's performance of "We Are the World" had been stopped short when someone backstage inexplicably cut off the sound, but that was swiftly and furiously denied by a spokesman for the show's organizers. The music blog *PopRevenge* disclosed that "Jackson's people" had been so inept that they allowed one of its reporters to infiltrate the chorus that was to perform with Michael: "Nobody asked if I could sing or dance or knew the song," the young woman told London newspapers.

By the time he returned to Ireland, Jackson was so distraught that he dispatched Bain to announce that he would not be traveling to Japan for a "premium Christmas party" event on December 20 that had been planned months earlier. Badly as he needed the $250,000 cash payment, Michael insisted that the event be canceled, resulting in a degree of excoriation he had never before experienced from the Japanese media. He promptly agreed to make a trip to Tokyo in the spring to "host" a buffet dinner and concert by Michael Jackson impersonators, but this did not entirely quell the criticisms of his "insensitivity to the Japanese people" that appeared on the editorial pages of newspapers.

By mid-December, the dank chill of the Irish winter was working its way into his bones, and the cold front that the London tabloids were sending his way across St. George's Channel made the temperature feel freezing. He began to long for heat and light, and to ask if perhaps he had been out of the United States long enough to be missed. Three days before Christmas, he helped his children finish packing, then called for the limousine that would carry them all, plus Grace, to Cork Airport. While preparing to go, Michael gave the Dunnings his television set, a box of toys that had been bought for Prince, Paris, and Blanket, and the collection of hats he had worn during his stay in County Westmeath. He signed a slice of tree trunk, just as all guests at Grouse Lodge were asked to do, and left a page-size signature in the visitors book. As Michael left, he thanked the Dunnings for never once asking him to moonwalk, then told Paddy and Claire that they were "the only people who have never asked me for a photograph." There were tears in his eyes as he walked out the door.

Two hours later, Michael, Grace, and the kids were aboard a private jet that flew into the setting sun. At least in America they would give him something to help him sleep.

PART THREE

WEST

12

Michael Jackson was wearing his standard travel disguise of sunglasses and a veil when he stepped off his jet in a private hangar at McCarran Airport in Las Vegas on the evening of December 23, 2006. The entertainer, his children, and Grace Rwaramba climbed into a limousine that skirted the towering lights of the Strip, carrying them instead to the upscale suburbs northwest of the city, stopping finally at 2785 South Monte Cristo Way, a gated Spanish mansion on ten acres of grounds in the "custom home community" of Summerlin. Michael had signed a six-month lease on the property—sight unseen—that required an advance payment of $1 million, more than five times what it was worth on the open rental market.

A large Christmas tree with dozens of brightly packaged presents beneath it waited in the living room of the Jacksons' new home, placed there by gaming dealmaker Jack Wishna and his wife, Donna. Wishna, best known for bringing Donald Trump to Las Vegas (he was now a partner in the Trump International Hotel and Tower), had arranged for the private jet that brought Jackson and his entourage to Las Vegas from Ireland and already was letting reporters know that he and Michael had been talking for weeks about staging the star's "comeback" in Las Vegas, possibly with a live show like the hugely successful one Celine Dion had been headlining for months at Caesars Palace. The two of them envisioned what would be a sort of Michael Jackson Hotel they could create either by transforming an existing property or developing a new one, Wishna said. Jackson had suggested that they use one of the statues left over from the *HIStory* promotion at the hotel, according to the businessman: "Michael says, 'I want the hotel to encase it in the wall and the nights I'm in performance the statue comes out to the center of the Strip so the world knows that I'm here.' It would come out on a conveyer belt." Jackson even wanted to design his own King of Pop slot machines. But that was just one of several projects under consideration, added Wishna, who answered a call from

Us Weekly by assuring the magazine's reporter that Jackson "is poised to return to the top of the entertainment world soon."

Michael himself stayed silent and out of sight, hidden behind his new home's gated entrance, except for a quick shopping excursion on Christmas Eve at the Forum Shops in Caesars Palace. The photographers and cameramen who missed him there attempted a series of drive-by shootings at the Monte Cristo compound but came away with nothing except pictures of the 16,000-square-foot mansion's red-tile roof.

Michael would make his first public appearance on American soil since the end of his criminal trial less than a week later, though, when he flew to Georgia for the funeral of James Brown. The seventy-three-year-old Brown had died of congestive heart failure on Christmas morning after being admitted to an Atlanta hospital with pneumonia. Two days later, his body was transported to Harlem for an open-casket viewing at the Apollo Theater that would last all day and into the evening of December 28 in order to accommodate the lines, in which some people waited as long as five hours in the cold for a look at the Godfather of Soul. By nine that night, Brown's remains were in the cargo hold of a private jet, on their way back to his hometown of Augusta, Georgia. Michael Jackson was flying toward Georgia also, and made it to Augusta's C. A Reid Sr. Memorial Funeral Home just after midnight on December 29, less than an hour after the arrival of James Brown's body.

The gold-plated casket was in the chapel when Mr. Jackson walked into his establishment at about 12:30 a.m., Charles Reid recalled, and he immediately asked that the funeral director raise the lid. Michael looked at James Brown's embalmed body lying in a bed of cream-color satin, dressed in a black jacket worn over a ruffled red shirt, then leaned over to kiss the corpse on the forehead. He ran his hands through Brown's freshly oiled pompadour and pulled a lock down onto the brow, in order to create the slightly disheveled look that he had seen so many times before, onstage and in photographs. Reid was preparing a moment later to reclose the lid of the casket. Michael Jackson, though, showed no sign of leaving. "Normally, a person comes in, views, and that's pretty much it," Reid explained, but Michael Jackson would remain beside James Brown's body for four and a half hours.

Mr. Jackson spent the first hour just standing and looking, Reid remembered. Gradually, he began to talk to the funeral director about how much Mr. Brown had meant to him, telling Reid that when he was six or so years old his mother used to wake him up any time James Brown was on television, just so he could watch his idol dance. The relationship that began back on the chitlin' circuit had fluctuated over the years but grew strong in 2003, when Brown had been among the first black celebrities to offer support after criminal charges were filed against Michael Jackson.

What took Charles Reid aback on that evening in late December 2006 was that after spending about an hour beside James Brown's casket Mr. Jackson began to ask the funeral director a series of very specific questions about the preparation of a dead body. He wanted to know "how it was done," Reid recalled. "What do you actually do?" Mr. Jackson made him go through the entire process in elaborate detail, Reid remembered. His famous visitor listened intently and interjected demands for the exact details as the funeral director described how one went about "setting the features" with eye caps and a needle injector. Michael Jackson didn't want the funeral director to stop there. "What types of fluids do you use?" he asked. "And how do you put them in the body?" Reid found himself describing the various processes of embalming, the sorts of things that almost no one outside the mortuary professions wanted to know. "Most people shy away when it comes to death," Reid would later explain to *New York Daily News* columnist Michael Daly. "They would be trying to head the opposite way. It was amazing to me he would talk about it the way he did. It's just out of the ordinary."

Mr. Jackson's questions weren't morbid in nature, though, Reid said, not at all. Mr. Jackson was humble in his curiosity, very respectful and genuinely kind. He just wanted to know. It was almost five in the morning when Michael finally told Reid to close the casket and then walked back out of the funeral home.

Michael Jackson was clearly the star attraction at Augusta's James Brown Arena the next day, where the funeral was staged. Al Sharpton and Jesse Jackson stood beside him as Michael stepped to the podium and spoke to the crowd of 8,500 over a microphone. In some way that was clear yet ineffable, Michael's appearance seemed to culminate a reassertion of himself as a black man that had begun back in 2003, shortly after the criminal charges were filed against him. A crowd that was largely African American had been swaying and singing along to such James Brown hits as "I Feel Good," "It's a Man's Man's Man's World" and yes, "Sex Machine," which had ended with Brown's casket being covered by the cape that had so often been laid over his shoulders at the end of his stage shows. The Reverend Sharpton delivered a stirring eulogy that recalled the impact of James Brown's 1968 song "Say It Loud—I'm Black and I'm Proud." "I clearly remember we were calling ourselves colored, and after the song, we were calling ourselves black," Brown had told the Associated Press in 2003. "The song showed people that lyrics and music and a song can change society." Sharpton devoted a surprising amount of his speech to an explanation of Michael Jackson's presence in Augusta. "I don't care what the media says tonight, James Brown wanted Michael Jackson with him here today," Sharpton boomed into the microphone. "He said . . . 'I love Michael.' He said, 'Tell him don't worry about coming home. They always scandalize those that have the talent. But tell him we need to clean up the music, and I want Michael and all of them that imitated me to come back and lift the music back.'"

Amid the squeals and shouts of the rapturous crowd, Michael, dressed in a fitted black leather jacket, his makeup streaked with tears, stepped to the microphone and spoke in the voice that only those who did business with him knew well, a voice far deeper and stronger than the sibilant whisper to which the American public had grown accustomed. "James Brown is my greatest inspiration," he told a crowd that deeply wanted to believe it. "When I saw him move, I was mesmerized . . . I never saw a performer move like James Brown . . . James, I shall miss you, and I love you so much. Thank you for everything."

Michael made his deepest impression on those who saw television footage of the funeral, though, when he bent once more over the gold casket, this time in broad daylight, to again kiss the corpse of James Brown, right on the lips.

By the middle of January 2007, word had begun circulate in Las Vegas that Michael Jackson was in talks with Steve Wynn, the opportunistic billionaire developer credited for the dramatic resurgence of the Strip in the 1990s, having either built or refurbished casino resorts that included the Mirage, Treasure Island, and the Bellagio. The two had some history. Steve Miller, the former prosecutor whose *Inside Vegas* blog made him the closest thing to a muckraking journalist the city had seen in recent years, reported that, "On the many occasions when Jackson was in Vegas, often in the company of small boys, he and the unchaperoned children slept and played together in a specially decorated suite in Steve Wynn's hotel and had free use of Wynn's private jet." Miller had reported extensively about the triangular relationship between Wynn, Jackson, and Michael Milken, the fabled "junk bond king" who had been convicted of illegal securities trading in 1990, then was visited more than fifty times in prison by Wynn (despite Nevada laws that forbade the association of gaming licensees with convicted felons). After Milken's release from prison, Wynn had helped the former Californian rehabilitate his public image as a resident of Nevada, and introduced the still enormously wealthy financier to Jackson when the three posed together on the pirate ship during the grand opening of the Treasure Island Hotel and Casino in Las Vegas. Relations had chilled in 2005, though, after Wynn was listed as one of the character witnesses for Jackson that Tom Mesereau might call to the stand at the criminal trial in California. Michael was hurt that Wynn dispatched his head of public relations to tell the local media in Las Vegas that the casino mogul had no plans to be a witness and "actually was surprised to see his name mentioned." Jackson and Wynn appeared to be on friendly terms once again, though, in January 2007, when they dined together in a private room at Alex, the most opulent of the gaming magnate's many restaurants. Immediately afterward, however, Wynn went out of his way to squelch a report that he and Jackson were on the verge of a deal that would have made Michael a sort of in-house entertainer at his hotels.

Jack Wishna's relief was short-lived. Yet another impresario, the flamboyant fat man Jeff Beacher, who had transformed the Hard Rock Cafe into his Madhouse at Hard Rock with the wildest and most lurid show ("think *The Original Kings of Comedy* combined with *Girls Gone Wild*," *Backstage West* had suggested) the Strip had ever seen, followed Wishna to *Us Weekly* in order to tell the magazine that he, too, was meeting with Jackson. Michael was so committed to making his comeback in Las Vegas, Beacher said, that he was already looking for the property that would become his new Neverland. Also in the mix was Simon Fuller, the producer-manager whose big piece of *American Idol* was supplemented by the fees he earned managing *Idol* stars Kelly Clarkson, Ruben Studdard, and Clay Aiken, as well as soccer player David Beckham. Fuller had set up a series of meetings between Jackson and his *Thriller* choreographer Kenny Ortega, who by now was better known for staging *High School Musical*. The "scenarios" involving Wynn, Wishna, Beacher, and Fuller would all come to nothing, but at least the various meetings and negotiations provided Michael with an excuse to avoid his father.

Joe Jackson had been living primarily in Las Vegas for more than a decade, having been gradually banished from the Hayvenhurst estate for various indiscretions. Foremost among these was Joe's close relationship with his illegitimate daughter, Joh'Vonnie, whose birth (the day after

Michael's sixteenth birthday) in 1974 had forced Katherine Jackson to acknowledge that the stories about Joe's infidelity were true.

Michael had made an explicit statement of his intention to be eventually reconciled to Joseph when he spoke at Oxford in March 2000. The occasion was one of several events intended to launch the humanitarian initiative that Michael Jackson pledged would be at the center of his life's work from that day forward: his Heal the World Foundation. Rabbi Boteach would later claim that he had written the speech for Michael "based on our interviews." The theme was forgiveness and the focus was on Michael's relationship with his father. He described Joe as "a tough man," but glossed over the physical abuse he had endured as a child. "I want to forgive him because I want a father and this is the only one that I've got. I want the weight of my past lifted from my shoulders, and I want to be free to step into a new relationship with my father for the rest of my life, unhindered by the goblins of the past."

That was easier said than done, of course. Michael might make Prince's middle name Joseph, just as Paris's was Katherine, and he could encourage his children to phone their grandparents on holidays, but he still almost never wanted to spend much time with anyone from his family.

During the past three decades, Michael had grown increasingly determined to distance himself from the sordid soap opera that was life among the Jacksons. The process of separation had been going on since 1974, when Katherine and the rest of the family had learned of Joe's relationship with twenty-five-year-old Cheryl Terrell, who gave birth to Joh'Vonnie Jackson later that same year. In 1982, when Marlon filed for divorce from his wife, Carol, Michael urged his brother to attend counseling sessions to try to save his marriage. He tried to be supportive as well when eighteen-year-old Janet eloped with James DeBarge, whom the rest of the family despised. Michael had thrown up his hands, though, by 1983, when Jackie's affair with Los Angeles Lakers cheerleader Paula Abdul blew up his marriage amid a series of scenes that culminated in Enid Jackson's breaking her husband's leg by running him over with a car after catching Jackie in bed with Abdul. In March 1987, Jermaine showed up for Marlon's birthday party carrying his three-month-old son by a young woman named Margaret Maldonado, while his thirty-four-year-old wife, the former Hazel Gordy, looked on with an expression of bewilderment. During their divorce, Hazel would allege Jermaine had attempted to rape her in front of their children. By 1990, Michael had moved to Neverland and was keeping his distance from the other

Jacksons. He made no comment when newspapers reported that Randy's wife Eliza was accusing him of beating her throughout her pregnancy and claimed that one of his girlfriends had phoned to say that she, too, was about to give birth to Randy's child. Eliza shook her head when Randy denied these accusations in court. The Jackson brothers were all just like Joe, Eliza told a reporter, except for Michael.

Michael's sister La Toya, meanwhile, would not be ignored. She'd been a problem without a solution for years. As a teenager, La Toya raged against being shut out of the spotlight, demanding to be put onstage and brought into the studio. Her ranting and raving was spectacular, but her talent nonexistent. Well, she could dance a little, Joe allowed, and he let her join the Jacksons' Las Vegas shows in 1974, if she promised only to lip-synch onstage.

La Toya began to get all the attention she craved in 1988, when she eloped with her Jewish manager Jack Gordon to Las Vegas and permitted him to arrange the press conference where she announced that she was posing for *Playboy*. La Toya's cover shot and nude pictorial in *Playboy*'s March 1989 edition made it the best-selling issue in the magazine's history. The other Jacksons were most concerned, though, by the news that La Toya had informed the press she was working on an autobiography that would reveal "the whole truth about my dysfunctional family."

When *La Toya: Growing Up in the Jackson Family* was published in 1991, the most scandalous revelation was La Toya's claim that Joe Jackson had sexually abused both her and her older sister Rebbie. What most stunned fans, however, was the book's scathing portrait of Katherine Jackson, whom her daughter described as "the guiding force behind the cruelty and abuse" in her family.

Katherine expressed more sadness about what was happening to her daughter than she did anger about La Toya's attacks on her character, and Mrs. Jackson's dignified response won her some admirers, even among the media. Michael, though, was shaken by La Toya's graphic description of his mother's 1980 physical assault on a young woman named Gina Sprague, whom Katherine suspected of having an affair with Joe. Michael's relationship with his middle sister was not completely shattered, however, until December 1993, when La Toya responded to the Jordan Chandler scandal by holding a press conference in Tel Aviv, Israel, at which she declared her belief that the accusations against her brother were true. "I can't remain silent," she squeaked into a bank of microphones. "I will not be a silent collaborator in his crimes against small, innocent children."

Within three years, La Toya would insist that she had been bullied and manipulated by Jack Gordon into saying and writing such terrible things about her family. Katherine impressed onlookers once more by accepting La Toya's disavowals and welcoming her daughter back to the Hayvenhurst compound with open arms. Michael, though, still did not want anything to do with his sister, or for that matter with any member of the Jackson family other than his mother. According to Bob Jones, when Michael went on tour he instructed his bodyguards not to let any of the other Jacksons near his dressing room.

That hard line softened after Michael's arrest on child molestation charges in 2003. Michael suddenly wanted his family near, and the Jacksons responded by closing ranks around the face of the franchise, rallying to his side when even the people he called his closest friends were keeping him at arm's length. Reporters mocked the emotional scenes of Michael walking into and out of the Santa Maria courthouse during the trial, surrounded by family members (with Joe Jackson usually at his right elbow), as a marriage of financial arrangement with performance art.

Those closer to the scene were especially nauseated whenever Jermaine showed up. A growing number of people knew that back in 2003, when Michael's world was collapsing all around him, Jermaine had gone to New York publishers with a "tell-all" book proposal in which he admitted believing his little brother might be a child molester. "I don't want to tell you my brother's innocent. I am not certain he is," Jermaine had stated in the eight-page proposal for a book he wanted to call "Legacy." Along with detailing his claims of Michael's dishonesty, drug abuse, cruel streak, and rampant anti-Semitism, Jermaine had described what he observed during a family gathering in the mid-1990s, after the death of Tito's ex-wife: He had walked into a bedroom where he found Michael sitting on the bed with three young relatives and holding them in a manner that left "the entire house shaken," the older brother told publishers, adding, "Yes, he has a thing for young children."

Some cynics questioned even Katherine Jackson's loyalty to her son. "Sure, his mother was in court every day," observed the black Los Angeles attorney and radio host Leo Terrell, whose familiarity with the Jacksons went back to his days as a Johnnie Cochran acolyte, "but I have heard that he had to pay her to be there. I'm sure Tom [Mesereau] wanted a united front, but I'm also sure that every one of them had his or her hand out. They all looked to Michael as an ATM machine."

That was literally true, according to Grace Rwaramba. When Sheikh Abdullah began to wire money from Bahrain during the trial, Michael instructed her to run it through her bank account, Rwaramba said. Upon learning about the money coming from the Persian Gulf, Grace recalled, Katherine Jackson immediately complained to Michael that she needed cash, and Michael ordered the nanny to give his mother her ATM card. Tens of thousands of dollars quickly disappeared, according to Rwaramba: "[Katherine] was cashing out of the machine every day." Soon she was told that "other Jackson relatives needed money, too," Grace said. "So Michael told me to give *them* my ATM card. They were taking cash out of the machine every day."

The Jackson brothers had needed less than a decade to blow through the millions they brought home from the *Victory* tour. By the time Michael returned to the United States from Ireland at the end of 2006, all of them were strapped, none more so than Marlon, who was about to lose his home to foreclosure and move into an extended-stay hotel. Marlon was fifty-one when Michael settled into his rented Las Vegas mansion, and he worked stocking shelves at a San Diego–area supermarket. Randy Jackson at age forty-six supplemented his savings by fixing cars in a Los Angeles garage owned by a family friend, while fifty-six-year-old Jackie had turned to managing his son Siggy, an aspiring rapper. Fifty-five-year-old Tito was the only Jackson brother besides Michael who continued to make music for a living, fronting a blues band that played occasional club gigs for a group fee that was usually under $1,000. Jermaine, his singing career kaput, was recovering from bankruptcy at age fifty-four by shuttling between his girlfriend's home in Ventura County and the Hayvenhurst estate, where Jackie and Randy also slept many nights. More than $5 million in federal, state, and local liens were on file against Jermaine, who was overjoyed to discover (right around the time Michael landed in Las Vegas) that he had won a place on the UK reality show *Celebrity Big Brother*, noting how difficult it would be for creditors to attach his earnings in England.

Most of the Jackson 5 had filed for bankruptcy. After Joe and Katherine were declared insolvent back in the late 1990s they had been followed to federal court by Tito and Marlon, and then by Jermaine, leaving Jackie as the only original member, other than Michael, who had avoided a Chapter 7 filing. And Jackie was barely holding on after an Internet clothing business he had launched three years earlier began to go belly up.

Joe Jackson had been hiding from creditors since 1987, when concert promoter Gary Berwin won a $3 million judgment against him for writing a bad check to purchase the former Hollywood Athletic Club. The *Segye Times* was awarded an even larger judgment against Joe, Katherine, and Jermaine a few years later for swindling the Moonie newspaper out of the money it had spent to try to arrange a Michael Jackson concert in Seoul. The bankruptcy court refused to discharge that debt, ruling that Joe, Katherine, and Jermaine were guilty of fraud. A former business partner named Henry Vaccaro also had a judgment against Joe and Katherine that had survived bankruptcy court and was chasing their hidden assets all over California. Vaccaro finally trapped them by issuing fake "rebate" checks in the amount of $50 made out to each family member. When Katherine Jackson deposited one of those checks into her bank account, Vaccaro followed a paper trail that led eventually to a pair of storage units in Oxnard where Joe and his estranged wife had stashed a huge trove of Jackson memorabilia. Since then, Joe had been living mostly on handouts from Katherine (who divvied up the $25,000 check Michael sent to her each month among various needy members of the family) and was incessantly looking for opportunities to draw his most famous son into assorted dubious business deals.

Michael had refused to discuss the financial problems of family members during a holiday gathering he hosted at his home in Vegas, shortly after returning from Ireland. He hardly said a word to anyone, afraid that his father and brothers would begin pestering him with propositions. To avoid eye contact, he kept his sunglasses on even during dinner. The Jacksons recognized it as an ominous sign. Wearing dark glasses indoors, the family knew, had long been Michael's way of signaling that he wanted to be more involved with whatever drugs he was taking than with the people around him.

The Santa Barbara district attorney's office had largely ignored a case against Michael Jackson for procuring and using prescription drugs that was far stronger than the one it filed charging him with child molestation. Tom Mesereau actually introduced more evidence about Jackson's "drug problem" at trial than the prosecution did, telling the jury early on that his client "had gotten a lot of prescriptions from various physicians" under assorted identities. Yet most of what Mesereau knew about Michael's use of painkillers and antianxiety medications had been gleaned from reports filed by police investigators working out of Santa Barbara and Los Angeles counties.

Court documents revealed that Jackson had used dozens of names to obtain prescription drugs since 1993. In 1998 alone Michael collected an assortment of drugs—mostly synthetic opiates, or "opioids"—under false names that included M. Johnson, Michael Scruz, Bill Scruz, Joseph Scruz, John Scruz, Omar Arnold, and Arnold Omar. He also had collected prescriptions in 1998 under the names of his employees Bill Bray and Bob Jones.

District Attorney Sneddon understood that a key job description for Jackson's security staff was the procurement of prescription drugs. Chris Carter, the entertainer's chief of security at the time of the raid on Neverland, told Santa Barbara County investigators that he regularly obtained Xanax prescriptions for Michael under an array of fictitious names, but occasionally resorted to using the names of Neverland employees like Frank Cascio, Jesus Salas, and Joe Marcus to get the drugs. Michael LaPerruque, who became Jackson's chief of security a year later, said that most of the drug prescriptions he saw Michael use were under the name Chris Carter. Joey Jeszeck, the blond surfer whom Michael had recruited to work for him after meeting the teenager in a Santa Barbara beach shop, told Sneddon's investigators that Jackson regularly sent him to the pharmacy to pick up prescriptions obtained under assorted names from doctors all over the country. When a pharmacy wouldn't release the drugs he wanted under one name, Michael would call the doctor and have the name on the prescription changed to the person standing at the counter, deputies were told by Jeszeck, who remembered dealing with a "Dr. Farshchian in Florida" in that regard on multiple occasions.

Dr. Alimorad "Alex" Farshchian was the founder of the Center for Regenerative Medicine in Miami, a clinic ostensibly devoted to helping patients recover from injury or arthritis. Farshchian had regularly traveled with Jackson during the years 2002 and 2003 and was with him during the baby-dangling incident in Berlin. Jackson spent time as a guest at Farshchian's home in Bay Harbor Islands and visited the doctor's office during his frequent stays at Miami's Turnberry Isle Resort. Carter described Michael to investigators as being sharp and "in tune" before his visits to Farshchian but "out of it" afterward. LaPerruque told Santa Barbara detectives that he believed Dr. Farshchian "may have been overprescribing medication" to Michael. Carter advised the same detectives that Farshchian had said Jackson was addicted to Demerol and that he was attempting to wean Michael off the drug. Michael was seeing Farshchian on an almost daily basis when the Bashir documentary aired in February 2003. The Florida doctor flew back to California with Michael a few days later, then stayed on at Neverland Ranch during that period when, according to Dieter Wiesner, Michael was so loaded on opioids that he couldn't feed himself. In the months before the criminal trial in Santa Barbara County, Farshchian told reporters that he was mainly prescribing vitamins for Michael and the press took to describing him, tongue in cheek, as "Jackson's vitamin doctor."

"My biggest gripe about the doctors around Michael is that they didn't treat him as a patient," said Marc Schaffel. "They just gave him stuff. And Farshchian is exactly who I'm thinking of."

Investigators in California had recovered a July 21, 2002, handwritten note from Farshchian to Jackson in which the doctor informed the star that he had just sent him a special "package." It was "a 5 to 7 day program that offers you the solution," Farshchian had written. "Buprenex is the potent narcotic I told you about last week, it is just like the D but better." The "D" Farshchian referred to was the highly addictive painkiller Demerol, investigators believed, and Buprenex, they knew, was a newly developed and even more powerful injectable analgesic.

For Dr. Farshchian, Schaffel said, "it wasn't about money so much, I don't think, as the glamour and excitement. I remember Farshchian and his wife had quite a bit of problems at one point, because she did not approve of him leaving his house and family in Miami to go hang out with Michael."

Before Farshchian, Jackson had relied upon Dr. Allan Metzger to provide his medications. Metzger, a specialist in the treatment of lupus, had accompanied Michael in 1996 on the entire *HIStory* tour and, according to Dieter Wiesner, "gave him whatever he asked for." Among Metzger's other duties on the tour had been videotaping the Michael Jackson–Debbie Rowe wedding in Australia. The Los Angeles County authorities that later reviewed Metzger's files found one labeled "Omar Arnold/Michael Jackson." In September 2000 the medical board of California had officially reprimanded Metzger for "fraudulent medical practice based on prescriptions written for an international entertainer, using a false/fictitious name." That "entertainer," though, was not Michael Jackson, but his sister Janet, according to Metzger, who insisted that he had not seen Michael Jackson "regularly" as a patient for several years.

Metzger and Farshchian were but two of the countless physicians who over the years had assisted Jackson in obtaining drugs. Helping Michael find doctors who would write prescriptions for him was a crucial task of the enablers who traveled with Jackson as part of his security staff. An MD who demanded anonymity would provide the *Las Vegas Review-Journal* with a snapshot of the methods Michael and his team used to make new drug connections. After being summoned to Jackson's hotel suite, supposedly to treat a sore throat, the doctor said, he quickly realized that the entire examination had been "staged" and that "they just wanted drugs." When he was asked to "call in all these pills under someone else's name," the doctor said, he refused and was immediately confronted by a hulking "handler" who gruffly asked, "What do you mean? They always do that." Frightened, he agreed to see what he could do, and headed for the door, but was stopped by the big bodyguard, who "put a finger in my chest and said, 'You do that.'"

Both the amounts and the combinations of the drugs Jackson asked for astounded any number of reputable doctors who treated him. Rabbi Boteach recalled an occasion when the Nobel laureate Elie Wiesel had asked his personal physician to attend to the back pain Jackson complained of during a stay at the Waldorf-Astoria. "One of New York's most prestigious doctors" emerged from Michael's bedroom "ashen faced" after about fifteen minutes alone with the star, Boteach remembered, and immediately announced that, "Michael has just asked me for a quantity of drugs that would kill a horse." When he went into the bedroom to ask if it was true, Boteach said, Michael calmly replied, "I have a very high tolerance. I'm used to this. I'll be fine." Orthopedic surgeon Mark Sinnreich, who treated Jackson at his clinic in Miami, reported that in 2000 Michael had asked for 200 milligrams of Demerol, four times the dose that would normally be administered to a patient his size. "But he said that he needs more since he had this burn," Sinnreich recalled. "And I know burns are very, very painful. He said that ever since he was in that Pepsi commercial and burned his hair that he had a lot of pain and that he had a very high tolerance to pain medication."

That was true, but as doctors who have studied the subject understand, a high tolerance for pain medication equates to a low tolerance for pain. Ordinary aches can become debilitating for a person who consistently refuses to feel them. Clinical studies have consistently shown that heavy use of pain medications changes brain chemistry in ways that profoundly affect perception and can result in a condition known as hyperalgesia, in which taking painkillers causes a person to actually feel pain more acutely. This can advance to the point in an addicted brain where getting off the drugs equates to a sense that one is committing suicide. Michael Jackson consistently described himself that way, telling one person after another that it wasn't a question of *wanting* drugs but rather of *needing* them. "If I stop using drugs, I'll die," he told one concerned friend. "I won't survive another day without them. No one understands that. I need to be here for my kids. There's no other way. There's just no other way."

Tarak Ben Ammar, a Tunisian film producer and distributor who managed the *HIStory* tour, said he was tempted to describe Jackson as a hypochondriac but hesitated because, "One never really knew if he was sick." Michael complained constantly of this condition or that one. He truly did suffer from a constellation of autoimmune disorders (most linked to childhood trauma) but whether these caused him real pain or merely discomfort was impossible even for a trained physician to know. Twenty years later, Michael was still using the small patch of scarring from the burn he had suffered during the Pepsi commercial filming as a reason why he needed a new prescription of pain medication. He also would say the rib he had broken while training for the *Dangerous* tour was bothering him, or that an ankle he had twisted during the *HIStory* tour was acting up again.

Back pain was what he most often cited when he asked for the opioids that were his drug of choice. Jackson regularly told people that he had fractured a vertebra years earlier. That wasn't true, though he did suffer from a mild case of arthritis in his lower back. Rabbi Boteach would recall how, after he was jostled by autograph seekers at a charity event in New York, Michael almost immediately began to complain that his back was injured and he needed pain medication. Jackson showed up in Britain for the Oxford speech with his foot in a cast and on crutches, Boteach remembered, claiming he had broken his foot while practicing dance moves at Neverland and needed to see a doctor who could give him Demerol. Over the next few days, he heard Michael tell a number of different stories about what had happened to his foot, the rabbi recalled, "but again, I made nothing of it, thinking that Michael was forgetful."

People constantly made such mental adjustments to accommodate Michael Jackson. No one showed more flexibility in that regard than his old friend Dr. Arnold Klein. In the process of becoming the most famous dermatologist on earth, Klein had explored the frontiers of pharmacology, an adventure he began right around the time he started treating people's skin. Back in 1972, one year after graduating Phi Beta Kappa from the University of Pennsylvania School of Medicine, Klein was credited as the coauthor of a book published by the University of Pennsylvania Press titled *Drug-Trip Abroad: American Drug-Refugees in Amsterdam and London.* During the next two years, while working as a resident at the hospital of the University of Pennsylvania, Klein made a number of trips to Mexico, where he was said to have experimented with and purchased a wide range of pharmaceuticals. He abandoned his Ivy League residency in 1974 under circumstances that were the subject of considerable rumor and speculation, nearly all of it involving the use and distribution of prescription drugs. Klein told colleagues (who did not know he was gay) that he was moving to the West Coast to marry a woman he had met there.

In 1975, Klein became the chief resident in dermatology at UCLA's School of Medicine. The young doctor swiftly discovered, though, that the skin care business in Southern California is fiercely competitive. Still working part-time at UCLA, he took a position with a small practice in the San Fernando Valley where he spent his time "giving light treatments and picking pimples," Klein recalled. As bored as he was ambitious, the young Dr. Klein used $18,000 in savings to "venture into the jaws of what was Beverly Hills," opening his own practice in an 800-square-foot office. The new practice flourished in part because Klein was so adept at developing personal relationships. He obtained his earliest referrals, the doctor remembered, by knocking on the door of every physician's office in Beverly Hills. Within a year, he had so many patients—many of them celebrities—that he opened a larger office and hired an associate. But television was what lifted him into the stratosphere of the medical business. Klein's first TV appearance, on *The Merv Griffin Show*, changed his life overnight. "The next day, people were asking for my autograph, and soon thereafter, I received ten thousand letters," he remembered.

By the time Klein went on television to discuss his experimentation with collagen injections his office was nearly ten times the size of the one he had started. The practice exploded after that. Within a couple of years Klein's client list included the largest assembly of stars boasted by any doctor on the planet (though the majority of his patients were merely rich people). That list continued to increase—in fame and wealth, if not in number—when he pioneered the field of Botox injection. His relationships with his celebrity clients, Cher and Dolly Parton among them, were the common currency of Hollywood in-jokes that made their way into at least two feature films, *Postcards from the Edge* (based on a book by his client Carrie Fisher) and *The First Wives Club*. He was best known around town, though, for his close personal friendships with two particular clients: Elizabeth Taylor and Michael Jackson.

Klein's relationships with Taylor and Jackson were forged through what the doctor had done to help Liz preserve her looks well past the age of fifty and how he had cured the acne that had tormented Michael all through his late teens and early twenties.

Klein was more than a physician to his most favored patients, however. Nothing said more about his relationship with Taylor, for example, than the note the actress had written in the copy she had given him of her book *My Affair with Jewelry*. "My beloved Arnie," it read, "I love you more than I can tell. I feel you have saved my fading life. I love and thank you forever. Yours, Elizabeth." The doctor's mastery of collagen and Botox injections were but two of the four pillars that supported his exalted status in Beverly Hills. The other two were Klein's intellectual sophistication and his sensitivity to client "needs." The doctor made no secret of his belief that pain, like need, was a highly subjective concept, and that achieving the proper chemical balance for the full enjoyment of life might involve the judicious use of pharmaceuticals.

How liberally Dr. Klein might be interpreting "pain" and "need" was first publicly suggested in the 1980s when Liz Taylor attempted to kick her by-then-voracious prescription drug addiction. During consultations with the physicians who supervised her rehabilitation, Taylor acknowledged that Dr. Klein—a man she dearly loved—had written her multiple prescriptions for various drugs that included Dilaudid and Ativan. Klein's name appeared in news columns a second time, in the autumn of 1993, when a deputy sheriff arrived at the doctor's office in Beverly Hills armed with a search warrant connected to the Jordan Chandler investigation. "Dr. Klein said that prior to the service of the search warrant on November 19, 1993, he removed Jackson's medical files from his office at [his lawyer's] direction and kept the files in his home and car," read the deputy's report of that encounter. During the 2003 investigation of the criminal charges filed against Jackson in Santa Barbara County, Klein admitted to police that he had prescribed Dilaudid and Ativan to both Michael and Liz Taylor. Tom Sneddon's office later listed Klein as one of the doctors who had prescribed Demerol to Jackson, under the name Ferdinand Diaz.

He and Michael had first met in 1983, Klein would recall, shortly after he sat in the audience that had cheered madly as Jackson introduced the Moonwalk during his performance of "Billie Jean" at the "Motown 25" show in Pasadena. A week later, he was "sitting in David Geffen's driveway," Klein would recall, when he saw Michael Jackson sitting in the backseat of a Lincoln Town Car, looking "very lonely." Geffen brought Michael to his office just days later, according to Klein, to look at the "butterfly rash" on his face that was accompanied by a severe crusting of his scalp. He had diagnosed Jackson with lupus that day, Klein said, and a relationship that would endure for more than a quarter-century was forged. "Michael was probably the purest person I ever met," Klein would tell *Vanity Fair*'s Mark Seal. "He did not have a mean bone in his body." Carrie Fisher saw the relationship in somewhat starker terms: "They each had something that the other desperately coveted," the actress would write in her book *Shockaholic.* "Arnie wanted to be friends . . . with the *biggest star on the planet* [and] Michael wanted access to the farthest reaches of the medical community 24-7."

In spite of rampant rumors about the kinds and amounts of drugs Klein was prescribing to Jackson, however, there was little if any follow-up investigation of Klein's role in Michael's life by police officials in either Los Angeles or Santa Maria, in either 1993 or 2003. Klein had become immensely wealthy and well connected. He demonstrated how willing he was to fight any accusations made against him during a lawsuit filed in 2004 by Irena Medavoy, wife of former TriStar Pictures chairman Morris Mike Medavoy, who accused the doctor of giving her Botox treatments that brought on crippling migraine headaches. Klein won the case even in the face of evidence that demonstrated how dependent his medical practice was on injection treatments, and that he had collected a good deal of money from Botox manufacturer Allergan. He was by then an eminence in Los Angeles, a cofounder with his friend Rose Tarlow (LA's most prominent interior designer) of the Breast Cancer Foundation at UCLA and a philanthropist credited with raising more than $300 million for HIV research. He was among Southern California's leading art collectors and delighted in mentioning that one of his patients had offered to name a new building at UCLA's School of Medicine for him, but that he had modestly declined, accepting an Arnold Klein teaching chair instead.

Klein was not only a prominent member of a profession that prides itself on self-policing, but projected enormous confidence that he knew where the line was between serving his patients' "needs" and feeding their addictions. He did not overprescribe, the doctor insisted, to Michael Jackson or anyone else. His friend and patient Marc Schaffel defended this claim as true. "When people go into Arnie's office, he's completely different than he is when they're in his home," Schaffel said. "I've never seen Arnie not be professional with any patient, including Michael." The problem in Jackson's case, though, was that Klein's relationship with Michael was just one among the dozens that the star maintained with doctors all over the country and in Europe, each of whom wrote him prescriptions for the medications and sleeping aids that Jackson carted around for years in a large black suitcase that was filled with preloaded syringes, IV bags, and a collapsible IV pole. None of them, individually, needed to overprescribe in order to keep Jackson's black suitcase full.

"I had lots of fights with these doctors," Dieter Wiesner would insist. "Michael didn't need it, that was the problem. When Michael was down you could talk to him, and he got a good feeling again, and everything was all right. But these doctors told Michael, 'Take this and take this, and you will feel good.' And Michael would do it. Money, money, money, that's what the doctors were about. That's all they wanted."

Jackson's drug problem had been a serious one ever since the first sex abuse charges were made against him by Jordan Chandler in 1993. The tabloids began reporting on Michael's prescription drug addiction in 1999, when the *National Enquirer* published an article claiming that the entertainer was feeding himself painkillers through an intravenous drip. After their 2000 civil filing against Jackson, Marcel Avram's lawyers submitted a document proving that two doctors in Munich, Germany, were owed $264,000 for "services rendered" that the concert promoter's attorneys suggested mainly involved the supply of prescription drugs during Jackson's *HIStory* tour. Avram's lawyers also introduced a monthly budget for Jackson that showed he was running up $10,000 per month in charges at the Mickey Fine Pharmacy, a legendary establishment just downstairs from Dr. Arnold Klein's offices on North Roxbury Drive in Beverly Hills. In 2003, Myung Ho Lee's attorneys had submitted documents to the court in Santa Barbara County demonstrating that Jackson owed the pharmacy $62,645. The most graphic evidence of Michael's drug use, though, was a photograph obtained by the *Daily Mail* in London that showed what an intravenous line being fed into Jackson's lower right leg had caused him after months of usage: a huge and horrific-looking black wound that doctors agreed was necrosis—a shin-size patch of dead tissue surrounded by dozens of puncture marks.

Jackson's self-medication became so sophisticated (at least in his own mind) over time that the IV lines he used were filled not with a single prescription drug but with the combinations of opioids, benzos, and sleeping aids that he called "mixes." Michael "always ate too little and mixed too much," according to Grace Rwaramba, who claimed that "I had to pump his stomach many times." Yet members of the Jackson family suspected that Rwaramba was more than a passive observer of Michael's drug addiction. For years she had been his closest adult companion, often the only aide who traveled with Michael and his children. Even when there was a larger entourage around Jackson, the nanny was the only one who had unfettered access to him. The police investigation would disclose that Rwaramba's name was used to rent the mailbox to which prescription drugs were shipped to

Jackson, and her credit card (unbeknownst to her, she claimed to police) was used to pay for those shipments.

Rwaramba's own story was that she had attempted on more than one occasion to curb Michael's addiction to prescription drugs and actually approached Katherine and Janet Jackson to help her persuade Michael that he needed to enter a treatment program. His response had been to accuse her of "personal betrayal," Grace recalled, and to dismiss her from her position as the children's nanny. Weeks passed before Michael yielded to the kids, who kept asking for her, Rwaramba said, and invited her to return. She never went behind his back again.

In early 2007, as Michael and the children were still settling into the house on South Monte Cristo Way in Las Vegas, the Jackson family decided that Grace was collaborating with Raymone Bain to keep Michael cooped up and under control and that the two believed his drug addiction made him more pliable. Whatever might be said about the Jacksons' financial interests, his family members were the only people who had consistently attempted to get Michael off drugs. As early as 2001, Janet, Tito, Rebbie, and Randy Jackson attempted an intervention in New York City, shortly before the "30th Anniversary" concerts. Their brother's response had been to tell them to leave him alone. "Look, I'll be dead in a year, anyway," Michael said.

Twelve months later, his sisters and brothers attempted a stealth intervention by showing up at Neverland unannounced, hoping they could take him directly from the ranch to a treatment facility. According to the story Rabbi Boteach heard from Joseph and Katherine Jackson, Michael found out ahead of time that the family was coming and fled the ranch before they got there; the Jacksons suspected that Grace Rwaramba had warned him to leave. Tito Jackson would tell a different story when he granted an interview to the London *Daily Mirror*. Six family members in all—he, Jackie, and Randy, along with Janet, Rebbie, and La Toya—pushed their way past Michael's bodyguards to gain access to Neverland. Tito said: "We bust right into the house, and he was surprised to see us, to say the least. We kept asking him if it was true what we had heard, that he was using drugs. He kept denying it. He said we were overreacting. We also spoke to a doctor [Tito declined to give the physician's name], and he assured us it was not the situation. He said he was there to make sure Michael was healthy."

The Jacksons believed that the pressure they were applying was at least part of what motivated Michael to kick his drug habit a couple of months later. He had come clean without rehab and was very proud of himself, but when the Bashir documentary aired just a few months later, Michael not only resumed the use of Demerol and Xanax that he had abandoned earlier but upped the dosages, never again getting completely free of drugs.

In December 2005, just six months after Jackson moved to Bahrain, the *National Enquirer* reported that Michael had suffered several drug overdoses and that the situation had "become critical." Raymone Bain promptly issued a written statement declaring, "That story is entirely false." Michael "is doing fine," Bain assured the media. "I have never seen him happier or healthier." Bain then added a threatening coda: "Mr. Jackson's tolerance [for such stories] has come to an end. The green light that people have thought they have had to willfully impugn Michael Jackson's character and integrity has now become red." Bain would be forced to revisit this promise thirteen months later when, in the second week of January 2007 (three weeks after Michael landed in Las Vegas), the Mickey Fine Pharmacy filed a lawsuit in Los Angeles County Superior Court claiming that Michael Jackson owed them $101,926.66 for "prescription medicines." This time, Bain informed the media simply that "the issue has been amicably resolved. Mickey Fine Pharmacy has been paid."

The Jackson family did not ignore the reports—or the signs—that Michael was once again flirting with disaster and in late January 2007 made what was at least their third attempt at a coordinated drug intervention. Multiple versions of what took place emerged, two stories put forth by people close to one or more Jackson family members, and another by Michael's team of bodyguards. By one account, Janet Jackson had visited Michael at his Vegas home on South Monte Cristo Way after the Mickey Fine lawsuit appeared in newspapers and was shocked by both her brother's appearance and the "creepy" environment in which he and his children were living. She phoned her brothers Jackie and Randy to come and convince Michael to get help but Michael ordered his bodyguards to turn the two away at the front gate, insisting that they needed to make "an appointment" if they wanted to see him. In the second version, Jackie and Randy got in the door, along with their sister Rebbie, but Michael became enraged when they suggested he was a drug addict and ordered them to leave. The bodyguards' version was that Michael refused to let any of his siblings inside his house, agreeing to meet with them only briefly outside in the security trailer. According to the bodyguards, Randy Jackson came back later with his girlfriend Taunya Zilkie, who had worked for a short time as Michael's PR person after his arrest in 2003. Randy tried to sneak past them as the gate was opening and closing during a delivery, the bodyguards said, and banged his vehicle against the iron bars as he wedged through. One of the bodyguards, Bill Whitfield, drew his gun. "Get that thing out of my face or I'll call the press," Randy snarled. When he realized he was confronting Mr. Jackson's brother, he put the weapon away, Whitfield said, and phoned the house. Michael was "not happy" to hear that his brother had showed up unexpectedly, according to Whitfield, and said, "Send him away." Furious, Randy backed his dented car into the street and drove off.

One story not in dispute was that Joe Jackson had showed up at the mansion on South Monte Cristo Way only a few days after Randy's attempt to gain access. Joe demanded a meeting with his son but was refused entry by Grace Rwaramba, who came out to meet Michael's father when the bodyguards phoned her. Michael did not want to see him, Grace told the elder Jackson, who sat in his car outside the gates for three hours, finally driving away when they did not open for him.

13

Managing the Michael Jackson news had become a more complex task for Raymone Bain after January 25, 2007, when the Associated Press went worldwide with the story that the entertainer had returned to the United States to live. "I can confirm that he is in the United States," Bain told the AP by telephone. "We don't want to give out information regarding our client's whereabouts because of safety and this is just an ongoing policy."

Even for those still in the dark about where Jackson had been living since his return to the United States, Las Vegas would have been a good guess. Michael's relationship with the city was a long one. His first residency in Vegas had been in April 1974, when the entire Jackson family settled in at the MGM Grand for a two-week stand of shows that Berry Gordy and Ewart Abner had predicted would result in humiliating failure. Instead, those Vegas performances had become a sell-out smash, as was the Jacksons' return engagement at the MGM Grand four months later. He had come back to the city again and again as he separated from his family, often to spend time with friends Siegfried & Roy, staying regularly at the Mirage, where the magicians were the resident act, and where the property was managed by his pal Steve Wynn. Jordan Chandler would allege that the first time he slept in the same bed with Michael was at the Mirage in 1993. That scandal was still in full flower when Michael returned with his family to the MGM Grand one year later for the taping of NBC's *Jackson Family Honors* special and the *Review-Journal* would report that "the show turned into more of a rally in Jackson's defense, led by Elizabeth Taylor." Michael had increasingly viewed Las Vegas as a sanctuary after that, the one place on American soil where he could always count on steadfast civic support. Just months after the airing of Martin Bashir's *Living with Michael Jackson* had made him an object of condemnation and ridicule in the American media, Las Vegas mayor Oscar Goodman presented Michael with the key to the city. He was spending almost as much time in Vegas as at Neverland by then, and was, of course, living in a villa at the Mirage in November 2003 when the authorities in Santa Barbara County raided Neverland and issued a warrant for Jackson's arrest. The spectacle of the next few days had become the most indelible memory that most in Las Vegas had of Michael Jackson, riding around in the backseat of Marc Schaffel's Navigator, surrounded by bodyguards, wearing a frightened, dazed expression, seemingly with nowhere left to hide as TV helicopters circled in the air above him. Still, it was Las Vegas he had chosen for his return to America in the last days of 2006, and in early 2007 he was already looking for the home that would replace the paradise he had created for himself in the Santa Ynez valley.

The media had jumped all over a December 2006 report on the Bravo channel program *Million Dollar Listing* that Jackson had put Neverland on the market. That was not true, but for the first time Michael was considering the sale of Neverland as part of the plan to fix his finances and subsidize the purchase of a new home in Las Vegas. The deal that, in principle, had been worked out months earlier between Sony and Fortress Investments was stalled because of the insistence by Fortress that all pending legal judgments and claims against Jackson be resolved before the refinancing agreement was finalized. The list of claimants and creditors was pages long and making deals with each and every person on the list had turned into a torturous task. As many as a dozen attorneys were working to get the mess cleaned up, but it was slow going, and in the meantime Jackson was still living from paycheck to six-figure paycheck. Serious shopping excursions were out of the question, and that he found nearly unbearable.

Michael would pick up a nice chunk of change, but by his standards no bonanza, when he tried to make up for his canceled Christmas show by appearing at a "buffet dinner and concert" featuring a series of Japanese Michael Jackson impersonators in Tokyo on March 8. Tickets were $3,500 per person but seating was limited. Michael's share was only about half of the $400,000 take. For that he had to spend "thirty seconds to one minute" with each of the paying guests and listen to a half-dozen impersonators perform his hit songs. Repairing his image in the country's media was supposed to be the main point of the trip, and Michael got off to a bad start by showing up an hour late for the event, leaving his paying guests standing outside in a cold drizzle until he arrived. He tried to make up for it by giving each of them a hug and a handshake and he invited one hundred orphaned or handicapped children to attend the dinner and concert as his guests. If he ever lost the Japanese, Michael knew, there would be no place left on earth for him. He arrived on time the next evening for what

the Tokyo newspapers described as "a fan appreciation event for lesser affluent fans" that cost only $130 per ticket. There were many more "lesser
affluent fans," of course, and Michael pocketed nearly another $200,000
for that appearance. He also hosted a "Fan Art Contest" in Tokyo during his
five-day stay and collected another, more modest, check for that. Before
leaving the country, he managed to garner some of the best publicity he
had gotten in years from the American media by paying a visit to three
thousand American GIs and their families at Camp Zama, a U.S. Army
post about twenty-five miles southwest of Tokyo on the Sagami River.

Back in Las Vegas, the deals that Jack Wishna had been touting since
December looked more and more like mirages that were dissolving into
the desert air. Jackson appeared "drugged up" and "incoherent" when he
tried to discuss business with him, Wishna complained; the guy was so
weak that he needed a wheelchair to get around.

The Las Vegas media closely followed his movements. Assorted realtors
claimed to be his agent in the search for his "new Neverland," and described
one luxury estate after another that he had inspected for its suitability.
The *Las Vegas Sun* published a breathless report that Jackson was "lined
up" to play a series of 250 concerts at a casino on the Strip, beginning in
the fall of 2008, then followed that with news that the deal had fizzled.
There was even bigger buzz around the story that Michael was working
with fashion designer Andre Van Pier on the costume and set designs for a
fifty-show "residency" at an unnamed Vegas hotel. The centerpiece of the
deal, according to Van Pier's partner Michael Luckman, was a fifty-foot-tall
Michael Jackson robot that would be turned loose in the nearby desert
as a sort of perpetual motion "monolithic advertisement" for the shows.
That plan changed when it was decided that the robot design should be
incorporated into the facade of a "Michael Jackson Hotel and Casino" by
turning the building's exterior into a King of Pop face that moved back
and forth shooting off "laser beam–looking lights."

It wasn't long before a disgruntled Wishna confided to *Las Vegas Review-
Journal* columnist Norm Clarke that Jackson had decided not to renew his
lease on the South Monte Cristo Way property. Michael and his kids had
trashed the place, according to Wishna. The master bedroom had been
turned into a "huge romper room," he said, where mattresses covered the
floors so that the four of them could bounce around together while music
blasted from the speakers in all four corners. The walls of the house were
covered with handprints and the carpets splattered with stains. Van Pier
and Luckman were still working on the design for the Michael Jackson

Hotel and Casino when they read in the newspaper that "Jackson has given up on trying to relaunch his music career in Las Vegas and is heading back to Europe. He feels his fan base in Europe and Asia is much larger than the United States and is planning a tour of the continents."

There was no "tour of the continents" in the works and Michael wasn't heading back to Europe, either, except for a quick trip to England to attend Prince Azim of Brunei's twenty-fifth birthday party at the Stapleford Park House. The truth was that Jackson was flat broke and couldn't afford now to even to rent a home in Las Vegas, let alone buy one. What he was looking for was that one "magic" person to help him mount the comeback that had become his last best hope.

Randy Phillips, CEO of AEG Live, flew to Las Vegas in spring 2007 to meet with Jackson and a team of advisors who all seemed to be jockeying for first position. AEG stood for Anschutz Entertainment Group, whose principal was Philip Anschutz, the thirty-first richest person in the United States. Anschutz had parlayed fortunes earned from oil drilling and farming into a sprawling financial empire that included Qwest Communications, which he had founded, and the Southern Pacific and Union Pacific railroad lines. Through AEG, he had cofounded Major League Soccer and purchased ownership positions in several of its teams, including the Los Angeles Galaxy. AEG also had pieces of the Los Angeles Lakers and the team's arena, the Staples Center. On top of that, he owned and controlled Regal Cinemas Corp., the largest movie-theater chain in America. A deeply religious conservative Christian, Anschutz's stated ambition was to restore family films to box-office dominance, and he had taken a big step toward that goal one year earlier with the release of *The Chronicles of Narnia: The Lion, the Witch and the Wardrobe,* a film produced in partnership with Walt Disney Pictures.

Randy Phillips had not come to Las Vegas to talk about motion pictures, but rather about the state-of-the-art 18,000-seat arena called the O2 that AEG was about to open on the banks of the Thames in London. Phillips and his company were looking for a star big enough to pack the place. Michael Jackson, in spite of everything that had befallen him in recent years, still fit that bill. The two sat down face-to-face for the first time in the wine cellar of a luxury condo that AEG had rented for the occasion. Michael showed up for the meeting wearing big sunglasses and an oversize hat, Phillips recalled, and did not seem particularly engaged by the conversation: "He was listening. He wasn't excited." Barely responding to the idea of a concert series at the O2, Michael told Phillips he loved Celine Dion's show at Caesars Palace (where Dion had already performed at more than six hundred sold-out shows on a stage built especially for her) and wouldn't mind creating a situation like that. Phillips agreed to consider the idea.

Only a short time later, though, Raymone Bain phoned to tell Phillips that Michael wasn't ready to perform even a single concert, let alone a series of them, at the O2 or in Las Vegas. Bain made a similar call to Michael's long-ago manager, Ron Weisner, who was producing the BET Awards show, scheduled to take place on June 27 at the Shrine Auditorium in Los Angeles. Weisner had invited Jackson to perform songs from his soon-to-be-released *Thriller 25* album during the show and to present a Lifetime Achievement Award to Diana Ross. Michael was "too incapacitated" to appear, Bain told the producer. That same week, Michael vacated the house on South Monte Cristo Way and flew to the Washington, D.C., area, supposedly to continue looking for the home that would replace Neverland.

The move east startled both Jackson fans and the Jackson family. Joe Jackson and his proxies were telling reporters that Bain wanted to separate Michael from his family, which was deeply concerned about his "health and welfare." Joe felt Raymone thought she could keep control of his son by relocating Michael to her power base in D.C.

Bain did indeed know her way around Washington, D.C. She had come to the capital in the 1970s as a campaign worker for Jimmy Carter, who had found her a position working in the Office of Management and Budget under Carter's ill-fated friend Bert Lance. Bain survived the scandal that soon swamped Lance and went on to graduate from Georgetown Law School, although she never passed the bar exam and was not licensed as an attorney. Instead she had taken a job representing the boxer Hector "Macho" Camacho in a contract dispute with Don King and impressed a good many people by collecting Camacho's money for him. She represented a number of other pugilists during the next decade, among them Muhammad Ali. Bain became a somebody in Washington, though, when she helped disgraced D.C. mayor Marion Barry recover from complete self-destruction. Barry had been caught on tape in 1990 smoking a crack pipe in the company of people he had no idea were federal agents. Bain signed on as Barry's spokeswoman in 1991 on the very day the ex-mayor entered prison and was still by his side during his 1994 campaign to win back his old job. When Barry was reelected as Washington's mayor, he appointed Bain as his press secretary. Jesse Jackson had by then become a close associate and helped Bain establish a public relations business that landed her an impressive list of black celebrities as clients, including Serena Williams, Deion Sanders, and Michael Jackson's little sister Janet. By 2005 Bain was the most prominent and influential black public relations spokesperson in the country. Now, at age fifty-two, she had the biggest client of her career, and not just as his spokeswoman, but also as his personal manager.

When Michael was spotted on Maryland's eastern shore in early July, it was Bain who told the *Washington Post* he was looking for real estate, and that all further inquiries about him should be made through her office. Jackson sightings were sporadically reported all across the metropolitan area during the rest of the month until the morning of July 25, when he was seen entering the downtown Washington offices of the powerful Venable law firm accompanied by "a pair of oversize bodyguards," as a *Washington Post* gossip columnist described them.

Bain had set Michael up at Venable, a firm that employed more than six hundred attorneys and was consistently ranked among the most influential in the country, with alumni who included a U.S. senator, a former U.S. attorney general, and assorted CEOs. The firm welcomed few clients who had the effect that a Michael Jackson did, though, and before his arrival a memo was sent to staffers warning them not to "gawk at clients."

Awaiting Jackson in the conference room was Howard King, there to conduct the first deposition of the defendant in the lawsuit brought by Dieter Wiesner, who was seated at the attorney's side. There would be no change of wardrobe this time; Michael wore the same black jacket, white shirt, black pants, white socks, and black loafers throughout and never removed his sunglasses. King was struck by the fact that Michael "seemed more clear-headed" than he had at the London deposition in the Schaffel case, and greeted Dieter far more warmly than he had Marc Schaffel.

Things got edgy early on, though, when Michael claimed to have forgotten signing the management contract with Wiesner, and suggested that it could have been because he was under the influence of prescription drugs.

"Were you impaired by the taking of prescription medications or something else at the time you signed these documents?" King asked.

"I could have been," answered Michael, who had never before gone on the record with an admission of his drug habit.

"How long in 2004 were you impaired because of the taking of prescription medication?" King asked a little later.

"I don't know," Michael told him.

"Was it most of 2003?" King asked.

"I'm not sure," Michael told him.

"Did Dr. Farshchian prescribe medication for you?" King inquired.

"No, it wasn't Farshchian," Michael answered, clearly uncomfortable. "I think it was a local."

"During the period of time you were impaired by the taking of prescription medication," King continued, "was this an impairment that lasted, like, all your waking hours, or did it come and go?"

"It comes and goes," Michael replied, "not all of the waking hours, of course not. Yes."

Michael had continued to smile at Wiesner even during this part of his interrogation and when it was done agreed with King's suggestion that he and Dieter go into a room alone and speak privately. "We talked about family and friends for a while," Wiesner remembered, "and then Michael mentioned that he wanted to work together again, and his voice changed. He told me that he had almost no money coming in, and that he was desperate." Dieter was among the few people Michael could tell that his only credit card, a black one from American Express with no limit on it, had been canceled a few weeks earlier and that he was unable to obtain a replacement. During his weeks on the East Coast, he had been asked to leave several hotels after using the canceled American Express card to check in. Tears welled up in Michael's eyes and his voice broke as he described the humiliation of these scenes and the expressions on people's faces as they watched him and his children march through the lobby onto the sidewalk outside. "He asked for help," Wiesner recalled. "I could see that it was a very, very hard time for Michael. He had nowhere to go and he was afraid. He felt they might make him go on tour, but he didn't want to do it. He didn't know what to do."

The only plan Michael seemed to have for his immediate future, Wiesner remembered, was to seek out sanctuary and wait to see what came his way.

The arrival of the Michael Jackson traveling party at the Cascio home in Franklin Lakes, New Jersey, during the first week of August 2007 startled not only the people next door, but also Grace Rwaramba. She had no idea where they were headed, Grace recalled, until they were almost there. The Cascios were used to it. Michael Jackson had been showing up announced on their front porch for nearly a quarter century. More than once, he had awakened them by knocking on the door in the middle of the night. These people he called his "second family" always welcomed him. In return, he had insisted that they fly out to California to be present for the births of each of his children; not a single Jackson family member was invited. Connie Cascio continued to be the only person other than Grace whom Michael trusted to take care of his kids. In recent years, he had spent many more holidays with them than with anyone from his birth family, including his mother Katherine.

Michael's relationship with the Cascios had weathered criticism and controversy beginning back in 1993 when the New York tabloids quoted Blanca Francia's claims about seeing Jackson naked with young boys, naming Frank as one of them. After Frank told his parents it was a lie, they continued to let him travel with Michael. Ten years later, when the allegations of Gavin Arvizo had turned into a criminal complaint by Santa Barbara County authorities, Dominic Cascio sat his children down and asked whether there had ever been any "improprieties" during their sleepovers. Frank, Eddie, and Marie Nicole all told him very firmly that there had not been. After documents surfaced showing that in 2002 Michael had loaned the Cascios $600,000 to start a restaurant, some suggested that it was a "payoff," noting that more than one year later no such restaurant existed. The Cascios dismissed the story and, by the time of Michael's acquittal in Santa Maria, were serving customers at their Brick House Italian restaurant in Wyckoff, New Jersey, just a short drive east from the family home on Franklin Avenue.

Michael settled quickly into the "cave" the Cascios created for him in their basement, right next to the wooden dance floor they had installed. Michael said he and the kids and Grace would be staying for "a while." The nanny didn't conceal her displeasure at being forced to share the Cascios' guest bedroom with all three of the kids. Her description of the Cascio home made the place sound small and shabby when in fact the house was a comfortable white brick and clapboard neocolonial on a raised lot in one of New Jersey's wealthiest boroughs, a suburban enclave that talk show host Kelly Ripa and assorted professional athletes called home.

Grace had been shaken and embarrassed by the experience of being asked to leave hotels in both Washington, D.C., and New York City after Michael's credit card was canceled. She noticed that Michael was trying to pass off the New Jersey visit to both the Cascios and to the kids as a late summer holiday. Privately, Michael told Grace that they were staying until they had some place else to go. "I felt so bad that we were staying such a long time at this family's small home," Grace said, as their holiday was extended week after week, but the Cascios didn't seem to mind. Even though they were only about the same age as Michael's oldest siblings, Dominic and Connie knew that he enjoyed being treated like their oldest son, returning home after a long absence. Michael especially enjoyed standing around the kitchen counter with the whole family, sharing memories and encouraging the Cascios, one at a time, to tell the others what he or she was most thankful for. Connie cooked the homemade pizzas and pastas Michael loved, and regularly served his favorite dinner, roast turkey with mashed potatoes and stuffing. He always insisted that they hold hands and say grace together at mealtime. As they always did when Michael came for a visit, the Cascios set up the theater-style candy counter that he loved to visit with his kids before settling down to watch a movie on TV.

Michael was happy to help out with the household chores, Connie Cascio recalled, loading and unloading the dishwasher and dusting the furniture. Michael seemed to delight in vacuuming the floors and would do it daily if asked. He made his own bed each morning and instructed the three children to do the same. He and his family understood better than anyone else how much this facsimile of ordinary life meant to Michael, Frank Cascio would say, how deeply he cherished it. "That's when he was himself," Frank said. Michael slept fine at their house, according to the Cascios, and was not using any drugs at all as far as they knew.

The children's tutor was staying at a nearby motel with the bodyguards and came to the house daily to teach "school." Afterward, they would spend hours splashing in the Cascios' backyard pool and seemed content. While they studied and played, their father was working with Eddie in the Cascios' basement recording studio.

Eddie Cascio had already made a name for himself—"Angel Cascio" he was called—in the music business. An article touting the young man's career had been published in the school newspaper at Drew University, where Eddie had graduated in 2004 with a degree in sociology. With the help of "a family friend with connections in the business," as Eddie described Michael in the article, he had begun selling songs to Sony/ATV while still an undergraduate. Soon he was working as a producer for 'N Sync on their song "Fallin'" and that landed him jobs working on the Luther Vandross album *Dance with My Father* and on Usher's *Here I Stand*. Before his graduation, Eddie had formed his own company, Angelikson Music. The parents who had started him off with piano lessons years earlier at Michael's urging paid for the construction of a recording studio in their basement that, while not state of the art, was well enough equipped to convince Michael Jackson that he and his young friend should lay down some tracks together. They recorded twelve songs in all, the most memorable (if not the best) being "Breaking News," an antitabloid screed in which Michael vented his rage and hurt over what had been done to him during his criminal trial, referring to himself repeatedly by name. He and Eddie had written the song together, with help from James Porte, an arranger and engineer who had worked with Eddie on the Luther Vandross album.

Within a couple of weeks of landing at the Cascios, Michael began venturing out, most often with Frank, who had been helping him work up disguises for years. The two shopped at malls all over the New Jersey suburbs without Michael being recognized, according to Frank. Michael ate out regularly with members of the Cascio family at the Brick House. The bodyguards who occasionally joined the group, though, were growing unhappy about not being paid, especially when they reflected on the size of the legal bills that were being forwarded to Michael. A complaint by Jackson's former attorney Brian Ayscough one year earlier had identified more than a dozen lawyers who claimed Michael owed them amounts ranging from $100,000 to $1.25 million. More names had been added to that list in the twelve months since and Jackson simply didn't have the money to pay them.

Michael's cash flow crisis was squeezing him tighter week-by-week. His only way out was the deal to refinance his debt, which had been delayed again by Fortress Investment's surprising decision to exercise its right to match any financing terms offered by another lender and thereby hold on to Michael's loans. In the meantime, the list of creditors pursuing him now included any number of people he had once considered close friends, along with his brother Randy and Randy's girlfriend Taunya Zilkie, who had each filed claims against him.

After September, Michael began demonstrating less concern about being recognized in public. On October 31, he showed up with Frank Cascio at the Halloween Store in the Boulder Run Mall wearing a disguise that consisted of only a baseball cap worn with sunglasses and a scarf that was wrapped around his neck and lower face. After picking out $200 worth of disguises that included a Mardi Gras mask and a king's robe, Michael stepped up to the counter and let the scarf slip below his chin. When the young woman ringing up his order saw who it was, she gasped. Less than a minute after Michael and Frank stepped out of the store, she was on the phone with the *New York Daily News*.

By the next morning, everyone in the metropolitan area knew that Michael Jackson had been staying for weeks with a family in Franklin Lakes, New Jersey. It was time to find another hiding place.

14

Michael departed the Cascios' three days later when he got a phone call from Jesse Jackson, who asked whether he was planning to attend the gala party planned for the reverend's sixty-sixth birthday at the Beverly Hilton. Michael had no choice but to explain that he didn't have the cash to pay for the trip, and couldn't use his credit card. Startled and slightly alarmed, the Reverend Jackson asked mutual friend Ron Burkle to fly Michael, the kids, and Grace—plus his three bodyguards—to Los Angeles and put them up in rooms at the Beverly Hilton for three nights.

Burkle was a "babe-chasing supermarket billionaire" (as the *New York Post* enjoyed describing him) best known as the close personal friend and business partner of former U.S. President Bill Clinton, who for years had jokingly referred to the billionaire's private Boeing 747 jet, famous for the number of supermodels who had flown aboard it, as "Air Force Two." Burkle maintained a wide array of friends and familiars, in large part due to his prominence as a fund-raiser for Democratic political candidates. In 2004, Burkle hosted a fund-raiser at his Beverly Hills estate, "Green Acres," a home built by silent-screen legend Harold Lloyd, where wealthy Democrats paid $100,000 per couple to attend.

It was Jesse Jackson who had introduced Burkle to Michael Jackson five years prior, encouraging the billionaire to help Michael deal with his fiscal circumstances. Michael first seriously discussed the subject of his finances with the supermarket mogul after they met at Johnnie Cochran's funeral in 2005. Like so many advisors before him, Burkle had attempted to persuade Michael it was time to curb his spending and go back to work at what would make him money. Burkle also hired forensic accountants (whom he paid for himself) to examine Jackson's finances, and in the process convinced Michael that various unnamed advisors were fleecing him. During a deposition in the Prescient Capital case that Jackson gave in Paris during 2006 (on his way to Ireland), Michael credited Burkle with protecting him from the assorted "sharks, charlatans, and imposters"—many of whom, he said, had been introduced by his brother Randy—who were pilfering his wealth. And now, at Jesse Jackson's birthday party in the grand ballroom at the Beverly Hilton, Michael asked again if Burkle could help him sort out the mess of his current cash flow crisis.

Burkle had responded, by all accounts, with extraordinary generosity, moving Michael and his children into the Green Acres mansion when their three days at the Hilton were up, and once again hiring accountants to examine Jackson's situation. It was a thicket, to say the least. The refinancing of Jackson's enormous debt was still not accomplished. Negotiations had dragged on for eighteen months and new claimants were joining the pool of creditors every week. Lawsuits against Jackson continued to proliferate. The security guard screening Michael's e-mails would say later that most of those demanding payment were attorneys, with many of the bills in seven figures. What Michael brought on himself was more than matched by the frivolous claims against him. The world was full of people who thought it was fair to carve another two or three or four million dollars out of Michael Jackson and there were enough large predators looking for eight figures to make his world a truly scary place. The family of Roc-A-Fella Records cofounder Damon Dash had sued Jackson ten times in the year 2007 alone. Damon's cousin Darien Dash was the principal in Prescient Capital, and the force behind the massive lawsuit that had nearly forced Jackson into bankruptcy.

An accountant hired by Randy Jackson had signed the deal with Dash— whether with or without Michael's consent was a matter of dispute—to arrange for a $272 million loan to replace the debt Jackson owed to Bank of America, plus find another $573 million in financing to purchase Sony's half of the Beatles song catalog. The contract had been executed in May 2005 just as Michael was approaching the climax of his criminal trial in Santa Barbara County, when he was most distracted and Randy Jackson's control was most absolute. Michael's refusal to honor the commitments made by his brother had cost Prescient Capital—and him personally— some $48 million, according to Darien Dash, who had been blocking the renegotiation of Michael's debt for months, demanding that the banks settle with him.

Other more arcane court filings multiplied the cost of being the King of Pop. A London woman who called herself Nona Jackson had sued Jackson in Los Angeles with the claim that she was the mother of all three of his children, demanding not only custody of the kids but compensation for the three thousand songs she claimed to have written for her "longtime lover." Up in Santa Barbara County, the family of an elderly woman who had died at the Marian Medical Center shortly after Jackson's stay at the hospital filed a lawsuit claiming her death was caused by being moved to free a room for the entertainer.

The lawsuit currently consuming the most in legal fees was the one that Sheikh Abdullah bin Hamad bin Isa Al Khalifa had filed against Michael in London just a few weeks earlier. The sheikh felt "a strong sense of personal betrayal," Abdullah's attorney Bankim Thanki had told the High Court justice who would be hearing the case, after advancing $7 million under the terms of a written agreement in which Mr. Jackson had promised to deliver a new album, an autobiography, and a stage play, only to see the entertainer renege on each of his obligations, then abandon not only these projects, but also the charity records promised to the victims of the New Orleans hurricane and the Indonesian tsunami. Prince Al Khalifa had fully expected Mr. Jackson to return to Bahrain to resume work on their projects after a brief trip to Japan in spring 2006, Thanki told the court, but neither saw nor heard from "Mikaeel" again. All that Abdullah had ever received by way of explanation was a letter faxed to him by Raymone Bain "aggressively seeking [the sheikh's] personal agreement to an express release of [Jackson] from his obligations." When Prince Al Khalifa refused, Thanki told the court, Bain followed with a letter informing him that Mr. Jackson did not intend to work with or for the sheikh and "was unwilling to perform or observe his obligations."

Unlike others who had sued Jackson, Abdullah refrained from any reference to drug use but did have his attorney advise the court that he believed the entertainer was "in grave danger of losing" both Neverland Ranch and his stake in the Sony/ATV Music Publishing catalog, and that the sheikh intended to join those who would claim a share in any liquidation of assets. Michael's attorneys replied with a terse claim that Sheikh Abdullah's case was based on "mistake, misrepresentation, and undue influence," and that any monies received by Jackson in Bahrain had been "gifts," not "advances." Furthermore, Prince Al Khalifa's description of Mr. Jackson as "an experienced businessman" was unwarranted, added Michael's attorneys, who claimed that their client had never read the terms of the document in question and was without independent legal advice when he signed. Thanki countered with a demand for an open court trial he estimated might last twelve days and would require Mr. Jackson's presence in London. The British tabloids, salivating over Michael Jackson's appearance before the High Court, were making Sheikh Abdullah's claims front-page headlines. All Burkle knew

Michael Jackson onstage in the early days of the Jackson 5. A star was born, particularly when Berry Gordy got the Motown machine primed. *(Mirrorpix)*

Those kids wouldn't be so popular if they didn't have a damn midget as their lead singer! The Jackson 5 circa 1966, in a publicity shot from their "chitlin' circuit" days. Clockwise from far left, Tito, Jackie, Jermaine, and Michael at bottom, with Marlon in the center. *(Gilles Petard/Redferns)*

1971: The Jackson family has moved to the Hayvenhurst estate in Los Angeles and Michael just graced the cover of *Rolling Stone* for the first time (not this image). He has also been schooled in showbiz truthiness, insisting he is two years younger than his actual age, thirteen. *(©Henry Diltz/Corbis)*

The Jacksons, no longer allowed to use the "Jackson 5" name after leaving Motown, in New York, February 1977. Jermaine, breaking with his brothers over the Motown split, has been replaced by fifteen-year-old Randy. Later this year, Michael will return to New York to shoot *The Wiz,* and have his first taste of independence. *(©Bob Gruen/www.bobgruen.com)*

Michael was escorted to the Golden Globes, for which he won Best Song for "Ben," by his parents in February 1973. Two months later Katherine would file for divorce from Joe, but wouldn't go through with it. *(© PHIL ROACH/IPOL/GLOBE PHOTOS INC.)*

Blame it on the boogie: The Jacksons around the time of *Destiny,* their first record for their new label. Their 1979 world tour would take them to nine countries and four continents. *(Gijsbert Hanekroot/Redferns)*

Michael had known Stevie Wonder since his early days at Motown, and appeared on several of Wonder's songs. Michael was in the studio here, along with his brothers, supplying backing vocals on Wonder's 1974 song "You Haven't Done Nothing." *(Todd Gray)*

Michael's arrival in New York allowed him to stretch his wings, and
he became a regular at Studio 54. Here he is with Woody Allen in April 1977.
(Russell Turiak/Liaison)

Michael dancing with Tatum O'Neal at a 1978 party in Los Angeles held in
celebration of the Jacksons' gold records. *(Brad Elterman/BuzzFoto/FilmMagic)*

Man in the mirror: Michael, New York 1977. The child frontman had become painfully self-conscious as puberty wreaked havoc on his skin and his brothers and father mocked his appearance. (©*Bob Gruen/www.bobgruen.com*)

Alone in a crowd—or onstage—Michael could put his introversion aside. (*Epic Records/courtesy Neal Peters Collection*)

Michael's love of movies and desire to act stayed with him all his life, as did his love of costumes, either as dress up or as disguise. Here he is (left) as Charlie Chaplin in London, 1979. *(Tony Prime/WpN)*

Dressing up as *The Wiz*'s Scarecrow (right) allowed Michael an excuse for his skin breakouts and inaugurated a lifelong dream of movie stardom. *(Richard Corkery/NY Daily News Archive/Getty Images)*

Michael with Andy Warhol in 1981, whom he befriended four years earlier while in New York for *The Wiz.* They both enjoyed watching the goings-on at Studio 54, but neither really participated. *(©Lynn Goldsmith/Corbis)*

We want Michael! Michael's success with *Off the Wall* made him the indisputable star of the Jacksons, and on the *Triumph* tour he'd started to adopt the signature look that would come to full flower with *Thriller* (rhinestone accents, long curly hair). He had also had his first rhinoplasty. *(©Lynn Goldsmith/Corbis)*

Michael and Diana Ross in 1981 on her TV special. Motown's first lady, Diana introduced the Jackson 5 at their Los Angeles debut, and taught Michael how to conduct himself as a star. (Rex USA)

Liza Minnelli was another Studio 54 friend with whom Michael maintained a lasting bond. She escorted him to the club's VIP area and, later, to Swifty Lazar's legendary Oscar party. (Ron Galella/WireImage)

She's even wearing his glove: Michael met actress Brooke Shields, a fellow survivor of childhood stardom, in 1984, and she became his constant companion at public appearances and a good friend. Passion? Not so much. *(©Sonia Moskowitz/Globe Photos/ZUMAPRESS.com)*

Michael in the "Beat It" jacket, with his sister La Toya, around the time she played his love interest in the "Say, Say, Say" video. *(Time & Life Pictures/Getty Images)*

"Dodgy to be someone's friend and then to buy the rug they're standing on": Michael with Paul McCartney in 1983. They wrote and recorded music together and bonded over their mutual love of collecting cartoons, but the friendship soured when Jackson bought the Beatles catalog. (©Bettmann/CORBIS)

When Michael acquired majority ownership in the Hayvenhurst property, his parents' home, from his father, he remade it, demolishing and rebuilding the house and assembling his own menagerie, including these deer, Prince and Princess. (Todd Gray)

Michael on November 30, 1983, with his brothers and Don King at a press appearance for the *Victory* tour. He had recently become friends with Emmanuel Lewis, the twelve-year-old star of *Webster,* also pictured. Three days later, the "Thriller" video was released. *(©Bettmann/CORBIS)*

Quincy Jones, producer of *Thriller,* was at Michael's side as he collected an arm-straining eight awards at the February 1984 Grammy Awards, a month after he was burned shooting a Pepsi commercial. *(AP Photo/Doug Pizac/Saxon)*

Michael showed the victory sign arriving at Heathrow with his manager
Frank Dileo. He was literally treated like royalty in London, entering
the Guildhall for a sumptuous fete in his honor by the royal entrance,
by special permission of the Queen. *(Mirrorpix)*

John Branca, Michael's attorney since 1979, with whom Jackson is pictured here
at Branca's 1987 wedding, negotiated some of his biggest deals and career moves.
(AP Photo/courtesy of John Branca)

The Changing Face

1976

1983

2000

2002

# of Michael Jackson

1988   1995

2005   2009

At Radio City Music Hall in 1992, Michael did press for the *Dangerous* world tour with Tommy Mottola of Sony Music (with beard) and Peter Kendall of Pepsi. (*Ron Galella/WireImage*)

When Sony sought promo ideas for 1995's *HIStory* tour, Michael suggested, "build a statue of me." Nine were built and distributed to select European cities including this one floating up the Thames on a barge. "Baldly vainglorious," said the *LA Times. (Associated Press)*

Jackson rallied outside the New York headquarters of his record company, Sony, on July 6, 2002, for failing to do enough to promote *Invincible,* and brandished a sign showing Tommy Mottola with devil horns. (*Mark Mainz/Getty Images*)

when he skimmed the articles was that this was going to get ugly and expensive and that settling the case would probably be the only way out of it.

What made Burkle's efforts so heroic—or baffling—was that an examination of Jackson's finances was certain to shock any lender. Michael boasted an annual income that averaged about $25 million, mainly from royalties and dividends paid from the Sony/ATV catalog. On the other hand, he had been spending between $10 million and $15 million more than he earned each year for the past decade, even as he fell steadily behind on the servicing of his debt and his investment obligations to Sony in connection to the ever-expanding song catalog. Michael had recently phoned songwriters Mike Stoller and Jerry Leiber to tell them how happy he was to have acquired the rights to Elvis Presley hits that included "Hound Dog" and "Jailhouse Rock," promising the two their work was in good hands, but it was Sony that had paid the full cost of that acquisition. The half of the purchase price on the Leiber-Stoller catalog that Michael owed was now just one more piece of a personal debt that was past $500 million and growing. On October 19, just four days after Abdullah's attorneys submitted the sheikh's lawsuit to the High Court in London, Fortress Investments had filed a $23 million default notice on Neverland Ranch in California, the first step toward foreclosing on the property.

The notion that any bank would give Michael Jackson a mortgage on a $50 million-plus property in Las Vegas under such circumstances was preposterous but Ron Burkle pledged to try to find one that would, and Burkle was a man who got things done. He proved that by prevailing on his friend George Maloof (best known, along with his brother, Gavin, as the owners of the NBA's Sacramento Kings franchise) to put Michael and his children up at the Maloofs' hotel in Las Vegas, the Palms, where the brothers had recently installed their fabulously equipped Studio X, making it the perfect location for Michael to resume work on his "comeback album." After spending Thanksgiving with Burkle in California, Jackson flew to Las Vegas and moved into the Hugh Hefner suite in the Palms' "Fantasy Tower." It was the finest and most secure accommodation he could offer, explained Maloof, who didn't realize until a week later that it was not the place for Michael Jackson. "I came in there one day and Michael had covered up all the nude pictures," George Maloof recalled. "This was because of the kids. He didn't want them looking at those pictures."

Maloof promptly arranged for Jackson and his children to move to a two-story Sky Villa just below the Hefner suite. He and Michael did all the lifting and toting, Maloof said: "No one else could help with this because nobody else knew he was at the hotel. It was just us, moving all of these belongings, carrying them down the stairs because he didn't want to use the elevator and risk someone recognizing him." Michael and the kids stayed in the Sky Villa for only a couple of days before Maloof informed Jackson that he would have to move again, to another Sky Villa one floor down, because the suite he was living in had been booked for months in advance by a high-roller who had reserved an additional three hundred rooms on the property. "Brutal," Maloof called this transition: "The second move was harder than the first because they'd brought more stuff in—but he understood our situation." He had no idea at the time that Jackson and his children would be staying at the Palms for four months, Maloof admitted. What made the whole thing bearable, Maloof would tell Larry King more than three years later, was Michael's good manners. "He would call me up and say, 'George, are you in the middle of something?' I'd say, 'No, whatever you need.' And he was always respectful. And a great guy."

By Christmastime, the Las Vegas media had discovered that Michael Jackson was back in town, living high atop the Palms. Comparisons were inevitably made to Howard Hughes: The "fading star" had stationed his bodyguards in the hallway outside his suite around the clock, it was reported, but no one ever seemed to enter or leave. It wasn't until early December when he and the kids were spotted, making a late-night stop at a bookstore just off the Strip. The bulky army coat, the dark glasses, the hat pulled low on his head, and the shawl wrapped around his neck like a scarf not only failed to keep him from being recognized, but didn't hide the small square bandages all around his chin and mouth. By the next day photographs of him had appeared in a British tabloid, accompanied by a story (under the headline "Plaster of Disguise") that he had been back to see his cosmetic surgeon. The article ended with Jackson being described as "looking stranger than ever." Internet reporters jumped the story immediately. On Christmas Eve, one Web site reported that "part of Jackson's upper lip collapsed" after Prince accidentally punched him in the face while they were roughhousing. "The mishap led a hysterical Jacko to make a beeline for the plastic surgeon for a bit of quick repair work," a second site reported later that same day. A third site chimed in just hours later, "Imagine how sensitive his face has become, that one touch and it breaks apart."

What many people didn't understand about Michael Jackson was how hard he tried to get it right. His early training had turned him into an artist who pushed himself and everyone around him to correct even the slightest imperfection in a performance. Michael's attitude in the studio was, "I am here to be the best in the world, to be better than best, in fact, and you had better try to do the same if you want to work with me." He would not tolerate shortcomings. That approach was what carried him to the overwhelming success he achieved with *Thriller,* and it was also what left him stuck there. He devoted more than four years to his follow-up album, *Bad,* determined, as he said at the time, to make the record "as perfect as humanly possible." He was confused when critics complained that it was as if he had tried to apply a thousand coats of aural lacquer to *Thriller,* to make pretty much the same album, only shinier. Jackson spent another four years on *Dangerous* and then read in the New York and Los Angeles newspapers that the album was an "overproduced" facsimile of *Bad.* It was as if he believed that polishing the surface of his work to a high gloss would blind people to the increasingly hollow core that lay beneath. Along the way, he lost interest in authenticity. What he wanted was flawless artifice. It was the same goal he pursued in the reconstruction of his face.

Michael's first two plastic surgeries resulted from a fall onstage that broke his nose. The initial operation in 1980 left him with a breathing obstruction, so he had a second surgery to correct the problem, this one performed by Dr. Steven Hoefflin. He was delighted with the cosmetic outcome and with Hoefflin.

Michael had been ashamed of his appearance ever since hitting puberty. All those "big nose" and "liver lips" taunts he heard from his father and brothers were like the soundtrack to a movie that ran in his mind, the one where he saw the expressions on the faces of strangers who were startled—even slightly horrified—by how blemished his skin had become. "I'd hide my face in the dark," he told Oprah Winfrey during their 1993 interview. To improve his complexion, Michael tried giving up the fried food he loved and went on a macrobiotic diet that at one point was reduced to seeds and nuts. At 120 pounds he was delighted by his sinewy "dancer's body." His face grew slimmer as well, and the weight loss seemed to bring his cheekbones to the surface of what had been an unusually chubby childhood face.

What actually conquered his acne, though, were the able hands of Dr. Arnold Klein. Beginning in the late 1980s, Klein applied a series of treatments to Jackson's skin that ranged from drainage and excision ("acne surgery") to corticosteroid injections of cysts and retinoid prescriptions. Chemical peels and dermabrasion smoothed the scarring on his cheeks and forehead. Even as Michael marveled at the improvement of his appearance wrought by Klein, though, he was shaken by the doctor's diagnosis of lupus, the mysterious autoimmune disorder that in Jackson's case manifested itself most notably as vitiligo, a condition that results in patchy depigmentation of the skin.

Treating any autoimmune disease is, like attempting to cure acne, a process rife with psychological implications. Numerous studies have indicated a link between childhood trauma, whether physical, sexual, or emotional, and lupus. Physicians who deal with the disorder invariably find that a sensitivity to the mind-over-matter aspect of lupus and the conditions that result from it is the largest part of their treatment program. The emotional bond that forms between doctor and patient in such cases stretches the definition of medical practice. As a result, Klein went along for nearly twenty years with the story that the steady lightening of Jackson's skin was entirely the result of vitiligo and the courses of treatment he applied to it.

Michael first revealed in his 1993 interview with Oprah Winfrey that his skin had become steadily more pallid as a result of the hydroquinone bleaching agents (such as Solaquin Forte, Retin-A, and Benoquin) prescribed by Dr. Klein to blend the discolorations caused by vitiligo. Michael had in fact begun to lighten his skin long before he met Klein. As early as the late 1970s he and his sister La Toya were using Porcelana, an over-the-counter skin bleaching cream marketed to black Americans. Arnold Klein's introduction to his life was still years away when Michael began to tweeze his eyebrows daily, and to wear eyeliner and mascara. He wasn't trying to be either white or a woman, merely a more finished product. "I do want to be perfect," he said in 1986. "I look in the mirror, and I just want to change to be better." He hated looking at pictures of himself between the ages of fifteen and twenty-one. "Ooh, that's horrible," he told Robert Hilburn when, while working together on a proposed book, they came across a photograph of Michael as a teenager. He quickly shoved it under a stack of papers.

The plastic surgeries continued for some time after he became a patient of Arnold Klein. Dr. Hoefflin gave Michael his third nose job immediately after the twenty-sixth Grammy Awards ceremony at which Michael had cleaned up for *Thriller*. He was upset by photographs he had seen of himself standing alongside Diana Ross; her nose was so thin and his was so fat, Michael explained to the doctor. Hoefflin, a plastic surgeon who up to that time had been best known for enhancing the breasts of Playboy bunnies, would undertake multiple cosmetic procedures on Jackson over the next decade and in the process become one of Michael's intimates well before the advent of Arnold Klein.

Public remarks about what Hoefflin was doing to Jackson's appearance were heard as early as his performance on the *Motown 25* special, but in 1983 those were mostly complimentary. Michael's lean and limber physique, slightly narrowed nose, Jheri curled hair, and lighter, smoother complexion were all part of what made him the first icon of a postracial reality. "Pretty" was perhaps a better word to describe him than "handsome," but he was no more androgynous than Mick Jagger. People were startled, though, when they saw him on the *Bad* cover in 1987. Michael had received a fourth nose job from Hoefflin in 1986, and a short time later decided he wanted to have a cleft in his chin. He followed this with a procedure to have permanent eyeliner tattooed around his eyes and another surgery to thin his lower lip. There was a sharp cut to his cheekbones that hadn't been there during Thriller Time, and Dr. Klein's bleaching creams had dramatically lightened his skin tone. Pancake makeup had been applied, and a pink tattoo defined the perimeter of his lipstick.

It didn't help that his antics in the tabloids had inaugurated the epoch of Wacko Jacko, or that he insisted on speaking in that breathy whisper so reminiscent of the one Marilyn Monroe had used when she serenaded Jack Kennedy at his birthday party in 1962. The really strange thing, to a lot of people, was that Michael seemed to flaunt his surgeries. After the cleft was cut into his chin, he made appearances all over LA in a surgical mask, wearing the thing like it was an accent to his wardrobe, akin to his black fedora and big sunglasses.

The public was getting queasy by the time *Dangerous* was released in 1992. Michael did a photo spread for *Rolling Stone* that showed him looking like the sort of Latin matinee idol gang members would call a *maricon*, with tightly drawn, slicked-back hair, dressed in a white tank top with striped white pants and patent leather Mary Janes. His skin was paler and his makeup thicker. He admitted in the accompanying article that he hid from the sun. Michael now had Joan Crawford's eyebrows and a nose almost as sharp as the blade on an ice skate, but at the same time his jaw had been dropped and the cleft in his chin was deeper. Was this guy ever going to stop?

Black America largely viewed Michael's physical transformation through the lens of race, and no wonder. The first single released from *Dangerous* was "Black or White," and most people, black *and* white, thought there should have been a question mark at the end of that title. Epic Records described

"Black or White" as "a rock 'n' roll dance song about racial harmony," but it generated little of that—even in his own family. Shortly after "Black or White" was released, Michael's brother Jermaine put out a single from his latest failed album that was titled "Word to the Badd!" and included these lines in the lyric: "Reconstructed / Been abducted / Don't know who you are . . . Once you were made / You changed your shade / Was your color wrong?" Michael had already made his reply in the most memorable line from "Black or White": "I'm not gonna spend my life being a color."

Jackson's perpetual makeover was motivated more by a refusal to accept limitation or definition than by a rejection of his African ancestry. "What he told me was, 'I would like to separate myself from the Jackson Five and become me, Michael Jackson,'" recalled his former video tech Steven Howell. What drove Michael was too complex to fit into any one or even any several categories. The discomfort with his racial identity—and disassociation from his racial roots—that rankled so many black people was part of the total equation, but even that was multifaceted. What he especially liked about the first nose job he got was that it left him looking a lot less like the man who had sired him. As a family friend named Marcus Phillips put it, "If he couldn't erase Joe from his life, at least he could erase him from the reflection in the mirror." Michael experienced Joseph Jackson as coarse, violent, and dishonest, sexually reckless and hard-hearted. To some degree, he imputed such qualities to black men in general, but he also fought against that tendency his whole life, and in the end overcame it. Since childhood, he had suffered from a fear of black men he described as "big, tall, mean guys," and yet he dealt with it by surrounding himself with big and tall black men to work as his bodyguards. Reporter and self-described "family friend" Stacy Brown was probably correct when he said that Michael had insisted upon having white children because "he did not want to take the chance that a child of his would look like Joseph." But Brown was overboard and off the mark when he added that Michael "hates people with dark skin." Anybody who ever saw him dance with James Brown knew that wasn't the case. The thing about Michael, though, was that he enjoyed dancing with Fred Astaire just as much.

It was true that at Neverland Ranch Michael was sometimes openly disdainful of black people—or at least a certain class of black people—referring to them as "splaboos," and using the word most often in exchanges with the young white boys who shared his bedroom. Perhaps it was also true that, as a Santa Barbara County sheriff's deputy who interviewed his household staff wrote in a 2003 affidavit, Jackson "bleaches his skin because he does not like being black and he feels that blacks are not liked as much as people of other races." But when Oprah Winfrey asked him about his racial identity in 1993, Jackson responded with a simple declaration: "I am a black American." Deepak Chopra's son, Gotham, who probably knew Michael a lot better than his father did, would say, "It was very disturbing to him that people thought he always wanted to be white."

As early as 1991, Michael admitted to the black musicians and producers who worked on *Dangerous* that he had gone too far with the cosmetic surgery and said, almost apologetically, that he wished he could reverse the process. That was impossible, so he continued to try to fix the fixes, submitting to the knife again and again until he seemed to some an alien life form.

"He came in approximately every two months," said Hoefflin's former associate Dr. Wallace Goodstein, who recalled multiple nose jobs, cheek implants, eyelid surgery, and the cleft implant. "It was about ten to twelve surgeries in two years (during the 1990s), while I was there."

Michael pitted doctors Hoefflin and Klein against each other, and in the process probably only exacerbated his problems. Hoefflin had for years enjoyed the status and the perks he derived from accompanying Michael on tour, billed as "Mr. Jackson's special traveling companion and personal physician." By around 1990, though, Klein succeeded in convincing Michael—at least temporarily—that he didn't need any more plastic surgery (particularly on his nose) and that he should rely on subcutaneous fillers instead. The danger of repeated surgical procedures, Klein warned (correctly), was that when enough blood vessels in the face were cauterized the blood stopped flowing and the skin eventually turned black and withered away or even fell off in pieces. "I remember times when Michael told Arnie he wanted to have a surgical procedure done, and Klein told him no," Marc Schaffel said. "Arnie would call the doctor and say, 'Don't do it.'" Hoefflin (a man who mentioned his "genius IQ" at nearly every opportunity) countered by telling Michael that the massive injections of collagen he was receiving from Klein were worsening his lupus. He continued to get the injections, though, and to schedule surgeries with Dr. Hoefflin. How many of those procedures actually took place remains an open question. In the mid-1990s, four of Dr. Hoefflin's nurses sued him for sexual harassment, alleging, among other things, that the plastic surgeon had handled and mocked the genitals of celebrity patients who had been placed under anesthesia. The nurses also claimed that for several years their employer had been staging elaborate hoaxes in which the doctor placed Michael Jackson under general anesthesia but only pretended to perform an operation. Jackson would wake up with his nose bandaged, the nurses said, convinced there had been a "touch-up" on his already tiny proboscis. Hoefflin denied the story and claimed not only that he had won a dismissal of the lawsuit, but also that he had received a letter of apology from the attorneys who had filed it and "a substantial sum of money" from the former colleagues he had countersued. Whether that was true or not remained in doubt, as records in a related case stated that each of the women who sued Hoefflin had received $42,000 in compensation. However that lawsuit had been settled, Hoefflin continued to serve as one of Michael Jackson's doctors.

Neither Hoefflin nor Klein wanted their work on Jackson detailed in public. In 2003, when the Santa Barbara County sheriff's department served search warrants on each doctor's office, deputies were informed that all records relating to Michael Jackson had been removed and that neither the doctors nor their attorneys would reveal where those records were now being kept.

By the time of his criminal trial in 2005, any number of psychologists who had never met Michael Jackson were diagnosing him on TV as suffering from "body dysmorphic disorder," a psychological condition in which a person loses all sense of how he or she is seen by others. Yet according to Deepak Chopra, Michael was acutely aware of what vitiligo had done to his appearance and "had, as a result, a very, very poor image of his body. He was almost ashamed of it. That's why he would cover it up. Why do you think he wore a glove and all that stuff. He would not go into the swimming pool in his own house with his clothes off. He would just jump into the pool at the last moment, you know, take his robe off, but he was ashamed that people would look at all the blotches on his skin." Jackson wept when the editor of *Us Weekly* told an interviewer that she could no longer put Michael Jackson on the magazine's cover because people found looking at him depressing.

Around the same time, London's *Daily Mail* published an interview with Professor Werner Mang, director of the renowned Bodensee Clinic in Lindau, on the German-Swiss border, a man who boasted of building his reputation by "making beautiful noses" for celebrity clients. In 1998, Mang said, Dr. Hoefflin had asked him to perform "reconstructive surgery" on Michael Jackson's nose. Mang flew to California for a consultation and discovered that the skin on Jackson's face was "parchment-thin," while the tip of the entertainer's nose was "unstable." He had fixed the latter problem, Mang said, by using some of Michael's ear cartilage to shore up the nose he was in danger of losing altogether. A couple of days later, David Letterman joked that Michael was now "deaf in his left nostril."

Hoefflin denied Mang's story and if the Swiss surgeon really *had* tried to save Michael Jackson's nose, he failed. Dr. Mark Sinnreich recalled Michael's first visit to the orthopedic surgeon's Florida office in 2002: "I had him take off his mask . . . It looked almost like he had two blow holes. No nose."

Michael made do with prosthetics. He kept them in his closet at Neverland, a big jar of fake noses—various shapes and sizes—surrounded by tubes of stage glue. "He told me they were for disguises," recalled Adrian McManus, one of his maids at Neverland Ranch. All Michael was disguising at this point, though, was what at least six rhinoplasty surgeries had left him with: a pair of nostrils surrounded by a rim of shriveled, shrunken, discolored cartilage. He had been a skilled makeup artist since his teens, and in fifteen minutes at the mirror could create an appearance that fooled most people. Plastic surgeons had been speculating on TV since as early as 1990 that the tip of his nose had been replaced by a prosthetic of either bone or plastic. By about 2001, though, the way his nose was changing from year to year—sometimes from week to week—gave him away.

Michael salvaged something from this personal disaster. At least now he could have the nose he had always wanted—Bobby Driscoll's. The most famous child star of the late 1940s and early 1950s, Driscoll had for years been an icon of Jackson's who rivaled Shirley Temple in importance. Bobby was the first actor Walt Disney ever put under contract, to play the lead character in 1946's *Song of the South*. His best-known role would be as Jim Hawkins in Disney's 1950 version of *Treasure Island*, but for Michael Jackson the most important part the boy had ever played was for Disney's 1953 animated film *Peter Pan*. Driscoll provided the voice of Peter Pan in the movie, but it was his work as the animators' "reference model" that captivated Michael. He admired the child actor's slim, athletic physique, straw-colored hair, and light spray of freckles, but what he adored was Driscoll's perfectly pyramidal, slightly upturned nose. It was a feature so unusual that it looked as if it belonged on the face of a pixie or some other preternatural creature, perfect for Peter Pan and, Michael believed, perfect for him, too. He began to appear in public with his Bobby Driscoll prosthetic right around the time *Invincible* was being released. There is footage from 2002 of Michael standing amid an enthralled crowd outside the Virgin Records store in Times Square in New York, arms open and hands extended as if embracing the applause and adoration that flows like a gust of wind through the scene, his chin lifted, Barack Obama–style, as he stands in profile to the camera, his Bobby Driscoll nose raised to the sky as if being displayed not just to those present, but to all of creation, seeming to declare in that moment, "I *am* Peter Pan."

Along with the acquisition of his nose, Michael had become a student of Bobby Driscoll's sad and lonely life. He knew all about the disappointments the young actor had suffered when the film part he had been promised as Tom Sawyer failed to materialize, and how crushed Bobby Driscoll had been when he met with Walt Disney after the release of *Peter Pan* and was told by his employer that he was probably more suited these days for roles as a young bully than for the part of an appealing protagonist. Nothing about Bobby Driscoll's life made Michael identify with him more than learning that the young actor's contract with Disney had been canceled immediately after his sixteenth birthday, because, according to a studio press release, the severe case of acne he had developed made him unwatchable. Michael knew all about how the teenage Bobby Driscoll had bounced around after that between various Los Angeles–area high schools, teased and tormented by other kids as a has-been who had played a bunch of cornball parts in hokey family films. He knew that Driscoll had begun to experiment with heroin when he was seventeen, was busted for possession of marijuana at the age of nineteen, then arrested for assault with a deadly weapon after he pistol-whipped a pair of hecklers, and incarcerated in 1961, at the age of twenty-four, in the California Institution for Men in Chino. Michael described for friends how, upon his release, Bobby tried to reinvent himself as an adult actor named Robert Driscoll, but met with little success. Michael had even researched Driscoll's 1965 relocation to New York, where he tried to find work on the Broadway stage and, failing that, joined Andy Warhol's Greenwich Village art community, the Factory. Driscoll's collages and cardboard mailers were considered outstanding by some people (and would be exhibited at the Santa Monica Museum of Art) but never earned him more than a few pennies, and Bobby was flat broke by the time he left the Factory in late 1967. A few months later, shortly after Driscoll's thirty-first birthday, two boys playing in a deserted East Village tenement found his lifeless body, but there was no identification on it, and photographs circulated through the neighborhood failed to turn up even a single person who recognized the dead man. The anonymous corpse was buried at Potter's Field. "His own family didn't know that he was the one in the pauper's grave with a heroin overdose," Michael would marvel. "He was a Disney giant, the voice of Peter Pan." And yet look what Bobby had come to. Michael had promised Shirley Temple that he would open a museum for child stars some day, and that the boy who had played Peter Pan would be given a featured display. In the meantime, though, all that was left of Bobby Driscoll, besides those early Disney films, was the nose on Michael Jackson's face.

15

In early 2008, Michael Jackson was subjected to the most invasive and thorough examination of his finances that had ever been performed, courtesy of Washington, D.C.–based accounting firm Thompson, Cobb, Bazilio and Associates. The good news was that Michael had credibly claimed a net worth of $236.6 million. The bad news was that only $668,215 of that wealth was liquid. Thompson, Cobb calculated that Jackson owned $567 million in assets, including $33 million in equity on Neverland Ranch, his $390 million share of the 750,000-song Sony/ATV catalog, and $20 million worth of cars, antiques, and collectibles, but that his total debts amounted to $331 million. Given his refusal to surrender his ownership of the song catalog, the only alternatives were to borrow more money or file for bankruptcy.

In the short term, London-based Barclays Bank saved him from the latter fate by assuming more than $300 million in Jackson debt held by Fortress Investments in a new loan secured by the Sony/ATV catalog. Additionally, HSBC bank and a hedge fund called Plainfield Asset Management were loaning Michael $70 million against MiJac Music, the company through which he controlled the rights to his own songs, as well as those of Sly and the Family Stone and others he had purchased before buying the Beatles catalog. The loan came with a 16 percent interest rate on terms that allowed him to defer payments for more than a year. None of that money would go into Jackson's pocket, though. Much of it had been used to settle thirteen outstanding lawsuits (not including Sheikh Abdullah's), among them the cases involving Marc Schaffel and Dieter Wiesner. In addition, Michael had agreed to pay John Branca $15 million to buy out the attorney's share of the ATV catalog (Branca had already earned an estimated $20 million from the ATV deal) and to sever their relationship. What remained, plus all dividends, profits, and payments from the two song catalogs, would be used to service Michael's debts. Sony had agreed to guarantee all of the loans through September 2011 in exchange for the right to purchase half of Jackson's share in the ATV catalog for just under $200 million and Jackson's agreement that the company could spend up to $400 million to purchase the 125,000-song Famous Music LLC catalog, which included rights that ranged from the *Footloose* theme song to Eminem's "The Real Slim Shady." What Michael would receive in exchange was the guarantee of a cash distribution of $11 million per year through 2011.

Among the obvious problems he was left with was that living on $11 million a year wouldn't work for Michael Jackson, not when his "personal expenses" were at least $8 million per annum and dozens of legal matters remained pending. Furthermore, he would have to discover a major new stream of income before September 2011 to avoid losing everything. On top of that, Fortress Investments still held the note on Neverland Ranch and intended to wring every penny from him that it could.

Still, encouraging signs were appearing in Michael's life. Most significant was the surprisingly successful release of *Thriller 25*. Sony had waited until November 30, 2007, to announce the release, timed to the exact date that the original version of *Thriller* had appeared in record stores a quarter century earlier. *Thriller 25* began showing up on shelves only a little more than two months later, in early February 2008, and Sony knew within days that it had struck at least a minor pocket of gold. The first week's domestic sales totaled 165,805 units, putting *Thriller 25* in the #1 spot on *Billboard*'s top pop catalog chart. If eligible, the album would have entered *Billboard*'s top 200 in the #2 spot. It was selling even better overseas. *Thriller 25* was eligible for full placement on foreign charts and within a week was #1 in France and Belgium; #2 in Germany, Australia, the Netherlands, Norway, Sweden, and Switzerland; #3 in the UK and Denmark; #4 in Spain; #5 in Spain, Austria, and Ireland; and #6 in Italy and the Czech Republic. Sensing what it had, Sony committed to a level of promotion for *Thriller 25* that few of the company's original releases received, making agreements in the weeks before the album went into distribution for midnight showings of John Landis's *Thriller* video at Odeon cinemas throughout the UK, followed by a forty-episode "ThrillerCast" Internet podcast, a "Thrillicious" Sobe Life Water campaign that would kick off at halftime of the Super Bowl, and the presentation of a Lifetime Achievement Award to Michael at the NRJ Awards in Cannes, among numerous other PR and advertising events. The largest retail music chain in Britain, HMV, planned to host an event featuring twenty-five Michael Jackson impersonators, plus the

"Thriller LIVE" dancers on the day *Thriller 25* CDs and vinyl records began appearing in its stores. Even the critics were being kind, especially to the remixes of "The Girl Is Mine 2008" (by will.i.am) and Akon's "Wanna Be Startin' Somethin' 2008." *Rolling Stone* was so impressed that it gave *Thriller 25* five stars, compared to four for the original version.

Michael's spirits were lifted to the point that he began to show real commitment to the long-promised "comeback album" he was recording at Studio X. Reports from those who were spending time in the studio with him verged on the ecstatic. "Michael Jackson is working day and night on this great, great record," will.i.am told the audience at the Cannes MIDEM conference. "I heard and seen him in the studio and he is creating a masterpiece . . . Before the year is over Michael Jackson will be back on top of the charts."

Reports that release of the comeback album was imminent had been appearing for months in the media. An HMV store in England had actually advertised the release date as November 19, 2007, under the title *7even*. There would be fourteen songs on the album, the promotional materials said, divided by half into an A side and a B side with Michael appearing on the cover shaped into the figure of a seven. That date passed without any sign of the record, of course, and one new scheduled release after another was postponed without explanation. The public was teased with leaks that came in tiny drips spaced far apart. Michael harmonizing with The Fugees' Pras on "No Friend of Mine" was posted briefly on the producer Tempramental's MySpace page and stirred a rhapsodic response from fans stunned by how smooth and powerful Jackson sounded. "Man, he still sings like a bird," will.i.am told MTV. The cut quickly disappeared. Michael's collaboration with Akon on a song called "Hold My Hand" was leaked to YouTube, and again fans went wild, but the cut was pulled from the Internet thirty-six hours later. Chris Brown, 50 Cent, Syience, and Carlos Santana all said they were hoping to work with Michael.

By the time Michael left the Palms at the end of February 2008 he had recorded more than a hundred new songs but still had not selected the ones he would include on his comeback album. Michael was nervous about the public reception and kept putting off the release. "It's tough when all eyes are on him and there is so much young competition out there," Ne-Yo explained to *Rolling Stone*. Michael had told him "this album needs to be better than *Thriller*," Ne-Yo added. Who could live up to that standard? "He needs killer melodies," Ne-Yo said. "He'll call me back and say, 'I really like song number three. Song number four, the hook could be stronger. Song number one, change the first verse. Okay, bye.' Click. And then I redo them and he's like, 'Okay, they're perfect. Send me more.' So I don't know what he's keeping and what he's getting rid of."

Michael refused to talk about the album with *Rolling Stone* or anyone else. All he would say even to those who were working with him was that whatever he came out with next had to be the best work he had ever done. Otherwise, the world would ask why he had even bothered.

When Michael left the Palms at the end of February in 2008, it was for the most modest residence he had called his own in many years. Not that the hacienda-style home at 2710 Palomino Lane was anything less than palatial, 20,638 square feet of luxurious living space that included a spectacular Spanish Chapel, set among gardens and trails that wound through a nearly two-acre lot set among the equestrian properties of an established community situated just west of downtown Las Vegas. Michael and his children wouldn't be living in the main house, though. Instead he had rented the property's 3,982 square foot guesthouse, agreeing to move in without having the premises painted or repaired. The monthly rent was $7,000, less than a tenth of what it had cost Michael to live in the Monte Cristo house; he paid $49,000 cash to cover the full six months of the lease agreement, including the security deposit, and for that price was able to negotiate use of the main house's 8,500 square foot basement for the storage of his memorabilia and art collections. The kids were happy that the property included a large swimming pool for them to splash around in and that the horse trails provided plenty of room for them to run with their new puppy, Kenya. There was room for a small security trailer just inside the front gates and neighbors likely would imagine that the Jacksons were living in the mansion, not the the guest quarters. Rancho Circle Shopping Center was within walking distance.

Michael was still hoping to buy the Sultan of Brunei's estate at 99 Spanish Gate Drive. Even Ron Burkle, though, had not been able to find a bank that would loan Jackson the money to buy the place. The 37,000-square-foot main house that the sultan's wastrel younger brother, Prince Jefri Bolkiah, had commissioned nearly a decade earlier remained unfinished and uninhabitable, needing "a million or so just to get the house up to par to a move-in condition," as one Las Vegas real estate broker described it. Underwriting a mortgage on the property—even at the reduced price of

$60 million—made no sense to anyone who looked at Michael Jackson's finances. Michael grew increasingly despondent, especially when Sony informed him it would be withholding his royalties from *Thriller 25* in order to cover what it was costing the company to service his share of the song catalog.

The person who signed the lease on the Palomino property was Michael Amir Williams, a Nation of Islam foot soldier who had taken responsibility for the fleet of automobiles that Jackson had assembled in Las Vegas. At a moment when Jackson was vulnerable, Louis Farrakhan had dispatched a small contingent of NOI members to Las Vegas. One of Farrakhan's own sons was installed in the Palomino guest house as the family's cook and Williams (whom Jackson and his children addressed as "Brother Michael") began identifying himself to other people not as the star's driver but as "Mr. Jackson's executive assistant."

"The Muslims made Michael nervous, and he got tired of having them around pretty quickly," said one of the several attorneys representing Jackson during 2008. "But he didn't want to offend Farrakhan, so he felt sort of stuck with them. And then I guess he started to trust Brother Michael."

Only after settling in at Palomino Lane did Michael finally acknowledge the looming catastrophe of a foreclosure on Neverland Ranch. Fortress Investments had given him until March 19, 2008, to ante up $24,525,906.61 or face an auction that day on the steps of the Santa Barbara County courthouse at which the ranch and everything on it would be sold to the highest bidder. One week before the scheduled sale, Londell McMillan told the Associated Press that Michael had worked out a "confidential" agreement with Fortress that would allow him to retain ownership of Neverland. The clock was still ticking, though, according to Fortress, which had given Michael just a few more weeks to find either a new lender or a buyer for the ranch. The timing was just right for another would-be white knight to gallop onto the scene, and an interesting candidate showed up at precisely the right moment, almost as if he had answered a cue.

Dr. Tohme R. Tohme was a cryptic character who complained constantly that his penchant for privacy was misread by a media that described him alternately as "mysterious" or "shadowy." Various news reports identified Tohme as a Saudi Arabian billionaire who had trained to be an orthopedic surgeon before becoming what the Associated Press would call "a financier with a murky past." In fact, Tohme was a Lebanese-American raconteur-slash-real estate investor whose principal place of business was the bar of the Hotel Bel-Air. There, Tohme exercised his extraordinary gift for facilitation, brokering assorted deals that drew alternately on sources of Middle Eastern or Southeast Asian money, as well as an impressive range of international contacts. Tohme had grown wealthy—or at least apparently wealthy—in the thirty-plus years since arriving in America by diversifying into almost every conceivable kind of business enterprise, working nearly always as a highly paid middleman.

"I have a relationship all over the world. I can find money," he modestly explained. "Doc," as he preferred to be known among his American friends, was a compact but broad-shouldered man in his late fifties whose heavy, broken features and rolling gait gave him the look of someone who had spent years boxing in the welterweight division. He wore custom-made suits but spiced his conversations with growls, barks, snarls, and singularly colorful curses. Many people in Los Angeles, when first introduced to Tohme, were intimidated by his gruff manner. He did not mind letting a person he had just met know he was tired of explaining that having the same first and last names was not uncommon among Middle Easterners, and yet could charm just about anyone on the rare occasion he chose to do so. As he told it, many wealthy Arabs and Asians, including members of various royal families, counted him among their friends. So did Jermaine Jackson, who saw an opportunity in his brother's distress.

He and Jermaine had been introduced by mutual acquaintances in the Los Angeles Muslim community, said Tohme, who was "intrigued but not impressed" when his new friend asked him, in April 2008, to meet with his brother Michael in Las Vegas. "Jermaine came to my house to see me and he said, 'Michael needs your help. His house is going on the auction block. You gotta help him save it,'" Tohme recalled. "I said, 'I gotta look what it is, then we'll see.'" In other words, he and Jermaine made some sort of deal.

Tohme traveled to Las Vegas the next day in a white Rolls-Royce driven by Jermaine. A story would spread later that Tohme provided the Rolls to Jermaine to secure a meeting with his brother. Both men deny this. What Tohme recalled best about their arrival in Las Vegas was being startled by the circumstances in which he found the world's most successful recording artist. "I couldn't believe that this is Michael Jackson living in an environ-ment like this and in a house like this," he recalled. "It was a pretty average place and it really needed to be cleaned and painted. It was messy. He was a single guy with three kids and there was a dog and he didn't have any housekeeper." Grace Rwaramba had been ordered out of Michael's life yet again shortly before they left the Palms, so "he was taking care of the kids and the dog and the place all by himself," Tohme recalled. "He had hurt his right foot and he couldn't move around too well, so stuff was piling up. He was sitting in a wheelchair when Jermaine introduced us, wearing pajama bottoms and two different-colored slippers."

Amid the squalor and disarray of the Palomino house, Michael's demeanor was plaintive. He seemed desperately lonely. According to the security guards, they had been the only guests, besides the nanny and the children's teacher, at Paris's tenth birthday party on April 3, and for them it had been a sad affair. Grace would say later that she had been forced to pay for the balloons they used for decoration with her own credit card and that the people she had brought in to clean the house for the party would not come back because they were never paid. "I am thinking, 'This is Michael Jackson! This is the King of Pop!'" Tohme recalled. "And he was so humble. I looked in his eye and I could tell he was sad. Not embarrassed, but *sad*. A combination of many things. I was really shocked about how he was living and I wasn't shy about it. I told him, 'This is not a place for you, Michael. What are you doing here?' And he said, 'Everybody abandoned me. I don't have anybody. I have no friends. They all turned their backs on me.' He wasn't feeling sorry for himself, though. It didn't sound like that at all.

"Michael told me, 'Please, please help me save Neverland.' He didn't want to go through the embarrassment of foreclosure, and he knew that the media hated him and would make a joke of him."

Tohme agreed to do what he could, shook hands, and left with Jermaine. They were driving back to LA, Tohme recalled, when his cell phone rang: "It was Michael. He said, 'I want you to come back and talk with me.' So we went back and he said to me, 'I have no one. I want you to be with me.'"

Tohme returned to LA again and began calling every big real estate investor he knew. One after another turned him down. "I got a couple of friends of mine to visit Neverland with me," he recalled, "but they said, 'No, I don't wanna do it. It's full of problems.'"

Finally, Tohme tried his American friend Thomas Barrack, a billionaire real estate investor for whom he had arranged financing on a previous deal. Barrack, who as a young man had served as a deputy undersecretary in Ronald Reagan's Interior Department, boasted a reputation as a prescient fellow. Donald Trump conceded that no one, including himself, had a better eye for the value of a property than Tom Barrack. Back in 2005, Barrack had told *Fortune* magazine that he was just about ready to get out of the U.S. real estate market because, "There's too much money chasing too few deals, with too much debt and too few brains." In 1991, Barrack founded the private equity firm Colony Capital, a company that had done more than $35 billion in transactions in the years since. "Tom was in Europe when I called," Tohme remembered, "and when I asked if he would like to buy the note on Neverland, he said no. When he came back to LA I went to see him and said, 'Come on, man, do it.' And he said no, he doesn't wanna be involved with Michael Jackson. So I said, 'Why don't I introduce you to Michael, so you can see what kind of human being he is.' Because, see, I know already that Michael still has that magic in him. You sit with him and he will take you over. He had that flair. So I convinced Tom to go to Las Vegas and meet Michael. And after just a few minutes I can see that Tom Barrack is becoming very interested in Michael Jackson."

He had been charmed by Michael's wit and surprised by his focus, Barrack would admit later. The polo-playing Barrack, whose own sprawling ranch in Santa Barbara County bordered Neverland on one side and Ronald Reagan's Western White House on the other, shared a laugh with Jackson about being next-door neighbors, given that their houses were eleven miles apart. His sons had attended a number of the "field day" events that Michael staged at Neverland, Barrack said, and came back each time raving about what a great time they'd had. Ten minutes into their meeting, the odd couple found that they liked each other. Ten minutes after that, Barrack agreed to see if he could swing a deal to rescue Neverland from the clutches of Fortress Investments, which had rescheduled its auction of the ranch for May 2008.

"Tom knows it's a fabulous property," Tohme observed. "He's not a stupid guy. But it was a long, hard negotiation, because there was one issue we got stuck on. Under the Fortress loan, whoever held the note on Neverland owned everything on the property: all of Michael's art, his books, his clothes—even his animals and his rides, whatever there is. I told Tom, 'This is not right. I gotta take everything out.' So we had a lot of back and forth, attorneys and stuff like that, but finally they agreed we can remove Michael's personal things."

In May, just days before Neverland was to be sold to the highest bidder, Colony Capital announced that Tom Barrack had personally written a check for $22.5 million to "save" Neverland as part of a deal the company had made with Michael Jackson. Under the terms of the agreement, Colony and Barrack agreed to defer Jackson's loan payments (for more money later) and to finance the refurbishment of the ranch with an eye toward selling it at a substantial profit. Tohme had cut himself in for a finder's fee. It was a Tom Barrack kind of deal. He had never been the sort of investor who wanted to "chase yield" by buying properties with secure tenants and predictable returns, preferring to seek out undervalued assets that could be rehabilitated and sold for a big profit. That was exactly how he'd made a killing on London's Savoy Hotel. Neverland Ranch, he imagined, might sell for as much as $50 million if it was marketed properly. Aside from being relieved of payment obligations, Michael was guaranteed to receive whatever profits were left after Colony deducted its investment in the note, plus accrued interest, management, upkeep expenses, and a 12 percent "success fee." If Barrack was right about the eventual sale price, Jackson stood to come away with as much as $20 million.

Michael had been wrestling with the problem of what to do with Neverland ever since arriving in Bahrain in the summer of 2005. During his long stay in Ireland, he had invited Bob Sillerman, the Wall Street deal maker who acquired Elvis Presley Enterprises, to visit him at Grouse Lodge to discuss ways they might make the ranch over into a fan destination. One tentative plan after another fell through, and it had looked almost certain that Fortress would sell the place out from under him before Barrack showed up in Las Vegas.

For Michael Jackson, Tohme Tohme became "my partner Dr. Tohme" after the Colony deal was sealed. "Michael was very happy," Tohme recalled. "He said, 'I want you to be in charge of everything.' He said, 'You and I, we are gonna make billions, not hundreds of millions.' He said, 'I trust you like nobody else, and I'm gonna give you a free hand to do whatever you want.'"

While the deal with Barrack seemed to have settled Michael's Neverland problem, it had barely chipped the giant boulder of debt that was going to crush Michael if he didn't begin to break it down. After reading through the refinancing agreement Michael had signed six months earlier, Tohme realized he would have to convince his prospective client that the day of reckoning would be upon him before he knew it. "I could see that this deal had put Michael in a position of losing the Beatles catalog and his own MiJac catalog—basically everything he had," Tohme recalled. "He only had until 2011 to fix his finances, or this will definitely happen. I told Michael, 'We need to eliminate as much of your debt as possible.'" The only way Tohme could see that happening, though, was to persuade Michael to mount another major tour. "But he doesn't want it," Tohme recalled. "He told me, 'I don't want to sing. I don't want to perform. All I want to do is make movies and do projects.'"

Filmmaking had become a fixation for Michael in the years following the *HIStory* tour. He came much closer to realizing the dream of owning his own movie studio than most people knew, according to Dieter Wiesner: "It was more than a dream, it was a plan." The acquisition of Marvel Comics was at the core of that plan and Michael had tried for three years to pull it off. Back in 1999, he met with the primary creator of Marvel's best-known characters, Stan Lee, to ask if they could be partners. "Michael wanted to make a Spider-Man movie long before there was a Spider-Man movie," Wiesner explained, "and he told Stan Lee about that." Lee, who was on the outs with Marvel at the time, has confirmed that such a conversation took place.

"Michael was thinking about playing Spider-Man himself," Wiesner continued. "He asked Stan Lee to help him run Marvel if Michael was able to buy the company, and Lee said he would. I really believed it would happen and it almost did." Michael actually retained the investment banking firm Wasserstein Perrella to negotiate a sale with Marvel's then-owner, Ike Perlmutter. "Michael thought this would be like his second buying of the Beatles catalog," Wiesner recalled. "It was that big for him." Reports at the time suggested the deal had fallen through because Perlmutter was demanding a billion dollars for the company. "That's not true," Wiesner said. "In 2002, Michael was willing to pay $1.4 billion for Marvel, which was the asking price then." The financing fell apart, though, Wiesner said, when Sony refused to let Jackson use the ATV catalog as collateral: "Sony was constantly blocking his projects. They wanted to have complete control over him. And today Marvel is worth $4 billion. The Spider-Man movies have made hundreds of millions of dollars. Michael was right."

As an alternative, Wiesner and Jackson had negotiated a deal with Cinegroupe, the famed animation studio in Montreal, that would have given Michael a 51 percent share of the company and creative control of its projects. Michael possessed "plane hangars full of footage" from the film and video shoots he had commissioned over the years, Wiesner explained, "and he said, 'Dieter, with the new technology we can make all of this—doesn't matter if it's *Thriller* tour stuff or whatever I have—we can make this completely new for the new generation. We can put everything together in a new light.'"

Michael was initially encouraged by friends that included Steven Spielberg and David Geffen, according to Wiesner, who promised to go in as partners with him on several film projects but never followed through: "He said they had taken his ideas, but didn't want him. He was always talking about this, about Spielberg especially. He was very hurt and angry with Spielberg. He said they promised him, Spielberg and Disney, but then they kept him out."

Michael had never really given up on his dream of becoming a movie star. His love of role play had actually triggered his separation from the Jehovah's Witnesses. A pair of elders were on the set of the "Smooth Criminal" video Michael had shot in 1987, shortly before the song was released as the seventh single from *Bad*, and had shaken their heads in disapproval as they watched Michael revel in the scene in which he had mowed down a battalion of alien invaders with a machine gun. Michael arrived late to the set the next day, his makeup artist Karen Faye would remember, and was obviously distraught. When she asked what was wrong, Faye recalled, Michael's eyes filled with tears. "Mother called last night," Michael answered, sobbing as he spoke. "The church called her and told her that I held and fired a gun yesterday. They ordered that I have to make a decision. I must leave the church or leave the entertainment industry." His mother "felt horrible," Michael choked out: "She told me it was up to me. She said she would stand by me with whatever I decided." So here he was, back on the set, Faye observed. "Yes," Michael told her, and prepared to shoot the day's scenes.

When *Phantom of the Opera* first opened on Broadway in New York, he had showed up backstage night after night to talk to Andrew Lloyd Webber about playing the lead part in a feature film. "He had a connection to that lonely, tortured musician," Webber would explain years later. Michael and *Flashdance* screenwriter Tom Hedley spent dozens of hours in a hotel room where the lamps were switched off and the curtains drawn, watching the 1939 black-and-white adaptation of Victor Hugo's *The Hunchback of Notre Dame* over and over again as they discussed a remake in which Michael would replace Charles Laughton in the role of the hunchback. "This is awfully dark, Michael," Hedley observed at one point. "Don't you want to think about maybe doing something lighter?" "I like the dark," Jackson replied. Even after those projects and others came to naught, Michael continued to take private acting lessons from Marlon Brando for years.

Michael made his most determined effort to become the screen star he believed he should be in 2000 when he learned that Warner Bros. was developing a remake of *Willy Wonka and the Chocolate Factory* with director Tim Burton. Working in secret, he recorded an original soundtrack for the film at a small studio in Los Angeles. "He wanted to play Willy Wonka in the worst way," explained Marc Schaffel. "He thought it was the perfect role for him, and he planned to use the soundtrack, basically, to bribe his way into getting the part." Schaffel attended several meetings at Warner Bros. to discuss the idea. "The execs at Warner were intrigued and went nuts over the soundtrack, absolutely loved it," he recalled. "But then they came back later and said, 'You know, this may not be the perfect marriage for us. But we would one hundred percent pay anything for the soundtrack.'" Michael demanded to know why the studio wouldn't give him a chance at the Willy Wonka role. "I think Tim Burton wanted Johnny Depp all along," Schaffel said, "but the reason Warner Brothers gave, when I pressed them, was, 'We can't have this guy starring in what would be a children's movie. As a marketable idea, it doesn't work.' I had to tell Michael, and he was very hurt, very upset. He said these people were ignorant, that they were still rehashing all that '93 stuff." Warner Bros. told Schaffel that if Michael would sell them the soundtrack he could name his price *and* they would find a part for him in the movie, just not the lead. "Michael said, 'If I can't have the Willy Wonka part, then they're not getting the soundtrack,' and he just basically shelved it. It was such a shame, because he had done an incredible job with that soundtrack. I'm sure it would have won him an Academy Award."

What ultimately gave Tohme leverage to get Jackson to commit to live performance again was a realization that the key to motivating Michael Jackson was his children. "Tohme, who has a large family of his own, pointed out to Michael that his children had never seen him perform, and that he owed them the opportunity," said Dennis Hawk, the attorney who was in the best position to observe the discussions between the two men. "Tohme also told Michael that unless he went back to work now—right now—he was in danger of having nothing to leave his kids. That got to Michael."

Several months would pass, though, before this approach took full effect. In the meantime Michael continued to list and drift, often without enough cash on hand to pay his bodyguards or entertain his children in anything like the style to which they had become accustomed. He was spotted out in public in Las Vegas only once that entire spring, on May 16, when he took the kids to an early showing of the second installment of the *Chronicles of Narnia: Prince Caspian*. "I can tell that part of what Michael needs is to get his oxygen back," Tohme recalled. "He needs to remember that he is the King of Pop. Michael knows this, but he doesn't *know* it. Because of the criminal trial and all the lies that were told about him, he wasn't sure how people saw him. I wanted him to go back out in public and look good doing it. I told him, 'Michael, no more wheelchair, no more umbrella, no more masks, no more of this two-colored slippers.'"

With Tohme's encouragement, Michael made his most public appearance in Los Angeles in nearly five years during the last week of May 2008,
flying in to attend the fiftieth birthday party of Christian Audigier, the
French designer behind the Ed Hardy label. Michael was photographed
dancing and smiling, wearing high-heel boots, black leather pants, and an
elaborate periwinkle tunic with white lace flowers strung like bandoliers
across the chest and sergeant's stripes on the shoulders. Audigier proposed
that the two of them collaborate on a clothing line, and Michael said it
sounded like a good idea, but then flew back to Las Vegas to face a financial
bind that was squeezing him tighter by the month.

On June 3, Jackson ate dinner with Tom Barrack in the Las Vegas Hilton's Verona Sky Villa and confessed that he knew he'd have to go back
onstage or risk losing the ATV catalog, the one asset that had propped
him up for years. Barrack had ideas. Colony Capital owned the Las Vegas
Hilton, the same hotel where Elvis had staged his famous 1969 comeback
concerts and performed for another seven years after that. Colony also
held a 75 percent stake in the Station Casinos that dominated the locals
market in Las Vegas. Michael could relaunch in Vegas as a headliner at
either venue, Barrack suggested, performing as often as he liked, up to
180 shows a year, and earning tens of millions in the process. Or, if he preferred, Michael could include his brothers in an extravaganza that would
be staged perhaps twenty or thirty times a year and still make him at least
ten million. Michael had no interest at all in the second idea, and very
little in the first, but was in desperate need of a patron, and so promised
Barrack that he would think about both proposals.

Michael's recognition that going onstage again was probably his only
way forward was, for Tohme, the fissure of hope that promised a breakthrough. "I was workin' on it, and I was workin' on him," Tohme recalled.
"Because he still wasn't really ready to say he would do it. But he said, 'See
what you can do. Keep continuing.' And I am telling him, 'Michael, you
have to do it. For the kids. For you. Show the world.' And he said, 'Yes,
yes, yes.'" More significantly, perhaps, Michael decided to suspend work
on the "comeback album," so that its release would be timed to whatever
event he chose for his "comeback concerts."

In July 2008, Michael certified his faith in Tohme by signing not one
but two separate powers of attorney (each witnessed by a lawyer) that
gave the Arab nearly absolute control over his financial and business affairs. One month later, the two men signed a service contract that named
Tohme as Jackson's manager and guaranteed him 15 percent of any deals

he negotiated. "Michael understands the love I have for him," Tohme said. "He knows I want only the best for him. Before we sign, we make an agreement: He will never interfere in any of my business decisions and I will never interfere in any of his artistic decisions."

There was considerable overlap in those two apparently discrete areas of interest, however, as Tohme would eventually discover. In the meantime, according to Michael Amir Williams, what most impressed Michael Jackson about his new manager was Tohme's claim of a close relationship with the royal family of Brunei. "This was the main reason Michael wanted Tohme around," Brother Michael said. "He thought that Tohme was associated with this family and could easily get him the [Prince Jefri Bolkiah's] Spanish Gate Drive estate."

"Michael really, really wanted that house," Tohme said. "Michael has vision, he wanted to make it a residence, but also a museum. All the stuff he was buying— and he was criticized in the media for it—but he wanted to have a place like Graceland that would be a monument to him while he was alive and after he died. And he knew it couldn't be Neverland." The Spanish Gate property had the space to accommodate even Michael Jackson's vast collection of art and antiques, by then spread out in warehouses that stretched from Santa Barbara to Santa Monica to Las Vegas. In addition to the immense main house, the estate Prince Jefri had created for himself included a 47,000-square-foot "sporting house" that featured an Olympic-size swimming pool, assorted fitness rooms, a squash court, a racquetball court, and a disco hall, plus two 4,500-square-foot guest villas. "I did my best to make it happen for him," Tohme explained. "I am very, very close friends with a high government official in Brunei. I called and told him, 'We're gonna do it like Graceland.' I eventually got the price down to $45 million. But then I find that financing for a place like that in Las Vegas is difficult. There are lots of houses that cost that much money in Los Angeles, but not so many in Las Vegas. They will finance maybe $20 million, maybe $25 million, but no more."

Collecting the money Michael would need to take possession of the Spanish Gate house became another carrot Tohme could use to motivate his client's return to the stage: "I told Michael, 'One more time. We're gonna conquer the world. You will be back on top and you will get that house, too.'"

In the meantime, Tohme was urging Michael to return to Los Angeles while they searched for the right concert package. "I told him, 'The action is all in LA. People don't want to come to Las Vegas to meet with you.' But Michael was reluctant."

Michael's resistance to the idea of leaving Las Vegas softened considerably after his fiftieth birthday. On August 28, dozens of British fans had showed up outside the gates of the Palomino hacienda to serenade Michael until the wee hours of the August 29. He was still glowing, despite not having slept a wink, when he did a telephone interview with *Good Morning America* that began before sunrise in Vegas and he was delighted to learn that millions of people had switched channels to ABC to catch some of it. "I'll probably just have a little cake with my children and we'll probably watch cartoons," he answered in reply to a question about how he intended to celebrate.

Michael's mood was shattered later that same day, though, when he received a letter that had been signed by many of his neighbors. "He called me and he was crying like a baby," Tohme remembered. "I said, 'Michael, what's wrong?' He said, 'They've sent me something saying they don't want a child molester living across the street.'" What especially hurt him, Michael said, were the complaints that Wasden Elementary School was just down the street, visible from the windows of Jackson's home, and that it did not seem fitting to have an accused sex criminal so close by. As a "concerned mother" explained to the *Review-Journal*, "Of all the residences he could have purchased—why one across from an elementary school? I understand he was never convicted of anything and can live wherever he wants, but . . ."

His new manager flew to Las Vegas the next day. "I told him, 'Michael, it's time to get the hell out of here,'" Tohme recalled. "I wanted him to come to Los Angeles. He was still not sure about that. So I said, 'Why don't you come to LA for a few days to meet my family, to stay with us?' So I brought him to my house, we had lunch, he stayed there, but then he went back to Las Vegas."

Not to the Palomino property, though. Although he continued to use the house as an enormous storage unit, Michael moved once again into the Palms, where his visits to the recording studio were both less frequent and more informal than during his previous stay. He'd roll in after noon with all three of his kids, leading Blanket by the hand, dressed in black jeans and a silk shirt, noodle at the keyboards, working on melodies and trying lyrics, then leave an hour or two later.

Back in Los Angeles, Tohme discovered an ally in his campaign to find the right "performance situation" for Michael when he took a call from Peter Lopez, one of the dozens of attorneys who had represented Michael in recent years. Like most of those who tried out for a role as "the one," Lopez had been left with unpaid bills. "Peter knew I was now Michael's manager," Tohme recalled, "and he told me, 'I'm owed money.' He asked if I could pay him. I said, 'At this time, there's no money. But if you are owed I will see you get paid. Prove it to me.' So he came to meet me at the Hotel Bel-Air. And I told him he had a chance to help me put Michael back on top. I told him, 'Forget all the rumors. Michael is gonna go back to work. Help me find the right concert series for him.' And I could see that he was a lot more interested in talking about that than about the money he was owed."

Lopez was the best-known Latin entertainment lawyer in Los Angeles. Among his closest friends was the new governor, Arnold Schwarzenegger, who had appointed Lopez to the State Athletic Commission. Lopez was married to former *Dukes of Hazzard* actress Catherine Bach and his list of clients, past and present, included the Eagles, Britney Spears, Jennifer Lopez, and Andrea Bocelli. But "Peter knew that nothing would compare to helping Michael Jackson make a comeback," Tohme recalled.

Lopez first set up a meeting with Live Nation that left Tohme unimpressed. "I don't like those guys," he recalled telling Lopez, who then suggested AEG. Tohme claimed to be unaware of Michael's previous meeting with Randy Phillips, who had never entirely given up on signing Michael to an AEG Live contract. What really moved things along was a phone conversation between a pair of billionaires, Barrack and Anschutz. Barrack told Anschutz how impressed he'd been when he met Michael Jackson in person. Anschutz pointed out that if Michael Jackson's public stature was elevated and his career reinvigorated, the value of Neverland Ranch could easily double. Beyond that, a series of shows at AEG's O2 could easily lead to some sort of resident performer arrangement in Las Vegas that might be staged at one of the Colony's hotels or casinos. Immediately after Anschutz got off the phone with Barrack, he called Randy Phillips and asked him to meet with the Colony Capital CEO to talk about what it would take to secure a commitment from Michael Jackson to perform a series of concerts at the O2 in London. Barrack passed Phillips on to Tohme, who suggested that the AEG Live chief meet him for a drink at the Hotel Bel-Air.

"So we sat, we talked, I liked him," Tohme recalled. "He will do anything to have Michael Jackson. He said that. I said, 'We need advances, we need this, we need that. Let me think about it and talk to Michael." Phillips's stock got a boost when Dennis Hawk, the attorney who had been brought in to assist Tohme in managing Michael's affairs, told Jackson and Tohme that Phillips was "a classy guy" who could be trusted to help put on a show that would be everything they hoped for.

Within days, a summit with Phillips and Anschutz had been scheduled to take place at the MGM Grand in Las Vegas, where the AEG principal owned a villa. "Michael and I talked a lot about it ahead of time," Tohme recalled, "and I told him, 'You gotta look sharp, show them who they're dealing with.'" AEG Live's "co-CEO" Paul Gongaware was advising his associates to take exactly the opposite approach to the meeting: Wear casual attire, he suggested to those who would be attending, "as MJ is distrustful of people in suits." Also, they should be prepared to talk some "fluff" with "Mikey," Gongaware added. Tohme, Hawk, and Lopez were already seated on one side of a conference table across from Anschutz, Phillips, Gongaware, and AEG corporate president Tim Leiweke when Michael arrived with Blanket. "He looked superb," Tohme remembered. "He was dressed in his best and he was in great shape, had great color, his expression was happy, and his eyes were clear. I could tell from the first second they were very impressed by him."

Phillips would admit later to being startled by how changed Jackson was from the distracted, uninterested star he had encountered at their previous meeting months earlier. Michael now seemed "very laser focused," Phillips said, intent not only on looking into the eyes of Philip Anschutz but also on working out some sort of deal.

Anschutz, a business titan most often described as either "reclusive" or "secretive" in the media, "seemed to me a very nice man," Tohme said, "a very honest man, a very kind man. I could see Michael felt it, too." They had agreed beforehand that, after some introductions and a brisk, general conversation about what he hoped to accomplish with a new live show, Michael would stand up again, shake everyone's hands, and say good-bye. "Because this is Michael Jackson," Tohme explained. "He doesn't sit there for hours talking to these guys. I always want to elevate him as much as I can, make him feel he's the King of Pop. We had already arranged for his security and his driver to be waiting right outside. As soon as he is gone, we start negotiating for a comeback concert at the O2. Michael had told me he would never do any concert in the United States."

By the time the guests left Anschutz's villa, they had a handshake agreement that Michael Jackson would perform a series of ten concerts at the O2 in London in the fall of 2009. Phillips and Tohme agreed on a presentation of the idea they believed would please the entertainer: "This way, Michael, fans from all over the world will be coming to you, instead of you having to go to them."

"And Michael Jackson did like the sound of that," Tohme recalled. "He was starting to fill his lungs again."

Two weeks later, Michael agreed to move back to Los Angeles and live there until he left for London. Tohme arranged for Michael to have a huge suite in the rear of the Hotel Bel-Air, "away from everybody," where the management would allow him to create a home studio, complete with a portable dance floor. Within a week of his arrival at the hotel, Michael began testing himself in sessions with a parade of musicians and dancers. He was eating regularly and sleeping better than he had in years. "It is a beautiful thing to see," Tohme recalled. "He wants to prove to the world that he is still Michael Jackson, the King of Pop. And I am watching it happen in front of my eyes." Tohme showed up at the hotel one day with Mina Shafiei, the finest tailor in Beverly Hills, best known for creating celebrity wedding dresses, to measure Michael for a wardrobe of silk jackets and the brocaded shirts he loved. "I want Michael to look like the biggest star in LA any time he steps out his front door," Tohme recalled. "I want him to *feel* like the biggest star."

Michael had been tremendously encouraged by the news that a compilation album called *King of Pop*, released on his fiftieth birthday, had charted in the top ten in every country where Sony made it available, and that the company intended to expand the *King of Pop* concept into a series of records. Spreading rumors of a Michael Jackson comeback also resulted in a slew of interview requests. Tohme refused to approve any publications that would not guarantee, in writing, that his client be identified on first reference as "Michael Jackson, the King of Pop." The number of musicians, producers, and songwriters calling to say they'd love to arrange a visit at the Hotel Bel-Air was doubling by the week.

"Michael became very happy," Tohme recalled. "He is working out every day, dancing, he looks fantastic, smiling all the time, always very sharp and clear. The wheelchair is gone, the umbrella and the two-colored slippers are gone. There are no drugs, no problems with sleeping. I know because I was there all the time. I was seeing him two, three times a day. We'd talk on the phone five, six times a day. I can see and hear him becoming better by the week."

Tohme appeared to be delivering in his role as Jackson's business manager, closing one deal after another. A "Michael Jackson Dance" application for MySpace and Facebook released three days before Michael's birthday had turned into a big seller online. In September, the German teen publication *Bravo* launched its Legends series with a special issue dedicated entirely to Michael Jackson. That same month, Hot Toys announced a deal for a new Michael Jackson action figure that would be released in Japan during the coming Christmas season. Four weeks later, the same company scheduled the worldwide release of a Michael Jackson Cosbaby line, seven small figurines that featured the star in various incarnations that ran the gamut from his *Motown 25* "Billie Jean" performance to the persona he had created for the *HIStory* tour. Tohme had also compelled Sony to pay Jackson $12 million in royalties from the worldwide sales of *Thriller 25*. "They really don't have a right to hold that money for servicing the catalog; they have to turn it over," Tohme explained. "Sony was not used to having someone representing Michael be so forceful with them, to threaten an audit or a lawsuit. But I don't care about my relationship with Sony. I don't care about my relationship with AEG. All I care about is my relationship with Michael Jackson. And that is what he needed." Jackson instructed his manager to hold on to everything that was left from that $12 million after-debt payments in what the two of them called "The Lockbox," a fund Michael would use to buy the Bolkiah Spanish Gate estate when the London shows were finished. The entertainer's new manager had already told AEG that a condition of any agreement they signed was that a certain sum (eventually $15 million was agreed upon) must be paid as an advance before Jackson began performing in concert, so that he would be certain of returning to the United States with enough money to complete the work on the abandoned Bolkiah's Las Vegas mansion.

Tohme understood by then that the promise of a new home that would replace Neverland motivated Michael more than anything else that had been offered to him. "He talked about it constantly, more than making a comeback or anything else," Tohme recalled. "It was his goal, his reward, and he was determined to reach it." Between now and the completion of the London shows, Michael told Tohme in the early autumn of 2008, he wanted every penny that came in from outside the AEG deal to go into the Lockbox with the *Thriller 25* royalties. "He said to keep it a secret," Tohme recalled. "He doesn't want anyone to know about it or touch it. He doesn't want to touch it himself. And especially he doesn't want his family to touch it. He made me promise they would never know about the *Thriller 25* money. He wanted no contact with his family, whatsoever. We were changing his phone number every two weeks so that they wouldn't be able to get it. He said they could have my number, they could contact him through me. And he was very kind. He said, 'Help them.' When one of his brothers calls and needs money, he says, 'Give it to him.' And he would always be generous to his mom. He loved his mother and trusted only her, no one else in the family. But even her he didn't want to have his phone number, because he said the others would use her to get things from him."

The family had picked up on the increase in the buzz around Michael, though, and in late October Tohme had felt obliged to issue a statement from Michael about the rumor that Jackson was about to embark with his brothers on a Jackson 5 reunion tour: "My brothers and sisters have my full love and support, and we've certainly shared many great experiences, but at this time I have no plans to record or tour with them. I am now in the studio developing new and exciting projects that I look forward to sharing with my fans in concert soon."

By November, the O2 negotiations were advancing rapidly, Randy Phillips recalled, and Michael seemed more enthusiastic by the week about resurrecting his career. During a meeting with Michael at the Hotel Bel-Air, Phillips recalled, "I asked him straight off, 'Why say yes to the tour now? Is it the money?'" Michael replied that cleaning up his finances was part of it, but the single biggest reason was that his children were finally old enough now to see him perform and understand why people chased him on the street. And he wanted people to start talking about his work again instead of his "lifestyle." In that meeting, Phillips for the first time sensed that Michael Jackson still harbored grand ambitions. He described the movies he wanted to make, spoke about the comeback album he would release in tandem with the O2 concerts, talked about how much he wanted to settle down again, about finding a new home, some place he loved enough to let go of Neverland.

Still, all of the people involved in working out the details of the contract for the London shows knew they were walking on eggshells. "Everybody said two things about him," Tom Barrack would tell *Fortune* magazine. "Firstly, if Michael Jackson came back it would be the greatest thing in music history. And secondly, it would never happen."

"People told me I was crazy, that I would get my heart broken," Randy Phillips admitted to *Rolling Stone*. "But I just believed in him. How many times in your career do you get to touch greatness?"

PART FOUR

SOUTH

16

It came as no surprise to the clerks at Santa Monica's Hennessey + Ingalls art and architecture bookstore that, in the autumn of 2008, they were among the first to learn Michael Jackson was once again living in Los Angeles. For most other people in the city, though, Jackson's intellectual curiosity had always been the least appreciated of his qualities. He kept over ten thousand books at Neverland and had read most of them. The owners of Book Soup on Sunset Boulevard and Dutton's in Brentwood had been selling to him by the box load for years. Michael was a quiet shopper who lingered longest in the poetry section but had a special affection for the all-embracing philosophy of Ralph Waldo Emerson and the nineteenth-century transcendentalists. He was extensively read in the works of Sigmund Freud and Carl Jung, the great psychoanalysts, whose work he was able to discuss with a sophistication that astonished acquaintances over the years.

Many in the media were amused by descriptions of the infamous *Last Supper* painting that hung over his bed at Neverland, a depiction of him sitting at the center of a long table flanked by Walt Disney on one side and Albert Einstein on the other, with Thomas Edison, Charlie Chaplin, Elvis Presley, John F. Kennedy, Abraham Lincoln, and Little Richard ("Tutti Frutti" was right up there with Tchaikovsky's "Danse des petits cygnes" in Michael's book, and Little Richard did his own dancing) spread out beside them. Very few knew that Michael had studied the biographies of each of these "inspirational heroes" and could recount their life stories in extraordinary detail. He had been fascinated for decades with celebrities who died young, and professed amazement as early as the mid-eighties that it was "the same things over and over again"—meaning drugs and sex—that had brought the lives of these stars to an early, tragic end.

Michael's multitasking attempts to learn and grow amid even the most chaotic circumstances touched and perplexed any number of people who came into his life. He peppered with numerous questions nearly everyone he met who boasted expertise in any area of human endeavor. Michael studied the field of medicine intently, and, with the help of Arnold Klein, among other doctors, had arranged to observe numerous surgeries at the UCLA Medical Center. Jackson and Marlon Brando, another omnivore, spent much of their time together comparing notes about the various scientific concepts and technologies they were studying. Deepak Chopra, who had encountered Michael for the first time backstage in Bucharest during the *Bad* tour, recalled, "He would be swarmed by crowds at the airport, perform an exhausting show for three hours, then sit backstage afterward drinking bottled water, glancing over some Sufi poetry as I walked into the room."

Gregory Peck had met Michael a decade earlier when, one afternoon, Jackson called him up and asked if he could stop by for a visit. Peck was stunned that Michael had memorized every line of dialogue from *To Kill a Mockingbird* and asked cogent, thoughtful questions about the film. The friendship that developed from this meeting was as enduring as it was surprising. Jackson and Peck (who had bought a working cattle ranch in northern Santa Barbara County back in the late fifties, when he was working on a movie called *The Bravados*) regularly went horseback riding together at Neverland Ranch and carried on conversations that lasted for hours. Michael was among the few people with whom Peck would discuss the 1975 suicide of his eldest son, Jonathan, and the first "Blanket" Michael ever met was the Pecks' dog. In December 2002, when the balcony-dangling incident with his own Blanket from the balcony of the Hotel Adlon in Berlin made Michael into an international pariah, Gregory Peck and his wife, Veronique, wrote an "Open Letter of Support" that was posted on Jackson's Web site.

When Gregory Peck died in his sleep at the age of eighty-seven in June 2003, Jackson created a minor scandal by arriving twenty minutes late (and dressed in a bright red jacket) to the actor's funeral in the Cathedral of Our Lady of the Angels. What most of those who chided him for attempting to upstage the most beloved of Hollywood's stars didn't know was that Michael had come to the Pecks' home in Bel Air the day after Greg's death to help his widow plan the memorial service.

Veronique Peck, still elegant in her seventies, was on Michael's arm the evening of October 29, 2008, when he made the public appearance that announced his return to Los Angeles. The occasion was a Halloween party hosted by Dixie Chicks lead singer Natalie Maines and her actor husband, Adrian Pasdar. Thinking he was an impersonator, the DJ at the party began to play "Thriller" when Michael walked into the huge room. Several people approached to say that his was absolutely the best Michael Jackson costume they'd ever seen, only to stop frozen in midsentence when they realized it *was* Michael Jackson. Maines would later tell shock-jock Howard Stern that Michael's eldest son was perhaps "the most well-adjusted" and "self-assured" child she'd ever met. She wasn't quite so complimentary toward the boy's father, who not only had failed to introduce himself after arriving at her home but also allowed his bodyguards to keep her away when she made the effort to meet him. "I think maybe he's stuck in time as a child," she told Stern. "I felt like maybe he's a child. He's got lots of handlers."

Michael wasn't wearing a mask on the evening of Maines's party, but he had been three weeks earlier, when he and his children were photographed leaving a comic book store on Melrose Avenue, each of the kids costumed as a Halloween character. The story that accompanied the photograph in London's *Daily Mail* (which remained interested in each and every Wacko Jacko sighting) described him as looking "scarier than ever in a surgical mask, giant black sunglasses, and a hooded jumper."

Tohme was furious: "I told him, 'No mask, Michael. Not again, ever, please. Remember who you are.'"

The newly minted manager, though, was learning quickly that who Michael Jackson was would mean fielding an unceasing swirl of false reports, scandalous claims, and vindictive rumors, whether he wore a mask or not. In Las Vegas, columnist Norm Clarke had just come out with a story that Jackson had turned down the opportunity to perform at the opening of Steve Wynn's new $2.2 billion Encore Tower "and everybody thought it was because Michael was sick or on drugs," Tohme recalled. The rumors that Jackson was seriously ill had been fueled by a claim made in Britain's *Sun* by Ian Halperin, who was claiming that "sources" had informed him the star's fading health had left him nearly blind in one eye and in need of a lung transplant that he "may be too weak to go through with." The absurd story had gained traction so quickly that Tohme had been forced to grant the *New York Daily News* an interview in which he declared it "a total fabrication." Just a couple of months earlier, the *Wall Street Journal* had published an article stating that Jackson was "holed up" in the "rural Nevada compound" of Pahrump, a dusty little census-created community on the edge of the Mojave Desert that was best known for its discount brothels. "Michael had never been near the place," a baffled Tohme would say. "And this is the *Wall Street Journal.*" The appearance of the Pahrump story had coincided with the resurfacing of Jack Wishna, who was playing a particularly unattractive version of the spurned suitor as he told the *National Enquirer* that reports Michael Jackson was about to mount a series of comeback concerts at Tom Barrack's hotels were wishful thinking. "Sadly, Michael's incapable of keeping promises, because he hasn't got the will to even show up anywhere, much less get himself into shape for a world-class performance," Wishna told the *Enquirer*. "He might drop by to wave at guests, or do a dance on top of a limo, but a long term show? That dream will never come true, I'm afraid."

The only good thing about all the stories coming out of Nevada was that they seemed to make Michael increasingly content to stay in Southern California, Tohme said. By the middle of November, Jackson was telling his manager that he wanted to start looking at houses in Bel Air. Tohme was delighted, until he discovered that the first home to capture his client's imagination was the most expensive on the entire LA market, a lavish estate that had just been built at the top of Bel Air's most exclusive street, Nimes Road, by the former owner of the Ritz-Carlton Hotels, Mohamed Hadid. "Le Belvedere," Hadid called his mansion, a 48,000-square-foot palace that offered 280-degree views and was barricaded by a thousand-foot-long, 36-foot-high wall made of stones imported from Jerusalem. The 2.2-acre grounds were breathtaking, heavy with specimen plantings that surrounded a "swan lake" and an infinity pool, all set against the property's majestic vistas. Among the home's many interior amenities, Michael's favorite was a sixty-seat home theater that was set up in the style of an opera house. Hadid had just put the place on the market for $85 million and Michael was trying to convince both the owner and his manager that he could afford it. "I told him, 'Michael, it's too much. It's not worth it,'" Tohme recalled. Hadid refused when Tohme asked if his client could rent Le Belvedere, but said he would allow Jackson to spend the night in the house with his children "in order to feel the place." It was agreed that Hadid and his son would vacate the property on Thanksgiving morning to spend that day and night in Santa Barbara. Tohme and his wife prepared a feast, then transported it, along with their own children, Michael, and Michael's children to Le Belvedere, where they all dined together. "We stayed late, then left Michael and his children and returned home," Tohme recalled. "The next morning I went and picked up Michael and his children and took them back to the Hotel Bel-Air. On the way Michael said he didn't want Hadid's house. He said he heard some bad voice there. Michael was a very spiritual guy, and he was guided by that in his decisions."

Over the next few days, Tohme convinced Michael that renting a home was the right move, at least until they returned from London after the O2 shows. With the help of a real estate broker friend named Joyce Essex, Tohme located an estate on Carolwood Drive in Holmby Hills, a neighborhood that—with Beverly Hills on one side and Bel Air on the other—formed the fabled "Platinum Triangle." The property's 17,171-square-foot, three-story, French chateau–style mansion belonged to Christian Audigier's senior partner in his Ed Hardy stores: Hubert Guez. Designed by Richard Landry, LA's reigning architect to the ultrarich, the home was situated on 1.25 acres enclosed by walls and gates, with a breathtaking slate-patioed pool. There were seven bedrooms, thirteen bathrooms, twelve fireplaces, a gourmet kitchen, a wine cellar, a theater and family rooms, a huge curving staircase, and a wood-paneled library that Michael adored the moment he saw it. He was also pleased that the house had formerly been the Los Angeles home of Sean Connery—Sir Sean Connery. Before being pulled off the market the property had been advertised at a price of $38 million. Quite a few people snickered, naturally, when Tohme Tohme said that Michael had moved into the Carolwood chateau, which was being rented for $100,000 per month, "to save money." But that *was* less than it cost to live full-time at the Hotel Bel-Air. Anyway, AEG was paying the bill, though Michael tended to forget that the cost was being subtracted from his future earnings. The chateau was actually a rather modest spread for this particular neighborhood, which encompassed Hugh Hefner's Playboy Mansion and the monstrous 57,000-square-foot, 123-room palace that TV producer Aaron Spelling had built after tearing down Bing Crosby's lovely old house on South Mapleton Drive.

What most who knew him wondered was whether Michael's move into the Holmby Hills mansion was a break from the past or a return to it. Much of his personal history was nearby. Gregory Peck's place and Berry Gordy's mansion were over the hill on the other side of Beverly Glen Drive. The house in which Jackson's former wife Lisa Marie Presley had grown up could be found just around the corner on Monovale Drive. The Hayvenhurst compound, where Michael had lived even longer than at Neverland, was a ten-minute drive from Carolwood when traffic was light. And the Guez chateau was much closer than that to the intersection in Beverly Hills where the Jeep Michael was driving one day in May 1992 had broken down, at Wilshire and Lindley, a location that for Jackson was loaded with more bad memories and dark juju than just about any other spot on the planet. It was the point, really, at which he had come to the beginning of his end.

*   *   *

An arresting sight it must have been on that sunny afternoon when thirty-three-year-old Michael Jackson, wearing a black turban fitted with a veil and large black sunglasses, stood in the right lane of Wilshire Boulevard, kicking the tires of his stalled Jeep. It must have *sounded* pretty strange to Mel Green, who took a phone call from his wife telling him whom she had just seen stranded in traffic. Sensing a moment of opportunity, Green sped to the rescue, then phoned Dave Schwartz, his boss at Rent-A-Wreck, a used-cars-for-hire agency situated about a mile away in West Los Angeles. He would be arriving within minutes, in the company of a very special guest, Green told Schwartz. "You sure it's not some impersonator?" the boss asked. Green seemed pretty certain, so Schwartz phoned his wife June and told her to get over to the shop and to bring their six-year daughter Lily and June's twelve-year-old son from a previous marriage, Jordan Chandler.

Jordie was a beautiful kid (a fact that would be employed against Jackson later) with caramel-colored skin, dark eyes, perfect white teeth, and flawless features. June Chandler Schwartz, born June Wong, was herself an exotic Eurasian with a hint of African blood, full lips, and lustrous black hair. At Rent-A-Wreck, she told Michael that Jordie was a big fan of his, had in fact sent him a drawing in 1984 after his hair caught fire filming that Pepsi commercial, then handed Michael a business card on which she'd written the family's home phone number.

In the weeks that followed, Michael began calling Jordie, as he had called many other boys over the years, and the two became phone friends. According to June, Jackson invited her son to visit him at his condo in Westwood—"the Hideout"—but she was unable to take him. Michael left on a three-month promotional tour a short time later (accompanied by two other boys, an eleven-year-old Australian named Brett Barnes and nine-year-old Prince Albert von Thurn und Taxis of Bavaria) but still found time to call Jordan Chandler on a regular basis. According to Jordie, Michael described the wonders of Neverland, "a place where boys have rights," and promised to have him there soon as a guest. The pledge was kept when Michael returned from his tour; Jordie, June, and half-sister Lily visited Neverland a number of times in late 1992 and early 1993. On the family's first visit, Jordie and Lily were treated to an after-hours shopping spree at Toys "R" Us in which the kids piled more than $10,000 worth of merchandise into their shopping carts. The next evening, Jordie would say, he and Michael took a ride together on the Neverland Ferris wheel, which stopped when their gondola was at the apex of its revolution.

"Do you know how much time I spend up here alone?" Michael asked the boy, sweeping his arms across the sea of lights beneath them. "I have all this, yet I have nothing."

"You have us now," Jordie replied, and slipped his arm around Michael's shoulder.

"My new little family," Michael said, and smiled, according to the boy's account.

Michael invited Jordie, June, and Lily back to Neverland the next weekend, and arrived personally at their front door in a limousine on Friday afternoon to take them to the ranch from Los Angeles. When he climbed into the limo, Jordie would say, he found Brett Barnes already inside, sitting on Michael's lap. Michael spoke mostly to Brett during the ride, according to Jordie and his mother, and when they arrived at Neverland instructed his staff to take the Australian boy's things to his own bedroom. Jordie, like his mother and half-sister, slept in a guest room. When Michael invited the family to join him on a trip to Las Vegas, though, that all changed, according to both Jordie and his mother. He and Michael watched *The Exorcist* together, Jordie said, and he was so frightened that he sought comfort in Michael's bed that night. "There was no physical contact" on that occasion, according to Jordie's sworn statement, but his mom was upset when she saw that the boy's own bed hadn't been slept in, questioned him about it, then warned her son, "Never do that again."

Jordie told Michael what his mother had said and, according to June, Jackson came to her wearing an injured expression. "How could you think I would hurt Jordie?" he asked. During the conversation that followed, June claimed later, Michael explained his theory that children were sexually innocent and remained that way until they were "conditioned" by adults to develop prurient thoughts. What he wanted for Jordie, Michael said, was that the boy remain "pure," free of the contamination with which adult society would try to ruin him. The very next day, Michael presented June with a $12,000 ruby-and-diamond bracelet from Cartier. "It's nothing," Michael told her, according to June. "I just love you."

After that, Jordie and Michael slept in the same bed every night they spent together. Michael was as innocent as a young child himself, June told her husband and friends: "I really don't think he has a devious bone in his body." Her ex-husband, Jordie's father Evan Chandler, expressed doubts, but seemed to have been swiftly won over by Michael's sweet personality and extraordinary generosity.

Evan, though, was a man of complex motives. He had been born in the Bronx in 1944 as Evan Robert Charmatz, and dutifully but unhappily followed his father and brothers into the field of dentistry, opening a practice in West Palm Beach, Florida, in 1973. Within the next few years he changed his last name to Chandler (he thought Charmatz "too Jewish-sounding"), married June Wong, whom he regularly introduced as "an ex-model," and moved to Los Angeles, where he hoped to establish a career as a screenwriter.

Chandler supported his family in the meantime by working at the Crenshaw Family Dental Center, a clinic catering to low-income patients on the edge of South Central Los Angeles. He got into trouble with the California Board of Dental Examiners in December 1978 for performing restoration work on sixteen of a single patient's teeth during one visit. An investigation of the work resulted in a judgment by the board that Chandler was guilty of "gross ignorance and/or inefficiency," and a ruling that his license be revoked. After an appeal, the revocation was reduced to a ninety-day suspension, plus thirty months of probation.

Chandler dealt with his suspension by moving back to New York to write a screenplay but was unable to sell it. By 1980, the year Jordie was born, the family had returned to Los Angeles, where Evan worked at a series of dentistry jobs and complained that each one made him more miserable than the last. Over the next few years, his marriage deteriorated, in large part, June claimed, because Evan couldn't control his violent temper. After their divorce in 1985, June Chandler was awarded full custody of their son and $500 per month in child support.

By 1990, both Jordie's mother and father had remarried, June to Dave Schwartz, Lily's father, and Evan to a corporate attorney named Nathalie who bore him two sons. Evan had a successful dentistry practice in Beverly Hills by then, but in 1991 found himself once again in trouble due to claims of carelessness or incompetence. A model he was contracted to do restoration work for had suffered severe damage to her teeth and sued him for negligence. Chandler claimed the woman had signed a consent form accepting the risks involved in the procedures he'd undertaken, but he was unable to produce it when subpoenaed, telling the court that the document had been stolen from the trunk of his Jaguar. Eventually the suit was settled out of court.

In 1993, right around the time his son Jordie met Michael Jackson, Evan finally found some success in Hollywood when one of his scripts was rewritten by Mel Brooks and turned into the film *Robin Hood: Men in Tights*. A lucrative career as a screenwriter did not result, however, and

Evan soon fell behind on his child support payments; eventually his debt to June approached $70,000, with interest. June would claim that her ex-husband had been largely an absentee father to Jordie, rarely spending time with his son until Michael Jackson appeared. Evan's brother Raymond disagreed. Evan tried to be a good dad, Ray insisted, and before Michael Jackson came into their lives, "Everybody liked everybody and the kids all played together, even though there were divorces."

There are conflicting accounts of what took place after Evan and Michael got to know each other. Michael's story—or at least the story his representatives put together for him—was told most authoritatively in an article for GQ magazine written by journalist Mary A. Fischer in close collaboration with Anthony Pellicano, the private investigator who was working for Jackson attorney Bert Fields and handling most of the early contacts with the Chandler family. Evan's brother Raymond (who would also change his name from Charmatz to Chandler) called Fischer "a dupe" and Pellicano "a thug," claiming that the two had combined to terribly "distort the picture" of Evan's behavior and Michael's as well. In police interviews and court testimony, June Wong Chandler Schwartz told yet another version of the story, one that disagreed in numerous ways with both Evan Chandler's account and Michael Jackson's. What Jordie Chandler himself said happened would eventually be laid out in interviews with psychiatrists and police officers.

Not in dispute is that early in the relationship between Michael and Jordie, Evan began to invite the two to spend time together at his home in Brentwood. "They hung out together, they talked about movies, about writing screenplays together, about writing songs together," said Ray Chandler. "Evan readily admitted that he fell under Michael's spell. He thought Michael was a highly intelligent, well-read, well-rounded guy. He liked Michael and he was excited about Michael and he really believed that he and Michael were going to do great work together and be friends forever." The Fischer/Pellicano account was that Evan pitched story ideas to Michael and suggested that Michael could pay him by building an addition onto the house, one that would create enough space to give them all more privacy. When zoning restrictions prevented that, according to Fischer and Pellicano, Evan proposed that Jackson simply build him a newer, larger home. Michael, Pellicano told Fischer, shrugged off that idea. Ray Chandler, though, said it was Michael who proposed to either build a new wing on the house, or to build a new house entirely, so that they could all live together.

What's known for certain is that in June 1993, Michael flew Jordie and June to Monaco with him to attend the World Music Awards. Photographs of the lovely woman and the beautiful boy seated with Jackson at the ceremony were published worldwide amid much speculation that June might be Michael's new girlfriend and Jordie his future stepson. "Michael's New Adopted Family" read the headline in the *National Enquirer*. "Evan began to get jealous of the involvement and felt left out," June's former attorney Michael Freeman would tell Fischer.

Evan invited Michael to spend five days at his house and allowed him to sleep in the same room with Jordie and his five-year-old half-brother Nikki. It was during this stay, Evan would say later, that he began to develop suspicions about Jackson's possible sexual misconduct. He never saw either Jordie or Michael without their clothes on, Chandler would admit, but he walked into the room one day and saw the two spooning on the bed with Michael's hand near Jordie's crotch. Evan called to tell his brother what he had seen, and in the same conversation told Ray that June intended to take Jordie with her on Michael's *Dangerous* tour.

By the end of June 1993, Evan Chandler was increasingly vocal and volatile about his "concerns." According to Evan, he finally confronted Michael, saying, "You and Jordie are having sex, aren't you? Just be a man and fucking admit it." Evan admitted that he was impressed by how well Michael maintained his composure, calmly replying, "That's preposterous. It never happened." Michael immediately cut off all contact with the man.

By early July, Evan was making it clear that he intended to challenge June's custody of Jordie. He discussed "the situation" in a phone call to Dave Schwartz that his ex-wife's new husband tape-recorded. The only publicly available transcript of that conversation is the one Anthony Pellicano provided to Mary A. Fischer, and it casts Evan Chandler in a very dim light.

The Pellicano/Fischer transcript had Jordie's father beginning the conversation with seemingly sincere expressions of concern for his son and of fury at both Jackson and June, whom he described (to her current husband) as "cold and heartless." He had tried to talk to June about his worries, Evan complained, but she replied by telling him, "Go fuck yourself." Chandler's tone changed, though, becoming almost whiny, as he shifted the conversation to his estrangement from Michael Jackson. "I had a good communication with Michael," Chandler told Schwartz. "We were friends. I liked him and I respected him and everything else, for what he is. There was no reason why he had to stop calling me. I sat in the room one day and talked to Michael and told him exactly what I want out of this whole relationship."

He had "been rehearsed" about what to say and not to say when he spoke to Jackson, Chandler told Schwartz, which was why he never mentioned the subject of money. Schwartz asked what Michael had done that so upset him. "He broke up the family," Chandler replied. "Jordie has been seduced by this guy's power and money." Each of the men confessed their failure to properly father Jordie, then suddenly Chandler confided that he was preparing to take action against Jackson. "It's already set," he said. "There are other people involved that are waiting for my phone call that are in certain positions. I've paid them to do it. Everything's going according to a certain plan that isn't just mine. Once I make that phone call, this guy is going to destroy everybody in sight in any devious, nasty, cruel way that he can do it."

Ray Chandler said that Pellicano, through Fischer, had selectively sampled the tape recording of the conversation to falsely create the impression that Evan was talking about a "win" that would put some enormous sum in his pocket. Anyone who listened closely to the entire tape, Ray said, would recognize that Evan was talking about getting custody of his son, not money from Michael Jackson.

What most made people doubt Ray Chandler's explanation was that the "guy" who had "rehearsed" Evan was Barry K. Rothman, a Century City attorney whom his client described to Dave Schwartz as "the nastiest son of a bitch I could find."

Many people in Los Angeles would have said that description was too generous. Rothman had once been a music lawyer of some note who negotiated contracts for the Rolling Stones, Little Richard, and the Who. Gold and platinum records decorated his office walls. He had a general practice these days and, Rothman's ex-wife once told her own attorney that Rothman made so many enemies over the years that she was amazed somebody hadn't killed him by now. Rothman was canny, though, and had layered his life with protections against the long line of people who despised him and the even longer line of people who claimed he owed them money. Many of the latter were former employees. Rothman had lots of those, because he went through office workers at an astounding rate, notorious both for verbally abusing the women he hired and for failing to pay their salaries. He'd taken to hiring temps as receptionists who usually lasted a couple of weeks before he ran them out of the office, cursing them as idiots as they fled from his presence in tears. The woman who was working as his legal secretary that summer, Geraldine Hughes, would characterize him as "a real life demon straight out of the pits of hell."

An investigator involved in one of the many lawsuits filed against Rothman called him "a professional deadbeat." When he fell behind on alimony and child support payments to his ex-wife, she threatened to attach his assets. When her attorney tried to put a lien on Rothman's home in Sherman Oaks after a year of nonpayment, it was discovered that the deed had been transferred to a Panamanian shell corporation called Tinoa Operations. He'd had $200,000 of Tinoa's cash robbed from a safe in his house, Rothman would claim, and had to make good on the loss by signing over the deed on his home. Only when the most prized of his possessions, a Rolls-Royce Corniche (with the license plate "BKR 1"), was towed away did Rothman pay his ex-wife what he owed her.

Documents from other cases filed at the Los Angeles Superior Court demonstrated that Rothman was operating behind a complex network of foreign bank accounts and shell companies (Tinoa Operations among them), several with the same address as a Chinese restaurant on Cahuenga Boulevard in Hollywood. Twenty lawsuits, multiple complaints to the state Labor Commission, and at least three disciplinary actions by the State Bar of California had been initiated against Rothman, but he managed time after time to avoid serious consequences. A year before Evan Chandler came to him, Rothman had been suspended for a year by the bar association for blatantly ignoring conflict-of-interest rules in a case involving a woman he had been representing in child support and custody proceedings. Rothman managed to have the suspension reduced to probation, then promptly had his law firm file for bankruptcy. When creditors demanded to know how a man who drove a Rolls-Royce could claim no assets, Rothman produced papers showing that the title to the car had been transferred to a subsidiary of Tinoa Operations.

So, as Pellicano explained to Fischer, Evan Chandler recognized Rothman at once as the perfect partner in his scheme to take down Michael Jackson. The truth, Ray Chandler countered, was that Rothman had been one of Evan's dental patients, and had offered to help him out—for free— when he expressed concern about June's plan to take Jordie on a world tour with Michael Jackson.

What Evan said about Rothman during his tape-recorded conversation with Dave Schwartz , though, was, "All he wants to do is get this out in the public as fast as he can, as big as he can, and humiliate as many people as he can. He's nasty, he's mean, he's very smart, and he's hungry for the publicity." Chandler spoke as if he hadn't yet decided to unleash

Rothman, but was leaning in that direction: "If I go through with this, I win big time. There's no way I lose. I've checked that inside out. I will get everything I want, and they will be destroyed forever. June will lose [custody of Jordie] and Michael's career will be over."

"Does that help Jordie?" Schwartz asked.

"That's irrelevant to me," Chandler replied. "It's going to be bigger than all of us put together. The whole thing is going to crash down on everybody and destroy everybody in sight. It will be a massacre if I don't get what I want."

Tensions between Chandler and his ex-wife came to a head at a middle school graduation ceremony where June dismissed Evan's allegations against Jackson, then informed him that she still intended to take Jordie out of school in the fall so that the two of them could join Michael on his *Dangerous* tour. "Michael was very good at sizing people up," a member of the Chandler family would observe later. "He looked for a family where some level of disconnect between the parents created a vulnerability that he could exploit. In this case, he saw that June was not in a marriage that she enjoyed. Dave held the purse strings. She wanted independence from that. She was not a woman who wanted to get up in the morning and go to work. A life of luxury and travel was what she dreamed of, and Michael offered her that."

When Evan began to spew threats, June told Michael, who then went to Bert Fields for help. Fields, who had completed the negotiations of Jackson's epic Sony contract that were begun by John Branca, brought in Pellicano, who listened to the tape of the conversation between Evan Chandler and Dave Schwartz and "knew it was about extortion," as he told Fischer. That same day, Pellicano went to the Hideout in Westwood, where Jordie and Lily were visiting. He asked the boy a series of "pointed questions," Pellicano would say, that included "Has Michael ever touched you?" and "Have you ever seen Michael naked in bed?" Jordie looked him in the eye and answered no to each such query, according to Pellicano.

Two days later, though, on July 11, Chandler moved forward with his "plan" by persuading June that Jordie needed some major dental work, then convincing her to let him have his son for an afternoon to get it done. The next day, according to Pellicano, Evan Chandler refused to return Jordie to his mother unless she put her signature on a document prepared by Rothman promising that she would not take Jordie out of Los Angeles County. Evan kept Jordie with him even after June signed the document, though, and on July 14, Rothman placed a phone call to a Beverly Hills psychiatrist named Mathis Abrams and presented what he called "a hypothetical situation" involving a thirteen-year-old boy and an adult celebrity. The next day, Dr. Abrams sent Rothman a two-page letter stating that "reasonable suspicion would exist that sexual abuse may have occurred" and that if this were *not* a hypothetical situation he would be compelled to report the matter to the Los Angeles County Department of Children's Services. On July 27, Rothman instructed Geraldine Hughes to type up a set of instructions for Evan Chandler explaining how to report child abuse to the authorities without exposing himself to liability.

A deeply religious young black woman who happened to be a Michael Jackson fan, Hughes was at once alarmed and suspicious about the "the incredible level of secrecy" her employer was imposing on his contacts with Evan Chandler and began to keep a written record of what she saw and heard. Chandler phoned the office as many as five times a day, Hughes observed, and each time Rothman retreated to his "Fort Knox of an office" to make sure that no one could listen in on the conversation. Even meetings with his associate attorneys were suspended so that Rothman could take calls from Chandler in private. It seemed "odd" to her, Hughes noted, that afterward there were never any memos to file. When Chandler came into the office, Hughes said, he always met with Rothman behind locked doors and no notes were made of their conversations. Curiosity overcame her one afternoon when Chandler showed up late at the office in an emotional state and was immediately pulled by Rothman into the conference room. She stepped to the door of the conference room to try to hear what was being said, Hughes would admit, but the two men inside kept their voices low except for a single loud outburst by Rothman in which he shouted, "We have to stick to the plan . . . we cannot deviate from the plan!"

Rothman did not accompany Chandler when Evan showed up with Jordie for a meeting with Jackson and Pellicano at the Westwood Marquis Hotel. According to Pellicano, Evan Chandler first gave Michael a hug, then pulled the letter from Dr. Abrams out of his pocket and began to read it aloud. At the point where his father began to quote the references to child molestation, Pellicano said, Jordie hung his head, then looked up at Michael with an expression of surprise. The meeting ended with Evan pointing his finger at Michael and telling him, "I'm going to ruin you." Pellicano came to Rothman's office that evening for a second meeting, at which (according to the private investigator) the attorney presented his client's demand for $20 million. Pellicano said that after he walked out in disgust, the demand was reduced to a payment of $5 million for four screenplay deals. According to Ray Chandler, the idea that Michael Jackson should pay off with a screenplay deal was Pellicano's, not Evan's, and his brother had been so incensed by the suggestion that he nearly came to blows with the private investigator.

By Pellicano's account, he returned to Rothman's office on August 13, to make an offer—$350,000 for a single screenplay deal if this whole thing went away. Rothman answered that it was three screenplays or nothing, according to Pellicano, who claimed he had phoned back later to say one screenplay deal for $350,000, take it or leave it. Geraldine Hughes recalled that Chandler's disappointment was apparent. "I almost had a $20 million deal," the secretary heard him tell Rothman.

Sometime between the August 13 meeting and a custody hearing scheduled for August 17 (at which the judge would almost certainly order Jordie returned to his mother), Evan Chandler took his son to see Mark Torbiner, the dental anesthesiologist who had introduced him to Barry Rothman in 1991. In Chandler's presence, Torbiner administered a dose of the so-called "truth serum" sodium Amytal to the boy, who, under questioning by his father, said Michael had touched his penis. At that point, it may not have mattered that most psychiatrists would agree that sodium Amytal is no truth serum (studies going back to 1952 show that it can be used to implant false memories), because all Dr. Mathis Abrams had to hear was that Jordie had made an accusation. Abrams heard that and plenty more from the boy in a three-hour session the next day, including descriptions of masturbation, kissing, nipple tweaking, and oral sex. As required by law, the psychiatrist immediately reported the accusations to a social worker at the Department of Children's Services, who then phoned the police. Learning that a criminal investigation had been initiated, the judge hearing the custody case between Evan and June delayed his ruling. Though she didn't yet know it, June had lost her son.

Five days after Abrams phoned the social worker and the social worker phoned the police, a freelance reporter in Burbank was tipped off that warrants had been issued allowing officers from the Los Angeles Police Department's Sexually Exploited Child Unit and deputies from the Santa Barbara County sheriff's office to enter both Neverland Ranch and the condo in Westwood to search for evidence that would support child sex abuse charges against Michael Jackson. The freelancer sold the story to the local NBC affiliate, which broke the news at four the next afternoon and set off a global media frenzy. Most papers redacted the boy's name but they all printed Michael's.

The pressure of it all—perhaps supplemented by simple greed—persuaded June and her husband Dave to change stories and switch sides. On August 18, when LAPD officers first interviewed her, June said she did not believe Michael had done anything inappropriate with her son. She began to waver, though, a few days later, when two LAPD officers told her that Michael Jackson was a perfect fit for "the classic profile of a pedophile." By September the Schwartzes were running scared, fearful that Evan Chandler and Barry Rothman would try to take custody of Jordie by claiming that June had been a neglectful parent. In October, the couple threw in with Evan Chandler and his impending lawsuit. June's attorney, Michael Freeman, told Mary Fischer that he resigned immediately in disgust. "The whole thing was such a mess," he would explain. "I felt uncomfortable with Evan. He isn't a genuine person, and I sensed he wasn't playing things straight."

On the advice of Bert Fields, supported by the strong opinion of Anthony Pellicano, Michael Jackson agreed in late August to the filing of extortion charges against Chandler and Rothman. Both men promptly hired high-priced criminal defense attorneys (Rothman's was future O. J. Simpson attorney Robert Shapiro) and began to sweat their exposure. According to Geraldine Hughes, Evan Chandler and his son spent one night sleeping in the conference room at Rothman's law firm to hide from the media and the next day she heard Chandler shout at the attorney, "It's my ass that's on the line and in danger of going to prison." Evan Chandler became completely paranoid after being punched in the face by a man (apparently a Jackson fan) who ambushed him outside his dental office. Chandler occasionally brought his son to the office with him, Hughes would recall, and "I understood why Michael Jackson was fond of the boy. He was very fun-loving, warm-spirited, and cute." Jordie was much more relaxed than Evan, Hughes noted, and actually "was the one who kept calming and consoling his father, who was a nervous wreck. It appeared as if the boy was protecting his father instead of vice versa."

Although the extortion charges were never seriously investigated (police in Los Angeles had already committed themselves to proving Jackson guilty), they did force Rothman to resign as Chandler's attorney. Gloria Allred was briefly retained and did what she does best—hold a news conference. "I'm ready and willing to go forward with the trial," she told the media, but then withdrew from the case without explanation just a couple of days later. Soon after, Larry Feldman agreed to become the Chandlers' attorney.

Feldman was, arguably, the most successful civil attorney in Southern California, a former head of the Los Angeles Trial Lawyers Association who was said to have won more multimillion-dollar cases than any lawyer in the county. Since graduating number one in his class from Loyola Law School in the late sixties, he'd risen to senior partner in a firm that employed more than six hundred attorneys in offices spread out from New York to Shanghai. The man was a stone-cold killer in the courtroom and perhaps the worst person in LA to have against you. On September 14, 1993, Feldman filed a $30 million lawsuit against Michael Jackson that accused the star of "1.) sexual battery; 2.) battery; 3.) seduction; 4.) willful misconduct; 5.) intentional infliction of emotional distress; 6.) fraud; and 7.) negligence."

Recognizing what he was up against and expecting criminal charges to be filed against Jackson any day, Bert Fields (who was primarily an entertainment lawyer) brought in his own high-profile trial attorney, Howard Weitzman, best known for helping auto magnate John DeLorean beat a federal case back in the early eighties that had at one point looked ironclad. Almost from the moment Weitzman became involved in the Jackson case, though, according to Fields and Pellicano, he began to push for a settlement. They resisted furiously, said Fields and Pellicano, convinced that the case against Michael was weak, even with Larry Feldman as the attorney prosecuting it.

Jackson was at that point in no position to make any good decisions. He had been in the midst of the Asian leg of the *Dangerous* tour when the Chandler allegations surfaced, already suffering from a variety of minor injuries incurred during his punishing schedule, and almost completely unable to sleep. Within days of learning what Jordie had reportedly said about him, Michael began mixing painkillers, antianxiety medications, and sleeping pills in combinations and doses that swiftly became a serious threat to his health. Jackson was unable to provide the deposition Feldman was demanding, according to one of Bert Fields's associates, because he was glassy-eyed, slurring his speech, could hardly stay awake, had difficulty even lifting a glass of water, and was unable to maintain focus for more than a few seconds at a time.

On November 12, 1993, Michael arrived in London in the company of Elizabeth Taylor to be examined by Dr. Beauchamp Colclough, who promptly arranged for Jackson's admission to an eight-week drug rehabilitation program. Eighteen vials of medications were found in Michael's suitcase when he checked into a clinic where he had booked the entire fourth floor. Doctors put him on a Valium IV to wean him off the painkillers and his management company canceled the remainder of the *Dangerous* tour, at a cost to Jackson of at least $10 million.

Feldman responded by filing a motion for trial preference that would force the case into court within 120 days, a request typically granted when a plaintiff is under the age of fourteen. He also filed to compel the deposition of Michael Jackson. The court granted both of Feldman's motions on November 23, and set a trial date in March 1994. During the hearing, Bert Fields, in an attempt to delay the civil suit, argued before a courtroom filled with reporters that a criminal indictment of Jackson seemed imminent, and that, of course, the criminal case should be tried before the civil one was heard. Howard Weitzman immediately told the media that Fields "misspoke himself," and the simmering tensions between the two boiled over. The next day, Fields and Pellicano resigned from the case.

Amid the chaos and mounting pressure, Weitzman recruited Johnnie Cochran to the defense team. Cochran and Weitzman agreed that the judge's 120-day trial ruling had been a "devastating" blow to the Jackson side, according to Carl Douglas, the top associate in Cochran's law office. "It pushed us to settle," Douglas recalled. An additional benefit of the 120-day ruling, according to Feldman, was that he had been able to use it to persuade the Los Angeles County district attorney's office to "let us take the lead in prosecuting the case. That put the defense in the position of having to defend the civil case knowing that a criminal case was behind it."

Feldman also vigorously opposed the defense request for a gag order, ensuring that the media would have full access to each of his highly detailed court filings. The defense lawyers felt increasingly harried by a tabloid media that continued to report only what made Jackson look guilty. "The British press was relentless," Douglas remembered. A woman who had been working as Jackson's maid at Neverland was quoted as saying that she had been sent to Michael's bedroom at Neverland with several others to gather up all his makeup, eyeliner, lipstick, creams, and gels, then crate them up, along with stacks of magazines and photographs, including one of Macaulay Culkin in his underwear. "My job was to hide all the bottles of women's perfumes," she explained. "Michael used only female fragrances, not male, and I guess someone thought that might look bad."

After Pellicano acknowledged in an interview that Jackson had spent at least thirty nights sleeping (innocently, the PI said) in Jordie's tiny bedroom at the Chandler house, a document was leaked to the media in which police investigators reported that Jordan had told them that Michael engaged in oral sex and mutual masturbation with him in both of his parents' homes, at the Hideout, in Monaco, and at Disneyland Paris. Evan Chandler portrayed himself as a father desperate to protect his son, who was being victimized by Jackson's defenders: His life had been threatened, a dead rat had been left in his mailbox, and his office had been ransacked, Chandler said. A statement from Jordie taken by a Santa Barbara County sheriff's deputy was published that included: "Jordan stated that Jackson told him that if Jordan ever told anyone about the molests, Jordan would be placed in juvenile hall and both Jordan and Jackson would be in trouble. Jordan said that Jackson told him he did this with other boys; however, Jackson said that 'he didn't go as far with them.'" "Peter Pan or Pervert?" read a headline in the *New York Post*.

As 1993 drew to a close, Weitzman and Cochran huddled with John Branca, who had been replaced by Bert Fields three years earlier but had been brought back aboard as Jackson's general counsel. All three men maintained that they believed Michael was innocent of the charges against him yet were inclined to advise him to settle the case. Branca worried that Michael might not be capable of withstanding a trial that could last six months. Cochran's concern was the racial divide that had opened wide in the wake of the Rodney King debacle and the Los Angeles riots in April 1992. Ethnic animosities might work against Michael if the case was tried in largely white Santa Barbara County, Cochran fretted, and even if the trial was held in Los Angeles County, Hispanics might resent Jackson for his money and blacks might dislike him for trying to be white. The kicker was that a settlement could forestall the criminal case if it prevented Jordan Chandler from testifying against Michael. "We wanted to do all we could to avoid the possibility that there would be a criminal filing," Carl Douglas admitted.

Cochran's long relationship with Los Angeles County district attorney Gil Garcetti (during the early 1980s the two had worked together on the district attorney team that investigated shootings involving police officers) enabled him to secure a promise that Jackson could return from London to Neverland without fear of arrest. As he emerged from the cocoon of rehab and began to make his way back to California during early December 1993, Michael was stunned by the immense media coverage the accusations against him were receiving. In the UK, the *Daily Mirror* set up a "Spot the Jacko" contest in which readers could win a trip to

Disney World if they correctly predicted where Jackson would show up next, while another paper reported that the entertainer was at a European clinic receiving a course of cosmetic surgeries that would render him unrecognizable. In the United States, Geraldo Rivera convened a mock trial with a jury composed of audience members to consider criminal charges against Jackson that hadn't even been filed. Michael's own sister La Toya offered to provide proof that he was a pedophile for a fee of $500,000 and a bidding war erupted among tabloids in both the United States and the UK before editors on both sides of the Atlantic realized that La Toya had nothing to sell.

The final blow that broke his will to fight was the warrant served on Jackson shortly after his return to the United States that permitted police to conduct a strip search of his body, giving officers from both Los Angeles and Santa Barbara counties the right to photograph and videotape "his penis, anus, hips, buttocks and any other part of his body." Failure to comply, the warrant stated, would be used in court as an implied admission of guilt. On December 20, 1993, at Neverland Ranch, Jackson was forced to stand naked on a raised platform for twenty-five minutes while his lower body was photographed from every conceivable angle, so that resulting prints could be compared to Jordie's description of Michael's genitalia. Michael nearly fainted several times and perhaps only got through "the most humiliating ordeal of my life" by keeping Arnold Klein in the room with him. In the end, the exercise proved to be a wash. While the several vitiligo splotches on Jackson's buttocks and the one on his penis were an approximate match to what Jordie described, Michael was not, as the boy had said, circumcised.

Larry Feldman stepped up the pace of his court filings, submitting one motion after another that demanded depositions of the defendant. "Each time Michael Jackson used the Fifth Amendment, we took the opportunity to be very specific about what he was not answering," Feldman remembered. "We described in detail why we were entitled to the photos of his genitalia. It almost didn't matter whether we won or lost—we were getting even."

Cochran, the lawyer Jackson most trusted, made the crucial decision to advise Michael that he should just pay these people and walk away. His insurance company wanted him to be done with this almost as much as he did, Cochran told Michael, and was prepared to write the check for their share of the cost. When Larry Feldman submitted a motion to the court in Los Angeles asking for the right to examine Jackson's finances, Michael told his attorneys, "I want this over."

Cochran and Feldman, who were quite familiar with one another (Feldman had represented Cochran as his attorney in a number of "personal matters"), arranged to conduct their settlement conference under the supervision of three retired LA County judges. Cochran and Weitzman regarded the photographs of Michael Jackson's genitalia as "the purple gorilla sitting in the room," recalled Carl Douglas, and were desperate to keep them out of Larry Feldman's hands. Fully aware of this, Feldman negotiated ferociously. "The numbers being discussed seemed fantastic," remembered Douglas, who believed that the turning point of the settlement conference came when one of the three retired judges observed that, "It's not about how much this case is worth. It's about how much it's worth to Michael Jackson."

On January 25, 1994, the day before Jackson's scheduled deposition by Larry Feldman, Douglas was assigned to carry the settlement papers to the bungalow at the Mirage Hotel in Las Vegas where Michael was staying, and witness his signature on an agreement that would cost him more than $20 million, including a $15.3 million annuity for Jordan Chandler, $1.5 million apiece for Evan Chandler and June Chandler Schwartz, and more than $3 million in fees for Feldman and his law firm. The media was informed that same day.

Tom Mesereau would say that settling the Jordan Chandler case on such terms was "the worst decision Michael ever made." Most of the media and the public took the news that Jackson had paid so many millions to the Chandler family as an implicit admission of guilt, even after he had made his emotional public statement of denial: "I am not guilty of these allegations. But if I am guilty of anything, it is of giving all that I have to help children all over the world. It is of loving children of all ages and races. It is of gaining sheer joy from seeing children with their innocent and smiling faces. It is of enjoying through them the childhood that I missed." Within a matter of weeks, Pepsi had canceled its endorsement contract and all of Michael's film projects fell through. The theme song he had recorded for the movie *Addams Family Values* was dropped from the soundtrack, the development of a line of his and hers fragrances bearing his name was abandoned, and plans for a Jackson-themed *Captain EO* attraction at Disneyland were scrapped.

Neither the Chandler case nor the Chandler story went away. Grand juries were convened by the district attorneys in both Los Angeles and Santa Barbara counties during the spring of 1994 to hear evidence that Michael Jackson was a pedophile. Frustrated by the refusal of Jordan

Chandler to appear before either grand jury, prosecutors dispatched police to find at least one other boy who would corroborate Jordie's sworn statement. Jackson and his attorneys waited out proceedings that dragged on for months while nearly two hundred witnesses testified and stacks of evidence were presented, including the description of Jackson's genitalia given by Jordie that was laid out next to the photographs of Michael's lower body.

Grand juries are generally a formality in California; nearly all such deliberations end in indictments. Only prosecutors can present evidence, and they are required to demonstrate no more than a "reasonable likelihood" that a crime has been committed. Yet in the summer of 1994, both grand juries refused to indict Michael Jackson. "There was no real evidence," a police officer involved in the investigation admitted to the *Los Angeles Times.*

Damaging allegations against Jackson continued to surface in the media (*Hard Copy* correspondent Diane Dimond was making something like a life's work of that project) but Michael was buoyed by polls that showed the majority of the public didn't believe the charges made against him by the Chandlers. He was determined to move on with his life and rehabilitate his image. Michael might have taken any number of different approaches to this task, ranging from going back into the studio to disappearing from public view. What he chose was to marry the daughter of the greatest pop icon of all time.

Lisa Marie Presley was nine years younger than Michael Jackson but already the mother of two children by her first husband, whom she had met when she joined the Church of Scientology. Lisa Marie had grown up as Elvis Presley's pampered daughter in Graceland, his estate in Memphis, Tennessee, until her parents divorced when she was three. She then moved back and forth between Tennessee and her mother Priscilla's home in Beverly Hills, which became the girl's full-time residence after Elvis died in 1977, when Lisa Marie was just ten.

Though she cut a demo in 1992, Lisa Marie had turned down the offer of a recording contract, put off by an executive at Sony who had told her she would "have to crawl before you walk," and could not realistically expect the production or promotion support of an established star. It was not long after this that their mutual friend, the painter and sculptor Brett Livingstone Strong, suggested that Lisa get together with Michael Jackson to explore putting out a record on Michael's new Nation Records label.

Lisa Marie was "taking courses" at Scientology's headquarters (or "Flag Land Base" as members of the church call it) in Clearwater, Florida, during early 1993 when Strong phoned her to suggest that putting out a record produced by Michael Jackson would give her the launch she hoped for. Lisa was excited by the idea, Strong recalled, but Michael was dismissive: "She can't sing." Strong insisted she could. "Get her to send me a tape," Michael told him. Lisa said she would bring Michael a tape in person, and arranged to play it for him at Strong's home in Pacific Palisades.

She and Michael had actually met once before, in October 1974, when Lisa was six and Michael was sixteen, backstage at the Sahara Tahoe, where the Jacksons were performing one of the last concerts of a nearly year-long world tour. Neither remembered that brief encounter and believed they were saying hello for the first time when Lisa showed up at Strong's house in January 1993 with her Scientologist husband, bass player Danny Keough, and a demo tape that persuaded Michael the young woman did, indeed, have some potential as a singer. He wasn't so impressed that he wanted to take the time to work with Elvis's daughter, though, at least not at that moment. Lisa, however, began calling Strong constantly, as the artist recalled it, to see if he could arrange another meeting with Michael. All Strong could get for Lisa Marie was a meeting with the head of Nation Records; Michael himself never showed.

Lisa eventually became resigned to the fact that nothing was going to happen at Michael's company, said Strong, who persisted anyway in playing matchmaker—at least at the professional level. On February 1, 1993, the artist arrived at the huge birthday party Lisa Marie's mother, Priscilla Presley, was throwing for her at the Six Flags Magic Mountain amusement park north of Los Angeles loaded with wrapped presents, among them an art book and a framed photograph of her introduction to Michael Jackson in Strong's living room. Strong had written the inscription in the book, but allowed Lisa to believe it was Michael's handwriting and that the book and the photograph were Michael's gifts to her. Lisa again began to express interest in meeting with Michael, and her interest now seemed as much personal as professional. In March 1993 Strong suggested that Michael escort Lisa Marie to the Academy Awards ceremony, just as he had Madonna the year before. Michael refused, saying he was not about to date a married woman. By the late spring of 1993, when Lisa inquired about Michael it was with "the passion of a woman who fell in love," according to Strong. "And Michael wasn't interested at all."

Sometime before late June of that year, though, when Michael would launch the European leg of his *Dangerous* tour, Michael himself arranged a face-to-face meeting between the two of them, Lisa Marie said. "He immediately went into this whole explanation of what he knew people thought of him, and what the truth was," Lisa Marie would tell *Rolling Stone* in 2003. "He sat me down and said, 'Listen, I'm not gay,'" Lisa Marie explained to Diane Sawyer that same year. "'I know you think this, I know you think that,' and he started cursing and started, you know, being a normal person. And I was like, 'Wow!'" What most struck her, Lisa would say in another interview, was that Michael spoke in a normal masculine voice and used the word "fuck."

She had no idea that her feelings for Michael were developing against the backdrop of the emerging Jordan Chander scandal. "I just want to say he's not stupid, he didn't get where he was because he's stupid," Lisa Marie would tell *Rolling Stone* almost ten years later. "It's unfortunate that not a lot of people know who he really is. He doesn't let anybody see it. And he has some idea about how he should represent himself in the public, which he thinks works for him, which is the sort of meek victim, meek-quiet thing that he does, which is not like he really is. So, he doesn't let a lot of people see that. When he wanted to lock into you, or intrigue you, or capture you, or, you know, whatever he wants to do with you, he can do it. He is very capable of doing that." She swooned at the thought that Michael was being real with her in a way he couldn't be with other people, as Lisa Marie told it. "So I get caught up in that, I'm pulled in right away," she would tell Sawyer. "Like, 'Wow, you're so misunderstood. Oh my God, you're this guy.' I fell into this whole, 'You poor, sweet misunderstood thing.'"

Those feelings intensified when the lawsuit on Jordan Chandler's behalf was filed in September 1993. "That whole shit hit the fan," Lisa Marie would recall in her 2003 interview with *Rolling Stone*, "and he was quick to call me and tell me what his side of the story was, so it looked like an extortion situation. I believed him, because he was so convincing. I don't know . . . I just believed everything he said, for some reason." After that first conversation, Michael began to spend hours with Lisa Marie on the phone nearly every day, sharing his distress and seeking her advice. "I believed he didn't do anything wrong, and that he was wrongly accused and, yes, I started falling for him," she would tell Diane Sawyer in 1995. "I wanted to save him. I felt that I could do it." Maybe it had something to do with her father, Lisa Marie would acknowledge years later; she still wasn't sure.

During the last months of 1993 and in early 1994, Michael was showering Lisa Marie with flowers and gifts, saying that without her and Liz

Taylor, he might have killed himself to escape the horror of what was happening to him. Lisa Marie confided in her childhood friend Myrna Smith about the developing relationship, but Smith recoiled, finding the whole thing both suspicious and ridiculous. "I can only guess what his motives were," Smith would tell author Suzanne Finstad, "and I could only tell you what I thought, what a smart businessman he was, and that he was only pursuing her for what she could do for him, and that he wasn't interested in women. And she told me he was."

Michael settled the Chandler lawsuit in January 1994, but was still under investigation by two grand juries and remained the object of an unstinting media investigation. Whether the goal was to remake his image or to create something that resembled a normal life, or both, he began to tell the people around him he was longing for family and children. During one of their phone conversations in April 1994, according to Lisa Marie, Michael asked, "If I asked you to marry me, would you do it?" She answered "I would do it."

On April 29, 1994, Lisa Marie announced her separation from Danny Keough. Barely more than two weeks later, on May 14, 1994, Michael and Lisa Marie exchanged marriage vows at a secret ceremony in the Dominican Republic in May 1994 at which no family or friends were present. Priscilla Presley was indignant and publicly accused Michael of using her daughter to repair his public image: "It's so obvious."

There were others, though, who believed the relationship was genuine. Donald Trump purported to be one of them. Michael hadn't been too convincing at the beginning, Trump admitted. Michael told him over dinner one evening that he had a new girlfriend, Trump recalled, and "I congratulated him and asked, 'Who is it?' He was very shy and looked down into his napkin, then put the napkin over his face and said, 'Trump, Trump, I don't want to talk about it. I'm so embarrassed.'" Later, Trump invited the couple for a stay at his Mar-a-Lago estate in Palm Beach, Florida. The couple stayed in separate bedrooms, which also did not encourage anyone to believe that this couple was enjoying any sort of romance. One afternoon, though, he happened to see the two of them walking the grounds of the estate, Trump said, Lisa Marie wearing a form-fitting black silk dress and Michael in a sharply tailored black suit with a scarlet dress shirt and black tie. Suddenly Michael dropped to one knee and kissed Lisa Marie's hand, Trump remembered. She pulled him to his feet and they kissed, staring into one another's eyes. Then Michael pulled a small box from his vest pocket and when Lisa opened it she found a string of pearls. "For awhile, those two were really getting it on," Trump would insist several years later.

Few others believed it. Among those who scoffed at the notion of a love affair was the man who had performed the couple's marriage ceremony. "Michael looked like a little boy lost," Judge Hugo Francisco Alvarez said a few weeks after the wedding. "He stared at the floor throughout the ceremony and when I pronounced him and Lisa Marie man and wife, he was reluctant to kiss her. There were no tears of happiness, no joy, no laughter. The ceremony had a somber tone. It was bizarre. I never heard him say he loved Lisa Marie."

The president of the Elvis Presley Fan Club in California, Terry Marcos, responded to news of the marriage by blurting, "Oh God, no! Are you serious?" Michael Jackson was "not even a man as far as I'm concerned," Marcos said.

Michael had tried repeatedly over the years to satisfy the fans who wanted him to have a real girlfriend, and the mother who wanted him to find a wife. Both Brooke Shields and Tatum O'Neal, whom Michael continued to describe as the loves of his life, acknowledged that he never made the slightest sexual advance toward them. Lisa Marie, though, was spreading a very different story. With her apparent encouragement, one of Lisa Marie's friends, Monica Pastelle, told a reporter that his new wife had described Michael as "very hot" in bed, albeit a bit kinky, given to dressing up in women's clothes and "role playing" during their sexual encounters. Lisa Marie appeared wearing only a towel around her waist in the video for his song "You Are Not Alone," and kissed him with apparent passion onscreen. In one of the few statements she ever made to the media about their relationship during that time, Lisa Marie described it as "a married couple's life . . . that was sexually active."

Michael's longtime PR chief Bob Jones, though, would call the marriage "nothing more than a publicity stunt. Michael had no desire for a woman," Jones would say shortly after his firing ten years later. "Not the natural desires that heterosexual men have, anyway." The odd thing was, though, that Lisa Marie seemed to sincerely care for Michael and to want the marriage to work, said Jones, who admired the young woman. "Lisa Marie was so down to earth," he said, yet remained "a tremendous supporter and believer" in Michael, even when it was obvious to him and everyone else, Jones said, that the feelings didn't run both ways.

Lisa Marie became hurt and angry when Michael began to disappear without warning, often for weeks at a time. She had no idea where he might be, his wife said, other than what she read in the press. As early as December 1994, London tabloids began reporting that Michael planned to file for divorce after complaining that his wife was "invading his space." By that point, Lisa Marie was spending almost no time at Neverland and when Michael came to stay at her house in the San Fernando Valley's Hidden Hills enclave, he always brought kids with him. "He would join them running around the house and creating havoc," Jones recalled. "They were out of control and she couldn't say a word."

According to Jones, Lisa Marie was becoming increasingly annoyed by the efforts Michael made to convince her he was worth just as much as the Elvis Presley estate she had inherited and to either impress or threaten her with a relationship to Princess Diana that did not actually exist. And she was more and more offended by what her husband told the press. In a September 1994 interview with London's *Daily Mirror*, Michael offered an entirely invented story about his marriage proposal, saying it had taken place when he and Lisa Marie were drinking wine in the living room at Neverland: "We had just finished watching *All About Eve*, starring Bette Davis. We both love that movie. I just walked over to her, reached into my pocket and pulled out this huge diamond ring. 'So what do you think?' I asked her. 'You want?' She screamed out, 'Yes, yes, yes.'" The voices of those who said he was just using her began to penetrate Lisa Marie's defenses. She became truly angry, and a little disgusted, when she read Michael's interview with *TV Guide* and saw that he had said, "Lisa Marie told me Elvis had a nose job." It was "absolute bullshit," Lisa Marie would tell *Rolling Stone*: "I think it justified something in his mind—they were asking him about his plastic surgery. I read that, and I threw it across the kitchen. 'I told you what?'"

Friends would say that the marriage began to truly sour shortly after Lisa Marie and Michael were interviewed by Diane Sawyer in June 1995. Lisa Marie watched the ABC interview afterward and was shocked and hurt by the moment when Michael had reached behind her to hold two fingers over the crown of her head, making devil horns. A month after the Sawyer interview aired, Lisa Marie left with her ex-husband Danny Keough and their children for a two-week vacation at Hawaii's Mauna Lani Bay resort, and tabloid reports described them as acting like a young couple in love, kissing and cuddling on the beach. A young waitress at one of the resort's restaurants told a reporter, "If they're divorced, then maybe all couples should split! They were just totally in love." Lisa Marie would tell Oprah Winfrey years later that, "I was very torn up because I broke up my family. I left my husband for Michael. I was having a hard time trying to process that."

By the end of their first year of marriage, Elvis's daughter seemed to be tiring of the whole charade. Monica Pastelle, the same friend who had spread the story that Lisa Marie said Michael was "very hot" in bed was now telling people that Elvis's daughter had become fed up with the hours and hours her husband spent in the bathroom applying and removing various cosmetics. She had never seen Michael when he wasn't wearing makeup, Lisa Marie complained; if they slept in the same bed, she'd find his pillow smeared with it in the morning.

In August 1995, the *Daily Mirror* reported that Lisa Marie was about to file for divorce. Lisa Marie denied the story, but she and Michael *were* separated. The two of them hadn't seen one another in nearly a month when Bob Jones and other Jackson representatives began calling her in September to say it was important that she show up at the MTV Video Music Awards ceremony in New York, where Michael was going to open the show with a twenty-minute long medley. She finally consented, Lisa Marie said, on the condition that she didn't have to walk the red carpet with Michael. Michael's people agreed, but when they delivered her to Radio City Music Hall on the evening of the event, she was dropped off right at the red carpet, where her estranged husband was waiting. "I was pissed. I just felt like I was being used at that point," Lisa Marie would tell *Rolling Stone*. It got worse when Michael said he was going to sing to her, and that he had a surprise for her. "He says, 'I'm gonna kiss you,'" Lisa Marie would recall in her interview with *Playboy*. "I was like, 'No, I don't want to do that. Do we have to? That's bullshit.' On the way there I kept saying, 'Do we have to?' I squeezed his hand so hard that I cut off the circulation. He wouldn't tell me when it was going to happen." It happened onstage, with a worldwide television audience watching. "And they said it wouldn't last," Michael said into the camera, then locked lips with Lisa Marie in one of the most awkward kisses ever caught on camera. "It looked awkward because I wanted out of my skin," Lisa Marie would tell *Playboy*. Afterward, "I remember my whole look was, 'Don't you come anywhere fucking near me,'" Lisa Marie would tell *Rolling Stone*, and Michael got the message. After his performance, "he didn't come over," Lisa Marie remembered. "I talked to him later and he said, 'I saw the look on your face and I knew that if I walked up to you, I didn't know what you were going to do to me.'"

Bob Jones would say he realized how little Lisa Marie truly mattered to Michael when the star collapsed onstage while rehearsing for an HBO special in December 1995 and was taken to the hospital. Michael was excited by the arrival of Diana Ross at the hospital (where his room was decorated with posters of Shirley Temple and Mickey Mouse) and welcomed his mother Katherine as well. But "Bill Bray had to talk him into letting his wife, Lisa Marie, visit," the publicist remembered. "Bill had to explain to Michael that the media would crucify him if he turned his own wife away." When she arrived at the hospital, Lisa Marie said, she was confused by the conflicting accounts of her husband's condition. "Every day there was a different report," she would explain to Oprah Winfrey. "I couldn't tell what was happening. Dehydration, low blood pressure, exhaustion, a virus . . . we were all a little bit in the dark." Eventually, "There was a bit of a showdown in the hospital," Lisa Marie would tell *Playboy*. "When I started asking too many questions about what was wrong, he asked me to leave. This is the real story. He said, 'You're causing trouble.' The doctors wanted me to go. I freaked out, because it was all too familiar. When he got out, I called him and said, 'I want out.'"

Michael had insisted from the beginning of their marriage that he wanted Lisa Marie to bear his child. Increasingly inclined to suspect that having a baby who was Elvis's grandson was part of Michael's motivation, Lisa Marie dreaded what she imagined would be a "custody battle nightmare" in the not too distant future, and refused to abide by Michael's plans for impregnating her. One morning over breakfast he told her that the nurse in Arnie Klein's office, "my friend Debbie," had offered to have his baby if Lisa Marie wouldn't. "Tell her to go ahead and do it," was Lisa Marie's level reply. The two separated for good shortly thereafter, but when Lisa Marie learned that Debbie Rowe was being artificially inseminated she made a last-ditch attempt at reconciliation. "Lisa Marie Presley actually had a thing for Michael Jackson, and for a time she wanted him back," Bob Jones would recall. "She not only would seek assistance from his family in trying to reunite with Michael, but Lisa Marie also often called me and Johnnie Cochran asking for help in her quest to get back her husband." When it was announced in late 1996 that Debbie Rowe was pregnant, though, Lisa Marie's "quest" ended.

Michael made slight pretense that he and Debbie were living "a married couple's life." He did, though, continue to either tease or try to please his fans with the illusion that he had healthy heterosexual appetites. Michael encouraged his fans to pass around the rumor that one of the boys who was often seen in his company during the late nineties, Omer Bhatti, was his "love child." The evidence collected to support this story included the fact that the entire Bhatti family had lived at Neverland for a time, and that Omer (who had begun performing a Michael Jackson tribute act that toured worldwide when he was still a preteen) began to appear regularly in public and onstage with Michael after about 1996. The boy, fans posted among themselves, was the product of a one-night stand Michael had with Omer's Norwegian mother, Pia. Look how dark the kid's skin is, more than one believer suggested. What those fans overlooked was that Pia's husband was a Pakistani named Riz Bhatti whose own complexion easily explained his son's. The Bhattis *were* very close to Michael, though. Many believed, with good reason, that Pia Bhatti was the biological mother of Michael's son Blanket. How the child had been conceived, and who the father might be, remained a matter of pure speculation. The only certainty was that the conception of Michael's youngest child had not occurred, as he liked to put it, "in the natural way."

Jackson repeated his determination to leave behind the Jordan Chandler scandal throughout the last years of the twentieth century. It would never happen. He might refuse to discuss the Chandler allegations following his interview with Diane Sawyer, but they would follow him everywhere he went, permanently tarnishing his image in the United States. After his marriage to Lisa Marie Presley ended, he left America more and more often, and was almost perpetually on the move. When he was in his home country, he spent at least as much time in New York, Florida, and Las Vegas as he did at Neverland Ranch, and a lot of time in Los Angeles. His *HIStory* tour set attendance records in Europe and Asia, but didn't make a single stop in the mainland United States—American fans had to be content with two concerts in Hawaii. And yet, as he prepared to take a last stab at the recovery of all he had lost, Michael was not simply returning to the country of his birth, but to the very city where, fifteen years earlier, it had all been taken from him.

17

The Christmas season of 2008 would be a wrenching one for Michael Jackson's three children. The woman who had raised them was out of their lives and this time, it seemed, for good. Grace Rwaramba had once again been dismissed from Michael's presence. The reasons were disputed. Rwaramba's enduring claim was that she and Michael were fighting constantly about his abuse of prescription drugs, but Michael had been injecting or ingesting drugs, often heavily, during most of the time she was in his employ. Grace also said that Michael hadn't paid her salary or her health insurance premiums in months, and that he gotten rid of her by sending Tohme to say that her pay was being cut by half. Jackson family friend Romonica Harris, a Chicago school teacher, would report that, shortly before her departure, Grace attempted to force Michael to marry her and that Rwaramba grew incensed when Jackson refused. The nanny denied the story and there was no evidence it was true other than Harris's claim.

Grace's support of Sheikh Abdullah's legal claim against Michael, though, was without doubt a sore point. "When Abdullah sued Michael last year, Michael said in the beginning, 'Oh, I never got money from him,'" Grace would explain not long after being sent away from the Carolwood chateau. Worried that she was being set up to take a fall for filching the more than $1 million that Abdullah had wired to her personal bank account, Grace turned for help to Katherine Jackson: "I said, 'You, Michael, and I—we will all go to jail! You know we didn't report to the IRS about that gift.' I told her I had all the documents. That worked. She immediately called Michael and he stopped denying that he knew about the money."

What Grace didn't know was that Michael had become convinced that *she* was stealing from *him*. Tohme Tohme and Dennis Hawk had flown to Manama in October to try to settle Sheikh Abdullah's claims against Michael. After reading the contract Michael and the sheikh had signed, Tohme explained, he realized that they could not close the deal with AEG until Abdullah gave Jackson a release. "Michael signed away his whole life,"

Tohme explained. "He cannot fart without the permission of Sheikh Abdullah." Tohme had traveled to Bahrain in the belief that his relationships in the Arab world and familiarity with Middle Eastern culture would form the basis of a dialogue with the Al Khalifas. Tohme was well connected in neighboring Oman, whose royal family were the Al Khalifas' closest allies in the region. "And also I understand three things," the manager explained. "One is that the Al Khalifas do not need the money. Two is that they do not want the publicity. Three is that it is not part of the Arabic tradition to fuck somebody who has been a guest in your home." On top of that, "Michael really liked Sheikh Abdullah," Tohme said, "and he felt the Al Khalifas had been very kind to him. I wanted to convey that to them personally, in the language we all speak." Within a couple of days, Tohme had convinced the Bahraini royal family to let their attorneys try to work out a settlement with Michael's lawyers that would release him from the 2005 contract and to accept something less than the $7 million they were demanding at the High Court in London. The Al Khalifas even agreed to permit Tohme and Hawk to remove the contents of the safe where Michael's jewelry and cash were being held. When they opened the safe, though, the two men found it empty. The Al Khalifa people insisted that only one person had been in the safe since Michael's departure, and that was Grace Rwaramba, who had shown up on her own in Manama, explaining that Michael needed some papers he had left behind. "I don't have any direct evidence that Grace took anything out of the safe," Hawk said, "but it was obvious the people in Bahrain thought she had."

Grace was never accused of any wrongdoing, but nevertheless Michael ordered the nanny gone soon after Tohme and Hawk returned from Manama. Grace swiftly compounded her employer's disaffection when she agreed to testify for Abdullah in London, where his lawsuit against Jackson was to come before the High Court in November 2008. The sheikh was the first witness on his own behalf and, as anticipated, Jackson's attorneys went after him with the accusation that he had exploited the performer's posttrial vulnerability and lack of good sense. Not so, Abdullah told the court: "Michael is an individual who is very switched on. He is a fantastic intellectual."

"There's nothing unusual about him?" Jackson's own attorney in London, Robert Englehart, asked.

"No!" Abdullah replied. The sheikh actually sounded at moments as if he still hoped Mikaeel would come back to him. But if he wasn't going to get what had been promised, Abdullah made clear, he expected repayment.

A court victory for the sheikh and his family looked likely after Grace Rwaramba took the witness stand to back Abdullah's story in almost every detail.

Michael was so desperate to avoid testifying in London that, Arnold Klein's assistant Jason Pfeiffer alleged in court, he prevailed upon Klein to supply the evidence of a staph infection that could be offered as an excuse for why he couldn't fly to the United Kindgom. Englehart, Jackson's attorney, told the court in London that his client was awaiting test results and that "even in a best-case scenario it would be unwise to travel," and requested that Michael be permitted to testify by video link from Los Angeles. Abdullah's attorney Thanki insisted he needed Jackson physically in London and suggested the star be "bandaged up" and brought to London. The ruse bought Michael a brief delay, but the judge ruled he would have to appear in person at the trial. As the appointed day drew near, Tohme arranged through Mohamed Al Fayed to fly Michael and the children to London aboard a private jet, and planned on coming along for the ride. He was with Jackson at the Hotel Bel-Air loading bags into the limousine that was to deliver them to the Burbank airport when his phone rang. "Michael really doesn't want to go," Tohme remembered. "He is terrified of being in court. He knows it will be a circus. And literally at the last second I get a call from overseas: 'Don't come, it's not necessary. We're gonna solve the problem.' So I told Michael, 'Okay, let's go back to the suite. We don't need to go to London.' And he was so happy."

After testifying for Sheikh Abdullah, Grace wouldn't be returning to Los Angeles any time soon. Shortly after Rwaramba left London, reports came out of Africa that she had married a man named Joseph Kisembo. Grace would not confirm this, but it was true that she had returned for a time to Uganda, where her fluency in Runyankole kept her in the good stead that endured on the reputation of her father Job Rwaramba, a man who had set up and ran medical dispensaries in rural areas all over the country after escaping with his large family from Rwanda. Early in 2009, Grace founded, and appointed herself chief executive officer of, a foundation called World Accountability for Humanity, which was pledged to "bridge the gap" between rich Western donors and poor African recipients. From Uganda, Grace could not keep in contact with the Jackson children even by telephone. It was the longest period of time in their lives that they had gone without speaking to her.

Michael let Dr. Tohme take the fall for sending Grace away. The children believed it and such a story seemed plausible even to the adults following the Michael Jackson saga. Amid widespread rumors that Jackson was on the brink of signing a contract with AEG to perform a series of shows at the O2, Tohme appeared to be in complete command of Jackson's world. Tohme and Peter Lopez were in discussions with the Nederlander Organization about putting together a Broadway musical for Michael, and for an animated television program based on the "Thriller" video. As the president of MJJ Productions, Tohme was also working out the details of a deal for an MJ clothing line that would include "moonwalk shoes." He had also retained the services of contract attorneys recommended by Tom Barrack to attempt a renegotiation of the Sony/ATV catalog deal. He intended to "secure the future" of Michael's children, Tohme told Lopez and Dennis Hawk, with spin-offs from the O2 concert series that would include a 3-D live concert film, a 3-D movie based on the "Thriller" video, and a three-year worldwide concert tour. In Las Vegas, reports surfaced that Tohme and Barrack were simultaneously fleshing out yet another plan to develop a Michael Jackson–themed gambling establishment—a "Thriller Casino"—and were well into discussions about converting Neverland Ranch into a Michael Jackson Museum "in the style of Elvis Presley's Graceland."

Reeling from a simultaneous collapse of the real estate and financial markets in fall 2008 that had already cost him an estimated $1.3 billion, Barrack was energized by the realization that at least one of his properties might actually be *increasing* in value. By January 2009, Colony Capital had hired eighty workers to complete Neverland's refurbishment, all with an eye to selling the place for up to four times what he had paid for it, as Barrack explained to the *Wall Street Journal*. And "should Michael Jackson's career be reaccelerated," Barrack observed to the *Journal*, "it will have substantial additional value."

Prior to the Colony crew's arrival, Tohme made a second visit to Neverland and returned to Los Angeles convinced that the removal of Michael's personal property from Santa Barbara County was imperative. "So many things were left lying around, broken," he recalled. "And people were taking things. Everybody has access. I went to the warehouse where much of Michael's stuff was being stored, and it was sad that all this money was being wasted. I told Michael and he really didn't care. He hated Neverland by then. He hated how they treated him in Santa Barbara during that trial. And he said, 'I don't ever want to set foot there again. Just get rid of everything.' I said, 'How about an auction?' And he said, 'Do it.'" Within a few weeks, Tohme made a deal with Julien's Auctions in Los Angeles to sell off everything that wasn't nailed down at Neverland in 1,390 lots of "memorabilia." The potential take, he was told, could easily surpass $10 million.

The "reacceleration" of Michael Jackson's career that Tom Barrack had spoken of in his interview with the *Wall Street Journal* began to look more and more likely after Michael signed the AEG "contracts" (actually, a letter of intent and a promissory note) on January 27, 2009. "Michael is very excited, but he is also very afraid that he won't be able to live up to what people expect from him. Michael Jackson does not wanna go on-stage and disappoint," Tohme recalled. "He still needs to be lifted up, to be convinced that he is still the one, the King of Pop, that no one has replaced him, that no one *can* replace him." Tohme continued to demonstrate that he understood how much even minor tributes meant to Michael's self-esteem. "Michael told me, 'I go to the store to buy a game for my kids, and everybody has a game except me.' So I told Sony, 'Michael Jackson, you have to make a game for him. Otherwise, nothing.' Because we were discussing doing a new *Off the Wall* album like they had done with *Thriller*. So they agree. They send someone to see Michael in Los Angeles and he was flabbergasted. He was so happy." The planned game would have a dance mat and be programmed with all of Michael's signature moves.

AEG had locked Michael in with language (tucked into a "miscellaneous clause") that stated the promissory note agreement was "final" and that by accepting a "loan" of $6.2 million from AEG Michael was backing his promise to perform in London with a lien against "collateral" that included every asset he owned. The document also acknowledged that a "definitive" contract was still to be prepared and signed. Tohme and Randy Phillips continued to barter back and forth about the terms of the "definitive" agreement all through February. It had become clear to Phillips that convincing Michael to extend his concert series far beyond what was initially agreed on might be the only way to meet the worldwide demand for a Jackson tour. Tohme understood that doing just ten shows in London would not produce enough revenue to pay down Michael's debts. Nevertheless, Michael still believed he would be performing only ten shows when he flew to London shortly after the first of March for the news conference at which the O2 concerts were to be formally announced. According to Tohme, the name for the concert series had been agreed upon just a couple of weeks earlier, when he and Michael were discussing the trip to London during a meeting in the living room at the Carolwood chateau. "Michael said, 'You know, this is it, this is the last show I'm ever gonna do,'" Tohme recalled. "And I said, 'So let's call it 'This Is It' then.' And he smiled and said, 'Yeah, I like that.'"

The trip to London was, for Tohme, the peak of his experience as Michael Jackson's manager. "It was beyond your imagination," he recalled. When he and Michael and the children arrived at the Lanesborough Hotel in Knightsbridge, where they would be staying, "it was below zero temperature and people were sleeping outside in the park across from the hotel just to get a glimpse of Michael getting in and out of the car," Tohme remembered. "I've never seen him happier than when he saw how his fans were running [and] greeting him."

The night before the March 5 announcement at the O2, Tohme commented on how fit Michael was looking, saying it was obvious he had added some bulk. Michael stripped to his underwear and stood on a bathroom scale that showed him weighing 157 pounds. "We were laughing," Tohme remembered, "because of stories in the newspaper about how skinny he is, that they just keep printing the old news, they don't even care what is true now. You should have seen Michael's legs. They were like an Olympic sprinter's, like steel bands from all the dancing. The guy is solid muscle."

Randy Phillips's appraisal of Jackson's condition the next day as they prepared for the press conference at the O2 Arena was not nearly so sanguine. "MJ is locked up in his room drunk and despondent," Phillips wrote in an e-mail to his boss Tim Leiweke.

"Are you kidding me?" was the reply Leiweke sent back minutes later. Just the day before, AEG's corporate chief had attended a music-industry symposium where he answered a question about Michael Jackson's readiness for a concert series by saying, "The man is very sane, the man is very focused, the man is very healthy."

"I [am] trying to sober him up," a frantic Phillips wrote to Leiweke, as the appointed time of the O2 press conference approached. "I screamed at him so loud the walls are shaking. He is an emotionally paralyzed mess riddled with self-loathing and doubt now that it is show time."

He and Tohme actually had to dress Michael to get him prepared for the press conference, Phillips wrote to Leiweke: "He is scared to death."

More than three years later, Tohme would say that Phillips's e-mails "exaggerated" Michael's condition. Dennis Hawk agreed. "He might have drunk a couple of glasses of wine to relax," Hawk said. "I wouldn't have blamed him if he drank a whole bottle, given how big the moment was for him. But if he'd make the kind of scene Randy described in those e-mails, I think I would have heard about it. I didn't."

Nearly four hundred reporters and more than seven thousand fans were assembled at the O2 when Michael arrived more than an hour-and-a-half late for the press conference. If Michael was either intoxicated or frightened, he hid it well behind a broad grin and an assured manner. The shows he would stage in the arena during the summer of 2009 would be called the "This Is It" concerts, because he intended to make them his final curtain call, Michael told the assembled crowd. "'This Is It' really means this is it," he declared into a bank of microphones. Many in the crowd remarked on how deep and resonant his voice seemed to suddenly become. "I knew the announcement of the London shows would be big news, but I had no idea how big," Tohme remembered.

Michael had asked Tohme to arrange for him to take his children to see the revival of *Oliver!* at the Drury Lane theater a couple of nights after the O2 press conference. "I leaked it to the media when we were going," Tohme said. "I wanted the public to know Michael will be there. Because I wanted Michael to get his oxygen back. I want him to know how much he is loved. I told the PR people working with me to leak it everywhere, to make sure his fans will know. But even I can't believe what it's like. There are thousands and thousands of people at the theater when we arrive. It was unbelievable how they reacted when they saw him coming. The love—I never saw anything like it. Michael is so happy, he cannot stop smiling. And the kids, they were shocked. They'd never seen this before, not like that. It's like they finally know who their father is."

Michael's mood would change dramatically when he discovered that Tohme and Phillips had already made a preliminary agreement that the number of O2 concerts might be increased if public demand warranted it. There was still some doubt within AEG about whether an audience for more shows existed, at least in London. Michael Jackson had not performed a major concert series since the end of the *HIStory* tour in 1997. Those forty shows had been hugely successful, raking in $90 million, but still finished second in total ticket sales that year to U2's take from their PopMart tour. Jarvis Cocker became a folk hero for farting on Jackson during his last London appearance and a great deal had happened in the intervening years, including a criminal trial for child molestation. The only album of new Michael Jackson material released since 1997 was *Invincible*, widely considered a commercial failure. All of that, combined with the string of canceled performances and appearances in Jackson's recent past, made the whole "This Is It" concept appear tenuous in the eyes of many.

Early on during the O2 contract negotiations, Randy Phillips confided to several associates that Jackson's lack of self-confidence was the most surprising—and worrying—thing he had observed about Michael. In London, Phillips tried to laugh off such worries: "If Mike gets too nervous to go on," he told a reporter from the *Daily Telegraph*, "I'll throw him over my shoulder and carry him onstage. He's light enough." The AEG Live boss, though, continued to harbor doubts about the investment his company was making. Immediately after the March 5 press conference in London, Phillips and Tohme agreed to test the waters by allowing fans to register for a "presale" drawing of tickets on Jackson's official Web site. The response was far beyond what either had imagined: Michael's site was overwhelmed by registrations that poured in at a rate of up to sixteen thousand per second. Despite the fact that hundreds of thousands of fans were unable to get through, nearly one million people had submitted applications within the twenty-four-hour window. Tickets not even printed yet were already being offered on eBay for $450 apiece.

Phillips and Tohme prepared plans to at least double the number of O2 concerts. When Michael discovered what they were up to, he burst into a tearful rage, insisting that ten shows was all that he had agreed to perform. The operatic scene he created initiated a series of high-drama meetings with Phillips, Tohme, and the two LA attorneys representing Jackson's interests in the AEG negotiations: Hawk and Lopez. Michael announced several times that he was canceling the O2 shows, but Tohme, according to one of the attorneys, had proven to be the first person in years who could force the star to acknowledge his circumstances. He would earn at most $20 million from the ten shows at the O2, Tohme explained to Jackson. Less than half that amount would remain after taxes, fees, and the cost of the settlement with Sheikh Abdullah. Even with what was in the Lockbox, there might not be enough to purchase the Bolkiah's Las Vegas property. He still owed AEG all the money they were advancing for rent on the Carolwood chateau and for his other expenses, Tohme reminded Michael, and in the meantime he was falling further and further in debt to Sony.

The reality of his financial situation was that Jackson had to earn *at least* $100 million before his financing arrangement expired in 2011, or face the liquidation of his assets—in other words, bankruptcy. Grudgingly, Michael agreed to twenty shows at the O2. Phillips then played what he had known all along would be his strongest card with Michael by pointing out that the first artist to perform at the O2 had been Prince, toward whom Jackson was well known to harbor both considerable ill will and an intensely competitive fascination. "As soon as Michael heard that Prince had done twenty-one shows at the O2, he insisted on doing more than that," recalled an attorney who had been part of every negotiating session with AEG. "Ten more, in fact." Within days, Michael's agreement to thirty-one concerts at the O2 had been increased to forty-five shows that would continue through the end of 2009. Shortly after this, Jackson, Phillips, and Tohme settled on an even fifty concerts, extending into February 2010.

Phillips helped Tohme persuade Michael to make such a commitment with a series of concessions that some thought ridiculously generous. "Randy really wanted to see these shows happen, and not just because he wanted to make money for AEG," said the attorney who was handling much of the communication between Phillips and Tohme. "He really did see this as his chance to resurrect the career of a great artist." Among the promises Tohme and Jackson were able to extract from Phillips were that $15 million would be placed in the "down payment fund" for the purchase of a new home in Las Vegas when the O2 concerts were finished; that an estate near London on a par with Paul McCartney's place—"sixteen-plus acres, running streams, horses," as Phillips recalled it—would be rented as a temporary home for Jackson and his children during the full run of the O2 concerts; that AEG would pay for a personal trainer and chef/nutritionist to prepare him for the concerts; and that the company would also hire a personal physician to attend to Michael's health from the moment he agreed to fifty shows until the last concert was finished. Michael also insisted that AEG had to arrange for the *Guinness Book of World Records* to document the entire concert series and include any records it broke in the next edition of the book. Phillips and AEG agreed that Jackson would receive 90 percent of all profits from the O2 concerts, and that the London shows would be outsized extravaganzas that included high-wire walkers, acrobats, jugglers, and magicians, something on the order of a Cirque du Soleil spectacle, with elaborately choreographed dance numbers set against constantly shifting multiscreen backgrounds of short films in an IMAX or 3-D format, enhanced by laser light shows. Michael would have to appear onstage himself for only thirteen minutes at a stretch during the concerts, it was agreed, and if his voice weakened, well, the O2 possessed the most sophisticated lip-synching technology on the planet.

On March 11, 2009, AEG began offering half of the seats for the first forty-five "This Is It" shows as "presale" tickets. Minutes after the two Web sites selling the tickets went online, more than a million Jackson fans attempting to log on crashed them both. Two hours after the sites were rebooted, 190,000 tickets had been sold. During the next sixteen hours, all of the 300,000-plus seats available had been snapped up, and more than a million and a half people who had tried but failed to purchase tickets were waiting for another chance. A week later, the other half of the seats for the first forty-five "This Is It" shows, plus all of the seats for the last five shows, went on sale to the general public and sold out within a few hours. With little effort and almost no marketing, AEG had sold 750,000 tickets to the "This Is It" concerts. That guaranteed a minimum gross revenue of $85 million, with a final tally of at least $125 million expected by the time the money from merchandising, a planned documentary film, and other ancillaries rolled in. Sony announced that sales of the *King of Pop* album it had released on Michael's fiftieth birthday were up 400 percent. Within days, tickets for the "This Is It" shows were being offered on eBay for up to $15,000 apiece.

Even the British newspapers that had for so long tormented Jackson were forced to genuflect in the face of the public response. "Michael Jackson has floored his critics," the *Times* of London acknowledged. An "astonishing comeback for a man who in recent years has been dogged by controversy," the *Guardian* said, acknowledging the speed and size of the ticket sales for the O2 shows. AEG had pulled off the "showbiz coup of the decade," conceded the *Evening Standard*.

The accolades Tohme and AEG posted on the official Michael Jackson Web site included a list of the records that had been established by the almost instantaneous sell-out of the O2 shows: "The biggest audience ever to see an artist in one city"; "The most amount of people to attend a series of arena shows"; "The fastest ticket sales in history." Randy Phillips and his company knew full well, though, even if Tohme did not, how dangerous it was to start counting chickens when Michael Jackson was involved. Everyone in the music business was aware of how Jackson had bailed on his heralded "Millennium Concerts" in Honolulu and Sydney back in 1999, even when warned that he was inviting the Marcel Avram lawsuit that eventually resulted in a $5.5 million judgment against him. Phillips and his associates also knew about Jackson's infamously aborted *One Night Only* special for HBO back in December 1995 when a worldwide audience expected to number 250 million had been disappointed after Michael collapsed during rehearsals and had to be rushed by ambulance to New York's Beth Israel Medical Center to be treated for "dehydration." The HBO special was canceled amid stories that Jackson had faked the whole thing in order to escape his commitment. Among those suggesting as much was Bob Jones, who said he had repeatedly observed Michael's "penchant for staging illness and other problems to get out of commitments and promises he had made." Grace Rwaramba would agree: "To Michael, to go to a hospital was never about being ill. It was all about avoiding a court appearance or a performance." Jones said he put some stock in the claim that "Michael often pulled these hospital stunts just to see how many gifts and flowers he'd receive."

Phillips and AEG had little choice but to hope and pray that Dr. Tohme would find a way to keep Jackson on track. Someone was already sawing a circle in the floor under Tohme's feet, however, and Michael's new manager wouldn't even hear the sound until the split second before he was in free fall.

In the newspapers, reports of how rapidly the O2 concerts had sold out were often accompanied by estimations of how much money Michael might earn from fifty shows in London. A total haul of $100 million was entirely realistic when all the ancillaries were included, Dennis Hawk believed. If Michael could be persuaded to follow up the O2 concerts with an Asian tour that turned into a world tour, Hawk had calculated, his client's earnings might climb to the vicinity of $400 million. AEG's own estimates of what Jackson would net from a world tour were considerably more conservative: $132 million was the amount the company's executives had reckoned Michael would walk away with, after his advances and expenses were deducted. "This is not a number that MJ will want to hear," Gongaware warned Phillips and Leiweke in an e-mail. "He thinks he is so much bigger than that." They should talk to Michael in terms of gross receipts, Gongaware suggested. Those would come close to the numbers being tossed about by Tohme and Hawk, who believed that if their client followed the world tour with a triumphant return to the United States that ended with a residency in Las Vegas, he could quite conceivably earn a billion dollars during a two- or three-year period.

Even if the eventual take was only a couple of hundred million dollars, that was still a gusher of chum in the water for the sharks who had surrounded Michael Jackson since the age of nine, and, as always, the pushiest snouts in the pack belonged to the members of his own family.

Michael was doing his best to avoid contact with the rest of the Jacksons as he prepared for the O2 shows, but that was impossible. Katherine could always get to him, and she did that spring, with a request made through Tohme Tohme that he purchase her a $750,000 motor home to take a trip back to Indiana. For the first time in years, Michael had millions of dollars of cash on hand, most of it tucked away in the Lockbox account controlled by Tohme that was intended to provide a down payment on his new home in Las Vegas. The rest was hidden beneath the carpets of the Carolwood chateau. "Michael tried to say no to his mother," recalled the individual who had been forced to serve as go-between in what became a complex transaction. "He wanted to say no. But in the end he couldn't." Dennis Hawk was able to take advantage of the deep recession washing over the country in early 2009 to negotiate with Marathon Coach, the Oregon company that produced the customized Prevost Katherine wanted, until the price was reduced to only a little more than half a million dollars, but even that amount made a significant dent in the Lockbox.

Joe Jackson intended to get a bigger piece of the action than that, and was already partnered up with a "promoter" named Leonard Rowe for precisely that purpose. Rowe was an ex-convict who had been arrested on multiple occasions for writing bad checks, and was sentenced to federal prison in the early 1990s after being convicted of wire fraud in the cashing of a bogus insurance payout. He was best known in Hollywood for initiating a class-action lawsuit that accused CAA and the William Morris Agency, among others, of racism for denying him the opportunity to promote concerts. The case dragged through the courts for six years before a judge finally ruled that, "No rational trier of facts could find for the plaintiffs on any of the myriad claims made in this action." Rowe continued to cast himself in the role of oppressed minority and one of the few to buy it was R. Kelly, who hired Leonard to promote his 2007 and 2008 Double Up tour. Both Kelly and his coheadliner Ne-Yo would successfully sue Rowe for defrauding them when the tour was over.

The campaign that "Joe and Rowe" would conduct to usurp Tohme Tohme had already been joined by Michael's former manager Frank Dileo. On November 26, 2008, at the instigation of Joe Jackson, Dileo had signed a binder agreement with a New Jersey concert organizer called AllGood Entertainment for a "Live Performance of the Jackson Family (Michael Jackson, Janet Jackson and Brothers, hereinafter referred to as the 'Jacksons')" at New Jersey's Giants Stadium. The guaranteed fee would be $24 million for a single show lasting "no less than 150 minutes" in which

Michael Jackson was to perform for "no less than ninety (90) minutes" and sing at least two songs with his siblings. The Jacksons were also to receive a percentage of the net earnings from various other "revenue streams associated with the event" that would include licensing royalties, merchandising, pay-per-view, broadcast or cable television, theatrical release, and sponsorships, as well as a concert DVD and CD that would be released through a distribution agreement with major retailers like Wal-Mart.

According to AllGood's chief executive, Patrick Allocco, he had contacted Dileo after a meeting with Joe Jackson at the New Orleans Casino in Las Vegas where Joe "told me that Michael was closely working with Frank Dileo and that Frank was managing his business affairs." At the time, Dileo had no business relationship with Michael Jackson. Dileo's story was that he never represented himself as Michael's manager and that he told Allocco from the first that Michael would never agree to perform with his family. Allocco recalled their conversations quite differently, insisting that Dileo *had* claimed that he managed Jackson. All he promised, Dileo said, was to present Michael and the Jackson family with a written proposal for the reunion concert deal, provided AllGood paid a $400,000 "deposit" up front (only $150,000 of that money, "for expenses," would go to him, Dileo later insisted). The agreement that Dileo and Allocco signed in November 2008, though, called for a $2 million check to be delivered to Dileo no later than December 31, 2008. Soon after signing the agreement with Dileo, Allocco said, he learned that Frank's partner Mark Lamicka had been named in a lawsuit that accused him of defrauding a promoter who had paid an advance fee on a promised concert deal that never materialized. He and Dileo met again on January 15, 2009, Allocco recalled. Frank said he was ready to move forward with the Jackson family concert deal, but only if he first received his $150,000 share of the advance deposit. Allocco, though, was "uncomfortable" with what he was hearing about Dileo and Lamicka, he said, and offered to put the money in a trust account. No, Dileo said, he would need the $150,000 in hand before he so much as spoke to Michael Jackson about the concert deal.

Right around this time, Leonard Rowe showed up in Allocco's office insisting that *he* was Michael Jackson's manager and could negotiate on behalf of the entire Jackson family. Rowe's claim was that he had been trying for months to put together a Jackson family concert tour. By the end of 2008, he and Joe Jackson had teamed up, intending, among other things, to cut Frank Dileo out of the AllGood deal. He quickly secured the agreement of all the Jackson siblings other than Michael to join the family concert tour, Rowe said, though not without struggling to convince Janet Jackson that she lacked the "drawing power" to headline such a tour. Rowe had at one point gathered Janet, Jermaine, Jackie, Marlon, and Tito at the gates to Michael's home, where they informed the security guard who met them that they wanted a meeting with Michael. The guard went inside the house, then came back outside to ask that each of them write his or her name on a piece of paper so that Michael would know who exactly was at his door. Fifteen minutes later, the guard led them inside to see Michael. By Rowe's written account: "I told him that we want him to reunite with his brothers and tour in America. Michael said, 'I just can't do it right now. I have other things I'm planning and working on.' We stayed there for a few hours trying to persuade him. I could tell that Michael was becoming irritable so we decided to leave."

In late January 2009, Allocco began to hear reports that Michael Jackson either had signed or was about to sign a deal with AEG for a concert series at the O2. Frank Dileo, who continued to represent himself as Michael Jackson's manager, Allocco said, "was telling us that the London shows were never gonna happen, and that Michael didn't have a deal with AEG." He and his partners were increasingly skeptical about Dileo, said Allocco: "One of my insiders got a call from a guy at AEG saying that they got a deal imminent to be signed with Michael—this was at the end of January. So this told me that Frank Dileo was a fraud."

Alarmed, Allocco promptly paid Leonard Rowe a $15,000 "retainer" to set up a meeting with Katherine Jackson, the one family member said to have her son Michael's ear. On February 3, 2009, Allocco met with Mrs. Jackson and Rowe at a restaurant in Encino, just down the hill from the Hayvenhurst compound. "I went through with her my vision for the show," Allocco recalled. Mrs. Jackson seemed to like what she was hearing, he remembered, because she didn't think Michael could or should do an entire concert series. "That is why our deal is very suitable," Allocco remembered Michael's mother saying, "one day of show with a substantial amount of money." Only a couple of days later, though, Allocco learned through sources at Sony that Michael Jackson was actually managed by someone named Dr. Tohme Tohme. He suggested that Rowe call Tohme on the telephone and try to arrange a meeting.

Tohme was now in an awkward position. He and the attorneys who negotiated the AEG Live contract on Michael's behalf had promised Randy Phillips that they would not publicly disclose or discuss that deal until a formal announcement of the O2 concerts was made in early March. Rather than meet with Allocco and Rowe himself, Tohme spoke to the two men briefly on the telephone, then sent them to Dennis Hawk, explaining that Hawk was Michael's main entertainment attorney. Allocco seemed a decent enough fellow, Tohme told Hawk, but Rowe was obviously a dolt; talk to one, ignore the other. However he handled it, Hawk was going to have to hear the two men out without letting on that Michael already had a deal in place with AEG Live.

Allocco and Rowe arrived at Hawk's office on February 12, and swiftly abandoned the Jackson family reunion concert concept to begin pitching a deal for a Michael Jackson solo concert with "guest appearances" by family members at the Superdome in New Orleans that would pay Michael as much as $30 million for a single performance. The meeting degenerated rapidly when Rowe began to loudly insist that he, not Tohme Tohme, was Michael Jackson's manager, that he was an intimate of the entire Jackson family, and that Michael would do whatever he told him to do. Rowe grew more and more out of control, shouting and swearing at Hawk, who merely sat listening until the two men were done talking, thanked them for coming by, and promised to deliver their proposal to Dr. Tohme. For the next few weeks, Hawk answered a number of phone calls from Allocco's attorney, who wanted to collaborate on a revision of the earlier document signed by Dileo. Hawk took one look at that "contract" (which had been written by Dileo himself) and knew it would never hold up in court. "The worst-drafted agreement I've seen in more than twenty years of practicing law," he later described it.

Hawk researched AllGood and discovered that the company had staged some successful concerts in the Caribbean, including a Bon Jovi performance that sold out the Coliseo de Puerto Rico and a music festival in Trinidad and Tobago where Stevie Wonder and Babyface, among others, had performed for 20,000 people. AllGood was no AEG Live, though, and, like Tohme, Hawk agreed with Randy Phillips that Michael needed to begin his comeback overseas, where he was beloved, before performing in the United States, where his public reception was certain to be more mixed. As much as Michael hated to hear references to the "rehabilitation" of his image, he was shrewd enough, Hawk knew, to recognize that an enormous success on the world stage would make it much more difficult for the American media to marginalize him.

Hawk and Tohme stalled until the O2 shows were officially announced by Michael himself at the press conference in London. Joe and Rowe immediately stepped up their offensive, showing up at the Carolwood chateau day after day for a solid week with demands to be admitted.

According to Rowe, Michael told him during a phone conversation on March 22 that he would consider hiring him as a tour manager. Finally, on March 25, Michael made the mistake of letting Joe and Rowe through the door of his home. "I have no money and it's your fault!" Joe shouted at Michael, all the while pushing him to sign some sort of agreement that would allow Rowe to negotiate a deal with AllGood Entertainment on the star's behalf. Rowe would claim that Michael *did* sign some sort of document that day, though he has been unable to present it.

Joe went where he always did after exhausting other options, to his estranged wife Katherine. Joe and Rowe worked Michael's mother on multiple fronts. Rowe began with a furious denunciation of her son's new so-called manager. This so-called "Dr." Tohme was an amateur shyster who knew nothing about the entertainment business and was using Michael to make himself rich, Rowe said. Tohme was in cahoots with AEG, working with them to cut Michael off from the rest of the world, including his own family. If Michael did the Superdome concert, Joe and Rowe said, Michael would pocket at least $20 million for one night's work, and the rest of the family would split another $20 million after the television rights were sold. Her share alone would be $2 million, Rowe promised Katherine Jackson, and all she had to do for that money was convince the son who loved her that there was a better deal for him on the table than the one he had made at AEG Live.

By the end of March, Katherine had begun to serve as Joe and Rowe's conduit to Michael Jackson. Michael had issued strict orders that neither his father nor his father's partner was to be admitted through the gates of the Carolwood chateau ever again, and he refused to speak to either of them on the telephone. His mother, though, always got through within twenty-four hours of calling. "Michael really only listened to Mrs. Jackson when it came to the family," said one of the attorneys who was representing him. "He didn't listen to his dad and he didn't listen to his brothers and sisters. The only one he wanted to help all the time was Mrs. Jackson. Whenever she wanted anything, we had to take care of it. And now she was doing everything she could to convince Michael to sign that AllGood deal."

Not *everything*. When Joe Jackson insisted that Katherine should prevail upon Michael to let her move into the Carolwood chateau in order to work on their son around the clock, she refused. "I have more respect for his privacy than that," she told Joe. Still, she continued to ask Michael every time she spoke to him on the phone why he wouldn't replace Tohme Tohme with Leonard Rowe and sign the AllGood deal.

It would be good for him and for the entire family, said Katherine, who had maintained for years that Michael's biggest mistake in life was to leave the Jackson 5.

"We were hearing about all of this," recalled Hawk, "and everyone was worried that Michael would sign an AllGood contract just because his mother wanted him to."

His siblings had long since fallen into step behind their parents, looking to be cut in on a deal that Patrick Allocco promised would be the biggest payday that any of them other than Janet had seen in decades. Jermaine was especially persistent in lobbying for a collaboration with Michael. "Jermaine called constantly. It was never-ending," said Hawk, who had become, grudgingly, the liaison between Michael and Dr. Tohme on the one hand, and Michael and the Jackson family on the other.

Meanwhile, Frank Dileo continued to spread the story that Tohme Tohme was a Svengali who had hypnotized Michael into obeying his will, even when it was clearly not in his best interest. He found a receptive audience among the Jacksons, who were eager to believe both that Tohme was keeping them away from Michael in order to maintain his control and that the new manager was in over his head. Perhaps he was. Several seasoned AEG executives noticed that Tohme appeared both enraptured and overwhelmed amid the adulation that surrounded Michael on the London trip for the O2 announcement. The starry look in the man's eyes, the AEG execs said, made them nervous. Also, Tohme didn't seem to grasp that his determination to protect his client from any outside demands or pressures, to mediate every one of Michael's business dealings, no matter how trivial, was alienating those who believed that access to the star was their ultimate validation.

By March 26, when Frank Dileo and Leonard Rowe met for the first time, at the urging of Katherine Jackson, attorney Peter Lopez had joined the chorus of people who were carping about Tohme. Lopez was convinced that it had been Tohme's decision, not Michael's, to name Dennis Hawk as Jackson's primary entertainment lawyer. Also unbeknownst to Tohme, Michael Amir Williams—"Brother Michael"—had formed a behind-the-scenes relationship with Dileo and began to make the complaint that Tohme was "mostly talk." Tohme's blustering tone and imperious manner, combined with his broken English, strange name, and Arab background, didn't win him any friends in the Jackson household or in the media. At the same time, there was a certain naïveté to Tohme, a curious inability to recognize that just because people were warm and friendly when they sat across the table didn't mean they weren't sticking pins in a voodoo doll as soon as you left the room. "I am from outside this business," Tohme explained. "I am a businessman, and I think I have played with the big boys, but I have never seen anything like the entertainment industry, where people will do anything to win, where there is no idea of honor or loyalty, where sneaking and backstabbing are just the ordinary way to do things. I couldn't believe it. I *didn't* believe it until it was already happening."

On April 2, 2009, the Celebrity/Access Web site published a column by Ian Courtney under the headline "Will Michael Jackson's Real Manager Please Stand Up?" that cited a press release in which Leonard Rowe claimed to have been hired as Michael's new manager. The article then quoted a spokesperson for Dileo saying that *Frank* was Michael's new manager, and that Mr. Dileo's company would be joining with AEG to issue a press release that challenged Rowe's misrepresentations. Tohme held his tongue, letting an e-mail sent from the offices of AEG Live speak for him:

> Ian, the only individual that AEG Live has dealt with from the onset of the recent negotiations that resulted in the unprecedented sales of 50 shows at the O2 Arena in London is Dr. Tohme. He has been in attendance at all my meetings with MJ and was instrumental in MJ's appearance at the now historic press conference in London. MJ has continued to refer to Dr. Tohme as his manager.
>
> I received one phone call from Leonard Rowe requesting a meeting that I, summarily, turned down after Michael Jackson told me, personally, that Rowe was not involved and disavowed that purported quote in the press release. That was my one and only interaction with Leonard Rowe.
>
> As far as Frank Dileo . . . we are not anticipating any press releases involving Mr. Dileo, nor are we in a business relationship with him.
>
> That is it in a nutshell.
>
> Randy Phillips

For Tohme, Phillips's written remarks were reassurance enough. "Even when I know that Frank Dileo is sniffing around, that Leonard Rowe is sniffing around, that John Branca is sniffing around, that others are sniffing around, I am not worried," he explained. "I am Michael's manager! I have the documents! He has given me complete control. So I think it does not matter what the others say. I have a lot to learn."

18

After the announcement of the O2 shows in London, the crowd of paparazzi tailing Michael whenever he ventured out in Los Angeles expanded three-fold. Jackson's only two regular destinations, the paparazzi knew, were Arnold Klein's office and Elizabeth Taylor's Bel Air home. By April, Michael was visiting Klein's office two or three times a week. The tabloid pack chasing the story naturally suspected that Jackson was collecting painkillers and spent a good deal of time sipping milkshakes at the counter in Mickey Fine's while they waited for him to emerge from Klein's offices. It was difficult to say whether Jackson was getting drugs from Klein, however, because according to a former assistant, the doctor had taken to writing prescriptions for certain patients under his own name. Records would later reveal that Klein had written at least twenty-seven new prescriptions to himself after Michael Jackson returned to the United States from Ireland, for Valium and Vicodin, as well as for the sedative midazolam and for modafinil, a drug used to treat narcolepsy that was said to improve wakefulness in people who didn't get enough sleep. Mickey Fine's motorcycle deliveryman was seen coming and going from the Carolwood mansion on a regular basis. Michael often went to Liz Taylor's directly from Klein's office, leading some of the paparazzi to speculate that the King of Pop was working as a drug courier.

While it could not be proven that Klein was providing Jackson with drugs, there was no doubt that he was working as Michael's doctor. By his own accounting, Klein provided more than $48,000 worth of medical services to Jackson in the three-month period between March 23 and June 22, 2009. The 179 procedures involved were minor compared to some of the work done on Michael in the past, but inventorying the sheer volume of foreign substances shot into or applied onto his face during those weeks was not for the squeamish. Michael had been injected fifty-one times with an intramuscular drug meant to prepare his skin for insertions of Restylane with the fine-line needle that Klein was using to fill

Jackson's wrinkles. Restylane is an acid-based substance that can not only cause headaches and nausea but also commonly results in tenderness at the injection points—a small price to pay, say those who extol its long-lasting results. Klein had also injected Michael with Botox around and under the eyes and in his forehead, not only eliminating what dermatologists like to call "expression lines" but also reducing his body's ability to cool itself with perspiration. Jackson received as well multiple applications at Klein's office of the ophthalmic solution Latanoprost, developed as a treatment for glaucoma but more popular for enhancing the growth, thickness, and darkening of eyebrow and eyelash hair. In addition, Klein had given Michael the eyelash lengthener and thickener Latisse, and a supply of the mouth plumper Nutritic Lips. There had been some new "acne surgery" in the doctor's office as well. Part of the explanation for the big bill was an emergency situation involving Jackson that required Klein to interrupt a weekend vacation to fly into Beverly Hills in a rented helicopter and to transport his staff in chauffeur-driven cars. It was believed by the Jackson stalkers among the paparazzi (who had not heard Michael was trying to get out of testifying in London) that it had something to do with a staph infection that had developed after work on Michael's nose.

For Klein, repairing the damage that Jackson had already done to himself was half the battle; helping Jackson stave off the effects of aging was the rest of it. Michael was unable to bear even the thought of growing old, let alone the process of it. He would be a recluse after the age of sixty, Jackson had said more than once. "You don't want people to see you growing old?" Rabbi Shmuley Boteach asked him back in the year 2000, when the star was about to turn forty-two. "I can't deal with it," Michael answered. "I love beautiful things too much and the beautiful things in nature and I want my messages to get out to the world, but I don't want to be seen now . . . like when my picture came up on the computer, it made me sick when I saw it . . . Because I look like a lizard. I wish I could never be photographed or seen." Watching Fred Astaire suffer the debilitation of old age had been one of the worst things he ever endured, Michael told the rabbi. "One day [Astaire] said to me, 'You know, Michael, if I was to do one spin right now, I would fall flat on my face. My equilibrium is totally gone.'" It was agony to watch the greatest glider ever move about his house at the end, Michael said: "Little tiny steps, and it broke my heart."

"I think growing old is the ugliest, the most—the ugliest thing," he had told Boteach. "When the body breaks down and starts to wrinkle, I think it's so bad . . . I never want to look in the mirror and see that." At age fifty, though, there it was. He would refuse to let it go all the way, Michael said. "I don't want to go out like Brando," he told Gotham Chopra that spring in Los Angeles. "I'd rather go out like Elvis."

In preparation for the O2 shows, Jackson was determined to surround himself with familiar faces. AEG Live was happy to support their star's clannish approach to the "This Is It" concerts. Randy Phillips had already gotten off to a good start with Jackson by embracing the fact that, when he prepared for a stage show, Michael thought of himself first and foremost as a dancer and was inclined to choose choreographers as his principal collaborators.

Kenny Ortega, with whom Jackson had been meeting on a regular basis almost from the moment he returned to the United States from Ireland in 2006, had choreographed both the *Bad* and *Dangerous* tours before going Hollywood. Ortega had come a long way since the days when he was teaching Patrick Swayze to dirty dance and transforming Madonna into a Marilyn Monroe who could twirl for her "Material Girl" video. Twenty years after the end of the *Dangerous* tour, Ortega was considered to be the person most responsible for turning *High School Musical* into one of the most lucrative franchises in Disney's history. That success, plus the ease of communication between Kenny and Michael, made the seven-figure fee Ortega was to receive as show director for the "This Is It" concerts seem to AEG a solid investment.

It was no surprise either that Michael wanted Travis Payne to help him design the dance routines. Payne had won an American Choreography Award back in the mid-nineties for his work on the music video for one of the angriest songs Jackson ever wrote, "Scream," a furious denunciation of the tabloid media. Jackson and Payne persuaded AEG to fly in hundreds of dancers from all over the world who would be winnowed down to the twelve chosen to perform onstage with Michael at the O2. Those who had worked with Michael in the past were impressed that he broke with his practice of screening the tryouts by video, so as to avoid meeting those he would reject, and insisted upon getting up close to each and every aspirant so that he could look them in the eye. The bean counters grumbled when eight of the twelve Michael selected turned out to be Americans, while two of the other four were Canadians. What exactly had been the purpose of spending tens of thousands of dollars on plane tickets to bring scores of people from Europe to Los Angeles? The accountants wanted to know.

Those expenses were peanuts compared to what Christian Audigier had in store for Jackson's concert wardrobe; Audigier's plan was to encrust Michael's outfits with 300,000 Swarovski crystals.

When it came time to choose the band, Michael selected a mix of familiar hands and fresh faces. The drummer he picked to drive the dance performances was Jonathan "Sugarfoot" Moffett, who had served as Michael's percussionist a quarter century earlier on the Jacksons *Victory* tour. For lead guitarist, on the other hand, Michael had chosen Orianthi Panagaris, a stunning twenty-four-year-old blonde Australian of Greek descent who was largely unknown outside the business. When she was eighteen, Carlos Santana had pulled her onstage to perform with him at a concert. Michael insisted Panagaris audition after seeing some of her YouTube videos and appeared overjoyed when she opened her live performance for him in Los Angeles with the solo from "Beat It," then delivered a version that measured up to the one Eddie Van Halen had produced more than twenty-five years earlier. He grabbed the young woman by the arm, walked her to the edge of the stage, and hired her on the spot.

For his personal trainer, Michael hired Lou Ferrigno, who had first come to his attention as the second-best-known bodybuilder (behind Arnold Schwarzenegger) of the early 1970s and later as the nonspeaking actor who played the giant green man on the popular TV show *The Incredible Hulk*. The two were training three times a week, always at the Carolwood chateau. "The paparazzi will follow me if I come to your house," Michael explained. Working with Michael required a whole different approach from the one he'd taken when he'd been hired to bulk Mickey Rourke up with muscle for his role in *The Wrestler*, Ferrigno recalled. Michael wanted flexibility and sinew, so they did exercises that involved rubber bands and an inflated ball, not free weights. Ferrigno had first worked with Michael almost fifteen years earlier when Jackson was preparing for the *HIStory* tour, back in the days when he was known to regularly push himself beyond his physical limits. The Michael Jackson he was spending time with these days seemed mellower and more measured, Ferrigno thought. Michael did every exercise he was asked to do, and was "very animated," Ferrigno said, but also seemed to have learned something about quitting while he was ahead.

Back in the nineties, Michael had confessed on a number of occasions how lonely his life was but he now seemed much more "fulfilled and happy," said Ferrigno, who could only stand and grin when Michael took a break from their workouts to play hide and seek with the kids: "He was like Mr. Mom."

Michael would show up for their training sessions in an all-black outfit, Ferrigno remembered: black slacks, shirt, shoes, and a jacket that Jackson removed on only a single occasion. Ferrigno looked at his arms and saw no needle marks.

Michael hadn't stopped using drugs, however. He ingested pills in a pattern that appeared random but was actually based on his mood. Boredom was a trigger for his drug use, as were anxiety and depression. When he resorted to a needle, it was most often below his waist where no one would spot the tiny stab wounds. He'd collapsed any number of veins over the years, which was why he preferred to have a physician supervising his injections.

Michael especially favored needles when he suffered crippling bouts of the insomnia that his anxiety and depression fueled. His struggle to sleep nearly always became a losing battle during periods of intense stress. Over the years, he had built up incredible tolerances to doses of antianxiety drugs like Xanax and Valium (not to mention opioids such as Demerol and OxyContin) that would have left an average man catatonic. More than twelve years after he had first sampled it, there was still only one drug he could count on to help him start the day feeling rested and renewed. A trained anesthesiologist and a clinical setting, though, were required to safely use propofol.

Cherilyn Lee, a registered nurse who visited Michael Jackson's home approximately ten times in early 2009, tried to remind him of that. Like any number of medical professionals before her, Nurse Lee was first summoned by Michael Jackson to tend to his children's "cold symptoms." When the entertainer began to question the nurse about her practice, Lee told him that she worked mainly as a nutritionist who, based on a person's blood chemistry, could mix up a vitamin and mineral concoction that would boost energy. She had done it for Stevie Wonder and she could do it for him, Lee said. Michael hired her to serve up a daily menu of invigorating all-natural cocktails, according to Lee, but let only a day go by before asking if the nurse might also give him an injection of Diprivan as a sleep aid. Taking that medication anywhere but in a hospital was dangerous, Lee replied. "He said, 'I don't like drugs. I don't want any drugs. My doctor told me this is a safe medicine,'" Lee recalled.

Michael gave Lee the impression that he had received propofol on only a single occasion, prior to a minor surgery of some sort. "I'd fallen asleep so easily that I wanted to have that experience again," Lee quoted him as saying. Jackson, however, had been put under with propofol on scores of occasions during the *HIStory* tour, and his request that Lee administer Diprivan to him was just one of many similar conversations that Michael had had with medical professionals in the twelve years since then. After returning from the tour in 1997, he had insisted that dermatologists and plastic surgeons arrange to have him anesthetized with propofol before any number of cosmetic procedures. That Michael believed the drug was safe seems clear from the fact that, in July 2008, while still living in Las Vegas, he prevailed upon a dentist named Mark Tadrissi to put Blanket under with Diprivan for two hours during an unspecified procedure in Tadrissi's office. Tadrissi would later tell investigators that he told Jackson he didn't have a permit to administer anesthesia but did so anyway at Jackson's insistence. Tadrissi also admitted to putting Michael on a propofol drip during a visit to his office.

Cherilyn Lee brought her copy of the *Physicians' Desk Reference* to the Carolwood chateau in order show Michael the dangers of propofol, the nurse said, but the star remained adamant that he wanted an injection of Diprivan. "He said, 'No, my doctor said it's safe. It works quick and it's safe as long as somebody's here to monitor me and wake me up.'" She again refused to administer Diprivan, Lee said, persuading Jackson instead to try one of her herbal soporifics and let her spend the night watching him while he slept. Once Michael was under the covers, though, Lee found it difficult to convince him to turn off the lights and sounds in his bedroom. He was watching Donald Duck cartoons on the computer he kept by the bed "and it was ongoing," the nurse recalled. "I said, 'Maybe if we put on softer music,' and he said, 'No, this is how I go to sleep.'" Mr. Jackson did doze off briefly as she observed him from a chair in the corner of the bedroom, Lee recalled, but then jumped out of bed and approached her with a "wide-eyed" stare. "This is what happens to me," he told the nurse. "All I want is to be able to sleep. I want to be able to sleep eight hours. I know I'll feel better the next day." Lee again refused to administer Diprivan and was not called back to the house after that.

Tohme Tohme first heard the name Frank Dileo in connection to one Arfaq Hussain—His Royal Highness Arfaq Hussain, as the man introduced himself when he showed up at the Hotel Bel-Air in late February 2009 in the company of a young Lebanese woman. The supposed prince had been preceded, Tohme remembered, by a letter from a London lawyer who wrote that he represented a member of the Saudi royal family interested in purchasing Neverland Ranch. "But when he shows up I am suspicious," Tohme explained. "Arfaq is not an Arab name. It sounds Indian or Pakistani. Also, I know just about every prince in Saudi Arabia, and I've never heard of him. So I brushed him off, but politely, just in case I was wrong."

HRH Hussain showed up again at the Lanesborough Hotel soon after he and Michael arrived in London to announce the O2 Arena shows, Tohme recalled, asking for a face-to-face meeting with Mr. Jackson. "Michael said he didn't know him and didn't want to meet with him," Tohme recalled.

It seems likely Michael must have at least recognized the name, given that during the past decade Arfaq Hussain had identified himself in London tabloids both as Michael Jackson's costume designer and as his perfumer. Whatever their past relationship was or was not, Arfaq Hussain became extremely interesting to Michael Jackson when Frank Dileo called to say that the Saudi prince wanted them to make movies together and had a fund of $300 million set aside for just that purpose. "Before, Dileo cannot even get Michael on the phone," Tohme said. "Dileo is going every day to Michael's mother, trying to contact Michael, about the AllGood deal at first. Michael wants nothing to do with him. But Michael is dying to make movies, and when his mother tells him about this prince with $300 million, he wants to talk to Dileo. That is Dileo's way in."

Tohme was concerned—not about Dileo, but about this HRH Hussain character. So he hired a former Scotland Yard inspector, "someone I know has access to government agencies at the highest levels," Tohme explained, to look into Arfaq Hussain's background. Shortly after that investigation was launched, however, Tohme discovered that his relationship with Michael Jackson was being tested by a new development that seemed to come out of nowhere.

On March 4, 2009, the day before the announcement of the AEG deal in London, Michael's longtime company MJJ Productions had filed a lawsuit against Julien's Auctions to stop the scheduled April 22 sale in Beverly Hills of the possessions Jackson had left behind in Santa Barbara County. Michael was "horrified," unnamed associates explained to the media, when he found the catalog for the auction on the Internet and saw what they were trying to take away from him. "It was Peter Lopez and Frank Dileo and that insect Brother Michael," Tohme said. "They told Michael, 'Look, he's selling your clothes. He's selling everything.' I wasn't even here when they moved the things out of Neverland. I was in Bahrain taking care of that problem. So then before we go to London, Michael said, 'I don't want the auction anymore.' I said, 'Fine, I'll cancel the auction.' But Julien doesn't want to cancel; we have a contract. So we have to file a lawsuit."

What Tohme didn't know was that Michael had begun voicing suspicions about his new manager within a month of signing the power of attorney that gave the Arab absolute authority over his finances and business affairs. In August 2008, Jackson had assigned Michael Amir Williams to find a private investigator who could "check this guy out." The PI, Rick Hippach, filed a report on August 23, 2008, that "Mr. Tohme has been both a defendant and a plaintiff in at least sixteen (16) civil lawsuits filed from 1986 to 2007, many of which involved contractual disputes," then added his own opinion that "this is not the best guy to do business with." Michael Jackson, who had been involved in considerably more than sixteen lawsuits during the past twenty-one years, wasn't terribly impressed by Hippach's report, but continued to worry that he had given Tohme too much control of his life.

"This guy, he just . . . has ways about him," Michael said during a tape-recorded phone conversation in September 2008. "There's a divide between me and my representatives, and I don't talk to my lawyer, my accountant. I talk to him and he talks to them . . . I don't like it. I wanna get somebody in there with him that I know and trust."

During late 2008 and early 2009, Williams had begun to make the case to Jackson that Tohme was a con man. It was increasingly obvious, Brother Michael said, that Tohme was not nearly as intimate with the royal family of Brunei as he claimed to be and was making little progress toward a deal to purchase the Bolkiah's Spanish Gate estate in Las Vegas. Williams was not able to produce any solid evidence of Tohme's deceptiveness, though, until his employer became distressed that his cherished "King Tut" project was not moving forward. "This was a film Michael wanted to do for years and [he] already had a full script," Brother Michael explained. "He told Tohme that he wanted Mel Gibson to direct the film. Tohme then told Michael that he grew up with Mel and that they are best friends. I remember Michael being excited, calling me, telling me that Tohme and Mel Gibson were best friends and he was going to send him the script. For some reason I didn't believe Tohme; I thought it was too big of a coincidence for him to be best friends with the man Michael wanted to work with. So I decided to try to get in touch with Mel Gibson myself. I reached out to Peter Lopez and asked Peter if he can get in touch with Mel Gibson for me. And he told me that Tohme just called him asking him if he knew Mel Gibson and if he could help him get in touch with him. That's when I told Michael, but Michael said, 'Let's just wait and see what happens.'"

Tohme insisted that the name Mel Gibson never came up in connection to the King Tut project. "Michael wanted Peter Jackson for that," he said. "Peter Jackson was the only person he would consider. And Brother Michael would have no idea what Michael Jackson and I discussed. He was never in our meetings. He was an errand boy. He went for coffee. If Michael saw him listening at the door he would tell him to go outside and close the door behind him."

Williams had Jackson's ear, though, when he began pointing out how suspicious it was that "Tohme just happened to know everyone Michael wanted to meet." Jackson was especially interested in collaborating with A. R. Rahman, the composer who had just won two Academy Awards for the *Slumdog Millionaire* soundtrack, Brother Michael recalled, and "Tohme told Michael that he had known Mr. Rahman for years and that they were good friends. I didn't believe him so I decided to do some research myself. The day before [Rahman and Jackson] were supposed to meet I reached out to [Rahman's] agent. His agent put me in touch with Mr. Rahman and I was able to speak with him. I asked him if he knew Tohme and he told me that he had no idea who Tohme was and that Tohme was making him go to the Hotel Bel-Air two hours before the meeting for drinks with him, and that Tohme and Mr. Rahman were to drive to Michael's house together. I then told Michael what I found out and I ended up setting up a private meeting with Michael and Mr. Rahman at Michael's residence without Tohme. Tohme was very upset at me but Michael and I had a good laugh about it . . . we realized that Tohme was doing this with almost everyone. He would meet them at the Hotel Bel-Air and then drive over to Michael's house with them to make Michael think that they had been good friends."

It was true that he arranged to meet Rahman at the Hotel Bel-Air, Tohme conceded, but not that he had claimed to be old friends with the composer. "Brother Michael was working for Dileo by then," he said, "but I didn't know it. Michael told me to fire him more than once. He told me Brother Michael was stealing from him. But Brother Michael cried that he had nowhere else to go and I kept him on. I was a fool."

Tohme was the one Jackson was planning to get rid of, Brother Michael retorted: "After Michael and I realized Tohme was a liar, I would ask Michael, 'Why don't you just fire him?' Michael's response would be, 'Brother Michael, when you're on a plane flying in midair, you don't get rid of the pilot in the air. You wait until you land and the job is done, then you can get rid of the pilot.'"

The deals Tohme had made for him in the first six months after becoming Michael's manager seemed to ease Jackson's concerns about the man, but those apprehensions were aroused again when he discovered that Tohme and Randy Phillips had been planning to expand the number of concerts he would perform at the O2 long before they told him about it. At almost the same moment, Michael's discovery that Tohme had authorized an auction where Darren Julien would be selling "priceless and irreplaceable" personal items, as Jackson's court filing described them, stoked his fury. MJJ Productions *had* "authorized the auction house to remove the items from Jackson's Neverland Ranch," Michael's suit alleged, "but not to sell them without Jackson's permission." That did not jibe with the recollection of Dennis Hawk, who had served as the main liaison between Tohme, Jackson, and Darren Julien. "I was there in the fall of 2008, when Michael was asked what he wanted to sell from Neverland," Hawk recalled, "and his answer was, 'Everything.' He said it twice: 'Everything.' Darren Julien handled the whole thing in the most professional way you could imagine. He sent a fleet of trucks up to Neverland to load everything, at his own expense, and also paid for it all to be stored at warehouses in Los Angeles. Then he prepared this absolutely beautiful catalog of the items for sale at an auction that would have netted Michael millions." Julien had begun selling $20 tickets to the auction in February, along with auction catalogs priced at $50 for a single volume or $200 for a five-volume boxed set. "Like Disneyland collides with the Louvre," he had described the contents. The man's money and his reputation were already on the line. But after making the deal for the O2 shows, Hawk said, "Michael wasn't so sure he needed the money, and all of a sudden he didn't want to sell 'everything' from Neverland. It put Julien in a terrible position."

Confronted by the lawsuit, Julien refused to return the property in his warehouses unless he was paid for time and costs, plus the share of profits he would be losing. It became a nasty public dispute that placed Tohme right in the middle. On one side, Michael Jackson was insisting that he had never intended to sell much of what had been removed from Neverland, that there were things in Julien's warehouse that meant more to him than money. On the other side, Darren Julien was warning Tohme that he'd better convince Michael Jackson to keep his commitment, or else come up with the $2 million in expenses he had run up preparing for the auction, plus some reasonable percentage of the commissions he would be losing if the event was canceled. In an attempt to settle the matter, Tohme dispatched his business partner, James R. Weller, to a private meeting with Julien. Weller was a legendary advertising man who had won a slew of major awards, including Clios, Emmys, Addys, and prizes from the Cannes and New York film festivals. *Ad Age* had listed him as the writer or creative director on two of the "10 Greatest Ad Campaigns of All Time." He had also served as the creative director for the presidential campaigns of Ronald Reagan and George H. W. Bush. Since 2005, Tohme and Weller had been partners in TRW Advertising, where Weller, who was in his seventies, ran the shop while Tohme functioned as the moneyman. Finesse was supposed to be Weller's strong suit.

A PR disaster was the last thing Tohme expected from a meeting where he was represented by Jim Weller. Yet shortly after the meeting (which, oddly, took place in a fast food restaurant on Wilshire Boulevard), Darren Julien filed an affidavit in Los Angeles Superior Court in which he alleged that Weller had threatened his life. "Weller said that if we refused to postpone [the auction], we would be in danger from 'Farrakhan and the Nation of Islam,'" Julien's sworn statement read. After stating that "those people are very protective of Michael," Julien claimed, Weller "told us that Dr. Tohme and Michael Jackson wanted to give the message to us that 'our lives are at stake and there will be bloodshed.'" (Weller later filed a declaration with the court in which he denied making any of the threats Julien alleged.) Julien and his partner Martin Nolan met with Tohme Tohme the next day at a Starbucks where, according to Julien's affidavit, Michael Jackson's manager "denied any knowledge of Weller's threats, and said that he accepted that the auction would need to proceed as agreed."

Tohme was shocked when gossip columnist Roger Friedman got hold of Julien's affidavit and turned it into a pair of columns that publicly eviscerated Michael Jackson's "mysterious new manager." Tohme could only blame himself for some of what Friedman wrote. His clumsy attempts to circumvent Michael's displeasure about the potential sale of his prized possessions made him sound (assuming Friedman reported his remarks correctly) at once craven and devious. "I did not set up the auction, the auction is not going through!" Friedman quoted him as saying. Tohme most certainly had set up the auction but compounded his problems by trying to make it sound as if he had merely been using Julien to transport and store "a lot of stuff" that had to be removed from Neverland when Colony Capital took possession. Darren Julian was understandably insulted by being described as the operator of a moving and storage service. He urged

Friedman to ask what exactly this "Dr. Tohme" was a doctor of. Quoting "sources" who said that Jackson's manager had "referred to himself as an orthopedist or orthopedic surgeon," Friedman asked Tohme if he was a licensed physician. "Not at this time," was Tohme's answer. When Friedman asked repeatedly what kind of doctor Tohme might once have been, he got no answer. "If you want to talk about Michael Jackson, fine," Tohme told Friedman. "The story isn't about me." After Friedman added the false suggestion that Tohme hadn't really set up the deal at AEG, Michael's manager came off looking dubious indeed. Friedman promptly followed with a second column that used Julien's story of his meeting with Weller to dredge up Michael Jackson's connections to the Nation of Islam, then reported that he had contacted someone at the Senegalese embassy in Washington who said he had never heard of any "ambassador at large" named Tohme Tohme. In fact, Tohme did possess a passport that had been personally signed by Abdoulaye Wade, the country's president since 2000, with a notation in Wade's handwriting that identified him as the country's "Ambassador at Large," but by then no one was very interested in looking at the thing. Michael himself was most upset by a final comment from Darren Julien that Friedman had added to his second column, in which the auctioneer spoke of voluntarily returning "certain items" that might "be embarrassing" to Jackson.

Michael's mortification and fury increased after the *Los Angeles Times* picked up the story and lent Friedman's inferences legitimacy. For the first time since the two had met, he began refusing to answer Tohme's phone calls. "I remember Michael saying, 'I am never talking to him again!'" recalled Patrick Allocco, who, like Frank Dileo and Leonard Rowe, was maneuvering to fill the opening created by Jackson's separation from his manager. Darren Julien, meanwhile, refused to back down, and scheduled an exhibition of 1,390 lots of property from Neverland beginning on April 14. That very day, literally at the last minute, the dispute was settled when Tohme presented Julien with a cashier's check for the full amount he demanded. "Where he got the money remains a mystery," the *Times* would report. It had come from the Lockbox and put a far bigger dent in Michael's house fund than the purchase of Katherine's deluxe motor home. Tohme Tohme declined to say another public word about the entire auction debacle but the damage to his reputation had been done, and the timing could hardly have been worse.

On April 2, Patrick Allocco had spent nearly an hour on the phone with Katherine Jackson, confirming Leonard Rowe's promise of a $2 million payment if she could convince Michael to sign the AllGood deal and repudiate his agreement with AEG. Allocco also urged Katherine to persuade her son that he should be represented by Leonard Rowe rather than Tohme Tohme. At least tell Michael he should sit down with Joe and Rowe one more time and hear what they have to say, Allocco told Mrs. Jackson. Katherine did as asked, and before the middle of that month had talked Michael into taking another meeting with his father and Leonard. It wasn't a coincidence that Joe and Rowe arranged to meet with Michael (and Patrick Allocco, who was there also) at the Sportsmen's Lodge in Studio City on the morning of April 14, less than ten hours before Darren Julien was scheduled to begin exhibiting his possessions ahead of the April 22 auction. "Let me say my piece," Joe began the meeting, then launched into a lengthy diatribe about his son's allowing himself to be controlled by AEG and its agents, particularly this Tohme. Leonard Rowe was a family friend, Joe said, who would look out for the Jacksons' interests, not AEG's, and see that Michael's earnings were protected. With his father literally standing over him, Michael signed a document that read, "Leonard Rowe is my authorized representative in all matters concerning my endeavors in the entertainment industry and any other of my endeavors as he may be assigned by me." Michael made a number of handwritten amendments to the letter before signing it, however, including one in which he stated that the authority he was giving Rowe applied to "financial overseeing *only*" and "can be revoked at any time."

At that same meeting, Michael signed a notarized "notice of revocation of power of attorney" that stripped Tohme Tohme of his control over the star's finances, then added the request that "all personal or professional property related to me, my immediate family, and all other related family in the possession of Dr. Tohme R. Tohme, including without limitation any passports or other documents, be returned to me immediately." Tohme would insist that he never received a copy of any such document and that his position in Michael Jackson's life was unchanged.

Frank Dileo was still out there, too, though, working every angle he could find that played off his relationship with Michael Jackson. On April 1, Dileo negotiated an AllGood Entertainment–like deal with a company called Citadel Events that promised to assist in putting on a Michael Jackson concert in Trinidad and Tobago during the fall of 2009. Unlike Patrick Allocco, Citadel's principals had been reckless enough to advance Dileo a $300,000 "binder" fee. No Michael Jackson concert in Trinidad and Tobago was ever going to happen but Citadel wasn't going to see its $300,000 again, either.

Dileo wasn't Michael Jackson's manager but the story of those hundreds of millions of dollars in movie money under the control of HRH Arfaq Hussain had helped him recapture a measure of Michael's attention. Dileo's first contact with Randy Phillips had come, the AEG Live chief executive recalled, in an e-mail, when "MJ orchestrated a conference call with Mr. Dileo, MJ, and me to discuss a fund that Frank had raised to make motion pictures with MJ. This was prompted by AEG's commitment to develop a shooting script for a 3-D live-action film based on 'Thriller.' MJ mentioned his fondness for Frank and that he wanted him to executive produce these films." Phillips still saw Dileo as a fringe player, though.

On April 11, Phillips responded to a cease-and-desist letter from AllGood Entertainment by stating, "Mr. Dileo doesn't involve AEG in any manner whatsoever." After learning that Michael Jackson had signed some sort of an agreement with Leonard Rowe on April 14, however, Phillips began to wonder if perhaps he shouldn't be in business with Frank Dileo after all—especially if Tohme Tohme was on shaky ground. And apparently Tohme was, given that on April 22, 2009, Michael signed a letter to AEG stating that Tohme would not serve as the production manager on the O2 "tour" as had been previously contemplated. The same letter, written by Frank Dileo, directed AEG not to pay Tohme for any work he did on this "tour" or any other. Phillips immediately requested a meeting with Dileo. Three days later, he sent Tohme an e-mail stating that Michael Jackson apparently did not want him to serve as the tour manager during the O2 concerts.

According to Patrick Allocco, Phillips had already begun to encourage Michael Jackson to replace Tohme with Dileo. "Randy Phillips wasn't able to control Michael the way he wanted to," Allocco explained, "and Randy Phillips was most definitely angry at us involving Leonard Rowe in Michael's life. Randy is the one who hired Frank Dileo." Michael himself told people close to him that Dileo had been hired by Phillips and said he was furious about it, insisting that he still believed Frank had stolen from him back in the 1980s.

Tohme, for his part, continued to insist that nothing had changed. "I still had not received anything from Michael saying I was not his manager, or that he didn't want me with him in London," Tohme said. "He still called me on the phone and told me he loved me. Randy Phillips still treated me as Michael's manager."

Tohme clearly recognized that his position was precarious, however, and began to backpedal furiously in his public statements, especially with regard to Neverland Ranch. In early April, based on what Michael had been saying for months, Tohme had told the *Wall Street Journal*, "Neverland is finished." By May, however, he was veering sharply toward his new position that Michael wanted to keep the ranch, that he envisioned Neverland as a "veritable city for children," one that would be "ten times bigger than Graceland."

Then a new complication surfaced that forced him to "distance myself from the situation," as Tohme put it. His private investigator's report on Arfaq Hussain had finally been delivered from London. Hussain was not a Saudi prince, the report stated at the outset, but had been born to a Pakistani family in England in July 1970. "He initially came to the attention of the law enforcement authorities when a series of allegations were received that his business practices were fraudulent and criminal," Tohme's investigator went on. That complaint was made by Michael Jackson's dear friend Mohammed Al Fayed, who told police that Hussain seemed to "come out of nowhere" when he approached the Harrods owner in the spring of 1998, boasting of acquaintance with "well-known Muslim figures in the worlds of show business, politics, and sports," and "also made much of an apparent close relationship with Michael Jackson."

In 2001, the report from London continued, Hussain "was arrested during a massive antidrugs operation by police in the North of England." After being criminally charged, the report explained, Hussain cut a deal with authorities and turned informant. His plea bargain resulted in a minimal sentence of four months' imprisonment, related to his fraudulent conduct in business activities.

"Having investigated this subject thoroughly," the report's conclusion began, "it is strongly recommended that your client should not enter into any commercial or social contact with Arfaq Hussain."

When he urged Jackson to send Hussain away, Tohme said, Michael refused, insisting that Frank Dileo said Arfaq really did have access to $300 million in Saudi money to finance film productions. "This is the first time I realize that Dileo has Michael's ear," recalled an indignant Tohme. "He came for weeks, trying to push himself in, but he couldn't, not until he got with Arfaq Hussain." Tohme detailed the efforts and the progress he'd made toward helping Michael realize his dream of creating big-budget motion pictures. He had been talking to major studios about Michael's cherished King Tut project, Tohme said, and had arranged meetings between Jackson and Andy Hayward, the creator of the *Inspector Gadget* series that Michael loved, to develop characters for an animated version of the "Thriller" video. "Things are moving along," Tohme insisted, but Michael believed the "fund" Frank Dileo had supposedly put together with the help of Arfaq Hussain would make it possible for him to proceed immediately. Finally, Tohme said, "I told Michael, 'I will never set foot next to you if you have that crook around.'" Michael just laughed.

According to Patrick Allocco, "Michael stopped all contact with Dr. Tohme" around the time of this conversation. Tohme himself insisted that, "Michael and I were still close. There is still love between us. I am still his manager." What almost everyone else observed, though, was that by the middle of May 2009, Tohme, the man who described his job as "protecting Michael Jackson from everyone and everything that can hurt him," was largely out of the picture.

In the eyes of an attorney who had been representing Jackson on and off for nearly twenty years, what was taking place seemed an obvious reification of the star's relationship with his father: "Michael had always done best in terms of his career when he had some powerful authority figure telling him what to do. He was conditioned to that at an early age. But at the same time he resented those authority figures, because they brought back memories of Joe, who he really hated deep down. So he eventually had to shatter the relationship and push away the one person who was driving him to succeed. Then he'd be on his own again, and he'd start drifting, usually into trouble."

Frank Dileo, Leonard Rowe, and the members of the Jackson family were not the only ones whose ears had perked up at the news of the O2 concerts and the enormous sums of money under discussion. Just as the franchise seemed to be cranking up to once again produce huge revenues, those who were Michael's collaborators back in Thriller Time began lining up in court to be cut in on the action. John Landis had put himself into first position on January 21, 2009, when the London shows were just a rumor, by filing a lawsuit that claimed back royalties from the "Thriller" video, plus a piece of the Nederlander deal. Michael's attorneys had seen it coming since late 2007 when stories about a possible series of Jackson concerts at the O2 began to appear in print and Landis complained to London's *Telegraph*, "Listen, Michael probably owes me $10 million because he's in hock to Sony so deeply. All the monies from the 'Thriller' video, which I own fifty percent, are collected by Sony. My deal is with

Michael's company, and he owes Sony so much that they keep the money." If Jackson was about to become flush again, though, there would be ways for Landis to collect. TheWrap.com's Andrew Gumbel, who announced the lawsuit two days before it was filed, reported that Tohme and other Jackson advisors had held a "council-of-war meeting" at the Bel-Air Hotel over the weekend to discuss the Landis suit. "We just wanted to make sure Michael wasn't upset or distracted," Tohme explained. That spring, Landis's claim against Michael would be joined by Ola Ray, the former *Playboy* centerfold who had been Jackson's costar in the "Thriller" video. Now a forty-eight-year-old single mom living in Sacramento, Ray's career had tailed off after a cocaine bust in 1992, and seventeen years later she was demanding to know why she wasn't receiving royalties from the twenty-fifth anniversary release of *Thriller.*

The lawsuits filed against him had always bothered Michael more than he let on. He hated conflict, and despised the attorneys who exploited it. His bodyguards recalled that near the end of one long day spent in a law office where he had been subjected to separate depositions, Michael was so overwrought that he grabbed one of their cell phones and hurled it through the glass of a conference room window.

"You have the same thousand parasites that float back in and try to take advantage of the situation," Tom Barrack told the *Los Angeles Times* near the end of May. If Barrack's comment was directed at anyone in particular, that person appeared to be Raymone Bain, who, on the same day as Ola Ray's California court filing, had submitted a lawsuit to the federal court in Washington, D.C., that demanded $44 million from Jackson for 10 percent of every bit of the entertainer's business she had ever touched, the AEG deal included. Those who had been involved in the negotiations for the O2 shows were incensed. "Raymone Bain was not at a single one of the meetings where the AEG deal was negotiated, not in person and not on the telephone," said an attorney who attended every one of them. Bain had been unable to so much as contact Michael by phone since 2008, when he changed numbers and insisted that the new one not be given to her. "Raymone Bain wasn't even *mentioned* during the meetings with AEG that resulted in the contract for the O2 shows," the attorney recalled. "She had absolutely nothing to do with that deal. But now she wants a piece of it." Bain, naturally, saw things differently. She had been in discussions with Randy Phillips and AEG long before Tohme Tohme arrived on the scene, and even if those discussions had not resulted in a deal, they gave her, Raymone believed, the basis for a claim.

Other lawsuits were coming. The only way to cope with it all was to keep Michael moving forward, looking straight ahead. Yet something in him suddenly wanted to reconcile with his past, to own up and pay out. Drugs could fog him over, but not make him truly forget. He seemed to believe he couldn't go forward without first going back. Out of nowhere he phoned Terry George in London.

George's story of Michael masturbating during a trans-Atlantic phone call back in 1980 had long been and still was the most credible of all the claims made against Jackson for inappropriate sexual conduct with a child. Who Terry George was and what he had become made him especially convincing; he didn't need money and had never sought attention. George was a multimillionaire businessman now, in his early forties, and remained, as he had been always, essentially a defender of Michael Jackson's reputation. When the Los Angeles police had contacted him back in 1993 during the Jordan Chandler investigation, George was very clear in telling them that Michael had never touched him in any sexual way, and insisted then, as he continued to do, that he did not believe Michael was a pedophile. He didn't know for certain, of course, since he hadn't seen or spoken to Jackson in three decades—at least not until he answered that "shock call" from the Carolwood chateau in the spring of 2009. Michael got quickly to the point and acknowledged what had happened during that phone conversation back in 1980, then said he wanted "to apologize and be forgiven," as George recounted their discussion. "But he insisted that his love for children was entirely innocent," George recalled. Yes, there had been accusations from a couple of boys over the years, but there was no truth to those stories at all, Michael said. He believed the kids had been forced to say things that they later regretted, and he really hoped they would some day be given a chance to say so publicly. He asked Michael how he was doing, and the star's only reply had been to say he had been "under a lot of pressure recently," George recalled. Michael thanked the Englishman again for being kind enough to forgive him, then said good-bye.

Perhaps Michael imagined he had wiped the slate clean. Or maybe he knew that really wasn't possible. Tom Mesereau believed that Michael had never really healed from the series of concussive blows he had absorbed back in 2003, 2004 and 2005. "I think he was bleeding internally the whole time," Mesereau said. "He was dying right in front of everyone, but nobody saw it."

19

On April 21, 2004, when a Santa Barbara County grand jury indicted Michael Jackson on ten felony counts related to his alleged sexual abuse of Gavin Arvizo, the entertainer's circumstances—legal, personal, and financial—had deteriorated so rapidly that even those who had been closest to him assumed the end was at hand.

The raid on Neverland Ranch and Jackson's subsequent arrest, in November 2003, had come at the worst possible time for Michael, and the district attorney who orchestrated the two events, Tom Sneddon, was fully aware of that. Sony had released *Number Ones* one day before the raid, sending the album into record stores at the very moment forensics experts, sheriff's deputies, and police videographers were inspecting every square inch of the main house at Neverland. In Las Vegas, Michael had been putting his final touches on a special for CBS television, featuring both new performances and a retrospective of his entire career, that was scheduled to air the following week. That the network would offer him such a platform (and the seven-figure fee that went with it) was testimony to how successful the "rebuttal video" broadcast on Fox had been both in debunking the Bashir documentary and in demonstrating Jackson's continuing ability to draw huge ratings. Michael was on the brink of a renaissance that exceeded what even his most ardent supporters had imagined possible a year earlier.

But within forty-eight hours of the raid, Jackson and those advising him had made two enormous mistakes that would put his future in serious jeopardy. One was to allow the Nation of Islam to move in and take almost complete control of his life. The other was to retain Mark Geragos as his criminal defense attorney.

Geragos was a controversial figure among many in the Los Angeles legal community, mainly because a lot of L.A. Lawyers believed he cared far more about getting his face on television than he did about winning cases. Geragos had become a fixture of the twenty-four-hour news cycle when he represented actress Winona Ryder after she was caught stealing $5,500 worth of designer clothes and accessories from the Saks Fifth Avenue store in Beverly Hills in December 2001. Geragos appeared on cable news shows almost nightly as the absurd farce dragged on, mainly because he and his client refused to accept a plea bargain and forced the case to trial. After Ryder was convicted of felony grand theft and vandalism, Geragos boasted before TV cameras that, instead of jail time, he had gotten his client a sentence of three years' probation, 480 hours of community service, $3,700 in fines, and $6,355 in restitution—the exact sentence the prosecution had asked for. His self-proclaimed ability to manage the media was why Geragos had been hired to represent California congressman Gary Condit when Condit was a public object of suspicion in the disappearance of a young woman named Chandra Levy in Washington, D.C. Condit was never charged with a crime, but that had absolutely nothing to do with Geragos's nightly appearances on television and everything to do with the fact that no evidence existed to link the congressman to Levy's disappearance. Just how successful Geragos had been in protecting his client's reputation was evident a short time later when Condit's thirty-year political career ended with an eighteen-point loss in the Democratic primary. And yet now, in 2004, after two very public failures, Geragos was the lead defense attorney not only for Michael Jackson, but also for Scott Peterson, whose pregnant wife Laci's dismembered body had been recovered from San Francisco Bay in April 2003. (That case would result in a trial at which Geragos promised to show that Laci Peterson's baby had been born alive, suggesting that she was a kidnap victim. No such evidence was ever presented and, after his conviction, Peterson was sentenced to death.)

The publicity that surrounded the Jackson and Peterson cases had made Geragos into the leading man of *Larry King Live*, but not into a skillful criminal defense attorney. Within days of taking the Jackson case, he made a pair of crucial errors. The least of these was to permit Jackson's appearance on *60 Minutes*. Michael told Ed Bradley on camera that he had been manhandled during his arrest by Santa Barbara sheriff's deputies, who dislocated his shoulders and bruised his forearms with overtightened handcuffs, then locked him up in a filthy bathroom where he was "taunted" for forty-five minutes. This story was a gross exaggeration, and the sheriff's department promptly proved it by, among other things, releasing an audiotape of Jackson's ride to the police station, where he was fingerprinted, booked, and released within just over an hour. Combined with the fact that he had lied to Martin Bashir about the extent of his plastic surgery, the *60 Minutes* appearance neither helped Michael's case nor improved his public standing. In fact, it damaged him on both fronts. Geragos's warning on *Larry King Live* that the sheriff's department would face "repercussions" for what it had done to his client only made matters worse.

More foolish was that Geragos had not only accepted but actually embraced the involvement of the Nation of Islam in the preparation of Michael's defense. Leonard Muhammad, the NOI's "chief of staff," stood directly behind Geragos at the first news conference called to respond to the molestation charges, and afterward was offered space in the attorney's law offices. The news that Jackson was affiliated with a blatantly racist and anti-Semitic organization did him no good with anyone outside a narrow spectrum of black America. More costly in the short term, though, was that Muhammad and his henchmen were destroying Jackson's relationships with almost everyone who had done anything to help him in recent years. The most expensive exclusions were those of Marc Schaffel, who had made Michael tens of millions of dollars in 2003 and had tens of millions more in the pipeline, and Al Malnik, who was closer than a lot of people realized to sorting out Jackson's financial problems.

Michael had first met Malnik when the movie director Brett Ratner invited him to see a house "so beautiful it will make you catatonic." Though described by old-money types in Palm Beach County as "gauche," Malnik's 35,000-square-foot mansion in Ocean Ridge (reputedly the largest waterfront home in the United States) overwhelmed Michael. So did Malnik's Asian art collection, which included carved mammoth tusks and an ivory sculpture featuring 8,000 separate figures, all with different faces. Like everyone who met Malnik, of course, Michael soon learned about the lawyer's "mob connections." Malnik had consorted with the likes of Meyer Lanksy and Sam Cohen as a younger man. *Reader's Digest* had described Malnik as Lansky's "heir apparent" when the biggest Jewish mobster of his era died in 1983, and that label (fairly applied or not) got Malnik banned from the casinos in Atlantic City. The fact that his Rolls-Royce was blown up in a parking garage in 1982 no doubt contributed to the attorney's spotty reputation.

In the years since, Malnik had made much of his immense fortune in the opportunistic (some would say predatory) title loan business. No matter what people said or wrote about him, Malnik had emerged as an undeniable eminence in Palm Beach County, where he was known as the developer of the Skylake Country Club and, especially, as the owner of the Forge, a legendary restaurant (*Wine Spectator* called it the best in the country) and nightclub in Miami Beach that had remained a major destination since the days when it was the South Florida haunt of Frank Sinatra and the Rat Pack.

Jackson and Malnik merged realities in the year 2000 within moments of a meeting that almost never happened. "I initially said no," Malnik recalled, "because I was not a fan, so I really didn't see the point of inviting him to come over and entertain him." Malnik's much younger wife had grown up with Michael Jackson posters on the wall of her bedroom, though, and insisted upon having the star over. In almost no time, Jackson and his children were living in Malnik's house for long stretches of time. Michael was maybe the easiest houseguest he ever had, Malnik would say later: "He liked to clean his own room and make his own bed, and he taught his kids to do that, too, much to our amazement." Malnik's older son Shareef soon formed a foursome with Michael, Ratner, and Chris Tucker. Malnik's triplets, who were about the same age as Jackson's two oldest children, quickly bonded with Prince and Paris. A year after Blanket was born, Michael asked Malnik to be the boy's godfather. When Malnik celebrated his seventieth birthday at the Forge, he sat with his wife on one side and Michael on the other. "Al made Michael part of his family," said Schaffel. "Michael stayed at his house for months on end and absolutely loved it there."

Jackson wrote dozens of new songs at the Malniks' enormous Ocean Ridge home, usually while walking around the place in pajamas and singing his lyrics a cappella. One of Malnik's favorite memories of Michael was the day he saw his houseguest walking up one set of stairs, then back down another, over and over again. "I asked him, 'What are you doing?' He said, 'I'm doing two songs at once. I am walking up this set doing one song, and when I walk down the other, I do the other song.'" When Michael asked him to install a portable dance floor, Malnik obliged. The biggest favors he did for Jackson, though, were financial. How much money he spent on Michael, Malnik wouldn't say, but it was substantial. "Al personally wrote checks to pay down a *lot* of Michael's bills," Schaffel recalled. "He really came to feel a warm affection for Michael. He felt that Michael was vulnerable and that people had taken advantage of him. And he really wanted to help him. But he understood the type of person Michael was. He knew that as well as cleaning up Michael's debt, he had to rehabilitate Michael's spending. Among other things, he tried to teach Michael to negotiate instead of just paying top dollar for whatever he wanted." Malnik demonstrated the art of haggling in his dealings with a number of Jackson's major creditors. Given Malnik's wealth, power, and reputation, very few of the people he telephoned were unwilling to hear him out. "Al called the head of Bank of America, and the guy immediately came to have dinner with Al at his house," remembered Schaffel, who was even more impressed by a conversation he listened to on speakerphone between Malnik and George W. Bush. The president of the United States was calling in the autumn of 2003 to ask for an introduction to rap mogul Russell Simmons, whom he hoped would help with "getting some of the black vote" in the 2004 election. "That's the kind of stature Al has," Schaffel observed. "And he used it to help Michael." By late 2003, after the disposition of the Myung Ho Lee and Marcel Avram lawsuits, "Al almost had Michael's finances to the point of a turnaround," Schaffel recalled, "and then it all just blew up."

It was Malnik who posted Jackson's bail following his arrest on the molestation charges in Santa Barbara County, but almost immediately afterward communication between the two ceased. "I told Michael that it was the worst mistake of his life when he allowed the Nation of Islam to come in and convince him to stop speaking to Al Malnik," Schaffel said. With Leonard Muhammad and associates whispering in Michael's ear, the relationship with Malnik deteriorated far beyond the point of not talking to one another. By the spring of 2004, Jackson, as drug-addled as he'd ever been, was convinced that Malnik was part of a conspiracy against him that included Sony, Bank of America, and Tom Sneddon, and that all of them were after the Beatles songs.

Many of the people surrounding Michael at that point were playing on both his sense of persecution and his delusional thinking. The Reverend Jesse Jackson was vying with Louis Farrakhan for first position. He saw something distinctly sinister in the way Bank of America had off-loaded Michael's debt to Fortress Investments, Jesse Jackson told USA Today. "Who was forcing the bank's hand and what did they stand to gain?" he asked. "That must come under scrutiny. I think the bank sold the loan rather than face the heat."

Louis Farrakhan wasn't going to be easily shouldered aside by the likes of Reverend Jackson, though, and he continued to work Michael's sensitivity on the subject of those "Hollywood Jews"—Steven Spielberg and David Geffen in particular—who had strung him along for years but were nowhere to be seen now, when he needed support and protection. Both Farrakhan and Michael appeared to have forgotten that back in Thriller

Time the Nation of Islam leader had denounced Michael for his "female-acting, sissified-acting expression," warning that "it is not wholesome for our young boys nor our young girls."

What Michael seemed not to understand was that whether or not he won black people over to his side would have absolutely nothing to do with what was going to happen to him in Santa Barbara County. Mark Geragos didn't get that, either, just one reason among many why it was so fortunate for Michael that Geragos, distracted by the Scott Peterson case, was on his way out as Jackson's lawyer.

Something like poetic justice imbued Johnnie Cochran's role as the key figure in selecting Geragos's replacement as Michael Jackson's defense attorney. It was Cochran, after all, who had persuaded Jackson to make the terrible and enduring mistake of settling the Jordan Chandler case for millions of dollars. "Michael never forgave Johnnie Cochran for that," Schaffel recalled. Cochran hadn't helped Michael's reputation much, either, with a subsequent comment that suggested Michael's insistence upon pleading the Fifth Amendment when asked about his relationships with young boys during a deposition in 1994 had been an implied admission of guilt. The attorney famed for helping O. J. Simpson avoid a murder conviction was on his deathbed in April 2004, wasting away rapidly from the effects of a fatal brain tumor, when Michael's brother Randy called Cochran to ask him to recommend an attorney to take Geragos's place. "If it was me," Johnnie said, "I'd want Tom Mesereau."

Imposingly tall and broad-shouldered, with a shoulder-length mane of white hair and ice-blue eyes, Mesereau looked as if he could hold his own with any movie lawyer onscreen. He had been raised as the son of a U.S. Army officer (and military academy football coach) and briefly pursued a career as a boxer before attending Harvard. Mesereau had become a nationally known attorney only a few months earlier, in the autumn of 2003, when his defense of actor Robert Blake on murder charges at a preliminary trial in Los Angeles Superior Court put his face on television for a solid month. Blake was accused of the 2001 murder of his wife, Bonnie Lee Bakley, as she sat in the car outside a Studio City restaurant where the two had eaten dinner. Convinced that the "egomanical" prosecutors on the case had decided Blake's guilt was so obvious it didn't need to be proven, Mesereau approached the prelim as if it were a real trial, and eviscerated the state's witnesses on cross-examination. The analysts on cable TV all agreed it had been brilliant work, especially after Blake became the first defendant charged with a special circumstances murder case in California to be granted bail.

Mesereau had taken a vacation in Big Sur after the prelim, and spent an entire week in November 2003 with his cell phone shut off. When he turned the phone back on during the drive back down 101 to Los Angeles, it began to ring repeatedly. "All these friends of Michael Jackson's were calling me from Las Vegas, begging me to come and see him," Mesereau remembered. One of the callers was Larry Carroll, who for more than twenty years had been the most prominent black newscaster in Los Angeles, until he was charged with securities fraud by a grand jury in San Bernardino County. Mesereau had represented Carroll at trial and won his acquittal. Of course he was intrigued by the idea of representing Michael Jackson, Mesereau told Carroll, but the Blake case was scheduled to go to trial in February and he needed to give that his full attention. The calls from Michael's friends kept coming, though. "They were in shock, I think," the attorney said. "You would turn down Michael Jackson?" they all said. Michael's brother Randy, now in control of the star's business affairs, had watched the entire Blake prelim on Court TV and was especially insistent, but Mesereau kept saying that he couldn't take on both of these cases at once.

Mesereau was familiar to the city's African-American elite not just because he lived with a former Miss Black Los Angeles—the cabaret performer Minnie Foxx—and was among the few white people seen regularly in the pews at the African Methodist Episcopal Church on Crenshaw Boulevard, arguably the most august institution in LA's black community. The attorney had made a virtual alternate career out of his pro bono work for poor black clients both in the Los Angeles Basin and in the Deep South. Nearly every African-American leader in the country, including Louis Farrakhan, was aware of the acquittal Mesereau had won for Terry Wayne Bonner, a homeless black man accused of murdering a white woman in Birmingham, Alabama. Mesereau was admired as well for persuading the San Bernardino district attorney's office to drop the rape charges it had filed against boxer Mike Tyson in 2001.

During Blake's pretrial hearings in early 2004, Court TV began to report on "growing tensions" between Blake and his defense team. One report had Blake unhappy with Mesereau's partner and cocounsel Susan Yu, insisting she be removed from the case at the same time Mesereau refused to attend court without her. Another story recounted Mesereau's frustration with his inability to control Blake, who had given an interview to Barbara Walters on ABC against the attorney's advice. There was also a story that Blake had hired private investigators that were to report directly to him, without consulting Mesereau, and another that the actor had accused his attorney of exploiting the case to promote his career by mentioning it repeatedly in an infomercial.

Mesereau has refused to explain why he asked the court, in February 2004, to let him be released from the Blake case, but does admit that he withdrew to his offices in a glum mood, realizing that in the course of a couple of months he had lost the two biggest opportunities of his career, the Robert Blake and Michael Jackson cases, and might soon be returning to relative obscurity. Less than two weeks after he withdrew from the Blake case, though, Mesereau received another call from Randy Jackson, who said, "Look, we still want you. Can you come to Florida and meet my brother?"

The attorney flew to Orlando the next day and was driven to a "secret location" where Michael and his large team of advisors waited. "Michael didn't say much of anything," Mesereau recalled. "He just observed me intensely while the others asked questions."

"We don't like what our attorneys are doing with the media," said Randy Jackson, who told a story about being shouldered aside by Geragos after a court hearing in the lawyer's rush to get to the microphones. In explaining that he was "not a Hollywood type," Mesereau found himself being, perhaps, a bit too forthcoming. He had never been much interested in show business, the attorney said, had always been something of a loner, to tell the truth, one whose favorite entertainment was to drive around Los Angeles, especially South Central LA, "just to see what's going on and feel the people." Other than a slight smile, Michael Jackson showed no visible response to all of this, and Mesereau walked away from the interview "figuring I was one of a hundred lawyers to come through, and might be the weirdest guy they'd talked to." He had his own reservations about taking the job, anyway, if it was offered: "People who cared about me were warning that this case would define me for the rest of my life, especially if I lost. I'd be the guy who let Michael Jackson die in prison." Two weeks later, though, after Michael spoke directly with Johnnie Cochran, Randy Jackson called Mesereau to tell him he had the job, if he wanted it, and the attorney immediately said yes.

Excited as he was, Mesereau soon began to impose conditions. The first was that Susan Yu would be his cocounsel. "No problem," Randy Jackson said. Mesereau knew he risked losing the case when he made his second demand, which was that the Nation of Islam disappear from Michael's life.

After spending some time in Santa Maria, the small city in northern Santa Barbara County where the trial would be held, Mesereau decided the entire subject of race must be removed from the case. Santa Maria was a mostly white, conservative, largely blue-collar community with a sizeable Hispanic minority but almost no black people. Mesereau spent a week hanging out in local bars and coffee shops wearing jeans and a leather jacket, and realized the place didn't precisely accord with the effete liberal bias against it. "What I discovered was that Michael was very well thought of by most of the people there," Mesereau recalled. "He was part of the community, employed a lot of people, and had been a good neighbor. Everyone I spoke to remarked that on the rare occasions when he came into the city he had been very polite and considerate. But the big thing that struck me was that people didn't see Michael Jackson in terms of race. He was the rare person, maybe the one person, who truly transcended race in people's minds. As an artist, white people loved him, Hispanics loved him, Asians loved him, everybody loved him. I admit I was surprised, but not a single person I spoke to brought up the subject of race. It just wasn't an issue where Michael was concerned."

Mesereau first publicly distinguished himself from Michael Jackson's previous attorneys when he supported the prosecution request for a gag order that Mark Geragos had opposed. "I didn't want to spend a lot of time talking to cameras and microphones," he explained. That didn't win him any friends in the media. Geragos's pal Geraldo Rivera was on TV every night telling his audience what a mistake it was to hire Mesereau, who had never handled a high-profile case other than Robert Blake's, and had lost that job before the actual trial began. Geragos himself was relentlessly lobbying members of the Jackson family, Jermaine in particular, to put him back on the case. Mesereau found an ally in Carl Douglas, who was now running Johnnie Cochran's Los Angeles law firm. The Scott Peterson case looked like a loser to him, Douglas would explain later, and "listening to people on TV say that Michael Jackson had the same attorney as Peterson concerned me," so he privately urged that Geragos be kept away from the case.

Mesereau's position remained tenuous, however. Big-name attorneys were arriving at Neverland by helicopter on a regular basis to make a pitch for the job. When Mesereau announced that he intended to try the case in Santa Maria, his media critics across the board began to scourge him. The attorney's refusal to do as suggested by the "experts" on Court TV and bus in jurors from the ostensibly more liberal city of Santa Barbara was offered up as evidence that he wasn't ready for prime time.

"I had discovered that the people in Santa Maria were conservative and very law and order, yes, but they were also quite libertarian," Mesereau explained. "I knew all those college professors and wealthy art patrons in the south were supposed to be more liberal than the people up north, but I wasn't sure they would be when it came to Michael Jackson. And I learned from talking to them that the people up north were very sensitive about being compared to the people in the southern part of the county. They lived up north because they couldn't afford the real estate in the south, and felt a deep sense of separation." The Santa Ynez Mountains created a natural geographical division in Santa Barbara County that had been embraced as a point of pride by the people up north. As the judge assigned to the Michael Jackson criminal trial, Rodney Melville, would put it, "The attitude is, what happens north of the mountains stays north of the mountains." For Mesereau, "What sealed it was when I found out that there had been two bills submitted to the state legislature where the north part of the county had tried to secede from the south. I had realized by then that a lot of people in the north identified Tom Sneddon with the south, because that was where he kept his offices, and where he lived. I had a feeling that if I played it right, Santa Maria was a perfect place to try Michael."

Mesereau was alarmed when he learned that Michael and Louis Farrakhan were talking about staging a second Million Man March through the streets of Santa Maria. "I told Randy, 'Look, this is crazy. The worst thing you can do in this community is make the Nation of Islam your most visible identifier.' Randy listened, and he went to Leonard Muhammad and explained the situation to him." The Nation of Islam acceded almost immediately and vanished from Michael Jackson's entourage. "It was Louis Farrakhan's call," Mesereau said. "He could have swayed Michael, I think. But I believe he really did care for Michael and wanted to see him acquitted even if it meant getting less publicity for himself. As opposed to some others. And yes, I mean Jesse Jackson."

While Michael himself accepted the departure of the black Muslims without protest, he remained vulnerable to the imprecations of Raymone Bain, who never stopped trying to sell him on the idea that bringing in prominent black leaders to raise the cry of racial injustice was a useful strategy. Mesereau identified Bain early on as an opportunist "who cared a lot less about what was best for Michael than about how she could promote herself as some sort of spokesperson for black America." One of the most difficult moments for the attorney during pretrial preparations came when Bain placed a phone call to Mesereau with Michael on the line. "Raymone did almost all the talking," Mesereau recalled, "and she began to tell me that 'Michael isn't just concerned about the outcome of this trial, he's also concerned about his legacy,' and that he thought it was important to bring in a series of important African-American leaders like her friends Jesse Jackson and Al Sharpton to remind America what Michael Jackson meant to the black community." He had to resort to deep breathing to keep control of his temper, Mesereau recalled, before explaining, for his client's benefit more than Bain's, "If Michael loses this trial, his legacy will be to die in a California state penitentiary. My only concern—which should be your only concern, Raymone—is to make sure that doesn't happen."

Bain backed away, but not for long. And she still had Michael's ear, Mesereau knew, which left open the clear possibility that he could be removed as Jackson's attorney at any time. "I never blamed Michael," he said. "When people are under that kind of stress—the worst stress imaginable—they turn to what they know and where they came from."

Jackson's mounting paranoia had surged just days after his arrest, when it was revealed that the owner of XtraJet, the private air transport company that flew him from Las Vegas to Santa Barbara to be arrested, had conspired with one of his maintenance workers to install microphones and a pair of hidden digital cameras that recorded a video they were marketing to television news shows.

The people out to get him had become, in Michael's mind, a lynch mob led by Tom Sneddon. Jackson and Sneddon had been obsessed with one another since 1993, and the contrasts between the two men could not have been more marked. Sneddon was a ruddy-faced Republican in his sixties who had graduated from Notre Dame, the father of nine children whose wife wrote abstinence manuals for Christian youth groups. The DA's determination to corroborate Jordan Chandler's accusations had carried him as far afield from Santa Barbara as Australia and England, where he made personal appeals to the families of boys he believed Jackson had molested, and Sneddon did little to hide his disappointment when they rebuffed him. Michael certainly hadn't eased any strain when he added a cut titled "D.S." to the *HIStory* album, which was released two years after the Chandler trial. The song was a barely disguised attack on Sneddon in which Jackson's only concession to Sony's attorneys had been to change his target's name to "Dom Sheldon." The lyrics were among the sloppiest and certainly the most infantile ever written by Michael Jackson, who had accented his attack on the "BS DA" by repeatedly chanting, "Dom Sheldon is a cold man."

In the ten years since the end of the Chandler case, the district attorney had granted interviews to newspapers on three continents, detailing his frustration with the failure to make a molestation case against Michael Jackson. He continued to describe his investigation as "open but inactive," and told one reporter after another that all he needed to initiate new grand jury proceedings was a single "cooperating witness." Sneddon and former Los Angeles County district attorney Gil Garcetti had persuaded the California Legislature to pass what became known as the "Michael Jackson Law," allowing district attorneys statewide to compel the testimony of a child they believed had been sexually abused. The Santa Barbara County DA made little secret of the fact that he was now prepared to pounce on the first viable victim he could find, cooperative or not, to make a case against Jackson.

After the first installment of Martin Bashir's *Living with Michael Jackson* documentary aired in the UK in early 2003, Sneddon issued a statement to the press saying that he and the county's sheriff, Jim Anderson, had agreed that "the BBC broadcast would be taped by the sheriff's department" and "anticipated that it will be reviewed." Michael Jackson's remarks about sharing his bed with children were "unusual at best," Sneddon said, and "for this reason, all local departments having responsibility in this are taking the matter seriously." The DA then urged any child who believed he had been sexually abused by Jackson to come forward. Just a few days later, someone in Sneddon's office leaked onto the Internet Jordie Chandler's 1993 affidavit that described in detail the alleged molestations by Jackson.

District Attorney Sneddon was but one of the faces who floated through Jackson's sense of déjà vu as a squadron of familiar foes lined up against him. Larry Feldman, the attorney who had extracted the huge settlement for the Chandlers, had been the first stop for Gavin Arvizo's family, in early March 2003, well before they ever contacted the police. Feldman had sent the Arvizos to Dr. Stan Katz, the very psychologist who had interviewed Jordan Chandler and his family at length during the preparation of the 1994 civil case against Jackson. It was Katz, after hearing from five-year-old Nikki Chandler that he had seen Michael "touch" his half-brother Jordie, who had reported the suspected abuse to law enforcement, setting off the grand jury investigations in both Los Angeles and Santa Barbara counties.

What Michael couldn't know in the summer of 2004 was that Katz's interview with Gavin Arvizo had actually produced plenty that was to the advantage of his defense. The boy had told the psychologist he knew all about the Jordan Chandler allegations, for example, and Mesereau would later use this to support his claim that the entire case was an extortion plot. The fact that Gavin's mother Janet Arvizo consulted with Feldman and Katz before talking to police would provide even stronger evidence for that argument. By the time Mesereau learned of all this, Janet Arvizo had already claimed that she first discovered her son's molestation on September 30, 2003, when Tom Sneddon and a team of investigators broke the news to her during a meeting at a Los Angeles hotel. The question of why, then, she took her son to Feldman and Katz months before that date was one the defense attorney particularly looked forward to asking in court.

In Michael's mind, the gallery of tormentors targeting him also included two woman journalists who had made exposing him as a pedophile their principal occupation during the past decade. Diane Dimond, formerly of *Hard Copy*, where she broke the Jordan Chandler story, was now at Court TV and willing to look at any sort of "evidence" she could use to prove Jackson guilty in the eyes of the American public. Dimond had managed to once again lower the bar of tabloid TV standards when she contacted a man who had a collection of Michael Jackson memorabilia, persuaded him to let her display a pair of soiled, twenty-year-old underpants on camera, then phoned Tom Sneddon to urge the prosecutor to take DNA samples from the item. It was believed by many in the media and out that someone in the DA's office had leaked the confidential settlement agreement in the Jordan Chandler case to Dimond shortly before the document was posted on the Internet in 2003.

The coziness of Dimond's relationship with Sneddon became an open secret when other reporters realized that she had known about the raid on Neverland Ranch well before they learned of it. The Associated Press would later report that Dimond had told her bosses at Court TV that Sneddon was working on a criminal filing against Michael Jackson months before a warrant was issued for the entertainer's arrest. During the press conference at which Sneddon announced the raid and the arrest warrant, the DA had responded to a question about the number of civil cases (involving allegations of sexual misconduct with children) that had been settled by Jackson since 1993 by saying, "Ask Diane. She knows everything about Michael Jackson." When Sneddon gave his first sit-down interview after the press conference, it was with Dimond.

Dimond commanded even more media attention a short time later when she told Larry King that prosecutors were in possession of a "stack of love letters" written by Michael Jackson to Gavin Arvizo. "Does anyone . . . know of the existence of these letters?" King asked her. "Absolutely," Dimond answered. "I do. I absolutely know of their existence." Had she read them? King wondered. "No, I have not read them," Dimond admitted. In fact, she had not even seen them. But she was certain there were such letters, having heard it from "high law enforcement sources." No such letters ever surfaced because no such letters existed.

Vanity Fair's Maureen Orth, meanwhile, was filing a series of lengthy articles that drew largely on anonymous or pseudonymous sources to portray Jackson in a light as lurid as anything the tabloids had ever cast upon him. The capstone of Orth's Michael Jackson oeuvre was the March 2003 article she wrote in collaboration with Myung Ho Lee shortly after the "financial advisor" filed his lawsuit against Jackson. Among the few bits of fresh information in Orth's piece was an allegation that Michael had used Coke cans filled with the white wine he called "Jesus juice" to aid in his seductions of a Japanese boy named Richard Matsuura. Matsuura's response was to tell an NBC reporter that those claims were "completely false" and that Michael had never behaved improperly around him. It was impossible, of course, to rebut or verify claims by Orth that Michael had bathed in sheep's blood or paid a voodoo chief from Mali named Baba to ritually sacrifice forty-two cows, but the outpouring of "information" on the Jackson case—true, false, and indeterminate—made clarity about any of it near to impossible.

Orth was just one among scores of journalists who had attempted to scrape together enough information about Jordan Chandler to paint a plausible portrait of a young man who was now nearing his mid-twenties and had done virtually everything possible to make himself invisible. While he believed that Jordie had grown up to be "normal," Evan Chandler's brother Ray said, the young man's life was anything but. "My big worry is that, you know, even when he is sixty he is still going to be 'that Jackson kid,'" Ray told Orth. "I don't think it will ever go away." He was urging his nephew to come to Santa Barbara and testify against Jackson at the criminal trial on the new charges, Ray Chandler said, "because it would be the final nail in Michael's coffin and Jordie would be a hero."

20

On January 31, 2005, jury selection began for Michael Jackson's criminal trial in Santa Maria. Judge Rodney Melville granted an exception to the gag order he had imposed on the case to allow Jackson to provide reporters with a video of a brief public statement that Mesereau had written. The attorney was incensed that his client had consented to an interview with Geraldo Rivera arranged by Raymone Bain, but broke his own ban on contact with the media when the transcripts of the grand jury proceedings in the Arvizo case were leaked just before Jackson's criminal trial was to begin. He would never be sure who the source of that leak had been, Mesereau said. "It could have been someone who had worked for me," he admitted, "someone who was upset about being fired and retaliated in this way. Whoever did it, I felt we had to reply, so I approved Michael's appearance in that video. It made him feel better, if nothing else."

Mesereau decided to ignore the advice of his jury consultant to exclude as many women as possible, the idea being that women—mothers in particular—would be especially hostile to a defendant in a sexual molestation case. "Susan and I wanted women," the attorney explained. "We thought they would be more open-minded about an eccentric artist like Michael Jackson, less prone to judge." Michael smiled just once during jury selection, when a prospective juror admitted, "I'm not so much into his music, but I sure like his moves." Before the end of February, Mesereau and Yu had collaborated with the prosecution to empanel a jury of eight women and four men. There were eight Caucasians, three Hispanics, and one Asian. They included a middle-aged man who believed Deepak Chopra was a rapper, an elderly lady whose grandson had been forced to register as a sex offender, and a younger woman who was divorced from a Santa Maria police officer.

Sneddon's opening statement on March 1 likened Neverland Ranch to a pedophile's lair, a virtual "Pinocchio's Pleasure Island": "The private world of Michael Jackson reveals that, instead of reading them *Peter Pan*, [he] is showing them sexually explicit magazines. Instead of cookies and milk, you can substitute wine, vodka, and bourbon. It's not children's books but visits to Internet porn sites." Sneddon offered explicit descriptions of masturbation scenes, Jackson's erect penis, and simulated sex with a mannequin.

Mesereau had focused his own opening statement on the young accuser's mother, Janet Arvizo, describing her as a serial con artist who had tried and failed to extract money from Jim Carrey, Mike Tyson, and Adam Sandler before finding her way to Michael Jackson: "The mother, with her children as tools, was trying to find a celebrity to latch onto. Unfortunately for Michael Jackson, he fell for it." Mesereau also hammered on the criminal indictment's bizarre timeline, something everyone involved in the trial recognized as the greatest vulnerability of the prosecution case. Shortly after Michael Jackson's arrest in November 2003, Tom Sneddon's office had produced criminal information alleging that the sexual assaults on Gavin Arvizo had occurred in early February 2003, right around the time the Martin Bashir documentary aired. In January 2004, Mark Geragos had appeared on NBC's *Dateline* to assert that his client had a "concrete, iron-clad alibi" for the dates on the prosecution's charge sheet. Soon after, Sneddon arranged for Michael Jackson to be rearraigned on a conspiracy charge, and moved the alleged molestation dates two weeks forward into mid-February 2003. In order to discredit the defendant's supposedly "iron-clad alibi," the district attorney was now attempting to make the case that Michael Jackson, in a panic after the airing of the Bashir documentary, had conspired to kidnap Gavin Arvizo and force him to deny acts of molestation that had not yet taken place, then somehow managed to recover his bearings long enough to commit those terrible acts at the very moment when the whole world was watching him. "Can you imagine a more absurd time for it to happen?" Mesereau asked, and at least a couple of jurors were seen shaking their heads.

Martin Bashir was called as the trial's first witness. Sneddon's brief direct examination, intended solely to authenticate *Living with Michael Jackson*, was sufficient to reveal Bashir's farcical pomposity. As *Rolling Stone*'s Matt Taibbi would observe, Bashir was the sort of media creature "who peers through the bedroom windows of famous people and imagines he is curing cancer." When a question described his productions as documentaries, Bashir sniffed that, "I call them *cultural-affairs programs*." On cross-examination, Bashir refused to answer nearly thirty questions about the footage he had left out of his documentary, based on the claim that he was protected by both California's journalist shield law and the First Amendment of the U.S. Constitution.

"I asked him one long-winded question after another, mostly of the 'Isn't it true . . . ?' variety," Mesereau recalled. "Basically, it allowed me to testify on my client's behalf." While Mesereau and Yu were pleased by Melville's warning that he would consider holding Bashir in contempt for his failure to answer questions, they were far more delighted by the judge's decision that the jury could view the videotapes of Bashir's outtakes. "I was pretty sure that they would eventually despise Bashir just as much as I did," the attorney said.

Sneddon next called to the stand Santa Barbara County sheriff's deputy Albert Lafferty, who had been responsible for videotaping and photographing the Neverland Ranch raid. This was in some ways the most difficult hour of the trial for Michael, Mesereau would say later. Lafferty had been part of a veritable army of law enforcement officers who arrived at Neverland at just after nine on the morning of November 18, 2003, and were still searching the premises fourteen hours later. The deputy narrated a twelve-minute DVD offering a virtual tour of Michael Jackson's private world that was far more detailed and invasive than anything that had been shown in Martin Bashir's hour-long "cultural-affairs program."

The exterior shots of Neverland's main house, arcade, train station, zoo, and amusement park were familiar to much of America, but very few people had ever peeked inside the guest cottage where Elizabeth Taylor and Marlon Brando stayed during their visits to the ranch, or gazed upon the fleet of Rolls-Royces and Bentleys that filled the garage.

Lafferty formally began his guided tour at the ornate wrought-iron entrance gate to the ranch that was staffed by life-size mannequin security figures. From that moment forward, who or what might be "real" became the fundamental, if unintended, theme of the deputy's video. More mannequins appeared in frame after frame once Lafferty was inside the main house, many of them child-size figures hiding in corners, or doing handstands and somersaults in hallways or foyers. There were white marble naked cherubs posed on the magnificent parquet floors along with blowups, cutouts, and papier-mâché statues of characters that included Superman, Batman, Spider-Man, and most of the cast of the *Star Wars* movies, along with Mickey Mouse, Michael Jordan, Tinker Bell, Indiana Jones, Bruce Lee, the Ninja Turtles, and assorted knights in shining armor. Life-size photographs of Shirley Temple, Charlie Chaplin, and the Three

Stooges were strewn among huge posters depicting the characters from *The Wizard of Oz, Pinocchio, Who Framed Roger Rabbit, Bambi,* and *Singin' in the Rain.* The stiff-backed members of a kitchen staff costumed in formal black-and-white outfits looked like mannequins themselves for a moment until one of them moved suddenly, drawing gasps from the jury and the courtroom gallery.

The piles of stuff cluttering the house, especially Michael's bedroom, were staggering: Christmas decorations, coffee-table books, tennis racquets, Game Boys, boom boxes, stuffed animals, stacks of books, heaps of DVDs, hats of every conceivable description, and hundreds of toys still in boxes, some half opened, others still sealed. Peter Pan was everywhere: There were giant posters and cutouts dangling from strings, there were photographs of Bobby Driscoll as Peter in the Disney film, and the camera took in a jewel-encrusted Peter Pan figurine. Lafferty showed his audience the bedroom filled with dolls, the huge gold throne where a mannequin of a child was doing a handstand in the seat, and the glass cases filled with the most valuable collection of Disney figurines not owned by Walt's relatives. The deputy's camera led them around a living room so large that it was hung with three crystal chandeliers, and lingered at length on the elaborately fashioned small-scale castle—complete with moat and guarded by child-size figurines—that took up much of the floor space. Lafferty had been equally attentive to the enormous paintings of Michael that hung all over the walls of the lower level of the main house, most depicting him as either a king or an angel. The deputy gave the courtroom crowd a long but blurry look at the sparkly blue comforter on Michael's bed and *The Last Supper* painting that hung above it. He then showed them the closet where Michael's clothing hung in color-coordinated sections, letting the jurors see that he possessed an apparently limitless supply of the crisp white dress shirts, striped black slacks, and brocade vests he wore to court each day.

After the courtroom's TV screen went blank Michael's lower lip trembled and tears smudged the makeup at the corners of his eyes. Mesereau stood to make the point that the authorities in Santa Barbara County had used more police manpower to raid Michael Jackson's home than had ever been used in the pursuit of a serial killer anywhere in the United States.

The first Arvizo called to the stand was Gavin Arvizo's eighteen-year-old sister Davellin, the most sympathetic and likeable member of her family. She told the jury about her family. While growing up poor in East Los Angeles, Davellin explained, her brother Gavin had been diagnosed with a mysterious but terrifyingly aggressive stage-four cancer that by the age of thirteen had cost the boy a kidney, his left adrenal gland, the tip of his pancreas, his spleen, and multiple lymph nodes. A sixteen-pound tumor had been removed from his abdomen and a double round of chemotherapy had left him throwing up blood in the middle of the night.

The girl described at length how the family had gained access to assorted celebrities through a "comedy camp" for inner-city kids held at the Laugh Factory on the Sunset Strip, and how her mother Janet passed along Gavin's "dying wishes" to the club's owner, Jamie Masada. At the top of that list was meeting his heroes Chris Tucker, Adam Sandler, and Michael Jackson. The Arvizos never got near Sandler, but were taken under the protection of both Tucker and Jackson, each of whom showered Gavin and his siblings with gifts and attention. Michael had seemed so kind and humble back at the beginning, Davellin remembered, regularly calling Gavin at his grandparents' home to tell the boy how to visualize his healthy cells eating up the cancer cells "like Pac-Man." After her parents split up and her father took off with the family car, Michael gave her mom a Ford Bronco she could use to drive Gavin to and from his doctor appointments.

Everything seemed to change, though, Davellin said, after the Bashir documentary aired on ABC. She and her family flew from California to Florida aboard Chris Tucker's private jet on the day that *Living with Michael Jackson* was to be broadcast. When they arrived at the Turnberry Isle resort near Miami, where Jackson was putting them up, Davellin recalled, Michael seemed "kind of, like, upset" and said he didn't want them to watch the program. Michael and Gavin met "privately" for several minutes, Davellin said, and afterward her brother began to act differently, "very hyper, very talkative, running around, very playful, more talkative, more jumpy."

As they prepared to return to Neverland, her brother was given a $75,000 watch and a rhinestone-studded jacket as gifts (Sneddon had called them "bribes" in his opening statement). Back at the ranch, Dieter Wiesner gave her and the rest of the family a list of "nice things" to say about Michael when they appeared in what would become known as the "rebuttal video," Davellin testified, and told them not to talk about "what goes on at the ranch." The girl then described walking into the wine cellar at Neverland to find Jackson pouring wine into cups for her brothers Star and Gavin, who were twelve and thirteen at the time.

Sneddon had already told the jury that it was during this stay at Neverland that Jackson began to sexually abuse Gavin Arvizo. How had her brother's behavior changed during that time? Sneddon asked Davellin.

"He didn't want to be hugged, he didn't want to be kissed," the girl replied. "It just hurts because I'm his older sister." Had she seen the defendant touch her brother inappropriately? Sneddon asked. "Michael Jackson was constantly hugging [Gavin] and kissing him on the cheek or on the head," the girl replied.

Davellin then described how the Arvizos were "held captive" (Sneddon's words) at the Calabasas Country Inn after leaving Neverland in spring 2003, under the constant observation of Jackson employees and Frank Cascio and Vinnie Amen. (Because Cascio and Amen had been named by Sneddon as "unindicted coconspirators," the two were prevented from testifying themselves.) "Vinnie and Frank said not to leave," the girl testified. "We couldn't leave the room, so we didn't even bother to ask [to go out] because we knew the answer would be no." It was for their own good, the family was told, according to Davellin: "There was one time when Frank told us there were death threats on us."

What Mesereau wanted the jury to hear was the audiotape of an interview the Arvizos had given to Mark Geragos's private investigator, Bradley Miller, back in February 2003. That interview had proceeded on two tracks, one in which the family praised "Daddy Michael's" kindness and generosity, and another in which it offered graphic descriptions of the "demonic ways" that characterized the children's biological father. Janet Arvizo and each of her children made David Arvizo, a warehouse worker for a supermarket chain, out to be a fiend who had beaten and abused them in every conceivable manner before disappearing from their lives. Davellin said David had broken her tailbone during one beating. Her youngest brother, Star, told Miller that his dad had kicked him in the head. Gavin Arvizo claimed that their father had knocked him around even when he was being given chemotherapy treatments. Janet described being slapped, punched, and thrown into walls. Clumps of hair had been torn from her head while the children watched, she said. The violence had been so extreme that she was granted a five-year restraining order that kept David away not only from her and the three children, but also from the family dog, Rocky, who had been abused every bit as terribly as the rest of the family.

Sneddon had reason to be pleased with this portrayal of David Arvizo, who had told reporters that he believed his wife was making the accusations of sexual abuse against Jackson because she wanted Michael's money. The thrust of the family's interview with Bradley Miller, though, was to contrast David Arvizo with the man who, as Janet described him on the audiotape, "delivered [us] from this evil." Michael Jackson had been the first person to show her children the meaning of "unconditional love," Janet had told Miller. On the Miller audiotape, Janet and her children spoke of how "safe" and "protected" they felt with Michael, how he had become "the father figure" the kids longed for and seemed intent only on making all of them "as happy as possible." It was Gavin who had first asked if he and Star could sleep in Michael's room at the main house, the family all told Miller, because he felt safer there than in the guest quarters, where David could get to him.

The Miller interview was conducted just two weeks after *Living with Michael Jackson* aired on ABC, and all of the Arvizos professed to be outraged and offended by what first Bashir and then the media had done to both Gavin and Michael. Now, only a little more than two years later, Davellin Arvizo was telling the jury in Santa Maria that she and her mother and her brothers had made it all up, having been coerced or manipulated into defending Michael Jackson as part of an elaborate plan to smother the truth.

During her cross-examination, Davellin insisted to Mesereau that no one in her family had ever seen the Bashir documentary, but the jury had already heard Janet Arvizo make a contradictory claim several times on tape. Mesereau let the girl explain that her mother had said a number of things that were exaggerated, then reminded Davellin that it was not only on the Bradley Miller audiotape or on the Marc Schaffel–produced "rebuttal video" that she and her family praised Michael Jackson, but also in interviews with state social workers. Some of what the Arvizos said was true, and some of it wasn't, Davellin explained. "So you'd lie about certain things, and tell the truth about certain things," Mesereau asked. "Yeah," Davellin answered.

The jury had viewed a section of the famous "rebuttal video" immediately before Mesereau began his cross-examination of Davellin and they would see more of the video each time the attorney prepared to interrogate another Arvizo family member. The panel had watched and listened as the purported victim's sister described Michael Jackson as "a loving, kind, humble man [who] took us under his wing when no one else would." More significantly, the rebuttal video was what had given the jurors their first look at the rest of the Arvizo family. They had seen and heard Star Arvizo say of Michael, "He actually seemed more fatherly than, like, our biological father." They had studied Gavin Arvizo as he said of the man he now accused of molesting him, "He was a loving, kind, humble man, and all he wanted to do was good and happiness." They had listened at length while Janet Arvizo lambasted both Martin Bashir and the media that had been sent into a frenzy by his documentary: "It breaks my heart because they're missing out on something very beautiful that they have tainted." The jury seemed to be paying especially close attention as Janet Arvizo recalled the day her son had asked Michael Jackson, "Can I call you Daddy?" Michael had kindly answered, "Of course."

Fourteen-year-old Star Arvizo was supposed to be a far more potent prosecution witness than his older sister. While Davellin had admitted that she never saw Michael Jackson touch either of her brothers in a sexual way, Star's claims in that regard were graphic. Among the things he had seen in the master suite at Neverland, Star said, were various pornographic sites that Michael Jackson and his friend Frank Cascio had shown him and his brother Gavin while Prince and Paris Jackson were sleeping on the bed nearby. He told Sneddon that when an image of a woman with large bare breasts flashed onto the screen, Michael had joked, "Got milk?" At another point, Star continued, Michael had whispered in his own son's ear, "Prince, you're missing some pussy." Michael also shared porn magazines with him and Gavin, Star said, and simulated having sex with a mannequin while he and his brother watched. Once, while he and Gavin were watching a movie in the bedroom, Michael waltzed in buck-naked, Star said: "Me and my brother were grossed out. [Michael] sat on the bed and said it was natural," then walked out of the room, still nude. Had he noticed anything "unusual" about Jackson's appearance on that occasion? Sneddon inquired. No, Star answered. Sneddon asked again, twice, before Star remembered that, oh, yes, Jackson's penis had been fully erect.

The jurors were squirming in their seats by the time Star told Sneddon about how Michael had given him and his brother wine while they were flying between Florida and California in a private jet. "He leaned over and handed it to me," Star said. "I thought it was Diet Coke so I didn't want to be rude. It smelled like rubbing alcohol. I asked him what it was and he said it was wine." During that same flight, he saw an intoxicated Jackson licking Gavin's head (a description that had appeared previously both in Jordan Chandler case documents and in Bob Jones's book *Michael Jackson: The Man Behind the Mask*) "for about six seconds," Star said. Just like his sister Davellin, he had seen Gavin drinking red liquid from a 7 Up can. After a few sips, Gavin "wasn't acting right," Star said. "He was, like, saying weird stuff that didn't make sense." Star also described a drinking game Michael made the Arvizo boys play in the master bedroom: Each of them had to make a prank call, and if the number they dialed didn't exist, they had to take a drink of wine. Michael usually called wine "Jesus juice," Star remembered.

Star echoed his sister's story of being held captive by the "unindicted coconspirators" in the case. Dieter Wiesner had told him "always say good things about Michael Jackson" before his appearance with his family in what became known as the rebuttal video, Star said. Frank Cascio had warned him that if he said anything he shouldn't say, there were "ways that my grandparents could disappear," Star testified.

When Star was asked by Sneddon if he had actually witnessed Jackson's molestation of his brother Gavin, the boy said he had, twice: The first time, "I saw directly onto the bed. I saw my brother was outside the covers. I saw Michael's left hand in my brother's underwears (sic)." Two days later, "I went upstairs," Star said. "The same thing was happening, but my brother was on his back. My brother was asleep and Michael was masturbating while he had his left hand in my brother's underwears (sic). I didn't know what to do. I just went back to the guest room where my sister was sleeping."

Sneddon finished with Star by asking if Michael Jackson had ever warned him to keep his mouth shut about what went on in the master suite at Neverland. Yes, Star said: "One time, me and my brother and Eddie Cascio were sitting on the bed and [Jackson] told us not to tell anyone what happened, 'even if they put a gun to your head.' He told us not to tell Davellin anything. He was afraid she might tell our mom what we were doing." What was it they were doing? Sneddon asked. "Drinking," Star answered.

Mesereau began his cross-examination by bringing back the image of the *Barely Legal* magazine that Star had identified (after Sneddon projected it onto a screen for everyone in the courtroom to see) as the one Michael Jackson shared with him and Gavin. Yes, that was the magazine, Star told Mesereau, who promptly pointed out that the date on the magazine was "August 2003"—months after Arvizo family's final visit to Neverland Ranch. Star began to squeeze his hands together. "I never said it was exactly that one," he testily told the attorney. "That's not exactly the one he showed us."

The defense attorney's cross-examination segued to the deposition Star had given in a civil case that had been brought by the Arvizo family against JCPenney some years earlier. Mesereau wanted to save the details of the case for Janet Arvizo's appearance on the stand, but the jury got the gist of it. Back in 1999, Gavin Arvizo had "taken" an item of clothing from a JCPenney store to try to "trick" his father into buying it. Security guards followed the Arvizos out of the store and then, according to the family, they roughed up and groped Janet Arvizo. The Arvizos eventually won a six-figure settlement, but it was now clear that the family had fabricated evidence and perjured themselves in depositions. Among the claims Star had made in that case was that his parents never fought and his father never hit him. "Were you telling the truth?" Mesereau asked. "No," Star admitted, far too readily. Mesereau asked why he had lied, and Star replied dismissively, "I don't remember. It was five years ago. I don't remember nothing." When Mesereau wondered if "someone" had told him to lie in the JCPenney case, Star gave exactly the same answer to the question that his sister Davellin had: "I don't remember."

With that, Mesereau moved to Star's claims that he had witnessed his brother's molestation by Michael Jackson, establishing immediately that the boy had not said a word about any of this to anyone until he and his family met with Larry Feldman, that Feldman had sent Star to see Dr. Stan Katz, and that it was Katz's complaint that had resulted in criminal charges being filed against Michael Jackson. The attorney probed a few small discrepancies between the boy's testimony on direct examination the previous day and what he had told Katz eighteen months earlier, then became steadily more specific—and graphic. Referring to the second alleged molestation, Mesereau asked, "Did you tell Stanley Katz that Michael Jackson had his hand on your brother's crotch?" Yes, Star answered, just as he had testified the day before.

"That's not really what you told him, is it?" Mesereau said.

"What are you talking about?" Star asked, and for the first time looked apprehensive.

"Well, you told Stanley Katz that Michael Jackson was rubbing his penis against Gavin's buttocks, didn't you?"

Star hadn't said anything like that during his direct examination. "No," he answered.

"Would it refresh your recollection if I showed you [Katz's] grand jury testimony?" asked Mesereau. The attorney retrieved a copy from the defense table, but Star refused to look at it, and insisted he had never said anything like that to Dr. Katz.

Star had earlier denied that he ever wanted to be an entertainer, but Mesereau quickly established that the boy had attended a dance school and a comedy school, and had asked Michael Jackson to help him become an actor. He and his brother had also entered the main house at Neverland "hundreds of times" without Jackson's knowledge. Michael had given them the house alarm code when they returned from Miami to California after the airing of the Bashir documentary, Star explained; he and Gavin could go anywhere they wanted in the house, including Michael's bedroom. Mesereau asked about a time when Star and Gavin had been caught drinking in the Neverland wine cellar during one of Jackson's absences, but the boy denied it, and the attorney appeared pleased that he had. Star's attitude grew increasingly arrogant and dismissive as the cross-examination continued. He visibly lost the sympathy of most members of the jury when he admitted carving up Michael's expensive, leather-bound guest book, the one that had been signed by all of his most famous houseguests. Jessica Simpson seemed to be the only guest Star could remember, and the boy seemed far from contrite about what he had done.

On direct examination, Star had said his nickname at Neverland was "Blowhole," and under Sneddon's questioning this sounded distinctly suggestive. On cross-examination, though, Star admitted that he had given himself the nickname. Mesereau produced a card Star had given to Michael Jackson on Father's Day in 2002, with an inscription that read, "Michael, we love you unconditionally, to infinity and beyond forever. Thank you, Michael, for being our family. Blowhole Star Arvizo." More than a dozen other cards and notes written to Jackson by the Arvizos were then offered into evidence. In one of them, Star had written, "When we get our hearts broken into tiny little pieces, we always still love, need, and care about you with every tiny little piece of our heart, because you heal us in a very special way." That note didn't mean anything, Star said: He'd copied the words from a card his grandmother had bought at the supermarket.

Fifteen-year-old Gavin Arvizo took the stand in Santa Maria looking nothing at all like the frail, sweet-faced boy the jury had seen in three separate videos. This Gavin Arvizo was a broad-shouldered, bull-necked adolescent who wore a blue button-down shirt and dark slacks and had a buzz cut that gave him the look of a recent Marine Corps recruit. He had obviously been shaving for some time and spoke in a voice that was deep even when he tried to make it soft. Nevertheless, the teenager melted the guarded expressions of several jurors at the beginning of his direct examination with a recapitulation of the ordeal his life had been during the years when he battled cancer in a one-bedroom East LA apartment that overflowed with the violent tumult of his parents' relationship. He thought Michael Jackson was "the coolest guy ever" when the star began to phone him at the hospital—more than twenty times, Gavin said—before they ever met face-to-face. That opinion held when Michael started to invite him and his family for weekends at Neverland.

Mesereau observed that the jurors began to take notes right around the first time Gavin contradicted what he had said on the rebuttal video, claiming in court that it was Jackson's idea to have him and his brother Star sleep in the master bedroom. He and Star watched *The Simpsons* on TV that first night, Gavin said, but became distracted when Michael and Frank Cascio began to show them "female adult materials." He repeated his brother's story about Jackson looking at topless women and joking, "Got milk?"

The recitation was oddly stilted and the boy's manner curiously detached. The only genuine emotion Gavin showed on the stand came when he recalled his next six visits to Neverland, and being told each time that Michael was either not there or not available. There was real hurt and anger in the boy's voice as he described how, on one of those occasions, he "bumped into" Michael after being told the star was away on business. Gavin also grew animated as he told the jurors that almost immediately after the interview with Martin Bashir was taped, Michael left Neverland and did not return until the Arvizos were gone. He never heard from Michael again, Gavin said, until the Bashir documentary aired in the UK.

Jackson's own emotions were on the surface all during Gavin's testimony, just as they had been when Davellin and Star occupied the witness stand. His fury had seemed to darken with each successive appearance by the Arvizo children, and he became increasingly agitated as Gavin sneered that Michael had coached him to tell Martin Bashir that "he pretty much cured me of cancer." Mesereau laid a hand on his client's arm, as if pressing him to remain seated, fearing, he would admit later, a repetition of what had happened during Davellin Arvizo's testimony. Just as the girl told the jury that she had seen the defendant repeatedly kiss her brother on the forehead, Michael abruptly stood and stormed out of the courtroom. Mesereau, looking flustered for the first time during the trial, had chased his client, then returned moments later, flushed and slightly disheveled, to tell Judge Melville, "Mr. Jackson had to go to the bathroom, Your Honor."

The drama of that scene was eclipsed on the morning of Gavin Arvizo's return to the witness stand. Just before court was to convene at 8:30 a.m., Mesereau took an emergency call from his client. "Michael said he had been up in the middle of the night, unable to sleep, and was walking around Neverland in the dark when he fell and hurt his back," the attorney recalled. Just moments later, Mesereau responded to Melville's incredulous "The defendant's not here?" question by answering, "No, Your Honor, Mr. Jackson is at the Cottage Hospital in Santa Ynez with a serious back problem . . . he does plan to come." Enraged, the judge warned that if the defendant was not in his courtroom within one hour he would issue a warrant for Jackson's arrest and revoke his bail. "I knew the judge meant it," Mesereau would say later. The defense attorney was so distraught that he barely seemed to notice the cameras and sound booms that followed him into the parking lot, where he paced nervously and could be heard repeating, alternately pleading and demanding, "Michael, you've got to get here now!" Michael's return to the courthouse in a big black SUV at five minutes past the 9:30 deadline would become the most emblematic moment of the entire trial. Amid a throng of feverishly concerned fans, Jackson emerged from the vehicle looking distinctly groggy and glassy-eyed as he tottered through the crush of the crowd wearing a blue blazer over a white T-shirt, iridescent blue pajama bottoms, and Gucci slippers.

"I had told Michael he couldn't go home to change," Mesereau explained. "We couldn't take the chance of bail being revoked. He had to get to court as quickly as he could. So we just threw a jacket over the pajamas. The funny thing is that the jurors told me later that they didn't even notice," Mesereau recalled. "Michael was sitting down at the defense table when they came in, and the fact that he had pajama bottoms on made no impression on them at all. When they heard about it later, they couldn't believe there had been so much fuss."

The "pain medications" Michael had taken at the hospital were probably what got him through a day of testimony in which Gavin Arvizo described the various acts of sexual abuse he claimed had been perpetrated on his person by Michael Jackson. It had all been set up, the boy insisted, when Michael served him wine on the private jet that carried them back to California from Florida the morning after the Bashir documentary aired on ABC. Michael continued to serve him alcohol during the Arvizos' subsequent stay at Neverland, where he and his brother Star spent the night in Michael's bedroom, Gavin testified, but Jackson did not touch him sexually. It was during this time that Michael began to call him "son," Gavin said, and he returned the favor by calling Jackson "Daddy." District Attorney Sneddon introduced as evidence a note Michael had written to Gavin that read, "I want you to have a good time in Florida. I'm very happy to be your DADDY. Blanket, Prince, and Paris are your brothers and sisters. But you really have to be honest in your heart and know that I am your DAD and will take good care of you. DAD."

"Nothing bad happened," Gavin continued, until after the taping of the rebuttal video on February 20, 2003. That very evening, Michael had walked naked into the bedroom where he and Star sat watching TV. In contradiction of his brother, though, Gavin said that Michael did not have an erection. The strangest quality of the boy's testimony continued to be the flat, rote tone of it. He might have been talking about what he had eaten for lunch as he described the evening when Michael began to talk about masturbation and told him it was "normal." "He told me that if men don't masturbate, then they can get to a level where they might rape a girl," Gavin told the jurors, who looked far more uncomfortable than the boy did. Michael asked him if he masturbated, and, "I told him that I didn't," Gavin went on. "And then he said he would do it for me . . . And I said that I really didn't want to." But Michael put his hands under the covers, reached inside his pajamas, and began stroking his penis. Eventually he ejaculated, Gavin said, then became embarrassed, but Michael again told him it was "natural," and they both fell asleep. Michael masturbated him again a few nights later, when they were sitting on the bed watching TV, Gavin continued. "He said he wanted to teach me. And we were laying there, and he started doing it to me. And then he kind of grabbed my hand in a way to try to do it to him. And I kind of pulled my hand away, because I didn't want to do it."

After Gavin told Sneddon that these were the only two instances of sexual molestation by Mr. Jackson, the prosecutor turned the boy over to Mesereau, who began by asking the witness to recall his years as a student at John Burroughs Middle School in Los Angeles, where he had twice told the dean that Michael Jackson "didn't do anything to me." Mesereau then walked Gavin through the litany of complaints from teachers at the school who had described the boy as "disruptive." Assorted memoranda that noted Gavin's bad behavior and refusal to do homework were introduced into evidence. The boy seemed barely able to suppress a smile when Mesereau read that a Miss Bender had complained he was regularly defiant, but disagreed vehemently when shown that the same teacher had written that he had "good acting skills."

Mesereau then played the entire rebuttal video for Gavin, stopping every few minutes to ask if what he and the other Arvizos had just said was true or a lie. The boy called himself and his family liars so many times that even Judge Melville became visibly disgusted with the witness, swatting away Sneddon's objections with a dismissive backhand.

When Mesereau asked Gavin about riding in chauffeured limousines and a Rolls-Royce, the boy offered a reply that cracked up the courtroom: "I only rode in a Rolls-Royce when I was escaping." After establishing that during his "escapes" Gavin had gone shopping at Toys "R" Us and visited an orthodontist who removed his braces, all at Michael Jackson's expense, Mesereau produced a sheaf of receipts (courtesy of Marc Schaffel) showing that while they claimed to have been held prisoner in Calabasas, the Arvizos had run up thousands of dollars of bills for cosmetics, designer clothing, spa and beauty treatments, expensive restaurant meals, and lodging, charging it all to Neverland Valley Entertainment.

Mesereau got Gavin to admit that he and his family had met with Larry Feldman before speaking to either the police or the district attorney's office about Michael Jackson's alleged misconduct. The boy insisted he did not know that he could profit financially by filing a lawsuit against Jackson before he turned eighteen. Gavin then acknowledged he had told detectives it was not Michael Jackson but *his grandmother* who said that men masturbate "so they do not rape women." Mesereau used a series of questions that he knew Sneddon would never permit the boy to answer to make the jurors aware that Gavin had been caught drinking alcohol at Neverland, searching for porn on the Internet, and masturbating during times when Michael Jackson was not at the ranch. The attorney finished by asking Gavin if he and his family were angry that after the boy's cancer went into remission, Michael Jackson had stopped inviting the Arvizos to the ranch. "You felt he had abandoned you, right?" Mesereau asked. "Yes!" Gavin answered. It was the most emotionally expressive moment of the boy's entire examination.

The media in general, and the cable television correspondents in particular, seemed to convince Sneddon that he was gaining ground with the jury when he was in fact losing it. "Again and again you'd see the TV reporters run outside to talk to the cameras when some salacious detail was presented," Mesereau recalled, "and they wouldn't even be in the courtroom when the witness was taken apart on cross-examination. One witness after another was shown to have a financial motive for testifying, or to have contradicted earlier sworn statements, or to have a shady background that made them suspect, but you weren't hearing a word about it from the media. The media was completely invested in convicting Michael Jackson, because that's where they thought the ratings and revenue were. And I could see that Sneddon believed he was winning the case because the media said he was winning the case. But the jurors couldn't run out of the courtroom after the direct examination. They had to sit through the cross-examination, and I could see that at least a couple of them were getting more and more disgusted with the prosecution witnesses. I didn't know about the rest, but I could see that at least a couple didn't believe a word Gavin Arvizo said."

Still, Mesereau refrained from saying as much to his client. "I don't know if Michael understood that the prosecution case was falling apart," Mesereau said. "I just know that he was very scared. Very scared. He would call me or Susan Yu at three or four in the morning, crying. He was always worried that somebody somehow would corrupt us. He said over and over again, 'Please don't let them get to you.' We didn't even know who 'they' were. Sony, I guess. Anyway, even though we were doing well, and he knew it, the trial turned into an immensely exhausting and painful experience for Michael, and for us. We were far from finished when Gavin Arvizo left the stand. Michael understood that. We all believed that the most dangerous prosecution witnesses were yet to come. But we were completely in the dark about who and what Sneddon was going to use to back up his claim that Michael had molested five other boys. And that was scary."

On March 30, 2005, Judge Melville ruled that the prosecution would be permitted to introduce into evidence the allegations against Michael Jackson involving Jordan Chandler and four other boys: Jason Francia, Wade Robson, Brett Barnes, and Macaulay Culkin. "I knew that three of those boys—Robson, Barnes, and Macaulay Culkin—were not going to testify for the prosecution," Mesereau recalled. "And I wasn't that afraid of Jason Francia. The Jordan Chandler allegations, though, those were of major concern. I knew we might win or lose this case on whether or not the jurors believed Michael had molested Jordie Chandler."

Mesereau was aware of the lengths to which the prosecution had gone to make Jordan Chandler a witness against Michael Jackson. Sneddon's most dedicated deputy, Ron Zonen, had flown to New York to personally threaten, cajole, and finally plead with Jordie to fly out to California to testify at the criminal trial. No one outside the district attorney's office knew that Zonen had been unsuccessful, and both the defense and the media were similarly unaware that the Santa Barbara County prosecutors had prevailed upon the FBI to assist them with their problem. In June 2004, Zonen and another deputy district attorney assigned to the case, Gordon Auchincloss, had flown to Virginia to meet with agents from the FBI's Behavior Analysis Unit to ask if the bureau might become involved in the case against Jackson, perhaps even initiate a federal prosecution. After an August 30, 2004, conference call between the BAU agents and the Santa Barbara prosecutors, as an FBI memo produced two weeks later recalled, it was agreed that the bureau's agent in Santa Maria would "open a case." In September, two FBI agents met with now twenty-nine-year-old Jordie Chandler at a hotel in New York City, but the young man was just as adamant about avoiding an appearance at Michael Jackson's trial as he had been when Zonen met with him. According the report filed by the FBI agents, Jordie said he "had no interest in testifying against Jackson" and "advised that he would legally fight any attempt" to compel him to do so. "I don't think Jordie was concerned with vindication or with what people thought about him," said his uncle Ray. "He was concerned with being left alone, with being safe."

Larry Feldman took the stand as a witness for the prosecution on April Fools' Day, less than forty-eight hours after the judge had ruled that the jury could hear evidence of alleged prior acts of sexual molestation by Michael Jackson. Sneddon left it to Mesereau to connect the Jordan Chandler case to Feldman, asking the attorney only about his 2003 meeting with the Arvizos. The family had come to him initially to discuss pursuing a case against Martin Bashir and ABC for taping the Arvizo children without their consent, Feldman said. Unable to make "heads or tails" of what he was hearing, Feldman said, he sent Gavin and Star to see Dr. Stan Katz. After the boys' second meeting with the psychiatrist, Katz had sent him a report stating that Gavin and Star were alleging that Michael Jackson had molested Gavin.

Feldman said he personally contacted the head of the Los Angeles County Department of Children and Family Services, who suggested he report the suspected abuse to someone in law enforcement. It was then that he phoned District Attorney Sneddon and initiated the process that ultimately led to Michael Jackson's arrest and the raid on Neverland Ranch. He was not involved in any civil lawsuit against Michael Jackson, Feldman said, and had no plans to become involved in such a lawsuit. In fact, he had formally resigned as the Arvizos' attorney in October 2003, shortly before the warrant for Michael Jackson's arrest was issued by the Santa Barbara County sheriff's department.

Mesereau immediately picked up where Sneddon had left off, compelling Feldman to agree that there was nothing to prevent him from representing Gavin and Star Arvizo in some future civil case, and that, irrespective of the outcome of the criminal case, Gavin and Star had until the age of eighteen to file a lawsuit against Michael Jackson claiming millions of dollars in damages. And if there was a conviction in the case now before the jury, "the only issue remaining would be how much money you get, correct?" Mesereau asked. "Probably. I think that's close enough," Feldman answered, and permitted himself a slight smile. A criminal conviction in this case would be crucial in offsetting the cost of the trial for the attorney, wouldn't it, suggested Mesereau, who got Feldman to admit that financing the investigation of the Jordan Chandler allegations back in 1993 had cost him a substantial part of the eventual settlement. When Feldman attempted to quibble over details, Mesereau used the opportunity to let the jury know that Michael Jackson had sued the Chandlers for extortion back in 1993 and that the eventual settlement had included language in which "neither side admits wrongdoing to the other." Mesereau left it to the jury to decide whether the fact that two attorneys and their associate psychiatrists who had been key players in the Jordan Chandler case in 1993 had also driven the prosecution of Michael Jackson for the abuse of Gavin Arvizo in 2003 was merely, as Feldman had it, "a coincidence."

Mesereau then began to flatter Feldman, who seemed pleased to agree that he was "one of the most successful plaintiffs' lawyers" in the country, an attorney who had won "numerous multimillion-dollar awards" for his clients. "Say it again for the press," Feldman replied, smiling. Mesereau then noted that while Feldman claimed not to be representing the Arvizo family, he had in fact appeared in court as the attorney for Janet Arvizo's mother "in an attempt to prevent us from seeing if [Janet] deposited money into her parents' account."

The prosecution case continued to be undermined by their own parade of witnesses who witnessed nothing, contradicted the Arvizos' claims of exhibiting good behavior at Neverland (former Neverland maid Kiki Fournier claimed Star had pulled a knife on her in the kitchen), and admitted peddling false stories to the media for money. Former Neverland house manager Dwayne Swingler almost came across as refreshingly honest by comparison to other witnesses when he replied to Mesereau's question about trying to sell stories to the tabloids by saying, "Look, I was going to cash in like everyone else." Even Sneddon seemed to realize he had lost momentum by the time he summoned the woman whom he anticipated—correctly in this instance—would be his most powerful witness.

Now nearly fifty, June Chandler was still an exotic beauty packaged in elegance, from the designer suit fitted to her slim but shapely figure to her graceful carriage and crisp enunciation. As June began to tell the sad and slightly sordid story of her life, however, the glow around her dimmed. Failed marriages to an abusive dentist and a man who rented used cars for a living had left her coarsened in some regretful way, and disillusioned.

When she described being swept up into the enchanted centrifuge of Michael Jackson's private world back in 1993, there was a distinct if unspoken sense that this lovely lady had at last been living the life she was meant for, and enjoying it so thoroughly that she was blinded to the costs and the consequences. A genuine fondness for the Michael Jackson she came to know in those first weeks and months still sounded in June's voice as she admitted being surprised and impressed by what "a regular guy" he was, so generous and polite and unassuming. There was still the faint echo of a thrill in her voice as June recalled the gifts Michael had lavished upon her and the trips aboard private jets to Monaco and Florida that she and Jordie and Lily made with their famous new friend. Both June's story and her tone grew colder and grimmer, though, as she described the next trip she and her children took with Michael, the one they made to Las Vegas later in 1993. She was shocked and alarmed, as June told it, by her discovery that Jordie had apparently spent the night sleeping in the same bed with Jackson.

Speaking through an emotional strain that was quite convincing, June delivered the most devastating moments of testimony against Michael Jackson that were heard during the entire trial. Shortly after telling her son that he would not be allowed to stay in the same suite with Michael unless they slept in separate bedrooms, June recalled, she heard a knock at the door of her own hotel room. It was Michael Jackson, June told the jury. He stood before her sobbing, she remembered, his cheeks bathed in tears, wanting to know if what Jordie had told him was true: "He was crying, shaking, trembling. 'You don't trust me?'" Michael asked her, according to June. "'We're a family! Why are you doing this? Why are you not allowing Jordie to be with me?' And I said, 'He is with you,'" June remembered. "He said, 'But my bedroom. Why not in my bedroom?'" Michael's "histrionic tantrum" had gone on for another half-hour, said June, before she finally caved in and agreed that Jordie could sleep in Michael's bedroom, and, as she told it, lost her son.

The icy ferocity with which Mesereau attacked the woman on the witness stand was an abrupt and startling transition from the adoration in which an obviously smitten Sneddon had bathed June Chandler. Michael's attorney immediately hammered June with a series of questions that suggested she and Dave Schwartz had been in dire financial circumstances back in 1993, deeply in debt and desperate for a way out. June's denials were shaky from the first and grew more uncertain as Mesereau bombarded her with dates and numbers. "I don't recall," became her answer to most of the attorney's questions, though she occasionally managed an "I don't think so." She could scarcely recall a single detail of the lawsuit that she and her two ex-husbands had filed against Michael Jackson back in 1994 and professed not to even be aware that Jackson had answered with a lawsuit that accused the three of them of extortion.

June appeared almost relieved when Mesereau changed the subject to her son Jordie's relationship with Michael Jackson, recalling with palpable pleasure and pride how, years before the two met, her son had taken to dressing up like Michael and would entertain her by imitating his dance moves. It was like a dream come true for Jordie when he actually got to meet Michael and become close to him, June agreed, and she had been particularly appreciative of the paternal interest Michael seemed to take in Jordie, especially since the boy's natural father, Evan Chandler, was barely involved in his life at that point. Yes, it was true that Michael had spent at least thirty nights at their little house in Santa Monica and that she had encouraged the entertainer's relationship with her son. Each of the jurors and everyone else in the courtroom were leaning forward in their seats, utterly silent, as June described Michael's joining the family at the dinner table, helping Jordie with his homework and playing video games with the boy for hours on end. She looked at Michael Jackson as being "like a child," June told Mesereau. Yes, it was Jordie who had insisted on staying in Michael's room whenever they visited Neverland, June said, complaining to her that other kids, including Macaulay Culkin, were allowed to sleep in "the big boys' room." Yes, Culkin's father was with him at Neverland, June agreed; most of the children who visited the ranch were accompanied by a parent. June's demeanor became increasingly flat and remote as she answered questions about flying with her son in private jets that belonged to Sony and to Steve Wynn, about the trips she and her children took with Michael Jackson to Orlando and Las Vegas, about meeting Elizabeth Taylor, Nelson Mandela, and Prince Albert of Monaco. She seemed to recognize that Mesereau was painting her as a gold digger, and yet could summon up no better response than to go numb. Several of the women on the jury wore reproving expressions when June admitted that her ex-husband Evan Chandler had suggested that the family's relationship with Michael Jackson could be "a wonderful means for Jordie not having to worry for the rest of his life."

Mesereau was still absorbing the realization that June would be the only Chandler called to testify in Santa Maria when Tom Sneddon summoned Janet Arvizo to the stand. "I had a feeling this would be the most important moment of the entire trial," Mesereau said later. "And I was right."

For weeks the jury and the gallery had been watching clips of Janet Arvizo from the rebuttal video that had been shot in the spring of 2003. Two years and twenty pounds later, there was no sign of the giggling coquette whose teased and permed curls, red-lipsticked mouth, and too-tight sweater had given her the look of an oversexed Kewpie doll. This real-life Janet Arvizo was a pear-shaped woman on the cusp of middle age, her broad face scrubbed clean. She wore a baggy pink sweatshirt and had straight dark hair that she had clipped into place with sparkly barrettes better suited for a six-year-old girl.

Judge Melville prefaced Janet's testimony by explaining that Mrs. Arvizo was invoking her Fifth Amendment right against self-incrimination and would refuse to answer any questions about welfare fraud or perjury. Mesereau had prepared the jury with an opening statement in which he alleged that Janet Arvizo was a professional scammer who illegally obtained months of welfare payments during a time when she had more than $30,000 in bank accounts, and now was the subject of a criminal investigation that had been initiated by the California Department of Social Services.

Sneddon delegated the task of rehabilitating Janet Arvizo in the jury's eyes to his assistant, Ron Zonen, who gave it a heroic effort. The prosecutor's questions led Janet through a tale of illness, poverty, and abuse that had filled most of her adult life, beginning with her marriage at age sixteen to a drug addict who beat her constantly, broke his own children's bones, and even tortured their pets. Eventually, though, Zonen had to turn his witness toward the subject at hand, the supposed "captivity" that Janet and her children had endured after Michael Jackson phoned to say he wanted the Arvizos to join him in Miami for a press conference to respond to the Bashir documentary.

In Janet's telling, Michael had said her family might be "in danger" after Living with Michael Jackson aired in early February 2003 and that he wanted to place them under his protection because there had been "death threats." Once they arrived in Florida, Michael decided that no press conference was necessary, but from that moment forward the entire family was under the control of Jackson's "people," Janet said. She described being "locked up" in Michael's huge suite at the Turnberry Resort, where her children spent all their time with Prince and Paris Jackson and the three Cascio kids, Frank, Marie Nicole, and Eddie. The entire time, Janet said, Michael and his adult associates were "scripting" the media response to the Bashir documentary that eventually became the rebuttal video.

Under Mesereau's cross-examination, Janet Arvizo used derivations of the word "script" as a verb, noun, or adjective in nearly every answer she gave, no matter how unrelated to the question.

"Now, Mrs. Arvizo, you said you and your children were neglected and spit on, right?" Mesereau began.

"Yes," she answered.

"And who were you referring to?" Mesereau asked.

"They took elements of my life and my children's life that were truthful, and they incorporated them into their script," Janet Arvizo answered. "And this happened in the initial meeting in Miami. They were already in the works on this. It took me a while to find out."

Mesereau pressed on: "Who neglected your family?"

"In this script, everything is scripted," the witness replied.

Mesereau tried again: "When you said your family was spit upon, who were you referring to?" the attorney asked.

"On this rebuttal thing, everything is scripted," Janet answered. "They took elements of mine and my children's life which were true, and incorporated them there."

"When you said, 'We weren't in the right zip code, and we weren't in the right race,' what were you referring to?" Mesereau inquired.

"This was all scripted," was Janet's only reply.

Janet insisted she had no idea that Gavin and his siblings had been interviewed on camera by Martin Bashir before *Living with Michael Jackson* aired. She conceded that she pursued, then abandoned, a lawsuit against Granada Television for using her children's images without permission. Janet vehemently insisted that the sexual abuse of Gavin had begun *after* the Bashir documentary aired, then admitted that she had never seen Michael Jackson do anything sexual with her son, other than lick his hair on the flight from Florida back to California.

Using a sheaf of receipts provided by Marc Schaffel, Mesereau took Janet through each of the expenses she had rung up while deciding whether to participate in the rebuttal video, allowing Michael Jackson to pay for her family's extended stay at the Calabasas Country Inn, where they spent

their days on shopping sprees and spa treatments, and ate in expensive restaurants nightly. During this period of what she called "captivity," she had
even taken her son Gavin to an appointment to have his braces removed
at Mr. Jackson's expense. Had Mrs. Arvizo considered calling the police to
report that she was being held prisoner while she sat in the orthodontist's
office for five hours? Mesereau asked. She hadn't contacted the authorities
because, "Who could believe this?" Janet explained.

Mesereau chose that moment to play outtakes from the rebuttal video.
The jurors appeared riveted by footage in which Janet Arvizo told her
children to sit up straight and behave themselves, and in particular a section of tape in which Janet suggested to the videographer that she and
Gavin hold hands, then urged the camera to move in for a close-up. Was
this footage "scripted," too? Mesereau asked. Jurors shook their heads as
Janet insisted that it was: "Everything on there was choreographed. It's all
acting." "I'm not a very good actress," she added a moment later. Mesereau
replied, "Oh, I think you are."

Janet Arvizo grew steadily more histrionic as the cross-examination
continued, turning to the jurors at one point to tell them, "Don't judge
me." Seemingly out of nowhere, she began to snap her fingers at the jury
to punctuate her points. "A number of the jurors told me later that they
wanted to tell her, 'Don't snap your fingers at me, lady,'" Mesereau recalled.

Jurors also said later that they were amazed by Janet's determination
to lie about even the smallest detail. During a discussion of her spa treatments in Calabasas, she insisted that she had gotten only a leg wax, then
sat sullenly when Mesereau showed her a receipt she had signed for a full
body wax. No, it was only a leg wax, Janet said after a few moments. So
the receipt was fabricated? Mesereau asked. Janet replied by pointing to
Michael Jackson: "He has the ability to choreograph everything."

To Mesereau, it seemed a good time to introduce records showing that
Janet Arvizo had collected $19,000 in welfare payments by making false
claims about her financial status. The attorney followed this by establishing
that the Arvizos had used money donated for Gavin's cancer treatments to
buy a big-screen TV, among other items, then introduced a newspaper article
in which Janet had claimed that the family was paying ten times the actual
cost of Gavin's chemotherapy sessions. A typo, Janet insisted. Mesereau
had saved for last the evidence he believed would completely destroy Janet
Arvizo's credibility in the jurors' eyes: She and her family had collected a
$152,000 settlement after suing JCPenney for alleged physical and sexual
assaults by store security guards, on the basis of lies and falsified evidence.

Mesereau focused at length on Janet's assertion in a deposition that one of the security guards had twisted her nipple between ten and twenty-five times. When Janet attempted to explain that there were "inaccuracies" in her deposition and that she had tried to get her attorney to make "corrections" before the case was settled, Mesereau turned her attention to the fact that both of her sons, Gavin and Star, had supported the nipple-twisting story. Star had gone so far as to state under oath that he had to put his mother's breast "back into her bra" after this abuse, and that he had seen one of the guards grope his mother's vaginal area. Janet had claimed that the guards punched her repeatedly, using their handcuffs as if they were brass knuckles, and had also said that she saw Gavin and Star being punched by the guards.

Shortly after these supposed assaults, she was booked into the West Covina city jail, where she was photographed and fingerprinted, recounted Mesereau, who then showed Janet police reports that noted that she showed no sign of injury and did not need medical treatment. Yet only two days later she showed up at an attorney's office claiming to have been physically and sexually assaulted, and was photographed displaying bruises that covered her arms and legs. Her son Gavin had been photographed at the same time with a broken arm. These photographs were the main evidence of her civil case.

Janet admitted to Mesereau that she had lied under oath; it was in fact her husband who had beaten her and Gavin. Mesereau also pointed out that each of the woman's children had testified on the witness stand at this trial that it had been their father who abused them and their mother, and that Janet Arvizo had obtained multiple restraining orders against her ex-husband. Gavin in fact had once accused his mother of assaulting him also, triggering an investigation by the Department of Children and Family Services. Janet's attempts at answering these questions became more and more incoherent, a series of non sequiturs that bore little connection to the questions she had been asked. She turned to speak directly to the jury several times and addressed Michael Jackson personally on a number of occasions.

As Mesereau excoriated Janet Arvizo for her ingratitude to Michael Jackson after all the man had done for her and for her family, the witness was roused to the first comprehensible reply she had made during the past two hours. Janet Arvizo's voice rose when she insisted that Michael Jackson "really didn't care about children, he just cared about what he was doing with the children." Glaring at the defendant, she continued,

"He's managed to fool the world. Now, because of this criminal case, now people know who he really is."

After watching Janet Arvizo's disintegration under cross-examination, Sneddon recognized that the time had come to play his ace in the hole—Debbie Rowe. Other than their fear that Jordan Chandler would show up in court, Mesereau and the defense team were more concerned about the testimony of Michael's ex-wife than they were with any other part of the prosecution case. What Mesereau, his associates, and their client knew that neither the media nor the public did was that Debbie had been working with Santa Barbara County law enforcement for months to prepare the criminal case against Jackson. She had provided Sneddon and his investigators with dozens of documents and scores of names and dates—anything they wanted. Most alarming was that Rowe had cooperated with Santa Barbara County sheriff's deputies to tape numerous phone conversations with the various "unindicted coconspirators," including at least a half-dozen with Marc Schaffel. Caught up in the excitement and drama of playing her part in an undercover police investigation, Debbie (who referred to the man she was dating at the time as "a murder cop") had described her ex-husband to the deputies as a shallow narcissist who saw his children as mere possessions, barely more real to him than the mannequins who populated the hallways at Neverland. As far as the kids who visited the ranch, Debbie added, they were nothing more than playthings to Michael, animated, life-size toys that he discarded as soon as they ceased entertaining him.

Mesereau had prepared twenty notebooks filled with the material he intended to use for his cross-examination of Michael's ex-wife, more than for any other single witness. "But moments after Debbie got on the stand, I started to push that pile of notebooks away," the attorney recalled. "I could see that as soon as she took one look at Michael, everything changed. The reality of it all hit her. It wasn't a game anymore. He was vulnerable, and she didn't want to hurt him."

Zonen knew he was in trouble only a few minutes after beginning his direct examination of Rowe. Debbie acknowledged speaking to Michael Jackson about appearing in the rebuttal video, but said there was no discussion of what she would say. Sneddon had promised in his opening statement that Jackson's ex-wife would characterize her participation in the rebuttal video as "completely scripted," but Rowe did exactly the opposite on the witness stand. Asked to describe her conversation with Michael Jackson, Debbie replied, "I asked him how he was. I asked him how the children were. And I asked if I could see them when everything settled down," she recalled. When Michael asked if she would appear in what became the rebuttal video, "I said, as always, yes," Debbie told Zonen. "I was excited to see Michael and the children when all this was over. I promised I would always be there for him and the children." Before arriving in court today, she had not seen Michael, Debbie admitted, since the day of the last divorce hearing in 1999. She had not seen Prince or Paris in that time, either. She came across as sad, but not angry.

Rowe described arriving at Marc Schaffel's house in Calabasas for the taping of the rebuttal video on February 5, 2003, accompanied by attorney Iris Finsilver, who had remained with her the entire time. When Zonen asked if she was given a script, Debbie answered tersely, "No." But she had been given a list of questions, Zonen asked, and moved forward in anticipation when she answered yes. The prosecutor was back on his heels a moment later, though, when Debbie added that she never looked at the list of questions and that nothing she said on the rebuttal video had been scripted. "I didn't want anyone to be able to come back to me and say my interview was rehearsed," she explained. "As Mr. Jackson knows, no one can tell me what to say."

Mesereau probed the subject of Debbie Rowe's legal dispute with Michael Jackson, but with a gentle approach that bore no resemblance to the attack for which he had prepared. Debbie's eyes filled with tears as she gazed at Michael during her questioning on the subject, as if trying to communicate how saddened she was that it had come to this. Her expression was a plea for acknowledgment. Michael refused to give it. "He knew she had betrayed him by working with the police," Mesereau recalled, "and he was not ready to forgive her for it."

Michael's attorney, though, recognized that Debbie was trying to do all she could to make amends. Rowe denounced the "unindicted coconspirators," Konitzer, Wiesner, and Schaffel in particular, as a pack of predators whose strategy was to give Michael Jackson as little information as possible about what they were up to. "In my past knowledge, [Michael is] removed from the handlers, the people who are taking care of business, and they make all the decisions, and there are many times when they don't consult him," Debbie said. "And you thought these three guys, Schaffel, Dieter, and Konitzer, were doing just that, didn't you?" Mesereau asked. "Very strongly," answered Debbie, who moments later described the three as "opportunistic vultures." She was especially tough on Schaffel, the only one of the three with whom she could claim anything like a friendship. Marc had boasted more than once about saving Michael's career, and making millions for himself in the process, she recalled scornfully: "He just bragged about how he had taken advantage of an opportunity. He said he was going to make sure Michael's career was saved. He's like everybody else around Mr. Jackson. He wouldn't tell him everything. Obviously, he's full of shit."

Debbie finished by telling Mesereau that everything she had said on the rebuttal video was honest and spontaneous, that she wanted the world to know that Michael Jackson was a good father, a family man at heart, and someone she still cared about. She gave her ex-husband one more imploring glance, but Michael still seemed to be looking through her.

21

On May 5, 2005, when the procecution rested its case in *People v. Michael Joe Jackson*, Mesereau asked for a recess to consider whether he should bother with putting on a defense. "I was pretty confident that we had at least a hung jury," he explained. "It was all over the faces of several jurors. But when I thought about it, I realized that a hung jury and a mistrial was not the outcome we wanted. I was certain that Sneddon would refile, and I was pretty sure that the next trial would be much tougher for us. I knew the judge was on the prosecution's side, and that he was unlikely to make some of the rulings that had helped us the first time around if there was a second trial. The prosecution would have been educated about the weaknesses of its case and would be much better prepared the second time around. Also, I was hearing from Randy Jackson and everyone else around Michael that he didn't have it in him to survive a second trial. I could see myself that it was true. Michael was getting weaker day by day. He wasn't eating. He went to the hospital several times." The only place Michael could sleep, Grace Rwaramba explained, was in a hospital room.

The strain was wearing Mesereau down as well. He was waking up at 3:30 every morning to a new stack of filings, reports, and information that were added to the tens of thousands of pages of documents already generated by the case of *People v. Jackson*. He had been braced for months against his possible dismissal as Michael Jackson's attorney. Randy Jackson had told him that Mark Geragos was pressing relentlessly to be reinstated, warning that Mesereau had no real concept of what a high-profile trial required. The three-ring circus of chaos that engulfed Michael Jackson was also a constant distraction. The wall of the sentry post at the entrance to Neverland was covered with the photographs of various undesirables, accompanied by captions like, "Has been loitering near the gate," "Believes she is married to Mr. Jackson," and "Might be armed."

Some of these same people had infiltrated the "Caravan of Love" formed by Michael's supporters outside the courthouse, who were every bit as

UNTOUCHABLE   353

obsessive as Mesereau had been told they would be. Amid the Michael
Jackson impersonators and the women who claimed to be the real Billie
Jean were hundreds of lost souls who had made the pilgrimage to Santa
Maria from all over the world, people for whom being Michael Jackson
fans was the most consuming reality of their lives. The wailing, shrieking,
and sobbing that rose from this crowd each morning as Michael emerged
from the big black Suburban that delivered him to the courthouse charged
the atmosphere with some weird blend of dread and delirium. The congratulations he could expect if he won this case, the defense attorney knew,
would be short-lived by comparison to the condemnations that would
follow him for the rest of his days if he lost it.

For Mesereau, who had refused to speak to the media from the beginning of the trial, the realization that some version of the mad scene
surrounding the courthouse had been Michael Jackson's reality since he
was ten years old engendered both pity and exhilaration. In this alternate
universe of supercelebrity, it seemed at once perverse and appropriate
that more than half the crowd was composed of the twenty-two hundred reporters, producers, and researchers who had been credentialed
by the Santa Barbara County authorities. Since only thirty-five of them
a day would be seated in the courtroom, the rest loitered amid the sea
of media tents, ready to chase down anyone who would serve them up
a dollop of drama.

From the start of the trial, most of the distractions Mesereau had dealt
with were produced by people who were supposed to be on his side. "Michael himself was the nicest client Susan and I have ever had," Mesereau
said. "The problem was the people around him. A lot of the time, we were
more at war with our own camp than with the other side. Celebrities in
general tend to be surrounded by those that try to keep them off balance, to
keep them scared, as a way to create a reason they're needed. And Michael
Jackson was probably the biggest target ever of those types of people."
Mesereau included Raymone Bain, Jesse Jackson, and Grace Rwaramba
prominently among those "types," and was increasingly concerned that
certain members of the Jackson family had become the instruments of
other parasites that were attempting to attach themselves to his client.

"That's what's so exhausting about a high-profile case," Mesereau recalled. "You have to spend half your time dealing with things that have
nothing to do with the actual trial happening in the courtroom."

Convinced as he was that the prosecution had failed to make its case
in court, Mesereau had to admit his doubts. "You think you know, but

you're not sure that you know," he explained. "I don't believe there's a lawyer alive who hasn't been surprised by a jury's verdict. Plus, Sneddon looked like he thought he had won the case, and the reporters were all fawning over him like they thought so, too."

Mesereau's dismantlement of Gavin Arvizo on cross-examination went almost entirely unreported on television or in newspapers. Big-city tabloids actually bannered proclamations that the testimony of the "victim" had cooked Jackson's goose. "SICKO!" howled the *New York Daily News* headline. "Jacko: Now Get Out of This One" gloated the *New York Post*. In London the *Sun* article describing Gavin Arvizo's appearance as a witness ran under the heading, "He's Bad, He's Dangerous, He's History," while the *Mirror* made its headline into a veritable endorsement of the accuser's story: "He Said If Boys Don't Do It They Might Turn into Rapists: Cancer Boy Gavin Tells Court of Jacko Sex."

For reporters like Diane Dimond and Maureen Orth, the revelation of Janet Arvizo's sleazy character served as little more than further evidence of Michael Jackson's guilt. "As I watched the mother on the stand," Orth wrote for *Vanity Fair*, "one thing seemed clear to me: Michael Jackson would probably never have spent more than a moment's time with this poor, dysfunctional family if he hadn't had an ulterior motive." Dimond chipped in with a *New York Post* article in which she pointed out that, "Pedophiles don't target kids with Ozzie and Harriet parents."

Mesereau tried not to hear the roar of impending doom sounding all around him, but that was not entirely possible. The attorney saw little choice but to mute the assurances he wanted to offer his client. "I felt sure I was right about where the case stood, but I wouldn't have been doing my job if I hadn't admitted that I could be wrong," Mesereau reflected. He was "terribly tempted" to rest without offering a defense case, the attorney said: "I knew Michael desperately wanted this to be over, but at the same time he understood that his life literally depended on the outcome of this trial."

The knowledge of the sentence he faced had overwhelmed Michael from the day the grand jury returned its indictment. "Discussing the specifics of that was probably the hardest part of the whole thing," Mesereau recalled. "The numbers were just so scary to Michael." If convicted on all charges, Jackson would be sentenced to at least eighteen years and eight months in state prison. Should the "aggravating circumstances" argued by the prosecution be factored in, Judge Melville had the right to impose a sentence of up to fifty-six years in prison.

"In the end, I decided that the stakes were just too high to do anything less than go all out," Mesereau decided. "We were going to put on our full defense."

Mesereau knew that his case would begin with a devastating rebuttal of the prosecution case that was also a high-risk proposition for the defense. Sneddon had told the jury during his opening statement that they would hear evidence that Michael Jackson had sexually abused five other boys besides Gavin Arvizo, and the prosecutor mentioned each of the five by name. Jordan Chandler's refusal to testify at trial had reduced Sneddon to the point of attempting to introduce an eleven-year-old document with a motion submitted under the heading: "Plaintiff's Motion to Admit Evidence that Jordan Chandler had Knowledge of, and Accurately Described Defendant's Distinctly Blemished Lower Torso and Penis in 1994; Declaration of Thomas W. Sneddon Jr.; Memorandum of Points and Authorities." In the end, Sneddon was able to call only one of those five boys, Jason Francia, to the stand, and Francia had been, at best, marginally effective. "He came across as someone who thought he deserved $2 million for being tickled," Mesereau recalled.

The defense attorney would be widely criticized for putting up as witnesses a series of young men who admitted they had spent the night in Michael Jackson's bedroom, but as Mesereau recalled, "Three of the five young men whom the prosecution described as 'Michael Jackson's other victims' were willing to testify for the defense that it wasn't true."

Wade Robson was a dancer who had joined Michael Jackson's world at the age of seven, during the Australian leg of the *Bad* tour, when he began performing with Michael onstage. Later he appeared in three Jackson music videos, traveling regularly with the star and staying with him at Neverland on and off for more than a decade. Robson was now twenty-two, lean and handsome, a "celebrity choreographer," according to the tabloid press, who was best known for being sexually involved with Britney Spears while she was married to fellow dancer Kevin Federline. He had slept in the same bed with Michael Jackson on approximately twenty separate occasions, Robson told Mesereau on direct examination. When the attorney asked what "activities" he engaged in while staying in Mr. Jackson's bedroom, Robson replied that they mostly played video games or watched movies. "We had pillow fights every now and again," he added, with a smile. "Mr. Robson, did Michael Jackson ever molest you at any time?" Mesereau asked. "Absolutely not," the young man answered in a tone that suggested he was more contemptuous of the suggestion than scandalized by it.

Brett Barnes was considerably more indignant about being named as one of Michael Jackson's playthings. "Has Mr. Jackson ever molested you?" Mesereau bluntly asked the young Australian shortly after he took the stand.

"Absolutely not!" Barnes answered loudly. "And I can tell you right now that if he had, I wouldn't be here right now!"

"Has Mr. Jackson ever touched you in a sexual way?" Mesereau went on.

"Never!" Barnes answered with even greater intensity. "I wouldn't stand for it!"

"Has Michael Jackson ever touched any part of your body in a way that you thought was inappropriate?" Mesereau continued.

"Never! It's not the type of thing I would stand for," answered Barnes, who seemed barely able to control his fury when Mesereau asked how he felt about being described by prosecutors as one of Michael Jackson's "victims."

"I'm very mad about that," replied Barnes, who obviously was. "They're pulling my name through the dirt, and I'm really, really not happy about it."

Macaulay Culkin was an even more effective witness. "I can't tell you how impressed I was by [him]," Mesereau recalled. "I met with him and his attorney and his manager and his agent beforehand, and he was the most relaxed person in the room. The others were all terrified and trying to convince him that it was a terrible idea for him to take the stand, that he shouldn't do it." But in the meeting with Mesereau, "Culkin just sort of shrugged and said, 'Look, if Michael needs me to tell people the truth, then I'm going to do it,'" the attorney recalled. "He was really a stand-up person, just like Chris Tucker—and unlike the rest of Michael's other so-called celebrity friends."

Now in his mid-twenties, Culkin appeared as relaxed on the witness stand as he had been in the meeting with Mesereau. He began his direct examination by saying that he was godfather to two of Michael Jackson's children, then tried to describe for the jury the nature of the unique bond he shared with Prince and Paris's father. There was a loneliness to the life of a child star that only other people who'd experienced it—people like him and Michael and Elizabeth Taylor and Shirley Temple—could understand, Culkin explained: "We're part of a unique group of people. [Michael had] been through that, so he understood what it was like to be put in that position I was in, to be thrust into it. Anyone who was a child performer, we keep an eye out for each other."

He'd been a guest at Neverland more than a dozen times between the ages of ten and fourteen, Culkin said, often accompanied by his younger brother, his two sisters, and his father and mother. He and the defendant remained friends to this day, and he had visited Michael as recently as a year earlier. When Mesereau turned to the matter at hand and described the allegations of former Neverland employees that they'd seen Michael Jackson touching him sexually, Culkin dismissed such stories with evident disdain.

"What do you think of these allegations?" Mesereau asked.

"I think they're absolutely ridiculous," Culkin answered. He hadn't learned of these claims from the prosecution, Culkin told Mesereau, but from a cable television news program. "I just couldn't believe it," Culkin recalled. "I couldn't believe that, first of all, these people were saying these things—let alone that it was out there, and people were thinking that kind of thing about me. And at the same time it was amazing to me that nobody approached me and asked me whether or not the allegations were true. They just kind of threw it out there, and they didn't even double-check it, basically. I mean if they assumed that I knew the answer, what got me was they didn't even ask."

"Are you saying that these prosecutors never tried to reach you to ask your position on this?" a wide-eyed Mesereau wondered.

"No, they didn't," Culkin replied.

"Are you aware that the prosecutors claim they are going to prove that you were molested by Michael Jackson?" asked Mesereau.

"Excuse me?" asked Culkin, whose expression of incredulity communicated a good deal more than his words did.

Mesereau called a couple dozen other witnesses, nearly all of them put on the stand to further discredit the Arvizos. The orthodontist and the dental assistant who had removed Gavin Arvizo's braces at Jackson's expense told the court that they saw no sign the Arvizos were being held against their will. They remembered Gavin Arvizo as an especially rude kid, the two said, one who rifled through drawers when their backs were turned, forcing them to throw out sterile items. Janet Arvizo insisted upon keeping her son's ruined braces, they remembered, because she intended to use them as evidence in a claim against the doctor who had put them on.

Chris Tucker's ex-girlfriend Azja Pryor testified that Janet Arvizo not only wasn't trying to escape from Michael Jackson, but complained repeatedly that Dieter Wiesner and Ronald Konitzer were keeping her family *away* from Michael. "They won't let us around him because they know the children tug at his heartstrings," Pryor remembered Janet telling her. A Neverland housekeeper backed Pryor's story, testifying that Janet Arvizo *had* complained about being held hostage, but only by Dieter Wiesner and "two others" who were "interfering" in her relationship with Michael. Neverland's housekeeping supervisor, Gayle Goforth, told the court that Janet Arvizo not only didn't want to leave Neverland, but begged for a job on the ranch and was furious about being turned down.

Neverland security chief Violet Silva testified that there was a directive issued that the Arvizo children not be allowed to leave the property, but said this was only because of their bad behavior and their mother's lack of supervision. Gavin and Star were "reckless" kids, Silva said, who regularly drove off in ranch vehicles without permission. Neverland property manager Joe Marcus not only confirmed Silva's testimony, but also told the court that *he* was the one who had issued that directive, because the Arvizo boys were stealing ranch vehicles whenever they got the chance, and he didn't want them on public roads. Marcus scoffed at the notion the Arvizos were being held hostage, telling the court they could have left at any time. On the one occasion when Janet said she wanted to return home, Marcus said, he allowed a ranch employee to drive her and her family in one of Mr. Jackson's Rolls-Royces. Marcus laughed when asked if this brief departure from Neverland could have been called an "escape." The Arvizos always seemed "excited" to be at the ranch when he saw them there, Marcus said.

A former security guard at Neverland described catching Gavin and Star in the wine cellar of the main house while Mr. Jackson was away from the ranch. The two had an open wine bottle, the guard said, from which "some of the contents were missing." One of Neverland's assistant chefs told the court about a time when Star Arvizo demanded that he mix liquor into a milk shake, and threatened to have him fired if he didn't. The chef described Gavin Arvizo as an astoundingly obnoxious kid who said things like, "Give me the fucking Cheetos." The chef said he had developed a "romantic relationship" with Davellin Arvizo, and that the girl never complained once about her family being held at the ranch against their will.

The judge and the jury grew restless under an onslaught of character assassination testimony that grew increasingly redundant. Some of the witnesses Mesereau called to the stand, though, provided testimony that was both more singular and of greater consequence. Irene Peters, the Los Angeles County Department of Children and Family Services social worker who interviewed the Arvizo family in February 2003, testified that Gavin Arvizo "became upset" when she asked whether he had had a sexual relationship with Michael Jackson. "Everybody thinks Michael

Jackson sexually abused me," Peters recalled the boy telling her. "He never touched me." Gavin also said that he never slept in the same bed with Michael Jackson, and described Mr. Jackson as someone who "was very kind to him" and behaved toward him like the father he had always wished for. Janet Arvizo had also described Mr. Jackson as a father to her children, "and she felt he was responsible for helping Gavin to survive his cancer," Peters told the court. She found the Arvizos entirely convincing, Peters said, which was why she filed a report stating that the allegations of sexual abuse by Michael were "unfounded."

A forensic accountant was called to testify that the Arvizo family received $152,000 from the settlement of its lawsuit against JCPenney, and deposited $32,000 of the money in an account in the name of Janet Arvizo's mother, then used some of the remaining money to buy a new vehicle. The Arvizos set off on a $7,000 shopping spree shortly after arriving at the Calabasas Inn in early 2003, the accountant testified, purchasing $4,800 worth of luggage and clothing in just two days and putting everything on Mr. Jackson's bill. The accountant also testified that Janet Arvizo had deposited the welfare checks she received from Los Angeles County into her then-boyfriend's account and used the money to pay their rent. After the accountant, an intake worker from the Los Angeles County Department of Public Social Services was called to the stand and described in detail the fraud Janet Arvizo had committed in her application for welfare payments.

An editor from the weekly *Mid Valley News* testified that she felt "duped" by Janet Arvizo into writing articles that raised money for her son Gavin's medical treatments. She had accepted Janet's claim that Gavin's chemotherapy sessions were costing $12,000 apiece, the editor said, only to discover that the real cost was $1,200 per session. After the editor stepped down, Janet's former sister-in-law took the stand to recall for the jury being so moved by the *Mid Valley News* articles that she had decided to start a blood drive for Gavin, but was rebuffed by Janet: "She told me that she didn't need my fucking blood, that she needed money."

The coup de grâce was delivered by a "surprise witness" Mesereau had promised the jury during his opening statement. Paralegal Mary Holzer took the stand to say that she had formerly worked at the law firm that represented the Arvizos in their lawsuit against JCPenney. In private conversation, Holzer testified, Janet confided that the injuries she was claiming had been caused by store security guards were actually inflicted by her husband on the night of the incident. When Holzer said she couldn't suborn perjury, Janet responded by warning that her husband's brother was in the Mexican mafia, "and that she knows where I live and they would come and kill me and my nine-year-old daughter." She became truly frightened of Janet, Holzer said, when she accompanied the woman to a doctor's appointment at which "she threw herself down on the ground, started kicking and screaming, carrying on that the doctors were the devil and the nurse was the devil and they were all out to get her." Janet also told her that she had enrolled the kids in acting classes so they could become convincing liars, Holzer testified: "She said she wanted them to become good actors so she could tell them what to say."

As Mesereau had planned from the first, the attorney used two and a half hours of outtakes from the Martin Bashir documentary to let his client speak directly to the jury without facing cross-examination. The British journalist had begun the interviews by flattering Michael Jackson as "the greatest musical artist alive today," then insisting that he wanted the world to know more about the international charity work the entertainer had done to help children all over the world. When Michael complained that the media reported only "negative things" about him, Bashir dismissed tabloid reporters as "scum," then described the recent stories he had seen about Michael as "disgusting" and promised that he would never produce such "rubbish."

The utterly strange and unique amalgamation of grandiosity and naive yearning in Michael's voice as he lamented the loneliness imposed upon him by stardom was mesmerizing. He never got to know what people were really like, he said, because "when people see Michael Jackson, they're not themselves anymore." In some ways, he felt more lonely when he was in a hotel room listening to the people outside chant his name than he did at any other time, Michael told Bashir a few moments later, and often cried during such experiences: "There's all that love out there. But still, you really do feel trapped and lonely. And you can't get out." Every once in a while he went to a nightclub, Michael said, but the DJs always played his music and the fans began begging him to dance and the whole thing started to feel like he was working, not playing.

Michael began to talk for the first time about a subject that related to the Arvizo accusations when he described the recoveries of several young cancer patients who'd visited Neverland. Just as he started to describe the curative powers of love and prayer, Bashir turned to his camera operator and said, "Cut."

Bashir ended the tape by telling Michael that making people aware of his dedication to children was what made this documentary so important:

"People are scum, and there's so much jealousy. The problem is, nobody actually comes here to see it. But I saw it here yesterday, the spiritual." Several jurors said after the trial that if Bashir had been in the courtroom that day, they might have spit on him.

Mesereau would say later that he believed the Bashir outtakes could have tipped the outcome of the trial from hung jury to outright acquittal. On the one hand, he remained certain that a hung jury was the worst outcome his client had to fear. On the other hand, the overwhelming public perception surrounding the trial was that Michael Jackson would soon be a California state prison inmate. Every doubt the attorney harbored about his ability to read a jury magnified and tortured his thoughts. "It's a terrible thing when you see a client suffering and you want to reassure them with a sense of certainty you don't have," Mesereau admitted. "No one has it in that situation. You just can't know."

The defense attorney at least had been able to deliver one last blow to Tom Sneddon on the final day of the trial. After the judge ruled that a videotape of Gavin Arvizo's police interview from two years prior could be shown to the jury, Mesereau demanded that the Arvizo family return to Santa Maria to face further questioning. Sneddon and his team were happy to comply, putting the Arvizos up in a "secure location" near the courthouse where the prosecutors spent hours prepping Janet and Gavin for a return to the witness stand. This would be a welcome opportunity to rehabilitate their star witnesses, the prosecutors believed, to show the jury that these people were not the low-life grifters Mesereau had made them into during his cross-examinations. When Sneddon finished his rebuttal case, though, Mesereau answered with just three words: "The defense rests."

The cable news programs were reporting that Gavin Arvizo's police interview had sealed the prosecution's victory. The district attorney and his team had already scheduled what amounted to a celebration dinner for the following evening, so certain were they that Michael Jackson would be found guilty of at least some charges. Ron Zonen made the prosecution's case to the jury, taking nearly two full hours to try to cement the conspiracy charges against Jackson before turning to the subject of child molestation. As Sneddon had done in his opening statement, Zonen returned in his final argument to the theme that Neverland Ranch was much like Pinocchio's Pleasure Island: "They rode rides, went to the zoo, ate whatever they wanted—candy, ice cream, soda pop. There was only fun . . . And at night they entered into the world of the forbidden. Michael's room was a veritable fortress with locks and codes that the boys were given . . . They learned about sexuality from someone only too willing to be their teacher . . . It began with discussions of masturbation and nudity. It began with simulating a sex act with a mannequin."

The Arvizos were a family with problems and issues, Zonen allowed, but "the lion on the Serengeti doesn't go after the strongest antelope. The predator goes after the weakest." Those of them bothered by Gavin Arvizo's demeanor on the witness stand should bear in mind how difficult it must be for a teenage boy to testify about being sexually abused by one of the most famous people in the world, Zonen told the jurors: "It is intimidating . . . He had been molested by a man he once held in high regard." Everyone in the courtroom knew that Janet Arvizo was less than a sterling character, Zonen conceded, but "for all her shortcomings, Janet, after learning Michael was giving her son alcohol, in thirty-six hours she had her children out of there." The defense had argued from the beginning and no doubt would argue again that Janet Arvizo was essentially a con artist out to fleece a wealthy celebrity, Zonen said, but the evidence showed that up to this very day, "Janet never asked for one penny from Michael Jackson. She never desired anything from him and she doesn't today."

Zonen's argument finished with an attack on the credibility and character of Michael Jackson's attorneys. Mark Geragos had accepted $180,000 from Michael Jackson during his first three weeks of representation, but couldn't seem to recall a single conversation with his client when he was on the witness stand. And Mr. Mesereau, during his opening statement, had recited a long list of famous people who would be testifying as to Michael Jackson's good character, Zonen observed. Yet almost none of those people had shown up in court.

It was a sore spot with Mesereau, who had been bitterly disappointed by the refusal of the many celebrities Michael had called his friends to speak for him publicly. The defense attorney channeled both his frustration and his fury into an introduction to his final argument that recounted the criticisms that Zonen had aimed at him personally. "Whenever a prosecutor does that, you know they're in trouble," Mesereau told the jury. This wasn't a popularity contest between lawyers, he added, it was a decision about the fate of a human being, about the application of justice under the law.

The jurors had heard enough from and about the Arvizos to know they were a family of "con artists, actors, and liars," Mesereau went on. Did any of them really doubt that a civil lawsuit would materialize when the criminal case was finished? "Everyone is looking for a big payday at the expense of Michael Jackson," he said. "There's going to be great celebration in this group if he's convicted of one single count in the case." Examine the motives of all the major prosecution witnesses, Mesereau urged: "Aren't they all after millions from Michael Jackson? Haven't you seen one person after another come in this courtroom who have sued Michael Jackson? They're all lined up." And the Arvizos were at the front of the line. Larry Feldman had acknowledged that a criminal conviction in this case meant certain victory in the civil case that was sure to follow. The Arvizos and their attorney "want the taxpayers of this county to establish liability for them," Mesereau told a jury of Santa Barbara County taxpayers. "For this to happen, you have to label [Michael Jackson] a convict. You have to label him a sex offender. You have to label him everything he is not."

Mesereau resorted to a visual display to emphasize what had always been the weakest link in the prosecution case, the contention that Michael Jackson had waited until the very moment that his relationship with Gavin Arvizo became the object of international media scrutiny to begin molesting the boy. Laying out charts and graphs to create a timeline of Jackson's relationship with the Arvizo family, Mesereau pointed out how many other, far better opportunities Jackson had had to try to seduce Gavin Arvizo into a sexual relationship. That Michael had passed those opportunities by to seize upon one that was almost certain to result in his exposure could make no sense to anyone who had any.

The Arvizos' proven pattern of lying under oath was by itself grounds for acquittal in this case, Mesereau told the jurors. It was a proven fact that the Arvizo children had lied at their mother's behest to further a civil lawsuit filed against JCPenney. And Gavin Arvizo had been the most persuasive among them in telling those lies: "He was very young, he was very street-smart, he had been schooled by his parents." The JCPenney lawsuit served as a training program for the Arvizos, Mesereau said, one that had prepared them to take down Michael Jackson in the "the biggest con of their careers."

The attorney knew that in the end he would have to bring his argument back to the character of the defendant. Mesereau told the jury: "If you look in your hearts, do you believe Michael Jackson is evil in that way?" Mesereau asked as he approached the end of his speech. "Is it even possible? It really is not. If you look deep in your heart, do you think it's even remotely possible that he's built that way?"

The judge had instructed them to bear in mind that this wasn't a civil case in which the issue before them was a preponderance of evidence, the attorney observed. Even by that standard, Michael Jackson should prevail. But at this criminal trial the standard was proof beyond a reasonable doubt, Mesereau reminded the jurors, meaning that, "If you have the slightest suspicion [about his guilt], Mr. Jackson must go home. He must go free."

Court TV's Nancy Grace, a pioneer in the transformation of criminal trial coverage into serial evening soap opera, flatly predicted that Michael Jackson would be found guilty on most if not all of the ten felony and four misdemeanor counts that had gone to the jury. And her counterpart on Fox News, former prosecutor Wendy Murphy, was every bit as sure: "There is no question we will see convictions here." Virtually no dissent from these opinions was heard on television or read in newspapers. Only a handful of commentators even admitted uncertainty.

"You have to remember how *invested* the media was in seeing Michael convicted," Mesereau said. "The story just wasn't as good if he was acquitted." Coverage of the Michael Jackson trial had rivaled the O. J. Simpson murder case in terms of media saturation. The twenty-four-hour coverage kicked in from the moment of the Neverland Ranch raid. Only CNN broke away from Michael Jackson coverage to a press conference shortly afterward at which George Bush and Tony Blair stood side by side to brief the world on a terrorist attack in Turkey. Within weeks of Jackson's arrest, ABC, CBS, and NBC all had churned out hour-long specials on the accusations against the entertainer. *Daily Variety* called the Jackson sex scandal "a godsend [for] cable new channels and local stations looking to pump up Nielsen numbers in the final week of the all-important November sweeps." On December 18, 2003, the date that the criminal charges against Michael Jackson were formally filed, Judge Melville's court administrator came outside with only five hundred copies and "had to be rescued by sheriff's deputies," as the judge recalled it, "after being overrun by the media."

The jury was still out on the evening of June 10, when Tom Sneddon and his team gathered for their "celebration dinner" at northern Santa Barbara County's top steak house, the Hitching Post in Buellton. Heady with the praise of their presentation that was being broadcast on one cable news network after another, the prosecutors not only toasted one another repeatedly but seemed to enjoy the audience of television correspondents who kibbitzed from the bar area. Mesereau and Yu, meanwhile, appeared to have gone underground. The defense attorneys wouldn't even answer their cell phones. "There really wasn't anything to do but wait," Mesereau explained. "We ate in our condos."

Over the weekend, as the jury's deliberations passed the one-week mark, cable news operations reported that the jury had been requesting "read backs" of testimony, mostly from prosecution witnesses. On MSNBC, Mesereau's friend Ron Richards, one of the few pundits who had predicted acquittals, said he was becoming "nervous for the defense."

Just after noon on June 13, 2005, word came that the jury had reached verdicts on all counts. Judge Melville ordered that the parties be present in his courtroom at 1:30 p.m.

Preparations for the media frenzy that would engulf the delivery of the jury's verdicts at the courthouse in Santa Maria would have suited the theaters either of the absurd or of the grotesque. A security detail that now included the Santa Maria Police Department, the Santa Barbara County sheriff's department, and the interagency Santa Barbara Mobile Field Force, replete with flak-jacketed SWAT teams and bomb-sniffing dogs, herded the hundreds of reporters who had been denied seats in the courtroom and the "overflow room" into the holding pens that surrounded the courthouse. An escalating scale of "County Impact Fees" were paid by those who won the four pool camera positions in the courthouse or the fifty-two TV camera stations outside the front entrance or the fifty kneeling-still camera spots in front of those. There was even a "helicopter pool." Plans were put together for a jury news conference, a prosecution news conference, and a defense news conference—as well as for camera positions at the county jail, should those be necessary. Gaining access to even the most remote fringes of the tented "Media Area" required reporters to run a staggering gauntlet of rules, regulations, signature sheets, and inspections.

As the appointed hour ticked past, the networks reported that Michael Jackson would be arriving late at the courthouse. Helicopter cameras tracked the motorcade of black SUVs that made its way from Neverland toward Santa Maria. The sheriff's deputies in charge of crowd control barked orders at the media horde and snarled commands to the legion of Michael Jackson fans that had arranged itself in assorted camps wherever there was open space near the courthouse. Fans pressed as close as they could to the Cyclone fence and steel gate that protected the entrance to the courthouse parking lot, awaiting the defendant's arrival. The fans appeared "apprehensive," one television correspondent after another told viewers. The crowd roused themselves to boo and jeer when Sneddon and the prosecution team arrived at the courthouse. They chanted, "Liar! Liar! Liar!" at various reporters and commentators who were considered to be especially prejudiced against Michael. Quoting "law enforcement sources," at least two cable channels reported that the Santa Maria authorities were concerned that the fans might attack certain members of the media if Michael Jackson was convicted.

Mesereau and Yu had come out of the courthouse to wait in the parking lot by the time Michael's black Suburban finally pulled through the gate. Many of the fans brandished either camcorders or cell phone cameras. The sunlight glinting off all that shiny metal, combined with the wailing cheer that erupted from their numbers when Michael stepped out of the SUV, produced atmospherics that suggested the siege of an ancient city.

Haggard, gaunt, and heavily made up, Michael moved forward in tiny steps, surrounded by bodyguards who seemed to be keeping him on his feet. Behind his mirrored sunglasses and beneath his black umbrella, he followed Mesereau and Yu to the courthouse entrance. Before walking through the doors, Michael turned to wave to his fans, summoning up a slight smile as their cheers and screams rose to deafening volume. That smile was gone, though, the moment he stepped inside.

"He was strained beyond description," Mesereau recalled. "He looked more emaciated, more frail, more out of it than I had ever seen him." The dazed expression and robotic movements evidenced an unprecedented level of self-medication. "I don't know if he was on drugs," Mesereau said, "but if he was, who could blame him?"

The six seats inside the courtroom reserved for the Jackson family were taken by Joe and Katherine, Randy, Tito, Rebbie, and La Toya, who managed to spend more time in front of the cameras that day than all the others combined. Janet Jackson waited outside.

Eleven deputies wearing sidearms spread out around the courtroom as the eight women and four men of the jury filed into their seats. At 2:10 p.m. the verdict envelopes were delivered to Judge Melville, who opened and read each one without expression. Tears welled in the eyes of several female jurors. "Every second seemed to last ten hours," Mesereau remembered. Melville finally handed the verdict sheets to his clerk, Lorna Ray, who read them aloud from the top. "Count One: Conspiracy—Not Guilty. Count Two: Lewd Act upon a Child—Not Guilty. Count Three ... Not Guilty." Michael Jackson had been acquitted on all counts.

The media at first couldn't believe it, then wouldn't believe it. An incompetent, overawed jury was the default explanation offered up by experts who had predicted multiple convictions. "Not guilty by reason of celebrity," was the way Nancy Grace described the verdict on Court TV. "I don't think the jurors even understand how influenced they were by who Michael Jackson is," Wendy Murphy chimed in on Fox News. In New York, the *Daily News* and the *Post* ran their stories on the verdict under the very same headline: "Boy, Oh, Boy!" Those newspapers were restrained by comparison to London tabloids, which baldly asserted that Jacko "got away with it" and excoriated "what they laughably call American justice."

On the morning after, Diane Sawyer of ABC's *Good Morning America* actually tried to convince jurors that Michael Jackson's enormous fame had overwhelmed them: "Are you sure? Are you sure this gigantically known guy walking into the room had no influence at all?" Tom Sneddon took to invoking "the celebrity factor" in each and every interview he gave, in which he also denied any personal responsibility.

In interview after interview, the jurors made it clear that they were insulted by questions about whether they had been swayed by Michael Jackson's celebrity, and insisted their verdicts had been based on the facts of the case. Jury foreman Paul Rodriguez said that the videotape of Gavin Arvizo's police interview had been the single most significant piece of evidence, and that he and the other jurors had viewed it multiple times. The boy simply hadn't been believable, Rodriguez explained. Nearly every one of the jury's eight women described Janet Arvizo as both despicable and dishonest. Several jurors said they saw the Arvizos as a family of professional grifters who had tried to frame Michael Jackson. Other members of the panel told reporters that there was no compelling proof of sexual abuse. A few complained that the prosecution had used tawdry evidence that had little relevance to the case before the court in order to mock, insult, and degrade the famous defendant.

The media's reporting (and posturing) held sway in the immediate aftermath of the verdicts. A Gallup Poll taken hours after Michael Jackson's acquittal showed that 48 percent of the country (and 54 percent of white Americans) disagreed with the jury's verdict. More than 60 percent said they believed Jackson's celebrity was a major reason the panel had voted not guilty on every count. A third of those polled said they were "saddened" by the verdict, and a quarter said they were "outraged."

"We were all oblivious to what was being said in the media that first afternoon and evening," Mesereau recalled. The Jackson family, along with Mesereau, Yu, and a handful of invited guests, headed straight back to

Neverland. They were awaited by the members of a staff that had lined the ranch's driveway, holding hands, only a couple of hours earlier, when they sent Michael off to the courthouse without knowing whether they would ever see him again.

The crowd of fans at the gate was so thick and so raucous that Michael's security team had to help Mesereau and Yu pass through. Inside the main house, though, the atmosphere was remarkably subdued. "It wasn't really a celebration," Mesereau remembered. "It was more spiritual, very quiet, very calm—almost serene. Everyone was thanking God." Mesereau believed that religious faith—Katherine's religious faith, really—had been what had most sustained Michael during the past nineteen months. "His mother would tell him in a soft voice, but very firmly, that God was with him," Mesereau recalled. "And I could see the way that soothed Michael. Joe would shake his fist and tell him to keep fighting, but I don't think that really did a lot of good. Michael wasn't that person. He wasn't a fighter. The gentle approach is what worked for him."

After letting "Michael's kids crawl all over me" for a couple of hours, Mesereau returned to his condo and went to bed early, so he could be up at 2 a.m. to begin an all-day schedule of television interviews. Neither Mesereau's triumph nor Jackson's deliverance were greeted with much enthusiasm, though, by either the American media or the American public. "You cost the worldwide media billions," Berry Gordy told Mesereau. "We have a less interesting story now," CNN head Jonathan Klein said to his lieutenants on the afternoon of the verdicts. Klein was proven correct that very evening, when three broadcast networks rushed Michael Jackson acquittal specials onto the air only to see them outperformed in ratings by Fox's rerun of *Nanny 911*.

The competence and integrity of the Jackson trial jury would be questioned for weeks, even months, after the verdicts were delivered. Wendy Murphy suggested that the jurors "should take IQ tests." Ron Zonen described the Jackson jury as inferior to those he usually dealt with in Santa Barbara County. The length of the trial meant that those who led full lives, people with important jobs and those who ran businesses, could not make the expected six-month commitment. "So we were left with the unemployed, the underemployed, and the retired," Zonen said. "It certainly wasn't a jury that was as educated or accomplished as I'm used to seeing."

Mesereau accused Zonen of calling the jurors "idiots" and retorted that the panel included a civil engineer, a man with a master's degree in mathematics, and a retired school principal. "I thought it was a very intelligent jury," Mesereau said. "They paid good attention, took excellent notes, and deliberated for almost nine days."

The district attorney's office had discovered later that some of the jurors read newspapers during the trial even though they were instructed not to, Zonen said, and that one juror was negotiating a book deal while the trial was in progress. Even if Michael Jackson had been convicted, Zonen said, the verdict would probably have been overturned. Judge Melville offered no opinion on that, instead simply observing the "incredible pressure" that the jury had coped with during the Michael Jackson trial. "We had jurors who reported being followed home by suspicious cars," Melville said, "and others who said that flowers were sent to their homes with notes attached inviting them to appear on this or that TV talk show."

Mesereau would be as taken aback as anyone else when, weeks after Michael Jackson's acquittal, two jurors appeared on MSNBC to say they thought Jackson was guilty, but had voted for acquittal because they felt pressured by other members of the panel. Three of their fellow jurors were such devoted Michael Jackson fans that they had made it clear early on they would never vote to convict him, Eleanor Cook and Ray Hultman said; one woman on the panel even referred to the defendant as "my Michael." They had caved, Hultman and Cook said, when the jury foreman threatened to have them removed unless they voted for acquittal. At the same time, both Cook, who was seventy-nine years old, and Hultman, who was sixty-two, admitted they had been shopping books and that their deals had fallen apart when Jackson was found not guilty. Cook revealed that she had brought in a medical text during deliberations in order to convince the other jurors that Jackson fit the definition of a pedophile.

Mesereau called the two jurors' televised remarks "absurd," and noted that they had been among the most outspoken proponents of Michael Jackson's innocence when he spoke with the panel immediately after the trial. "The other jurors were upset with them, to put it mildly," Mesereau recalled.

The guest of honor was nowhere to be seen at the Jackson family celebration of Michael's acquittal held at the Chumash Casino Resort near Santa Ynez on the evening of June 17. Tito and his band performed and Janet shook hands with her brother's fans, while Katherine Jackson assured them, "We couldn't have done it without you." Nearly every news organization that took note of the party, though, led with the report that one of the jurors had attended, and was quoted as saying she had blinked back tears when "Beat It" began to play on the sound system.

At Mesereau's urging, Michael had left Neverland less than forty-eight hours after his acquittal. "I just had this gut feeling that the authorities in Santa Barbara weren't going to let it go, that they were going to find a way to make a new case against Michael," Mesereau said. In fact, Sneddon and his associates were already discussing how they might charge Jackson for obtaining prescription drugs under false names. A preliminary investigation of this possibility would last well into the next autumn. After a series of phone conversations with Grace Rwaramba and other intermediaries, Mesereau spoke to Michael on the evening of June 15: "I told him, 'Michael, I know how much Neverland means to you. And that it's a glorious, enchanted place, and that you've known real peace there. But I really believe that its time in your life is passed. We all have to move on. You have to move on. I don't think you'll ever be really safe there again. Go somewhere else.'"

Two days later, Jackson's passport and the $300,000 posted to secure his bail were returned to him and he began to make plans to travel overseas. He had become convinced by then that he was no longer really welcome in the United States.

As a *Washington Post* editorial put it, "An acquittal doesn't clear his name, it only muddies the water." Wendy Murphy described Jackson on Fox News as "a Teflon monster," and accused jurors of "putting targets on the backs of all—especially highly vulnerable—kids that will now come into Michael Jackson's life." In the *New York Post*, Diane Dimond wrote that Jackson was more dangerous now than ever before: "He walked out of court a free man, not guilty on all counts. But Michael Jackson is so much more than free. He now has carte blanche to live his life any way he wants, with whomever he wants . . ." Maureen Orth reported in *Vanity Fair* that Michael Jackson was in discussions to put together a world tour called "Framed!" in order to restore his shattered finances. "That was the most ridiculous of all the things reported about Michael," said Dieter Wiesner. "A world tour was the very last thing Michael would have wanted to do."

"To me, it was like watching them stick knives in his open wounds," Mesereau said. "Michael had been drained of his strength, of his happiness, of his hope. He was so hurt by what had been said and written about him. He had been accused of things that he wasn't even remotely capable of doing. He had told Martin Bashir that he would rather die than hurt a child, and I believed him. But he knew that many people—most of the people in the media—didn't believe him. I really think that by the time the trial was over Michael wasn't sure he wanted to live anymore. If not for his children, I'm not sure he would have lived as long as he did."

On June 19, Michael flew with his children and Grace Rwaramba to Paris. Mesereau didn't even know that his client had left the country until more than a week later, when Grace phoned Susan Yu to say they had settled in Bahrain. "I think he wanted to get as far away from Santa Barbara County as he could," Mesereau said. "I think he was looking for the sort of safety, the sense of sanctuary that he had felt at Neverland. I didn't think it was a bad idea. But at the same time, I think I just assumed that he would come back to the United States eventually. I mean, this was his country."

22

On May 20, 2009, AEG Live announced that the debut of Michael Jackson's "This Is It" concert series had been pushed back five days, to July 13, and that three other July dates would be rescheduled for March 2010. For thousands of people who had already purchased tickets and made travel plans, it was devastating news. Stung by the "We told you," gibes from Roger Friedman and others, Michael lashed out as he left the Burbank Studios after one of his infrequent rehearsal appearances, saying he was angry at "them" for "booking me up to fifty shows when I only wanted to do ten."

Marc Schaffel and Dieter Wiesner told each other they had seen this coming. "As soon as I heard fifty concerts," Wiesner recalled, "I knew it would never happen."

"My guess was that Michael would quit after three shows," Schaffel said. "And I knew there was no way he would do those London concerts on the schedule they wanted. It would have taken much longer, at the very least. I think he realized he had to do it, but the less he had to perform, the better Michael liked it."

For years, Michael had insisted (to Wiesner and Schaffel, among others) that he found it far more satisfying to work on a movie, or even a video, than to perform in concert. He was forced to do an enormous amount of work to prepare for a concert, Michael complained, "but when it's over, it's over." There was nothing captured, nothing permanent, nothing you could show your children. Live performances were here and gone. Afterward, you felt like you'd wasted your energy.

In London, the tabloids reported that Jackson was still hardly ever leaving the Carolwood chateau, even when the "This Is It" dancers and musicians began their intensive, seven-days-a-week practice sessions at CenterStaging. He preferred to work from home, Michael told Kenny Ortega and Randy Phillips. "I know my schedule," he crisply informed Ortega, then added that he was still working out three times a week with Lou Ferrigno and getting in shape for the shows. Like Randy Phillips,

Ortega was hearing reports that while Jackson wasn't showing up at rehearsals, he was still making at least a couple of trips every week to see Arnold Klein. Michael would remain inside Klein's office for up to five hours at a time. The paparazzi who had staked the place out reported that on at least a couple of occasions Michael had emerged from the Bedford building so incapacitated that his bodyguards literally had to carry him to his vehicle. British tabloids that knew Klein had been giving the entertainer injections of Demerol since the 1990s began running stories about Jackson's drug use "spiraling out of control."

For Phillips and AEG Live, Jackson's health—physical as well as mental—had become the biggest issue hanging over the preparations for the O2 shows. Insurers were understandably reluctant to underwrite a policy that would cover a production headlined by a performer whose collapses and no-shows had torpedoed one extravaganza after another during the previous fifteen years. Rumors that Michael was suffering from an assortment of major medical issues had been dogging plans for the London concerts ever since the previous December. Publicly, Phillips waved away worries about his star's health. "Making up rumors about Michael Jackson is a cottage industry," he told a London reporter. "We were having dinner when I got a Google alert that he had a flesh-eating disease. He was sitting opposite, healthy as ever."

What Phillips did not tell reporters was that AEG still had not found insurers for all fifty of the O2 concerts (less than thirty were covered so far) and might have to write its own policy for the rest. And the company had only obtained what insurance coverage Lloyd's of London was willing to extend by convincing Michael to submit to a nearly five-hour battery of medical tests. The examination had been conducted by Dr. David Slavit, a New York City–based ear-nose-and-throat specialist best known for his work with opera singers, and resulted in a certificate of health stating that the doctor had found nothing more serious than a slight case of sniffles attributed to hay fever. Yes, he was aware that Mr. Jackson had cancelled past performances and tours, Slavit noted in his report, but this had been the result of "dehydration and exhaustion"—easily avoided if he received appropriate medical care. All in all, Michael Jackson was in excellent health, and more than fit enough to perform the London concerts, AEG announced shortly after receiving Slavit's report. The company didn't mention that the policy Lloyd's had issued (under the pseudonym "Mark Jones") specifically stated that, "This insurance does not cover any loss directly or indirectly arising out of, contributed to, by or resulting from . . . the illegal possession or illicit taking of drugs and their effects." Nor did anyone at the company take public note of the fact that, on the questionnaire he completed as part of his medical examination, Michael had responded to the query, "Have you ever been treated for or had any indication of excessive use of alcohol or drugs" by circling "no."

In order to prepare Michael physically for the O2 shows, AEG had agreed to pay for the services of a chef/nutritionist named Kai Chase who would live full-time at the Carolwood chateau. Like Lou Ferrigno before her, Chase reported that no matter how concerned others might be about his sporadic appearances at the CenterStaging show rehearsals, Michael was embracing the disciplines of health and fitness at home. He had sworn off the KFC chicken dinners he loved and was eating only healthy food during the run-up to the O2 shows, Chase said—meals like spinach salad with free range chicken for lunch and seared wild tuna for supper. He needed a diet that would help him avoid cramping up when he was performing, Michael told Chase, who was as struck as others had been that he referred to himself constantly as a dancer, but only rarely as a singer. The one meal of the day at which neither Chase nor the children saw Michael was breakfast, because the specially mixed fruit drinks and organic granola the chef prepared for him were always carried upstairs by the only member of the staff who was admitted to the master bedroom: Dr. Conrad Murray.

Of all the demands that Michael Jackson made during the negotiation of the contract for the O2 shows, his requirement that AEG pay for the services of a "personal physician" had been the one that Randy Phillips and the company attorneys resisted most vigorously. Jackson's refusal to compromise on this point suggested that his sense of self-importance had made a comeback every bit as extraordinary as the one Randy Phillips hoped to see onstage at the O2. "Look," Michael told Phillips, "my body is the mechanism that fuels this entire business. Just like President Obama, I need my own doctor attending to me twenty-four/seven." Paul Gongaware remembered Jackson pointing to himself and saying, "This is the machine. You have to take care of the machine." Frank Dileo pointed out to Phillips and Gongaware that hiring a personal physician might be a good way to separate Michael from Arnold Klein, whom all three men believed to be Jackson's primary drug supplier. AEG agreed to pay for a private physician, even yielding to Michael's demand that he alone be permitted to pick the MD who would live with him.

The doctor Jackson selected was Conrad Murray, a Las Vegas cardiologist whose services had first been arranged more than a year earlier by Michael Amir Williams. Brother Michael had urged his employer to hire a black physician. Supposedly, Dr. Murray had treated Jackson and his children for flu symptoms shortly after the move from Ireland. A native of Trinidad who had attended Meharry Medical College in Nashville, Murray was living large in a 5,268-square-foot home with a spectacular pool near the Red Rock Country Club in Vegas when he and Jackson met. He had been running Global Cardiovascular Associates out on East Flamingo Road since 2000 and had just opened the Acres Homes Cardiovascular Center in Houston, Texas. Behind that facade of success, though, Conrad Murray was something of a deadbeat.

Murray had first come to the attention of Nevada authorities back in 2002, when a child support case out of California's Santa Clara County that followed the doctor through three states finally caught up with him in Las Vegas. By spring 2009, when he received the call inviting him to work as Michael Jackson's physician, Murray was under siege from a phalanx of creditors. Capital One bank had won a default judgment against Murray in October 2008, and in March 2009, HICA Education Loan Corporation was awarded a $71,332 judgment against the doctor for his failing to repay student loans that dated back to his days in Nashville. Separate lawsuits filed by Citicorp Vendor Finance and Popular Leasing USA had ended with judgments against Murray totaling $363,722, and the doctor was still facing court claims lodged in Las Vegas by Digirad Imaging Solutions and Siemans Financial Services that demanded another $366,541 for unpaid debts.

The call that came out of nowhere offering him a job as Michael Jackson's personal physician must have seemed to Murray a miracle cure for all that ailed him. Murray, though, showed no sign of that to Michael Amir Williams, who had phoned to say that Jackson "very much wanted" the doctor to be part of his London concert tour, then explained that the deal would have to be negotiated with AEG. When Paul Gongaware called, Murray represented himself as a highly prosperous medical professional who would have to be very well compensated if he was going to not only abandon a successful medical practice but also close thriving clinics in Las Vegas and Houston. He would need $5 million a year, Murray told the AEG executive. "I told him there was no way that was going to happen," Gongaware recalled. Murray eventually agreed to work for $150,000 per month, but even then insisted to AEG attorney Kathy Jorrie that his contract would have to guarantee such payments for at least ten months, from May 2009 to March 2010. "One hundred and fifty thousand dollars is a lot of money," Jorrie told Murray, who eventually agreed to be paid on a month-to-month basis. During their negotiations Murray told her that Michael Jackson was "perfectly healthy" and in "excellent condition," remembered Jorrie, who passed this reassuring news on to Gongaware and Phillips.

Murray himself was "giddy with excitement" once the deal was made, recalled one of his friends from Las Vegas. The doctor's assorted creditors, like the Nevada legal authorities, would have a tough time finding him in Los Angeles, and no chance at all once he traveled with Michael to London. If the O2 shows turned into a world tour, as everyone involved hoped, Murray would be out of reach for the next couple of years. In the meantime, he would not only be making $150,000 per month, but also have plenty of free time for a personal life during the evenings when Michael was in rehearsals. Dr. Murray fancied himself as quite the ladies' man, and almost immediately after making the move to LA became a regular at the kind of clubs where sticky-haired, hot-bodied young women flocked to a fellow who could introduce himself as Michael Jackson's personal physician.

At least one of Jackson's entertainment lawyers saw it as significant that Dr. Murray's entrance into Michael's life had coincided with Dr. Tohme's exit. "There's no way Murray would have gotten in the door if Tohme had still been around," that attorney said. "Tohme would have driven Murray away the moment he met him. But Tohme had been pretty much destroyed by what Frank Dileo and Leonard Rowe and Michael's father were able to do through Mrs. Jackson. Joe Jackson and Rowe were using Katherine Jackson to bad-mouth Tohme nonstop."

Still, that attorney was among several people startled by a copy of a letter that arrived at his office during the middle of May 2009, sent to him by Brother Michael. Jackson's Muslim aide phoned first, the attorney recalled, to say that Tohme Tohme had been fired as Michael's manager and was being replaced by Frank Dileo. The letter, dated May 5, 2009, was delivered a short time later, informing its recipients that Michael Jackson had dispensed with the services of Dr. Tohme and that all future correspondence and communication should be sent through Frank Dileo. Among the several odd things about the letter was that, although it read as if written by Michael personally, Dileo had actually composed and typed it. Stranger still was that no copy had been sent to Tohme himself. When he finally saw the letter more than a year later, Tohme took one look at the signature and pronounced it a forgery. "I was never fired," he insisted.

"I continued to represent Michael. I was still handling his business. I had millions of dollars of Michael's money. If he had fired me, don't you think he would have asked for that money back?"

Frank Dileo, though, had a letter dated May 2, 2009, and signed (apparently) by Michael Jackson that appointed him as "one of [my] representatives and tour manager." After an absence of more than twenty years, Dileo's restored presence in Michael's life was undeniable.

The pillow-bellied, gravel-voiced Dileo had achieved a soft landing in the years immediately following his 1989 dismissal as Michael Jackson's manager. He'd used a reported $5 million severance package to purchase the forty-acre Tookaroosa Ranch near Ojai, California, where he was raising Tennessee Walking Horses. Even more satisfying, his old pals Robert De Niro and Joe Pesci had convinced Martin Scorsese to give Dileo the part of Tuddy in the film *Goodfellas*. Though he'd bought in as a partner in De Niro's New York restaurant, the Tribeca Grill, Dileo's career in the entertainment business hadn't exactly soared in recent years. Managing people like Taylor Dayne and Laura Branigan hardly measured up to being Michael Jackson's main man, and his Dileo Entertainment Group (formed around Frank's purchase of a Nashville recording studio) was strictly small-time. Dileo did better for himself by taking advantage of his unique appearance (at a height of five feet, two inches, he weighed nearly three hundred pounds) and raspy voice to win minor roles in *Wayne's World* and *Wayne's World 2*. Jackson had little good to say about Dileo after dismissing him in 1988, but Frank had won his way back into Michael's good graces during the spring of 2005, when he showed up to offer support during the criminal trial in Santa Maria. Tears had welled up in Michael's eyes when Dileo walked into the courtroom one day and he embraced his former manager warmly and publicly. Dileo had been trading on that moment ever since, and four years later intended to take full advantage of it.

He made an ally of Randy Phillips by persuading the AEG Live president that he could handle the Jackson family and keep Michael focused on performing in London. According to Dileo, after the phone conference in which the two men were introduced by Jackson, Phillips called back to remark that "Michael seems to have a real comfort level with you." Phillips also liked that Dileo seemed more committed than Tohme to the idea that Michael should not only complete the entire series of fifty concerts at the O2, but also be persuaded to continue with a world tour. Deep down, Dileo and Phillips agreed, Michael wanted to return in triumph to the United States before hanging it up. Together, they had the moxie to make that happen.

The attorneys who had put together the deal for the O2 shows read the writing on the wall when they learned in early May that Dileo was now working out of an office at AEG Live. "I don't blame Randy," one of them said. "For him and for AEG, it was all about protecting their investment. But Tohme was getting screwed in the process. He had made a fantastic deal for Michael. It was literally going to rescue his life and protect his kids and save the Sony catalog, all at once. And Tohme worked night and day on this thing—I witnessed it. But all the knives came out when people saw the potential for a huge success and big, big money. They didn't know Tohme, and he had a funny-sounding name and a funny-sounding accent, so they all went after him. And Tohme didn't realize that Dileo was moving him out until it was too late. Tohme's a pretty savvy guy, but he's not savvy in terms of the entertainment business, which is far more cutthroat than the Middle East."

Dennis Hawk, who had been handling a double-load as Michael's attorney since the dismissal of Peter Lopez, recalled that from the second half of May 2009, "It was like there were two parallel worlds going on at the same time. Dileo phoned me four or five times and he wanted to know about a document concerning the movie deal he was involved in. But he never said he was Michael's manager, and he never mentioned Dr. Tohme. It was odd. It was like he had positioned himself, but he hadn't really closed the deal. He was there, he was part of the 'team,' but he didn't seem to have any formal title."

Even with Dileo in position, though, the question of Michael Jackson's commitment to the O2 shows continued to concern Randy Phillips and the other executives at AEG. None of them was happy to learn that on the evening of May 14, Michael had arrived with his children at the Indian restaurant Chakra in Beverly Hills to join a celebration dinner marking Joe and Katherine Jackson's sixtieth wedding anniversary, which, strangely, was being held six months before their actual anniversary in November. Michael, the AEG execs had learned from Tohme, always became susceptible when he was trying to convince Prince, Paris, and Blanket that they belonged to a large and loving family. That evening at Chakra, surrounded by every one of his brothers and sisters plus more than a dozen of his nieces and nephews, Michael had allowed Katherine to convince him to join her the next day for a lunch meeting with Joe and Rowe at the Beverly Hills Hotel. Was this the actual reason for the celebration dinner all along? Whatever the case, when Randy Phillips and Paul Gongaware learned of the scheduled meeting, they insisted upon joining it.

On the afternoon of May 15, at a table in the Polo Lounge, Phillips and Gongaware listened glumly as Joe Jackson explained that AllGood

Entertainment had agreed to schedule the "Jackson Family Reunion Concert" at the Dallas Cowboys' football stadium on July 3, which would give Michael plenty of time to get to London and prepare for the O2 shows. Patrick Allocco was ready to guarantee the family a fee of $30 million. His brothers really needed their piece of that money, and "I do, too," Joe told his son. Leonard Rowe pointed out that Michael would be much better paid, on an hourly basis, for that one AllGood concert than he would be for fifty shows at the O2 Arena. "Who's paying *you?*" Phillips demanded of Rowe at one point during this conversation. "It's none of your concern," Rowe answered. Flanked by Phillips and Gongaware, Michael explained that the deal he had signed with AEG Live was an exclusive one. He couldn't perform anywhere else until he had finished the concerts in London. With Katherine urging her son to listen, Joe spent most of an hour trying to convince Michael that, at the very least, he and Leonard should be cut in on the AEG deal. "You owe me!" Joe shouted at one point, startling people at nearby tables. Again, Michael said that what his father asked was impossible.

"But we all knew how hard it was for him to say no to Mrs. Jackson," explained one of the attorneys who had negotiated the AEG contract. "And they were coercing him so hard that we worried he might just go ahead and sign something to please his mother and make his father go away, which would have been a disaster. It might have cost him the AEG deal, and it certainly would have given either AEG or AllGood, or both, grounds for a successful lawsuit. Thankfully, though, Michael listened to reason and refused to sign."

Michael went further than that. First, he insisted that his brothers issue a public denial of their involvement with AllGood Entertainment in a Jackson 5 reunion concert that was supposedly to take place in Texas on July 3. Then on May 25, five days after the postponement of the O2 shows, Leonard Rowe received a letter in which Michael informed his father's partner, "You do not represent me and I do not wish to have any oral or written communications with you regarding the handling of my business and/or personal matters."

"No one was sure whether Tohme had been fired and whether Dileo had been hired or what was going on," said one of the attorneys who had received the earlier letter that was supposedly from Michael but had actually been written by Dileo. "Was Dileo just writing letters and sending them out? Was he getting Michael's okay? Or was he just putting something in front of Michael and telling him to sign it? Was that even really Michael's signature? The whole thing was very mysterious."

"Basically," said one of those who remained in Jackson's employ, "the situation surrounding Michael was such that you were either creeping around with a knife in your hand, or you were holding your breath, waiting to see when you'd be stabbed in the back."

The O2 Arena concerts were "a do or die moment" for Michael Jackson, Randy Phillips observed in a May 30 interview with the *Los Angeles Times*: "If it doesn't happen, it would be a major problem for him, career-wise, in a way that it hasn't been in the past."

Sending a warning through the media was not, in general, an effective tactic for dealing with Michael Jackson. Phillips was smart enough to know that, but the AEG Live boss was beginning to feel the stress of a highly leveraged and increasingly exposed position. As costs quickly consumed the $12 million budgeted for preproduction, then more than doubled that figure, the joke Phillips had cracked to the London *Telegraph* back in March about making Phil Anschutz "into a millionaire from a billionaire" did not sound nearly so amusing. Michael's absences from the CenterStaging rehearsals continued and what the *Los Angeles Times* referred to as Jackson's "track record of missed performances and canceled dates" began to loom larger by the day.

"We finally made Mohammed come to the mountain," an exuberant Phillips had told the London newspapers at the announcement of the O2 shows back in March. Making Mohammed climb that mountain, though, was another task entirely. "In this business, if you don't take risks, you don't achieve greatness," Phillips had gamely asserted in the *Los Angeles Times*. By the end of May, though, AEG Live's head man was looking to cut corners and tie up loose ends. He refused his star's request to shoot Victoria Falls from a helicopter equipped with an IMAX camera as part of the environmental theme that Jackson wanted for the O2 shows, insisting that it was an expense the company couldn't afford. And when Michael proposed arriving onstage for the jungle section of the show by riding with three live monkeys on the back of an elephant, accompanied by panthers led on gold chains while a flock of parrots and other exotic birds flapped in the air around him, Phillips was grateful for the objections of animal rights activists from both sides of the Atlantic.

Phillips and AEG Live had begun reminding Jackson that he had put up his own assets as collateral on the $6.2 million they had already advanced to him, and that he would be on the hook for a lot more if the O2 concerts were canceled because of his failure to perform. When a promoter involved with the O2 concerts questioned Jackson's ability to deliver on his promise of fifty concerts, Phillips wrote back, "He has to or financial disaster awaits."

"We [need to] let Mikey know just what this will cost him in terms of him making money," Gongaware wrote to Phillips. "We cannot be forced into stopping this, which MJ will try to do because he is lazy and constantly changes his mind to fit his immediate wants." The performer needed to be reminded regularly that, "He is locked," Gongaware added. "He has no choice . . . he signed a contract."

Michael understood his position, according to his longtime makeup artist Karen Faye: "He was scared to death because AEG was funding everything. He said he would have to work at McDonald's if he didn't do these shows." Phillips's "do or die moment" comment, though, was AEG's first public attempt to get tough, to demand that Michael commit himself fully to the preparations for a show that was scheduled to open in a little more than a month. The stakes were now truly enormous. The CEO of the UK's biggest secondhand ticket seller, Seatwave, told the BBC that "There's gonna be somewhere near on a billion pounds' worth of economic activity brought to London through hotels, restaurants, shops, pubs, people coming to see Michael Jackson. It's the Michael Jackson economic stimulus package." AEG Live was now out of pocket nearly $30 million and its commitments to the O2 concerts amounted to a good deal more than that. As the preparations for the staging of the show in London mounted toward a climax, Randy Phillips was relieved to hear from his director that the star of the show at least appeared to have a clear vision of what he wanted to achieve at the O2.

All along, Kenny Ortega said, he and Michael had imagined the O2 concerts as a Broadway musical on a giant scale. He wanted to make his initial appearance onstage in a number constructed around "Wanna Be Startin' Somethin'," Michael told Ortega, and "I don't want to hold anything back. I want this to be the most spectacular opening the audience has ever seen. They have to ask themselves, 'How are they going to top that?' I don't even care if they're applauding. I want their jaws on the ground. I want them to not be able to sleep because they are so amped up from what they saw."

The enormous stage for the "This Is It" concerts was being designed and built by Michael Cotton, who had designed the sets for the *HIStory* tour, in close collaboration with Bruce Jones, whose visual effects for *The Spirit* had impressed Michael, even though the film was widely regarded as a failure. Jones and Cotton, plus lighting designer Peter Morse and art director Bernt Capra, were filling the four biggest soundstages at the Culver Studios (235-feet-by-150-feet-by-45-feet tall—the same stages used to create the burning of Atlanta in *Gone with the Wind*) with, among other things, the largest LED screen ever assembled: 100 feet wide. The screen was to provide a background of 3-D videos for the O2 shows that would run throughout the concert, designed to create a hologram effect by blending seamlessly with the real sets and the live dancers performing in front of them so that, during the "Thriller" number, "live" wolves and ravens would be running through and flying around a cemetery set that Capra had populated with mummies, zombies, and a decomposed pirate.

The crew had been given five weeks to make the transition from conceptual design to working set, an overwhelming task that left, as Capra put it, "no margin for error." Integrating elements that were not only physically immense but also at the extreme edge of technology required degrees of both exactitude and flexibility that had never before been demanded of anyone involved in the production. The stage at the O2 Arena would have to be equipped to accommodate a cherry picker as tall as a two-story building that would be used to fly a spinning Michael Jackson through the air above his audience while a video and light show literally played inside his clothing—his costume made of a high-tech fabric rigged with circuitry. The stress of coordinating dozens of complex effects in such a tight window might have been unbearable if not for the fact that Michael seemed so confident they could pull it off, said Capra, who was collaborating with the star on restaging scenes from five Jackson music videos that stretched from the early 1980s to the late 1990s: "Thriller," "Smooth Criminal," "The Way You Make Me Feel," "They Don't Care About Us," and "Earth Song."

As was so often the case among those who worked with him for the first time, Capra had been bowled over by the level of Michael's intellectual and artistic literacy. He was stunned and delighted, the art director said, when Michael began their meeting on the "The Way You Make Me Feel" video with a dissertation on one of his favorite photographers, Lewis Hine, a social worker who had made his name during the Great Depression with photographs of young children working in mines and mills. He wanted to base both the set design and the choreography for "The Way You Make Me Feel" on the photos Hine had taken of men constructing steel beams for the Empire State Building, Michael explained: The whole thing should feel like it was happening among a group of workmen taking a lunch break atop a half-finished skyscraper.

Michael had showed up every day at the Culver Studios between June 1 and June 11 to shoot footage for what became known as the "Dome Project," the adaptation of the music videos he had worked out with Capra, plus a pair of short 3-D videos. One was "MJ Air," in which a 707 jet rolled into the frame just as a hole opened in the screen, allowing Michael to enter and board the jet, which then flew away. The other new video, "The Final Message," featured a young girl from an Amazon rain forest tribe embracing the Earth. Michael brought his three children to the set one day and sat them all in director's chairs to watch the scene from "Smooth Criminal" where he would be chased by the likes of Edward G. Robinson and Humphrey Bogart. "This is the first day that we've seen Daddy on a movie set," Paris told Kenny Ortega. At that moment, Ortega remembered, Michael walked over and asked, with real concern, if the kids were "behaving."

During the third week of June, Michael was working out his choreography with Travis Payne in two-a-day sessions, one held in the afternoon at the Carolwood chateau, the other in the evening at the Los Angeles Forum, where rehearsals for the O2 shows had been moved to give the performers more space. John Caswell, the co-owner of CenterStaging, said that the move to the Forum was due entirely to the enormous scale of the production. "By the time he left my facility, he had graduated through several studios and was on a soundstage taking up ten thousand square feet," Caswell explained—and even that wasn't big enough. It wasn't Michael Jackson's health or erratic attendance at rehearsals that had delayed the opening of the London concerts, Caswell insisted, but rather the stupendous nature of what the entertainer was attempting: "He was trying and succeeding in structuring the biggest, most spectacular live production ever seen . . . The show was getting so damn big, they couldn't finish it in time. That's why they had to delay."

There was still an ambient skepticism on the sidelines, of course, and plenty of cause for concern among the attorneys and accountants clustered around the preparations for the O2 shows. On June 12, AllGood Entertainment filed a $40 million lawsuit against Michael, AEG Live, and Frank Dileo, claiming that there had been multiple breaches of Jackson's "contract" to perform at a Jackson family reunion concert, including Michael's promise not to appear onstage anywhere else before that event or for three months after it. When AllGood's lead attorney told Britain's *Guardian* that the lawsuit could be settled by cutting the company in on the O2 shows, the newspaper rattled London with a headline on its article that read: "Michael Jackson Comeback Concerts in Jeopardy?"

Internet gossip columnists warned that Jackson was nowhere near ready to perform in London, and wondered if he was even really trying after Michael skipped rehearsals to spend the afternoons of June 9 and June 16 at Arnold Klein's office in Beverly Hills. Karen Faye would later say that Michael was "self-sabotaging" with drugs because he didn't believe he could do all fifty shows for AEG. Some of the most cold-eyed number crunchers involved with the O2 project, though, claimed to be impressed by the level of focus with which Michael was engaging the financial opportunities presented by his London concerts. During May, he had met with representatives of the Universal Music Group's merchandise division, Bravado, to sketch out designs for more than three hundred items—from jigsaw puzzles and children's games to leather handbags and rhinestone dog tags—that would be sold in conjunction with the "This Is It" concerts. "He really did understand the opportunity he had to repair his finances if he fulfilled his contract for the London shows," said one of the entertainment attorneys working with him that spring. Simply by performing all fifty concerts at the O2, Michael would stabilize his finances through the end of his contract with Sony, this lawyer was advising him. If he did a world tour, he could likely eradicate most, if not all, of his debt and regain control of the Beatles catalog. With a U.S. tour, he might once again aggregate a net worth of a billion dollars. "He got it, he really did," the attorney said. "I think he was ready to do what he had to do." Kenny Ortega agreed: "There are those out there who say, 'Michael didn't want to do "This Is It," he wasn't capable.' Michael didn't just want to do it—his attitude was, 'We *have* to do it.'" After nearly two solid decades of ridicule and excoriation over his lawsuits and plastic surgeries, his sham marriages and sperm donor–sired children—not to mention the molestation allegations against him—Jackson's excitement about the London shows "was giving him back something that had been sucked out of him," Ortega said, "his dignity as an artist."

Marc Schaffel and Dieter Wiesner remained "out there" among the doubters: "Just because Michael knew something was good for him didn't mean he'd do it," Schaffel said. "Performing the same songs the same way, night after night, Michael would be very unhappy," Wiesner observed. "He didn't like to do what he had done already. I know he was mad at them for making him."

After his visit to Arnold Klein's offices on June 16, Michael again skipped rehearsal. Frank Dileo already had suggested to a fretting Randy Phillips that they reassemble the "old team" by inviting John Branca back aboard as Michael's entertainment attorney. "I'm pretty sure Dileo wanted to bring Branca in as a way of protecting himself," said one of the attorneys that was being pushed out the door. "He knew he had some legal exposure here, and not just from the AllGood deal. Dileo was planning to take the entire AEG commission and that was a deal Tohme had done. But if he brought Branca in, he had to figure John would help protect him. I mean, John wasn't going to be taking an hourly fee. He was going to take his five percent commission and make a big killing. He would owe Frank."

Branca's recollection was that Dileo had phoned him in late May to say, "Michael wants you to come back. He wants you to give some thought to what you can do for him, what kind of deals." He spent three weeks drafting an "agenda" that detailed his plans for a concert movie, books, and assorted merchandising deals, Branca said, then drove to the Forum on the evening of June 17 to present it to Michael during a break in rehearsals. At least five years had passed since the two men had seen each other, and their reunion was "very emotional," as Branca recalled it: "We hugged each other. He said, 'John, you're back.'" Branca's account sounded more than a little strange to people who had heard Michael repeatedly denounce Branca as a devil in recent years.

Tohme claimed that Michael had made it overwhelmingly clear he did not trust Branca. The attorney had arranged to be introduced to Jackson's new manager by Randy Phillips at the 2009 Grammy Awards ceremony, and afterward Branca phoned to arrange a lunch meeting, Tohme said. When he told his client about it, though, "Michael told me I had to cancel the lunch. He said, 'You can't have anything to do with Branca. I don't want him near me.'"

Michael Amir Williams, who by the middle of April 2009 was almost exclusively handling the details of Jackson's business affairs, said he never once heard the name John Branca, and was not aware of any meetings with the attorney or communications with him of any kind.

Whatever the arrangement was between Branca and Dileo, picturing Michael Jackson flanked by the two men who had steered the entertainer's affairs during the most financially successful period of his (or any other artist's) career was reassuring to Randy Phillips and the executives at AEG Live, who also encouraged the hiring of Michael's former accountant, Barry Siegel. AEG execs were distraught, though, when Jackson failed to show for rehearsal on the evening of June 18. Randy Phillips was furious when he received an e-mail from Kenny Ortega suggesting that if the star of the show wasn't going to come to rehearsals it might be time they "pulled the plug." Phillips drove to the Carolwood chateau for a meeting in which he demanded, in the presence of Dr. Murray, that Michael stop seeing Dr. Klein and stop taking any drugs that Klein had provided. It was almost ten p.m. when Michael arrived at the Forum looking "very shaky," as one person who was present put it.

The frustration of the AEG executives now extended to Ortega. Only a couple of weeks earlier, during "The Dome Project" shoot, the director had told them that Jackson appeared to be responding to the pressure of a deadline by accelerating the pace of his preparations, and that his focus was sharpening as the cast and crew prepared for the move to London. Now, though, Ortega said he was watching Michael go off the rails again. He was seeing "strong signs of paranoia, anxiety, and obsessive-like behavior," Ortega wrote to Phillips, adding "it is like there are two people there. One (deep inside) trying to hold on to what he was and still can be and not wanting us to quit on him, the other in this weakened and troubled state."

The show's music director Michael Bearden advised AEG that, "MJ is not in shape enough yet to sing this stuff live and dance at the same time." Production manager John Hougdahl wrote after he watched Jackson stumble and mumble through a rehearsal at the Forum, "He was a basket case. Doubt is pervasive."

Scores of other observers on the scene, though, had maintained all along that Michael Jackson wasn't either strong enough or sane enough to pull off a comeback at this stage of his life. Michael's physical health was the main concern of those who actually cared about him. He had been losing weight at an alarming rate since the announcement of the O2 shows in London, and those who hadn't watched it happen gradually were especially startled when they saw him for the first time after several months. Michael's filmmaker friend Bryan Michael Stoller was one of them. Stoller and Jackson had become friends twenty years earlier after Jackson saw *The Shadow of Michael*, the young director's short-film parody of the infamous 1984 Pepsi commercial. Stoller had paid his last visit to Michael just before the beginning of May, and recalled that when he greeted his old friend, "It was like hugging bones. After seeing him, I never thought he would complete the tour." From the high of 157 pounds he had reached at the time of the announcement of the AEG deal, Michael's weight fell as low as 130 pounds that spring. "We did talk a lot about his weight," Kenny Ortega admitted. "We would always try to get him to eat something, but he said, 'I'm a dancer and this is how I like to feel.'" Michael showed Ortega photographs of Fred Astaire at the height of his career, pointing out that his old friend Fred had been just as thin back then as he was now. Newspapers reported that Ortega was literally fork-feeding Jackson his chicken and broccoli dinners. "It's not true," the director said. "I would unwrap his plate and slide it over in front of him. But I didn't feed him."

Also back in the picture were that pair of powerhouse women Tom Mesereau had tried to warn his client about back in 2005; Raymone Bain and Grace Rwaramba. Bain and her Washington, D.C., attorneys had attempted to take advantage of Michael's absorption in preparing for the O2 shows and long-standing inattention to legal affairs by filing a ten-day notice of application for a default judgment at the federal courthouse in Washington, D.C. With just forty-eight hours left on the ticking clock, a team of three attorneys from the New York offices of Dewey and LeBoeuf appeared in court pro hac vice alongside a D.C.-based colleague to inform the judge hearing the case that a response to Bain's suit would be entered before the deadline passed. Among the many ironies of the day's legal drama was that the attorney Michael had put in charge of dealing with Bain was Londell McMillan, the same lawyer that Raymone herself had brought in to represent Michael (in the Marc Schaffel case, among others) more than two years earlier. Once the default judgment motion was set aside, Bain's only real hope for a payoff would be to harrow or exhaust Michael into a settlement that saved him the cost of defeating her in court. And Raymone's friend McMillan was the very attorney who had counseled Michael against settling cases on that basis, urging his famous client to battle every one of them through to a jury verdict.

Grace Rwaramba had been given formal notice of her dismissal as the nanny to Michael's children in early April, when she received a letter signed by Paul Gongaware that read: "It is with regret that I must inform you that your employment with Michael Jackson will be terminated as of Monday, April 20, 2009 . . . In an effort to try to reduce the impact of this termination, the company has worked out a severance arrangement that will pay you a final sum of $20,000." Shocked and angry, Grace had accepted an invitation from "celebrity interviewer" Daphne Barak to sojourn at Barak's expense in London. For that hospitality, plus an undisclosed fee, Grace had agreed to spend several days spilling secrets in a series of interviews (some videotaped) that painted her former employer as a drug-addled incompetent so lost in a chemical haze that he really believed his contract with AEG Live was for ten shows at the O2 Arena, not fifty. "He didn't know what he was signing," Rwaramba told Barak. "He never did." At the same time, Michael was impossibly controlling, Grace told the interviewer, and did all he could to prevent her from developing a relationship with anyone who was important to him. While they were staying in New Jersey with the Cascios, "I tried to develop a friendship with Frank's mother, just to tell them thank you, but when Michael saw we were getting friendly he said, 'Don't trust her. She is not interested in you. She just talks to you because of me.'" Grace was even scoffing at Michael's image as a doting father. She and she alone had provided the three kids with a stable and loving environment, Grace told Barak: "I took those babies in my arms on the first day of each of their lives. They are *my* babies . . . I used to hug and laugh with them. But when Michael was around they froze." The nanny described an afternoon when Blanket had put on a concert of Michael Jackson songs, singing and dancing for her and the two older children. "I was laughing so hard. Prince and Paris were playing around. It was such a happy moment. Then suddenly Michael walked in. He surprised us. Usually, the security would alert me that he was about to come. Blanket immediately stopped. The kids looked frightened. Michael was so angry. I knew I would be fired. Whenever the children got too attached to me, he would send me away."

Any number of times during the months they lived in Las Vegas, Grace said, she had been forced to keep the children away from their father so they wouldn't see the pathetic state he was reduced to by his drug addiction. In the weeks after she was first ordered out of the Carolwood chateau at the end of 2008, Rwaramba went on, she regularly received distress signals from security guards and other members of the staff concerned about Michael and the kids: "These poor babies . . . I was getting phone calls that they were being neglected. Nobody was cleaning the rooms because Michael didn't pay the housekeeper. I was getting calls telling me Michael was in such bad shape. He wasn't clean. He hadn't shaved. He wasn't eating well. I used to do all this for him, and they were trying to get me to go back." Without her, their former nanny lamented, those three kids were essentially alone in the world, and so was their father, even if he didn't realize it.

Friends who ranged from Deepak Chopra's daughter Mallika to Marc Schaffel would insist later that Grace had been "tricked" into giving Barak those interviews. "Daphne is a vulture," Schaffel said. "She waits and watches to see who is in trouble." The Israeli-born, British-based Barak was a determined and resourceful vulture, though, one who over the years had induced women as varied as Hillary Clinton, Mother Teresa, and

Benazir Bhutto to speak into her microphone. Giving Barak the time of day made you a "dear friend" in her self-flattering autobiography, and the list of famous people she counted among her intimates was pages long. Back in 2003, Barak had persuaded Jackson's parents to cooperate with her (for a substantial fee, of course) on a documentary broadcast in the UK (part of it aired in the United States on CBS) under the title *Our Son: Michael Jackson*. Barak and Joe Jackson followed Michael around for weeks, attempting to get him to speak to Barak on camera. "I had to have her kicked out of the lobby of the Mandalay Bay in Las Vegas when she showed up with Joe," Schaffel recalled. "She had offered him money to get an interview with Michael, and refused to go away when Michael said he wasn't going to do it. He didn't want anybody to talk to Daphne about him, and was very upset when he found out his parents had taken her money to do it anyway."

Michael would have been even more upset to learn that Rwaramba— who knew far more about the past fifteen years of his life than his parents ever would—had done the same thing. Grace's stay with Daphne Barak went undetected, however, and the ex-nanny began telling people that she and Michael were back in business. "In late May, Grace sent a message through a mutual friend that she wanted my new phone number," Schaffel recalled. "She said Michael wanted to speak with me. I said, 'Of course.' But it was Grace who called. She said she was in London looking for a house for Michael that she was going to help set up for him."

The escalating intensity of the demands that he prepare for the London shows had, among other things, worsened Michael's insomnia. His obsessive-compulsive tendencies were always exacerbated by pressure, and what would preoccupy him was never predictable. Around the middle of June, he began to make phone calls in the night to talk for hours on end about apocalyptic imagery from the Bible and its associations with predictions of the world's end in 2012 that had been extrapolated from the ancient Mayan calendar. "We only have a little time left," he kept saying.

What made slumber even more difficult for Michael as the move to London approached was that his stress was now shot through with an accelerant of excitement. He was simply, as Frank Dileo put it, "too wound up" to turn off his thoughts when he got into bed. "I didn't get much sleep last night," was Michael's constant refrain even after he began attending rehearsals regularly. His principal creative collaborators, Kenny Ortega and Travis Payne, both suffered from insomnia themselves and so were less troubled than others might have been by Michael's calls at three or four in the morning to talk through the ideas that had come to him during yet another sleepless night. Such middle-of-the-night conversations seemed to him a normal part of being "immersed in the process," Payne said: "That was when we'd be able to get a lot done because the phones weren't ringing and we didn't have a schedule." Ortega offered a more ethereal memory of Michael's predawn phone calls: "He would say, 'I'm channeling. I'm writing music and ideas are coming to me and I can't turn it off.'"

Over time, though, even Ortega grew concerned about the noticeable drop in his star's energy level on the days when Michael reported to rehearsals—or, more often, failed to report—complaining that he hadn't slept the night before. Maybe he should "hold off" working on writing new songs until after they opened in London, the show's director suggested. "He would say when the information was coming, when the idea was coming, it was a blessing," Ortega recalled, "and he couldn't turn his back on a blessing . . . I would say to him, 'Can't you make a little pact with your higher power to have this put on the shelf for you until a later date? We need you healthy. We need you nourished.' He'd laugh at me and say no. 'When they come, you have to be ready for them and you have to take advantage of them when they're there. Or they won't be yours.'"

After a few hours of tossing in his bed at home, though, the star wasn't so sanguine about his sleeplessness. Michael turned to his old friend from the *HIStory* tour Dr. Allan Metzger, pleading for "some form of an anesthetic," as the doctor recalled it. Metzger sympathized, having learned from the time they spent together on tour that after the high of a performance Michael simply "could not come down." Sleep medications that were fine for other people simply did not work for Michael Jackson, Metzger would explain. During a meeting at the Carolwood chateau, Dr. Metzger remembered, Michael had attempted to sway him by explaining how "fearful" he was that the O2 concerts would fail because he wasn't well rested enough to perform the way he needed to in London. Metzger, though, by his account, would write a prescription only for what the doctor's attorney later described as "a mild sleeping pill." When Arnold Klein also refused to prescribe anything beyond sedatives, painkillers, and muscle relaxants, Michael began seeing a second plastic surgeon, Dr. Larry Koplin, hoping that the nurse who administered anesthesia in Koplin's office would help him obtain propofol. That effort, too, apparently failed.

He was getting getting plenty of other drugs, though, from somewhere. Michael appeared "groggy and out of it," as one witness put it, when, after nearly a full week's absence, he showed up for rehearsals on the evening of June 19. "He didn't look well," Kenny Ortega would testify later. "Michael was chilled and soft-spoken . . . He wasn't in the kind of condition to be at rehearsal." AEG executives were infuriated again when "This Is It" site coordinator John Hougdahl sent an e-mail to Phillips and Gongaware on the evening of June 19 telling them that Jackson had been sent home because he "was a basket case and Kenny was concerned he would embarrass himself onstage, or worse yet—get hurt." Ortega was at once graphic and distraught in the e-mail he sent to Phillips a short time later to describe Michael's condition: "He appeared quite weak and fatigued this evening. He had a terrible case of the chills, was trembling, rambling, and obsessing . . . I was told by our choreographer that during the artist's costume fitting with his designer tonight they noticed he's lost more weight." He had personally wrapped Michael in blankets and massaged his feet to calm him down, Ortega wrote Phillips, and was truly concerned that Michael might be slipping into a downward spiral.

According to one person in a position to know, AEG's executives were unhappy that Ortega had instructed Michael to just go home and come back when he was ready to work. "We have a real problem here," Randy Phillips wrote to Tim Leiweke. After conferring with his bosses, Phillips told Frank Dileo to make sure his client understood what was at stake, reminding him of language in the contract that required Michael Jackson to put on a "first-class performance" in London while maintaining a "positive public perception." Phillips also got Conrad Murray on the phone and told the doctor he needed to keep a closer watch on his patient. Michael needed to be kept away from Arnold Klein, Phillips told Murray and kept off whatever drugs Klein was giving him. Dileo left a voice mail on Murray's iPhone in which he told the physician, "I'm sure you are aware he had an episode last night. He's sick. I think you need to get a blood test on him. We got to see what he's doing."

Ortega, though, thought Michael might need a different kind of doctor. "My concern is now that we've . . . played the tough-love, now-or-never card is that the artist may be unable to rise to the occasion due to real emotional stuff . . . everything in me says he should be psychologically evaluated," the director warned Phillips. "It's going to take a strong therapist as well as immediate physical nurturing to help him through this." He was concerned that there was apparently no one taking care of Michael Jackson "on a daily basis," Ortega wrote to Phillips: "There were four security guards outside his door, but no one offering him a cup of hot tea."

He thought it was "important for everyone to know" that Michael truly wanted the O2 shows to happen, Ortega ended his e-mail to Phillips. "It would shatter him, break his heart if we pulled the plug. He's terribly frightened it's all going to go away. He asked me repeatedly tonight if I was going to leave him. He was practically begging for my confidence. It broke my heart. He was like a lost boy. There still may be a chance he can rise to the occasion if we get him the help he needs."

Back in his bedroom at the Carolwood chateau, Michael made more of the early morning phone calls that had become almost a ritual during the past couple of weeks. "He kept telling people he was saying good-bye," Arnold Klein's office manager Jason Pfeiffer recalled. "Everyone was creeped out by it."

Even Michael's daughter was becoming concerned about him. It seemed strange to her that Daddy always had a big fire going, even on the warmest days, Paris would explain later. She and the new nanny, Sister Rose, would come into a room where he was sitting and "it would be so hot," the girl recalled, but Daddy would keep saying he was cold, that he couldn't get warm.

Cherilyn Lee was convinced that Michael had secured a supply of propofol after she received a phone call from the Carolwood chateau on the evening of June 21, just as the "This Is It" cast was about to begin full dress rehearsals at the Staples Center in Los Angeles. According to Lee, the caller was a member of Jackson's staff who said that Michael needed to see her right away. "I could hear Michael in the background: 'Tell her. Tell her that one side of my body is hot, it's hot, and one side of my body is cold, it's very cold,'" Lee remembered. "I knew somebody had given him something that hit the central nervous system." You have to get him to the hospital, the nurse told the man who had phoned her. Michael wouldn't do it, the caller replied. Why should I go to the hospital when I have my own doctor on call? Michael wanted to know.

Conrad Murray had been spending nights at the Carolwood chateau since at least May 12, 2009, the date the physician had used a Visa card to pay $865 (plus $65 for FedEx shipping) to Applied Pharmacy Services in Las Vegas for a supply of Diprivan in 20-milliliter and 100-milliliter bottles. Included in the May 12 package sent to Los Angeles were three vials of antianxiety sedatives from the benzodiazepine family, plus a vial of Flumazenil, an "antidote" to the benzos that could counteract their effects in case of an overdose. During the next few weeks, Murray would make several more purchases of Diprivan from the Las Vegas pharmacy, gradually collecting enough propofol (some of it in 1,000-milliliter bottles) to last well into the London concert series.

According to Dr. Murray, he spent six weeks using an IV to feed 50 milligrams of Diprivan into Jackson's veins after the performer returned home from rehearsals, enough to let Michael "sleep" (it's more accurate to describe patients under propofol as unconscious than as asleep, anesthesiologists say) for at least a few hours, then wake up feeling not just rested, but actually exhilarated. Kai Chase, Michael's chef, would say she knew nothing about any sleep medications, but did see Dr. Murray carry a pair of oxygen canisters downstairs each day after his morning consultation with Mr. Jackson in the master bedroom. Oxygen is one of the two medical gases (nitrous oxide being the other) that are commonly mixed with anesthesia in continuous-flow machines during surgeries.

The degree to which Murray had assumed control of all decisions being made about Michael Jackson's physical well-being was evident to Kenny Ortega and Randy Phillips when they showed up for a meeting on June 20 that the doctor had demanded. Dr. Murray insisted that Michael was "physically and emotionally fine," Ortega remembered, and seemed infuriated by the decision to send Michael home from rehearsal on the previous evening: "He said I should stop trying to be an amateur doctor and psychologist and be the director, and leave Michael's health to him."

He was reassured when Dr. Murray "guaranteed us that Michael would get into it," recalled Phillips, who sent out an e-mail that afternoon in which he expressed his confidence in Murray, "who I am gaining immense respect for as I get to deal with him more."

"This doctor is extremely successful (we check everyone out) and does not need this gig," Phillips added, "so he [is] totally unbiased and ethical."

23

The last ten days of rehearsals in Los Angeles had been shifted to the Staples Center because even the Forum didn't have enough ceiling height to accommodate the production's gargantuan scale. According to Kenny Ortega, Michael Jackson responded to the move with a determined effort to demonstrate that he could still, as the show director had put it, "rise to the occasion."

Just three nights after an exasperated Ortega had sent him home, Michael arrived at the Staples Center for the first full dress rehearsal of the O2 show, on the evening of June 22, "in this new kind of place," the director recalled, and his enthusiasm was infectious. Suddenly "everyone was just kind of believing," Ortega said. "I think there was this feeling in the room, in the air, we all could feel it, like we were on a plane. 'We're packed, we're going.' You could see London, we could smell it, we were ready."

They had all seen the mercury in Michael's personality during the past few weeks, moments when he was illuminated by a flash of insight and expected that his dancers and musicians get it without a great deal of explanation. He might coax them at first, but turned insistent within moments, flashing his temper when one of the performers frustrated his demand for an adjustment in tempo, or pouting and stalking off when another answered his instructions with a look of incomprehension. But now, a little more than a week before they were scheduled to leave for London, Michael seemed suddenly to love everything he saw and heard. "Beautiful, beautiful," he kept telling people.

Watching it all through the lens of her camera, Sandrine Orabona was entranced by the sense of communion that enveloped Michael, his musicians, and the dancers as they worked out their performance of "Human Nature." A strange but beautiful intimacy appeared to have developed among all the performers, the videographer remembered. Everything onstage started moving at lightning speed and people began to speak in what Orabona described as "creative shorthand," so focused that they could understand each other completely with only a couple of words and a gesture. When Michael told the musicians, "Make it sound like you're dragging yourself out of bed," they all seemed to know exactly what he meant and "were spot on," the videographer recalled. The atmosphere on the stage that evening, Kenny Ortega would say later, became a kind of shared breath in which the entire production team understood exactly what would be possible when they took the stage in London. "Everyone in a Michael Jackson show is an extension of Michael Jackson," Ortega had shouted at the dancers any number of times during rehearsals, and now it was as if they had known all along precisely what he meant.

On the following evening, June 23, Tohme Tohme showed up at the Staples Center to make his first-ever visit to rehearsals for the London shows. Ten days earlier, Tohme and Katherine Jackson had met at the Coffee Bean on San Vicente Boulevard in Brentwood. Tohme's claim was that Mrs. Jackson wanted the meeting to tell him that Michael was deteriorating physically and to beg him to intervene. Mrs. Jackson's story was that Tohme was asking her to help him get his job back. She had never liked the man, Michael's mother said, ever since he had insisted that her grandchildren who were living in the Lindley Avenue condo should pay rent on the place. Whoever was telling the truth about the Coffee Bean meeting, what was certain was that Tohme hadn't seen his erstwhile client face-to-face in five weeks. And was horrified, Tohme said, when Michael ran forward to wrap him in an embrace: "I felt his bones. I was shocked to see the weight he had lost. I asked him, 'Michael, what's happening with you?'" Michael just laughed off the question about his weight, and went back to rehearsals. Only minutes later, though, he pulled Tohme aside to complain tearfully that, "They're torturing me." He asked what was wrong, Tohme recalled, "and all Michael told me is that they're asking him to put things in his ears. He hates things in his ears—the microphone, you know, he doesn't like that." It felt like someone sticking a fist in his ear, Michael said, but they wouldn't let him take it out. "I said, 'Michael, just don't wear it if you don't want to. You are the star.' But he said, 'They're making me.'" Within moments, though, Michael was back onstage performing, and looked as if there was nothing at all bothering him. "It was confusing," Tohme recalled.

Tohme would say later that whatever doubts he harbored about his own status were soothed by that visit to the Staples Center. Randy Phillips introduced him to everyone as "Dr. Tohme, Michael's manager," and placed a bracelet around his wrist that would allow Tohme access to the Staples Center rehearsals any time he wanted to show up. At one point,

Michael waved to Frank Dileo and said, "Come here and give your boss a hug." Dileo responded by walking away, and Tohme asked Randy Phillips, "What's that guy doing here?" They kept Dileo around, Phillips answered, according to Tohme, "because he makes Michael laugh."

When Michael returned to the Carolwood chateau that evening, there was already an IV drip set up in his bedroom. Dr. Conrad Murray would claim later that he had grown concerned about fostering a propofol addiction in Jackson, and was especially bothered by hearing Michael refer to the white liquid Diprivan solution as "my milk." He had decided that Jackson should be "weaned" from his reliance on propofol, Murray said, and sometime after midnight, gave Jackson a Diprivan dosage of 25 milligrams—just half of what Michael had been taking—then supplemented it with two of the prescription sedatives that had come in a package delivered from Las Vegas. It was enough, Murray claimed, to let the performer sleep until after the sun rose the next morning.

On June 24, 2009, Michael arrived at the Staples Center at about 6:30 p.m. for a meeting with Randy Phillips, Tim Leiweke, and Grammy Awards show producer Ken Ehrlich. Frank Dileo sat in, listening with Phillips and Leiweke as Jackson and Ehrlich discussed their ideas for a Halloween television special that would incorporate clips from Michael's live performance of "Thriller" at the O2 Arena into the network premiere of his film *Ghosts*. Phillips's promise of support for Michael's attempt to create a career in movies, the AEG executives knew, had been a major motivator in winning his agreement to the O2 concerts; the airing of *Ghosts* would satisfy that promise in a big way.

The understanding that a success in London was going to reinvigorate Michael Jackson's career across the board—as a live performer, as a recording artist, as a filmmaker, and as a cultural phenomenon—seemed at last to be sinking in, Phillips thought. Michael was humming with excitement as he left his meeting with Ehrlich to spend the next hour reviewing the 3-D effects for the "This Is It" shows. What the production team had done with the music videos of the Dome Project had him giddy with excitement. Michael's idealism and his vainglory each would be on full display in this series of "short films." But what the fans would wildly love was certain to invite an equal measure of derision from his critics.

Those who mocked him could be counted on to sneer at a montage that placed Michael among a parade of his icons: Princess Diana, Mother

Teresa—and now the face of Barack Obama. Anyone with an even slight sense of perspective could only squirm while imagining what the likes of Jarvis Cocker might say about the eleven hundred CGI soldiers who would march down the Champs-Élysées to the tune of "They Don't Care About Us" before arriving at an Arc de Triomphe that had been bent into an *M* shape. Jackson-lovers and Jacko-haters were certain to be polarized by the effects that would accompany Michael's performance of "Earth Song," the spiritual centerpiece of the "This Is It" show. The song would end with a recapitulation of that famous man-versus-tank scene from Tiananmen Square, only at the O2 it would be a dewy young native girl facing down a bulldozer in the Amazon rain forest—soon to be replaced by Saint Michael standing up for her against the villains of corporate pillage. On the other hand, the 3-D effects that would be incorporated into "Thriller" were going to flood the arena with adrenaline, and the sight of Michael in his white pinstriped suit dashing through the reworked video for "Smooth Criminal"—dodging a come-hither look from Rita Hayworth's Gilda in one frame and ducking a Humphrey Bogart scowl in another—was both electrifying and hilarious.

"I want people to scream for miles!" he had told Ed Alonzo, the magician-comedian that had been hired to help him stage the two big set-piece illusions of the London shows. Jackson was delighted by what he and Alonzo had come up with for the introduction to the concert's opening number, "Wanna Be Startin' Somethin'." As Michael stood on the darkened stage, a luminous glass globe would hover in the air, then float all around his spacesuit-encased body before flying out above the audience, growing steadily brighter as it zoomed over the heads of the fans then spun back toward the stage, skimming across the floor before it climbed again and landed in Michael's open palm, exploding into incandescence as it disappeared from sight. The other piece of stagecraft Alonzo had created was a prelude to Michael's performance of "Dirty Diana." The stunt was to take place on and around a flaming mattress. Michael would be pursued about the bed by a pole-dancing aerialist "fire woman" who would raise a burst of "flames" (fluttering strips of scarlet and crimson fabric) each time she touched the stage. She would catch her prey eventually, of course, and then, leering, use her golden ropes to lash Michael like an unwilling partner to the tall posts of the bed. A semisheer sheet of billowing red fabric would fall over the scene, allowing the audience to see only Michael's struggling silhouette until finally the red sheet fell—revealing the fire woman as the one tied to the bed, just as Michael materialized in the center of the stage, standing alone.

A planned practice session for the magic acts would be postponed until the next evening, but Alonzo was still waiting and watching when Jackson finished his chicken and broccoli dinner and took the stage at just about nine p.m. on the evening of the twenty-fourth. Michael complained that he had laryngitis, Alonzo remembered, and people glanced at one another, wondering if he was joking. There was no sign that he was ill when Michael began what turned into a run-through of the numbers he would perform at the O2. "He looked great and had great energy," Alonzo recalled. "He wasn't singing at full level, but it was as beautiful as ever."

To what degree sweet emotions or wishful thinking—or even self-interest—might have colored the memories of those who were present in the Staples Center that night is impossible to gauge. Still, there was a persuasive unanimity in the recollections of witnesses.

"Bioluminescent," was the word Kenny Ortega used to describe the Michael Jackson he saw on the stage at Staples.

"He came onstage and was electric," agreed the show's lighting designer Patrick Woodroffe.

"It was fantastic, he was so great," said Randy Phillips.

"I watched in awe," said Michael's personal photographer Kevin Mazur. "Every track he sang sounded terrific. Michael was back and in real style."

"The hair on the back of my neck stood up," Ken Ehrlich said. "I wasn't watching Justin Timberlake or Chris Brown or Usher or any of the hundreds of acts that have taken from Michael, the modern inheritors of his art. It was *him*."

During Michael's performance of "Billie Jean," Sandrine Orabona would recall, "I turn the camera around and it's like fifteen crew and dancers on the floor [standing and] watching, and they can't believe what they are seeing."

"We all looked at each other and there was something that said he really had it," Woodroffe remembered. "It was like he had been holding back, and suddenly he was performing as one had remembered him in the past."

"I honestly could not wait to see the show," Mazur chimed in.

Ehrlich alone leavened his recollections of Michael's performance with something that resembled objective reporting: "What I saw that night was a person who was still in the process of learning the show. I watched Kenny Ortega walk him through some stage directions. I know his method and there's a certain reticence when he's not in full makeup and wardrobe . . . I've seen him in rehearsal mode several times over the years. Michael is extremely methodical. He's not going to give it all until he knows he's got it all. But sometimes he'd jump into it, and it was really exciting.

As he got more comfortable with the props and where the dancers were, he got more animated . . . He wasn't giving it full out, but vocally he had started to really project."

For several others, the most impressive thing about Michael's passage through the songs he would perform in London, from the opening salvo of "Wanna Be Startin' Somethin'" right on through the show's closer, "Man in the Mirror," was that he never hesitated. "He didn't even take a moment to grab a bottle of water or take a rest," remembered Ed Alonzo. "He went from one number to another." According to Ken Ehrlich, Michael "performed virtually nonstop for two hours and ran through about a dozen greatest hits. He stopped just a couple of times to tweak arrangements and work on moves with dancers."

Michael did pause once for a few minutes to inspect the props that would be employed during his performance of "Thriller" at the O2, and was especially taken with the giant spiders Bernt Capra had created for him. Then he went right on to the next number.

The most transcendent moment of the evening, those who were there would say, was Michael's rendition of "Earth Song." He had placed his own composition at the very heart of the program he planned for London, and intended it to be the climax of the concert. His performance of "Earth Song" *was* the climax of that last rehearsal, according to the people present in the Staples Center, the one moment of the evening when Michael truly cut loose and gave full voice. The homiletic lyrics of "Earth Song" might easily have been dismissed (and were, by any number of critics) as cloying clichés, targeted to the sort of emotional manipulation that is the essence of sentimentality. Yet as he finished the song amid the sounds of crying whales and images of a ravaged rain forest, "We all had goose bumps," Randy Phillips said. "I had never seen such exultation in the cast and crew."

Everyone stood stunned for a while, Kenny Ortega remembered. Moments later, it seemed, the rehearsal was over, but no one wanted to break the spell by leaving: "When he finished, we all stayed there, just pressing around." Finally, as the other performers started to move offstage, he and his star stood out front, Ortega recalled, and "Michael said, 'This is the dream. We did it good, Kenny. We did it. Very good.'"

"There was this anticipation of tomorrow, this anticipation of London and this great feeling about what we'd accomplished over the past couple of nights," Ortega remembered. "He told me he was happy. He had nothing creatively or critically to say to anyone other than, 'I love you, thank you, everyone's doing a great job and I'll see you tomorrow.'"

It was after 12:30 a.m. when Michael began to make his way out of the arena. One of the producers stopped him to say thanks for all the work he'd done to finish the videos. A moment later, the man came running over to tell Ortega, "You won't believe what Michael just said to me: 'Make sure those ghosts come through the screen.'"

Randy Phillips walked Michael outside to his car. According to Phillips, "He put his arm around me and said to me in that kinda soft, lilting voice of his, he said, 'Thank you for getting me here. I got it now. I know I can do this. I'll take it from here.'"

Michael Jackson had left the Staples Center in Travis Payne's words "ec-static and excited." The sensations he carried with him out of the rehearsal were still charging Michael's nervous system at 1:30 a.m., when he began trying to settle down in his bedroom at the Carolwood chateau. Sleep would not come easily.

Dr. Conrad Murray, though, at least by his account, was determined to continue weaning Michael from his reliance on Diprivan. As he had the night before, Murray said, he decided to attempt a gradual induction of sleep in Michael without using any anesthesia at all. He began, the doctor said, with a tablet of diazepam, a benzodiazepine drug most commonly marketed as Valium. Diazepam is principally an antianxiety drug, though it is also used to treat insomnia and epileptic seizures, as well as muscle spasms, restless leg syndrome, and alcohol withdrawal. Valium is frequently administered to hospital patients who are about to undergo such relatively minor procedures as a colonoscopy, and is sometimes used before more major surgeries, not only to relax patients, but also because its hypnotic effects tend to induce a specific state of amnesia that permits people to forget what it was like to be cut open. It's a valuable drug, but also a highly addictive one. Symptoms of withdrawal from long-term use can include convulsions, tremors, and hallucinations.

Michael Jackson had been taking Valium regularly for almost a quarter-century, and the 10-milligram dose Dr. Murray claimed to have given him during the early morning hours of June 25 was not going to put this patient to sleep, at least not all by itself. In fact, according to Murray, the Valium had very little effect at all. At around 2 a.m., as he recalled, using the IV that was hooked up to his patient nightly, Dr. Murray gave Michael a slow injection of lorazepam, a stronger, fast-acting benzo that is most often marketed as Ativan. Like diazepam, lorazepam acts on the central nervous system and is employed mainly to treat anxiety but can also be used to ease insomnia or epileptic seizures. In hospitals, Ativan is regularly administered to patients doctors deem "aggressive." Its principal properties are classified as "sedative-hypnotic" and "anterograde amnesia," a medical description of the loss of the ability to form a new memory without affecting long-term recall. Ativan is even more effective than Valium at helping people forget unpleasant experiences. It's also even more addictive, and withdrawal from lorazepam can bring on not only insomnia and seizures, but also a full-blown (albeit temporary) psychosis. Kicking an Ativan addiction is a lot like withdrawing from long-term alcohol abuse, drug treatment specialists say. Also, using lorazepam over a lengthy period of time can actually increase anxiety in a person, not to mention inducing confusion, depression, dizziness (losing balance and falling are quite common), hyperactivity, hostility, agoraphobia, and suicidal thoughts. The 2 milligrams Dr. Murray said he shot into Michael Jackson's veins that morning was actually the minimum recommended dose for treating insomnia, though of course that didn't take into account the diazepam already in his system. "Polypharmacy" is the pejorative term that doctors use to describe such mixing of drugs.

At 3 a.m., Dr. Murray remembered, he administered another "slow push" through the IV, this time sending the benzodiazepine drug midazolam (the specific brand name was Versed) into Jackson's veins. Midazolam is stronger than lorazepam and considerably more potent than diazepam. The hypnotic and amnesic effects are each more powerful. Rectal administration of midazolam has become a preferred treatment for children suffering seizures because it is so fast-acting and so effective at erasing all memory of a disturbing event. Midazolam is also more dangerous than either diazepam or lorazepam, however, and has caused both respiratory and cardiac failures that have resulted in patient deaths, as well as cases of hypoxic encephalopathy, an interruption in the supply of oxygen to the brain that can result in permanent damage. Manufacturers as well as medical associations strongly urge that midazolam not be used outside a hospital setting where resuscitative drugs are readily available, and that patients who have received it by injection be constantly monitored by their doctors. The recommended initial dose of midazolam is 1 or 2 milligrams. According to Dr. Murray, he gave Michael Jackson 2 milligrams.

"Four o'clock came and four o'clock went, and he was still awake," Conrad Murray would explain to a police investigator later. "And he complained, 'I got to sleep, Dr. Conrad. I have these rehearsals to perform. I must be ready for the show in England.'"

By 5 a.m. Michael was tossing and moaning, insisting again and again he had to get some sleep. "He said, 'Please, please give [me] some milk so that I can sleep, because I know that this is all that really works for me,'" Dr. Murray recalled. Again he refused to give his patient propofol, the doctor said, and instead administered another 2 milligrams of Ativan in a slow push through the IV. Michael still couldn't sleep.

The sun had already been up for more than an hour at 7:30 a.m. Michael was by then in an agony of sleeplessness, according to Dr. Murray, who claimed to have given him one more IV injection, this time pushing another 2 milligrams of Versed into his patient's veins. He remained at Jackson's bedside after this, Murray would claim, constantly monitoring his patient's condition with a device called a pulse oximeter connected to Michael's index finger that provided a steady readout of his pulse rate and oxygen levels.

Even by Dr. Murray's account, his patient by then had a combination of drugs in his system that would have put even those with the hardiest drug tolerances to sleep for hours—perhaps forever. Michael Jackson, though, was still wide awake and begging for his "milk." At 10:40 a.m., Murray said, he told Michael that he would need to wake up around noon. Michael again demanded propofol. "He said, 'Just make me sleep, doesn't matter what time I get up,'" Murray recalled. He finally gave in, the doctor said, feeding 25 milligrams of Diprivan into Jackson's IV. Michael closed his eyes, his breathing slowed, and he went to sleep—technically he was unconscious—just moments after the propofol entered his bloodstream.

Conrad Murray was already in trouble with the law at that moment. The Clark County district attorney's office in Las Vegas had filed a case against the doctor for his failure to pay back child support two weeks earlier on June 10. His legal jeopardy would magnify exponentially during the next few hours.

He waited at Michael Jackson's bedside, reading the pulse oximeter, for about ten more minutes, Dr. Murray later told the police, before deciding at about 10:50 a.m. that he could permit himself a brief bathroom break. A public record that includes the recollections of other witnesses calls into question nearly every one of Murray's claims about what happened from this point forward, but the doctor's story (according to police) was that he returned to the master bedroom of the Carolwood chateau after an absence of only about two minutes and discovered Michael Jackson was no longer breathing. That claim would leave Murray trying to explain how nearly another ninety minutes passed before a 911 call was made. His attorney Ed Chernoff would later insist that the police misunderstood, that Dr. Murray did not discover that Michael Jackson had stopped breathing until nearly an hour after he returned to the master bedroom.

What can be known for certain is that Conrad Murray made three cell phone calls between 11:18 a.m. and 11:51 a.m. on the morning of June 25, 2009. The first was to his medical clinic in Las Vegas and lasted thirty-two minutes. The second was to leave a recorded message in a very calm, somewhat exhausted-sounding voice for a patient named Bob Russell: "Just wanted to talk to you about your results of the EECP. You did quite well on the study. We would love to continue to see you as a patient, even though I may have to be absent from my practice for—uh . . . because of an overseas sabbatical." The final call was to a Houston cocktail waitress named Sade Anding. Dr. Murray asked her how she was doing and she spoke for "a few minutes" in reply, Anding recalled, before realizing the doctor was no longer on the phone, even though he hadn't disconnected. "I just remember saying, 'Hello, hello, hello! Are you there?'" said Anding. She realized that Conrad had dropped the phone, Anding said, when she began to hear the sounds of a "commotion," then coughing and "the mumbling of voices."

According to Chernoff, the doctor, realizing that his patient had stopped breathing, "rushed over to [Jackson], felt his body to see if he was warm. He was looking for a pulse, found a weak pulse, and started performing CPR." Assuming all of that was true, Michael Jackson probably could have been revived in a hospital setting. Heart and blood pressure monitors would have alerted doctors the moment the patient's breathing ceased and a defibrillator would have been available to restart his heart. Conrad Murray, though, had no heart and blood pressure monitors on hand, and no defibrillator either. It did not help matters, according to medical experts, that Dr. Murray resorted to "nonstandard" CPR. Rather than pulling Michael Jackson's body off the bed to the hard surface of the floor and performing chest compressions with two hands, what Murray did was place one hand under Michael's body between the shoulder blades and use his other hand to compress the chest. Approximately twenty-five minutes passed between the time Murray broke off his cell phone conversation to begin administering CPR and the time a 911 call to emergency services was made at four seconds past 12:21 p.m.

According to Chernoff, Murray spent between five and ten minutes simultaneously trying to perform CPR and call 911. The doctor was "hindered," his attorney explained, because there was no landline in the

Carolwood chateau and Murray didn't believe he could call 911 on a cell phone. Dr. Murray did phone Michael's security trailer, Cheroff said, but there was no answer. He also placed a call to Michael Amir Williams's downtown LA apartment, and left a voice mail message: "Call me right away, please, call me right away. Thank you." Finally, the doctor ran downstairs shouting for help.

Kai Chase was in the kitchen preparing lunch for the Jackson children and wondering why the Tuscan white bean soup she had prepared for Mr. Jackson's dinner sat untouched in the refrigerator, she recalled, when, sometime between 12:05 p.m. and 12:10 p.m., "Dr. Murray runs down the steps and screams, 'Go get Prince!'" Prince ran toward the sound of the shouting and was in the den's doorway when Dr. Murray told him in a panicked voice, "Something may be wrong with your dad!"

"From that point on," the chef remembered, "you could feel the energy in the house change."

Chernoff would say that his client told Chase to "get security" up to Mr. Jackson's bedroom, but the chef did not recall that. Sometime after 12:10, Michael Amir Williams returned Dr. Murray's call. Michael Jackson was having "a bad reaction" to some medication, said the doctor, who told Brother Michael to get to the Carolwood house. Dr. Murray sounded frantic, Brother Michael remembered: "I knew it was serious."

Michael Jackson's "logistics director" Alberto Alvarez was in the security trailer outside Mr. Jackson's home when his phone rang at 12:17 p.m. Brother Michael was calling to say that Mr. Jackson was in trouble, recalled Alvarez, who immediately sprinted into the house, up the stairs, and through the open door to the master bedroom. What he saw left him "frozen and stunned," Alvarez said. Michael Jackson was lying on his back in the middle of his bed with an IV tube attached to his leg, arms outstretched, eyes and mouth wide open, as Dr. Murray performed one-handed chest compressions, his other hand under Michael's body. "Alberto, Alberto, come quickly," Murray called, according to Alvarez. "He had a reaction. He had a bad reaction."

The doctor became increasingly frantic and at one point attempted mouth-to-mouth resuscitation while Alvarez took over the job of performing chest compressions. Another security guard, Faheem Muhammad, was in the room by then, and saw Dr. Murray on his knees by the side of the bed, looking wild-eyed as he pushed again and again on Michael Jackson's chest. "Does anyone in the room know CPR?" Muhammad remembered the doctor shouting.

Prince and Paris Jackson stepped into the bedroom moments later. Both of them began to cry as they watched Murray and Alvarez struggling to revive their father. Paris fell down on her hands and knees; she began to sob and scream, "Daddy!" over and over again, Muhammad remembered. "Get them out! Get them out!" Murray shouted at the security guards. "Don't let them see their father like this!" Alvarez called for the nanny, who quickly ushered the two children out of the room and back down the stairs.

It was 12:20 by then and still no call to 911 had been made. Somehow, though, Murray managed to send text messages at 12:03 and 12:04, and data packages—possibly photos or other media—at 12:15 and 12:18. According to Alvarez, Dr. Murray delayed making the call to emergency services so that he could disconnect the IV line (in which "a milklike substance" showed through the tubing) from Mr. Jackson's leg, then gather up the drug vials strewn about the bedroom. Dr. Murray handed the vials and the IV line to him, Alvarez recalled, then said to load the whole lot of it into medical bags and place the bags in the closet.

It was Alvarez himself who finally made the 911 call at 12:21 p.m. and engaged in the following one-minute-and-fifty-six-second conversation:

911 operator: Paramedic 33, what is the nature of your emergency?

Alvarez: Yes, sir, I need an ambulance as soon as possible.

911 operator: Okay, sir, what's your address?

Alvarez: Carolwood Drive, Los Angeles, California, 90077.

911 operator: Is it Carolwood?

Alvarez: Carolwood Drive, yes (inaudible).

911 operator: Okay, sir, what's the phone number you're calling from and (inaudible) and what exactly happened?

Alvarez: Sir, we have a gentleman here that needs help and he's not breathing, he's not breathing and we need to—we're trying to pump him but he's not . . .

911 operator: Okay, how old is he?

Alvarez: He's fifty years old, sir.

911 operator: Okay, he's unconscious and he's not breathing?

Alvarez: Yes, he's not breathing, sir.

911 operator: Okay, and he's not conscious, either?

Alvarez: No, he's not conscious, sir.

911 operator: Okay, all right, is he on the floor, where is he at right now?

Alvarez: He's on the bed, sir. He's on the bed.

911 operator: Okay, let's get him on the floor. Let's get him down to the floor. I'm gonna help you with CPR right now, okay?

Alvarez: (inaudible), we need to . . .

911 operator: We're on our way there. We're on our way. I'm gonna do as much as I can to help you over the phone. We're already on our way. (inaudible) did anybody see him?

Alvarez: Yes, we have a personal doctor here with him, sir.

911 operator: Oh! You have a doctor there?

Alvarez: Yes, but he's not responding to anything. He's not responding to CPR or anything.

911 operator: Okay, okay, we're on our way there. If you guys are doing CPR instructed by a doctor you have a higher authority than me. Did anybody witness what happened?

Alvarez: Just the doctor, sir. The doctor's been the only one here.

911 operator: Okay, did the doctor see what happened, sir?

[Alvarez can be heard beginning to ask the question before he's cut off by someone speaking angrily in an uncommon foreign language (many residents of Conrad Murray's home country speak "Patois Trinidad," which was first identified as a language by Christopher Columbus in 1498.]

Alvarez: Sir, you just—if you can please . . .

911 operator: We're on our way. I'm just passing these questions on to my paramedics while they're on their way there.

Alvarez: Okay. He's pumping his chest but he's not responding to anything, sir. Please . . .

911 operator: Okay, we're on our way. We're less than a mile away. We'll be there shortly.

Three minutes and seventeen seconds later, the paramedics came in through the front door of the Carolwood chateau and ran toward the stairs leading to the master bedroom.

"I walked into the hall, and I saw the children there crying," Kai Chase recalled. "The daughter was crying. I saw paramedics running up the stairs."

At 12:26 p.m. the paramedics arrived at the bedside of Michael Jackson, where they found him unconscious, not breathing, and in full cardiac arrest. He thought at first that the man on the bed was much older than fifty, recalled paramedic Richard Senneff. The fellow looked like a hospice patient, almost skeletal and with feet that were a disturbing shade of blackish blue. He was startled, Senneff said, when someone told him this was Michael Jackson. Senneff and his partner, Martin Blount, quickly pulled Jackson's body to the floor and began performing the standard form of CPR the way it should have been done from the beginning.

Kai Chase, along with the children's nanny and one of the housekeepers, held hands and formed a circle with Prince, Paris, and Blanket in the hallway at the foot of the stairs. "We were all praying," Chase remembered. "'Help Mr. Jackson be okay.' Then everyone was quiet."

It was obvious to the paramedics within moments that they had arrived too late, Senneff and Blount recalled. Senneff had asked as he came into the bedroom how long the man on the bed had been "down" and was told by the doctor that, "It just happened." He and Blount, though, agreed that based on Mr. Jackson's dilated pupils, dry eyes, and cold skin, the man had gone into arrest quite some time ago. Dr. Murray, who was sopping wet with sweat, insisted to the two paramedics that he had phoned 911 one minute after noticing that Michael was no longer breathing.

At 12:57 p.m., the paramedics received permission over the telephone from Dr. Richelle Cooper at the Ronald Reagan UCLA Medical Center to pronounce the patient dead. Dr. Murray responded by kneeling over the body and laying two fingers on the inside of one elbow. He could feel a pulse, Murray told Senneff and Blount, and was refusing to accept a pronouncement of death. Urged on by Murray, the paramedics attempted to restart Michael Jackson's heart with a defibrillator and deployed an air pump to inflate his lungs. When that failed, Murray got on the phone with Dr. Cooper and her colleague Dr. Than Nguyen, who instructed the paramedics to inject adrenalin directly into Michael's heart. It had no discernible effect.

At 1:07 p.m., nearly forty-two minutes after their arrival at the Carolwood address, the paramedics loaded Michael Jackson's body onto a stretcher and carried him to the ambulance, followed by Conrad Murray, who would ride with his patient to UCLA. According to Dr. Murray, Michael still had a faint pulse.

It was about 1:30, Kai Chase said, when security guards ordered her and the rest of the staff to leave the property because "Mr. Jackson was being taken to the hospital."

Frank Dileo had been eating lunch at the Beverly Hilton Hotel when he received a cell phone call from a Michael Jackson fan who said there was an ambulance in front of the Carolwood house. Dileo immediately phoned Michael Amir Williams to ask if that was true. It was, said Brother Michael, who added that he was on his way to Carolwood right now. After taking the elevator upstairs to change from shorts into long pants, Dileo returned to the hotel lobby, then went out front to retrieve his car from valet parking. He was already driving toward Holmby Hills, Dileo said, when he phoned Randy Phillips, who lived very close to Carolwood Drive. Phillips was at the dry cleaners when he answered the call. He headed quickly outside to his car and started driving to Holmby Hills.

Tohme Tohme was at home in Brentwood when he took a cell phone call from an Internet reporter who asked if it was true that Michael Jackson had had a heart attack. "I said, 'You gotta be out of your mind,'" Tohme remembered. "And then I got a call from NBC asking the same thing. Then I got a call from ABC. So I told my son to turn the TV on." The first image that came onscreen was of an ambulance parked in front of the Carolwood house.

Dileo got lost on his way to Carolwood Drive and found the gates to Michael's house flung wide open with a group of security guards standing out front when he finally arrived. The ambulance had already left with Michael, the guards said. Figuring that the ambulance was headed to Cedars-Sinai Medical Center, Dileo began driving in that direction. While on the road, he again phoned Randy Phillips, who said he was following the ambulance to the hospital. No—it was UCLA, not Cedars, Phillips told Dileo. Moments later, Dileo got a call on his cell phone from the Hayvenhurst estate. It was Katherine Jackson. "I heard they took my son to the hospital," she said. "I don't know what's going on," Dileo told her. "Give me a minute to find out and I'll call back." He was still headed toward UCLA three minutes later, Dileo said, when Mrs. Jackson's driver called to ask what he should do. "Bring her to UCLA Medical Center," Dileo told the driver.

The seven-minute ride to the hospital's emergency room was "unbelievable . . . like the Rose Parade," Richard Senneff remembered. "People running down the street, taking pictures, random cars passing the ambulance. It was insane."

By the time Dileo arrived at the UCLA Medical Center, the main lobby was filled with security guards and nobody could get through. He made his way through a crowd to the emergency room, Dileo recalled, and found Randy Phillips waiting. Randy said he wasn't sure what was going on. The staff in emergency knew who he and Randy were, Dileo said, and permitted the two men through the security door that led back to the room where a team of doctors surrounded the gurney on which Michael Jackson lay. "Outside the room, we heard them working on him," Dileo recalled. "We thought he was alive. Then—no."

Dr. Cooper and Dr. Nguyen agreed that Michael Jackson was officially dead an hour and twelve minutes after his body's arrival at the hospital. Frank Dileo and Randy Phillips walked back out to the emergency room lobby, where they arranged for the wheelchair, the cardiologist, and the social worker who would be waiting when Katherine Jackson arrived at the hospital a short time later.

"It was madness at the hospital when I got there," Tohme Tohme remembered. "Police, fans, media. The police are keeping everybody back, but they knew me and let me in. I walked in by myself and then I saw Randy Phillips. He told me, 'We lost him.' I said, 'I wanna see him.' So they took me in a room, he was in a small room, a viewing room. I saw him and it broke my heart. Then I saw Katherine and the kids come in. Everybody was crying. I just couldn't stand it. I didn't know what to think or do. I just hugged the kids and started to leave. But Randy Phillips came to me and said, 'Doc, we need you.' He and someone else from AEG, I don't even remember who they were, said we need to go to the conference room to sign some document. I didn't even know what it was. I was in a daze. I just signed it. Randy said we needed more security at the house, so I called for that. Then Randy said we had to go talk to some administrator at the hospital. As we were walking by he introduced me to Dr. Murray. I said, 'Who the hell is Dr. Murray?' And Randy said, 'This was Michael's personal doctor.' The first time I heard they hired a doctor for Michael was the first and only time I saw Dr. Murray. Dr. Murray came in the conference room with us and there was a conversation I can't talk about. Murray left, and then they said we had to make an announcement to the media."

The group remaining in the conference room decided that Tohme would introduce Jermaine Jackson, and that Jermaine would address the media.

Michael Jackson had been dead for nearly four hours when his older brother Jermaine, wearing a crisp white shirt and a remarkably calm expression, stood before the cameras and microphones to read a prepared statement that someone else had written.

"This is hard," he began: "My brother, the legendary King of Pop, Michael Jackson, passed away on Thursday, June 25, 2009, at 2:26 p.m. It is believed he suffered cardiac arrest in his home. However, the cause of death is unknown until the results of the autopsy are known.

"His personal physician, who was with him at the time, attempted to resuscitate my brother—as did the paramedics who transported him to Ronald Reagan UCLA Medical Center. Upon arriving at the hospital at approximately 1:14 p.m., a team of doctors, including emergency physicians and cardiologists, attempted to resuscitate him for a period of more than one hour. They were unsuccessful.

"Our family requests that the media please respect our privacy during this tough time," Jermaine went on, then added his own addendum: "May Allah be with you, Michael, always. Love you."

As respectful of Michael's "personal physician" as the prepared statement had been, a number of those at the hospital already harbored suspicions about Conrad Murray. The doctor was "spinning . . . moving around, nervous, sweating, multitasking," remembered Richard Senneff, who told the emergency room doctors that Murray had initially told him Mr. Jackson was "dehydrated," then admitted to giving Michael some Ativan to sleep, but made no mention of any other drug.

Murray would say later that he was upset because Paris Jackson had wept to him that she was now "an orphan." He told Michael's daughter that "I tried my best," Murray said, and the girl answered, "I know you tried your best."

Even before the public announcement of Michael Jackson's death, Murray asked at least two people for rides back to the Carolwood chateau. Brother Michael, who had followed the ambulance to the hospital, recalled that shortly after Michael Jackson was pronounced dead Dr. Murray said he needed to return to the Carolwood chateau, "so that he could pick up some cream that Mr. Jackson has so that the world wouldn't find out about it." (Dozens of tubes of skin-whitening creams were later found, along with a large quantity of Diprivan, in a medical bag that had been stashed in a cupboard of a closet in Michael Jackson's bedroom.) Faheem Muhammad, also at the hospital, remembered that Dr. Murray told him he was hungry and wanted to leave. He suggested the doctor eat at the hospital, Muhammad recalled, but watched as Murray walked out of the building anyway.

Travis Payne was driving on Sunset Boulevard, headed to the Carolwood chateau for his 2 p.m. private rehearsal with Michael Jackson, when his cell phone rang. It was a cousin from Atlanta, calling to say he had heard that Michael Jackson had been rushed to the hospital and might be dead. He thought it was just "another big story," Payne recalled, but when Payne's mother phoned a few minutes later and said she had heard something similar, "I started to worry," he admitted. He still figured the whole thing was another hoax, the choreographer said, but decided to drive to the Staples Center to see what was happening there.

"We were getting a lot of rumor calls," remembered Kenny Ortega, who was already at Staples when Payne arrived. "My phone was just ringing constantly." He was waiting for Randy Phillips to call from the hospital and tell him "what was really happening," Ortega said: "Of course, what I wanted to believe was that this was another of those days in the life of Michael where rumor and exaggeration take over."

He and Kenny agreed that they should just begin getting ready for rehearsal like they always did, Travis Payne recalled. First, though, Ortega gathered the entire production team around him—musicians, dancers, the musical director, the vocal coach, the dance coach, the production and lighting designers, even the technicians—and led them in a prayer that Michael would "return to us in a strong state of health," as the show director recalled it.

Only a few more minutes passed, though, before Ortega got that call from the hospital. "I just saw Kenny's face drop," Payne remembered. They all knew what had happened before Ortega said a word, the choreographer recalled: "Everyone went silent."

People were slow to react, Travis Payne remembered: "No one wanted to believe it. Finally, we all realized it must be true." The entire group gathered again, dimmed the lights, lit a candle, and watched the flame flicker in the dark.

PART FIVE

REMAINS

24

The Michael Jackson show was still going on, even bigger in his absence than it had been while he was around. New media and old were seized by the revelation of his passing on a scale and to a depth that surpassed all understanding. Order would not be easily restored.

The Los Angeles–based "entertainment news" purveyor TMZ.com claimed credit for breaking the story of Michael Jackson's death with a terse bulletin it had issued at 2:44 p.m. Pacific Daylight Time. CNN needed two full hours after TMZ's initial report to confirm the news. Word of Michael's death had first gone public twenty-three minutes before TMZ announced it, however, with a Facebook status update posted at 2:21 p.m., five minutes before the official announcement by the UCLA Medical Center. By the time the media was alerted, a crowd of praying, chanting, clamoring fans had already formed at the main entrance to the hospital, serenaded by Michael's own performance of his song "Human Nature," played repeatedly on speakers that had been stacked in the windows of the Sigma Alpha Epsilon fraternity house across the street.

People had begun to gather even earlier outside the gates of the Carolwood chateau, where, in an only-in-Los Angeles moment, a celebrity homes tour bus happened to pull up outside Michael Jackson's rented home at the very moment the entertainer's body was being driven through the open gates in a cherry-red ambulance. Several passengers disembarked right there and became the nucleus of a crowd that by three o'clock was swollen with grief-stricken fans who sobbed to Michael's music, many already dressed in various renditions of his wardrobe. Among them was Marie Courchinoux, one of the dancers Michael had selected for his London shows, who wore a single white glove and explained through tears that she simply didn't know where else to go. A second tour bus passed by and many of the passengers demanded to be let off to join the mourners.

An even thicker crush of people had assembled outside the wrought iron gates of the Hayvenhurst estate, holding signs and carrying portable music players that blasted Michael's greatest hits. Many wore an outfit of one white glove, a fedora hat, and big sunglasses.

Joe Jackson was in Las Vegas but had written himself into the story early on, even before the Facebook announcement of Michael's death. As early as 1 p.m., Joe informed *E! News* that his son had gone to the hospital by ambulance and was "not doing well." At 1:50 p.m. Joe again spoke to *E! News* by phone, informing a reporter that Michael had suffered a heart attack and "is not okay." Joe would keep talking all afternoon.

Long before CNN gave the story of Jackson's death the stamp of its weakened authority, news organizations were reeling from what they had watched occur in cyberspace during the first minutes and hours after the doctors at UCLA made it official. TMZ's ringmaster Harvey Levin was crowing that, "No matter what they say, people know we broke this story." The surge of online traffic so overwhelmed Google that it began to respond as if under attack, answering "Michael Jackson" searches either with "error" messages or the squiggly letters of a "captcha" screen. Wikipedia reported a crash within the first hour after Jackson's death. Twitter messages had doubled within seconds of the first TMZ bulletin, the company said, increasing to 5,000 per minute by mid-afternoon. Wikipedia reported that there had been nearly a million visitors to its Michael Jackson biography within a single hour, the most in the online encyclopedia's history by far. The *Los Angles Times*, which had put out the story of Jackson's death at almost the same moment CNN did, said its Web site was subsequently swamped by nearly 2.3 million page views in an hour, more than it had seen on the day of Barack Obama's election. Facebook announced that its status updates tripled during the first hour after the news of Jackson's death went public. The 16.4 million unique visitors to Yahoo! News easily eclipsed the 15.1 million total that had been reached on the day of the presidential vote. At AOL Instant Messaging, which had collapsed for forty minutes in the immediate aftermath of Michael's death, company officials issued a message saying that, "Today was a seminal moment in Internet history. We've never seen anything like it . . ."

Cameras and microphones poked through the mob pressed against the barriers at UCLA Medical Center, where the hospital was in full lockdown mode. The scene was almost as frantic inside the building as tense administrators attempted to forestall a scandal like the one that had erupted a year earlier when nineteen of its employees were caught snooping through the private medical records of Britney Spears, presumably with an eye toward cashing in the way their colleague Lawanda Jackson had when she sold the tabloids information lifted from Farrah Fawcett's files. A group of sobbing girls that blocked the hospital's emergency room driveway was ushered aside by police as Michael Jackson's body was surreptitiously loaded into the helicopter that would fly it to the Los Angeles County medical examiner's office.

By nightfall there were huge crowds outside the Apollo Theater in New York; at Hitsville U.S.A., the old Motown headquarters in Detroit; and at the Rock and Roll Hall of Fame in Cleveland, where a memorial wall was posted with photos that chronicled Michael's career from his days as the lead singer of the Jackson 5 right up through the *HIStory* tour. In Gary, Indiana, flags were lowered to half-mast and the people who stood singing and crying outside what was once the Jackson family residence included the city's mayor. Back in Los Angeles, crowds gathered at the GRAMMY Museum in downtown Los Angeles and at the Staples Center farther south. A group of women locked arms and marched down the Walk of Fame on Hollywood Boulevard singing "We Are the World." Farther north, people were already making pilgrimages to the gated entrance at Neverland Ranch.

By the morning of June 26, there were Michael Jackson shrines and crowds of mourners at the Angel de la Independencia monument in Mexico City, on the square in front of the Cathédrale de Notre-Dame in Paris, and outside the U.S. embassies in Moscow, Tokyo, Nairobi, Odessa, and Brussels. In London, after the Liberal Party prime minister Gordon Brown issued a brief statement reading: "This is very sad news for the millions of Michael Jackson fans in Britain and around the world," his Conservative Party opponent David Cameron promptly answered with: "I know Michael Jackson's fans in Britain and around the world will be sad today. Despite the controversies, he was a legendary entertainer." Nelson Mandela made a rare public appearance to salute Michael's ability to "triumph over tragedy on so many occasions in his life." Two separate ministers of the national government in Japan issued statements expressing their sadness at this "tragic loss," while former South Korea president Kim Dae-jung proclaimed that, "We've lost a hero to the world." Imelda Marcos said she cried when she heard the news. In Paris, French culture minister Frédéric Mitterrand told reporters, "We all have a Michael Jackson within."

Back in the United States, politicians remained more circumspect. While California governor Arnold Schwarzenegger praised Jackson as "one of the most influential and iconic figures in the music industry," he was careful to add mention of the "serious questions about his personal life" that remained unanswered. Barack Obama declined to pay homage with a personal appearance, sending press secretary Robert Gibbs out to tell White House correspondents that the president saw Michael Jackson as "a spectacular performer," but also believed there were "sad and tragic" aspects to the entertainer's life. The U.S. House of Representatives paused for a tribute moment of silence, which spared them and the American public from anything they might have spoken out loud. The Associated Press dredged up a memorandum written by U.S. Supreme Court Justice John Roberts back in the 1980s when he was working as a young White House attorney that objected to a letter being sent to Michael Jackson on behalf of President Ronald Reagan: "Frankly, I find the obsequious attitude of some members of the White House staff toward Mr. Jackson's attendants, and the fawning posture they would have the president of the United States adopt, more than a little embarrassing." The atmosphere was such that the AP actually imagined Justice Roberts might want to clarify his remarks.

At the Wimbledon tennis tournament in London, both Serena Williams and Roger Federer began the press conferences marking their third-round victories by answering questions about Michael Jackson. "What did Michael Jackson mean to you personally?" was the first query put to Williams, who would take eleven more MJ-related questions before hearing one about tennis.

Even people who hadn't exactly been on friendly terms with Jackson in recent years felt obliged to assure the world of their love and admiration for him. "I feel privileged to have hung out and worked with Michael," read Paul McCartney's press statement. "He was a talented boy-man with a gentle soul. His music will be remembered forever and my memories of our time together will be happy ones." Former arch-foe Tommy Mottola described Jackson's death as "one of the greatest losses" ever, then added, "In pop history, there's a triumvirate of icons: Sinatra, Elvis, and Michael . . . Nothing that came before him or that has come after him will ever be as big as he was."

The *Wall Street Journal*, of all newspapers, heartily agreed. "The Age of Celebrity died with Michael Jackson's heart," wrote the *Journal's* deputy editorial-page editor, Daniel Henninger: "Michael is the last celebrity because he rose to fame in the 1980s, and in the 1980s there was no World Wide Web. We didn't have a thousand cable TV stations . . . It has taken some time to see how modern media squashed the life out of genuine celebrity." As if to prove Henninger's point about the degraded nature of modern celebrity, stars such as John Mayer, Miley Cyrus, and Demi Moore all took the opportunity to tweet their deep feelings and shallow thoughts about Michael Jackson's passing.

Missing from the cacophony of competing voices was insight from someone who actually *knew* Michael Jackson, but no such thing was forthcoming.

"There were a number of people who went on Larry King after he died and professed their great love for Michael Jackson and their great sense of loss," Tom Mesereau recalled, "who I happen to know would not step forward and help him when he needed it during the trial. With friends like that, Michael didn't need enemies."

Elizabeth Taylor, one of the few women who had been close enough to Michael Jackson to say anything meaningful about him, begged off, explaining through a spokesperson that she was "too devastated" to comment. In the end, the most incisive public observation came from another of Michael's female friends, Liza Minnelli: "When the autopsy comes, all hell's going to break loose, so thank God we're celebrating him now."

25

In the morgue at the Los Angeles County coroner's office in Lincoln Heights, Chief Medical Examiner Lakshmanan Sathyavagiswaran and his staff were confronted by the corpse of a very thin but not quite emaciated middle-aged man who was nearly bald beneath a black wig that had been stitched into the fuzzy strands of his closely cropped white hair. The skin beneath was covered by what Dr. Christopher Rogers, who performed the autopsy, described as a "dark discoloration" that stretched from ear to ear, apparently a tattoo intended to camouflage the burn scars on the dead man's scalp. There were also dark tattoos under the eyebrows and around the eyelids, and a pink tattoo on his lips, all of them clearly cosmetic. A bandage covered a nose so cut away that, without a prosthetic, it looked like little more than a pair of slightly ridged nostrils. Dr. Rogers and those who assisted him counted thirteen "puncture wounds" on the body, spread from one side of the neck to both arms and both ankles, suggesting recent needle insertions. The only real signs of trauma, though, were deep bruises covering the chest and abdomen, apparently inflicted during a desperate attempt to resuscitate the man with CPR. Several ribs were cracked, either by chest compressions or by the balloon pump that had been inserted into the lungs. The penis was sheathed by an external urine catheter, as it might have been for a patient suffering severe incontinence, or one who was heavily sedated.

The most remarkable finding of the autopsy performed on the body of Michael Jackson during the morning of June 26, 2009, was that the entertainer had been in far better physical condition than the public had been led to believe. He had suffered from a slight case of arthritis in his lower back and a mild buildup of plaque in the blood vessels of his legs. The allergies that Michael battled for years probably explained the chronic inflammation in his lungs where "respiratory bronchiolitis, diffuse congestion, and patchy hemorrhage" had been noted by the medical examiners. Such symptoms probably made it difficult to take a deep breath, but were far from life-threatening. At the age of fifty, the man's heart had been strong, his internal organs clear, his muscle tone excellent. He had weighed 136 pounds at the time of death, on the low end of the normal range for a male adult who stood slightly under five feet, ten inches tall. Michael Jackson had a body that, if he had tended to it properly, he could have lived in for another thirty years.

The medical examiners were but the first links in a lengthy chain of investigators who would eventually be joined in the complex criminal case resulting from Michael Jackson's death. Even as Jackson's body reposed at the morgue, Dr. Conrad Murray's car was being towed away from the Carolwood chateau by a forensics unit of the Los Angeles Police Department armed with a warrant stating the vehicle might contain "medication or other evidence" related to the demise of Mr. Jackson. The same search warrant permitted LAPD detectives to search the bedroom of the home, where they recovered medical bags from a compartment of Michael Jackson's clothes closet that contained a virtual pharmacy of drugs, including large quantities of propofol, along with lorazepam, diazepam, temazepam, trazodone, Flomax, clonazepam, tizanidine, hydrocodone, lidocaine, and Benoquin.

Detectives discreetly requested that Conrad Murray make himself available for an interview the following evening. By then, the LAPD had heard from both the paramedics who responded to the 911 call and the doctors in the emergency room at the UCLA Medical Center that Dr. Murray had said nothing to them about propofol being in Michael Jackson's system, admitting only that his patient had taken some Ativan.

Murray was accompanied by attorney Ed Chernoff on the afternoon of June 27 when he arrived at the Ritz Carlton Hotel in Marina Del Rey to be interviewed by LAPD detectives Orlando Martinez and Scott Smith. Chernoff, a senior partner in the Houston firm of Stradley, Chernoff & Alford, was obscure outside Texas but touted as a big gun for hire in Harris County. He had established himself while in the employ of the district attorney's office, where, his firm boasted on its Web site, he had lost just one felony jury trial out of the forty he had prosecuted. It was Chernoff who provided most of the information the media had about what transpired during Conrad Murray's LAPD interview. His client was in no sense the suspect in a crime, according to Chernoff, but rather "is considered to be a witness to the events surrounding Michael Jackson's death." Dr. Murray was cooperating fully with LAPD investigators and had answered "every and all" questions put to him, Chernoff said, in order to "clarify some inconsistencies."

The LAPD's spokesperson simply stated that Dr. Murray had not been accused of any criminal wrongdoing. The coroner's investigators reported no evidence of foul play but were listing the cause of death as "deferred" until more tests were completed.

The Jackson family, though, was already building its own case against the doctor. In the first day or two after Michael's death, various family members and spokespersons (Jesse Jackson among them) had suggested that Michael died because his doctor left him unattended. The Jacksons had already arranged for an "independent" autopsy to be performed by a privately retained pathologist, Dr. Selma Calmes, just a few hours after Michael's body was released from the Los Angeles County morgue. Dr. Calmes could do little to satisfy her clients, however, because the county's medical examiners had stitched up Michael's body and returned it to the Jackson family without the brain, which would be kept in a jar of formaldehyde as the main piece of forensic evidence in a sprawling investigation that would force the LAPD to seek assistance from the California Department of Justice, the DEA, the FBI, Interpol, and Scotland Yard.

Forty-eight hours after his death, the real dissection of Michael Jackson was just beginning. What the entertainer had left behind, along with his three children and body of work, was one of the largest and most complicated estates in California history. A crush of creditors and claimants recognized that the fortune they were after was growing at a rate no one could possibly have foreseen. Within hours of Jackson's death, *Thriller* was the #1 album on iTunes and Michael Jackson's albums occupied all fifteen of the top spots on Amazon.com's best-selling-albums list. Overall, Michael's record sales were up eighty-fold by the end of that day. In the next two weeks, nineteen of his albums would make the top twenty on iTunes in the United States, while fourteen claimed top twenty places on the Amazon.co.uk list. Six would chart in Japan and nine in Argentina. In Australia, Michael Jackson songs occupied thirty-four spots in the top one hundred. Thirteen countries in total pushed *Number Ones* to the top of their iTunes charts. *Thriller 25* was the #1 album in Poland, where it was quickly displaced by *King of Pop*, which was also topping the chart in Germany. In America, Michael was breaking assorted records at *Billboard*, where his albums filled the first twelve spots on the magazine's top pop catalog chart. Digital sales, though, were what made Michael's passing an economic event that far exceeded the deaths of Elvis Presley and John

Lennon. More than 2.5 million Jackson songs had been downloaded in the four days after his death in a world where no other musical act ever had its songs downloaded even a million times in a week. When this was added to the 800,000 albums sold in the seven days after Michael died, it became clear that he had staged the posthumous revival of an entire depressed industry. And that was just the leading edge in an avalanche of commercial possibility that would exploit his image on T-shirts, coffee cups, and wherever else it could be fitted.

The King of Pop was going to be worth a billion dollars again, maybe two billion, maybe more, and the Jackson family intended to make sure they held first position in the collection line. They had begun demonstrating this within hours of Michael's death, when the women of the clan initiated what became a week-long occupation and search of the Carolwood chateau.

The family, and La Toya in particular, would later accuse Tohme Tohme of looting the house where Michael had died, but Tohme never set foot on the property that day, or in the days that followed. At the behest of AEG, Tohme had done his best to make the Carolwood chateau off-limits to everyone outside law enforcement. After Randy Phillips suggested that they needed to lock down both the Carolwood house and the Hayvenhurst compound, Tohme had placed a call to Ron Williams, a former agent with the U.S. Secret Service who now operated Talon Executive Services, an Orange County company that provided security and performed investigations for dozens of major corporations and a good many celebrities. Tohme wanted Williams because he knew Williams was a man people trusted.

The Talon chief immediately dispatched teams of operatives to both the Carolwood chateau and the Hayvenhurst compound, and drove to the Holmby Hills house himself. At Tohme's instigation, Williams also sent a team to Las Vegas to secure the Palomino hacienda where many of Michael's most valuable possessions remained in storage in the basement.

He and his people were kept outside the gates of the Carolwood property for a full five hours, Williams recalled, while the LAPD photographed the premises, searched the master bedroom, and interviewed Michael Jackson's security staff. It was dark when the Talon chief got a call from his lead man in Las Vegas informing him that a group of Michael Jackson's former bodyguards had been caught trying to sneak out of the Palomino hacienda with assorted valuables and were being detained by the police. "Secure the perimeter and let no one inside," Williams told him.

It was about 10 p.m. when the security staff at the Carolwood chateau were allowed to leave. The police prepared to vacate just minutes later. Williams and his people were met outside the front gate by Ron Boyd, the Los Angeles Port police chief, who said he was working with the Jacksons as a family friend and would walk the Talon agents onto the property. To Williams, it said something about the position of the Jackson family in Los Angeles that the first black chief in the history of the port police was on hand to personally protect their interests.

About an hour after Williams and his people had stationed themselves along the perimeter of the Carolwood property's inside wall, La Toya Jackson and her boyfriend Jeffre Phillips showed up and demanded to be admitted to the house. Tohme had told him that "no one" was to be allowed onto the property or permitted to remove anything from it, Williams recalled, "but La Toya and her boyfriend said, 'We're family and we should have access to the house.' And Ron Boyd gave them tacit permission." Williams phoned Tohme, who was not pleased. "I knew Michael Jackson's sister and her boyfriend were in the house taking everything they could," Tohme Tohme said, "but I didn't know what to do. It was up to the police." Three hours after La Toya and Phillips were let into the house, Katherine Jackson arrived and went inside after them.

It was mid-morning in London, where Grace Rwaramba was staying with Daphne Barak, when the nanny received a call from Mrs. Jackson. According to Rwaramba, Katherine began the conversation this way: "Grace, the children are crying. They are asking about you. They can't believe that their father died. Grace, you remember Michael used to hide cash at the house? I'm here. Where can it be?" Rwaramba described Michael's standard practice of hiding his cash in black plastic garbage bags tucked under the carpets of whatever house he was living in. "But can you believe it?" she asked Barak after hanging up. "This woman just lost her son a few hours ago and she is calling me to find out where the money is!" Talon employees said it was La Toya Jackson, though, along with her boyfriend, who loaded black plastic garbage bags filled with cash into duffel bags and placed them in the garage. La Toya would later insist that nearly all of Michael's money was gone by the time she arrived at the Carolwood house. All she found, La Toya said, were a few wrappers from the bundles of cash that someone else had removed from the premises and a couple of twenty-dollar bills they had dropped on their way out.

Ron Williams and his agents had remained outside the house, at La Toya's insistence. It was impossible, Williams said, for anyone to know what Michael's sister and her boyfriend were doing inside, or what Katherine Jackson was doing after she entered the Carolwood chateau. And he couldn't account either, Williams added, for whatever had taken place inside the house in the nine and a half hours that had passed between the time that Michael Jackson was carried to an ambulance and when the Talon team had been permitted to secure the Carolwood property.

It did not become absolutely obvious to Williams and his people that the Jacksons intended to remove whatever valuables were inside the house until the next morning, when Janet Jackson arrived at the front gate, explained that she had just flown in from out of town, and demanded that the gate be opened to admit the moving van that was following behind her. The van had just backed up to the doors of the garage when La Toya came out of the house and insisted that Williams and his agents move their perimeter to the *outside* of the walls, so that the family would have privacy.

It was an awkward moment for Williams. He was in the employ of Tohme and AEG, both of whom had made it clear that they did not want anyone, including the Jackson family, on the property. Williams had supervised Secret Service details that protected four U.S. presidents, Queen Elizabeth, and Pope John Paul II, but he found it "pretty hard to tell the Jackson family, after their brother and son had died, to 'Get your ass off this property.'" So he withdrew his agents to the outside of the walls and gave the Jacksons "unfettered access to the house." A couple of hours later the moving van rolled back through the front gate with Jeffre Phillips at the wheel. Katherine Jackson and her daughters, though, made it clear they wouldn't be leaving any time soon. "They camped out for most of a week," Williams recalled, coming and going "whenever they felt like it."

Talon agents remained at the walls of the Carolwood property for three weeks, dealing mainly with "fan types and paparazzis" that attempted to climb the walls. They kept a log of everyone who entered or exited the front gate and never once saw Tohme Tohme. "The Jackson family let it be known that they didn't want him around," Williams recalled.

For several days, it appeared that Michael Jackson had died intestate. In the absence of a will, his entire estate belonged to his children and would be placed into a court-administered trust until the three came of age. This, of course, meant that custody of the children would be the only way any adult could have access to Michael's wealth. The Jacksons announced their claims on both Michael's children and his fortune to the media assembled outside the Shrine Auditorium for the BET Awards ceremony on June 28. When CNN's Don Lemon attempted to interview

Joe Jackson for the first time after Michael's death, a publicist was summoned to read a prepared statement saying that only Michael's parents "have the personal and legal authority to act, and solely Katherine and I have authority for our son and his children." Joe then gestured to his partner Marshall Thompson, former lead singer of the Chi-Lites, to tell the CNN reporter all about their new record company. The *Los Angeles Times* would describe the scene outside the Shrine Auditorium as one in which "camps began to form for what could be extended battles over Jackson's children, his money, and his legacy."

Katherine Jackson initiated the process by filing petitions with Los Angeles County Superior Court Judge Mitchell Beckloff to be granted temporary custody of Prince, Paris, and Blanket, and to be named as the administrator of her late son's estate, so as to ensure that the children would be its beneficiaries. Judge Beckloff granted the temporary guardianship of the children, but scheduled a hearing for July 6, to rule on an estate petition that would give Katherine nearly absolute control of Michael Jackson's rapidly growing fortune. Beckloff also agreed to determine at that same hearing whether to grant Mrs. Jackson permanent guardianship of the three children.

A story in the next morning's *Los Angeles Times* described Katherine's court filing as "the first legal volley in what is anticipated to be a protracted battle over custody of the children and control of Michael Jackson's estate," then added that "some legal experts believe the pop star's former wife, Debbie Rowe, is most likely to receive final custody of the two older children." Katherine and her attorneys clearly felt that concern, describing Debbie's whereabouts in their court petition as "unknown," then adding that Prince and Paris "have no relationship with their biological mother." In the space where they were to identify Blanket's mother, Mrs. Jackson's petition had answered "None."

At the same time the Jacksons closed ranks around Katherine Jackson's bid to control both the children and their inheritance, the family began to signal that it was organizing to mount some sort of a wrongful death claim. In an interview with the ABC affiliate in Los Angeles, Joe Jackson advised the channel's reporter that, "I'm suspecting foul play somewhere." La Toya told two London newspapers that a "shadowy entourage" of manipulative handlers was responsible for "murdering" her brother. She complained to the *Sunday Mail* and the *News of the World* that more than $1 million in cash and a valuable collection of jewelry had "somehow" disappeared from the Carolwood chateau, then implied that the "bad circle" around Michael was probably responsible for that, as well.

The British newspapers and later *People* and *Us* magazines had translated La Toya's remarks into an implicit accusation against the "Lebanese-born, self-appointed business manager" Tohme Tohme, noting her accusation that Tohme had abruptly "fired all the staff" at the Carolwood chateau on the evening of Michael's death. "At 11 p.m. on the day he dies, all the staff are fired?" she said. "That raised my suspicions."

As Tohme knew, at 11 p.m on the day Michael Jackson died, La Toya and her boyfriend had arrived at the Carolwood house to begin searching it, a full hour after the staff had been excused by LAPD investigators. Tohme was less astonished by how brazen La Toya could be, though, than by the realization that he was being set up as the villain who had brought about Michael Jackson's death. "I am in the media as a murder suspect!" Tohme recalled. "I am 'the mysterious Dr. Tohme'! People are calling my kids to ask if I'm in jail."

Tohme voluntarily turned over the $5.2 million that had been left in the Lockbox account after the settlements with Sheikh Abdullah and Darren Julien, and was still vilified. "Nobody asked for it. Nobody even knows about that money," he said. "I gave it to the estate because it is Michael's money." Dennis Hawk confirmed this claim. He had advised Tohme—not as his attorney, but as a friend, Hawk said—that he probably had a right to hold on to those millions, as an advance against the much greater sum he was owed in management fees. Tohme, though, insisted that it should be returned. "Whatever anybody says about Tohme, it was clear to me in that moment that all he wanted was to do the right thing," Hawk recalled. "And he thought the right thing was to give back the money. I'm pretty sure nobody else involved with Michael would have done that." Jeff Cannon, who had worked as Michael Jackson's primary accountant during most of the last two years of his life, agreed with Hawk that Tohme's conduct had been above reproach. Cannon, who had been brought aboard by Ron Burkle's company well before Tohme arrived on the scene, said he had kept track of every dollar that came in or went out for more than twenty months and knew to a certainty that Tohme had been scrupulous about accounting for both the money spent and the money set aside. He was kept informed of what was in the Lockbox "to the penny," Cannon said, and like Hawk was impressed that Tohme had turned over the entire $5.2 million, since he seemed to have every right to hold on to it.

Yet only a couple of hours after Tohme delivered the $5.2 million, gossip items and blog posts began to appear that made Michael's manager out to be a swindler who was caught trying to hide his client's money, then surrendered the cash only because he was being threatened with legal action. "All I am trying to do is make sure everything is open and above-board," he recalled, "and suddenly they are calling me a thief."

Sensing that this was the moment when his rival could at last be brushed aside, Frank Dileo had seized the opportunity to tell NBC's Jeff Rossen that he had recognized Tohme as one of those "wrong people" in whom Jackson had invested his trust during recent years. "He controlled Michael's life. He controlled everything . . . He kept his accounts. He deposited the money in the accounts. He signed the checks," but Michael had eventually rebelled, Dileo added: "He said [Tohme] tried to tell him who he could see and when he could see them. He said he did not like that."

Tohme still fancied himself a tough guy who shrugged off punches. "I refused to talk to the media because I thought, 'I know better. I know what I did for Michael,'" he explained. "And Michael had just died. I had just lost a beautiful friend. Me, my wife, and my children, we were all heartbroken. Michael loved my family, loved my kids, loved my wife. He loved us all and we loved him. My family didn't want me to talk to anybody. So I tried not to pay attention. But it was overwhelming. The media was all over my house. I had to climb a fence into my neighbor's yard to leave. Everybody was attacking me. Even people I thought were my friends stabbed me in the back. I couldn't believe what was happening." The climax of the drama for Tohme came a week after Michael's death when he collapsed in the living room of his home and was transported by ambulance to Saint John's Hospital in Santa Monica. Doctors at first thought he had suffered a heart attack but concluded it was simply an intense stress reaction. "After that I just withdrew into my family," Tohme recalled. "I didn't want to see anybody else. I didn't want to talk to anybody else. I let them say whatever they wanted about me. I didn't care. I was numb."

There were plenty of other people for the media to interview. So many were putting themselves forward as spokespersons for "the Jacksons" that TV reporters spun dizzily from one to the next, offering the microphone to just about anyone who beckoned for it. Jesse Jackson was at once vying and collaborating with Al Sharpton for some unspecified but not entirely imaginary position that appeared to involve a blend of spiritual direction and racial politics. As Leo Terrell would observe, Jesse Jackson had positioned himself more shrewdly this time around, making sure he was seen as standing by Katherine Jackson, while Sharpton let himself be publicly identified as Joe Jackson's wingman. The two reverends were actually spending a good deal of time together in Los Angeles in the week after Michael's death, and their public comments seemed to involve the development of insinuations directed at Conrad Murray, AEG, and Tohme Tohme on the one hand, and a repudiation of any custody claim that Debbie Rowe might make on the other. For Terrell, the most amusing moment of the media frenzy was one he observed from a table at the Ivy restaurant in Beverly Hills. "I saw Jackson and Sharpton walking out the front door as happy as can be, laughing and joking, and then the moment they saw the cameras pointed at them their faces fell and suddenly they were grieving. I mean, it was just that fast. What a pair of actors those two are. I laughed so hard I almost fell off my chair."

Ken Sunshine, the veteran PR consultant who had actually been retained as the official Jackson family spokesperson, told the *Los Angeles Times* he was stunned by all the people who were being identified on television as "an authority" on the clan's inner workings. "Where are the standards of choosing somebody to go on camera?" Sunshine wondered. "The so-called experts, who the hell *are* these people?"

No single moment so begged that question as the appearance of Leonard Rowe on an Atlanta television station that permitted him to tell the story of how he had been "hired in March by Michael Jackson to oversee his comeback tour in England." When he "last saw" Michael, he sensed the star was in danger, Rowe told the Channel 2 *Action News* reporter: "I felt something like this was coming if there wasn't an intervention. I felt something was coming and I hated it." Rowe went on CNN's *Larry King Live*, described himself Michael Jackson's "manager," then quoted from a statement that had Michael proclaiming, "I am very pleased that Leonard has accepted my offer to manage my business affairs during this important period in my career . . . Leonard Rowe has been a longtime friend and business associate whose judgment I have come to trust." Given that Michael's most recent communication with Rowe had been a letter reading, "This is to inform you that you do not represent me," it was difficult not to be impressed by the man's sheer gall. It wasn't long before Rowe announced that he was working on his own Michael Jackson book, based on his "long relationship" with the star.

In death, Michael Jackson was serving as the most encompassing tabula rasa in the history of celebrity worship. His passing had created a global community of mourning unlike anything the world had seen before or was likely to see again. "Car windows were open all over the city, and just about every station on the radio dial had switched to an all–Michael Jackson format," wrote Kelefa Sanneh in the *New Yorker*. "For the first (and for all we know, the last) time, it felt as if absolutely everyone was listening to the same songs." It was like that also in London and Sydney and Berlin and Tokyo. There were Michael Jackson memorials being created in Bucharest and Baku. The mayor of Rio de Janeiro announced that the city would erect a statue of Jackson on the favela of Dona Marta. *USA Today* ran a photograph of Pakistani girls lighting candles at a King of Pop shrine in Hyderabad. Jesse Jackson addressed the fans assembled at a musical tribute to Michael being staged back in Gary, where the city's mayor unveiled a seven-foot-tall memorial to him. On the Internet, views of Michael Jackson music videos had increased from an average of 216,000 per day to more than 10 million. ABC's *World News*, the *CBS Evening News*, and NBC's *Nightly News* devoted more than a third of their broadcast coverage for an entire week to Michael Jackson. *Time* was just one of more than a dozen U.S. magazines that produced commemorative editions featuring Jackson on the cover.

The media's obsession with Michael itself became both a story and a study in America's self-contradictions. According to the Pew Research Center, more than two-thirds of people polled felt that the coverage of Jackson's death had been excessive; at the same time 80 percent of them admitted being fascinated by it. The inevitable backlash forged strange alliances: Rush Limbaugh joined Al Sharpton in decrying the speculation about the cause of Michael Jackson's death, while Fox News commentator Bill O'Reilly and Venezuelan president Hugo Chavez each objected to the hours that CNN was devoting to the story. The attraction of such opposites was in its own way compelling evidence of how utterly Michael transcended race, creed, and color.

For most of his adult life, Michael had been described as "strange," "weird," and "bizarre." Only now, after he was gone, did people realize that he was what they had in common.

26

The Jackson family celebration of Judge Beckloff's ruling placing custody of the children and control of the estate into the hands of their matriarch lasted less than seventy-two hours. On the morning of July 1, 2009, a certified copy of a document titled "Last Will of Michael Joseph Jackson" was filed in Los Angeles Superior Court by two of the three executors named in the document, John Branca and John McClain, the latter a record company executive who had a long history with the Jackson clan. The signature on the will had been officially witnessed by McClain and Barry Siegel, the former Jackson accountant who was the third executor named in the document, as well as Trudy Green, who had been Michael's manager at that time. A handwritten annotation stated that this had taken place in Los Angeles at 5 p.m. on July 7, 2002. According to Branca, who produced the document, Michael's will had been sitting in the files of his law firm, Ziffren Brittenham, LLP, for the seven years since.

By the time the will and a related trust agreement arrived at the courthouse in downtown Los Angeles, Branca had already retained the services of two powerful and highly paid allies. One was Howard Weitzman, who during the years since he helped Johnnie Cochran persuade Michael Jackson to settle the Jordan Chandler case had become arguably the most influential attorney in Los Angeles. After establishing himself in the early 1980s as a top criminal defense lawyer, Weitzman had branched out into areas that included entertainment, intellectual property, family law, civil rights, antitrust, regulatory, and probate issues. He had represented every single one of the major movie studios and his long list of celebrity clients included the current governor of California. Weitzman was as well connected to the city's political, financial, academic, media, and cultural power centers as anyone in LA, and as formidable a litigator as there was in the country.

Branca's other top hire, Mike Sitrick, was less well known but even more feared. "The Ninja Master of the Dark Art of Spin" was how the

Web site Gawker had recently described Sitrick, an ultra-expensive "crisis manager" whose career in media manipulation stretched from helping Exxon cope with the catastrophic Valdez oil spill in Alaska's Prince William Sound to advising the Roman Catholic archdiocese on how to defend itself against allegations that it had protected priests accused of sexually abusing children. In between, he had managed the assorted PR disasters of such celebrities as Paris Hilton, Michael Vick, and Rush Limbaugh. Sitrick's skill at mounting counterattacks (or "smear campaigns" as people on the receiving end tended to call them) against those who criticized or accused his clients, however, was the main stuff of his legend. The man's ability to produce a preemptive strike of news leaks, press releases, and blog posts that simultaneously destroyed an opponent's reputation and shaped the public perception of a controversy before the local media so much as started to report the story had been dazzling and terrifying onlookers for two decades. People lived in terror of being placed on what Sitrick liked to call his "Wheel of Pain." That Branca had put Weitzman and Sitrick on his payroll even before producing Jackson's will was evidence of two things: one, Branca believed he was in for a public fight with the Jackson family; and two, he intended to win that fight.

The will itself was most striking to the national media for the way it addressed the subject of Debbie Rowe. The first two sentences of the document's Article I read: "I am not married. My marriage to DEBORAH JEAN ROWE has been dissolved." The last line of Article VI stated: "I have intentionally omitted to provide for my former wife, DEBORAH JEAN ROWE JACKSON." Clearly, the intention was to ensure that Debbie didn't get a dime—or custody of Michael's kids. Katherine Jackson was emphatically designated as the children's guardian, though if Katherine was unable to serve in that capacity Michael had named Diana Ross as the first alternate. Ross was reported to be in shock, telling friends she didn't know any of the three children, hadn't been in Michael's life for years, and was well past the age where she wanted to take on the task of raising young children; she most definitely would not oppose Debbie Rowe's bid for custody if it came to that.

How the money, property, copyrights, and trademarks would be divided was what most concerned the interested parties, and that was detailed in a separate document. According to the Michael Jackson Family Trust agreement that was submitted to the court by John Branca, 40 percent of Michael Jackson's estate was to be held in the Michael Jackson Children's Trust for Prince, Paris, and Blanket, then released to the three in steps as they reached the ages of thirty, thirty-five, and forty. Another 20 percent of the Family Trust would be assigned to various charities; the trust agreement seemed to permit Branca and McClain to choose which charities those were. The other 40 percent would be held by an entity called the Katherine Jackson Trust. Funds from that trust were to be used to support Mrs. Jackson, but there was no provision for Joe Jackson or for Michael's siblings. The most notable thing about the trust agreement, though, was that it gave Branca (and McClain) "absolute discretion" to decide how the money from the Katherine Jackson Trust would be distributed. Knowing that the provision would send a shiver through the family, Branca arranged to meet with the Jacksons at Jermaine's house on the day after the will was filed in court. Every member of the immediate family, other than Joe, had been in attendance, according to Branca, who insisted afterward that what he had to say was greeted with resounding approval. "They applauded three times when they were told who got the property," he said.

Katherine Jackson remembered the meeting rather differently. According to her, the atmosphere had gone from quiet to glum. She personally was offended that John Branca never once said how sorry he was for her loss, nor expressed any sign that he mourned Michael's passing. The man was cold, Mrs. Jackson thought, just as her son had described him. "My son had told me and the kids that he never wanted Branca to be any part of his business ever again," Katherine Jackson said.

Branca himself professed to be astonished when Katherine Jackson's attorneys filed a motion asking the court to give Michael's mother control of her son's wealth, based on "conflicts of interest" and "other factors" that compromised the ability of Branca and McClain to administer the estate. The deals with Sony and AEG were specifically referenced.

Katherine had already won a key concession from Judge Beckloff, who ruled that a provision in the will that would punish anyone who attempted to challenge the document with exclusion from the estate should not limit Mrs. Jackson's ability to oppose the executors. Branca instructed Howard Weitzman to see if a deal could be reached that would avoid a hearing in open court. The prospects for that did not look good when Katherine Jackson's attorneys responded by asking Judge Beckloff for the power to subpoena Branca and McClain in order to question them publicly about their involvements with AEG and Sony. Branca and his legal team countered by pressing the judge to move forward swiftly, alleging that this court battle was delaying an "urgent probe" into what had happened to millions of dollars in "missing" funds and properties that belonged to the Michael Jackson estate. Branca's attorneys said they had reason to believe valuable items were already being offered for sale by members of the Jackson family. A rumor was circulating that these items included a computer hard drive filled with Michael Jackson songs, many of them duets recorded with big-name artists.

He would answer these requests, and more, Judge Beckloff told attorneys for both sides, at the hearing already scheduled for July 6, a court date that suddenly loomed as the decisive battle for control of the Michael Jackson estate.

By then it appeared obvious that the amount of money at stake would far exceed the $236.6 million estimate of Jackson's net worth that Thompson, Cobb, Bazilio and Associates had made back in 2007. The chief of Platinum Rye, the world's largest buyer of music and talent for corporations, would tell *Forbes* magazine that Jackson's share of the Sony/ATV catalog alone was worth at least $750 million, considerably more than the accounting firm had valued it at back in 2007. Earnings of $80 million per year on Michael's half of the catalog would be a reasonable expectation, *Forbes* reported. The burgeoning value of Michael's music and image, though, were what lifted the potential size of his estate well above the billion-dollar mark. Demand for his records in the United States would remain strong week after week, making Michael Jackson the best-selling musical artist in the country for 2009, with 8.2 million albums sold. Sony sold 21 million copies of Michael's albums worldwide in the first eight weeks after his death, and nearly this many again in the eight months after that. *Thriller*, which had remained the best-selling album ever internationally (with more than 100 million copies sold), was closing the gap between it and the best-selling United States album, the Eagles' *Greatest Hits*, with 28 million copies shipped domestically, compared to 29 million for the latter album. Sony held a great deal of unreleased Michael Jackson material in its vaults but what the record company had was just a small portion of the work Michael had left behind. Dieter Wiesner and Marc Schaffel, who had probably gained greater access to Michael's personal film and music archives than any other two people alive, agreed that there were at least a thousand songs and thousands of hours of film and videotape stored away in warehouses. The potential earnings from its exploitation were incalculable.

Neverland was now worth considerably more than the $22 million Tom Barrack had paid to save it from foreclosure, and the huge collection of valuables that were removed from the ranch and warehoused by Darren

Julien had at least tripled in value, and might be worth ten times what they had been before. The day after Michael's death, Julien's had placed twenty-one items of Michael Jackson memorabilia purportedly belonging to David Gest on the block at a previously scheduled auction in Las Vegas. Prior to the event, the entire lot had been estimated to sell for $10,500. When the very first two items (a promotional display for a 1973 Jackson 5 album and an autographed copy of the Jackson 5 TV special *Goin' Back to Indiana*) sold for $27,500, it became obvious that the take was going to be at least ten times what Julien's had anticipated. By the end of the day, the take was nearly $1 million. On eBay, sellers were offering domain names like michaelthekingofpopjackson.com for $10 million. The pot of gold at the end of Michael Jackson's rainbow was not only real, it was also apparently bottomless.

Branca was in court, but Katherine Jackson was not, when Judge Beckloff convened the hearing that would decide the disposition of the Michael Jackson estate. The introduction of the various attorneys involved took nearly as long as the oral arguments. Branca had surrounded himself with a team of high-priced legal talent. Howard Weitzman informed the court that he was working in association with Joel Katz and Vincent Chieffo of the megafirm Greenberg Traurig. The Atlanta-based Katz was the chairman of Greenberg Traurig's global media and entertainment practice and perhaps the only music attorney in the country whose practice rivaled Branca's. Chieffo, based in Los Angeles, was the cochairman of the firm's national media and entertainment litigation group. Also present in court on behalf of Branca were three attorneys from Hoffman, Sabban & Watenmaker, a small but powerful LA firm that specialized in trusts and estates. One of the three, Jeryll S. Cohen, had been much in the news during the previous year when she helped Britney Spears's father James Spears gain temporary control of the singer's estate after the pop star was admitted several times to a psychiatric hospital.

⁃ Londell McMillan appeared as Katherine Jackson's principal attorney. McMillan had simply showed up at the Hayvenhurst house immediately after Michael's death, Mrs. Jackson would explain months later, insisting that her son would have wanted him to protect the family's interest. "He just put himself there," she recalled. At the July 6 court hearing, McMillan was accompanied by two other attorneys from the Los Angeles office of his law firm Dewey & LeBoeuf: John E. Schreiber and Dean Hansell. Also representing Katherine Jackson as her probate attorney was Burt Levitch, a partner at the Beverly Hills firm Rosenfeld, Meyer & Susman. Present in court as well was Las Vegas criminal defense attorney David Chesnoff, best known for being partners with former Las Vegas mayor Oscar Goodman and for representing a huge roster of celebrities and organized crime figures. He was there as an observer, Chesnoff explained to the court, and as the representative of Michael Jackson's brothers and sisters.

The last lawyer to identify himself to the judge was Joseph Zimring, a deputy in the California attorney general's office who explained that his office was required to involve itself whenever unnamed charitable institutions could receive assets from an individual's estate. The 20 percent of Michael Jackson's estate that had been assigned to unnamed charities potentially totaled hundreds of millions of dollars.

When the hearing finally got under way, it was clear that there would be no real objection to the will itself. According to Branca, the original document had been drafted in 1997 by an attorney at his firm who specialized in wills and trusts. He had no personal involvement, Branca assured the court. All he knew was that Michael did not want a family member in control of his estate and did not feel obligated to take care of his brothers and sisters. The will had been rewritten and signed again in 2002 because of Blanket's birth, Branca explained.

Though no one was publicly voicing doubts about the authenticity of the will, a number of people were privately asking rather pointed questions. One of these was why Branca and his law firm had retained an original copy of the will. At the time Branca was fired as Michael Jackson's attorney in early 2003, he presumably had received a letter that explicitly requested the return of his client's documents. Why hadn't Branca turned over the will then? Others pointed out that Barry Siegel had removed himself as an executor of the estate after he was discharged as Michael Jackson's accountant in 2003. This was the proper thing to have done, according to various interested parties, yet Branca had chosen to remain an executor of the will even after he was dismissed as Michael's attorney.

The "complete and unfettered discretion" that the trust document gave Branca and McClain over Michael Jackson's estate was particularly bothersome to the husband-and-wife probate attorney team of Andrew and Danielle Mayoras, authors of a serialized online analysis of the battle for control of the star's fortune. "They have total power and control over Katherine Jackson," Andy Mayoras explained. "This is unusual—because Michael Jackson's affection and trust and support of his mother was publicly displayed in the past, plus she has his kids. This is not normal for an adult beneficiary." Even more bothersome was the "exclusion clause" under which anyone who challenged the document risked being cut out of the estate. Since the only person named a heritor of the estate—besides Prince, Paris, and Blanket—was Katherine Jackson, the exclusion clause suggested that Michael had intentionally and specifically blocked his beloved mother from arguing that the will might be invalid.

Because the estate would not begin disbursing funds to Michael Jackson's children until they reached the age of thirty and would not finish until the last child, Blanket, turned forty, Branca and McClain (each in his late fifties) would continue to be paid millions of dollars a year to administer the estate for decades to come, if they remained executors. Katherine Jackson almost certainly would not live to see even her oldest grandchild turn thirty. "When you look at the potential for the trustees to reprofit from Michael Jackson's trust, you have to look at the trust with an extra-careful eye," Danielle Mayoras said, "because the ones who are profiting significantly from the trust are the trustees." Her husband complained that it was improper for Branca to be named as the executor and trustee of Michael Jackson's estate in a will and trust agreement that had been prepared by his own law firm. "Because these are the docs that put John Branca in a position to earn so much money," Andy Mayoras said, "as such, John Branca's firm should not have been the one to prep these docs." (Upon hearing of such complaints, Branca would retort through Howard Weitzman: "We are not aware of any ethical prohibition on an attorney both drafting a will and serving as an executor . . . To the contrary, California's Probate Code expressly contemplates an attorney drafter serving as either a trustee or executor.")

Tohme Tohme and several members of the Jackson family went so far as to question whether the will Branca had submitted to the court was actually signed by Michael Jackson, but none of them mounted a formal challenge. Concerned that Mrs. Jackson might forfeit the 40 percent of Michael's estate that had been left to her, Katherine's attorneys made no objection to the will, but did complain that the trust agreement gave John Branca—a man Michael Jackson had regularly professed to distrust—almost total control of the estate.

She would not have been so concerned, Mrs. Jackson was saying privately, if she believed John McClain was capable of providing a counterbalance to Branca. McClain, though, according to Branca's attorneys, was suffering from some unidentified affliction that kept him housebound. Howard Weitzman described McClain in court as physically disabled but mentally sound. He was reportedly a diabetic who had suffered a stroke that impaired both his mobility and his speech, but this was never confirmed by evidence submitted to the court. For someone so prominent in the music industry, McClain had long maintained a remarkably low profile. A blade-thin black man who in 1990 cofounded Interscope Records with Jimmy Iovine and Ted Field, McClain had worked before that as an executive at A&M Records, where he helped launch Janet Jackson's career.

McClain's decades-long relationship with the Jackson family was complex. During the mid-eighties, Janet formally affirmed her break with Joe Jackson by hiring McClain away from A&M to work as her manager. At the time, Joe had accused McClain of deviously luring his daughter away from him. "I've worked hard for my family," he said. "The problem comes, though, when others come in behind you and try to steal them away." Few, however, doubted the wisdom of Janet's decision when her next album, *Control*, turned into the breakthrough hit she so longed for, selling six million copies and establishing the youngest Jackson as a commercial force in the record industry. McClain, *Control*'s producer, was given enormous credit for the album's success. One of those who admired what he'd done for Janet Jackson was her brother Michael, who soon hired McClain away to work for *him*, reportedly on the condition that he have nothing further to do with his sister's career. Katherine Jackson was fond of McClain and told those around her that she believed he could be trusted. Joe Jackson doubted that, but like his estranged wife was far more concerned about Branca, who both he and Katherine believed would long outlive his coexecutor. "I told [Michael] all the time to watch John Branca, and that John Branca was no good," Joe said.

Only Katherine had standing before Judge Beckloff, though. "Frankly, Mrs. Jackson is concerned about handing over the keys to the kingdom so quickly," her attorney Schreiber told the judge at the July 6 hearing, making reference once again to "conflicts" that might affect John Branca's ability to make decisions most favorable to the Michael Jackson estate. If anyone's judgment was going to be clouded by conflicts, countered Paul Gordon Hoffman, it was Katherine Jackson, who would be more interested in spreading the wealth throughout her family than in building the fortune that Prince, Paris, and Blanket Jackson would eventually inherit.

After acknowledging that, "we're getting off to a bit of a rocky start here," Judge Beckloff ruled in favor of the executors named in the will. "Someone needs to be at the helm of the ship," the judge explained, and for now that would be Mr. Branca—and Mr. McClain if he was able to assist.

Under the circumstances, Beckloff's decision made sense. Weitzman and the other attorneys representing Branca in court had argued effectively that a singular level of knowledge and acumen would be required to sort through the mountain of debt and scores of lawsuits that Michael Jackson had left behind while at the same time managing the assets of his enormous—and enormously complicated—estate. Regardless of what enemies said about Branca's character, few disputed that he was a brilliant lawyer and a masterful deal maker. In the years since he had helped Michael Jackson secure the ATV catalog, Branca's negotiations of sales involving the copyrights of Kurt Cobain and Nirvana; Steven Tyler's Aerosmith publishing catalog; Julian Lennon's share of the Beatles' royalties; Berry Gordy's Jobete Music; and the catalog of the legendary Leiber and Stoller songwriting team each had established new precedents in the valuation of musical properties. Branca had helped Don Henley of the Eagles and John Fogerty of Creedence Clearwater Revival regain copyrights and secure royalties they'd lost years earlier. The unprecedented deal he brokered that made Korn partners with the band's record label, EMI, had become the industry standard. That Branca would put millions of dollars into his own pockets if permitted "unfettered" control of the Michael Jackson estate was a given, but it appeared reasonable to assume that the attorney would do this by "maximizing the estate," as Weitzman put it.

In his ruling, Judge Beckloff not only removed Katherine Jackson as the administrator of her son's estate, but also formally revoked his earlier order giving her power over her son's possessions, meaning that Branca could demand the return of anything that had been removed from the Carolwood chateau. While Beckloff left Mrs. Jackson's temporary custody of Prince, Paris, and Blanket Jackson in effect, the judge put off a decision about permanent custody until the end of the month, a ruling that was clearly intended to permit time for challenges.

The Jacksons recognized immediately how precarious their position had become. "Family attorney" Londell McMillan stood shoulder-to-shoulder with Branca outside the courthouse pledging to work with the estate's executors to ensure the futures of Michael's children. "We have no reason to believe that this is going to turn into a nasty fight over millions of dollars," McMillan told the assembled media.

For the moment, John Branca was no longer the Jacksons' main concern. The greatest threat to their grasp on Michael's fortune now, they knew, was Debbie Rowe.

One competing report after another about the parentage of Prince and Paris had surfaced during the days immediately following Michael's death. *Us*

Weekly published an article that identified Arnold Klein as the biological father of Prince and Paris, and suggested he would demand some say in deciding custody. Dr. Klein's denials, made to ABC's *Good Morning America* and on CNN's *Larry King Live*, were at the very least equivocal. "I think, to the best of my knowledge, I am not the father," Klein told King, then conceded a moment later that he had "once donated sperm" at Michael Jackson's request. He would not take a DNA paternity test, Klein insisted on both programs: "It's no one's business," he told King. Yet the doctor was quite willing to make suggestions that sounded vaguely like demands about the upbringing of the Jackson children. Debbie Rowe, their natural mother, should be involved in raising the two older kids, Klein said, and Grace Rwaramba should be included as well, since she was the caregiver all three of the children knew best. Within weeks, he would be dispatching an attorney to a courtroom filled with reporters with the demand that he be permitted to play a role in rearing Michael's children, a request Judge Beckloff dismissed as "quite bizarre."

Even as Klein's comments were being batted about in the United States, Mark Lester was telling newspapers in the UK that he could very well be the father of Paris and might be Prince's father as well. It was at Michael's request that he had donated his sperm at the Harley clinic in London (where Jackson had undergone a number of cosmetic procedures), Lester said, back in early 1996, about eight months before Michael's marriage to Debbie Rowe, and eleven months before the birth of Prince. It was to Paris, though, that he had always felt a "definite bonding," Lester said. "I think there's a definite possibility that she's part of me," he said. "Paris is very pale, with blue eyes," the former child actor pointed out. "All my daughters, apart from my eldest, are fair with blue eyes." When the Lester and Jackson families went on holiday together, he noted, people commented regularly upon how alike Paris and his daughter Harriet looked. He was only speaking out publicly, Lester said, because the Jackson family had cut him off from contact with all three children. "With Michael's mother now their legal guardian, it's like the kids are being isolated," he complained. "I'm their godparent, and Michael was the godparent to all my four kids. Our two families spent a lot of time together, and had a lot of fun together. Now I'm not able to have any communication with the children. My repeated phone calls aren't returned and e-mails go unanswered . . . I think it's cruel that I've been excluded." Uri Geller, who had been Jackson's friend for years and remained friends with Lester, confirmed that Michael had mentioned to him when they were in New York together that "he wanted Mark to help him father a child for him." Lester had offered to take a DNA test to settle the question of his paternity and Geller urged the Jackson family to allow it. "That would solve everything," he observed.

The Jacksons, though, categorically refused to acknowledge that there was any question about who had fathered Prince, Paris, and Blanket. "These genetic lottery attempts aren't going anywhere," Londell McMillan told reporters. Jermaine and Tito Jackson each insisted, in separate interviews with British tabloids, that Michael was the biological father of all three children. "People say things just to get attention, but those are definitely Michael's children," Jermaine told the *News of the World*. "You can look at the kids and tell that they are Michael's kids." Tito echoed his brother in a paid interview with the *Daily Mirror*: "They are [Michael's] children. Blanket is Michael's, I can tell. Those eyes don't lie. Them eyes are Michael's all over again. I see a lot of Michael in him." Prince and Paris were Michael's offspring as well, Tito went on: "Yes, they are. Just because they look white doesn't mean they are not his."

The motivations for the Jacksons' claims were obvious to many cynics. "What people don't understand is how powerful those kids are," Leo Terrell observed. "Those kids are the key, because the money goes wherever they go. And that means *all* the money, except what's being given to charity. Believe me, all the players know that.

"The provisions of the will hold initial weight, but not long-term weight," added Terrell, who had read the document closely. "Celebrity aside, no court is going to allow Michael Jackson to dictate from the grave who is the best parent for his kids. Will or no will, Debbie Rowe has the inside track, in front of Katherine Jackson."

Biology was a trump card in California custody contests and it was obvious that the Jacksons had been advised of this by their attorneys. On July 2, four days before the court hearing at which control of the estate and guardianship of the children was to be decided, Debbie Rowe had told the NBC affiliate in Los Angeles that she would seek a restraining order to keep Joe Jackson away from the kids. "I want my children," she told a reporter for the channel. "I am stepping up. I have to." A friend of Rowe's told *Us Weekly* that Debbie also planned to seek custody of Blanket, so that the children could stay together. Iris Finsilver, the attorney who had represented Rowe in her custody disputes with Michael Jackson, told the same magazine, "They are her children. She loves them and always has."

A private viewing of Michael Jackson's body for his family at Forest Lawn and a public memorial at the Staples Center were scheduled for July 7.

At Forest Lawn, Jackson's corpse had been prepared for its final public appearance by Karen Faye and Michael Bush, the makeup artist and costume designer who had been with him for years. The two spent nine hours blinking back tears and gagging on the reek of formaldehyde as they worked on the body as it lay next to the casket on a mortuary table. Faye applied a thick coat of the Lancome Dual Finish Powder that Michael had carried in a compact for years. Bush dressed his longtime client in a black tunic that was specially crafted for the occasion, draped with white pearls and accented by a gold belt that La Toya would liken to a boxing champion's. The costume designer had also helped to lift the body into the coffin. "The work me and Karen did with Michael at Forest Lawn, that bonded us for life," he would say later.

After the Jackson family had admired the work of Faye and Bush and said a private goodbye to Michael, his closed casket was transported to the Staples Center, the same venue where the final rehearsals for the "This Is It" concerts had been held, and where AEG would get its chance to put on a blockbuster Michael Jackson concert after all. The company had hired Ken Ehrlich and Kenny Ortega to work as the memorial's producers in consultation with the Jackson family. The assembly of those who would speak or perform was inevitably fraught with opportunism and exaggeration. Brooke Shields was among those chosen to deliver a eulogy even though she had had no relationship with Michael during the previous quarter century and not much of one before that. Perhaps in anticipation of Debbie Rowe's potential claim on both Michael's children and his estate, the Jacksons were loading the deck with race cards, asking that Reverend Al Sharpton, Representative Sheila Jackson Lee (D-Texas), and the children of Martin Luther King Jr. all be invited to speak. Berry Gordy, whose only contact with the deceased in recent years had been through the attorneys handling the lawsuits they filed against one another, was on hand to describe Michael as "like a son to me." By contrast, Marlon Jackson was genuinely affecting when he stood to say of his brother, "We will never understand what he endured . . . being judged, ridiculed. Maybe now, Michael, they will leave you alone." Eleven-year-old Paris upstaged everyone who had appeared before her when she stepped to the microphone at the end of the event to make a short speech that the memorial's producers insisted was unscripted and unplanned: "I just want to say that ever since I was born, Daddy has been the best father you can ever imagine. And I just want to say I love him so much."

In all its false notes and true ones, the Michael Jackson memorial had been suffused with a sense of uplift, and it would be remembered as yet another demonstration that Michael was far more loved than hated. After only 8,750 pairs of tickets were awarded, at random, from among the 1.6 million members of the general public who applied for them, the City of Los Angeles had braced for what they feared might be a stampede of the perimeter its police department had set up around the Staples Center. Instead, the atmosphere that surrounded the event was hushed. The 31.1 million television viewers in the United States who had tuned in to Michael's memorial made it the third-most-watched send-off in TV history, just behind the 33.2 million Americans who had watched Princess Diana's funeral in 1997 and the 35.1 million who had seen Ronald Reagan's burial in 2004.

Internet video streams that had not existed in 1997 and were nascent in 2004 attracted another 33 million views at the Web sites of the three major cable news networks (CNN, Fox News, and MSNBC) alone. Worldwide, the memorial collected the biggest television audience ever to watch a farewell to a public figure. More than 6.5 million British viewers had tuned in, which was still only about a third of the 18.7 million people who watched it in Brazil. Every one of Japan's networks covered the service, and 7 million of that country's viewers had tuned in to a live broadcast that was running simultaneously in Germany, France, and at least a dozen other countries. Politicians in Los Angeles who attempted a public objection to the estimated $1.4 million in costs associated with what one city councilman called a "private memorial for a celebrity singer" were quickly sent scurrying for cover when economists pointed out that the event had added at least several times that amount to the revenues of local businesses for three days, during which nearly every hotel room in the city was occupied.

Marlon Jackson's hope that his brother would finally be left alone was, of course, futile. Michael Jackson's death provided British tabloids with a freedom from their country's restrictive libel laws that they had never enjoyed while he was alive and they intended to take full advantage. As debate raged within the family and among Jackson's fans over the prospect of Michael's interment at Neverland, the tabloid media rushed to fill the void of decision with round after round of ghoulish speculation. One British tab reported that Jackson had long been "interested in having his body frozen in the hope he could be brought back to life." Because of the autopsy, however, "It is now too late for his wish to be granted as the freezing process—cryonics—must be initiated almost immediately after death." Another tabloid reported that "Michael Jackson will live on as a 'plastinated' creature'" preserved by the controversial German anatomist Gunther von Hagens, whose Body Worlds exhibition of human corpses had already shocked and fascinated more than 26 million visitors in cities around the world. The tabloid quoted von Hagens as declaring that, "An agreement is in place." The doctor had spoken to representatives of the Jackson family months earlier, a spokesman explained, and it was agreed that Michael's body would be plastinated and placed next to Bubbles, his late pet monkey, plastinated years ago and now on exhibit in the Body Worlds and the Mirror of Time exhibition at the O2 Arena.

On the day of Jackson's public memorial, the coroner's office released his death certificate. No cause for Michael's demise was listed. That determination would likely take weeks, it was explained, while various toxicology tests were completed. The coroner's office did for the first time acknowledge that it retained possession of Jackson's brain—or at least part of it—for neuropathology tests, adding that it would return the organ to his family when the testing was finished.

The question of what would be done with Michael's corpse continued to fill news columns, especially in the UK. What had kept so many Jackson fans at Neverland was, according to a London tabloid report on June 30, that Michael's family had scheduled a "public viewing" of his body at the ranch. This was entirely untrue, but the Jacksons *were* feeling the pressure of an enormous fan base that was insisting Michael should be buried at Neverland. Many local residents in Los Olivos were already unnerved by the vigil that had been taking place outside the gates of the ranch since the day of Michael's death. Two-lane Figueroa Mountain Road was bottlenecked by satellite news trucks, while vendors hawking T-shirts and spring water trailed hundreds of fans (and dozens of reporters) who appeared ready to camp out there "until it's all over," as one of them put it to the *Los Angeles Times*. The young clerks at the Corner Coffee House in Los Olivos enjoyed collecting business cards from journalists who had arrived from Germany, Belgium, Poland, and Venezuela, but most of the property owners in the community fretted about what the traffic and noise would do to their bucolic community if Neverland became Graceland West.

Jermaine Jackson and his father Joe were the two family members pushing hardest for a "shrine" at Neverland that would far exceed both the scale and appeal of the Elvis attraction in Tennessee. The creation of a private memorial park at the ranch would ensure a revenue stream that even Michael's music catalog couldn't match, Jermaine argued. Tohme Tohme had arranged for a helicopter to fly Jermaine to Santa Maria in order to make a direct appeal to local officials. All of the other Jackson brothers supported plans for a Michael Jackson memorial at Neverland, Tohme said. Tohme was also trying to negotiate an arrangement with Tom Barrack and Colony Capital, which still held the note on Neverland. Sensing an opportunity, Barrack ordered the work crews at the ranch to step up their pace. The main grounds were cleared and close to the condition in which Michael Jackson had left them within a few days of his death. The flower beds were "pristine," as *Fortune* magazine had it, while the mansion, guesthouse, and movie theater were all thoroughly refurbished, with fresh candy placed at the concession stand.

Barrack himself began quietly working to persuade county authorities to permit a burial at the ranch but learned quickly that California state regulations about the disposal of human remains were quite restrictive. Graves on private property were disallowed if even a single neighbor objected, and the last thing a majority of the people in the Los Olivos area wanted was an international tourist destination with a 10,000-vehicle parking lot in their backyard.

Katherine Jackson was resisting the idea of a Neverland burial. As it dawned on her that she held all the real power in the Jackson family, Mrs. Jackson seemed to be finding the voice that had been shouted down by Joe for so many years, and her character was shining through. Michael had never gone back to the ranch after leaving it in 2005, his mother pointed out, and associated Santa Barbara County mostly with humiliation and pain. And the suggestion by his brothers that Michael's body should be driven through the streets in an open coffin, so that mourners could throw flowers, just as they had for Princess Diana, was "ghoulish," Katherine said. Rebbie and Janet, the next two most influential family members, agreed that Michael's funeral should not turn into "the Jackson Four's greatest performance," as Frank Dileo described the brothers' plan. The scales tipped further when Michael's favorite nephew, Tito's son Taj Jackson, phoned Katherine to say that putting his Uncle Mike at Neverland was the wrong thing to do. All the magic of the place had been destroyed for Michael after the police raid in 2003, Taj said, and Katherine agreed. Michael would be laid to rest somewhere else.

Even after Neverland was rejected, the family spent another two months deciding how and where to arrange Michael's burial. As fans and family debated the subject, on the Internet and in the privacy of the Hayvenhurst

compound, the subject of Michael's spirituality percolated into a mean-
dering yet intense undercurrent of the conversation. What was the fitting
ceremony for someone who meant so many different things to so many
different people? All three of the major monotheistic faiths made claims
upon him, but Michael had not only worshiped as a Christian, a Jew, and
a Muslim, he had also persistently dabbled in witchcraft, regularly retaining sorcerers and shamans whose rituals were rooted in the polytheistic
Yoruba faith that originated in what is today Nigeria. Michael Jackson,
his former confidant Uri Geller explained, "believed in it all," from ghosts
and séances to Jungian archetypes and Einstein's Theory of Relativity.
His reach across all boundaries of belief had echoed especially loudly in
the international response to his death. "For us, this is a very great loss," a
young Russian fan standing outside the U.S. embassy in Moscow had told
the state news agency Novosti. "To us, he became a symbol of the spiritual
world. It's hard to convey how great a loss this is." Some of his countless
"spiritual advisors," Deepak Chopra and Rabbi Boteach among them, saw it
as tragic that, above all else, Michael believed in "magic," and that enduring
fame was the greatest proof of who possessed it. During his regular stays
at Geller's London home during the 1990s, Michael had insisted upon
taking time each day to pray or meditate in the family room, where one
of the main features was a large wooden sculpture of Elvis Presley holding a guitar. "Michael liked to sit near it," Geller remembered. Perhaps his
most enduring memory of Michael, Geller said, had come one day when
he paused in the doorway after dimming the lights in the family room,
so that he could observe his friend undetected. "I saw Michael lift up his
right hand and hold Elvis Presley's hand, with his head bowed," Geller
recalled. "That was how he prayed."

It was Katherine Jackson, of course, who would have the final say about
how and where the star was laid to rest, and Mrs. Jackson insisted that her
son had remained a Christian. Little more than a week after Michael's death,
Katherine advised the family that Michael's coffin would join those of the
other great stars in the Great Mausoleum of Forest Lawn Memorial Park, in
Glendale not far north of the "Hollywood" sign. Mrs. Jackson had instructed
Michael's brother Randy to find a place where Michael's grave would not
be disturbed by either overzealous fans or paparazzi ghouls, and Randy had
reported back that Forest Lawn was the one graveyard in all of Southern
California where the security was sufficient to protect a celebrity corpse of
even Michael Jackson's stature. Keyed entries and armed guards preserved
the peace amid the private sanctuaries of Forest Lawn's three hundred acres.

Katherine decided her son should be encrypted in the Great Mausoleum, which was designed in the style of Genoa's Campo Santo and used such similar elements as blind arches on the outer walls and a main entrance crowned by a Gothic tabernacle. Its marble replicas of Michelangelo's *The Pieta* and *Moses* were full-scale and stunningly precise, but not nearly as impressive as the gigantic (thirty-feet-long-by-fifteen-feet-high) rendition of *The Last Supper* in which da Vinci's masterpiece had been reproduced as a luminous stained-glass window.

Employing the Campo Santo's building-within-a-building design, the Great Mausoleum was divided into various "terraces" where the tombs of the rich and famous were connected by seemingly endless marble corridors lined with burial drawers. Among the stars whose remains were interred within the Great Mausoleum were Clark Gable, Humphrey Bogart, Jimmy Stewart, Nat King Cole and Sammy Davis Jr. W. C. Fields was there as well, and so was Michael's old pal Red Skelton, who had befriended him after the Jackson 5 appeared on the comic's television variety show. Out back, concealed by a hedge, was an exquisite flower bed where the cremated remains of Michael's hero Walt Disney had been spread. An adjacent plaque read, "Ashes scattered in paradise."

Upon John Branca's consent, Michael's mother had decided that his coffin should repose in the most impressive of the remaining crypts in the Great Mausoleum, at the end of the main hallway of Holly Terrace, in an area known as the Sanctuary of Ascension. Framed by three tall stained-glass windows that depicted the Ascension of Christ to Heaven and featuring a marvelously detailed free-standing marble sarcophagus, the Sanctuary of Ascension had remained empty for fifty years, due to its extraordinary cost (more than $600,000 for purchase and maintenance), and was said to be the last truly grand burial place in all of Forest Lawn.

Michael's coffin would be a near duplicate of the one in which James Brown had been buried: a solid bronze, gold-plated, blue-velvet-lined "Promethean" model from the Batesville Casket Company. That was Katherine's decision as well.

The King of Pop's body would repose in that Batesville casket for more than nine weeks, however, while fans worldwide awaited his funeral and burial. As the Jacksons bickered amongst themselves over the implementation of various competing projects, Michael's remains lay largely unattended in the Great Mausoleum's main hall, directly beneath that magnificent stained-glass reproduction of *The Last Supper* in the main entrance. Visitors were no longer welcome to view the work in a half-hourly unveiling. The tableau that met the eyes of those few who crept in to sneak a peek—mostly Forest Lawn employees—was at least as true to who Michael Jackson had been and to how he had lived as the Staples Center show that had been viewed by a worldwide audience of more than one billion. Michael had been lonely most of his life. Now, he was truly alone.

Before the end of July, the family's fortunes seemed to have been secured by an unexpected deal with Debbie Rowe that gave Katherine permanent custody of Prince, Paris, and Blanket. After word spread that Debbie had hired Eric George, the son of California Supreme Court Justice Ronald George, as her attorney, the debate in the media was entirely between those who believed Rowe would attempt to gain custody of the kids through the courts and those who insisted she would wring an eight-figure settlement from the Jackson Family Trust with the threat of such legal action. Debbie did neither.

Marc Schaffel served as the "intermediary," as he described it, in working out the agreement between Katherine Jackson and Debbie that settled the custody question. Convinced that John Branca still bore him enmity over the attorney's firing in 2003, Schaffel recognized that he would need the Jackson family's cooperation if he was going to salvage—and profit from—the projects he and Michael had developed together over the years, in particular the "What More Can I Give?" recordings. Demonstrating how effective he could be as a middleman was a way to win a seat at the table, Schaffel hoped. Beyond that, though, Marc was genuinely fond of Katherine Jackson and surprisingly protective of Debbie, given the things she had said about him during Michael's criminal trial.

Schaffel's relationship with Rowe had been renewed after Michael Jackson's death by a TMZ report that included confidential footage from his 2003 interview with Debbie for the "rebuttal documentary" broadcast. The portions that had been held back from Fox included materials subject to a joint consent agreement between Schaffel and Rowe. This footage had been seized when the Santa Barbara County sheriff's office executed a search warrant on Schaffel's home in Calabasas. All of that material was returned after Michael Jackson's criminal trial acquittal but somehow TMZ obtained copies and used the portion of the tapes in which Rowe spoke about using sedatives herself. In the interview, Debbie had stated that she used drugs to deal with stage fright, but the TMZ broadcast had tied her remarks to Michael's apparent death by drug overdose.

Schaffel and Rowe joined in a demand that the confidential outtakes be removed from TMZ's report. According to Howard King, TMZ at first replied that it had obtained the footage from a British TV station, then admitted that it had come from the Santa Barbara sheriff's department, and finally rescinded both claims, insisting its source was confidential and that the inclusion of the Rowe interview in its report fell under "fair use" provisions of the law. Schaffel, joined by Rowe, filed a lawsuit against TMZ that claimed the outtakes had "an estimated value of potentially millions of dollars, the exact amount of which shall be proved at trial," as King's moving papers put it.

Having secured his relationship with Rowe, Schaffel set about persuading Debbie and Katherine Jackson to meet privately without first informing their attorneys. The two got together for a preliminary conversation on July 10, and several other meetings followed. "Debbie's lawyer found out afterward and he was really cool with it," Schaffel recalled. "Katherine's lawyer, though, wasn't too happy." The upshot of the meetings had been an agreement that included no financial payments to Rowe and regular visits with the children. Debbie's only absolute condition was that Joe Jackson be allowed very little contact with the children, none of it unsupervised. Joe had already made a number of unnerving public comments about the potential show business careers of Michael's children. "I keep watching Paris. She . . . wants to do something," Joe told ABC News, then added, "And as far as I can see, well, they say Blanket, he can really dance." Debbie's custody agreement with Katherine mandated Joe to sign a separate document promising that he would stay away from the kids except during family gatherings. "It keeps him completely out of the picture," Schaffel said.

The custody agreement between Debbie and Katherine had also solidified Grace Rwaramba's position in the Hayvenhurst household. "Debbie has no problem with the kids living there with Katherine and Grace," Schaffel explained. "But if Grace left, things might change." The complications of the situation's shifting dynamics were rapidly apparent. In mid-July 2009, La Toya Jackson told reporters that she had "a lot of questions about Grace" and in fact was "highly suspicious" of the ex-nanny's motives. Soon after this, the *National Enquirer* reported that Rebbie Jackson and Rwaramba had actually come to blows during a dispute that resulted from Grace's criticisms of Katherine's parenting style. "Not exactly accurate," Schaffel said. "I mean, it was mostly Rebbie. Even Katherine pushed Rebbie back a little. Katherine and Grace are fine with each other. I think

Grace knows that Katherine is really a great person. But she's up there in age, and trying to make sure everybody is taken care of has really taken a toll on her. She needs to be in a situation where she can take it a little bit easier. The kids do, too."

Rebbie had so far been Katherine Jackson's main support in rearing the three children, actually sleeping on a cot next to Blanket's bed for the first few nights after the boy arrived at the Hayvenhurst estate and said he was scared to sleep alone. Some did not see the oldest Jackson sister's motives as entirely pure. "Rebbie tried to jump in at the beginning, because she thought she was gonna take the kids," said one family advisor. "Rebbie's got this deadbeat husband, and one of her first comments, right after Michael died, was, 'Well, the kids should move with me to Vegas and the estate should buy me a mansion to raise them in.'" What alienated Prince and Paris, the advisor said, was that Rebbie had been so insistent about indoctrinating the children with her religious beliefs. "Rebbie's like a born-again Jehovah's Witness," he said. "I mean, really off the edge. And she was trying to push this on the kids. And the kids just said, 'We don't want this.' So at one point Katherine had to say, 'I appreciate your help, Rebbie, but I'll handle it.'"

The three children were coping with life at Hayvenhurst in very different ways. Prince had withdrawn into a private world, rarely speaking except to answer questions, and then only in monosyllables. He was losing himself for hours on end playing video games on his PlayStation, something he had never been permitted to do while his father was alive. "No one could really tell what was going on with him," said the advisor. Paris appeared to make a much smoother transition. She was a sociable girl who didn't mind being alone when she was pursuing her favorite activities: reading and painting. Paris had turned her bedroom into an homage to "Daddy," rejecting Katherine's suggestion that she decorate with pictures of flowers and ballerinas and instead covering the walls with photographs and drawings of her father. "I always want to be able to see him," Katherine quoted the girl as saying. Blanket continued to cry at night and to wander about during the day wearing a lost expression for the first week or so after arriving at the Hayvenhurst compound, but seemed to slowly relax as he drew closer to his grandmother.

When the Jacksons invited Grace to join the children at the Hayvenhurst estate, some reasonably appraised it as a calculated move on at least two fronts. First, ensconcing Grace in the Hayvenhurst compound would further cement the family's claim that they offered the most stable and familiar environment for the three children. Secondly, all the Jacksons knew that there were tabloids that would be happy to hand over a small fortune for a tell-all about Michael and his family and that no one had more to tell than Grace. Keeping her close to them was clearly in the family's best interest.

Schaffel, who had helped negotiate the rapprochement between Grace and Katherine, insisted that Michael's mother's motives were pure. "All Katherine wants is what's best for those kids," he said. "And that's the reason she brought Grace back, to provide them with a sense of continuity. Say whatever you want about Katherine and Grace, but they both love Michael's children."

Soon after settling in at the family compound, though, Grace discovered what Katherine Jackson already knew: The biggest obstacle to creating a healthy environment for Michael's children was Hayvenhurst itself. As many as twenty people at a time were sleeping under the roof of the mansion, and even the home's 11,000 square feet weren't enough to comfortably contain them all. In addition to Prince, Paris, and Blanket, Jermaine's two youngest children, thirteen-year-old Jaafar and nine-year-old Jermajesty, were in residence, along with their two older half-siblings (fathered by Randy Jackson) Genevieve, twenty, and Randy Jr., eighteen. The mother of all four children was Alejandra Oaziaza, a forty-year-old Colombian woman who had been married to and divorced from both Randy and Jermaine, giving birth along the way to two children by each Jackson brother. That Alejandra's kids referred to Jermaine, the second Jackson brother she married, as "Uncle Daddy" had been a source of great amusement for Michael Jackson.

Also living in the estate's main house was seventeen-year-old Donte Jackson, whose parentage was unclear. The original explanation for Donte's presence was that he was Alejandra's son by Randy. This was dismissed by people who pointed out that the child had been born less than eight months after Alejandra gave birth to Randy Jr. and that no one had ever heard Donte address Randy as his father. There had also been rumors for years that Donte's biological father was actually Joe Jackson. Joe had in fact fathered at least four and perhaps as many as six children out of wedlock, according to Jackson family insiders. "When I was traveling with Michael, there were always these strangers coming up to him and acting like they were related," Schaffel recalled. "And Michael would say, 'Oh, that's my half-brother' that Joe had fathered with some other woman. I remember there was this Thai or Filipina maid Joe had gotten pregnant, and a bunch of other women." The *Sun* reported that Donte was the product of a "brief fling" between Michael Jackson and a "mystery woman" who might be Alejandra. Schaffel was certain this was not the case. "Michael used to joke that Alejandra had slept with all of the brothers except him," Schaffel recalled. "He said she was trying to work her way up to him."

The twenty-five-year-old "Norwegian rapper" Omer Bhatti, who was known as "Monkey" among the Jackson family, also called Hayvenhurst home, though how exactly he had been included in the household wasn't clear even to those, like Schaffel, who had ready access. "Omer sort of tried to go along with this tabloid story that Michael was his father, but nobody bought it, so he eventually gave up," Schaffel said. "But Katherine let him stick around. I don't know why." Katherine was genuinely fond of the young man, one of her advisors said, and determined to look out for him.

Even after Grace Rwaramba moved onto the estate, a Nation of Islam woman named "Sister Rose," the nanny Michael hired while living in the Carolwood chateau, also remained in the house. Michael's brothers Jermaine and Randy spent nights at the Hayvenhurst estate, as did La Toya, while other Jackson siblings visited from time to time and often left their children there. Besides Grace and Sister Rose, there was a number of live-in staff.

What just about everyone who knew the inside story agreed upon was that Alejandra Oaziaza had been the epicenter of turmoil within the Hayvenhurst estate for years. The South American beauty had been bewitching various Jackson men since first becoming involved with Randy when she was sixteen. After more than twenty years in residence at Hayvenhurst, the woman Prince, Paris, and Blanket called their aunt seemed to specialize in serving as a disruptive force.

"What really started up the problems at the house," Schaffel said, "was Alejandra undermining everything that Grace did, because Alejandra was looking at Michael's kids as her meal ticket. Alejandra was basically trying to instill in the children that she was the next best thing to their mother. Any time Grace would say, 'Do your homework. Don't watch TV. Go to bed,' Alejandra would say, 'Oh, stay up as late as you want. Don't listen to Grace. She's not your family, I am. She's just hired help.' And Alejandra's cool, right? She'll basically let them stay up all night, eat ice cream, cruise the Internet, whatever they want."

Michael had refused to allow his children to go online, and was quite restrictive about what they could watch on television as well. "He made them read," recalled Tohme Tohme. "I never saw them when they didn't have a book in their hands. They were reading constantly. Michael wouldn't let them go on the computer or any of that. Always a book."

"The kids were brought up to be very well mannered," Schaffel said. "They always said hello, good-bye, please, thank you, you're welcome, because that was what Michael taught them. But when they went to live at Hayvenhurst, their world changed dramatically. They had the Internet there, and all the kids had computers. The kids got on the computer, their parents got on the computer. It was just the way things were. And so with Alejandra's permission or encouragement they started reading shit about Debbie, and about Michael being a pedophile, and they had never been exposed to any of this information before."

Among the worst effects on Prince, Paris, and Blanket of what Alejandra (and the Internet) had done, Schaffel said, was how difficult it became for the kids to develop a relationship with their biological mother. "The kids didn't want anything to do with Debbie, even though Debbie really wanted to get to know them. It was very painful for her."

Katherine Jackson said she had no idea what to do. "She didn't want to cut the Internet off at the house because there was Genevieve and the other kids, Donte and Randy Jr., and they claimed they needed the Internet for their schools and their lives," Schaffel explained. "And meanwhile Michael's kids are watching the rude and nasty way that Alejandra's two youngest kids, Jaafar and Jermajesty, are treating Grace. They were always swearing at her and saying, 'You're the hired help.' And Prince and Paris started giving her a little lip themselves. Then whenever she laid the law down, Alejandra would undercut her. So it wasn't very long before Grace was saying that she didn't know how long she could stay at Hayvenhurst with Alejandra in the house. What it all boiled down to was that Katherine started realizing she was going to have to find another house where she could raise Michael's kids separately."

Nothing quite revealed how the Jackson family functioned—or dysfunctioned—as the announcement that Michael's funeral, scheduled to take place on his fifty-first birthday, was being postponed. Ken Sunshine delivered the news but gave no reason for the delay. Joe Jackson told reporters only that the family "had things we need to take care of first." What he didn't say was that those things involved appearances by family members at various events where they had been promised hefty fees. Joe himself was scheduled to spend the morning of Michael's birthday with La Toya at the Nokia Theater in Times Square in New York, where they would greet fans at a $25-per-ticket "birthday celebration" for Michael called "Long Live the King!" Joe would then immediately jet to Las Vegas to appear with Robin Leach at the installation of the Brenden Theaters "Celebrity Star" at the Palms.

The funeral finally took place on the evening of September 3, 2009, a date of no special distinction other than that no one in the Jackson family had any paying gigs to attend. Raging wildfires in the Angeles National Forest lit the northern horizon and turned the sky into a startling, spooky frieze of smoky vermilion. From a distance, the entire affair created a scene that might have been an outtake from the "Thriller" video. It seemed appropriate that the fleet of Rolls-Royces delivering the Jackson family to Forest Lawn should all be Phantom models.

A motorcade of more than twenty long black vehicles had made the trip from the Hayvenhurst estate to Glendale. Those who emerged from the assorted limousines and made their way toward the Great Mausoleum included Lisa Marie Presley, Quincy Jones, Berry Gordy, Chris Tucker, Macaulay Culkin and his actress girlfriend Mila Kunis, Kenny Ortega and Travis Payne, the Reverend Al Sharpton, and federally indicted home run champion Barry Bonds. The most notable guest of all was seventy-seven-year-old Elizabeth Taylor, who had scorned the public "hoopla" of the Staples Center memorial but arrived early at Forest Lawn, pushed in a wheelchair that was positioned at the end of one row before most of the other guests arrived. Joe Jackson came separately as well, but took a seat in the front row next to his estranged wife and alongside his sons, who showed up dressed in black tuxedos brightened by red ties and pocket handkerchiefs, accented by the same single silver glove that each of them had worn at the public memorial. The most notable absences were Stevie Wonder, who had stayed away so as not to be "a distraction," and Debbie Rowe, who had received an invitation but remained at home.

Owing to the suffocating heat of an evening on which the temperature didn't drop below ninety degrees until well after sunset, the service itself was to be conducted in a garden space just outside the Great Mausoleum, from which Michael's gold-plated casket was carried to the specially built stage, then adorned with and surrounded by enormous bouquets of white lilies and white roses. Two large painted portraits of the star, both from Thriller Time, flanked the stage.

The funeral's opening prayer was delivered not by a Jehovah's Witness but by Pastor Lucious Smith of Pasadena's Friendship Baptist Church, who began by reading Ecclesiastes 3:7. "A time to tear and a time to mend; a time to keep silent and a time to speak." Gladys Knight's performance of the gospel hymn "His Eye Is on the Sparrow" moved most to tears, while

Clifton Davis delivered a heart-stopping rendition of the Jackson 5's "Never Can Say Goodbye." Lisa Marie wept throughout and seemed in some way conjoined to Katherine as mourners in chief. His death had transformed Lisa Marie's attitude toward Michael in ways that seemed at once predictable and surprising. The last time Michael had called her, in 2005, shortly after his acquittal on the criminal charges against him, "He asked if I still loved him," Lisa Marie would tell Oprah Winfrey a year later. Michael said "he wanted to tell me that I was right about a lot of the people around him, that it had panned out to be exactly what he and I had talked about years ago," Lisa Marie recalled. Michael "was trying to throw a line out to see if I would bite emotionally, and I wouldn't," she said. To his question about whether she still loved him, "I told him I was indifferent," Lisa Marie remembered, "and he didn't like that word, and he cried." But still, for some reason she had sobbed all during the day of Michael's death, Lisa Marie told Winfrey, even before she heard the news: "I was in England and I don't know why but it was the strangest day of my life . . . I was trying to work and I came home and I was literally cutting my food, eating my dinner, crying. And I wanted to go upstairs and watch something mindless on TV and stop crying. I looked at my husband and said, 'I don't know what's wrong with me, I just can't stop,' and then an hour later the call came and I heard." She was still crying more than two months later. She had spent the time since Michael's death "trying to gain clarity," Lisa Marie would tell Winfrey, "because at some point I pushed it away and I just had to move on with my life and when that happened it was like a tidal wave brought it all back."

When Elizabeth Taylor rose from her wheelchair to speak, the choke in her voice gave the simple words a complex power: "We shouldn't have to be here. It shouldn't have happened! He shouldn't have passed away." Joe rambled on about the people who had tried to "cheat" Michael and warned that he and the rest of the family would find those responsible for his son's death and make them pay, but Michael's father's thinly disguised avarice was forgotten moments later when a young man who had scar tissue for features stood to speak.

David Rothenberg had become a public figure back in 1983 when, as a six-year-old boy, he was the victim of a crime that shocked Southern California to a depth that few other events of the eighties would reach. David's monstrous father Charles Rothenberg, seeking revenge against his ex-wife during a bitter custody dispute, had doused his son with kerosene and set him afire as the boy lay sleeping in a hotel room bed. David survived, but third-degree burns covered more than 90 percent of his body, leaving him so horribly scarred that no amount of plastic surgery could give him a face.

Protected by his mother from the pitying looks of adults who shuddered involuntarily the first time they saw him, the boy still glimpsed the terrified expressions on the faces of children he met outside burn wards. He had just turned seven and was still cycling in and out of surgery when he was first invited to visit Michael Jackson at home, David Rothenberg recalled, at the height of Michael's *Thriller* success. Michael looked him in the eye and hugged him on that occasion, and every time they met afterward, the young man recalled. He had visited Neverland Ranch many times over the years, and if he was certain of anything in this world, it was that Michael Jackson would never hurt a child. "Michael was always there for me," David Rothenberg finished. "Through everything, he never let me go."

Michael's own three children sat in front-row seats throughout the service. Before it began, they had been permitted to approach the casket together and lay a golden crown at its head. By the end, Prince and Paris were so spent that they fell asleep against each other's shoulders in the backseat of a Rolls-Royce. Blanket, though, remained awake and continued to sob as the children were driven back out onto the street.

The mourners were gone by the time Michael's casket was carried back to Holly Terrace and installed in the Sanctuary of Ascension, where it would remain, Forest Lawn had promised the family, as long as the building stood.

On August 27, 2009, one week before Michael Jackson's funeral, the Los Angeles County coroner's office had officially ruled his death a homicide.

"Acute propofol intoxication with benzodiazepine effect," was the cause cited in the coroner's report, which listed the drugs in Jackson's system as "propofol, lorazepam, midazolam, diazepam, lidocaine, and ephedrine." The implicit indictment of such reckless polypharmacy was about as clear an indication as could be offered that Dr. Conrad Murray was going to be charged with responsibility for Michael's death.

LAPD Chief William Bratton had told reporters as early as July 9 that his detectives were investigating a possible homicide but would have to wait for the coroner's toxicology reports. A finding that the benzos in his system had contributed to Michael Jackson's death would certainly complicate matters. The *Los Angeles Times* quoted a senior law enforcement official as saying that even if the coroner ruled that Jackson's death had been a homicide, it was possible no charges would be filed, given the entertainer's well-documented history of drug abuse. If the coroner ruled that propofol was what had killed Mr. Jackson, the *Times* source added, then Murray and any other doctor involved in providing or administering the drug could very well face involuntary manslaughter charges.

In addition to the independent investigation being conducted by the Los Angeles County coroner's office, at least seven state, local, federal, and foreign agencies were working with LAPD detectives. That the U.S. Drug Enforcement Administration had been called in was not simply the result of DEA "expertise," but also because the agency had the power to operate across jurisdictional boundaries. News that the police departments in Las Vegas and Houston were cooperating in the investigation of Conrad Murray was no surprise, but word came that the New York police department, the Dade County sheriff's department in Florida, Scotland Yard in London, and Interpol were also involved. California State attorney general Jerry Brown told reporters that his office was mining its computer database for information about prescription drugs that had been provided to Michael through various doctors and pharmacies under any number of aliases. A team of physicians had also been assembled through the medical board of California to make a determination about whether Conrad Murray and/or other doctors had been guilty of negligence in their treatment of Michael Jackson, a finding that would have to be reached in order to sustain a manslaughter prosecution in the case.

As early as July 4, the *Los Angeles Times* had reported that investigators were "focusing on at least five doctors who prescribed drugs to Michael Jackson." None of those physicians was named, but it didn't require inside sources to know that one of them was Arnold Klein. Among the first search warrants executed by the DEA was one that ordered the Mickey Fine Pharmacy to turn over "all records, reports, documents, files, inventories, and written information" in connection to its distribution of controlled substances. The raid on Mickey Fine appeared to have been targeted primarily at the dermatologist whose offices were just upstairs, and any doubt was removed when Los Angeles County assistant chief coroner Ed Winter showed up at Dr. Klein's door to serve a subpoena demanding information about medical files in his possession.

Klein had been answering tough questions since the afternoon of Jackson's death, when Debbie Rowe called the doctor and, according to Jason Pfeiffer, "started screaming at him. I heard her say, 'What did you give him?' And Klein said, 'I wasn't there. I haven't given him Demerol for a couple days.'"

Ed Winter would say he had become interested in Dr. Klein when he examined the more than thirty vials and packages of medications that had been recovered from Michael Jackson's master suite at the Carolwood chateau. "We located prescription slips in the names of Omar Arnold, Peter Madhonie, and other names," Winter recalled. "These were specifically from Klein." Winter promptly filed a subpoena for Dr. Klein's medical records, and by the time the coroner's investigator visited Klein's offices in mid-July reporters were already chasing the story.

In public, Klein seemed self-assured as ever, initiating a media offensive the moment his name began to be raised in connection to the criminal investigation. Though unwilling to reveal much about the prescriptions of Demerol and Dilaudid he had written for Michael Jackson over the years, and refusing to say a word about the twenty-seven occasions on which he had self-prescribed controlled substances between the time of Jackson's return to the United States from Ireland in 2008 and his death in 2009, Klein wanted to make it clear that he had never prescribed propofol for Michael or anyone else. "I didn't give him the crap they're talking about," he snapped at an interviewer on ABC's *Good Morning America*. "How am I going to prescribe Diprivan when I don't understand how to use it." Klein's claim seemed convincing when he added that whoever *had* provided and administered propofol to Michael should be treated as a criminal: "It becomes nothing more than manslaughter, or something worse than that."

By August, Klein was just one of at least a dozen physicians who were either flinching from or responding to stories that they had provided Michael Jackson with controlled substances. Subpoenas had been served to obtain the medical records of not only Arnold Klein, but also of Mark Tadrissi, the dentist who had acknowledged giving Michael and his son Blanket propofol; Dr. David Adams, a Las Vegas physician who reportedly admitted to the LAPD that he gave Michael Jackson propofol before Conrad Murray did; and Dr. David Slavit, who had conducted the independent medical examination of Michael for AEG. Assistant Chief Coroner Winter arrived unannounced at Dr. Larry Koplin's clinic in Beverly Hills with a search warrant shortly after his first visit to Arnold Klein's shop just down the street, demanding to examine the records of a nurse who had worked as an anesthetist in Koplin's office during the time Michael Jackson was his patient. Winter also visited Dr. Randy Rosen at the Spalding Pain Medical Clinic in Beverly Hills, a high-end outpatient surgery center where Arnold Klein had reportedly required the services of the clinic's anesthesiologists while he performed an assortment of cosmetic procedures, including, perhaps, some on Michael Jackson. The Spalding Pain Medical Clinic was also, it turned out, where Debbie Rowe had given birth to Paris Jackson in 1998. Knowing that he might be visited next, Dr. Allan Metzger sent forth his celebrity attorney Harland Braun to tell reporters that while his client "did give Mr. Jackson a prescription for a mild sleeping pill in 2009, because Michael was complaining of not sleeping," Dr. Metzger "turned Michael Jackson down" when the entertainer asked for propofol. The doctor had not seen Mr. Jackson since an April 2009 visit to Michael's home, Braun added, which was the occasion "when he said no to Michael's request for Diprivan." Even without a search warrant served upon him, Dr. Metzger was cooperating fully with authorities, the attorney added: "We have turned over all of Dr. Metzger's records to the LAPD."

Alex Farshchian, on the other hand, was resorting to a duck-and-cover strategy, refusing even to admit that he was one of the doctors being targeted by the investigation into Michael Jackson's death. Plenty of other people, though, were talking to investigators about allegations that the Miami doctor had "overprescribed" antianxiety drugs to Jackson at a time when Michael was downing as many as forty Xanax pills a day. LAPD detectives confided in off-the-record interviews that they were convinced Farshchian had supplied Jackson with Demerol over a period of years.

Even as Farshchian kept silent, a number of other doctors who were not implicated in the investigation chose to be proactive with the media and to make it clear that they were not among Michael Jackson's enablers. Tokyo-based physician Eugene Aksenoff, who had treated both Michael and his children during their visits to the city, told the *Japan Times* that he had steadfastly refused Michael's requests for stimulants (though he said nothing about any requests for sleeping medications) and hypothesized that Michael's overuse of skin-whitening medications had contributed to the symptoms that plagued him in later years, including his insomnia. Deepak Chopra, who had been licensed as an internist and endocrinologist long before he became a celebrity self-help guru, was outspoken in criticizing the doctors who had fed Michael's drug habit. "We put drug pushers in jail, but give licenses to doctors who do the same thing," Chopra said in one of many interviews. "I know personally that they write multiple prescriptions and they even use false names . . . This cult of drug-pushing doctors, with their codependent relationships with addicted celebrities, must be stopped."

Physicians and pharmacists weren't the only ones sweating the investigation into Michael Jackson's drug history. At least two dozen former and current employees or entourage members were suspected of having in some way facilitated Jackson's procurement of controlled substances, mostly by letting him use their names on prescriptions and/or picking up the drugs at various pharmacies in Los Angeles, Beverly Hills, Santa Barbara, Las Vegas, and Miami. Whether people like his ranch managers Joe Marcus and Jesus Salas had deniability was unclear, and the same might be said of Frank Cascio, whose real name and his alias Frank Tyson had both been used on prescriptions. The names of at least two of Michael's employees at the time of his death, Kai Chase and Michael Amir Williams, were listed among the "aka's" in the search warrants served on Conrad Murray's home and office, as were Paul Farance, Bryan Singleton, Jimmy Nicholas, Roselyn Muham-mad, Faheem Muhammad, Fernand Diaz, and Peter Madonie. The name of Michael's oldest son, Prince, as well those of the long-dead novelist Jack London and the legendary 1930s cabaret performer Josephine Baker were also listed on search warrants as among those Jackson was suspected of using to get prescription drugs during the last months of his life. Items seized in the raid on Conrad Murray's office included a CD inscribed "Omar Arnold," the name Michael had used for years on his drug prescriptions. Even those like Joey Jeszeck who had cooperated with authorities and described Mi-chael's drug use freely back in 2003 and 2004 were being forced to submit to further questioning from various law enforcement agencies, with the threat of prosecution if they failed to disclose all they knew.

Dr. Murray, though, continued to be the primary target. On August 28, 2009, the day after the coroner's report officially ruling that Michael Jack-son's death had been a homicide, the LAPD announced that it was referring the case to prosecutors who would decide whether to file criminal charges. Murray was left to twist in the wind for weeks afterward while the media speculated endlessly about the strength of the case. Jackson's history of drug abuse, which had long predated Murray's presence in his life, was mitigat-ing but not exculpatory. Of far greater concern to the Los Angeles County district attorney's office was that the LAPD had not secured the Carolwood chateau in the days after Michael's death, permitting Jackson family members to reportedly remove not only the cash secreted under the rugs but entire truckloads of other property, which was certain to raise chain-of-custody issues at a criminal trial. Among the missing items was Michael's personal computer.

Murray remained free on his own recognizance and was living in Hous-ton that November when he made his first public comments in connec-tion to the case to the fellow members of his Galilee Missionary Baptist Church. "I know what trouble is," the doctor told them, then attempted to paint himself as a well-intentioned physician who was being made into a scapegoat: "I, with my compassion, was only trying to help my fellow man. But it appears I was at the wrong place at the wrong time." He had not been convicted of any crime, and was still licensed to practice medicine, Murray reminded the parishioners; he would continue to see patients at his clinic in the Acres Homes area. His attorney Chernoff explained why, in a statement issued that same day: "Because of deteriorating financial conditions and prompting by many of his beloved patients . . . Dr. Murray plans to attend to patients in both Las Vegas and Houston. His decision to first return to practice in Houston was made because of the greater need these low-income patients have for his services and the prohibitive cost of reopening his clinic in Las Vegas."

The effect in Los Angeles was stepped-up pressure on authorities to initiate a process that would, at the least, strip Murray of his medical license. In January 2010, as leaks out of the DA's office suggested charges were imminent, Chernoff posted a statement on his Web site announcing that his office was "negotiating with the district attorney's office the surrender of Dr. Murray." On February 8, 2010, Murray was officially charged with involuntary manslaughter, a crime that carried a maximum sentence of four years in state prison. After a plea of not guilty was entered at his arraignment, the district attorney's office revealed that it would use the public forum of a preliminary hearing rather than the private setting of a grand jury proceeding to bring Dr. Murray to trial.

The Jackson family had long since decided that Conrad Murray wouldn't be the only one to pay. It had taken the Jacksons little time to come to a collective recognition that claims of "foul play" were not necessarily their best hope for profiting from Michael's death. The suggestion that Tohme Tohme was the ringleader of the "cabal" who were behind it all was undercut by the family's gradual realization that Tohme had not been around during the last weeks of Michael's life. While Murray was the primary target of law enforcement, a civil lawsuit against the doctor was unlikely to yield any payday at all, given the number of creditors who had already filed claims on the man's rapidly diminishing assets. As the summer of 2009 drew toward an end, the vague outline of a legal strategy was emerging from the family's garbled insinuations. Joe Jackson began to suggest that Michael had been "driven" to his death by people intent upon exploiting his talent, and reminded reporters that AEG, not his son, was Dr. Conrad

Murray's employer. As if picking up on a cue, La Toya Jackson confided to a British reporter that Paris Jackson believed her father had been pushed to a breaking point by the producers of the "This Is It" shows: "She said, 'No, you don't understand. They kept working him and Daddy didn't want that, but they worked him constantly.' I felt so bad."

The family had watched with obvious discontent as it dawned on them that, rather than being stuck with the $30 million in losses reported in the media in the days after Michael's death, AEG was likely to make a substantial profit from the "This Is It" deal. A coroner's finding of death by drug overdose might make it difficult for AEG to collect insurance payouts to recoup the estimated $25 million it had invested in preparations for the London shows, but the company shrewdly offered ticket holders for the O2 Arena shows the choice between a full refund and a special "souvenir" ticket that featured a three-dimensional image of Michael Jackson. As many as half of the nearly one million people given this option had chosen the souvenir ticket, meaning that AEG could keep nearly 50 percent of the $85 million it had collected. The high-definition video footage of Michael's rehearsals for the "This Is It" shows held in an AEG vault at the Staples Center set off a bidding frenzy among Hollywood studios when it was offered up as the raw material of a motion picture. Sony put up a bid of $50 million right out of the gate. AEG was also said to be considering a televised tribute concert at the O2 that would incorporate the staging and the choreography of the "This Is It" shows, a spectacle that could run for weeks or even months and produce millions more in profits.

Patrick Allocco and AllGood Entertainment were now locked in a legal battle with the Jackson estate, demanding $300 million that the company argued should be paid out of profits from the planned "This Is It" movie and out of revenues from the Sony/ATV catalog. AllGood's claim that Frank Dileo, representing himself as Michael Jackson's manager, had made a written promise that Jackson would tour for the company created some potentially complex problems. Dileo hadn't been Michael's manager at the time of the AllGood agreement, according to the Jackson estate, which was currently paying Dileo for supposedly serving as the entertainer's manager during the run-up to the O2 shows—a deal that had been negotiated entirely by Tohme Tohme, whom the estate wasn't paying at all. Also named as a defendant in the AllGood lawsuit was AEG Live, which continued to be in business with the Jackson estate and was keeping Dileo tucked comfortably under its wing, knowing he might be needed as a witness in the separate lawsuits the company anticipated would be filed against it by both Tohme and the Jackson family. In the end, the fact that the AllGood contract was so badly written, and that the company had failed to make the initial binder payment promised in that agreement, rendered all other issues moot, and the case was dismissed in federal court on a motion for summary judgment made by Howard Weitzman.

It would not be so easy, though, for AEG and the estate to free themselves from claims by the Jackson family and Tohme Tohme. AEG had seen the Jacksons coming almost from the start, and recognized that the family was using both Michael Jackson's enormous fan base and the media to develop a PR case against the company. "It's easy to make us look like corporate villains who took advantage of Michael Jackson," Randy Phillips complained to *Fortune* magazine in October 2009. "It's quite the opposite—we were the people who empowered Michael Jackson and gave him his dream back." Key witnesses Frank Dileo and Kenny Ortega were clearly allied with AEG. Each man had made multiple public comments about how fit and ready Michael Jackson appeared to be in the final days and weeks of his rehearsals for the O2 shows. "I saw a guy that wanted to perform," Dileo told ABC. "But he wanted to do it right. And he was strong enough. He was working out every day. If he wasn't healthy, if there was something wrong, I would have stopped him. There was nothing to stop." Recalling that final "great week" of rehearsals, Ortega recalled a Michael Jackson who "couldn't wait to get to London," and described Michael's death as "an accident": "I don't think that everybody contributed to his life in the most positive way," Ortega allowed in one interview, "but I don't think you can hold those people responsible. Michael was a fifty-year-old man. A father. A professional. A businessman." With Dileo already in their pocket, AEG and the estate had seemingly secured Ortega as well by endorsing him as the director of the *This Is It* film being made from the rehearsal footage.

The *This Is It* film itself presented a Michael Jackson to the world who was, as always, different things to different people. Many reviewers and fans agreed with the Wrap.com description of the star as "a surprisingly spry and energetic presence, bounding around the stage and exhorting the backup dancers and musicians to give their all—a far cry from the Howard Hughes–like figure withering away in his final days that had been portrayed in the tabloids." Others who knew Michael personally, though, said that it pained them to see how diminished he had looked in the film. "He was doing the very same things he had done on the *HIStory* tour," complained Dieter Wiesner. "I could see in his eyes how sad that made Michael, to be doing the same thing all over again, only not so well." Tohme Tohme said that he had seen a Michael who was shockingly more gaunt and fragile-looking than the entertainer he had traveled to London with in March 2009. "In the film he was dancing mostly with his hands, he could barely move his lower body," Tohme said. "He was not the same Michael I saw in March and April."

Remarks such as that might have made Tohme an excellent witness for the Jacksons in a claim against AEG, but Michael's former manager was far from disposed toward the family, still convinced that Joe and Katherine had conspired with Dileo and Leonard Rowe against him, and that by doing so had contributed to their son's death. "If I am there, no way will this Dr. Murray be in that house," Tohme said. "I would never have let Michael lose so much weight. I would not have let that happen to him. He would still be alive if those people hadn't separated him from me."

Tohme's adversarial relationship with the Michael Jackson estate, and with the estate's three general counsels—John Branca, Howard Weitzman, and Joel Katz—had also hardened as the end of 2009 approached. Branca and his legal team were backing Frank Dileo's claim that he had been Michael Jackson's manager "in life and in death." It was widely reported that the estate was putting Dileo up at the Beverly Hilton and paying him some undisclosed sum of money for services that were not detailed in public records.

Tohme felt betrayed that Randy Phillips now seemed to be going along with the story that Dileo was Michael Jackson's manager. Without Phillips, there was no way that Frank Dileo would have been credited as a producer on the *This Is It* movie, Tohme knew. "I alone made the *This Is It* deal," he said. "Randy knows that. He has said so in public. And yet Dileo is the one who receives credit and money for the movie." Tohme was unsettled by his belated discovery that Phillips had given Dileo an office at AEG during the last weeks of Michael Jackson's life, and even more disturbed to learn that AEG was still taking care of Dileo in an assortment of ways, even using the company's cars and chauffeurs to carry Frank to various music industry events, including the Grammy Awards ceremony. Phillips had told various media outlets, including *Rolling Stone* magazine, that Tohme remained Michael's manager right up to the end. It was Randy, Tohme pointed out, who had insisted he should be the one to join Jermaine Jackson at UCLA in announcing Michael's death. That day, Phillips introduced Tohme to people as Michael Jackson's manager, but in his dealings with Branca and the estate, Phillips was reportedly not so sure. Under pressure from AEG's attorneys not to comment, Phillips would only say of the dispute over who managed Michael Jackson that "There was a great deal of confusion, some of it created by Michael himself."

27

The competing schemes, hidden agendas, and factional conflicts that churned and seethed beneath the superficially united front of the Jackson family provided all the points of vulnerability that John Branca required to break down their challenge to his administration of the Michael Jackson estate.

By the late summer of 2009, Randy Jackson was leading the opposition to Branca, in coordination with his father. Both men, and most of the Jackson family for that matter, were suspicious of the July 2, 2002, will and the Michael Jackson Family Trust document that Branca had produced out of his law firm's files. They had what several attorneys told them were solid reasons for that suspicion. Branca's possibly questionable decision to permit his own firm to prepare a will that named him as the executor of an estate that included one of the most valuable properties in the entire entertainment industry—a half-share of the Sony/ATV catalog—was just one of several potential fault lines.

Attorneys who specialized in probate law agreed almost unanimously on how badly drawn both the will and the trust appeared to be. Each document was much shorter, much simpler, and much less detailed than one would have expected in the disposition of such a large personal fortune. The absence of provisions that would have protected Michael Jackson's estate from tax burdens was perplexing to a number of lawyers who had read the trust agreement. The failure was so glaring that it raised questions about a breach of fiduciary duty, several of them said. Then there was the fact that the trust had been prepared and executed in March 2002, nearly four months before the date on the signature page of the will. Commonly (though not always) a person's will and his trust agreement are executed on the same day.

The observation that resonated most loudly among Michael's family, though, was that his children had not been listed by their proper legal names. The oldest boy's name in the will was written "Prince Michael

Jackson, Jr." when in fact his name is Michael Joseph Jackson, Jr. (no "Prince"); the girl's name in the will omitted the hyphen between Paris and Michael, and the youngest was identified as "Prince Michael Joseph Jackson II" when it is actually Prince Michael Jackson II (no "Joseph"). Every one of the Jacksons, along with most of those who had spent any time with Michael during the previous decade, understood how particular he was when it came to his kids. "Michael would never sign something where his kids' names were not spelled right," Joe Jackson said, and for once his entire family agreed with him.

The biggest questions of all, though, continued to be how and why John Branca had managed to remain in possession of Michael Jackson's will and trust agreements until July 2009. Jackson lawyer Brian Oxman had secured a copy of the letter with which Michael had dismissed Branca as his attorney in February 2003. In it, Branca had been "commanded" to "deliver the originals" of "all of my files, records, documents, and accounts" to the new attorney, David LeGrand. He did in fact deliver several boxes of papers to LeGrand. In 2004, after LeGrand was dismissed, Brian Oxman took possession of those documents. "I had access to every file and I had to go through them," he said. "And I did. There was no will. There was no trust. It just showed up after he died." Randy Jackson said (and eventually signed a sworn statement to this effect) that he had made a follow-up demand to Branca for Michael's documents in 2004, specifically mentioning the will. Branca had told him he would turn over the documents still in his possession only if he was paid monies he claimed to be owed for recent services. Under United States law, an attorney is obligated to turn over all documents upon request whether bills have been paid or not. Branca never sent the will, Randy Jackson said.

Branca's failure to turn over the will the first time he was asked to surrender all documents would have been a reasonable basis for referring him to the State Bar for disciplinary action, Oxman said. That he had refused two subsequent requests for his former client's documents nearly ensured that Branca would have faced some sort of investigation from the bar, added Oxman, who was in a position to know, having been twice suspended by the State Bar himself for failing to follow proper procedures.

The Jacksons knew about Oxman's reputation in the local media for unseemly pursuit of television airtime. The family also knew, though, as did a good many attorneys in Los Angeles, that however bad his personal judgment might be, Oxman was a smart lawyer and a terrific researcher. When he suggested hiring a team of private investigators to see if there were still more reasons to be suspicious of the Michael Jackson will that Branca had submitted to Judge Beckloff, Randy Jackson agreed and so, eventually, did the rest of the family.

In October 2009, Janet Jackson hosted the family meeting at which the contents of the report were revealed. The very first fact laid out on the table was the most startling: Michael Jackson had been in New York City on July 7, 2002, the date on which, according to the handwritten annotation on the signature page of the will, he had executed that document in Los Angeles.

The date in question had fallen right in the midst of the four days in the summer of 2002 when Michael Jackson was laying a very public siege to Sony Music and its chairman, Tommy Mottola, a period in which he had been seen, photographed, and written about as he rolled up Madison Avenue in a double decker bus packed with protesters from Harlem organized by the Reverend Al Sharpton, waving a photograph of Mottola upon which he had drawn horns and a pitchfork. All of the city's daily newspapers, including the *New York Times*, had chronicled the entire drama. News photographs of Michael Jackson had been taken in New York on July 6, July 8, and July 9, but, oddly, not on July 7. Michael had spent most of that day hiding out in his hotel suite, his bodyguards said, blistered by the backlash against him throughout the recording industry and in the national media. He had, however, attended a meeting in Harlem during the afternoon, according to Al Sharpton.

The private investigators had also gotten hold of the Interfor report that was commissioned by Michael Jackson (through David LeGrand) back in late 2002. "Interfor's investigation found a tight relationship between Branca and Tommy Mottola," the second paragraph of the report on Branca began, "primarily in regard to the affairs of Jackson. Interfor had begun investigating the flow of funds from Jackson through Mottola and Branca into offshore accounts in the Caribbean," the company stated in the dossier provided to Jackson, but there was no actual evidence provided to support Interfor's claim of "a scheme to defraud Jackson and his empire by Mottola and Branca by diverting funds offshore." Even Brian Oxman recognized that Interfor was making accusations against Branca that the company couldn't back up, while at the same time pleading for "additional time and a proper budget." What he himself could prove, though, Oxman said, was that Michael had terminated Branca a short time after the Interfor report was delivered to him because he firmly believed that his attorney was in cahoots with Tommy Mottola.

All the Jacksons knew was that Michael had spent most of the next six years insisting that he wanted nothing to do with the attorney and that no one who was in business with him should also be in business with Branca. "Even after Michael died I found notes that he had written to himself," Katherine Jackson said: "John Branca has nothing else to do with my business from this day on, from this day forward, nothing." Was it reasonable to believe that in June 2009, just days before his death, Michael would suddenly do an about-face and hire Branca back? Taking all of what they knew together, there was plenty of evidence to challenge John Branca's right to serve as the administrator of the Michael Jackson estate, Oxman told the Jacksons. This was a winning case, in his opinion.

Armed with all the facts that Oxman and the private investigators had assembled, it looked as if Katherine Jackson and her children might be poised to try to push John Branca aside and seize at least partial control of the estate and its assets. The family's facade of a united front, though, was cracking into pieces. The world outside the Hayvenhurst compound might not see it, but Branca did.

The weak points were several, and located mainly in the characters of the Jackson brothers. Randy was the one pushing hardest to take Branca down, but the rest of the family was concerned that Randy also imagined that he might take Branca's place as a trustee. Branca and his attorneys were continually telling people what a rotten character Randy was. And in fact the Jacksons themselves viewed Randy as the most selfish and conniving among them. He was a chip off the old block, visitors to the family compound said, far more like Joe than any of his brothers—and no one intended that to be a compliment. His brothers and sisters all remembered that Michael had accused Randy not only of entangling him in dirty deals and mismanaging his affairs during 2004 and 2005, but also of stealing from him. Katherine knew Randy as the son who came to visit only when there was something he wanted, even though he had two children living in the Hayvenhurst house. She wasn't about to let him take over running things.

Jermaine, as always, could be gotten to. He was weak for women, but took little responsibility for the children they bore him. Margaret Maldonado, the former common-law wife who had borne him two sons, said she had never received a penny from Jermaine, even with a court order allowing her to collect it. "I just said, 'Forget it,'" explained Maldonado, who supported her sons by setting up an agency that represented photographers and stylists in Hollywood. "It wasn't worth going to court and fighting with him." Alejandra and her attorneys, though, had kept careful track of the more than $90,000 Jermaine owed her. The estate was unwilling to clean up Jermaine's child support arrears (or Randy's either) but sent a message that it might help him earn the money to do it himself. Joel Katz suggested that he might be able to get Jermaine a recording contract at Universal. Branca sent a message that the estate could find a place for Jermaine in the Cirque du Soleil show deal they were negotiating, performing live with Janet and collecting fat checks, but of course only if he was on board with the men in charge. We should try to work with Branca and them, Jermaine began telling Katherine.

Jackie was the son who visited Hayvenhurst most often, spending nearly every other weekend there, and was in some sense the estate's inside man. Jackie had been friends with his former high school classmate John Mc-Clain since the two were teenagers and was the one who introduced Mc-Clain to the Jackson family. Now each nearly sixty, the two men continued to speak on the phone almost daily and it was McClain who had helped Jackie win the right to make a profit from his failing clothing business by selling Michael Jackson designer T-shirts. Branca and the estate would only let Jackie sell five hundred shirts at a time, but that was enough to bring in $10,000, $15,000, or even $20,000 a month, which was a lot better than Jackie had been doing before. And McClain said he was working on Branca to let Jackie expand, that it would come in time.

McClain was also talking regularly to Katherine Jackson, calling her just about every morning to chat for a few minutes. He still called Mrs. Jackson "Mother," just as he had done decades earlier, and promised that he was looking out for her interests. According to Katherine, McClain professed to dislike Branca every bit as much as any of the Jacksons did, and told her he was protecting her from the man and his law dogs. "I'm on your side, Mother," John McClain told her. "I'm there for you."

Katherine was starting to wonder. McClain had sent an air treatment system he raved about to the Hayvenhurst estate that sat boxed in the utility room for weeks. He kept calling to ask if the Jacksons had set it up, and "seemed really intent on making sure they did," a family advisor said. Suspicious that there was some sort of listening device secreted inside, Joe and Randy had convinced Katherine to move the box, still unopened, out into the garage.

Unable to comprehend the financial analysis of the estate submitted by Branca and his cocounsels, Katherine's confidence in her own repre-sentation was being shaken by the constant complaints of Joe and Randy Jackson. Her probate attorney Burt Levitch, widely regarded as one of the best lawyers in Los Angeles, was actually preparing to take exactly the sort of aggressive actions Joe and Randy urged, including one court filing that accused the executors of submitting a fraudulent will and another that demanded the appointment of a Jackson family member as the estate's third executor. Doubts about what Levitch was up to intensified within the Jackson family during October when the estate requested a hearing on its motion to greatly expand the powers of Branca and McClain, allowing the two executors the right to negotiate deals and settle debts at their own discretion. Not long after the hearing was scheduled, Randy Jackson convinced his mother to fire Levitch for dragging his feet and to hire Adam Streisand, a partner at Loeb and Loeb who had been involved in courtroom battles over more celebrity estates than just about any other lawyer in the country, including those of Marlon Brando, Ray Charles, William Randolph Hearst, and Michael Crichton. That Streisand was best known as a litigator appeared to signal that Mrs. Jackson was about to go to war. The new man didn't exactly get off to a scintillating start in his first appearance as Katherine's attorney, though, when Streisand missed most of the October 22 hearing at which Judge Beckloff had already agreed to expand the administrative powers of Branca and McClain. After listening to Howard Weitzman explain that the executors had initiated deals that would bring in at least $100 million in earnings to the estate, much of that money resulting from the *This Is It* movie that would premiere the following week, Beckloff ruled that the pair should have greater freedom to settle with creditors and negotiate new contracts. "I want this estate to move forward," the judge said.

His client Mrs. Jackson continued to feel that the executors were keeping her in the dark about both the deals they had made and their plans for the future, Streisand told Beckloff when he finally arrived in court. She and the entire Jackson family were frustrated with their inability "to get this case going," Streisand told Beckloff, seeming to suggest that Katherine Jackson still intended to challenge Branca's control of the estate. The judge's response was not encouraging. Branca and McClain were in charge of the estate for now and would remain in charge for the time being, he said, "And while we are proceeding in this posture, I want Mrs. Jackson to have information about what is going on, and I don't want to be in court all the time."

Local TV stations reported that Streisand had been hired because of "new evidence" that questioned the signature on Michael Jackson's will, and that the attorney would be presenting it to the judge in his next court appearance. And in fact, Streisand doubted the will's legitimacy, according to Katherine Jackson. The attorney also told her, though, Mrs. Jackson said, that she'd be well advised not to challenge the document. If she did not prevail, Katherine could be cut out entirely, Streisand said. Even should she prevail in court, if Michael was found to be intestate his estate was likely to be thrown into probate and chewed up by whatever bank was chosen to run it. Challenging John Branca was not necessarily a smart move either; Branca probably understood the value of Michael Jackson's assets and how to expand that value better than anyone else alive. All things considered, allowing him to remain in charge might be the lesser of evils. The best course, Streisand said, according to Katherine, was to make peace with the man and to begin working with the estate. Perhaps Branca could win her "a seat at the table" by arranging for a Jackson family member to be named as the third executor.

Katherine suggested that her grandson Taj might be that person; one of Michael's favorite nephews (along with Tito's two other sons), Taj was a solid, dependable young man with good sense. Branca flatly refused, claiming that to name a Jackson family member as an executor would create a clear conflict of interest. By early November, Streisand had convinced Mrs. Jackson that continuing the fight was counterproductive and that Braca was prepared to make certain concessions, including an increase in her monthly allowance, if she ended it. Also, Streisand wanted her to distance herself from Joe, who seemed determined to draw Katherine into his own bid for a piece of the estate.

Joe Jackson remained intent on putting his one truly talented son to work for him, even in death, and his campaign continued to be the featured program of the ongoing family drama as it played out in the media. One day after the *This Is It* movie made its debut and raked in $20 million at the box office, Joe told the TV program *Extra* that his son was "worth more dead than alive." For once, Joe seemed to realize what had just come out of his mouth and quickly added that, "I'd rather see him alive." Three days after this, the Jackson patriarch was filing a petition in Judge Beckloff's court to request "his own independent family allowance" from an estate that had "earned more than $100 million in the first seven [7] weeks following Michael Jackson's death." He needed $15,425 per month to cover his expenses, Joe's moving papers claimed, including $2,500 per month for eating out, $2,000 for air travel, and $3,000 for hotel bills. Joe had worked out some sort of contingency arrangement with the one attorney he knew would accept an opportunity to stand before the TV cameras in lieu of a cash retainer: Brian Oxman.

Joe was demanding that Katherine weigh in on his behalf, but Streisand was only one among many who warned her that would be a mistake. Being seen as attached to Joe would not only alienate fans, but also provide ammunition to anyone who wanted to argue that she should not have custody of Michael's children. It was time to come to terms with Branca and get on with things.

On Tuesday morning, November 10, 2009, Streisand arrived in Judge Beckloff's courtroom to make the stunning announcement that Katherine Jackson was withdrawing her objections to John Branca and John McClain's continuing to serve as the estate's administrators. His client felt that it was "high time that the fighting end," Streisand told the judge, and was making this decision in the best interests of her grandchildren. "She feels that Mr. Branca and Mr. McClain have been doing an admirable job," Streisand went on. "We're going to try to partner with them and work closely with them to make sure that the estate is doing the best that it can for the legacy of Michael Jackson, for the kids, most importantly."

He and Mrs. Jackson had reached this decision independently, Streisand told the judge. His client had actually kept it a secret from the rest of the family until a meeting with them all on the previous Saturday, and he was pleased to report that the Jacksons all agreed with what she was doing. Well, no, not Joe Jackson, Streisand told Beckloff; he hadn't been invited to the meeting, but the entire rest of the family was present, and not one of them had objected to Mrs. Jackson's decision.

Brian Oxman was objecting, though, loudly and angrily when he stepped out of the courtroom to speak to the media horde. Katherine Jackson's reversal was "one of the most despicable displays" he'd ever seen in a legal proceeding, Oxman declared. By making a secret deal with Branca and the estate attorneys behind her husband's back, Katherine had "reneged on her obligation to her family," Oxman added. Neither he nor Joe was going to simply stand by and let it happen.

Streisand shot back by telling reporters that this accusation of a secret deal was "not only baseless, but just a product of Mr. Oxman's imagination." There was no deal and Mrs. Jackson's decision had been just as much of a surprise to the estate as it was to the rest of the Jackson family. "Before I announced my decision [to the estate's lawyers], Mrs. Jackson and I were the only two people in the world who knew what I was going to say." As for Joe Jackson, Streisand added, "He has no rights in the assets of the estate."

At the same time he'd denied Joe's right to challenge the executors, Judge Beckloff had ruled that Michael Jackson's father could pursue his petition for an allowance, though the judge could scarcely conceal his amusement when Brian Oxman told him, "The executors discriminated against my client by not giving him an allowance and giving one to Katherine Jackson." A hearing to consider the matter was scheduled for December 10, 2009, then postponed until January 2010.

Through Adam Streisand, Katherine let it be known that she wouldn't oppose Joe's request for his own allowance. The lawyer who had just been appointed to serve as the guardian *ad litem* (legal representative) of Michael Jackson's children, however, insisted that Joe Jackson had no right to any money from the estate. Margaret Lodise, one of the top trust and estate attorneys in Los Angeles, argued that Joe was not entitled to any stipend for the same reason he was not permitted to challenge the executors: Michael had not named him as a beneficiary of the estate. Lodise quickly lined up as a John Branca ally, siding with the estate administrator when Katherine Jackson objected to elements of the merchandising and memorabilia deals that Branca had made with Bravado, and again when Branca insisted that Mrs. Jackson had to sign confidentiality agreements before she was allowed to see any of the contracts he had either negotiated or was in the process of negotiating. Judge Beckloff ruled in Branca's favor on both points. So far, the judge had come down on the executors' side every time a member of the Jackson family challenged Branca. On the question of Joe Jackson's petition allowance, though, Beckloff announced he was putting off a decision until May 2010.

With both momentum and the judge on their side, Branca seized that moment to submit a request to Judge Beckloff that he and John McClain, in their capacities as the special administrators of the Michael Jackson estate, be permitted to collect and split a 10 percent commission on the earnings of the estate, twice what they had been getting and more than triple the statutory fee for executors. They were asking for such "extraordinary compensation," Branca and McClain told the court, because they were providing "extraordinary services," in part compelled by the relentless efforts of Joe Jackson to collect an inheritance that had not been left to him, and by Katherine Jackson's attempts to gain control of the estate for herself. Added to that, they had been forced to deal not only with the eleven lawsuits that were pending against Michael Jackson at the time of his death, but also with the dozens of others that had been either filed or threatened in the months since.

The estate had in fact swiftly dispatched the two most grandiose court claims, made by AllGood Productions and Raymone Bain. The latter lawsuit was dismissed in May 2010 by a New York court judge who scarcely bothered to conceal his disdain for such a meritless money grab, ruling that the release document Bain had signed on December 27, 2007, in exchange for a payment of $488,820.05 had "unambiguously covered 'all monies, known or unknown,' owed under 'any and all agreements whether written or verbal.'" The estate had not even needed to show the court that Bain was not involved in making the deal with AEG for the O2 Arena shows. Still, the onslaught of court filings, in particular those made by the Jackson family, had created a working climate in which their own "business reputations and the character and reputation of Michael Jackson were repeatedly assaulted by personal and unfounded attacks," the executors explained (through Howard Weitzman) to Judge Beckloff, forcing them to answer back publicly in order to protect the Michael Jackson brand. To a lot of onlookers, it appeared as if Branca was concerned about protecting himself, but as the man running the estate, Branca could claim that the complaints made against him were actually assaults on Michael Jackson and Michael Jackson's children.

The executors were also being forced to sort through scores of financial claims being made against the estate, Weitzman told the court. The executors were offsetting such payments, Weitzman explained, by pursuing millions of dollars in funds that had been "improperly lost" when various business partners took advantage of Michael Jackson's drug addiction. Their work on all of this was complicated, the executors pleaded to the court, by the fact that Michael Jackson had neglected to pay taxes during the years 2006, 2007, and 2008, and made no quarterly payments in 2009.

Even as the executors unwound Mr. Jackson's debt and sorted through the myriad claims made against him and his legacy, Weitzman pointed out, Branca and McClain were negotiating deals that would yield hundreds of millions of dollars to the estate. At the same time, they were required to engage the dozens upon dozens of people who were attempting to profit from either real or imagined relationships with Michael Jackson. Christian Audigier insisted that he and Michael had collaborated on a collection of T-shirts, jackets, and sequined gloves that he was anxious to put into production, and produced assorted e-mails as documentation. At the same time, the estate was forced to involve itself in such sleazy situations as the one created by Eric Muhammad, a former member of Michael Jackson's security detail who had been caught on videotape attempting to sell a surgical mask he said was worn by the entertainer the night before he died. "This is a very personal item," Muhammad had told the businessman to whom he offered the mask at a price of $150,000. "This is the only way I could, you know, preserve it. This was *his* and you are more than welcome to DNA it. It still has his makeup on it. It still smells like him."

Dealing with all of that, and more, had forced the executors to keep a seven-days-a-week, fourteen-hours-a-day work schedule, Branca and McClain pleaded to Beckloff when they requested that the judge allow them to collect 70 percent of what they were owed, pending the court's approval of the full amount. In addition, the two added, they needed more than $3 million to pay the assorted law firms who had handled matters for the estate that ranged from probate issues to extortionary demands.

What Weitzman didn't mention (along with the fact that his was one of the firms collecting those enormous legal fees) was that increasing the combined commission paid to the executors from 3 percent to 10 percent would potentially add tens of millions of dollars to their individual earnings—possibly hundreds of millions if they remained in charge for a decade or two. Weitzman defended the arrangement as one by which the executors had forfeited guaranteed compensation to gamble on their ability to make the estate profitable: "Basically, the coexecutors only get paid if they generate income for the beneficiary of the estate."

Branca and McClain achieved total victory when Judge Beckloff not only granted each of the requests they had made in their petition for extraordinary compensation as "special administrators" of the Michael Jackson estate, but also agreed that they should be paid immediately. He was making this decision in part, the judge noted, because Katherine Jackson had decided to abandon her efforts to supplant Branca and Mc-Clain, and now seemed anxious to work with them. Finally, they could all get on with things, the judge said.

While he awaited a ruling on his allowance petition, Joe was trying to make ends meet promoting his record company whenever a microphone was placed in front of him. He had also been meeting in Las Vegas with Gary, Indiana, mayor Rudy Clay to discuss plans for the "Jackson Family Project," a museum, hotel, and performing center complex that a spokesperson for the mayor conceded was still in "the proposal and concept stage." Brian Oxman filed an appeal of Judge Beckloff's ruling that Joe had no standing as a representative of Michael's estate, but it was clear by early January that the attorney and his client had come to believe that cobbling together some sort of wrongful death claim was now their best shot at achieving both a big money award and a continuing presence on cable television.

In late January 2010, Oxman filed a motion in Los Angeles Superior Court demanding that Michael Jackson's medical records be turned over to his father, so as to ascertain the exact cause of death. The filing also complained that the Michael Jackson estate was refusing to file a case on Joe Jackson's behalf, forcing Michael's father to incur further expenses, which, Oxman argued, should be paid by the estate. Attorneys for the estate questioned Joe's "intentions" by implying what everyone already knew for certain: If they found any basis for a wrongful death claim, Joe and his attorney were certain to make such a claim.

The two were already moving in that direction by March 29, 2010, when Oxman began to outline the case he would be making against Dr. Conrad Murray, beginning with the claim that doctors at the UCLA Medical Center had briefly detected a heartbeat in Michael Jackson's chest while trying to save him. This indicated that, if paramedics "had been called right away, chances are he could have been revived," Oxman observed. Two days later, the attorney pledged that his client would file a lawsuit against Dr. Murray within the next ninety days. Describing what he knew about the variety and quantity of the drugs that had been injected into Michael Jackson's bloodstream, Oxman told reporters that it was like playing Russian roulette with a revolver that had bullets in all of its chambers.

Most observers assumed that Joe's real aim was to somehow bind himself to Katherine and collect a piece of whatever came her way. Katherine and Joe would be reunited that spring when they were named, along with Jermaine, as codefendants in a court claim made by Reverend Sun Myung Moon's *Segye Times* newspaper. Reverend Moon and his Unification Church had been waiting almost fifteen years for this opportunity. Back in the early 1990s, the Moonies had filed lawsuits that demanded the return of all the money and gifts they had doled out in their campaign to stage a concert tour of South Korea headlined by Michael Jackson. Michael himself had settled with the *Segye Times* back in 1992. Katherine and Joe, though, failed to show up when the case against them went to trial in 1994 and the Moonies had won a $4 million judgment against the couple. Two years later, in 1996, the Unification Church moved to take possession of the Hayvenhurst estate. Joe and Katherine transferred ownership of the estate to Michael and La Toya, then in 1999 listed the Moonies' judgment against them as part of a $24 million bankruptcy filing. The property transfer to La Toya, though, had provided the basis for a fraud claim that exempted the Moonies' judgment from discharge in bankruptcy court. The Reverend Moon's attorneys let the claim lie dormant for years, but then pressed it vigorously in the late summer of

2009 when they learned that Katherine Jackson had, arguably, inherited 40 percent of the Michael Jackson estate. They wanted the full amount of the original judgment against the Jacksons, plus interest, the Moonies demanded in their 2010 Los Angeles court filing, which brought the total balance due to more than $13 million. In order to collect, they moved once again to foreclose on the Hayvenhurst property.

Through Howard Weitzman, Branca offered a shaken Katherine Jackson a way to both separate herself from Joe and to insulate herself from the Moonies claim: The estate would agree to pay the $5 million mortgage on the Hayvenhurst mansion if ownership of the property was transferred to the estate. Katherine would be guaranteed the right to live at Hayvenhurst free of cost for the remainder of her natural life, and would be well taken care of without possessing any assets that could be attached by the Moonies.

It was his bitterness about his sense that Katherine was being taken care of while he was cast aisde, sources close to the family said, that had prompted Joe to sit down with the *News of the World* in early June 2010 for a presumably paid interview in which he seemed to blame his estranged wife for their son's death. When they had visited the mortuary where Michael's body was being prepared for burial, they saw their son's corpse lying on a table and Katherine broke down into sobs, Joe said, "but I didn't give her a hug because I was mad at her for crying." She could have saved Michael if she had listened during May 2009 when he told her their son was "looking kinda funny and frail," Joe said. He asked Katherine to spend some time with Michael and "keep him cheered up," Joe went on, and the two of them argued after Katherine refused because she didn't want to invade her son's privacy. After Michael's death, "I said, 'This would never have happened if you had went and been with him.'"

Adam Streisand replied on Katherine's behalf by observing, "The world knows who Joe Jackson is, and he seems bent on never letting us forget it."

Joe Jackson's lawsuit against Conrad Murray was filed by Brian Oxman on a date the two knew was certain to maximize media coverage—June 25, 2010, the one-year anniversary of Michael Jackson's death. Sure enough, the court claim became the lead-in for any number of TV news stories about the events of the day, which had included the first real mingling of fans and Jackson family members at Michael's grave site. The Jacksons had pulled their private security guard from the Sanctuary of Ascension back in February, six months after Michael's interment, arranging for Forest Lawn security to monitor the crypt for as many as twelve hours out of every day. By early March, though, the memorial park's management had decided that dedicating its manpower to the observation of a single burial spot was unreasonable and instructed its guards to patrol as usual. In early May, Lisa Marie Presley had visited Michael's tomb and afterward expressed dismay at the empty space surrounding it, posting a plea on her MySpace page for fans to fill that space with sunflowers, Michael's favorites. The owner of the sunflowerguy.com Web site was quick to seize the opportunity and delivered three hundred bushels of sunflowers in black vases. Lisa Marie had returned with her own bushel of sunflowers, in a purple frame inscribed with the words, "I will always love you." Some of Michael's fans brought flowers also, but just as many arrived at Holly Terrace with the Sharpies they used to inscribe the sarcophagus with various dedications. Security was out in force at the Great Mausoleum on June 25, to enforce strict rules on fan decorum that included no releasing of doves or balloons, and no sale of memorabilia.

On September 15, 2010, Katherine Jackson and her attorneys filed their own eighteen-page wrongful death lawsuit, accusing AEG of being responsible for Michael Jackson's death. Mrs. Jackson's suit alleged that the company had failed in "multiple duties of reasonable care," and named its causes of action as breach of contract, fraud, negligence, negligent inflic-tion of emotional distress, and employer responsibility. Among the few indisputable passages in Mrs. Jackson's court filing was a description of the deal between her son and AEG: The company would "put up the funds and production expenses" for the O2 concerts while Michael provided "the talent and fame to make the venture a success." The claim grew murky, though, when Katherine's attorneys alleged that AEG had advanced large sums of money to Michael Jackson (and provided him with the Carolwood chateau) because they knew that if the London production flopped, the company could seize Michael's assets, including his stake in the Sony/ATV song catalog, to recover its losses. This was, the lawsuit contended, a way of forcing Michael to hold up his end of the deal despite serious health problems. AEG became upset when Michael missed "some rehearsals" in spring 2009, the lawsuit went on, and insisted that he separate himself from his "treating physician," Arnold Klein, then hired Conrad Murray to take Klein's place. "By injecting themselves between Michael Jackson and his treating physician, and telling Michael Jackson what to do medi-cally," Mrs. Jackson's attorneys concluded, "AEG committed independent negligence against Jackson." Specifically, AEG was accused of failing to provide "key lifesaving equipment" (a defibrillator) that should have been available to the physician attending to Michael Jackson in his home and of inadequately monitoring the cardiologist it had hired to take care of him.

Michael himself was portrayed in his mother's lawsuit as a helpless, hapless pawn of corporate malfeasance, one who was "confused, easily frightened, unable to remember, obsessive, and disoriented" in the weeks preceding his death. "He was cold and shivering during the summer rehearsals for his show, and as shown in photographs of him, he uncharacteristically wore heavy clothing during the rehearsals, while other dancers wore scant clothing and were perspiring from the heat," according to the court filing. However, instead of cutting back on Michael's rehearsal schedule, AEG had "insisted that he attend every rehearsal in a grueling schedule, threatening that if he missed even one more they would cancel the tour," the lawsuit went on, all this so that the company "could reap staggering profits from the tour."

The "great trauma and emotional distress" that Michael Joseph Jackson Jr. had suffered by witnessing the injuries "caused by AEG" that led to his father's death was cited as a basis for damages. Paris also had been present in her father's bedroom as Conrad Murray attempted to revive Michael Jackson on the morning of June 25, 2009, but, curiously, her pain and suffering were not listed as a cause of action. No precise amount of money was claimed in Katherine Jackson's lawsuit, but the demand for economic, noneconomic, and punitive damages meant that AEG could be on the hook for hundreds of millions of dollars if Michael's mother's claims were sustained at trial.

"The purpose of this lawsuit is to prove to the world the truth about what happened to Michael Jackson, once and for all," the attorney who had filed it on Katherine Jackson's behalf, Brian J. Panish, said in a statement released to the press. Money might enter into it as well, of course, given that Panish was best known for having won the biggest personal injury and product liability award in United States history, $4.9 billion, in a lawsuit that found the General Motors Corporation guilty of selling Chevy Malibus with faulty fuel systems.

AEG's own attorneys denounced the lawsuit as "meritless." Contrary to the description of Michael Jackson in his mother's claim, AEG's attorneys wrote in an answer filed with the court more than three months later, the entertainer "was not helpless or incompetent; he lived in his own home, negotiated his own contracts, engaged his own attorneys, and cared for his own family." Jackson "controlled his own medical care and hired his own longtime personal physician," the company's papers stated. AEG "did not choose or hire Dr. Murray, it merely conducted negotiations aimed at retaining him as an independent contractor on the tour." All AEG's executives knew of Dr. Murray, aside from the fact that Michael had chosen him, the company's attorneys argued, was that he was "a licensed physician with no history of malpractice." Clearly it was unforeseeable that Dr. Murray would administer propofol in a personal residence "and that Michael Jackson would die as a result." This lawsuit should be thrown out immediately, AEG's attorneys argued, finally, because Katherine Jackson and her grandchildren "lack standing to bring these claims other than as wrongful death theories" and their action had been filed, in effect, on behalf of Michael Jackson himself. Another month passed before Judge Yvette Palazuelos denied AEG's motion to dismiss, though she also ruled that Katherine Jackson's attorneys would have to show actual evidence of fraud, negligent infliction of emotional distress, and civil conspiracy to prevail at trial: "If the object was to get him to rehearsals, I don't see that as a wrongful or illegal act."

Among the many specters raised for AEG by the Katherine Jackson claim was that, if the case ever reached the point of determining damages, the company might have no choice but to argue that Michael Jackson was, as Joe Jackson so choicely observed, "worth more dead than alive." *Billboard* estimated that Michael Jackson had generated $1 billion in income in the first year after his death, an amount that exceeded what all but a handful of artists produce in their entire careers. The Jackson estate had collected more than $250 million of those earnings, approximately five times what was taken in that same year by the most valuable estate in the history of the entertainment industry: Elvis Presley's. The 31 million Michael Jackson albums sold worldwide in 2009 had far eclipsed that of any other recording artist, and the 8.3 million of those albums sold in the United States were nearly twice the number sold by the second best selling artist, Taylor Swift. Sony had paid the estate an advance of $60 million for the rights to the *This Is It* film, which grossed $261 million worldwide. The merchandising deal with Bravado and the dance game licensed through Ubisoft Entertainment had earned the estate a $26 million advance. The MiJac Music catalog had spun off payments of $25 million on the copyrights to Michael's own compositions, due to radio play that had increased ten-fold after his death. Sony/ATV had paid the estate the $11 million due under its agreement with Michael, and John Branca was said to be negotiating a new deal that would pay twice that amount annually. The reissue of Michael's autobiography *Moonwalk*, plus his piece of

AEG's commemorative ticket sales and other ancillary income, had added another $25 million to the coffers. No one knew how much the estate would earn from the two Michael Jackson–themed shows it had licensed to Cirque du Soleil, but $250 million was the guarantee on the contract that Branca eventually negotiated with Sony. The deal gave the company the right to distribute Michael's recordings through 2017, along with ten Jackson albums that would be made up of unreleased material, remixes, and reissues of his classic albums, plus DVDs of Michael's music videos. Not only was the Sony contract worth more than twice the $120 million that Madonna would earn from the "blockbuster" deal she had made with Live Nation, but the Jackson estate had retained control of the enormously valuable merchandising and "likeness" rights that Madonna was forced to surrender. And of course Michael would not be touring, as Madonna was required to do to earn her millions.

What was most startling about Michael Jackson's postlife success was how completely death seemed to have rehabilitated his public image. "His sainthood began the moment that he died," David Reeder, a vice president at GreenLight, the licensing agency that handled the estates of Johnny Cash and Steve McQueen, among others, observed to the *New York Times*. "That's been beneficial for the estate. They haven't had to overcome a lot of obstacles that might have made him less desirable commercially." John Branca wanted to make sure that he and John McClain received credit for how redeemed Michael was in the eyes of the American people. "We felt we needed to restore Michael's image," Branca told the *Times*, "and the first building block of that was the movie. People came away from that movie with a completely different view of Michael. Rather than being this out-of-control eccentric, they saw him as the ultimate artist, the ultimate perfectionist, but at the same time respectful of other people." The estate's executors were praised in the *New York Times* for having made maximum use of both the passion and the fascination that people felt for the entertainer. "What they've done brilliantly is that they've taken advantage of the emotion surrounding the tragic and unexpected passing of Michael Jackson," said the Elvis Presley estate's Robert F. X. Sillerman, "and [they've] done it in a way that's tasteful yet profitable, and that's challenging."

Not everyone was impressed. "What they've done, anyone could have done," scoffed Tohme Tohme. "They're selling Michael Jackson to a world that wants Michael Jackson. It's not difficult."

28

Descriptions of life inside the Hayvenhurst compound varied considerably from visitor to visitor. "Camp Jackson," Paris Hilton's mother Kathy described it to *People* magazine, which quoted another "insider" who painted a picture of three happy children whose devoted grandmother had helped them settle into a life that was "simple and sweet." "On a typical day the kids get up early and romp around the grounds with their dogs, Jackson and Kenya, before drifting over to the pool," *People* told its readers. "Indoors, they watch movies, play Pictionary and horse around with Grandma." Arnold Klein saw things rather differently: "The Sodom and Gomorrah show in Hayvenhurst," he called the Jackson family home. He was so disgusted with them all, Klein told TMZ, that he had lost interest in anything beyond the "the welfare of the children."

Amid the dueling characterizations, there was at least some agreement about how the three kids were dealing with life after Michael. Prince was still withdrawn, but visitors to the Hayvenhurst compound also sensed a resolute composure in the boy, an iteration of the poise Natalie Maines had remarked upon one year earlier. He didn't want to talk much about his father, or anything else for that matter, and continued to spend silent hours at a stretch playing video games, but what little he did say suggested that Prince had been paying close attention to what was going on around him. A couple of his uncles were quite uncomfortable with some of the questions the boy was asking about his inheritance. Paris summoned up memories of her father far more frequently than both of her brothers combined. She seemed to find comfort in recalling the day Daddy had introduced their puppy Kenya into the family, or that evening when he took them all to the tower of the Luxor Hotel in Las Vegas, where they stood eating Snickers bars and looking out on the phantasmagoria of colored lights. She was becoming interested in fashion and developing a sense of personal style; when she needed new eyeglasses, she posed in more than a hundred different frames before choosing the one that suited her. Blanket still seemed to be suffering, but not so intensely. Only seven when his father died, the youngest child continued to cry out for Daddy during the night for weeks after his arrival at the Hayvenhurst house. He wanted to be held often. Katherine Jackson's fundamentally loving nature was a blessing to the boy, most visitors to the family compound said, and he was increasingly devoted to her.

Michael's siblings, though, squabbled regularly and often loudly over the disposition of Michael's estate, and in particular about what it had cost to make peace with John Branca. All of Katherine Jackson's children, but Randy most aggressively, were complaining that she had accepted a deal with Branca that cut them out of the estate entirely. Katherine herself was increasingly unhappy with the stingy allowance she received. While John Branca and cocounsels were responding generously to any request that directly benefited Michael's three children (by its accounting, the estate had shelled out $115,000 for a "family vacation" during the second half of June and the first part of July in 2010), they were providing Katherine Jackson with a monthly cash allowance of just $3,000, and the entire family were up in arms about it. Almost nothing was left over for Katherine's children, and that was as intended, according to Branca, who said that Michael Jackson had made it very clear that he did not intend to provide for his siblings. Even when Branca upped Mrs. Jackson's monthly stipend to $8,000, several of her surviving children continued to complain vociferously, demanding that Katherine mount a genuine challenge to the estate's administration.

The clamor for action grew deafening after the estate trustees submitted to Judge Beckloff's court their preliminary accounting of "disbursements" during the sixteen months between Michael's death and October 31, 2010. The three-page document showed that nearly $29 million had been paid out to people working for the estate. John Branca's first two hires were being well taken care of: More than $600,000 had been paid to Sitrick and Company, which was still only about a third of the nearly $1.8 million that had been collected by Howard Weitzman's law firm. All told, nearly $6 million had been paid to attorneys working for the estate. Greenberg Traurig had recieved more than $2.1 million, while Hoffman, Sabban & Watenmaker had collected just about $1.6 million. Branca's own firm had received only a little more than $100,000 for its services, but Branca himself had done far better than that, as had John McClain. Under the heading "Co-executive and Creative Director Compensation," nearly $18 million in payments were listed between February 2, 2010, and October 8, 2010, indicating that Branca and McClain had each pocketed nearly $9 million in a period of eight months. Even if those payments were for the full sixteen months of work, it meant that Branca and McLain were averaging nearly $600,000 per month in compensation. And meanwhile Branca wants you to thank him for raising your allowance to $8,000 a month, Joe and Randy Jackson told Katherine.

The anger among Michael's siblings, nieces, and nephews was increasingly matched by a mood of apprehension as they came to understand that Katherine Jackson would be able to collect even this pittance from the Jackson Family Trust only for as long as the eighty-year-old woman remained healthy enough to serve as the three children's guardian. Rebbie and Janet were the only two Jacksons considered fit to replace their mother in the event of serious illness or death, but Janet had no real interest in the kids beyond "arranging photo opportunities with them," as one of Katherine's advisors put it, while Prince and Paris were outspoken about rejecting Rebbie's extreme religiosity, and did not want to live with her. The brothers and La Toya were certain to be shut out if Katherine passed, a fact that only intensified the fractious nature of the family's relations. And of course there was still the question of Joe, constantly circling the compound, sneaking in at every opportunity to look for whatever levers he thought might turn things his way.

The inclusion of Grace Rwaramba in the household was intended to provide a stabilizing effect, but it seemed to have quite the opposite effect. La Toya now appeared to have recognized Grace as a serious threat to the Jacksons' hegemony. "The family has mixed feelings about her," La Toya told a British reporter. "Mother says she wants to be with the kids, but I warned her to be careful. It's not like the children like or dislike her. They like everyone. Mother is gullible and feels sorry for her." La Toya seemed to believe that it was Grace herself who had spread the story that she was Michael's girlfriend and was quick to dispute it. "I have a lot of questions about Grace," La Toya had told a British tabloid not long after Rwaramba landed at Hayvenhurst. "She was instrumental in keeping the family away. All of a sudden she is back, listening and watching the family. I think her behavior is odd."

Learning what Grace had said to Daphne Barak was what cooled the affections of Prince and Paris, according to some reports from the compound. Others said the real problem was that Grace persisted in overplaying her hand. The nanny knew that her presence at Hayvenhurst had been a determining factor in Debbie Rowe's decision to yield custody to

Katherine, these sources explained. And over time, several family members had interpreted various remarks she made as implicit threats to tell the world what she knew about the Jacksons, Michael included.

In late August word emerged from the Hayvenhurst estate that Michael's three children would be enrolling in the fall at the exclusive Buckley School. Prince, who was pushing to explore the world outside the Hayvenhurst compound, wanted to attend class with other kids. All three of Tito's children had attended Buckley, whose recent alumni included Paris Hilton, Nicole Richie, and Kim Kardashian. When September came, though, Katherine decided to continue homeschooling the kids. It was what they were used to, she said. The estate administrators approved funds to convert the theater into a classroom and to create an actual schoolyard within the family compound, complete with a volleyball court, so that their curriculum could include PE class. The kids would take field trips and have a regular lunch, as well.

Things turned ugly a couple of months into 2010. On the first day of March, a team of officials from the Los Angeles County Department of Children and Family Services arrived at the Hayvenhurst compound, having been called to investigate a report that Jaafar Jackson had purchased a stun gun online and was experimenting with it on his young cousin Blanket. ABC News posted an online story that Jaafar had ordered at least one, and perhaps two stun guns off the Internet, then shared the 3,000-volt weapon with the other children in the house for three days before they were caught chasing Blanket around the house with it. After receiving a phone call from an alleged witness, DCFS had dispatched a team of investigators, who arrived at the Hayvenhurst estate shortly before 11 p.m.

Adam Streisand was on the scene the next morning to refute the ABC story, acknowledging that Jaafar Jackson had ordered a stun gun (Streisand incorrectly described it as "a Taser") online, and had "opened it in his bathroom and tested it on a piece of paper." Katherine Jackson and a security guard at the house heard the sound, followed it to Jaafar's bathroom, and promptly confiscated the weapon, Streisand said: "Blanket Jackson never saw or heard the Taser. Neither did Paris Jackson. Prince saw the Taser in possession of security." DCFS officials had taken possession of the gun and removed it from the house, said Streisand, who quickly added that he saw no reason why the incident should be brought before Judge Beckloff.

The Jackson family was less concerned about what the judge might think of the stun gun story than with how Debbie Rowe might react to it. The cordial relations that appeared to have resulted from Rowe's agreement not to contest Katherine Jackson's custody of the children had chilled considerably in August when Katherine's attorneys opposed Debbie's petition to have the Michael Jackson estate pay the nearly $200,000 in legal fees she owed to Eric George, calling the amount "unreasonable." The Jacksons *had* reportedly complied with their agreement to inform Prince and Paris that Debbie was their biological mother, and to retain a child psychologist who would structure and monitor her visits with the two older children. People who purported to speak for Rowe, however, suggested that the Jacksons were making it difficult to arrange those visits by repeatedly claiming conflicts with other scheduled events. Debbie did not believe the Jackson family welcomed her, these sources said. Tito Jackson insisted this was not the case: "She can definitely have rights to visit, hang out, and be part of the family," he said. "After all is said and done, they are her kids. I would like to see her be part of the Jackson family. There is enough love for everybody."

The stun gun incident, however, ratcheted up concerns among the Jacksons about whether Rowe and her attorney might bring her concerns before Judge Beckloff. DCFS wasn't doing much to ease the family's anxiety, sending investigators to the Hayvenhurst estate repeatedly during the next two days to question each of the fourteen people who had been living in the house at the time, as well as all security guards and other employees. Within twenty-four hours, TMZ began raising questions about Adam Streisand's description of what had taken place. Apparently, there was a "conflict" between the accounts offered by the Jackson family and those that came from employees at the Hayvenhurst compound, TMZ reported: "We know some members of the staff will tell DCFS that the stun gun was there for several days before a member of security went upstairs and allegedly found Jaafar and other kids playing with the gun and pointing it at Michael's son Blanket."

Tensions inside the compound spiked again in early May 2010, when Radar Online, a Web site affiliated with the *National Enquirer*, posted "WORLD EXCLUSIVE VIDEO: Shocking Violence Inside Jackson Home." What the video showed was Jermajesty speaking into a camera for a moment, then Jaafar stepping into the frame with a furious scowl and cursing his younger brother as a thief, then slapping Jermajesty across the face with enough force to send the boy sprawling to the ground. At least that's what the editors at Radar Online saw. A perhaps more persuasive interpretation was that a couple of goofy kids had staged what they hoped might be a massive YouTube hit before some opportunistic adult got hold of it. Radar Online, though, found a clinical psychiatrist to analyze this "brutal" scene. "It shows a cycle of violence, knowing about family history," opined Dr. Joseph Haraszti. "When he hits his brother so hard that he falls flat out, it looks like he knocks him out. There may have been violence towards him to make him behave that way." As for the stun gun incident, Dr. Haraszti went on, "it shows lack of supervision. It seems that the children are out of control. Which begs the question, where are the adults? Who is in charge?"

Debbie Rowe was asking the same question, Radar Online reported, after catching Debbie outside a Barnes and Noble at a shopping mall in Calabasas that very evening. "Of course I'm concerned about Blanket," an emotional Rowe replied to a question about the stun gun imbroglio. "I'm concerned about my children. Who wouldn't be?" Debbie also took the opportunity to tell the world that, despite the Jacksons' supposed suggestion that she could be a member of the family, she still had yet to set foot on the Hayvenhurst property. "I have never been to the house," she said, blinking back tears.

Within the gates of the family compound, the questions that Katherine and the other Jacksons asked were: Who snitched us out to the DCFS? And who gave that video to Radar Online? The paparazzi agency X17 was reporting that Grace Rwaramba had done both. Grace's call to DCFS had been the result of an ongoing "feud" between the children's nanny and their grandmother over who was really raising Prince, Paris, and Blanket, according to X17. Even though Katherine knew that Grace was responsible for both calling DCFS and selling the video to Radar Online, X17 reported, the Jackson family "is afraid to get rid of Rwaramba because she has been threatening to write a tell-all book."

In fact, Grace would leave the Hayvenhurst compound before May 1. It wasn't the Jacksons who compelled her departure, though, but rather Alejandra Oaziaza. "That whole mess, with the stun gun and all of it, was really about just one person," Marc Schaffel said. "Alejandra's the one Katherine wanted out of the house." Mrs. Jackson tried to persuade Alejandra to depart with her two youngest children during the last months of 2009. "What Katherine did originally was tell Alejandra she was going to remodel Hayvenhurst—which it definitely needed," Schaffel recalled. "There were toilets that didn't work and doors falling off hinges. And Alejandra almost went, but then she said, 'Well, how do I know you're gonna let us come back?'" After the stun gun incident, though, DCFS had made a "strong recommendation" that Michael's children needed to be separated from their cousins, especially Jaafar and Jermajesty. This time, Katherine tried to entice Alejandra into vacating the Hayvenhurst compound with an offer that she and her children could live, all expenses paid, in the Encino condominium that Michael had transferred to his mother years earlier. "It's a beautiful condo," Schaffel explained. "Katherine had it completely remodeled and it was like brand-new. But Alejandra wasn't happy. She wanted to know who was going to cook and clean for them. So Katherine, being the woman that she is, said, 'Well, I'll send some of the staff members over there a couple of days a week.' And get this, Alejandra says, 'Why would I want that when I already have full-time help here?'"

On TMZ, it was claimed that Alejandra was responsible for both the call to DCFS and the appearance of the slapping video on Radar Online, each move made as a way of letting the Jacksons know she would not leave Hayvenhurst quietly. Family members blamed Alejandra for the story that Grace had decamped from Hayvenhurst because she and Paris were fighting constantly, forcing Katherine to ask the nanny to pack her bags and go. "The only reason Grace left was because she couldn't take the abuse that Alejandra and her kids were putting her through," Schaffel said.

In the months since their father's death, it had become obvious that Prince, Paris, and Blanket were destined to live out their singularly strange childhoods as the objects of a never-ending soap opera written in tabloid headlines and lit by flash attachments. They would be envied and pitied, enabled and adored, and never left alone, except when they didn't wish to be. And the people who wanted to protect them were the ones they really had to watch out for.

At least their grandmother seemed sincerely committed to normalizing the lives of Michael's children. The kids were allowed to spend their first Christmas without Daddy at the Cascios' home in New Jersey. Katherine might not celebrate the holiday herself, but she wouldn't keep Michael's children from doing so. Six months later, on the first anniversary of her son's death, Mrs. Jackson lamented that Prince, Paris, and Blanket "don't have any friends," during an interview with the *Daily Mirror.* "They don't go to school, they have private lessons at home—but that will change in September." True to her word, Katherine enrolled both Prince and Paris in the Buckley School for the fall term. Prince had been increasingly insistent upon getting the chance to mix with other kids. Paris, at first reluctant, became enthusiastic after a visit to the school. Blanket would continue to be homeschooled for a time, but perhaps in a year or two would join his brother and sister at Buckley, Katherine said.

The lawyers running the estate would accuse Mrs. Jackson of exploiting her grandchildren later that autumn, though, when she and the other Jacksons made Prince and Paris the point persons in a family campaign against the first posthumous Michael Jackson album. Cobbled together from the bits and pieces of the "comeback album" he had been working on since his 2006 stay in Ireland, plus other cuts that went back decades, the new album, titled *Michael*, was under attack weeks before its Christmastime 2010 release. The loudest complaints had to do with three songs that had been recorded in the basement of the Cascio family's New Jersey home. When "Breaking News" was previewed for fans during late October on michaeljackson.com, the Jacksons promptly objected that the voice featured on the track was not Michael's, then offered his two oldest children as exhibits A and B. Prince had told them he was upstairs listening while his father recorded with Eddie Cascio, the Jacksons said, and the boy insisted that none of what he heard matched the tracks that Sony was including on the new album. Paris was said to be especially "adamant" that the voice singing lead on "Breaking News" was not her dad's. Sony executives grumbled anonymously that the kids were being "manipulated" by Katherine Jackson. As was his practice, John Branca remained silent and out of sight, dispatching Howard Weitzman to tell reporters that the estate had hired forensic audiologists to verify the tracks recorded in the Cascio basement and that all of them agreed they heard Michael's voice on "Breaking News" and the two other songs. Eddie Cascio himself sounded more hurt than angry when he insisted, "It is Michael's voice. He recorded right there in my basement."

Randy Jackson, though, said that the first time he heard the Cascio tracks, "I knew it wasn't [Michael's] voice." The objections of other Jackson family members were echoed by will.i.am, who called the release of the new album "disrespectful." "Now that he is not part of the process, what are they doing?" he asked. "Why would you put out a record like that?" Quincy Jones's argument was perhaps the most persuasive: Michael was too much of a perfectionist to have put out such a rough and unfinished record.

Branca and the estate answered with a report stating that "six of Michael's former producers and engineers, who had worked with Michael over the past thirty years—Bruce Swedien, Matt Forger, Stuart Brawley,

Michael Prince, Dr. Freeze, and Teddy Riley—all confirmed that the vocal was definitely Michael." Riley, the most credited of the several producers on the new album, protested that "without any proof" it was unfair to call the Cascio tracks frauds. "You can hear the authenticity in his voice, and you can hear the natural part of him," Riley said.

Sony shipped 900,000 units of the new album domestically when it went into stores during December 2010. Just 224,000 copies of *Michael* sold in its first week of release, placing it at #3 on the charts behind albums by Taylor Swift and Susan Boyle, and well behind the 363,000 copies of *Invincible* that had sold in the first week of that album's 2001 release. The initial single released from the new album, Michael's "Hold My Hand" duet with Akon, had peaked at #39 on the *Billboard* Hot 100. Radio and record company executives were in agreement that questions about the authenticity of the tracks on *Michael* were the main reason for such a disappointing commercial performance.

The critics weren't much kinder. "Breaking News," the track from the new album that had gotten the most media attention, was dismissed as "self-referential rehash that spotlights all that was wrong with" Michael Jackson. In some ways, the saddest thing about *Michael* was that the two best cuts on the album, "Behind the Mask" and "Much Too Soon," had been performed and produced back in the 1980s. "Behind the Mask" was especially excellent, a strangely psychedelic, lushly orchestrated R & B reworking of a track off the Yellow Magic Orchestra's 1979 album *Solid State Survivor* for which Michael had written fresh lyrics, then sung them with a ferocity that he hadn't matched since his *Dangerous* days. A number of critics noted how much the more recent cuts suffered by comparison.

Sony was spared this suffering by strong international sales of the new album. Questions about the Cascio tracks hadn't received the same sort of publicity overseas, where Michael Jackson continued to be more popular than he was in his native land. *Michael* had shipped platinum in thirteen countries outside the United States and gold in another seventeen, making its debut at #1 in Germany, Italy, the Netherlands, and Sweden. First-week sales in the UK were the highest for any Michael Jackson album since *Dangerous* and in Japan it joined *Bad*, *Thriller*, and *This Is It* as the only Jackson albums to debut in the top three. The deal Sony had made with the estate might yet pay off, but only if the company got Michael's kids and his mother in their corner. That looked less and less likely to happen.

*   *   *

It was scarcely a surprise that conspiracy theories flourished in the aftermath of Michael Jackson's demise. Sudden celebrity deaths from Elvis Presley's to Tupac Shakur's had generated stories of arcane plots and elaborate hoaxes, and this one would as well. The difference in Jackson's case was that the decedent himself had long been convinced there was a conspiracy to destroy him. Even in the run-up to the "This Is It" shows, Michael refused to abandon his belief that Sony and a somewhat fluid cast of accomplices were behind the criminal charges that had been filed against him in Santa Barbara County, and that gaining full control of the Beatles catalog was the cabal's motivation. "Michael Jackson was afraid for his life throughout the entire time I knew him," Raymone Bain said. "Michael always thought that his property and his possessions—particularly his publishing—were going to be the cause of his death."

Sony execs Tommy Mottola and Marty Bandier were nearly always among those Michael accused of plotting against him, as well as his former manager Trudy Green and her boss Howard Kaufman, of HK Management. A paragraph in the Interfor report that claimed Al Malnik had been involved with John Branca in a scheme that used Mr. Jackson's money was not substantiated by the slightest offer of evidence, but nevertheless had made Michael suspicious of the Florida attorney. The Nation of Islam fed that suspicion and also persuaded Michael to include Charles Koppelman and Brett Ratner among "the Jews" on his enemies list. Tom Sneddon was their partner and their pawn in the plot, as Michael and the NOI had it.

A surprising number of people from outside the family—some of them substantial figures—had bought into the Sony conspiracy theory during recent years. Tom Mesereau believed "a case could be made" that the company assisted the prosecution in Santa Barbara County in order to gain greater control of the ATV catalog. Tohme Tohme declared himself "convinced there was a conspiracy against Michael—not necessarily to kill him, but to weaken him, to make him cancel the shows and to use that to get control of the catalog." Said an attorney who had dealt with Branca, Tohme, Frank Dileo, and Randy Phillips in connection to the AEG contract and the disposition of the Michael Jackson estate, and who had dealings as well with Leonard Rowe and the Jackson family, "Oh, there was a conspiracy certainly, but what kind of conspiracy, who was involved, and how they were involved is difficult to know."

Of course, the story that Michael was still alive became the one most welcomed by his legions of fans. It had arisen within twenty-four hours of the death pronouncement at UCLA, when a photograph of someone who was supposedly Michael climbing out of an ambulance in the parking garage of the Los Angeles County coroner's office had appeared on cable television. Literally thousands of descriptions of how Michael had faked his death surfaced in the months afterward. "I get at least twenty e-mails a week from people who say Michael is not dead," reported Uri Geller. "I'm not kidding you."

Michael *was* dead, though, and the one person in the world certain to answer for it continued to be Dr. Conrad Murray. As he prepared for a preliminary hearing that was scheduled to begin during the first week of 2011, Murray was left with just a few flickers of hope that he might escape from criminal liability. Among these was that Michael Jackson's parents appeared to have recognized that they and the doctor shared certain common interests. Joe Jackson had actually written a letter asking Michael's fans not to assault, verbally or physically, either Murray or his supporters during the doctor's preliminary hearing. "By calling names, we are lowering ourselves to their level," read the letter, which itself served as a sort of preamble to the complaint against AEG Joe lodged with the medical board of California one month later. Joe's accusation in this filing was that AEG had practiced "unlawful corporate medicine." He supported the charge by claiming that Conrad Murray had repeatedly asked for both a defibrillator and an attending nurse at the Carolwood chateau, and was denied by executives who refused to pay the cost. Court filings being made in Katherine Jackson's wrongful death lawsuit indicated that the very same claims were going to be at the heart of her case against AEG. What this meant, among other things, was that Dr. Murray himself might be the plaintiffs' most important witness. Murray indicated he was willing to play ball by encouraging unidentified "friends" to spread the word that he had retained copies of e-mails sent to AEG asking for both the resuscitation apparatus and a registered nurse, and that the doctor blamed Michael's death on the company's refusal to comply. "I could have saved Michael if I had the right equipment," Murray was quoted as saying. "I have the paperwork to prove it."

As the Los Angeles County district attorney's office prepared to present its case against Murray at his preliminary hearing, Michael's siblings made comments suggesting a growing sympathy for the physician. "Dr. Murray's the fall guy," Jermaine Jackson told reporters after one court hearing. "This is bullshit!" It surprised no one when La Toya issued a statement that amplified her brothers' remarks: "Michael was murdered, and although he died at the hands of Dr. Conrad Murray, I believe Dr. Murray was part of a much larger plan. There are other individuals involved, and I will not rest and I will continue to fight until all of the proper individuals are brought forth and justice is served."

The case took an even more unexpected twist when Murray's attorneys filed court papers suggesting that Dr. Arnold Klein was at least partially responsible for Michael Jackson's death. Klein "prescribed or may have overmedicated Michael Jackson, including to such point that AEG Live read Michael Jackson the proverbial 'riot act' to get him to stop subjecting himself to overmedication by Dr. Klein," read the filing. Joe Jackson's attorneys promptly demanded to know "why, given these allegations, Dr. Arnold Klein is not a required party to be added to accord proper relief." For the first time since Michael Jackson's death, Klein had declined to reply publicly to an allegation against him. Other people *were* talking, though. Michael's longtime hairdresser Karen Faye told police investigators that Michael almost always "exhibited signs of drug use" after seeing Dr. Klein. According to Faye, she had noticed about a week before Michael's death that he seemed more lucid and asked Frank Dileo if he knew why. "'Cause Klein is out of town," had been Dileo's reply, Faye said.

The knowledge that he had become the target both of a state investigation and of Dr. Murray's defense strategy did not prevent Klein from submitting claims against the Michael Jackson estate that demanded both $48,522.89 owed for cosmetic dermatology procedures performed on the entertainer in the last months of his life and the return of a $10,000 green Gianfranco Ferre jacket that he had loaned Michael back in the spring of 2009. Those who had read documents Klein had submitted in his demand for payment were asking the doctor some sharp questions. By his own tally, Klein had injected Michael Jackson with either Restylane or Botox at least three times a week during April 2009, a month when he had also injected Jackson with 2,475 milligrams of Demerol. The same records showed that Klein had injected Michael with another 1,400 milligrams of Demerol during a two-week period in May. A number of anonymous medical professionals were quoted as questioning whether the Botox and Restylane injections listed on the medical billings were nothing more than "cover" for the Demerol injections Jackson wanted. Klein insisted he had performed every one of the procedures he had billed for and defended the Demerol injections by explaining, "You have to understand, Michael Jackson was incredibly needle-phobic. I had to sedate him."

As questions persisted about his alleged "overmedication" of Michael Jackson, however, Klein grew increasingly mute, hunkered down with his attorneys, it was said, against the possibility that either the California attorney general's office or the medical board of California might take action against him. Further complicating matters was that Conrad Murray's accusations against Klein seemed to fly in the face of the claims in Katherine Jackson's lawsuit that AEG had become responsible for the death of her son by replacing his upstanding "treating physician" Arnold Klein with the recklessly incompetent Dr. Murray. How it would all sort itself out was impossible to predict. The only surety was that the criminal case against Murray would be decided before any settlement of the civil claims against AEG.

The prosecution case laid out by Deputy District Attorney David Walgren on January 4, 2011, the first day of Dr. Conrad Murray's preliminary hearing in downtown Los Angeles, was a surprise to no one. Not only had Murray's administration of the anesthesic propofol to Michael Jackson during the early hours of June 25, 2009, been an "extreme deviation from the standard of care," Walgren told the court, but the doctor compounded matters by delaying his emergency phone call to 911 while he improperly performed CPR on his dying patient, then concealed the fact that he had injected propofol into Jackson's bloodstream from both paramedics at the scene and doctors at the hospital.

Kenny Ortega was summoned to the stand as the first prosecution witness, called mainly to describe how upset the doctor had been when the "This Is It" show director sent Michael home early from rehearsal on the evening of June 19, 2009. During a meeting the next day at the Carolwood chateau, Ortega recalled, Dr. Murray insisted that only he should make such decisions, and maintained that Michael was "physically and emotionally fine." Murray's attorney Ed Chernoff asked if Ortega had read Michael "the riot act" before sending him home on the evening of June 19, but Ortega (who had been named in the original filing as a defendant in Katherine Jackson's lawsuit against AEG) denied it.

Michael Amir Williams followed Ortega to the stand and told the court about Murray's approaching him at the hospital to say he needed to get back to the house to retrieve tubes of skin-whitening cream in Michael's room. The next witness was Faheem Muhammad, who testified that Dr. Murray had told *him* he wanted to leave the hospital because he was hungry and needed something to eat. Alberto Alvarez described once again being instructed by Murray to remove the IV bag filled with some milky-white substance and of being ordered as well to load bottles filled with a similar milky-looking liquid into a medical bag before the paramedics arrived.

The two EMTs who had been the first responders to arrive at the Carolwood chateau, Richard Senneff and Martin Blount, were especially damning witnesses. Senneff estimated that Michael Jackson must have been dead for at least twenty minutes before the first call to 911 was made. He and Blount agreed there was absolutely no chance of revival, Senneff remembered, and yet Dr. Murray insisted he felt a pulse and refused to pronounce Mr. Jackson dead. When he and the other paramedic asked if Mr. Jackson had been taking medications, Senneff recalled, the only one the doctor mentioned was Ativan; he never uttered a word about propofol and described his patient's main problem as dehydration. Blount described Murray as soaked with perspiration when he first spoke to the paramedics and remembered the doctor insisting that he had waited only one minute after Michael Jackson stopped breathing to call 911. Blount echoed Senneff's frustration at the doctor's refusal to pronounce death.

The doctors from UCLA, Richelle Cooper and Thao Nguyen, said that Dr. Murray refused to recognize that Mr. Jackson was dead even though they could find no signs of life when the body arrived at the hospital's emergency room, and that he implored them to "try to save the patient." The doctors also remembered that Murray had told them Michael was taking Ativan, but made no mention of propofol.

Elissa Fleak, an investigator from the coroner's office, testified that she found not only twelve bottles of propofol in the closet of Michael Jackson's bedroom, but along with them a virtual pharmacy of other drugs, including lorazepam, diazepam, temazepam, trazodone, Flomax, clonazepam, tizanidine, hydrocodone, lidocaine, and Benoquin, as well as a quantity of syringes, needles, IV catheters, and vials, both opened and unopened. A pharmacist from Applied Pharmacy Services in Las Vegas followed with testimony that Dr. Murray had made six separate orders of Diprivan between April 6 and June 10 in 2009, for a total of 255 vials of the drug, and that he had all of it, as well as the benzodiazepine drugs he wanted, shipped to an apartment in Santa Monica.

LAPD robbery-homicide division detective Orlando Martinez testified that during the interview with Conrad Murray he conducted two days after Michael Jackson's death, the doctor had said he was attempting to "wean" Mr. Jackson off of propofol, but that during the early morning hours of June 25, Michael had literally "begged" for the drug to help him sleep. Feeling "pressure" from his patient, Murray said, he gave Mr. Jackson a reduced dose of propofol—with the patient's help. Michael liked to "push in the propofol himself," Murray explained, and said "other doctors let him do it." Murray also told him that he had gone to the bathroom for only two minutes, Detective Martinez testified, and that he saw that Mr. Jackson wasn't breathing as soon as he returned. Los Angeles County assistant medical examiner Dr. Christopher Rogers said on the stand that he believed Dr. Murray had lied to Detective Martinez about the size of the propofol dose that was administered to Michael Jackson. If it had been a mere 25 milligrams of propofol, as Murray said, then the patient would have awakened after as little as three to five minutes of sleep, testified Dr. Rogers, who added that it was inappropriate to use propofol to treat insomnia and that he considered the medical care provided to Michael Jackson by Dr. Murray to have been "substandard."

The prosecution appeared to be holding powerful evidence in reserve. A pair of phone company representatives were put on the stand to testify that Conrad Murray did a great deal of texting and calling between the time he discovered Michael Jackson had stopped breathing and the first 911 call. Who Dr. Murray had been texting and calling, along with what he had said to them, was not revealed. A connection between a couple of the cell phone calls Murray made and two women from the doctor's office in Texas who had gone to a storage facility to retrieve boxes was implied but not explored.

The failure of the LAPD to secure the Carolwood chateau in the immediate aftermath of Michael Jackson's death was the one real advantage the defense possessed. Conrad Murray's attorneys indicated they might exploit that area of vulnerability in the future but for now there was no doubt that Conrad Murray would be ordered to stand trial on a charge of involuntary manslaughter. Before Judge Michael Pastor adjourned to prepare his decision, however, the California deputy attorney general who represented the medical board of California wanted to ask that the judge also suspend Dr. Murray's license to practice medicine. Murray's attorneys hastened to argue that this would deprive the doctor of the ability to mount a defense if he went to trial. It certainly would deprive him of the ability to pay their fees.

A little more than an hour later, Judge Pastor ruled that Murray would stand trial, and that his license to practice medicine would be suspended as a condition of his bail. The doctor was given twenty-four hours to notify the medical boards in Texas and Nevada of the judge's decision.

29

Katherine Jackson's determination to drive Alejandra Oaziaza and her children out of the Hayvenhurst compound had mounted to the point that she finally went to John Branca and Howard Weitzman for help with it. The estate's request for an eviction order was filed three days into Conrad Murray's preliminary hearing and was the culmination of a struggle that had gone on for more than six months. Mrs. Jackson had made her first attempt to force Alejandra out back in June 2010 and was reportedly stunned when the mother of four of her grandchildren by two of her sons responded by hiring an attorney who made it clear she would fight to stay. Katherine and the Jacksons tried negotiation, offering to give Alejandra the title to the condominium where she had earlier been encouraged to live rent-free. Alejandra refused to sign the confidentiality agreement that was part of the deal, however, insisting she wanted to keep the option of writing a tell-all book. At that point, Katherine had turned to the estate executors, urging *them* to get Alejandra off the property.

"One thing Katherine really didn't like was that the other children were preventing Michael's kids from making friends," Marc Schaffel explained. "Jermajesty and Jaafar, and Randy Jr.—all these other kids—were telling Prince and Paris, 'We're your family. We're the only ones who care about you. Don't trust anyone else.' Even Omer Bhatti would be telling them, 'I'm your only friend. The rest just want your money.' These poor kids were getting really distracted and Katherine could see it. But it was difficult for her, because those other kids were still her grandchildren. So she let the estate take over trying to get rid of Alejandra. They arranged to fumigate the house a couple times, and they even went so far as to change the locks. But Alejandra kept coming back and getting in."

By the summer of 2010, at the urging of Los Angeles County social workers who wanted Prince, Paris, and Blanket separated from Jaafar and Jermajesty, both Katherine and the estate had accepted that she would have to find another place to raise her grandchildren. Katherine, who had stayed several times with the children at Schaffel's house out in Calabasas, decided that she loved the area, and asked Marc to drive her around to look at vacant properties. Eventually she would settle on (and into) a 12,670-square-foot mansion in a gated community perched in the hills just a block from Britney Spears's home. The rent was $26,000 per month. She and Prince and Paris and Blanket would live there until the work at Hayvenhurst was completed—maybe longer, Katherine said.

Alejandra, though, was digging in at Hayvenhurst. She was described as "a squatter" by TMZ. "She basically stays in the house full-time," reported one of Katherine's closest advisors in March 2011, "because she's afraid they're gonna change the locks on her again." Exhausted and fed up, Katherine had eventually phoned the police to ask that they escort Alejandra off the property. Alejandra's attorney intervened, however, convincing the cops that they could not remove a woman who had been in residence for more than two decades without a formal eviction order. A filing to evict Alejandra was made by the estate one week later.

Alejandra's ability to inflict pain on any Jackson who crossed her, though, was being demonstrated even in that moment. Some weeks earlier, Jermaine had traveled to Africa with a passport that was about to expire. Through her attorneys, Alejandra made the U.S. State Department aware that Jermaine owed her $91,921 (including interest and penalties) in back child support, which meant that, by law, he could not be allowed to renew his passport and return home to the United States until the full amount was paid. The American embassy in Ouagadougou, the capital city of the volatile, land-locked West African nation Burkina Faso, was being asked to issue temporary papers so that Jermaine could return home and attend to his obligations, but if the embassy refused, he would be stuck in Africa until Alejandra was paid. At Jermaine's request, Katherine had gone to the estate to plead for the money he owed to Alejandra so that he would be allowed to return to the U.S. from Burkina Faso. The estate responded with a loan of $80,000.

The other Jacksons shuddered at the thought of what Alejandra might say or do before March 15, 2011, when the hearing on the eviction order was scheduled to take place in court. "Katherine's in a horrible situation," Schaffel said. "She's got two sons who have children they're not taking responsibility for. Jermaine doesn't pay a penny in child support and Randy didn't for a long time. So Katherine's stuck feeling she has to take care of these kids, but she doesn't have the financial backing from the estate to do it."

Both Alejandra's tenacity and her gall were on full display when she showed up for the March eviction hearing with an attorney who argued that Michael Jackson had wanted to ensure that the mother of his niece and nephews was taken care of, and intended that she be provided for by the Jackson Family Trust. "Alejandra actually had the nerve to complain that Katherine had taken the staff with her to Calabasas and that there was no one to take care of her needs in the manner to which she was accustomed," Schaffel marveled. "She even claimed that she was receiving no grocery money and that Katherine and the estate were trying to starve her out. And she got a temporary stay on the eviction order."

The power of the role that Alejandra had carved out for herself within the Jackson family was nowhere more evident than in the deal by which John Branca and Howard Weitzman had settled matters between Alejandra and Katherine on one hand, and between Alejandra and Jermaine on the other. The essential ingredient in the negotiation during early April 2011 was the loan by the estate relieving Jermaine of his child support arrears.

Katherine was becoming increasingly outspoken about her displeasure with Branca's imperious attitude. During her interview for the *Oprah* show, Katherine had complained that Branca was willfully ignoring what he knew had been her son Michael's wishes. After the interview aired in November 2010, Mrs. Jackson made a public statement that she was upset with Oprah Winfrey and her producers for caving in to threats from Weitzman and the estate attorneys, delivered shortly before the show was to run, that including Mrs. Jackson's remarks about Branca might result in legal action. "Oprah relented and did not air the segment about the executors at all!" Katherine complained.

Mrs. Jackson's rhetoric heated up as she was drawn into the court battle for control of her son Michael's Heal the World Foundation. Katherine publicly sided with the young woman to whom Michael had delegated responsibility for the charity, Melissa Johnson, and railed against the legal asault on Johnson that Branca and his attorneys had launched. The blow that landed heavy on Branca's chin was the one Katherine delivered in early April 2011, just a week before the Heal the World lawsuit was to go to trial, when Mrs. Jackson's signed declaration was filed with the court. "It is not my desire, nor would it be the desire of my son Michael, to continue this lawsuit against the Heal the World Foundation," Mrs. Jackson had written. "Michael would be very upset if he knew that our charity was being torn apart by people who say they are doing what he wanted." Katherine's declaration singled out Branca as the one responsible for "bringing this lawsuit," then stated publicly what she had been telling people privately for months: "Mr. Branca was a man my son was very worried about. Michael told me on more than one occasion that he did not like this man and did not trust him. He told me that John had stolen from him. This lawsuit is exactly the type of awful thing that Michael said he was capable of doing . . . These people say that I have been manipulated by Melissa Johnson and that we are exploiting my grandchildren, because we joined Heal the World, all while the executors convince people they are only doing what Michael wanted or what is in my best interests by suing everyone who helps us. Please do not believe them. It's not true . . . Michael did not want his charity to be destroyed or lost; he wanted Ms. Johnson to run it for him."

Melissa and her partner Mel Wilson were "good and selfless people and I have grown to trust them very much," Mrs. Jackson went on. "They have done a remarkable job with my son's charity and they have made me happy to be a part of their work . . . Michael's children absolutely do want to carry on their father's legacy of giving and healing and to demean and distort that desire, for greed, is as awful as you can get."

Branca and his cohort struck back immediately with a statement that dismissed the assertions in Katherine Jackson's declaration as "pathetic" and "full of lies." At the same time, though, the estate lawyers attempted to avoid a direct confrontation with Michael's mother by leaking a story to TMZ that Mrs. Jackson hadn't actually made any of the personal attacks on John Branca that appeared in her declaration. Those slanders had come from "people who have Katherine's ear [and] have it out for the estate," as TMZ reported it.

Adam Streisand made a fateful decision when he chose to chime in later that same day, telling TMZ that Mrs. Jackson "denies signing any statement to the court that makes accusations against the executors of any wrongdoing with respect to her son or his estate," then adding, "She did not and would not make any such statements about the executors."

The headlines that Streisand's assertions produced infuriated those who surrounded Katherine Jackson (who had, in fact, made those statements, and signed the declaration as well). "Basically, Adam Streisand was saying that his own client was either a liar or a fool," one of Mrs. Jackson's advisors said.

The following morning, Adam Streisand received a letter by courier from Mrs. Jackson that read, "I have spent many hours reflecting on my goals and objectives with regards to my son's estate and I have decided to move in a different direction. Therefore effective immediately I am hereby terminating the services of you and your law firm."

Streisand was indignant. "My partner Gabreille Vidal and I spoke with Mrs. Jackson and her assistant Janice Smith," the attorney said, "and Mrs.

Jackson told us that she did not sign a copy of the declaration that had the false accusations against the executors saying that they stole money from the estate, among other things, and she agreed to precisely what I was going to do and what I did issue as a statement about it." But Mrs. Jackson had *not* accused the executors of stealing money from the estate in her declaration. "I never called Mrs. Jackson a liar," Streisand insisted, but it sounded very much like he *was* calling her a liar now. "There is no doubt in my mind that after I issued the statement, Randy and Joe and probably others were very upset about it, and made that very clear to Mrs. Jackson. I have no doubt in my mind that she agreed to terminate our relationship as a way of disavowing responsibility for the statement."

His statement wasn't the only reason Streisand had been let go, however. More significant was that Katherine Jackson had decided she needed an attorney who believed she had a better choice than to accept Branca's control of the estate and to be appreciative of whatever generosity he could be persuaded to extend to her. She wanted a lawyer who would fight Branca, one who believed that Branca could be dislodged from his positions as executor, special administrator, and co–general counsel of the Michael Jackson estate, and perhaps be made to repay every penny he had earned from those positions.

Within hours of firing Adam Streisand, Mrs. Jackson had hired an attorney who told her very convincingly he could do that.

Perry Sanders Jr.. was a "big-time litigator," as TMZ put it in the first report of his appearance on the scene. Most famously, he had filed the wrongful death lawsuit against the City of Los Angeles that accused LAPD officers of involvement in the murder of rapper Christopher Wallace, aka Notorious B.I.G., aka Biggie Smalls. Sanders had also played the pivotal role in securing song-publishing rights worth hundreds of millions of dollars in an action against Master P and the No Limit Records catalog. Gaining control of a disputed music publishing catalog was, for obvious reasons, a particularly impressive achievement in Katherine Jackson's eyes.

Sanders suggested that Katherine direct any questions she might have about his performance as an attorney and his trustworthiness as an individual to Voletta Wallace, Notorious B.I.G.'s mom, herself a Jehovah's Witness, a woman of great faith and impressive character. The day before she dismissed Streisand, Michael's mother and Biggie's mother spent four hours on the phone together. By the end of that conversation, Katherine said, she was sold on Perry Sanders.

Sanders is an athletically built man in his late fifties, with chiseled features, a shaved head and face, and barely any eyebrows; he suggests an actor hired to play Lex Luthor as a protagonist. Raised in Louisiana as the son of one of the South's best-known Baptist preachers, Sanders's big grin and down-home colloquialisms (he was usually "fixin'" to do one thing or another) masked a capacity for cold-blooded cunning and creative strategies that was matched by few attorneys in the country. According to one of Mrs. Jackson's advisors, Sanders had explained to Katherine at their second meeting that his main tactic in a situation like the one he had inherited from Adam Streisand was fairly simple on the surface: He approached his adversaries with the peacemaking offer of a fair deal in one hand and a brick in the other. He offered the deal first. If they didn't take it, he hit them in the head with the brick, then asked if they'd like to reconsider. Of course, Sanders added, you wanted to make sure you had a real solid brick before you began that kind of conversation.

Sanders realized he had the makings of a blunt instrument to his liking as soon as he read a copy of a filing that Brian Oxman had made in Judge Beckloff's court several months earlier. "Joseph Jackson's Objection to the Appointment of John Branca and John McClain as executors of the Estate of Michael Jackson" was the heading on a lengthy document that began with detailed allegations of fraud and possible forgery by Branca. Oxman had listed seventeen separate occasions between July 1, 2009, and September 29, 2009, when he claimed the executor had perjured himself by testifying that the will submitted to the court was "correct," asserting that Branca and McClain "have conducted themselves in a fraudulent deceptive manner where their veracity can no longer be trusted."

While Oxman's filing detailed the doubts about the authenticity of the will and trust agreement raised by his investigation, Joe's attorney had been shrewd enough to recognize that the smart move was not to try to invalidate those documents. Rather, Sanders saw, the play was to challenge Branca's decision to retain the originals of those two documents after he was fired as Michael Jackson's attorney, and to attack his failure to resign from his position as executor. "In violation of his fiduciary duties, Branca concealed the purported will and concealed his refusal to resign," Oxman charged, and in so doing had deceived and defrauded both Michael Jackson and the court. On the one hand, "Branca never accounted to Michael Jackson regarding his conduct, nor disclosed his books and records to Michael Jackson." On the other hand, Branca's failure to inform Judge Beckloff that he had been fired as Jackson's attorney because Michael believed he was guilty of "embezzlement" was a fraud upon the court, Oxman had written.

Sanders had been warned that Oxman was a bit of a publicity hound, but Katherine's new attorney was impressed by the largely technical accusations of fraud, conflict of interest, self-dealing, and failure of fiduciary duty that made up most of the court filing submitted on Joe Jackson's behalf. The document was filled with accusations involving "the thousands of licensing agreements that Branca and his law firm had entered into on behalf of Michael Jackson and the Sony/ATV Trust," as well as details about the 2006 deal in which Michael had bought out Branca's interest in the Sony/ATV music publishing catalog for $15 million.

The two-page business plan that Michael had "supposedly" signed a week before his death was itself "a continuation of the concealment, conflicts of interest, and violations of fiduciary duties which plagued Branca's conduct for years," Oxman had concluded.

The filing was the stuff of a potent lawsuit, Sanders thought, but the merits of the case had never been heard. Judge Beckloff's preemptive ruling had been that Joe Jackson was not a named beneficiary of his son Michael's will and therefore "doesn't have any interest in the estate." Sanders's client Katherine Jackson, though, *was* a named beneficiary of the will, meaning that the judge would be compelled to hear any claim he brought against Branca on her behalf.

Even before being hired as Mrs. Jackson's attorney, Sanders had been discussing how to mount an attack on Branca with other high-profile litigators, among them Paul V. LiCalsi, who had long represented the Beatles' company Apple Corps Limited and John Lennon's widow Yoko Ono. At the same time, he was collecting information that raised ever more intriguing questions about Michael Jackson's will and John Branca's conduct. Branca had thus far avoided answering questions* about who at

---

*In late August 2012, after sixteen months of refusing to answer any questions at all, despite multiple offers of the opportunity to do so, John Branca, through his attorney Howard Weitzman, agreed to respond to questions from me, if they were "put into context." Essentially, Branca and Weitzman wanted me to reveal what I had. Despite the fact that this book had already gone into production, my publisher and I agreed and I responded with an e-mail to Weitzman in which I outlined the four major areas of question or controversy: questions involving the preparation and signing of the 2002 will; questions about the circumstances of Mr. Branca's termination as Michael

his law firm had prepared the Michael Jackson will and trust agreement submitted to Judge Beckloff, or about why he and his law firm had retained the originals of those documents after they were "commanded" to return them in 2003. Branca had also declined to respond to any questions about where and when Michael Jackson signed the will that had been submitted to Judge Beckloff. On Branca's behalf, Weitzman emphasized that Michael Jackson's 2002 will had been approved by the probate court, but Weitzman himself offered no details about where and when the will had been signed, though he did insist that the signature was genuine and that all three witnesses had been present when Jackson signed his name.

Jackson's attorney in February 2003; questions about whether Michael Jackson, at the time of his death, actually wanted John Branca to serve as his executor; and questions about whether John Branca was in fact rehired as Michael Jackson's attorney in June 2009. I also invited Mr. Branca to respond to the criticism of him by members of the Jackson family for the degree to which he had been personally enriched by his administration of the Michael Jackson estate.

Weitzman responded forcefully and persuasively to the question about whether Branca was rehired in 2009, first by arranging for a conference call with Michael Kane, who had been hired as Michael Jackson's business manager shortly before his death and who continued to serve in that capacity for the estate. Kane told me that he had personally witnessed the meeting between Branca and Jackson at the Forum, and had in fact participated in some of it. Weitzman also arranged a conference call with Joel Katz, who had been hired as Jackson's entertainment lawyer in the spring of 2009, and Katz told me he was certain that Branca and Jackson had met as claimed, because he had spoken to Michael Jackson about the meeting a short time afterward. He had asked Michael if he minded John joining the team, Katz said, and Michael had told him he did not. Not long after this, Katz said, he saw a document signed by Michael Jackson that approved a business plan that would be directed by John Branca. Members of the Jackson family and critics of John Branca retorted that Kane and Katz were employees of the estate and allies of Branca. I see no legitimate basis for insulting Mr. Kane and Mr. Katz with the suggestion that they would lie at John Branca's behest and I accept that Branca did in fact meet with Michael Jackson at the Forum and likely was rehired as one of Jackson's entertainment attorneys. For me, that controversy has been settled in Mr. Branca's favor.

Howard Weitzman had no real answers to offer, though, about the other three areas of question and controversy I submitted to him. On the question of why the will shows that it was signed in Los Angeles on July 7, 2002, a date when Michael Jackson was in New York City, Mr. Branca was choosing not to reply, Weitzman told me. Weitzman claimed that he himself had not been given an explanation for the discrepancy, stating that he had heard different stories from different people. Weitzman, of course, insisted the July 7 will was not fraudulent and was signed by Michael Jackson in the presence of three witnesses. Unbeknownst to me at the time, Branca was talking to a reporter from *Forbes* named Zack O'Malley Greenburg, who had just written a story for his magazine that would be published even as Weitzman and I were talking. "The

Howard Weitzman refused to go on the record with TMZ or anyone else in the media about whether the will had been signed in New York or Los Angeles. Sanders himself spoke to Jackson's former accountant, Barry Siegel, who said the will had been signed "in California." Yet Siegel's friend Dennis Hawk said he understood from Barry that the will was signed in New York.

After Katherine Jackson told Sanders that Adam Streisand had said he believed the Michael Jackson will submitted to Judge Beckloff's court was questionable, Mrs. Jackson's business partner Howard Mann advised Sanders that he could produce a court-certified handwriting expert who

Scandalously Boring Truth About Michael Jackson's Will," the article was titled. In it, Greenburg explained that even if the 2002 will had been found to be invalid, there were two other Michael Jackson wills in John Branca's possession, one executed in 1997 and the other in 1995, that would have become the successor documents. And both of those wills, as Greenburg reported, named John Branca as one of Michael Jackson's executors. So Branca had absolutely no motive to submit a fraudulent 2002 will, Weitzman pointed out to me after he recited the facts that were the basis of the Greenburg article. What both Weitzman and Greenburg somehow ignored, though, was that in February 2003, when he was terminated as Michael Jackson's attorney, Branca had been ordered to surrender "all" documents in his possession, not just the 2002 will, but the 1997 and 1995 wills as well. If Branca had done what he was supposed to do, he would have had *no* Michael Jackson wills in his possession at the time of Michael's death, a fact that renders both Weitzman's argument and Greenburg's thesis irrelevant.

Weitzman had no reply to offer from Branca to the question of why he had failed to surrender the originals of Michael Jackson's wills in 2003. Again Weitzman told me that his client was declining to answer any questions on that subject. When I pointed out that Branca's refusals to answer questions about the problems with the will itself and about his failure to return it to Michael Jackson in 2003 were inevitably going to raise suspicions, Weitzman said he understood this, but had to obey his client's instructions. Weitzman did attempt at one point to suggest that perhaps Branca had simply handed off the 2003 termination letter from Michael Jackson to an assistant who had somehow failed to include the will (or wills) in the documents returned to Jackson. I pointed out that this was implausible. If the will had surfaced months after Michael's death when files were being moved into storage or something such as that, then the story that the failure to return the will was an oversight by an assistant would perhaps be believable, I told Weitzman. But the fact was that Branca knew he had the 2002 will at the time of Michael Jackson's death and immediately began the process of producing it for certification, then presented it to the court within a week of Jackson's death. And if Branca knew he had the will, I pointed out to Weitzman, then he knew he had failed to do as he had been instructed to do by his former client back in 2003. And that, by the standards of the State Bar, was not ethical. Weitzman didn't like hearing this from me, but he had no answer for it, either.

could challenge the Michael Jackson signatures on the trust agreement. Raising further doubts about the validity of the will, at least in Sanders's mind, was that the signature page produced by Branca was entirely separate from the body of the document, making it impossible to say whether it was the same document that Michael Jackson had signed in July 2002. Even Barry Siegel had admitted to Sanders that he had no way of knowing.

Sanders was even more interested to learn that in the spring of 2009 Michael had been in conversations about his need for an estate planner,

---

Weitzman quite reasonably pointed out that John Branca couldn't be expected to respond to claims about the things that Michael Jackson had said about Branca during the more than six years that passed between his 2003 termination and Michael's death. What startled me, though, was how exercised Branca and Weitzman were by the subject of the 2003 Michael Jackson will that named Al Malnik as executor. Weitzman said he had spoken to Malnik and that Malnik had told him that will "was never filed." Later Weitzman stated that Malnik had told him the will "never existed." That was strange. My initial knowledge of the Malnik will had come from Marc Schaffel, who told me he had been one of the two witnesses to Michael Jackson's signature at Malnik's home in Florida. I would have been a little shaky if all I'd had to base my belief in the 2003 will was on Schaffel's statements. But I had discovered that on the day of Michael Jackson's death, Malnik had given not one but two telephone interviews to journalists in the Miami Beach area in which he stated that, as of 2004, he was the executor of Jackson's estate, on the basis of a document signed in 2003. The first interview was given to *Palm Beach Post* columnist Jose Lambiet and the second to a reporter at the CBS affiliate in Miami, Lisa Petrillo. The Petrillo interview had been tape-recorded and played on the air during an evening broadcast. When I sought counsel from attorneys about what could be motivating Malnik to claim there never had been a 2003 will, if he was in fact saying that, two of them did bit of legal research for me and reported that, Malnik, as an attorney, had been obligated by the California Probate Code to produce any Michael Jackson will in his possession within sixty days of Michael's death. If Malnik had possessed such a will and failed to produce it, he might face some legal consequences. What this all comes to I have no certain knowledge. I am convinced, though, that the 2003 Michael Jackson will did exist and I told this to Howard Weitzman.

Weitzman's replies to the questions concerning whether Branca was rehired and to those who have criticized him for using his own law firm to prepare a will that named him as executor of the Michael Jackson Estate were incorporated into the text in an earlier chapter of this book.

In the letter that Weitzman sent to me and my publisher in John Branca's formal reply to my questions, the attorney stated: "Mr. Branca and Michael Jackson had a long and multifaceted personal and professional relationship that, admittedly, was interrupted at certain points in their careers for various reasons. Those who harbor no bias or animus against Mr. Branca acknowledge his contributions to Michael's career, and recognize his role and that of his co-executor in the stunning financial turnaround of the estate after Michael's death." No argument here.

and in the process had convinced his representatives, Dennis Hawk and Tohme Tohme, that there was no valid will or trust agreement in existence. "That was my distinct impression," said Hawk, who in March 2009, right around the time that the "This Is It" shows were announced, had been asked by Jackson and Tohme to find an attorney who could prepare an estate plan for Michael that included a will and trust agreement. Both Hawk and Tohme saw the Neverland Trust agreements (naming Katherine Jackson as the trustee of the estate and making no mention of John Branca) that had been prepared in 2006 during Raymone Bain's reign as Michael's manager, and assumed those would be the templates of any new estate documents. Hawk reportedly had contacted Sean Najerian, a lawyer who had prepared such documents for other clients of his.

Najerian said Dennis had indeed called to ask if he would consider the scope of an estate plan for Michael Jackson, whether he would be capable of preparing documents that included a will and trust agreement, and what he would charge in terms of a flat fee to do so. Tohme followed up, and there were a number of conversations during March and April, Najerian said, but then the calls simply stopped. The reason for that, apparently, was Tohme's estrangement from Jackson during the Julien Auctions imbroglio. "I can tell you that in 2009 Michael didn't think he had any will," Tohme said two years later.

What made the whole situation even more confusing was that Michael Jackson had signed at least one other will and trust agreement subsequent to July 2002—in Florida during 2003. Those documents named Al Malnik as the executor of Michael's estate, and as guardian to Michael's youngest child, Blanket. Marc Schaffel was one of the two official witnesses to Michael's signature, at Malnik's home in Ocean Ridge. He recalled that this trust agreement was much longer and more elaborate than the one submitted by Branca to Judge Beckloff, Schaffel said. Malnik had in fact acknowledged the existence of such a will in a brief interview with the *Palm Beach Post*'s "Page 2" columnist Jose Lambiet on the day after Jackson's death, adding that he also had agreed to be the guardian of MJ's youngest child Blanket. "There could always be a superseding document he signed since then," Malnik told Lambiet. "I haven't heard anything yet, but it's probably too early." After that, though, Malnik had gone silent, refusing to talk to the reporters who called to ask about it. And no 2003 will had surfaced.

There had been just two copies of that will and trust agreement, as Schaffel remembered it, one for Malnik's files and one for Michael's. If anyone had discovered a copy of the Malnik will in Michael Jackson's files after his death, though, they weren't saying. Malnik himself refused to speak on the record but told Schaffel that he wasn't interested in producing his copy of the will Michael had signed in 2003. "Al is an eighty-year-old billionaire who doesn't want to be bothered with all this," Schaffel explained. "He certainly doesn't need the money, and his feelings were hurt when Michael turned on him back in 2003, after the Muslims came in. Plus, he told me he'd probably have hired Branca to run the estate anyway, because he knows more than anybody else about it."

By late April 2011, Sanders seemed to think he had formed a brick that was solid and sizeable enough to carry into a conversation with the estate. Some members of the Jackson family, though, Joe and Randy in particular, were complaining that this new lawyer looked like yet another guy who wanted to get in bed with Branca. They weren't pleased by Sanders's first public statement after the news of his hiring as Katherine's attorney broke: "Bottom line—I am going to do anything in my power to tone down the rhetoric that has happened to date to the extent possible." At a lunch meeting in Beverly Hills the next day, Sanders assured Howard Weitzman that he would much rather work with the estate than fight against it. Within the week, he had proven this by settling the Heal the World Foundation lawsuit, orchestrating a deal that guaranteed Katherine Jackson and Melissa Johnson seats on the charity's board of directors but gave John Branca ultimate control.

Joe and Randy renewed their complaints about Sanders, telling other family members that they believed Katherine's lawyer was really working for the estate. He was ready to go to war with Branca if he had to, Sanders assured Mrs. Jackson, but an amicable settlement was clearly preferable. He would be meeting with Howard Weitzman again, this time for dinner, to determine if that was possible.

Sanders refused to say afterward what had transpired during his dinner with Weitzman, but it was obvious in the days that followed that a deal had been struck. Katherine Jackson was back to describing Branca as "a very able man." Perry Sanders said that he admired Weitzman and respected Branca. "Katherine is being taken care of," he said.

Among those who were oblivious to Sanders's machinations, the good news was that Michael's children seemed to thrive after their move to Calabasas and enrollment at the Buckley School. "They're making tons of new friends and Katherine is really happy about it," Marc Schaffel said. "Paris is having sleepovers, and she's been going out. Prince has finally started to do things. Before, he was very in his shell, but now he's playing sports and making friends." When Prince showed up at a Los Angeles Lakers basketball game in January 2011, the buzz around the boy was far louder than for any of the many other celebrities seated inside the Staples Center. Familiar faces that ranged from George Lopez to Khloe Kardashian hurried over to have their photographs taken with Michael Jackson's son. What made his grandmother happiest was seeing how easily Prince chatted with Lakers forward Ron Artest. "The most amazing thing to everyone is that he's getting really talkative," Schaffel explained. "It's made a world of difference to get away from that whole bad influence crowd. I think they might want to get close to Debbie, too, before very long."

He already saw a lot of Debbie in Paris, Schaffel added: "Paris loves horses. She's a dog person. She's really into animals. There's no doubt in my mind the two of them are going to develop a relationship around that."

Though the media wouldn't touch it, a much-discussed subject on the Internet, after Katherine appeared with Michael's children on the *Oprah* show, was how curious it had been to see these white kids being raised by a black family. It no doubt would have surprised a lot of people to learn that all three of the children continued to firmly believe that Michael Jackson was their biological father. The Caucasian complexions of the two oldest kids might appear to clearly contradict this belief, but before the end of 2010 Prince had developed a condition that convinced the entire Jackson family he truly was Michael's son: The boy had vitiligo; spotting was heavy around his knees and under his right armpit.

"All I can tell you is that those kids believe completely that Michael was their father," Schaffel said. "There's no doubt at all in their minds."

30

For the moment, it wouldn't matter what questions remained about the will or the signature on the trust. It wouldn't matter whether John Branca failed to resign as the executor of the Michael Jackson estate as he should have or kept Michael's will if he had an obligation to return it. It wouldn't matter what had happened to the will that made Al Malnik the executor of the Jackson estate, or why Michael had asked in the spring of 2009 for the creation of a new will and trust agreement that made no mention of John Branca or John McClain. It wouldn't matter whether Branca really had been hired back as Jackson's lawyer a week before Michael's death.

All of those questions were moot because in the end the struggle wasn't about right or wrong, good or evil, justice or injustice. It was about money, Michael Jackson's money, and there was enough of that to go around for everyone—everyone except Michael himself, of course. There'd never been enough money for *him* because what he wanted and needed most, money couldn't buy.

Nearly as often as he lamented the childhood he lost to celebrity, Michael had cursed the day he bought the Beatles catalog. He regularly compared himself to the boy with the golden goose: Everyone he met wanted to take it away from him. His mother Katherine said it was Michael's wealth far more than his fame that had set him apart from the rest of the family and then separated the rest of them from one another. The resentment, the infighting, the scheming—all of that had been much more about Michael's millions than his superstar status, Mrs. Jackson said. Michael and his mother had always been so much alike, full of the same sweetness and sentiment, and so similarly blind to their own contradictions. In much the same tone in which Michael mourned the carefree youth he had never really known, Katherine reminisced about their days back in Gary, and said again and again that they had really been so much happier then, so much more of a family. She would never have gone back if given the choice, of course, and neither would Michael, but it was lovely to imagine for a moment a world in which they might have.

His mother wasn't the only one in his family Michael loved, but she was the only one he trusted, and for years it was through her that his generosity had been distributed to the other Jacksons. Now, when he was gone, it was Katherine who would decide exactly how they divided whatever would ultimately be obtained for the Katherine Jackson Trust—half of Michael's estate after the donations to charity, according to Mrs. Jackson's advisors. It was a burden, Katherine said. They would all be coming after her, all trying to tell her what she should do and how she should do it. She already felt a clearer sense of what it must have been like for Michael.

In fact, family intrigues were already set in motion. For reasons of his own, John McClain had leaked the news to the oldest Jackson son, Jackie, that this new lawyer of Katherine Jackson's had cut some sort of deal that might potentially give Katherine control of hundreds of millions of dollars in Michael Jackson estate assets. Some of Mrs. Jackson's advisors believed that McClain was trying to scuttle the deal, fearful that if it went through Katherine would discover that he had been less than candid with her about how much money he was making as an executor of the estate. Whether that was true or not, Jackie had passed along what he heard from McClain to his father and brothers. Joe and Randy immediately began lobbying to stop the deal Perry Sanders had made, whatever it was, insisting that to leave Branca in charge was a mistake, that the only way to go was to take him down and gain control of the estate themselves.

In early May 2011, Joe won a sort of victory over Katherine when his wrongful death lawsuit against Conrad Murray was tied to Mrs. Jackson's lawsuit against AEG. Judge Yvette Palazuelos, who was already hearing Katherine's case, had scheduled a May 3 hearing on the "notice of related cases" filed by Brian Oxman on Joe's behalf. Katherine's attorneys fiercely opposed the attempt to tie Joe's suit to hers, insisting to Judge Palazuelos that Mrs. Jackson's claim "has distinct factual and legal issues of AEG's direct negligence and whether or not it employed Dr. Conrad Murray." AEG also objected to joining the two cases. "Whereas the vast majority of the factual allegations in Joseph Jackson's complaint concern the day of Michael Jackson's death and subsequent events, the allegations in Katherine Jackson's complaint almost entirely concern events prior to Michael Jackson's death," the company's attorneys argued in court. The judge, though, had sided with Oxman's argument. Joe was now certain to be a major player in whatever went forward and to have his own piece of the action. It was likely that, in order to streamline the process and cut down on the cost of litigation, the two "related cases" would eventually be combined into a single lawsuit.

Other family members and factotums looked to cash in on different fronts. Janet, Jermaine, and La Toya all published books. Frank Cascio had announced a book, too, and Dieter Wiesner said he was working on one also.

Frank Dileo intended to write his own tell-all book as well, but was confronted with a chapter he hadn't expected to write. The sixty-three-year-old Dileo, who had suffered from heart problems for years, checked into a hospital near his home in Pittsburgh in March 2011 to prepare for open-heart surgery that included a bypass and valve replacement. "Complications" had swiftly ensued and Dileo suffered a heart attack on the operating table that caused an interruption in the supply of oxygen to his brain. He remained in a coma for weeks, and never fully regained consciousness before his death on August 24, 2011.

Dr. Arnold Klein had no immediate plans for a tell-all book though at that point in his life could have used the revenue. Confined mostly to a wheelchair and denying reports he was afflicted with multiple sclerosis, Arnie was also broke. According to Klein, his assistant Jason Pfeiffer had teamed up with his accountant Muhammad Khilji to clean him out. Klein was claiming embezzlement in reports to the Beverly Hills police department, but Marc Schaffel doubted it was quite that cut and dry. "I know for a fact that every Friday they used to give Klein a packet of papers to sign—payroll, checks, documents, and basically anything they put in front of him, he signed. He didn't even look at what it was." It sounded eerily like Michael Jackson. "But I don't think even Michael was that careless," Schaffel said.

Among the papers bearing the doctor's signature were powers of attorney that had allowed the two men not only full access to all of his bank accounts, Klein said, but also the ability to take out equity loans on all of his homes: the historically registered $9 million mansion on Windsor Square in Los Angeles, the $12 million Frank Gehry–designed beach house in Laguna, and the $1.9 million desert retreat in Palm Springs. Pfeiffer and Khilji had leased themselves Bentleys in his name, the doctor said, and had opened credit card accounts billed to their employer with spending limits so high they could cover purchases well into six figures. In January 2011, Dr. Klein was forced to file bankruptcy.

Desperate, Klein had gone to the FBI, claiming wildly that his accountant, Khilji, had stolen his money to turn it over to a terrorist organization.

"Arnie's lost it a little bit," Schaffel said. "He's saying, 'Those weren't my signatures,' then he's saying, 'I didn't know what I was signing.' He thinks he's gonna sue them civilly and get the money back. I said, 'Arnie, the money's gone. They've spent this money like water.' Not only is all his money gone, but they left him ten million in debt. They mortgaged all his properties, dried up all his cash. He owes his medical supplier $250,000 and can't afford to pay it."

Pfeiffer and Khilji insisted that it was Arnold Klein's profligacy, not any scheme by them, that had driven him into bankruptcy. Klein's disregard for the bottom line had caught up with him after 2007, when his two top-grossing medical partners left the practice, Khilji said, and by 2011 his reported gross monthly revenue of $90,872 was a far cry from the $20,000 a day he had boasted of in a 2004 interview with the *New York Times*. "To say I'm a thief? He still owes me $50,000 from outstanding invoices," the accountant told the Daily Beast and promised to sue Klein for slander.

Klein, for years as admired a raconteur as Beverly Hills could boast, now lived in dread of the Conrad Murray trial. The defense had subpoenaed Klein's medical records going back to the beginning of his relationship with Michael Jackson and clearly intended to build a case around the argument that the dermatologist had been encouraging Jackson's drug abuse for decades.

"I used to consider Arnie the most intelligent person I've ever met," said a saddened Schaffel, "and Michael saw him the same way. You could learn so much from a conversation with Arnie. He was so articulate and well-read. But now he's less and less coherent. He babbles, something he never did before."

Perhaps nothing left Klein so distraught as the fact that Liz Taylor had cut him off from contact during the last months of her life. Taylor had been furious when Klein gave an interview that seemed to support Jason Pfeiffer's claim that he had been Michael Jackson's lover, and in May 2010 she had openly denounced Arnie on her Twitter account for the treachery she saw in his public comments about Michael's sexuality: "It seems he supplies not only women, but men too . . . how convenient. Just what we want in our doctors. And then to say he did not betray Michael's confidence. No wonder he has death threats . . . I thought doctors, like priests, took an oath of confidentiality. May God have mercy on his soul."

Klein would retract his statements about Michael Jackson and Jason Pfeiffer, and apologize for suggesting things that weren't true. It was too late, though, to repair his relationship with Liz. "Arnie tried to call her but she wouldn't take his calls," a mutual friend said. "Arnie sent her Christ-mas gifts, she returned them. When she went into the hospital [in March 2011], Arnie sent her flowers, but Liz rejected them. Arnie tried to go over to see her at the hospital before she died, but they wouldn't let him in."

Klein at least had been able to enjoy the public humiliation of his long-time rival Dr. Steven Hoefflin. Thanks in large part to Michael Jackson's old nemesis Diane Dimond, Hoefflin now owned a reputation for weird-ness that matched anything the reporter had ever attributed to Jackson.

Dimond had gotten hold of a Los Angeles police department report that chronicled a recent history of "delusional" behavior by Hoefflin that, she reported, had resulted in officers from the LAPD Threat Assessment Unit being assigned to monitor him. Dimond went on to detail a sequence of bizarre behavior which, if true, indicated Hoefflin was in serious need of psychiatric help. What distressed Arnold Klein was that, despite this, Hoefflin claimed to be the Jackson family's "authorized medical repre-sentative" in the weeks after Michael's death, sitting in with the family as they discussed plans to file wrongful death lawsuits against various physi-cians (Dr. Klein among them) as well as Lloyd's of London and AEG Live. Jackson family insiders denied Hoefflin's claim to this title.

In Las Vegas, the Palomino hacienda was being offered as "Michael Jackson's Last Las Vegas Residence." The brochure didn't mention that Michael and his children had lived in the guesthouse, instead emphasiz-ing the "lower level" of the home where Michael had stored "his vast collection of memorabilia, book collection, and art, and also kept his personal studio and art room," which sounded a far cry from the dingy basement and oppressive clutter that Tohme Tohme and others recalled from their visits to the house while Michael lived there. Still, the price of $8.8 million was a pittance compared to the $29 million that Hubert Guez wanted for the Carolwood chateau where Michael Jackson had come to the end of his life.

Even the cash-strapped State of California was looking to cut itself in on the booming market in Michael Jackson–related real estate. At a time when the new governor, Jerry Brown, was moving to close down any number of state parks, Assemblyman Mike Davis was proposing to add a new one, introducing a bill to finance a study to determine the feasibility of letting the California Department of Parks and Recreation join in a public/private partnership with Colony Capital to run Neverland Ranch as a state-sanctioned tourist attraction. The owners of Oxnard-based Channel Island Helicopters certainly believed there was still widespread interest in Michael Jackson's former home. The company announced that on June 25, 2011, the second anniversary of Michael's death, it would begin offering half-hour flights over Neverland at a cost of $175 per person.

Enduring as the fascination with Michael Jackson seemed to be, there was reason to wonder whether his estate could sustain the fantastic earning power it had demonstrated in the first year after the star's death. Sales of Jackson's classic records had subsided during 2010 to approximately the level they had been at before his death. After more than 33 million Jackson albums had been purchased worldwide in 2009 (most of them in a six-month period) sales had dipped to less than 6 million units through the first eleven months of 2010 and the disparity was even greater domestically. From 12.6 million downloads of Michael songs in the United States during 2009, the number had fallen to 1.1 million in 2010. Sony was disappointed by sales of the *This Is It* soundtrack but that album had sold more than twice the number of copies that *Michael* did. In the third, fourth, and fifth weeks of its release, *Michael*'s domestic sales dropped to 27,000 units, then 18,000 units, and finally to 11,000 units, making it evident that Sony would have what *Billboard* called "an inventory liability problem" on its hands.

The estate reported that Michael's enormous debt had only been partially paid off, even though most of what the estate had earned thus far, John Branca said, had been dedicated to that purpose. Money was still pouring in, of course, largely as a result of the contracts that Branca had negotiated prior to the release of *Michael*. The executors' public report at the end of 2010 listed $310 million in profits for the Michael Jackson estate during the past eighteen months. The total value of the deals that the estate had made in just the first twelve months after Michael's death was estimated at $756 million, and continued to pay off at the rate of tens of millions per month. "There's something unique about Americans," Robert F. X. Sillerman told the *New York Times*. "We root against people and look for the negative while they're alive, and then we're very forgiving, whether they deserve it or not, and we celebrate their success in death."

Other observers, though, wondered whether Michael Jackson's estate really would continue to be the most valuable in the entertainment industry. "The question is: Is he Elvis or is he not?" Bob Lefsetz, the former entertainment lawyer whose blog *The Lefsetz Letter* was widely read throughout the music industry, told the *Times*. Personally, he didn't think so, Lefsetz said, not without some Graceland-like destination for fans to flock to. The failure to make a Michael Jackson monument of Neverland Ranch, Lefsetz believed, would cost the estate hundreds of millions of dollars over the long term.

Potential revenues were no doubt a good reason to reconsider the question of a King of Pop shrine at Neverland Ranch, but perhaps not the only one. The debate that arose from the possibility of a final return to Neverland encompassed the complexity of Michael Jackson's legacy like no other public discussion possibly could. On one side was that for nearly fifteen years Michael had cherished Neverland in a way that he never did and never would again love any other place on earth. The ranch was a universe custom-fitted to his character and, as Tom Mesereau put it, "the only place he had ever really felt comfortable." It was his vision as well as his home. The other side of the argument was that Michael had told one person after another during the last four years of his life that Neverland was lost to him, describing his former residence as a ruin of faded hopes and forgotten dreams that he would always associate with suffering and humiliation, and with the profound sense of betrayal that had shredded the last fibers of his trust in people. Neverland had been Michael Jackson's fantasy land and his true-life residence, an imaginary redoubt of eternal youth and an actual repository of the questions about the star's "personal life" that would shadow his memory far into the future.

At Neverland, Michael Jackson had learned that "going on" with what remained of his life after the settlement of the sex abuse charges against him in 1994 would take far more from him than he had bargained for. And it was of little if any consolation to him that the man on the other side of that deal had been even more destroyed by it than he was.

In the Chandler family narrative, the characterization of Michael Jackson was surprisingly sympathetic even though they all agreed, without reservation, that he was a pedophile. "Michael had needs," one of the Chandlers (speaking anonymously) would explain shortly before the second anniversary of the star's death. "Among these was to love and be loved, to touch and be touched. He had sexual urges. It was just that his emotional growth in that area was stunted because of his childhood experiences. Michael was the most sensitive one among the Jacksons. And as the most sensitive one, he was the one most affected by what he saw and felt.

"With Jordie and with the others, he was just trying to meet his needs. To a normal heterosexual male, having sex with a twelve-year-old is icky. To Michael, having sex with an adult was icky. That was who he was. From his point of view he wasn't trying to hurt anybody."

This version of Michael owed much to the research and thought of Evan Chandler's younger brother Ray, who had put together a portrait of the star that other members of the family adopted, with varying degrees of condemnation. Ray was also the one person in the family—the one person on earth, perhaps—who insisted on a compassionate portrait of Evan.

In the years since the settlement with Jackson, members of the Chandler family—Ray in particular—had repeatedly pointed out that neither Evan nor Jordie ever said a single public word about what had happened in 1993 and 1994. "Everything people heard came from the Jackson camp," one member of the family noted. "They began staging these worldwide media events, and that's what whipped up the press." The Chandlers remained most unforgiving of the "smear campaign" they accused Jackson of allowing his representatives to run against them during those weeks and months. "When Michael was faced with what he'd done, he had a choice to make," one of them explained. "If he truly loved Jordie he would not have done what he did by setting his dogs on the family like that."

By the time the $20-million-plus settlement was made, the Chandlers said, they were a fragmented family made up of frightened individuals. During a meeting with the deputy district attorney and the lead detective who were handling the criminal investigation in Los Angeles, Evan and Ray were told, "You'll be looking over your shoulder for the next ten years," then warned that, "It only takes one nut with one bullet to kill you." The relentless barrage of threats against not only Evan and Jordie, but every member of the family, sent them all into hiding. "The British were by far the worst," recalled one of the Chandlers. "They were actually coming here to the States to hunt us down."

It would be reported years later in *Vanity Fair* that Jordie's life had been "completely broken by his association with Michael Jackson," while a UK newspaper described him as "a lonely, introverted young man." But that might have been nothing more than another way of saying that he had spent the subsequent ten years hiding from reporters and photographers. Jordie *had* endured a great deal, though, and "broken" was certainly a fair description of his family.

The "Jackson saga" had grown "like a cancer in the family," Ray Chandler would say in 2009, "and it affected us all." No one was more decimated than Evan, in Ray's telling. "Evan was at one point the most vilified person on the planet," his brother explained, "because he had accused the most loved person on the planet of something heinous. And when you are the most vilified person on the planet, it affects you. All of the adults who were touched by this came out of it broken and ruined, but Evan was the most broken and ruined. He spent the rest of his life being afraid."

When Jordie was still thirteen, his father had won custody of the boy by claiming in court that his ex-wife June had, effectively, prostituted her son to Michael Jackson. Even Ray wouldn't defend his brother's decision to abandon his two young sons, Nikki and Emmanuel, when he headed east with Jordie. The relationship with the boys' mother Nathalie had turned so nasty that he couldn't bear to deal with her, Evan explained, but he intended to remain in his sons' lives. He would come out to visit them, Evan promised, more than once, but he never did. After more time passed, he said he would develop a relationship with the boys when they got older, but that didn't happen either. In the Chandler family chronicle of events, Nikki and Emmanuel were just two more of Michael Jackson's victims.

Evan fled with his oldest first to Germany, then to a Long Island beach community, before returning the boy, at age fourteen, to Los Angeles, where Jordie found some sense of family in the home of his former step-mother Nathalie, his two half-brothers, and Nathalie's new husband, the screenwriter Robert Rosen, who by all accounts was doing stellar work as a stepfather. The teenager refused to have any contact with his mother, though. The skateboard that June had delivered to her son on his birthday in 1996 sat for years untouched in the garage of the Brentwood house where he lived.

Jordie paid his own way through the Crossroads School, an exclusive and expensive arts-oriented academy in Santa Monica whose alumni roster was well stocked with celebrities (Zooey Deschanel, Taylor Locke, and Spencer Pratt were among Jordie's schoolmates during his years there). One of the first major business investments Jordie made was in the very school he was attending; after contemplating his $20,000-plus annual tuition and the prime piece of property that encompassed the campus, the boy had become one of Crossroads' owners. He was successfully playing the stock market by the time he graduated from high school and then enrolled at UCLA, grow-ing wealthier year-by-year with the assistance of a vice president at Santa Monica Bank who had become his financial advisor. By the time Jordie had transferred to New York University, he was hiring the best private instructors and became a skilled skier and windsurfer whose lifestyle included regular snorkeling adventures in the Bahamas and winter sojourns in Taos and Vail. He appeared to be thriving. His stunning looks, cheerful personality, and willingness to pick up one check after another made him popular among fellow students in both high school and college.

Still, Jordie's existence remained a furtive one. Threats against his life were regularly posted on the Internet by Michael's most rabid fans. Evan Chandler had refused to return to Los Angeles after 1994, the year a twenty-four-year-old British woman began stalking him at home and at work. Other more aggressive fans had taken her place and everyone related to Jordie knew they had to watch out for both him and themselves. "We're coming to take your blood. Your blood and your shitty little son's blood," was just one of the many frightening messages that had been left on Evan's answering machine, according to Ray. After receiving a package at his dental office that contained a decapitated rat and a note reading, "You're next," Ray said, Evan arranged for his son to take shooting lessons at the Beverly Hills Gun Club. The tabloids put their own sort of bounty on Jordie's head, offering six figures for candid shots of the boy.

By the time he turned twenty, Jordie was once again living mainly in New York, where he felt safer. He had developed by then into a young man who was every bit as good-looking as he had been as a thirteen-year-old boy. He owned luxury properties on both coasts and was enormously wealthy, having more than doubled his payout from the Michael Jackson settlement by investing in Mobil, Chevron, and Texaco at the exact moment when oil company stocks were about to enter a period of explosive growth. He moved between his beachfront house in West Hampton and his apartment in a Manhattan building that featured a rooftop swimming pool and an indoor running track, working briefly as a dancer, interning at a record company, and dabbling as a songwriter in collaboration with a young Greek-American woman named Sonnet Simmons who wanted to be a pop star. As long as he stayed out of the media's eye, life was good. People around the young man were protective. Jordie was increasingly disturbed, though, by what was happening to his father.

What the public knew Evan Chandler best for during those years were his legal conflicts. He was accused in 1994 of attacking and beating Dave Schwartz in Larry Feldman's office for calling him an extortionist. Two years later, Evan filed a $60 million lawsuit that accused Michael Jackson of violating the terms of their confidentiality agreement in his interview with Diane Sawyer and in the lyrics of a song from the *HIStory* album.

Along with the demand for money, Evan had insisted that he be permitted to release his own album, to be titled *EVANstory*, with songs that included "DA Reprised," "You Have No Defense (For My Love)," and "Duck Butter Love." The lawsuit was thrown out in 1999.

Handsome as he was (a better-looking version of Rob Lowe was how one relative described him), Evan had been unable to form another relationship with a woman after leaving Nathalie. He spooked the few he got to know. Though diagnosed as bipolar, Evan refused to take his medicine, complaining that it turned him into a "zombie." Both his depressions and his manic episodes grew more pronounced as he aged. He could be vaguely dangerous and definitely scary when he transitioned from one state to the other. He also became nearly as addicted to plastic surgery as Michael Jackson. Inordinately vain and spectacularly insecure, Evan had subjected himself to at least nineteen separate cosmetic procedures in the years after the Jackson settlement. Evan would claim that part of the reason for his repeated surgeries was that he wanted to alter his appearance to avoid being recognized by the Jackson fans that were constantly promising online to chase him down and do him in. This, however, didn't explain why he injected himself on a monthly basis with Botox and cosmetic facial fillers. The result of all this "work" was a face that still appeared remarkably striking and youthful from a distance, yet eerily smooth up close. People who met him for the first time got the impression of an old man who was wearing the unbearably tight mask of some youthful movie character they couldn't quite place.

Evan was also growing financially depleted, regularly asking his much wealthier son for loans that he never repaid. Money was a constant source of friction between the two.

The filing of criminal charges against Michael Jackson in 2003 was viewed by some of the Chandlers—Ray in particular—as an opportunity for vindication. In the run-up to the trial, the media began dredging up information about the Chandler case that had never been reported earlier, and almost all of it reflected badly on the accused.

Among the many unfortunate developments afflicting Michael was that Lisa Marie Presley's debut album, *To Whom It May Concern*, was released in early 2003, when the effect of the Bashir documentary was still being felt. Lisa Marie, the one person in the world who was in a position to speak the truth about Michael's sexuality, had agreed to a series of national interviews to promote her album and was distressed but probably not surprised to discover that the subject most interesting to reporters was her marriage to Michael Jackson. To her credit, she never suggested that Michael might be a child molester—quite the opposite—but her wish to distance herself from her ex-husband, combined with whatever residual ache she felt about it all had resulted in some edgy observations about Michael's ability to manipulate people by pretending to be someone he was not.

"You think he used you?" Howard Stern asked her.

"Mmm . . . you know, sketchy," she answered.

"Sketchy?" Stern asked.

"Mmm. Timing-wise," Lisa Marie replied.

In a one-on-one interview with Diane Sawyer, Lisa Marie described herself as "naïve as hell," when she married Michael: "I never thought for a moment that someone like him could actually use me for any reason like that. It never crossed my mind, and I don't know why—I'm sure it crossed everyone else's."

The most devastating observation about Michael, though, was the one she offered to GQ in early 2004, two months after his arrest: "He's somewhat asexual, but he can be whatever he wants to be when he wants to be."

The impact of Lisa Marie's remarks was mild in comparison to the blow NBC delivered with its *Michael Jackson Unmasked* special that ran on *Dateline* around the same time that the first single from *To Whom It May Concern* was released. The program featured a Chicago private detective named Ernie Rizzo who had worked on the Chandler case. Rizzo gave NBC the names of multiple witnesses who agreed that back in 1993 Michael had gotten into the habit of phoning Jordie every weekday at 3:15 p.m., the moment the boy got home from school, and that the two of them regularly stayed up late into the night talking on the telephone. Several witnesses corroborated Rizzo's claim that he had seen "lots of love notes" written by Michael to Jordie, and that Michael liked to play a game with children that he called "Rubba"—"You rubba me and I rubba you."

NBC quoted lines from Jordie's sworn statement to the police that had never been seen or read before by the public, including those that described what had happened during their trip to Monaco for the World Music Awards. Jackson had rented two hotel suites, the boy said, one for his mother and Lily, the other for him and Michael. It was in that hotel suite, Jordie had claimed, that Michael first sexually seduced him.

The same file of police reports included Evan Chandler's recollection that when he confronted Jackson about the relationship with Jordie, Michael's reply had been, "It's cosmic. I don't understand it myself. I just know we were meant to be together."

NBC had also found the maid who worked for Evan and Nathalie Chandler back in 1993, Norma Salinas, who described the "strange things going on" in the Brentwood house after Michael Jackson began to spend the night. Michael usually showed up "all by himself, no bodyguards or anyone," Salinas recalled. Jordie introduced the star to her as "my best friend," the maid remembered: "They were hugging, laughing. They looked very happy, like a couple." On the first Friday night that Michael stayed over, Nathalie told her to pull out the trundle beneath Jordie's bed, Salinas recalled, because that was where Michael would be sleeping. The two of them, man and boy, had spent nearly the entire weekend behind the closed door of the bedroom Jordie normally shared with his half-brother Nikki, according to the maid, who remembered coming into the room on Saturday morning to discover that the trundle had not been slept in.

Nothing delighted the Chandlers so much as the fall of Anthony Pellicano, whom they regarded as the person most responsible for spreading lies about their family. Almost a year before the November 2003 raid on Neverland Ranch, FBI agents had swarmed Pellicano's offices in Los Angeles, searching for evidence that he was behind a threat against *Los Angeles Times* reporter Anita Busch, who had discovered a dead fish with a rose in its mouth and a sign reading "Stop" on the cracked windshield of her car. The FBI obtained its warrant to search Pellicano's offices after learning that Busch had been working on a potentially shocking story about the private investigator's client, the actor Steven Seagal. During their search, FBI agents found two military practice grenades modified to serve as homemade bombs and enough C-4 explosive to take down a jumbo jet, along with illicit telephone recordings of Tom Cruise speaking on the telephone to his estranged wife Nicole Kidman. Pellicano had pleaded guilty to illegal possession of dangerous materials and was sentenced to thirty months in federal prison. By the time Michael Jackson was preparing to go to trial in Santa Barbara County, federal authorities were already deep into an investigation that would result in wiretapping and racketeering charges against Pellicano, and an additional federal prison sentence of fifteen years.

Ray Chandler began asking reporters if they still thought Mary Fischer's GQ article about Evan Chandler's dealings with Michael Jackson was so great.

It became much easier to believe people like Robert Wegner, Neverland's former chief of security, who told NBC that during the police search of the ranch back in 1993, he had received a phone call from Pellicano ordering him to collect all records involving guests who had slept in

Michael's bedroom and to delete the files from his computer. *Dateline* also quoted anonymous sources who said that Pellicano had been tape-recorded begging Neverland employees not to talk to the police, and reported that some of these people had been so shaken by Pellicano's subsequent threats that they "still cower when they speak of him."

Ray Chandler would create a similar if slightly smaller sensation with the publication of his book *All That Glitters: The Crime and the Cover-Up*. He had been moved to pen his "exposé," Evan's brother said, when he saw the Martin Bashir documentary. Among the fresh revelations in Ray's book was that the first to realize what was happening between Michael and Jordie was Nathalie Chandler, who had shouted at her husband one afternoon, "Can't you see what's going on? They're in love!"

Ray also produced a list of "six wishes" that he said Michael had given Jordie, telling the boy to repeat them three times a day to make them come true. These were:

1. No wenches, bitches, heifers, or hos.
2. Never give up your bliss.
3. Live with me in Neverland forever.
4. No conditioning.
5. Never grow up.
6. Be better than best friends forever.

The most significant impact of all, though, was the publication of Jordan Chandler's detailed and undeniably disturbing description to police investigators of how a sexual relationship had developed between Michael Jackson and him:

"Physical contact between Michael Jackson and myself increased gradually. The first step was simply Michael hugging me. The next step was for him to give me a brief kiss on the cheek . . . He then started kissing me on the lips, first briefly, and then for a longer period of time. He would kiss me while we were in bed.

"The next step was when Michael put his tongue in my mouth. I told him I didn't like that. Michael started crying. He said there was nothing wrong with it. He said that just because most people believe something is wrong, doesn't make it so . . . Michael told me another of his young friends would kiss him with an open mouth . . .

"We took a bath together. This was the first time we had seen each other naked. Michael named certain of his children friends that masturbated in front of him . . . Michael then masturbated in front of me. He told me that when I was ready, he would do it for me. While we were in bed, Michael put his hand underneath my underpants. He then masturbated me to a climax. After that Michael Jackson masturbated me many times both with his hand and with his mouth . . .

"He had me suck one nipple and twist the other nipple while he masturbated. On one occasion when Michael and I were in bed he grabbed my buttock and kissed me while he put his tongue in my ear. I said I didn't like that. Michael started to cry . . .

"Michael told me I should not tell anyone what had happened. He said this was a secret."

All that saved Jordie, Ray Chandler would say, was that "Evan separated him from Michael before it got to anal sex."

Evan Chandler's brother took satisfaction in seeing former Michael Jackson defenders turn on the star. Among these was young actor Corey Feldman, who completely contradicted what he had told reporters back in 1993. "I started to look at each piece of information, and with that came this sickening realization that there have been many occurrences in my life and in my relationship with Michael that have created a question of doubt," Feldman explained to Martin Bashir, who interviewed him for ABC's *20/20*.

What "occurrences" were those? Bashir inquired: Was there "anything inappropriate"?

"If you consider it inappropriate for a man to look at a book of naked pictures with a child that's thirteen or fourteen years old, then your answer would be yes," Feldman replied. It had happened during a stopover at the Hideout on the way to Disneyland, Feldman said: "We went to his apartment, and I noticed a book that he had out on his coffee table. The book contained pictures of grown men and women naked. And the book was focused on diseases and the genitalia." When he asked what it was all about, Michael sat down with him and began to explain the pictures, Feldman recalled. "I was kind of grossed out by it," he said. "I didn't think of it as a big deal. And for all these years I probably never thought twice about it . . . But in light of recent evidence, I have to say that if my son was fourteen years old, thirteen years old, and went to a man's apartment that was thirty-five, and I knew they were sitting down together talking about this, I would probably beat his ass."

Ray Chandler didn't see it as especially significant that Feldman had followed up by admitting that Michael "never did anything out of line" and that "the closest he ever came to touching me was maybe slapping me on the leg once." Evan's brother simply dismissed boys like Ahmad Elatab, a New Jersey teen who said he had begun to spend extended periods of time at Neverland in the mid-1990s, when he was nine years old. After a New York columnist wrote that Jackson disliked Middle Easterners, Elatab recalled, Michael had arranged to bring a bunch of Arab kids to a private studio in New York City where he explained that this was not true. He and Michael developed a phone relationship, Elatab said, and eventually started "hanging out" at Neverland. He slept in the same room with Michael on multiple occasions, Elatab said, and knew any number of kids who had spent the night in the same bed with Michael. Those evenings had been nothing more than really fun slumber parties, Elatab told CBS News: "He's not sexual with kids. He's not a molester. He's not a pedophile. He just likes to help children."

Ray retorted that, "Michael only made sexual advances to a select few of the boys he spent time with. He was quite selective." During Jackson's criminal trial, Jordie's uncle was employed by the networks as a sort of self-made authority on pedophiles, having read dozens of books and spoken to nearly that many psychiatrists about the subject. He liked to quote Sam Vaknin, whose writings on the "roots of pedophilia" sounded to some people like a personality profile of Michael Jackson. "Sex with children is the reenactment of a painful past," Vaknin had asserted. "Children are the reification of innocence, genuineness, trust, and faithfulness—qualities that the pedophile wishes to nostalgically recapture . . . Through his victim, the pedophile gains access to his suppressed and thwarted emotions. It is a fantasylike second chance to reenact his childhood." Ray noted that pedophile "profiles" described common characteristics that sounded like an inventory of life at Neverland Ranch, such as a "fascination with children and child activities," a tendency to refer to children "in pure or angelic terms using descriptives like 'innocent,' 'heavenly,' and 'divine,'" the cultivation of "childlike hobbies such as collecting popular expensive toys and keeping reptiles or exotic pets," the use of "childlike decor," and a preference for "children close to puberty who are sexually inexperienced but curious about sex." Ray particularly liked pointing out that pedophiles commonly targeted single-parent familes. "What made Michael different," Evan Chandler's younger brother said, "is that the average pedophile can only offer candy and video games. Michael offered the world."

He was perplexed by the fact that his brother Evan and nephew Jordie were unhappy with him for going on television, Ray admitted. The two of them wanted nothing to do with the criminal case in Santa Barbara

County. Jordie was especially displeased when his Uncle Ray publicly implored him to testify in court against Michael Jackson. He was not going to sacrifice his privacy—not to mention risk his physical safety—to take the stand in California, the younger Chandler said. "Jordie's attitude is, 'Think what you want. I don't care. Just leave me alone,'" explained one of his relatives. During the trial, Jordie tried to hide out at a Lake Tahoe ski chalet in the company of school friends who included Sonnet Simmons but was photographed on the slopes wearing a big smile and expensive ski wear, an image of cavalier indifference that caused him to be more hated than ever among Michael's fans.

By the time of Michael's acquittal in June 2005, Jordie and Evan were sharing a luxury apartment on the sixteenth floor of the Liberty Towers in Jersey City. Tall windows offered a magnificent view of the Manhattan skyline, but Evan was largely indifferent to it. He was sixty-one now but looked much older, despite the Botox and wrinkle filler injections. What made Evan age faster than other men was the degree of his suffering. The agony he experienced did indeed come from deep inside, as so many of those who despised him suggested it should, but the primary source of Evan's hurt was a rare genetic disorder called Gaucher's disease. In Gaucher's patients (an unusually high percentage of whom are Ashkenazi Jews), the deficiency of an enzyme that disperses lipids causes a fatty substance to accumulate in white blood cells. Among the most common symptoms are bone lesions that eventually result in constant racking pain.

The ache in his bones made Evan increasingly irritable and exacerbated the mood swings of his untreated bipolar condition. Jordie was his only companion but relations between the two grew more and more strained. Evan would explode into rages and blame his son for all that had happened to him and to the family. In September 2005, Jordie filed a motion with the Hudson County Family Court for a restraining order against his father, claiming that Evan had attacked him from behind with a twelve-pound barbell, sprayed him in the face with a can of Mace, and then attempted to choke him. When Evan refused to leave the apartment, Jordie did, moving back into Manhattan by himself.

By the summer of 2009 Evan was sixty-five years old and a virtual hermit. The only people he conversed with were the staff at the Colanta Hematology and Oncology Center in Bayonne, New Jersey, where he went for his pain medication prescriptions. His Gaucher's disease had progressed to the point that Evan found it impossible to make it through even part of a day without being doped up. He wasn't living, he was existing, Evan told his brother Ray during one of their infrequent phone conversations.

Now almost thirty, Jordie spent much of his time in California, taking guitar and surfing lessons. He had cowritten a frothy song with Sonnet Simmons called "You're So Good for Me" that became a minor pop sensation. In Los Angeles, Jordie was surrounded by friends and family. He and his two half-brothers remained close, supporting one another in their refusal to have anything to do with the man who had fathered each of them.

Neither his sons nor anyone else knew what Evan Chandler made of Michael Jackson's death, because by that time even his brother Ray had stopped speaking to the man. Alone with his agony and unwilling to swallow another pill, Evan allowed himself to feel the pain in his bones for a few hours on a day in the middle of November 2009, not quite four months after Michael Jackson's passing. It might have been the fourteenth or the fifteenth—nobody would ever be sure. He sat on his bed in the Liberty Towers apartment with the inspiring view of the Manhattan skyline and held a snub-nose .38 revolver, a pistol he had purchased years earlier to protect himself against a feared attack by some deranged Jackson fan. He wrote no note before raising that revolver to his head and pulling the trigger.

The Liberty Towers concierge found his body sprawled across the bed, the gun still in his hand, late on the afternoon of November 17, 2009, after doctors from the Colanta Center phoned to say that Mr. Chandler had missed his regular appointment.

Ray Chandler would chafe at Internet reports that Evan had taken his own life out of remorse over what he had done to Michael. "It had absolutely nothing to do with Michael Jackson," Ray said. "That was the last thing on his mind. He was just in a lot of pain. He and I had talked a lot about euthanasia, about how if either of us got in the position of being in a hospital bed with the tubes and all that, that we would see to it that the plug was pulled. Evan just decided to pull his own plug while he still had the strength to do it."

When a reporter phoned him from London's *Daily Mail*, Ray said he was waiting to hear about the funeral arrangements, but by then Evan's body had already been cremated. "Actually, no one was there," a staff member at the Jersey City funeral home where the cremation had taken place told the *Mail*'s reporter. "We were instructed that no one would want to go. It was very sad. They still haven't decided what to do with the ashes."

Evan Chandler's bleak end occasioned cruel celebration among dozens of Michael Jackson fans who posted about it online. "Good riddance, you piece of shit," wrote one. "Hope you rot in hell!!" Evan was "a very, very evil man," wrote another fan. "He should have been punished. This seems the easy way out."

One of Jordie's relatives said the young man hoped that the successive deaths of Michael Jackson and Evan Chandler might be "two very important events for him, because he thought that people would finally lay off of him, that it would all die down and he'd finally get some anonymity." It quickly became clear this wouldn't be the case. The postings on Jackson fan sites were as vicious and threatening as they had ever been. "Jordan Chandler, I hope you dream of Michael every night. Nightmares for the rest of your life. Guilt should rack your soul forever," wrote one. Added another, "If I ever see him he'd better run . . . a brick will be headed for his bitch-ass head."

Jackson fans posted the Old Meadow Boulevard address of Jordie's $2.35 million West Hampton home on the Internet and warned him not to return there. They created a "tracking" blog where people described various sightings of the young man and listed the places he frequented in both New York and Los Angeles, urging one another to keep up the "hunt" for him.

Shortly after a British tabloid offered $300,000 for a photograph of "the Michael Jackson boy," Jordie left LA and headed for Europe. A supposed "confession" by Jordie that Michael had never molested him and that he only made such a claim because "my father made me do it" popped up on dozens of Web sites. The confession was a fraudulent attempt at solace sent to Katherine Jackson by someone posing as Jordan Chandler. The Jackson family insisted that it was authentic, though, and after Jermaine Jackson arranged its dissemination in cyberspace Jordie's "confession" achieved a kind of de facto substantiality. The young man himself refused to comment, telling those closest to him that people could believe whatever they wanted to believe, he didn't care.

A week after the discovery of Evan Chandler's body in the Liberty Towers apartment, his two youngest sons gathered with friends and family for a Thanksgiving dinner at their mother's house in Los Angeles. A Hollywood producer at the table was taken aback by the animosity that Nikki and Emmanuel expressed toward Michael Jackson. "They literally couldn't speak his name without cursing him," the producer said. "They blame him not only for what they believe he did to their brother, but also for what they believe he did to their family."

None of the Chandlers had recanted their conviction that Michael Jackson was a child molester, and they weren't alone. Ron Zonen, years removed from the prosecution of Michael in Santa Barbara County, remained convinced that the defendant had been guilty as charged. During a September 15, 2010, Los Angeles Bar Association "Frozen In Time" symposium, Zonen betrayed a barely suppressed bitterness about the outcome of the criminal trial and a dogged insistence that justice had not been done. In front of an audience that included Tom Mesereau, Larry Feldman, Carl Douglas, and Judge Rodney Melville, Zonen told his audience about what a fine young man Gavin Arvizo had turned out to be.

After moving out of state and changing his name, Zonen said, Gavin became a high school football star, until his identity was revealed by a Michael Jackson fan who had linked his Myspace page to the social network connections of every other student at his school, then posted a lengthy attack on the teenager's character. Gavin was twenty years old now, Zonen said, and in his third year at a prominent East Coast university where he was an honor student with a 3.5 GPA pursuing a double major in history and philosophy. He wanted to become, of all things, a lawyer. Gavin was deeply religious, Zonen told the crowd, and had been in a relationship for the past three years with the daughter of a minister. He continued to refuse to accept so much as a penny from the numerous media organizations that were offering him six-figure sums for an interview and was paying his way through school with a half-scholarship supplemented by student loans. That Gavin had risen so far above his family background to develop into such an admirable person spoke volumes, in Zonen's opinion, about the truth of his accusations against Michael Jackson, accusations that he had never withdrawn.

Mesereau frowned and shook his head. The crowd observed an uncomfortable silence.

31

_____

"Michael was a good person, of that I'm certain," Tom Mesereau said shortly after the star's death. "He was one of the most sensitive and kindest people I've ever encountered. He really wanted what was best for everyone. He *wanted* people to do well. And he was remarkable with children and the elderly, one of the most considerate, if not *the* most considerate people I've ever met in that regard."

Kenny Ortega said that if you had been there to see what it was like to be on tour with Michael in the 1980s, before those allegations about him first made by the Chandler boy, if you had seen him hurrying to visit one orphanage or children's hospital ward after another between performances, in city after city, all over the world, you would have understood that the accusations against him simply *could not* be true. He had spent months at a stretch in constant contact with Michael Jackson, over a period of more than two decades, Ortega noted, and in all that time, "I've never seen Michael do anything to embarrass, harm, insult, or hurt anyone, ever."

What was perhaps most remarkable about Michael Jackson—more remarkable even than his tremendous talent—was that the overwhelming testimony to his goodness, to his sensitivity and kindness and generosity and resilience, could be so completely convincing and yet not cancel out the voices of those who gave the world reasons to wonder what lay underneath, or alongside, that goodness. The conundrum was as perplexing as any in the history of celebrity. Proof beyond a reasonable doubt about what Michael had or had not done would never be possible. Questions would remain. He didn't have to live with them anymore, but those he had left behind did.

"Please tell the world my son was not a pedophile," Katherine Jackson told me in the spring of 2011. "He was not and people need to know that about him." I could only say that *I* didn't believe Michael was a child molester.

Later I thought that perhaps it was a pity Mrs. Jackson had decided her son should not be interred at Neverland Ranch. What her decision had cost was more than a pilgrimage site for the fans or a row of ticket booths for the estate. The greater loss, it seemed to me, was that within the main house at Neverland existed the most fitting of all possible crypts for the King of Pop, the one perfect place in the world to contemplate the abiding mystery of Michael Jackson.

This hidden space was a custom feature of the main house that the dozens of deputies who swarmed the ranch back in November 2003 had almost overlooked. Behind a screen of stage uniforms in the back of a closet in the master bedroom was a trapdoor that opened onto a narrow carpeted stairwell lined with rag dolls, descending to a tiny eight-foot-by-seven-foot cubicle that seemed like a small child's bedroom. There were toys and games stacked on shelves. The walls were decorated with photographs of diapered babies. A large stuffed doll with big eyes and red hair reclined at the head of the single bed, leaning against pillowcases imprinted with the face of Walt Disney's Peter Pan—the one with Bobby Driscoll's features—and the word "Neverland." A Mickey Mouse telephone sat on the nightstand, next to a framed photograph of Macaulay Culkin signed, "Don't leave me in the house alone."

This, according to the Santa Barbara sheriff's department, was where Michael Jackson brought boys to sexually molest them. There was some basis for believing it might be true. The three deadbolt locks on that trapdoor, for instance. Michael wanted his privacy when he came down those carpeted stairs to the room with baby pictures on the walls, obviously. But for what? Those who arrested and prosecuted Jackson have yet to explain how it was that, out of the hundreds of boys who spent the night with him at Neverland Ranch, only two (or three, if Jason Francia is counted) ever accused him of sexual molestation, and that in each case the circumstances of those charges was at least as suspicious as anything Michael ever did or said. The detectives and the district attorneys haven't explained, either, how it could be that even those accusers never claimed Michael took them to the secret room to abuse them.

Marc Schaffel had purchased the photographs of the little boys in diapers that hung on the walls of Michael's most private place. It had started after Michael saw a poster-size photograph of a little blue-eyed blond boy in a diaper on the ceiling of a store they visited together, Schaffel recalled, and sent him back to buy the picture, whatever it cost. He remembered being instructed also to locate and obtain a book that featured naked toddlers done up as cherubs, Marc said. Schaffel admitted he had no idea whether such images stirred sexual feelings in Michael, but it was in this secret room where Michael had hidden from his father, his mother, and his brother Jermaine back in 2001, when they were trying to get him to the sign the contract promising them another $500,000 for showing up at thirtieth anniversary concerts. Prince and Paris had been with Michael on that occasion, noted Schaffel, who found it impossible to believe his friend would have brought his own children to a room where he had sexually molested others.

Alternate theories deserve consideration. One legitimate possibility was that the secret room was where Michael Jackson came to join those babies on the wall, to be one among them, not necessarily wearing a diaper or sucking on a milk bottle (though such notions couldn't be simply dismissed in Michael's case), but to travel back in time as far as it was possible to go, to that point where he could imagine being born again as the child he had so long yearned to be, the one who had grown up on the other side of the window, not in the studio, but on the playground.

Michael himself had been trying to tell people something like this for the last thirty years of his life. "One of my favorite pastimes is being with children—talking to them, playing games with them in the grass," he told an interviewer from *Melody Maker* shortly after the release of *Off the Wall*. "They're one of the main reasons I do what I do. They know everything that people are trying to find out—they know so many secrets—but it's hard for them to get it out. I can recognize them and learn from it."

Ultimately, no one could be certain of *the* truth. Admitting that, though, did not change the fact that the tiny hidden room behind the closet and down the stairs was the best spot on the planet to acknowledge *a* truth: Of all the answers one might offer to the central question hanging over the memory of Michael Jackson, the one best supported by the evidence was that he had died as a fifty-year-old virgin, never having had sexual intercourse with any man, woman, or child, in a special state of loneliness that was a large part of what made him so unique as an artist and so unhappy as a human being. In that room, a person could choose to mourn for the Michael Jackson who had lived his last fifteen years convinced that he had been found guilty in the court of public opinion, and to permit him the presumption of an innocence he spent his whole life trying to reclaim.

In that room it would be possible, perhaps, even to grant him the wish that he isn't sleeping alone tonight.

"I wanted to save him. I felt that I could do it": Michael clung to Lisa Marie Presley for support in the wake of the Chandler allegations, and the two were married in May 1994. They divorced in 1996. *(Pool ARNAL/PAT/Gamma-Rapho via Getty Images)*

From surrogate mother to wife: Michael with Debbie Rowe in 1997 during a visit to France. Prince (Michael Joseph Jackson, Jr.) had recently been born and Rowe would become pregnant with Paris later that year. *(AAR/SIPA)*

Michael (here, with Prince and Paris circa 2001) was a proud father—and by all accounts, a devoted and responsible one. *(© www.splashnews.com)*

Michael with Sean Lennon on the set of the "Bad" video, 1987. Lennon appeared in the accompanying movie, *Moonwalker*. *(Ron Galella/WireImage)*

Jimmy Safechuck was Michael's young friend in 1988, four years before Jordan Chandler. At the time, it was considered odd but harmless. Later every one of Michael's friendships with young boys would be examined. *(Ron Galella/WireImage)*

Michael with Jordan and Lily Chandler in Monaco for the World Music Awards, May 1993. Jordie stayed in the same hotel suite as Michael, while Lily and their mother, June, stayed in another. *(Nikos Vinieratos/Rex USA)*

Michael in Times Square, November 2001, at his first ever in-store appearance, at the Virgin Megastore for *Invincible*. Jackson seemed to be wearing the nose of his idol Peter Pan. *(©SUZANNE PLUNKETT/AP/Corbis)*

Jackson dangling Blanket, face obscured, from the balcony of Berlin's Hotel Adlon in 2002, where he was accepting a Bambi Award. The incident would provoke an international outcry. (*©Tobias Schwarz/Reuters*)

Something in common: Michael and Elizabeth Taylor, with whom he shared a painful childhood as a child star and breadwinner, with Arnold Klein, the dermatologist who was friend and doctor to both, at an amFAR event. *(Gregg DeGuire/WireImage)*

Michael with Al Malnik's hands on his shoulders. Malnik was one of several financial advisors who attempted to turn around Jackson's spending and debt. At left is Brett Ratner, the film director who introduced Jackson and Malnik. In the center is producer Robert Evans. *(Ray Mickshaw/WireImage)*

Ron Burkle, the supermarket billionaire and investor, was one of Michael's financial rescuers. Here, they attended an MTV Movie Awards afterparty in 2003, along with Sean "Diddy" Combs. *(Celebrityvibe.com)*

Dieter Wiesner was Michael's manager in the early 2000s, until the criminal trial when the Nation of Islam forced him out. Behind him in the doorway is Leonard Muhammad. *(AP Photo/Kevork Djansezian)*

Do you want fries with that? Marc Schaffel, one of Michael's business partners, delivered cash to him in paper bags, which Jackson would call "Supersizing it." Lack of a paper trail on these payments cost Schaffel some of what he'd hoped to recover in his suit against Michael. *(AP Photo/Nick Ut)*

Tom Mesereau and Susan Yu, the legal team who represented Jackson in the Gavin Arvizo case. Mesereau to this day is a staunch defender of Jackson's reputation. *(Dave Hogan/Getty Images)*.

Tom Sneddon, District Attorney of Santa Barbara County, in the middle of Jackson's criminal trial. Sneddon continued to refer to the Jordan Chandler case as "open but inactive" years after the grand jury refused to indict Jackson in 1994. *(Aaron Lambert-Pool/Getty Images)*

Michael had made his own private world at Neverland Ranch in Santa Ynez, California. At top, the main house *(John Roca/NY Daily News Archive/Getty Images)*; from here, visitors could catch a train to the Neverland amusement park (below), with its own carousel and fairground rides, cinema with a working candy counter, and sound system embedded in the landscaping. *(Jason Kirk/Getty Images)*

During Gavin Arvizo's testimony at his criminal trial, Jackson was hospitalized, and nearly had his bail revoked for failing to show up the following morning. Here he is shown entering the courtroom, wearing a blazer thrown over his pajamas and walking aided by bodyguards. *(Kimberly White/WireImage)*

By the end of the trial "he was strained beyond description," according to Tom Mesereau, who is shown here with his client and Susan Yu leaving the courthouse after Michael was acquitted on all charges. Jackson, far from celebrating, was barely eating or sleeping and was hospitalized that night. *(Kevork Djansezian/WireImage)*

With Neverland raided and ruined for him, Jackson left it behind. Sheikh
Abdullah bin Hamad al-Khalifa, prince of Bahrain, offered him a place to
crash. Here, he and Sheikh Abdullah (left) traveled to Dubai and posed with
Emirates motor rally driver Mohammed Ben Sulayem. (©epa/Corbis)

Grace Rwaramba reporting to the High Court in London in November
2008, to testify in Sheikh Abdullah's suit against Michael for failing to
deliver on the album and other projects for which, the Sheikh said,
he had paid him advance money. (©ALASTAIR GRANT/AP/Corbis)

Tohme Tohme became
Michael's manager in 2008 and
set up the O2 shows.
(courtesy of Tohme Tohme)

Michael visits with
Japanese children from an
orphanage, invited specially
for a Tokyo fan event.
(Eric Talmadge/AP/Corbis)

Michael walks in Beverly Hills
with Paris, Prince, and Blanket, 2009.
The kids hated wearing masks,
but said after his death that
they understood he'd done
it to protect them.
(Ciao Hollywood/Splash News)

James Brown's funeral in Atlanta was Michael's first public appearance after returning to America from Ireland, and a chance to say goodbye to a "chitlin' circuit" friend whose moves had inspired him, and who had spoken out on his behalf in 2003. Here, Michael is sandwiched between Al Sharpton and Jesse Jackson *(Brett Flashnick/WpN)*; below, he approaches the coffin. His goodbye kiss on the Godfather of Soul's lips would be a minor scandal. Michael would himself be laid to rest in the same model casket as Brown. *(TAMI CHAPPELL/Reuters/Corbis)*

In 2011, Prince, Blanket and Paris (wearing a distinctive "Thriller" video jacket just like her dad's) joined Jermaine and La Toya onstage in Cardiff, Wales, for a Michael Forever tribute concert. *(Samir Hussein/WireImage)*

After Michael's death, fans flocked to his residences in Los Angeles and childhood home in Gary, and to scores of impromptu memorials all over the world. Here, fans mark the year anniversary of his passing at his star on the Hollywood Walk of Fame. *(Frazer Harrison/Getty Images)*

Jackson's children Prince, Blanket, and Paris (L-R) with Katherine Jackson and Justin Bieber at a 2012 Grauman's Chinese Theatre Hand & Footprint Ceremony. The kids would use their father's sequined glove and dance shoes to "immortalize" him in the forecourt of the theater. *(Lester Cohen/WireImage)*

This memorial, erected by fans in Prague's Old Town Square a few days after Jackson died, demonstrates that grief for him stretched across the globe. *(STRINGER/AFP/Getty Images)*

Moonwalker: Michael Jackson doing his signature move onstage
at Wembley during the *Bad* tour in 1988. *(©Harrison Funk/ZUMApress.com)*

AFTERWORD

The theme of the trial of the man accused in Michael Jackson's death was the same one that had played out so poignantly in Michael Jackson's life: Where did the fault lie, in what had been done to Michael, or in what he had done to himself? It had been made clear months in advance that the defense would take the second position, while the prosecution assumed the first.

In a case where both sides had revealed their strategies well ahead of time, the biggest surprise was that there *were* any surprises. The most significant had come even before a jury was selected, when Conrad Murray's defense team was blindsided by a ruling from Judge Michael Pastor stating that he would not permit the testimony of as many as a dozen people the defense had described as "key witnesses," among them Tohme Tohme and Dr. Arnold Klein. "As much as possible," Judge Pastor explained, he intended to "limit" the trial to the last seventy-two hours of Michael Jackson's life.

The media was nearly as disappointed by the judge's decision as were Murray and his attorneys. The reporters covering the trial had anticipated that its juiciest moments would come during an examination of Dr. Klein and his medical records. The defense team hadn't kept it a secret that they intended to convince the jury that Michael Jackson had been reduced to a pathetically vulnerable condition by Klein's overprescription of narcotics, especially Demerol. As Michael built up greater and greater tolerances to Demerol, Murray's attorneys planned to argue, his addictive personality had driven him to seek out stronger drugs that included the anesthetic propofol, and eventually to self-administer a fatal overdose.

Drugs prescribed by Klein *had* been recovered from Jackson's home. Those turned out to be muscle relaxants, though, not narcotics. Klein acknowledged administering Demerol to Michael in his office on a regular basis, but continued to insist this had been simply his way of prepping his "needle phobic" patient prior to Botox and Restylane injections. DEA agents spent weeks comparing the narcotics scripts they removed from Klein's office with the triplicate copies filed with the California attorney general's office and the state's medical board was reportedly preparing to initiate an action to suspend Klein's license. What really had both the media and the Murray defense team salivating, though, was the counterclaim that Jason Pfeiffer had filed against Klein with the bankruptcy court in August 2011, a month before the criminal trial was scheduled to begin. Pfeiffer's allegations about both Klein's medical practice and his personal life achieved a whole new level of lurid.

The most significant of Pfeiffer's claims in the eyes of the defense lawyers was that Klein regularly sent Michael Jackson out of his office so loaded on Demerol that the star couldn't walk out the door under his own power. "Several times, Klein told Pfeiffer to help Michael down to the car because Michael was too drugged up and disoriented to stand on his own," the lawsuit stated. He and the nurses "were worried that Michael was being 'overmedicated' by Klein," according to Pfeiffer, who claimed to have expressed concern for Jackson's "safety" and been told by Klein to "keep his mouth shut." The lawsuit also claimed that Klein had attempted to sneak scripts for muscle relaxants to Jackson by writing Pfeiffer's name on the prescriptions and that the doctor helped Michael try to "get out of a court appearance" (the one scheduled to take place at the Sheikh Abdullah trial in London) by issuing a note based on a fabricated test that his patient was suffering from a staph infection.

What the Internet media most appreciated were Pfeiffer's relevations about Klein's debauched lifestyle: "Dr. Klein searched obsessively for sex partners online and otherwise. From home, his medical offices, and elsewhere, Klein usually spent hours per day online searching for sex. Once home from work, Klein typically stayed awake until 2:00 a.m. or later . . . Klein required that Pfeiffer stay awake with him late into the night dictating e-mails Mr. Pfeiffer was required to send for Dr. Klein to potential sex partners . . . Pfeiffer repeatedly told Klein that he did not want to assist . . . that he needed to sleep. Klein responded by bellowing at Pfeiffer that this was his job, that Pfeiffer would do what he told him, and that Pfeiffer would be fired if he refused. On occasions when Pfeiffer dared to doze off in a chair while Klein was searching the Internet, Dr. Klein threw things at him to wake him up . . .

"Throughout Mr. Pfeiffer's employment, Dr. Klein required that Mr. Pfeiffer prepare him for sexual encounters with masseurs, paid escorts and prostitutes, and others. Mr. Pfeiffer was required to prepare Dr. Klein for sex frequently as Dr. Klein generally had several sex partners each week and on occasions multiple partners daily. Klein required that Mr. Pfeiffer wash Klein's groin, administer Klein's Cialis, Viagra, and similar prescription drugs, greet and accompany Dr. Klein's masseurs and other sex partners when they arrived at the Los Angeles or Laguna Beach homes and, as they were leaving, pay masseurs and others on Klein's behalf.

"After Dr. Klein had purchased his home in Palm Springs, Klein dispatched Pfeiffer and another employee into the Warm Sands Drive neighborhood to find a man with whom Klein could have sex. [They] returned with a large-bodied homeless man for Klein and a smaller homeless man for the other employee . . ."

His refusal to submit to Klein's "unwelcome, unwanted, offensive" sexual advances on him, Pfeiffer claimed, had made him into a target for Klein's cruel and crude jokes: "In Pfeiffer's presence, Klein told other male employees that they should urinate on Pfeiffer. 'Let's throw Jason in a bathtub and piss on him,' Klein said, laughing at Pfeiffer. 'He'll love it.'"

Pfeiffer was being quite public about his intention to ruin Arnold Klein. He provided the Daily Beast with prescriptions from two Beverly Hills pharmacies (Mickey Fine being one) that Klein had allegedly written identifying Pfeiffer as his patient and told reporters that he'd never received any such drugs. On his blog, Pfeiffer was not only excoriating the man he called "FrankenKlein," but also soliciting complaints about Dr. Klein's professional practices that could be submitted to the medical board of California. Skip Miller, Dr. Klein's Los Angeles attorney, replied to the filing against his client with the statement that, "All of Jason Pfeiffer's allegations are false and will be demonstrated to be baseless in court."

Reporters assigned to cover the Murray trial imagined that at least a little of this stuff would be admitted into testimony, but such hopes were dashed when Judge Pastor refused to allow even Dr. Klein's medical records into evidence. Pastor's ruling meant that what had promised to be a deliciously scandalous trial would now be reduced to "expert testimony," the outcome hanging on the dry recitations of a pair of physicians whose outlandish egos were their most remarkable qualities.

The judge "essentially gutted our defense strategy," Ed Chernoff moaned. Some in the media recognized that Pastor and the prosecution had even done their best to eradicate the most intriguing subtext to the trial, the impact of these proceedings on the wrongful death lawsuit Katherine Jackson had filed against AEG. Within moments after the first AEG executive called as a witness, Paul Gongaware, took the stand, it became obvious that the questions and answers had been choreographed, and that Gongaware would not be asked to say anything that might jeopardize his company's defense against Mrs. Jackson's civil action.

Gongaware, though, was preceded to the witness stand by Kenny Ortega, and there was no way to prevent the "This Is It" director from providing fodder for Mrs. Jackson's attorneys. Prior to the criminal trial, Katherine Jackson's lawyers had removed Ortega's name from the list of defendants in the wrongful death lawsuit, leaving the director with little incentive to skew his testimony in AEG's favor. The highlight of Ortega's appearance on the stand was his reading of the June 20, 2009, e-mail to Randy Phillips in which Ortega expressed his mounting concern about Michael Jackson's mental condition. When the director read aloud, "Everything in me says he should be psychologically evaluated," then went on to the parts of his e-mail where he pleaded for the intervention of "a strong therapist" and some "physical nurturing," AEG's executives only had to observe the triumphant expressions on the faces of the Jackson family to imagine the impact of Ortega's words on the civil trial to come. The prosecution attempted to provide immediate relief by swinging the weight of Ortega's testimony toward Conrad Murray. Deputy District Attorney David Walgren prompted the director to recall the meeting with the doctor at which Murray had told him, essentially, to stand aside and let his physician determine whether or not he was ready to work.

When Gongaware followed Ortega to the stand, the AEG executive was encouraged by the prosecutor to lay the blame for Michael Jackson's deterioration and death entirely at the feet of Dr. Murray, and at the same time permitted to put the responsibility for Murray's employment on Jackson himself. He had argued that Jackson should hire a British physician, Gongaware said, but Michael insisted, "I want Dr. Murray." Gongaware's description of Murray's initial demand for a salary of $5 million per year supported the prosecution's portrait of a physician who was both greedy and reckless. The AEG executive ended his testimony, though, by giving both the prosecution and the defense grist for their mills. His recollection of a meeting with Michael Jackson shortly after rehearsals for the O2 shows began, Gongaware said, was that "Michael had been "a little bit off. His speech was just very slightly slurred and he was a little slower than I'd known him to be." Jackson said he had just come from seeing his doctor, Gongaware remembered, but the AEG executive couldn't recall whether the physician in question was Conrad Murray or Arnold Klein.

From the prosecution's perspective, Gongaware's recollection folded nicely into its presentation of an audio file recovered from Murray's iPhone. He was merely giving them "a taste" of the recorded conversation between Michael Jackson and Conrad Murray, Deputy District Attorney David Walgren had told the jurors when he played it for them during his opening statement. What those in the courtroom heard was Jackson speaking in a voice that was considerably more that "just very slightly slurred" as he attempted to explain what the London concerts were all about. Sounding like a man whose mouth was filled with marbles and molasses, Michael told Murray that the young people of the world were in a state of depression that he intended to treat with the biggest pediatric care facility on the planet, the Michael Jackson Children's Hospital.

"My performances will be up there helping children and always be my dream," Michael mumbled slowly, his words barely comprehensible. "I love them. I love them because I didn't have a childhood. I had no childhood. I feel their pain. I feel their hurt. I can deal with it. 'Heal the World,' 'We Are the World,' 'Will You Be There,' 'The Lost Children' . . . these are songs I've written because I hurt, you know. I hurt."

Children "don't have enough hope, no more hope," he went on, sounding like a record on a turntable that had been unplugged and was slowly coming to a stop. "That's the next generation that's going to save our planet, starting with—we'll talk about it. United States, Europe, Prague, my babies. They walk around with no mother. They drop them off, they leave . . . They reach out to me: 'Please take me with you.'"

For all the abandoned children, for his own children, for the child he himself had wanted to be, "We have to be phenomenal [in London]," Michael said, then digressed into a grandiosity that was rendered pathetic by his fading voice. "When people leave this show, when people leave my show, I want them to say, 'I've never seen anything like this in my life. Go. Go. I've never seen nothing like this. Go. It's amazing. He's the greatest entertainer in the world.'"

The audio file would be submitted as evidence that the accused was fully aware of Michael Jackson's "state" even as he continued supplying the entertainer with more and stronger drugs, Deputy DA Walgren explained.

When Walgren's examination of Paul Gongaware was finished, the prosecutor summoned AEG lawyer Kathy Jorrie to the witness stand so that she could tell the jury, "Dr. Murray told me repeatedly that Mr. Jackson was in perfect health."

With the formal introduction of the iPhone evidence, the prosecution revealed that Dr. Murray's phone had also yielded the voice mail left by

Frank Dileo on the morning of June 20, 2009, the one in which Dileo had told the doctor, "I'm sure you are aware he had an episode last night. He's sick."

In addition to voice mails and audio files, the iPhone had also provided a record of the e-mails and text messages sent and received by Conrad Murray on the morning of Michael Jackson's death. At 7:03 a.m., while his sleepless patient was still thrashing about in bed, jurors learned, a pair of e-mails had been delivered to Dr. Murray by lawyers working out the details of his $150,000-per-month contract. Even more jarring was the evidence that, at 9:45 a.m., well before Murray knew Jackson was in any distress, he had been reviewing medical records sent from his Las Vegas practice that referenced the care of a patient named "Omar Arnold," which the jury already knew was the most commonly used of Michael's drug aliases. Most startling of all, though, was the e-mail Murray had sent to a London insurance broker at 11:17 a.m., more than half an hour after the doctor, by his own account, had administered the dose of propofol that resulted in Jackson's death: Press reports about the precarious condition of Michael's health were, Conrad Murray wrote, "fallacious."

Before the prosecution moved on from the subject of Murray's dubious character to the forensic evidence at the heart of its case, David Walgren wanted the jury to hear from the doctor himself, and played the two-and-a-half-hour tape-recorded interview that LAPD Detective Scott Smith and his partner Detective Orlando Martinez had conducted with Murray in a small office off the banquet hall of the Ritz-Carlton Hotel in Marina del Rey on June 27, 2009.

The Conrad Murray that the jurors heard on the tape bore little resemblance to either the frenzied, sweaty man described by witnesses to the events surrounding Michael Jackson's death or the wide-eyed, frightened one they now saw at the defense table. The Murray on the tape was measured, suave even, a distinguished physician seemingly convinced he could explain to everyone's satisfaction what had happened. The doctor's expression as he listened to himself in court, though, made it clear he understood now that the LAPD interview had trapped him in a corner from which there was little chance of escape. Murray's story of trying to ease the suffering of a patient who was desperate for sleep with benzodiazepine drugs and then finally caving in to Jackson's pleas for his "milk" with a dose of propofol that was just half the amount Michael normally took was already familiar to most of the people in the courtroom, as was the doctor's claim that he had left Jackson's bedside for no more than two minutes while he went to the bathroom, only to return and find that Michael was no longer breathing. On the tape, Murray's voice grew louder and more intense only when the detectives began to ask why he hadn't called 911 sooner. Talking to the operator at a time when his patient needed him to be resuscitated would have been a form of *neglect*, the doctor insisted. Murray also denied taking the time to gather up medicine bottles and the IV bag before calling 911, something that previous witnesses had described in compelling detail. Murray seemed especially intent during the LAPD interview on making the detectives understand that Michael Jackson had been using propofol for years and was very familiar with the anesthetic. He was quite amazed by Mr. Jackson's "pharmacological knowledge," the doctor said, and had attempted to use it to his advantage as he weaned Michael off propofol.

Chernoff made tiny dents in the prosecution case by eliciting an acknowledgment from Detective Smith that the interviews with Michael Amir Williams, Alberto Alvarez, and Faheem Muhammad—all three devastating to Dr. Murray as prosecution witnesses—had taken place days after the coroner's office made public its finding that Michael Jackson's death was a homicide. Smith also admitted to Chernoff that he had not said anything to Dr. Murray about propofol found in an IV bag. The defense attorney's most penetrating questions were about why the LAPD had permitted the Jackson family the run of the Carolwood house for more than twenty-four hours before the coroner's investigators showed up to retrieve the medical evidence. Smith had no good answers, other than that "given the circumstances" it should hardly come as a surprise that the house had not been locked down.

The defense attorney's brief moment in the sun was swiftly clouded over by the appearance on the witness stand of Dr. Christopher Rogers, the medical examiner who had performed the autopsy on Michael Jackson. Dr. Murray's own words led him to rule out the possibility that Michael Jackson had given himself a lethal dose of propofol, Rogers explained: The two-minute bathroom break that Murray claimed was his only absence from his patient's bedside was simply not a long enough time for any propofol Mr. Jackson might have self-administered to take effect. The more likely scenario, the medical examiner testified, was that Dr. Murray had mistakenly administered a much larger dose of propofol than he realized, one that was lethal to his patient. And anyway, even if Michael Jackson had himself taken the fatal dose of propofol, Rogers added, the cause of death would remain, in the judgment of the coroner's office, an unsatisfactory standard of care by his doctor.

Jurors were shown an autopsy photo of Michael Jackson's body (a fuzzily gruesome image that somehow made its way to TMZ) as Dr. Rogers reiterated the results of his report: Though Michael Jackson was quite slender, his weight was in the normal range and he was actually in above average health for a man of fifty; he could have lived for decades longer with proper care.

Rogers was followed to the stand by two more physicians, a cardiologist and a critical care specialist, both of whom told the jury that Dr. Murray's treatment of Michael Jackson violated the standard of care. After them came the prosecution's final and most important witness, Dr. Steven Shafer, a professor of anesthesiology at Columbia University. Shafer made it clear that he did not believe Conrad Murray had given Michael Jackson only 25 milligrams of propofol on the morning of his death. For one thing, the orders of propofol that Murray had placed with his pharmaceutical supply company in Las Vegas were "an extraordinary amount to purchase to administer to a single individual," Shafer told the jury. His calculations showed that the more than four gallons of Diprivan shipped to Los Angeles at Dr. Murray's request averaged out to nearly 2,000 milligrams per day, nearly fifty times the amount that Murray said was the largest daily dose of propofol that he ever gave Michael Jackson. The only plausible scenario of Mr. Jackson's death, in his expert opinion, Shafer said, was that Dr. Murray had used an entire 1,000-milligram bottle of Diprivan to begin the drip into Michael Jackson's veins, and had somehow managed to leave the drug running into Mr. Jackson's bloodstream even after his heart had stopped beating.

Shafer then listed a dozen "egregious" violations of the standard of care by Dr. Murray—actions that posed a foreseeable danger to his patient's life. "Each one, individually, could be expected to lead to a catastrophic outcome, including death?" David Walgren asked. "Absolutely," Shafer answered.

Chernoff attempted an aggressive cross-examination, forcing Dr. Shafer to acknowledge that he could not be absolutely certain that Michael Jackson hadn't awakened and with his own hand removed the clamp on the IV line that had stopped the propofol drip. Such a scenario, however, was "in no way exculpatory," Shafer added, because it meant that Dr. Murray had set up the IV drip of a dangerous drug and left his patient alone with it. Even if Murray had done what his attorney was suggesting, "it would still be considered abandonment."

Without Arnold Klein, Tohme Tohme, and the rest of the cast of excluded characters, the defense case amounted to little more than quibbling. A records custodian for the Beverly Hills police department was summoned to testify that the 911 call from Michael Jackson's home had been delayed by forty-six seconds because it was routed through her agency before reaching the city's fire department. A pair of LAPD detectives acknowledged that Alberto Alvarez had only mentioned key details about Dr. Murray's attempted cover-up two months after Michael Jackson's death, and that Alvarez made two separate drawings of the IV bag in which he said the propofol was stashed, a year and a half apart, which were "significantly different."

Unable to compel Dr. Klein's appearance on the witness stand, Murray's defense lawyers settled for Dr. Allan Metzger, who was called to testify that, during an April 18, 2009, meeting at the Carolwood chateau, Michael Jackson had complained of chronic insomnia and asked for "some form of anesthetic." Under cross-examination by Walgren, though, Metzger said he advised Michael against using anesthesia to combat insomnia, warning that intravenous administration of such drugs outside a hospital setting was dangerous. Was there "any amount of money" that would have persuaded him to give Jackson propofol at his home? Walgren asked Metzger. "Definitely not!" Metzger answered. Even those who doubted Dr. Metzger on this last point understood that he had been a far better witness for the prosecution than for the defense.

The same was essentially true of Cherilyn Lee. The nurse's story of Michael's pleas for Diprivan ended as it had every time she told it—with her at once refusing and warning him that the drug was dangerous. The prosecution had already made the point that Michael Jackson believed his risk was nullified by having a doctor attending to him.

In the end, Murray's defense team decided that it had little choice but to prosecute Katherine Jackson's lawsuit against AEG. As the Jackson family looked on in undisguised anticipation, Ed Chernoff proposed to introduce the contract for the O2 shows as evidence of the pressure that Michael Jackson was under to perform. A man already $400 million in debt, Chernoff explained to the judge, would have been required to pay AEG at least $30 million if he was unable to deliver as expected in London; the stress of his situation gradually drove the entertainer to inject himself with a lethal dose of propofol in a desperate attempt to sleep between rehearsals. Judge Pastor had already ruled that the defense would not be permitted to introduce evidence of Jackson's financial circumstances, and prosecutor Walgren urged a similar ruling on the contract. "At every turn," Walgren told Pastor, "Conrad Murray, through his attorneys, have (sic) put the blame for his failures on Michael Jackson and this is just another attempt to do the same."

The judge agreed. "This is not a contractual dispute," Pastor told Chernoff. "This is a homicide case."

The defense responded by summoning Randy Phillips to the stand, a decision that accomplished little more than to provide AEG with one more opportunity to defend itself against Mrs. Jackson's civil suit. "Motivated, energized, and receptive" was how Phillips described the Michael Jackson he had encountered in the autumn of 2008, when they first met to begin planning the O2 shows. And it was absolutely untrue, Phillips said, that Michael had been "forced" by AEG into agreeing to perform at more than ten shows. Thirty-one shows were planned from the start, Phillips testified, and Michael agreed to nineteen more concerts "in twenty minutes."

The judge rebuffed Chernoff's attempt to use this testimony to get the contract into evidence, creating a strange moment of theater in which the Jackson family were openly supporting the attorney for the man accused of killing Michael. As Katherin Jackson observed the judge's ruling with an expression of dismay, Joe snorted his indignation. Janet Jackson rolled her eyes and shook her head.

The Jacksons were whispering among themselves with infuriated expressions as Phillips continued with his testimony, explaining that while he was concerned by his star's absence from rehearsals for the O2 shows, "no one on our end was ever contemplating pulling the plug." After Kenny Ortega sent Michael home from the June 19 rehearsal, Phillips said, he was reassured by what Conrad Murray had to say at the meeting the next day, when the doctor "guaranteed us that Michael would get into it."

The Jacksons were still shaking their heads when Phillips added that after the very last rehearsal on the evening of June 24, Michael had thanked him for the help in getting this far, then added, "Now I'm ready. I can take it from here."

Chernoff eked out a moment of minor triumph from Phillips's appearance as a witness: After the AEG Live chief made several references to the contractual obligations of both sides for the O2 shows, Judge Pastor permitted the defense attorney to ask if Michael Jackson was "ultimately responsible" for the production costs of the concerts. "Yes," Phillips replied. Chernoff seemed to sense an opening when Phillips denied that there was ever any thought of canceling the O2 concerts, but admitted that Michael Jackson's problems with "focusing" might have resulted in further delays.

"At some point the shows could have been postponed to the point that production would not be possible?" Chernoff asked.

"I can't speculate on that," a poker-faced Phillips answered.

By then, Conrad Murray's hopes for a hung jury were reduced to a series of patients called as character witnesses and two physicians who would try to cancel out the testimony of Dr. Steven Shafer. The former patients at least offered a portrait of Conrad Murray that was very different from the one created by the public record. "That man right there is the best doctor I've ever seen," said an elderly gentleman who had been treated for a heart condition in 2002. "I'm alive today because of that man." Another patient described appointments with Murray that lasted more than four hours, recalling that after each one the doctor had phoned his wife to explain his condition. An eighty-two-year-old woman named Ruby Mosley told the jury that if Dr. Murray had been greedy, he never would have set up a clinic in Houston's Acres Homes neighborhood, where three-quarters of the population lived in poverty. David Walgren countered by establishing that when his patients in Houston were sedated prior to a procedure performed by Dr. Murray, this had taken place in hospital settings where there was monitoring equipment and backup personnel.

The first of the defense's expert witnesses was Dr. Robert Waldman, a specialist in medical addiction who testified that Michael Jackson had "probably" been turned into a Demerol addict by Dr. Arnold Klein. He had consulted with dermatologists who told him that shots of Botox and Restylane were not so painful that a patient needed Demerol, Waldman said, then told the jury that his examination of Dr. Klein's medical records suggested Michael Jackson was getting as much as 375 milligrams of Demerol in a ninety-minute period, more than seven times the recommended dose. Walgren then asked the defense's doctor: "If a patient asks you to administer a dangerous drug, a drug that could be harmful . . . would you refuse to administer that drug to the patient?"

"Absolutely," Waldman answered.

The appearance of the defense's second expert and final witness, Dr. Paul White, provided the most enlivening moments of the entire trial. White, it turned out, had been one of Steven Shafer's medical school professors and later a personal friend. He was not speaking highly of his former student these days, however. "I am going to take the high road, not the low road with him," E! Online had quoted White saying of Shafer, whom he had reportedly called "a scumbag" for ridiculing his calculation of probabilities in the Conrad Murray case.

Judge Pastor insisted upon chiding the witness prior to his testimony, lecturing the doctor at length about why he had "no business making any of those comments." White then denied calling Shafer a scumbag, but

Pastor announced anyway that he was scheduling a hearing after the trial to determine whether the doctor should be held in contempt of court.

Dr. White appeared determined to impress the viewing public. After presenting his credentials as an anesthesiologist who had conducted clinical trials of propofol back in the 1980s that had led to FDA approval of the drug, White took issue with the math models Shafer had used to show that Dr. Murray might have given Michael Jackson more than forty times the dosage of propofol that the doctor claimed. The problem with such models, White sniffed, was that while they might describe the general population, they were not applicable to "a specific or particular individual." Michael Jackson was obviously an exceptional person who had consumed prodigious amounts of drugs long before Conrad Murray became his physician. His tolerances were most unusual. Furthermore, the amount of propofol found in Jackson's bloodstream during his autopsy clearly contradicted Dr. Shafer's theory that Dr. Murray had left the propofol drip running until there were as many as 1,000 milligrams of the drug in Michael Jackson's bloodstream. Dr. Shafer had called White's self-injection hypothesis a "crazy scenario." His former professor returned the favor by describing Shafer's theory as "underdeveloped."

His own review of the circumstances of Mr. Jackson's death, in light of the entertainer's background and other factors, Dr. White said, suggested to him that the entertainer had probably inadvertently ended his own life by injecting himself with a dose of propofol while his doctor was distracted by phone calls and not keeping a close eye on him.

The most significant moment of White's testimony might have come when the defense used him to acknowledge that it would not be challenging the claim that Dr. Conrad Murray had violated the standard of care, but rather simply arguing that this violation was not severe enough to warrant a manslaughter conviction. "Let's deal with the elephant in the room here," Chernoff's associate counsel J. Michael Flanagan told Dr. White. "Conrad Murray has been accused of infusing a dose of propofol and leaving his patient. Can you justify that?"

"Absolutely not," answered White. Nevertheless, other than his failure to remain alert at Michael Jackson's bedside, nothing else about the way Dr. Murray had dealt with the patient was to his mind improper, White said. He was, for example, not at all certain that adminstering propofol as an insomnia treatment was unreasonable, said White, citing a Chinese study of using the anesthesia to help people with sleep disorders that had produced some flawed but "very interesting" results. And while he agreed with prosecution witnesses that Michael Jackson had swallowed at least several tablets of lorazepam—Ativan—White said, he did not at all agree that combining the sedative with the anesthetic propofol had created the "perfect storm" that killed Mr. Jackson. Would the drugs Dr. Murray admitted administering to Jackson—relatively light injections of sedatives followed by a half-dose of propofol—have created "a dangerous situation?" Flanagan asked. "Not at all," White told him.

By the time the prosecution took over questioning, White seemed to be enjoying himself on the witness stand. He was amused that both Flanagan and Judge Pastor had repeatedly referred to him as "Dr. Shafer," and suggested in an aside to the jury, "I should get a name tag." Pastor and Walgren were each visibly furious with White a few minutes into his cross-examination, but the doctor himself appeared nonchalant. The prosecution had begun by attempting to elicit Dr. White's admission that propofol was a potentially life-threatening drug. "Without careful bedside monitoring, it *could* be dangerous," White allowed.

"Could it result in death?" Walgren asked.

"If the infusion somehow came opened up widely . . . certainly you could achieve a significant effect that could result in cardiopulmonary arrest," White replied.

Clearly irritated by the answer, Walgren demanded to know if Dr. White had ever administered propofol in someone's bedroom. "No, I have not," White answered.

"Had you ever heard of someone doing that prior to this case?" Walgren asked.

"No, I had not," White said.

Walgren's satisfied nod turned into head-shaking incredulity only seconds later, though, when Dr. White said he was not inclined to criticize Dr. Murray for letting twenty minutes pass between the time he noticed that Michael Jackson was not breathing and the time of the call to 911. Yes, he personally would have called sooner for an ambulance, White said, but Dr. Murray "reacted as many physicians would."

By his own admission, Dr. Murray was holding a cell phone in his hand, Walgren noted: "Are you saying he wasn't capable of pressing 911?" White shrugged at the question and told the prosecutor that Michael Jackson would have died that day no matter what time the ambulance arrived.

The exchange between the prosecutor and the witness became truly testy when White began to make reference to information he had gleaned from "two extensive conversations" with Dr. Murray. Judge Pastor had ruled prior to White's testimony that he would not be allowed to mention his conversations with Murray. "Please listen carefully to the prosecutor's questions," Pastor told White the first time the witness mentioned his conversations with Dr. Murray. When White made another reference to his conversations with Murray just moments later, the judge sent the jurors out of the courtroom.

Walgren was indignant, protesting that the witness was intentionally dropping mentions of his conversations with Conrad Murray in front of the jurors, in direct defiance of the judge's ruling. Flanagan countered that Dr. White couldn't be expected to specifically remember what information he had ascertained from Dr. Murray's police interview and what information had come from his meetings with the doctor. "Nice try," Pastor told the defense attorney. "This is so obvious . . . He's trying at every juncture to add in other material. It's deliberate. I don't like it. It's not going to happen again." Dr. White would face a second charge of contempt at his hearing on November 16, the judge ruled.

White's self-confidence did not seem seriously shaken. When the jury returned, Walgren asked if Conrad Murray had violated the physician's oath of "First, do no harm."

"I think he was providing a service to Mr. Jackson, which Mr. Jackson had requested, in fact insisted upon," White replied. When Walgren seized upon the word "service," White amended his answer: "Well, 'medical care' is a better word than 'service.'"

Walgren began to use questions as testimony. Michael Jackson was attached to both an IV stand and a urinary catheter at the time of his death, the prosecutor noted, which obviously made it more plausible that Dr. Murray had injected his patient with propofol and later lied about the amount he gave. "It's possible, if he wanted to potentially harm Michael Jackson," White replied.

"If Michael Jackson did it, was he doing it to harm himself?" Walgren demanded.

"I don't think he realized the potential danger," White answered.

Walgren was at the end of his patience. "You keep throwing out these kind of rehearsed lines," he snapped. When the defense objected, the comment was stricken, but the judge refrained from admonishing the prosecutor.

How much was he being paid to testify on Conrad Murray's behalf? Walgren demanded of White. He had received $11,000 so far, White answered. Did he expect additional compensation for attending court? the prosecutor wanted to know. Well, his normal day rate was $3,500, White replied, but he doubted a further payment would be forthcoming. The defendant, he explained, "has limited financial resources."

The prosecution replied by bringing back Steven Shafer to tell the jury that his former professor's analysis had relied on an outdated study, and that more recent research "absolutely" supported his own opinion that Michael Jackson could not have self-administered the fatal dose of propofol.

But even if Michael Jackson *had* injected himself with the propofol that stopped his heart, David Walgren told the jury in his closing argument, Conrad Murray was still responsible. The jurors had heard Dr. Murray tell detectives that Jackson liked to "push" the drug into his own veins, which meant he had to be aware that his patient might inject himself if left alone. A "foreseeable consequence" was all that was required to arrive at a verdict of guilty, Walgren said, but this case also offered clear evidence of the defendant's "consciousness of guilt" on multiple fronts. Most damning was Murray's failure to inform paramedics and emergency room doctors that he had administered propofol to his patient. Equally significant, though, was that Murray had not documented his "pharmaceutical experiment" of using propofol to treat insomnia with a single medical record. The prosecutor reminded the jurors of the converstion recorded on Dr. Murray's iPhone weeks before Mr. Jackson's death. They had heard for themselves "the tragic, sad voice of Michael Jackson in some sort of drug-induced, slurred stupor," Walgren told the panel. "After hearing this voice, after hearing Michael Jackson in this condition, what does Conrad Murray do? He orders the largest shipment of propofol."

Did anyone in the courtroom believe that Conrad Murray left his patient's bedside for only two minutes to go to the bathroom, then returned to find his patient no longer breathing? "How long Michael Jackson was there, by himself, abandoned, we'll never know," Walgren said. "Did he gasp? Did he choke? Were there sounds? We don't know, and we'll never know."

At this point, Conrad Murray's attorneys needed someone else to blame. Targeting the victim, though, was looking less and less like a winning tactic. Chernoff pointed first to the media, and to a political establishment that seemed to answer to the media. "Somebody's got to say it," Ed Chernoff told the jury. "If it were anybody but Michael Jackson, would this doctor be here today?"

Chernoff decried Walgren's decision to repeatedly show jurors photographs of Jackson's children. "It's heartbreaking to see those kids, you know that and I know that," the defense attorney said. "That's why they showed those kids. There's a tremendous desire to see Dr. Murray as this perfect victim."

But Conrad Murray was just "a little fish in a big dirty pond," Chernoff went on, one who had no knowledge of the other doctors his patient was seeing or of the drugs they were giving him. All Dr. Murray saw was a man overwhelmed by stress who desperately needed rest. Chernoff called out the corporate bogeymen of the Anschutz Entertainment Group. "Michael Jackson was under a tremendous, abnormal, impossible amount of pressure from AEG," the defense attorney said, and Dr. Murray saw no way to relieve that pressure but to help his patient get some much-needed sleep.

Only at the end did Chernoff ask the jury to consider what responsibility for his own death might belong to the so-called victim: "Was Dr. Murray supposed to watch Michael Jackson to save him from himself at all times? At what point do you draw the line for Dr. Murray's responsibilities for a grown-up?"

During the jury's deliberations, the Los Angeles Criminal Courts Building demonstrated one more time that it could stage a show like none other in the country. The scene was strange but familiar. Michael Jackson fans screamed in the faces of Conrad Murray supporters; one fan was a woman who held a sign reading, "Turn away from addiction." Some sport drove by in a Mercedes coupe holding a license plate out the window that read, "Love4MJ," and was wildly applauded. A young woman who had traveled all the way from Copenhagen kept telling everyone she met how much it hurt her to know that Michael was no longer in the world. Easily the most surreal moment came when a group of protesters from the Occupy Los Angeles encampment across the street marched over to the courthouse and began shouting, "We are the ninety-nine percent!" only to be answered by Jackson fans who shouted back, "This Is It!"

The Jackson family had been putting on its own show since day one of the trial, entering and leaving the courthouse like they were walking a red carpet amid an uproar of cheers, questions, camera clicks, and cries of sympathy. Eighty-three-year-old Joe Jackson had stalked into the courtroom on the first day snarling, but by the time Paul Gongaware took the stand the old man had closed his eyes and appeared to be napping. Eighty-one-year-old Katherine Jackson was "harrumphing incredulously," as the *Wall Street Journal*'s reporter had it, when Ed Chernoff used his opening statement to present Conrad Murray to the jury as a sympathetic figure who had been pressured and manipulated by his famous patient. As witnesses began to testify, La Toya and Rebbie sat on each side of their mother, repeating into her ears what each person was saying; La Toya made sure she had the better camera angle. Jermaine, who had recently come out with the story that his brother Michael was planning to flee to the Middle East if convicted at his criminal trial in 2005, continued to insist that he was the second-most-famous member of the Jackson family. Jackie, Tito, and Marlon, as usual, preserved a measure of personal dignity by staying away and leaving the spotlight to the others. Also as usual, Katherine's genuine displays of emotion silenced the snickering of cynics. The tears in her eyes and the pain on her face were entirely convincing as Michael's mother listened to the full four-minute recording of her son talking to his doctor back in May 2009. "Mmm, mmm," was all Murray could be heard replying as Michael mumbled on and on and on about how he understood the pain of the world's children and intended to build them the biggest hospital in the world after reestablishing himself as the greatest entertainer on earth. When Michael suddenly went silent, though, a concerned Murray had asked, "You okay?" There was a long pause, then Michael answered, "I am asleep." It was Mrs. Jackson, though, who closed her eyes.

After three and a half days of deliberation, the jury informed the judge on the morning of November 7, 2011, that it had reached a decision. "Verdict is FINALLY IN!!!" La Toya had tweeted to her followers. "I'm on my way! I'm shaking uncontrollably!" Joe and Katherine and Jermaine arrived at the courthouse just after noon, pushing through a crowd that was slightly outnumbered by the media horde as they made their way to the courtroom on the building's ninth floor.

"This is not entertainment, not a circus, not a spectacle," a young woman from Denmark told the *Los Angeles Times*. "This is real life." By LA standards perhaps.

The jury had unanimously found Conrad Murray guilty of involuntary manslaughter. This did not mean he would serve time in a state prison, as Los Angeles County district attorney Steve Cooley readily acknowledged. California's budget crisis had resulted in, among other things, a "prison realignment bill" called AB 109 that was sending minor felons without criminal records to local jails rather than state prisons, and the jails in turn were permitting more and more of those criminals to serve their sentences at home under house arrest.

District Attorney Cooley sought consolation in the knowledge that, as a convicted felon, fifty-eight-year-old Conrad Murray would be losing his license to practice medicine in California. The truth, though, was that other states were under no legal obligation to honor California's decision, and some other countries almost certainly would not. It was entirely possible that by the age of sixty Murray would be working as a physician somewhere in the world.

Judge Pastor had done his best to show the public that such an outcome would not be *his* doing. He was denying the defense request that Dr. Murray remain free until his sentencing, the judge announced after the verdict was delivered. "This is not a crime involving a mistake of judgment," Pastor told both the courtroom and the camera. "This is a crime where the end result was the death of a human being."

"Public safety demands that he be remanded," Pastor declared as his bailiffs prepared to handcuff Conrad Murray and place the doctor behind bars.

The judge was talking even tougher when Murray returned to his courtroom on November 29, 2011, to face sentencing. He was outraged, Pastor let it be known, by the paid interview Murray had provided to NBC for a documentary that was to run partially on the *Today* show and in full on MSNBC. When asked about leaving Michael Jackson alone in his bedroom attached to an IV line filled with propofol, Murray had insisted to his interviewer that he had no reason to think that his patient was in danger. "Had I known what I know today, in retrospect, that Mr. Jackson was an addict, that might have changed things. Addicts may behave in a way that is unreasonable and I would have taken that into consideration," Murray said. But he had no such knowledge because Michael Jackson had hidden it from him. "I only wish that maybe in our dealings with each other, he was more forthcoming and honest in telling me things about himself," Murray explained. "Certainly, he was deceptive by not sharing with me his whole medical history, doctors he was seeing, treatment that he might have been receiving."

Said Murray, "I went there to take care of a healthy man who said he was fine, to just keep surveillance. But once I got in there I was entrapped."

Making out that he, not Michael Jackson, was the victim in this case had been just one more example of Conrad Murray's deficient character, in Judge Pastor's opinion.

At least Murray had provided John Branca with an opportunity to become the indignant defender of Michael's reputation. Branca and John

McClain had signed a letter to MSNBC demanding that the network not "give Conrad Murray a platform to shift the blame, postconviction, to Michael Jackson . . ."

Before passing sentence, Judge Pastor blasted Murray for his part in the "faux documentary" that made him out to be nothing more than a "bystander" in Jackson's death, one who was "betrayed" by his patient, rather than the other way around.

"Talk about blaming the victim," Pastor said. "Not only isn't there any remorse, there's umbrage and outrage on the part of Dr. Murray against the decedent, without any, *any* indication of the slightest involvement in the case."

The judge expressed even greater offense at the audio file of the conversation between Jackson and Murray that had been entered into evidence during the trial. That recording had been "your insurance policy," Pastor told Murray. "It was designed to record this patient surreptitiously at that patient's most vulnerable point." He not only viewed this as a "horrific violation of trust," the judge told Murray, but wondered if the recording might have been offered for sale some day. After more talk about Murray's "cycle of horrible medicine" and his "pattern of deceit and lies," the judge gave him the maximum sentence allowed: four years, in county jail.

Outside the courtroom, Katherine Jackson told a Los Angeles TV station that, "Four years is not enough for someone's life. It won't bring him back, but at least he got the maximum."

In reality, as Judge Pastor knew, AB 109 would automatically cut the four-year sentence by half, and there would be an additional reduction for time served. A spokesman for the Los Angeles County sheriff's department, which ran the jail, stood by with a statement that Murray's (now two-year) sentence would be reduced by no more than the forty-seven days he had already served and that the doctor was not eligible for early-release electronic monitoring or house arrest.

Most likely, Conrad Murray would spend at least twenty months behind bars, which was about the worst that California could do to a first offender convicted of involuntary manslaughter. Whether or not this was justice was the sort of question lawyers and cable talk show hosts would enjoy debating for several days, but Conrad Murray was telling friends and family that he had already moved on. Murray said that he had no regrets about cooperating with the producers of the documentary that had run on MSNBC, various sources close to the doctor told the media, because at least it allowed him to put out his side of the story. The same sources described Murray as "surprisingly upbeat." One friend quoted the doctor as saying, "I'm just relieved it's finally over," then adding, "Don't worry, I'm fine, and I'll be out soon."

The long arm of the law was still wrapping itself around various other Michael Jackson advisors and employees.

Dr. Arnold Klein was feeling the squeeze. Well before the Conrad Murray trial had begun, Klein was advising friends that he had been summoned to a hearing before the medical board of California to answer accusations that he overprescribed dangerous drugs to Jackson. With friends fleeing and his Beverly Hills practice dissolving, Klein had hired a $20,000-per-month publicist in the homes of "re-branding," but the effort was not met with success and patients continued to abandon him in ever-increasing numbers. By the end of 2011, the doctor's finances had contracted to the point where not only were all three of his homes up for sale, but he was also auctioning off the memorabilia he had collected from friends who included Michael Jackson and Elizabeth Taylor. Bonhams & Butterfields was offering Klein's invitation to Taylor's eighth wedding (to Larry Fortensky, at Neverland) at an opening price of $350, while the bidding on the hat Jackson was wearing when he left the hospital after being treated for the burns suffered during the Pepsi commercial in 1984 was to start at $10,000. Also on the block was Princess Leia wig that had been worn to a party by one of Klein's few remaining friends, Carrie Fisher, who around Christmas time would loan Klein $150,000 to hire a new bankruptcy lawyer.

The medical board, meanwhile, continued to tighten its grip, questioning dozens of witnesses about Klein's alleged use of aliases on prescriptions, his reported distribution of drug samples to patients and the claim that Klein regularly prescribed narcotics to himself. His attempts at self-defense accomplished little more than to make him an object of derision and animosity. On his Facebook page, in a post titled "The California Medical Board: A Novel by Kafka," Klein had claimed that the Board's chief investigator was guilty of "elder abuse" for the ferocity with which he was tracking his prey. The medical board had responded on May 2, 2012 by ordering Klein to "undergo a physical examination, a mental examination, including psychological testing, and to submit to testing to detect the presence of illicit drugs," warning that the failure to comply might likely result in the revocation of his license to practice medicine. That very same day, the former lover of Liberace had suggested to *Entertainment Tonight* that he and Michael Jackson had also been lovers, dredging up the defense Klein had made of Jason Pfeiffer's earlier claims about a relationship with Michael, just when the subject seemed to be fading from tabloid headlines.

It would be one thing after another, though, with Dr. Klein, as the tabloid press by now clearly understood. In mid-May 2012, the real estate company that owned the Beverly Hills mansion he had rented for $60,000 per month went to court once again to get him out of the house. Klein had earlier won a stay of his eviction because he was in bankruptcy proceedings. YHL 26 Holdings, though, was now arguing that the stay should be lifted and Klein forced to move, because he "has taken advantage of the protection of the automatic stay to maintain a lavish personal lifestyle at the expense of his creditors." In June, Klein went to the Los Angeles County District Attorney's office with a request that they file charges of criminal theft against photographer David LaChapelle. Klein alleged he had returned a "painting-like" photograph he owned that depicted Michael Jackson as Jesus Christ to LaChapelle for repairs, after it was damaged in the 2010 fire at his Windsor Square mansion. LaChapelle *had* repaired the piece, Klein complained, but instead of giving it back LaChapelle arranged to exhibit it in galleries worldwide. After due consideration and no small amount of eye-rolling, the district attorney's office had declined to file charges. For the time being, the photograph would remain in a police evidence vault. As for the case itself, said LAPD Art Theft Det. Hrycyk, "I'm glad to get rid of it."

Raymone Bain had spent the summer of 2011 dealing with the IRS, which in June had charged her with failing to file tax returns or to make tax payments during the years from 2006 to 2008, when she was earning $30,000 per month as the president and general manager of the Michael Jackson Company. After Bain pleaded guilty, the feds asked U.S. Magistrate Judge Alan Kay to lock Bain up for eighteen months to show how the government dealt with tax scofflaws. At her sentencing hearing in Washington, D.C., on October 25, 2011 (right around the time Randy Phillips was testifying at the Conrad Murray trial in Los Angeles), Bain had tearfully pleaded for mercy, explaining to the judge that during that three-year period she had been overwhelmed by dealing with the affairs of a mother who was dying of Alzheimer's and of her erratic and demanding pop star employer. Bain appeared to skate when Kay sentenced her to five years' probation and payment of $202,422 in federal and local back taxes. Back in LA, though, Tom Mesereau was saying that it was Raymone who had been responsible for Michael Jackson's failure to pay taxes during those same years, and that the Jackson estate should take a hard look at holding her responsible.

Brian Oxman, of whom Mesereau did not speak highly either, was facing perhaps even more serious consequences. In March 2011, the State Bar of California had recommended that Oxman be suspended from the practice of law for two years, with a third year of suspension stayed if Oxman attended and completed the State Bar's ethics and client trust accounting schools. This latest action against Oxman had resulted from the attorney's failure to pay sanctions related to a divorce case he had handled and a finding that Oxman, along with his wife and partner Maureen Jaroscak, had refused to surrender money from the trust account of a client who had died. The bar had also found that Oxman and Jaroscak commingled their personal funds with those of clients, used client trust accounts to hide money from creditors, and "lacked candor" when questioned about these and other matters by investigators. Oxman had won a temporary stay of his suspension by appealing to the State Supreme Court. It was a risky maneuver, but Oxman reasoned that at least he might continue his representation of Joe Jackson and join Joe in riding piggyback upon Katherine Jackson's wrongful death action against AEG.

What Joe's lawyer apparently failed to recognize was that the State Bar could not only choose to sustain its recommended punishment, but to impose an even more severe sanction. And that the bar would do, arriving at a decision in the early summer of 2012 that Oxman would be permanently disbarred, effective on July 27.

It was a particularly painful moment to have been jettisoned from the wrongful death case. For months, various people, including attorneys from the estate, had been attempting to convince Katherine Jackson that continuing with the lawsuit against AEG was a futile endeavor. The problem wasn't that they didn't think she could prevail in court, those who had Katherine's ear told her, it was that they didn't believe she would be collecting much in the way of damages. Joe's throwaway line about Michael being "worth more dead than alive" had been borne out by earnings that continued to far exceed what he had been making in the last years of his life. The entire "loss of support" aspect of the claim against AEG was, as a result, looking like a weak one. But the appearance at Conrad Murray's trial of that June 19, 2009, e-mail to Randy Phillips in which Kenny Ortega had described the star's pitiful condition and urged the company to "get him the help he needs" had changed the minds of a number of people about how strong the claim against AEG might be. In the months after the trial, the discovery of the Ortega e-mail had been followed by other, less public revelations of what Katherine Jackson's attorneys believed a jury would see as bullying, threats, and callousness on AEG's part in its dealings with Michael Jackson. Brian Panish and his partner, Kevin Boyle, were looking more and more likely to take the case all the way to trial and to have a shot at a gigantic judgment.

The result was a heightening of tensions between the Jackson camp and the estate. Branca and his cohorts wanted the lawsuit against AEG to go away so that they could join forces with the company in compelling Lloyd's of London to pay off on the $17.5 million "This Is It" insurance policy. In early 2011, Lloyd's had asked the court in Los Angeles to declare it null and void, claiming that Michael Jackson had lied about his medical history and drug addiction. The company had insured only "losses resulting from accident," Lloyd's' lawyers argued, and the official cause of Mr. Jackson's death was "homicide." The estate's August cross-complaint argued that the policy remained in effect because Michael Jackson never intended to die; suicide would have nullified the policy, but homicide did not. For good measure, the estate's attorneys had added a demand for punitive damages, which was certain to send a chill through Lloyd's' London offices. An arrangement whereby Katherine Jackson and her grandchildren would receive some sort of significant compensation from the estate for dropping the AEG lawsuit had been in the works, according to Mrs. Jackson's advisors, but now was rapidly falling apart.

This was in part because several of Katherine's children had heard from Howard Mann about the tape recording he possessed of a telephone conversation between Joel Katz, Henry Vaccaro, and Vaccaro's attorney in which Katz and the other attorney at one point could be heard chuckling about the fact that Joe and the rest of the Jacksons would get nothing when Katherine died. In the minds of the Jacksons, this confirmed their suspicion that the estate intended to delay the funding of the Family Trust in the hope that their eighty-two-year-old mother would die before collecting her forty percent of the estate.

Perry Sanders, by then, was hearing regularly from his client and her advisors that Michael's siblings were unhappy that he wasn't moving against the estate, and against Branca in particular. Sanders actually *was* increasingly impatient with Branca and his lawyers, more inclined by the week to suspect that they were in fact stalling, and for exactly the reasons that Katherine's children claimed.

Just six months earlier, Sanders had been assuring Mrs. Jackson and her advisors that settling with the Internal Revenue Service and dealing with Tohme Tohme's claims were the only two remaining major obstacles to a final settlement of the estate and a funding of the Family Trust. The largest problem previously had been the *Segye Times* judgment against Katherine Jackson, but in the late summer of 2011 Sanders himself had negotiated a settlement with the Moonies that involved a payment of $6 million, less than half of what the *Segye Times*'s attorneys had been demanding. Branca and the estate were persuaded to advance that money in the form of a loan that Mrs. Jackson was obligated to pay within one year. In its negotiations with Sanders, the estate had agreed to charge an absurdly low rate of interest on that loan, .16%, to be exact. It was assumed that Mrs. Jackson would be able to pay back the $6 million from her half-share of the $30 million that the estate described as a "preliminary distribution" to the Family Trust. That money could not be released, however, Branca and Weitzman had told Sanders, until the estate had settled with the IRS.

When the Conrad Murray trial began in September 2011, Katherine Jackson and John Branca had seemed to still be members of the same team. Mrs. Jackson and her grandchildren, Prince and Paris, had flown to Montreal at the estate's request for the October 2 world premiere of the Cirque du Soleil's *Michael Jackson THE IMMORTAL World Tour,* afterward telling television cameras how "fantastic" and "amazing" the show had been. Sanders, meanwhile, was praising Branca at every opportunity. Whatever deal had been cut seemed to be satisfying everyone involved. That deal had been an oral one only, though; nothing had been committed to paper. Like the Jackson children, Sanders had watched with displeasure as Branca and Weitzman appeared to do nothing to discourage the story that they had paid $30 million to his client and her grandchildren, all the while holding the money back until the IRS situation and "other outstanding issues" were resolved. Also, like his client's children, Sanders had been startled when Branca and Weitzman agreed to be interviewed by Piers Morgan on CNN and told the TV host that Michael's stake in the Sony/ATV catalog alone was worth more than a billion dollars, an amount that did not even include the MiJac catalog and other music publishing properties. When Morgan observed that Jackson's "publishing rights alone, by the sound of it, were worth several billion dollars" at the time of his death, Branca did not disagree and neither did Weitzman, who was seated beside him. The clamor among Katherine's children that Sanders find some way to collect their mother's share of the estate grew louder and more threatening.

By the spring of 2012, Sanders's conversations with Weitzman were no longer friendly ones, and he was once again meeting with Paul LiCalsi to outline the case that could be made against Branca and McClain, insisting to Mrs. Jackson's advisors that it was far stronger than their questions about the will. Nothing alienated affections between the Katherine Jackson side and the estate side, though, like Sanders's decision in the late spring of 2012 to join Brian Panish and his law firm in prosecuting the wrongful death lawsuit against AEG. Branca and Weitzman were shrewd enough to recognize that Sanders could and would use that position to conduct discovery of their dealings on behalf of the estate without having to file a lawsuit against them. He already had found evidence of what he believed to be a conflict of interest involving AEG, Sanders told his client, and was looking for proof of actual collusion, along with an accounting of just how much Branca and McClain, along with Weitzman and the other lawyers, had collected from the estate since Michael's death.

Sanders still generally gave Branca credit for taking care of business. Katherine's lawyer would admit to being most impressed that Branca had negotiated a deal to reduce the interest on Michael's debt by more than three-fourths, from seventeen percent to less than four. The estate's special administrator had negotiated a deal with Pepsi that was richer even than the ones he'd made on Michael Jackson's behalf in the 1980s. The soft drink manufacturer was licensed to use the star's image on special souvenir cans of Pepsi and in a campaign that would coincide with the re-release of *Bad*, it was reported, even "resurrecting" him in a TV commercial. The estate's attorneys, meanwhile, were dealing with everything from settling Ola Ray's claim against royalties from the "Thriller" video, to the handwritten lawsuit a woman named Kimberly Griggs had filed in San Diego that demanded $1 billion for inspiring Michael to write songs for *Thriller, Bad,* and *Dangerous,* in the course of a years-long "romance."

Neither Sanders nor his client was happy, though, when it was reported that the estate had obtained permission from Judge Beckloff to sell Hayvenhurst. After checking in with Weitzman, Sanders was telling TMZ that "the motion to sell Hayvenhurst was withdrawn and this is merely for permission to buy a different place"—the Calabasas estate—"for the beneficiaries to reside." The estate in fact *had* retained the right to sell Hayvenhurst, however, and was in the eyes of the Jackson family once again demonstrating to Michael's mother who wielded the real power.

Still, there was little obvious basis for arguing with the claim that Branca had, as promised to Judge Beckloff nearly three years earlier, "maximized" the value of the Michael Jackson estate. Documents filed with Judge Beck-loff showed that the estate had generated gross earnings in excess of $475 million through May 2012 and that nearly all of Michael's debts had been paid off. What Michael's brothers and sisters wanted to know, though, was how much of that money Branca and McClain and their attorneys were putting in their own pockets. Sanders's associate Sandra Ribera would tell the Jacksons that the first accounting provided to the court back in November 2010 showed that Branca and McClain had paid themselves $9 million apiece in a seven-month period, and that another $13.6 million had gone to attorneys who included Katz, Weitzman, and Branca's own law firm. Sanders said the accounting statements weren't entirely as clear as that, but also told his client and her advisors that Branca and McClain might have made even more than Ribera was saying. Without a truly exhaustive audit, Sanders admitted, it would be impossible to say with certainty what Branca, McClain, Weitzman, Katz, and the rest were collecting.

Katherine's children, Randy and Janet in particular, were insisting that they wanted more than an audit—they wanted Branca taken down. Randy had never ceased scheming and plotting with his father how to seize control of the estate, and Janet was becoming increasingly stressed by her role as the Jacksons' new Michael. Though her wealth was still in the tens of millions, Janet had grown increasingly frugal—even stingy some of her siblings thought—in the aftermath of her 2000 divorce; ex-husband Rene Elizondo had walked away with $15 million, a five-bedroom beach house in Malibu, and a piece of his ex-wife's song royalties. The family had gotten a good look at the new Janet in July 2003 when they were preparing to celebrate their patriarch's eighty-fourth birthday with what they had decided to call "Joe Jackson Day" (an event Michael allowed to take place at Neverland, even though he skipped it). The family had decided to present Joe with a fishing boat and a trailer—"nothing big, maybe a fifty-thousand dollar purchase," recalled one of Michael's associates who was involved in planning the event. Janet, though, refused to put up her share of the money to pay for the boat until Michael had coughed up his share. And in the summer of 2009, Katherine Jackson had complained to confidants that Janet's demands to be repaid the $49,000 deposit that she had paid to secure the burial spot at Forest Lawn, which was reserved in Janet's name, had caused the initial postponement of Michael's funeral. Katherine had been so frustrated that she asked Marc Schaffel to help her obtain a credit card with a high enough limit to pay Forest Lawn herself.

(Through her attorney, Janet Jackson denied this story.) Almost three years later, Janet was increasingly put out by the carousel of brothers, sisters, nieces, and nephews coming to her for handouts. She wanted them to have their own money.

Randy, though, remained the driving force of the campaign to unseat Branca and was loudly complaining that Perry Sanders should be fired if he wasn't going to take action. The atmosphere enveloping the Calabasas estate that had replaced Hayvenhurst as Jackson Family Central was increasingly murky approaching the third anniversary of the death of its brightest star.

Michael might have found comfort in the knowledge that the inheritors of his estate all seemed to be coming into their own. His mother Katherine, her attorneys and advisors said, was increasingly sure of her own mind and less vulnerable to being swayed by Joe. She wouldn't hear a bad word about any of her children, even the one she knew was bent on making trouble, Randy, but Mrs. Jackson nevertheless refused to yield to her youngest son's unceasing demands that she hire new lawyers who would go after Branca. The relationship between Michael's mother and his children was "a moving thing to see, very deep and loving," Katherine's attorney Sandra Ribera said, and the two oldest, the teenagers, actually seemed to enjoy spending time around a grandmother who was almost seventy years their senior.

Prince was still a quiet boy, but he was making the force of his personality felt. On the trip to Montreal for the premiere of the Cirque du Soleil shows, he had confronted Sanders with the complaints he was hearing from some of his aunts and uncles, speaking so forcefully that other people on the trip said the usually unflappable Sanders was struggling to find words "and looked actually intimidated" as one of Mrs. Jackson's advisors described it. Only a little more than a week before, Prince had traveled to Germany with Katherine's advisor Lowell Henry and a camera crew dispatched by Mrs. Jackson's business partner Howard Mann for the "Tribute to Bambi" charity event at The Station in Berlin, where he was to present the handwritten lyrics of "Billie Jean," "Bad," and "Smooth Criminal" for an auction to raise money for seriously ill children. Dieter Wiesner had accompanied the traveling party to the event, and even when Henry and the others began to believe that Wiesner had set the whole thing up as a form of self-promotion, Prince had continued to conduct himself with impressive grace. Dressed in a black suit, red shirt, black tie, and red armband—the same ensemble Michael had worn when he collected the Bambi

Award in 2002—he told the crowd he intended to "try to build on what my father did. I want to try to help and change things, just like he did."

Paris was growing up to be a beauty, every bit as self-assured as her older brother, and a good deal more gregarious. Shortly before Christmas in 2011, Paris had appeared on the Ellen DeGeneres show to talk about her first acting role in a film, *Lundon's Bridge and the Three Keys*, admitting that she had lobbied hard to convince her grandmother to let her be in the movie. When she was asked about wearing a mask as a child, the girl admitted that she had chafed against it: "I'm like, 'This is stupid. Why am I wearing a mask?' But I kind of realized the older I got, like, he only tried to protect us. And he'd explain that to us, too." What she liked best about school was being treated like everyone else, Paris had explained to DeGeneres: "When I came to Buckley, they didn't know who I was. I was like, 'Yes! I have a chance to be normal.'"

In the run-up to the third anniversary of Michael's death, Paris was being asked regularly about the objections of her Aunt Janet to her niece's insistence on seeking work in movies. "We've spoken about the fact that you're only a child once," Janet had told the magazine *Prevention*. "I think there's a time for everything, and now is not the time [to act in films]." Paris had stood strong in letting Janet know she could think for herself, people at the Calabasas house said, and Janet hadn't seemed to like it much. Two weeks before the anniversary of her father's death, Paris had appeared on Oprah Winfrey's new show to confess that a number of her fellow students at Buckley weren't too happy about having Michael Jackson's two oldest children among them, once they realized who the new kids were. Was she picked on by the other kids? Winfrey asked. "They try, but it doesn't always work at school," Paris had answered. "And some people try to cyberbully me. They try to get to me with words, but that doesn't really work." She remained wary of making new friends, the girl admitted: "If I feel someone is being fake to me, I will just push away."

While the two older children seemed to embrace the public nature of their lives, the youngest, Blanket, continued to be home-schooled, sheltered by his grandmother from a world of prying eyes he wasn't prepared to face. No one at the Calabasas house wanted the now ten-year-old boy to know that in April his father's former bodyguard Matt Fiddes had told tabloid reporters he was Blanket's father and intended to try to prove it in court in order to obtain visitation rights. "More than anything," Fiddes said, he wanted the boy to meet his biological mother, who was at the moment battling cancer. This wasn't about money, Fiddes insisted: "I'm a self-made man. I don't want or need their cash." The Jacksons weren't buying it.

Paris was in the lead paragraph of nearly every article about the June 25 anniversary. Five days before, she had posted online a photograph of Michael Jackson kissing Debbie Rowe on the cheek, above the caption, "Mommy and Daddy!" On the anniversary itself, she had tweeted, "RIP Michael Jackson . . . Dad you will forever be in my heart<3 i love you."

Conrad Murray was also featured in articles about the anniversary. Murray was now lodged in the Segregation Unit at the Los Angeles County Men's Jail, where his neighbors included disgraced major league baseball star Lenny Dykstra and the first man Janet Jackson had ever married, James Debarge. Debarge, it was reported, had actually become friendly with Murray. A week before the anniversary, his new attorney quoted the doctor as saying the conditions of his incarceration were destroying his health. He only got fresh air once a month and clean underwear just once a week, Murray had complained to her, and was suffering from a constant headache he feared might be a brain tumor. "I may not make it out of here alive," the lawyer quoted him as saying. "This is a very dangerous place. I'm in here dying. The system is intent on killing me."

Murray had chosen June 25 as the day on which he once again protested his innocence, insisting through his lawyer that he was not responsible for Michael Jackson's death. Her client's one regret, the lawyer said, was that he hadn't testified on his own behalf, and Murray remained intent upon resuming his career as a physician when he was released.

June 25, 2012, was also the date that the surviving members of the Jackson 5 had chosen for a major promotion of a "Unity" concert tour performing Jackson 5 and Michael Jackson material, which would stretch from coast to coast and include at least twenty stops. "The brothers don't know this," Jermaine told London's *Daily Telegraph* on the anniversary date, "but I've broken down several times and cried during rehearsals."

Katherine Jackson was at least as excited about the Unity tour as any of her sons. Mrs. Jackson was planning to "be a sort of groupie," as one of her advisors put it, going on the road with her faithful caretaker, Joe Jackson's nephew Trent Jackson, in the Prevost motor home Michael had purchased for her shortly before his death. She and Trent would be seated in the front row at each of the concerts in the southwest region, beginning in Albuquerque on July 17 and including dates in Phoenix, Las Vegas, and Southern California, traveling from city to city in the Prevost. She might even follow her sons north to Saratoga, California, Katherine said, and maybe even on to Lincoln City, Oregon. What Mrs. Jackson didn't know, of course, was that some of her children and grandchildren had a whole different surprise prepared for her.

The opening act of the craziest Jackson family drama since Michael's death would begin on July 14, 2012, when Dr. Allan Metzger arrived at the Calabasas estate at the behest of Janet Jackson and was introduced as an associate of Katherine Jackson's longtime Beverly Hills physician, a woman doctor whom she trusted, literally, with her life. Her doctor wanted her to receive a physical before she set out on this road trip, Mrs. Jackson was told. Metzger conducted a brief examination, then told Katherine that her blood pressure was elevated. It really wouldn't be a good idea, the doctor said, to make this trip in a motor home. To avoid placing strain on her heart, Metzger explained, Mrs. Jackson should fly to Albuquerque.

Though terribly disappointed, Katherine agreed to leave the next morning, Sunday, July 15, on a commercial jet out of LAX, accompanied by her daughter Rebbie, Rebbie's daughter Stacee Brown (no relation to the ghostwriter), and Mrs. Jackson's personal assistant, Janice Smith. Not until they were at the airport did Mrs. Jackson realize they weren't headed to Albuquerque, but rather to Tucson, where she had been booked into a room at the nearby Miraval Spa resort. Janet Jackson was waiting at Miraval. Her doctor had decided she needed bed rest, Janet and the others explained on the way to Miraval, where Katherine was checked into a room in which the telephone had been disconnected and the television was not working. Lots of sleep and no disturbances, Janet and Rebbie explained, were what the doctor had ordered. Rebbie took her mother's cell phone from her, "so you won't be bothered by calls." Confused, but touched by her children's concern, Katherine settled into her room at Miraval.

Back at the Calabasas house, there was no worry. Katherine had been taking a motor home trip about once a year since Michael's death. During those trips, and on the rare other occasions she traveled by air without her grandchildren, Prince, Paris, and Blanket were left in the able care of their thirty-four-year-old cousin Tito Joe "TJ" Jackson.

TJ and his brothers, Taryll and Taj, had been Michael Jackson's favorite nephews. Even more than most in the family, Michael had credited that to the boys' mother, Delores "Dee Dee" Martes Jackson, a daughter of Dominican immigrants whom Tito had begun dating in 1968, when they were sophomores at Fairfax High School in Los Angeles, and married in

1972, when the Jackson 5 was just past the peak of its success. In 1994, a year after her divorce from Tito, Dee Dee had been murdered by the man she was dating, Donald Bohana. Her sons had been unable to persuade the district attorney to prosecute until they filed their own wrongful death lawsuit; Bohana was convicted of first-degree murder three years after Dee Dee's death.

Michael Jackson had always been supportive of Tito's sons, putting each of the three through the Buckley School. He became especially close to the young men, though, after their mother's death, agreeing to produce their first album, *Brotherhood*, and to release it on his MJJ Music label in 1995. *Brotherhood* was a considerable success, spinning off five singles and eventually selling more than six million copies. That success was mostly due to the fact that Michael had performed a duet with 3T on the album's best-selling single, "Why," and had sung backing vocals on the second best-selling single, "I Need You." When 3T brought out a second album without Michael's involvement nine years later, it wasn't even released in the United States and disappeared quickly overseas.

Relations between Michael and the two older brothers had cooled somewhat when he declined to continue working with them in the late 1990s, but TJ had remained loyal to his uncle, appreciative of the help and support that Michael had offered them all after their mother's death. He was also the closest to his grandmother of any of Tito's sons, and had been the first and the most generous about offering to help her with Michael's children after his death. Though he was heart-stoppingly handsome and still best-known for being the first serious boyfriend of fellow Buckley School student Kim Kardashian, TJ had turned into a solid family man, fathering three sons by his wife, Frances, and by 2010 was the closest thing to a father that Prince, Paris, and Blanket had left in the world. "He's so good with them, so kind and patient," Sandy Ribera said. "TJ is like a male version of Mrs. Jackson." For months it had been TJ who took the kids to the doctor, rode with them to school, helped them with their homework, met with their teachers. They were fine with being left in his care, but more than a little confused by the fact that they hadn't heard from their grandmother; she had never before gone twenty-four hours without checking in with them.

By midday Tuesday, everyone at the Calabasas house sensed that something was up. The media were reporting on a letter that had been signed by five of Michael Jackson's siblings—Randy, Janet, Jermaine, Rebbie, and, astonishingly, Tito—then sent to John Branca and John McClain.

"We insist that you resign effective immediately," the letter began, "as executors from the estate of our brother, Michael Joe Jackson." The letter promised to reveal the reasons why Branca and McClain should resign "in the coming weeks," but then proceeded to state the main one: the will that had named them as executors was "fake, flawed, and fraudulent." After describing how Branca had at first presented the will to them without a signature page, the letter cut to what the siblings apparently believed was their strongest argument, at least in the court of public opinion: "Michael was absolutely not in Los Angeles, California, on the date of his signature reflected in the will at-hand."

The next paragraph detailed what had always been the real and seething contention within the family about why Branca, in particular, but McClain as well, should not be the executors of Michael's estate: "Our brother told us, in no uncertain terms and without hesitation in the months prior to his death, that he despised both of you and that he did not want either of you to have anything to do with his life or estate for that matter. We know that and you knew that. We believe you relied on the presumption that no one would be so bold as to suggest that you would perpetrate such unconscionable deceit; but you were wrong."

The argument that followed was a rough—very rough—approximation of what both Sanders and Ribera had also come to believe: the executors were deliberately dragging things out in the hope that Mrs. Jackson would die before they had to pay her money she could leave to her children. "Even worse still," the letter to Branca and McClain read, "is what you have done and continue to do to our mother since you fraudulently assumed the position as the executors of the estate of her son. You keep lying to her, you manipulate her, and you make promises that you know will never happen . . . She's an eighty-two-year-old woman."

It was a legitimate *reason* to take the executors on, Sanders had tried to explain, but not an effective *basis* for a filing against them in court. The permitted time period in which to challenge the will had passed long before he became Katherine's attorney, Sanders had said for what seemed to him the hundredth time, so that was a moot point. Only ego or ignorance, he and Ribera agreed when they read the Jackson siblings' letter, could explain a course of action by Katherine's children that was sure to work against their own best interests.

Sanders and Ribera were startled by the next paragraph: "Your actions are affecting [our mother's] health, and on top of that, we've just found out she recently had a mini-stroke," the letter to Branca and McClain went on. "Please understand, she's not equipped to handle the stress load you are putting on her. She feels, as she has said, 'I'm stuck in the middle.' She too knows and acknowledges that the will was forged. She wants to do the right thing, and move in the direction of justice for her son and family, yet she fears the POWERS THAT BE."

Like Sanders, the people holding down the fort in Calabasas were shaken when they read the paragraph after that, which laid much of the blame for the failure to go after Branca and McClain at the feet of three of the four people who had become Katherine's closest advisors: Lowell Henry, Perry Sanders, and Trent Jackson. These three were "telling her to disregard what she knows as fact," the siblings' letter accused. "Instead, her so-called advisors are convincing her to let them negotiate 'deals' with Branca and McClain on her behalf, or is it on the behalf of all of you?"

AEG was the letter's next target: "AEG has been very vocal about how they are going to destroy [Katherine] and her family publicly and blame her for Michael's death. Since then, they've wasted no time harassing each and every family member, including Michael's children in a barrage of depositions, where they are asking personal, inappropriate, and disrespectful questions that, to say the least, have nothing to do with his passing."

All in all, it was a very sloppy letter, and couldn't possibly have been written by or even with the help of a competent attorney, thought Sanders, one of the ten people who had been cc'd at the bottom of the last page (along with Randy Phillips, Paul Gongaware, Tim Leiweke, Trent Jackson, Lowell Henry, Howard Weitzman, Martin Bandier, Phil Anschutz, and Tom Barrack). Sanders wasn't even pleased to see that Michael's brothers and sisters had made a point he himself had said was of supreme significance: Branca and McClain had written a letter to Judge Palazuelos, who was still presiding over the wrongful death lawsuit, "asking her to keep all documents handed over by AEG under court seal, clearly protecting AEG, but not protecting our mother nor our niece and nephews Paris, Prince, and Blanket. Who are you working for? What is it that you don't want to be known?"

The letter got truly nutty in the last paragraph, though, in the opinion of Katherine's attorneys, when it warned that the Jacksons were "considering retaining the law firm, Baker Hostetler, who have advised us on the potential criminal misconduct in your actions. We will hand this over to the proper authorities." If you plan to bring the authorities in, Sanders would remember thinking, you damn sure don't tell people about it ahead of time.

Sanders's associate Ribera was dispatched to the Calabasas estate that afternoon, not long after Trent Jackson had left for Albuquerque, where he was supposed to meet Katherine prior to that night's concert at the Hard Rock Hotel & Casino. It was almost dark when Trent phoned to say that Mrs. Jackson had never showed up. "That's when we started getting really worried," Ribera recalled.

In her room at Miraval, Katherine Jackson was frustrated mainly that she couldn't get anyone to come and fix her television. She liked to fall asleep with the TV on, she explained, but the thing was absolutely dead, no picture, no sound. Yet no repairman came, despite her repeated requests for one, so she spent hours playing the word game Scramble with Friends on her iPad. It had become something of an obsession with her in recent weeks; she'd gotten TJ into it and the two of them played daily. But when Rebbie came to check on her, she asked her mother if it was possible to send messages on an iPad. Katherine told her it was and began to show her daughter how. Rebbie immediately took the iPad from her, Mrs. Jackson would recall, saying that she needed rest, not stimulation.

Prince and Paris had been alarmed by the claim in the letter signed by their five aunts and uncles that Mrs. Jackson had suffered a "mini-stroke." That certainly hadn't happened before she left on her trip. Ribera suggested calling Mrs. Jackson's doctor's office. When they did, the doctor told them she had no association with Dr. Metzger and had never sent him to see Mrs. Jackson. "That's when we knew for certain that something was going on," Ribera recalled. "We started to talk about Dr. Metzger and that was like an 'Oh, my God' moment." For the first time, they realized that this was the same Dr. Allan Metzger who had been called as a defense witness at the Conrad Murray trial. The same Dr. Metzger who had been reprimanded by the state medical board for writing prescriptions for Janet Jackson under fraudulent names. The same Dr. Metzger who had accompanied Michael on the *HIStory* tour in 1996. The same Dr. Metzger who, after Michael's death, had sent his attorney out to tell the media that in the spring of 2009 Michael had asked him to provide propofol, and to insist that the doctor had refused to prescribe anything more than a mild sleep medication, and whose records had been subpoenaed by investigators from the coroner's office during the investigation into Michael's death.

At Miraval, Katherine Jackson was being visited regularly by Rebbie, who was in the room next door, and by Randy, Janet, and Jermaine, who were stopping by every other day or so for visits. She would ask them how the children were doing, Mrs. Jackson said, and they would tell her the kids were fine, everything was good at the house, nothing to worry about, just get some rest.

Shortly after the Dr. Metzger connection was made, Paris took to Twitter, responding to a tweet from her Uncle Randy that read, "We ask that everyone respects that this is a serious matter that will be handled by the proper authorities." Paris tweeted back, "i am going to clarify right now that what has been said about my grandmother is a rumor and nothing has happened, she is completely fine. i'd like to know who made up the rumor . . . i will defend my beloved family member with all i have, even if it means from other family members." She also shot a tweet directly to Randy that read, "hello dear FAMILY member I don't appreciate you telling people things that aren't true thank you very much." As word of Paris's tweet spread on the Internet, the tabloid media swarmed, convinced they were now chasing a big story.

In its initial response to the letter signed by the five Jacksons, the estate had trotted out the familiar contention that any questions about the validity of the will and Michael's selection of his executors had been "thoroughly and completely debunked two years ago when a challenge was rejected by the Los Angeles Superior Court, the California Court of Appeals, and, finally, the California Supreme Court." Remarkably, not a single member of the media pointed out that *none* of the questions about the validity of the will or the selection of Branca and McClain had been settled by those courts. The only thing that had been settled was that Joe Jackson lacked the standing to challenge Branca and McClain. If the executors and their attorneys felt contempt for reporters in general, it certainly seemed justified. Saddened as they were by the "false and defamatory accusations grounded in Internet conspiracy theories [that] are now being made by certain members of Michael's family, whom he chose to leave out of his will," the estate executors and their attorneys pledged to continue their efforts to secure the financial futures of Michael's children. By the next day the estate had produced a more politic pronouncement, one that focused less on the executors' reputations and more on "the welfare of Mrs. Jackson, and most particularly with Michael's minor children. We are concerned that we do what we can to protect them from undue influences, bullying, greed, and other unfortunate circumstances."

At the Calabasas house, people were commenting that, stressful as the situation was, it was nice at least not to have Katherine's assistant Janice Smith in town. Ribera and Trent Jackson regarded Smith as an especially corrosive force. She continued to work out of an office in the Hayvenhurst mansion, although Katherine no longer resided there, and had been placed on the estate's payroll. That and her relationships with Joe and Randy Jackson had resulted in widespread suspicion about her loyalties. The previous April, Smith had joined Randy Jackson in filing a complaint of financial elder abuse against Trent Jackson at the Los Angeles County sheriff's station in Malibu. Katherine Jackson had "emphatically denied" this claim, but sheriff's investigators had continued to interrogate several people who frequented the Calabasas house, Ribera among them. The attorney had gotten on Smith's bad side when she attempted to resolve a sexual harassment complaint involving Smith and a security guard, and seemed more sympathetic to the bodyguard than to Katherine's assistant. sheriff's deputies said that Smith had complained about her also, Ribera recalled, "and so they started investigating me, too." Prince and Paris told Ribera and TJ Jackson that their nanny and the chef had been whispering in each other's ears all day, and when they'd sneaked a look at the cell phones of the chef and the nanny, the two teenagers said, they discovered they were exchanging text messages with Janice Smith about what was going on at the house, and what the kids should be told. Ribera and TJ made the decision on Thursday, July 20, that they would put all of the staff—except for the security detail—on paid leave. "After that, it was just me and Trent and TJ and Prince and Paris and Blanket," Ribera recalled. "We were the core group hunkered down there at the house." Prince and Paris were calling their grandmother almost hourly on their cell phones and getting no answer. Ribera and TJ Jackson tried communicating with her through the Scramble with Friends game, but again there was no reply.

By then, Ribera, Trent, and TJ Jackson had become convinced that the five siblings who were behind whatever was going on intended to somehow gain a conservatorship over Katherine Jackson, possibly by demonstrating her incompetence to serve as the guardian of Michael's children. The money, as everyone knew, would follow those three kids.

That very day the children's court-appointed attorney, Margaret Lodise, went to Judge Beckloff to recommend that Katherine Jackson be stripped of her guardianship of Prince, Paris, and Blanket, temporarily, until a determination could be made about whether she was able to responsibly care for them.

On Friday, private investigator Tom Grant joined the group at the Calabasas house. A former L.A. sheriff's Department investigator, Grant "really calmed everyone and got us focused," Ribera recalled. He also convinced the people at the Calabasas house they should bring in law enforcement.

On Saturday, July 21, Trent Jackson went to the Malibu station of the L.A. County sheriff's office, the same building where Randy Jackson and Janice Smith had filed their complaint against him a year earlier, to report Katherine Jackson as a missing person. When someone at the sheriff's department leaked that to the media, the story went international.

In the United States, every cable news outfit and all three broadcast networks were chasing the story, mainly by following the tweets of Paris Jackson. "Yes, my grandmother is missing i haven't spoken with her in a week i want her home now," Paris told her more than 500,000 Twitter followers on the morning of Sunday, July 22. TJ Jackson made his first public pronouncement on what was taking place in a tweet to Paris that read, "I know it's completely unfair for them to do this to you and your brothers. We will keep trying. I love you." Jermaine's attempt at media management was to send out his own tweet: "I want to reassure everyone (incl all sudden medical experts) that Mother is fine but is resting up in AZ on the orders of a doctor, not us." Paris answered with a tweet that read, "the same doctor that testified on behalf of dr murray saying my father was a drug addict (a lie) is caring for my grandmother . . . just saying."

On Sunday afternoon, the sheriff's investigators called to say that Mrs. Jackson had been located in Arizona but wouldn't divulge her exact location. Local law enforcement had spoken to her, the Los Angeles sheriff's investigators said, and Mrs. Jackson had told them she was fine. Ribera, the daughter of a San Francisco police chief, ascertained that the authorities in Arizona had only spoken to Mrs. Jackson while she was surrounded by members of her family. "You have to get her away from them and ask her what's been going on without them hovering over her," Ribera said. "That's the protocol." The sheriff's investigators said they would be flying to Arizona aboard a chartered jet early the next morning and would check on Mrs. Jackson's condition themselves when they arrived. Ribera asked to come along, but the request was refused.

That evening "it became really serene at the house," Ribera recalled. With the staff gone, and especially with Janice Smith out of the picture, "everyone was calm and peaceful," Ribera said. "The kids . . . had had their nanny in their ear, their cousins, their aunts and uncles, a lot of people trying to manipulate them, but now they were thinking for themselves. You could see it. . . . And TJ was amazing."

The most outlandish developments thus far, though, would take place on Monday, July 23. First, the sheriff's investigator in charge phoned from Arizona to say that Janet Jackson's security detail had met them at "the location" and had told them they could not see Mrs. Jackson. "And I said, 'Well, why'd you stop there?'" Ribera recalled. "And they said, 'We didn't have jurisdiction because it's Arizona.' I said, 'Why didn't you bring in local law enforcement?' And they said, 'Well, we thought she was fine.' I said, 'If you thought she was fine, why did you go to Arizona in the first place?' And they just said, 'Oh, well, Arizona took care of it. We did all we could.' They were pathetic."

"8 days and counting. something is really off, this isn't like her at all . . . i wanna talk directly to my grandmother!!<|3" Paris Jackson tweeted to her followers. Jermaine answered with a tweet that insisted Prince and Paris were not "being 'blocked' from speaking with Mother . . . She is merely an 82-year-old woman following doctor's orders to rest up and de-stress, away from phones and computers."

The adults at the Calabasas house gathered to try to figure out where in Arizona Katherine might be. TJ got La Toya on the phone, but "La Toya wanted to be Switzerland, totally neutral," Ribera remembered, and wouldn't get involved. Must be the only time in her life that La Toya didn't want to talk to the media when they wanted to talk to her, someone at the house observed, and they all shared a chuckle. La Toya did tell them, though, that she thought her mother might be at Miraval.

Shortly after 1 p.m., Prince and Paris were in an SUV returning to the Calabasas house through the double gates that defended the driveway when another SUV, loaded with passengers, pulled up right on its bumper. Randy Jackson was at the wheel of the tailing SUV, which got in through the main gate and made it to the inner gate just as the steel barrier was coming down. "He just drove through and broke the arm off," recalled Ribera, who was watching from the property's pool house. The SUV braked to a stop in the driveway, and "all of a sudden the doors open and there's this swarm of people pointing cameras all around," Ribera remembered. She thought it was paparazzi at first, Ribera said, then recognized that the cameras were cell phones and that the people in the driveway were Randy Jackson, Janet Jackson, Jermaine Jackson, and several of Prince, Paris, and Blanket's cousins, including Randy's oldest daughter, Genevieve, and Jermaine's two youngest sons, Jaafar and Jermajesty. It was friendly at first, hugs and handshakes all around, though of course everyone wondered why Janet, Randy, Jermaine, and the others were aiming their phone cameras at them, even as they said hello.

Rebbie's son Austin, who had come to "visit" a little earlier, joined the others in the driveway. "They had actually planted cousins in the house to sort of spy and report," Ribera would marvel later, "to manipulate the kids and try get them to leave the property without security. That hadn't worked, so they came in themselves."

Trent and TJ Jackson stood confused for a few moments, until they realized that the other Jacksons were there to take Michael's children. The timing of this guerilla action, though, was not propitious. Only two security guards at a time were supposed to be on duty at the Calabasas house, but the guards had called a meeting that day and eight of them were in attendance. None of the guards were anxious to get into a physical altercation with Katherine Jackson's children, though, and so they mostly stood by with their palms raised, waiting for someone to tell them what they should do.

Janet Jackson went for her niece Paris, while Randy approached Prince and Jermaine engaged the guards, all three of them still using their cell phones as video cameras. When Janet and Randy told Paris and Prince they were coming with them, both teenagers flatly refused. Prince turned his back on Randy, but Jermaine pulled the boy aside and told him that this was something that had been in the planning for three years and that it was important for him to join in with the rest of the family. Prince shrugged off Jermaine and continued walking toward the house. Paris, meanwhile, made it clear to Janet that she wouldn't be leaving the Calabasas estate. When Janet tried to snatch Paris's cell phone, the same phone the girl had been using to tweet to the world, Paris pulled it away and turned a shoulder to protect it. Janet spoke to her briefly, then reached for the phone again and Paris took another step back. TMZ would initially report, based on anonymous sources, that Janet told Paris she was a "spoiled little bitch" and that Paris answered, "This is our house, not the Jackson family house. Get the fuck out!" TMZ also said the two exchanged slaps. TMZ recanted, though, when Janet threatened legal action. It's obvious from the video of the confrontation between Janet and Paris that there were no slaps. What was said remains a matter of dispute. CNN would report that Janet "scolded her niece for using her phone to write about family issues on Twitter," and the network was not threatened with a lawsuit.

Eventually TJ and Trent realized that the other Jacksons had come to the Calabasas house to take Michael's children off the property (then on to Arizona, they would learn later) and ordered the security guards not to let that happen. When the guards blocked his way, Randy, who had been smiling up until then, began to snarl warnings about not interfering in a family matter. One of the guards suggested that perhaps he should leave the property and Randy became enraged, cursing in the man's face, which was when Trent Jackson grabbed him. The two grappled for a moment, then the bull-strong Trent put Randy in a headlock and subdued him. Jermaine, cursing at the top of his lungs, came briefly to his brother's aid and would claim later that Trent grabbed him by the throat and punched him in the face.

Whatever was true about that, the scuffle ended quickly when Trent withdrew with Prince and Paris into the house. Those who were staying at the Calabasas house would say later that the saddest thing about the entire scene was the way Jermaine had used his sons. "I mean, Jermaine is cursing as bad as you can curse in front of these kids and fighting and doing all this stuff, and he's telling his kids to videotape it," Ribera recalled. "And Jermajesty . . . is just sobbing. His face is covered in tears. He's taping, but he's sobbing." TJ Jackson approached the boy to tell him, "Go upstairs. You shouldn't be here. You shouldn't be doing this." "But my Dad told me I have to," the weeping boy replied.

While five or six of the security guards faced off against Randy, Janet, Jermaine, and the cousins in the driveway, two other guards and Trent Jackson led Prince and Paris out the backdoor of the house and into a gulley that ran along the rear of the property, trying to get them away before the invading Jacksons came after them.

A sheriff's car answering a 911 call arrived at the front gate at almost that exact moment and everyone froze in place. After noting various accusations of battery and trespassing, the sheriff's deputies persuaded Randy, Janet, and Jermaine, and their group to leave the property. "Gotta love fam," Paris tweeted to her followers shortly after they were gone.

Shortly after Randy, Janet, and Jermaine departed, Ribera phoned the estate's probate attorney Jeryll Cohen to tell her what had taken place. "I normally would never want to ask for the estate's help, but it was a situation," Ribera explained. "For one strange moment in time our interests were aligned." Since the Calabasas house was being rented by the estate, it was up to the estate to lock the place down. Not long after Ribera spoke to Cohen, Margaret Lodise called to say she would be coming out in the evening to talk to the children.

Perry Sanders had remained at his home in Colorado Springs all during the drama thus far, trying to convince himself—and Ribera—that staying out of this family dispute was the wisest course. Until he had spoken to Katherine Jackson, Sanders was insisting to the reporters who called him, he would make no statements nor form any firm opinions. Privately, he was all but certain that what Ribera, along with Trent and TJ Jackson, believed to be taking place probably was. He phoned Tito's lawyer to say, "I don't know what I've done to piss your client off, but I'll be happy to talk to him about it and see if we can clear this up." Tito was in fact already backtracking, telling his sons that he really hadn't known what he was signing when he put his signature to that letter, but had just gotten "caught up." Randy was very persuasive, Tito explained: He had thought he was just closing ranks with the others against Branca. He hadn't meant to go after Trent or Perry Sanders, didn't know there was anything about them in the letter, and didn't know either about this claim that his mother had suffered a "mini-stroke."

By Sunday, July 22, the day after the missing person's report was filed, Sanders had realized there was a battle taking place and that it was largely being waged in the tabloid press, the Internet news media, and the Twittersphere. TMZ was the central clearinghouse, but Roger Friedman's Showbiz 411 column was almost as important. The X17online Web site was also a player, but they seemed to have become, like ABC News, a public relations vehicle for Randy and Janet Jackson. That had been made clear on that Sunday when X17 posted a photo provided by Janet and Randy that showed Katherine Jackson smiling and playing Uno with her family in Arizona, accompanied by text that mocked the idea she was a "missing person." Sanders warned X17 management that they had better start doing a better job of telling the truth. He continued to provide "deep background" to the TMZ staff, but was mostly talking to Roger Friedman. Friedman was the smartest tabloid reporter he'd ever spoken to, Sanders would explain, and maybe the only one who seemed to have some actual interest in reporting the truth. By the evening of the July 23, Friedman was at the cutting edge of reporters on the story, the first to describe in any detail the process by which Katherine Jackson had gotten to Arizona and the circumstances of the assault on the Calabasas estate.

Ribera and those keeping vigil in Calabasas, TJ especially, were heartened when Tito Jackson issued a statement that read, "I completely retract my signature from the July 17 letter sent to the executors of my brother Michael's estate and repudiate all the claims made against them," then added, "I don't want any part of that letter whatsoever."

The four siblings whose signatures had not been withdrawn could feel the tide turning. The media was sticking it to them with evident relish after the bungled attempt to remove Prince, Paris, and Blanket from the Calabasas estate. Within a few hours of the debacle, Sandy Ribera issued a statement to reporters that, "Jackson family members ambushed Katherine Jackson's home after their vehicle tore through security gates on the tails of the SUV containing Michael Jackson's children," and then suggested that perhaps the FBI should get involved in this case, since Katherine Jackson had been transported across state lines. That evening Paris tweeted, "days are counting, something is really off, this isn't like her, all i want to do is talk directly to my grandmother." That evening, Roger Friedman produced a column about the day's events with a headline that wondered if Janet Jackson had "Lost Her Mind." The next day, Friedman's column ran under a headline that identified Randy Jackson as "Michael's Delusional Brother." Paris sent out a tweet that read, "days are counting and help me God, i will make whoever did this pay." Articles began appearing in newspapers that suggested Katherine Jackson and been "kidnapped" or "abducted" by members of her own family. ABC was reporting that Margaret Lodise was preparing to file court papers that would "demand that Katherine Jackson be allowed contact with the children."

Janet, Randy, and Jermaine tried to fight back with their own publicity campaign. Jermaine issued a statement that the questions about his mother's whereabouts were nothing more than "a conspiracy to deflect attention from a letter we wrote asking for the resignation of [the] executors." Randy proved he was not yet a complete pariah by turning to the one media personality who would still take him seriously, Al Sharpton. Speaking by phone, Randy immediately told Sharpton that his mother was "doing great," then repeated the story that she was in Arizona only because "her health was ailing and her doctors ordered that she get immediate rest, isolate herself from the outside world and rest." He parroted Jermaine's line about deflecting attention from the letter to Sharpton, who, rather than asking probing questions, jumped on the opportunity to explain his own important role in this part of the drama. "Now, just for complete disclosure," Sharpton told his viewers, "I want to show people the date that is being in question, that weekend that Michael Jackson was to have signed that will in Los Angeles, he was, in fact, in Harlem with me that weekend. And I am showing that video now." When Sharpton asked him again, "Why all this drama that we are hearing in the media in your opinion?" Randy sounded like he was enjoying himself for the first time in days. "Well, because executives of the estate, John Branca and John McClain, are doing—they are using the children to try and put pressure on my mom to try and come out and get her to say things in their favor, to kind of clean up their image. They know they have been caught, they know that they falsified the document. And they know that there are questions that we want answered."

Janet, meanwhile, continued to deploy ABC News reporters as her unpaid PR spokespersons. It was through ABC that she and her siblings had first responded to Trent Jackson's trip to the Los Angeles County sheriff's department with a statement that read, "This fallacious missing persons report was created by the very person and persons we are trying to protect our mother from. We feel that there is a conspiracy to deflect the attention away from a letter we wrote asking for the resignation of the executors, John Branca and John McClain, as well as some of her 'advisors' and 'caregivers.'" Now Janet's people were talking to ABC about arranging an interview with Katherine Jackson, so that the "missing" woman could tell the world she was just fine.

At the Calabasas house, the main concern had become the issue of custody. Margaret Lodise had scheduled a hearing before Judge Beckloff on the morning of July 25 to try to temporarily suspend Katherine Jackson's guardianship of Prince, Paris, and Blanket. On the afternoon and evening of July 24, Ribera was dealing with that all by herself, "because Perry was like MIA," she recalled.

Unbeknownst to his associate, Sanders had finally made phone contact with Janet and Jermaine Jackson, and after a series of difficult conversations had convinced them, he thought, that letting him speak to Katherine would staunch the flow of bad publicity. He exercised no control over Sandy Ribera, who maintained her own law firm, separate from his, and had, in fact, repeatedly cautioned her about speaking out before she had more information, Sanders said. "All I want is to talk to my client and confirm her condition," he told Janet and Jermaine, again and again.

Katherine Jackson's condition by that point was one of advanced confusion. That afternoon, her television's sound had suddenly come on. There was still no picture, but the first words she heard were people talking about her being missing and possibly having been "abducted." When she asked what was going on, her children and Janice Smith blamed it all on media sensationalism and an attempt by Trent Jackson to get even with Randy by filing a missing persons report with the police, then joining with Sandy Ribera to spread the rumor that her own children had kidnapped her. They said Trent had actually attacked Randy when he went to the Calabasas house to try to explain to Prince, Paris, and Blanket what was happening, and then had gone after Jermaine when he tried to protect his brother. The security guards seemed to think they were working for

Trent and had backed him even after he had physically assaulted two of her sons, Mrs. Jackson was told. Then the police had arrived, called either by TJ or that Sandy Ribera, and not only refused to arrest Trent, but actually threw *her own children* off the property. Prince and Paris had seen the whole thing; it must have been terrible for them, Katherine was told. And now the media was turning on them like the pack of animals they were.

The media weren't the only ones turning against Randy, Janet, Rebbie, and Jermaine, however. Their brothers Marlon, Jackie, and Tito appeared on CBS's *The Insider* that evening to make it clear they weren't in league with their siblings in Arizona. "All I know is there's somebody who made the decision that my mother cannot talk to me, and whoever that person is, they've got to answer to me, because I'm going to see my mother and I'm going to bring her home," Marlon said, and then choked up. "I'm going to get to the bottom of this. I am."

While the three brothers were talking to CBS, Perry Sanders was flying to Tucson aboard a chartered jet, having been promised by Janet and Jermaine that he would be permitted to speak with their mother and confirm that she was well.

Janet and Jermaine landed at Tucson Airport aboard a commercial jet at almost the same moment Sanders's private jet set down. By cell phone, the two instructed him to meet their hired car near baggage claim. When Sanders's own driver pulled the Lincoln Town Car he was riding in up behind the limousine where Janet and Jermaine were waiting, they told him to get in and have his car follow theirs to Miraval Spa.

What he believed about who was running this operation was confirmed for Sanders when Janet and Jermaine refused to discuss the situation until they had put Randy on speakerphone, and then let the youngest Jackson brother do most of the talking. All three siblings were sticking to the official story that Katherine was under doctor's order to rest and "de-stress" by staying away from phones and computers, and that they had wanted to remove Michael's children from the Calabasas property for no other reason than to reassure them that their grandma was being taken care of. Sanders kept nodding and saying he understood, repeating once again that all he wanted was to have a conversation with his client in order to dispel the rumors and gossip that were flying around the Internet. When Sanders asked about what had happened at the Calabasas house earlier that day, Jermaine showed him a scratch on his neck and insisted that Trent Jackson had attacked him for no reason. Janet, speaking in a breathy murmur that was eerily similar to the one her brother Michael had put on in public, said she was deeply wounded by the false report on TMZ that she had cursed at Paris and slapped the girl, and that her lawyers would be taking action. Over the phone, Sanders assured Randy that he was no friend to John Branca and was not in league with the estate. At one point during the drive, Janet, still speaking in that whispery voice, told the driver to pull over to the side of the road, then asked Sanders to step outside so that they could speak privately "as a family." Sanders was invited back into the car a few minutes later and driven on to Miraval. When they arrived, though, Janet suggested that Sanders must be famished and should get a bite to eat while she and Jermaine checked on their mother. Sanders had just finished his meal when two of Janet's security team arrived at his table to tell him, "You won't be needed tonight," then walked away. "I was dismissed," he recalled.

His pilot said he was required by FAA regulations not to fly again until the next morning. There was nothing to do but go back to the airport, find a hotel room and get a few hours sleep before he had to fly to Los Angeles for the guardianship hearing that had been scheduled for 8:30 a.m.

It was only a short time later that Katherine Jackson phoned the house in Calabasas to say that she was firing Trent Jackson and every member of the security detail at the house. The people at Calabasas recognized that Mrs. Jackson was on a speakerphone and could hear the murmurs of other people in the room with her, "whispering into her ear and telling her what to say," Ribera recalled. TJ Jackson said he wasn't even sure at first that it *was* his grandmother, because she sounded literally like a different person. She was taking long pauses between sentences and using words he had never heard her use before, TJ would tell Judge Beckloff the next morning: "I've never heard my grandmother talk like that. She wasn't sharp. Some *words* seemed a little sharp." He almost wondered if his grandmother was "speaking in code," TJ added.

Then Mrs. Jackson said she wanted to talk to Sandy. "After she fired Trent and security, the estate immediately hired them back," Ribera said, "so that they didn't leave the house." But if Katherine fired Ribera, "the estate wasn't going to hire me back, and I knew it." Instead of handing the phone to Ribera, though, TJ told his grandmother that Jackie and Marlon were there and asked if she didn't want to speak to them, then waved his two uncles forward and let them finish the conversation with Katherine. Ribera would say later that TJ had saved her job.

Over the telephone during the early morning hours of the July 25, Ribera and Sanders worked out a plan to request that TJ be named the

children's temporary guardian, until Mrs. Jackson was allowed to return home. Margaret Lodise was amenable, and so was Judge Beckloff once he had been informed that TJ Jackson was named in Katherine Jackson's will as her "successor guardian" to Michael's children. After Sanders described his thwarted attempt to see Katherine in Arizona, Beckloff agreed to appoint TJ as the children's temporary guardian, noting he did not believe Katherine Jackson had done anything wrong and was acting solely out of concern about "the actions of third parties." The law required him to apply for permanent custody, the judge told TJ Jackson, but that process could be delayed if Mrs. Jackson came home. "The children's primary concern is that they get their grandmother back," Lodise told the judge.

At Miraval, Janet and her handlers had arranged for ABC's *Nightline* to tape a statement from Mrs. Jackson that she read off a teleprompter, seated between Rebbie Jackson and Stacee Brown, with Janet Jackson, Jermaine Jackson, and Janice Smith standing behind her. "Hello, I'm Katherine Jackson, and there are rumors going around about me that I have been kidnapped and held against my will. I am here today to let everybody know that I am fine and I am here with my children, and my children would never do a thing like that, holding me against my will. It's very stupid for people to think that. But anyway, I am devastated that while I've been away, that my children, my grandchildren, have been taken away from me, and I'm coming home to see about that, also." There was more, but it was obvious that every word Katherine said had been dictated (as Mrs. Jackson would confirm once she was back home). The strangest part of the entire scene was the expression on Janet Jackson's face, a bizarre combination of shame, regret, and cornered animal calculation that contrasted vividly with the fixed smiles of those who sat and stood with her.

Katherine Jackson's speech "reminded me not just a little bit of a hostage reading her kidnapper's message to the press," Roger Friedman wrote in the column posted online shortly before midnight. Marlon Jackson tweeted, "I'm tired of not knowing where my mom is. I did speak with her last night, but she didn't sound like herself. I was told by Janet, Randy, and Jermaine that I could not see my mom. Doctor's order. But see them on television with her. How come they could not call me so I could be with her as well?" Paris Jackson tweeted, "they promised my grandmother would be home YESTERDAY. why isn't she home?"

Katherine was already on her way by then, riding in a car with Rebbie, Janice Smith, and two of her grandchildren that sped across the desert in the dead of night. Shortly after the car crossed into California, Mrs.

Jackson woke Sanders with a phone call and asked if she could meet him at the Calabasas house the next day. The car carrying her back arrived at Calabasas at just before 3:30 a.m. "grandma's here! #thankyougod<33" Paris tweeted.

The big news the next morning, though, was that Prince Jackson had finally made his entrance into the Twittersphere drama. After thanking his father's fans, telling them how much his father appreciated their support, and that he did too, Prince explained he had been "waiting a long time to reveal my side," but at last was ready: "As long as I can remember my dad had repeatedly warned me of certain people and their ways. Although I am happy my grandma was returned, after speaking with her I realized how misguided and how badly she was lied to. I'm really angry and hurt." He had sent group texts to his relatives demanding to know what was going on, and when Janet replied-all to the group, got a rude awakening about what they were saying to each other, including about him and his sister. Prince then spoke to those people directly: "For this whole time, we were denied contact to our grandmother. 'If you continue with your lies, I will continue with the truth.'" He signed off as "Michael Jackson Jr."

When Sanders arrived at the Calabasas house on July 26, he had stepped through the front door expecting to be fired. Instead Katherine greeted him warmly, and it did not take long before Sanders could see that his client understood at least the rough outline of what had taken place. By the time their meeting was done, she had readily agreed to reinstate Trent and the security staff. Katherine was not going to publicly criticize her children, though, Sanders realized, or permit anyone else to criticize them, either. Sanders made it clear he wasn't there to assign blame. The main thing to get done, he told Katherine, was her reinstatement as the children's guardian.

Immediately after the meeting with Mrs. Jackson, Sanders issued a statement that, "I am pleased to report that she is fine and laughed at the widely published report that she had suffered a stroke."

Roger Friedman predicted that Katherine would find a way to avoid facing the unpleasant truth about what had taken place during the previous ten days. "'Ignorance is bliss' has been her motto." Sandy Ribera, though, said Mrs. Jackson understood completely how she had been deceived: "It breaks her heart, I think, but she maintains loyalty to her family."

Randy Jackson certainly remained in denial, unable to grasp either that it was too late to challenge the July 2002 will or that he had lost not just this battle, but the entire war. Shortly after Sanders told the media that Katherine was laughing at reports she had suffered a stroke, Randy tweeted seven bulletin points to his followers:

1) When TJ asked my mother if he should ask for temporary guardian-ship, my Mother told TJ NO—twice.
2) The estate denied Rebbie, Janet, and Jermaine access to the house when they returned home to Calabasas with a letter written by Howard Weitzman, who is not a resident of the home.
3) The estate is trying to isolate my mother from her family JUST LIKE THEY DID TO MICHAEL, in order to propagate their lies, financial agendas, and to protect a fraudulent will.
4) The same people that are trying to manipulate my mother are the same people that were involved with my brother when he died.
5) In order to obtain temporary guardianship, TJ lied to the court. Reb-bie, Janet, Jermaine, and I would never harm our mother and we are doing our best to protect her and the estate knows that. I want to know why Perry Sanders would consider a negotiation based on lies.
6) It is clear that anyone who stands up against the executors of the estate—John Branca, John McClain and their attorney Howard Weitzman—is denied access to my mother.
7) It is my fear and belief that they are trying to take my mother's life.

It was with Katherine Jackson's explicit permission, however, that Sand-ers, TJ Jackson, TJ's attorney Charles Schulz, and Margaret Lodise met to work out an agreement under which TJ would be named permanent coguardian of the three children. It was "a good deal all around," Sanders said when he announced the agreement that afternoon, because TJ already handled duties like household management and security arrangements, and now Mrs. Jackson would be officially free to focus on the emotional lives of Prince, Paris, and Blanket.

That night, Katherine showed up at the Unity tour concert in Saratoga, California, accompanied by all three of Michael's children. Yes, Jermaine was one of those onstage, Sanders said, but so were Jackie, Marlon, and Tito, and Katherine wanted to be there for them.

Mrs. Jackson wouldn't be seeing Jermaine—or Randy or Janet or Reb-bie—at the Calabasas house any time soon. On July 29, the estate issued an order banning those four siblings, plus their children and Jermaine's wife from entering the property. Also banned were Janice Smith "or anyone else who was involved in the recent events that led to Mrs. Jackson's separation from and inability to communicate with Michael's children."

The order, written by Weitzman, added that "Joe Jackson is precluded from entering the property." While Joe had been all but invisible during the previous two weeks, Ribera and others at the Calabasas house heard that he had been "squatting" at Hayvenhurst during that period, and had met with Randy there. Ribera and Sanders each assumed that Joe had been involved in some way.

Weitzman had also written that "Howard Mann, who is in litigation with the estate and is working with the Jackson siblings that wrote the 'letter' should also not be allowed on the property." Mann was flabbergasted that a number of Web sites credited him with drafting the letter, a notion that Weitzman had encouraged. "Randy *hates* me," a mournful Mann said. "He's been trying to convince Katherine to cut me off almost since the day we met." Randy Jackson's dislike of Mann paled by comparison to what Branca, McClain, and Weitzman felt toward him, though. The trial over what the executors and their lead attorney described as Mann's attempt to create "a shadow estate" through his business relationships with Katherine, Prince, Paris, and Blanket Jackson was scheduled to begin in early September and promised to become an especially vicious courtroom battle. Weitzman and Branca were still steaming from a letter Mann had written more than a year earlier in which he demanded they submit their resignations and promised that if they didn't he would see them put in prison. That letter had been sent not long after Mann described their administration of the estate to TMZ as "a fraudulently obtained dictatorship" and shortly before he helped craft the affidavit in which Katherine Jackson stated that her son Michael had told her more than once that he disliked Branca and believed the attorney "had stolen from him." Katherine and Joe Jackson were both scheduled to testify on Mann's behalf at the trial and Mann was making it clear to the other side that he intended to put the claims that the will was a forgery and that Branca had made up the story about being rehired as Michael Jackson's attorney front and center in court.

Branca had once more been proven lucky in his enemies. Inexplicable mistakes by Mann's legal team in the documents they had filed to compel Branca's deposition had enabled the estate's attorneys to force a refiling. The attorney Mann had assigned the task of filing the new deposition demand had failed to respond in a timely manner, meaning that Branca would again avoid being questioned under oath about the will that had named him as Michael Jackson's executor and the various questions that still surrounded his assumption of that position. At the end of the first full week of August, the federal judge hearing the case had ruled massively in the estate's favor on a summary judgment motion, gutting Mann's claim to intellectual property rights and almost certainly guaranteeing that Branca would not even have to answer questions on the witness stand. For the Jackson side, the only blessing was that Perry Sanders had refused to let Katherine join the case as anything other than a witness. The estate could claim a victory over her business partner, but not over her personally.

At the Calabasas estate Michael's children were in the happiest environment they had known since their father's death, according to Ribera. "The combination of TJ and Mrs. Jackson makes the kids really happy. They love their grandmother and don't want to leave her, but they also love TJ, and he's so good to have around, because he does the fun things." The day before, TJ had taken Paris shopping for an electric guitar, and when the two returned they had performed a version of Michael's song "Black or White" for his mother, Ribera recalled, "and Mrs. Jackson was like, tapping her foot in time with them. It was just so nice."

By August 1, Jermaine had decided unconditional surrender was the only course left to him. He declared his new position with a tweet that began by describing "a phone call with my son Jaafar that broke my heart. He asked, 'Is it true that we cannot visit grandmother's house as a family anymore?' Enough has become enough . . . After much soul-searching, it is clearly time for us to live by Michael's words about love not war. In this spirit, I offer this statement by way of extending an olive branch. Accordingly, I rescind my signature from the letter which was sent to the estate, and which should never have gone public." That last part was pretty amusing to those who knew that it was Randy, Janet, and Jermaine who had sent copies of the letter to various media. Blaming his excesses on "questions of whether we stepped off him too much or whether we did enough to help when the corporate world surrounded him," Jermaine made a plea for understanding: "When it comes to the well-being of loved ones, and especially our mother, we are perhaps understandably and un-apologetically over-protective."

The next day, August 2, the world learned what had otherwise occupied La Toya during the conflict in the family: She was negotiating with the Oprah Winfrey Network for a reality show that was to be titled, "Life with La Toya."

Those who imagined that capitulations from Janet, Randy, and Rebbie would soon follow were startled when, on August 4, Janet's lawyer Blair

Brown issued a statement on behalf of all three Jacksons that was essentially a double down on the bad bet they had made almost three weeks earlier. The statement, of course, began with the claim that their only concern had been the well-being of their mother, Katherine, and their brother Michael's three children, then went on to say, "The negative media campaign generated by the executors and their agents has been relentless. In recent weeks the media has received preposterous reports—all now proven to be false—of a purported kidnapping of Katherine Jackson and of physical and verbal abuse of a child." All that banning Janet and the others from the Calabasas estate had accomplished was "to damage fundamental family relationships," the letter asserted, and "also to isolate Katherine Jackson from anyone questioning the validity of Michael's will."

It was at the very least a remarkable coincidence that on the very same day an affidavit signed by Katherine Jackson was submitted to Judge Beckloff in which Mrs. Jackson effectively accused her children of doing the very things they were so vehemently denying. The affidavit began by describing how she had been held incommunicado at Miraval, with her room phone and television set shut off, her cell phone and iPad taken from her. She had never been told that Perry Sanders had flown to Tucson to meet with her, the affidavit continued, or that Janet and Jermaine had prevented him from going any further than Miraval's lobby. She was particularly upset that she had been prevented from speaking to her grandchildren for ten full days, noting that it was not until the night she left Miraval that "I was permitted" to speak to them. "I trusted the people I was with to be honest with me," the affidavit concluded. "They clearly were not. I never would have gone such a long time without communicating with [my grandchildren]."

Signing the affidavit had been the price Katherine was forced to pay to regain her guardianship of Prince, Paris, and Blanket. "She doesn't want to hear or say anything bad about any of her kids," Ribera said, "even Randy. But nothing is more important to her than Michael's children."

Perry Sanders followed shortly by granting a brief interview to TMZ in which he stated that Mrs. Jackson had "absolutely" no plans to press charges over the incident: "This chapter of chaos is closed and we are supportive of family unity in spite of recent events and arguably poor decisions."

A new chapter of chaos would undoubtedly open soon enough, but Sanders, who had already outlasted the tenures of Burt Levitch and Adam Streisand as Katherine Jackson's attorney, hoped he could survive long enough to show even the likes of Joe and Randy that he was preparing not just a well-made brick but a suit-case sized nuclear bomb for John Branca—and Howard Weitzman as well. Even as the letter sent to Branca and McClain was raising tabloid headlines to banner heights, the estate and its attorneys had been given far greater reason for concern by the request Sanders had made for "all supporting documents" of the "Second Account Current" the estate had filed with Judge Beckloff, covering the period between November 1, 2010, and December 31, 2011, with a particular emphasis on its dealings connected to AEG and on third-party payments. Branca and Weitzman certainly were smart enough to see where this was heading. In its submission to Judge Beckloff, the estate's accounting was extensive but opaque, divided into broad categories of "disbursements" such as "Payroll," "Public Relations," "Attorney Fees," "Legal Fees" and, of course, "Co-Executive and Creative Director Compensation." There were some startling figures that indicated the scope of Michael Jackson's properties; the automobiles he had kept in Las Vegas alone were valued at more than $675,000, while the bills for the moving and storage of his possessions alone had come to more than $1.5 million in a nineteen-month period. The estate also reported that it had employed more than a dozen law firms in London, Tokyo, Berlin, Munich, Hamburg, New York, Chicago, Las Vegas, Washington D.C., Cleveland, and Los Angeles, but that the largest shares of legal fees had gone to the firms of Howard Weitzman ($4.28 million) and Joel Katz ($3.71 million).

Sanders had hired the best forensic accountant he could find to go through the estate's documents piece by piece, looking for evidence of conflict of interest, self-dealing, and failure of fiduciary responsibility. Katherine's attorney was clearly targeting anything that might suggest collusion between the estate and AEG. He already possessed perhaps enough ammunition, Sanders believed, to file a claim based on conflict of interest that targeted Branca and Weitzman personally for the estate's failure to either file its own lawsuit against AEG or to join in the case filed by Katherine Jackson, and was prepared to make this known at the August 10 hearing before Judge Beckloff.

In apparent anticipation of such a move, the estate in early August had requested and received a postponement of the "Second Account Current" hearing before Judge Beckloff, putting it off until September 20. He had no problem with that, Sanders said; it would give him time to complete his audit of the estate's dealings, once the "supporting documents" were turned over. On August 20, however, the estate had filed nine separate objections to Sanders's request for documents, characterizing it as "vague and ambiguous" and "unduly burdensome." The estate's lawyers also claimed that some of the information sought by Katherine Jackson was "highly confidential" or was protected by attorney-client privilege and as attorney work-product. The demand Sanders had made on Mrs. Jackson's behalf clearly infringed upon Branca and McClain's "rights to privacy," argued the estate's attorneys, who also objected to the demand for documents in the "control of third parties" and assumed "the existence of certain documents" without proof that they did in fact exist.

In short, the battle had been joined even before war was declared.

The fight was starting undetected by the media, and while Katherine Jackson was off on that motor home trip that had been delayed by her diversion to Arizona. It had been a grueling month for a woman whose next birthday would be her eighty-third. On top of all that her children had put her through, Mrs. Jackson had been greeted on the day of her return home to Calabasas with a public invitation from Conrad Murray to visit him in jail. "I've been told that she has a desire to speak with me before she departs this life," Murray had explained in a statement to CNN. "Seeing that she is up in age and in questionable health, and the fact that she is the mother of a very dear departed friend, it would give me great pleasure to sit with her one on one and answer any questions she might have." Three days later, the attorneys handling Murray's appeal of his conviction had gone to court to ask that it order a forensic analysis on the residue in a drug vial that had been a key piece of prosecution evidence at his trial. Murray's fingerprint had been found on the bottle, which prosecutors maintained was the one that had contained the propofol that killed Michael Jackson. If that argument could be disproven, then the court would have to find that Jackson had, after all, injected himself with the fatal dose of the anesthesia, Murray's attorneys argued. Infuriated by his persistence, Katherine took a pass on Murray's offer and hit the road with her most faithful companion, Trent Jackson, seeking relief together from the fractious drama of recent weeks. That series of clumsily plotted scenes had left her brood more divided than it had ever been before, and the matriarch was still suffering the sadness of it all, those closest to her said. She needed a break.

It was a comfort to Mrs. Jackson to know that, in the end, they would all be together again. Katherine's deal with Forest Lawn to acquire the crypt in the Sanctuary of Ascension had included the purchase of eleven other burial spots on Holly Terrace, ensuring that in death Michael Jackson would be closely surrounded by the members of a family he had tried to keep at a distance for most of his life. Michael may have been one of a kind, but he was sharing with the world one last lesson in the common lot: There is no escape from family.

TIMELINE

July 26, 1929	Joseph Walter Jackson born in Fountain Hill, Arkansas
May 4, 1930	Kattie B. Scruse/Katherine Esther Scruse born in Barbour County, Alabama
May 29, 1950	Maureen "Rebbie" Jackson born in Gary, Indiana
May 4, 1951	Sigmund Esco "Jackie" Jackson born in Gary
October 15, 1953	Tariano Adaryl "Tito" Jackson born in Gary
December 11, 1954	Jermaine LaJuane Jackson born in Gary
May 29, 1956	La Toya Yvonne Jackson born in Gary
March 12, 1957	Marlon David Jackson born in Gary
August 29, 1958	Michael Joseph Jackson born in Gary
October 29, 1961	Steven Randall Jackson born in Gary
1961	Jackie, Tito, and Jermaine begin to perform as a singing group
1962	Marlon joins the group
1963	Michael performs "Climb Ev'ry Mountain" at his kindergarten, begins singing with his brothers
August 29, 1965 (MJ's 7th birthday)	As the Jackson 5, brothers win "Tiny Tots' Back to School Jamboree" at Big Top Department Store in Gary with their performance of "Doin' the Jerk"
Spring 1966	Jackson 5 wins talent show at Roosevelt High School in Gary
May 16, 1966	Janet Dameta Jackson born in Gary
Late 1966 to early 1967	Jackson 5 joins the chitlin' circuit
Early 1967	Jackson 5 wins talent show at Chicago's Regal Theater three times in a row
August 1967	Jackson 5 win Amateur Night contest at Apollo Theater in Harlem
January 31, 1968	Steeltown Records releases the Jackson 5's first Record, with "Big Boy" on side A

July 23, 1968	Jackson 5's Motown Records audition, Detroit
July 26, 1968	Jackson 5 signs with Motown
August 11, 1969	Jackson 5 introduced by Diana Ross at the Daisy in Beverly Hills, California
October 1969	Jackson 5's "I Want You Back" is released by Motown
December 14, 1969	Jackson 5 appears on *The Ed Sullivan Show*
December 18, 1969	Jackson 5's first Motown album, *Diana Ross Presents the Jackson 5* is released
October 10, 1970	Jackson 5 perform "The Star Spangled Banner" at Game 1 of World Series, Riverfront Stadium, Cincinnati
October 17, 1970	Jackson 5 become first group to have first four singles top the pop charts when "I'll Be There" reaches #1
February 25, 1971	Joe and Katherine Jackson purchase estate at 4641 Hayvenhurst Drive in Encino, California
April 29, 1971	Michael Jackson on the cover of *Rolling Stone*
September 11, 1971	*The Jackson 5ive* animated series debuts on ABC
January 24, 1972	First Michael Jackson solo album, *Got to Be There*, released
August 4, 1972	Second Michael Jackson solo album, *Ben*, released
October 29, 1972	Jackson 5 arrive at Heathrow Airport, London, to begin first European tour
March 9, 1973	Katherine Jackson files for divorce from Joe Jackson, Los Angeles Superior Court
February 19, 1974	Michael Jackson meets Rodney Allen Rippy at first annual American Music Awards ceremony
April 9, 1974	Jackson 5 open at MGM Grand in Las Vegas
June–July 1975	Jermaine leaves Jackson 5, Randy joins the group
July 1975	Jackson 5's Motown contract expires; they sign with CBS and become the Jacksons
June 16, 1976	*The Jacksons* variety show debuts on CBS
Spring 1977	Michael Jackson meets thirteen-year-old Tatum O'Neal at On the Rox club in Los Angeles
July 1977	Michael Jackson moves to New York to begin work on *The Wiz*
December 1978	Michael Jackson begins recording *Off the Wall* in Los Angeles
December 17, 1978	The Jacksons *Destiny* album released
Spring 1979	Michael breaks his nose in fall onstage; has first rhinoplasty surgery

Late 1979	Dr. Steven Hoefflin corrects previous nose job; relationship continues for more than twenty-five years
April 14, 1979	The Jacksons begin their *Destiny* North American tour in Cleveland
August 10, 1979	Michael Jackson's *Off the Wall* released
Autumn 1979	Michael Jackson hires John Branca as his attorney
July 8, 1981	The Jacksons begin *Triumph* tour in Memphis
April–November 1982	With Quincy Jones producing, Michael Jackson records *Thriller* in Los Angeles
November 12, 1982	Katherine Jackson files second time for divorce from Joseph Jackson in Los Angeles Superior Court
December 1, 1982	Michael Jackson's *Thriller* released
March 25, 1983	*Motown 25* special taped at Pasadena Civic Auditorium
Early April 1983	Michael meets Dr. Arnold Klein
October 1983	Michael Jackson meets Emmanuel Lewis during shooting of "Thriller" video
December 2, 1983	"Michael Jackson's Thriller" video debuts on MTV
January 27, 1984	Michael Jackson's scalp burned while filming Pepsi commercial at Shrine Auditorium in Los Angeles
February 7, 1984	Michael Jackson's first date with Brooke Shields
February 28, 1984	Michael Jackson wins record-tying eight Grammy Awards for *Thriller*
January 21, 1985	Michael Jackson, assisted by Lionel Richie, finishes lyrics and music for "We Are the World"
January 22, 1985	"We Are the World" recording sessions begin at Lion Share Recording Studio in Los Angeles
Autumn 1985	Michael Jackson purchases the ATV Music Publishing Company for $47.5 million
June 1986	For first time, Michael seen in Los Angeles wearing a surgical mask
September 16, 1986	Michael on cover of *National Enquirer* in a hyperbaric chamber
Early 1987	Michael buys Century City condominium that will become known as "The Hideout"
January 5–July 9, 1987	*Bad* album recorded at Westlake Studio in Los Angeles
April 1987	Michael withdraws from Jehovah's Witnesses
August 31, 1987	Michael Jackson's *Bad* released
September 12, 1987	*Bad* world tour kicks off in Tokyo
April 20, 1988	Michael Jackson's autobiography *Moonwalk* released

June 23, 1989	The Jacksons CBS/Epic Records contract expires; without Michael as a member of group, contract is not renewed
October 7, 1991	Elizabeth Taylor and Larry Fortensky are married at Neverland Ranch
November 14–15, 1991	Video for Michael's "Black or White" released
November 21–22, 1991	Michael Jackson's *Dangerous* released
1992	Deepak Chopra introduces Grace Rwaramba to Michael
May 1992	Michael meets Jordan Chandler in Los Angeles
January 1993	Michael introduced to Lisa Marie Presley at Brett Livingstone Strong's home in Pacific Palisades
January 19, 1993	Michael Jackson sings "Heal the World" at 1992 Inaugural Gala for newly elected president Bill Clinton
January 25, 1993	Jordan Chandler visits "Hideout" condo in Westwood for first time
January 31, 1993	Michael Jackson performs at halftime show of Superbowl XXVII at the Rose Bowl in Pasadena
February 10, 1993	Michael appears on *The Oprah Winfrey Show*, speaks for the first time publicly about being abused as a child by his father
February 27–28, 1993	Michael invites Jordan Chandler, his mother June, and sister Lily to Neverland for first time
March 28–30 1993	Michael takes Jordan Chandler, June, and Lily to Las Vegas
Early May 1993	Evan Chandler invites Michael to sleep over with Jordie at his house
May 9, 1993	Michael checks into the Hotel de Paris in Monaco with Jordie, June, and Lily, accompanied by Bob Jones
Early July 1993	Evan Chandler retains Barry Rothman; Michael's attorney Bert Fields hires Anthony Pellicano
August 17, 1993	The LAPD officially opens a criminal investigation of Michael Jackson
August 21, 1993	Michael arrives in Bangkok to begin the third leg of his *Dangerous* world tour; the LAPD serves search warrants on Neverland Ranch and the Century City condo
August 30, 1993	Michael collapses backstage at concert in Singapore
August 31, 1993	Michael undergoes brain scan in Singapore hospital; Gloria Allred is retained to represent Jordie Chandler in Los Angeles

September 14, 1993	Gloria Allred resigns as Jordie's attorney, is immediately replaced by Larry Feldman; a civil suit is filed against Michael Jackson in Los Angeles Superior Court that day
November 12–14	Via Canada and Iceland, Michael flies with Liz Taylor and Larry Fortensky to London, where he checks into a private detox clinic
November 16, 1993	In Los Angeles, a strip search warrant is obtained to examine Michael Jackson's genitals
November 24, 1993	Trial date of March 21, 1984, is set for Jordan Chandler's civil suit against Michael Jackson
December 20, 1993	Johnnie Cochran replaces Bert Fields on Michael's legal team; that same day Michael submits to a strip search and examination of his genitals at Neverland Ranch
January 24, 1993	The Los Angeles County District Attorney's office announces that it does not have enough evidence to charge Evan Chandler with extortion
January 25, 1993	Larry Feldman, Carl Douglas, Howard Weitzman, and Johnnie Cochran strike a deal to settle the civil case
February 1994	District Attorneys Gil Garcetti and Tom Sneddon each initiate grand jury proceedings to investigate criminal charges of child molestation against Michael Jackson
Late February 1994	Michael checks into the Trump Tower in New York City, where he will begin recording the *HIStory* album at the Hit Factory Studio
May 25–26, 1994	Michael Jackson and Lisa Marie Presley arrive at the Casa de Campo in the Dominican Republic, where they are married in a secret ceremony
September 24, 1994	Tom Sneddon and Gil Garcetti announce that, due to Jordan Chandler's refusal to testify, they have not been able to present enough evidence to convince the grand juries in either Los Angeles or Santa Barbara counties to indict Michael Jackson for child molestation
June 14, 1995	Michael and Lisa Marie are interviewed by Diane Sawyer for *Primetime Live*
June 15, 1995	*HIStory* is released amid the fanfare of huge Michael Jackson statues going on display in European cities
November 1995	Michael and Sony merge their song catalogs, which are estimated to be worth $600 million
December 6, 1995	Michael collapses while rehearsing for the HBO concert special and is rushed to Beth Israel Medical Center in New York

January 18, 1996	Lisa Marie Presley files for divorce
February 19, 1996	Michael's performance of "Earth Song" at the Brit Awards in London is interrupted by Jarvis Cocker
May 1996	Debbie Rowe becomes pregnant with Michael Joseph Jackson Jr.
November 14, 1996	Immediately after a concert in Sydney, Michael marries Debbie Rowe
February 13, 1997	Debbie Rowe gives birth to Michael Joseph Jackson Jr. in Los Angeles
November 25, 1997	Debbie Rowe announces she is pregnant with a girl, who will be born Paris Michael Katherine Jackson
April 3, 1998	Debbie Rowe gives birth to Paris Michael Katherine Jackson at the Spalding Pain Medical Clinic in Los Angeles
August 29, 1999	On his forty-first birthday, Michael cancels the Millennium concerts scheduled to take place on December 31 in Seoul and Honolulu
June 23, 2000	Marcel Avram files a lawsuit against Michael for cancelling the Millennium concerts
August 27, 2000	Gavin Arvizo pays his first visit to Neverland Ranch
March 6, 2001	Michael delivers his speech at Oxford
June 2001	Michael and Marc Schaffel meet at Dr. Arnold Klein's home
September 7 & 10, 2001	Michael performs at his "30th Anniversary" concerts at Madison Square Garden
September 16, 2001	Michael announces that "What More Can I Give?" will be released as a charity record to benefit the victims of the 9/11 terrorist attacks, with Marc Schaffel producing
October 15, 2001	Michael completes the recording of "What More Can I Give?"
October 17, 2001	Debbie Rowe is in Family Court in Los Angeles to surrender her parental rights to Prince and Paris
October 30, 2001	Michael Jackson's *Invincible* released
February 21, 2002	Michael's youngest child, Prince Michael Jackson II, aka Blanket, is born to an unidentified surrogate mother at the Grossmont Hospital in San Diego
June 11, 2002	At dinner in London, Uri Geller introduces Martin Bashir to Michael Jackson
July 6, 2002	Michael arrives riding atop a double-decker bus at Sony's New York headquarters, where his fans are demonstrating

July 7, 2002	Apparently, Michael is in Los Angeles to sign the will that names John Branca, John McClain and Barry Siegel as his executors
June 6, 8, 9, 2002	Michael is photographed in New York City
July 30–31	Martin Bashir arrives at Neverland Ranch to begin shooting the documentary that will be *Living with Michael Jackson*
November 19, 2002	Michael arrives in Berlin with Dieter Wiesner, Marc Schaffel, Grace Rwaramba, and his children to accept his Bambi Award; he creates international outrage by dangling Blanket from the balcony of his hotel
February 3, 2003	Bashir's *Living with Michael Jackson* premieres on ITV in Britain to huge ratings
	Michael fires John Branca as his attorney
February 4, 2003	Michael fires Barry Siegel as his accountant
February 5, 2003	Janet Arvizo and her three children arrive in Miami aboard a private jet with Chris Tucker, check into the Turnberry Isle resort where Michael and his entourage are staying
February 6, 2003	Jordan Chandler's 1993 sworn statement describing his alleged sexual abuse by Michael Jackson is leaked to the Smoking Gun Web site
	Living with Michael Jackson airs in America on ABC
February 7, 2003	Mark Geragos is hired as Michael's attorney
February 14, 2003	The Los Angeles County Department of Family and Children's Services opens an investigation into Michael's relationship with Gavin Arvizo
February 18, 2003	The Santa Barbara sheriff's department opens an investigation into Michael's relationship with Gavin Arvizo based on complaints by Gloria Allred and Carol Lieberman
February 20, 2003	*Take Two: The Footage You Were Not Meant to See* airs on Fox
March 2003	Michael Jackson reportedly signs a will naming Al Malnik as his executor
March 14, 2003	A jury awards Marcel Avram $5.3 million in his lawsuit against Michael Jackson
April 16, 2003	The Santa Barbara sheriff's department reports that it does not have probable cause to arrest Michael Jackson
	The Arvizo family meets with Larry Feldman
May 15–29, 2003	At Larry Feldman's behest, the Arvizo children meet with Dr. Stan Katz

June 13, 2003	Larry Feldman and Stan Katz report the allegations of child molestation made against Michael Jackson by Gavin and Star Arvizo to the Santa Barbara County authorities
August 26, 2003	Barry Siegel sends letter removing himself as an executor of Michael Jackson's estate
August 29, 2003	Michael's forty-fifth birthday celebration party in downtown Los Angeles
October 24, 2003	Michael arrives in Las Vegas with Dieter Wiesner, Marc Schaffel, and Stuart Backerman to promote "What More Can I Give?" and is given the key to the city by Mayor Oscar Goodman
November 18, 2003	*Number Ones* is released
	The search warrant raid on Neverland Ranch is executed
November 19, 2003	Tom Sneddon and Santa Barbara County sheriff Jim Anderson announce that an arrest warrant for Michael Jackson has been issued
Early/mid December 2003	The Nation of Islam takes over Michael's security, and all contact with Wiesner and Schaffel is cut off
December 18, 2003	Prosecutors formally charge Michael Jackson with seven counts of committing lewd acts against a child
Late December 2003	Michael abandons Neverland to move into a rented home in Beverly Hills
December 31, 2003	Debbie Rowe files to reinstate her visitation rights to the children
January 15, 2004	Gloria Allred asks the Department of Child and Family Services to remove all of Michael's children from his care
January 16, 2004	Michael is arraigned at the courthouse in Santa Maria and enters a plea of not guilty
February 1, 2004	Michael is at Ron Burkle's house in La Jolla, where he watches Janet's "Nipplegate" halftime performance at the Super Bowl
February 7, 2004	Michael hires Raymone Bain to replace Stuart Backerman, who has resigned
March 19, 2004	The DCFS announces that it has no cause to remove Michael Jackson's children from his care
March 25, 2004	A grand jury is empanelled in Santa Barbara County to hear evidence against Michael Jackson
April 21, 2004	Michael is in Orlando when he learns that he has been indicted by the grand jury in Santa Barbara
April 25, 2004	Michael fires Geragos as his attorney and replaces him with Tom Mesereau

September 13, 2004   Ray Chandler's *All That Glitters* published

November 4, 2004   Joseph Bartucci files his sex abuse lawsuit against Michael in New Orleans

November 16, 2004   Howard King files a civil complaint on behalf of Marc Schaffel in Los Angeles

January 31, 2005   Jury selection in *People v. Michael Joseph Jackson* begins

February 28, 2005   Tom Sneddon makes his opening statement

March 1, 2005   Tom Mesereau makes his opening statement

June 2–3, 2005   Ron Zonen and Tom Mesereau deliver their closing arguments

June 14, 2005   Michael Jackson is acquitted on all counts

June 29, 2005   Michael, Grace, and the kids fly to Bahrain

July 11, 2005   Prescient Acquisitions sues Michael Jackson for $48 million

September 23, 2005   Michael arrives at the Dorchester Hotel in London for his deposition in the Schaffel case

October 27, 2005   Michael files a countersuit against Marc Schaffel

November 12, 2005   Michael is escorted by police after a scene in the ladies room in the Egyptian Court of the Ibn Battuta Mall in Dubai

December 9, 2005   *National Enquirer* reports that Michael is in critical condition after overdosing on prescription drugs and alcohol

January 15–22, 2006   Michael travels to Orlando, Florida, meets with Lou Pearlman

January 26, 2006   Michael, Grace, and the children fly to Hamburg, settle in at the Schleiter home

February 15, 2006   The California Court of Appeals rules that Debbie Rowe's parental rights were not terminated by an earlier ruling and that she can seek custody of Prince and Paris

Late March/ early April 2006   Michael and his children work with Tony Buzan; Michael's "aide" is stopped with a suitcase full of OxyContin at the airport in Manama

April 13, 2006   A statement is issued that Michael Jackson has restructured his finances in a deal with Fortress Investments

April 17, 2006   The Bartucci lawsuit is dismissed

April 19, 2006   Michael meets with King Hamad bin Isa Al Khalifa at Safriya Palace

May 20–21, 2006   Sheikh Abdullah sees Michael for the last time

May 22–23, 2006   Michael arrives in London for the second deposition in the Schaffel case

May 24, 2006	The California Supreme Court refuses to hear Michael's appeal in the Debbie Rowe case
May 26, 2006	Michael, Grace, and the kids arrive in Tokyo for the MTV Japan Awards
June 14–22, 2006	Michael and his party are at the New York Hotel at Disneyland Paris; tour the Jardin des Plantes
June 23–25, 2006	The Jackson party flies to Cork, Ireland, and settles at Blackwater Castle
June 28, 2006	The *Schaffel v. Jackson* trial begins in Santa Monica
July 3, 2006	Michael and his party settle in at Ballinacurra House in Kinsale, Ireland
July 14, 2006	The verdict in the *Schaffel v. Jackson* case is a split decision; Schaffel is awarded $900,000 and Jackson $200,000
August 29, 2006	Michael and his party are at Luggala Castle in County Wicklow, Ireland, as he celebrates his forty-eighth birthday
September 29, 2006	Michael and his party are at Grouse Lodge when his attorneys and Debbie Rowe's reach a confidential settlement of their legal dispute
October/November 2006	After Michael tells Raymone Bain he has no valid will or trust agreement and needs one, she initiates the creation of the "Neverland Trust," which appoints Katherine Jackson trustee
Early October 2006	Michael is working with Will.i.am at Grouse Lodge on "comeback album"
October 15, 2006	Billy Bush interviews Michael for *Access Hollywood* at Grouse Lodge
November 15, 2006	Michael's abbreviated performance at Earl's Court during the World Music Awards ceremony
December 23, 2006	Michael, Grace, and the kids fly from Dublin to Las Vegas aboard a private jet that is met at the airport by Jack Wishna; he and Grace and the kids move into the house on Monte Cristo Drive
December 29, 2006	Michael's vigil at the casket of James Brown
December 30, 2006	Michael speaks at James Brown's funeral
January 25, 2007	Associated Press reports that Michael Jackson has returned to the United States
Later February	Joe and Randy Jackson make separate attempts to gain entry to Michael's Monte Cristo property and are turned away

March 31, 2007	Thompson, Cobb, Bazilio and Associates audit shows Michael Jackson has a net worth of $236 million
April 2007	Randy Phillips flies from Los Angeles to Las Vegas to meet with Michael about performing at the O2 in London; Raymone Bain calls a short time later to say Michael isn't ready to perform
April 17, 2007	Sony/ATV acquires the Leiber-Stoller catalog
June 18, 2007	Just as jury selection is about to begin at the U.S. District Court in Manhattan, Michael's attorneys settle the Prescient Acquisitions lawsuit
Late June to early July 2007	Michael is sighted in Washington, D.C., area
July 2007	Following the cancellation of his only credit card, Michael and his children are forced to leave hotels shortly after checking in
July 25, 2007	Michael is deposed by Howard King in the Dieter Wiesner lawsuit at the offices of the Venable law firm in Washington, D.C.
Mid August 2007	Michael, Grace, and the children show up at the Cascio's house in Franklin Lakes, New Jersey
October 15, 2007	At the High Court in London, Sheikh Abdullah files a lawsuit against Michael Jackson demanding approximately $7 million
October 31, 2007	Michael is recognized shopping with Frank Cascio at the Halloween Store in New Jersey
November 7, 2007	Michael, Grace, and children fly to Los Angeles for the sixty-sixth birthday party of Rev. Jesse Jackson
Mid-November to early December 2007	Michael, Grace, and the kids are the guests of Ron Burkle; Michael refuses to take calls from Raymone Bain
December 31, 2007	The refinancing of the loans against Michael's share of the Sony-ATV catalog is finalized
February 11–13, 2008	*Thriller 25* is released in Europe and the United States
February 20, 2008	Fortress Investments issues notice of default on Neverland Ranch
February 27–March 2, 2008	Michael and children move from the Palms to the Palomino property; Jermaine Jackson introduces Michael to Tohme Tohme
April 2008	Fortress Investments schedules May auction for Neverland Ranch and all property on premises
Early-mid May 2008	Colony Capital announces that it has acquired the note on Neverland Ranch and the threatened auction is averted

Early July 2008	Tohme Tohme officially becomes Michael Jackson's new business manager
August 28–29, 2008	Michael is interviewed by *Good Morning America*, serenaded by British fans gathered at gates of Palomino property, and receives a copy of letter circulated by neighbors expressing concern that an accused child molester is living among them
Early September 2008	Tohme begins consulting with Peter Lopez about setting up a new concert tour for Michael
Late September to early October 2008	Michael and Tohme meet with Phil Anschutz at the MGM Grand in Las Vegas
Mid-late October 2008	Michael and children leave Las Vegas and check into the Bel Air Hotel, without Grace
October 21, 2008	Patrick Allocco of Allgood Entertainment flies to Las Vegas to meet with Joe Jackson about a "Jackson Family Reunion Concert"; Joe sends Allocco to meet with Frank Dileo
Late October to early November 2008	Negotiations of the O2 deal continue; Grace comes to Los Angeles, but is sent packing
October 31, 2008	Michael and his children attend Halloween party at Natalie Maines's house with Veronique Peck
November 17, 2008	The Sheikh Abdullah lawsuit trial begins in London's High Court
November 20–21, 2008	Patrick Allocco meets with Frank Dileo in Nashville
November 23, 2008	Michael and Tohme are preparing to fly to London when word comes that the Sheikh Abdullah lawsuit has been settled
November 26, 2008	Frank Dileo and Patrick Allocco sign a "binder agreement" for the Jackson Reunion Concert
Early December 2008	With help from Barrack, Tohme convinces Michael to commit to ten concerts at the O2; Tohme, Lopez, and Dennis Hawk initiate negotiations with Randy Phillips
Later in December 2008	Michael and his children move into the Carolwood Drive chateau
January 1, 2009	Allgood Entertainment hires Leonard Rowe as a "consultant"
January 26, 2009	At the Carolwood chateau in Beverly Hills, reportedly surrounded by Phil Anschutz, Tim Leiweke, Paul Gongaware, and Randy Phillips of AEG, Michael signs a deal to perform ten concerts at the O2 Arena in London

February/March, 2009	After Michael tells them he has no will and needs one, Tohme and Hawk consult with attorney Sean Najerian about preparing a will and trust agreement for Jackson
February 3, 2009	Leonard Rowe and Patrick Allocco take Katherine Jackson to lunch, explain the Reunion Concert proposal and tell her she will be paid if Michael signs a contract
February 9, 2009	Tohme's partner James Weller meets with Darren Julian at a fast food restaurant on Wilshire Boulevard
February 12, 2009	Leonard Rowe and Patrick Allocco meet with Dennis Hawk at Hawk's office
March 4, 2009	MJJ Productions files a lawsuit against Julian Auctions, demanding that it halt the scheduled April 22, 2009, auction of Michael's property
March 5, 2009	Michael announces the "This Is It" concert series (ten shows) at the O2 in London
March 6–11, 2009	Michael discovers that Tohme and AEG are talking about increasing the number of shows at the O2; eventually he is persuaded by Tohme and Phillips to commit to thirty-one shows
March 11, 2009	Ticketmaster's "pre-sale" of Michael Jackson's O2 shows produces an astounding response
March 13, 2009	The number of scheduled concerts at the O2 has been increased to fifty; the tickets for all seats at every show sell out within four hours
March 16, 2009	Roger Friedman column questions Tohme and voices opinion he is not really a doctor
March 24, 2009	Roger Friedman publishes column in which Darren Julian describes being threatened by James Weller
March 25, 2009	Joe Jackson and Leonard Rowe gain entry to Michael's Carolwood chateau
March 26, 2009	Leonard Rowe and Frank Dileo meet for the first time, at the urging of Katherine Jackson
March 27, 2009	Leonard Rowe sends out a press release claiming he has been hired as Michael's new manager; Michael stops taking calls from Rowe
	Allgood Entertainment sends a cease and desist letter to Randy Phillips at AEG, claiming that Frank Dileo is Michael Jackson's manager and has signed an agreement with them
April 6, 2009	Dr. Conrad Murray places an order for propofol from Applied Pharmacy Services in Las Vegas

April 12, 2009	Michael asks Cherilyn Lee if she can obtain and administer propofol
April 13–15, 2009	Auditions for the "This Is It" show dancers are held at the Kodak Theater in Hollywood
April 14, 2009	Julian Auctions is scheduled to begin exhibiting Michael Jackson property at the Beverly Hilton ahead of the scheduled April 22 auction
	Michael Jackson meets with Joe Jackson, Leonard Rowe, and Patrick Allocco at the Sportsmen's Lodge; Michael signs letter stating that Rowe is his "authorized representative"; Michael also signs a revocation of Tohme's power of attorney
	Tohme strikes a deal with Darren Julian that settles the lawsuit and prevents the auction of Michael's property and delivers the check that pays Julian off; it's not enough, as Michael cuts off all contact with Tohme
Late April to early May 2009	Michael is regularly absent from the rehearsals at Center Staging
April 21, 22, 23, 25, 27, 28, 30, 2009	Paparazzi trail Michael to Dr. Klein's office in Beverly Hills
May 2, 2009	Letter apparently signed by Michael Jackson goes out to various associates announcing that Frank Dileo has been appointed as "one of [my] representatives and tour manager"
May 5, 2009	Raymone Bain files a $44 million lawsuit against Michael in Washington, D.C.
	Ola Ray files a lawsuit against Michael in Santa Monica
	Letter written by Frank Dileo and apparently signed by Michael Jackson is sent out to various associates stating that Michael has dispensed with the services of Tohme Tohme
May 8, 2009	AEG reaches an oral agreement to hire Dr. Conrad Murray as Michael Jackson's personal physician; Murray begins spending the night at Michael's home
May 12, 2009	Conrad Murray places an order for propofol and assorted benzodiazepine drugs with Applied Pharmacy Services in Las Vegas
May 14, 2009	Michael and his children attend sixtieth anniversary dinner for Joe and Katherine Jackson at Chakra restaurant in Beverly Hills
May 15, 2009	Michael's brothers issue a denial of any involvement in a reported Reunion Concert to be put on by Allgood Entertainment

	Michael, Randy Phillips, Paul Gongaware, Leonard Rowe, Joe and Katherine Jackson meet at the Beverly Hills Hotel
	In the afternoon, Michael goes to Dr. Klein's
May 20, 2009	AEG announces postponement of "This Is It" shows
May 25, 2009	Michael sends his "you do not represent me" letter to Leonard Rowe
Late May 2009	Randy Phillips tells the *Los Angeles Times* that the O2 shows are "a do or die moment" for Michael Jackson
June 1, 2009	"This Is It" rehearsals move to the Forum
June 17, 2009	According to John Branca, he meets with Michael and Frank Dileo at the Forum
June 18, 2009	Michael doesn't show for what will be one of the last two rehearsals at the Forum; Randy Phillips drives to the Carolwood chateau to demand, in the presence of Dr. Murray, that Michael stop seeing Dr. Klein and stop taking the drugs he believes Klein is giving him
June 19, 2009	Michael arrives for the last evening of rehearsals at the Forum "a basket case" and is sent home by Kenny Ortega
June 20, 2009	Randy Phillips tells Frank Dileo he needs to bring his client into line; Dileo leaves a voice mail for Conrad Murray that Michael is "sick" and needs a blood test "to see what he's doing"; Murray demands a meeting with Ortega and Phillips at the Carolwood chateau
June 22, 2009	Michael shows up for the first day of full dress rehearsals at the Staples Center "in this new kind of place," according to Ortega
June 24, 2009	Michael arrives at the Staples Center around 6:30 p.m., delivers a "bioluminescent" performance, in Ortega's words, and leaves for home exhilarated
June 25, 2009	Michael Jackson is pronounced dead at UCLA Medical Center

A Note on Sources

It's difficult to acknowledge people you can't name. That's why none of us—neither readers nor writers—likes to rely on anonymous sources. It all comes down to a question of trade-offs. Is the access and the information worth sacrificing the reader's knowledge of exactly who is saying what? I decided that, in a few cases, it was.

Two of my most valuable sources insisted upon absolute confidentiality. They would not allow me even to quote them anonymously or to identify them as sources in any way. One of them, a person I'm going to refer to as Anonymous Source 1 (AS1 hereafter), was absolutely essential to me in tracking the movements and activities of Michael Jackson (MJ hereafter) during a period of time that stretched from his acquittal at his criminal trial in Santa Barbara during June 2005 to his long stay at the Cascio family home in the late summer and early autumn of 2007. This individual also told me a great deal about MJ's relationships with family members and other personal details. The second person, Anonymous Source 2 (AS2 hereafter) was key to understanding MJ's legal, financial, and business affairs. I dealt with the insistence of these two sources on total anonymity by making a decision that I would not use anything significant or potentially controversial that they told me unless I could find at least one other independent source that substantially verified what they were saying. Both of these individuals (but AS2 especially) were quite good about directing me to where I could obtain such verification, which was often in the public record. I also used them to confirm or deny things I'd heard from other sources. The only instances in which I relied solely upon these two particular anonymous sources had to do with context and atmosphere—where and when something took place. I did of course pay close attention to what the two of them—AS1 in particular—told me about MJ's emotional condition and state of mind.

Two of my other sources allowed me to quote them, but not by name. I'm going to refer to them in my notes as Confidential Source 1 (CS1) and Confidential Source 2 (CS2). Each of these two persons worked with and for MJ, off and on, for a lengthy period of time: more than twenty years in one case and nearly fifteen in the other. One was an attorney, the other worked both with and for MJ. I identify them in this way when they are quoted. CS2 was someone I felt certain would agree eventually to be quoted by name, but this person died before I finished the book. Since it was never renegotiated, I have kept my promise not to identify or quote this individual by name.

In addition, there were two people who advised me midway through the course of multiple interviews that they did not want to be quoted by name. My practice in this regard is that I will not identify a source by name from the point in time when such a request is made and I agree to it, but that I remain free to quote anything they said prior to that time, and to attribute it to them. That is how I dealt with the requests of these two sources, each of whom is quoted by name in some instances and anonymously in others.

On top of all this, I also made what amounted to unilateral decisions not to quote a couple of other people by name. In one case, I made use of remarks uttered by an advisor of Katherine Jackson's during the course of what could conceivably be called a business meeting. This individual (who also has a long association with Joe Jackson) knew I was writing a book about Michael Jackson, and never said his words were off the record, but he also never explicitly told me that what he said was for attribution. I elected to quote him a handful of times in the book, but not to use his name. Also, what this person told me about MJ's siblings probably left as deep an impression as anything else I heard or read. In the other case, a producer with whom I was involved in a business relationship having nothing to do with this book or its subject matter told me about eating Thanksgiving dinner with Jordan Chandler's stepmother and two half-brothers in 2009, and how they had reacted when he spoke MJ's name. Weeks later, he told me he didn't want to be quoted. I agreed only not to quote him by name.

The most painful of the confidentiality demands made upon me were those I heard as the book was being prepared for publication. Nearly all of these came from sources in show business who had provided a snippet of information or the recollection of a glancing encounter with MJ. In the summer of 2012, one after another were telling me that they had shared this story or that one simply for my edification, not because they imagined I would use it in the book, and either pleaded or demanded that I not. Their reasons often seemed absurd to me, but most often came down to either a concern that they had violated a confidence by telling me something they shouldn't have or that they would be dragged into the swamp of legal claims as various people angled for a piece of the MJ action. Generally, I refused to take things out of the book (though several times I gave in even on that point), but conceded that I would not quote these sources by name. What really hurt was removing the two funniest MJ-related stories I ever heard from the book.

It will be obvious that I spoke directly with members of the Chandler family; I'll explain that situation in my chapter notes when we come to that section of the book.

I didn't quote Katherine Jackson's business partner and close advisor Howard Mann by name in this book, even though I consider him to be a significant source. Mann has been terribly vilified on the Internet. Whatever anyone writes or reports about Mann, though, there is no question that from late 2009 until the present he has been one of Mrs. Jackson's two closest advisors and that because of this relationship knows as much as anyone about what has taken place within the Jackson family since MJ's death, and a good deal, as well, about what took place during MJ's life. That said, I'm still not sure how unfair the accusations against Mann have been. I often found him to be forthright and earnest. I also found him to be less than accurate on occasion and relied on four separate individuals affiliated with Katherine Jackson to fact-check his assertions for anything exaggerated or erroneous. One I can't name. The other three were Marc Schaffel and Mrs. Jackson's attorneys Perry Sanders and Sandra Ribera.

I should note that I permitted Sandy Ribera to read the entire first-draft manuscript of this book before publication. I recognize that this is unusual, but felt I owed it both to Katherine Jackson and to my readers. Sandy replied with two long "comments and corrections" e-mails that did point out some slight but not insignificant errors, and offered her view of how things operate within the Jackson family. She also took the opportunity to argue passionately against the negative portrait of Katherine Jackson others had put forth, and had some effect; I either deleted or softened several descriptions of Mrs. Jackson's complicity in the financial exploitation of her son. I retained most of that material, however, because the evidence of its accuracy was too strong to discount.

I think Katherine knows that I liked her the moment I met her; she really is a lovely woman, both funnier and more vulnerable than I anticipated. I came to believe, and still do, that she is not a devious person.

There is a kind of dishonesty that takes the form of denial, however, and the evidence continues to tell me MJ's mother is guilty of that, at least in certain regards.

Sandy Ribera also shared with me her insights and the observations she made while attending the trial of Conrad Murray, and those were helpful.

I should disclose that Perry Sanders is a friend of mine and that I made the introductions that resulted in him being hired as Katherine Jackson's attorney. He did share certain information with me "to make sure you don't get off track," but it was all given in confidence with the agreement that I would need to obtain it independently from another source to use it in this book. Katherine Jackson's former attorney Adam Streisand also told me things that contributed to my understanding of the dynamics of the Jackson family.

Howard Mann told me one story that I know to be mostly true and that I feel should be told, even though it was omitted from the main body of this book: In the fall of 2009, Mann made a deal to acquire the trove of Jackson family memorabilia, videotapes, photographs, and music recordings that Henry Vaccaro called "The Michael Jackson Secret Vault." Among those items was what had long been the most speculated about piece of physical evidence ever possessed by the Santa Barbara County District Attorney's office. This was a box of "salacious materials" that would become the object of a frenzied hunt in the weeks after Michael's death. When the British tabloids discovered that these "materials" were now in Mann's possession, they began a bidding war that, according to Howard, resulted ultimately in an offer of seven figures. (I know there was a bidding war, but doubt the amount offered ever approached a million dollars.) Whatever amount of money it was that the British tabloids offered, it's a fact that instead of selling these objects he conveyed the box and its contents to the Hayvenhurst compound and presented it to Katherine Jackson. It was an attempt at forging a relationship with a woman he had never met. "I told Mrs. Jackson I didn't think it would be right or smart to sell this stuff to a tabloid that would trash her son's reputation," Mann explained to me, "and that I was giving it to her to do with as she saw fit." Katherine opened the box, looked inside, closed her eyes for a moment, then thanked Mann profusely for his kindness and consideration. "It was very good of Howard," Mrs. Jackson said months later, after he had become her business partner and personal advisor.

Mann told me that the box of "materials" had been packed by Marc Schaffel and delivered to Michael Jackson back in 2002. "Michael asked me to send some of the movies I'd made," Schaffel explained when I asked him about this. The "exotic" sex toys in the box, more than the gay porn films, were what the tabloids had coveted. "I threw that stuff in to make him laugh," said Schaffel. No, he didn't believe Michael was gay, Marc said: "At least I never saw any sign of it." Michael often commented that he found this or that woman attractive, admiring the curve of her hips or the shape of her posterior, but Schaffel never knew him to engage in anything more than a brief and superficial flirtation with any female. He certainly never slept with one during the years Marc spent with him. So why did Michael want him to send that box of gay porn films? I wondered. "He was curious," Schaffel said. "Michael was interested in everything. He looked at straight films, gay films, tranny films—you name it. He wanted to see it all. I took it as him trying to know about things he wasn't experiencing in his own life."

Another disclosure: I briefly worked with Mann on an (apparently) aborted documentary about the Michael Jackson estate (tentatively titled *Stealing Michael Jackson*) and in that capacity was able to view footage and obtain transcripts of interviews with Joe Jackson, Katherine Jackson, Brian Oxman, Raymone Bain, and Dick Gregory, among others, that inform certain sections of this book.

After that first documentary was shelved, Mann began to develop a different documentary about Michael Jackson, tentatively titled *Luv U More*. Through him, I was made aware of a trove of tape-recorded interviews with Michael that were conducted in the late 1980s. Mann obtained these recordings from the husband of a former Neverland Ranch employee who claims Michael gave them to him. These recordings, now in Mann's possession, are just as compelling as the ones that Rabbi Shmuley Boteach compiled. I can't quote directly from them, but must admit that I was influenced by the harsh things Michael had to say about his family, especially with regard to their financial exploitation of him. Even his mother was not spared. It's the only occasion I know of in which Michael has made critical remarks about Katherine. Those tapes were a secondary but significant source of information that contributed to what I wrote about Michael's life prior to the accusations made against him by Jordan Chandler in 1993. They also illustrated to me how changed Michael was by the sexual abuse charges leveled at him.

The amount of information—and misinformation—available about Michael Jackson is staggering. As those who examine my bibliography will observe, I couldn't keep myself from exploring it. How to attribute reports in this Internet age is problematic. I wasn't always sure whether an article had appeared in print before it was posted online. There were several times, with *Los Angeles Times* stories, for example, where I discovered that the online version of an article was running under a different headline than the one on the same article I had clipped from the actual newspaper. Also, I was at times uncertain about how much of a story posted online by one of the American television networks (or by the BBC) had appeared on air, or if it had been expanded in the Internet version. I've cited my sources taking into account how the reader might locate them, if interested, and also how the material appeared first or in most detail, but if I've erred in that respect, I apologize.

The postings on various Michael Jackson fan sites were also a significant source of information for me. To those who arch their eyebrows I will point out that quite often the only "reporters" to whom Michael and those around him allowed access were people running these fan sites, and that members of Michael's staff and household often passed on information about his movements and activities to these fan sites with his full knowledge and consent. I'm still amazed by the accuracy of the "Michael Jackson Timeline" on allmichaeljackson.com, something that was compiled in real time, as Michael lived through the days, weeks, and months the timeline encompasses. AS1 was among those who passed along information about Michael to fan sites.

I have rendered some of the chapter notes that follow in a narrative fashion, because in my mind they are part of the story. I will, however, attach a list of specific citations to each chapter section. Where a source is from the Internet, radio or television, or a press release/other public relations communication, it will be indicated in the source list with (I), (RT), or (PR), respectively.

I'll acknowledge and thank further sources as I come to the relevant chapters, and in some cases explain my relationships with them. One person I want to single out in advance, though, is Tom Mesereau, an honest and decent man who I believe tried sincerely and scrupulously to answer every question I put to him in the course of at least twenty separate conversations. I'm not sure I can make that unqualified statement about any of my other sources. Tom was also tremendously helpful, making introductions, sharing information that I would never have discovered without him, even providing me with a sympathetic ear when I was frustrated by the conflicting stories I was hearing from various people who had been in Michael Jackson's life. The truth is that every single person I spoke to or communicated with or even attempted to interview while researching this book was attacked or criticized by others among my sources—except Mesereau. His reputation and his reputation alone was not impugned by a single person. Pretty remarkable, I think. I'm particularly grateful to Tom for the DVD of the Los Angeles Bar Association's "Frozen in Time" symposium on the sexual abuse allegations made against Michael Jackson that he sent me. I thank him also for directing my attention to the two excellent essays that Charles Thomson wrote for the *Huffington Post* about the biased media coverage of Michael Jackson's criminal trial. To this day there is no more ardent or persuasive defender of Michael's reputation than Tom Mesereau.

I want to thank Morgan Entrekin for supporting my decision to expand an overgrown magazine article into a book, and for his patience in giving me time to complete it. I enjoyed the benefit of two talented editors working with me on this book. Brando Skyhorse, a talented author in his own right, was generous enough to put his own work aside to focus on mine up to the point of producing a workable draft of *Untouchable*. Amy Hundley took over from there and did a prodigious amount of the work to bring this book to the finish line. Brando and Amy consistently provided me with the sort of sound advice I need a lot more than I like to admit. For being good angels on both my shoulders, I am grateful to them both.

BIBLIOGRAPHY AND CHAPTER NOTES

GENERAL

DVD

Frozen in Time: A Riveting Behind-the-Scenes View of the Michael Jackson Cases. Los Angeles County Bar Association, September 15, 2010 (Tom Mesereau, Ron Zonen, Judge Rodney Melville, Larry Feldman, Carl Douglas).

BOOKS

Bego, Mark. *On the Road with Michael* (Pinnacle, 1984).
Boteach, Shmuley. *The Michael Jackson Tapes* (Vanguard Press, 2009).
Cadman, Chris, and Halstead, Craig. *Michael Jackson: For the Record* (Authors OnLine, 2007).
Campbell, Lisa. *Michael Jackson: The King of Pop's Darkest Hour* (Branden Books, 1994).
Cartman, Shirley. *A Teacher Remembers the Jacksons* (Gabriel Publishing, 1987).
Cascio, Frank. *My Friend Michael* (William Morrow, 2011).
Chandler, Raymond. *All That Glitters* (Chanadon Publications, 2004).
Dannen, Frederic. *Hit Men* (Random House, 1988).
Dimond, Diane. *Be Careful Who You Love* (Atria Books, 2005).
Finstad, Suzanne. *Child Bride: The Untold Story of Priscilla Beaulieu Presley* (Three Rivers Press, 2006).
Foster, David. *Hitman* (Pocket, 2008).
George, Nelson. *The Michael Jackson Story* (Dell, 1984).
Grizzuti-Harrison, Barbara. *Visions of Glory* (Robert Hale, 1980).
Haden-Guest, Anthony. *The Last Party: Studio 54, Disco, and the Culture of the Night* (New York, William Morrow, 1998).

Haney, Lynn. *Gregory Peck: A Charmed Life* (Da Capo Press, 2005).

Heymann, C. David. *Liz: An Intimate Biography of Elizabeth Taylor* (Atria Books, 2007).

Hughes, Geraldine. *Redemption: The Truth Behind the Michael Jackson Child Molestation Allegations* (Hughes Publishing, 2004).

Jackson, Katherine. *My Family, the Jacksons* (St. Martin's Press, 1990).

Jackson, Jermaine. *You Are Not Alone* (Simon and Schuster, 2011).

Jackson, Janet with David Ritz. *True You* (Gallery Books, 2011).

Jackson, La Toya. *Growing Up in the Jackson Family* (Dutton, 1991).

Jackson, La Toya, with Jeffré Phillips. *Starting Over* (Gallery Books, 2011).

Jackson, Michael. *Moonwalker* (Random House, 1988).

Jefferson, Margo. *On Michael Jackson* (Pantheon, 2006).

Jones, Aphrodite. *Michael Jackson Conspiracy* (iUniverse, 2007).

Jones, Bob, with Stacy Brown. *Michael Jackson: The Man Behind the Mask* (SelectBooks, 2005).

Posner, Gerald. *Motown: Music, Money, Sex, and Power* (Random House, 2005).

Rowe, Leonard. *What Really Happened to Michael Jackson the King of Pop* (Linell-Diamond Entertainment, 2010).

Schechter, Daniel, and Erica Willheim. "The Effects of Violent Experience and Maltreatment on Infants and Young Children." In *Handbook of Infant Mental Health*, 3rd Edition, Charles H. Zeanah (Ed.) (Guilford Press, 2009).

Shorter, E. *A Historical Dictionary of Psychiatry* (Oxford University Press, 2005). See especially the chapter "Benzodiazepines."

Singleton, Raynoma Gordy. *Berry, Me, and Motown* (McGraw-Hill, 1991).

Sitrick, Michael. *Spin: How to Turn the Power of the Press to Your Advantage* (Regenery Publishing, 1998).

Taraborrelli, J. Randy. *Elizabeth* (Grand Central Publishing, 2006).

———. *Michael Jackson: The Magic and the Madness* (Birch Lane Press, 1991).

———. *Michael Jackson: The Magic, the Madness, the Whole Story, 1958–2009* (Grand Central Publishing, 2010).

———. *Motown—Hot Wax, City Cool, Solid Gold* (Doubleday, 1986).

Vaknin, Sam. *Malignant Self Love: Narcissism Revisited* (Narcissus Publications, 2001).

White, Timothy (Tony Wills). *A People for His Name* (Vantage, 1968).

TIME LINES

"Michael Jackson Timeline," allmichaeljackson.com.

"MJJ Timeline," mjjtimeline.blogspot.com.

Daily Mail, August 13, 2012.

PROLOGUE

Interviews: Marc Schaffel, AS1. Jackson family Anniversary Concert compensation: pleadings in *Schaffel v. Jackson*. Secret room: descriptions by sheriff's deputies, Neverland staff member interviews in *People v. Jackson*. Ribera to Sullivan letters (see below) attributed Mrs. Jackson's participation to pressure from Joe and Jermaine.

COURT FILES

Criminal

1133603 (Santa Barbara Superior Court) *The People of the State of California v. Michael Joe Jackson*, December 18, 2003 (hereafter cited as SBSC 1133603).

Civil

SC083501 (Los Angeles Superior Court) *F. Marc Schaffel v. Michael Jackson*, November 16, 2004 (hereafter cited as LASC SC083501).

SECRET ROOM

"Michael Jackson's Secret Room." *Popdirt.com*, November 19, 2003 (I).
"Police Find Secret Room in Michael Jackson Raid." *Extra*, November 19, 2003 (RT).

CHAPTER 1

Interviews: AS1, AS2, CS1, CS2, Tom Mesereau, Marc Schaffel, Tohme Tohme, Schaffel, Liam Sheehan. Katherine Jackson, re. Michael's religion. Dick Gregory: to van Susteren, interview for *Stealing Michael Jackson*. Bahrain: AS1, Mesereau, Tohme. Scene at Neverland/hospitalization: AS1, Mesereau, Gregory, AP, Access Hollywood. Center for Well Being, Crillon: AS1. MJ-Rwaramba relationship: AS1, Mesereau, Tohme, Schaffel, Sheehan, CS1, CS2; Rwaramba to Daphne Barak (published in *News of the World* and *Times* of London online; I cite full versions on Barak's Web site). Stacy Adair/"marriage of convenience": "Secret girlfriend"/*Daily Mirror*. Sheikh Abdullah background: AS1, Tohme, media below. "Flabbergasted," "it blew my mind": Rwaramba High Court testimony as per British press, esp. The *Independent* and *Guardian*. MJ-Abdullah travels: AS1; also, Mesereau paraphrasing Susan Yu, Tohme. London/*Schaffel v. Jackson*: AS1, Schaffel, Mesereau, Howard King and Dieter Wiesner. Schaffel/Jackson financial transactions: sources as above, and Al Malnik. *Schaffel v. Jackson* court file, and evidence and testimony in *People v. Jackson*. Attending church with KJ during *People v. Jackson*: AS1, Mesereau, Stacy Brown to Dan Abrams. "A psychological state that he required in order to function": Schaffel as quoted by King in a court pleading. Marlon Brando "a god": phone message, MJ to Schaffel. John Branca/ MJ, esp. 2001–3 and "What More Can I Give?": Schaffel, King, Wiesner, *Schaffel v. Jackson* court file, Phillips/*LA Times*, Carter/*New York Times*, Gunderson. Mark Wahlberg/White Plains: Schaffel, AS1. Branca-MJ relationship: Taraborrelli, Branca to *California Lawyer* magazine, Schaffel, King, Wiesner, Phillips/*LATimes*. Interfor Report: my own review of document; Schaffel, King, and Mesereau; testimony of David LeGrand in *People v. Jackson*. Sony: Schaffel, Wiesner, *New York Times* July 2002, Phillips/*LA Times* 2002. Cascio family: Schaffel, Wiesner, Mesereau; Cascio/MJ interviews in Boteach book; and sources below. "Cascio kids" music video incident: Schaffel, AS1. Trudy Green would not speak with me. Mask story: Schaffel, Wiesner and AS1. Adlon Hotel: Schaffel, Wiesner. Martin Bashir: interview with Uri Geller, who introduced them, Schaffel, Wiesner, and Mesereau, and sources below. *People v. Jackson*: pleadings, testimony, transcript/ examination of Bashir. Payments for *Home Movies* interviews: *Schaffel v. Jackson* court file. As described in Chapter 20, Bashir used the journalist shield law when asked about refusal to show Jackson footage, etc. Nation of Islam: Schaffel, Wiesner, Mersereau. "Conversion" to Islam: Although at least five newspapers in London and New York reported that MJ had made the *shahada* at the Hollywood Hills home of Steve Porcaro, the former Toto keyboardist and a Muslim convert, David "Dawud" Wharnsby (credited with urging MJ's conversion) has issued a statement that he never even met MJ, and Yusef Islam (formerly Cat Stevens, who supposedly witnessed it) flatly denies attending any ceremony where MJ converted to Islam. The *Daily News* article that infuriated MJ was the "Pedophilia charges ruining his career . . ." one listed below. I should disclose that in the spring of 2010, while negotiating a contract to serve as the host and executive producer of a television show for the Oprah Winfrey Network, I was represented by King's law firm. That deal had nothing to do with this book.

COURT FILES

Criminal

SBSC 1133603

Civil

SC026226 (Los Angeles Superior Court) *J. Chandler, a minor, v. Michael Jackson*, September 14, 1993 (hereafter cited as LASC SC026226).

2:04—CV—2977 (United States District Court Eastern District of Louisiana) *Joseph Thomas Bartucci, Jr., v. Michael J. Jackson*, November 1, 2004. LASC SC083501.

DOCUMENTS

"RE: Letter of Direction." Letter from Michael Jackson to Sony/ATV Publishing LLC. December 23, 1998.

"RE: Representation of Michael Jackson and Sony/ATV Music Publishing LLC." Letter from John Branca to Michael Jackson. August 14, 2002 (hereafter cited as Branca to Jackson, 8/14/02).

"RE: Sony/ATV/Leiber-Stoller." Letter from John Branca to Martin Singer, Esq. August 27, 2002 (hereafter cited as Branca to Singer, 8/7/02).

"RE: Michael Jackson/Sony-ATV Music Publishing." Letter from Martin D. Singer to John Branca. September 10, 2002 (hereafter cited as Singer to Branca, 9/10/02).

Interfor Report on John Gregory Branca, entered as an exhibit in 1133603 (Santa Barbara Superior Court) *The People of the State of California v. Michael Joe Jackson*, December 18, 2003; and in BP117321 (Los Angeles Superior Court) *Joseph Jackson v. The Estate of Michael Joseph Jackson*, November 10, 2009 (hereafter cited as Interfor Report on John Gregory Branca).

"Discontinuance of Service." Letter from Michael Jackson to John Branca. February 3, 2003 (hereafter cited as Jackson to Branca, 2/3/03).

"RE: Marc Schaffel." E-mail from Howard King to Randall Sullivan. February 1, 2010 (hereafter cited as King to Sullivan, 2/1/10).

"Statement of Grace Rwaramba" to Los Angeles Police Department. September 12, 2009 (hereafter cited as Rwaramba, 9/12/09).

"Comments/Corrections." E-mail from Sandi Ribera to Randall Sullivan. November 9, 2011 (hereafter cited as Ribera to Sullivan, 11/9/11).

"Comments/Corrections." E-mail from Sandi Ribera to Randall Sullivan. November 13, 2011 (hereafter cited as Ribera to Sullivan, 11/13/11).

FROM CALIFORNIA TO BAHRAIN

CIA World Factbook: Bahrain. March 8, 2011.

"Jackson Dropped from Hospital Lawsuit." Associated Press, April 10, 2008.

"Michael Jackson Sued over Woman's Death." *Access Hollywood*, February 20, 2007.

Van Susteren, Greta. "Dick Gregory: 'It Happened So Fast.'" *On the Record*, Fox News, June 26, 2009 (RT).

GRACE RWARAMBA

Barak, Daphne. "Fired Nanny's First Interview Ever." daphneBarak.homestread. com (hereafter cited as Barak Rwaramba interview) (I).

Batty, David. "Michael Jackson Nanny Says Star Had Stomach Pumped Many Times: Nanny Gives Grim Account of Singer's Final Months, Detailing Drug Abuse, Out of Control Spending, and Nomadic Lifestyle. *Guardian*, June 28, 2009.

Friedman, Roger. "Michael Jackson Can't Wed Nanny: She's Married." Fox News, June 19, 2006 (I).

Gould, Lara, and Will Payne. "Jackson's Secret Girlfriend Was His Children's Former Nanny Grace Rwaramba." *Daily Mirror*, July 5, 2009.

"Grace Rwaramba's High School Yearbook." *TMZ* (I).

SHEIKH ABDULLAH AND BAHRAIN
(INCLUDING MJ'S "CONVERSION" TO ISLAM)

Adams, William Lee. "Michael Jackson Settles Out of Court with Sheikh." *Time*, November 24, 2008.

Booth, Robert, and Michael Cragg. "Michael Jackson, the Sheikh and the Comeback Album That Came Too Late." *Guardian*, June 26, 2009.

Foster, Patrick. "Sheikh 'Wanted Michael Jackson to Sing His Songs.'" *Times*, November 18, 2008.

"Genealogy of the Al-Khalifa Dynasty." Royal Ark (I).

Hari, Johann. "The Dark Side of Dubai." *Independent*, April 7, 2009.

Howard, Stephen. "Sheikh 'Felt Personally Betrayed' by Jackson." *Independent*, November 18, 2008 (hereafter cited as Howard, "Personally Betrayed").

"Jacko Is on the Verge of Converting to Islam." earthtimes.com, March 30, 2006 (from *Panorama*) (I).

Lewis, Paul. "Songwriting Sheikh Sues Michael Jackson for 4.7 Million Pounds." *Guardian*, November 18, 2008.

"Michael Jackson Impressed by Nakheel Projects." albawaba.com, September 1, 2005 (I).

"Michael Jackson Visits Kingdom Hall with his Mother." watchtowerinformationservice.org, June 13, 2005 (I).

Pipes, Daniel. "If the King of Pop Converts to Islam." *New York Sun*, March 7, 2006.

"Stacy Brown Interview." *Abrams Report*, MSNBC, March 10, 2005 (RT).

Worth, Robert F. "Laid-Off Foreigners Flee as Dubai Spirals Down." *New York Times*, February 11, 2009.

BARTUCCI LAWSUIT

Gumbel, Andrew. "Sex, Drugs and Abduction by Limo—the Claims Against Jackso That Even His Enemies Won't Buy." *Independent*, July 31, 2005.

WHAT MORE CAN I GIVE?

Carter, Bill. "At Jackson's Request, ABC Cuts a Song Out of a Concert Tape." *New York Times*, November 1, 2001.
Gundersen, Edna. "Jackson Charity Single Tied Up in Limbo." *USA Today*, July 18, 2002.
———. "Jackson's 9-11 Single Produced by Gay-Porn Maker." *USA Today*, July 14, 2002.
———. Michael Jackson Writes, Casts a Benefit Ballad." *USA Today*, September 16, 2001.
Philips, Chuck. "New Spin on Collapse of Jackson's Charity Project." *Los Angeles Times*, June 13, 2002.
———. "Producer Sells the Rights to Jackson Project." *Los Angeles Times*, July 17, 2002.

JOHN BRANCA

Hillburn, Robert. ""Attorney John Branca: He's Equally as Brilliant . . ." *Billboard*, July 21, 1984 (hereafter cited as Hillburn, "Equally as Brilliant").
Sinberg, Stan. "The Prince of Rock." *California Lawyer*, August 2011 (hereafter cited as Sinberg).

SONY/INVINCIBLE/TOMMY MOTTOLA

Guzman, Isaac, George Rush, and Lola Ogunnaike. "Pedophilia Charges Ruining His Career, Says Music Exec." *New York Daily News*, July 9, 2002.
Holson, Laura M. "Recording Industry Questions a Bitter Attack by a Pop Star." *New York Times*, July 8, 2002 (hereafter cited as Holson, "Bitter Attack").
———. "Star's Costs Mount as Album Sales Slump." *New York Times*, November 20, 2003.
Holson, Laura M., and Lynette Holloway. "Sony and Its Star Go to War over the Promotion of an Album." *New York Times*, July 10, 2002 (hereafter cited as Holson and Holloway, "Sony and Its Star").
Siklos, Richard. "The fight over Michael Jackson's Millions." *Fortune*, October 23, 2009 (dated November 2009 elsewhere; hereafter cited as Siklos).

MJ FINANCES AND CAREER/SCHAFFEL V. JACKSON

Hong, Peter. "Jackson Trial Ends with Dual Awards." *Los Angeles Times*, July 15, 2006.

"Jackson Hit with $3 Million Lawsuit." *Smoking Gun*, November 17, 2004 (I).

CASCIOS

Winfrey, Oprah. "The Cascios on Their Secret Friendship with Michael Jackson." *Oprah*, December 6, 2010 (hereafter cited as Winfrey, "Secret Friendship") (RT).
———. "How the Cascios Became Friends with Michael Jackson." *Oprah*, December 6, 2010 (hereafter cited as Winfrey, "How the Cascios") (RT).

BERLIN

"Michael Jackson and Halle Berry Pick Up Bambi Awards in Berlin." *Hello*, November 22, 2002.

"Michael Jackson Honored with Germany's Bambi Award Following Baby Dangling Snafu." *Jet*, December 9, 2002.

Vineyard, Jennifer. "Michael Jackson Calls Baby-Dangling Incident a 'Terrible Mistake.'" MTV, November 20, 2002 (RT).

BASHIR/REBUTTAL VIDEO/NEVERLAND RAID/MUSLIMS/AFTERMATH

Bashir, Martin. "Living with Michael Jackson." Granada Television, February 6, 2003; rebroadcast in a slightly different version, ABC News, February 6, 2003 (RT).

"Gloria Allred." vindicatemjj.wordpress.com, March 6, 2012 (I).

Jensen, Elizabeth. "Michael Jackson Close-Up, Times 2." *Los Angeles Times*, February 6, 2003.

Roth, Kristin. "Michael Jackson Strikes Back with 'Take Two' TV Special: Singer Counters Allegations in Recent TV Documentary with Show of His Own." MTV, February 12, 2003 (RT).

Silverman, Stephen M. "Michael Jackson Readies Video Rebuttal." *People*, February 12, 2003.

"Take Two: The Footage You Were Never Meant to See." Fox, February 20, 2003.

CHAPTER 2

An essential source for this chapter was Taraborrelli's *The Magic and the Madness*. Whether Taraborrelli was as familiar with the Jackson family during their rise to fame as he claims is something I can't know, but I've done my best to check his secondary sources and court files, which seem to have provided a great deal of his material. I'm grateful to Alison Weinflash for providing me with hard copies of every article about MJ that was ever published in *Rolling Stone*, dating back almost forty years. I found that Taraborrelli had been consistently accurate in his use of the information and quotations from the articles and court files I was able to access. In particular, he drew heavily on Katherine Jackson's first two divorce filings against Joe Jackson, in 1973 and 1982; the 1976 lawsuit against Berry Gordy and Motown in which MJ was the lead plaintiff; and the 1983 lawsuit filed against MJ by the Carlin Music Corporation. The Motown court file is especially rich with MJ's descriptions of his early life and career. I did disagree with Taraborrelli on several factual points, noted below. Taraborrelli and I both owe a considerable debt of gratitude to the work of his former colleague at *Soul* magazine, Judy Spiegelman (she was the reporter to whom ten-year-old MJ insisted he was eight).

I relied extensively on the quotations attributed to Michael in Rabbi Shmuley Boteach's *The Michael Jackson Tapes*. I am well aware of the controversy Rabbi Boteach's book has engendered but reject claims that Boteach invented quotes or tape-recorded MJ without his knowledge. Independent witnesses have assured me that Boteach collected many hours of tape recordings of Michael and that he did so with full consent. I believe in the accuracy of the recorded comments Boteach attributed to MJ and consider them to be, along with the tapes of MJ now in Howard Mann's possession, the most reliable record of what MJ remembered and believed—far more convincing, in my opinion, than what he wrote in his autobiography *Moonwalker*.

Among television productions, I want to single out the VH-1 documentary (hosted by Dave Walsh) *The Secret Childhood of Michael Jackson*, which featured many interviews and affectingly described the emotional damage done to MJ by his father.

Evelyn LeHaie, interviewed in the *Times of Northwest Indiana*, corrected Taraborrelli on a few points. LeHaie said the Big Top was a department store, not a grocery, where she was putting on a fashion show, for example; she also said the group was calling itself the Jackson Brothers by the time of that first gig and that she was the one who put on that first citywide talent show the group won a short time later.

MJ dancing to the washing machine/"Climb Ev'ry Mountain" anecdote (which Jermaine, to Larry King, placed at PTA meeting): Katherine Jackson's *My Family*. Tito's recollections, Etta James anecdote: Taraborrelli. MJ's description of Joe as father: his own words in Boteach, to Oprah Winfrey, and in tape-recorded interviews that now belong to Howard Mann. "He told me how to work the stage . . .": to Gerri Hirshey/*Rolling Stone*; "if you didn't do it the right way": MJ to Martin Bashir. Quotes from Michael ("I'd be sleeping . . ."/"It makes me shy . . .") re. the Jacksons's early career: MJ to Paul Theroux. "If I did a great show . . .": MJ's Oxford Union speech. Joe never telling MJ he was loved: Oxford Union speech, Boteach. MJ quote about staring out at the playground across the street: MJ to Boteach (p. 73). "They were so big . . .": KJ to Mark Bego. Gordon Keith's description of the Jackson 5's audition: interview on "Gordon Keith" Wikipedia entry, run by Katherine Jackson for verification. Motown/Gordy: As above, plus Raynoma Gordy Singleton.

COURT FILES

Civil

42680 (Los Angeles Superior Court) *Katherine Jackson v. Joseph Jackson*, March 9, 1973 (first divorce filing; hereafter cited as LASC 42680).

C139795 (Los Angeles Superior Court) *Michael Jackson et al. v. Motown Record Corporation of California et al.*, March 30, 1976 (hereafter cited as LASC C139795).

D076606 (Los Angeles Superior Court) *Katherine Jackson v. Joseph Jackson*, November 12, 1982 (second divorce filing; hereafter cited as LASC D076606).

C347206 (Los Angeles Superior Court) *Carlin Music Corporation v. Michael Jackson*, February 28, 1983 (hereafter cited as LASC C347206).

DOCUMENTS

Raw interview footage directed and provided to the author by Howard Mann, intending for *Stealing Michael Jackson*, a documentary that was never completed.

Ribera to Sullivan, 11/9/11.

Ribera to Sullivan, 11/13/11.

WIKIPEDIA

"Gordon Keith."

JOE JACKSON/UPBRINGING

Byrne, Bridget. "Michael Jackson." *Los Angeles Times Magazine*, October 1, 1987.

"Oprah Talks to Michael Jackson's Mother, Katherine, and Visits with His Children." oprah.com, November 8, 2010 (hereafter cited as Winfrey, "Katherine and children") (I).

Walsh, Dave, Walter Yetnikoff, Theresa Gonsalves, J. Randy Taraborrelli, et al. "Michael Jackson's Secret Childhood." VH-1, February 7, 2005 (hereafter cited as VH-1, "Secret Childhood") (RT).

White, Timothy. "The Man in the Mirror." *Penthouse*, March 1987.

Winfrey, Oprah. "Katherine Jackson–Oprah Interview." youtube.com, November 24, 2010.

——— "Michael Jackson Interview with Oprah: Parts 1–8." youtube.com, posted July 5, 2009. Interview took place February 10, 1993.

JACKSON 5/MICHAEL'S EARLY CAREER

Deavers, Melissa. "Valpo Resident Who Named Jackson Five Recalls Time with Michael." *Northwest Indiana Times*, June 28, 2009.

Fong-Torres, Ben. "The Jackson 5: The Men Don't Know but Little Girls Understand." *Rolling Stone*, April 29, 1971.

Hirshey, Gerri. "Michael Jackson—Life in the Magical Kingdom." *Rolling Stone*, February 1983 (hereafter cited as Hirshey 2/83).

"The Jackson Five." *Look*, August 25, 1970.

King, Larry. "Interview with Jermaine Jackson." *Larry King Live*, CNN, November 30, 2003 (RT).

Spiegelman, Judy. "A Close-Up of Jackie." *Soul*, June 15, 1970.

———. "Jackson Five Finish Concert Tour." *Soul*, October 1, 1971.

———. "Jackson Five vs. Osmond Brothers." *Soul*, March 22, 1971.

———. "Jermaine Jackson." *Soul*, July 13, 1970.

———. "The Many Sides of Tito Jackson." *Soul*, June 29, 1970.

———. "Marlon Jackson: To Know Him . . ." *Soul*, July 27, 1970.

———. "Michael and Marlon Tell All . . ." *Soul*, August 6, 1973.

———. "Toriano Jackson: His Many Moods." *Soul*, September, 1971.

———. "What Does the Future Hold for the Jackson Five?" *Soul*, February 14, 1972.

Theroux, Paul. "My Trip to Neverland, and the Call from Michael Jackson I'll Never Forget." *Daily Telegraph*, June 27, 2009 (hereafter cited as Theroux).

OBITUARIES AND RETROSPECTIVES

Boucher, Geoff, and Elaine Woo. "Michael Jackson: Michael Jackson's Life Was Infused with Fantasy and Tragedy." *Los Angeles Times*, June 26, 2009.
"Michael Jackson's Life and Legacy: The Eccentric King of Pop (1986–1999)." VH1.com, July 2, 2009.
Pareles, Jon. "Tricky Steps from Boy to Superstar." *New York Times*, June 26, 2009.
Shanahan, Mark, and Meredith Golstein. "Remembering Michael." *Boston Globe*, June 27, 2009.

CHAPTER 3

Interviews: AS1 described nearly every one of the events I've written about in this chapter. Additional interviews: Howard King (countersuit vs. Schaffel, audio tapes, Wiesner suit), Tohme (Sheikh Abdullah), Wiesner (his lawsuit). "The positive and the negative"/*Billy Elliot* quotes: Mark Lester to Elizabeth Sanderson. "Pretty tolerant of everybody": King. Abdullah on "He Who Makes the Sky Gray": Almezel/*Gulf News*. "Ladies toilet incident"/aftermath: AS1, Tohme, sources below. Tohme said he had a photo of MJ in his abaya but I never saw it. Death of Bill Bray/"cried alone in his room": AS1. *Segye Times* suit: court file, Taraborrelli, interview with Perry Sanders, details verified by Sandra Ribera. MJ not wanting to do the moonwalk at fifty: Wiesner.

COURT FILES

Civil

CV 90 4906 KN (United States District Court for the Central District of California) *Segye Times, Inc., v. Joseph Jackson, Katherine Jackson, Jackson Records Company, Inc., Jackson Family Concerts International, Jerome Howard, Kyu-Sun Choi, Mi Rae Choi, Michael Jackson, Jermaine Jackson, Bill Bray, and Ben Brown dba Jackson Marketing and Distributing Company,* October 17, 1990 (hereafter cited as USDC-CA CV 90 4906).
LASC SC083501.

DOCUMENTS

Ribera to Sullivan, 11/9/11.
Ribera to Sullivan, 11/13/11.
King to Sullivan, 2/1/10.

LONDON STAYOVER/MARK LESTER

"Michael Jackson Lawyer Rejects Mark Lester Claim He Is Paris' Father." *Daily Telegraph*, August 10, 2009.

Sanderson, Elizabeth. "Michael Jackson Asked If I Wanted to Be Blanket's Godfather: Friend Mark Lester Gives a Touching Insight into the Tortured Singer." *Daily Mail*, June 27, 2009 (hereafter cited as Sanderson).

Thompson, Jody. "Michael Jackson's Close Friend Mark Lester Says He's Spoken to the Star's Children Since His Death and 'They Are Fine.'" mirror.co.uk, June 29, 2009 (I).

SCHAFFEL/WIESNER/KING/ANTI-SEMITISM CHARGES

"ADL Demands Michael Jackson Apology." Associated Press, November 23, 2005 (I).

Hiscock, John. "The Baffling Case of Jacko, Gay Porn King and Bags of Cash." *Independent*, July 2, 2006.

Masters, Kim. "Michael Jackson's Strange Final Days Revealed in Dueling Lawsuits." *Hollywood Reporter*, July 19, 2012.

"Michael Jackson Admitted: 'I Took Painkiller Medication' in Lawsuit Evidence." *Daily Telegraph*, September 15, 2009.

"Michael Jackson Pleads for Money on Tapes." *Good Morning America*, ABC, November 22, 2005 (RT).

Riemenschneider, Chris. "Jackson Will Re-Record 'Care' Lyrics. Pop Music: Michael Jackson Apologizes and Says He Plans to Change the Words in 'They Don't Care About Us' That Some Considered to be Racial Slurs." *Los Angeles Times*, June 23, 1995.

Smith, Dinitia. "Jackson Plans New Lyrics for Album." *New York Times*, June 23, 1995.

———. "Michael Jackson Apologizes for Hurt Caused by Lyrics." *New York Times*, June 17, 1995.

Weinraub, Bernard. "In New Lyrics, Jackson Uses Slurs." *New York Times*, June 15, 1995.

———. "Jewish Response to Jackson." *New York Times*, June 16, 1995.

BAHRAIN/CHARITY RECORD/SHEIKH ABDULLAH

Al Mezel, Mohammad. "Michael Jackson Attends Dubai Desert Rally Awards Tuesday," *Gulf News*, November 14, 2005.

———. "Song Calling for World Peace to Be Launched." *Gulf News*, November 15, 2006.

Tumposky, Ellen. "Lawyer: Michael Jackson to Testify in His Defense in Lawsuit Filed by Prince of Bahrain." *New York Daily News*, November 20, 2008.

BILL BRAY

Friedman, Roger. "Jacko Loses Daddy No. 2." Fox News, November 16, 2005 (I).
"Thread—Michael, Bill Bray, Bob Jones: What Happened?" positivelymichael. com (I).
"Statement of Michael Jackson Regarding the Death of Mr. Bill Bray." MJPortal. com, November 19, 2005 (PR).

TOILET CROSS-DRESSING INCIDENT

Agarib, Amira. "Michael Jackson's Toilet Faux Pas in Dubai." khaleejtimesonline.com, November 13, 2005 (I).
"Caught in a Toilet: Arab Women Go Berserk Against Michael Jackson." *Evening Post*, November 15, 2005.
"Michael Jackson Caught Applying Makeup in Ladies Toilet." *Evening Post*, November 14, 2005.
"Michael Jackson to Build Mosque in His New Home of Dubai—Ladies Room Cross-Dressing Incident Leads to Demands He Be Jailed." militantislammonitor.org, November 27, 2009 (I).

CHAPTER 4

The famous speech at Oxford was written by Rabbi Boteach, as the rabbi ultimately acknowledged, "based on" his conversations with MJ. MJ's assertion that he never had a childhood was made many times, but I chose the one from the Oxford speech. Boteach and I exchanged a couple of e-mails, but never spoke.

KJ background, Jehovah's Witnesses, KJ and early Jackson 5: Taraborrelli, Mrs. Jackson's 1990 book, *The Jacksons—My Family*. "Kattie B. Screws": a source who did not want to be quoted by name. Michael/Jehovah's Witnesses: MJ's statements/writings, Beliefnet essay, MJ to Boteach. KJ and Joe/infidelity: Taraborrelli, Boteach, off-record sources. KJ "an abused woman": Sanders, Ribera. MJ young life on the road, strip clubs, etc., and parents ("the only person . . .", "would never touch me or hold me . . .", "I did not want to go", "Joseph," ". . . I will drop you like a hot potato"), Joe's beatings:

Boteach. Groupies: MJ to Oprah, KJ divorce filings, Taraborrelli, Tohme. MJ reading to the prostitutes from his Bible: *The Secret Childhood of Michael Jackson* (see Chapter 2 notes). Jacksons/Motown, move to CBS: Taraborrelli, Motown case file. MJ/lothario stories, O'Neal: Taraborrelli, *Secret Childhood of Michael Jackson* (see Chapter 2 notes). New York/Studio 54: as below, and my one visit to the club. I recommend the Web site lacienegasmiled. wordpress.com for reminiscences about MJ and photos of MJ. Destiny: Taraborrelli, court files in re. Motown and Carlin Music. MJ's sexuality/ gay rumors: interviews, including AS1, CS1, Schaffel, Wiesner, and Tohme; MJ to Boteach; Taraborrelli, *Secret Childhood* (see Chapter 2 notes), Oprah interview and accompanying articles. Quincy Jones quotes/*Off the Wall*: Jones *LA Times* essay, except "innocence": *Wall Street Journal*; "driven" and "determined": Haley/*Playboy*. According to Jones (in *LA Times*) he suggested that MJ should include "a black 'My Sharona' " on *Thriller* and MJ himself brought back "Beat It." Hiring of John Branca: Branca interviews in Taraborrelli. Hilburn remarks: his *LA Times* article. Condo: Schaffel, KJ advisor interviews. Gerri Hirshey's first article about MJ for *Rolling Stone* (see Chapter 2 notes) probably moved me more than anything I had ever read or heard about MJ up to that time; he opened up to her as he perhaps did to no other interviewer. Yetnikoff remarks: *Secret Childhood* (see Chapter 2 notes). Hayvenhurst: Hirshey (see Chapter 2 notes). La Toya on MJ working on *Thriller*, interview quoted by Taraborrelli. *Thriller*: Taraborrelli, esp. Branca interviews, *Playboy*, Jones/*LA Times*, Landis interview/*Daily Telegraph*; quotes from Swedien: interviews, Yetnikoff: Taraborrelli, Hoefflin: his Web site, except "three minutes": *Sun* interview. The Web site quotes may have been from an earlier interview but were not attributed. "Billie Jean"/groupies and Jones's wanting it off the album: 1996 MJ interview in Thailand, cited as rerun on MTV. MJ borrowing KJ's jacket: Jermaine, interviewed by Jimmy Fallon (see contactmusic.com cite). Leaving Jehovah's Witnesses: MJ (esp. Beliefnet essay), Jehovah's Witness publications, La Toya, Firpo Carr. MJ on "pioneering": Oxford Union speech; Cain and Abel, etc.: Boteach. KJ/birthday gifts: AS1, *Secret Childhood* (see Chapter 2 notes). MJ on loneliness, wandering the streets, approaching strangers, party life, Disneyland: quotes from Boteach. AS1 told me how MJ loved to ride the Pirates of the Caribbean attraction at Disneyland over and over, and about being led around the park through secret passageways by security staff. There's a marvelously weird "Michael Jackson Disneyland Sightings" folder at rhythmofthetide.com that includes much of this material.

Joe Jackson/"white help," MJ reply: *Billboard*. Joe's financial difficulties/ concealment of assets: CS1, 1982 divorce action, 1999 bankruptcy filing,

Tarraborrelli. JJ fired as manager: CS1. Frank Dileo: obituaries below, Tarabor-relli. I never spoke to Dileo; at almost the moment I reached out to him he lapsed into a coma. I did speak to his wife Linda, but that had to do with events surrounding the "This Is It" concerts, his health problems, and his relationship with John Branca.

Victory tour/KJ intervention: Taraborrelli, Mrs. Jackson's attorneys. Delsen-er and Cooley/crowd safety, Don King problems: *Rolling Stone* "Trouble in Paradise" article. Brooke Shields/tongue: AS1, La Toya/*Growing Up*. laciene-gasmiled.wordpress.com's Brooke Shields file contains nearly every word published on the relationship.

COURT FILES

Civil

LASC 42680.
LASC C139795.
LASC D076606.
LASC C347206.
05113 (Los Angeles Superior Court) *Petition to Nullify Marriage, Janet Dameta DeBarge*, January 30, 1985 (hereafter cited as LASC 05113).
D157554 (Los Angeles Superior Court) *Enid Jackson v. Sigmund E. Jackson (aka Jackie Jackson)*, January 8, 1986 (hereafter cited as LASC D157554).
D202224 (Los Angeles Superior Court) *Hazel Gordy Jackson v. Jermaine Jackson*, October 9, 1987 (hereafter cited as LASC D202224).
USDC-CA CV 90 4906.
LASC SC083501.

DOCUMENTS

Ribera to Sullivan, 11/9/11.
Ribera to Sullivan, 11/13/11.

JACKSON FAMILY/EARLY YEARS AT MOTOWN

"Can Michael Jackson's Demons Be Explained?" BBC, June 27, 2009 (RT).
Hilburn, Robert. "Michael Jackson: The Wounds, the Broken Heart." *LATimes. com*, June 27, 2009 (I) (hereafter cited as Hilburn, "The Wounds").
Jackson, Michael. "My Childhood, My Sabbath, My Freedom." Beliefnet, De-cember, 2000 (I).

MJ IN NEW YORK/*THE WIZ*/STUDIO 54

Canby, Vincent. "When Budgets Soar over the Rainbow." *New York Times,* November 26, 1978.

MJ'S DEVELOPMENT AS A SOLO ARTIST/*OFF THE WALL*

Fusilli, Jim. "Quincy Jones on How Michael Jackson Did It." *Wall Street Journal,* July 1, 2009.
Haley, Alex. "The Playboy Interview: Quincy Jones." *Playboy,* July 1990.
Jones, Quincy. "Quincy Jones on Michael Jackson: 'We Made History Together.'" *Los Angeles Times,* June 29, 2009.

THRILLER TIME/FRANK DILEO

"Bruce Swedien on *Thriller.*" *GearSlutz,* January, 2009.
Glentzer, Molly. "The Steps That Made Michael Jackson Great." *Houston Chronicle,* July 1, 2009.
Hillburn, Robert. "CBS Group President Walter Yetnikoff . . ." *Billboard,* July 21, 1984.
———. "An Interview with Quincy Jones . . ." *Billboard,* July 21, 1984.
———. "Manager Frank Dileo: Taking Care of Business . . ." *Billboard,* July 21, 1984.
———. "The Saga of Michael Jackson." *Billboard,* July 21, 1984.
"Michael Jackson Dances Alone." *Rolling Stone,* February 17, 1983.
"Michael Jackson Wore Mother's Jacket for Moonwalk Debut." *Contactmusic.com,* June 28, 2012.
Noland, Claire. "Frank Dileo Dies at 63; Michael Jackson's Manager." *Los Angeles Times,* August 25, 2011 (hereafter cited as Noland).
Pond, Steve. "Former Motown Stars Return for Birthday Bash." *Rolling Stone,* May 26, 1983.
Senior, Mike. "Bruce Swedien: Recording Michael Jackson, Legendary Engineer on *Thriller,*" *Sound on Sound,* November 2009.
Sisario, Ben. "Frank Dileo, Michael Jackson's Manager, Dies at 63." *New York Times,* August 24, 2011 (hereafter cited as Sisario 8/24/11).
"Three Minutes to Pen 'Billie.'" *The Sun,* July 26, 2009.
Vena, Jocelyn. "Michael Jackson Answers Fan Questions in 1996 Thailand Interview." mtv.com, July 6, 2009 (I).
Williams, Janette. "Michael Jackson Left Indelible Mark on Pasadena." *Whittier Daily News,* June 25, 2009.
———. "Michael Jackson Stopped the Party Cold." *USA Today,* April 11, 1984.

"THRILLER" VIDEO/JEHOVAH'S WITNESSES

Carr, Firpo. "Michael Jackson and Jehovah's Witnesses." *Los Angeles Sentinel*, July 23, 2009.

Lee, Marc. "Michael Jackson's Thriller, Interview with Director John Landis." *Daily Telegraph*, July 8, 2007 (hereafter cited as Lee, "Landis").

"Michael Jackson Interview." *Awake!* May 22, 1984.

VICTORY TOUR/DON KING/MJ'S SEPARATION FROM BROTHERS

Goldberg, Michael, and Christopher Connelly. "Trouble in Paradise." *Rolling Stone*, March 15, 1984.

Swertlow, Frank. "How Michael Jackson and Don King Get Along." *Los Angeles Herald Examiner*, March 3, 1984.

PEPSI SET ACCIDENT/BURNS

Cackler, Jaime. "Jackson's Burns Caused by Bad Timing." *Los Angeles Herald Examiner*, January 30, 1984.

Seiler, Michael. "Pop Star Michael Jackson Burned." *Los Angeles Times*, January 28, 1984.

Townsend, Dorothy. "Singer Michael Jackson Released . . ." *Los Angeles Times*, January 29, 1984.

Woodyard, Chris. "Michael Jackson Seriously Burned . . ." *Los Angeles Herald Examiner*, January 28, 1984.

Yorkin, Nicole. "Jackson Released from Burn Center." *Los Angeles Herald Examiner*, January 29, 1984.

Zoglin, Richard. "Too Much Risk on the Set?" *Time*, February 13, 1984.

ECCENTRICITIES/WACKO JACKO

McGrory, Mary. "Reagan Has Moves Michael Might Envy." *Los Angeles Times*, May 16, 1984.

"Why Michael Hid Out in a White House Men's Room, and Other Tales of the Day Power Played Host to Fame." *People*, May 28, 1984.

RODNEY ALLEN RIPPY

"Rodney Allen Rippy Talks About His Friend Michael Jackson." KABC–Los Angeles, June 26, 2009.

EMMANUEL LEWIS

Hall, Jane. "Emmanuel Lewis Got a Boost from Michael Jackson, but as Web-ster He Stands on His Own." *People*, April 9, 1984 (hereafter cited as Hall, "Emmanuel Lewis").

TATUM O'NEAL

"Michael Denies Sex Change; Says He Is Not Gay and Did Not Swim Nude with Tatum O'Neal." *Jet*, September 22, 1977.
Stern, Marlow. "Tatum O'Neal Opens Up." *Daily Beast*, June 14, 2011 (I).
"Tatum O'Neal Contradicts Jackson's Seduction Story." WCVB-TV, February 10, 2003 (RT).
"Tatum's Tell-All Teaser Released." *Sydney Morning Herald*, October 13, 2004.

BROOKE SHIELDS

"Archive for the '1981–1984 Brooke Shields' Category." lacienegasmiled. wordpress.com, December 21, 2009 (hereafter cited as lacienegasmiled. wordpress.com Brooke Shields) (I).

BAD/ALBUM, VIDEO, AND TOUR

DeCurtis, Anthony. "Michael Debuts His New Show in Kansas City." *Rolling Stone*, April 7, 1988.
Goldberg, Michael, and Christopher Connelly. "Is Michael for Real?" *Rolling Stone*, September 24, 1987.
Hilburn, Robert. "A Good—and Bad—Night." *Los Angeles Times*, March 4, 1988 (hereafter cited as Hilburn, "Good—and Bad—Night").
McKenna, Krista. "The Moonwalker's Strange Quest for Perfection." *Los Angeles Times*, November 6, 1988 (hereafter cited as McKenna).
Steigerwald, Bill. "Buckle Debacle." *Los Angeles Times*, November 8, 1987.

CHAPTER 5

MJ/ Sony Dubai meeting: AS2, who was involved, and AS1; O'Brien, Siklos (see Chapter 1 notes), Duhigg. Wilkinson and Crawford were the first to warn of MJ financial distress. "Psychologically shattered": Mesereau interview. ATV catalog acquisition: see Chapter 6. Paul McCartney: McCartney interview/ *Rolling Stone*; additional quotes: Jack Doyle/pophistorydig.com, Taraborrelli.

McCartney's role in acquisition of Beatles catalog: MTV McCartney biography, Letterman interview. MJ/Tommy Mottola/determination to hold on to Sony/ATV share: AS1 and AS2; Maureen Orth "Neverland CSI" article tells it similarly. "Jacko Bombshell" impact on MJ: AS1.

Bahrain/Christmas, Dubai, $250,000 from Abdullah, Cascio and Lester visits: AS1, court evidence/testimony before High Court, November 2008; including Grace Rwaramba account, Lester interviews. Frank Cascio/pranking: Boteach; water-balloon fights: *VIBE*. "Mounting impatience," 2 Seas Records, Katrina song: High Court trial in London, AS1 and AS2, Tohme. Abdullah quotes: Linda Deutsch/Associated Press interview with MJ/Abdullah. This was MJ's only interview with a U.S. journalist during his time in Bahrain; Tohme and Mesereau both told me that MJ was rewarding her for treating him fairly during his criminal trial.

Orlando: AS1. David Siegel quotes: "The Timeshare Authority" interview; he didn't respond to my request for an interview. Jane Carter quote: Bryan Burrough's "Mad About the Boys," the comprehensive account of Lou Pearlman's fall. Orlando was among the few of MJ's movements not described by the "Michael Jackson Timeline," an indication to me that MJ was keeping it on the down low. Pearlman said he was "negotiating" a deal with MJ that seemed to involve a good deal more than the Katrina record (Pearlman local Orlando TV interview), but I relied mainly upon AS1 in reporting that MJ left Florida quickly after getting wind of the Pearlman investigation.

Abdullah quotes on MJ's return to Bahrain: High Court testimony. Legacy of "We Are the World": AS1, Wiesner. "A black hole for Michael watchers": Hirshey, "The Sound of One Glove Clapping." Yetnikoff quote: *The Secret Childhood of Michael Jackson* (see Chapter 2 notes). Other "We Are the World" sources below; the anecdote about MJ needing a young friend to tell him who Michael Jordan is: Bob Jones, *The Man Behind the Mask*.

SONY/DUBAI MEETING/REFINANCING OF DEBT

Crawford, Krysten. "Michael Jackson to Lose Beatles Catalog?" *Money*, May 5, 2005.

Duhigg, Charles. "Michael Jackson Advisors Try to Stave Off Default." *Los Angeles Times*, December 21, 2005.

O'Brien, Timothy. "What Happened to the Fortune Michael Jackson Made?" *New York Times*, May 14, 2006 (hereafter cited as O'Brien).

Orth, Maureen. "C.S.I. Neverland." *Vanity Fair*, July 2005 (hereafter cited as Orth 7/05).

Wilkinson, Peter. "Is the King of Pop Going Broke?" *Rolling Stone*, April 25, 2002.

ATV CATALOG/PAUL McCARTNEY

Doyle, Jack. "Michael and McCartney." *Pophistorydig.com*, July 7, 2009 (I).

Hilburn, Robert. "The Long and Winding Road." *Los Angeles Times*, September 22, 1985 (hereafter cited as Hilburn, "Long and Winding Road").

McCartney, Paul, interviewed by David Letterman. *Late Show with David Letterman*. CBS, July 15, 2009 (RT).

"Paul McCartney Biography." MTV, March 3, 2009 (RT).

White, Timothy. "Paul McCartney: A Backstage Look at His U.S. Tour." *Rolling Stone*, January 8, 1990.

BAHRAIN/SHEIKH ABDULLAH/HURRICANE KATRINA
SONG/CHRISTMAS GATHERING

Bain, Raymone. "Michael Jackson Statement on Drug Overdose Rumors." December 10, 2005 (PR) (hereafter cited as Bain, "Overdose Rumors").

Basnett, Guy. "I'm the Real Father of Michael Jackson's Girl, Claims Mark Lester." *News of the World*, August 9, 2009.

Butterfield, Alan. "Jacko Bombshell." *National Enquirer*, December 9, 2005 (hereafter cited as Butterfield, "Bombshell").

Deutsch, Linda. "Six Months Later, Jackson's Katrina Song Ready." Associated Press, February 17, 2006.

"Jackson's Katrina Song Said to Be Ready." *Billboard.com*, June 23, 2007 (I). Sanderson.

"Unbreakable: Michael Jackson Interview." *VIBE*, March 2002.

Winfrey, "How the Cascios." (RT)

Winfrey, "Secret Friendship" (RT)

ORLANDO VISIT/LOU PEARLMAN

"Boy Band Founder to Plead Guilty in $300M Suit." Associated Press, March 4, 2008.

Burrough, Bryan. "Mad About the Boys." *Vanity Fair*, November 2007.

"Jackson Considered Moving to Orlando." *Fox News 13*, June 27, 2009 (RT).

Tremblay, Jason. "Orlando Timeshare Developer Played Landlord to Michael Jackson." *Timeshare Authority*, July 3, 2009.

"WE ARE THE WORLD"

Hillburn, Robert. "Behind the Scene of a Pop Miracle." *Los Angeles Times*, March 24, 1985.

Hirshey, Gerri. "The Sound of One Glove Clapping." *Rolling Stone*, January 1986.
Loder, Kurt, and Michael Goldberg. "Inside the USA for Africa Sessions." *Rolling Stone*, March 28, 1985.

CHAPTER 6

Break from Quincy Jones: confidential sources, Jones–Katie Couric interview; from Dileo: confidential sources, Taraborrelli, Dileo obituaries. Snake anecdote: Dileo interview in Taraborrelli. John Branca: Hilburn/". . . equally as brilliant (see Chapter 1 notes)," Taraborrelli, for whom Branca was a major source. Acquisition of the Beatles catalog: Hilburn, Knoedelseder/*LA Times*, Branca *California Lawyer* profile (from which Branca quotes come), Taraborrelli, other sources as below. Sony/ATV letters in "Documents" (confirm cause and nature of agreement under which MJ and Sony exchanged majority/minority positions in the deal, and Branca as main MJ-Sony liaison until 2003 dismissal): Joe Jackson's suit against the executors of the Michael Jackson estate. Quotes from Branca ("Part of him may be a ten-year-old . . ."), Dileo ("a cross between ET and Howard Hughes"): 1980s interviews quoted by Taraborrelli from a British newspaper. Neverland Ranch purchase: Taraborrelli. Description of Neverland: Santa Barbara County Sheriff's department video. *Dangerous LA Times* quote: Chris Willman; Ron Wilcox Sony quote: 1991 Hilburn/Phillips *LA Times* article.

Michael's financial transactions, amassing and squandering wealth: Avram lawsuit, press coverage, esp. Siklos (see Chapter 1 notes), O'Brien (see Chapter 5 notes), Orth. Schaffel quote: interview. MJ on Chandler scandal: Boteach. For the Chandler affair generally see Chapter 16 and its source notes. Dan Beck quote: O'Brien/*New York Times* (see Chapter 5 notes). Sony/ATV renegotiation/expansion: AS2, CS2, Tohme, Hawk, Mann, Sanders; Joe Jackson suit against estate executors; un-bylined *Rolling Stone*, the *New York Times*, and *Jet* articles; TheWrap.com series on MJ/Branca. Film/video projects: AS2, CS2, Schaffel, Wiesner; MJ to Boteach; O'Brien (see Chapter 5 notes), Day. Loan refinancing agreements: Avram case file, with Myung Ho Lee interviews and additional info from Orth "Losing His Grip." These renegotiated loans also constituted a major point of discussion on talks I had with two attorneys who were considering filing lawsuits against John Branca and the Michael Jackson estate.

Al Malnik quotes: deposition in the Avram lawsuit. Boteach on MJ's extravagance: *The Michael Jackson Tapes* (p. 30). Celebrity Costumes bill:

evidence in Avram lawsuit. $75,000 perfume: Fragrance Depot Web site (not known whether the purchase definitely occurred or he merely allowed it to be reported). Purchases and nonpayments: Orth, from Avram trial evidence. Description as "bizarre" of projects introduced by MJ's advisors including Wiesner/Konitzer: Malnik deposition. Wiesner and his former associate Ronald Konitzer obviously do not agree with suggestions that they took advantage of MJ financially. Dieter emphatically denied it to me in an interview, and neither man has ever been charged with any crime in connection to their involvement with MJ. Michael LaPerruque: Gerald Posner, police investigators in Santa Barbara County. Joey Jeszeck and Chris Carter: Posner, based mainly on information from *People v. Jackson*; Jeszeck's and Carter's interviews with investigators are part of the court file. Chris Carter: Las Vegas daily newspapers, via Posner's "Jackson's Shady Inner Circle," *People v. Jackson* court file, coroner's and LAPD investigations included in *People v. Murray*. Backerman quotes: the *Sun* (of London). Backerman forced out by the Nation of Islam: Schaffel. Avram trial info and forensic accountant's report: the court file. Schaffel's quotes: interviews; Dieter Wiesner confirmed the story of money advanced at the casino in Las Vegas.

COURT FILES

Civil

BD 497718 (Santa Barbara County Superior Court) *Marcel Avram v. Michael Jackson*, June 14, 2000.

DOCUMENTS

"RE: Operating Agreement." Letter from Michael Jackson to Sony/ATV Publishing LLC. November 7, 1995.
"RE: Representation of Michael Jackson and Sony/ATV Music Publishing LLC." Letter from John Branca to Sony/ATV Music Publishing LLC. August 14, 2002 (hereafter cited as Branca to Sony/ATV, 8/14/02).
Singer to Branca, 9/10/02.

BEATLES CATALOG/SONY-ATV

Brown, Mick. "Michael Jackson, Death by Show Business." *Daily Telegraph*, June 27, 2009.
Hillburn. "Long and Winding Road."

Knoedelseder, William. "Beatles Song Catalogue Acquired." *Los Angeles Times*, August 15, 1985.

"Michael Jackson and Sony Enter Joint Publishing Venture Valued at $600 million." *Jet*, November 27, 1995.

"Michael Jackson Buys Rights to Eminem Tunes and More." *Rolling Stone*, May 31, 2007.

"Michael Jackson Sells Beatles Songs to Sony." *New York Times*, November 8, 1995.

Sinberg.

QUINCY JONES, FRANK DILEO, JOHN BRANCA, AND DAVID GEFFEN

Couric, Katie. "Quincy Jones: 'I Miss My Little Brother.'" CBS News, July 8, 2009 (RT).

Grover, Ronald. "David Geffen Tries Out a New Act." *Business Week*, June 29, 1992.

Noland.

Rosenfield, Paul. "David Is Goliath." *Vanity Fair*, March, 1991.

Roberts, Johnnie L. "Michael Jackson Nearly Lost His Prized Music Catalog." The Wrap, December 5, 2010. (I).

Sisario 8/24/11.

CAREER/DECLINE

Christgau, Robert. "Michael Jackson Albums Review." robertchristgau.com (I).

Goldberg, Michael. "Michael Jackson: The Making of the King of Pop." *Rolling Stone*, January 9, 1992.

Hirshey, Gerri. "Michael Jackson." *Rolling Stone*, June 11, 1992.

Harrington, Richard. "Jackson's 'Dangerous' Departures; Stylistic Shifts Mar His First Album in 4 Years." *Washington Post*, November 24, 1991.

Orth, Maureen. "Losing His Grip." *Vanity Fair*, April 2003 (hereafter cited as Orth 4/03).

Pareles, Jon. "Michael Jackson in the Electronic Wilderness." *New York Times*, November 24, 1991.

Stevenson, Richard W. "'Thriller,' Can Michael Jackson Beat It?" *New York Times*, November 10, 1991.

Willman, Chris. "Michael Jackson's 'Dangerous': Michael Jackson Serves Up Something for Everyone in His Relatively Tame—and Wildly Unfocused— New Album." *Los Angeles Times*, November 24, 1991.

WEALTH/SPENDING/FINANCIAL EXCESS AND DEBT

Day, Elizabeth. "Off the Wall, but Still Invincible." *Guardian*, March 8, 2009 (hereafter cited as Day, "Off the Wall").

Hillburn, Robert, and Chuck Philips. "Sony Deal Will Give Jackson Big Share of His Own Success." *Los Angeles Times*, June 18, 1991.

Leeds, Jeff, and Andrew Ross Sorkin. "Michael Jackson Bailout Said to Be Close." *New York Times*, April 13, 2006 (hereafter cited as Leeds and Sorkin).

"$100,000 Michael Jackson the King of Pop Fragrance." *Fragrance Depot*, October 8, 1998 (I).

Posner, Gerald. "Jackson's Shady Inner Circle." *Daily Beast*, July 10, 2009 (I) (hereafter cited as Posner, "Inner circle").

———. "Michael's Missing Millions." *Daily Beast*, August 2, 2009 (I) (hereafter cited as Posner "Missing Millions").

OTHER

Boucher, Geoff. "To Michael Jackson on his 45th Birthday." *Los Angeles Times*, September 1, 2003.

"Michael Jackson Adviser Says Nation of Islam Took Over His Life." *Sun*, July 7, 2009.

CHAPTER 7

Sheikh Abdullah's displeasure: AS1, Tohme's account of visit to Bahrain, Sheikh Abdullah and Grace Rwaramba testimony at the High Court trial. Trip to Germany: AS1.

Anton Glanzelius/Sweden material and quotes: Glanzelius *Göteborgs-Posten* interview. Schleiter stay, Wolfgang Schleiter: AS1, Friedman. MJ/Germany generally: Wiesner, Kloth. Italy and London: AS1. Mesereau's resignation as MJ's attorney: interviews, plus press release. MJ's return to Bahrain: AS1, testimony at the High Court trial, Tohme. Chris Tucker quote: *Playboy*. Tony Buzan/mind mapping: AS1, Buzan in UK press, payment information from High Court case. Buzan's quotes: unbylined *Sunday Times* article "The extraordinary life of Michael Jackson's children." Manama airport/OxyContin: AS1, *Sunday Times*. Abdullah (with Jermaine Jackson's encouragement) pushing 2 Seas deal signing: AS1, AS2, Tohme; quotes and specific info: press release. MJ-Abdullah strained conversations: AS1, Tohme; Rwaramba to Barak (see Chapter 1 notes);

testimony at High Court trial. MJ's complaints about shuttling from property to property: Rwaramba to Barak. Second deposition in London: Schaffel, King. Departure from Bahrain for Japan: Abdullah and Rwaramba testimony at High Court trial.

BAHRAIN/ABDULLAH

Fleming, Michael. "Playboy Interview: Chris Tucker." *Playboy*, August, 2007. Leeds and Sorkin.
"Thomas Mesereau Releases Statement." February 24, 2006 (PR).
"Raymone Bain Releases Statement." March 17, 2006 (PR).

GERMANY/THE ANTONS

Friedman, Roger. "Jackson Staying at Home of Wolfgang Schleiter." Fox News, January 30, 2006 (I).
"Interview with MJ's Former Pal, Anton Glanzelius of *My Life as a Dog* Fame." *Göteborgs-Posten*, June 27, 2009.
Kloth, Hans Michael. "Deutschland's King of Pop." *Spiegel Online*, June 29, 2009 (I).
"Michael Jackson Visits Germany." *Hello!* January 30, 2006.

TONY BUZAN/MIND MAPPING

"The Extraordinary Life of Michael Jackson's Children." *Sunday Times*, September 13, 2009.

CHAPTER 8

MJ beloved in Japan: AS1, AS2, CS1, and below. Kabuki: AS1 and CS1 on educated Japanese seeing MJ as a sort of global Kabuki performer, Deborah White blog, research on role-playing in "young man Kabuki." Brunei stopover: Tohme told me that MJ's visit "was not that big a deal" to the Brunei royal family. Abdullah/representatives unreturned calls: High Court trial. American in music business whispering in Abdullah's ear: Tohme, based on statements from Sheikh Abdullah's people in Manama. MJ's possessions sent to the hotel, stay in Manama: Tohme, AS1, Rwaramba to Barak (see Chapter 1 notes). Money and jewelry left behind: Tohme and Dennis Hawk, from their trip to Manama. Visit to Europe: AS1 and Rwaramba. Departure from Bahrain, relocation to Europe, Raymone Bain's elevation to business manager: AP's "Jackson fires business managers" and press release it was based on.

Tracking MJ's six-month-long stay in Ireland (interrupted by a ten-day foray to New York that I left out of the narrative) was made difficult for two main reasons. One was obfuscatory press releases that the media (*Ebony* in particular) swallowed whole. The other was that the media proved even more susceptible to the story that MJ spent his time in Ireland "mooching" off Michael Flatley, as Roger Friedman reported it. The *Daily Mirror*'s "CRAIC-O JACKO" was the story that stated MJ would attend the Bob Dylan concert. Blackwater Castle rumor: blogger James Galvin. Blackwater Castle stay: Liam Sheehan, Patrick Nordstrom 2009 press interviews, Blackwater Web site; Nordstrom was caring for a wife dying of cancer and could not be interviewed. Leprechaun theme park quote: *Daily Mirror*; AS1 told me that MJ really did believe in leprechauns, or at least encouraged his children to do so. Tensions between MJ and Grace, antique buying in Florence: AS1, Rwaramba to Barak. Debbie Rowe–MJ relationship: Marc Schaffel, AS1, AS2, Bob Jones book, Lisa Marie Presley interviews. Confidentiality agreement, Rowe's concerns about children: Iris Finsilver declaration on the Smoking Gun Web site. Jones quotes on birth of Prince and Paris: his book. Rowe-Jackson prenuptial agreement: court records; payment: "reported," though Katherine Jackson used the same figure. MJ-Rowe disputes and resolution: AS2, who has direct knowledge; resulting MJ-Grace disagreements: AS1. "Abducted" claim, other quotes re. custody dispute: court documents. Sheehan told me he had no idea the custody dispute was ongoing while he was living in the same home with MJ. He was also the first to tell me what a dedicated father MJ had been, something I hadn't known and which was repeated again and again by other people. I think it was immediately after talking to Sheehan that I decided my magazine article was going to become a book.

DOCUMENTS

"Declaration of Iris Joan Finsilver." February 3, 2005.

JAPAN

Masters, Coco. "Big in Japan: Tokyo Mourns Jackson's Death." *Time*, June 26, 2009 (hereafter cited as Masters. "Big in Japan").

Kageyama, Yuri. "Michael Jackson Had Loyal, Generous Fans in Japan." Associated Press, June 26, 2009 (hereafter cited as Kageyama).

White, Deborah. "Michael Jackson as Kabuki Theater." thecrazywoman.com, July 5, 2009 (I).

PARIS

"Michael Jackson Fires Business Managers." Associated Press, June 27, 2006.
 "Michael Jackson en Disneyland Paris." flickr.com, June 17, 2006 (I).
"Michael Jackson Visits Paris Garden." justjared.com, June 23, 2006 (I).

IRELAND ARRIVAL/DYLAN/FLATLEY

Burnhill, Eleanor. "CRAIC-O JACKO; Superstar and Kids Jet into Ireland for
    Bob Dylan Gig." *Daily Mirror*, June 24, 2006.
"Jacko Is in Cork." jamesgalvin.com, June 24, 2006 (I).

BLACKWATER CASTLE

Browne, Bill. "Jackson's Cork Hideaway." *Corkman*, July 2, 2009.
Kelleher, Olivia. "'He Just Wanted the Best for His Children.'" (*Irish*) *Inde-
    pendent*, June 29, 2009.
McCarthy, Louise. "Magic Tricks with Michael Jackson and His Kids." *Cork-
    man*, July 2 2009.
Martin, Paul. "Leprechaun Land; You'll Never Believe It but Wacko Jacko Is
    Planning a Theme Park Full of Celtic Myths and Legends Called . . ." *Daily
    Mirror*, September 15, 2006.

GRACE RWARAMBA/DEBBIE ROWE

Heath, Chris. "Lisa Marie Presley." *Rolling Stone*, April 20, 2003 (hereafter
    cited as Heath, "Lisa Marie Presley").
"*Playboy* Interview: Lisa Marie Presley." *Playboy*, August 2003 (hereafter cited
    as *Playboy*, "Lisa Marie Presley").

CHAPTER 9

Schaffel v. Jackson: Schaffel, King, Mesereau, who had previously represented
MJ in the matter; juror quote: unbylined UPI articles; Bain and McMillan
remarks: Bain press release; King quotes: interviews. Ballinacurra: AS1, Des
McGahan press interviews and his Web site; MJ "dancin' on the grass": *Independent* interview.
    Luggala: AS1. Neverland fire: press release/Raymone Bain. Puppet theater
outing: Eugene Lampert to *Sligo Champion*. Grouse Lodge: AS1; Paddy Dunning press interviews; unfortunately, Dunning would not give me an interview.
Important detail including Grace Rwaramba's scouting expedition, arrival at

Grouse Lodge, attempt to keep his stay secret (including Dunning's "Yeah, so is Elvis Presley" remark), the Elvis wax statue in the woods, protective attitude of local farmers: Luke Bainbridge, the *Guardian*. Will.i.am/"apple picking": to starpulse.com. Other comments of artists and producers: "What's the Scoop on Michael Jackson's New Album?" (collected from dozens of publications and press conferences). Thanks much, R.J. Dr. Patrick Treacy: Mesereau, who recounted a phone conversation with Treacy; Treacy quotes: web interviews; acknowledgment he/his clinic gave MJ propofol during a procedure: interview with Deborah Kunesh, Catherine Gross, CastTV. Treacy insisted to Kunesh that MJ understood that he couldn't use propofol without an anesthesiologist and "would never have done so." Supposed photos of MJ in the south of France: AS1, Bain interview for *Stealing Michael Jackson*; *Daily News*, MJ/Bain response: entertainmentwise.com. Billy Bush/dialogue between MJ and camera operator: Gawker. Insomnia/recording machine with three clocks: Todd Gray interviews posted on amazon.com, Essence.com, Huffington Post. Frank Cascio's gathering up MJ's prescription drugs at night: Cascio to ABC News. MJ–Lisa Marie Presley letter about not sleeping for four days: Lucina Fisher/ABC; the letter came to light when Julien Auctions placed it up for bid in early 2012. When Lisa Marie protested, Darren Julien agreed not to sell it after all.

I'll have to be careful what I write about my knowledge of MJ's propofol use. I can say with certainty that he was using it on the HIStory tour. Dieter Wiesner was the only one who told me that on the record, though, and didn't want to say the name of the doctor who was providing it to MJ. An anonymous source did name a doctor, one who has been the subject of investigation since MJ's death. A second anonymous source told me that the propofol was provided by a pair of German anesthesiologists Wiesner had hired. As noted, Wiesner emphatically denied this. Schaffel and Wiesner both talked to me about the lengths to which MJ went to get some sleep, and of course a great deal of that information came out in connection to the criminal charges and trial of Dr. Conrad Murray. AS1, though, told me the most about this.

Bedsores: AS1, MJ autopsy report. MJ more free of drugs in Ireland than in years: AS1, Mesereau, Patrick Treacy interviews and MJ's hosts' insistence that he did not seem to be on drugs. Tullamore story: The [Irish] *Independent*. Anxiety about World Music Awards: AS1, Raymone Bain, and Patrick Treacy.

DOCUMENTS

Autopsy Case Report—Case No. 2009-04415, *Jackson, Michael Joseph*, Los Angeles County Department of Coroner. June 25, 2009 (hereafter cited as Autopsy, 6/25/09).

SCHAFFEL V. JACKSON

"Accusations Fly in Lawsuit Against Jackson." UPI, July 12, 2006.

Caldwell, Tanya. "Jury Views Jackson Deposition in Lawsuit." *Los Angeles Times*, July 7, 2006.

Deutsch, Linda. "Michael Jackson's Frantic Messages Played." Associated Press, July 6, 2006.

Hong, Peter Y. "Trial Delves into Odd Finances of Pop Star." *Los Angeles Times*, July 12, 2006.

"Raymone Bain Releases Statement Regarding Trial Against Schaffel." July 15, 2006 (PR).

"Two Jackson Personalities Emerge in Suit." UPI, June 30, 2006.

BALLINACURRA HOUSE

Carty, Ed. "Irish Trip Revealed Down-to-Earth Family Man." (*Irish*) *Herald*, June 27, 2009.

"Fit for a King of Pop: Family's Luxury Hideaway." (*Irish*) *Independent*, June 27, 2009.

Fitzpatrick, Tom. "Mary Recalls Day Michael and His Three Kids Visited Her Kinsale Shop." *Evening Echo*, June 27, 2009.

WICKLOW CASTLE

Bain, Raymone. "Fire Engulfs Neverland Valley Ranch." August 28, 2006 (PR).
———. "Michael Jackson Takes on Legal Conspiracy." August 8, 2006 (PR).

Gray, Jim. "Jackson Was a 'Down to Earth, Doting Father' Recalls Sligo Puppeteer." *Sligo Champion*, July 1, 2009.

"Michael Jackson to Buy Wicklow Castle." *Hot Press*, September 18, 2007.

Woollard, Deidre. "Michael Jackson in Retreat at Irish Castle." *Luxist.com*, September 2, 2006 (I).

GROUSE LODGE/COMEBACK ALBUM/INSOMNIA

Aughey, Olga. "Paddy Dunning Talks of the Famous Grouse." *Westmeath Examiner*, April 28, 2009.

Bainbridge, Luke. "Michael Jackson's Irish Hideaway." *Guardian*, August 14, 2010.

"Billy Bush Seduced by Michael Jackson's 'B' Game." *Gawker.com*, October 16, 2006 (I).

Bush, Billy. "The Return of the King of Pop." *Access Hollywood*, November 2, 2006 (RT).

"Creepy Michael Jackson Dresses as a Woman." *New York Daily News*, October 11, 2006.

Fisher, Lucina. "Michael Jackson's Sleepless Letter to Lisa Marie Presley." abcnews.go.com, May 30, 2012 (I).

Friedman, Roger. "Who's Funding Jackson's Retreat to Irish Recording Studio?" Fox News, October 21, 2006 (I).

Gray, Todd. "Michael Jackson's Photographer Todd Gray Shares Intimate Moments with the King of Pop." *Essence.com*, October 27, 2009 (I).

"King of Pop Felt at Home in Westmeath's Grouse Lodge." *Westmeath Independent*, July 2, 2009.

Lee, Chris. "Pop King's Planning His Return." *Los Angeles Times*, October 1, 2006.

"Michael Jackson's Irish Retreat for Rent." *Irish Times*, June 6, 2010.

"Michael Jackson Spotted in Tullamore Centre." *(Irish) Independent*, October 28, 2006.

Monroe, Brian. "A Q & A with Michael Jackson: In His Own Words." *Ebony*, December 2007.

"A Q & A with Todd Gray, Author of *Michael Jackson: Before He Was King*." Amazon.com (I).

R.J. "What's the Scoop on Michael Jackson's New Album?" michaeljacksonbeat.blogspot.com, April 22, 2009 (I) (hereafter cited as "What's the Scoop").

Topel, Fred. "Will.i.am Goes Apple Picking with Michael Jackson." starpulse.com, May 4, 2009 (I).

"Will.i.am on Working with Michael Jackson." *Rolling Stone*, September 24, 2007.

"You Docs: Propofol Probably Not a Factor in Michael Jackson's Death." Syndicated column, July 15, 2009.

PATRICK TREACY/DUBLIN

Gross, Rev. Catherine. "A Place in Your Heart: Interview with Patrick Treacy." blogtalkradio.com, September 24, 2010 (RT).

Kunesh, Deborah. "The Michael I Knew . . . Patrick Treacy Shares His Reflections on Michael Jackson." reflectionsonthedance.com, 2010 (I).

"Patrick Treacy on Michael Jackson's Death." *CastTV*, June 26, 2009 (RT).

WIKIPEDIA

"Anterograde Amnesia."

"Propofol."

CHAPTER 10

1988 visit to London: contemporaneous coverage; coverage alongside 1996 Brit Awards; coverage in 2009. I also used interviews, coverage related to 2006 World Music Awards appearance. 1988 Guildhall dinner: Paul Cole, *Sunday Mercury*; original research. *Bad* tour: press coverage of Japanese and Australian legs, esp. the *Age*; Hilburn and McKenna/*LA Times* (see Chapter 4 notes), Pareles/*NY Times*, Frith/*Village Voice* (posthumous publication). MJ's weirdness due to curiosity: my own interpretation, but his mother, at least, agrees with it. Skid Row: Gina Sprague (Joe's secretary), to Taraborrelli. Antiques store incident: Atlanta Police Department "deputy" to Taraborrelli. "Daringly thin disguise": Hirshey/*Rolling Stone* (see Chapter 2 notes). MJ on disguises/"Pioneering": Beliefnet essay, Boteach (p. 104). David Foster story: *Hit Man*. "Bizarre" image: Frank Dileo press interviews, Taraborrelli. Jimmy Safechuck: Taraborrelli. More than fifteen years later, Bob Jones and his cowriter Stacy Brown attempted to retroactively infer impropriety from Jones's claims that MJ remained financially generous to boys like Jimmy Safechuck and Jonathan Spence. More recently, blogger Desiree Hill has undertaken to prove that MJ's relationship with Safechuck and other boys was somehow sinister. She's done a good job of pointing out the inconsistencies in La Toya Jackson's recent disavowals of the claims she made against her brother in *Growing Up Jackson*, but her other contentions are not persuasive. At the criminal trial in 2005, Tom Mesereau told the jury that Jimmy Safechuck had been married at Neverland. In his conversations with me, Tom was unable to recall where he had heard that. Based on what I've been told by sources I can't identify, I don't think it's true. But again, there is no evidence that Safechuck ever accused MJ of any improprieties.

Emmanuel Lewis relationship: VH-1/*Secret Childhood* (inc. interviews w/ Rippy, George; see Chapter 2 notes); also, Bashir/*Secret Life of Michael Jackson*, Lewis to Howard Stern, Taraborrelli. In each of the few instances he has spoken about this on the record, Lewis has insisted that there was no sexual contact of any kind. "All we did was watch comedy and cartoons," he told Bashir. "Could anything negative happen between the two of us? The answer to that question is hell no!!" Baby bottles and nipples: *The Man Behind the Mask*; photo: *In Touch*, March 2005. 1984 public perception of Lewis relationship: *People* article about Lewis (see Chapter 4 notes). Alfonso Ribeiro/Ricky Schroeder relationships: VH-1/*Secret Childhood* (see Chapter 2 notes). Again, there have been no suggestions of impropriety by either of them, as boys or men. Corey Feldman has given two very different descriptions of his relationship with MJ, one in 2003 to Larry King, the second in 2005 to Martin Bashir. He has since come back around to a pro-MJ position. Seven Dwarfs at Hayvenhurst: Taraborrelli, *Secret Childhood* (see Chapter 2 notes).

Brooke Shields/"no big romance": Shields to Joan Rivers, others in lacienegasmiled.com file (see Chapter 4 notes). MJ/Rivers sparring, "Boy George" press conference: Taraborrelli, my own recollection. MJ himself continued to perpetuate the myth of hot and heavy romances with Shields and O'Neal into the twenty-first century. In his interviews with Boteach, he called Shields "one of the loves of my life" and O'Neal "my first girlfriend." Suggestion MJ should play Peter Pan: Jane Fonda to Gerri Hirshey. MJ on Shirley Temple (incl. quotes used): Boteach.

Elizabeth Taylor's relationship with MJ was very real, as unlikely as it seemed to some people. Sources: Taraborrelli, MJ to Boteach, Theroux/*Daily Telegraph* (see Chapter 2 notes), Marikar/ABC. MJ/real estate agent: Dimond/*Be Careful Who You Love*. Taylor at *Victory* tour concert, first meeting w/Bubbles: MJ/other sources to Taraborrelli (rev. ed.). Liz and MJ incognito moviegoing: Theroux (see Chapter 2 notes), AS1. Picnic spot: Theroux (see Chapter 2 notes). Taylor giving elephant Gypsy to MJ: Schaffel; video from *Home Movies* project; MJ's return gift: Theroux (see Chapter 2 notes). "Michael did a lot more giving": AS1, CS1, pleadings and evidence in *Schaffel v. Jackson*. Wedding at Neverland: *People*. Shrine to Taylor: reported as *National Enquirer* in other outlets, orig. story not found. Debunking of shrine story: Frank Dileo to *People*, Schaffel. Liz, MJ, red string: msnbc.com among others. Role of drug use in Taylor/MJ relationship: Taraborrelli/*Elizabeth*, Posner/*Daily Beast*. Thousand prescriptions: Taraborrelli ("In the five-year period between 1980 and 1985, she was given prescriptions for more than a thousand different drugs ranging from sleeping pills to painkillers to tranquilizers.") Posner quoted a "good friend" of MJ's who said he had warned MJ that his relationship with Liz was "toxic"; "teetering": Posner, per "a witness" at the 1993 American Music Awards. Elizabeth Taylor herself acknowledged her problems with prescription drugs, but was never so specific. I heard a good deal about this subject from AS1, but that information was mostly secondhand. MJ going straight from Klein's offices to Taylor's home during 2007–2008 LA visits; presumption they were sharing drugs; Klein response: AS1; Ben Evenstad, head of paparazzi agency National Photo Group, to Posner; Craig Williams; Klein has admitted to prescribing Demerol and turned over documents to the medical board showing when and how much.

MJ's ideal woman a fusion of Mother Teresa and Princess Diana is something he spoke about frequently, including to Boteach. MJ told Boteach how turned off he was by hard or coarse women, such as Madonna (cf. his description of Taylor to Theroux, see Chapter 2 notes). KJ "like a saint," Taylor "playful and youthful," ". . . if we ever did anything romantically . . .": MJ to Boteach. Captain EO set: firsthand from Todd Gold/*People*, Taraborrelli. Jonathan Spence/ MJ never acting inappropriately: Mesereau, court file. Gifts to Spence: Dimond/*Be Careful*, court file. Rolls-Royce to Jimmy Safechuck's parents; Dileo/MJ conversation: Taraborrelli (others said car was a Mercedes). Jury's Hotel bar/reporters: firsthand from Sam Smyth/*Belfast Telegraph*.

MJ's "crotch grab" is something anyone who watched him perform in the late '80s and early '90s has seen. Audience reaction: Taraborrelli. Reflexive response to the music: MJ to Boteach. Controversy about the crotch grab/what it signified: personal experience. Terry George story: British press from time of Chandler case onward; it did not really cross the Atlantic (at least in media reports) until after MJ's arrest. Account here: George to Nick Owens/*Daily Mirror* after MJ's death. In 2005, Britain's Channel 4 reported that George would be testifying for the prosecution at the criminal trial and quoted him as saying, "I can believe that the latest allegations are true because of what happened to me." According to Sky News, the FBI also interviewed George about his allegations. But George didn't testify at trial, something Mesereau cited as evidence either that the story was exaggerated or that George did not in fact believe MJ was a child molester.

DOCUMENTS

"Michael Jackson's Home Movies" raw interview footage provided by Marc Schaffel.

LONDON 1988/*BAD* TOUR

Cole, Paul. "Michael Jackson: The Day Our Man Came Face-to-Face with King of Pop." *Sunday Mercury*, June 26, 2009.
Frith, Simon. "Wack Attack." *Village Voice*, August 16, 1988.
Pareles, Jon. "Michael Jackson Opens Tour." *New York Times*, February 24, 1988.

BOYS/CHILDLIKE BEHAVIOR

Bashir, Martin. "*The Secret Life of Michael Jackson.*" ABC, March 7, 2005 (RT).
Cole, Rob. "FBI Probed Jackson 'Sex Call' to Brit Teen." *Sky News Online*, December 22, 2009 (RT) (hereafter cited as Cole, "Brit Teen").
Hill, Desiree. "Jimmy Safechuck Findings." desireespeakssolisten.blogspot.com, November, 2011 (I).
"Interview: Terry George About His Friendship with Michael Jackson." *Skynews*, July 29, 2009 (RT) (hereafter cited as "Terry George").

King, Larry. "Corey Feldman Interview: 'Nothing Inappropriate Happened.'"
     CNN, November 21, 2003 (RT).
Lewis, Emmanuel, interviewed by Howard Stern. *The Howard Stern Show*,
     January 9, 2003 (RT).
"Michael Jackson and Emmanuel Lewis." *In Touch*, March 2005.
Owens, Nick. "First Target of Michael Jackson's Obsession with Boys Says:
     'What He Did Was Wrong . . . but I Forgive Him.'" *Daily Mirror*, June 28,
     2009 (hereafter cited as Owens, "First Target").
Smyth, Sam. "Jacko and Jimmy at Jury's Hotel, 1988." *Belfast Telegraph*, June
     27, 2009.
"Terry George (40) Will Appear at Jackson's Trial." (British TV) Channel 4,
     January 24, 2005 (RT).
"When Jacko and 'Best Pal' Jimmy (10) Came to Cork." (*Irish*) *Independent*,
     June 18, 2005.

BROOKE SHIELDS

"Rivers—Brooke Shields Exploited Jacko's Death." TMZ, August 4, 2009.

ELIZABETH TAYLOR

Marikar, Sheila. "Elizabeth Taylor and Michael Jackson: Hollywood's Odd
     Couple, Now Gone." ABC, March 25, 2011 (RT).
Park, Jeannie. "He Does, She Does—They Do!" *People*, October 21, 1991.
Posner, Gerald. "The Jackson-Liz Drug Link." *Daily Beast*, July 6, 2009 (I)
     (hereafter cited as Posner, "Drug Link").
Walls, Jeannette. "The King of Kabbalah?" msnbc.com, June 23, 2005 (I).

CHAPTER 11

Jarvis Cocker/Brit Awards: dangerousminds.com's retrospective of coverage
of MJ's 2006 return to London; video of the performance and Cocker's interruption (dailymotion.com). *HIStory* promotional campaign and backfire/
MJ reduced status: Willman/*LA Times*, Nisid/*Entertainment Weekly*, Hillburn
poll/*LA Times*, Pareles/*NY Times* review. The most complete and balanced
account of both the promotional campaign and the release of the album itself,
though, is the one found on pophistorydig.com.

Response to Diane Sawyer's MJ–Lisa Marie Presley interview, negative: Orth/
Vanity Fair; positive: *Jet*; middle America: Bark/*St. Louis Post-Dispatch*. Cocker
recalling Brit Awards thirteen years later: Cocker to British Press Association.

"Diva demands"/2006 World Music Awards: msnbc.com cataloging British press; demands and performance fiasco: "Michael Jackson booed . . ."/*NME.* "Truly macabre figure," "so prone to panic attacks," "germaphobe": Alison Boshoff/*Daily Mail.* Bain containing damage: November 16 and 17 press releases and statement. *Pop Revenge* reporter quote: "Michael Jackson Booed at World Music Awards"/artistdirect.com, a good general description of the events and immediate aftermath. Postponement of Japan trip: AS1, Bain press release December 4, 2006; reaction in Tokyo: Adamu/mutantfrog.com. MJ restlessness and discomfort on return to Grouse Lodge: AS1. Departure from Grouse Lodge (incl. gifts, signing of slice of tree, "you are the only ones . . ."): AS1, Dunning interviews.

HISTORY/ABC INTERVIEW

Bark, Ed. "Michael Jackson Interview Raises Questions, Answers." *St. Louis Post-Dispatch*, June 26, 1995.

Hajarl, Nisid. "The King of Pap." *Entertainment Weekly*, September 20, 1996.

Hillburn, Robert. "King of Pop Is Now a Commoner, Poll Says." *Los Angeles Times*, October 22, 1995.

"Michael Jackson and Lisa Marie Presley Reveal Intimate Side as Lovers, Parents and Best Friends." *Jet*, July 3, 1995.

Orth, Maureen. "The Jackson Five." *Vanity Fair*, September 1995.

Willman, Chris. "Michael Jackson Takes Off the Glove and Rails at Attackers with New Songs That Take the King of Pop from 'Bad' to Sad—Very Sad." *Los Angeles Times*, June 18, 1995.

LONDON 1996/JARVIS COCKER

"Brit Awards 1996: Jarvis Cocker vs. Michael Jackson." dailymotion.com, September 25, 2009 (I).

"Jarvis Cocker Breaks His Silence over Michael Jackson's Death." Press Association, July 3, 2009.

"When Jarvis Cocker Met Michael Jackson." dangerousminds.com, January 21, 2011 (I).

LONDON 2006/WMA APPEARANCE

Bain, Raymone. "Michael: Performing 'Rumour' Was 'Misunderstanding.'" November 16, 2006.

———. "World Music Awards Appearance Had Sound Off—Head of Public Relations Baffled." November 17, 2006.

Boshoff, Alison. "Is This Jacko's New Wife?" *Daily Mail*, November 10, 2006.

"Michael Jackson Booed at World Music Awards." artistdirect.com, November 16, 2006 (I).
"Michael Jackson Booed During London Live Comeback." *NME*, November 16, 2006.
"Michael Jackson's Diva Demands @ World Music Awards." msnbc.com, November 16, 2006 (I).

WMA AFTERMATH

Adamu. "ZAKZAK on Why Michael Jackson cancelled His Xmas Party in Japan." mutantfrog.com, December 20, 2006.
"Raymone Bain Releases Statement—Michael to Attend Christmas Celebration in Tokyo." November 21, 2006.
"Raymone Bain Releases Statement Refuting Neverland Sale Claims." December 21, 2006.

CHAPTER 12

Arrival in Las Vegas, including MJ's travel disguise: AS1, unnamed inside source to *US Weekly*. Property address: documents shown to me by CS2; $1 million in advance for rent: widely reported, confirmed to me by three separate sources. Everyone aware of what MJ paid was outraged by the inflated figure. Christmas tree and presents, Celine Dion–like Las Vegas act: Wishna to *Us* magazine. Wishna and MJ opening a hotel together, slot machines and statue: Wishna (two interviews) to Norm Clarke/*Las Vegas Review-Journal*. Statue details: Wishna to E!online. James Brown's funeral: AS1. Brown's death, remains at Apollo, transport of body: Associated Press, Vogel/*Columbia Spectator*. MJ at C.A. Reid Funeral Home: Daly/". . . grim fascination . . ."/*New York Daily News*, Tune/WRDW, original research into mortuary. Brown's casket: press reports, KJ's statement that her son was laid to rest in the very same model. Description of MJ at funeral: video of funeral, Reid/mtv.com. Early conversations with Steve Wynn: AS1, *Review-Journal*, Leach. MJ/Wynn background and Milken: former prosecutor Miller/"Inside Vegas." Beacher: Beacher to *Us*. Fuller meetings with MJ (and Ortega): Leach/Luxe Life blog. MJ avoiding his father: a half-dozen sources, Wishna to *Access Hollywood*. I know that Joe Jackson has been living mainly in Las Vegas since the 1990s from an assortment of people who have been involved with the Jackson family then and now, and that Joe's infidelities, and his relationship with his illegitimate daughter Joh'Vonnie in particular, were the main reason for that.

I believe Rabbi Boteach's imprint is heavy on the part of the Oxford speech that involved MJ's determination to forgive Joe.

That MJ avoided his family as completely as possible has been attested to by numerous employees, associates, managers, and attorneys, from Bob Jones, who was working for him when MJ moved to Neverland, to Tohme Tohme, who was MJ's manager until two months before his death. Except during his criminal trial, MJ spent very little time with his family during the last twenty-five years of his life. Schaffel and Wiesner both told me that MJ instructed his security staff at Neverland not to let his father or his siblings onto the property; Schaffel recalled that MJ specifically barred his sister Janet from his home.

Jackson "soap opera" material Orth/"CSI Neverland," (Jackie/Enid/Abdul, Jermaine/Maldonado, Hazel allegations, Eliza allegations): court files of brothers' divorce actions, Taraborrelli, Bob Jones. Jackson brothers all alike except MJ: Eliza Jackson to Taraborrelli. Problem La Toya posed for her family: Schaffel, Taraborrelli, off-record sources. Jack Gordon, *Growing Up in the Jackson Family*: multiple accounts, including *Jet, People*. KJ/more sadness than anger about La Toya's accusations: KJ to *Jet* and confidential sources, who have expressed amazement at how willing Katherine has been to forgive her daughter. The two of them are actually pretty close these days, and La Toya spends more time in her mother's home than any of the children, except Jackie. 1993 Tel Aviv press conference in which La Toya promised to "prove" Michael's guilt: video via YouTube, *Washington Post, Houston Chronicle*. La Toya recanting accusations against MJ/her family, blaming Jack Gordon: Larry King 2003, 2008 interviews with a Danish television network and, of course, her most recent book, *Starting Over*, in which she paints herself even more graphically as Gordon's victim.

It should be noted that all of La Toya's more lurid accusations against Gordon have been made since his death in 2005. Before he died, Gordon denied La Toya's claims that he battered her into posing nude, dancing topless, and defaming her family. Gordon insisted that La Toya told him that everything she wrote in her first book was true and said also that the only violent encounter between the two of them took place when she came after him with a broken bottle and he held her off with a chair.

MJ's dislike of his family: Bob Jones ("made it perfectly clear that he didn't want his family around," "ordered his staff to stay away from them and keep them at arm's length," and "had more than an active dislike for the Jacksons; he acted as if he despised his family"). This accords with what I heard from virtually everyone I spoke to who was close to MJ during the last two decades of his life, his love for his mother being the exception.

Jermaine wasn't publicly outed for his attempt to sell his brother out until the spring of 2006, when Michelle Caruso of the *New York Daily News* got hold of the proposal for "Legacy" that MJ's brother had been shopping back in 2006. Jermaine went on Larry King's show immediately after Caruso's story ran to insist he never tried to sell a book that disparaged his brother, and blamed the entire controversy on Stacy Brown, Bob Jones's coauthor, who had contracted to do the actual writing of Jermaine's book. He was going to sue Brown, Jermaine said. Brown responded by going to Caruso to tell her about the tape recordings he had made of his conversations with Jermaine, he said he had turned them over to an attorney and was considering suing Jermaine for slander. Neither ever filed a suit against the other, and Jermaine has done all he can to pretend the entire episode never took place. But CNBC show host Donny Deutsch also obtained a copy of the "Legacy" book proposal and all but called Jermaine a liar on the air. Shortly after MJ's death in 2009, Roger Friedman found his own copy of the "Legacy" proposal and wrote that it described MJ in even harsher terms than had been previously reported. Jermaine kept his mouth closed. In a 2011 interview with muzikfactorytwo.blogspot.com, Stacy Brown confirmed again that all of the terrible things said about MJ in the book proposal came from Jermaine's mouth. In fact, Brown said he had written the proposal for a "positive" book, which didn't sell, and Jermaine himself changed it to empha- size all those terrible things he had said about MJ. Brown also revealed that the publisher Judith Regan had given MJ a copy of the proposal, leading to a confrontation between the brothers, and that the rest of the family agreed MJ had "sabotaged the book because of his disdain for Jermaine." Randy Jackson and Rebbie's husband Nate both called Brown, fearing that he would release the tapes he had made of his conversations with Jermaine, and Brown promised not to "as long as Jermaine stopped lying."

Leo Terrell's comments: Terrell. Terrell knows more about the Jacksons than he can say, and told me more than I can print; most of his insight derives from work for Johnnie Cochran sorting out assorted legal peccadilloes involving the Jacksons. Grace Rwaramba/Jacksons using ATM card: Rwaramba's High Court testimony, Rwaramba to Barak (from which quote is taken; see Chap- ter 1 notes). Jackson brothers' financial distress/reduced professional status: bankruptcy court files, sources with authoritative knowledge of the family's finances, Brown/Fanelli/*New York Post*, Ditzian/mtv.com. Gary Berwin judg- ment against Joe: Jacksons' bankruptcy file, Taraborrelli. *Segye Times* lawsuit, "Michael Jackson's Secret Vault"/Henry Vaccaro: Joe/KJ bankruptcy file. MJ legal claim against Vaccaro, dismissal: Mariant/Associated Press. I know a great deal more about both the *Segye Times* lawsuit and Vaccaro's dealings with the Jackson family than I wrote into the text, having observed the process by which Perry Sanders settled the Moonies' claim against Katherine Jackson on the one hand, and having been provided with the truly arcane details of Vaccaro's pursuit and acquisition of the "Secret Vault" (through the same storage unit paper trail described in Chapter 12) by Howard Mann, who eventually took possession of those assets from Vaccaro.

The Jacksons's 2006 holiday gathering (incl. MJ's dark glasses): AS1. A couple of the Jacksons have spoken about that get-together themselves in interviews, but I'm reluctant to put much stock in their accounts, so this is a rare occasion in which AS1's account is the primary source.

I know that the Santa Barbara District Attorney's office was running a drug investigation against MJ after his acquittal at the criminal trial from a confidential source who did not want to be quoted; it is in the public record as well. Tom Sneddon's office actually filed documents alleging that a large stash of prescription drugs had been seized when police raided Jackson's Neverland ranch in 2003, including bottles of Vicodin, OxyContin, Versed, Promethazime, Xanax, and Valium. Some of that information is detailed in Lorenzo Benet's *People* article. The DA's office in Santa Barbara continued the drug investigation for some months after MJ left the United States, but for reasons unknown to me never filed charges and eventually let the entire matter lapse. No one involved in the investigation will comment on it. Mesereau on MJ drug use: *People v. Jackson* court transcript. Drug procurement by MJ's security staff: reports and files in *People v. Jackson*, Posner/"Jackson's Shady Inner Circle" (see Chapter 6 notes) "Jackson and the 'Pill Mills,'" Waxman/TheWrap.

Farschian material: court file documents as above, investigative documents that have been produced since MJ's death, Schaffel, Wiesner. Carter and La-Perruque quotes: statements in criminal investigation. The handwritten note referencing Buprenex and "D" surfaced during the more recent investigation into doctors who enabled MJ's drug addiction. I believe the first journalist to obtain it was Kyle Munzenrieder of the *Miami New Times*, whose article included a photocopy of the note.

Allan Metzger: investigative files (most generated in connection to the Conrad Murray criminal case), media reports, Wiesner. Wiesner told me Metzger was with MJ during the entire *HIStory* tour. Lisa Marie Presley also identified Metzger as being with MJ on the *HIStory* tour: her interview for criminal investigation. She named as well a second doctor, New York anesthesiologist Dr. Neil Ratner, as being part of the tour. I simply don't have enough information about Dr. Ratner's role to do more than note his presence. Maureen Orth reported that Myung Ho Lee had claimed that he had paid Ratner to put MJ through a detox program in Seoul in 1999. When I mentioned Ratner's name to Dieter Wiesner, Dieter gave a slight gasp and said, "Ah, so you know about him." Unfortunately, I really don't. A number of articles have reported that Metzger was reprimanded (but retained his license) for prescribing drugs to Janet Jackson under an alias, and Metzger has acknowledged that he treated

MJ in the 1990s. Metzger videotaping MJ/Debbie Rowe wedding: "Friendly Docs"/TMZ.

MJ staff attempting to use a doctor visit to procure drugs: Clarke/"Doctor . . . Jackson's suite." Elie Wiesel's doctor: Boteach. Sinnreich quotes: Sinnreich via vitals.com. Relationship between pain, addiction, and perception: my research; in particular, Nutting/"Understanding Addiction Cycles," opioids911. org. "If I stop using drugs I'll die": Taraborrelli/*Daily Mail*. Ammar quote: Boshoff/"Michael Jackson was so high . . ."*Daily Mail*. Claims of injury or pain: Boteach in his book, Deepak Chopra in interviews.

Klein-MJ relationship: innumerable articles, investigative reports, and court filings; Schaffel, who was generally quite sympathetic to Dr. Klein; and AS1, CS1, and CS2, none of whom spoke favorably of Klein. Because these last three chose to be anonymous sources, I've given their recollections less weight than Schaffel's. Dieter Wiesner also spoke about Klein, though more obliquely, simply lumping him in with "the doctors" who had prescribed drugs to MJ over the years. Klein background/University of Pennsylvania: Posner/"Jackson's Doc's Drug Dealing Past," Seal/*Vanity Fair*. Founding and expansion of practice: Klein via drarnoldklein.com. How and why Klein became so popular in Beverly Hills: Schaffel, stories I've heard about Klein going back decades. Taylor book inscription to Klein: Seal. Taylor telling doctors in rehab Klein had prescribed her Dilaudid and Ativan: Posner/" Jackson-Liz Drug Link" (see Chapter 10 notes), off-record sources. That said, Schaffel is not the only one who has insisted that Klein was not a "drug-dealing doctor"; Carrie Fisher (who knows a lot about drug dealing doctors) has said so as well. Amount of drugs Taylor consumed, Taylor and MJ sharing drugs: Posner (see Chapter 10 notes), Heymann/*Liz* (which reported that Taylor had received more than three hundred prescriptions for thirty separate drugs in 1981 alone, and that she received a prescription for six hundred pills on the occasion of MJ's birthday party a few years later. Klein hiding medical files involving MJ, admitting to police prescribing Dilaudid and Ativan to MJ and Taylor, Sneddon listing him as one of doctors prescribing Demerol to MJ (as Ferdinand Diaz): deputy's report, other docs in court file of *People v. Jackson*, "Jacko Doc Hid Medical Records . . ."/ TMZ.

Klein meeting MJ through Geffen: Seal. Little follow-up investigation of Klein: 1993, 2003 lines of inquiry petered out. That Klein's wealth and connections (and litigious nature) helped to protect him is an inference, but it was the only explanation I heard from the people I asked about this. Irena Medavoy case: Seal, and contemporaneous media reports. Klein-Tarlow relationship: arnoldklein.com, UCLA.

Frank Cascio on collecting MJ drugs: Cascio, *My Friend Michael*. I will disclose here that I did not read all of Cascio's book, only the ABC News web story about it, which included a couple of brief excerpts. I have used those quotes and others from a Cascio interview here and in the insomnia section. Schaffel quotes: Schaffel. Drugs in black suitcase: AS1, Wiesner, Orth (see Chapter 5 notes). *National Enquirer*/intravenous drip: "Jacko Bombshell" (see Chapter 5, which refers to unavailable 1999 one). Avram material: Avram court file. Myung Ho Lee: Orth/"Losing His Grip" (see Chapter 6 notes), Los Angeles media covering the court case. *Daily Mail* photo: cited below; the photo is still posted. "Ate too little and mixed too much": Rwaramba to Barak. Jackson family suspicions of Grace: family members in public and private statements, based largely on the fact that she spent more time with him than anyone else. Post office box and credit cards in Rwaramba's name: Rwaramba LAPD statement.

Grace Rwaramba has denied that she ever enabled Michael Jackson's drug use (and also dismisses the suggestion that she pressured Michael to marry her). But she at one point also denied being interviewed by Daphne Barak and Barak replied by posting video of her interviews with Rwaramba online. Grace then issued a public statement in which she stated "I have never spoken to the *Times* online, the original source of the story that has now been picked up worldwide." That was disingenuous. Grace *had* spoken at length to Daphne Barak, who sold the story to the *Times'* parent company, as Rwaramba knew. Grace's statement labeled as "outrageous and patently false" the "claim that I routinely pumped [Michael Jackson's] stomach after he had ingested a dangerous combination of drugs." This disavowal of the remarks attributed to her by Barak, though, came after Rwaramba had been summoned to an interview with the LAPD at which she would be questioned about her knowledge of Michael's drug use and whether she had, in fact, pumped his stomach. Obviously, I have no direct knowledge of whether Grace pumped Michael's stomach, enabled his drug use or pressured him to marry her. That said, I think the evidence pretty strongly indicates that Barak's account of their conversations is far more reliable than Rwaramba's. I'm basing Grace's defense of herself in part on what I've been told she's said to the Jackson family and, especially, what I read in her September 12, 2009, statement to the LAPD.

Claims of Bain and Rwaramba collaborating to control MJ: Joe Jackson to fan sites, late spring and summer 2007; confidential sources told me other family members, including KJ, agreed at the time. Raymone and Grace jockeying for control: Mesereau. Jackson family's attempted interventions: family members in interviews; others have said that the Jacksons did try at various times to get MJ off drugs. Mesereau, Schaffel, and Wiesner all said they believed it, and I do also. See also Boteach on Katherine and Joe seeking his help to intervene; Tito Jackson to Fricker. In this case, I think the Jacksons deserve much of the credit they're trying to claim. Drug use spiraling after Bashir documentary: firsthand from Schaffel and Wiesner. *National Enquirer* claim of overdose in Bahrain: "Jacko Bombshell" (see Chapter 5 notes), response: Bain, "Overdose Rumors" (see Chapter 5 notes). Mickey Fine lawsuit: TMZ. 2007 Jackson family intervention attempt: *Rolling Stone, People,* bodyguards to ABC. Joe Jackson trying to get in: AS1, reported by Roger Friedman who clearly had a source inside MJ's entourage. Again, AS1 denied being that source.

COURT FILES

Criminal

SBSC 1133603.

Civil

C383387 (Los Angeles Superior Court) *Gina Sprague v. Joseph Jackson, Katherine Jackson, Randy Jackson, and Janet Jackson (a minor),* September 21, 1981.
LASC D076606.
LASC 05113.
LASC D157554.
LASC D202224.
USDC-CA CV 90 4906.
NWC55803 (Los Angeles Superior Court) *Katherine Jackson v. Jack Gordon and La Toya Jackson aka La Toya Gordon,* February 28, 1990.

DOCUMENTS

Audiotapes of interviews with Michael Jackson from "Michael Jackson's Secret Vault" provided by Howard Mann.
Rwaramba, 9/12/09.

ARRIVAL IN LAS VEGAS

Clarke, Norm. "Michael Jackson Landing on Strip?" *Las Vegas Review-Journal,* December 24, 2006.
English, Whitney, and Natalie Finn. "'It's Going to Be a Disaster': Associate Says Jackson Too Weak for Major Comeback." *E!online.com,* July 10, 2009 (I).
"Jackson Confidant Jack Wishna Opens Up About Michael and the Tour that Never Was." *Access Hollywood,* January 8, 2010 (I).
Leach, Robin. "In a World Exclusive Interview, Michael Jackson Talks About His New Life in Vegas and His Comeback." *Luxe Life,* February 5, 2007 (I) (hereafter cited as Leach, "Vegas").
"*US* Exclusive: Michael Jackson's New House." *Us,* December 24, 2006.

JAMES BROWN'S DEATH AND FUNERAL

Daly, Michael. "Michael Jackson's Grim Fascination with Death, Odd 5-Hour Vigil over James Brown." *New York Daily News*, June 28, 2009.

"'Godfather of Soul' James Brown Dies at 73." Associated Press, December 26, 2006.

"Michael Jackson Speaks at James Brown Funeral." YouTube, December 30, 2006 (I).

Reid, Shaheem. "James Brown Saluted by Michael Jackson at Public Funeral Service." mtv.com, December 30, 2006 (I).

Tune, Melissa. "Funeral Director Recalls Night Michael Jackson Spent Viewing James Brown's Remains." wrdw.com, July 6, 2009 (I).

Vogel, Sara. "James Brown Lies in State at Harlem's Apollo Theater." *Columbia Spectator*, January 16, 2007.

JACKSON FAMILY

Brown, Stacy, and James Fanelli. "Jackson 'Dive': Once-Mighty Music Family Goes from Riches to Rags." *New York Post*, March 23, 2008.

Caruso, Michelle. "Jackson Tell-All Book Pitch: Thought Jax Was Guilty, Feared Suicide; His Brother Admits Jacko's 'Thing for Young Children.'" *New York Daily News*, March 5, 2006.

———. "Tell-All Writer Warns Jax Bro Rants Were Recorded: Jermaine's Dis on Tape." *New York Daily News*, March 8, 2006.

"Confirmed! Jermaine Jackson Did Write a Disparaging Book About Michael Jackson." musikfactorytwo.blogspot.com, July 20, 2011 (I).

"Danger Zone: La Toya Jackson's Marriage Becomes a Danger Zone." *People*, May 3, 1993.

Deutsch, Donny. "Stacy Brown Interview About Jermaine Jackson's Book 'Legacy.'" CNBC, March 7, 2005 (RT).

Ditzian, Eric. "Michael Jackson's Family Tree: Janet, Rebbie, Marlon and More." mtv.com, June 26 2009 (I).

Friedman, Roger. "Jermaine Jackson Told All in Shocking 2003 Book Proposal." *Showbiz411.com*, August 12, 2009 (I).

———. "Michael Jackson's Nanny Locks His Father Out." Fox News, January 31, 2007 (I).

"Jacksons Refute La Toya's Charge Michael Kept Boys with Him at Family Home—La Toya Jackson's Views About Child Sexual Abuse Investigation of Michael Jackson." *Jet*, December 27, 1993.

King, Larry. "Interview with La Toya Jackson." CNN, March 9, 2003 (RT).

————. "Interview with Jermaine Jackson." CNN, May 6, 2006.

"La Toya: Charges Are True; Family Says Jackson Never Molested Kids." *Washington Post*, December 9, 1993.

"La Toya Jackson Interview, Go' Aften Danmark," TV2, May 19, 2008 (I).

"La Toya Jackson Says Michael Committed Crimes Against Boys." *Houston Chronicle*, December 9, 1993.

"La Toya Jackson Tel Aviv Press Conference 1993." YouTube (I).

Netter, Sarah. "Michael Jackson Bodyguards Dish on Living with Eccentric King of Pop." abcnews.com, March 8, 2010 (I) (hereafter cited as Netter, "Jackson bodyguards").

"Stacy Brown Breaks His Silence About Jermaine Jackson Book Excerpts and Michael Jackson's Death." musikfactorytwo.blogspot.com, May 19, 2011 (I).

VH-1, "Secret Childhood" (RT).

"Wedding Bells Were a Hoax, La Toya Says." *Deseret News*, September 8, 1989.

Yazmeen. "Katherine Jackson and Howard Mann: The Whole Story." musikfactorytwo.blogspot.com, March 1, 2011 (I).

————. "Katherine Jackson and Melissa Johnson: The Whole Story." muzikfactorytwo blogspot.com, April 15, 2011 (I).

MJ AND DRUGS/DR. KLEIN AND LIZ TAYLOR

Benet, Lorenzo. "The Neverland Drug Case That Never Was." *People*, July 23, 2009.

Boshoff, Alison. "Michael Jackson Was So High on Painkillers That He Spent Days in a Stupor." *Daily Mail*, June 26, 2009.

"Drugs and Alcohol: Jackson Family Attempted Vegas Intervention." *People*, June 26, 2009.

Fricker, Martin. "Michael Jackson Was Confronted by Family over Drugs." *Daily Mirror*, July 15, 2009 (hereafter cited as Fricker).

"Grace Rwaramba Michael's Biggest Enabler?" *News of the World*, October 16, 2009 (hereafter cited as "Biggest Enabler").

"Help for Safely Using Opioids." Opioids911.org.

"Jacko Sued for Not Paying for His Meds." *TMZ*, January 12, 2007 (I).

"Jackson Doc Hid Medical Records, Deputy Says." *TMZ*, July 13, 2009 (I).

"Jackson Drug Aliases." *TMZ*, July 20, 2009 (I).

"Jackson's Knack for Picking Friendly Docs." *TMZ*, July 11, 2009 (I).

James, Susan Donaldson. "Friend Says Michael Jackson Battled Demerol Addiction." abcnews.go.com, June 26, 2009 (I).

King, Larry. "Interview with Dr. Arnold Klein." July 8, 2009 (RT) (hereafter cited as King, "Klein").

Klein, Dr. Arnold. "In the Beginning." drarnoldklein.com (I) (PR).

Kreps, Daniel. "Report: Janet Jackson Planned Intervention for Michael in 2007." *Rollingstone.com*, July 9, 2009 (I).

Munzenrieder, Kyle. "Miami Beach Doctor Prescribed Michael Jackson Drugs, but Was He Trying to Help?" *Miami New Times*, July 10, 2009 (I) (hereafter cited as Munzenrieder).

Nutting, John Blight. "Understanding Addiction Cycles." www.voice-dialogue-inner-self-awareness.com (I).

Posner, Gerald. "Did the Doctor Do It?" *Daily Beast*, July 24, 2009 (I).

———. "Jackson and the 'Pill Mills.'" *Daily Beast*, July 12, 2009 (I) (hereafter cited as Posner, "Pill Mills").

———. "Jackson's Doc's Drug Dealing Past." *Daily Beast*, July 16, 2009 (I) (hereafter cited as Posner, "Jackson's Doc").

"Quotes by the Michael Jackson Doctors." spotlight.vitals.com, July 3, 2009 (I) (hereafter cited as "Quotes").

Seal, Mark. "The Doctor Will Sue You Now." *Vanity Fair*, March 2012 (hereafter cited as Seal, "Doctor Will Sue").

"Shocking Pictures Which Show Michael Jackson's Drug-Ravaged Legs as Police Say They Are Treating His Death as a Homicide." *Daily Mail*, Muly 16, 2009 (hereafter cited as "Drug-Ravaged legs").

Taraborrelli, J. Randy. "I Saw in His Eyes He Was Dying." *Daily Mail*, June 29, 2009.

"UCLA Announces New Endowed Chair: The Arnold Klein, M.D., Chair in Dermatology." Newsroom.ucla.edu, July 23, 2004 (PR).

Waxman, Sharon. "Exclu: 5 Doctors Named in 2004 Police Report." *Thewrap.com*, July 6, 2009 (I) (hereafter cited as Waxman, "Doctors Named").

CHAPTER 13

The AP's "Michael Jackson Returns to U.S." story had been set up as an announcement of MJ's trip to Japan and some newspapers made that the headline; most though, led with MJ's coming back to America. That his location was being kept secret is evident from the "Michael Jackson Sets the Record Straight" allmichaeljackson.com post. MJ's long relationship with Las Vegas: Weatherford. Gordy, and Abner predicting failure for the Jacksons's 1974 Vegas shows: Taraborrelli. Scene after 2003 raid on Neverland: Schaffel. *Million Dollar Listing* of Neverland: Bain's press release February 7, 2007. Considering sale of Neverland, refinancing deal stalled due to pending legal claims: AS2, Boshoff, Siklos (see Chapter 1 notes). MJ unhappy about inability to shop, spend freely: AS1 and AS2. Japan trip details: Talmadge/AP, allmichaeljackson.com, Bain PR releases, Michael Jackson Timeline. "Drugged up," "incoherent": Wishna to Duke/Saeed/CNN shortly after MJ's death. Movements, plans in Las Vegas: Clarke, Katsomiletes. Condition of Monte Cristo house: Wishna in Clarke's "Jackson changes Las Vegas address." Assorted brokers: Zar Zanganeh promotes himself as MJ's Las Vegas real estate broker, and he was the one who arranged the Monte Cristo rental, but MJ used a number of other brokers to search for properties. MJ robot: first appearance seems to be NME.com March 2007. "Heading back to Europe": Clarke/"Michael Jackson is leaving Las Vegas." Prince Azim's birthday party: AS1; also Tohme (who heard about it later). Randy Phillips on meetings with MJ: interviews pre- and immediately post-MJ's death, including Lee-Ryan/"Deep pockets"/*LA Times*, Adams/"Final decline"/*Independent*. Description of initial meeting and Phillips's "He was listening": Hoffman/*Rolling Stone*. MJ and Phillips discussing something like Celine Dion's show: Tohme, secondhand; a Dion-like residency was being reported almost from the time MJ arrived in Las Vegas. Declining BET Awards: AS1, Friedman/"Michael Jackson Moving to Virginia," later in Posner/"Michael's Missing Millions" (see Chapter 6 notes). "Too incapacitated": Ron Weisner; Raymone Bain denied saying this: starpulse.com. Jackson family concerns about Bain's attempts to control MJ: Mesereau, Tohme, Friedman/"Michael Jackson's Family Calls for Help." Raymone Bain background: Wiltz, *Washington Post* (flattering); confidential sources (less so). MJ looking at real estate in D.C. area: Bain to *Post*'s Argetsinger/Roberts. Venable: venable.com. Memo warning staffers not to "gawk": Howard King; Argetsinger/Roberts. Venable deposition: King, Wiesner; King also permitted me to read and take notes from his transcript. Roger Friedman apparently got a copy, also, because he quoted dialogue exactly in his "Michael Jackson Admits Drug Use in Testimony" column.

Stay with Cascios: Cascios interviews with Oprah Winfrey (see Chapter 1 notes), ABC, *New York Daily News*; Rwaramba to Barak (see Chapter 1 notes); Rwaramba statement to LAPD, Friedman, MJ to Dieter Wiesner, AS1, Mesereau; Taraborrelli/"Jacko the hobo" also contributed. I think it should be obvious which is which, certainly in the case of Rwaramba's recollections. Dominick and Connie Cascio quotes: Oprah; Frank remarks: ABC; Eddie: *Drew Today*. Bodyguards' concerns about not being paid, MJ kicked out of hotels: interviews with ABC. Ayscough claim: Ayscough's complaint, confidential source. Claims by Randy Jackson and Taunya Zilkie: claims that became part of estate probate case. Halloween Store: *Daily News*. Departure from Cascios: AS1, who told me in separate conversations that MJ left because he knew the media had found him, and because of Jesse Jackson's birthday party.

COURT FILES

Civil

BP 117321
YCOF2627 (Los Angeles Superior Court), *Ayscough & Marder v. Michael J. Jackson*, July 25, 2006.

DOCUMENTS

Deposition of Michael Jackson by Howard King in the Dieter Wiesner lawsuit at the offices of the Venable law firm in Washingtyon, D.C. (not actual title, document reviewed by author).

MJ AND LAS VEGAS

Weatherford, Mike. "Michael Jackson's Relationship with Las Vegas Started at Young Age." *Las Vegas Review-Journal*, June 26, 2009.

EARLY LAS VEGAS STAY/MONTE CRISTO HOUSE PERIOD/FINANCIAL STRAINS

Bain, Raymone. "Brand New Music from Michael Jackson." February 12, 2007 (PR).
Boshoff, Alison. "Michael Jackson—the Man Who Blew a Billion." *Daily Mail*, November 24, 2008.
Clarke, Norm. "Jackson Changes Las Vegas Address." *Las Vegas Review-Journal*, July 3, 2007.
Duke, Alan, and Saeed Ahmed. "Portrait of Jackson's Pill Consumption Emerges." cnn.com, July 10, 2009 (I).
"John Katsomiletes Stamps Out a Rumor with the Help of a Man Who Put His Stamp on Las Vegas." *Las Vegas Sun*, March 4, 2007.
Littlefield, Christina, and Sito Negron. "After Arrest, Pop Star Takes Crowds for a Ride." *Las Vegas Sun*, November 2003.
"Michael Jackson Denies BET Awards Snub." starpulse.com, July 6, 2007 (I).
"Michael Jackson Returns to U.S." Associated Press, January 26, 2007 (I).
"Michael Jackson to Build Robot Replica in Las Vegas?" *NME.com*, March 27, 2007 (I).

Miller, Steve. "Inside Vegas: Vegas Is a Second Chance Town." AmericanMafia. com, June 20, 2005 (I).

"Raymone Bain Releases Statement." February 7, 2007 (PR).

"Statement from Raymone Bain Regarding Lawsuit." January 13, 2007 (PR).

JAPAN TRIP/RETURN

Talmadge, Eric. "Jackson 'Wouldn't Change a Thing.'" Associated Press, March 8, 2007.

DEPARTURE FROM LAS VEGAS/EAST COAST STAY

Adams, Guy. "Michael Jackson: The Final Decline of a Pop Legend." *Independent*, June 26, 2009.

Argetsinger, Amy, and Roxanne Roberts. "The Return of Jacko." *Washingtonpost.com*, July 27, 2007.

Clarke, Norm. "Michael Jackson Is Leaving Las Vegas." *Las Vegas Review-Journal*, July 2, 2007.

Friedman, Roger. "Michael Jackson Admits Drug Use in Testimony." Fox News, October 25, 2007 (I).

———. "Michael Jackson Evidently Moving to Rental Home in Virginia." Fox News, July 3, 2007 (I).

———. "Michael Jackson's Family Calls for Help." Fox News, June 29, 2007 (I).

Lee, Chris, and Harriet Ryan. "Deep Pockets Behind Michael Jackson." *Los Angeles Times*, May 31, 2009 (hereafter cited as Lee and Ryan, "Deep Pockets").

Netter, Sarah. "Michael Jackson Bodyguards: 'We Were Asked to Leave Hotels.'" abcnews.com, March 8, 2010 (I).

Wiltz, Teresa. "Keeper of the Famed." *Washington Post*, October 8, 2006.

CASCIO STAY/NEW JERSEY

"Alumnus Lands Three Tracks on King of Pop's New CD Ad a Spot on Oprah's Couch." *Drew Today*, December 14, 2010.

Friedman, Roger. "Jacko Lived with New Jersey Family for Three Months." Fox News, November 19, 2007 (I).

Netter, Sarah. "Befriending Michael Jackson—Longtime Pal Says King of Pop Yearned for Normalcy." abcnews.com, July 7, 2009 (I).

Taraborrelli, J. Randy. "Jacko the Hobo's Worldwide Trail of Debt." *Daily Mail*, December 11, 2007.

Winfrey, Oprah. "Michael Jackson Recorded Music in the Cascio Home." *Oprah*, December 6, 2010 (RT) (hereafter cited as Oprah, "Cascio Home").
———. "Secret Friendship" (RT).
Yaniv, Oren, and Adam Nichol. "Michael Jackson Hid with Kids in Jersey." *New York Daily News*, December 12, 2007.

CHAPTER 14

MJ–Ron Burkle relationship: AS2, CS2. Stay with Burkle, Jesse Jackson involvement: *New York Post*. Burkle background (incl. Green Acres fund-raiser, Jesse Jackson): "The Complete Ron Burkle." Details of financial assistance Burkle gave MJ: AS2, Friedman/"Billionaire to the rescue," Siklos (see Chapter 1 notes), Gawker. MJ was deposed in the Prescient case at Versailles, passing through France on his way to Ireland. Prescient deposition: Friedman/"Michael Jackson Will Lose Beatles Catalog." MJ actually said far harsher things about his brother Randy than I reported here; see the "Mijac Claimed on 18.June.2007, Brother Randy Stole His Money" article at michaeljackson.com. MJ meeting Burkle at Cochran's funeral/Fortress Investments pressure on MJ: Siklos article (see Chapter 1 notes), the most comprehensive account of the financial machinations around MJ in this period (AS2 first suggested that I read it). MJ paying lawyers but not paying bodyguards: their interviews with ABC. Details of the Prescient case: documents provided to me, Friedman, Siklos (see Chapter 1 notes). Nona Jackson, Manuela Gomela Ruiz (the elderly woman who died in the hospital): complaint filings. Sheikh Abdullah lawsuit: court filings, AS2, CS2, and Tohme, who dealt with the Al Khalifas personally in negotiating a settlement of the case. Quotations in that section: court testimony (as reported by the British press; see articles regarding Rwaramba testimony in Chapter 1 notes), pleadings.

Leiber-Stoller catalog: AS2, CS2, Butler/*Billboard*. Call to Leiber and Stoller; Sony paying full cost of the purchase: AS2, Siklos (Siklos reported that it was only Stoller MJ called, which may be correct; see Chapter 1 notes). Danger of losing Neverland to Fortress in a default: Friedman, Siklos (see Chapter 1). Burkle introducing MJ to George Maloof: AS2. Maloof on MJ's stay at the Palms: Maloof to Katsilometes, except where attributed to Larry King interview in the text. "Plaster of Disguise": Moodie/*Daily Mail*; follow-up quotes: contactmusic.com, finditt.com, hollyscoop.com.

I acknowledge that the long plastic surgery section in this chapter could be described as interpretive, perhaps even as opinionated. It was the result of nearly three years of research and dozens of conversations with people who knew MJ. The point of view is my own, but it's an informed point of view.

Among those things that informed me was the footage for the "What More Can I Give?" video that was shot by Marc Schaffel in 2001 and is now in the possession of Howard Mann. I doubt that MJ ever looked worse than he does in those harshly lit scenes, and his discomfort with himself and with being seen in person for the first time by some of the musicians and singers he had chosen as collaborators was palpable to me. I actually found his onscreen sadness almost unbearable to watch.

MJ's perfectionism: multiple reports, including from collaborators such as Lenny Kravitz, Akon, and others who worked with him in the last year of his life. Making *Bad* "as perfect as humanly possible": MJ to *Rolling Stone*, Taraborrelli. *Bad* "over-produced": *Rolling Stone* managing editor Will Dana in 2009, summarizing critical reaction at the time. MJ's first two plastic surgeries, Dr. Hoefflin: Taraborrelli. Arnold Klein work on MJ: billing and medical records, Dr. Wallace Goodstein to *People* ("Michael Jackson's Plastic Surgery"). Klein diagnosing vitiligo: Klein to Seal/*Vanity Fair* (see Chapter 12 notes), and elsewhere. Vitiligo and lupus background, emotional implications of treatment, link to childhood trauma: my research, in particular, "What is Vitiligo?"/ National Institute of Arthritis and Musculoskeletal and Skin Diseases pamphlet; Deepak Chopra to *People*. Porcelana, "I do want to be perfect," third nose job/comparison to Diana Ross: Taraborrelli. Reaction to old photograph: Hilburn/"The wounds, the broken heart (see Chapter 4 notes)."

Hoefflin has never acknowledged the extent of the surgeries he performed on MJ (perhaps to protect his patient's privacy), but there is a substantial public record (incl. information from nurses' lawsuit against Hoefflin, Dr. Goodstein to *People*). Cleft in MJ's chin: stories I recall from LA gossip columns from living there in 1986; MJ acknowledging it: Taraborrelli.

What I write about MJ's plastic surgery and his feelings about race are, ultimately, my own conclusions, based on my reading of the evidence. "If he couldn't erase Joe from his life": Marcus Phillips to Taraborrelli; I heard more or less the same thing from Schaffel, Wiesner, and Tohme years later. MJ on separating from the Jackson 5 to "become me": Steven Howell in *Secret Childhood*. "Big, tall mean guys": MJ to Boteach; although MJ wasn't specifically speaking about Joe, I think it's pretty clear that's where the fear he was talking about originated. Stacy Brown observations: *Man Behind the Mask*. "Splaboos" to do more with class than race: Schaffel, Tohme. MJ disturbed people thought he wanted to be white: Gotham Chopra in *People*'s "Deepak Chopra: Michael Jackson Had Lupus." Admissions he'd gone too far with plastic surgery: *Rolling Stone*'s 1991 "The Making of the King of Pop" (cited earlier).

MJ playing Hoefflin and Klein off against one another: both doctors in interviews; lawsuits against each other. Klein trying to prevent MJ from more

Hoefflin operations: affirmed by Schaffel. Klein-Hoefflin rivalry: Seal/*Vanity Fair*, Ryan/*LA Times* on Klein's lawsuit against Hoefflin. Nurses' lawsuit vs. Hoefflin: *People, LA Times* (by two different women with very similar names); "Ugly face of beauty"/*Independent*. Hoefflin claims of vindication: his Web site. Court documents showing $42,000 payments to nurses: Diane Dimond/Daily Beast. Hoefflin and Klein withholding law enforcement access to files: *People v. Jackson* court file. Chopra on MJ's "poor body image": *Time*'s MJ commemorative issue. MJ weeping when *Us* magazine editor "could no longer put him on the cover": AS1. Werner Mang claims: "Jackson's Nose Patched Up"/*Daily Mail*; Hoefflin denial of Mang claims: contactmusic.com. Sinnreich/"blow holes": vitals.com (see Chapter 12 notes). Prosthetic noses: multiple sources; Adrian McManus comments: *Daily Mail* (may have run first in the *Mirror*). I heard the story about MJ's nose falling off long before it was published in *Rolling Stone*, from Will Dana. MJ on Bobby Driscoll: MJ to Boteach. Driscoll life story: Beck, Larson. That the nose MJ wore during the last years of his life was Bobby Driscoll's should be obvious to anyone who looks at side-by-side pictures of the two.

JESSE JACKSON PARTY/RON BURKLE/FINANCES

Banfield, Ashleigh, and Angela Ellis. "Michael Jackson: Inside His Family and Finances." abcnews.go.com, March 10, 2010 (I).
Butler, Susan. "Sony/ATV Acquires Lieber and Stoller." *Billboard*, April 16, 2007.
"The Company Ron Burkle Keeps." *Gawker.com*, July 1, 2008 (I).
Friedman, Roger. "Billionaire to the Rescue for Jacko." Fox News, April 25, 2005 (I).
———. "Michael Jackson Will Lose Beatles Catalog in '08." Fox News, March 9, 2007 (I).
Horowitz, Jason. "The Complete Ron Burkle." *New York Observer*, April 12, 2006.
"Jacko, Kids Squat with Burkle." *New York Post*, November 20, 2007.

PALMS/MALOOFS

Katsilometes, John. "Michael Jackson Recorded New Song 'Hold My Hand' at Palms, but Had 'Artistic Differences' with Playboy Suite." *Las Vegas Sun*, November 12, 2010.
King, Larry. "Interview with George Maloof." CNN, August 19, 2011 (RT).

PLASTIC SURGERY

Chopra, Deepak. "Remembering Michael." *Time,* June 2009. Special "Michael Jackson 1958–2009" commemorative issue.

Dimond, Diane. "It's Getting Even Weirder." *Daily Beast,* August 5, 2009 (I) (hereafter cited as Dimond, "Even Weirder").

"Jackson Has 'Surgery' After Hit by Son." *Contactmusic.com,* December 24, 2007 (I).

Messer, Lesley. "Deepak Chopra: Michael Jackson Had Lupus." *People,* June 27, 2009.

"Michael Jackson Gets a Beating." hollyscoop.com, December 24, 2007 (I).

"Michael Jackson Needs Surgery After Being Whacked by Son Prince." finditt.com, December 24, 2007 (I).

"Michael Jackson Wore a Fake Nose, and It Was Missing as He Lay in the Morgue." *Daily Mail,* July 25, 2009.

Moodie, Clemmie. "Plaster of Disguise: Bandaged Michael Jackson Goes Shopping in Las Vegas." *Daily Mail,* December 21, 2007.

O'Neill, Anne-Marie. "Under Scrutiny." *People,* November 24, 1997.

O'Neill, Ann W. "Doctor Files Suits Alleging Defamation." *Los Angeles Times,* November 12, 1997.

Orr, Deborah. "The Ugly Face of Beauty." *Independent,* February 19, 1999.

"A Photographic History of Michael Jackson's Face." anomalies-unlimited.com (I).

"Plastic Surgeon Steven M. Hoefflin Is Cleared and Vindicated of All Legal Claims Against Him." Hoefflin Center for Plastic Surgery, hoefflin.com (PR).

Ryan, Harriet. "Michael Jackson's Dermatologist Sues Another Physician." *Los Angeles Times,* September 16, 2009.

Seal, "Doctor Will Sue."

Triggs, Charlotte. "Inside Story: Michael Jackson's Plastic Surgery." *People,* July 10, 2009.

"What Is Vitiligo?" niams.nih.gov, November 2010 (I).

Wigmore, Barry. "Jackson's Nose Patched Up with Ear." *Daily Mail,* August 23, 2004.

BOBBY DRISCOLL

Beck, Marilyn. "With Re-Release of Disney Film—Child Star's Tragic Death Described." North American Newspaper Alliance, July 14, 1971.

Larson, Donna. "Bobby Driscoll Won't Be Around for Reissue of Song of the South." *Los Angeles Times*, February 13, 1972.

CHAPTER 15

Thompson, Cobb, Bazilio, and Associates audit: I was able to read and make notes, but don't have a copy. I haven't listed it among my sources for that reason; I don't recall the specific title of the document or the exact date on the cover letter. Associated Press reporter Stevenson Jacobs apparently saw it as well. MJ's only choices (besides selling his share of the Sony/ATV catalog) to borrow more money or file for bankruptcy: Tohme, Hawk, AS2, CS2, among others. MJ's refinancing details: same sources, plus Siklos (see Chapter 1 notes), who had details about HSBC and Plainfield involvement in Mijac loan. Refinancing money to settle lawsuits, pay off John Branca: Tohme, Hawk, AS2, CS2, Siklos (see Chapter 1 notes). Deal with Branca: documents in Joe Jackson lawsuit against Michael Jackson Estate. "Obvious problems": my analysis of Thompson, Cobb audit and refinancing details, plus Hawk, AS2, and, especially, Tohme. Promotion and success of *Thriller 25*: Sony press releases collected on MJ MySpace, Facebook pages, michaeljackson.com, "Charts and Certifications"/Wikipedia, Herrera/*Billboard*, "Artist Chart History." "Working day and night": Will.i.am in michaeljacksonbeat.blogspot.com collection of artist quotes on comeback album (see Chapter 9 notes). Thanks again to R.J. 7*even*, leaking of Pras and Akon duets: michaeljackson.com, michaeljackson-beat.blogspot.com (which also has Will.i.am MTV interview, quotes from Chris Brown, 50 Cent, Syience, and Carlos Santana, Ne-Yo's *Rolling Stone* interview; see Chapter 9 notes). Ne-Yo, Will.i.am and Akon were among the many who spoke about MJ's insistence that there was no point in putting out another album unless it was the best work he had ever done.

Palomino lease: original lease agreement, signed by Brother Michael on MJ's behalf. Description of property: Tohme, also Hawk, CS2.

MJ actually stayed at the Bolkiahs' Spanish Trail estate briefly in summer 2007, between leaving Monte Cristo and leaving for the East Coast. Jefri Bolkiah's wastrel ways: Seal/*Vanity Fair*. Condition of Spanish Trails house, MJ's determination to purchase it: Tohme, Brother Michael, AS1. Sony with-holding *Thriller 25* royalties: Tohme. Farrakhan's son as MJ's cook: Hawk, Tohme. Brother Michael's position in household: Hawk, Tohme, CS2. Because of a promise of confidentiality, I can't name the attorney quoted about MJ and the Muslims. Foreclosure and refinancing of Neverland: primarily Tohme, who ultimately brokered the deal that kept it in MJ's possession; comprehensive account: Lee/Ryan "Deep pockets behind"/*LA Times*; risk of losing it, foreclosure, auction notice: Friedman, foreclosurelistingsca.com. McMillan boasting on "confidential" arrangement: McMillan to Moody/AP.

I anticipate that Tohme Tohme will be the most controversial of my sources. Since Tohme was indispensable to me as a source, and because our relationship illustrates how complicated my investigation of Michael Jackson's last days became, I'm going to explain it at length here. This is how I met Tohme: Tom Mesereau told me I should talk to Dennis Hawk, who had been Michael's main attorney during the final year of his life and was a good man. After I interviewed Dennis a couple of times, he said he'd like to attempt an introduction to Michael's "mysterious" manager, Tohme Tohme. Dennis described Tohme as terribly misunderstood and said the man had been treated more unfairly by the media than just about any other significant figure in the Michael Jackson story. Tohme and I eventually met three times at Hawk's office in Santa Monica and, irascible as he is, I liked him. Also, I recognized it as a coup that he was speaking to me at such length and in such detail. I knew that lots of network correspondents and various national media had been trying to score an in-depth interview with Tohme and that he'd turned them all down. (I especially enjoyed hearing from Tohme about how "Barry King" kept trying to take him to lunch at Spago.) "You are the only one I trust," Tohme told me. Naturally, that was pleasing to my ears. Michael's former manager and I began to talk regularly on the phone and to meet for drinks whenever I was in LA. As I worked to verify what he was telling me, though, I heard more and more people question Tohme's professional manner and credibility. Howard Mann, for example, shared information about Tohme with me that he believed cast him in a bad light.

In a long and threatening letter sent to me by Howard Weitzman, co-general counsel for the Michael Jackson estate and John Branca's right-hand man, there were a number of assertions that challenged statements Tohme had made to me. Tohme had answers to most of these claims and Dennis Hawk largely backed him up but at the very least Weitzman had stirred waters that were looking increasingly murky. And the estate's attorney had referenced a number of documents concerning Michael Jackson's separation from Tohme that I found did, in fact, exist and that were, in a couple of cases, indisputably valid.

The fact that Frank Dileo was indisposed complicated matters. I was and am absolutely certain that Dileo resorted to various devious ploys while angling to reenter Michael Jackson's life in the spring of 2009 and that a number of these were intended to separate Michael from his then-manager, Tohme. Still, I had heard Tohme's version of events in great detail, but hadn't spoken to Dileo, who fell into a coma right around the time I began trying to make contact with him. I spoke to his wife Linda to check on something Tohme had told me about Frank and Mrs. Dileo insisted, convincingly, that it wasn't true. Her husband never recovered, so in the end I had to rely on the public record and on what Frank Dileo had said in various interviews, including with the police, to get his side of the story. It didn't make him look good—there were a number of things he'd said that I knew were false—but it bothered me that I couldn't offer him a chance to respond to accusations I was hearing from Tohme and others. I was certain that Randy Phillips knew the whole truth about what had transpired, but Phillips was claiming that he couldn't talk to me about any of that without the approval of AEG Live's legal counsel, Marvin Putnam, who told me that, because of Katherine Jackson's wrongful death lawsuit, he was compelled to advise Mr. Phillips not to speak to me at this time. Other than the e-mail in which Phillips asserted that there was "much confusion" surrounding the subject of Michael Jackson's management, "much of it caused by Michael himself," I got no help from the AEG Live boss.

Meanwhile, Howard Weitzman and Mike Sitrick, both representatives of John Branca, were defending Dileo to me while attacking Tohme. Branca, though, declined to answer any questions about his personal dealings with either man. Then, in the early summer of 2011, I introduced Tohme to Perry Sanders and sat in on a couple of meetings between the two. At the time, I was trying to help Tohme settle his differences with both the Jackson family and the Michael Jackson estate (and, of course, collect whatever useful information might surface in the process). Sanders started out liking Tohme, but became increasingly skeptical about the man. They met at least once when I wasn't present, and Sanders began to tell me he didn't trust Tohme because he'd caught the man in several "internal contradictions," meaning that Tohme had told different versions of the same story in separate conversations. Sanders also said that Tohme had "outright lied" on at least a couple of occasions. These "lies" sounded petty to me—more akin to braggadocio than to some grand deception, but still. And I was bothered when Katherine Jackson made it clear she didn't trust Tohme, suggesting he was a con man who had taken advantage of her son Michael. Mrs. Jackson also seemed to put some stock in the accusations made by other members of her family—most notably La Toya—that Tohme had looted the Carolwood chateau after Michael's body was removed from it, that he had made some sort of under-the-table deal on the Neverland refinance, and that he might even be complicit in Michael's death. Many of my concerns in these regards were swept away by my first interview with Ron Williams, the former Secret Service agent whose company was charged with securing the Carolwood property on the evening that Michael Jackson died. Williams backed Tohme's story of what happened on the day of Michael Jackson's death in every detail and made it clear that if anything had been taken from the Carolwood house, it was likely by the Jackson women, led by La Toya herself.

My concerns about Tohme were revived when I began to hear things from Michael Amir Williams—Brother Michael—that called the man's character into further question. Learning that Michael Jackson had agreed to have Tohme's background examined by a private investigator and that, according to Brother Michael, Tohme had been caught in a number of claims about his relationships with the rich and famous that were either exaggerated or untrue, raised fresh doubts. I've reported Brother Michael's claims, and the fact that Tohme disputes them. I think that Brother Michael has possibly garbled things he heard about mostly secondhand, but that there is a good deal of truth in his account.

It's my understanding that the Michael Jackson estate (which is to say John Branca and Howard Weitzman) also hired private investigators to look into Tohme's background. Among other things, those investigators recovered a couple of pieces of historical flotsam that I don't consider to be of any real significance but that have threatened this very proud man with embarrassment. Although I don't believe that either of these minor revelations is anything Tohme should be ashamed of, he pleaded with me to leave them out of this book and I decided to do as he asked. I don't believe I'm covering up for him, merely sparing the man some needless humiliation. I feel compelled to report, though, that Internet reports that Tohme used to be married to Randy Phillips's sister are untrue. I should also add that Tohme refused to tell me what kind of "doctor" he was. I'm pretty sure he has never possessed a medical license.

I was, of course, more concerned about suggestions by Brother Michael, by members of the Jackson family, and by the Michael Jackson estate that Tohme had cheated Michael Jackson financially. I agree that Tohme did, as Brother Michael said, make side deals with Jermaine Jackson and Tom Barrack prior to Colony Capital's takeover of Neverland Ranch, but to the best of my knowledge those were merely finder's fee arrangements that appear to be lucrative but legitimate. Also, Tohme fully disclosed the deal with Barrack to both Michael's attorney and his accountant. Dennis Hawk was adamant that Tohme had been "pristine" in his handling of Michael Jackson's business and financial affairs, but Brother Michael, like Howard Mann, answered that Tohme and Hawk were cooperating. The one person that I knew would be able to speak authoritatively on the subject of how Tohme had dealt with Michael Jackson's business, financial, and legal affairs was Jeff Cannon, who had served as Michael's accountant for most of the last two years of his life. Cannon, I knew, was not Tohme's man. He had gone to work for Michael initially at the behest of Ron Burkle's company, well before Tohme was on the scene, and had remained an independent agent. Cannon told me very clearly that Tohme had been utterly above board in his handling of Michael's affairs and had not made any attempt to benefit financially from their relationship, other than through the earnings he was to make as Jackson's manager, and never actually received even that money before Michael's death. Cannon agreed with Dennis Hawk that Tohme had been very careful about spending Michael's money, going so far as to rent a tiny office in West Los Angeles for a thousand dollars a month at a time when he was being told by his client to spend $50,000 per month on a suite of offices in Beverly Hills. Cannon also said that Tohme had been exceptionally scrupulous in handling the money that Michael set aside in the "Lockbox" as a down payment on a new home. He had been fully aware of that money, the accountant said, had kept track of it "to the penny," and was absolutely certain that Tohme handed over every cent of it to the estate. Cannon also agreed with Dennis Hawk that Tohme was probably not legally obligated to return that money, that Tohme could have simply kept it as an advance against the management fees he was owed, and that his decision to surrender it anyway demonstrated an exceptional degree of integrity. The money Tohme turned over to the estate (on the assumption that it would come back to him later) also included the $2.3 million fee he received for brokering the Neverland Ranch deal with Tom Barrack. Again, neither Hawk nor Cannon felt that Tohme was obligated to surrender that money, and were impressed that he had done so.

After my conversations with Jeff Cannon and Ron Williams, I was feeling much better about the trust I'd placed in Tohme. I was also becoming convinced that Brother Michael was the one who needed to answer some tough questions. Ron Williams told me that nearly two weeks after Michael Jackson's death, Brother Michael and Joe Jackson had showed up at Michael's house in Las Vegas to try to remove property and valuables. Williams's Talon Executive Services operatives were at the Palomino Drive property (by then Talon was working for the Michael Jackson estate and refused to allow Joe Jackson or Brother Michael inside the Palomino house). A shouting scene ensued, I was told, but the Talon operatives held firm. Brother Michael, through Perry Sanders, insisted that he had never gone to the Las Vegas house after Michael Jackson's death, with Joe Jackson or anyone else. He *did* accompany Katherine and Janet Jackson to the Carolwood chateau on one occasion after Jackson's death, according to Brother Michael, but Ron Williams didn't recall that. I hold Ron Williams in high regard as a witness, but all I can say for certain is that he and Brother Michael are telling very different stories. I was also told by at least three sources that Brother Michael had somehow come into possession of Michael Jackson's navy blue Cadillac Escalade, which he was seen driving around Los Angeles for months after Jackson's death. A number of stories were told to me about why Brother Michael was in possession of the vehicle, though no one showed me any persuasive evidence. Brother Michael himself insists that he never had the Escalade and that the stories being repeated about him are untrue.

What I'm sure of is that Tohme Tohme was the central figure in Michael Jackson's business and personal affairs for much of the last fifteen months of Michael's life and that he possesses knowledge of what took place during that period that no one else has. This makes him a valuable source. I don't pretend to be unaffected by the fact that I'm the only person with whom Tohme has shared much of that information, and I don't deny that I'm slightly concerned that there may be facts about Tohme that will emerge over time to undermine his credibility. Howard Weitzman has said that he has information that could get Tohme locked up (just as Tohme has told me he has information that could send John Branca to prison "for years"). No one has shown me any proof that either claim is true, and I tend to agree with Tom Mesereau that this sounds like the sort of posturing that takes place when people are lining up against each other in civil litigation. All I can report is that a number of independent sources, among them Dennis Hawk, Jeff Cannon, Tom Williams, and Sean Najarian, have consistently confirmed things I've heard from Tohme. In the end, I've relied heavily on Tohme's version of events, but have tried to make clear, where I had no confirming source, that these are his claims, not certifiable facts.

"Financier with a murky past": Deutsch. Tohme's background: Tohme, Hawk, CS1; public record of his business dealings, including with Tom Barrack. Tohme quotes throughout chapter: interviews with me, except where indicated. Tohme giving Jermaine use of the Rolls-Royce: Brother Michael, Mann. Birthday party: security guards to ABC (see Chapter 12 notes). Grace paying for balloons: Rwaramba to Barak (see Chapter 1 notes). Tom Barrack background: Tohme, Tully/*Fortune*, including Trump acknowledgment, "too much money chasing too few deals"; Barrack appeared in much coverage of Neverland refinance and O2 shows. Barrack charmed by MJ and the things the two discovered they had in common: Tohme, Barrack to Lee/Ryan/*LA Times*, to Siklos/*Fortune* (see Chapter 1 notes). Deal between MJ and Barrack with Tohme as middleman, Sillerman's trip to Ireland: Siklos (see Chapter 1 notes). MJ determined to focus on moviemaking over music: Schaffel, King, Wiesner, Tohme. Attempt to buy Marvel: Dean/*Comics Journal*, which had confirmation and specifics of the deal Dieter Wiesner had described to me; web reporting. Cinegroupe deal, anger at Spielberg and Geffen, Wiesner quotes generally: Wiesner interviews. Stan Lee confirmation of MJ's intention to buy Marvel and play Spiderman: Lee to comicsalliance.com. MJ separating from Jehovah's Witnesses over "Smooth Criminal" video: Karen Faye's "A Life Intersected" blog. Andrew Lloyd Webber on MJ/*Phantom*: Webber to *Daily Telegraph*. Tom Hedley/*Hunchback*: Phoebe Larmore, literary agent for Hedley's close friend Tom Robbins, via my manager Jeanne Field. MJ-Brando private acting lessons: Schaffel. Determination to play Willy Wonka, soundtrack he wrote and performed: Schaffel, Wiesner. To my knowledge, it's never been publicly disclosed before now. Christian Audigier's birthday party/Audigier generally: Tohme, photos and video on YouTube, at popsugar.com. Dinner with Barrack: Tohme, date/location: Michael Jackson Timeline. Barrack Hilton and Station Casinos ideas: Tohme, Siklos (see Chapter 1 notes). MJ not that interested: Tohme. MJ liking Tohme's Brunei ties: Brother Michael e-mail via Perry Sanders. Spanish Trails estate: Tohme, Clarke/"Michael Jackson Waving Goodbye," "Slashes Price to $25 Million"/*Wall Street Journal*. Troubles with Palomino house neighbors: Tohme, Clarke/"Michael Jackson living near school"; also, Hawk, CS2. 2008 work at the Palms: CS1, Elfman/*Las Vegas Review-Journal*. Meeting with Peter Lopez: Tohme; Lopez did not disagree, to my knowledge, though he and Tohme disagreed about other things. As an aside, I know quite a bit about Peter Lopez's law practice as my longtime entertainment attorney was one of Peter's law firm partners. Out of respect for the man's family I've left the subject of his suicide alone; I established to my own satisfaction that the rumors that Peter didn't really kill himself and that his "suspicious" death was somehow connected to MJ's were without basis.

Hawk calling Randy Phillips "a classy guy": Tohme, during an interview with Hawk present. "Summit" between MJ and Anschutz at the MGM Grand: primarily Tohme; also, Hoffman, Siklos, Phillips to *Rolling Stone*, *Fortune*; Gongaware at Murray trial. "Laser focused": Phillips to Siklos (see Chapter 1 notes). "Fans coming to you": Phillips; MJ pleased by the idea: Tohme. *King of Pop*'s success: *Billboard*, allmichaeljackson.com. Journalists required to identify MJ as the "King of Pop": Tohme. "Michael Jackson Dance," the Bravo *Legends* series, and the Hot Toys deals, releases and successes: allmichaeljackson.com. Lockbox account set up: Tohme, confirmed by MJ accountant Steve Cannon, Hawk. Continuing desire for Spanish Gate estate, reliance on Tohme to get it done: Brother Michael. MJ-AEG terms: the agreements (two separate ones were signed), much related e-mail correspondence. Tohme was the source of the statement issued on MJ's behalf about touring with his brothers. Negotiations with MJ/"Why say yes to the tour now?": Randy Phillips to *Daily Telegraph*. MJ wanting to be known for his work and not his "lifestyle" and "People said I was crazy": Phillips to Hoffman/*Rolling Stone*. "Everybody said two things about him": Barrack to Siklos (see Chapter 1 notes).

COURT FILES

Civil

BP117321 (Los Angeles Superior Court) *Joseph Jackson v. The Estate of Michael Joseph Jackson*, November 10, 2009 (hereafter cited as LASC BP117321 11/10/09).

BC445597 (Los Angeles Superior Court) *Katherine Jackson, Michael Joseph Jackson Jr., Paris-Michael Katherine Jackson, and Prince Michael Jackson II v. AEG Live LLC, Anschutz Entertainment Group, Brandon Phillips (aka Randy Phillips), Kenneth Ortega (aka Kenny Ortega), Paul Gongaware, and Timothy Leiweke*, September 15, 2010 (hereafter cited as LASC BC445597).

BP117321 (Los Angeles Superior Court) *John Branca and John McClain, Co-Executors of the Estate of Michael Jackson v. Tohme R. Tohme*, February 17, 2012 (hereafter cited as LASC BP117321 2/17/12).

DOCUMENTS

"Dear Michael." Letter from John Branca (and his law firm). April 15, 2006 (hereafter cited as Branca 4/15/06).

"Original Lease of 2710 Palomino, Las Vegas, Nevada," signed by Michael Amir Williams and James Beasley. February 28, 2008.

"Julien Auctions LLC Consignment Agreement" for Michael Jackson's personal property to be removed from Neverland Ranch, signed by Darren Julien and Tohme Tohme, August 7, 2008 (hereafter cited as Julien and Tohme, 8/7/08).

"Promissory Note." Loan Agreement between Michael J. Jackson and AEG Live. January 26, 2009 (hereafter cited as "Promissory Note" 1/26/09).

E-mail from Michael Amir Williams to Arlyne Lewiston, executive assistant to Brandon K. Phillips, president and CEO of AEG Live. April 27, 2009 (hereafter cited as Williams to Lewiston, 4/27/09).

E-mail from Arlyne Lewiston to Michael Amir Williams. April 27, 2009 (hereafter cited as Lewiston to Williams, 4/27/09).

"RE: E-mail to Michael Sitrick, Dated March 24, 2011." Letter from Howard Weitzman to Randall Sullivan and Morgan Entrekin. March 31, 2011 (hereafter cited as Weitzman to Sullivan and Entrekin, 3/31/11).

"RE: Michael Jackson Book." E-mail from Randy Phillips to Randall Sullivan. April 4, 2011 (hereafter cited as Phillips to Sullivan, 4/4/11).

"RE: Weitzman." E-mail from Mike Sitrick to Randall Sullivan, April 7, 2011.

"Michael Jackson hired Tohme." E-mail from Michael Amir Williams to Perry Sanders, November 3, 2011 (hereafter cited as Williams to Sanders, 11/13/11).

Thompson, Cobb, Bazilio and Associates audit.

FINANCES/AUDIT/NEVERLAND FORECLOSURE

Friedman, Roger. "Michael Jackson's Lawyer Says Deal Will Save Neverland Ranch from Auction." Fox News, March 13, 2008 (I).

———. "Michael Jackson's Neverland on Verge of Foreclosure." Fox News, January 11, 2008 (I).

Jacobs, Stevenson. "AP Exclusive: Jackson Said Net Worth $236 Million in 2007." Associated Press, June 30, 2009 (I).

Moody, Nekesa Mumbi. "Jackson Saves Neverland Ranch from Foreclosure." Associated Press, March 13, 2008.

THRILLER 25

Herrera, Monica. "Michael Jackson: King of Billboard's Pop Charts." June 25, 2009.

"Artist Chart History—Michael Jackson." Billboard.com (I).

"Thriller 25." Michaeljackson.com (I)

"Thriller 25." Michael Jackson Facebook (I).

"Thriller 25—Charts and Certifications." wikipedia.

COMEBACK ALBUM/PALMS

Wardrop, Murray. "Michael Jackson: The Unreleased Album." Daily Telegraph, June 27, 2009.

TOHME DEALS/KING OF POP

"Bravo Legends." allmichaeljackson.com, September 10, 2008.

"Hot Toys Announces New Michael Jackson Figurines." allmichaeljackson.com, September 25, 2008.

"King of Pop Album." allmichaeljackson.com, September, 2008.

"Michael Jackson Makes History on Euro Charts." Billboard.com, July 16, 2009.

"Michael Jackson Japan Charts, 1979–2009." Billboard.com.

"Will.i.am Helps Jacko." mtv.co.uk, January 4, 2007 (I).

PALOMINO HOUSE/SPANISH GATE ESTATE/BIRTHDAY PARTY

Banfield, Ashleigh. "Michael Jackson's Secretive Life." ABC, March 9, 2010 (RT).

Clarke, Norm. "Michael Jackson Waving Goodbye." *Las Vegas Review-Journal*, July 4, 2007.

"Michael Jackson at Christian Audigier Birthday Party." YouTube, May 24, 2008 (I).

"Photos of Britney Spears and Michael Jackson at Christian Audigier's Birthday Party." popsugar.com, May 26, 2008 (I).

Seal, Mark. "The Prince Who Blew Through Billions." *Vanity Fair*, July 2011.

"Massive Las Vegas Estate Slashes Price to $25 Million." *Wall Street Journal*, October 22, 2010.

MOVIES/MARVEL

Burkeman, Oliver. "Brando Became Close Friend of Michael Jackson." *Guardian*, September 24, 2004.

Dean, Michael. "How Michael Jackson Almost Bought Marvel." Excerpted from *Comics Journal* #270, August 17, 2005.

Faye, Karen. "August 29." karenfayeblog.com, August 29, 2010 (I).

"Stan Lee on Michael Jackson's Desire to Buy Marvel and Play Spiderman." comicsalliance.com, May 23, 2012 (I).

Webber, Andrew Lloyd. "Michael Jackson to Appear in *Phantom of the Opera*." *Daily Telegraph*, June 27, 2009.

TRANSITION TO LA/RETURN TO PALMS

Clarke, Norm. "Michael Jackson Living Near School." *Las Vegas Review-Journal*, September 14, 2008.

Elfman, Doug. "Shhh! Music Stars Work in Secret at Palms Studio." *Las Vegas Review-Journal*, January 25, 2010.

TOHME/BARRACK/ANSCHUTZ/AEG MEETINGS

Deutsch, Linda. "Jackson's Mysterious Advisor Opens Up." Associated Press, July 4, 2009 (hereafter cited as Deutsch, "Mysterious Advisor" 7/4/09).

Hoffman, Claire. "The Last Days of Michael Jackson." *Rolling Stone*, July 22, 2009 (hereafter cited as Hoffman, "Last Days").

Lee and Ryan. "Deep Pockets."

Mason, Rowena. "Randy Phillips Profile: Michael Jackson's Promoter Is Making

All the Right Moves." *Daily Telegraph*, March 14, 2009 (hereafter cited as Mason, "Phillips Profile").

Tully, Shawn. "I'm Tom Barrack and I'm Getting Out." *Fortune*, October 31, 2005.

CHAPTER 16

Visit to Hennessey + Ingalls, Los Angeles bookstores: Kellogg/"Michael Jackson, the bookworm," supplemented by Tohme, Mesereau (another book collector). "Last Supper" painting: viewable on web; best quality: debbieschlussel.com. "Same things over and over": Taraborrelli. Reading habits, omnivorous curiosity: Bob Sanger, one of MJ's many attorneys, to *LA Weekly* (possibly the catalyst for Kellogg's story). Watching operations at UCLA, fascination shared with Brando for scientific/technological breakthroughs: AS2, CS1, Wiesner. "Glancing over some Sufi poetry": Chopra/"Tribute to My Friend." MJ–Gregory Peck relationship: Haney/*Gregory Peck* (incl. first meeting, conversation about *To Kill a Mockingbird*, horseback rides); Peck bio/imdb.com (incl. MJ late entrance at Peck's funeral); "Gregory Peck and Michael" file/michaeljackson.com (placed there at MJ's request, including Pecks naming dog Blanket). My manager Jeanne Field was at one time married to Gregory Peck's son Steve and we did discuss the Peck family (about which she had absolutely nothing negative to say), including Veronique. Letter of support of MJ: mjfanclub.net.

Natalie Maines's party: theboot.com, Maines to Howard Stern. Masks and costumes on Melrose Avenue: "Halloween comes early . . ."/*Daily Mail*. As earlier, Tohme's quotes are from interviews with me except where specified otherwise. MJ/Steve Wynn: Clarke. Halperin's claim MJ was near death/Tohme response: *Daily News*. MJ in Pahrump: Ethan Smith/*Wall Street Journal*. Wishna's comments to *National Enquirer*: starpulse.com. MJ interest in "Le Belevedere": Tohme; details of the property: Ayers profile of Hadid, *Angeleno* (Tohme scoffed at Hadid's claims of a relationship with MJ). Rental of Carolwood chateau: Tohme; relevant documents in file of wrongful death lawsuit against AEG; details of property: Cohen/Associated Press. That AEG guaranteed to Guez $1.2 million in rent on the chateau I know from a review of documents that are part of the wrongful death suit. Description of the neighborhood: in large part derived from living for several years on North Beverly Glen Drive; proximity of Carolwood chateau to Lisa Marie Presley's childhood home: stardriveways.com.

Chandler case: court documents, articles published as the scandal was unfolding, and of course Fischer/"Was Michael Jackson Framed?"; also, Ray Chandler, who was willing to speak on the record about his brother Evan, and about Michael Jackson, but not about his nephew Jordie. MJ's breakdown in Beverly Hills, ride to Rent-A-Wreck: Fischer; address: court file; turban and veil/sunglasses: Taraborrelli/"Lisa Marie . . . passionate lover." Driving a Jeep: Taraborrelli, confirmed by CS1 (Fischer said it was a van). How Jordie, his sister, and mother got to Neverland: Fischer; court records. "Do you know how much time I spend up here . . .": Taraborrelli/*Daily Mail* (he doesn't identify his source but a very similar account is in the leaked file of the grand jury proceedings). MJ and Jordie watching *The Excorcist*, spending night in same bed: Fischer, Orth, court file, June Chandler testimony in *People v. Jackson*. Conversations between June and Jordie/between June and MJ: June in court file and in *People v. Jackson*. "Don't think he has a devious bone": Fischer, court file. Evan Chandler background, marriage to June: Fischer (information via Pellicano), adjusted by me based on Ray Chandler. Some of that information is in the court file, but most is not. "Everybody liked everybody": Ray Chandler to David Jones/*Daily Mail*. I complied with Ray's request that I would try to quote his previous statements to the media rather than what he said to me, whenever possible.

When I state that Fischer wrote her article "in close collaboration" with Pellicano, I don't mean to suggest she did no other reporting—she did a great deal. But the key information clearly came from Pellicano, and there's no doubt in my mind he was using Fischer to get the MJ defense side of the story out. Bert Fields wouldn't talk to me; I can't help but believe that this was because of his concern that he could be dragged into Pellicano's mess. June's story is in the court file and I also look at her testimony at the criminal trial. Some of Jordie's account is in the court file, but most of it is from documents that were leaked to journalists.

"They hung out together": Ray Chandler. Evan Chandler on MJ's sleepovers at his home: court file, *All That Glitters*, Chandler family members. "You and Jordie are having sex . . .": court documents, *All That Glitters*, media including Taraborrelli/*Daily Mail*. Chandler/Schwartz tape-recorded conversation: transcript in Fischer, Orth; key evidence in extortion investigation of Evan and Rothman. Ray Chandler claims about Pellicano and Fischer: Ray Chandler interview, *All That Glitters*. First reporting on tape and contents: Phillips/Ferrell/*LA Times*.

Rothman background, incl. Tinoa Operations: Fischer (via Pellicano). Other attorneys described Rothman similarly and when I checked his status with the State Bar while working on this book I found that his license to practice law had once again been suspended. Even Ray Chandler did not dispute that Rothman was an unsavory character. Hughes's description of Rothman, and all quotes from Hughes below except as indicated: Hughes/*Redemption*.

Rothman–E. Chandler relationship/former patient: Ray Chandler. "Michael was very good at sizing people up . . .": a member of the Chandler family I can't name. Jordan Chandler has never made any public statements about his relationship with Michael Jackson and has made it clear that he does not want any of his relatives to make such public statements, either. Fields and Pellicano brought in/interview with Jordie: Fischer via Pellicano. Evan moving forward with "plan": Fischer, documents in court file. Evan going to Dr. Abrams to get the story into the media: Bert Fields; Ray Chandler vehemently disagrees with this claim. Pellicano's account of MJ-Evan-Jordie meeting: Fischer; court records. Pellicano-Rothman meeting: Fischer. "$20 million deal": Hughes/book. Torbiner/sodium amytal: Fischer/Pellicano. Torbiner himself has stated to investigators that if he did give the boy sodium amytal, it was "for dental purposes." Department of Children's Services: leaked document/The Smoking Gun. Dr. Abrams's report getting to police and to freelance reporter: Fischer, court record. June Chandler manipulated by police: Fischer. Fields/Pellicano convincing MJ to file extortion charges: Fischer, Hughes. Gloria Allred, replacement by Feldman: Orth, coverage from the time. Feldman background: Mesereau, who thinks Feldman is one smart lawyer.

I'm told (by Mesereau, among others) that Howard Weitzman insists privately that he did not push MJ to settle and in fact refused to be part of the settlement. Mesereau mentioned this to Carl Douglas, who pulled out the settlement agreement and made sure Weitzman's signature was on it (it was).

No one disputes that Fields made his statement about an imminent criminal indictment of MJ, but not everyone thinks it was the "blundering" mistake Orth described in her article. Sources: Fischer, Nazario/*LA Times*. Carl Douglas on pressure to settle: Douglas at LABA "Frozen in Time" symposium, as are all Douglas and Feldman quotes in this section. (I owe my possession of the DVD on which Douglas and Feldman discuss the 1993 case to Mesereau.) Maid collecting makeup, etc., from MJ's bedroom: Taraborrelli/*Daily Mail*; likely via criminal case court file. Pellicano admissions re. MJ sleeping in Jordie's bedroom: Pellicano to CNN; this interview was alongside Brett Barnes and Wade Robson, who said they had slept with MJ and had not been subjected to any sort of sexual behavior. This was, as Orth put it, Pellicano's "most controversial action." Leaked document describing Jordie's sexual contacts with MJ: Dimond; it's in the court file and now widely available online. Evan as victim of MJ fans: Ray Chandler; also, press at the time, Fischer, *All That Glitters*, coverage of Evan's suicide. Jordie's statement reported by the Santa Barbara sheriff's deputy: court file; also, press coverage, Dimond's book, *All That Glitters, The Magic and the Madness* (updated edition). I should note that Jordie made several separate statements to police investigators and was interviewed by at least three psychologists and/or psychiatrists about his claim that MJ had sexually molested him. The one who really got him talking was Deputy Rosibel Ferrufino, and she isn't the deputy referenced here.

Branca brought in: Fischer; in her account Branca, along with Weitzman and Cochran, maintained a belief in MJ's innocence. I'm not sure, based on what I know, that Weitzman and Cochran really did believe in MJ's innocence, but I agree that they claimed to. Johnnie Cochran's concerns were explained by Carl Douglas at the "Frozen in Time" symposium. Garcetti-Cochran working relationship: because the first time I met Cochran was when Garcetti introduced him to me in a hallway just outside their side-by-side Los Angeles County District Attorney offices, when the two were heading the team that investigated police officer involved shootings. Garcetti promise MJ could return without immediate arrest: Carl Douglas. "Spot the Jacko" contest: Fischer; Geraldo's "trial" (MJ was acquitted, by the way): personal experience. La Toya/tabloid bidding: press at the time; also see notes to Chapter 12; her claims are most thoroughly vetted in Campbell/*Michael . . . Darkest Hour* and *The Magic and the Madness* (updated edition). Strip search details: confidential source; also, "Boy's Lawyer Seeks Photos"/*LA Times*, "Photos May Contradict"/ *USA Today*; Feldman and Douglas/"Frozen in Time." Taraborrelli gives a detailed account that my source agreed with in most details, though not all, in the updated version of his book. "Most humiliating ordeal . . .": a statement MJ made from Neverland Ranch two days after the search; reproduced on mjliveson.com, in BBC story on Chandler case (2003), quoted in Pareles/"Michael Jackson is Angry, Understand?" Feldman on court filings: "Frozen in Time" symposium. The most reliable source I have about how Johnnie Cochran advised MJ in the Chandler case is the same confidential source who told me about the strip search, but Fischer's article largely agrees with this description of Cochran's role, and so did Carl Douglas's presentation at the "Frozen in Time" symposium, although it was more implicit in that instance. Demand to examine MJ's finances/MJ wanting it over: Douglas and Feldman. Feldman representing Cochran in "personal matters": Feldman. Settlement discussions/three retired judges: Feldman, Douglas. Douglas delivering settlement to MJ in Las Vegas: Douglas.

The terms of the settlement with the Chandlers are disputed. The Smoking Gun Web site obtained a copy of the document, but it was heavily redacted. That Web site states that the entire cost of the settlement to MJ was $15,332,250, but that was in fact the amount to be placed in trust for Jordie Chandler. What's been blacked out, according to AS2, are the amounts paid to Feldman and to Jordie's parents. I went with the numbers AS2 gave me.

"Worst decision he ever made": Mesereau. "I am not guilty . . .": MJ December 22, 1993, statement. Loss of the Pepsi contract, other business setbacks: Fischer. 1994 grand jury investigations; "no real evidence": Fischer, Newton/*LA Times*. I doubt anybody would dispute my assertion of Diane Dimond's doggedness. Campbell's book reports on the various polls that supported MJ; one of these was on the syndicated TV program *A Current Affair*, which had been relentless in making the case that MJ was a pedophile; more than 80 percent of its respondents said they believed MJ not the Chandlers.

MJ's marriage to Lisa Marie Presley has been chronicled as much in primetime television interviews as in print coverage. Lisa Marie Presley background: rhythmofthetide.com, Harrington/*Washington Post* piece, yahoo.com bio, Behar/*Elvis*, Finstad/*Child Bride* (latter includes initiation of MJ's relationship with Lisa Marie; Brett Livingstone Strong quotes are all from Finstad). Dennis Hawk is Strong's attorney and did his best to help me pin Brett down on some subjects, but that effort was largely unsuccessful. Lisa Marie on first one-on-one with MJ: Presley to *Rolling Stone* (see Chapter 8 notes), *Playboy* (see Chapter 8 notes). Recollection of how MJ explained Chandler situation: *Rolling Stone*. Description of MJ proposal: Presley to Diane Sawyer/ABC. "Very hot" in bed, "role playing," "sexually active": Presley to Monica Pastelle, in Taraborrelli/*Daily Mail*; also, *Magic and Madness* (updated). Trump on MJ's "new girlfriend"/Lisa Marie at Palm Beach estate: *Trump: The Art of the Comeback*. Description of MJ–Lisa Marie marriage by Judge Alvarez: Bob Jones book, from a newspaper interview. Terry Marcos: rhythmofthetide.com. MJ's disappearances/Lisa Marie hurt: Presley to *Rolling Stone* (see Chapter 8 notes), *Playboy* (see Chapter 8 notes), Diane Sawyer, Oprah Winfrey. MJ complaints of Presley "invading his space": *Daily Mirror* via rhythmofthetide.com. "Publicity stunt," "no desire for a woman," "so down to earth," "tremendous supporter," MJ and kid friends "running around the house": Jones book. Makeup on pillow: Taraborrelli/*Daily Mail*, also *Magic and Madness*. MJ boasts to Lisa Marie of wealth and Princess Diana: Jones book. MJ invented marriage proposal: MJ to *Daily Mirror* via lacienegasmiled.com. Lisa Marie reaction to *TV Guide* interview: Presley to *Rolling Stone*. Trip to Hawaii with Danny Keough: via lacienegasmiled.com. Lisa Marie "torn up" over leaving Keough: Presley to Oprah, 2010. MJ and Lisa Marie/MTV Music Video Awards: *Playboy* (see Chapter 8 notes), *Rolling Stone* (see Chapter 8 notes). Lisa Marie visiting MJ in hospital/Bill Bray: Jones book; also, Presley to *Playboy* (see Chapter 8 notes) and Oprah, 2010. MJ wanting to father Elvis's grandchild/"custody battle nightmare," "tell her to do it": Presley to *Playboy* (see Chapter 8 notes). "Had a thing" for MJ/"get her husband back":

Jones. Omer Bhatti/MJ encouragement of "love child" story: Schaffel, CS1; fan speculation: multiple MJ fan sites. Joe Jackson (whose reasons no one can guess) actually told the black television network TV One that Omer was MJ's child (see *Daily Mail* below), which Omer felt compelled to publicly rebut (see hollywoodgossip.com below). The closest thing to a comprehensive story on this subject appeared in Britain's the *Sun*, which gave the background on MJ's relationship with the Bhattis, the arguments pro and con, and even got Riz Bhatti to comment—or not comment, actually. I have it on the highest authority that Omer is *not* MJ's child.

COURT FILES

Criminal

SBSC 1133603.

Civil

LASC SC026226.

DOCUMENTS

"Statement of Declination Issued Jointly by the District Attorney's Offices of Los Angeles and Santa Barbara Counties." September 21, 1994 (hereafter cited as Statement of Declination, 9/21/94).

LOS ANGELES–LAS VEGAS TRANSITION

Ayers, Chris. "Surreal Estate: Mega-Spec Developer Mohamed Hadid." *Angeleno Magazine*, August 13, 2010.
Chopra, Deepak. "Tribute to My Friend, Michael Jackson." chopra.com, June 26, 2009 (I).
Clarke, Norm. "Jacko Turns Down Wynn Encore Gig." *Las Vegas Review-Journal*, November 2, 2008.
Cohen, Sandy. "AP Exclusive: Contents of MJ's Final Home for Sale." Associated Press, November 9, 2011.
Darden, Beville. "Michael Jackson Surprises Guests at Dixie Chick's Party." theboot.com, November 5, 2008 (I).
"Halloween Comes Early as Jacko's Wacko Clan Descends on LA Comic Store." *Daily Mail*, October 9, 2008.
Kellogg, Carolyn. "Michael Jackson, the Bookworm." *Los Angeles Times*, June 27, 2009.

"The Last Home of Michael Jackson." stardriveways.com (I).

"Letter of Support for Michael Jackson by Gregory and Veronique Peck." mjfanclub.net, December, 2002 (I).

"Michael Jackson 'Needs Lung Transplant.'" *Daily Telegraph*, December 22, 2008.

"Natalie Maines on *The Howard Stern Show*." November 3, 2008 (RT).

Roberts, Randall. "Michael Jackson's Lawyer, Bob Sanger, Talks to West Cost Sound About the Pop Star, His Life—and His Reading Habits." *LA Weekly*, June 25, 2009.

Smith, Ethan. "Michael Jackson: The Next Elvis?" *Wall Street Journal*, June 13, 2008.

Wishna, Jack, to *National Enquirer*, via "Promoter Says Jackson Isn't Capable of Las Vegas Show." starpulse.com, May 29, 2008 (I).

CHANDLER AFFAIR

"Anthony Pellicano, Brett Barnes, and Wade Robeson." CNN, August 26, 1993 (RT).

"Boy's Lawyer Seeks Photos of Michael Jackson's Body." *Los Angeles Times*, January 5, 1994.

Fischer, Mary A. "Was Michael Jackson Framed?" GQ, October 1994 (hereafter cited as Fischer, "Framed").

"Jacko: The Original Child Abuse Allegations." *Smoking Gun*, November 18, 2003 (I).

Jones, David. "Killed by the Curse of Michael Jackson: What Drove the Father of Jordy Chandler to Put a Gun to his Head?" *Daily Mail*, November 20, 2009 (hereafter cited as Jones, "Killed by the Curse").

"Michael Jackson's Statement from 22nd December, 1993." MJliveson. December 22, 1993 (I).

Nazario, Sonia. "Jackson Sued by Boy Who Alleged Sexual Molestation." *Los Angeles Times*, November 15, 1993.

Newton, Jim. "Grand Jury to Convene in Jackson Case Law: Sources Close to the Investigation Say a Panel in Santa Barbara Will Hear Testimony Next Week About Alleged Molestation of Boy." *Los Angeles Times*, February 5, 1994.

"1993: Michael Jackson Accused of Child Abuse." BBC, February 8, 2003 (RT).

Orth, Maureen. "Nighmare in Neverland." *Vanity Fair*, January 1994.

Phillips, Chuck, and David Ferrell. "Tapes Used to Allege Plot to Extort Jackson Released." *Los Angeles Times*, August 31, 1993.

"Photos May Contradict Michael's Accuser." *USA Today*, January 28, 1994.

HISTORY/LISA MARIE/POST JORDIE

Harrington, Richard. "The Princess of Rock Makes a Name for Herself." *Washington Post*, May 6, 2005.

"Joe Jackson Confirms Omer Bhatti Is Michael's Son as Katherine Wins Custody of Other Three Children." *Daily Mail*, August 1, 2009.

"Lisa Marie Presley Biography." yahoo.com (I).

"Lovechild in the Front Row at Memorial." *Sun*, July 8, 2009.

"Michael Jackson–Lisa Marie Presley." rhythmofthetide.com, January 8, 2012.

Pareles, Jon. "Michael Jackson Is Angry, Understand?" *New York Times*, June 18, 1995 (hereafter cited as Pareles 6/18/95).

Sawyer, Diane. "Interview with Michael Jackson and Lisa Marie Presley." *ABC/Primetime*, June 14, 1995 (RT).

———. "Lisa Marie Presley Talks Marriage, Elvis." *ABC/Primetime*, April 3, 2003 (RT) (hereafter cited as Sawyer, "Lisa Marie Presley").

Taraborrelli, J. Randy. "Lisa Marie Presley Said He Was a Passionate Lover. So What WAS the Truth About Jackson's Sexuality?" *Daily Mail*, July 1, 2009.

Winfrey, Oprah. "Lisa Marie Presley Opens Up About Michael Jackson." *Oprah*, October 21, 2010 (RT) (hereafter cited as Oprah, "Lisa Marie Presley).

———. "Priscilla and Lisa Marie Presley's First Mother/Daughter Interview Together." *Oprah*, March 28, 2005 (RT).

CHAPTER 17

Rwaramba-MJ relationship/comings and goings: assorted confidential sources, Tohme; Rwaramba to Barak (see Chapter 1 notes), Rwaramba LAPD statement. Fighting with MJ about drug use: Rwaramba to Barak and LAPD. Insurance premiums/salary cut: Barrack; Tohme told me, "Michael knew he was paying her too much and he wanted her gone." Romonica Harris claim: the now-defunct *News of the World*. Grace's denial of pressuring MJ to marry her: Schaffel, other sources connected to her/Jackson family. Grace re. MJ/Abdullah money/Jackson family: Barak as quoted; facts as stated in High Court testimony. Trip to Bahrain to intervene with Al Khalifa/safe empty/Al Khalifa's people implicating Grace: Hawk, Tohme. As earlier, all Tohme and Hawk quotes except where indicated are from our interviews. MJ feelings of betrayal at Grace's High Court testimony: Tohme, among other sources; everyone seemed to agree that she had done nothing more or less than tell the truth. Abdullah-Englehart exchange: trial testimony. Pfeiffer claims about Klein supplying evidence of staph infection: Pfeiffer counterclaim; Seal/*Vanity Fair*; aftermath: "Jackson 'too sick' for court case"/BBC, Tohme. Grace–Joseph

Kisembo marriage, Uganda background, charity: newvision.co.ug, majimbo-kenya.com; charity also: Friedman/"Jacko Nanny Starts Her Own Charity." Grace described this period to Barak as the longest MJ's children had gone without seeing or speaking to her. Schaffel also recalled her saying it. As to the suggestion that Rwaramba stole money and jewelry that Michael Jackson had left behind in Bahrain, I doubt it. People close to Grace have told me convincingly that she has hardly any funds and basically depends on the generosity of friends to stay afloat. The purpose of including the story from Tohme and Hawk about their conversations in Bahrain was that Michael Jackson had heard it from those two men long before I did and used it either as a reason or as an excuse to send Grace away for the last time.

Tohme taking the fall for sending Grace away: Tohme, CS2 (who said Tohme *was* responsible). Nederlander discussions (see also lawsuit against the MJ estate, broadwayworld.com), animated TV program: Tohme, CS2. Deals negotiated by Tohme: Tohme, court file of his lawsuit against estate, "Tohme Tohme, Michael Jackson's Close Friend and Manager" (placed on the Internet, I'm fairly certain, by Tohme himself). "Secure the future": Tohme to Deutsch. Depletion of Barrack's net worth: Tohme, "Deep Pockets"/*LA Times*; work on Neverland Ranch: Tohme, "Makeover"/*Wall Street Journal*. "Substantial additional value": Barrack to *Wall Street Journal*. "Letter of Intent" and "Promissory Note": review of documents, but each is available online. Tohme is not the only one to claim credit for naming "This Is It"; Kenny Ortega has, too, and probably so have others. Trip to London: Tohme; also, British press coverage. Announcement of O2 shows: Tohme, London press.

Growth of concert series from ten shows to fifty: multiple sources, including KJ lawsuit against AEG, Tohme lawsuit against MJ estate and countersuit. Randy Phillips's doubts audience for more shows: Phillips to London newspapers; filings in AEG lawsuit; Hawk, CS2. Hawk was quite generous in his appraisals of both Tohme and Phillips, but acknowledged MJ's anger at each of them when he discovered more concerts were being planned. CS2 was less positive in his descriptions of the two men, especially Tohme. Phillips surprised by MJ's lack of confidence: Phillips to Tohme, Hawk, and "Michael Jackson's promoter . . . moves"/*Daily Telegraph* (incl. "If Mike gets too nervous"). "Presale" tickets: Hawk, CS2; also, "Thirteen applications per second"/*Daily Telegraph*, "Fans fury"/*Daily Mail*, "Michael Jackson doubles London shows"/*Herald Sun*, "1.5m fans crash sites"/*Evening Standard*, Kreps/*Rolling Stone*; MJ's Web site. "Operatic scene," "high-drama meetings," Tohme convincing MJ to face reality of his circumstances: Hawk, CS2. MJ fiscal situation, including need to earn at least $100 million by 2011 or face liquidation: Tohme, Hawk, CS2. MJ-Prince rivalry persuading MJ to increase number of shows, "Randy really wanted . . . shows happen": either Hawk or CS2. "Sixteen-plus acres," *Guinness Book of World Records*: Phillips's testimony in Conrad Murray trial; KJ lawsuit against AEG. Chef and trainer agreement: KJ lawsuit against AEG, but also reported in media. Division of profits, staging of show: documents in AEG lawsuit; also reported at the time. "This Is It" ticket sales: same articles noted above, as well as NME, Moore/*Daily Telegraph*, MJ official site. Accolades: still posted on official MJ site at time of MJ's death; they remained for some time, but apparently have been removed. Millennium Concerts: Avram lawsuit. "One Night Only": Bob Jones, coverage of O2 shows; hospital room decorated with Shirley Temple and Mickey Mouse posters: *Jet*. Rwaramba on MJ/hospitals: Rwaramba to Barak. "See how many gifts and flowers": Jones, attributed to Neverland maid Blanca Francia. Total haul of $125 million . . . a billion dollars: Hawk.

The record is replete with examples of the Jackson family encircling MJ in the hope of exploiting him financially. Motor home, which remained in MJ's name and is now the property of the Michael Jackson estate: Tohme and Hawk. "Tried to say no to his mother": confidential source. Leonard Rowe background: Friedman, July 21 and 22. R. Kelly/Ne-Yo lawsuits against Rowe: primarily Cohen-Grossweiner/celebrityaccess.com, also Friedman. Rowe re-filed his lawsuit against William Morris (see court filings below) in June of 2012, claiming "newly discovered favorable evidence." In regards to my assertion that Rowe cast himself in the role of oppressed minority, here's what Kelly had to say on the day he was awarded a $3,397,410.38 judgment against Rowe: "I agreed to let Leonard Rowe promote my tour because he convinced me he was an underdog who deserved a chance to prove himself. Like the saying goes, no good deed goes unpunished." A number of other lawsuits were filed against Rowe by investors who accused him of selling them non-existent shares in the Double-Up tour. In his ruling in the R. Kelly case, the judge ordered Rowe to take full responsibility for every one of those lawsuits. Return of Frank Dileo (and Rowe): Patrick Allocco interview, other material/muzikfactorytwo.blogspot.com. Binder agreement in AllGood deal: review of document. Allocco–Joe Jackson–Dileo meetings: Allocco to muzikfactorytwo blogger Yazmeen; also, Allocco filing against Dileo/MJ estate. Lamicka lawsuit: Allocco to Yazmeen. Allocco quotes throughout these notes will be from this interview except as otherwise cited. Yazmeen actually obtained a copy of that lawsuit (in which Lamicka was accused of falsely identifying himself as a representative of the rock group KISS and bilking an Oklahoma company out of $50,000). That lawsuit ended when the plaintiffs were awarded a default judgment of $250,000 after Lamicka failed to show up in court. Allocco account of Lamicka/aftermath and Dileo/AEG deal: muzikfactorytwo, Allocco filing against Dileo/MJ estate. Rowe claim of agreement with MJ siblings (after convincing Janet she lacked "drawing power"), gathering at MJ's gate, forcing MJ into a meeting (incl. Rowe quotes): Rowe, *What Really Happened.* I was told by a source I trust that this meeting actually took place. Allocco/Rowe approaching Tohme/Hawk, Rowe/Hawk/Allocco meeting/Rowe's aggressive behavior, AllGood background: primarily Hawk, also Tohme. Need to relaunch career overseas (which Randy Phillips has acknowledged in interviews), stalling Allocco and Rowe: Hawk, Tohme. Joe and Rowe forcing their way into Carolwood, "I have no money and it's your fault": Friedman, March 26 and 30, 2009; also Tohme, via secondhand sources. Rowe claim that MJ signed an agreement: Rowe press release. Joe and Rowe going to KJ, persuasion tactics: Hawk, Tohme, CS2; also, confidential sources close to Mrs. Jackson; much of that information has been adduced by KJ/AEG lawsuit. Tohme heard about the pressure being applied to MJ and how MJ was dealing with it in some of their last real conversations in late March of 2009. Joe-Katherine conversations: confidential sources, also reported when Joe blamed KJ for MJ's death (interview, 2010). KJ rationale for why MJ should sign AllGood deal: confidential sources. Two of these sources told me Mrs. Jackson insisted then and continues to insist that MJ's biggest mistake was leaving the Jackson 5.

Dileo campaign against Tohme: confidential sources; Dileo made many of the same accusations in interviews immediately after MJ's death (Dileo to NBC and Raffles Van Exel). The best public record source of information about all of this, though, is the "Frank Dileo wasn't rehired by Michael Jackson!" article Yazmeen posted on muzikfactorytwo. Tohme appearing out of his depth in London: several off-record sources. MJ complaining about Tohme/control: assorted sources, including Brother Michael, MJ–June Gatlin tape, confidential source involved in AEG deal from the beginning. Dileo-Rowe meeting: muzikfactorytwo, esp. interview with Allocco, who was at the time in constant contact with Dileo and Rowe. Peter Lopez on Tohme, Brother Michael–Dileo relationship: CS2. Brother Michael/Tohme "mostly talk": Brother Michael (in e-mail communications with me via Perry Sanders—see Brother Michael to Sanders e-mails). Tohme alienating people: Hawk, CS2, among others. Celebrity Access: see below. Randy Phillips e-mail (sent to *Celebrity Access*'s Ian Courtney): given to me by Tohme, who claims it was given to him by Phillips.

COURT CASES

Civil

LASC BP117321 2/17/12.
98 CV 8272 (United States District Court, Southern District of New York) *Rowe Entertainment v. William Morris Agency*, June 12, 2012.

DOCUMENTS

Julian and Tohme, 8/7/08.

"Binder Agreement" between Dileo Entertainment and Touring Inc. and AllGood Entertainment. November 21, 2008 (hereafter cited as Binder Agreement, 11/21/08.

Rwaramba, 9/12/09.

"Letter of Intent" for Agreement between Michael J. Jackson and AEG Live. January 26, 2009 (hereafter cited as Letter of Intent, 1/26/09).

"Promissory Note," 1/26/09.

"Michael Jackson Manager." E-mail from Randy Phillips to Ian Courtney, *Celebrity Access*. April 1, 2009 (hereafter cited as Phillips to Courtney, 4/1/09).

AL-KHALIFA LAWSUIT/GRACE RWARAMBA

Friedman, Roger. "Jacko Nanny Starts Her Own Charity." *Showbiz411.com*, May 29, 2009 (I).

"Biggest Enabler."

"Jackson 'Too sick' for Court Case." BBC, November 18, 2008 (RT).

"Michael Jackson's Uganda Nanny Comes from Bushenyi." newvision.co.ug, June 29, 2009 (I).

Seal, "Doctor Will Sue."

"Ugandan Born 'Ms. Grace Rwaramba,' Michael Jackson's Nanny, Could Get Custody of the Children." majimbokenya.com, June 29, 2009 (I).

AEG DEAL/ANNOUNCEMENT OF O2 SHOWS/
TOHME/BARRACK/DEALMAKING

Allen, Nick. "Thirteen Applications per Second for Michaeldate." *Daily Telegraph*, July 6, 2009.

Cable, Simon. "Fans' Fury as Touts Sell Michael Jackson Concert Tickets for Up to £16,000 a Pair on Black Market." *Daily Mail*, March 13, 2009.

Day. "Off the Wall."

Deutsch, "Mysterious Advisor" 7/4/09.

"Dr. Tohme Tohme, Michael Jackson's Close Friend and Manager." freearticles227.blogspot.com, February 3, 2011 (I).

Kreps, Daniel. "Michael Jackson's 'This Is It!' Tour Balloons to 50-Show Run Stretching into 2010," *Rolling Stone*, March 12, 2009.

Lee and Ryan. "Deep Pockets."

Mason. "Phillips Profile."

"Michael Jackson London O2 Ticket Warning Issued." *NME*, March 5, 2009.

"Michael Jackson Recovers After Collapsing in New York." *Jet*, December 25, 1995.

Miranda, David. "Michael Jackson Doubles London Shows After 2 Million Seek Tickets." *Herald Sun*, March 12, 2009.

Moore, Matthew. "Michael Jackson O2 Ticket Website Attracting 16,000 Visits a Second." *Daily Telegraph*, March 6, 2009.

"1.5M Fans Crash Sites in Rush for Jacko Gig." *Evening Standard*, March 11, 2009.

Rossen, Jeff. "*Today* Investigates: Mystery Man Behind Michael Jackson." *NBC/ Today Show*, August 23, 2009 (RT) (hereafter cited as Rossen, "Mystery Man").

Schmidt, Veronica. "Michael Jackson Sells Out London Concerts and Adds More Shows." *Times*, March 11, 2009.

Singh, Amar. "Detoxing Brand Jacko." *Evening Standard*, March 13, 2009.

Smith, Ethan. "Economic Reality Prompts a Makeover at 'Neverland.'" *Wall Street Journal*, June 13, 2009.

Yazmeen. "Frank Dileo Wasn't Rehired by Michael Jackson!" muzikfactorytwo. blogspot.com, November 29, 2010 (I) (hereafter cited as Yazmeen, "Dileo").

JOE AND JACKSONS/LEONARD ROWE/FRANK DILEO/ALLGOOD DEAL

Cohen, Jane, and Grossweiner, Bob. "R. Kelly Awarded Multimillion Dollar Judgment Against Promoter Leonard Rowe." celebrityaccess.com, October 7, 2008 (I).

Friedman, Roger. "Jacko's Dad Still Wants Piece of Pie." Fox News, March 30, 2009 (I).

———. "Jacko's Dad Wants Back in Good Graces." Fox News, March 26, 2009 (I).

———. "Joe Jackson's Partner Has Sketchy History." *Showbiz411.com*, July 21, 2009 (I).

———. "Joe Jackson's Partner: Jail Sentences and Lawsuits on Résumé." *Showbiz411.com*, July 22, 2009 (I).

"Michael Jackson Appoints New Manager: Leonard Rowe, Legendary Promoter, to Steer Singer's Latest Comeback." March 26, 2009 (PR).

"Michael Jackson–Reverent June Gatlin Mystery Audio Tape Today." YouTube, August 26, 2009 (I).

Van Exel, Raffles. "Raffles Van Exel Interviews Frank Dileo." November 4, 2009 (I) (hereafter cited as Van Exel, "Dileo").

"Will Michael Jackson's Real Manager Please Stand Up?" *Celebrity Access*, April 2, 2009 (I).

Yazmeen. "Interview with Patrick Allocco—President of AllGood Entertainment." muzikfactorytwo.blogspot.com, May 24, 2011 (I) (hereafter cited as Yazmeen, "Allocco").

CHAPTER 18

Surge in paparazzi tailing MJ: Tohme, Craig Williams, also widely reported. MJ visits to Klein's office/Taylor's home: primarily, Craig Williams (part of the pack following MJ in last weeks, one of the few to have relationships with Jackson family members), Posner/Daily Beast (see Chapter 10 notes); also McConnell/*Daily Mail*, Seal/*Vanity Fair*, Ryan/"Troubles mount"/*LA Times*. MJ-Klein relationship, prescription of Demerol: lawsuit filings by Klein's former assistant Jason Pfeiffer. Klein's own bills to the Michael Jackson estate describe forty-one separate Demerol injections for MJ in 2009. Klein writing prescriptions in own name to provide drugs to others: former Klein assistant and live-in lover Paul Gohranson to Radar Online. Klein writing twenty-seven prescriptions to himself after MJ return to United States: Dimond/"The Secret World of Arnold Klein"; confirmed by documents adduced in Conrad Murray trial, State Medical Board of California investigation of Klein. Mickey Fine deliveryman coming and going from MJ's house: multiple sources, including Craig Williams; the deliveryman also spoke about making many deliveries to MJ's home of pharmaceuticals prescribed under assumed names (see x17video.com below); also, Murray trial, Medical Board investigation. Straight from Klein's office to Taylor's house: Posner (see Chapter 10 notes), McConnell, confirmed by Williams. Klein 2009 work on MJ, including "emergency situation": Klein bill to MJ estate. MJ hatred of aging (incl. quotes): MJ to Boteach. "I'd rather go out like Elvis": MJ to Gotham Chopra, in Deepak Chopra's "Tribute" to MJ. "This Is It" preparation: Tohme, but it should be noted he was essentially absent from the scene from early April until shortly before MJ's death. Selection of musicians: "Michael Jackson Band" file/MJ official site. MJ thinking of self first as a dancer: Tohme, among many others. MJ–Kenny Ortega meetings: Leach (see Chapter 12 notes). Ortega background: imdb.com bio. Ortega seven-figure fee: CS2; solid investment: "Michael Jackson enlists"/NME. Travis Payne résumé, "Scream": imdb.com. Selection of dancers: "Comeback Gig Dancers"/Sky News, MJ's own Web site. Audigier/crystal-encrusted costumes: "Extra . . . tickets"/NME. Panagiris "Beat It" solo/hiring: Panagiris to Gottlieb/*Boston Herald*. Ferrigno-MJ: Dobuzinskis/Reuters, unbylined/*People*. "Fulfilled and happy," "Mr. Mom": Hoffman/*Rolling Stone*. No needle marks: multiple Ferrigno interviews, including Van Susteren.

MJ's drug use has been thoroughly and depressingly documented since his death, dating back to the time he checked into rehab in London in 1993, before and during his criminal trial and in the last months of his life. Schaffel and Wiesner both told me that boredom was one of the things that motivated MJ's drug use, although I'm sure they'd both agree that emotional distress was a far bigger part of it. Karen Faye, who knew MJ longer if not as well as those two, voiced the opinion (in her LAPD interview, via TMZ) after MJ's death that he was "self-sabotaging" during May and June of 2009 in order to get out of his commitment to the O2 shows. Gerald Posner made the same contention (based on an interview with a source he didn't identify) in his Daily Beast article "Jackson's Final Panic." There may be something to that. Injecting mostly below waist: AS1; see also necrosis photo/*Daily Mail* (see Chapter 12 notes); autopsy found needle marks both above and below MJ's waist; confidential source told me that could be explained by the fact that a doctor was administering his drugs during the last weeks of MJ's life. Two sources who have been quoted by name in this book but don't want to be on this subject told me that MJ liked to have a doctor supervise his injections, but would do it himself if there was no other choice. Resort to needles due to insomnia: same two sources, who said that when he went two or more days without sleep he was willing to try almost anything to get some rest. MJ drug tolerances: evidenced by quantities Conrad Murray *admitted* to administering; see also Wiesel's doctor, Chapter 12. Propofol preferred when desperate for sleep: circumstances of death/Murray trial. Cherilynn Lee–MJ meeting/propofol, including quotes: Lee to Elber/Associated Press; Lee witness testimony at Murray trial (unimpeached); also, other Lee interviews. Furthermore, a confidential source in a position to know has told me her story is true. Tadrissi: document presented but not allowed into evidence in Murray trial, later part of Coroner's Office/Medical Board investigations; also, see Chapter 26 notes.

Dileo-Arfaq Hussain, Hussain's arrival: Tohme. Perfumer: London tabloid reports on MJ ordering two bottles of $75,000 perfume (which Hussain was selling); he also later identified himself as MJ's "costume designer," but I found no verification. Tohme's private investigator reported that Hussain approached Mohamed Al-Fayed years earlier with the claim he was one of MJ's associates, but it was clear that Al-Fayed, his head of security and Tohme's investigator all thought that was untrue. Julien Auctions lawsuit/controversy: court file, *LA Times*, Tohme, Hawk. Hippach report on Tohme/reaction: review of document, provided by Brother Michael, who I believe dealt with Hippach for MJ; Brother Michael, confidential source. Tape-recorded conversation: MJ to "the Reverent" June Gatlin. (I conducted a lengthy, amusing, and ultimately frustrating interview with Gatlin, prompted by Tohme's claim that the tape recording was "a fake" and that it wasn't MJ's voice. Gatlin refused to say who had introduced her to MJ, when they met, how often they spoke, or to offer any other information that would corroborate a connection to MJ and the authenticity of the tape recording. In the end, though, I decided the tape recording was authentic, based on a conversation with a confidential source who was in MJ's household and told me that MJ had spoken on the phone with Gatlin twice, but never actually met her face-to-face. I'm pretty sure MJ had no idea he was being recorded.)

Michael Amir Williams (Brother Michael) attempts to expose Tohme/Tohme retorts: Brother Michael via Sanders, Tohme. MJ pleased with Tohme deals: CS2 (CS2 was no fan of Tohme and felt he deserved credit for some of those deals), Hawk, Jeff Cannon. Julien Auctions imbroglio causing end of MJ-Tohme relationship: nearly everyone I spoke to; CS2, though, said it was also due to Tohme's involvement in raising the number of O2 concerts to fifty. "Priceless and irreplaceable," other MJ quotes re. Julien lawsuit: initial court filing. Hawk re. Julien: Hawk. "Like Disneyland collides with the Louvre": Julien in Hoffman/*Rolling Stone*, probably from Julien's promotional materials. Julien's demands: lawsuit filings, Tohme, Hawk, CS2. Tohme sending James Weller to Julien: Tohme, who described Weller as "a complete gentleman" who would never threaten anyone. Weller background: résumé/TRW site, Raine/*San Francisco Chronicle*. Julien on Weller meeting, including location, Weller denial: Julien affidavit and Weller declaration/court file. Friedman evisceration of Tohme: Friedman, March 16 and 24, 2009. Tohme will no doubt be unhappy with me for accepting Friedman's account of their conversations, but I think his story holds up in this instance. I have seen Tohme's Senegalese passport, signed by Abdoulaye Wade, with a notation in the president-for-life's handwriting identifying him as the country's "Ambassador at Large." Allocco on MJ reaction: Allocco to muzikfactorytwo. Julien-MJ face-off: Smith/*Wall Street Journal*, Villarreal/*LA Times* (incl. "where he got the money"), Friedman. Money from Lockbox: confidential source; I think but can't confirm that specific payment may have been out of the advance promised to MJ by AEG. Allocco-KJ April 2 conversation, Sportsmen's Lodge meeting: Allocco to muzikfactorytwo. Rowe authorization letter: via two sources who have copies; Allocco described MJ signing it to muzikfactorytwo. "Notice of Revocation of Power of Attorney": review of document; Tohme's denial of receipt: Tohme. Dileo/partner Citadel agreement: review of document. The one excellent account of all this is in the three Yazmeen articles listed below. "Orchestrated a conference call": Phillips e-mail to Ian Courtney; Phillips's acknowledgement of Dileo's promise of movie money via Arfaq Hussain is among the few helpful pieces of information I got from him. Dileo as a fringe player: Phillips dismissal of connection to Dileo, response to AllGood cease and desist. Phillips's changing attitude toward Dileo/

agreement with Rowe: Allocco to muzikfactorytwo, Tohme, Hawk confidential sources. I know that the attorneys representing Katherine Jackson in the AEG lawsuit have asked whether Randy Phillips and AEG hired Dileo without MJ's permission. April 22 letter purportedly signed by MJ: review of document; letter written by Dileo: Dileo to Van Exel; details/Phillips reaction confirmed by confidential sources (plus Allocco). Phillips e-mail to Tohme terminating "tour manager" duties: document. Allocco on Phillips-Dileo relationship ("wasn't able to control Michael"): Allocco to muzikfactorytwo; his account confirms those of Tohme, Hawk, CS2, and even Leonard Rowe. "Neverland is finished": Tohme to Smith/*WSJ* ("Michael Jackson auction is cancelled"). "Veritable city," "ten times bigger than Graceland": Deutsch/AP; this was shortly after MJ's death, but two confidential sources close to the situation in the spring of 2009 told me that Tohme was talking about saving Neverland in May, because, they believed, he was trying to impress MJ. As above, all Tohme quotes are from our interviews except where otherwise noted. Arfaq Hussain investigative report: quotes from the document. Tohme on film-industry inroads on MJ's behalf: Tohme, confirmed by contracts, documents, and e-mails he showed me; Randy Phillips has confirmed, in the Ian Courtney e-mail among other places, that the renewal of Dileo relationship was due to the imagined access to the motion picture fund. "Stopped all contact": Allocco to muzikfactorytwo. "Protecting Michael Jackson": Tohme, but similarly stated in (spring/summer 2009) interviews. "Michael had always done best": confidential source. John Landis lawsuit: court file, Gumbel; Landis quotes: as indicated. Ola Ray lawsuit (and current circumstances): *Daily News*, TMZ; Tohme and I also discussed it. MJ personal reaction to lawsuits: Tohme, Mesereau, others. Hurling cell phone through window: bodyguards to ABC. "Same thousand parasites": Barrack in "Deep pockets"/*LA Times*. Raymone Bain lawsuit: TMZ May 6, Friedman May 7; "Raymone Bain was not at a single one of the meetings": confidential source. Bain's position: court file, Mesereau, sources present when she spoke about it to Katherine Jackson, with whom Bain remains on good terms. MJ call to Terry George: George to Owens/*Daily Mirror* (see Chapter 10 notes); also, Cole, Sky News (see Chapter 10 notes); I also discussed the relationship between George and MJ with an MJ attorney who did not want to be quoted about it. "Dying right in front of everyone": Mesereau.

COURT FILES

Criminal

SA073164 (Los Angeles Superior Court) *The People of the State of California v. Conrad Robert Murray*, February 8, 2010 (hereafter cited as LASC SA073164).

Criminal Investigation

09MJ1897 (United States District Court for the Central District of California, Western Division) "Warrant for Inspection" *In the Matter of A&M Gross dba Mickey Fine Pharmacy, 433 North Roxbury Drive, Beverly Hills, California 90210*, August 21, 2009 (hereafter cited as USDC-CA 09MJ51897).

Civil

SC101420 (Los Angeles Superior Court) *Levitsky Productions, Inc.* (John Landis) *v. Optimum Productions and Michael Jackson*, January 21, 2009.

BC408913 (Los Angeles Superior Court) *MJJ Productions, Inc. v. Julien's Auction House, LLC, and Darren Julien*, March 4, 2009.

LASC BP117321 11/10/09.

CV10 4734 (United States District Court for the Central District of California) *Joseph Jackson v. Conrad Murray, Acres Home Heart and Vascular Associates and GCA Holdings*, June 25, 2010 (hereafter cited as USDC-CA CV10 4734).

2:11-ap-02407-RN (United States Bankruptcy Court, Central District of California) *Arnold W. Klein, M.D. v. Muhammed Khilji and Jason Roger Pfeiffer*, June 27, 2011 (hereafter cited as 2:11-ap-02407-RN 6/27/11).

2:11-ap-02407-RN (United States Bankruptcy Court, Central District of California) *Jason Roger Pfieffer's Counterclaim Against Plaintiff and Defendant Arnold W. Klein*, August 3, 2011 (hereafter cited as 2:11-ap-02407-RN 8/3/11).

LASC BP117321 2/17/12.

DOCUMENTS

"Criminal and Civil Case History: Tohme R. Tohme." Star Investigations, Santa Clarita California, Rick R. Hippach, chief investigator. October 2008.

"Binder Agreement" 11/21/08.

"Letter of Intent" 1/26/09.

"Promissory Note" 1/26/09.

"Full Background Enquiry of Arfaq Hussein in London." Private investigator's report to Tohme Tohme. April 2009.

Phillips to Courtney, 4/1/09.

"Binder Agreement" between Frank Dileo and Citadel Entertainment to promote a Michael Jackson concert in Trinidad and Tobago. April 1, 2009.

Notice of Revocation of Power of Attorney to Dr. Tohme R. Tohme by Michael J. Jackson, notarized by Rebecca Lopez. April 14, 2009.

Letter (apparently signed by Michael Jackson) informing AEG that Tohme Tohme will not serve as production manager on the "This Is It" tour. April 22, 2009.

E-mail from Randy Phillips to Tohme Tohme informing Tohme that Michael Jackson does not want him to serve as manager on the "This Is It" tour. April 25, 2009.

Letter (apparently signed by Michael Jackson) appointing Frank Dileo as "one of [my] representatives and tour manager." May 2, 2009.

Michael Jackson "To Whom It May Concern Letter" regarding Dr. Tohme R. Tohme. May 5, 2009.

Phillips to Sullivan, 4/4/11.

Williams to Sanders, 11/3/11.

MJ SEPARATION FROM TOHME/JULIEN AUCTIONS

Deutsch, "Mysterious Advisor" 7/4/09.

Friedman, Roger. "Claim: Jacko's Rep Threatened Harm from Nation of Islam." Fox News, March 24, 2009 (I).

———. "Jacko's Mystery Manager Revealed." Fox News, March 16, 2009 (I).

"James R. Weller, Worldwide Creative Director." trw—adv.com (I).

Raine, George. "Creating Reagan's Image / S.F. Ad Man Riney Helped Secure Him a Second Term." San Francisco Chronicle, June 9, 2004.

Smith, Ethan. "Michael Jackson Auction Is Canceled." Wall Street Journal, April 15, 2009.

Villarreal, Yvonne. "Michael Jackson auction canceled." Los Angeles Times, April 15, 2009.

Yazmenn, "Allocco."

Yazmeen. "Did Michael Hire Leonard Rowe as His Manager?" muzikfactorytwo.blogspot.com, February 22, 2011 (I).

———. "Dileo."

MJ AND ARNOLD KLEIN

Dimond, Diane. "The Secret World of Arnold Klein." Daily Beast, August 25, 2011 (I) (hereafter cited as Dimond, "Secret World").

"Delivery Guy at Mickey Fine Pharmacy Interviewed About Michael Jackson, Dr. Klein Spotted Leaving in Rolls-Royce." X17video.com, June 30, 2009 (I).

"Interview with Paul Gohranson." Radaronline.com, July 15, 2009 (I).

McConnell, Donna. "Michael Jackson Visits Doctors for Third Time in a Week as Fan Backlash Begins over Concert Cancellations." Daily Mail, May 22, 2009 (hereafter cited as McConnell, "Doctors").

Posner, Gerald. "Jackson Doc."

————. "Jackson Doctor Subpoenaed." *Daily Beast*, July 9, 2009 (I).
————. "Jackson's Final Panic." *Daily Beast*, June 30, 2009 (I).
————. "Jackson's Needle Problem." *Daily Beast*, July 8, 2009 (I).
Ryan, Harriet. "Troubles Mount for Michael Jackson Doctor." *Los Angeles Times*, January 1, 2012.
Seal, "Doctor Will Sue."

PREPARATION FOR "THIS IS IT"

Dobuzinskis, Alex. "The Hulk Trains Michael Jackson Ahead of London Concerts." Reuters, June 19, 2009.
"Extra Michael Jackson O2 Arena Tickets Made Available." *NME*, June 23, 2009.
Gottlieb, Jed. "Guitarist Orianthi Panagaris Gets Screen Time in 'This Is It.'" *Boston Herald*, October 23, 2009.
"Lou Ferrigno Training Michael Jackson for Tour." *People*, June 18, 2009.
"The Michael Jackson Band." michaeljackson.com (I).
"Michael Jackson Enlists *High School Musical* Director for London O2 Shows." *NME*, May 12, 2009.
"This Is It: Jacko Picks Comeback Gig Dancers." Sky News, May 19, 2009 (RT).
Van Susteren, Greta. "Personal Trainer Ferrigno in 'Shock' over Allegations About Jackson's Health." Fox News, July 2, 2009 (RT).

DRUGS/INSOMNIA/PROPOFOL

Elber, Lynn. "AP Exclusive: Michael Jackson, Bedeviled by Insomnia, Begged for Drug, Says Nurse-Nutritionist." Associated Press, June 30, 2009.
"Michael Jackson: Do You Want Fries with That?" *TMZ*, February 14, 2011 (I) (hereafter cited as "Do You Want Fries?").
"Drug-Ravaged Legs."
Van Exel, "Dileo."

LEGAL TANGLES/TERRY GEORGE

Dillon, Nancy. "Gloves Are Off! 'Thriller' Co-Star Ola Ray Sues Michael Jackson for Royalties." *New York Daily News*, May 6, 2009.
Friedman, Roger. "Jacko Sued by Manager Who Made Him Millions." *Showbiz411.com*, May 7, 2009 (I).
Gumbel, Andrew. "John Landis Slaps Singer with 'Thriller' Lawsuit." *Thewrap.com*, January 27, 2009 (I).

"Terry George."

Lee, "Landis."

"Michael Jackson Estate Settles War with Thriller 'Date.'" *TMZ*, May 10, 2010 (I).

"Michael Jackson Sued by Former Flack." *TMZ*, May 6, 2009 (I).

Netter, Sarah. "Michael Jackson Bodyguards Speak on Protecting the King of Pop." abcnews.go.com, March 8, 2010 (I).

CHAPTER 19

MJ's circumstances at time of Neverland raid/arrest: Schaffel, Wiesner; they and Stuart Backerman were the people most involved in his life/career then. Timing of raid: Tom Sneddon denied back then (in response to an accusation from Backerman) that he had deliberately timed it to ruin the release of *Number Ones* (Broder/*New York Times*); subsequent revelations suggested that Sneddon was, indeed, aware of the record's release. Schaffel, Wiesner, and Tom Mesereau all said they were certain the prosecutor intentionally dampened the release of *Number Ones*, and that MJ was absolutely certain of it. Sneddon had retired by the time I began work on this book and his chief assistant, who was in many senses the lead prosecutor on the case, Ron Zonen, declined to speak to me. I have his thoughts and comments only because of the *Frozen in Time* DVD. Las Vegas/CBS special: Schaffel, Wiesner. (A CBS press release the day of the raid announced that the special had been cancelled "given the gravity of the charges against Mr. Jackson.")

Geragos reputation in Los Angeles: my brother Brady, a criminal defense attorney in LA; a number of other attorneys, including Tom Mesereau, who had a lot to say about the Peterson case. Geragos's failures in the Winona Ryder, Gary Condit, and Scott Peterson cases were all very public. Ann Coulter wrote a devastating assessment of Geragos's ability to fail upward ("We're the Lose-Lose People!") that encompassed the Ryder, Condit, and Peterson cases; Mesereau and a number of other attorneys who did not want to be quoted by name said the same sorts of things. Also, Susman/*Entertainment Weekly* on Ryder, Nieves/*New York Times* on Condit's election loss. Geragos can rightly point out that I didn't note his earlier victory in another high-profile case, the one against Susan McDougal.

60 Minutes appearance a disaster for MJ: Mesereau, Orth/*Vanity Fair*. Exaggeration of "abuse" by sheriff's deputies: the audiotape, Branigin/*Washington Post* (the reporter was at the station when MJ arrived and until his departure). Cooperation with Nation of Islam a mistake: Mesereau, Schaffel,

Wiesner, Backerman to *Vancouver Sun*. I should note, though, that it wasn't Geragos's idea to bring the NOI in—that came from Jermaine Jackson. Alienation from Schaffel/Malnik costing MJ: my own conclusion. "So beautiful it will make you catatonic": Ratner in Orth/"CSI Neverland"/*Vanity Fair* (see Chapter 5 notes); Malnik has acknowledged Ratner introduced him to MJ in his remembrance (almalnik.com). Description of house: Schaffel, page2live. com, homesoftherich.com. Malnik declined to speak with me, mainly because, as I understand it, he did not want to answer any questions about MJ's 2003 will. He did communicate with me a bit through Schaffel, though, and made it clear that he appreciated my effort to hear his side of things. In the end, I found that the lengthy recollection of MJ he posted on his Web site gave me everything I needed—except an answer to what happened to that will. Malnik background/alleged "mob connections": Bob Norman/*New Times*, Orth/"CSI Neverland" article (see Chapter 5 notes). Malnik on meeting/relationship with MJ and MJ's finances: Web site remembrance (incl. all quotes); I also read Malnik's deposition in the Marcel Avram case; see also Malnik to Vieira. All Schaffel quotes except as indicated are from our interviews. Malnik posting MJ's bail: Schaffel, Wiesner, Mesereau, who told me in that order; Friedman reported it at the time. Malnik/MJ's imagined conspiracy: MJ via Schaffel, Mesereau; KJ, who still believes it to be true. Jesse Jackson's role in this part of MJ's life: Mesereau. "Who was forcing the bank's hand": *Guardian*/"Michael Jackson's bad fortune."

Farrakhan/"Hollywood Jews": Schaffel and, especially, Wiesner; Backerman on Farrakhan reaction to his being Jewish: Backerman to *Vancouver Sun*. "Female-acting, sissified": *Los Angeles Herald-Examiner*, 1984. Geragos dropped because distracted by Peterson case: MJ in contemporaneous accounts; see Waxman/ *New York Times*. Johnnie Cochran as person most responsible for decision to settle Chandler case: Schaffel, Wiesner, multiple off-record sources. Cochran/"I'd want Tom Mesereau": Randy Jackson via Mesereau. I understand some might say Mesereau is burnishing his own legend, but as I've noted earlier I consider him the most reliable source I have. Mesereau background: allamericanspeaks. com bio, *USA Today* profile published immediately after MJ's acquittal, and more than two dozen conversations. Robert Blake–Bonnie Lee Bakley case: Mesereau, Tru TV's "crime library." Description of how Mesereau left that case: primarily, Tru TV; of course, I noted what Mesereau said on that subject. Mesereau/Randy Jackson conversations, taking up MJ case, assessment of Santa Maria and strategy: Mesereau; all quotes from Mesereau were from interviews except where indicated. Douglas backing Mesereau: Douglas/"Frozen In Time." Difficulties Mesereau faced, Raymone Bain: Mesereau. XtraJet: facts from *LA Times*, plus Mesereau on how episode fed MJ's paranoia. Sneddon background:

trial coverage, esp. Matt Taibbi/*Rolling Stone*. I don't think anyone disputes that "D.S." is about Sneddon—the prosecutor made jokes about this during the trial. "Open but inactive": Sneddon statement released immediately after Bashir documentary aired in UK (see CNN's "Jackson tries 'shooting the messenger' British TV network says" story below). Sneddon/Garcetti and "Michael Jackson Law": Mesereau; it was discussed at "Frozen in Time," and though that is not the formal title of the law, everyone referred to it that way. Garcetti and Sneddon were already working on this new law when they issued their "Statement of Declination" in the Chandler case in September of 1994. Sneddon's office taping Bashir's documentary: same statement (above/"Shooting the messenger"/CNN); the full text is available on various MJ-related Web sites, including mjjr.net. Neither Sneddon nor anyone from his office has admitted leaking Jordie Chandler's deposition. However, see CNN's story below on the apology over his press conference remarks that Sneddon was compelled to offer.

Feldman report of alleged molestion of Gavin Arvizo: Feldman testimony, affidavits/court file. Katz interview, Janet Arvizo timeline of discovering alleged molestation: court file; Janet Arvizo was compelled to acknowledge these facts on the witness stand. MJ perception of Dimond/Orth out to get him: MJ via Mesereau; the two women sat together all during the trial, and have publicly maintained their belief in MJ's guilt. Dimond reporting/commentary on sexual abuse allegations against MJ: see MJ's own Web site, michaeljackson.com, and various other pro-MJ Web sites (obviously, the presentation there is slanted against Dimond in every way imaginable, but the accounting of the underlying facts is largely accurate). Dimond defends her work on her own Web site, dianedimond.com, but those who want a report on this that is both sympathetic and penetrating should perhaps read Lola Ogunnaike's *New York Times* article "A Dogged TV Reporter Defends Herself in the Jackson Case." Dimond/love letters: Larry King/"Analysis of the Michael Jackson Arrest"/CNN. Nonexistence of letters: Wichita District Attorney Nina Foulston to Greta Van Susteren. I believe even Dimond now acknowledges that those "love letters" never existed. Myung Ho Lee: Orth/"Losing His Grip" (see Chapter 6 notes). Matsuura denunciation of Orth: via Mike Taibbi (explow.com/Mike_Taibbi). "My big worry": Ray Chandler to Orth/"Neverland's Lost Boys."

COURT FILES

Criminal

SBSC 1133603.
Criminal Investigation
USDC-CA 09MJ1897.

Civil

LASC SC026226.

1007622 (Santa Barbara Superior Court) *Marcel Avram v. Michael Jackson,*
June 23, 2000.

DOCUMENTS

Statement of Declination 9/21/94.

ARREST/RAID

Branigin, William. "Jackson Arrested on Child Molestation Charges." *Washington Post,* November 20, 2003.

Broder, John M. "Michael Jackson Faces Arrest on Charges of Child Molesting." *New York Times,* November 20, 2003.

"Michael Jackson Special Canceled—CBS." November 19, 2003 (PR).

GERAGOS/MESEREAU

"Biography of Thomas Mesereau." allamericanspeakers.com (I).

Coulter, Ann. "We're The 'Lose-Lose' People!" anncoulter.com, December 15, 2004 (I).

Kasindorf , Martin, and Jayne O'Donnell. "Mesereau New 'Go-To Guy' for Celebs in Trouble." *USA Today,* June 14, 2005.

King, Gary C. "Who Murdered Bonny Lee Bakley?" TruTV Crime Library (I).

Nieves, Evelyn. "Condit Loses House Race to Former Aide." *New York Times,* March 6, 2002.

Susman, Gary. "Shopgirl: Winona Shoplifted Three Times Before, Prosecutor Told Judge." *Entertainment Weekly,* November 11, 2002.

Waxman, Sharon. "Jackson Says 'Full Attention' of Legal Team Was Lacking." *New York Times,* April 27, 2004.

AL MALNIK

Friedman, Roger. "Jacko's Bail Paid by Reputed Mobster?" Fox News, November 21, 2003 (I).

Lambiet, Jose. "Weird People, Nice Rich People at the Malnik Crib." page2live. com, April 20, 2009 (I).

"Michael Jackson—Al Malnik Friends." almalnik.com, 2009 (I).

"More Pics of Al Malnik's Ocean Ridge, Fla., Mega Mansion." homesoftherich. com (I).

Norman, Bob. "Mutual Benefits Con Man Joel Steinger Spent a Lifetime Getting Mobbed Up." *New Times: Broward-Palm Beach*, May 28 2009.

———. "Reputed Mobster Al Malnik Says He's Executor of Michael Jackson's Will and Blanket's New Dad." *New Times: Broward-Palm Beach*, June 26, 2009 (hereafter cited as Norman, "Reputed Mobster").

Vieira, Meredith. "Al Malnik Interview." *Today/NBC*, June 30, 2009 (RT).

JESSE JACKSON/LOUIS FARRAKHAN/MUSLIMS

Burkeman, Oliver, and David Teather. "Michael Jackson's Bad Fortune." *Guardian*, June 14, 2005.

Mackie, John. "Stuart Backerman Remembers Michael Jackson." *Vancouver Sun*, June 26, 2009.

"Muslim Leader Isn't Thrilled." *Los Angeles Herald Examiner*, April 12, 1984.

TOM SNEDDON/DEVELOPMENT OF CASE

Harris, Art. "Tom Sneddon: Jovial Press Conference Was 'Inappropriate.'" CNN, November 26, 2003 (RT).

"Jackson Tries 'Shooting the Messenger' British TV Network Says." cnn.com, February 10, 2003 (I).

Krikorian, Greg, and Richard Winton. "XtraJet Executive Called FBI Informant. Jeffrey Borer Denies the Reports. Agency Denies Any Role in Videotaping Michael Jackson on Jet." *Los Angeles Times*, November 27, 2003.

Orth, Maureen. "Neverland's Lost Boys." *Vanity Fair*, March 2004 (hereafter cited as Orth 3/04).

Taibbi, Matt. "Inside the Strangest Trial on Earth." *Rolling Stone*, April 7, 2005 (hereafter cited as Taibbi, "Strangest Trial").

———. "The Nation in the Mirror: The Face of George Bush's America at the Michael Jackson Trial." *Rolling Stone*, June 30, 2005.

DIANE DIMOND/MAUREEN ORTH

Foulston, Nola, interviewed by Greta van Susteren. "On the Record with Greta van Susteren." *Fox News*, November 24, 2003 (RT).

King, Larry. "Analysis of Michael Jackson Arrest." CNN, November 24, 2003 (RT).

"Michael Jackson–Diane Dimond." dianedimond.net (I).

"Michael Jackson–Diane Dimond." michaeljackson.com (I).

"Mike Taibbi." explow.com/Mike_Taibbi (I).

Ogunnaike, Lola. "A Dogged TV Reporter Defends Herself in the Jackson Case." *New York Times*, June 16, 2005.

"Wichita DA: Michael Jackson Love Letters 'Patently False.'" *Popdirt.com*, November 25, 2003 (I).

CHAPTER 20

MJ video statement: his Web site, where it can still be found; see also Chawkins/ *LA Times*. Rationale for seeking permission for the statement: Mesereau; throughout this section Mesereau quotes are either statements made in court, or from interviews with me—it should be fairly clear from context which is which. I cite below any exceptions as well as when our interviews informed what I wrote without being directly quoted. Jury selection: primarily, "Jackson jury from diverse backgrounds"/ cnn.com, also, Mesereau, Aphrodite Jones/ *Michael Jackson Conspiracy*.

I read the entire transcript of the trial, reviewed most of the affidavits, statements, pleadings, and other documents (most of the actual evidence had been returned after MJ's acquittal, but there were complete listings and descriptions in the court file) and my reporting on what took place is based almost entirely upon what I discovered there. I confess that I knew very little about the trial beforehand. I did read both of Matt Taibbi's *Rolling Stone* articles, but it was only when I read the full transcript that I realized how weak the case against MJ had been. I was about halfway through the transcript when Mesereau and I began talking about it, as we did on a regular basis for the next two-plus years. Aphrodite Jones's book offers little more than can be found in the trial transcripts, although her observations of courtroom dynamics were somewhat helpful. The accounts of Ron Zonen and Judge Rodney Melville are derived from their presentations at the "Frozen In Time" symposium. When I draw on any additional sources I will note them, but other than that I'm going to simply repeat that the information comes from the trial transcripts and the exhibits introduced in support of it.

Opening statements: entirely court transcript, plus exhibits (prosecutor's original information, Geragos on *Dateline*, prosecution filings in "re-arraignment").

Bashir's testimony: trial transcript, Mesereau (all the quotes from interviews), Taibbi/"Nation in the Mirror." Lafferty video: viewed most of it; also, Aphrodite Jones, Orth/"CSI Neverland" (see Chapter 5 notes). MJ reaction:

Jones, followed up with Mesereau. Davellin testimony: trial transcript, except "most sympathetic and likeable": based on Mesereau.

I introduced the Bradley Miller interview with the Arvizos in a somewhat different order than it was introduced at trial, for reasons of narrative flow. It's not directly germane to this case, but in June of 2012 Miller was sentenced to a year in jail, plus probation and fines, for obstructing justice in a rape case; O. J. Simpson trial judge Lance Ito is the one who sentenced him.

"Rebuttal video": I viewed it and pegged what was on it to the Arvizos's related testimony. Star Arvizo testimony: trial transcript and exhibits introduced testimony only; some influence from Mesereau re. his demeanor, Schaffel on him and his family. Gavin Arvizo testimony: trial transcript and exhibits. Physical description via Jones, Orth (see Chapter 5 notes), and Taibbi, plus Mesereu, who was taken aback by it. MJ bolting from courtroom, Mesereau reaction: Orth (see Chapter 5 notes), trial transcript; Mesereau to a lesser extent. Mesereau/judge: transcript; description of conversations with MJ re. back injury, hospital trip, and late arrival: Mesereau. Mesereau stated MJ was at "the Cottage Hospital" incorrectly; he was at Marian Medical Center, per the Manuela Gomela Ruiz lawsuit/related articles (see Chapter 1). I should perhaps note that the "litany of complaints" from Gavin's teachers introduced during Mesereau's cross-examination was much more extensive than I've reported here. Judge slapping away Sneddon's objections: Mesereau, similar descriptions in trial coverage. Providing receipts Mesereau used to impeach Arvizos: Schaffel, Mesereau. Media behavior: Mesereau; see also Charles Thomson. Ron Zonen trip to NYC to meet with Jordie Chandler: adduced during trial, Mesereau; FBI role did not come out until December 2009, when 343 pages of FBI materials involving MJ were released, including memos concerning meetings between prosecutors and the BAU and between FBI agents and Jordie Chandler. See"FBI Took Shot At Jackson"/Smoking Gun, including September 14, 2004, memo re. meeting and conference call. "I don't think Jordie": Ray Chandler, spoken before he told me he did not want to be quoted about his nephew. Larry Feldman testimony, cross-examination: trial transcript, supplemented by Mesereau, Jones. June Chandler testimony: trial transcript, supplemented by Mesereau, plus Orth (sympathetic), Jones (not). Janet Arvizo description: principally Mesereau, plus Orth, Jones. Judge Melville statement, Janet Arvizo direct and cross-examinations: trial transcripts. Zonen's heroic effort: Mesereau told me several times that Zonen was a far more formidable opponent than Sneddon. Jury reaction to Janet: Mesereau, also Jones, and Orth, who alone among the three was offended by the jurors's attitudes. Jurors amazed by Janet lying about even little things: Mesereau. Debbie Rowe testimony, taping of phone conversations: primarily Mesereau, also transcripts. "Murder cop": Rowe to Wetheridge/*Daily Mail*.

COURT FILES

Criminal

SBSC 1133603.

DOCUMENTS

"Michael Jackson Trial Press Release." County of Santa Barbara, California. February 6, 2003.

Federal Bureau of Investigation "Case Opening" Synopsis, Case ID #305B-LA-239204, Michael Joe Jackson. September 14, 2004.

"Sensitive Case." Summary by Jennifer Hottenroth, Assistant Regional Administrator, Department of Children and Family Services. November 26, 2003 (hereafter cited as "Sensitive Case" Summary 11/26/03).

TRIAL

Chawkins, Steve. "Jackson Rails Against Leaks in Abuse Case." *Los Angeles Times*, January 31, 2005.

"FBI Took Shot at Jackson." *Smoking Gun*, December 22, 2009 (I).

Marquez, Miguel, and Dree De Clamecy. "Jackson Jury from Diverse Backgrounds." cnn.com, February 24, 2003 (I).

Taibbi, "Strangest Trial."

Thomson, Charles. "Michael Jackson: It's Time for Outlets to Take Responsibility in Covering the Rock Star." *Huffington Post*, March 2, 2010 (I) (hereafter cited as Thomson, "Responsibility").

———. "One of the Most Shameful Episodes in Journalistic History." *Huffington Post*, June 13, 2010 (I) (hereafter cited as Thomson, "Shameful").

Wetheridge, Annette. "My Life as the Mother of Michael Jackson's Children, by Debbie Rowe." *Daily Mail*, February 8, 2008.

CHAPTER 21

Mesereau strategy re. proceeding with defense case, presentation strategy: Mesereau. MJ only sleeping well in hospital: Rwaramba to Barak (see Chapter 1 notes); she said the two of them checked in regularly so that he could get some rest. Unwanted people lurking about Neverland: Mesereau, but specific language of photo captions is from Theroux/*Daily Telegraph* (see Chapter 2 notes). Scene at the courthouse: Mesereau, YouTube videos shot by people who were there, Jones, Orth (see Chapter 5 notes), Thomson. Again, Mesereau's quotes are from interviews with me: as in Chapter 20, it should be clear which Mesereau quotes are from court; all quotes looking back on it are from interviews (and are not individually cited) unless stated. Tabloid headlines: Thomson/Huffington Post; they are still online. "As I watched the mother": Orth/"CSI Neverland" (see Chapter 5 notes). "Pedophiles don't target kids": Dimond/"Real World Walks"/*NY Post*. Wade Robson/Brett Barnes testimony/examination: trial transcript; their emotional reactions: Mesereau, to me and to Jones. Mesereau praised Macaulay Culkin and Chris Tucker equally in our interviews, and was quite scathing in his criticisms of various celebrities who refused to show up on MJ's behalf. Culkin quotes: entirely from trial testimony. Azja Pryor, Violet Silva, Joe Marcus quotes: all from trial transcript. I either summarized or omitted the testimony of other witnesses between Culkin and Pryor, and after Marcus. Anything in quotes is from trial testimony. Irene Peters's testimony should perhaps be read in the context of the "Sensitive Case" summary written by her superior Jennifer Hottenroth.

I summarized, obviously, the testimony of the forensic accountant, the Social Services intake worker, the weekly newspaper editor, and Janet Arvizo's sister-in-law. Mary Holzer testimony: trial transcript. Martin Bashir recalled to witness stand, outtake excerpts played to the jury: trial transcript and exhibits in support, aided by Jones's detailed account, Mesereau. Jurors recalling wanting to spit on Bashir: Mesereau. Conclusion of defense case, frustration of prosecution's wish to recall the Arvizos: Mesereau (he could scarcely hide his enjoyment, even five years later). Zonen and Mesereau closing arguments: entirely from trial transcript.

Media coverage observations: my own reading of it four, five, and six years after the fact, Thomson, Mesereau; numbers and logistics of coverage: redorbit. com. "Had to be rescued by sheriff's deputies": Judge Melville/"Frozen in Time." Mesereau/Yu underground: Mesereau. "Nervous for the defense": Richards on MSNBC's *The Abrams Report*. Scene at courthouse the day of verdict: Mesereau, foremost, also multiple YouTube videos, Jones. Media reactions to verdict: Thomson, also still online. Jury foreman Rodriguez/Gavin Arvizo not believable: Rodriguez to Nancy Grace. Polls on trial verdict: Thomson, most also still online. Berry Gordy comment: via Mesereau. Klein quote, ratings victory of "Nanny 911," Wendy Murphy on jurors: Thomson. Murphy, by the way, still insists MJ was guilty. Zonen description of jury, Mesereau response, Judge Melville/"incredible pressure": "Frozen in Time." Jurors Hultman and Cook remarks: "Rita Crosby: Live and Direct." Mesereau response: Mesereau. Jacksons's celebration, KJ quote: *LA Times, NY Daily News*; juror Pauline Coccoz almost starting to cry: *Daily News* only. Mesereau conversations with

MJ, Rwaramba, and others: Mesereau. Wendy Murphy, Diane Dimond, *Washington Post* editorial: again, Thomson, all still online. "Framed!" tour: Orth/"CSI Neverland" (see Chapter 5 notes); Wiesner response: Wiesner.

COURT FILES

Criminal

SBSC 1133603.

DOCUMENTS

"Sensitive Case." Summary 11/26/03.

TRIAL/AFTERMATH

Crosby, Rita. "2 Jurors Say They Regret Jackson's Acquittal." *MSNBC/Live and Direct*, August 9, 2005 (RT).

Dimond, Diane. "Real World Walks into Jacko Trial." *New York Post*, March 6, 2005.

Haberman, Maggie. "Ex-Juror Parties at Jacko's." *New York Daily News*, June 19, 2009.

"Interview with Jackson Jury Foreman." *Nancy Grace Show, Headline News*, June 15, 2005 (RT).

"Jackson Jury Deliberations." *MSNBC/ Abrams Report*, June 10, 2005 (RT).

Lin II, Rong-Gong, and Monte Morin. "Jackson Fans at Victory Bash." *Los Angeles Times*, June 18, 2009.

Thomson, "Responsibility."

———. "Shameful."

"2,200 Journalists Await Jackson Verdict." redorbit.com, June 10, 2005 (I).

CHAPTER 22

Postponement of O2 shows: AEG Web site; *NY Daily News, Daily Mail, NME*, Roger Friedman columns (three, including "We Told Ya"), others. MJ's anger re. fifty shows: musicradar.com. Wiesner/Schaffel reaction, MJ preference for movie/video work: Wiesner, Schaffel. "When it's over, it's over" MJ quote: Boteach. MJ staying home and missing rehearsals: McConnell/*Daily Mail*, other London papers not cited. MJ "I know my schedule": via Ortega to Hoffman/*Rolling Stone*. MJ's visits to Klein's offices: McConnell/*Daily*

Mail among others; Bedford building paparazzi stakeout: Craig Williams, also, Posner (see Chapters 10 and 12 notes). MJ carried out of Klein's offices: Jason Pfeiffer court filing; also, bodyguard Faheem Muhammad testimony/Murray trial testimony. O2 shows insurance issues and AEG/Lloyds of London/Michael Jackson estate: file of KJ lawsuit against AEG; conversations with Mrs. Jackson's advisors, plus confidential sources on the three-way battle; also, Michaels/*Guardian* story and Ryan/*LA Times*, which drew on a copy of the policy. Predictions O2 concerts would be cancelled: Friedman, Perez Hilton, others. "Making up rumors": Phillips to Mason/*Daily Telegraph*. Dr. Slavit examination, certificate of health, details of insurance policy: AEG lawsuit documents, which also informed Ryan's *LA Times* article. Dr. Slavit also noted MJ's lupus/vitiligo symptoms, but those were not considered a threat to his health. Hiring of chef, physical trainer: AEG "Letter of Intent" and "Promissory Note," e-mails between AEG and MJ representatives. Kai Chase description of diet, MJ seeing self as dancer, only Murray allowed into MJ bedroom: "Jackson chef recalls doctor's role, final days"/Associated Press. Phillips/AEG resistance to Murray demands/recompense: Murray trial testimony, e-mails admitted into evidence. "Just like President Obama": Phillips to Hoffman/*Rolling Stone*. "This is the machine": Gongaware testimony/Murray trial. Dileo on hiring a doctor to separate MJ/Klein: Murray trial testimony/evidence, AEG lawsuit documents. Dr. Murray hiring: Michael Amir Williams testimony/Murray trial, evidence given by same to KJ attorneys in AEG lawsuit. Murray background: trial, Haynes, and Harasim/*Las Vegas Journal-Review*; it's only because of Harasim that I know Murray is from Trinidad, not Grenada, as has been widely reported. Brother Michael and Gongaware communications with Dr. Murray; Gongaware, Jorrie quotes: Murray trial testimony. Dr. Murray ladies' man, nightlife, strip clubs: preliminary hearing, Harasim article (in which a "promotions girl" recalled that he liked to pose shirtless with women twenty years younger). Assertion Tohme would have kept Murray out: confidential source. May 5 letter signed, apparently, by MJ, circumstances of its arrival, reaction: review of document, via same source, interview. Letter actually written by Dileo: Dileo admitted this (Van Exel) before his death. Tohme insistence the letter was forged, he never received it, etc.: Tohme. As noted earlier, I have a copy of the May 5 letter and of the May 2 letter in which MJ apparently names Dileo as "one" of his representatives. Dileo bio: multiple sources; Tookaroosa Ranch/Tribeca Grill investment: Todd Gold's *People* article. Phillips-Dileo relationship: both attorneys who represented MJ in the last year of his life, Allocco to muzikfactorytwo; it's also the subject of inquiry by attorneys representing Katherine Jackson in the AEG lawsuit. 2009 Beverly Hilton Hotel Mann-Dileo conversations: Mann.

"Comfort level": Dileo quoting Phillips to Van Exel. Potential world tour: Dileo, Phillips in interviews. "I don't blame Randy . . .": confidential source. Hawk on conversations with Dileo: Hawk. Concern re. MJ's commitment to O2 shows: e-mails to and from him admitted into evidence at trial, others via my sources; Phillips at Beverly Hills Hotel meeting, Allocco interview, other sources. Katherine/Joe Jackson anniversary dinner: confidential source, but time and place coincide with "Michael Jackson Timeline"; KJ to *Daily Mirror*. Date discrepancy: Katherine and Joe were married November 5, 1949. Perhaps the anniversary dinner was held in May to honor their first date, not their marriage, or perhaps, as was suggested to me by an anonymous source, the event had been arranged as an opportunity to convince MJ to meet again with Joe and Rowe to talk about cutting them in on the deal.

MJ more vulnerable to family when with his children/AEG knowledge: Tohme. KJ convincing MJ to come to Beverly Hills Hotel meeting: confidential source. Phillips and Gongaware flanking MJ at meeting, what was discussed: Allocco (to muzikfactorytwo/later in complaints against MJ & estate), Rowe; also, confidential source not present at the meeting but who heard a good deal about it later. "But we all knew how hard it was": confidential source. Brothers' public denial, letter to Rowe: review of both May 15, 2009, press release issued by the Jackson brothers and May 25 letter to Rowe. "No one was sure," "stabbed in the back": confidential sources. "Do or die": Randy Phillips in "Deep pockets"/*LA Times*. Preproduction costs to AEG: primarily, introduced in defense in Murray case (though most of it was kept out); significant part of KJ lawsuit against AEG; also widely reported at the time. "Millionaire from a billionaire": Phillips in "Promoter . . . right moves"/*Telegraph*. "Track record of missed performances": "Deep pockets/*LA Times*; "Michael Jackson Rehearses Near Burbank Airport" also referenced "his reputation for flaking out on performances and business deals." "We made Mohammed come to the mountain": Phillips to *Telegraph*. "In this business": Phillips in "Deep pockets." Wish to "recreate" Victoria Falls: Phillips to contactmusic.com. Phillips added, "We were able to talk him out of that"; I was told by a confidential source that Phillips was a bit more forceful than that in his refusal. Elephant, monkeys, etc., objections of animal rights groups: Jamieson/*Telegraph*; Phillips's gratitude for the protests: confidential source. Phillips reminding MJ his own assets were collateral: same confidential source. "He said he would have to work at McDonald's": Karen Faye to LAPD, reported in "Do You Want Fries with That?"/TMZ. "Michael Jackson economic stimulus": Seatwave president to BBC 6 Music via metro.co.uk. AEG out about $30 million: documents associated with AEG lawsuit; Phillips has acknowledged that, more or less, to Contact Music and other interviews.

"I don't want to hold anything back": Ortega to Hoffman/*Rolling Stone*. Work on sound stages at Culver Studios, Bernt Capra quotes: Wiseman/*Topanga Messenger*; also, Associated Press. Two-a-day sessions with MJ: Travis Payne to Raffles Van Exel. John Caswell quotes: to Kaufman/mtv.com. All-Good lawsuit: review of documents, also, widely reported at the time; see Michaels/*Guardian*. June 16 and 19 absences from rehearsal: tabloids and Internet at the time, evidence in Murray trial, documents connected to AEG lawsuit. "Self-sabotaging": Karen Faye to LAPD/reported on TMZ. That accountants and lawyers were impressed by MJ's focus when it came to business matters I heard from a lawyer and an accountant, neither of whom I can identify by name; Bravado's CEO made the same point in "Singer's Last Big Product Push"/*LA Times*, which enumerated the merchandise to be sold at O2 shows. London shows/potential to repair MJ finances: confidential source. "There are those," "his dignity as an artist": Kenny Ortega to McLean/*Times* of London. Schaffel and Wiesner doubts: Schaffel, Wiesner.

Dileo suggesting bringing Branca aboard: confidential source associated with the lawsuit against AEG. "I'm pretty sure Dileo wanted to bring Branca in": confidential source. "Michael wants you to come back"/emotional reunion: Branca quoting Dileo to Deutsch/Associated Press. At least a dozen people (including Katherine Jackson) have told me that MJ denounced Branca in the strongest possible language during the last years of his life. Tohme introduction to Branca/ lunch date/breaking date at MJ insistence: Tohme; Randy Phillips, on the advice of Marvin Putnam, refused to comment; I also asked Branca, through Mike Sitrick, and got no reply. Michael Amir Williams (Brother Michael) has been very clear about the fact that he never heard Branca's name or heard about any meetings between MJ and Branca or that MJ had rehired Branca as his attorney.

AEG encouraging hiring of Siegel (they nearly succeeded): e-mails between Brother Michael, Randy Phillips's assistant Arlyne Lewiston and Siegel. John Hougdahl (inc. "very shaky" quote): e-mail to Phillips and Gongaware. AEG execs furious: testified to at Murray trial, documents associated with AEG lawsuit, confidential source; this source also told me Ortega reassured Phillips and Gongaware during the shooting of the Dome project. "Hugging bones": Stoller in "Shocking End"/*People*. Weight 157 pounds in London: Tohme, who put MJ on the scale in his hotel suite. "We did talk a lot about his weight": Ortega to Lang/The Wrap. Fork-feeding: Phillips to Hoffman/*Rolling Stone*. "It's not true": Ortega to the *Times* of London. Bain filing for default judgment: June 4, 2009; the appearance on his behalf in D.C. took place shortly before his death; see the Blog of Legal Times, report largely based on *National Law Journal*; also, MJ fan clubs covered this. Gongaware-Rwaramba letter: Rwaramba LAPD statement, review of document. I believe the quotes attributed to Rwaramba by Barak are accurate, which is why I've used them. At the same time, I did feel obligated to acknowledge those (Mallika Chopra and her father Deepak in particular) who have claimed Grace was tricked into giving those interviews, and to note Schaffel's "vulture" opinion. Please see notes to Chapter 12 for more on Grace's interviews with Barak. Grace calling Schaffel in late May 2009: Schaffel.

MJ/worsening insomnia: attested to at Murray trial, media coverage; close advisors of KJ have said his own children told their grandmother they were aware he wasn't getting enough sleep. Late night calls/end of world at hand: confidential sources associatged with KJ/Jackson family, also, Jason Pfeiffer to *Woman's Day*. "Too wound up": Dileo to Rossen/NBC, Van Exel. Payne and Ortega on insomnia/late night calls: Payne to Van Exel, Ortega ("I'm channeling") to the *Times* of London/("information was coming") to Lee/*LA Times* blog., Dr. Allan Metzger/propofol: Lee/*People* (see also Chapter 26). MJ "fearful" O2 concerts would fail due to his exhaustion: Metzger testimony, Murray trial. Klein refusal to prescribe anything beyond sedatives, painkillers, and muscle relaxants: Klein to investigators from coroner's office and medical board/*People v. Murray* court file. I believe him; the only drugs prescribed by Klein in MJ's home after his death were muscle relaxants. Dr. Larry Koplin: subpoena of medical records, L.A. County Coroner; in the subpoena Grace Rwaramba ("Owanda") identified Koplin as "the last physician to treat Jackson." Koplin denied providing MJ with propofol and no evidence has been offered to the contrary. "Groggy and out of it": confidential source, a witness in the AEG lawsuit. Kenny Ortega testimony: Murray trial. Ortega to Phillips e-mail: dated June 20 below, admitted into evidence/Murray trial. AEG execs furious Ortega sent MJ home, Phillips telling Dileo to remind MJ of his contractual obligations: evidence obtained by plaintiffs side/AEG lawsuit. Phillips call to Dr. Murray: Phillips testimony, Murray trial. Dileo voicemail: played in court, evidence. "My concern is" and all Ortega direct quotes and paraphrases in paragraph: Ortega's June 20, 2009, e-mail to Phillips. "He kept telling people": Pfeiffer, *Woman's Day*. MJ inability to get warm: Paris Jackson to KJ, recounted in documents from AEG lawsuit. "I could hear Michael in the background": Lee on *Anderson Cooper 360*.

Conrad Murray drug purchases: evidence (including receipts), preliminary hearing and trial. Benzodiazepine drugs: Wikipedia, associated medical journal articles; "Benzodiazepine" chapter/Shorter/*Historical Dictionary of Psychiatry*. Wikipedia can admittedly be risky, but I found the entries there to be astonishingly thorough and thoughtful. Claims attributed to Murray: interview with LAPD Detectives Martinez and Smith, a significant piece of evidence at the trial. Murray carrying oxygen canisters: Kai Chase to Deutsch/Associated Press, later, to *Larry King Live*, also, Chase to police investigators, Murray trial. June 20, 2009, meeting with Murray: Ortega and Phillips testimony/Murray trial.

COURT FILES

Criminal

LASC SA073164.

Criminal Investigation

USDC-CA 09MJ1897.

Civil

USDC-CA CV10 4734.
LASC BC445597.
2:11-bk-12718-RN (United States Bankruptcy Court, Central District of California) *Bankruptcy Petition of Arnold Klein*, January 20, 2011 (hereafter cited as 2:11-bk-12718-RN).
2:11-ap-02407-RN 6/27/11.
2:11-ap-02407-RN 8/3/11.
LASC BP117321 2/17/12.

DOCUMENTS

"Letter of Intent" 1/26/09.
"Promissory Note" 1/26/09.
Williams to Lewiston, 4/27/09.
Lewiston to Williams, 4/27/09.
E-mail from Barry Siegel, managing partner, Provident Financial Management, to Michael Amir Williams. April 27, 2009.
E-mail from Barry Siegel to Michael Amir Williams. April 28, 2009.
E-mail from Michael Amir Williams to Barry Siegel. April 30, 2009.
E-mail from Barry Siegel to Michael Amir Williams. April 30, 2009.
E-mail from Michael Amir Williams to Barry Siegel. May 1, 2009.
E-mail from Barry Siegel to Michael Amir Williams. May 1, 2009.
"Dear Patients and Friends." Letter sent by Dr. Conrad Murray to announce his "decision to cease practice of medicine." June 15, 2009.
E-mail from John Hougdahl to Randy Phillips and Paul Gongaware. June 19, 2009.

E-mail from Kenny Ortega to Randy Phillips. June 20, 2009.

"Statement by Jermaine Jackson" announcing Michael Jackson's death. June 25, 2009.

"Los Angeles Police Department Internal Affairs Group Transcript of Recorded Interview with Dr. Conrad Murray." June 27, 2009.

Weitzman to Sullivan and Entrekin, 3/31/11.

"RE: Your Letter of March 28, 2011." letter from Lee H. Durst (Howard Mann attorney) to Jeremiah Reynolds (Howard Weitzman associate). April 3, 2011 (hereafter cited as Durst to Reynolds, 4/3/11).

POSTPONEMENT/MJ HEALTH

Connor, Tracy. "Michael Jackson Denies Skin Cancer Report; Star Still Set to Perform at London Comeback Concerts." *New York Daily News*, May 16, 2009.

Friedman, Roger. "Jacko Shows Delayed, but Are Definitely On." *Showbiz411. com*, May 11, 2009 (I).

———. "Jacko Shows Might Be Delayed." *Showbiz411.com*, May 4, 2009 (I).

———. "Jacko Start Date Pushed Back—We Told Ya." *Showbiz411.com*, May 21, 2009 (I).

McConnell, "Doctors."

"Michael Jackson Fans Launch Petition over O2 Arena Postponement." *NME*, May 21, 2009.

Rogerson, Ben. "Jackson 'Angry' at 50-Date O2 Run." musicradar.com, June 2, 2009 (I).

Ryan, Harriet. "Jackson Was Scheduled for a Second Physical." *Los Angeles Times*, August 7, 2009.

DILEO/TOHME/ALLGOOD

Gold, Todd. "Dumped by Michael Jackson, Former Manager Frank Dileo Bounces Back as One of Hollywood's Goodfellas." *People*, October 22, 1990.

"Jacksons Deny Any Involvement with Planned Jackson 5 Reunion Show in Texas with Brother Michael and Sister Janet." May 15, 2009 (PR).

"Michael Jackson's Mum Remembers Her Son a Year On and Reveals What Life Is Like for His Children." *Daily Mirror*, June 20, 2010 (hereafter cited as "Jackson's Mum Remembers").

Yazmeen, "Allocco."

PREPARATIONS FOR "THIS IS IT"

Chmielewski, Dawn C. "Singer's Last Big Product Push." *Los Angeles Times*, July 9, 2009.

Cooper, Anderson. "Michael Jackson's Last Days: Jackson's Nurse Speaks Out." CNN, June 30, 2009 (RT).

Hoffman, "Last Days."

"I Was Jacko's Secret Lover." *Woman's Day*, August 14, 2009.

"Jackson Wanted Victoria Falls Onstage." contactmusic.com, October 16, 2009 (I).

Jamieson, Alastair. "Michael Jackson Wants to Ride an Elephant on Stage at His Concerts, Reports Claim." *Daily Telegraph*, March 25, 2009.

Kaufman, Gil. "Michael Jackson's Last Tour Rehearsals Filed for Possible Release." mtv.com, June 29, 2009 (I).

Lang, Brent. "Kenny Ortega Talks About Michael Again." *Wrap*, December 2, 2009 (I).

Lee, Chris. "Michael Jackson: He Was Channeling God." *LATimes.com*, October 27, 2009 (I).

Lee and Ryan. "Deep Pockets."

Mason. "Phillips Profile."

McLean, Craig. "Kenny Ortega on Michael Jackson's Final Days." *Times*, October 24, 2009 (hereafter cited as McLean, "Ortega").

"Do You Want Fries?"

"Michael Jackson Finally Takes the Stage in D.C. Court." *Legaltimes.typepad. com*, June 19, 2009 (I).

"Michael Jackson in 'Billion Pound' Boost to Economy." metro.co.uk, May 8, 2009 (I).

"Michael Jackson Shocking End, 1958–2009." *People*, July 13, 2009.

"Michael Jackson Wrapped Secret Film Project 2 Weeks Before He Died." Associated Press, July 1, 2009.

Michaels, Sean. "Michael Jackson Comeback Concerts in Jeopardy?" *Guardian*, May 12, 2009.

———. "Michael Jackson Concert Insurer Refuses $17.5 M Payout." *Guardian*, June 8, 2011.

———. "Michael Jackson Sued for O2 Arena Residency." *Guardian*, June 12, 2009.

Rossen, "Mystery Man."

Ryan, Harriet, and Chris Lee. "Michael Jackson Rehearses Near Burbank Airport." *Los Angeles Times*, May 12, 2009.

Van Exel, Raffles. "Dileo."

———. "Interview with Travis Payne." YouTube, June 27, 2009 (I) (hereafter cited as Van Excel, "Travis Payne").

Wiseman, Cassandra. "Tour Set Dies with Michael Jackson." *Topanga Messenger*, July 16, 2009.

DR. CONRAD MURRAY

Deutsch, Linda. "Jackson Chef Recalls Doctor's Role, Final Days." July 29, 2009 (hereafter cited as Deutsch, "Jackson Chef").

Harasim, Paul. "Cardiologists Link Hurting Energy Drink." *Las Vegas Journal-Review*, July 19, 2009.

Haynes, Brian. "Michael Jackson's Doctor Has History of Legal, Financial Woes." *Las Vegas Journal-Review*, June 27, 2009.

DRUGS/PROPOFOL

Lee, Ken. "Doctor Warned Michael Jackson About Propofol in April." *People*, July 31, 2009.

King, Larry. "Breaking News Investigation into Michael Jackson's Death." July 30, 2009 (RT).

WIKIPEDIA

"Benzodiazepine."
"Diazepam."
"Lorazepam."
"Midazolam."
"Propofol."

CHAPTER 23

Move to the Staples Center to accommodate scale of production: Caswell to *USA Today*, also, Ortega and Phillips testimony/Murray trial. "Rise to the occasion": Ortega June 20 e-mail to Phillips. "In this new kind of place": Phillips to Eric Ditzian/MTV. MJ's mercurial nature: multiple sources, including *This Is It*. "Beautiful, beautiful": Ortega to UPI. Orabona quotes: Orabona to Trey Borzillieri/Huffington Post, which Borzillieri sent me. Thanks, Trey. Other performers "an extension" of MJ: recalled by Orabona, Ortega (in different language), *This Is It*. Tohme's visit to Staples Center: Tohme (who showed me the All Access bracelet); Phillips, again on the advice of Marvin

Putnam, declined to comment. Tohme-KJ meeting: Tohme, KJ, her advisors, who obviously agree with her version. Dr. Murray "treatment" of MJ June 23: Murray's June 27, 2009, interview with LAPD detectives Martinez and Smith. June 24 meeting at Staples Center: Ortega and Phillips testimony/ Murray trial, Ken Ehrlich to Lee/Ryan/*LA Times* and Gunderson/Breznican/ *USA Today*, Hoffman/*Rolling Stone*; all accounts describe MJ as happy and excited, esp. about Dome project. MJ-AEG agreements re. "Ghosts": AEG lawsuit, referenced at Murray trial. Descriptions of videos: *This Is It*. "I want people to scream for miles," description of illusions: Alonzo to Gunderson/ *USA Today* article. MJ complaining of laryngitis, "He looked great . . .": Alonzo in "Last Rehearsal"/*LA Times*. "Bioluminescent": Ortega to Hoffman/*Rolling Stone*. "Was electric," "We all looked at each other": Woodroffe to BBC Radio 4, quoted in Gunderson/*USA Today*. "It was fantastic": Phillips to *LA Times*. "I watched in awe," "I honestly could not wait": Mazur to BBC. "The hair on the back of my neck," "What I saw that night": Ehrlich in "Last Rehearsal"/*LA Times*. Orabona: Borzillieri. "He didn't take a moment," MJ stopping to look at spiders: Alonzo in "Last Rehearsal." "Earth Song" performance: Hoffman, *Rolling Stone*. Goose bumps: Phillips to *LA Times*. "When he finished": Ortega to Hoffman/*Rolling Stone*. "This is the dream," "There was this anticipation": Ortega to Ditzien/MTV. MJ leaving Staples around 12:30: Ortega, Phillips, Travis Payne, others. Ghosts coming through the screen: Ortega to McLean/ the *Times* of London. Walking MJ to car, "He put his arm around me . . .": Phillips to Hoffman/*Rolling Stone*. "Ecstatic and excited": Payne to Van Exel.

Murray account of trying to put MJ to sleep: his interview with detectives Martinez and Smith; questions about the doctor's truthfulness are dealt with in the trial section (see Afterword notes). Effects of Valium, Atavin, and Versed: Shorter, Wikipedia pages, medical journals; I also spoke to my own physician, James Biemer, about the effects of benzodiazepine drugs. Clark County warrant for Murray's arrest for failure to pay child support: *Las Vegas Sun*. Pulse oximeter, no longer breathing: Murray to detectives Martinez and Smith. Chernoff claim that police misunderstood: press conference after Murray's police interrogation. Murray phone calls: testimony and evidence in preliminary hearing and criminal trial; messages themselves were played in court. Anding-Murray conversation: Anding testimony, preliminary hearing. "Rushed over to Jackson": Chernoff press conference. Williams message from Murray: Williams's testimony, criminal trial. Murray running downstairs and shouting, Chase quotes: Chase to Deutsch/AP, except Tuscan bean soup: testimony/criminal trial. Chernoff/"get security": press conference, chef did not recall: Chase testimony. Brother Michael, Alberto Alvarez, Faheem Muhammad accounts: their testimony in court. Prince and Paris entering bedroom: Alvarez, Muhammad testimony. Text messages, data packages: prosecution evidence at trial. 911 call, transcript, and exact times: prosecution evidence; this is the entire transcript of the conversation. "I walked into the hall": Chase to Deutsch/AP. Paramedics exact time of arrival, MJ's condition: testimony by paramedics, Senneff and Blount (as all further Senneff/Blount recollections). "We were all praying": Chase to Deutsch/AP. Murray behavior and response to paramedics: paramedics testimony. Chase ordered to leave, etc.: Chase to Deutsch. Dileo–Brother Michael call, subsequent actions: Dileo to Van Exel. Tohme recollections: Tohme. Time of death: Dr. Cooper and Dr. Nguyen testimony, also noted in documents in evidence at Murray trial. Jermaine Jackson announcement of MJ's death: transcript, but also available on YouTube. Murray encounter with Paris Jackson: Murray to detectives Martinez and Smith. Murray asking for a ride: Brother Michael, Muhammad testimony. Travis Payne account, "I saw Kenny's face drop," "No one wanted to believe": Payne to Van Exel. "A lot of rumor calls," production team gathering to pray: Ortega to the *Times* of London, as his for MJ's return "in a strong state of health." Payne and Ortega both recalled the candle lighting in interviews.

COURT FILES

Criminal

LASC SA073164.

Civil

USDC-CA CV10 4734.
LASC BC445597.

LAST DAYS

Borzillieri, Trey. "Michael Jackson's This Is It—Behind the Camera with Videographer Sandrine Orabona." Huffington Post, November 19, 2009.
Ditzian, Eric. "'This Is It' Director Kenny Ortega on Michael Jackson's Final Rehearsals: 'This Is the Dream. We Did It Good, Kenny, We Did It,' Ortega Remembers MJ Saying." mtv.com, October 27, 2009 (I).
Hoffman, "Last Days."
"Kenny Ortega: Michael Jackson Never Thought He Lost His Crown." UPI, October 24, 2009.
McLean, "Ortega."

LAST DAY

Deutsch, "Jackson Chef."

German, Jeff. "Warrant Sought for Michael Jackson Doctor over Child Support." *Las Vegas Sun*, October 7, 2009.

Gundersen, Edna, and Anthony Breznican. "Inside Michael Jackson's Last Show: The Magic Was Back." *USA Today*, June 30, 2009.

Lee, Chris, and Harriet Ryan. "Michael Jackson's Last Rehearsal: Just Beaming with Gladness." *Los Angeles Times*, June 27, 2009.

"Photographer on Jackson Rehearsals." BBC, June 30, 2009 (RT).

Van Exel, Raffles. "Dileo."

———. "Travis Payne."

CHAPTER 24

I arrived in Los Angeles shortly after MJ's death and stayed through the memorial service, all on the dime of *Rolling Stone* magazine. The all-consuming coverage was especially overwhelming in LA, but one also had the sense of its global scale. It was the first time, I think, that I understood how international was MJ's celebrity.

TMZ gloating about breaking story: TMZ; perspective on claims: "Turning Point"/*LA Times.*; see also *Daily Telegraph* on TMZ "scooping the world," *Daily Mail*'s "How Michael Jackson's death shut down Twitter," "Outpouring"/*Christian Science Monitor*, David Sarno/"Michael Jackson–related traffic," Shea Bennett. Scene at hospital, fraternity house, helicopter flying MJ's body to the morgue (incl. girls blocking ER driveway): "Michael Jackson dead at 50"/*LA Times*. "No matter what people say": Harvey Levin in "TV misses out . . ."/*LA Times*. Scene outside MJ's house: *LATimes* blogs, "Tourists flock to Michael Jackson sites"/*LA Times*, "Michael Jackson dead"/CNN, "Michael Jackson fans in shock"/*Daily Mail*. Scene at Hayvenhurst: *LA Times* blogs, "Fans can't stop crying, dancing"/NBC local. Joe Jackson remarks/their timing: "How . . . shut down Twitter"/*Daily Mail*, from *LA Times* blogs. Concern about medical privacy/Britney Spears and Farrah Fawcett outrages: Molly Hennessy-Fiske (which revealed MJ's records were improperly accessed), also, *LA Times* blogs; Lawanda Jackson was being prosecuted for violating medical privacy laws when she died at the age of fifty.

Impromptu MJ memorials: *LA Times* blogs, Harvey/*Times* of London, "Tributes are pouring in…"/*LA Times*, "Outpouring"/*Christian Science Monitor*, "Michael Jackson fans in shock . . ."/*Daily Mail*, Wikipedia. Women marching on Hollywood Boulevard, exodus to Neverland: *Times* blogs. International reaction: "Fans around the world"/Associated Press, "Fans worldwide"/ *LA Times*. Kim Dae-Jung, Imelda Marcos: "Shock and Grief"/Sharon Otterman/ *NY Times*. Gordon Brown, David Cameron: BBC. Japanese ministers: Masters/ *Time* (see Chapter 8 notes), Kageyama/Associated Press (see Chapter 8 notes). Frederic Mitterrand: Alexis Griffith/WorldMeetsUs. Nelson Mandela: his foundation. Arnold Schwarzenegger, Barack Obama/Robert Gibbs, John Roberts memo: Malcolm/*LA Times*. Pause in Congress: *Politico*. Serena Williams, Roger Federer: *USA Today*. McCartney, Mottola: issued through publicists and reported by the *New York Times*, *LA Times*. President Obama eventually did speak for himself about MJ and sent the Jackson family a letter of condolence; see msncbc.com below. Henninger comments: "Michael: The Last Celebrity"/ *WSJ*; David Segal made many of the same points in his earlier *New York Times* piece. John Mayer, Miley Cyrus, Demi Moore: "Celebrities mourn Michael Jackson's death via Twitter"/ *Latimes.com*. "With friends like that": Mesereau. Liz Taylor too devastated to speak: Natalie Finn. Liza Minnelli quote: Andrew Gumbel/"Police focus on doctor"/the *Guardian*.

Bates, Claire. "How Michael Jackson's Death Shut Down Twitter, Brought Chaos to Google . . . and 'Killed Off' Jeff Goldblum." *Daily Mail*, June 26, 2009.

Bennet, Shea. "How the Internet Died with Michael Jackson." mediabistro. com, June 26, 2009 (I).

"Brown 'Saddened' by Jackson Death." BBC, June 26, 2009 (RT).

"Celebrities Mourn Michael Jackson's Death via Twitter." *LATimes.com*, June 25, 2009 (I.)

Chu, Henry. "Fans Worldwide Grieve for Michael Jackson." *Los Angeles Times*, June 27, 2009.

Collins, Scott, and Greg Braxton. "TV Misses Out as Gossip Website TMZ Reports Michael Jackson's Death First." *Los Angeles Times*, June 26, 2009.

Collins, Scott and Meg James. "Michael Jackson May Be Turning Point for TMZ." *Los Angeles Times*, June 28, 2009.

"Fans Around the World Mourn Michael Jackson." Associated Press, June 26, 2009.

"Fans Can't Stop Crying, Dancing on Hayvenhurst." KNBC, July 16, 2009 (RT).

Finn, Natalie. "Liz Taylor 'Too Devastated' to Comment on Jackson's Death; Liza Minelli, Brooke Shields React." *E!online*, June 25, 2009 (I).

Gavin, Patrick. "Congress Pauses for Michael Jackson." *Politico*, June 26, 2009 (*Politico.com*).

Griffiths, Alexis. "Jackson: The Tragic 'Genetically Modified' Icon of Globalization." *WorldMeetsUs.com*, June 27, 2009 (I).

Gumbel, Andrew. "Police Focus on Doctor Who Was with Michael Jackson as He Died." *Guardian*, June 27, 2009 (hereafter cited as Gumbel, "Police Focus").

Harvey, Michael. "Fans Mourn Artist for Whom It Didn't Matter If You Were Black or White." *Times*, June 26, 2009.

Hennessy-Fiske, Molly. "Michael Jackson's Medical Records at UCLA Were Improperly Accessed, Source Says." *LATimes.com*, June 10, 2010 (I).

Henninger, Daniel. "Michael: The Last Celebrity." *Wall Street Journal*, July 3, 2009.

Malcolm, Andrew. "In Death, Michael Jackson Gets Politicians' (Cautious) Admiration." *Los Angeles Times*, June 27, 2009.

Martin, Hugo, and W. J. Hennigan. "Tourists Flock to Michael Jackson Sites; Tour Buses Adjust Their Routes." *Los Angeles Times*, June 27, 2009.

Metz, Rachel, and Daniel B. Wood. "Outpouring over Michael Jackson Unlike Anything Since Princess Di." *Christian Science Monitor*, June 27, 2009.

"Michael Jackson Dead at 50 After Cardiac Arrest." CNN, June 25, 2009 (RT).

"Michael Jackson Fans in Shock as the World Mourns the King of Pop." *Daily Mail*, June 26, 2009.

Murray, Mark. "Obama on Michael Jackson's Death." msnbc.com, July 2, 2009 (I).

Otterman, Sharon. "Around the World, Shock and Grief over Jackson." *New York Times*, June 26, 2009.

Ryan, Harriet,; Chris Lee, Andrew Blankstein, and Scott Gold. "Michael Jackson Dead at 50." *Los Angeles Times*, June 26, 2009.

Santa Cruz, Nicole, and Ari B. Bloomekatz. "Tributes Are Pouring in for Jackson." *Los Angeles Times*, June 29, 2009.

Sarno, David. "Michael Jackson–Related Traffic Doubled Twitter's Update Frequency, Tripled Facebook's." *Los Angeles Times*, June 25, 2009.

Segal, David. "After Jackson, Fame May Never Be the Same." *New York Times*, June 28, 2009.

"Serena Williams Pays Tribute to Michael Jackson at Wimbledon." *USA Today*, June 26, 2009.

CHAPTER 25

Description of MJ's body: autopsy report, death certificate. Better health than expected: see Snead/*LA Times* on false story in Britain's *Sun* ("8 st. 1 oz"); Fox News, *NY Daily News* on actual autopsy. Early investigation, police focus on Conrad Murray: "Michael Jackson's doctor interviewed"/*LA Times*, Gumbel/ the *Guardian* articles, Steinhauer/"Medication a Focus," Ryan/"Police seize medical CD"; all of that and more came out later at Murray's criminal trial. Also, Associated Press on search warrants executed after MJ's death, *Daily Mail* on questions to be answered. Matt Alford put himself forth as Murray's attorney initially (see Gumbel/"Michael Jackson doctor hires lawyer"), but Chernoff was already on the scene (Chernoff to Andrew McCartney/Associated Press; Murray to detectives Martinez and Smith—Chernoff was present; transcript). Chernoff bio: his firm's Web site, Ryan/"Unlikely lawyer," accounts of attorneys present during Murray's criminal trial. "Considered to be a witness," "every and all questions": Chernoff press conference, see Chapter 26 notes. LAPD, coroner statements: issued to media. Jacksons promptly hiring Dr. Calmes: "Michael Jackson's doctor interviewed"/*LA Times*, "Michael Jackson's doctor hires . . ."/*Guardian*, *Observer*. MJ's brain, or at least most of it, retained by the coroner's office: reporting at the time, autopsy and toxicology reports. Involvement of federal and international law enforcement: *LA Times*, court file in Murray case.

The size and value of the MJ estate is still being debated (between the estate's attorneys and the IRS, among others) and is something I know a great deal about, thanks to people associated with the struggle to control it, and to the lawsuit filed by Joe Jackson against the estate, as well as the extensive media coverage. I'm drawing on all of that when I make generalizations. MJ's album sales: Keith Caulfield and June 21, 2010/*Billboard*; in first three weeks after death: Lee/Lewis/*LA Times* (they actually got Amazon to account for its music sales); online sales: Lewis/*Times* online; see also, Sisario/*New York Times*, Sexton/*Billboard*, *Entertainment Weekly*, the *Times* of London, *NME*, BBC, and Business Wire comparison of record sales in 2009 and 2008. I base my assessment of MJ's imminent net worth on my knowledge of the estate and its assets.

As I described earlier in these notes, I made a thorough investigation of the claim that Tohme looted the Carolwood house and swiped MJ's money and found it to be utterly without foundation. Ron Williams, whom I regard as an unimpeachable source, described what he observed at the Carolwood house on the evening of MJ's death and in the days and weeks that followed in interviews with me. Grace/transatlantic phone call from KJ: Rwaramba to Barak (see Chapter 1 notes), who was with Rwaramba when she answered that call. La Toya/garbage bags of money: verbally that very day, via *Rolling Stone* (through Gerri Hirshey; it ran in Hoffman/"Last Days"); paper wrappers and spilled twenties claim: Craig Williams. I should note that Perry Sanders defended Katherine Jackson's presence at the house as nothing more than a mother attempting to protect her dead son's property from potential looters, and also said that Katherine was there to retrieve clothing and other personal items that belonged to MJ's children (Paris wanted a shirt that "smelled like daddy"), as well as the Cadillac Escalade that was "used to transport the children."

No will surfaced in the first week after MJ's death and I've been advised by Katherine Jackson's close advisors that she had no knowledge that a will existed. Joe Jackson/CNN interview: witnessed firsthand outside the Shrine Auditorium; for the shock and disgust it inspired, see Steve Harvey/theTimes, Associated Press on Sharpton. Early hearings before Judge Beckloff re. MJ estate, custody of children: firsthand witness, also *LA Times*, Associated Press on hearings/pleadings. "First legal volley"/ "Michael Jackson's mother granted temporary guardianship"/*LA Times*. Description of Debbie Rowe/her relationship with Prince and Paris, identity of Blanket's mother in papers: verbatim from petition. Joe Jackson KABC interview: via *Daily Mail* June 28, 2009. "Shadowy entourage": La Toya paid interview/*News of the World*, see also list. Tohme didn't fire the staff; they were held at the house and interviewed by the LAPD, then told they could go late that evening. All of this was observed by Ron Williams. AEG was actually Williams's employer at that time, and it was AEG's decision that the Talon people should be placed in charge of security at the Carolwood chateau and that MJ's security staff should be told not to return to the property. Tohme quotes: Tohme; Tohme returning "lockbox" money: confirmed by Hawk, Cannon. Accusations against Tohme: widely reported. "Wrong people": Dileo to Rossen/"Today," which also introduced the Reverent June Gatlin claiming she was MJ's spiritual advisor and that MJ was afraid of Tohme. As elsewhere, all Tohme quotes (incl. descriptions of the strain this placed on him) are from interviews unless otherwise stated. Jackson and Sharpton: *People*, Associated Press, many others; they were with the Jacksons in nearly every public appearance in the days immediately following MJ's death. Leo Terrell quotes: Terrell. Sunshine quote: "Jackson Media Frenzy Faulted"/*LA Times*. Rowe: see his *Action News* and *Larry King Live* appearances; "you do not represent me": see Chapter 22. Rio de Janeiro: Cobo/*Billboard*; Pakistani girls: Associated Press photo via *USA Today*. Scene at former Jackson home in Gary: Keagle/local paper. MJ media coverage, surge in airplay/Internet play of music and videos: Jeff Poor, Randy Lewis. Pew Research Center poll: see below for poll and other analysis. I don't listen to Rush Limbaugh, but the radio host described his agreement with Al Sharpton on his own Web site. I didn't see the Bill O'Reilly "rant" either, but see the Yahoo story. Hugo Chavez comment: *El Universal*.

COURT FILES

Criminal

LASC SA073164.

Civil

LASC. BC44597
USD-CA CV10 4734.

DOCUMENTS

Autopsy 6/25/09.

"Recorded Interview of Conrad Murray," Los Angeles Police Department Internal Affairs Group. June 27, 2009.

Certificate of Death, Jackson, Michael Joseph, County of Los Angeles Department of Health Services., July 7, 2009 (hereafter cited as Certificate of Death, 7/7/09.

AUTOPSY/PRELIMINARY INVESTIGATION

Blankstein, Andrew, Rong-Gong Lin II, Harriet Ryan, and Scott Gold. "Michael Jackson's Doctor Interviewed by LAPD." *Los Angeles Times,* June 28, 2009.

"Edward M. Chernoff." houstoncriminallaw.com (PR).

Gumbel, Andrew. "Michael Jackson Doctor Hires Lawyer as Family Hires Pathologist." *The Guardian,* June 28, 2009.

———. "Police Focus."

Harris, Paul. "Michael Jackson's Family 'Ask for Second Autopsy.'" *Observer,* June 28, 2009.

McCartney, Anthony. "Lawyer for Doctor: Jackson Had Pulse When Found." Associated Press, June 28, 2009.

McKay, Hollie. "Michael Jackson Balding, Incredibly Thin and Had Tattooed Facial Features." Fox News, February 9, 2010 (I).

Parker, Nick, and Steve Kennedy. "8 st. 1 oz., no food just pills in his stomach, bald, bruised . . ." *The Sun,* July 3, 2009.

———. "The Shock Findings of the Michael Jackson Autopsy." *Sun,* July 3, 2009.

Ryan, Harriet. "Police Seize Medical CD Labeled with Jackson Pseudonym." *Los Angeles Times,* July 29, 2009.

———. "The Unlikely Lawyer in Conrad Murray's Corner." *Los Angeles Times,* September 12, 2011.

Sears, Neil, Julie Moult, and Arthur Martin. "Michael Jackson's Death: The Questions Still to Be Answered." *Daily Mail,* June 29, 2009.

Siemaszko, Corky. "Michael Jackson Autopsy Report Confirms Singer Suffered from Vitiligo, Wore Wig, Had Tattooed Makeup." *New York Daily News,* February 10, 2010.

Snead, Elizabeth. "What Killed Michael Jackson, Where Will He Be Buried, Where's His Brain?" *Los Angeles Times*, July 7, 2009 (hereafter cited as Snead, "What Killed Michael Jackson?").

Steinhauer, Jennifer. "Medication a Focus of Jackson Inquiry." *New York Times*, June 27, 2009.

Watkins, Thomas. "Unsealed Search Warrants Reveal Heavy-Duty Anesthetic and Skin-Whiteners Found in Michael Jackson's Home." Associated Press, March 27, 2010.

Post-Death Career Boom/Estate

Caulfield, Keith. "Fans Snap Up 1.1 Million Michael Jackson Albums in One Week." *Billboard*, July 14, 2009.

———. "Michael Jackson Breaks *Billboard* Charts Records." *Billboard*, June 30, 2009.

Christman, Ed, Ann Donahue, Gail Mitchell, Glenn Peoples, and Ray Waddell. "How Michael Jackson Made $1 Billion Since His Death." *Billboard*, June 21, 2010 (hereafter cited as Christman, Donahue, Mitchell, Peoples, and Waddell).

Lee, Chris, and Randy Lewis. "Michael Jackson's Record Sales Top 9 Million Since His Death." *Los Angeles Times*, July 16, 2009.

Lewis, Randy. "Michael Jackson Album Sales Highlight Physical, Digital Merits." *LATimes.com*, July 14, 2009 (I).

Morgan, Piers. "John Branca and Howard Weitzman Discuss Michael Jackson Estate." CNN, October 3, 2011 (RT) (hereafter cited as Morgan, "Branca and Weitzman").

Sexton, Paul. "Michael Jackson Scores Eight of Top 10 Euro Albums." *Billboard*, July 16, 2009.

Sisario, Ben. "In Death as in Life, Michael Jackson Sets Music Sales Records." *New York Times*, July 2, 2009 (hereafter cited as Sisario, "In Death").

"2009 U.S. Music Purchases Up 2.1% over 2008; Music Sales Exceed 1.5 Billion for Second Consecutive Year." *Business Wire*, January 6, 2010 (PR).

JACKSON FAMILY OPPORTUNISM/TOHME ACCUSATIONS

Harris, Paul, and Jo Clements. "Michael Jackson Death Was 'Foul Play,' Claims Father Joe." *Daily Mail*, June 28, 2009.

Harvey, Steve. "Joe Jackson Condemned over Reaction to Death of Son, Michael." *Times*, June 30, 2009.

Rossen, "Mystery Man."

CUSTODY/COURT/DEBBIE ROWE

Dolan, Maura, and Jessica Garrison. "Debbie Rowe Considers Bid for Custody of Michael Jackson's 2 Older Children." *Los Angeles Times*, July 2, 2009.

Kim, Victoria, and Andrew Blankstein. "Michael Jackson's Mother Granted Temporary Guardianship of His Three Children." *Los Angeles Times*, June 29, 2009.

McCartney, Anthony. "Michael Jackson's Mother Seeks Custody of His Children." Associated Press, June 29, 2009.

JESSE JACKSON/AL SHARPTON/LEONARD ROWE

Clark, Champ. "Jackson Family Has Questions." *People*, June 28, 2009.

"Al Sharpton Spins Joe Jackson's Bizarre CNN Interview." Associated Press, June 29, 2009 (I).

King, Larry. "Michael Murdered? Interviews with Joe Jackson and Leonard Rowe." CNN, July 20, 2009 (RT).

"Metro Atlanta Mourns Michael Jackson's Death." *Action News*, WSB-TV, June 25, 2009 (RT).

INTERNATIONAL OUTPOURING/UNIFYING EVENT/EXCESSIVE COVERAGE

Cobo, Leila. "Michael Jackson Remains a Global Phenomenon." *Billboard*, July 2, 2009.

———. "We Are the World: Brazil." *Billboard*, July 11, 2009.

"El Rushbo Supports Justice Brothers in Case of Media v. Michael Jackson." Rushlimbaugh.com, June 29, 2009 (I).

Fernandez, Maria Elena, and Scott Collins. "Jackson Media Frenzy Faulted." *Los Angeles Times*, July 4, 2009 (hereafter cited as Fernandez and Collins).

"Hugo Chavez Scolds CNN for Coverage of Michael Jackson's Death." *El Universal*, June 25, 2009.

Keagle, Lauri Harvey. "Fans Paying Respects to the King of Pop at Boyhood Home." *The Times of Northwest Indiana*, June 26, 2009.

Lewis, Randy. "Radio Airplay for Michael Jackson: Off the Chart." *LATimes.com*, June 29, 2009 (I).

"Most Americans Believe Jackson Coverage Excessive." Pew Research Center, July 2, 2009 (I).

"O'Reilly Provokes Outrage with Jackson Rant." *Yahoo News*, July 2009 (I).

Poor, Jeff. "Jacko Telethon: Primetime Broadcast Network Coverage Devotes One Third of All News to Pop Star's Death." *NewsBusters*, July 10, 2009 (I).

Sanneh, Kelefa. "Postscript: Michael Jackson." *New Yorker,* July 6, 2009.
"*Time* Magazine to Publish Special Jackson Issue." *People,* June 27, 2009.

CHAPTER 26

I have a copy of the will that was handed out at the courthouse in Los Angeles
on the day of John Branca's first appearance before Judge Beckloff. Details of
its filing: "Executors Named by . . .", *LA Times, New York Times*. Branca retaining Sitrick, Weitzman: Mike was already speaking for Branca on the day the
will surfaced; Weitzman represented Branca from his first court appearance.
Weitzman bio: his firm's site, my own observations of him from the time of the
DeLorean trial. I met Mike Sitrick for the first (and only) time at his Fourth
of July party in Malibu, three days after the MJ will arrived at the courthouse
in LA. We were introduced by my friend Ron Kaye, the retired editor of the
Los Angeles Daily News, who told me a good deal about Sitrick's place in the
LA power structure. We've only communicated by e-mail since then. Sitrick's
"Wheel of Pain": an attorney who deposed him (claiming to be the only one
who ever had) in a lawsuit; Sitrick career: Nolan/Gawker, see also Sitrick's book
Spin. I know people are afraid of him because they've told me they are. Media
interest in Debbie Rowe cut out of MJ's will: see Associated Press headline;
local news in Los Angeles led with it, too. Diana Ross/no interest in raising MJ's
children: sources close to KJ; note also *Daily Mail*. I also have a copy of MJ's trust
agreement. Sandra Ribera, who is intimately familiar with the terms of both the
trust and the will, and an attorney to boot, pointed out what she thought was
some misunderstanding of the will on my part and suggested changes to the
manuscript that I made. "They applauded three times . . ."/Branca account of
meeting with Jacksons: Deutsch/"Jackson had long history"; Katherine Jackson
told quite a different story. "My son had told me": KJ at a meeting the two of
us attended together at a hotel in the San Fernando Valley. Branca astonished:
expressed through Howard Weitzman at the hearing to consider Mrs. Jackson's
motion to make her the executor of MJ's estate, observed firsthand. "Key concession" Katherine had won, Branca/Weitzman deal attempt, Jackson side request
for the power to subpoena Branca/McClain, Weitzman/delaying "urgent probe"
into missing assets: attorneys and advisors working for Mrs. Jackson, who have
shown me court documents. See also Mayorases Web site, Ryan and Kim/*LA
Times,* blow-by-blow in Julie Garber/ about.com "wills" blog, law.com article.
The *Forbes* article (see below) about the value of MJ's holdings was not written until late 2010, but it was based upon the status and performance of the
estate in 2009. Continued surge in sale of MJ's music: the *Times* of London,

Guardian, New York Times. Quantity and opinion of "incalculable" value of warehoused music, film, and video footage: Schaffel, Wiesner. I was fortunate to avoid an embarrassing mistake in connection to the Julien's auction of the MJ memorabilia supposedly belonging to David Gest (as reported by *LA Times* day of and day after the auction); it was only by chance that I saw that Gest disavowed ownership and expressed his fury (Contact Music). It turned out that they had been consigned from someone who obtained them from Gest earlier. MJ domain name on eBay for $10 million: saw firsthand. July 6 hearing/ long introduction of all the attorneys: firsthand observation; see law.com and Ryan and Kim/*LA Times*, which both described the various attorneys' backgrounds). How McMillan came to represent KJ: KJ. Branca's representations about the will: in court. To my knowledge, he has never identified the attorney who actually prepared the will, or offered any details about the signing. Questions about the will: various attorneys, observers, and advisors of Katherine Jackson. Termination letter MJ sent to Branca with instructions to return all documents, Barry Siegel (fired at the same time as Branca) removing himself as executor: from the documents. "Complete and unfettered" language: from trust document; see Mayorases relevant blog posts below; Mayoras quotes also come from interviews for *Stealing Michael Jackson.* Observations about exclusion clause and KJ: blog posts and film interviews. Authenticity of the will: Tohme, KJ/advisors, filings from Joe Jackson vs. estate. Katherine advice from attorneys and what she was thinking herself: KJ personally, in greater detail from her advisors and attorneys.

McClain long Jackson family association: KJ advisors/ attorneys. McClain "disability": not specified by Weitzman in remarks to court (at least in my presence); diabetic/stroke explanation: KJ advisors/attorneys, but as conjecture. McClain background: lalate.com profile and Taraborrelli (incl. Joe Jackson on losing Janet as client). KJ fondness for McClain (a high school friend of Jackie's), Joe's wariness: Jacksons's advisors/attorneys. KJ concern about Branca: KJ. Joe Jackson re. Branca: *Stealing Michael Jackson* interview. Schreiber expressing KJ concerns about Branca, Hoffman answer, Beckloff ruling: observed firsthand. My assessment of why this seemed reasonable, because of Branca's abilities, is based on my knowledge of his career successes and the concessions made to me even by people who dislike him that he is, as I wrote, "a brilliant lawyer and a masterful dealmaker." Branca has already earned millions of dollars by administering MJ's estate, and there are certainly people who think he deserves it. "Maximizing the estate": Weitzman, July 6 hearing, in my presence. Judge's ruling: also present; the details are confirmed by Ryan/Kim/*LA Times.* I was standing almost shoulder-to-shoulder with them when Branca and McMillan stood shoulder to shoulder outside the courthouse.

Jacksons's chief concern Debbie Rowe: family advisors, public statements, court documents. Klein named (for the second time) as father of Prince and Paris: *Us*; the headline had to do with the denial by Klein that morning on *Good Morning America* (also below); Klein's quotes: via *Larry King*. Mark Lester claims/possible father of Paris: London tabloid interviews (see Chapter 3 notes); Tito and Jermaine answer: "Jackson family anger," "Michael Jackson was confronted." Geller quotes here: same articles. Leo Terrell's observations and quotes, biology as trump: Terrell. Debbie Rowe July 2 interviews with KNBC and *Us*: see below; all quotes as attributed. Faye/Bush preparing MJ for viewing at Forest Lawn: "Michael Jackson's Inner Circle Addresses Rumors"/ABC.

Michael Jackson memorial event at the Staples Center, kindly arranged by Claire Hoffman, but ended up giving it away to an imploring mixed-race woman who had flown all the way from London. Only later did it occur to me that without something that identified her as me she probably wouldn't get in. So I watched it on television, just like the billion other people who tuned in, and my observations are based on that perspective. Ehrlich/Ortega putting memorial together: Gunderson/*USA Today*, *LA Times*. Number of tickets issued, concerns about impact on city, short-lived controversy over costs: *LA Times* July 4 through July 9. Jacksons's debate over interment: family advisors/attorneys, Tohme. Report MJ had wanted to be frozen (not true, insofar as I know) and would now be made into a Body World display (not true either, obviously): see *Daily Mail* below. I have a copy of MJ's death certificate. Coroner's investigator/ keeping brain: Snead/*LA Times*, later, *Guardian*. Public viewing of MJ's body at Neverland (wrong again): *Daily Mail*. Fan vigil at Neverland, local concern: Bloomekatz/*LA Times*, Tohme. Interment debate, conversations with Barrack: Tohme. Work at Neverland, Barrack maneuvers: Siklos/*Fortune* (see Chapter 1 notes). I heard Katherine Jackson's rather different point of view on it all later, from her advisors and attorneys, and I must admit that how she handled herself in this moment is what made me really start to admire Katherine. See also Ryan/ Blankstein/*LA Times* (which had Taj Jackson input). "Jackson Four's greatest performance": Dileo to *Daily Mail*. MJ praying with Elvis statue: Geller. Russian fan: Novasti via WorldMeetsUS. Final say on MJ funeral and burial place: I heard about Mrs. Jackson's point of view well after the event; also, Alexander/ *Time*, which reported Randy Jackson's role (though not how Randy looked in the eyes of the other Jacksons). Forest Lawn description: the Memorial Park's own Web site, seeing— stars.com "Grand Mausoleum" page, plus Alexander, Manning, Dimond, Ditzien, Kreps, Burks blog. Branca's permission to purchase Sanctuary of Ascension crypt/cost, etc.: KJ advisors, articles cited above. Same model casket as James Brown: KJ. Jacksons "bickering" about funeral date, MJ's remains largely unattended: same sources mentioned previously.

KJ-Debbie Rowe custody deal: Schaffel, who helped broker it. Debbie hiring Eric George and what it likely meant: Leo Terrell, followed by other attorneys including Mesereau and later media reports. Schaffel may have overstated the importance of his role, but he was the one who first brought Katherine Jackson and Debbie Rowe together. That Marc was attempting to show people how useful he could be is an inference I drew based on conversations with him; he never said that explicitly. Schaffel-Debbie reconnecting: Schaffel, see also Reuters article on lawsuit against TMZ; King quote: court filing. Schaffel bringing Katherine and Debbie together: Schaffel, unchallenged by other sources, including Sandra Ribera. Hayvenhurst goings-on: Schaffel, other sources; he was the only one who didn't ask not to be quoted by name. What Marc was telling me was almost exactly what I was hearing from the others, except that they thought they knew a lot more about what was going on than he did. The other advisors may not like it, but Katherine has confided a good deal to Schaffel and Mann. The advisor I quoted anonymously wasn't Mann. Re. the source I quoted referring to Rebbie's husband as a "deadbeat": I'm not calling him that. Nathaniel Brown has supported his family by working as, among other things, a letter carrier; by all accounts he is a decent, hardworking man, just one that doesn't have a great deal of money. Children dealing with new situation: via KJ advisors/attorneys, "Michael's Last Wish"/ *People*. Jacksons keeping Grace close: an inference based on what I was told by multiple sources; as noted, Schaffel had another view. He was involved in opening the line of communication between Grace and Katherine, but I don't think he was quite as critical as in the link between Katherine and Debbie Rowe. Living conditions at Hayvenhurst: sources who were regular visitors to the house/KJ confidants, Children's Services report prepared after the stun gun incident. Alejandra's kids referring to Jermaine as "Uncle Daddy": KJ advisor close to Jackson family for many years. Again, Schaffel is the one quoted most often about the situation in the house, and about Alejandra, because he was the only one who never asked me not to use his name. Rumors about Donte and Omer: KJ advisors, also British tabloids including the *Sun*. Alejandra Oaziaza: sources associated with KJ/Hayvenhurst household; I also drew on information contained in a lengthy letter about Alejandra published by TMZ and attributed to a "Jackson insider." I'm pretty sure I know who that person is and I'm very sure that person would be in a position to know just about everything there is to know about Alejandra and her dealings with the Jackson family. That letter has since been posted on desireespeakssolisten.blogspot. com (cited earlier), where it can still be found. I verified with at least one of my own sources whatever information I drew from it. Schaffel/Tohme quotes: Schaffel, Tohme. Reasons for delaying MJ's funeral: confidential sources; the timing speaks for itself. Ken Sunshine nonexplanation: "Jacksons Postpone Michael's Burial Again"/Associated Press; Joe Jackson: to TMZ; Jacksons' other obligations: Yahoo, manhattanlivingmag.com. Funeral: I happened to be in LA and observed the scene from a distance; also, *Time* magazine, *Daily Telegraph*, *Daily Mail*, MTV, Friedman, "Gloves Off on Cost"/*LA Times*, two sources who attended. Lisa Marie's last conversation with MJ: to Oprah 2010; sunflower request/ sunflowerguy.com donation: TMZ, X17.com. David Rothenberg: *Larry King Live* (9/3 Special Edition); I was told by someone who was there that Rothenberg spoke almost exactly the same words at the funeral. I knew his story well because I was a newspaper columnist in Los Angeles when that particular horror was perpetrated. Jacksons purchasing other burial spots: "Gloves Off"/*LA Times*, confirmed by a source I trust later.

Coroner's homicide ruling: The Smoking Gun, which effectively jumped the story three days earlier via affidavit executed by Orlando Martinez; also, "Ruled a Homicide"/*New York Times* and *LA Times*. Chief Bratton's early re-marks/homicide investigation: Bone/*Times*. Murder charges unlikely: Leonard/Ryan/*LA Times* 7/19/09. Involvement of agencies including DEA: Natalie Finn/E!Online July 2, 2009. Scope of investigation, five doctors: *LA Times* July 3 and July 4. Mickey Fine search warrant: review of document, which is inextricably linked to the investigation of Dr. Klein. Vials and packages from MJ's bedroom: "Medication Removed"/ABC. Ed Winter affidavit/Klein: "Evidence Piling Up"/Fox News, *People*, CNN; Winter's second visit: Radar Online. Execution of the search warrant at Mickey Fine's: TMZ. Winter quotes: Seal, *Vanity Fair*. Klein media offensive: *Good Morning America*, *Larry King Live*; quotes: *GMA*. One of a dozen doctors: *LA Times* July 4 (five doctors), the *Times* of London July 5 thirty people being examined, *LA Times* July 17; names of doctors being looked at by investigators emerged slowly over time, in connection to Murray case and state medical board probe. Dr. Tadrissi first named, Dr. Adams's records subpoenaed: August 24 "Lethal levels"/ *LA Times*. Dr. Adams denied to the *Las Vegas Review-Journal* the allegation by Conrad Murray that Adams had administered propofol to MJ. Adams's name was back in the news in May of 2011, when TMZ got hold of the summons issued by Murray's attorneys that would force Adams to testify about the fact that he had, in fact, administered propofol to MJ. Adams did admit that he administered propofol, which was testified to by Det. Martinez at Murray trial. And an e-mail was introduced as evidence to show that Adams wanted to join "This Is It" tour as MJ's resident anesthesiologist. Dr. Slavit's only involve-ment in the case was the physical he gave MJ in early 2009 for his insurance policy. Winter visiting Dr. Koplin: TMZ July 29, 2009; newspapers next day. Randy Rosen: TMZ July 23, 2009. Dr. Metzger read the writing on the wall and sending forth his attorney Braun to tell the media about MJ's attempt to get propofol from him in the spring of 2009; see Nancy Grace report. Dr. Farschian: Waxman/"5 Doctors"; the first significant reporting to implicate Farschian was his letter to MJ about Buprinex being better than Demerol: *Miami New Times* blog; first suggestion Farschian was a target of investigation: Posner/"Jackson and the 'Pill Mills'" (see Chapter 12 notes); Fox News four days later. It would be revealed eventually that a number of MJ's former bodyguards were talking to investigators about Farschian overprescribing drugs, in particular Demerol, to MJ. I was hearing about it from Schaffel and Wiesner, among others. Dr. Aksenoff refusing requests for stimulants: *Japan Times*. Deepak Chopra: to Gerald Posner. MJ drug aliases: Winter warrant, which hit media June 30, 2009; see *Guardian* below. Joey Jeszeck and others targeted as witnesses in 2009 investigation: confidential source who has access to the records of the investigation; see also Posner (see Chapter 12 notes). LAPD announcement referring case to district attorney/timing with coroner ruling death a homicide: Reuters. Prior drug use mitigating at best, potential chain of custody issues: confidential source cited above. MJ computer was missing: Tohme, confirmed later by my confidential source. Murray's address to Galilee church: click2houston.com. Chernoff's statement: "Feds Raid"/*Nightline*. Official charges: CNN February 8; Fox News had reported August 19 that Murray would be charged with manslaughter within two weeks, among other media speculation. Not guilty plea, preliminary hearing: Blas/*USA Today*.

Jacksons' "foul play" allegations (see Chapter 25 notes); Tohme eliminated as target, realization Murray would likely be unable to pay: confidential inside sources; process by which Joe ("Michael was driven hard") and La Toya made their case in the media, and were joined by Jermaine: "The Michael Jackson Conspiracy"/Tru TV. La Toya quoting Paris/"working him": to Britain's Channel 4 via *Daily Telegraph*. Eventually, of course, the Jackson's arrived at the realization that AEG was the only really viable target. I don't mean to suggest that Katherine Jackson's lawsuit against AEG isn't valid—the more I've learned about it the more I think there is a case to answer. Basic outline of claim eventually filed against AEG: "Michael Jackson Overexerted Himself "/ABC. Evolution of AEG self-presentation/portrayal of in media: see *LA Times* online June 25 ("in the lurch"), "counts cost" /the *Times* of London June 26; full refunds to ticket holders June 29: *Daily Mail, LA Times*; "Jackson death may prove boon" July 3 Lee; souvenir ticket: digitalspy.com July 3; "Promoter's Show Must Go On"/*Billboard* July 11. Lee's article was the first to report that between sales of the souvenir tickets, insurance claims and the sale of the "This Is It" rehearsal footage AEG could actually profit. Sony/$50 million for footage/possible televised tribute: Lee July 20, see also

Denver Business Journal. Again, though, Yazmeen's reporting was the best in terms of the background on the AllGood situation and the truth about how Frank Dileo had positioned himself (and been positioned later by the estate). I give Dennis Hawk credit for telling me months in advance that the AllGood lawsuit would be dismissed, and on exactly what grounds; he was right on every point. The contrast of Hollyscoop's "Michael Jackson Estate Hit" article announcing the lawsuit and the headline on the Associated Press article reporting the suit's dismissal demonstrate how effective the estate was in framing this as a personal attack on MJ. Randy Phillips/"corporate villains": Siklos/*Fortune* (see Chapter 1 notes). "I saw a guy": Dileo in "Final Days Timeline"/ abcnews.go.com. "Couldn't wait to get to London," "accident": Ortega to Lang/The Wrap. "I don't think everybody contributed": Ortega to McLean/the *Times* of London.

I'm sure AEG had good reasons other than securing his support for hiring Ortega as the director of the *This Is It* film, but I don't think anybody close to the situation doubts this was a consideration. "Surprisingly spry": Lang. Wiesner/Tohme quotes: Wiesner, Tohme. Tohme attitude toward Jacksons, estate, Dileo: Tohme. Dileo at Beverly Hilton for most of the first two years after MJ's death: multiple sources, including Friedman; estate paying for it: Tohme, Mann (who had several conversations with Dileo while both staying there), numerous confidential sources; the estate's own accounting shows payments to Dileo for services and to cover his expenses, but is no more specific than that. Phillips supporting story that Dileo was MJ's manager: Tohme inference from *This Is It* credits and other things he was learning. AEG office, company car to Grammys: Tohme, confidential sources. I was told by an editor at *Rolling Stone* that Phillips referred to Tohme as MJ's manager when interviewed for both the May 24 and June 29 stories. It's clear from the Knopper article that the magazine—or at least the writer—understood that Tohme was MJ's manager right up to his death. Phillips sending Tohme to address media on day of MJ's death as MJ's manager: video footage; Ron Williams also told me that the AEG execs told him Tohme was MJ's manager. When I asked about all of this almost two years later, though, Phillips wouldn't talk about it, except for "There was a great deal of confusion": Phillips e-mail to me.

COURT FILES

Criminal

LASC SA073164.

Criminal Investigation

USDC-CA 09MJ1897.

Civil

BP 117321 (Los Angeles Superior Court) "Petition for Letters of Special Administration" submitted by John Branca and John McClain, July 1, 2009.

BP 117321 (Los Angeles Superior Court) "Ex Parte Application to Vacate the Court's Order Appointing Katherine Jackson as Special Administrator" submitted by John Branca and John McClain, July 1, 2009.

BP 117321 "Opposition to (1) the Branca and Mclain Petition for Letters of Administration, and (2) Motion to Vacate the Order Appointing her as Special Administrator" submitted by Katherine Jackson, July 1, 2009.

BP 117321 (Los Angeles Superior Court) *Joseph Jackson's Objection to Appointment of John Branca and John McClain as Executors of the Estate of Michael Jackson*, November 9, 2009 (hereafter cited as LASC BP 117321 11/9/09).

LASC BC445597.

2:11-ap-02407-RN 6/27/11.

2:11-ap-02407-RN 8/3/11.

DOCUMENTS

Autopsy 6/25/09.

Certificate of Death, 7/7/09.

State of California, County of Los Angeles, "Search Warrant and Affadavit (Det. Orlando Martinez)." August 24, 2009.

Phillips to Sullivan, 4/4/11.

WILL AND TRUST

Arango, Tim, and Ben Sisario. "Despite a Will, Jackson Left a Tangled Estate." *New York Times*, July 6, 2009.

Bronstad, Amanda. "Lawyers Abound at Probate Hearing on Michael Jackson's Estate." law.com, July 8, 2009 (I).

Deutsch, Linda. "Jackson Had Long History with Estate Administrator." Associated Press, August 14, 2009.

"Executors Named by Michael Jackson File Last Will in Los Angeles County Superior Court." July 1, 2009. (Sitrick and Co. attachment to will) (PR).

Garber, Julie. "Michael Jackson's Will vs. the Michael Jackson Family Trust." about.com, July 6, 2009 (I).

Gardner, David. "Will Diana Ross Care for Michael Jackson's Three Children?" *Daily Mail*, July 2, 2009.

"Howard Weitzman." kwikalaw.com (PR).

"John McClain Interscope!" lalate.com, July 1, 2009 (I) (hereafter cited as "McClain Interscope").

Mayoras, Danielle, and Andrew Mayoras. "The Crazy Claims of the Michael Jackson Estate." probatelawyerblog.com, April 18, 2010 (I) (hereafter cited as Mayoras, "Estate Deal").

—— and ——. "Katherine Jackson's Shocking Change of Heart." probatelawyerblog.com, November 12, 2009 (I) (hereafter cited as Mayoras and Mayoras, "Change of Heart").

—— and ——. "Michael Jackson's Estate Teaches Important Planning Lessons." trialandheirs, April 26, 2011 (I) (hereafter cited as Mayoras and Mayoras, "Planning Lessons").

—— and ——. "Michael Jackson's Mother Won't Administer His Estate." probatelawyerblog.com, July 7, 2009 (I).

—— and ——. "New Evidence Coming in the Michael Jackson Estate Case." trialandheirs.com, October 26, 2009 (I) (hereafter cited as Mayoras and Mayoras, "New Evidence").

—— and ——. "New Jackson Estate Deal Reported." probatelawyerblog.com, November 23, 2009 (I) (hereafter cited as Mayoras and Mayoras, "Estate Deal").

McCartney, Anthony. "Michael Jackson's Will Cuts Out Ex-Wife Deborah Rowe." Associated Press, July 1, 2009.

Nolan, Hamilton. "Mike Sitrick: Ninja Master of the Dark Art of Spin." *Gawker. com*, July 9, 2008 (I).

Ryan, Harriet. "Michael Jackson Will Surfaces." *Los Angeles Times*, July 1, 2009.

Ryan, Harriet, and Victoria Kim. "Michael Jackson Estate: Mother Loses Control, but Retains a Say in Major Decisions." *Los Angeles Times*, July 7, 2009.

CUSTODY/DEBBIE ROWE/ARNOLD KLEIN

"Arnold Klein: Not Michael Jackson Sperm Donor 'to the Best of My Knowledge.'" *Us Weekly*, July 8, 2009.

"Debbie Rowe Breaks Her Silence: 'I Want My Children.'" *Us*, July 2, 2009. Fricker.

Gardner, Eriq. "TMZ Sued over Leaked Debbie Rowe Interview." Reuters, February 3, 2010.

Henry, Chuck. "Jackson's Ex Rowe Says, 'I Want My Children.'" KNBC (Los Angeles), July 2, 2009 (RT).

King, "Klein."

Sawyer, Diane. "Michael Jackson's Doctor Says He's Not the Father of Jackson's Kids." *ABC/Good Morning America*, July 8, 2009 (RT).

Thomas, Liz. "Jackson Family Anger as *Oliver!* Star Lester Claims, 'I'm the Daddy.'" *Daily Mail*, August 10, 2009.

MICHAEL'S CHILDREN/HAYVENHURST DRAMA

Samson, Pete. "Is This Secret Son of Jacko?" *Sun*, July 16, 2010.

Tresniowski, Alex, and Rennie Dyball. "Michael's Last Wish." *People*, August 17, 2009 (hereafter cited as Tresniowski and Dyball).

ESTATE/FINANCES

Adams, Tim. "Michael Jackson: Now for the Encore." *Guardian*, October 4, 2009.

Boyle, Catherine. "Michael Jackson's Post-Death Music Sales Outstrip Elvis and John Lennon." *Times*, July 1, 2009.

"Gest to Sue over Jackson Auction Row." *Contactmusic.com*, June 29, 2009 (I).

Greenburg, Zach O'Malley. "Michael Jackson: Secret Business Genius?" *Forbes*, January 25, 2011.

"Judge Dismisses Promoters' Lawsuit Against Michael Jackson." Associated Press, August 19, 2009.

Keep, David A. "Celebrity Deaths Can Send Collectibles Prices Soaring." *Los Angeles Times*, June 27, 2009.

Knopper, Steve. "Michael Jackson's Legacy Includes Tangled Financial Web." *Rollingstone.com*, June 29, 2009 (I).

Lang, Brent. "Ortega: Jackson Planned 3D 'Thriller' Feature Film." *Thewrap. com*, (I).

McLean, "Ortega."

"Michael Jackson Estate Hit with $300 Million Lawsuit." hollyscoop.com, October 17, 2009 (I).

"Neverland on the Block: Inside the Michael Jackson Auction." *Rollingstone. com*, May 24, 2009 (I).

Sisario, "In Death."

Whitcraft, Teri, Kristin Pisarcik, and Kimberly Brown. "Timeline: Michael Jackson's Final Days." abcnews.go.com, June 23, 2010 (I).

Yazmeen. "Dileo."

———. "Allocco."

MEMORIAL/BURIAL/NEVERLAND

Alexander, Bryan. "Jackson's Funeral: Family and Friends Say Goodbye." *Time*, September 4, 2009.

———. "Picking Jackson's Burial Place: Security Was Key." *Time*, September 3, 2009.

Bloomekatz, Ari B. "Michael Jackson Fans Stick It Out at Neverland Ranch." *Los Angeles Times*, July 4, 2009.

Burks, Lisa. "Sleeping in Beauty—Rest in Peace, Michael Jackson." typepad.com, September, 2009 (I).

Coleman, Mark. "Michael Jackson Finally Laid to Rest in Los Angeles." *Daily Telegraph*, September 4, 2009.

Collins, Scott. "Jackson Memorial Seen as a Landmark." *Los Angeles Times*, July 9, 2009.

Diaz, Joseph. "Michael Jackson's Inner Circle Addresses Rumors." ABC, June 25, 2010 (RT).

Dillon, Nancy, and Corky Siemaszko. "Michael Jackson's Mother Katherine Doesn't Want Jackson Buried at Neverland." *New York Daily News*, July 8, 2009.

DiMassa, Cara Mia, Richard Winton, and David Zahniser. "L.A. Aims to Limit Jackson Crowd." *Los Angeles Times*, July 4, 2009.

Dimond, Diane. "Michael's Foreverland." *Daily Beast*, August 31, 2009 (I).

Ditzian, Eric. "Michael Jackson's Burial: Details on Forest Lawn Mausoleum." mtv.com, September 4, 2009 (I).

"Florist Donates $5,000 Worth of Sunflowers to Michael." *X17.com*, May 15, 2010.

Friedman, Roger. "Jackson Funeral Travesty: Ex-Con 1st Speaker." *Showbiz411.com*, September 4, 2009 (I).

Graham, Caroline, and Daniel Boffey. "Jackson Family Fallout: Exclusive Interview with Manager Reveals Rift over Funeral." *Daily Mail*, July 5, 2009.

"The Great Mausoleum—Forest Lawn." seeing—stars.com (I).

Gundersen, Edna. "The Man Behind the Jackson Tribute." *USA Today*, July 9, 2009.

"Jacksons Postpone Michael's Burial Again." Associated Press, August 21, 2009.

Kaufman, Gil. "Michael Jackson's Kids Lay Golden Crown on His Casket at Funeral." mtv.com, September 4, 2009 (I).

King, Larry. "Special Edition: Michael Jackson's Funeral." CNN, September 3, 2009 (RT).

Kreps, Daniel. "Michael Jackson Burial Scheduled for August 29 at Forest Lawn." *Rollingstone.com*, August 18, 2009 (I).

"Lisa Marie Presley Wants Flowers at Michael Jackson Tomb." *TMZ*, May 12, 2010.

"Long Live the King! A Birthday Celebration for Michael Jackson." manhattanlivingmag.com, July 29, 2009 (I).

Manning, Sue. "Michael Jackson's Resting Place Among Greats: Forest Lawn Glendale." Associated Press, September 4, 2009.

"Michael Jackson's Body 'Will Have Public Viewing at Neverland Ranch Before Funeral on Sunday.'" *Daily Mail*, June 30, 2009.

"Michael Jackson's Burial Postponed, Daddy Says." *TMZ*, August 20, 2009 (I).

"Michael Jackson Set to Be Embalmed at the O2 Centre After Missing the Deadline for Cryogenic Freezing." *Daily Mail*, June 26, 2009.

"Michael Jackson's 51st Birthday Celebrations." yahoo.com, August 29, 2009 (I).

Reston, Maeve, and Ari B. Bloomekatz. "Gloves Off on Cost of Jackson Rite." *Los Angeles Times*, July 9, 2009.

Sheridan, Emily. "Exhausted and Emotional: Michael Jackson's Children Sleep After Saying Goodbye to Their Father at Funeral Service." *Daily Mail*, September 5, 2009.

Oprah. "Lisa Marie Presley."

WIKIPEDIA

"Forest Lawn Memorial Park."

RELIGION AND SPIRITUALITY

Blinova, Yekaterina. "Russian Fans of Michael Jackson Still Devastated." *WorldMeetsUs.com*, June 28, 2009 (I).

Carr, Firpo. "'Saint' Michael (Jackson)?" *Los Angeles Sentinel*, October 15, 2009.

DEATH INVESTIGATION/DRUGS/DOCTORS

"Anesthesiologist's Records Taken by Coroner." TMZ, July 23, 2009.

Blas, Lorena. "Michael Jackson Doctor Pleads Not Guilty to Manslaughter." *USA Today*, February 8, 2010.

Bone, James. "Jackson Death May Have Been 'Homicide,' Says Police Chief." *Times*, July 10, 2009.

"Coroner's Office Investigators Are Back at Dr. Arnie Klein's Office." radaronline.com, August 19, 2009 (I).

"Coroner Visits Another Beverly Hills Doc." *TMZ*, July 29, 2009 (I).

"DEA Raids Mickey Fine Pharmacy." *TMZ*, August 21, 2009 (I).

"Doctor Who Gave Michael Jackson Propofol in Las Vegas Forced to Testify for Dr. Conrad Murray in Manslaughter Case." *TMZ*, May 12, 2011 (I).

"Dr. Conrad Murray Visits Church." click2houston.com, November 22, 2009 (I).

Duke, Alan. "Investigator Visits Jackson Dermatologist Office." CNN, July 14, 2009 (I).

"Feds Raid Michael Jackson's Doctor Conrad Murray's Home and Office." *Nightline*, ABC, July 28, 2009 (RT).

Finn, Natalie. "Jackson Doc on the Move Again as Investigation Continues with State Attorney, DEA's Help." *E!Online*, July 2, 2009 (I).

Fisher, Luchina, and Russell Goldman. "Medication Removed from Michael Jackson's House as Part of Coroner's Investigation." abcnews.go.com, June 29, 2009 (I).

Glover, Scott, Rong-Gong Lin II, Cara Mia DiMassa, Andrew Blankstein, and Kimi Yoshino. "Michael Jackson Investigation Focuses on Doctors." *Los Angeles Times*, July 4, 2009.

Grace, Nancy. "Another Doctor Says Jackson Asked for Propofol." CNN, July 31. (RT).

King, "Klein."

Leonard, Jack, and Harriet Ryan. "Murder Charges in Michael Jackson Case Are Unlikely, Source Says." *Los Angeles Times*, July 19, 2009.

"'Lethal Levels' of Drug Killed Jackson." *Smoking Gun*, August 24, 2009 (I).

Matsutani, Minoru. "Tokyo Doctor Refused Jackson Stimulants: Late 'King of Pop' Asked for Drugs in 2007." *Japan Times*, July 16, 2009.

Meyer, Josh, and Andrew Blankstein. "LAPD Seeks DEA's Expertise for the Investigation." *Los Angeles Times*, July 3, 2009.

Michaels, Sean. "Michael Jackson Aliases Revealed." *Guardian*, June 30, 2009.

Moore, Solomon. "Jackson's Death Ruled a Homicide." *New York Times*, August 28, 2009.

Mower, Lawrence. "Anesthesiologist Calls Murray's Statements False." *Las Vegas Review-Journal*, August 27, 2009.

Munzenrieder.

"Police Target 30 in Hunt for Michael Jackson's Drug Suppliers." *Sunday Times*, July 5, 2009.

Posner, Gerald. "Deepak Chopra: How Michael Jackson Could Have Been Saved." *Daily Beast*, July 2, 2009 (I).

Ryan, Harriet, and Kimi Yoshino. "Investigators Target Michael Jackson's Pseudonyms." *Los Angeles Times*, July 17, 2009.

Sawyer, Diane. "Michael Jackson's Doctor Arnold Klein Denies Dangerous Drugs." *ABC/Good Morning America*, July 8, 2009 (RT).

Seal, "Doctor Will Sue."

Snead, "What Killed Michael Jackson?"

"Source: Michael Jackson's Doctor to Be Charged with Manslaughter." Fox News, August 19, 2009 (I).

Tauber, Michelle. "Evidence Piling Up Against Michael Jackson's Dermatologist." *People*, August 28, 2009.

Tourtellotte, Bob. "Jackson Death Ruled Homicide, Focus on Doctor." Reuters, August 28, 2009.

Waxman, "Doctors."

Winter, Jana. "At Least Nine Doctors Who Treated Michael Jackson Under Investigation." foxnews.com, July 15, 2009 (I).

———. "Evidence Is Piling Up Against Dermatologist to the Stars in Jackson Death." Fox News, August 27, 2009 (I).

Winton, Richard, and Harriet Ryan. "Jackson's Death Ruled a Homicide." *Los Angeles Times*, August 28, 2009.

Yoshino, Kimi, and Andrew Blankstein. "'Lethal Levels' of Anesthetic Propofol Killed Michael Jackson." *Los Angeles Times*, August 24, 2009.

JOE AND LA TOYA LEAD THE CHARGE

"Michael Jackson 'Was Worked Too Hard' Claims Daughter." *Daily Telegraph*, October 1, 2009.

Quinn, Delores. "The Michael Jackson Conspiracy: His Relatives Suspect Foul Play." trutv.com (I).

AEG

Connelly, Chris, and Lauren Sher. " Michael Jackson Overexerted Himself in Tour Rehearsal, Insiders Say." ABC, July 2, 2009 (I).

Flint, Joe. "Michael Jackson's Death Leaves AEG in the Lurch." *LATimes.com*, June 25, 2009 (I).

Gordon, Sarah. "Michael Jackson Fans Will Get Refund from Tour Operators." *Daily Mail*, June 30, 2009.

Harden, Mark. "Michael Jackson's Death Ends London Comeback Concert Series by Anschutz's AEG." *Denver Business Journal*, September 26, 2009.

Lee, Chris. "Jackson Death May Prove a Boon to AEG." *Los Angeles Times*, July 3, 2009.

———. "Michael Jackson Rehearsal Footage Draws Bids." *Los Angeles Times*, July 20, 2009.

"Michael Jackson Concert Promoter AEG to Refund Tickets." *LATimes.com*, June 29, 2009 (I).

Parks, Tim. "AEG to Release Jackson Memorial Ticket." Digitalspy.com, July 3, 2009 (I).

Sherwin, Adam. "O2 Arena Counts Cost as Curtain Closes on the Greatest Show of All." *Times,* June 26, 2009.

Waddell, Ray. "Promoter's Show Must Go On." *Billboard,* July 11, 2009.

CHAPTER 27

I know a great deal about the schemes, agendas, and conflicts of the Jackson family—more, I'd dare to assert, than anyone in the media does—based on my access to the advisors and attorneys who have been most involved in sorting it all out. None of them wants to be on the record (well, Howard Mann and Marc Schaffel may be exceptions) so I won't be making attributions by name. I will, though, note public record evidence for some of what I'm describing. Randy Jackson (along with Joe) leading family opposition to Branca (past and present): my sources; the estate knows it as well, as is demonstrated by the tape-recording of a phone conversation between Joel Katz, Henry Vaccaro, and Vaccaro's attorney that came into my possession (cited below), on which, among many other things, Katz says Randy and Joe are the ones making it difficult for the estate's attorneys. Mainly, though, I trust my sources.

I've spoken to or heard from the attorneys who have advised the Jacksons, from a number of attorneys who represented MJ in the last years of his life, and from a number who have simply been observing or commenting upon the controversies that have been raised about the will, the trust, and the estate. The Mayorases have been most critical of Branca for allowing his own law firm to prepare a will that named him as executor, and have done this publicly, most adamantly in the interviews they gave Howard Mann for *Stealing Michael Jackson.* Other attorneys who have or are representing MJ and his mother wagged their fingers at this, but described it only as questionable, not as illegal or even as unethical. Criticism of the quality of the will and the trust documents was something I heard from every attorney I spoke to about them, and breach of fiduciary duty was the basis for a complaint in this regard that one after another mentioned. All agreed, though, that this would be a difficult case to make on its own. The Mayorases were fairly outspoken in pointing out the difference in the dates on the will and trust documents, but other attorneys said it was unusual but not extremely unusual and would not be a significant legal issue unless it was part of some larger picture. That MJ's children are not identified by their legal names is something that clearly aroused the suspicions of the Jackson family and it's something that has bothered attorneys who have given the Jacksons counsel. Sandy Ribera went to pains to make me aware of the children's legal names and I have a copy of Paris's birth certificate. Joe's quote: interview for *Stealing Michael Jackson*.

I don't purport to be a legal arbiter, though I clearly see the validity of some of the arguments put forward—Branca's failure to return the will when he was "commanded" to by MJ being the most glaring. I have a copy of the letter in which MJ issued that command and every attorney I spoke to agreed that unless there is an explanation they don't know about, this is something that could result in Branca facing discipline from the State Bar. LeGrand getting documents from Branca: LeGrand testimony/*People v. Jackson*; Oxman searching through documents and not finding will: interview for *Stealing Michael Jackson*. Randy demanding documents from Branca, in particular the will: Randy Jackson sworn statement in Oxman/Joe Jackson filing objecting to the appointment of Branca and McClain as executors; all attorneys I spoke to agreed that Branca should also have returned the will then, if that was true. Oxman suspended from State Bar twice: Oxman disbarment ruling. Oxman appetite for face time on TV: "Media Frenzy Faulted"/*LA Times*, multiple other sources including Mesereau; Mesereau does acknowledge Oxman's intelligence, research, and writing abilities. Oxman and Randy hiring private investigators: some of sources above. Family meetings, discussions, and decision to investigate/hiring PIs: Rowe, presumably via Joe Jackson/possibly KJ, to Radar Online; Rowe's attempt to portray himself as a central figure was scoffed at by my sources. PI findings re. MJ in New York July 6–10, 2002: claims in Joe Jackson filing against Branca/McClain; it cannot have taken much investigating, see *New York Times* on Sony drama July 7, 8, and 10 (Chapter 1), though it is striking that there were pictures of MJ on July 6, 8, and 9, but not on July 7. Marc Schaffel was with MJ on that trip and was one of two people who told me MJ spent July 7 holed up in his hotel room. Though it certainly seems unlikely, the possibility that MJ got aboard a private jet and flew back to LA to sign the will can't be entirely dismissed. What's odd, though, if this is the case, is that Branca and the estate haven't simply said so and killed the entire controversy over the date on the will in a single stroke. TMZ was the first to report on this issue in an October 21, 2009, story that quoted Al Sharpton's spokeswoman as saying, "We have reason to believe that Michael may have been in New York on July 7 and Reverend Sharpton will address this after he discusses it with the Jackson family." One of Mrs. Jackson's advisors told me Sharpton signed a sworn statement that MJ had been at a meeting with him on the afternoon of July 7, but another said Sharpton was talking about a meeting on July 6.

Interfor report quotes: from document. What Oxman believed was important and not about the document: clear from filing against Branca and McClain. The only one of the Jacksons I've personally heard speak about MJ's excoriation of Branca is Katherine, though I've seen Joe on videotape doing so; one attorney or associate after another who was involved with MJ during the last six years of his life. It was only when Howard Weitzman produced a witness to the meeting between MJ and Branca, and then arranged a phone conversation with Joel Katz, who said he had spoken with MJ about that meeting afterward, that I concluded the meeting had taken place and that Branca likely had been hired as one of MJ's entertainment attorneys a week before MJ's death.

Up until the time that this book went into production, my attempts to elicit answers from John Branca about MJ's will and trust agreement, and about his relationship with MJ, have all been ignored. Other than the long and threatening March 31, 2011, letter from Howard Weitzman that denounced Tohme and Mann, my only communications with the estate were through e-mails exchanged with Mike Sitrick. I repeatedly offered Branca the opportunity to address the questions that have arisen about his position and performance as the executor of Michael Jackson's estate, and he declined. Howard Weitzman made a number of phone calls to various sources—Tohme, Dennis Hawk, and Tom Mesereau, among others—demanding to know if they are speaking to me (and implicitly discouraging them from doing so), but did not communicate with me personally until late August 2012.

Even after my conversations with Weitzman, John Branca, to my knowledge, has not answered a single challenging question about Michael Jackson's will being prepared by his law firm or how it is that Branca retained the original of the will after he was fired as Michael's attorney and received a command to return all documents. Branca also refuses to answer questions about the time, location, and circumstances under which Michael Jackson signed the will that was submitted to Judge Beckloff on July 1, 2009. Sitrick and Weitzman have attempted to suggest (to me and others) that all of those questions were settled when the court rejected the claims made in Joe Jackson's lawsuit against the estate. In fact, the court did not reject those claims. What it rejected was Joe Jackson's standing to make such claims, since he is not a named beneficiary of the estate. If Katherine Jackson had filed the same lawsuit, those claims almost certainly *would* have been heard by the court and Branca would have been compelled to answer. To date, he never has been.

Allegations against Branca (and Mottola) made in the Interfor report are cited not because I know or even believe them to be true but because they clearly influenced MJ and were a significant part of what soured his relationship with Branca. When Tom Mesereau questioned David LeGrand at the criminal trial in Santa Maria, LeGrand testified that he didn't have any independent knowledge that the claims made about Branca in the Interfor report were accurate. I don't know whether MJ himself had independent information that backed up the Interfor accusations, or whether he simply embraced them because they fit with what he already believed, but the latter possibility seems most likely.

I'm not personally accusing Branca of anything. I'm merely stating that there are legitimate questions surrounding his position as executor of the Michael Jackson estate and that he has refused to publicly address them.

Internal divisions among Jacksons/how Branca exploited them: mostly but not entirely from confidential sources. Estate attitude to Randy Jackson: Katz in tape recorded conversation with Vaccaro; Howard Weitzman said pretty much the same thing, in even stronger language, when I spoke to him on the telephone. My sources have described Randy in much the same way that Katz and Weitzman, and have said other Jacksons call him "Joe Jr." behind his back. MJ accusing Randy of stealing: MJ deposition wording/Prescient case could be and *was* construed that way in media; note Contact Music headline below; it's also true, though, that a 2007 press release (Bain on MJ's behalf, posted on "Friends of Randy Jackson"/Facebook) denied he had ever accused Randy of this, see also starpulse.com. Jackson family *awareness* that MJ accused Randy of stealing from him: my sources; Tohme also told me that MJ warned him that Randy was the member of his family he most had to watch out for, and that MJ said Randy had stolen from him in large ways and small, and that MJ was especially upset about an expensive watch he claimed Randy had stolen. I have no certain knowledge of whether Randy stole from MJ or not, but I am convinced that MJ told people he had, the 2007 press release notwithstanding. I've offered Randy the opportunity to respond to the stories told about him, including claims about what took place when he tried to get a meeting with MJ in Las Vegas in 2007. Matt Fiddes, who perhaps had a longer relationship with MJ than anyone who had worked security for him since Bill Bray, told Britain's *Sun* that MJ ordered his security guards to shoot Randy (see the TMZ story about that below). Randy denied that happened, but not to me. Through Taunya Zilkie, he declined the opportunity to discuss these matters with me.

Jermaine: sources cited above, observation of Jermaine's public statements/behavior. Weakness for women, child support arrears: KJ advisor. Maldonado quotes: Friedman July 24, 2012. Estate offering to help Jermaine get a record contract at Universal: same source as child support issues, Katz (whose standing at Universal is equal to Branca's at Sony) to Vaccaro. Offer to work in Cirque du Soleil, Jermaine joining pro-estate side (which he later abandoned): three separate sources. I have collapsed time here for purposes of narrative flow; the Cirque du Soleil opportunity came well after the Universal deal was proposed. Jackie-McClain relationship, past and present, arrangement with estate/T-shirt business: same sources. KJ-McClain relationship: same sources, KJ in my presence. Air purifier: a single source, but one who knows more about what goes on in the Jackson family than anyone who is not a member of it and most of those who are. KJ hiring Adam Streisand, KJ account of McMillan's advice: KJ herself, her advisors, other attorneys. Streisand's first hearing appearance, family push to challenge will/Branca as executor: Alan Duke/CNN October 22 and 23, 2009, from which quotes from October 22 hearing come; local TV stations/"new evidence" likely drew from this. Streisand questioning will but advising not to challenge: KJ (Streisand never expressed those doubts to me); all of Mrs. Jackson's main advisors say that she reported at the time that Streisand had made these statements. Taj Jackson as possible additional executor, Branca response, KJ attorney's advice to distance herself from Joe, KJ decision to drop fight against estate: confidential sources (Taj Jackson part may have been reported). I also discussed these matters with Adam Streisand. "Worth more dead than alive": Joe Jackson to *Extra*. Joe petition for an allowance: Ryan/November 7, 2009. Joe demand that Katherine weigh in on his behalf: through Oxman in open court, my sources. Streisand convincing Mrs. Jackson to drop objections and work with executors: explained in open court, and Streisand to me, KJ/her advisors. Events and all quotes at hearing of November 10, 2009: *LA Times* and CNN, other media who had reporters present. Executors' filing for "extraordinary compensation": review of document, TMZ (December 15 and 17, 2009). Weitzman presentation of request: public record. The probate case before Judge Beckloff is one court file I've broken into parts in my source list, separating out the various actions.

Raymone Bain claim against estate/outcome: Mesereau, TMZ April 19, 2010, "Raymone Bain's Claim Denied" report on mjworld.net. AllGood lawsuit: Hawk, see also "AllGood Socks Jackson Estate Hard," "It's All Good For Michael Jackson"/TMZ. Weitzman arguments: open court. Audigier claim: public record. Eric Muhammad: "Bodyguard Tries To Sell Mask"/mjworld.net.

Sums paid to Weitzman's law firms/others: estate's accounting, which I've seen. Joe/"Jackson Family Project": Judd/*Glendale News-Press*. Joe demand for MJ's medical records, complaint against estate for failing to file: examiner.com January 1, 2010, public record, probate case court file. Oxman's claim doctors detected MJ heartbeat at hospital, other quotes and claims in this regard: March 29, 2010, press conference, see Duke/CNN. *Segye Times* claim/KJ: court file, Friedman June 28, 2010; case/how dealt with by KJ/estate: confidential sources, and to some degree Perry Sanders, who eventually settled the matter on Mrs. Jackson's behalf. Joe attempt to blame KJ for MJ's death in *News of the World*, Streisand quote: *New York Daily News*, TMZ. Joe Jackson lawsuit against Murray on one-year anniversary: Associated Press,

BBC. Jacksons pulling private security from MJ gravesite, Forest Lawn actions: *Sydney Morning Herald*, Friedman/"Michael Jackson Vultures"; graffiti on MJ's tomb: *National Ledger*, June 25 scene: ABC story on the one-year anniversary. KJ filing against AEG: CNN, X17 stories; all quotations: verbatim from the filing. Brian Panish statement: see below. AEG response: Associated Press. Judge Palazuelos decision not to dismiss lawsuit, and comments on case: Julie Garber wills blog/about.com.

MJ post-death career success: *Billboard* June 21, 2010, also Tim Adams/ *Billboard*. Reeder, Branca, and Sillerman quotes, growth of the estate in its first year (and all due credit to Branca): Sisario/*New York Times*. Tohme retort: Tohme.

COURT FILES

Civil

CV-09-07084 (United States District Court, Central District of California) *John G. Branca, Special Administrator of the Estate of Michael J. Jackson; John McClain, Special Administrator of the Estate of Michael J. Jackson; and Triumph International Inc., a California Corporation v. Heal the World Foundation, et al.*, September 29, 2009 (hereafter cited as USDC-CA CU-09-07084).

LASC BP 117321 11/9/09.

BP 117 321 (Los Angeles Superior Court) *Ex Parte Application for Order Shortening Time for Notice of Hearing on Petition for Order Allowing and Approving Payment of: 1) Extraordinary Compensation to Special Administrators and Attorneys for Special Administrators; 2) Reimbursement of Costs and Compensation to Guardian Ad Litem; Memorandum of Points and Authorities*, December 15, 2009 (hereafter cited as LASC BP 117321 12/15/09).

CV 11-00584 DDP (United States District Court, Central District of California) *John Branca and John McClain, Executors of the Estate of Michael J. Jackson v. Howard Mann, et al.*, January 20, 2011 (hereafter cited as USDC-CA CU 11-00584 DDP).

LASC BP117321 2/17/12.

DOCUMENTS

"Certificate of Live Birth," Paris-Michael Katherine Jackson, State of California, County of Los Angeles, Department of Health Services. February 13, 1998 (hereafter cited as "Birth Certificate" 2/13/98).

"Amended and Restated Declaration of Trust, Michael Joseph Jackson." March 2, 2002 (hereafter cited as Declaration of Trust, 3/2/02).

"Last Will of Michael Joseph Jackson." July 7, 2002 (hereafter cited as Last Will 7/7/02).

Branca to Jackson, 8/14/02.

Branca to Sony/ATV, 8/14/02.

Branca to Singer, 8/7/02.

Singer to Branca, 9/10/02.

Interfor Report on John Gregory Branca.

Jackson to Branca, 2/3/03.

"Discontinuence of Services." Letter from Michael Jackson to Barry Siegel. February 4, 2003 (hereafter cited as Jackson to Siegel, 2/4/03).

"RE: Michael Jackson Insurance Trust, Michael Jackson Family Trust, Last Will of Michael Joseph Jackson." Letter from Barry Siegel, CPA, to Michael Jackson, John G. Branca, Esq., and John McClain. August 26, 2003 (hereafter cited as Siegel to Jackson, Branca, and McClain, 8/26/03).

Branca 4/15/06.

Tape recording of phone conversation between Joel Katz (co–general counsel of Michael Jackson Estate) and Henry Vaccaro. August 2009 (hereafter cited as Katz and Vaccaro, 8/2009).

Weitzman to Sullivan and Entrekin, 3/31/11.

Durst to Reynolds, 4/3/11.

"FWD: Will and Trust." E-mail sent from Howard Mann to Randall Sullivan. April 9, 2011 (hereafter cited as Mann to Sullivan, 4/19/11).

"FWD: New Video for Jackson Secret Vault About HTWF." E-mail sent from Howard Mann to Randall Sullivan. April 9, 2011 (hereafter cited as Mann to Sullivan "Secret Vault," 4/9/11).

"RE: Katherine Jackson." E-mail from Adam Streisand to Randall Sullivan. June 27, 2011 (hereafter cited as Streisand to Sullivan, 6/27/11).

Williams to Sanders, 11/3/11.

Ribera to Sullivan, 11/9/11.

Ribera to Sullivan, 11/13/11.

YEAR ONE (BEFORE JUNE 25, 2010)

"AllGood Socks Jackson Estate Hard." *TMZ*, October 16, 2009 (I).

"Bodyguard Tries to Sell Mask." mjworld.net, November 29th 2009 (I).

Duke, Alan. "Attorney: Michael Jackson Had Heartbeat at Hospital." CNN, March 29, 2010 (I).

———. "Jackson Family Lawyer Hints at 'New Evidence' in Battle for Estate." CNN, October 23, 2009 (I).

———. "Katherine Jackson Replaces Lawyers in Estate Battle." CNN, October 22, 2009 (I).

Fernandez and Collins.

Friedman, Roger. "Michael Jackson Estate Wouldn't Pay Randy and Jermaine's Owed Child Support." *Showbiz411.com*, July 24, 2012 (I) (hereafter cited as Friedman. "Owed Child Support").

———. "Michael Jackson: Moonies Want Millions from His Parent." *Showbiz411.com*, June 28, 2010 (I).

Holson. "Bitter Attack."

Holson and Holloway. "Sony and Its Star."

"It's All Good for Michael Jackson." *TMZ*, August 19, 2010 (I).

"Jackson Executors—Beyond the Call of Duty." *TMZ*, December 17, 2009 (I).

"Jackson's Will—Randy Says Not MJ's Signature." *TMZ*, October 21, 2009 (I).

"Joe Jackson Blames Katherine for Michael's Death." *TMZ*, June 13, 2010 (I).

"Joe Jackson: Michael 'Worth More Dead Than Alive.'" *Extra*, October 28, 2009 (RT).

Judd, Amy. "Gary, Indiana, Hosts Michael Jackson Tribute June 25, 2010." *Glendale News-Press*, June 25, 2010 (hereafter cited as Judd, "Gary, Indiana").

Kim, Victoria. "Michael Jackson's Mother No Longer Objects to Estate Executors." *Los Angeles Times*, November 10, 2009.

Lueck, Thomas J. "Record Industry Is Attacked by a Top Star." *New York Times*, July 7, 2002.

Martin, Brandy. "Michael Jackson's Dad Demands Medical Records." examiner. com, January 1, 2010 (I).

Mayoras, Danielle, and Andrew Mayoras. "Crazy Claims."

——— and ———. "Change of Heart."

——— and ———. "Planning Lessons."

——— and ———. "New Evidence."

——— and ———. "Estate Deal."

"McClain Interscope."

"Michael Jackson Accuses His Brother of Stealing from Him." *Contact Music*, June 18, 2007 (I).

"Michael Jackson Denies Stories About Illness and Brother Randy Stealing from Him." starpulse.com, June 29, 2007 (I).

"Michael Jackson's Executors—Pay Us Now!" *TMZ*, December 15, 2009 (I).

"Michael Jackson's Will Fake, Says His Former Advisor." *Radar Online*, June 21, 2010 (I).

"MJ Bodyguard Claims Singer Ordered Hit on Randy Jackson." *TMZ*, May 8, 2012 (I).

"MJ Estate to Publicist: You're Not Getting a Cent!" *TMZ*, April 19, 2010 (I).

"Raymone Bain's Claim Denied." mjworld.net, May 8, 2010 (I).

Roberts, Soraya. "Michael Jackson's Father, Joe, Claims Wife, Katherine, Is to Blame for Their Son's Death." *New York Daily News*, June 14, 2010.

Ryan, Harriet. "Michael Jackson's Father Seeks Allowance from Singer's Estate." *Los Angeles Times*, November 7, 2009.

"Statement by Michael (2007) Regarding Rumors Saying Randy Stole Michael's Money." Facebook/Friends of Randy Jackson, January 3, 2011 (I).

YEAR TWO (AFTER JUNE 25, 2010)

Adams, Tim. "Taylor Swift Edges Susan Boyle for 2009's Top-Selling Album." *Billboard*, January 6, 2010.

"AEG Live Responds to Katherine Jackson's Lawsuit." Associated Press, September 17, 2010.

Bourke, Philippa. "Michael's Gravesite No Longer Guarded." *Sydney Morning Herald*, March 10, 2010.

Christman, Donahue, Mitchell, Peoples, and Waddell.

Eager, Sophie. "Jackson Fans Graffiti Tomb." *National Ledger*, July 14, 2010.

Friedman, Roger. "The Michael Jackson Vultures Circle June 25th for 1st Attack." *Showbiz411.com*, June 11, 2010 (I).

Hernandez, Miriam, and Melissa MacBride. "Michael Jackson Mourned on Death Anniversary." abcnews.go.com, June 25, 2010 (I).

"Jackson Family Suing AEG in Wrongful Death Lawsuit." *X17*, September 15, 2010 (I).

McCartney, Anthony. "Joe Jackson Sues Murray for Wrongful Death." Associated Press, June 25, 2010.

"Michael Jackson's Father Files Wrongful Death Suit." BBC, June 25, 2010 (RT).

"Panish Shea and Boyle LLP Files Lawsuit Against AEG for Wrongful Death of Michael Jackson." psandb.com, September 15, 2010 (PR).

Sisario, Ben. "A Year Later, Jackson Estate Is Prospering." *New York Times*, June 23, 2010 (hereafter cited as Sisario, "A Year Later").

Wilson, Stan. "Father of Michael Jackson Accuses AEG of Singer's Death." CNN, June 18, 2010 (I).

CHAPTER 28

I have, obviously, heard a great deal about life inside the Hayvenhurst compound, and about life at Katherine Jackson's new home in Calabasas. I tried to draw as much as possible, though, on published reports and public records.

The fact that most of my sources of information (Schaffel and Mann being notable exceptions, along with Adam Streisand) have requested confidentiality is the principle reason for this. Where I'm drawing on my own sources will be acknowledged.

"Camp Jackson"/life inside compound: Tresniowski/"Michael's Last Wish"/ *People*. Children's circumstances/behavior: Tresniowski/"Michael's Kids: Inside Their World." "Sodom and Gomorrah": Klein in "Joe Jackson's a Hypocrite!"/ TMZ. Prince and Paris descriptions: confidential sources close to the family, plus Tresniowski, TMZ staff, La Toya to *Daily Mail*. MJ bringing dog Kenya home, eating Snickers atop Luxor: Paris to Oprah Winfrey (see Chapter 2 notes), others. Squabbling among Jacksons: confidential sources, Duke, Dimond. Randy leading opposition to Branca, KJ unhappy with allowance: confidential sources. Branca's response/upping of allowance: same, but also probate file documents. Estate payments for vacations, etc.: accounting statements, also Friedman. Pressure from children (especially Randy and La Toya) for KJ to challenge estate: confidential sources. Apprehension among Jacksons/estate ending payments if KJ died or was unable to continue as guardian: confidential sources; that mood was amplified when some of them either heard, or heard about, the taped conversation between Joel Katz and Henry Vaccaro, in which Katz and Vaccaro's attorney can be heard chuckling about the fact that the Jacksons would be cut off completely when Katherine died. Rebbie and Janet only candidates to raise kids if Katherine died: confidential sources.

La Toya on Grace: to *Daily Mail*. Grace's departure from Hayvenhurst, explanations: "overplaying her hand": my sources; due to Barrack interviews: other sources; children's fear of losing Grace: "Jackson Kids Secret Terror"/ *National Enquirer*; Paris having Grace fired: see below. Grace's presence influencing Debbie: Schaffel, other sources. Grace suggesting (or perceived as) that she might do a tell-all: confidential source, see also X17.com below. Buckley School plan/change of plan: TMZ, Tresniowski's second *People* article; confidential sources. Department of Children and Family Services/stun gun: ABC online; Streisand refutation of story: Associated Press, others. Debbie Rowe custody situation: Schaffel, *NY Daily News, Us*. Rowe petition for legal fees: estate case file, Contact Music (including Tito quote). Stun gun incident /TMZ questions re. Streisand account: TMZ cited below. "World Exclusive" video, Haraszti comment: Radar Online below. Debbie's concern about kids, never having been to Hayvenhurst: March 4 story. I've heard otherwise, but perhaps a visit came later; see also Friedman June 21, 2010. Jacksons's questions/accusations about leak of stun gun/video: confidential sources; X17 on Grace as "snitch"/"threatening to write a tell-all book": "Stun Gun Snitch." Schaffel said Grace wasn't the snitch; he was not my only source who said Grace wasn't fired but left Hayvenhurst of her own volition, because of Alejandra, and what Schaffel knows comes mainly from KJ. "Strong recommendation" of Department of Children and Family services (DCFS): Schaffel, other sources I regard as equally or even more reliable. Claim Alejandra called DCFS/sold slapping video: "Jackson insider" letter/TMZ (see Chapter 26). Observations about MJ's children's reality/lack of privacy: my own. Kids at Cascios' for Christmas: confidential sources; I don't know that it's been reported. "Don't have any friends": KJ to *Daily Mirror*. Enrollment at Buckley: TMZ August 27; insistence of Prince, reluctance of Paris, Blanket remaining homeschooled: confidential sources.

Michael controversy: media (more below) and confidential sources close to Jackson family; in this instance I'm pretty sure the estate's position was the true one—at least with regard to whether that was MJ's voice or not. The back and forth, and how people involved with the album on the one hand, and with MJ in the past on the other, divided between the two sides, was widely reported. Michaels/*Guardian* gave an account very close to the one I heard from my sources. Teddy Riley account: Nicholson/*Guardian*. Best source on assembly of album, review of music: Pareles "After Death, the Remix" (though I think he should have given "Behind the Mask" a little more respect). Existence of "Breaking News": MTV. Commercial performance, radio response, first to predict the controversy: Friedman, who reported the heck out of the story. Eddie Cascio: to "Oprah," *NY Daily News*. MJ's children saying it wasn't his voice: first, TMZ; see also TMZ video more than a year later of Paris Jackson telling friends (one of whom clearly sold her out) "It's *not* him . . . the whole album isn't even him!" Weitzman defense of album, especially "Breaking News," Dileo, Riley quotes: Sisario/*New York Times*. KJ/Randy Jackson complaints: Michaels/*Guardian*. Will.i.am: to *Rolling Stone*. Quincy Jones: to *Us*. Estate's defense of album: Sisario article on Howard Weitzman. Disappointing sales Gail Mitchell's *Billboard* international success Friedman's December 22, 2010, column. "Self-referential rehash": Infantry/*Toronto Star*. I stand by my own opinion of "Behind the Mask."

MJ's belief in conspiracy to take ATV catalog from him: Mesereau (who remembers MJ constantly begging him not to "let them get to you"), Schaffel, Wiesner, Tohme, Bain in *Stealing Michael Jackson* interview, La Toya to *Independent*, Orth (see Chapter 5 notes), confidential source; based on things she said in my presence, KJ believes it's all or mostly true. Conspiracy theories surrounding MJ's death: *Daily Telegraph*; David Icke's Web site has some truly arcane theories, and other sites picked up the one that the CIA was behind MJ's "assassination." David Rothenberg really MJ in disguise: *Sun*. MJ alive at coroner's office: photographs as described in text, also, YouTube videos purported to show it. Geller comments: Geller. Joe Jackson's letter telling MJ fans to lay off Conrad Murray: TMZ. Joe describing Murray as "fall guy": Duke/CNN story, months earlier and well before Jermaine would. Joe's complaint to the California Medical Board: Associated Press; similar allegations have been and are being made in AEG wrongful death suit, per documents filed in connection to it. Murray on how he might have saved MJ: the now-defunct *News of the World*, via *Times of India*. "Fall guy," "Michael was murdered": CNN story on La Toya's *Piers Morgan Tonight* appearance. Murray's lawyers' claim Arnold Klein overmedicated MJ: court file/Murray trial. MJ showing signs of drugs after seeing Klein, Dileo's remark: Faye statement to LAPD, used in "Do You Want Fries With That"/ TMZ. I've seen the claims Dr. Klein submitted to the Michael Jackson estate and all of the details about the treatment Klein provided to MJ are from one of those documents. "Needle-phobic": Klein to Ephron/Daily Beast. The attorney general's office was just one of a number of agencies investigating the relationship between Klein and other doctors with MJ. Klein himself was the first to announce (on Facebook.com/arnold.klein) that he was being investigated by the California Medical Board. "Upstanding physician": first filing by KJ attorneys in wrongful death lawsuit against AEG.

Conrad Murray preliminary hearing: almost entirely from testimony and evidence; a few pieces of information were from the media but I mainly read those to see how the hearing was being covered. Kenny Ortega, as noted in the text, was named as one of the defendants in the original filing in the AEG suit, but did not remain among them for very long and is now likely to be called, as I understand it, as a witness for the plaintiffs. Though I refer to it as Katherine Jackson's lawsuit, Prince, Paris, and Blanket are also plaintiffs; Katherine was the one who initiated it. Obviously, assertions such as that the paramedics were powerful witnesses and that the testimony of the phone company representative indicated that the prosecution was holding evidence in reserve were my own. The same is true of the statement that the failure to secure the evidence at the scene provided an opening for the defense. In fact the defense did attempt to take advantage of that at trial, but not very effectively.

MJ'S KIDS/HAYVENHURST

"Arnie Klein—Joe Jackson's a Hypocrite!" *TMZ*, June 14, 2010 (I).

Dimond, Diane. "The Jackson 8's Family Feud." *Daily Beast*, August 13, 2009 (I).

Duke, Alan. "Michael Jackson Estate Fight Becomes Public Family Dispute." CNN, November 11, 2009 (I).

Friedman, Roger. "Michael Jackson's Kids: Spending Time with Debbie Rowe." *Showbiz411.com*, June 21, 2010 (I).

Graham, Caroline. "Michael Was Murdered . . . I Felt It from the Start." *Daily Mail*, July 13, 2009.

"Jackson Kids' Secret Terror." *National Enquirer*, October 22, 2009.

"Jackson's Mum Remembers."

"Katherine and MJ's Kids—Pilgrimage on Anniversary." *TMZ*, June 19, 2010 (I)

"Katherine Jackson: Michael's Kids Have No Friends." *TMZ*, June 20, 2010 (I).

"Michael Jackson's Kids Could Turn Preppy." *TMZ*, August 23, 2009 (I).

"Michael Jackson's Kids Get School." *TMZ*, August 27, 2010 (I).

"Paris Jackson Has Nanny Fired." tribute.ca, May 27, 2010 (I).

Tresniowski and Dyball.

Tresniowski, Alev. "Michael Jackson's Kids: Inside Their World." *People*, September 17, 2010.

"The Jackson Kids' Education—Home Works." *TMZ*, September 8, 2009 (I).

STUN GUN AND SLAPPING INCIDENTS/DEBBIE, ALEJANDRA, AND GRACE

Chernikoff, Leah. "Debbie Rowe Concerned for Safety of Michael Jackson's Kids After Reports of Stun Gun Threat." *New York Daily News*, March 5, 2010.

"Debbie Rowe Wants Jackson Estate to Pay Bills." *Contact Music*, September 9, 2010 (I).

"Debbie Rowe 'Worried' After Jackson Kids Stun-Gun Reports." *Us*, March 5, 2010.

Goldman, Russell. "Jackson Nephew, 13, Investigated for Playing with Stun Gun." abcnews.go.com, March 2, 2010 (I).

"Jackson Stun Gun Snitch Exposed." *X17*, March 4, 2010 (I).

McCartney, Anthony. "Child Services Probes Stun Gun at Jackson Home." Associated Press, March 3, 2010.

"Michael Jackson's Ex Debbie Concerned About Blanket." *Radar Online*, March 4, 2010 (I).

"The Story of Alejandra Oaziaza Jackson?" desireespeakssolisten.blogspot.com, June 10, 2010 (I).

"World Exclusive Video: Shocking Violence Inside Jackson Family Home." *Radar Online*, March 5, 2010 (I).

MICHAEL ALBUM

Friedman, Roger. "Michael Jackson: 'Secret' Work Tapes Will Prove It's His Voice on Tracks ('Hold My Hand' Now Available)." *Showbiz411.com*, November 14, 2010 (I).

———. "Michael Jackson's New Album Finishes at Number 3 in U.S., but It's an International Hit." *Showbiz411.com*, December 22, 2010 (I).

———. "New Michael Jackson Album May Pose Legal Problems." *Showbiz411. com*, May 3, 2010 (I).

Infantry, Ashante. "Review: Michael Jackson's New Single Is Bad News." *Toronto Star*, November 17, 2010.

"Michael Jackson Kid—They FAKED My Dad's Voice on 'Michael' Album." *TMZ*, Feburary 29, 2012 (I).

"Michael Jackson's Kids: It's Not Daddy's Voice." *TMZ*, November 1, 2010 (I).

Michaels, Sean. "New Michael Jackson Songs Are 'Fake,' Says His Mother." *Guardian*, November 8, 2010.

———. "Randy Jackson Denounces Michael Album Tracks as Fakes." *Guardian*, November 19, 2010.

Mitchell, Gail. "Michael Jackson's 'Michael' Album Sales Pale Next to 'This Is It.'" *Billboard*, January 21, 2011 (hereafter cited as Mitchell, "Album Sales").

Nicholson, Rebecca. "The Row Behind the New Michael Jackson CD." *Guardian*, December 12, 2010.

Pareles, Jon. "After Death, the Remix." *New York Times*, December 12, 2010.

"Quincy Jones: Lady Gaga Is 'Madonna Jr.'" *Us*, November 22, 2010.

Roberts, Soraya. "Michael Jackson Recorded Album of New Music with Eddie (Angel) Cascio in November 2007." *New York Daily News*, May 3, 2010.

Ryan, Chris. "New Song: Michael Jackson, 'Breaking News.'" mtv.com, November 8, 2010 (I).

Sisario, Ben. "'Breaking News': Lawyer Says, It's Michael Jackson's Voice." *New York Times*, November 11, 2010.

"Will.i.am Explains His 'Disgust' for New Michael Jackson Album." *Rolling Stone*, December 13, 2010.

Oprah. "Cascio Home."

CONSPIRACY THEORIES

Bingham, John. "Michael Jackson Death: Conspiracy Theories and Unanswered Questions." *Daily Telegraph*, June 26, 2009.

Hodge, Katie. "Michael Jackson Murdered for Hit Catalogue, Claims LaToya." *Independent*, June 24, 2010.

"Michael Jackson Still Alive After Transport to Coroner." YouTube, August 25, 2009 (I).

Sloan, Jenna. "Is Jacko Posing as a Burns Victim?" *Sun*, May 11, 2010.

"Why the CIA Murdered Michael Jackson." forum.davidicke.com, August 25, 2009 (I).

CONRAD MURRAY PRELIMINARY HEARING

Duke, Alan. "Joe Jackson: Dr. Murray 'a Fall Guy' in Michael's Death." CNN, February 9, 2010 (I).

"Do You Want Fries?"

Ephron, Amy. "The Michael Jackson Trial That Wasn't." *Daily Beast*, September 29, 2011 (I) (hereafter cited as Ephron, "Trial").

"Joe Jackson: Don't Attack Conrad's Supporters." *TMZ*, May 12, 2010 (I).

McCartney, Anthony, and Thomas Watkins. "MJ's Doc Requested CPR Gear, Nurse for London Gig." Associated Press, June 17, 2010.

"Michael Jackson Was Murdered, Sister La Toya Tells Piers Morgan." cnn. com, June 21, 2011 (I).

"MJ Could Have Been Saved, Says Doc in Dock." *Times of India*, September 13, 2010 (I).

CHAPTER 29

KJ/estate effort to get Alejandra to leave Hayvenhurst: confidential sources close to KJ; also, information in the court file. June 2010 attempt/KJ stunned at Alejandra hiring an attorney/staying: my sources, see also (including Katherine attempting to convince Alejandra to move into MJ's former condo) hollywoodgossip.com June 2010, Perez Hilton November 2010; most of the Internet media did not join in until the estate filed to evict Alejandra in January 2011. Confidentiality agreement/tell-all book: my sources, eventually reported on the Internet—see Perez Hilton January 7, 2011. I'm quoting Schaffel in part because he was the only one who didn't ask me not to use his name, and also because he was a confidant to Mrs. Jackson as all this was playing out. Most of what he is reporting to me was told to him by Katherine and other people in her household. DCFS workers urging KJ to separate MJ's kids from cousins: Schaffel and other sources (see Chapter 28); implied but to my knowledge not explicitly stated on TMZ. KJ staying at Schaffel's in Calabasas/liking the neighborhood: Schaffel, confirmed by other sources. Details of Calabasas house: "Hangin' in Britney's Hood"/TMZ, visitors to the property. "She basically stays in the house," KJ calling police/Alejandra response: confidential/advisor of KJ, as well as Schaffel on latter story. Jermaine stuck in Africa: confidential sources, TMZ and IANS, January 8–9, 2011. I do not know that Alejandra's attorneys intended to trap Jermaine in Africa (two of my sources said they did) or whether they had filed a previous notice with the State Department that Jermaine was in child support arrears and that kicked in when Jermaine presented an expired passport in Burkina Faso. KJ going to the estate for money for Jermaine: confidential/her closest advisor; also, Friedman.

Jacksons's concerns about what Alejandra might say in court: multiple sources, including Schaffel. Account of court hearing: Schaffel, TMZ, Radar Online. Estate deal to settle KJ-Alejandra-Jermaine issues: confidential sources who were spending a good deal of time in the Jackson household/with KJ as it was happening; see also entertainmentrundown.com, TMZ, Radar Online. What Jermaine told other family members about dealings with Branca: confidential source/KJ's closest advisor. KJ complaints to Oprah Winfrey about Branca/estate: Mann, who was present at Hayvenhurst during the interview. Mann does bear no small animus toward Branca (and vice versa, I'm told) but his story about this was supported by others, and by KJ's sworn declaration filed in the lawsuit between the estate and the Heal the World Foundation, from which KJ's words come about Winfrey "relenting."

A little about the Heal the World lawsuit, Streisand, and Sanders: I saw a draft of Mrs. Jackson's declaration before it was even signed and received blow-by-blow reports as it all went down. I was at the time staying at the Beverly Hilton Hotel, and so was Perry Sanders, who was in town to deal with matters relating to the Notorious B.I.G. wrongful death lawsuit. Sanders and I got to know each other through the Notorious B.I.G. case: My article for *Rolling Stone* was the catalyst for the lawsuit, and we spoke on the phone while I was writing *LAbyrinth*, my book about the murders of B.I.G. and Tupac that sprung from that reporting. While I was working on a second *Rolling Stone* article about the case, we spent some time together in Colorado and became friends. So when we were both at the Beverly Hilton I asked Sanders to look at some of the documents I was being shown, in particular those connected to the Joe Jackson–Brian Oxman effort to remove Branca and McClain as executors, and tell me what he thought of them in terms of legal argument.

I was also meeting at the hotel with various people, including Tohme Tohme and Howard Mann, who wanted to hire me to write and possibly perform the narration for the *Stealing Michael Jackson* documentary. At one point, Mann stated that Katherine Jackson needed a new attorney who would be more aggressive in representing her and I suggested a meeting with my friend Perry. I had never had any contact with Adam Streisand up to that point in time and certainly bore him no ill will. Several meetings followed between Sanders and Katherine Jackson's advisors; I sat in on most of them. Sanders and I were looking at the same documents and hearing the same stories. All of this led to a meeting that was attended by Katherine and her two closest advisors, as well as her constant companion Trent Jackson, plus Sanders and myself. I did ask

Katherine a number of questions about her legal representation, why this or that decision had been made in dealing with MJ's will and estate, and about her dealings (and MJ's) with John Branca, among other things, but I also told her that Perry Sanders was an attorney I believed she could trust. The very next day, or perhaps it was the day after that, the public drama generated by Mrs. Jackson's declaration in the Heal the World lawsuit erupted and Adam Streisand was quoted as saying that Katherine denied making the statements in that declaration. I heard before the end of the day that he was out and that Mrs. Jackson wanted to hire Perry Sanders (after speaking to Voletta Wallace). "Either a liar or a fool": confidential/advisor present at the meeting where Sanders was introduced to Mrs. Jackson. TMZ articles containing estate response/Streisand: "Fraud," "Pathetic," April 12, 2011. (There have probably been more volleys fired through Harvey Levin than through Judge Beckloff at this point.) KJ firing of Streisand: I saw the letter, and eventually made contact with Adam to hear his side of the story; his quotes are all from e-mails he sent me in a back and forth dialogue. It was my analysis that Streisand, whether he wanted to say so or not, was effectively calling Mrs. Jackson a liar: Katherine *had* signed that declaration. Streisand is right that Joe and Randy wanted him gone, but they weren't the only ones. There was general agreement on the Jackson side that Branca needed to be taken on (though not all of Joe and Katherine's children thought so).

Sanders and I were together constantly during that week at the Beverly Hilton, but things did change after he formally took the job as Mrs. Jackson's attorney. He told me less and what he did say was confidential. Fortunately, he was telling Katherine's advisors everything and they were passing most of it on to me, including his brick and deal approach. "Big-time litigator": "Let's Be Fair"/TMZ. Phone meeting between KJ and Voletta: I knew about this before, during, and after it took place. Joe Jackson/Brian Oxman filing, Sanders's review: The first time he went through it I was sitting right next to him and we were discussing it point-by-point; I have a copy of the filing and all supporting documents; all quoted material is from Oxman's filing. Sanders warned that Oxman is a publicity hound: by me and others; I also told him that Oxman was not stupid and he agreed after reading the filing.

Assertion that Joe's suit against the executors would have been heard if it had been filed on behalf of KJ: opinions from Sanders and other attorneys; I've made the same point to Branca and Weitzman and they haven't disputed it. Sanders conferring with Paul LiCalsi/other attorneys: learned during week at Beverly Hilton. Questions about preparation and signing of will/why Branca hadn't returned it to MJ when fired: raised in Oxman's filing. Weitzman assertions about will's approval by the court, signatures of witnesses: Weitzman to Reuters. As noted in the text, Weitzman has never stated whether the will was signed in New York or Los Angeles; I've given both him and Branca the opportunity to do so. Sanders–Barry Siegel conversation: Sanders; Hawk, unaware of that conversation, told me that Siegel told him the will was signed in New York. Handwriting expert (Bart Baggett): witnessed Sanders and Mann discussing it. I don't pretend to know what to make of the accusations (and there are several posted online) that MJ's signatures on either the will or the trust are forgeries. I do know that MJ's signature varied considerably, and Dennis Hawk was just one of several people who told me that MJ often signed documents without even looking at them. I think Sanders was as skeptical about the whole handwriting analysis approach as I was, but he did seem to think it was significant that the signature page was separate from the rest of the document. Sanders learned from me that MJ was actively seeking to create a new will and trust in early 2009. I learned it from Tohme, confirmed it with Hawk, and then confirmed it again with Sean Najerian. "That was my distinct impression": Hawk. Tohme was much more blunt and certain, insisting that MJ made it clear he thought he had no will and didn't think the one naming Branca as an executor still existed. Hawk was much more reluctant to say anything that would sound like an accusation against Branca. 2006 Neverland Trust agreements: described by Tohme, Hawk, two other sources; eventually I saw copies myself. Najerian confirmed everything I had been told by Tohme and Hawk and voiced the opinion that the process was interrupted by the Julien Auctions imbroglio; Hawk agreed. "I can tell you": Tohme. 2003 will naming Al Malnik as executor: Schaffel, one of the two witnesses to the signing of the document; I later discovered that the day after MJ's death Malnik had told the *Palm Beach Post*'s "Page 2" columnist Jose Lambiet that he was indeed the executor of MJ's 2003 will and had agreed to be the guardian of MJ's youngest child, Blanket. A reporter for the local CBS affiliate in Miami, Lisa Petrillo, interviewed Malnik that same day and reported that Malnik had also told her that as of 2004 he was the executor of MJ's estate and the designated guardian of Blanket. Reporters who called to ask/did not get Malnik to comment: South Florida reporters Bob Norman and Joe Weisenthal. Malnik hasn't spoken to anyone on the record about the will since June 26, 2009, and wouldn't talk to me. Malnik's position as summarized in the text ("doesn't want to be bothered," etc.): Schaffel, who tried to communicate with Malnik on my behalf; the part about hiring Branca to run the estate makes sense. In our conversations in August of 2012, Howard Weitzman claimed he had spoken to Malnik and told me first that the will "was never filed" and then later wrote a letter to me in which he claimed

Malnik had told him that the will never existed. Perry Sanders believed that Malnik should have produced any will in his possession for inspection by the court within sixty days of MJ's death.

Sanders's spring 2011 assessment of his "brick": Sanders, before he stopped sharing so freely with me; also, Mann, other KJ advisors. Joe/Randy displeasure re. Sanders's preference for a deal: multiple sources. "Bottom line": Sanders to TMZ . Sanders-Weitzman lunch and dinner: Sanders; he did not say what it was about or what was discussed, but other confidential sources with relationships with KJ did. Settlement of Heal the World lawsuit: all of the documents, provided to me by one of KJ's advisors, also discussed with Sanders; it was a moment of contention between us because I didn't think Melissa Johnson had been dealt with fairly. Perry made it very clear he felt otherwise.

Joe and Randy accusing Sanders of working for the estate: multiple sources; actually, Joe insisted that *I* was the estate's "plant" and had arranged for Sanders's introduction at the behest of John Branca, who will no doubt be amused to read about it. Sanders convincing KJ of benefits of negotiating fair deal: multiple sources. What took place at Sanders-Weitzman dinner: per KJ advisors, Sanders made some sort of threat and that Weitzman decided that he, too, believed a deal was better than a battle. "A very able man": KJ via secondary source. Sanders on Branca: Sanders told me Branca was "super-competent" and a reasonable man. "Katherine is being taken care of": Sanders. How well MJ's children were in Calabasas: several sources, again only Schaffel willing to be on record. Prince/Lakers game: "Gets His Game On"/TMZ. Prince developing vitiligo: Schaffel, also reported in media; see *Daily Telegraph* November 2009, *NY Daily News* July 2010 (first US mention); Jermaine told *Extra* six or seven months after I'd first heard.

COURT FILES

Civil

USDC-CA CV-09-07084.
LASC BP 117321, 11/9/09.
LASC BP 117 321, 12/15/09.
USDC-CA CV 11-00584 DDP.
LASC BP117321, 2/17/12.

DOCUMENTS

Birth Certificate, 2/13/98.
Declaration of Trust, 3/2/02.

Last Will, 7/7/02.
Branca to Jackson, 8/14/02.
Branca to Sony/ATV, 8/14/02.
Branca to Singer, 8/7/02.
Singer to Branca, 9/10/02.
Interfor Report on John Gregory Branca.
Jackson to Branca, 2/3/03.
Jackson to Siegel, 2/4/03.
Siegel to Jackson, Branca, and McClain, 8/26/03.
Branca, 4/15/06.
Weitzman to Sullivan and Entrekin, 3/31/11.
Durst to Reynolds, 4/3/11.
Mann to Sullivan, 4/9/11.
Mann to Sullivan "Secret Vault," 4/9/11.
Streisand to Sullivan, 6/27/11.
Williams to Sanders, 11/3/11.
Ribera to Sullivan, 11/9/11.
Ribera to Sullivan, 11/13/11.

OTHER

Katz and Vaccaro, 8/2009.

HAYVENHURST DRAMA/ALEJANDRA

"Alejandra Jackson Agrees to Move Out of Family Compound." *Radar Online*,
    April 9, 2011 (I).
"Alejandra Jackson Refuses to Leave Michael Jackson's Encino Estate." *Radar
    Online*, March 15, 2011 (I).
"Alejandra Jackson to Move Out—Book Deal Imminent." *TMZ*, April 8, 2011 (I).
Free Britney. "Katherine Jackson Really Wants Former Daughter-in-Law,
    Grandkids Out." hollywoodgossip.com, June 17, 2010 (I).
Friedman, "Owed Child Support."
Hilton, Perez. "Katherine Jackson Wants Relatives to Move Out!" perezhilton.
    com, November 9, 2010 (I).
———. "Tell-All Book at Center of Jackson Family War!" perezhilton.com,
    January 1, 2011 (I).
"Jermaine and Randy Jackson's Ex-Wife Refuses to Leave Katherine's Home."
    entertainmentrundown.com, March 3, 2011 (I).
"Jermaine Jackson—Stuck in Africa." *TMZ*, January 8, 2011 (I).

"Jermaine Jackson Trapped in Africa After Passport Expires." *IANS*, January 9, 2011 (I).
"Katherine Jackson—Hangin' in Britney's Hood." *TMZ*, December 16, 2010 (I).
"Katherine Jackson: The Declaration Is a Fraud!" *TMZ*, April 12, 2011 (I).
"MJ Estate—Katherine's Accusations Are 'Pathetic.'" *TMZ*, April 12, 2011 (I).
"MJ Estate to Alejandra—Move Out Already!!!" *TMZ*, March 11, 2011 (I).

ESTATE/KATHERINE JACKSON/LAWYERS

Dobuzinkskis, Alex. "Michael Jackson Administrators Dismiss Questions About Legal Will." Reuters, October 21, 2009.
"Katherine's New Lawyer to Estate: Let's Be Fair." *TMZ*, April 15, 2011 (I).
Lambiet, Jose. "Palm Beacher Could Be Guardian of Michael Jackson's Son." *Palm Beach Post*, June 26, 2009.
Norman, "Reputed Mobster."
Petrillo, Lisa. "Interview with Michael Jackson Friend Al Malnik." CBS4/Miami, June 25, 2009 (RT).
Weisenthal, Joe. "Alleged Mobster May Control Jackson's Estate." business-insider.com, June 28, 2009 (I).

PRINCE MICHAEL JACKSON

Black, Rosemary. "Like Father, Like Son? Prince Michael Jackson May Have Vitiligo, Which Dad Michael Claimed He Had." *New York Daily News*, July 1, 2010.
Laing, Aislinn, and Nick Allen. "Michael Jackson: Son Prince Has Inherited Vitiligo Skin Condition, says La Toya." *Daily Telegraph*, November 17, 2009.
Lopez, Johnny. "Michael Jackson's Son Gets His Game On." *TMZ*, January 26, 2011.
"Jermaine Jackson Says Prince Michael Showing Signs of Vitiligo." *Extra*, September 26, 2011 (RT).

CHAPTER 30

As stated in the text, none of the questions surrounding MJ's will and estate have been answered. And it still seems likely they never will be. It was widely reported in September of 2011 that Katherine Jackson and MJ's children were to receive a $30 million distribution from the estate. Simply from reading the headlines on those stories it's clear the reporters believed that Katherine and the kids were to have that money in their accounts very soon. One year later, they still don't. When Weitzman appeared with Branca on CNN's *Piers Morgan Tonight*, he was careful about how he answered the host's question about the $30 million, saying, "It's only a preliminary distribution. You know, the court has a certain process we have to go through. You deal with IRS issues, state of California estate issues. But ultimately the executors, John Branca and John McClain, decided that it was time for a preliminary distribution. Thirty million dollars went into Michael Jackson's family trust." Neither Weitzman nor Branca can be accused of misleading Morgan or the media in general. MJ's family trust, though, has not actually been funded, meaning that none of that $30 million is available to Katherine or MJ's children. This has naturally stoked suspicion among some in the Jackson family, and even among Mrs. Jackson's attorneys, that Katherine will die before the estate has to pay her.

MJ cursing the day he bought the Beatles catalog/golden goose; KJ saying MJ's wealth created more difficulties with his family than his fame, happier back in Gary: confidential sources close to Mrs. Jackson. KJ the only one in the family MJ trusted: same sources, also Schaffel, Tohme, Hawk, others. KJ on understanding better how it must have been for MJ: the confidential sources just mentioned. John McClain telling Jackie about Sanders estate deal (before Katherine told the rest of the family), Jackie passing the news on, Joe/Randy lobbying to stop deal: multiple sources close to Mrs. Jackson. (This was when Joe started telling people I was an estate "plant"). My sources believed (as did Perry Sanders) that McClain was for some reason trying to scuttle the deal. I don't know that this last part is true, but it was clearly the consensus opinion of those around Mrs. Jackson. Jackie Jackson, by the way, is now being paid as a consultant to the estate. Judge Palazuelos tying Joe's wrongful death lawsuit to Katherine's, process by which Oxman accomplished: *Beverly Hills Courier*, May 3, 2011; later, my confidential sources. Janet, Jermaine, La Toya, Frank Cascio books: see bibliography, all were published in 2011. Wiesner's book: *Michael Jackson: The True Story*, published in 2011 in Germany; I was told by someone close to Wiesner that the estate either had sued or was threatening to sue Dieter Wiesner for copyright infringement. I haven't seen such a lawsuit. Dileo "tell-all": Dileo to *NY Daily News*. Dileo health problems: see Radar Online on illness, *Variety* obituary, among others. I also discussed this subject with his wife Linda while her husband was in the hospital.

Arnold Klein financial problems: Schaffel, Klein's bankruptcy filing, claim and counterclaim between Klein and Jason Pfeiffer, media reports. Klein's wild claim re. Khilji using his money to finance terrorist organizations: Schaffel, court file, Seal/*Vanity Fair*. I am in no sense suggesting that claim is true. "To

say I'm a thief": Khilji to Dimond/"The Secret World of Dr. Arnold Klein."
Subpoena of Klein's medical records by Murray defense: public record; some
of them were introduced as evidence at trial; see also reporting on subpoenas
of Klein's records issued by AEG and the California Medical Board. The effort
of the Murray defense to build its defense around the claim that Klein was
responsible for turning MJ into a drug addict was blocked by Judge Pastor.
Pfeiffer's claims he and MJ had been lovers: Pfeiffer to *Woman's Day*; Klein
backing Pfeiffer: Klein to *Extra* (appearing with Pfeiffer), later to TMZ; see
also hollywoodgossip.com. Klein apology: posted on Klein's Facebook page;
he said he was sorry for having repeated a story he now believed was "fabricated by a ghost writer" working with Pfeiffer, and wrote, "I do not at this
time believe there is any evidence that [MJ] was gay" (see lipstickalley.com
story). Taylor's tweet denouncing Klein: Seal, "Dramatic fall"/*Daily Mail*.
Taylor's rejection of Klein's rapprochement attempts: confidential source.
Hoefflin travails: Dimond/"It's Getting Even Weirder." Hoefflin as Jackson
family "medical representative": Hoefflin claim; KJ advisors largely dismissed
it. Hoefflin has never, to my knowledge, spoken publicly about these events.
I should note that Klein sued Hoefflin in September of 2009 for remarks
Hoefflin made to Britain's the *Sun* suggesting that Klein must have instructed
Conrad Murray in how to administer propofol and mostly likely was Murray's
source of the anesthetic. Hoefflin attempted to have the lawsuit dismissed on
free speech grounds but Judge Amy Hogue ruled against him after Klein's
attorneys showed evidence that Hoefflin had been warned beforehand that
he was about to make a false accusation. The case is apparently now in arbi-
tration, see Ourweekly.com below.

Palomino house sales data: promotional brochure from when it went onto
the market in spring 2010; the house is still for sale (see zillow.com listing),
but the price has been substantially reduced and the new listing acknowledges
that MJ lived in the guesthouse. Proposal to make Neverland Ranch into a state
park: *LA Times*; plans for helicopter tours: Bly/*USA Today*. Drop in MJ record
sales in 2010: Sisario/*New York Times*; much other information about the decline from 2009: Christman, Mitchell/*Billboard*. "Inventory liability": Mitchell.
Sillerman and Lefsetz: to Sisario. I used the $756 million figure for the value
of the deals generated by the MJ estate in the first year after his death because
it was the most widely published estimate, based on the examination of those
deals by *Billboard*, as the *NY Daily News* story listed below acknowledges. But
an estimate it is. That figure didn't include merchandising deals or the earnings
from the Mijac catalog. *Billboard*'s claim that MJ had made $1 billion in "earn-
ings" in the first year after his death may be closer to the mark. There will be no
way of knowing for certain unless the estate is subjected to a truly independent

audit. The same is true of the $310 million (an amount that increased to $475 million in the "Second Account Current") in "profits" reported by the estate. Back when he seemed to believe he had made a deal with the estate and was speaking well of Branca, Perry Sanders told me that Branca had done a brilliant job of reducing the estate's debt, including a remarkably successful renegotiation of the interest on MJ's loans. Sanders also told me that there was no way to be certain what Branca and McClain had paid themselves without an audit. Sanders said that such an audit would take place. "Only place he had ever really felt comfortable": Mesereau, our very first interview. Neverland ruined for MJ: just about everyone I spoke to who dealt with MJ in the last five years of his life agreed on this; he repeatedly said he would never go back, not even for a visit, and Katherine Jackson said her son's statements in that regard were why she blocked any attempt to bury him there. MJ talked about "going on" with his life in the very first interview he gave after the Chandler settlement, and it was a phrase he repeated again and again, according to those who represented him as attorneys, advisors, and business associates.

As noted earlier, I did speak to members of the Chandler family. None of them wanted to be quoted by name, though Ray Chandler didn't say that until past the midpoint of our second and final interview and, as I explained earlier, my position is that my obligation not to quote him by name didn't take effect until he made that request. Still, I did try to respect his wish that he not be quoted about Jordie and tried to use his quotes from earlier interviews or from his book when I could. That said, nearly all of the quotes attributed to Chandler family members in this section are from my interviews with them, though some of Ray's quotes are from David Jones's *Daily Mail* article on Evan Chandler's suicide. I'll note those.

"Looking over your shoulder for the next ten years": via Ray Chandler. "Completely broken": Orth, "Neverland's Lost Boys"; that's certainly not the description of Jordie I heard from two people outside his family who have had lengthy relationships with him. I can't name them or even describe the nature of those relationships (other than that they were quite protective of Jordie) without compromising their identities, and both wanted to speak only on background. "Lonely, introverted": *Daily Mirror* on Evan's suicide; probably from Gumbel/*Independent*, 2003; again, that doesn't really correspond to the descriptions I've heard, although the people I spoke to agreed that Jordie lives in a certain amount of fear and is wary of strangers—for good reason in their opinions. "Like a cancer": Ray Chandler to Jones/*Daily Mail*. "Most vilified person on the planet": Ray Chandler. Prostituted her son: Evan's fundamental claim in custody battle with June was failure to protect Jordie because she was being treated to the lifestyle she longed for. Evan's promises to maintain a relationship with two younger sons, excuse for poisonous nature of relationship with Nathalie: Ray Chandler; according to family members I spoke to, the producer mentioned earlier, and two other persons familiar with Jordie, Nikki, and Emmanuel were deeply wounded by their father's abandonment and as adults had refused any contact with him, including arranging or attending a funeral. It was clear to me that even Ray had a difficult time forgiving his brother for turning his back on his sons. Evan and Jordie fleeing to Germany, then settling on Long Island: Chandler family member. Praise of Nathalie/Robert Rosen home and parenting: several people, including my producer friend, who told me Rosen had been a terrific step-father and that because of that Nikki, and Emmanuel had turned out well. I also learned not long after this, though, that Rosen and Nathalie had separated. Jordie refusing contact with June: June testified to this in *People v. Jackson*, saying she hadn't seen him since 1994; the skateboard in the garage: probably first reported by Kevin Smith, 1997; see also vindicatemj.wordpress.com. A particularly rich though entirely slanted source of information about Jordie and the Chandlers is the "Michael Jackson Is Innocent" file at lacienegasmiled.wordpress.com, which has been written by a young woman who claims to have attended NYU with Jordie (a claim I'm told is true). Anyway, I was told by family members that the skateboard story was true, but that it was actually one of Jordie's siblings who put it in the garage. Jordie's growing wealth and investments: Chandler family members, other sources, *Daily Mail* (including investments in oil stocks), Smith/*People*, Gumbel 2003; the bank vice president who became Jordie's financial advisor was Jeffrey Hahn. Jordie/Evan terror of MJ fans, stalking: British MJ fan Denise Pfeiffer was sent to jail in Los Angeles for making threats against both of them, before being bailed out by the actress Lynn Redgrave: *Evening Standard*, 1994; I heard a good deal from Ray about how threatened Evan felt by Pfeiffer/other MJ fans. "We're coming to take your blood" phone message: basis of a complaint to the police in Beverly Hills; Ray Chandler told me that there were many other, equally disturbing messages. Jordie taking shooting lessons: *All That Glitters*. Tabloids' bounty on Jordie's head: widely reported (see vindicatemj.com for links). Jordie's adult life/living circumstances: Chandler family members, Jones/*Daily Mail* (including building with rooftop pool/indoor track, work as record company intern), other published reports. Sonnet Simmons was identified as Jordie's "girlfriend" in the 1997 Kevin Smith article, when they were both still still in high school; they also attended the same college. One source told me they were "just friends," but I didn't make a great deal of effort to determine if that was so. As noted earlier, the people I spoke to who had relationships with Jordie were quite protective of him and felt he was living a good life, other than feeling hunted by the media and certain MJ fans. Evan's attack on Dave Schwartz: Fischer/ GQ, Larry Feldman/*Frozen in Time*. Evan's 1996 lawsuit against MJ: widely reported at the time; see "On This Day"/BBC, posts on vindicatemj.com, which obviously take MJ's side. Evan handsomeness: agreed upon by pretty much all who knew him; "a handsomer Rob Lowe": unnamed source to *New York Post* on his suicide. Evan unable to form another relationship after the one with Nathalie ended: Ray Chandler, another source (also reported in Jones's story); bipolar diagnosis, avoidance of medicine/"zombie": Ray Chandler; another family source, though, had more to say about how Evan's condition worsened, and that he became increasingly unstable and frequently frightening. Evan's plastic surgery: Jones; Ray merely acknowledged that what I had read was true. Another source described it more vividly, in the context of both Evan's fragile psyche, his insistence that he was trying to maintain anonymity (which Ray mentioned also) and how difficult to look at he became. Evan and Jordie fighting over money: Jones, acknowledged by Ray, also an aspect of Jordie's family court complaint against his father. Opportunity for vindication: Ray told me how convinced he was that the criminal filing against MJ would offer this, and how disappointed he was when it didn't.

"Sketchy," "naïve as hell," "somewhat asexual": Presley to Stern, Sawyer, GQ as below. *Dateline*/Ernie Rizzo: see Mankiewicz/NBC, broadcast September 2004. "It's cosmic": reported by *Dateline* from a chronology Evan wrote for Barry Rothman. Salinas, Rizzo quotes: *Dateline*. Fall of Anthony Pellicano: I cite simply the lengthy reports of Pellicano's conviction on racketeering and wiretapping charges (see *LA Times, New York Times*), but the *LA Times* reported much more, as did *Dateline*. Ray Chandler clearly feels that what came out about Pellicano should have created greater sympathy for his family and greater skepticism about the Fischer article. He described Fischer as "a dupe" in an interview with me. Ray moved to write his book after seeing the Bashir documentary: Ray Chandler in 2004 and to me. "They're in love!," "six wishes": *All That Glitters, Dateline*. Sworn declaration in which Jordie described MJ's alleged sexual seduction: now widely available online, see "Michael Jackson's lover tells all"/ Michael Jackson Forum/topix.com. "Before it got to anal sex": Ray Chandler. Corey Feldman quotes: Feldman to Bashir. Ray Chandler dismissal of Feldman's prior "no inappropriate contact" account, similar stories from others: Ray Chandler. Elatab: "New Jersey Teenager"/CBS. Retort that MJ was "selective": Ray Chandler. Vaknin/roots of pedophilia: Vaknin, *Malignant Self-Love*. "What made Michael different": Ray Chandler. Ray acknowledged that Jordie and Evan were unhappy with him for going on TV (and for seeking publicity) and said that neither wanted to be associated with the criminal case—out of fear for their safety, Ray said. Photographs of Jordie on the ski slopes: I remember seeing them during the trial but they're not easy to find these days. Some were posted by a bulletin board user at somj.org ("Sisterhood of Michael Jackson"). Liberty Towers: description and accompanying photographs/Jones/*Daily Mail*. Evan/Gaucher's disease: Jones probably first to report, likely via Ray, who told me. As with drugs earlier, I used Wikipedia and its outbound links to research the disease. Evan's rages: Ray Chandler acknowledged, but another source described them more vividly. Attack on Jordie: public record, reported at the time by Friedman, Caruso/*NY Daily News*. Evan's last days: Jones, Ray Chandler. Surfing and guitar: Jordie continued to spend money on lessons right up to the time of MJ's death; according to confidential sources, he was studying surfing and guitar in Los Angeles when MJ died, but left town shortly thereafter. "You're So Good For Me": Jordie is credited as the lyricist; Simmons performs under her first name only. Jordie's life in 2009: based on confidential sources, as earlier. Death of Evan, discovery thereof: Jones, Ray Chandler. "Absolutely nothing to do with Michael Jackson . . . euthanasia": Ray Chandler; Ray/funeral arrangements, funeral home staffer quote: Jones/*Daily Mail*. MJ fan quotes about Evan's suicide, threats against Jordie: various MJ/gossip Web sites (perezhilton. com, popcrunch.com, and gossipjacker.net had the nastiest ones); I'm sure they're buried beneath many others by now. Address published, tracking blogs: floacist.wordpress.com, mjkit.forumotion.net. Tabloid/$300,000 for a photo of Jordie: Ray Chandler, another source; also, reported at the time.

It will disappoint and possibly infuriate some MJ fans when I write that Jordan Chandler most definitely did not write a letter Katherine Jackson received, confessing that he made up the story that MJ molested him. Jordie has not written any letters or made any public statements about his relationship with MJ since 1994. The story got traction mainly because Jermaine took it to starpulse.com. He may believe it's true. Katherine Jackson does, or at least says she does; she said it to me in April of 2011.

I described at the beginning of these notes the circumstances under which I heard the story of the producer who ate Thanksgiving dinner with Jordie's family. This is someone who had no agenda himself, and who knew I was pretty much convinced at that point that the abuse allegations against MJ were false. As noted, he asked me some time after that conversation not to quote him; I agreed only not to quote him by name. Obviously the family will know who it is.

Zonen demeanor during presentation at "Frozen in Time": "Frozen in Time" DVD; I'm pretty certain Mesereau will agree with my assessment. I'm paraphrasing Zonen's remarks, obviously, but this is almost exactly what he said, in a compressed form.

COURT FILES

Criminal

SBSC 1133603.
LASC SA073164.

Civil

LASC SC026226.
LASC BC445597.
2:11-bk-12718-RN.
2:11-ap-02407-RN, 6/27/11.
2:11-ap-02407-RN, 8/3/11.

DOCUMENTS

Mann to Sullivan, 4/9/11.
"RE: Oxman." E-mail from Howard Mann to Randall Sullivan, May 2, 2011.

ESTATE/AEG

"Katherine Jackson to Manage Wrongful Death Case Filed by Her Husband
    Joe." *Beverly Hills Courier,* May 3, 2011.
"Michael Jackson Estate to Distribute $30 Million to Katherine Jackson and
    the Children." *Huffingtonpost.com,* September 14, 2011 (I).
Morgan, "Branca and Weitzman."
Yoshino, Kimi. "Katherine Jackson, Kids to Get $30 Million from the Michael
    Jackson Estate." *LATimes.com,* September 14, 2011.

FRANK DILEO

"Frank Dileo, Michael Jackson's Manager, Touts Tell-All Book About the Pop
    Star, Controversial Album." *New York Daily News,* January 5, 2011.
"Michael Jackson's Ex-Manager Frank Dileo Hospitalized, Fighting for His
    Life." *RadarOnline,* March 30, 2011 (I).
Morris, Christopher. "Frank Dileo Dies at 64." *Variety,* August 24, 2011.

KLEIN/PFEIFFER/BANKRUPTCY/CHARGES/HOEFFLIN

"Arnold Klein: I Did Not Betray Michael Jackson." *TMZ,* May 1, 2010.
Dimond, Diane. "Even Weirder."

———. "Secret World."

"The Dramatic Fall of Michael Jackson's Dermatologist." *Daily Mail*, January 3, 2012.

"Jacko's Secret Lover."

"Jason Pfeiffer Alleges Gay Affair with Michael Jackson; Dr. Arnold Klein Backs Him Up." thehollywoodgossip.com, May 3rd, 2010 (I).

"King of Pop's Secret Lover: 'I Was Michael Jackson's Boyfriend." *Extra*, April 29, 2010.

"Michael Jackson Was Not Gay—Arnold Klein." lipstickalley.com, April 20, 2011 (I).

"More Lawsuits Surface Regarding Michael Jackson's Death." ourweekly.com, June 25, 2010 (I).

Seal, "The Doctor Will Sue."

Willets. David. "Michael Jackson 'Dead 47 Minutes' as Doc Made 3 Phone Calls." *Sun*, August 27, 2009.

MJ BONANZA

Bly, Laura. "Neverland: Michael Jackson's Former Ranch Keeps Grip on Ffans." *USAtoday.com*, June 21, 2011 (I).

Chawkins, Steve. "Neverland Ranch as a State Park?" *Los Angeles Times*, July 14, 2010.

Christman, Ed. "U.S. Album Sales Dropped 12.8% Last Year, Digital Tracks Post Small Gain." billboard.biz, January 5, 2011 (I).

Christman, Donahue, Mitchell, Peoples, and Waddell.

Mitchell, "Album Sales."

Sisario, "A Year Later."

"2710 Palomino Ln., Las Vegas, NV 89107—Michael Jackson's Last Las Vegas Residence from 2007 Through 2009." zillow.com, March 2009 (I).

CHANDLER CASE

Barnes, Brooks. "Pellicano and a Lawyer Convicted in Wiretapping." *New York Times*, August 29, 2008.

Bashir, Martin. "Corey Feldman Speaks Out Against Jackson." *ABC-20/20*, February 10, 2005 (RT).

Caruso, Michelle. "Jax Accuser Abuse Claim. Kid Paid Off in '93 Sez He Was Harmed—by Own Dad." *New York Daily News*, September 5, 2006.

Fischer, "Framed."

Friedman, Roger. "Ex-Jacko Accuser in Court Against Dad." Fox News, August 19, 2006 (I).

Gumbel, Andrew. "Accusing Jackson of Sex Abuse Ruined the Life of Jordy Chandler." *Independent*, November 22, 2003.

Hall, Carla, and Tami Abdollah. "Pellicano Found Guilty of Racketeering." *Los Angeles Times*, May 16, 2008.

Hodgson, Liz, and Pat Malone. "Jackson Stalker Put on Probation." *Evening Standard*, May 25, 1994.

"Jermaine Jackson: 'Abuse Victim Claims Michael Jackson Never Molested Him.'" starpulse.com, November 26, 2009 (I).

Leung, Rebecca. "New Jersey Teenager Reveals Secrets at Neverland Ranch." cbsnews.com, November 22, 2003 (I).

"Lisa Marie Presley Interview." GQ, January 2004.

Mankiewicz, Josh. "Inside Look at the 1999 Jackson Case." *NBC/Dateline*, September 12, 2004 (RT).

"Michael Jackson Forum: Michael Jackson's Lover Tells All." topix.com, January 7, 2011 (I).

"Michael Jackson Is Innocent." lacienegasmiled.wordpress.com, August 9, 2010 (I).

"On This Day, August 24, 1993: Michael Jackson Accused of Child Abuse." BBC (RT).

Orth 3/04.

Sawyer, "Lisa Marie Presley."

Smith, Kevin. "Jordy Made a Fortune Out of Michael Jackson . . . Now He's Alone and Abandoned." *People* (London), February 16, 1997.

Stern, Howard. "Lisa Marie Presley Interview." *Howard Stern Show*, February 25, 2003.

EVAN'S SUICIDE

Jones, "Killed by the Curse."

Parry, Ryan. "Michael Jackson Sex Case Dad Evan Chandler Wanted Justice but Ended Up Destroyed." *Daily Mirror*, November 19, 2009.

Perone, Tim, Lisa Stasi, and David K. Li. "Jacko Molest-Rap Dad Kills Himself." *New York Post*, November 18, 2009.

WIKIPEDIA

"Gaucher's Disease."

CHAPTER 31

"Michael was a good person": Mesereau. Ortega on MJ's trips to orphanages and hospitals, "never seen Michael . . . embarrass, harm": Ortega to McLean/ the *Times* of London. Katherine Jackson asked me to "tell the world" MJ was not a pedophile near the end of that meeting where she was introduced to Perry Sanders. Schaffel told me about being sent to purchase the photo and books in one of our last interviews. Three deadbolt locks/secret room: reports police investigators made on the day of the raid on Neverland, part of the court file (as is the fact that MJ installed a chime-sounding alarm to notify him whenever someone was approaching the door of his bedroom). His desire for privacy, as I acknowledged in the text, is undeniable. In the end, I can only say that the feelings I developed for MJ in the course of researching and writing this book were almost entirely tender ones, and that I do sincerely wish he is resting in peace.

COURT FILES

Criminal

SBSC 1133603.

Civil

LASC SC026226.

REFLECTIONS

Demorest, Steve. "Michael in Wonderland." *Melody Maker,* March 1, 1980 (hereafter cited as Demorest).
McLean, "Ortega."

AFTERWORD

Trial of Dr. Conrad Murray section: facts and quoted statements are from court record. I happened to be in Los Angeles when the trial began, as were Katherine Jackson's attorneys Perry Sanders and Sandra Ribera, who both shared their observations and analysis of what was taking place. Sandy was in court the first day of the trial, seated with the Jackson family, and not only discussed what she had seen but gave me a copy of the notes she made in court. Nevertheless, I relied mainly upon daily reporting from the courthouse: Ryan and Kim/*LA Times*, TMZ bulletins. TruTV's "In Session" program asked me to join their team of reporters and commentators covering the trial, but I declined.

Arnold Klein had admitted more than once that he administered Demerol to MJ in his office. "Needle phobic": to Amy Ephron (see Chapter 28); Ephron also recapitulated the work of DEA agents and California Medical Board investigators, some of which was also reported by her colleague Diane Dimond, among others. Pfeiffer's official claims against Klein: counterclaim against the doctor's lawsuit against him; Pfeiffer's unofficial claims (and references to the doctor as "Frankenklein"): postings on his blogspot. Klein prescriptions to Pfeiffer: provided by Pfeiffer for use in Daily Beast articles listed below. Judge Pastor's ruling that most of the Klein stuff would not be admitted into evidence was made before the trial began. "Essentially gutted our defense strategy": Chernoff to Ephron (see Chapter 28), though he said nearly the same thing to the *LA Times*. My opinion that the testimony of the AEG executives had been choreographed was shared by Sanders and Ribera. I can say for certain that the surfacing of the Kenny Ortega e-mail gave the attorneys representing Mrs. Jackson in the AEG lawsuit the sense that they might win that case after all. Gongaware testimony, playing of iPhone message, testimony that follows, etc.: evidence and testimony offered at trial. The autopsy photo of MJ did indeed appear on TMZ's Web site; I'm not going to cite it. Jackson family reaction to Phillips's testimony: sources in court, media reporting. Walgren, Pastor, White, Schafer, Waldman: transcripts/open court. "Scumbag": see below. Scene at courthouse, and appearance of Occupy protesters: Esquival and Rojas/*LA Times* Web site. "Harrumphing incredulously": Smith, *Wall Street Journal* blog. Positioning of La Toya and Janet: observers in court, media. Jermaine story/MJ planning to flee if found guilty: TMZ, which also reported Mesereau's reaction ("Calls BS"). The quote here, though, was made in a conversation with me. Observations about the Jackson family: my own, though I certainly spoke to people close to the family who shared them. La Toya's tweet: still online. Scene at the courthouse: again, Rojas and Esquival. Verdict/meaning in terms of sentencing: Blankstein/day of the verdict, ABC/next day; actual sentencing: CNN, *USA Today*. Murray remarks: "Michael Jackson and the Doctor"/MSNBC. Estate's attempt to block the documentary: *LA Times*. "Four years is not enough": KJ to Los Angeles ABC affiliate, reported on the network's Web site November 29, 2011. "Upbeat," "I'll be out soon": TMZ, same day as the sentencing.

Medical Board questioning Klein: first reported by Dr. Klein himself on Facebook, later, Dimond/Daily Beast, Perpetua/rollingstone.com. Hiring publicist: Ryan/*LA Times*. Klein's practice shrinking: Schaffel, later, Ryan, Seal. Auctioning off memorabilia: Heger/radaronline.com. Klein's Facebook posts, still online: Seal. Medical Board demands on Dr. Klein, Klein response: Klein's lawsuit in Sacramento's Superior Court. *Entertainment Tonight*/Liberace's former lover: see eonline.com. Landlord attempt to evict Klein: Heger/radaronline.com. Klein's battle with LaChappelle, quote from Detective Hrycyk: Ryan/*LA Times*. Raymone Bain guilty plea/sentencing: Mather/*LA Times* Web site; Mesereau on Bain being held accountable for MJ's failure to pay taxes: Mesereau. Oxman suspension/Jaroscak/related issues: State Bar Court of California Review Department ruling, Mesereau. Permanent disbarment: Friedman, Oxman's State Bar profile; it was made final after this book was completed.

AEG lawsuit/strategy, impact of Kenny Ortega e-mail and other information discovered in the lawsuit: confidential/KJ attorneys/advisors. MJ estate vs. Lloyds of London: TMZ; I heard a good deal more than they know about that from confidential sources closer to the action, especially about the backdoor communications on this matter between the estate and AEG. Katz-Vaccaro-Vaccaro's-attorney taped conversation: see chapter 27; I have a copy of that recording. Pressure on Perry Sanders, *Segye Times* lawsuit settlement: KJ advisors, Sanders; also re. settlement, TMZ, including information about the loan I wasn't aware of. Tax issues facing MJ's estate: *Tax Notes*, which thoroughly explained the issues that surround valuation of a dead celebrity's estate. Branca/Weitzman *Piers Morgan Tonight* appearance: watched first airing, discussed with my sources, who agreed that the IRS must have been made aware of the claims about the value of MJ's publishing rights. Settlement terms/*Segye Times*/loan from estate: confidential sources as above; the deal with the estate included some sort of provision for KJ and kids to fly to Montreal and enthuse about the Cirque du Soleil show. Sanders praising Branca: I was among those to whom he did. As noted previously, Sanders's tone was changing again, and so was the attitude of Mrs. Jackson's advisors, in the spring and summer of 2012. Sanders-LiCalsi meeting, Sanders-KJ meeting and advice about Branca/McClain: confidential source. Sanders's spring 2012 questions for estate/Weitzman: Sanders, people involved in AEG lawsuit. Sanders praise of Branca for renegotiating MJ debt: Sanders, others to whom he spoke about it. Pepsi deal, Ola Ray settlement: contactmusic.com, others. Kimberly Griggs lawsuit, right to sell Hayvenhurst: TMZ; Sanders's displeasure and estate explanation: Sanders, to me and to TMZ. Estate accounting statement: copy of document filed with Judge Beckloff, notated by Sandy Ribera. Jackson siblings' questions about executor earnings, mounting pressure on Sanders: confidential sources, Sanders. Ribera précis to clients of accounting statement: Ribera, confidential source; Sanders needing a full accounting: confidential sources, Sanders. Randy/ Janet pressure to take Branca on in court: my sources, as it was happening. The two youngest Jacksons have long been closer to each other than to others in the family. Janet/divorce: a number of people told me about how changed she was by her settlement with Elizondo—even Mesereau had heard about it. Divorce terms: papers and settlement via SmokingGun.com. Janet's demand that Michael put up for boat first: two anonymous sources. $40,000 Forest Lawn deposit: Katherine Jackson told a number of people who later told me about Janet's insistence on being repaid before MJ could be buried; the only one I can name is Schaffel; Janet wishing her siblings had their own money: same sources. What might appear to be hard-heartedness on Janet's part should probably be placed in the context of her two divorces; she allowed herself to be taken advantage of financially by her ex-husbands to a degree that may be unmatched by any other female celebrity in U.S. history.

KJ personal growth early 2011 through third anniversary of MJ's death: Sanders and Ribera; others remarked upon it also. KJ refusal to hear criticisms of Randy/her other children, refusing Randy's demands re. replacing her lawyers: same confidential sources. Ribera quotes: Ribera. Description of Prince: consistent across confidential sources; Prince questioning Sanders in Montreal: Mann, a confidential source. Prince's trip to Berlin: Mann, who sent along a film crew; another source. Paris quotes: to DeGeneres and Winfrey. Janet Jackson quote to *Prevention*: below. Fiddes claim to be Blanket's father: Fiddes to the *Globe* via contactmusic.com, aol.com. Paris's tweets and online posts: Goldberg, CNN. Murray at Los Angeles County Jail: TMZ, including Murray's quotes, contactmusic.com.

Promotion of *Unity* tour, Jermaine quote: "Michael Jackson Remembered By Brothers"/*Daily Telegraph*. KJ preparing to go on the road to follow her sons: KJ advisors, Ribera. KJ disappearance in July of 2012 and return home: Sanders and especially Ribera; also, Mann/one of his attorneys on their litigation with the estate. I also spoke to one of Mrs. Jackson's other advisors. The entire debacle was thoroughly chronicled in the tabloid media and on the Internet and the hearing before Judge Beckloff where KJ regained custody and the facts of her disappearance were entered is part of the BP 117 321 court file. Roger Friedman and TMZ led the way, as described in the text, relying heavily on what they heard from Sanders and Ribera, who were telling me a lot more than they were telling anyone else. All that came from secondary sources should be obvious to anyone reading the list of citations below.

COURT FILES

Criminal

LASC SA073164.
Civil
2:11-bk-12718-RN.
2:11-ap-02407-RN, 6/27/11.
2:11-ap-02407-RN, 8/3/11.
07-O-11968;08-O-12328;07-O13696;09-O12276 (State Bar Court of California, Review Department) *In the Matter of Rickey Brian Oxman and Maureen Patricia Jaroscak,* January 13, 2012.
34-2012-80001201 (Sacramento County Superior Court) *Arnold Klein, M.D. v. Medical Board of California,* July 17, 2012.
BP 117 321 (Los Angeles Superior Court) *Second Account Current and Report of Status Petition for Settlement Thereof, Estate of Michael Joseph Jackson,* July 2, 2012.
BP 117 321 (Los Angeles Superior Court) *Response of Executors John Branca and John McClain to Katherine Jackson's Request for Production of Supporting Documents for Account Current,* August 20, 2012.

DOCUMENTS

"Brian Oxman—CA State Bar Profile." February 10, 2012.
"Request for Production of Supporting Documents" submitted by Perry R. Sanders Jr. on behalf of Katherine Jackson to the Michael Jackson Estate, June 29, 2012.

PRE-TRIAL/KLEIN/PFEIFFER

Dimond, Diane. "Secret World."
"Dr. Klein Hands Over Michael Jackson's Records." *TMZ,* April 6, 2011 (I).
Ephron, "Trial."
Pfeiffer, Jason. "The Truth According to Jason: Desperate Times Call For Desperate Measures." jasonpfeiffer.blogspot.com, April 2, 2010 (I).
———."The Truth According to Jason: I Have Not Said a Lot Lately . . ." jasonpfeiffer.blogspot.com, November 14, 2011 (I).
———. "The Truth According to Jason: Trapped Like a Rat." jasonpfeiffer. blogspot.com, March 20, 2012 (I).
———. "The Truth According to Jason: What Goes Around Comes Around . . . Is It Mr. Klein Yet?" jasonpfeiffer.blogspot.com, December 10, 2011 (I).

———. "The Truth According to Jason: Your House of Cards . . ." jasonpfeiffer. blogspot.com, August 16, 2011 (I).

Ryan, Harriet, and Victoria Kim,. "Another Setback for Murray's Defense Strategy." *Los Angeles Times*, August 29, 2011.

Seal, "Doctor Will Sue."

TRIAL

Finn, Natalie, and Baker Machado. "Conrad Murray Defense Witness Calls Propofol Expert a 'Scumbag.'" *E!online.com*, October 20, 2011 (I).

Kim, Victoria. "Michael Jackson Trial: Day 2 to Start with 'This Is It' Producer." *LATimes.com*, September 28, 2011 (I). (These articles by Kim are cited chronologically.)

———. "Conrad Murray, in Taped Interview, Recalls Being Hired by Jackson." *LATimes.com*, October 7, 2011 (I).

———. "Conrad Murray Trial: Whether Jackson Swallowed Sedative Is Debated." *LATimes.com*, October 7, 2011 (I).

———. "Conrad Murray Trial: Detective Questioned on Propofol Bottle." *LATimes.com*, October 11, 2011 (I).

———. "Michael Jackson Autopsy Photo Shown to Jurors During Testimony." *LATimes.com*, October 11, 2011 (I).

———. "Testimony Strikes at Heart of Jackson Doctor's Defense." *Los Angeles Times*, October 11, 2011 (I).

———. "Witness: Conrad Murray More Like Employee Than Doctor to Jackson." *LATimes.com*, October 19, 2011 (I).

———. "Witness: A 'Possibility' That Michael Jackson Caused Own Death." *LATimes.com*, October 21, 2011 (I).

———. "Conrad Murray: Judge Issues Another Blow to Defense." *LATimes. com*, October 25, 2011 (I).

———. "Conrad Murray Witness: Jackson Wanted Unorthodox Sleep Drug." *LATimes.com*, October 25, 2011 (I).

———. "Conrad Murray Patient: 'I Am Alive Today Because of That Man.'" *LATimes.com*, October 26, 2011 (I).

———. "Conrad Murray Trial: Caving In to a Patient's Demands?" *LATimes. com*, October 27, 2011 (I).

———. "Michael Jackson 'Probably' Addicted to Demerol—Defense Witness." *LATimes.com*, October 27, 2011 (I).

———. "Defense Expert Concedes Conrad Murray Violated Medical Care Standards." *LATimes.com*, October 31, 2011 (I)

———. "Key Conrad Murray Witness Faces New Contempt of Court Charge." *LATimes.com*, October 31, 2011 (I).

———. "Conrad Murray's Fate Soon to Be in Jury's Hands as Testimony Ends." *LATimes.com*, November 1, 2011 (I).

———. "Defense Calls Conrad Murray a Victim as Case Goes to Jury." *LATimes.com*, November 3, 2011 (I).

———. "Conrad Murray Lied to Police About Jackson's Death, D.A. Says." *LATimes.com*, November 3, 2011.

———. "Conrad Murray's Defense Employed 'Junk Science,' D.A. says." *LATimes.com*, November 3, 2011 (I).

———. "Conrad Murray Guilty Even If Jackson Injected Himself, D.A. says." *LATimes.com*, November 3, 2011 (I).

———. "Lawyers for Conrad Murray Seek Test of Drug Vial." *Los Angeles Times*, July 31, 2012.

Kim, Victoria, and Harriet Ryan. "Conrad Murray Trial: Jackson Doctor Makes Frantic Call, but Not to 911." *LATimes.com*, September 28, 2011 (I). (These articles by Kim and Ryan are cited chronologically.)

——— and ———. "Jackson Begged for 'Some Milk,' Murray Says in Recording." *Los Angeles Times*, October 7, 2011.

——— and ———. "Witness: Murray Gave Jackson 40 Times More of the Drug Than He Told Police." *LATimes.com*, October 20, 2011 (I).

——— and ———. "Michael Jackson Probably Caused His Own Death, Witness Testifies." *Los Angeles Times*, October 29, 2011.

——— and ———. "Conrad Murray Trial: Prosecution to Cross-Examine Defense Expert." *LATimes.com*, October 31, 2011 (I).

——— and ———. "Murray's Defense Ends with Him Taking the Stand." *Los Angeles Times*, November 2, 2011.

Kim, Victoria, Harriet Ryan, and Andrew Blankstein. "Murray's iPhone Offers Snapshot of Jackson's Final Weeks." *LATimes.com*, October 6, 2011 (I).

"MJ's Lawyer Calls BS on Jermaine Jackson." *TMZ*, September 11, 2011 (I).

Ryan, Harriet and Victoria Kim. "Michael Jackson Was Too Sick to Dance at Rehearsals, Director Says." *LATimes.com*, September 27, 2011 (I). (These articles by Ryan and Kim are cited chronologically.)

——— and ———. "Michael Jackson 'Fearful' About Comeback Tour, Doctor Testifies." *LATimes.com*, October 24, 2011 (I).

——— and ———. "Defense Witness Describes a Confident Michael Jackson." *Los Angeles Times*, October 26, 2011.

——— and ———. "Conrad Murray Trial: Final Defense Witnesses to Testify Thursday." *LATimes.com*, October 27, 2011 (I).

———— and ————. "Conrad Murray Drug Expert May Hold Key to Doctor's Defense." *LATimes.com*, October 28, 2011 (I).

VERDICT AND SENTENCING

Avila, Jim, Alyssa Newcomb, and Luchina Fisher. "Michael Jackson Doctor Will Serve Only Half of Sentence." abcnews.go.com, November 29, 2011 (I).

Blankstein, Andrew. "Conrad Murray Trial: Odds 'Heavily Stacked' Toward Guilty, Experts Say." *LATimes.com*, November 7, 2011 (I).

"Conrad Murray—I'm Glad I Did That Documentary." *TMZ*, November 30, 2011 (I).

Dolak, Kevin, Jim Avila, and Christina Ng. "Conrad Murray Verdict: Will He Go to Prison?" abcnews.go.com, November 8, 2011 (I).

Duke, Alan. "Conrad Murray Sentenced to Four Years Behind Bars." CNN, November 30, 2011 (I).

Esquivel, Paloma. "Conrad Murray: Occupy L.A. Protesters Go to Courthouse." *LATimes.com*, November 7, 2011 (I).

Kasindorf, Martin. "Conrad Murray Sentenced to Four Years in Jackson death." *USA Today*, November 30, 2011.

Kim, Victoria, and Harriet Ryan. "Conrad Murray Guilty in Death of Michael Jackson." *LATimes.com*, November 7, 2011 (I).

"latoyajackson: Verdict is FINALLY IN!!!" twitter.com, November 7, 2011 (I).

"Michael Jackson's Estate Demands MSNBC ax Conrad Murray Documentary." *LATimes.com*, November 9, 2011 (I).

"Murray Talks About the Day Jackson Died in MSNBC Ddocumentary." entertaiment.msnbc.com, November 8, 2011 (I).

Rojas, Rick. "Conrad Murray Trial: Colorful Crowd Awaits Verdict at Courthouse." *LATimes.com*, November 7, 2011 (I).

Smith, Ethan. "Conrad Murray Trial: How Michael Jackson's Family Is Holding Up." blogs.wsj.com, September 28, 2011 (I).

POSTTRIAL/ROUNDUP/THE USUAL SUSPECTS

Crawford, Bridget J., Joshua C. Tate, Mitchell M. Gans, and Jonathan G. Blattmachr. "Celebrity, Death and Taxes: Michael Jackson's Estate." *Tax Notes*, October 19, 2009.

Dimond, Diane. "Michael Jackson Dermatologist Arnold Klein Under Investigation." *Daily Beast*, December 5, 2011 (I).

Friedman, Roger. "Brian Oxman Disbarred, Former Michael Jackson Lawyer —Sort Of." *Showbiz411.com*, July 6, 2012 (I).

———. "Michael Jackson's Ex-Lawyers: One a Hero, the Other Disbarred." *Showbiz.411.com*, July 9, 2012 (I).

Heger, Jen. "Bankrupt Dr. Arnold Klein Auctioning Off Michael Jackson, Liz Taylor Memorabilia." *Radaronline.com*, January 2, 2012 (I).

———. "Michael Jackson's Bankrupt Former Dermatologist Accused of Stiffing Landlord." *Radaronline.com*, May 16, 2012 (I).

"Liberace's Former Lover Details Romance." Etonline.com, May 2, 2012 (I).

Mather, Kate. "Michael Jackson's Former Manager Pleads Guilty to Tax Charges." *LATimes.com*, June 22, 2011 (I).

Perpetua, Matthew. "Michael Jackson's Dermatologist Investigated by Medical Board: Dr. Arnold Klein May Have Overprescribed Demerol to the Late Pop Star." *Rollingstone.com*, December 5, 2011 (I).

Ryan, Harriet. "A-List Doctor's Star Has Faded." *Los Angeles Times*, January 1, 2012.

———. "Prosecutor Rejects Case over Michael Jackson Artwork." *Los Angeles Times*, June 22, 2012.

JACKSON FAMILY'S DISCONTENT/ESTATE/PERRY SANDERS

"Janet Jackson Divorce Drama." *Thesmokinggun.com*, January 1, 2002 (I).

"Michael Jackson Estate Judge Approves Move to Sell Michael's House." *TMZ. com*, February 23, 2012 (I).

"Michael Jackson Estate to Katherine Jackson—Here's SIX MILLION." *TMZ*, October 5, 2011 (I).

"Michael Jackson Estate Will Work with Pepsi Again to Promote the *Bad* Album's Re-Release." *Contactmusic.com*, May 4, 2012 (I).

"Michael Jackson Sued for $1 Billion in Weird, Handwritten Lawsuit." *TMZ*, June 7, 2012 (I).

"MJ Estate to Lloyd's of London: This Is It. Now Pay Up!" *TMZ*, August 17, 2011 (I).

THIRD ANNIVERSARY/MJ'S CHILDREN/MURRAY FROM JAIL

DeGeneres, Ellen. "Ellen Talks to Paris Jackson About Growing Up." NBC, December 15, 2011 (RT).

Fiddes to the *Globe* via "Michael Jackson Bodyguard Matt Fiddes Claims He's Blanket's Father, Fights for Visitation Rights." blog.music.aol.com, April 26, 2012 (I).

Fiddes to the *Globe* via "Michael Jackson's Bodyguard to Fight for Blanket Visitation Rights." contactmusic.com, April 27, 2012 (I).

Goldberg, Stephanie. "Family, Fans Mark Michael Jackson's Death Three Years Later." cnn.com, June 25, 2012 (I).

"Lenny Dykstra, Conrad Murray, James DeBarge—Jailbird Homies." *TMZ. com*, May 6, 2012 (I).

"Michael Jackson Remembered by Brothers." *Daily Telegraph*, June 25, 2012.

Newman, Judith. "Janet Jackson, Living Joyfully." *Prevention*, May 2012.

Winfrey, Oprah. "Oprah Interviews Paris Jackson and 50 Cent." OWN, June 17, 2012 (RT).

KATHERINE JACKSON'S DISAPPEARANCE AND RETURN

"'Drugged' Katherine Jackson Demanded That Heads Roll." *TMZ*, July 25, 2012 (I).

Duke, Alan. "Conrad Murray Invites Katherine Jackson to Visit Him in Jail." cnn.com, July 27, 2012 (I).

Friedman, Roger. "LAPD Sheriff: Two Jackson Family Members in 'Minor Scuffle' at Home." *Showbiz411.com*, July 23, 2012 (I). (These articles by Friedman are cited chronologically.)

————. "Katherine Jackson Lawyers: 'Plan in Place for Three Years to Remove Her from Her Home and Grandchildren." *Showbiz411.com*, July 24, 2012 (I).

————. "Guardian Gambit Worked: Katherine Jackson on Way Back to Los Angeles." *Showbiz411.com*, July 25, 2012 (I).

————. "Katherine Jackson Speaks to Grandchildren at Last!" *Showbiz411. com*, July 25, 2012 (I).

————. "Katherine Jackson Suspended as Grandkids' Guardian." *Showbiz411. com*, July 25, 2012 (I).

————. "Someone's Lying About Katherine Jackson: Miraval Allows Cell Phones and Has Landlines in Every Room." *Showbiz411.com*, July 25, 2012 (I).

————. "TJ Jackson Is Named in Will as Successor Guardian." *Showbiz411. com*, July 25, 2012 (I).

————. "Katherine Jackson Arrives Home: 82 Year Old Driven 516 Miles Overnight." *Showbiz411.com*, July 26, 2012 (I).

————. "Katherine Jackson reads 'Hostage Statement' and ABC News Lets Her." *Showbiz411.com*, July 26, 2012 (I).

————. "Will Katherine Jackson Understand What Happened? The Family Lives in Denial." *Showbiz411.com*, July 26, 2012 (I).

————. "Lawyer: Katherine Jackson 'Laughed' at Report of Stroke." *Showbiz411.com*, July 27, 2012 (I).

———. "Katherine Jackson Will Let Grandson TJ Be the Permanent Co-Guardian of Michael's Kids." *Showbiz411.com*, July 27, 2012 (I).

———. "Michael Jackson Estate Bars Randy, Jermaine, Janet, Rebbie and Joe Jackson from Kids' Home." *Showbiz411.com*, July 30, 2012 (I).

———. "Katherine Jackson Tells Court About Kidnapping: iPad Taken Away, Room Phone Disconnected." *Showbiz411.com*, August 2, 2012 (I).

Watkins, Jade. "'She Is Just Heartbroken': Katherine Jackson Does Not Want to See Her Children Janet, Randy and Rebbie Following Family Drama." *Daily Mail*, August 13, 2012.